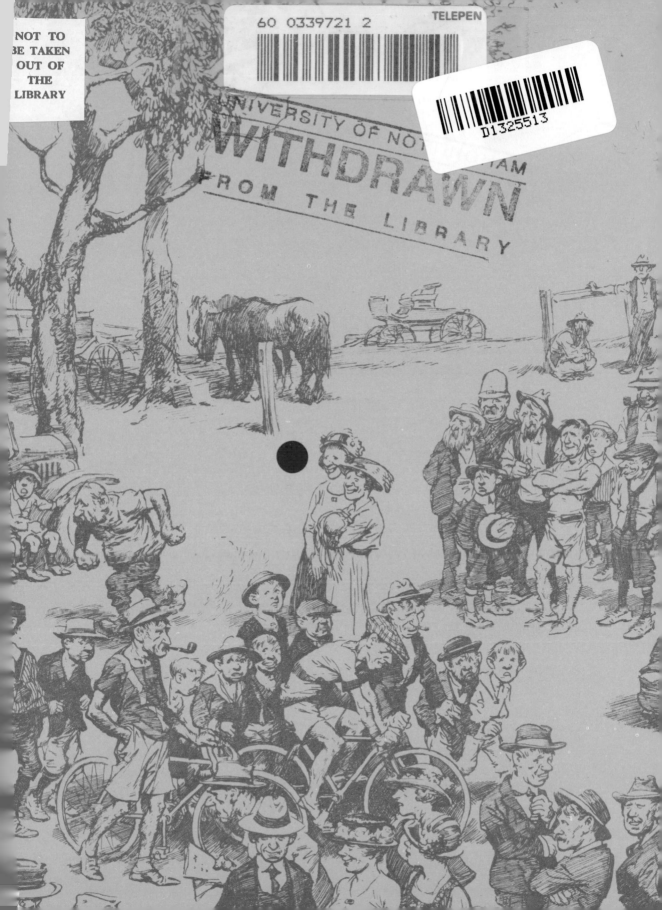

A DICTIONARY OF
AUSTRALIAN
COLLOQUIALISMS

A DICTIONARY OF
AUSTRALIAN
COLLOQUIALISMS

G. A. Wilkes

Sydney University Press

SYDNEY UNIVERSITY PRESS
Press Building, University of Sydney
UNITED KINGDOM, EUROPE, MIDDLE EAST, AFRICA
HB Sales, Enterprise House, Ashford Road, Ashford, Middlesex TW15 1XB, England
NORTH AND SOUTH AMERICA
International Specialized Book Services, P.O. Box 1632, Beaverton, Oregon 97075
United States of America

National Library of Australia Cataloguing-in-Publication data

Wilkes, G. A. (Gerald Alfred), 1927– .
A dictionary of Australian colloquialisms.

New ed.
ISBN 0 424 00113 6.

1. English language – Australia – Terms and phrases. I. Title.

427′.994

First published 1978
Second edition, revised and reset 1985
© M. O. Wilkes 1985
Printed in Australia at Griffin Press Limited, Netley, South Australia

Introduction

WHILE ON STUDY LEAVE in Oxford in 1968, I was asked by an English scholar whether there were any distinctively Australian proverbs. My first response was that there were not, although I could think of expressions like *game as Ned Kelly*, *the biggest liar this side of the black stump*, or *we've got two chances, ours and Buckley's*, that might be difficult for anyone other than an Australian to understand. Some of them might be found in dictionaries, but others – expressions of stoic resignation such as *I suppose it's better than a poke in the eye with a burnt stick*, or *If it was raining palaces, I'd get hit on the head by the dunny door* – almost certainly would not. Having always been interested in Australian idiom, I began to note such expressions when I encountered them, encouraged as I went on by the view of the Oxford authority on proverbs, the late Professor F. P. Wilson, that a man may value an occupation that 'keeps him busy and interested when he is too tired to do anything else'.[1]

As the list of 'proverbial' expressions grew, it became increasingly difficult to explain them without first explaining the colloquial vocabulary they depended upon. *Humping the drum* calls for an explanation of *drum*, which carries a different meaning in *give someone the drum* (or in *run a drum* in racing parlance), and means something else again in a reference to a Cairo *drum* in an Australian war novel. The need was for a collection of Australian colloquialisms.

Colloquialisms are a particular area of Australian English, not the whole field. A dictionary of colloquialisms omits much that a general dictionary of Australian English would include – the names of most plants, animals, trees and fish, for example – while giving more scope to informal usage than a standard dictionary can normally allow. The indispensable pioneer survey of Australian vocabulary in the nineteenth century, Edward E. Morris' *Austral English*[2] is not strong in colloquialisms, partly because it was being compiled in the years just before the vernacular idiom of writers like Lawson and Furphy had become established, and partly because of the compiler's preoccupation with flora and fauna at the expense of other things. The balance was redressed in the twentieth century in the work of Sidney J. Baker, from his early *A Popular Dictionary of Australian Slang*[3] to the revised edition of *The Australian Language*.[4] It is a matter for regret that Baker did not digest all his findings into a comprehensive dictionary of Australian English. The indexes to his books provide

---

[1] 'The Proverbial Wisdom of Shakespeare' in *Shakespearian and Other Studies*, Oxford 1969, p. 144.
[2] *Austral English A Dictionary of Australasian Words Phrases and Usages*, London 1898, facsimile reprint Sydney 1972.
[3] *A Popular Dictionary of Australian Slang*, Melbourne 1941.
[4] *The Australian Language*, Sydney 1966.

alphabetical lists, and *The Drum*[5] includes a dictionary of a kind, but we do not have in tabular form both the words and the supporting quotations needed as a guide to their usage and currency. All later workers in the field must none the less owe a substantial debt to Baker.

What is a colloquialism? It has its existence in familiar speech rather than in the language of the printed page, but the border between the two is constantly shifting. It is obviously a colloquial usage to say *nong* rather than 'simpleton', *come the raw prawn* instead of 'impose upon', *shickered* instead of 'drunk' or *shouse* instead of 'lavatory'. (Colloquialisms are not only less formal, but often also less respectable than 'standard' English.) But the boundaries remain inexact. The word *squatter* (imported from America) began life in Australia as a colloquial term for an unauthorized occupant of land, became 'standard' and respectable when it was defined in government regulations, and in the later nineteenth century asserted itself as a colloquialism again in a slightly hostile way of referring to a 'pastoralist' or 'grazier' – the hostile implication lingers in *squattocracy*. The history of *bushranger* is similarly complex. A dictionary of colloquialisms would not include *kangaroo* or *bandicoot*, which are standard terms, but would include the verb *kangaroo* for the jerky movement of a car and the verb *bandicoot* for stealing potatoes while leaving the surface soil apparently undisturbed, besides such expressions as *kangaroos in the top paddock* and *like a bandicoot on a burnt ridge*. Given that rigid divisions are not enforceable, I have tended to include rather than reject, just as in choosing citations I have not discarded any because they seemed amusing.

The difficulty of deciding what is colloquial is matched by the difficulty of deciding what is 'Australian'. As the example of *kangaroo* indicates, the discovery of Australia added some new words to the English language. The first 'Australianisms' were the words taken over from the Aborigines. Allowing that *bandicoot* is an Indian word, *emu* is Portuguese, and that *piccaninny* is West Indian, there is no difficulty in accepting terms like *boomerang, billabong, corroboree, bingey, humpy, gibber, mulga* and *warrigal* as Australian English, especially as all have been adopted colloquially by whites. Other terms arose as a patois evolved in attempts at communication between black and white – the 'pidgin' to which might be assigned *walkabout, mary* (for a woman), *sugar bag* (wild honey) and other words (e.g. *monaych, nanto*) which no lexicographer seems to have picked up.

As English experience of Australian conditions expanded during the nineteenth century, this stock of words was augmented by the necessity to describe the new circumstances encountered – hence *southerly buster, running a banker,* going *on the wallaby track*. The use of *cockatoo* as a sentinel no doubt arose from observing the habits of cockatoos, as perhaps did *cockatoo* for a small settler. A *pure merino* became someone insistent on his social status; *post-and-rails* was a nickname for a coarse bush tea. The *government stroke* had been observed by the mid-nineteenth century, as had the institutions of *smoko* and (later) *heading them*. The development of the vocabulary becomes a partial record of social history as this process goes on. I have found no record of *bottle-oh* until the turn of the century; *susso* belongs to the Depression; the *toastrack tram* and the *six o'clock swill* occur between the wars; the *brown bomber* and the *reffo* come a little later, and the *Pitt Street farmer* later still – though all may now seem *as Australian as a meat pie*.

Other terms are identifiable as Australian because they derive from persons or place-names, or from figures in Australian folklore. Examples would include *Jacky*

[5] *The Drum Australian Character and Slang*, Sydney 1959.

Howe (for a sleeveless shirt), *furphy, doing a Melba, up there Cazaly, Hay or Hell or Booligal,* the *Barcoo spews* or the *Barcoo salute.* A particular expression like *Sing 'em muck* is associated with Dame Nellie Melba, just as *tall poppies* was given currency by J. T. Lang. We approach the region of folklore with *Buckley's chance, beyond the black stump, Blind Freddie* and *Jimmy Woodser,* although in each case historical evidence has been adduced. There are also a number of rather synthetic Australian expressions fostered by comic strips (e.g. *stiffen the lizards*) or by entertainers (e.g. *Cop this, young 'Arry*) which have become part of colloquial usage as life imitates art. The most recent example is the vocabulary of Barry McKenzie (e.g. *go for the big spit*), described by its inventor as a pastiche in which 'words like *cobber* and *bonzer* still intrude as a sop to Pommy readers, though such words are seldom, if ever, used in present-day Australia'.[6]

Indigenous expressions, wherever they can be certified as such, are the first category of colloquialisms within Australian English. A second consists of terms that did not so much begin life in Australia as find a new life here. Words like *dinkum, bowyangs* and *damper,* as W. S. Ramson has shown, had their origin in England, but have so fallen into disuse there that an Englishman encountering them in Australia may have to ask their meaning. They are most often dialect words, sometimes surviving in parts of England, but in Australia having no restriction of class or region. When the twelve-volume Oxford dictionary was completed in 1928, the word *skerrick* was not included. When the first *Supplement* appeared in 1933, *skerrick* was entered as 'Austral. colloq. A small fragment' with a citation from Ion L. Idriess. It had already been recorded in the *English Dialect Dictionary* in 1905, with citations going back to 1863, in exactly the 'Austral.' sense: 'a particle, a morsel, scrap, atom', and it was this dialectal usage which had become established in Australia. Australian English may have no particular claim to *skerrick,* still used in parts of England, although its use in Australia is more widespread. But it indicates how the currency of a word, rather than its point of origin, may persuade a lexicographer how to classify it. Terms that pass completely out of currency in Britain may eventually survive as part of Australian English alone. This may already have appeared with *dinkum* and *bowyangs,* and words like *shanghai, larrikin* and *ringer* have a similar history.

Sometimes the source is not so much a dialect as the language of a particular class. The convicts brought with them the thieves' slang of England, which instead of remaining the property of criminals often passed into general use – for example *plant* in the sense of 'hide', *school* for a collection of gamblers, or *skinner* for a betting coup in racing. The practice of *scaling* a ride on trams may have gone out with the Sydney trams themselves, but a character in a Patrick White play still uses *shake* in the sense of 'steal'. Similarly the technical language of gold-mining, much of it brought from America, has made *pan out* an expression that no one would now connect with the wash-dish, just as the adjective *nuggety* (itself of dialectal origin) would not now recall the goldrush of the 1850s. The practice of *chiacking,* apparently the prerogative of costermongers in nineteenth-century England, is in Australia available to all.

To the same general category belong words of overseas origin which in Australia have undergone a change or extension of meaning. The use of *bail up* for securing a cow for milking derives from the English word *bail,* but in Australia *bailing up* came especially to be applied to the activities of bushrangers, while a city-dweller even now may run the risk of being *bailed up* in the street by a talkative acquaintance. *Swag* was originally an English word for the booty of a thief; in Australia it is extended to the

[6] Barry Humphries, 'Barry McKenzie', *Times Literary Supplement,* 16 September 1965, p. 812.

legitimate baggage of an itinerant. *Spell* is commonly used in England for a turn of work; in Australia it is more commonly used for an interval of rest. *Bastard* in England either imputes illegitimacy or serves as a general term of insult; in Australia it can be an affectionate mode of address.

All these words have therefore acquired particular Australian senses, not shared by the linguistic community from which they came. The same holds for words of foreign derivation absorbed into Australian idiom. *Swy* (for 'two-up') is from the German *zwei*, as *spieler* is from *spielen* and *shicer* from *scheissen* (possibly mediated through English and American slang); *shickered* and *put the moz on* are from Yiddish; *donah* and *bimbo* are from Spanish and Italian, though probably not directly; *hoot* (for 'money') has been traced to Maori and *donga* to South African. All have developed meanings here not found in the original language, much as the original language may help to explain them.

The second general category of Australianisms therefore consists of words of overseas origin which have either survived here while becoming obsolete elsewhere, or else have undergone semantic change. The third category is the most uncertain. It consists of words which do occur in the same sense in other linguistic communities, but on which the information is lacking that would establish priority or relative currency. *Swamper* is recorded in American English in 1850 as a 'road-breaker, who is constantly employed in keeping the roads open', especially in logging operations, and in 1870 as 'a man who goes with the driver of a 10, 12 or 14-mule team as his assistant'. This sufficiently antedates the Australian use of the word (which again develops in a slightly different way) to establish that *swamper* came into Australian English from North America. The same would apply to *corduroy, rouseabout* and *shinplaster*. But what of *knock* in the sense of 'disparage'? It is recorded in Australia in 1892, in America in 1896, in Canada in 1906 and thereafter in England. It has a general currency in Australia, and has been taken as referring to a national characteristic (a book was published in 1972 with the title *Knockers*), but it is not an Australianism of the same order as the other two categories I have distinguished. For a modern colloquialism, *knock* is comparatively well documented: for dozens of other terms there is hardly any guide at all, except that Partridge, Mathews or other chroniclers of slang elsewhere do not record them. Is *go for the doctor* used in racing parlance outside Australia? Did the advice *bum to mum* really originate with sporting coaches in Victoria? Did the ironical expression *That'll be the day!* arise first in New Zealand, and then find its way to the United States? The colloquial language is not well enough documented at present for these questions to be answered. One can only record the occurrence of the expressions in Australian English for the benefit of researchers elsewhere.

The problem of what to include or exclude is complicated by the ephemerality of colloquialisms themselves. We no longer use *logs* for gaol, offer *flash your dover* as an invitation to eat, or refer to canned meat as *tinned dog*. As these expressions may be encountered by readers of Marcus Clarke or Henry Lawson, a dictionary of colloquialisms should explain them. A reader born since World War II may be mystified by *the man outside Hoyts, more arse than Jessie,* or *like a pakapoo ticket* (as a synonym for untidiness). The future biographer of Prince Charles will no doubt be able to understand his reported remark at an Australia Day dinner in 1973 that 'all the faces here this evening seem to be bloody Poms', but may be puzzled by the Prince's joke about having his name linked romantically with 'the naughty Nullarbor nymph'. Even so short-lived a phenomenon as *the Nullarbor nymph* has found its way into the colloquial language, and so should be recorded.

The value of any survey of colloquialisms will rest finally on what it records. This dictionary is planned, in a modest way, 'on historical principles'. It seeks to record the history of each word, through examples of usage. The citations are the most important part of the dictionary, as the evidence on which it rests. To have simply listed the words themselves, with definitions, would have been to risk giving them all the same status. It is important to see that examples of *bonzer* fall mainly between 1900 and the 1940s, and that by 1969 the word is being described as 'an anachronism'. On the other hand *beaut* has gained in popularity, with its allied expressions *you beaut!* and *beauty* (pronounced *bewdy*, and conveying full agreement or approval). Any historical record of usage is uncertain, as the first occurrence of a term is usually beyond recovery, and the printed evidence on which one has to rely is always in arrears – thus *root* (for intercourse) was used in speech long before it came to be recorded in print. But it is possible to gain some impression from the quotations given of the period to which *brickfielder* and *humping the drum* chiefly belong, when *compo* and *sickie* came into vogue, how *bush telegraph* and *crawler* developed different meanings.

I have not attempted to distinguish levels of colloquial usage in the way that was still possible for Partridge in his invaluable dictionary of slang, by the use of terms like 'low' or 'vulg.'. At a time when the four-letter words are gaining common acceptance, the exercise has little point. More sensitivity is now attached to terms like *abo*, *boong* and *poofter*, and I have found a continued usefulness in the old-fashioned labels *derogatory* and *jocular*. Thus *reffo* and *silvertail* would have a *derogatory* implication; examples of *jocular* usage would be found in expressions of interstate rivalry: *the coathanger*, *the only river in the world that flows upside down*, *Bananalander*, *sand-groper*. Most colloquial terms for non-Australians are derogatory, although the gradations are subtle. A *Pommy bastard* is viewed with disfavour, but one who comes to be described as *not a bad poor bastard* has won grudging acceptance.

All dictionaries are tentative, and a colloquial dictionary is most tentative of all. Comments and further information from readers will be welcomed, and may contribute to the full *Dictionary of Australian English* being prepared by the Australian Language Research Centre at the University of Sydney. I am indebted to the expertise of my research assistant, Miss E. Morrell, at an important stage in the assembling of material, and for help at other stages to Miss Jennifer Urquhart and Mrs Jan Kociumbas. A draft of the entries from H to Z, as it then stood, was deposited with the *Oxford English Dictionary Supplement* in May 1975, when the *Supplement* editor, Mr R. W. Burchfield, generously provided access to the material in his charge – a courtesy that has continued in correspondence since. For the deficiencies that remain in the present text, I am of course responsible alone.

G. A. Wilkes
University of Sydney   1978

Preface to Second Edition

The appearance of a second edition of the *Dictionary*, considerably revised and enlarged, gives me an opportunity to thank all those who offered comments and suggestions on the first edition. While my correspondents are too numerous to be listed individually, I am particularly grateful for the interest taken by Mr D. C. Griffiths, Sir Paul Hasluck, the late Professor H. J. Oliver, and Mr E. G. Whitlam. I have relied on the continuing research assistance of Georgina Bitcon, with help in the earlier stages of the work from Susan Bridekirk, and in the later stages from Jennifer Evans.

G. A. W.

Abbreviations

Acland	L. G. D. Acland, 'A Sheep Station Glossary' (1933) in *The Early Canterbury Runs*, Christchurch 1951.
Baker 1941	Sidney J. Baker, *A Popular Dictionary of Australian Slang*, Melbourne 1941.
Baker 1943	Sidney J. Baker, *A Popular Dictionary of Australian Slang*, 2nd edn, Melbourne 1943.
Baker 1945	Sidney J. Baker, *The Australian Language*, Sydney 1945.
Baker 1953	Sidney J. Baker, *Australia Speaks*, Sydney 1953.
Baker 1959	Sidney J. Baker, *The Drum Australian Character and Slang*, Sydney 1959.
Baker 1966	Sidney J. Baker, *The Australian Language*, Sydney 1966.
Barrère and Leland	A. Barrère and C. G. Leland, *A Dictionary of Slang, Jargon and Cant*, 2 vols, Edinburgh 1889–90.
EDD	*The English Dialect Dictionary*, ed. Joseph Wright, 6 vols, Oxford 1898–1905.
Franklyn	Julian Franklyn, *A Dictionary of Rhyming Slang*, 2nd edn, London 1961.
Grose	Francis Grose, *A Classical Dictionary of the Vulgar Tongue*, London 1785, 1788, 1790, 1811.
Hotten	John Camden Hotten, *A Dictionary of Modern Slang, Cant and Vulgar Words*, London 1859, 1860, 1864.
HRA	*Historical Records of Australia*, Series I, 33 vols, Sydney 1914–25.
HRNSW	*Historical Records of New South Wales*, 7 vols, Sydney 1892–1901.
HRV	*Historical Records of Victoria*, 3 vols to date, Melbourne 1981–.
Lawson *Prose*	Henry Lawson, *Collected Prose*, ed. Colin Roderick, 2 vols, Sydney 1972.
Lawson *Verse*	Henry Lawson, *Collected Verse*, ed. Colin Roderick, 3 vols, Sydney 1967–9.
Mathews	M. M. Mathews, *A Dictionary of Americanisms*, Chicago 1966.
Morris	Edward E. Morris, *Austral English A Dictionary of Australasian Words Phrases and Usages*, London 1898; facsimile reprint Sydney 1972.
O'Brien and Stephens	S. E. O'Brien and A. G. Stephens, 'Materials for a Dictionary of Australian Slang 1900–1910', Sydney, Mitchell Library MS Q427.9/0.
obs.	obsolete
OED	*The Oxford English Dictionary*, 13 vols, Oxford 1933; *Supplement*, 3 vols to date, 1972–.
Partridge	Eric Partridge, *A Dictionary of Slang and Unconventional English*, 2 vols, London 1970.
Ramson	W. S. Ramson, *Australian English An Historical Study of the Vocabulary 1788–1898*, Canberra 1966.
SND	*The Scottish National Dictionary*, 10 vols, Edinburgh 1932–76.
Turner	G. W. Turner, *The English Language in Australia and New Zealand*, 2nd edn, London 1972.
Vaux	'A Vocabulary of the Flash Language' (1812) in *The Memoirs of James Hardy Vaux*, ed. Noel McLachlan, London 1964.
V.F.L.	The Victorian Football League
Wentworth and Flexner	Harold Wentworth and Stuart Berg Flexner, *Dictionary of American Slang*, 2nd Supplemented edn, New York 1975.

A

abo *n. & a.* Australian Aboriginal. Not always intended as derogatory, but now increasingly taken to be so [abbr.]

1922 *Bulletin* 5 Jan. 22: I was sheltering from a hailstorm under the verandah of the pub, and among my fellow refugees was an abo. who had been to the mission school.

1934 Jean Devanny *Out of Such Fires* 18: 'Wouldn't take long to get back to the abo state. A few hundred years, perhaps?'

1944 *Salt* 8 May 19: 'Abo Paints his World' [article on Albert Namatjira]

1958 Gavin Casey *Snowball* 118: 'You wait till he gets a bit older. Them abos always go t' the pack,' a cynic told him.

1966 Peter Mathers *Trap* 185: 'You're sure it's not La Perouse, the Abo settlement, you want?'

1970 Barry Oakley *A Salute to the Great McCarthy* 79: 'What ya do out there? Play in bare feet, like the abos?'

1982 *Sun-Herald* 14 Nov. 70: In Moree, the Aborigines are 'the dark community' or, more crudely, 'the Abos'.

abos, give it back to the   As for **give it back to the blacks** q.v.

1951 Dymphna Cusack and Florence James *Come in Spinner* 126: 'This house is a hundred years old.' 'Then it's time they gave it back to the Abos.'

acca   An academic

1977 K. S. Inglis *Meanjin* 90: Accas and Ockers: Australia's New Dictionaries [heading]

1982 *Sydney Morning Herald* 3 Sep. 12: N.S.W. University market day ... Intended for the whole community, not just accas (academic persons).

1984 *Age* (Melbourne) 23 Mar. Weekender 10: Ackers up from the university who read Saturday's 'Sydney Morning Herald' (it used to be the 'Guardian') at half-time.

accord, the   The 'Statement of accord by the Australian Labor Party and the Australian Council of Trade Unions regarding economic policy' foreshadowed by Mr R. J. Hawke in his election policy speech on 16 February 1983, and adopted by a union conference on 21 February. The document has been broadly interpreted as guaranteeing wage restraint by the unions in return for full wage indexation, as part of a prices and incomes policy.

1983 R. J. Hawke *Sydney Morning Herald* 17 Feb. 12: As a result of the months of painstaking consultation, discussion and work, we, the representatives of the incoming Labor Government, have reached an historic accord with the trade union movement which will form the basis for a firm, genuine and workable prices and incomes policy for this nation. [election policy speech]

1985 Robert Haupt *Sydney Morning Herald* 26 Jan. Mag. 16: The ritual elements of the Accord – the Hawkus-pocus – are stressed almost in the Prime Minister's every speech. By feats of logic-chop and circular argument, pretty well anything from Geneva arms talks to the America's Cup

1

victory can be pressed into service as omens or totems of the Accord.

ace   Probably a variant of *arse*: the expression **on one's ace** means 'alone, left to one's own resources', and could be associated with the score of 'one' in dice.
  1906 Edward Dyson *Fact'ry 'Ands* 298: 'Would yeh believe it, that tin was tickin' like forty watches, 'n' when Sniff stirred it, you'd think it was full iv live dried peas, 'n' was rattlin' on its ace.'
  1908 E. G. Murphy *Jarrahland Jingles* 58: Brim's in London on his 'ace'.
  1934 Archer Russell *A Tramp Royal* 213: 'They're capable of good work at times,' said a 'boss cattleman' to whom I had applied for his opinion of the merits and demerits of the aboriginal as stockman, 'but you've got to be with them. Send 'em out "on their ace" and they'll probably "go camp" under the first shady tree they come to.'
  1953 Baker 131: *ace, on one's* On one's own. [as prison slang]
  1984 *Age* (Melbourne) 31 Mar. 11: It's either a Waltham Cross or a Gordo Blanco if you happen to be a viniculturist and fascinated by these matters; or a sweet white grape if you happen to just tread on some and fall ace over elbow in the middle of them.

ace it up   Stop it: *rare* [unexplained]
  1965 Graham McInnes *The Road to Gundagai* 164: 'Hey, ace it up Bill, that hurts.' Bill grinned and loosened the tourniquet slightly.

Achiever, the Quiet   see **Quiet**

acid, to put the ~ on   To make the kind of demand (for money, information, or sex) that will either yield results or eliminate that possibility [f. *acid test*]
  1906 Edward Dyson *Fact'ry 'Ands* 215: Evidently it was Mr Cato's intention to try the acid on Feathers again. Ibid. 210: ''E [the Toucher] puts ther acid on so't yeh think it's the milk iv 'uman kindness.'
  1919 W. H. Downing *Digger Dialects* 40: *To put the acid on* (1) Ask. (2) Test. (3) Put a stop to.
  1925 Arthur Wright *The Boy from Bullarah* 16: 'He owes me anything up to a score of quids . . . I'm going to put the acid on.'
  1942 Leonard Mann *The Go-Getter* 234: Somehow they had learned Carkeek's share in this business, but when they had put the acid on him they had found he could not help them.
  1948 Ruth Park *Poor Man's Orange* 165: 'I'll tell every feller I know she's easy, and she won't be able to go down the street without having the acid put on her.'

1966 Patrick White *The Solid Mandala* 147: 'And a woman like that, married to such a sawney bastard, she wouldn't wait for 'em to put the acid on 'er.'
see **hard word**

acre (acher)   Buttocks, backside [? f. appearance]
  1938 Heard in conversation.
  1966 Baker 169: *acre* the anus. [as World War II slang]
  1971 Frank Hardy *The Outcasts of Foolgarah* 18: Wiping between his toes [after a shower] and falling on his acre. Ibid. 94: 'I'll give you a free kick up the acher if you're not careful.'
  1973 Roland Robinson *The Drift of Things* 164: Because they used to surf in the nude and lie among the flowering tea-trees on the sides of the valley sunbathing, one shack dweller . . . called his shack 'Sunburned Acres.'

Acre, the Dirty Half   see **Dirty Half Acre**

act, to put on an   To indulge in a tantrum, make a fuss (esp. with an implication of pretence or over-statement) [f. *act* (a role)]
  1945 Margaret Trist *Now That We're Laughing* 96: She groaned agonizingly. 'Get her something, quick,' cried Joyce. 'It's only Daffy putting on an act,' said Pearl.
  1949 Lawson Glassop *Lucky Palmer* 60: 'You should have seen me put on an act when they gave me a rocking horse for Christmas.'
  1957 Judah Waten *Shares in Murder* 58: 'Don't put on an act,' he said half pleading, half angry.
  1962 Criena Rohan *The Delinquents* 113: 'Do you think she's stacking on an act?' asked the younger cop. 'Or do you think she's sick, or in the D.T.'s?'
  1983 Georgia Savage *The Tournament* 61: That ability of a woman to not only put on an act, but while she was in the process of it to believe the act was the genuine thing, always knocked me out.

Adelaide River Stakes   The exodus from Darwin to the Adelaide River following the Japanese bombing raid of 19 February 1942
  1966 Douglas Lockwood *Australia's Pearl Harbour* 143: Men unquestionably ran away, but they were not only airmen. The leaders in what later became known as the Adelaide River Stakes included civilians who had not been under direct attack.

adjective, the great Australian   see **Australian**

Adrian Quist   see **Quist**

Adventure, the Great   see **Great**

aerial pingpong   Australian Rules Football: *jocu-*

lar [f. the long kicks and high leaps which are features of the game]

1965 Frank Hardy *The Yarns of Billy Borker* 43: Melbourne Mick would say, 'Australian Rules draws bigger crowds in Melbourne than Rugby in Sydney.' 'What?' Sydney Sam would say, 'that's not football, mate, it's aerial ping-pong.'

1973 *Sun* (Sydney) 4 Apr. 93: Aussie Rules, or aerial pingpong as it is sometimes called, is being telecast live from Melbourne by Nine.

1980 *West Australian* (Perth) 2 Apr. 7: The game cynics call 'aerial ping-pong'.

1984 *Australian* 20 Mar. 10: I was dismayed to read in your editorial (12/3) the reference to Australian football as 'aerial ping pong'. Perhaps you could explain to me the similarity between Australian football and table tennis.

aerialist

1970 Barry Oakley *A Salute to the Great McCarthy* 30: The high and mighty MacGuinness, the aerialist who drew the crowds and then fell.

after Afternoon, superseded by **arvo** q.v. [abbr.]

1933 Norman Lindsay *Saturdee* 193: 'So what price comin' a walk with me this after?'

1939 Leonard Mann *Mountain Flat* 242: 'This after we'll go for a swim.'

Akubra Hat [brand name]

1930 *Bulletin* 23 Jul. 16: Hamlet himself stirs pity in the soft-hearted boy, who is overheard to remark that the 'Prince is taking a bit of a risk getting about in the cold without his Akubra.'

1972 Patrick White *The Eye of the Storm* 450: The solicitor was looking at her from under the brim of his Akubra.

1977 *Southerly* 51: He ... took his leprous Akubra from a table near the door, perched it on top of his straggling grey hair.

1981 *Australian* 11 Mar. 9: These days, even plain clothes demons don't wear the snap-brim Akubras which villains found such a useful tip-off.

alas! milfissed the balfastards see **balfastards**

Albany Doctor A cool and refreshing breeze [place-name in W.A.]

1922 Edward Meryon *At Holland's Tank* 162: The south breeze, better known in those parts as the Albany Doctor, had arrived.

1937 A. W. Upfield *Mr Jelly's Business* 57: The 'Albany Doctor' people called it, because the strong cool wind from Albany way swept clear the bodily and mental languors brought on by the heat of the long day.

1979 Dorothy Hewett *The Man from Mukinupin* 90: 'The Albany doctor'll be blowing up soon.'

1983 John K. Ewers *Long Enough for a Joke* 105: The nights cool with often a blustering southerly

the locals called 'the Albany doctor'.

see **Fremantle doctor**

Alberts, Prince Rags wound about the feet in place of socks [f. the alleged poverty of Prince Albert before he became Victoria's consort: listed by Partridge as nautical]

c. **1888** 'Sam Griffith' *Old Bush Songs* ed. Stewart and Keesing (1957) 203: I knew his feet were blistered/From the Alberts that he wore.

1903 Joseph Furphy *Such is Life* (1944) 39: Unlapping from his feet the inexpensive substitute for socks known as 'prince-alberts', he artistically spread the redolent swaths across his boots to receive the needful benefit of the night air.

1912 G. H. Gibson *Ironbark Splinters* 44: 'Prince Alberts' ain't the fashion now,/The shearers all wears socks.

1949 John Morrison *The Creeping City* 112–13: 'I once walked all the way from Nar-nar-goon to Thargomindah with nothing on me feet but Prince Alberts!'

Al Capone Telephone [rhyming slang]

1980 *Weekend Australian* 20 Dec. 14: Our colleague got on the Al Capone and harangued the store.

alec, aleck A stupid fellow, an ass [f. *smart alec* U.S. 1865 Mathews]

1944 Lawson Glassop *We Were the Rats* 168: 'I reckon if I got stomach ache all you alecks would know almost before I did.'

1946 Margaret Trist *What Else is There?* 90: 'If a man goes on the booze and belts you up, you know where you stand. But when they start in preachin' I kind of feel a big aleck.'

1962 Alan Seymour *The One Day of the Year* 64: 'He looked such a big aleck, marching along as though he'd won both wars single-handed.'

1962 Stuart Gore *Down the Golden Mile* 96: 'Don't be an aleck!' the other returned brusquely. 'There haven't been any boongs – not real myalls – around here since Adam was a boy!'

Alf The uncultivated Australian (the opposite to **Roy** q.v.) now being superseded by **ocker** [see quot. 1965]

1960 Murray Sayle 'As Far As You Can Go' *Encounter* May 28: The Australian worker, the 'Alf' as we call him.

1965 E. Morris 'Reliques of Sope' [Neil C. Hope, d. 1964] *Nation* 27 Nov. 21: Middle-class 'Roys' in sports cars and yachting jackets, and red-necked 'Alfs' who want to fight those who swear in front of ladies. (It was Sope who invented the now-ubiquitous term.)

1968 Craig McGregor *People, Politics and Pop* 163: Alf is always someone else, the bloke in the

bungalow, Fred down the road, dead from the neck up, a talking beer gut from the neck down.
1974 *Australian* 23 Nov. 21: He does not want to show his films in the film workshop-co-op settings and they are too way out for your ordinary Alf.
1980 *Weekend Australian* 18 Oct. Mag. 7: Trendies must own a colored television set, preferably with a small screen and rabbit-ear antennas. Remote control selectors are Alf.

Alf-land   Australia
1971 Craig McGregor *Don't Talk to Me about Love* 130: 'We're all expatriates here, living an expatriate life in the middle of Alf-land.'

Alfred, Royal   An elaborate swag [? f. Alfred, Duke of Edinburgh who toured Australia 1867–8]
1902 Henry Lawson 'The Romance of the Swag' *Prose* i 501–2: The weight of the swag varies from the light rouseabout's swag, containing one blanket and a clean shirt, to the 'Royal Alfred', with tent and all complete, and weighing part of a ton.

Alfreds, Prince   As for **Prince Alberts**
1896 Henry Lawson 'Stragglers' *Prose* i 92–3: Occasionally someone gets some water in an old kerosene tin and washes a shirt or pair of trousers, and a pair or two of socks – or foot-rags (Prince Alfreds, they call them).

Alice, the   1   Alice Springs N.T.; more recently 'Alice'
1901 F. J. Gillen *Diary* (1968) 92: I was sleeping on a canvas covered stretcher which I procured at the Alice.
1933 R. B. Plowman *The Man from Oodnadatta* 140: 'I just dropped on them quite unexpectedly. I didn't know they had left the Alice.'
1944 Frank Clune *The Red Heart* 16: Arrived at 'The Alice' by plane, I decided to investigate the rumour of Lasseter's resurrection.
1953 *The Sunburnt Country* ed. Ian Bevan 75: When, years ago, I first visited that part of the world, a journey to 'the Alice' was a journey indeed.
1959 Lyndon Rose *The Country of the Dead* 159: 'I'll let them know in at Alice and out at the mission.'
1961 Jack Danvers *The Living Come First* 16: 'I met them in Alice a while back.'
1979 *Age* (Melbourne) 31 Oct. 11: Housing issue splits 'Alice' [heading]
1982 *NT News* (Darwin) 1 May 28: Alice swings toward home units [heading]
2   Train running between Sydney and Alice Springs
1984 *Australian* 16 Jan. 1: The Alice, a new rail service operating weekly from Sydney to Alice Springs, was due to leave tomorrow, but has also been cancelled.

alkie   An alcoholic [abbr.] [also U.S.]
1964 Bruce Beaver *The Hot Sands* 16: Ben Tickell, the regular night porter, was an alkie if ever she had seen one.
1971 Rena Briand *White Man in a Hole* 31: Kind-hearted, he'd share ... his last cigarettes with the alkies at the Front Bar.
1975 Elizabeth Riley *All That False Instruction* 126: 'Tried to think what I'd feel like if I was a sixty-odd alkie.'

all about   Collective term for workforce on a station, esp. Aborigines [Pidgin]
1908 Mrs Aeneas Gunn *We of the Never-Never* 302: Cheon was announcing dinner in his own peculiar way. 'Din-ner! Mis-sus! Boss! All about!' he chanted.
1935 Mary and Elizabeth Durack *All-About The Story of a Black Community on Argyle Station, Kimberley* [book title]
1951 Ernestine Hill *The Territory* 443: All-about (Pidgin) Everyone. Everywhere.
1956 Tom Ronan *Moleskin Midas* 235: 'What this yarn allabout got where you going to send my boy to whitefeller school?' she demanded.

all alone like a country dunny   see **dunny, shouse**

all prick and ribs like a drover's (shearer's, swaggie's) dog   i.e. lean but eager
1971 Frank Hardy *The Outcasts of Foolgarah* 35: To see them at work, Little Tich all prick and ribs like a swaggie's dog.
1981 *National Times* 25 Jan. 24: He was like a drover's dog, all —— and ribs.

alley   A marble [f. *alley* a choice marble or taw OED 1720–1865]
1   *To pass (toss) in one's alley* To give in, die
1916 C. J. Dennis *The Moods of Ginger Mick* 109: But if I dodge, an' keep out 'uv the rain,/An' don't toss in me alley 'fore we wins.
1924 *Truth* 27 Apr. 6: *Alleys, to toss in the* To give in.
1933 Norman Lindsay *Saturdee* 23: 'This book says a bloke kicked the bucket, an' Bill says it means a bloke pegged out, so what's it mean?' 'Means a bloke passed his alley in.'
1937 Vance Palmer *Legend for Sanderson* 31: 'Too much beer over the weekend, wasn't it, Neil? First time I've known you to toss in the alley.'
1960 Jack McKinney *The Well* in *Khaki Bush and Bigotry* ed. Eunice Hanger (1968) 228: 'Don't sling in yer alley, missus. There's a good time comin'.'
2   *To make one's alley good* To make the grade, improve one's status or prospects
1924 C. J. Dennis *Rose of Spadgers* 160: That 'e

4

'ad swore to get me one uv those / Fine days, an' make 'is alley good with Rose.

1952 T. A. G. Hungerford *The Ridge and the River* 109: 'That's all right,' Shearwood said soberly. 'It makes Wilder's alley good, but it doesn't win any popularity stakes for you.'

1964 *Sydney Morning Herald* 10 Aug. 2: 'Hey, Tom! Joe is making his alley good with Nelly Bli down be th' crik.'

1975 Xavier Herbert *Poor Fellow My Country* 362: Berated Pat for taking up the cause of a scab in order to make his alley good with a designing female.

see **marble**

alt   Follower of an alternative lifestyle

1981 *Age* (Melbourne) 15 Sep. 11: The North Coast is the heart of alternative lifestyles, but there are no visits to communes. We are efficiently informed that there are no votes in hippies and 'alts'.

1984 *Sydney Morning Herald* 8 Feb. 9: Dozens of long-haired and bearded 'new settlers' hang around outside the Rainbow Cafe [at Nimbin] with babies on their hips, or lie in the cool of the park. Although they call themselves new settlers, most other people refer to them as alternatives, or alts.

amateur players, a trap for   see **trap**

amber fluid, liquid   Beer

1959 *Bulletin* 4 Feb. 35: Dutchy and I were still wary of the amber fluid, but were getting a bit gamer with it.

1965 John Beede *They Hosed Them Out* 185: We grogged on till closing time; it was evident that we all had one thing in common – a liking for the amber liquid.

1976 Dorothy Hewett *This Old Man Comes Rolling Home* 77: 'Drown yer sorrows, drown yer sorrows in the amber fluid.'

1980 *NT News* (Darwin) 24 Jan. 6: There'll be 360 meat pies and 30 kilos of snags to demolish, washed down with 40 cartons of amber fluid.

America's Cup, Home of the   see **Home**

amster, ampster   Confederate of the manager of a sideshow, with the task of attracting custom [rhyming slang *Amsterdam* = *ram* q.v.]

1941 Kylie Tennant *The Battlers* 181: As soon as the showman begins to shout: 'All right, the show is commencing Roll up! Roll up!' ... the amster rushes eagerly up to the ticket window and says: 'Right-o, mister, I'll have a ticket.' He pretends to pass his money over, and is handed a ticket. His brother-amsters form into an impatient queue behind him and file into the tent at the head of the multitude who, like sheep, will follow the leader, but will not be the first to pay their money.

1957 D'Arcy Niland *Call Me When the Cross Turns Over* 101: Barbie, playing ampster, went up and bought a bottle.

1975 Hal Porter *The Extra* 244: A shady Soho club patronised by dips, amsters, off-duty prostitutes.

angora   sc. goat, usually in the phrase 'act (play) the angora': *obsolescent*

1899 *Truth* 8 Oct. 5: Refrain from playing the giddy ox, the antic angora, and the cowardly, foul-mouthed dirty devil generally.

1908 Henry Fletcher *Dads and Dan between Smokes* 61: But ther cove wot piles up a big fortchin fer others ter spend is a double-barrelled angora.

1922 Henry Lawson 'The Last Rose of Winter' *Prose* i 906: He had that lovable expression of a Bushman admiring his mate making a giddy angora of himself.

1937 Vance Palmer *Legend for Sanderson* 27: 'Don't be an angora, Leo. What d' you take me for?'

1945 Cecil Mann *The River* 142: 'And you, Clarkey – you, you great angora – standing there, leaning on the rail, scared stiff.'

animal   A term of contempt, esp. since World War II

1892 William Lane *The Workingman's Paradise* 80: There we were, poor, ragged, hungry wretches ... and that animal ran up a great wall in our faces so that we couldn't see the grass.'

1945 Baker 156: *animal* A term of contempt for a person. [World War II slang]

1946 K. S. Prichard *The Roaring Nineties* 317: 'To hell with Sir John Forrest and any other animals like him!'

1955 John Morrison *Black Cargo* 19: 'I had mates starved in that strike, and that animal ...'

1959 Dorothy Hewett *Bobbin Up* 57: 'I've never met a copper yet was any good. They're all a lotta animals.'

1968 Geoffrey Dutton *Andy* 58: 'Where did you two animals come from? Anybody'd think we were in the bloody Army.'

1974 David Ireland *Burn* 141: I reckon he knew about the other officers tossed overboard on the way home for their bastardry ... Paid in full for the animals they were.

ankle-biter   Child

1981 *Sun-Herald* 2 Aug. 167: The middle-aged Petula Clark does the Julie Andrews bit, skipping and trilling over the edelweiss with the Von Trapp ankle-biters.

1984 *Sydney Morning Herald* 26 Jan. 9: Travelling overseas with an ankle-biter has its advantages. It keeps you out of museums, cathedrals and temples and shows you the raw side of life: playgrounds, supermarkets, laundrettes and public toilets.

Anthony Horderns, Thursday or see **Thursday**

Anzac The code address adopted by General Birdwood in Egypt for the Australian and New Zealand Army Corps in 1915, and used by him in naming the landing-place at Gallipoli 'Anzac Cove'. Used colloquially in various senses:
1   The beachhead, or the campaign more generally
1915 C. E. W. Bean *Diary* 29 Apr. in *Gallipoli Correspondent* (1983) 83: The jealousy that existed between N.Z. and Australia in Cairo vanished at one blow on the first day at Anzac – vanished utterly as far as the men were concerned.
1916 Tom Skeyhill *Soldier Songs from Anzac* 26: But it's different 'ere at Anzac; / Mr Turk! 'e ain't arf slick.
1936 Miles Franklin *All That Swagger* 447: They remain incapable of instructing the rising generation that the glories of Anzac were as empty as all military glory down the centuries, symbolised by a tattered flag or a suit of rusty armour in a silent museum.
1944 Rex Ingamells *Selected Poems* 32: Our boast that Federation made a nation; / our boast that Anzac proved it with our blood / are tragic fictions.
1970 Donald Horne *The Next Australia* 153: One even hears rumours of homosexuality at Anzac.
2   A member of the Australian and New Zealand Army Corps
1916 Let. in Bill Gammage *The Broken Years* (1974) 156: So three cheers for the Anzac and the early ending of this sinful game.
1919 Edward Dyson *Hello Soldier* 18: Little Abdul's quite a fighter ... / But the Anzacs have him snouted.
1939 Herbert M. Moran *Viewless Winds* 163: The only other drinker was a grey-haired man with a hard cadaverous look who wore the badge of an original Anzac.
1962 Alan Seymour *The One Day of the Year* 73: 'When we went in there we was nobody. When we come out we was famous. [*Smiles*] Anzacs.'
1978 Patsy Adam-Smith *The Anzacs* [book title]
3   An Australian soldier in a later war, esp. on service overseas (sometimes close to 4)
1943 *Khaki and Green* 107: Greetings such as 'You'll do me, you big bronzed Anzac' are not encouraged.
1970 Richard Beilby *No Medals for Aphrodite* 169: 'Get on the big, bronzed Anzac, will yer!' Darcy mocked.
1982 *Sydney Morning Herald* 6 Feb. 3: Smaller role for Anzacs in Sinai [heading] Australia's contribution to the Sinai peace-keeping force will

be only about half as big as originally planned. see **bronze gods**
4   A stereotype of the Australian male
1957 Randolph Stow *The Bystander* 21: 'It's just the way I am. The lean bronzed Anzac type. Don't you agree?'
1965 Eric Lambert *The Long White Night* 8: Most of them had come to the hall straight from the pubs. They were dinkum diggers and bronzed Anzacs all over again. They were perpetuating the Australian Myth.
1974 *Sun-Herald* 15 Sep. 43: Although tarnished over the years, the Australian image of the healthy, bronzed Anzac still lingers as part of our folklore.
1982 *Sydney Morning Herald* 21 Jan. 17: Not so long ago, male cosmetics and skin care products were a definite no-no for the average bronzed Anzac.
5   See quot. 1980
1980 *Sun* (Sydney) 26 Feb. 37: In the food game, an Anzac is a chicken, lamb, porker or calf that has lost a limb, or been badly damaged (wounded in action) on the processing line.

AO The Australian Opera
1984 *Australian* 15 Aug. 8: Not every opera lover stays an AO supporter [heading]

aorta Strine version of 'they ought to'
1971 Frank Hardy *The Outcasts of Foolgarah* 129: *They* ought to (in strine, aorta) give a man a fair go – but they won't. So what do you do? ... tell them aorta go and get well stuffed.
1982 Ross Gittins *Sydney Morning Herald* 3 Jun. 6: It is not good enough for us PAYE captives to sit around tut-tutting and crying 'aorta do something.

Apple Isle, the Tasmania [f. crops]
1947 C. K. Thompson *Yes, Your Honour!* 231: Sir Richard must have had a terrible set on Tassie, because in 1836 he again tried to push Kinchela on to the Apple Isle as a puisne judge.
1965 *Australian* 10 Feb. 14: Smallest state in the Commonwealth – the 'Apple Isle' of Tasmania.
1971 *Sunday Australian* 13 Jun. 7: Apple Isle dumps a million bushels.
1981 *Weekend Australian* 31 Jan. 13: Not everything is rosy on the Apple Isle [heading] If Tasmanians hadn't previously felt the disadvantages of living in the smallest state they are certainly doing so now.

apples, everything's In good order, under control [? f. *apple pie order,* or rhyming slang *apples and spice = nice*]
1952 T. A. G. Hungerford *The Ridge and the River* 44: 'How's it going, Wally? Everything apples?'
1961 Frank Hardy *The Hard Way* 132: 'For Pete's

sake keep mum about it. 'She's apples,' the worker replied, with another demonstrative wink.

1966 Hal Porter *The Paper Chase* 251: 'Listen, mate, here's the problem. Mascot at five thirty. Passport photographs first – here's the address. While that's happening, can you collect my luggage at Usher's, buy me sixty cigarettes, and pick me up at the photographer's?' Sydney taxi-drivers are the world's best. 'She'll be apples, mate.'

1975 *Sydney Morning Herald* 24 Jun. 6: No one reckons it's 'apples' in the battle for Bass.

see **sweet, jake**

aristocracy, bunyip   see **bunyip**

arse   1   Effrontery, 'cheek', as in the phrase 'more arse than Jessie' q.v. [? f. 'hide']

1963 John Cantwell *No Stranger to the Flame* 76: 'The johns'd never have the arse to frisk every house in a dump like this – people'd feel their word was being doubted.'

1979 John Singleton *Bulletin* 11 Sep. 86: Since the place was set up 25 years ago there have been less than 200 visitors in total and I only got there through sheer arse and lots of it.

2   Equivalent to 'tail' (U.S.): sexual access to women (quot. 1958 also includes sense 3)

1958 Frank Hardy *The Four-legged Lottery* 188: 'See all the snooker balls going the pockets – he had more arse than a married cow playing snooker, I can tell you.'

1972 John Bailey *The Wire Classroom* 145: He used to have as many as twenty of them in his room stark naked romping all over him. The natives didn't mind it, of course. A bit of arse comes naturally to the blacks.

1979 Colin Johnson *Long Live Sandawara* 53: The only thing he doesn't like is that it is keeping the girls from plying their trade openly, and that means less free arse.

3   Good luck

1963 Frank Hardy *Legends from Benson's Valley* 73: 'They've had the luck of Eric Connolly all night,' Darky said sheepishly. 'Our turn for a bit of arse.'

arse, get the; be arsed out   To be dismissed

1966 Baker 366: *Got the arse at Bulli Pass* [as one of a number of sayings based on place-names]

1969 William Dick *Naked Prodigal* 19: 'What's up?' I asked. 'They give me the arse,' he answered loudly.

1974 John Powers *The Last of the Knucklemen* 50: 'I'm not worth a day's pay a week. I'm lucky Tarzan doesn't give me the arse out of the place.'

1983 Laurie Clancy *Perfect Love* 238: 'She's been playing around with half the town. So I went home and gave her the arse.'

arsehole, to   To dismiss someone peremptorily

1965 William Dick *A Bunch of Ratbags* 153: 'It's orright when yuh young, but when yuh get a bit old and yuh can't keep up . . . they'll arsehole yuh!'

1974 David Ireland *Burn* 125: They want to clear us right out. Arsehole us completely.

arseholes, ugly as a hatful of   see **hatful**

arsey   Lucky [f. *arse* 3]

1968 Stuart Gore *Holy Smoke* 30: 'The old man come up on the lottery or something?' 'No . . . He'd have to be pretty arsey, wouldn't he?'

1978 Richard Beilby *Gunner* 87: 'Just lie back an' take it easy. Ya got a homer, mate, you arsey bastard.'

Arthur or Martha, not to know whether one is   A state of confusion

1957 D'Arcy Niland *Call Me When The Cross Turns Over* 52–3: 'Don't try the Barcoo spews. A cow of a thing. Get a feed into you, and then you want to chuck it up again. You chuck it up and you're right as pie till you eat again. And so it goes on. You don't know whether you're Arthur or Martha.'

1965 John Beede *They Hosed Them Out* 104: 'Probably freeze your knackers off,' said Bill sceptically. 'I only tried swimming once over here and didn't know if I was Arthur or Martha when I came out.'

1971 Frank Hardy *The Outcasts of Foolgarah* 76: 'The boys don't know whether they're Arthur or Martha, what with all this talk about Red plots, there, and the latest telegram from Judge Parshall.'

1980 Jessica Anderson *The Impersonators* 192: She flopped into a chair and fanned herself with a hand. 'I still don't know whether I'm Arthur or Martha.'

1984 *Sun-Herald* 15 Jan. 118: More than ever, the British rock star Boy George must be wondering whether he is Arthur or Martha. Last week he was voted second most desirable bachelor in the world. This week, he came 10th in a list of the world's worst-dressed women. Still, it's all good publicity for a bloke who describes himself as a poof with muscles.

see **bored or punched**

artist   Expert, specialist, addict, esp. in expressions like 'bull artist', 'booze artist' [f. *artist* an adroit rogue; a skilful gamester U.S. 1890 OED]

[**1895** Cornelius Crowe *The Australian Slang Dictionary* 4: *Artist* a cunning thief or gamester.]

1919 W. H. Downing *Digger Dialects* 9: *Artist* 'One-star artist' – a second lieutenant.

1938 Xavier Herbert *Capricornia* 379: 'We'll take a couple of bottles with us. Joe's a champion

booze-artist.'
1941 Baker 14: *Bull artist* A braggart, an empty-headed blitherer.
1946 Rohan Rivett *Behind Bamboo* 395: *Bash artist* guard always beating up P.O.W.s.
1951 Dal Stivens *Jimmy Brockett* 49: Bill was fond of telling us he'd be able to retire in a few years, but he'd always been a bull artist.
1960 Murray Sayle 'As Far As You Can Go' *Encounter* May 27: Education, if he [the Australian worker] thinks of it at all, seems to him a childish trick whereby the 'bullshit artist' seeks to curry favour with the boss and thus get a better job.
1970 Patrick White *The Vivisector* 456: Decent people left the two derelicts plenty of room to pass; drunks, or more probably, metho artists.
1976 Helen Hodgman *Blue Skies* 93: 'Proper grog artist, I was. A regular flaming piss artist, that was me all right.'
1981 *Weekend Australian* 21 Nov. 7: Wran is a bull artist, says Aboriginal leader.
see **merchant**

arvo Afternoon [abbr.]
1927 *Sun* (Sydney) 9 Oct. 'Sunbeams' 1: I told young 'Ocker' Stevens to come up and say that so I could go shooting with him with his new pea rifle this arvo.
1958 H. D. Williamson *The Sunlit Plain* 41: 'Going up to see the cricket match this arvo?' Hattie asked, yawning.
1965 Patrick White *Four Plays* 121: 'Later on this arvo I'm gunna take Ernie out and buy him a good time.'
1973 Ward McNally *Man from Zero* 65: 'See you this arvo,' he said, turning and walking towards the docks.
1980 Craig McGregor *The Australian People* 131: For most people life begins at five o'clock on Friday arvo.

ashtray on a motorbike, useful as an   see **useful**

Ash Wednesday Wednesday 16 February 1983 (Ash Wednesday) day of bushfires in S.A. and Victoria, with the loss of 71 lives
1983 *Sydney Morning Herald* 18 Feb. 2: The Ash Wednesday Disaster [heading]
1984 *Weekend Australian* 28 Jan. Mag. 4: The threat of more devastating Ash Wednesdays is always part of the Australian landscape.

Aspro 1 Associate-professor, in academic slang [abbr.]
2 A nickname
1983 *Newcastle Herald* 1 Jun. 3: Various lazy people scattered through the Hunter Valley [are] called Aspro, Morphia and Opium: the slow working dopes.

Athens of the North, South Any Australian city with cultural pretensions, esp. a University city, as ironically viewed by any other
1983 *Weekend Australian* 26 Feb. 12: Armidale, 'the Athens of the north', is still seething since last year's street demonstration, when 3000 locals protested over a Fraser Government order to amalgamate the University of New England with the nearby College of Advanced Education.
1983 *Weekend Australian* 6 Aug. Mag. 20: It's not as though the leading intellectuals in the Athens of the South are taking hemlock: more your local Claytons, on the basis that the next Adelaide Festival is the one you have when you're not having one, according to some local pessimists.

Auntie The Australian Broadcasting Commission; from 1983 the Australian Broadcasting Corporation [f. nickname of the BBC]
1967 Heather Chapman *Sunday Mirror* (Sydney) 12 Mar. 84: But in the case of Miss Cobb people know she's never stuffy, pretentious, dull or high falutin'. She is, in fact, one answer to the ABC's Old Aunty image.
1972 *Australian* 1 Jul. 12: 'Auntie turns 40'. [heading to an article on the fortieth anniversary of the ABC]
1975 *Sydney Morning Herald* 23 Aug. 1: That wicked act which aborted the Third Test produced one clear winner – the A.B.C. . . . Tuesday's abandonment of play saved Aunty some $16,000.
1981 *Age* (Melbourne) 29 Jun. 2: To be surprised that Auntie ABC is no longer a financial virgin is about as ridiculous as suggesting that corporate underwriting will make her a whore overnight. It might be wise, however, for the Government to lead her from promiscuity and, if their poverty forces her to sleep around, persuade her, at least, to take proper precautions.
1982 *Sydney Morning Herald* 27 Mar. 16: Auntie at 50 faces the menopause with a quiet courage [heading]
1984 *Sydney Morning Herald* 5 May 1: Its managing director, Mr Geoffrey Whitehead, spoke of getting dynamism into the ABC, and said: 'If she is going to be Auntie, then she will be Auntie Mame.'

Aussie *n. & a.* 1 An Australian, usually with nationalistic overtones, as in phrases like 'a dinkum Aussie', 'a dinky-di Aussie' [abbr.]
1918 *Aussie The Australian Soldiers' Magazine* 18 Jan. 1: In short, make him a dinkum Aussie.
1934 Steele Rudd *Green Grey Homestead* 191: He's sure she's selected the right man for her husband – 'a good, industrious, God-fearing dinkum young Aussie.'
1940 Arnold Haskell *Waltzing Matilda* 164: Unlike so many who find success, she [Melba] remained a 'dinkum hard-swearing Aussie' to the

end.

1951 Dal Stivens *Jimmy Brockett* 80: We would show them that a dinkum Aussie was worth ten of anyone else.

1971 Hal Porter *The Right Thing* 51: 'Both of them [the housekeepers] fell for dad, first the Pommy one, and then a dinky-di Aussie one.'

1980 *Sunday Mail* (Brisbane) 21 Sep. 13: Helen said it was quite acceptable in Europe for men to cry or show their feelings in other ways. 'But here, it's contrary to the image of the strong, active, bronzed Aussie', she said.

2 Australia

1918 *Aussie The Australian Soldier's Magazine* 18 Jan. 1: To the Australian Soldier the name Aussie stands for his splendid, sea-girt, sun-kissed Homeland, and his cobbers are always Aussies.

1928 Arthur Wright *A Good Recovery* 110: And together they had set out for Aussie.

1945 Diary 16 Sep. Stan Arneil *One Man's War* (1980) 264: We embark tomorrow morning to go to dear old Aussie.

1974 *Australian* 15 Aug. 10: 'Cheers from A Sunburnt Country!' the advertisement trumpets. 'Toast your Pommie mates with a gift from good old Aussie! Great beers, Hardy's fine wines, and Vegemite for the kids!'

Aussie Rules Australian Rules Football (first played in 1858)

1963 R. and E. Wordley *How to Play Aussie Rules.* [book title]

1973 Max Harris *The Angry Eye* 63: Aussie Rules remains in its condition of benign stagnation.

1983 Wally Lewis *National Times* 13 May 50: 'A lot of people will bag Aussie Rules, calling it a sheila's game, but the guys that are playing it are top class sportsmen, there's incredible skill involved.'

Australia, the The Hotel Australia, built in 1891, demolished in 1971, long regarded as the leading Sydney hotel

1900 Henry Lawson 'Mr Smellingscheck' *Prose* i 234: We had a well-to-do whisky together, and he talked of things in the abstract. He seemed just as if he'd met me in the Australia.

1959 Jon Cleary *Back at Sunset* 118: 'I'll be waiting for you in the Long Bar of the Australia, with a beer on the counter.'

1968 Stuart Gore *Holy Smoke* 47: 'Here they are still standin' up . . . as cool as if they all had a foot on the brass rail in the Australia.'

1979 Patrick White *The Twyborn Affair* 107: Her youthful caper with Eadie Twyborn when they crashed that supper dance at the Australia.

1981 Maxwell Grant *Inherit the Sun* 360: He hoped Sir James hadn't found anywhere more satisfactory. 'Not unless you're rebuilding the old

Australia', Red said.

Australia for the Australians A slogan used in a variety of contexts:

1 As a call for national unity or individuality

1868 Archbishop John Bede Polding *Pastoral Letter* [responding to anti-Catholic feeling at the attempted assassination of the Duke of Edinburgh] in *Documents in Australian Catholic History* ed. P. O'Farrell (1969) i 428: The unhappy creature, who attempted the life of our Prince and guest, professes to be a Catholic . . . But will any man of sense believe that his crime was Catholic? . . . Australians we should all be. We owe it to each other, we owe it to duty, we owe it to Christianity. And I say, Australia for the Australians, our sole and sufficient nationality under the rule of our ever good and gracious Queen, whom with her Royal Family may God in his infinite mercy long preserve to us.

1891 Edward Kinglake *The Australian at Home* 155: 'Australia for the Australians', is a cry very often heard. It is a healthy, good, and laudable watchword, because Australia is always ready to hold out the hand of friendship to honourable men, ready to work as her own sons work, and welcomes them gladly to the ever increasing ranks of the Australians.

1898 A. B. Paterson 'Johnny Riley's Cow' (A Ballad of Federation) in *Singer of the Bush* (1983) 306: It's Australia for the Australians – one people east and west.

1908 C. H. S. Matthews *A Parson in the Australian Bush* 307: All true Roman Catholics were bound to take the anti-Socialistic side. How did the Roman Catholics reply? By an immediate appeal to the popular Australian catchword, 'Australia for the Australians.' . . . 'We are not Europeans,' they cried, 'but good Australians, therefore this document [an encyclical against Socialism] leaves us entirely untouched.'

2 As a plea for the interests of the native born

1889 A. B. Paterson *Australia for the Australians.* [pamphlet opposing the concentration of land in the hands of a few, and advocating protective tariffs]

1911 E. M. Clowes *On the Wallaby Through Victoria* 172: Australia . . . needs to open its arms, to enlarge its sympathies, and to get rid, once for all, of that 'precious only child in the world' idea by which it seems each year to grow more completely engrossed – I mean the 'Australia for the Australians' ideal.

3 As an expression of anti-imperialist sentiment

1888 *The Republican* 8 Feb. 5: Australia for the Australians. [article on the Australian Republican league, which advocated the abolition of the office of Governor, nationalization of the land, federation of the colonies under republican rule]

1901 Henry Lawson 'Lord Douglas' *Prose* i 492: The Royal Hotel at Bourke was kept by an Irishman, one O'Donohoo, who was Union to the backbone, loudly in favour of 'Australia for the Australians', and, of course, against even the democratic New South Wales Government of the time.

1902 A. G. Stephens 'Australia for the Australians' *Bulletin* 25 Jan. Red Page [article questioning the influences of the British in Australia: 'Let young Australia come to the front with the motto of Australia for the Australians. This question of independent national development overshadows all others.']

4   As expressing opposition to coloured immigration: the motto of the *Bulletin* from 21 April 1888 (following the anti-Chinese issue of 14 April) to 30 April 1908

1888 William Lane *White or Yellow?* in *Boomerang* 31 Mar. 9: 'Australia for the Australians!' shouted Colonel Withers ... 'We'll teach the yellow rascals which race has got to go!'

Australia for the White Man   Motto of the *Bulletin* from 7 May 1908 until 30 November 1960, indicating support for the White Australia policy

1974 Desmond O'Grady *Deschooling Kevin Carew* 122: Australia for the white man. He should have shown the note to the dumb Chink without letting it out of his hand.

Australian adjective, the great   Bloody q.v.

1894 *Bulletin* 18 Aug. 22: The *Bulletin* calls it the 'Australian adjective' simply because it is more used, and used more exclusively by Australians, than by any other allegedly civilised nation.

1899 W. T. Goodge *Hits! Skits! and Jingles!* 115: '——!' / *(The Great Australian Adjective!)* [poem title]

1939 *Daily Telegraph* (Sydney) 23 Jan. 7: Legal opinion upholds the ruling of Mr Atkinson S. M. that the Great Australian Adjective is sometimes offensive but not indecent.

1944 *Daily Telegraph* (Sydney) 7 Jul. 8: The great Australian accent, and the greater Australian adjective, are two of the best advertisements Australia has in other parts of the world.

Australian as a meat pie   see **meat pie**

Australian dream, the great   The hope of owning one's own home

1981 *Sun-Herald* 22 Nov. 55: The Labor Party of today is firmly committed to the great Australian dream of owning one's own home.

1982 *Australian* 8 Jan. 5: The great Australian dream is as pervasive in Lowe as anywhere else in the country, and two-thirds of the houses and flats in the area are owned or in the process of being paid off.

1984 Jim Kemeney *The Great Australian Nightmare* [book title]

Australian joke, the great   See quot. 1911

1911 C. E. W. Bean *'Dreadnought' of the Darling* 330: The Great Australian Joke is far too old a chestnut to be pardonable amongst Australians. But in case there are still any English readers that have not heard it, it may be said that it is the story of the sad and final breach between two mates who had been carrying their swags in company for some time along the interminable road that leads always to the horizon. Early one morning, up a creek-bed to the side of them, they passed a big black object which, whatever it was, had clearly been dead some days. About midday Bill took his pipe out of his mouth. 'D'jer see that dead ox?' he grunted. The shadows of evening were closing around them, when Jim spat solemnly into the camp fire. ''Tweren't an ox. 'Twas a 'orse,' he said. After that he turned in and slept eight well-deserved hours. When he awoke there was no sign of Bill or Bill's swag. Bill was clearly gone. Only a grimy note was left stuck in a cleft stick. 'There's too much argyment in this here camp,' it said.

Australian novel, the great   The novel that is always still to be written, or identified

1941 A. J. A. Waldock *Southerly* Nov. 34: Do people still muse on 'the great Australian novel' for which we wait? Casey, I believe, has it in him to write it.

1948 A. W. Upfield *An Author Bites the Dust* 133: 'Her work is much appreciated by the discerning and we are still expecting her to produce the Great Australian Novel.'

1966 Hal Porter *The Paper Chase* 70–1: The result is, of course, to be the Great Australian Novel.

1970 Patrick White *The Vivisector* 112: 'Well, good luck to you, kid! I'm going to write the Great Australian Novel.'

1980 *Weekend Australian* 20 Dec. Mag. 13: Helen Garner ... hasn't written the Great Australian Novel, but yet in her own frame of reference is tackling more than most.

Australian salute   The movement of the hand in brushing away flies

1972 Ian Moffitt *The U-Jack Society* 65: I flopped a hand at the flies (the Australian salute).

1976 *Australian* 9 Mar. 3: A sexually-mutated blowfly developed by CSIRO scientists in Canberra could lead to the demise of the great Australian salute.
see **Barcoo salute, Queensland salute**

Australian Ugliness, the Great   A phrase developed from the title of Robin Boyd's book of 1960, on the vulgarity of design in the ordinary Australian environment, from architecture to automobiles: since applied mainly to suburbia

1960 Robin Boyd *The Australian Ugliness* [book title]

1981 Leonie Sandercock and Ian Turner *Up Where, Cazaly?* 130: In the 1950s the spread of car ownership reinforced and multiplied those tendencies and that preference for low density living, otherwise known as suburban sprawl or, by some, as the Great Australian Ugliness.

Australia's national game   see **national game**

awake   see **wake up**

axe-handle   A unit of measurement, in country areas: *obsolescent*

1977 *Australian* 11 Apr. 6: A big woman, but not a big man, would be described as being 'two axe handles across the arse'.

1978 John Hepworth *His Book* 110: All the fine big cornfed girls with their bold eyes and the broad hips. Three axehandles across – good breeding stock.

1979 Sally Morrison *Who's taking you to the Dance?* 199: She shouldn't wear that suit. Two axe handles across the beam if you ask me.

1982 *Sun-Herald* 19 Dec. 127: 'There was this giant Yugoslav bodyguard there, about four axehandles across the chest and he had to wrestle with them to keep them away.'

ay   see **eh**

B

babbler, babbling brook   Cook, esp. one cooking for a number of men, as in the army or in the outback [rhyming slang]

1919 W. H. Downing *Digger Dialects* 9: *Babbling Brook; Babbler* An Army cook.

1924 *Truth* 27 Apr. 6: *Babbling brook* A cook.

1932 Leonard Mann *Flesh in Armour* 96: The new tins hadn't been properly cleaned out by the babbler.

1935 H. R. Williams *Comrades of the Great Adventure* 172: Peter perched upon a chair minus a leg, entertaining the 'babbling brooks' with a lecturette on the handling of horses.

1940 Ion L. Idriess *Lightning Ridge* 59: We were craftily diplomatic in our dealings with the Babbling Brook. All bush cooks are touchy.

1956 Ruth Park and D'Arcy Niland *The Drums Go Bang!* 71: The shearers ... drew as their lucky last a wizard cook from Sydney who could throw cream-puffs together with one hand and carve the roast with the other, while he washed up with his feet. Or so it seemed. He was voted one of the best babbling brooks in the business.

1964 *Sydney Morning Herald* 25 Apr. 11: 'If I keep this pretty woman babbler on my books next year I'll have to get an older team.'

1981 *Sunday Mail* (Brisbane) 9 Aug. Color Mag. 10: Local good cooks asked for the recipe, but minds boggled at the quantities the army's babbling-brook recited for their benefit.

babbling

1962 *Sydney Morning Herald* 24 Nov. 12: Gaily aproned women do the 'babbling' (cooking) now instead of cranky, gingery-whiskered old blokes.

bach   see batch

bachelors' hall   Another term for **barracks** q.v.: *obs.*

1881 A. C. Grant *Bush-Life in Queensland* i 56: The fourth side [of the square of buildings at the head-station] was filled up by the building John had dined and slept in, and which was called 'The Bachelors' Hall'.

bachelor's tart   An improvised bush delicacy: N.T.

1951 Ernestine Hill *The Territory* 426: Dessert was ... 'bachelor's tart' – damper and jam.

back block   1   A block of land further from water or grass, and so less favourable to settlement

1872 Anon. *Glimpses of Life in Victoria* 31: We were doomed to see the whole of our river frontage selected and purchased ... The back blocks which were left to us were insufficient for the support of our flocks, and deficient in permanent water supply. [Morris]

1874 Rolf Boldrewood *My Run Home* (1897) 265: 'A regular "back block", if ever there were one – all rock and mountain.'

1883 W. A. Brodribb *Recollections of an Australian Squatter* 132: There are always what are called 'back blocks' for sale, varying from 25 up to 100 square miles. Each block is capable of grazing from 4,000 to 6,000 sheep, when supplied by artificial means, with permanent water, by making tanks and digging wells.

2 *The backblocks* Regions remote from settled areas

1888 Overlander *Australian Sketches* 65: Jim Brandon's Christmas on the Back Blocks and what came of it [story title]

1902 Henry Lawson 'The Shearer's Dream' *Prose* i 312: They were part of a theatrical company on tour in the Back-Blocks.

1908 Mrs Aeneas Gunn *We of the Never-Never* (1966) 140: 'Back blocks!' he said in scorn. 'There ain't no back blocks left! Can't travel a hundred miles nowadays without running into somebody!'

1925 Seymour Hicks *Hullo Australians* 198: 'You haven't seen Australia if you haven't seen the back blocks.'

1944 Gilbert Mant *You'll be Sorry* 31: Bill was a gawky lad from the back-blocks who had this day seen Sydney for the first time.

1970 Barry Oakley *A Salute to the Great McCarthy* 78: 'Where ya from, kid? The backblocks? Flash boy from the paddocks?'

back blocker   An inhabitant of the back blocks

1870 *Argus* 22 Mar. 7: 'I am a bushman, a back blocker, to whom it happens about once in two years to visit Melbourne.' [Morris]

1898 David W. Carnegie *Spinifex and Sand* 149: Strong and hard, about thirty-five years of age, though, like most back-blockers, prematurely grey.

1907 Alfred Searcy *In Australian Tropics* 125: If a crowd of overlanders and backblockers happened to be present, things would be made lively, for . . . they would hardly give up all the liquor without a strong protest.

1957 Sydney Hart *Pommie Migrant* 161: He would . . . brew up his old billy-can on one of the furnace fires – a regular back blocks veteran, who preferred his own way to that of the moderns.

back country   The areas remote from settlement, usually further inland [U.S. 1746 Mathews]

c. **1801** Gov. Hunter *HRNSW* iii. 820n.: A report which some artful villain in the colony had propagated amongst the Irish convicts lately arrived, 'That there was a colony of white people at no very great distance in the back country – 150 or 200 miles – where there was abundance of every sort of provision without the necessity of so much labour.'

1863 Samuel Butler *A First Year on Canterbury Settlement* 116: Blocks . . . are frequently bought with a view to their being fenced in and laid down in English Ear grasses. In the back country this has not yet commenced, nor is it likely to do so for many years.

1888 Overlander *Australian Sketches* 1: 'You want to know how I first took to the roads and the back country, do you?'

1893 Simpson Newland *Paving the Way* 198: I presume you will continue the examination of the back-country with all the hands available, it is useless trying to track her in that thick scrub.

1903 Joseph Furphy *Such is Life* (1944) 34: 'I wish you could talk to him. Lots of information in the back country that never gets down here into civilisation.'

1911 C. E. W. Bean *The 'Dreadnought' of the Darling* 98: This back country along the Darling produces some of the very best wool in the world.

1921 K. S. Prichard *Black Opal* 69: His father, James Henty, had taken up land in the back-country, long before opal was found on Fallen Star Ridge.

1945 Tom Ronan *Strangers on the Ophir* 58: It was a feature of the development of the Back Country [of western Queensland] that when a man reached the frontier his past and all it signified were forgotten.

1956 A. W. Upfield *The Battling Prophet* 140: 'Us people from the Back Country can always look after ourselves. How long have you been in Australia?'

back, Mediterranean   see **Mediterranean**

back of Bourke   see **Bourke**

backside, sparrows (geese, peacocks, swallows) flying out of one's   see **sparrows**

back to the cactus   see **cactus**

back up *v.*   To repeat an action, esp. in obtaining a second helping of food

1932 Let. 2 Feb. in *The Wasted Years?* ed. Judy Mackinolty (1981) 120: It appears that owing to men backing up and getting double issues, by means of visiting two towns at short distances apart on dole days, the police were ordered to make dole issuing orders between the hours of 11 o'clock and 12 o'clock.

1966 Elwyn Wallace *Sydney and the Bush* 79: 'They were all backing up for a second lot so I thought I'd go one better and have a third go.'

1972 W. H. Gunning in G. C. Bolton *A Thousand Miles Away* 307: At the other end of the dining room there was a tub of hot water to wash your plate, etc. before backing up for the sweets.

1981 *Sydney Morning Herald* 14 Sep. 7: On Friday night . . . Ian is a barman at a restaurant at the Rocks from 7 pm to 12.30 am. He backs up on Sunday afternoon.

back up *n.*   A second helping

1946 Rohan Rivett *Behind Bamboo* 330: *Backup,* second helping. *Backup king,* man always chasing second helpings.
1953 T. A. G. Hungerford *Riverslake* 199: He raised the blackened tray above his head ... 'Who'll be in a back-up?'
1971 Frank Hardy *The Outcasts of Foolgarah* 19: 'We fed yer. Right? And we know you appreciate it because you always have a back up of everything.'

bag To disparage, 'knock'
1975 *Australian* 11 Nov. 10: 'He [the TV critic] said his wife loved the show and I said yeah but you're always bagging it and he said, yeah but we've got to sell papers somehow.'
1977 *Sydney Morning Herald* 23 Sep. 7: He is now bagging Mr Fraser at every opportunity, saying he is the worst Prime Minister the Liberals have ever had.
1981 *Australian* 20 Oct. 3: It pains me to report that Choice, journal of the Australian Consumers' Association, bags Vegemite for having too much salt in it.

bagarup see **bugger**

bag, get a Reproach to a cricketer who has dropped a catch
1925 Seymour Hicks *Hullo Australians* 246: If a man who is fielding misses a catch they tell him to get a bag.
1969 Leslie Haylen *Twenty Years' Hard Labor* 70: When annoyed at some bad play Evatt yelled out 'Get a Bag'.
1975 Xavier Herbert *Poor Fellow My Country* 1239: 'Sometimes you'd think you were listening-in to a commentary on a cricket-match or something, and expect someone to yell *Get a Bag!*'

bag, in the See quot. 1982
1941 Baker 7: *Bag, in the* (Of a horse) not intended to win.
1982 Joe Andersen *Winners Can Laugh* 148: Sam rejected many offers from the smart bookmakers to put him in the bag, meaning that, in return for preventing a horse from winning, a rider received a percentage of the money the bookmaker won on the race as a result of the arrangement.

bagman 1 An itinerant carrying his possessions with him. This is the broadest sense of the word, covering both the tramp (cf. *swagman*) and the traveller on horseback (*bagman* 2).
1904 Henry Lawson 'The Last Review' *Verse* ii 63: Thought he [Steelman] was an honest bagman.
1910 C. E. W. Bean *On the Wool Track* 220: When a man says he met a 'traveller' or a 'bagman' in the bush he does not mean a commercial traveller. He

means a man making his way from station to station, probably a man on horseback with his kit in his bag.
1941 Kylie Tennant *The Battlers* 19: 'Well, this (*adjective*) song was about an (*adjectival*) bagman who was getting himself a bit of meat ... The busker nodded somewhat contemptuously. 'Waltzing Matilda, the Australian National Anthem.'
1971 Keith Willey *Boss Drover* 45: You were likely to find a bagman anywhere. Some of them walked right around the country.
2 A mounted swagman: esp. in N.T. and W.A.
1911 E. S. Sorenson *Life in the Australian Backblocks* 72: Two terms that are often confused one with the other are swagman and bagman. The first is a footman, the other a mounted man who may have anything from one to half a dozen horses. Though both are looking for work, they move on very different planes; the latter is considered a cut above the former, and looks down with a mildly contemptuous eye on the slowly plodding swagman.
1951 Ernestine Hill *The Territory* 429: In those vast distances where no man could foot walk, the swagman became a bagman with a riding-horse, a packhorse and couple of spares, travelling from station to station, from creek to creek.
1966 Tom Ronan *Once There Was a Bagman* 31: The bagmen, the horse-borne wanderers, the one purely unique type Australia ever produced.
3 An unemployed itinerant in the depression of the 1930s
1931 Let. of 8 Dec. in *The Wasted Years?* ed. Judy Mackinolty (1981) 116: It is a common occurrence to see bagmen jumping the rattler from this siding.
1935 Kylie Tennant *Tiburon* 19: Mrs Malloy, who had made herself the council's curse for many years by her generosity to that 'undesirable element', the travelling unemployed. It was she who had built the sheltershed, and ... it had saved many a bagman from lying stiff with rheumatism under a bridge.
1962 Ron Tullipan *March Into Morning* 11: The bagman sprawled out in the shade ... waiting for the mixed goods and passenger train that went through there twice a week.
1965 Frank Hardy *The Yarns of Billy Borker* 49: 'I joined the army when war broke out. Came straight off the track. The sixth Divvy was made up mainly of bagmen, first steady job we ever had was getting shot at.'
1979 George Stewart *The Leveller* 20: The depression was upon the country and I had met some young bagmen and was fired with the excitement of joining them. A bagmen was an unemployed person whose only possessions were bags: a water bag, a tucker bag, flour bags washed and sewn together called a Wogga.

Bagman's Gazette A fictitious publication containing news and rumours; graffiti left by itinerants [f. *bagman* 2]
1954 Tom Ronan *Vision Splendid* 266: 'If the Bagman's Gazette,' decided Mr Toppingham, 'was an actual news sheet and not just a figure of speech, I'd advertise for the old beggar in the agony column.'
1957 W. E. Harney *Life Among the Aborigines* 183–4: We passed the windmills and tanks that stretch along the way to water the herds as they travel, and on the big black iron sheets of the squatters' tanks one could read the 'Bagman's Gazette' which is the escape channel for the grievances of the travellers as they go by . . . Each tank we passed had its 'news', and only when a boss passed by and saw his name in a headline would he get the tank re-tarred.
1968 *The Barry Humphries Book of Innocent Austral Verse* 130: Bagman's Gazette. [poem title]

bag of shells see **shells**

bag, out of the As for **out of the box**
1954 T. A. G. Hungerford *Sowers of the Wind* 44: 'It was all done with one bloody bomb – that's what makes it one out of the bag. One place that's been skittled is like any other, otherwise.'
1961 Tom Ronan *Only a Short Walk* 135: She was something out of the bag, was Hetty.

bag-swinger A street prostitute
1953 Baker 124: *Bag swingers* who solicit custom from sailors are said to *cover the waterfront*.
1968 Stuart Gore *Holy Smoke* 79: 'What they call a bag-swinger, down in the city'.

bag system, the In the depression of the 1930s, the issue of a bag of groceries each dole day to the unemployed
1963 Frank Hardy *Legends from Benson's Valley* 176: Ernie Lyle read two of the small signs 'Work not Charity', 'Down with the Bag system'. A chord in his heart responded: bags of groceries at Ambler's store, margarine, bulk tea, the cheapest brands thrust into your hand without choice or ceremony.

bag your head, go and Expression of disagreement, rejection, dismissal
1930 J. S. Litchfield *Far-North Memories* 168: 'Why didn't you tell that lunatic old government to go and bag its silly old head?'
1938 Xavier Herbert *Capricornia* 83: She flushed and snapped, 'Garn – bag y'r 'ead!'
1951 Dymphna Cusack and Florence James *Come In Spinner* 246: 'Aw, go bag your head. It makes me want to puke when I hear you fellows going on with all this purity bunk.'

1976 Dorothy Hewett *This Old Man Comes Rolling Home* 42: 'Ah! Go and bag your 'ead!'
1982 *Sydney Morning Herald* 19 Aug. 7: Fraser the cynical vote-buying survivor told Fraser the nice guy to go bag his head.

bags, rough as Uncouth, to outward appearance
1919 W. H. Downing *Digger Dialects* 42: *Rough as bags* See 'Rough stuff'. *Rough stuff* An undisciplined, reckless, indecent, disorderly or disrespectful person or thing.
1929 K. S. Prichard *Coonardoo* 22: 'Ted was as rough as bags,' Geary said; 'a good-looking, good-natured bloke who could neither read nor write.'
1938 Eric Lowe *Salute to Freedom* 318: 'Rough as bags. Cleared his throat – you know the way he does – and spat, just missing a pile of ribbons.'
1948 Patrick White *The Aunt's Story* 34: Tom Wilcocks was as rough as bags. His neck was red and strong. The pollard had caked hard on his hard hands.
1955 John Morrison *Black Cargo* 184: 'Only a few acres here and there settled at all – berry-farming and wood-cutting. Everything rough as bags.'
1967 Joan Lindsay *Picnic at Hanging Rock*: 'Rough as bags, young Crundall, but no fool and a first-rate man with the horses.'
1970 Cynthia Nolan *A Bride for St Thomas* 133: She was a good organiser, but as a nurse she was rough as bags.
1984 Marian Eldridge *Walking the Dog* 89: 'Rough as bags', people said of Raelene, and in the same breath, 'heart of gold.'

bail, I'll go Equivalent to 'I warrant' or any other expression guaranteeing the credibility of a statement: *obsolescent* [listed as a characteristic Irish expression in P. W. Joyce *English as We Speak it in Ireland* (1910) 9–10. ? f. *hail* = security]
1832 *The Currency Lad* 6 Oct. 4: 'I'll go bail she will be better.'
1847 Alexander Harris *The Emigrant Family* (1967) 47: 'Only leave it in their way, and I'll go bail you never clap eyes on it again.'
1870 Marcus Clarke *His Natural Life* ed. S. Murray-Smith (1970) 411: 'I'd cut the biggest iron you've got with this; and so would he and plenty more, I'll go bail.'
1880 Rolf Boldrewood *The Miner's Right* (1890) 43: 'There's something in that lead, I'll go bail.'
1928 Miles Franklin *Up the Country* (1966) 142: 'I'll go bail it's some of the mean things he's always saying about other people that are making him bilious.'

bail up All the senses illustrated seem to have been current simultaneously, although 3 gained more currency as 'bailing up' came to be associated more with highways

1 'To secure the head of a cow in a "bail" while she is milked ... *Austral.* and N.Z.' (OED 1847–1950)

2 In bushranging, to hold the victims under guard, confine them or tie them up

1843 *Sydney Monitor and Commercial Advertiser* 21 Jan. 2: On last Wednesday week, two armed bushrangers went into Grovenor's public house ... they pulled out pistols, 'bailed up' the whole of the family and proceeded to plunder the house ... about 10 o'clock, Mr Grovenor was enabled to free himself.

1843 John Hood *Australia and the East* 178: Bailing up is the term used to express their usual mode of proceeding in these occasions; which is this ... one of them goes in with his gun pointed and cocked, his finger upon the trigger, and with the muzzle disagreeably near your person, invites you to retire into the corner, while his companion inspects your property, and helps himself to anything which you may happen to have and he to lack.

1843 'Billy Barlow' *Old Bush Songs* ed. Stewart and Keesing (1957) 53: But by bushrangers met, with my traps they made free, / Took my horse, and left Billy bailed up to a tree.

1844 Louisa Meredith *Notes and Sketches of New South Wales* 132: The plan usually pursued by the bushrangers in robbing a house ... is to walk quietly in, and 'bail up' *i.e.* bind with cords, or otherwise secure, the male portion, leaving an armed guard over them, whilst the rest of the gang ransack the house.

1852 G. C. Mundy *Our Antipodes* i 179: The coachman was then compelled to take his horses off, the passengers were ordered severally to get out and to 'bail up' like cows prepared for milking at the fence side.

1862 Horace Earle *Ups and Downs* 82: A plan at that time not unusual amongst bushrangers in their dealings with their victims, namely 'bailing them up', or securing them to trees, and leaving them thus to starve.

1863 R. Therry *Reminiscences* 2nd edn 125–6: We had still a further ordeal to pass through, which is termed '*baling up*'. This sort of ordeal consisted in our being grouped together on the roadside, whilst one of the three bushrangers was placed as a sentinel over us, with instructions from the captain to shoot the first man that stirred without permission.

3 Equivalent to the highwayman's 'Stand and deliver'

1852 G. C. Mundy *Our Antipodes* i 179: 'Bail up – or you're a dead man,' resounded from behind a thick tree, through a fork of which a double-barrelled gun covered the driver's head.

1853 Mrs C. Clacy *A Lady's Visit to the Gold Diggings of Australia in 1852–53* 127: I cannot quite realise the terrified passengers being driven through the Black Forest, but can picture their horror when ordered to 'bail up' by a party of Australian Turpins.

1895 Rolf Boldrewood *The Crooked Stick* 6: As the coach came abreast of them the man on the grey turned towards it, and, with a raised revolver in his hand, shouted, 'Bail up!'

4 More generally, to hold at bay, arrest the progress of, 'corner'

1859 Henry Kingsley *Recollections of Geoffry Hamlyn* iii 152: And they [the bushrangers] were bailed up in the limestone gully; and all the party were away after them.

1870 Rachel Henning *Letters* ed. D. Adams (1963) 239: [The creek] had risen so that he could not get back, and was 'bailed up' in Stroud for two days.

1908 Henry Fletcher *Dads and Dan between Smokes* 127: He'll bail up ther fust bottle-oh he meets an' ask him who lets out vans.

1919 W. K. Harris *Outback in Australia* 3: Five miles further on ... a road maintenance man bailed me up. 'The mailman said he saw your roan colt tied up near my shanty. Did you have a feed?'

1949 Ruth Park *Poor Man's Orange* 91: Brought up in Surry Hills, she felt there wasn't a drunk in the district she couldn't have handled if he bailed her up.

bake it See quots [services slang]

1968 Geoffrey Dutton *Andy* 14: 'I'm going to need to use one of them latrine buckets pretty soon' ... 'Will you *shut up* and just bake it for a minute or two.'

1970 Richard Beilby *No Medals for Aphrodite* 167: No movement round the lines except to the latrines and then only in dire necessity – 'Bake it, fella if you don't want your head shot off.'

baker, floury see **floury baker**

balander See quot. 1978 [f. Macassarese]

1946 W. E. Harney *North of 23°* 121: He [the Malay] would land on the beach, and, advancing to the spot where Alf sat resplendently dressed ... would thrice bow his head to the 'ballander'.

1978 *Australian* 6 Oct. 7: Balander ... is an Aboriginal name for a white man – corruption of the word Hollander. The tribes of Arnhem Land knew the tough, phlegmatic Dutchmen of the East Indies before Cook was born. Now a balander means any white man.

1982 Alan Powell *Far Country* 36: The word 'balander', originally referring to the 'Hollanders', was adopted widely in Arnhem Land to designate all white men.

balfastards, alas! milfissed the An exclamation

indicating the failure of some action, from an anecdote 'A hulfunting we will golfo' current among Australian soldiers in World War II (communicated by L. Bottomley). Another version is given in Baker (1945: 274).

c. **1944** A rififleman jumped into a trulfuck with his gulfang to shoot dulfucks swilfimming on the walfater, he raised his rififle and ailfaimed at the dulfucks. Balfang! balfang! went the rififle. Flalfap! flalfap! went the dulfucks. 'Alas! milfissed the balfastards!' said the rififleman.

Another version is reported by Mr O. C. Uden of Glenunga S.A., from an RAAF source. A man goes to the doctor to be treated for stuttering, and as he can pronounce 'alf' without a stutter, he is encouraged to insert that in each word. He later gives an account of a hunting trip: 'Halfow Dalfoctor. I was walfading along a ralfiver stalfalking dalfucks...'

ball-bearing cowboy   See quot.
1980 Rod Ansell *To Fight the Wild* 46: That's one thing about being a 'ballbearing cowboy', for having taken to chasing cattle in a vehicle instead of on a horse.

ball of muscle, style   [analogous to *ball of fire* OED 1821]
c. **1914** A. B. Paterson 'Racehorses and Racing in Australia' in *The World of Banjo Paterson* ed. C. Semmler (1967) 321: The handicap king, Moonlighter, bounds along, a ball of muscle, in last place.
1939 Kylie Tennant *Foveaux* 160: Rolfe was again 'a ball of muscle', as he termed it, working on the Slum Abolition Committee.
1945 Cecil Mann *The River* 137: Spider Hayes, who's a ball of muscle, one of the fittest of the whole bunch.
1947 Margaret Trist *Daddy* 171: 'The missus isn't ready yet,' he greeted his mother-in-law. 'She'll be a ball of style when she's through, if you can count on the preparations.'
1951 Dymphna Cusack and Florence James *Come In Spinner* 251: 'Hullo,' he said pleasantly, 'you look a ball of muscle tonight.'
1960 Ron Tullipan *Follow the Sun* 30: 'This old bus isn't exactly a ball of style, but it's handy while I'm building.'
1965 Patrick White *Four Plays* 239: 'That Miss Scougall's a ball of ego.'

ball tearer   Someone or something exceptional, for good or bad qualities
1973 Jim McNeil *The Chocolate Frog* 25: 'I mean you bein' pinched for street fightin' ... yer must be a real little ball-tearer.'
1974 Barry Humphries *A Nice Night's Entertainment* (1981) 146: This Leonard French is a little balltearer. It's got luxury *built in*, not tacked on,

and I can fix you up with this model in all wanted colours and with all the optional extras thrown in.
1978 *National Times* 27 May 29: He [Mr Neville Wran] gets to the theatre, and of what he's seen lately Ron Blair's play about the Christian Brothers stood out as a 'ball-tearer'.
1984 *Sydney Morning Herald* 26 Mar. 2: He [Nick Greiner] thought the Opposition might have done better in the country and not quite as well in the city. 'The result in the city shows that corruption is a ball-tearer in the city.'

Balmain boys don't cry   Statement by N. K. Wran at the NSW Conference of the ALP on 11 June 1983
1983 *Sun-Herald* 12 June. 2: Premier Neville Wran yesterday told of the 'anguish and indignity' the Street Royal Commission was causing him ... 'You know Balmain boys don't cry – we're too vulgar and too common for that and probably vote Labor anyway.'
1984 Nick Greiner *Sydney Morning Herald* 25 Feb. 12: We all know that Balmain boys don't cry, but they certainly bleat a lot.
1984 *Age* (Melbourne) 21 Sep. 13: Queensland Liberal backbencher Don Cameron said it was obvious the Prime Minister did not come from Balmain – a reference to Neville Wran's tough comment ... that 'Balmain boys don't cry'.

Balt   An immigrant to Australia from the Baltic countries (and Poland and Holland) after World War II: *derogatory* [f. *Balt* a native or inhabitant of one of the Baltic states OED 1878: not used pejoratively]
1949 *Sydney Morning Herald* 11 Aug. 1: Yesterday Mr Calwell launched a campaign to get Australians to drop the terms 'D.P.s', 'Displaced Persons' and 'Balts' and to call these migrants 'New Australians'.
1953 T. A. G. Hungerford *Riverslake* 32: A dozen of them, six Poles and the rest a mixture of Lithuanians and Ukranians and Latvians and Estonians, big and small, old and young, dark and fair, but indistinguishable now in their nonentity. Balts.
1957 Randolph Stow *The Bystander* 134: 'Will she mind so much, that a bloody Balt marries her cousin?'
1959 Dorothy Hewett *Bobbin Up* 150: 'Look at them bloody Balts, all with their heads down and their arses up,' old Betty grumbled ... 'They'll never be Aussies while they keep that up. They'll work us all outa a job.'
1963 Bruce Beaver *The Hot Summer* 32: 'You're taller than most of those Balts' ... He knew she meant the migrant construction gangs working on an electrification project there.
1981 Peter Corris *White Meat* 45: When the migrant rush from Europe got going after the war

we called them all 'Balts' wherever they came from, but this one looked like the genuine article.

Bananaland   Queensland: *jocular* [f. crop]
1893 Henry Lawson 'Hungerford' *Prose* i 106: The post office is in New South Wales, and the police barracks in Bananaland.
1946 *Sun* (Sydney) 4 Aug. Suppl. 15: They reckon as he [Captain Cook] sailed away he gave one look back at the coast of Bananaland and said: 'Strewth, I'm glad to give that dump back to the blacks.'
1973 Patrick White *The Eye of the Storm* 185: 'Don't yer remember that, Florrie, from Banana land?'

Bananalander   Queenslander: *jocular*
1887 *Bulletin* 26 Feb. 67: He made all the arrangements for being married on that day, and his friends rallied up to congratulate him, and see him through, after the custom of the simple Bananalanders.
1911 E. S. Sorenson *Life in the Australian Backblocks* 66: The Bananalander's[1] pet [swag] is short and plump.[1]Queenslander's.
1968 Kit Denton *A Walk Around My Cluttered Mind* 3: 'I c'n tell a bananalander any time. I c'n pickem. You come from Queensland 'n' I *know* it!'

Banana-bender, Banana city, Banana curtain, Banana man
1976 Robert Drewe *The Savage Crows* 61: 'Banana-benders of course, look at that mob of classic Queenslanders over there in the shade.'
1981 *Sun* (Sydney) 11 Jun. 62: You've got to hand it to the banana benders. Not only are they pushing for big Artie to coach Australia against the French, but there are rumblings up north he should captain the side too.
1893 J. A. Barry *Steve Brown's Bunyip* 181: He had, he flattered himself ... been making rapid progress with the damsels of the Banana city.
1979 Hugh Lunn *Australian* 28 Dec. 1: We know the Fleet Street system, Henry. Even up here behind the banana curtain.
1886 Percy Clarke *The 'New Chum' in Australia* 66: A Queenslander is ... distinguished by the title of 'banana-man'.

bandicoot *n.*   Used in phrases suggesting misery or destitution [f. the animal]
1845 R. Howitt *Impressions of Australia Felix* 233: 'Poor as a bandicoot,' 'Miserable as a shag on a rock,' & c.; these and others I very frequently heard them make use of.
1859 Henry Kingsley *Recollections of Geoffry Hamlyn* iii 83–4: 'That Van Diemen's bush would starve a bandicoot.'
1877 Rolf Boldrewood *A Colonial Reformer* (1890) 442: He hadn't had a soul to talk to for

three weeks, since the muster began, and was as miserable as a bandicoot.
1885 *The Australasian Printers' Keepsake* 75: I crouched beside him 'as miserable as a bandicoot.'
1913 Henry Lawson 'The Hairy Man' *Prose* i 697: 'I've been feeling as lonely and dismal as a bandicoot on a burnt ridge.'
1934 Steele Rudd *Green Grey Homestead* 18: 'Spring Gully!' he'll snarl. 'That country is no good for you; 'twouldn't feed a bandicoot!'
1946 K. S. Prichard *The Roaring Nineties* 81–2: 'Was as miserable as a bandicoot, felt like chucking up prospecting and trying to get a job ... on the mines.'
1951 Dymphna Cusack and Florence James *Come In Spinner* 22: 'Hiya, Blue?' she said, stepping in. 'Miserable as a bandicoot.'
1969 Osmar White *Under the Iron Rainbow* 111: At first he looked as miserable as a bandicoot.
1980 Densey Clyne *Sydney Morning Herald* 12 Aug. 7: I don't know where the term 'miserable as a bandicoot' came from. They do wear rather long faces, but it's through bone structure rather than disposition.
see **boudoir bandicoot**

bandicoot *v.*   To remove potatoes from below the surface, leaving the top of the plant intact [f. the animal's burrowing habit]
1898 George Dunderdale *The Book of the Bush* 102: 'You bandicooted my potatoes last night, and you've left the marks of your dirty feet on the ground.'
1916 Joseph Furphy *Poems* 15: You may forgo your stylish duds, / And trade away your pin and studs, / To live on bandicooted spuds; / But you Must Never Whine.
1944 M. J. O'Reilly *Bowyangs and Boomerangs* 2: There was a general rule in our district ... that swagmen might be allowed to go into the paddocks and 'bandicoot' potatoes. The interpretation of 'bandicooting' is that the swaggie could scratch a hole round the potato plant, pick out a few big ones, and hill up the plant again to allow the remainder to mature.

bandicoot on a burnt ridge, like a   A state of loneliness and deprivation
1900 Henry Lawson 'Joe Wilson's Courtship' *Prose* i 546: I mooched around all the evening like an orphan bandicoot on a burnt ridge, and then I went up to the pub and filled myself up with beer, and damned the world.
1935 H. R. Williams *Comrades of the Great Adventure* 36: Abdul, shorn of his finery ... low in condition, like a bandicoot on an ironstone ridge.
1963 Marien Dreyer *Bandicoot on a Burnt Ridge* [play title]

bandy, knock someone To worst completely, leave flabbergasted [listed by Partridge as 'tailors': from ca. 1860]

1899 W. T. Goodge *Hits! Skits! and Jingles!* 165: 'You can talk about yer sheep dorgs,' said the man from Allan's Creek, / 'But I know a dorg that simply knocked 'em bandy!'

1908 E. S. Sorenson *Quinton's Rouseabout* 88: 'Joe was reg'lar knocked bandy.'

1934 F. E. Baume *Burnt Sugar* 59: 'You're seventeen, and could knock me bandy.'

1948 Ruth Park *Poor Man's Orange* 174: 'If I hear you slinging off at her again, I'll knock you bandy, honest to goodness I will!'

1968 Craig McGregor *People, Politics and Pop* 43: What do most of his [the taxi-driver's] passengers feel about the heat? 'Why, it knocks 'em bandy,' he says.

bang like a dunny door see **dunny**

bange, banje *n. & v.* Rest: *obs.* [f. *benge* to lounge lazily EDD Fr. *baigner*]

1847 Alexander Harris *Settlers and Convicts* ed. C. M. H. Clark (1954) 105: Stray hands wandering back were already dropping in every now and then at some of our pits for a few days' 'bange' (rest) on their way to Sydney.

1850 B. C. Peck *Recollections of Sydney* 98: Having scrambled down the rocks we may enjoy a quiet 'bange' on the greensward.

1873 J. C. F. Johnson *Christmas on Carringa* 16: So Sunday, Monday, Tuesday / I jogs upon my way / With a little banje* or whaling / To just fill up the day. *Banjing is bush slang for sleeping or lying full length under a tree.

bangtail *v.* To dock the tails of cattle or horses

1908 Mrs Aeneas Gunn *We of the Never-Never* 160: He ... suggested bang-tailing the cattle during the musters.

bangtail muster See quots 1888, 1938

1888 W. S. S. Tyrwhitt *The New Chum in the Queensland Bush* 61: Every third or fourth year on a cattle station, they have what is called a 'bang tail muster'; that is to say, all the cattle are brought into the yards, and have the long hairs at the end of the tail cut off square ... the object of it is, to take a census ... unless marked in some way, it would be impossible to distinguish those that have been through the stockyard from those that have not.

1901 *The Bulletin Reciter* 157: And the day we got the buster was just after bangtail-muster.

1938 Francis Ratcliffe *Flying Fox and Drifting Sand* 331 n.: In a bangtail muster every beast rounded up has the tuft of its tail docked to prevent its being counted twice. This is the only

way of getting an accurate tally on an unfenced run several hundreds or thousands of square miles in area.

1951 Ernestine Hill *The Territory* 391: 'We're sellin' Merryfield, an' now the buyers have asked for a bang-tail.'

1957 R. S. Porteous *Brigalow* 187: I had decided to make this a bangtail muster, a form of stock-taking where the brush was cut from the tail of every beast before it was passed down the dip crush to be dipped and tallied.

banje see **bange**

Banjo, the The pen-name of A. B. Paterson (1864–1941), used in his contributions to the *Bulletin* from 12 June 1886; nickname of anyone surnamed Paterson

1896 *Bulletin* 3 Oct. Red Page: An English weekly declares that Becke is popularly known as the Kipling of the Pacific. 'Banjo' and Lawson have also been identified as more-or-less Kiplings.

1903 Joseph Furphy *Such is Life* (1944) 348: Sir Francis Head, one of the five exceptions to this rule – Gordon being the second, 'Banjo' the third, 'Glenrowan' the fourth, and the demurring reader the fifth.

banjo 1 A frying pan [f. shape]

1900–10 O'Brien and Stephens: *Banjo* a bush name for a frying pan.

1 A shovel

1919 W. H. Downing *Digger Dialects* 10: *Banjo* – a shovel. *Swing the banjo* – dig.

1924 *Truth* 27 Apr. 6: *Banjo* a shovel.

1942 Gavin Casey *It's Harder for Girls* 224–5: All his mother's big ideas, and mine, too, wouldn't keep him off the handle of a banjo if that was what he was suited for.

1973 Donald Stuart *Morning Star Evening Star* 110: He was alongside me swinging his banjo.

1983 *Sun-Herald* 9 Oct. 71: 'My dad and I laid our 80 to 90 yards of gravel a day, working with a banjo (shovel) and a two-horse dray.'

3 A shoulder of mutton

1919 W. K. Harris *Outback in Australia* 146: Called at his particular station for the proverbial free ... 'banjo' (shoulder) of mutton.

1925 *Sydney Worker* 3 Jun. 13: The mutton was not of super-excellent quality, but Johnny was rarely known to part with a 'banjo' without getting good value in return.

4 Popular name for the fiddler ray [f. shape]

1979 *Age* (Melbourne) 2 Nov. Weekender 21: Their haul included banjo and gummy sharks.

banker A river with the water up to or overflowing its banks, esp. in the expression 'run a banker'

1848 W. H. Haygarth *Recollections of Bush Life in*

Australia 129: Now that I take a second glance at the river, its waters look very muddy, which is a sure sign of its being high, not to say a 'banker'.
1868 C. Wade Brown *Overlanding in Australia* 19: Nothing but a large river, running a 'banker' can stop them, and that they are soon made to swim.
1877 Rolf Boldrewood *A Colonial Reformer* (1890) 410: The river was high, had come down a 'banker', and any further rainfall might bring down a flood such as the dwellers in those parts had not seen for many a day.
1889 Henry Lawson 'The Ballad of the Drover' *Verse* i 27: Till the river runs a banker / All stained with yellow mud.
1908 Henry Fletcher *Dads and Dan Between Smokes* 21: 'I tell yer, Wayback, her tears run a fair banker.'
1927 Steele Rudd *The Romance of Runnibede* 88: The Station Creek rose to a banker – rose till it spread itself a quarter of a mile on either side, carrying down logs and uprooted trees and the carcases of dead bullocks.
1934 Thomas Wood *Cobbers* 27: 'That night she was running a banker, with sheep, trees – Oh anything you like coming down, and the water a mile wide.'
1956 Kylie Tennant *The Honey Flow* 209: Cobberloi Creek was running a banker.
1963 A. W. Upfield *The Body at Madman's Bend* 17: 'It's going to run again soon . . . Going to run a banker?'
half-banker
1925 E. S. Sorenson *Murty Brown* 59: In a few minutes he was baulked by the creek, which was running half a banker.
1951 Ernestine Hill *The Territory* 444: *Half-banker* A river in half flood.

Bankie   See quot. 1979
1979 Kathy Lette and Gabrielle Carey *Puberty Blues* 4: I decided he was a bit of a Bankie. You didn't have to come from Bankstown to be a Bankie. It just meant anyone who was uncool.

bar, can't stand (won't have) a ~ of   Can't tolerate on any terms [? f. *bar* in music]
1945 Margaret Trist *Now that We're Laughing* 25: 'I can't stand a bar of these people that visit you and must have a bath every day to show you how clean they are.'
1954 T. A. G. Hungerford *Sowers of the Wind* 1: 'You're right, I couldn't stand a bar of the animal myself.'
1962 Gavin Casey *Amid the Plenty* 149: 'Not that I'd have a bar of a bloke who'd lie to his mates, but it's different with that other mob.'
1973 *Australian* 4 May 2: Dr Arnold said that doctors would be violently against direct billing. 'They won't have a bar of it,' he said.

barb   A breed of sheep-dog [see quots 1908, 1945]
1908 W. H. Ogilvie *My Life in the Open* 162: The barb is a larger dog. Perfectly black in colour, stout and square in build, he too has the best points of the kelpie; the broad, almost bulldog forehead, the small feet and the short smooth hair. The barb dogs are all prick-eared and have a peculiar crouching and watchful carriage. They too are wonderfully enduring, though they are heavier dogs than the kelpies . . . This breed is supposed to have originated from a black dog given to one of the early squatters on the Lachlan River by a blackfellow, and is supposed to be related to the wild dogs or dingoes.
1915 Vance Palmer *The World of Men* (1962) 30: During the day . . . he spent the time talking to his dog, a black and white barb that sat all day near the door, watching him out of its sleepy eyes.
1926 K. S. Prichard *Working Bullocks* 262: Mark remembered dog-fights he had seen. Blue barbe and bull-terrier, that was the fight stuck in his mind.
1945 Baker 73: One of these pups [of a kelpie] was given to a stockman who named him *Barb* after the 1866 winner of the Melbourne Cup. He proved such an excellent sire that he, also, gave his name to a breed.
1952 *Sydney Morning Herald* 29 Mar. 7: The kelpie proper is generally used in the open, the barb for penning and yarding.

barbecue, a chop short of a   As for a shingle short q.v.
1984 *Sunday Independent* (Perth) 6 May 36: The tragedy of that premise is that it automatically assumes that all in charge of prisons are a chop short of a barbecue.

barbed wire   Fourex beer, esp. in Darwin [f. **XXXX** symbol]

barbie   A barbecue [abbr.]
1976 *Australian* 14 Aug. 20: He propounded the natural and national virtues of the Aussie beach barbie with beer and prawns, and the big chunder.
1981 *Age* (Melbourne) 19 Jun. Weekender 4: The barbie glows hotly in the cool, river-scented night air as the volunteer short order cook prepares to bung on the snags, hamburgers and giant T-bones.

Barcoo challenge   See quot. [f. river and district in Queensland]
1933 Acland: *Barcoo challenge* (1) To scrape the points of the shears on the floor or wall, or (2) to throw the belly over another shearer's head, indicating a challenge for the day's tally.

Barcoo rot   A skin ulceration similar to scurvy
1870 E. B. Kennedy *Four Years in Queensland* 46:

Land scurvy is better known in Queensland by local names, which do not sound very pleasant, such as 'Barcoo rot', 'Kennedy rot', according to the district it appears in. There is nothing dangerous about it, it is simply the festering of any cut or scratch on one's legs, arms or hands. [Morris]

1886 Percy Clarke *The 'New Chum' in Australia* 302: One of the most extraordinary features attendant on such a state of the body is the skin complaint known as the 'Barcoo rot'.

1903 Joseph Furphy *Such is Life* (1944) 201: The backs of his hands were pretty bad with the external scurvy known as 'Barcoo rot' produced by unsuitable food and extreme hardship.

1933 F. E. Baume *Tragedy Track* 45: A case of oranges ... was decided on as an antidote for scurvy which, in its barcoo rot form, was playing havoc with any tiny wounds on face, body or limbs.

1968 Walter Gill *Petermann Journey* 57: He has broken out in clusters of sores on hands and wrists. 'Barcoo rot' undoubtedly.

Barcoo salute   See quot. 1973
1973 Patsy Adam Smith *The Barcoo Salute* title page: 'I see you've learnt the Barcoo salute,' said a Buln Buln Shire councillor to the Duke of Edinburgh. 'What's that,' said His Royal Highness, waving his hand again to brush the flies off his face. 'That's it,' said the man from the bush. [quotation dated 1953]

1974 *Sydney Morning Herald* 23 Apr. 6: The humble, if ubiquitous, bushfly is not only responsible for our national habit, the Barcoo salute, but is also the feature of Australia most often commented on by overseas visitors.
See **Australian salute**, **Queensland salute**

Barcoo sickness (spews, vomit)   See quots
1898 Morris: *Barcoo Vomit* painless attacks of vomiting, occurring immediately after food is taken, followed by hunger, and recurring as soon as hunger is satisfied.

1925 E. S. Sorenson *Murty Brown* 56: I've had the barcoo, an' other upheavals.'

1927 M. M. Bennett *Christison of Lammermoor* 62: One of the great hardships of those days [the 1860s] was the sickness brought on by the monotonous food and bread made from tainted flour, every settler supposed it peculiar to his district, and named it accordingly Burdekin, or Belyando, or Barcoo sickness.

1935 H. H. Finlayson *The Red Centre* 50: A gastric disorder, known to the settlers by the crude but expressive term 'barcoo spews' is common in summer.

1966 *Australian* 3 Jan. 6: The unending irritations of the shearer's life ... barcoo spews and purgatorial insects.

bardie 1 An edible wood grub [*Bardistus cibarius*]
1946 K. S. Prichard *The Roaring Nineties* 200: Kalgoorla brought her toasted bardies to eat. Sally recognized the fat white grubs Maritana used to devour with such relish.

1955 F. B. Vickers *The Mirage* 69: 'Black fella tucker good.' 'Arrah! Bardies and goannas.'

1968 Stuart Gore *Holy Smoke* 82: 'They've been stuck out in the mulga for nearly a week ... livin' on lizards and bardies.'

1979 *Advertiser* (Adelaide) 30 Mar. 21: The bardie grub is proving to be a good bait for cod.

1983 T. A. G. Hungerford *Stories from Suburban Road* 41: He loved to eat the bardies my father cooked every time we went out for wood – the big, white fat grubs you found in every banksia when it split, with hard brown heads the size of a pea ... He would heat the blade of a shovel over the tea fire and drop a handful of bardies onto it and stir them around with a stick until ... they were done.

2   The exclamation 'Starve the bardies!' (a variant of 'Starve the lizards!') more often encountered in lists of Australianisms than in actual conversation
1941 Baker 8: *Bardies! Starve the*: A popular W.A. ejaculation, synonymous with 'Stone the crows!'

1969 *Pocket Oxford Dictionary* 1020: *Starve the bardies!* excl. of surprise or disgust.

bare, so ~ you could flog a flea across it   see **flea**

bark, short of a sheet of   As for **a shingle short** q.v.
1885 Mrs Campbell Praed *Australian Life* 199: He had always understood that Richard Murray was short of a sheet of bark – the Australian equivalent of 'a tile loose'.

Barker, a Bishop   A long glass of beer [f. Frederick Barker, Bishop of Sydney 1845–81, 6′ 5½″ in height]
1886 Frank Cowan *Australia: A Charcoal Sketch* 32: Long sleever, Bishop Barker, and Deep-sinker, synonyms of the Yankee Schooner.

Barlow, Billy   The inexperienced immigrant who meets with misadventures in the colony [f. the ballad 'Billy Barlow': see *Old Bush Songs* ed. Stewart and Keesing (1957) 53–5]
1843 'Billy Barlow' *Maitland Mercury* 2 Sep. 4: When I was at home I was down on my luck. / And I yearnt a poor living by drawing a truck; / But old aunt died and left me a thousand – 'Oh, oh / I'll start on my travels,' said Billy Barlow / Oh dear, lackaday, oh; / So off to Australia came Billy Barlow.

Barn, the Old   The Sydney Stadium (closed in 1970)
1973 *Sydney Morning Herald* 13 Feb. 15: It would

never have happened at the Old Barn.
see **Tin Shed**

barney *n.* An argument, disagreement, fight [f. *barney* A disturbance, dispute, altercation EDD 1891]
1858 Charles Thatcher *Colonial Songster* 68: A barney first commences / With a little bit of 'skiting', / But calling names is not enough, / And so it ends in fighting.
1875 Rolf Boldrewood *The Squatter's Dream* repr. as *Ups and Downs* (1878) 12: 'Well, we had a sair barney, weel nigh a fight, you might be sure.'
1893 Henry Lawson 'Brummy Usen' *Prose* i 77: 'She was just as self-opinionated as the neighbours, and many a barney she had with them about it.'
1920 Louis Esson 'The Woman Tamer' in *Dead Timber* 19: 'Had a barney, Chopsey?'
1938 Xavier Herbert *Capricornia* 379: 'Joe always plays tunes like that when there's been a barney with the men.'
1942 Sarah Campion *Bonanza* 45: That started such a hullabaloo and general barney among one and all.
1981 *Business Review* 11 Jan. 2: Andrew Peacock is planning to pull on a barney with the unions. If he wins the face of industrial relations may never be the same again.

barney *v.* To argue, dispute
1876 Rolf Boldrewood *A Colonial Reformer* (1890) 183: 'If you go barneying about calves, or counting on horses that's give in, he'll best ye, as sure as you're born.'
1888 E. Finn *Chronicles of Early Melbourne* i 85: The queer old Crown Prosecutor ... used to be very loud in his talk at times to those about him, and one day he and Chief-Constable Sugden were 'barneying' about some hitch in a criminal case. Their recrimination attracted the attention of the judge.
1947 Vance Palmer *Hail Tomorrow* 63: 'No more barneying with pannikin bosses about the length of a smoko or whether the sheep's wet or dry.'

Barney's bull see **bull**

barra Barramundi [abbr.]
1979 *Courier-Mail* (Brisbane) 6 Apr. 20: Controls on barra recommended [heading] The giant perch, or barramundi, one of Australia's top sporting and table fish, may be in danger of being fished out.
1982 *NT News* (Darwin) 17 Apr. 38: The Easter period proved a bonanza for barra fishermen in quite a few Top End spots.

barrack *v.* 1 To indulge in noisy comment; to subject to banter; to ridicule, jeer at [f. *barrack* to

brag, to be boastful of one's fighting powers N. Irel. EDD. Quot. 1878 may be from *baragouin* (*barrikin*) language so altered in sound or sense as to become generally unintelligible; jargon, 'double-Dutch' OED 1613]
[**1859** Hotten 3: *Barrikin* jargon, speech, or discourse, 'we can't tumble to that *barrikin*', we can't understand what he says.]
1878 T. E. Argles *The Pilgrim* iv 39: Douglass mumbled over a 'petition' intended for presentation to Parliament, for the edification of assembled toughs and larrikins, but it was received with noisy insult and cries of 'cheese your barrickin'' and 'shut up'.
1885 *The Australian Printers' Keepsake* 121: The same old rubbishy gibes that had been vogue for centuries were raked up again ... the customers enjoyed the barracking.
1893 Henry Lawson 'For'ard' *Verse* i 259: There's a broken swell amongst us – he is barracked, he is chaffed.
1907 Nathan Spielvogel *The Cocky Farmer* 29: Grant had been barracking Joe about some girl.
1915 C. J. Dennis *The Songs of a Sentimental Bloke* 22: Me! that 'as barracked tarts, an' torked an' larft, / An' chucked orf at 'em like a phonergraft!
1934 Vance Palmer *Sea and Spinifex* 285: He had never liked being barracked, he was beginning to lose his temper.
2 In sport, to interject in favour of one side or against the other; to support
1891 Henry Lawson 'At the Tug-of-war' *Verse* i 114: It gave the old man joy / To fight a passage through the crowd and barrack for his boy.
1903 Joseph Furphy *Such is Life* (1944) 34: 'Toffs is no slouches at barrackin' for theyre own push.'
1913 John Sadleir *Recollections of a Victorian Police Officer* 278: They yelled and shouted, some 'barracking' for Jack, some for the sergeant.
1924 C. J. Dennis *Rose of Spadgers* 91: ''Oo was it tried to stoush that rat-face mutt? / 'Oo was it barracked for me in the fight?'
1934 Tom Clarke *Marriage at 6 a.m.* 200: When Arthur Gilligan's Test Team came out he 'barracked' for Australia.
1969 William Dick *Naked Prodigal* 93: 'He barracks for the Magpies though, same as me.'
1971 David Ireland *The Unknown Industrial Prisoner* 135: This was great fun for the audience, who barracked loudly for the two men after each trick was done.
1981 *Canberra Times* 5 Aug. 8: Mr Cahill, SM sentenced a man to six month's jail yesterday after telling him he had been silly to wear an Essendon football jumper as Mr Cahill 'barracked' for Collingwood.

barrack *n.* 1 The product of 'barracking'; but see

barrack v. quot. 1859
1899 *The Rambler* 13 Feb. 2: Bits o' Barrack [heading to column]
1947 Vance Palmer *Cyclone* 14: Donolly was jollying the child about the shriek she had let out, but she did not respond to his barrack.
2 Baroque pearl
1962 Jock Marshall and Russell Drysdale *Journey Among Men* 138: Perhaps more interesting than ordinary pearls, though far less valuable today, are those locally known as 'barrack'. This expression is a corruption of 'baroque'. 'Barrack' pearls may be of fantastic shapes. They are sometimes formed by pearly deposits over fishes, crabs, and other small marine animals that have invaded the shell and died there.

barracker   One who 'barracks'
1892 G. L. James *Shall I Try Australia?* 129: In Victoria also, the people are 'football mad', and the youths wear the colours of their favourite club, in a profusion which is apt to mystify the new arrival, these are the 'barrackers', the verb 'to barrack' meaning to audibly encourage their own favourites, and comment disparagingly upon the performance of their opponents, a proceeding which frequently leads to an interchange of compliments between the 'barrackers' themselves.
1910 Henry Lawson 'Roll up at Talbragar' *Prose* i 751: Maybe some of the big, simple souls had a sort of vague idea that the departed would stand a better show if accompanied as far as possible by the greatest possible number of friends – 'barrackers', so to speak.
1914 Arthur Wright *In the Last Stride* 8: She followed the games, and with the colours of her favourite club pinned to her breast, graced the ladies reserve at all the big matches, applauding her champions at times to such an extent as to be in danger of being classed as a 'barracker'.
1925 Seymour Hicks *Hullo Australians* 246: A place they call the Hill is occupied by thousands of barrackers, not soldiers, but fellows who are sure they understand cricket better than the umpires.
1933 Norman Lindsay *Saturdee* 34: A prominent barracker for the local team, and deep in its polemics.
1945 Herbert M. Moran *Beyond the Hill Lies China* 100: On their own local ground 'barrackers' would sit or lie on the grass and make jeering remarks about the player who missed a catch or mulled a pass.
1969 Alan O'Toole *The Racing Game* 169: 'Like the football days, eh, Bill? You can't beat having a few barrackers.'

barracks   Building on a station for the accommodation of the jackeroos, etc., and marking a division in the social hierarchy
1876 Rolf Boldrewood *A Colonial Reformer* (1890) 100: At a short distance from 'the house', Mr Jedwood's cottage, or hut, as the residence of the proprietor was indifferently designated, stood a roomy, roughly finished building known as the 'barracks'. Here lived the overseer . . . Three of the numerous bedrooms were tenanted by young men . . . neophytes, who were gradually assimilating the lore of Bushland. To the barracks were also relegated those just too exalted for the men's hut, while not eligible for . . . 'the cottage'. Such were cattle dealers, sheep-buyers, overseers of neighbouring stations, and generally unaccredited travellers whose manners or appearance rendered classification hazardous.
1903 Joseph Furphy *Such is Life* (1944) 254: Being a little too exalted for the men's hut, and a great deal too vile for the boss's house, I was quartered in the narangies' barracks.
1942 Jean Devanny *The Killing of Jacqueline Love* 3: A hundred yards from the house the low wooden barracks, the home of the overseer and jackeroo and occasional workmen, stood with its back to . . . the edge of the scrub.
1963 John Naish *That Men Should Fear* 57: 'You want the barracks or the house?' asked the driver, with a suddenness that caught me unawares.

barrakin   see **barrack**

barrel   To fell or 'flatten', esp. in a football tackle
1966 Baker 169: *barrel*, to shoot and kill [from army notebook of 1940–5]
1972 John de Hoog *Skid Row Dossier* 106: 'I'll barrel her . . . The only thing that stopped me shovin' her through the window was a charge of assault.'
1973 Alexander Buzo *Rooted* 84: 'Remember that last football match, the grand final when Davo got barrelled?'
1975 *Bulletin* 26 Apr. 46: 'Some mug picked Punchy for a mark and barrelled a king at him at the bar.' . . . (Barrelled; to throw a punch. A king is a king hit; a punch thrown without warning.)

Barrett's twist   A chewing or pipe tobacco [f. brand name]
1870 Marcus Clarke 'Arcades Ambo' in *A Colonial City* ed. L. T. Hergenhan (1972) 70: When he rides over to the little public-house and is condescendingly blasphemous towards the publican, the best brandy – *without* the Barrett's twist at the bottom of the cask – is brought out in his honour.
1885 *The Australasian Printers' Keepsake* 84: Ever and anon extracting from a cavernous pouch a huge roll of Barrett's twist, like a bludgeon, from which he would bite off a Gargantuan quid.
1898 Alfred Joyce *A Homestead History* ed. G. F.

James (1969) 106: The tobacco [in 1847] was always of one kind, Barret's twist, in long square twisted sticks, sixteen to the pound.

barrow To start or finish off a sheep for a shearer, as a way of learning to shear [? f. Gaelic *bearradh* shearing, clipping]
1904 E. S. Sorenson *A Shanty Entertainment* 94: It's a good while since we started, you and me, to get a shed; / 'Ow you barrowed that first year for Marty Kell.
1933 Acland: *Barrow* To shear or partly shear a sheep for a shearer. 'No barrowing allowed on the board' was at one time a rule which the Shearers' Union got into the award. Boys often finish or begin a sheep for a shearer, who, of course, is responsible for its being properly shorn.
1964 H. P. Tritton *Time Means Tucker* 39–40: On the advice of the boss of the board, I spent most of the afternoon watching and 'barrowing', that is, finishing off. Bill would shear a sheep to the 'whipping side' then pass it to me and as it was straight going, seven or eight blows would complete the job ... Soon I was holding my own with the other learners.
1975 Les Ryan *The Shearers* 126: 'Though I had done only a bit of barrowing here and there, I fluked a learner's pen.'

bart A girl: *obs.* [unexplained]
c. **1882** *The Sydney Slang Dictionary* 1: *Bart* A girl, generally applied to those of loose character.
1899 W. T. Goodge *Hits! Skits! and Jingles!* 150: And his lady love's his 'donah', / Or his 'clinah' or his 'tart' / Or his 'little bit o' muslin', / As it used to be his 'bart'.
1941 Baker 8: *Bart* A girl. Now practically obsolete.

bash, have a, give it a Make an attempt at (as in 'give it a burl')
1959 David Forrest *The Last Blue Sea* 183: 'Yair, it's somebody else's turn to have a bash,' said Lincoln.
1969 William Dick *Naked Prodigal* 179: 'Reckon you'll be able to do it? I mean it's pretty hard.' 'I hope so. I'm gonna give it a bash, anyway.'
1972 Richard Magoffin *Chops and Gravy* 106: *give a bash* have a go, give it a trial, attempt.
1973 Max Harris *The Angry Eye* 106: They did have a bash at the weather, I remember.
1979 *National Times* 21 Jul. 15: The news director said 'We're a journo short – want to have a bash?'

bash the ear To harangue, talk incessantly [f. *earbasher*]
1971 Rena Briand *White Man in a Hole* 26: Other days I'd ... drown my sorrows at the Front Bar

and bash Johnny's ear with my tale of woe.
1975 Xavier Herbert *Poor Fellow My Country* 30: 'They told me that I'd be lucky if you talked to me at all ... and just as unlucky if you did' ... 'They mean you'd regret it, because then I'd bash your ear?'

bashing, poofter- see **poofter**

basket weavers from Balmain See **basket-weaving**
1982 *Sydney Morning Herald* 27 Oct. 24: Mr Unsworth is not alone in hurling the cutting insult at the defenceless trendies. Paul Keating disparagingly referred to them as 'basket-weavers from Balmain'.

basket-weaving The activity identifying the Left wing of the Labor party and its new ideology, in the view of their opponents
1983 Patrick Cook *National Times* 17 Jun. 51: Back in Australia, the various ALP conferences convened, keeping hundreds of disturbed people off the streets, absorbed in ideological basket-weaving.
1984 Mungo MacCallum *Sun-Herald* 8 Apr. 52: He marched down to the leafy bower where the Left held its meetings. In it were three or four old men practising their basket-weaving.

bastard None of the senses distinguished is exclusively Australian, but all are so much a part of the colloquial language as to be remarked upon by overseas visitors.
1 Derogatory, but not necessarily suggesting illegitimacy
1892 Henry Lawson 'The Captain of the Push' *Verse* i 187n: 'Here's the bleedin' push, me covey – here's a bastard from the bush! / Strike me dead, he wants to join us!' said the captain of the push.
1929 A. B. Piddington *Worshipful Masters* 46: *Digger* [paraded before an English officer trying to discover who called the regimental cook a bastard] 'You keep on asking us who called that cook a bastard; what we want to know is, who called that bastard a cook?'
1939 Kylie Tennant *Foveaux* 170: 'A man ought to heave the bastard out on his ear.'
1958 H. D. Williamson *The Sunlit Plain* 128: 'Have you ever heard of a bloke being one of Nature's gentlemen?' I says. 'Why, yes,' he says, grinning all over his fat mug. 'Well,' I says, 'you're one of Nature's bastards.'
1960 Donald McLean *The Roaring Days* 199: 'I want a few quid for th' school tonight, so don't be a bastard.'
1974 E. G. Whitlam [addressing the Canberra branch of the ALP] *Sunday Telegraph* 9 Jun. 2: 'I do not mind the Liberals, still less do I mind the

Country Party, calling me a bastard. In some circumstances I am only doing my job if they do. But I hope you will not publicly call me a bastard, as some bastards in the Caucus have.'

1979 *Sydney Morning Herald* 2 Mar. 6: A backbencher quoted Mr Robinson as saying, of his relations with the Prime Minister, that he could not work with bastard.

1980 *Weekend Australian* 16 Aug. 13: When told that Premier Bjelke-Petersen was still on the miners' side in their housing tax fight with Canberra, Mr Tanzer replied: 'You can't help but like the old mongrel sometimes. It's a pity that he's such a rotten, radical, reactionary tory bastard.'

2 Compassionate, indicating a grudging acceptance

1903 Joseph Furphy *Such is Life* (1944) 31: 'Seen better days, pore (fellow),' observed Cooper sympathetically, as the ripple of water into the pannikin indicated that the whaler was at the tap.

1931 William Hatfield *Sheepmates* 269: 'I've knocked around a bit in my time, and I'll tell them that don't know him he's a decent sort of a poor bastard.'

1934 F. E. Baume *Burnt Sugar* 249: 'And not a bad old bastard either. Been here twenty-two years.'

1953 T. A. G. Hungerford *Riverslake* 24: 'Not such a bad sort of a poor old bastard, but the grog's got him.'

1962 Stuart Gore *Down the Golden Mile* 159: Conlon ... replied casually: 'Ah, he's not such a bad poor bastard.'

1981 David Ireland *National Times* 25 Jan. 25: He wasn't a bad poor bastard, it's just that he wasn't anything in particular and people could take him or leave him.

3 Friendly, affectionate

1882 A. J. Boyd *Old Colonials* 62: 'Now then, Harry, you old ——, what the —— is it going to be? Give it some —— name or other!'

1935 H. R. Williams *Comrades of the Great Adventure* 64: One of the things often remarked on by other British troops was the frequent use by the Australians of the word 'bastard'. In the A.I.F. this expression had a very elastic meaning. So much so that between pals it became almost a term of endearment.

1944 Lawson Glassop *We Were the Rats* 168: 'G'day, ya old bastard,' said Jim, and I was amused again that the Tommies could never get used to our main term of endearment.

1964 H. P. Tritton *Times Means Tucker* [recalling period 1905–6] 109: A short-necked man, with a chest like a barrel, and arms reaching to his knees, forced his way through the crowd, put his hand out and said, 'Frank, you bloody old bastard!' ... They pumped his hand, smacked him on the back, swore at him and each other, then took possession of most of the bar.

1969 Patsy Adam Smith *Folklore of the Australian Railwaymen* 218: There was a Welsh fellow with us, a lay preacher, and ... a ganger called him a Welsh bastard. It was friendly you know. But Taffy didn't know and told us that he had evidence of the marriage of his parents. The ganger got heated and said if he himself didn't mind being called a bastard why was this Welsh bastard complaining and with that Taffy up and jobbed him.

1974 *Sydney Morning Herald* 13 Mar. 7: The Charmhaven Branch of the Australasian Order of Old Bastards will meet tonight.

1981 *Business Review* 18 Jan. 5: When being chummy, don't refer to them as 'you old bastard' or some such. Americans aren't used to being abused as a sign of friendship.

4 Impersonal

1915 Ion L. Idriess, diary in Bill Gammage *The Broken Years* (1974) 77: Of all the bastards of places this is the greatest bastard in the world.

1944 Lawson Glassop *We Were the Rats* 169: It's like one of your mates going out on patrol and not coming back. It's a bastard, but you can't do anything about it.'

1962 Alan Marshall *This is the Grass* 128: Sometimes a man began with a question seeking an explanation of my crutches: 'What's wrong with you?' 'Paralysis.' 'Bastard, isn't it ... ?'

1974 John Power *The Last of the Knucklemen* 11: 'The air-conditioner's ... on the blink. Bastard's not worth two bob.'

1981 *Sydney Morning Herald* 10 Oct. 39: 'People used to say it's a bastard of an industry, but it's not really, it's a business with a lot of bastards in it.'

1983 Arthur Cannon *Bullocks, Bullockies and Other Blokes* 98: In bullocky language: 'There is a tide in the affairs of men, which, taken at the ebb, turns into a real bastard.'

see **Pommy bastard**

bastard, the big see **big bastard**

bastard from the bush, the An uncivilized interloper who imposes himself on the society he enters. [f. Lawson's poem 'The Captain of the Push' and variants of it; the lines most often quoted are not by Lawson: 'Will you have a cigarette, mate?' said the Captain of the Push / 'I'll have the flaming packet!' said the Bastard from the Bush.]

1892 Henry Lawson 'The Captain of the Push' *Verse* i 187n: Till he gave an introduction – it was painfully abrupt – / 'Here's the bleedin' push, me covey – here's the bastard from the bush! / Strike me dead, he wants to join us!' said the captain of the push.

1962 Stuart Gore *Down the Golden Mile* 216: 'Don't think they'd have a bar o' me any other place, I suppose. Not cultured, eh? The bastard from the bush!'

1964 Dan Reidy *The Road to Tabuggerie* (1967) 79: 'Things get lively here at times when all the bastards from the bush come in and get tanked up.'
1975 Xavier Herbert *Poor Fellow My Country* 1079: 'It's you're the bastard . . . The Bastard from the Bush. Get back where you belong!'

bastard, happy (lucky) as a ~ on Father's Day Unhappy, unlucky
1958 Frank Hardy *The Four-Legged Lottery* 128: 'I've got about as much luck as a bastard on Father's Day.'
1967 Frank Hardy *Billy Borker Yarns Again* 20: 'The Parrot would be happy being talked out of seven winners in succession?' 'Happy as a bastard on Father's Day. Tears his ticket into confetti.'
1974 *Sunday Telegraph* (Sydney) 9 Jun. 30: Those words of the Bank of NSW's Russell Prowse – 'bankers are as miserable as a bastard on Father's Day' provided a touch of humour not normally associated with banks.

bastardization Term applied to initiation ceremonies at colleges, schools etc.
1969 *Australian* 20 Sep. 5: Mr Barnard also asked if the terms of reference of the board of inquiry into Duntroon were wide enough to look into whether 'bastardisation' at the college was condoned by some of the permanent military staff.
1971 *Sydney Morning Herald* 29 Oct. 10: The report said: 'Organised initiation ceremonies, a formal pattern of bastardisation or any form of patterned violence or misbehaviour have never been a part of the program, official or otherwise, at Leeuwin.'
1972 *Sunday Telegraph* (Sydney) 27 Aug. 1: A brutal bastardisation ceremony at Australia's oldest public school has forced a boy to leave school only two months before his matriculation examination.
1979 *Advertiser* (Adelaide) 7 Mar. 3: Senior cadets at the Fort Largs Police Academy have committed 'bastardisation' outrages on several junior cadets, says the Melbourne 'Truth'.
1983 Gerald Walsh *Sydney Morning Herald* 13 Apr. 1: 'Bastardisation, or the systematic hazing of junior cadets, has been back at Duntroon for 10 years.'
see **bishing**

bastardry See quot. 1945 [f. *bastard* 1]
1945 Baker 156: *bastardry* ill-treatment, injustice, anything unpleasant, especially when done at the whim of a superior officer [World War II slang]
1948 Sumner Locke Elliott *Rusty Bugles* in *Khaki, Bush and Bigotry* ed. Eunice Hanger (1968) 95: 'You see . . . bastardry all the way along the line.'
1950 *Meanjin* 222: Bastardry, Bastardry, Bastardry [review of Frank Hardy's *Power without Glory*]
1953 T. A. G. Hungerford *Riverslake* 2: They even acknowledged a perverted sort of pride in the sheer virtuosity of his bastardry, telling each other about things they had seen him do.
1962 David Forrest *The Hollow Woodheap* 195–6: 'As one expert to another, Mr Lucas, I have to admire your particular brand of bastardry.'
1974 David Williamson *Three Plays* 165: 'Now come on! That's just plain bastardry.'
1982 David Wilson *Weekend Australian* 6 Feb. 17: For more than a decade, taxpayer financed cultural bastardry has flourished in the name of experimental theatre at Melbourne's Pram Factory theatre.

bastards, keep the ~ honest The role perceived for the Australian Democrats (by their leader Senator Don Chipp) in holding the balance of power in the two-party system
1980 *Sydney Morning Herald* 10 Oct. 7: He [Senator Chipp] maintains that he hates politics but that there is a great need for the Democrats. The cynical realism of the catchcry 'keep the bastards honest' also appeals to an electorate noted for its disdain of politicians.
1981 Russell Schneider *The Colt from Kooyong* 112: Chipp . . . tramped around the countryside to form a new political movement dedicated to 'keeping the bastards honest', the Australian Democrats.
1984 *Age* (Melbourne) 25 Jul. 12: One aspect of the Mick Young affair that is intriguing is the silence of the Democrats. What has happened to Senator Chipp's election promise to 'keep the bastards honest'?
1984 *Sydney Morning Herald* 13 Oct. 38: I'm not sure why Senator Chipp was included [in the TV programme). Maybe it was to keep the bastards hypothetical.

bastards, run over the Reported instruction of the N.S.W. premier, Mr R. Askin, when demonstrators lay on the road before President L. B. Johnson's motorcade in Sydney in 1966
1968 *Sydney Morning Herald* 24 Jul. 4: Mr Askin was clapped and cheered yesterday when he told a luncheon meeting [of the American Chamber of Commerce] that he had advised a policeman to run over demonstrators trying to block President Johnson's motorcade in Sydney in 1966. He had turned to the policeman and had said 'Run over the bastards.'
1971 *Sydney Morning Herald* 20 Mar. 3: Mr D. Chipp [Minister for Customs and Excise, reported addressing a dinner of the American Chamber of Commerce in Canberra] 'I would like to think that men of goodwill of my generation have more in

common with the agonised student movement than with some of the extreme nigger-flogging reactionaries of the establishment complete with their "run-the-bastards down" philosophy.'

1981 *Sydney Morning Herald* 18 Jul. 12: I am going to go down (in history) as the bloke who said: 'Ride over the bastards'. – *Sir Robert Askin, in hospital.*

bat the breeze   To engage in idle talk [cf. U.S. *fan the breeze*]

1945 Baker 154: *to bat the breeze*, to gossip or talk. [World War II slang]

1953 T. A. G. Hungerford *Riverslake* 75: 'I've got no time to stand here batting the breeze with you.'

1963 Jon Cleary *A Flight of Chariots* 246: 'What have you two been batting the breeze about?'

batch   To do one's own cooking and housekeeping (of a man) [f. *bach* abbr. of *bachelor* U.S. 1870 Mathews]

1882 William J. Sowden *The Northern Territory As It Is* 154: Supposing he lives in a hut and 'batches', this is the kind of bill he is confronted with.

1892 G. L. James *Shall I Try Australia?* 116: Boarding-houses soon spring up, where he can be very well fed at about 2/- daily; but if he elects to 'batch'* himself, I have heard many declare they can live well for 7/- weekly. *A common expression for finding yourself in food, derived perhaps from the word 'batchelor'.

1896 Henry Lawson '"Dossing Out" and "Camping"' *Prose* i 164: He had a partner. They batched in the office, and did their cooking over a gas lamp.

1908 E. S. Sorenson *Quinton's Rouseabout* 61: 'Batching in a lonely wilderness for twenty-five bob a week!'

1911 F. M. Clowes *On the Wallaby through Victoria* 234: I remember one beautiful young man 'batching' there for years – cooking his own dinner, doing the housework, such as it was, washing up the dishes and working meanwhile like fury on his little fruit farm.

1936 William Hatfield *Australia Through the Windscreen* 234: Rooms in which men 'batch' with all the untidiness of men left to look after themselves in single blessedness.

1947 Margaret Trist *Daddy* 163: 'Now this poor young man, his brother is dead and he batches with his father.'

1955 *Sydney Morning Herald* 6 Sep. 1: 'When I'm batching,' he writes, 'I put on the electric kettle, cook the eggs in it, make the tea, shave and wash up with the same water.'

1971 David Ireland *The Unknown Industrial Prisoner* 278: 'How are you getting on, batching? You going to get married again?'

1983 John Morrison *Overland 93* 36: I'd been baching in Sherbrooke with a mate.

bathers   Swimming costume

1936 H. Drake-Brockman *Sheba Lane* 91–2: He appeared, as he had threatened, in his bathers, and was greeted with cries of 'Bright idea' from everybody.

1942 Gavin Casey *It's Harder for Girls* 152: Most of them were wearing trunks, and my old bathers were baggy as well as out-of-date.

1972 Richard Magoffin *Chops and Gravy* 49: I mean the style of bathers – like bikinis and the such.

1983 Mr Justice Rowland *West Australian* (Perth) 6 Aug. 4: 'It is the magistrate's task to decide whether the mere standing in a pathway to the beach in summer time with bathers down and penis in hand offends against contemporary standards of propriety.'

see **cossie**

battle (battling)   1   To struggle for a livelihood; to work in low-paid employment (usually with an implication of praiseworthiness or self-congratulation)

1907 Henry Lawson 'The Strangers' Friend' *Prose* i 731: 'The fellers as knows can battle around for their bloomin' selves, but I'll look after the stranger.'

1923 Jack Moses *Beyond the City Gates* 128: When you're cockyin' and battlin' and live on what you grow.

1939 Kylie Tennant *Foveaux* 178: All her life Mrs Thompson had been what she called 'battling for a crust.'

1959 Dorothy Hewett *Bobbin Up* 58: 'Battled all me life Al and for what ... a humpy on the Lachlan.'

1969 Alan O'Toole *The Racing Game* 156: 'That money would make all the difference between battling and being comfortable.'

1973 Max Harris *The Angry Eye* 32: Ideas come into the realm of the settled refinements of life, and 'battling', the Australian *modus vivendi*, is conducive to athletic greatness only.

2   To cadge, subsist by hawking homemade artifacts; used esp. of itinerants. Not derogatory, from respect accorded those down on their luck or able to live by their wits.

1902 Henry Lawson 'On the Tucker Track' *Prose* i 227: They were tramping along the track towards Bourke, they were very hard up and had to 'battle' for tucker and tobacco along the track.

1941 Kylie Tennant *The Battlers* 75: 'I'm going back to battle for some more rum.'

1944 Alan Marshall *These Are My People* 157: 'I'd been on a bad track and I knew this town was a hard town to battle, so I pulled up a bo and asked him if he knew where I could get a hand-out.'

battle of Brisbane   see **Brisbane**

battle of Cairns   see **Cairns**

battle, on the   Working as a prostitute
1944 Lawson Glassop *We Were the Rats* 93: The girl was still staring. Perhaps she was, as Eddie would say, 'on the battle'. I had been told some of those girls hung about this lounge.

battler   1   A toiler, one who struggles for a livelihood. Anyone so styling himself asserts his apartness from the affluent class.
1896 Henry Lawson 'Stiffner and Jim' *Prose* i 127: I sat on him pretty hard for his pretensions, and paid him out for all the patronage he'd worked off on me . . . and told him never to pretend to me that he was a battler.
1911 E. S. Sorenson *Life in the Australian Backblocks* 100: He was dressed like an ordinary battler, swinging a billy can.
1949 Lawson Glassop *Lucky Palmer* 150: 'I'm no big shot,' he had said. 'I'm a battler. Just a battler having a good trot.'
1958 Frank Hardy *The Four-Legged Lottery* 164: Sparks was a typical Australian battler, tall and angular, a sardonic wit, a kindly cynic who favoured the underdog . . . Tom Sparks had tried every way known to man of making a 'more or less honest quid', from gold prospecting to inventing gadgets. Now he eked out a living punting horses and, during a bad trot, 'turned over a quid' as a salesman.
1964 Donald Horne *The Lucky Country* 25: Australians love a 'battler', an underdog who is fighting the top dog, although their veneration for him is likely to pass if he comes out from under.
1967 John Yeomans *The Scarce Australians* 24: She and her husband owned no land anywhere, she explained. They were, in Australia's expressive slang, battlers – people for whom life is a daily battle . . .
1975 *Australian* 12 Aug. 9: There are no signs that the forthcoming Federal Budget will give any help to the small Aussie battler.
2   Someone making a living, not just by toil, but by ingenuity [f. *battle* 2]
1935 F. D. Davison and B. Nicholls *Blue Coast Caravan* 157–8: We met two members of the genus 'battler' . . . they were side-show artists, travelling from one country show to another.
1941 Kylie Tennant *The Battlers* [book title]
3   A prostitute
1898 *Bulletin* 17 Dec. Red Page: A *bludger* is about the lowest grade of human thing, and is a brothel bully . . . A *battler* is the feminine.
1956 Ruth Park and D'Arcy Niland *The Drums Go Bang!* 142: The landlord shrugged casually. 'We got a battler in there,' he said. A battler is

Sydneyese for prostitute.
4   See quots
1895 Cornelius Crowe *Australian Slang Dictionary* 7: *Battlers* broken-down backers of horses still sticking to the game.
c. **1914** A. B. Paterson 'Racehorses and racing in Australia' in *The World of 'Banjo' Paterson* ed. C. Semmler (1967) 310: A battler is a turf hanger-on who has not capital enough to be a backer, not personal magnetism enough to be a successful whisperer, and not sense enough to get work.
1922 Arthur Wright *A Colt from the Country* 118–19: Professional punters and racetrack battlers, who manage to make a living of sorts out of the game.

Bay, the   1   In N.S.W., Long Bay Gaol
1918 J. Vance Marshall *Jail from Within* 16: 'If yer lucky yer might get a bite at the Bay tonight,' said the officer with brutal unconcern.
1939 Kylie Tennant *Foveaux* 350: 'They can't send you out to the Bay on a Sunday, so you spend Sunday yarning with the chaps at Central and then Monday morning at six you get out to the Bay and put in your week.'
1967 B. K. Burton *Teach Them No More* 169: 'You could serve the whole five years, and you could do the lot at Grafton, or the Bay.'
1971 Frank Hardy *The Outcasts of Foolgarah* 34: The waterfront police [inquired] why his attic was full of smuggled transistors, and gave him a seaside holiday at the Bay.
2   In Victoria, Port Phillip Bay
1855 William Howitt *Land, Labour and Gold* i 29: On the left the Yarra winding down towards the Bay.
1915 C. J. Dennis *The Songs of a Sentimental Bloke* 81: We're honeymoonin' down beside the Bay.
1934 Vance Palmer *The Swayne Family* 1: Hurrying over breakfast so that they should not miss a moment of the slow approach up the Bay.
1979 *Herald* (Melbourne) 21 May 1: Searches were going on today for a boy missing in rugged alpine country and a father and son missing on the Bay.
3   In Queensland, Cleveland Bay
1979 *Courier-Mail* (Brisbane) 21 Jul. 28: 'Bay' champ to try it again [heading] Trainer Ray Birse expects eight-year-old Windy Lane to cap an outstanding racing career by winning his second Cleveland Bay Handicap at Townsville today.
4   In N.T., Fannie Bay gaol (now a museum), or racecourse
1946 W. E. Harney *North of 23°* 115: The cells of the 'Bay' reminded me of old medieval castles, with clanging doors, huge locks and thick stone walls painted black.
1980 *NT News* 25 Jan. 20: Bay turns it on for its

bettors [heading] It's free beer again tomorrow at Fannie Bay and then pony and train rides on Monday.

Bay of Biscay country   see **Biscay**

Bay 13   See quot. 1981
1981 *Sun-Herald* 11 Jan. 9: Bay 13 is to cricket lovers in Melbourne what the Hill is to their counterparts in Sydney. Both are traditional territory of yobbos who love cricket and alcohol in more-or-less equal amounts.
1984 *Age* (Melbourne) 30 May 39: The notorious Bay 13 produces shafts of Shavian wit like 'Go home ya Pommie mug'.

Bays, the   In S.A., the Glenelg Australian Rules team
1979 *Advertiser* (Adelaide) 19 Jun. 20: Norwood rattled by last quarter Bay revival [heading] Norwood withstood a spectacular revival by a gallant Glenelg to win a thrilling match by nine points at Football park.

Bazza-land   Australia, as represented by Barry (Bazza) McKenzie, hero of the comic strip by Barry Humphries
1973 *Sunday Telegraph* (Sydney) 25 Nov. 89: The losers: The Australian composers we won't hear now, the ticket holders, and above all Bazza-land itself.
1974 *Sydney Morning Herald* 23 Nov. 11: Who's who and who's not in Bazzaland. [review of *Who's Who in Australia*]

B-bus   The booze bus, q.v.
1982 *Australian* 21 Dec. 9: Just as one of the brightly lit B-buses was locking up for the night on a main highway at about 2 am, a car came weaving towards it, and pulled up sharply. From it emerged a more than slightly tipsy driver, and pounded on the bus door. 'What is it?' said a weary cop. Said the driver: 'I'd like two hamburgers and a can of Coke please, mate.'

bean, pork and   see **pork**

bear, teddy   see **teddy bear**

bear up, do a   To pay court to a woman: *obs.* [OED 'U.S. *colloq.*' n.d.]
1899 Henry Lawson 'The Hero of Redclay' *Prose* i 297: 'I'd been getting on all right with the housemaid at the Royal ... I thought it was good enough to do a bit of a bear-up in that direction.'
1942 Sarah Campion *Bonanza* 208: 'I was all set to lay another fiver on your chances o' gettin' hooked – you looked to be bearin' up proper, an' no mistake.'

1974 Donald Stuart *Prince of My Country* 63: 'Can you imagine old John doin' a bear-up to a young dolly?'

Bears, the   1   The North Sydney Rugby League team [f. club emblem]
1975 *Sydney Morning Herald* 18 Aug. 9: Gallant Bears skinned.
2   The police, in the argot of long-distance road hauliers [U.S.]
1976 *The Sun* 28 May 7: *Bear* Policeman. *Wall-to-Wall Bears* High concentration of police.

beaten favourite, head like a   see **head**

beaut   1   Applied to something which is exceptional in its class, and therefore usually deserving admiration; vague term of commendation [abbr. *beauty* U.S. 1866 Mathews]
1905 Randolph Bedford *The Snare of Strength* 223: At the sound all the stallion's senses were ... bent in his direction. 'He's a bute,' said Dunphy. 'Quick as a flash; his nerves are all on ball-bearings.'
1907 Nathan Spielvogel *The Cocky Farmer* 42: 'Them's Piggy Howe's cows. Best milkers on the plains. That big Allerney gives a heap of milk a day. She's a beaut.'
1911 Edward Dyson *Benno and some of the Push* 123: 'Ain't he a beaut?' vociferated Benno. 'Good man, Brophy! It's twenty t' one on yeh!'
1930 L. Lower *Here's Luck* 266: 'An all I get out of it is a black eye. Look at it!' 'What a beaut!' exclaimed Stanley admiringly.
1944 *Coast to Coast 1943* 156: Everything had been beaut that spring.
1969 Thomas Keneally *The Place at Whitton* 214: 'I'm a specialist in loneliness. Your mate down there's a beaut as far as loneliness goes.'
1973 Alexander Buzo *Rooted* 46: 'It was a beaut design ... He did this incredible white obelisk anchored into a beaut welter of blue streaks on a sheet of black strips with this incredible screen of pink flecks on a beaut steely surface.' 'Sounds beaut.'
1976 *Sydney Morning Herald* 6 Aug. 3: 'It's been beaut,' the Prime Minister, Mr Fraser, said yesterday of his four-day fishing holiday.
1982 Thomas Shapcott *Sydney Morning Herald* 31 Jan. 38: Brisbane is a beaut place to bring kids up in.
2   In the phrase 'You beaut!', as an interjection of approval
1944 Lawson Glassop *We Were the Rats* 212: 'You beaut!' I cried. 'You bloody beaut!'
1951 Dal Stivens *Jimmy Brockett* 184: 'You beaut!' he said. 'There's a fortune in it.'
1962 Gavin Casey *Amid the Plenty* 206: 'I've got a job,' he said. 'You bloody little beaut!' the grocer

roared.

3   Indicating reproach or disapproval
  1909 Arthur Wright *A Rogue's Luck* 35: 'You're a beaut,' he said, 'leavin' 'er cobber like that.'
  1948 H. Drake-Brockman *Sydney or the Bush* 201: 'Mum,' his reproach met her, 'you're a beaut. Wher've you been?'
  1953 T. A. G. Hungerford *Riverslake* 238: 'You must've thought I was a beaut, not sticking with you.'

beaut, the you ~ country   Australia [f. *beaut* 2, and the 1961 series of paintings by John Olsen called *You Beaut Country*]
  1964 *Australian* 3 Oct. 15: The pale sunniness of the Heidelberg painters ... will undoubtedly prevail and celebrate 'you beaut country'.
  1971 Craig McGregor *Don't Talk to Me About Love* 18: 'Australia? She's the You Beaut Country. It's so You Beaut even Olsen has to get out of it every year or so.'
  1972 Germaine Greer *Sun-Herald* 23 Jan. 103: Notwithstanding, if you are poor in the 'You Beaut' country, it is your fault.

beauty   Expression of full agreement and approval, often pronounced 'bewdy'
  1969 Thomas Jenkins *We Came to Australia* 243: Ask if they want to go swimming and they [the children] grin from ear to ear, leap up and down and yell: 'Yair!' (yes), 'Bewdy!' (beauty, meaning great idea).
  1974 *National Times* 15 Apr. 6: It is not unfair to see Mr Snedden ... thinking to himself at the beginning of this campaign, 'I shall ask the people to give me the opportunity to lead Australia to greatness.' And the answer he would want from the electorate is 'Bewdy, Bill.'
  1981 *Australian* 15 Dec. 14: Marsh was everyone's hero when he declared: 'I'm an Australian, not a bloody Pom.' Bewdy, Marshy.

Bedourie shower   see **shower**

beer-up   See quots
  1919 W. H. Downing *Digger Dialects* 10: *Beer-up* A drunken orgy.
  1924 *Truth* 27 Apr. 6: *Beer-up* A drinking bout.
  1941 Kylie Tennant *The Battlers* 314: 'If he's on a real proper beer-up,' the Stray whispered, 'he may go on for days.'
  1971 Frank Hardy *The Outcasts of Foolgarah* 200: 'He moved in today and they're havin' a big beer-up tonight to celebrate.'

Bee's Nest   See quot.: N.T. and W.A.
  1951 Ernestine Hill *The Territory* 424: *The Pleiades* are the Bee's Nest.

beg pardons, no   No apologies, no quarter
  1906 Edward Dyson *Fact'ry 'Ands* 198: ''Twas quick business down below here, 'n' no beg-pardons with Bunyip. He downed on his victim like er flash'.
  1932 Leonard Mann *Flesh in Armour* 96–7: The Fritzes began to put up their hands – too late for most of them. No 'beg pardons'.
  1965 Jack Dyer *'Captain Blood'* 27: There was little of the present-day spite ... simply he-man encounters, straight-out fights and no beg pardons.

beggars in the pan, on the coals   Small damper (see quots): *obs.*
  1846 G. F. Angas *Savage Life and Scenes in Australia and New Zealand* i 161: Our cook had not been idle: there were 'dampers', 'dough-boys', 'leather-jackets', 'johnny-cakes', and 'beggars-in-the-pan'.
  1848 Charles Cozens *Adventures of a Guardsman* 140–1: There is another sort of bread made when in a hurry, called 'beggars-on-the-coals' which is made very thin like our girdle bread, and merely placed in the hot ashes, and afterwards turned, about five minutes will suffice to make it.
  1908 Giles Seagram *Bushmen All* 94: Over the grilled chops and 'beggars-on-the-coals' the probability of meeting wild blacks was discussed.
  1934 P. H. Ritchie and H. B. Raine *North of the Never Never* 164: I decided to make some johnny cakes, commonly known by most old bushmen as 'b – s on the coals'.
  see **devils on the coals**

behind   In Australian Rules football, a kick that does not pass cleanly through the goal posts, or that goes between the goal post and the behind post: worth one point
  1880 'The Opening Ball' *Comic Australian Verse* ed. G. Lehmann (1975) 2: 'Forward Carlton!' is now the cry, / And we rush it like the wind, / A roar from ten thousand throats go up, / For we've kicked another behind.
  1980 *Mercury* (Hobart) 8 Apr. 22: North kicked 10 behinds in the first quarter and eight in the last in a shocking display.

behind, further ~ than Walla Walla   see **Walla Walla**

behind like Barney's bull, all   see **bull**

Beliander (Belyando) spew   See quots [f. place-name]
  1889 C. Lumholtz *Among Cannibals* 58: Beliander is also a common disease in Queensland, without the slightest apparent cause, a person is suddenly seized with vomiting, but is relieved just as

suddenly.
1918 C. Fetherstonhaugh *After Many Days* 58: All the ills that flesh is heir to in a new and tropical country . . . fever and ague, Moreton Bay rot (skin scurvy), Belyando Spue (pyrosis or water brash), sandy blight, bungy eyes, and dysentery.
see **Barcoo sickness**

bell sheep   A sheep taken from the pen just as the bell rings to signal the end of a shift (important to a shearer trying to increase his tally)
1900 Henry Lawson 'A Rough Shed' *Prose* i 464: He [the shearer] is not supposed . . . to take a sheep out of the pen *after* the bell goes (smoke-ho, meals, or knock-off) but . . . he times himself to get so many sheep out of the pen *before* the bell goes, and *one more* – the 'bell-sheep' – as it is ringing . . . The shearers are racing each other for tallies.
1911 E. S. Sorenson *Life in the Australian Backblocks* 245: There is also hard cutting among greedy persons for a bell sheep (the one caught just as the bell is about to ring off.)

bendy bus   An articulated bus: See quot. 1983
1983 *Sun* (Sydney) 25 Aug. 13: 29 more 'bendies' coming [heading] The first bendy bus initially had been opposed by the Government bus union but had now been running successfully on North Shore bus services for several months . . . The buses, which are joined by a telescopic section in the middle carry around 69 seated passengers and 27 standing.

Benghazi Handicap (Derby)   See quots
1944 Lawson Glassop *We Were the Rats* 135: The confusion that was the retreat to Tobruk early in 1941 – we always called it the Benghazi Handicap – has rarely been equalled in the history of a war full of confused retreats.
1952 Eric Lambert *The Twenty Thousand Thieves* 103–4. The Ninth Division and the remnants of a British armoured division reached Tobruk. The Benghazi Derby was over. In Tobruk they turned to stand before Rommel.

berley *v. & n.*   To scatter bait on the surface of the water to attract the fish; the bait so thrown [unexplained]
1855 G. C. Mundy *Our Antipodes* i 388: Anchoring the boats in about thirty feet of water, the first operation was the baiting of the spot – locally termed 'burley-ing' with burnt fish, and with the eggs of sharks when any have been caught.
1882 J. E. Tennison-Woods *Fish and Fisheries of New South Wales* 75: It is usual to wrench legs and shell of the back [of the crabs], and cast them out for berley.
1907 Ambrose Pratt *The Remittance Man* 9: 'They don't seem to be biting this morning,' said the boy.

'You should give 'em some burley.'
1937 Vance Palmer *Legend for Sanderson* 124–5: They had burleyed all their favourite fishing-grounds, mixing a sardine paste and scattering it over the sea-floor.
1965 Thomas Keneally *The Fear* 160: The man had worked considerably closer to us, and was hunting blood worms with a sugar-bag full of berley.
1981 *Sunday Mail* (Brisbane) 12 Jul. 55: Handfuls of mixed sand and chopped weed used as burley will often help bring the fish on the bite.

Berries, the   The Canterbury-Bankstown (N.S.W.) Rugby League team
1974 *Sydney Morning Herald* 9 Sep. 11: Berries just pip Sharks.
1975 *Sunday Telegraph* (Sydney) 15 Aug. 44: Berries' bliss. Form back with a vengeance.

bet like the Watsons   see **Watsons**

better than a poke in the eye with a burnt stick   see **poke**

bewdy   see **beauty**

bib, to stick one's ~ in   To interfere, intrude
1952 T. A. G. Hungerford *The Ridge and the River* 57: Here was Wilder, almost a schoolboy amongst them, sticking in his bib.
1960 Jack McKinney *The Well* in *Khaki, Bush and Bigotry* ed. Eunice Hanger (1968) 265: 'What's it got to do with you? Who asked you to stick yer bib in?'
1974 *Sydney Morning Herald* 28 Dec. 8: 'Sayings of the Year'. Sir Robert Askin: I would thank Mr Chipp and his pussyfooting Victorians to keep their bibs out of N.S.W.
1975 Xavier Herbert *Poor Fellow My Country* 523: 'You, eh, Delacy, stickin' your bib in.'
1980 *Sun-Herald* 20 Apr. 46: Then a fourth-grade kid put his bib in. 'She's my girlfriend', he said.

Bible, the Bushman's   see **Bushman's**

bible-basher   A clergyman, missionary or any devout person: *derogatory* [variant of *bible-banger, – pounder, – puncher*]
1944 Lawson Glassop *We Were the Rats* 124: 'I doan want any bible-bashing bastard who's never seen me before mumblin' any bull – over me.'
1950 Frank Hardy *Power Without Glory* 32: Devlin would have left him alone if it hadn't been for the 'bible bashers' who spoke from the pulpit and wrote to the press demanding action against the gambling mania.
1961 Xavier Herbert *Soldiers' Women* 271: 'Then there's the god cops, the bible-bashers.'

1975 Xavier Herbert *Poor Fellow My Country* 254: 'The bigger the case, the more the publicity. That's what the Anthrops and the bible-bashers want.'

1976 Alan Reid *The Whitlam Venture* 58: The National Country Party Premier of Queensland, Joh Bjelke-Petersen, whom Whitlam in a fit of petulance described publicly as that 'Bible-bashing bastard'.

bickies, big (small)   Applied to sums of money, esp. in sport
1981 Barry Humphries *A Nice Night's Entertainment* 188: They might look a bit shonky, but they're prepared to invest big bickies in up-grading the Arab image over here.
1983 Bob Simpson *Sun-Herald* 9 Oct. 72: Boycott also was probably one of the first cricketers to sense the possibilities of big bickies in endorsements and commercialisation and go after them.
1984 *National Times* 13 Jul. 31: Doctors' dilemma – big or bigger bickies? [heading]

Big Australian, the   Broken Hill Proprietary Ltd
1979 *Australian* 20 Jul. 11: All eyes on the Big Australian . . . BHP itself has shown some sensitivity to this [public criticism of price increases and record profits], especially with the institution over the last six months of a massive corporate publicity campaign aimed at extolling the virtues of its size in terms of international presence and its positive contribution at the local level.
  This campaign has reached its height, of course, in the sponsorship of the weekly 60 Minutes current affairs program, which features the company as the 'Big Australian'.
1981 *Age* (Melbourne) 25 Jun. 17: BHP set to report another top profit . . . The Big Australian should easily eclipse the $500 million profit mark – the first time for any Australian enterprise.
1984 *Bulletin* 6 Mar. 100: A new tilt at the Big Australian [heading]

Big Bastard, the   Malcolm Fraser, the Prime Minister 1975–83
1981 Russell Schneider *The Colt from Kooyong* 77: Peacock told anyone who wanted to listen how the 'big bastard' had been 'screwed'.
1984 John Somerville-Smith *Toorak Sunday* 10 Jun. 24: With affection, we have always called Big Mal, that 'Big Bastard' . . . We must get the Big Bastard back, who is still a lot younger than the little bastard.

big bickies   see **bickies**

Big Brother   The Barrier Industrial Council at Broken Hill
1981 *Australian* 3 Nov. 7: Since 1916 the BIC –

also dubbed Big Brother – has ruled on all wage negotiations and, few doubted, controlled the workings of the town.

Big Fella, the   J. T. Lang (1876–1975) Labor Premier of N.S.W. 1925–7, 1930–2 [? f. nickname given to Michael Collins, Irish republican hero, and the height and presence of Mr Lang]
1971 *Sydney Morning Herald* 5 Jul. 3: 'Big Fella' rejoins ALP after 28 years.
1975 *Sunday Telegraph* (Sydney) 28 Sep. 2: John Thomas Lang known to his friends and enemies as the Big Fella, died in St Joseph's Hospital, Auburn, after being admitted ten days ago for a rest.

Big Mal   see **Mal**

big man (men)   A powerfully built Australian Rules footballer, often playing in a special position (e.g. ruckman); any Australian Rules player
1963 Lou Richards *Boots and All!* 24: Most of the big men are tough, but very rarely do you see two big men clashing or knocking each other down . . . Take Jack Dyer, for instance. He was a very tough big man who broke the collarbones of seven players during his long career, but I'm led to believe that most of these blokes were only about 5 ft. 2 in. and could have played with an African pigmy team.
1965 Jack Dyer *'Captain Blood'* 177: He has to play to his ruckmen because the big men are the key to the game.
1982 *Australian* 26 Feb. 1: The big men clash over who will star at the footy [heading]
1984 *Age* (Melbourne) 26 Sep. 40: Michael Byrne vacated a forward pocket and took over the leading bigman role. He has . . . become respected as one of the new breed of quick, highly skilled ruckman [sic] who have replaced lion-hearted workhorses.
see **fly**

Biggles   Nickname of Senator Gareth Evans as Attorney-General in the Hawke Government, after he had authorized RAAF spy flights over the projected Franklin dam in 1983 [f. the aviator in the stories by W. E. Johns]
1983 *Australian* 28 Dec. 9: Gareth Evans: Biggles (after the spy flights) or Garrulous Gareth.
1985 *Weekend Australian* 5 Jan. 10: Among the 'exceptional circumstances' under which 'Biggles' released drug crim Peter Fulcher was, I suppose – 'It seemed like a good idea at the time'.

big-note man   A bookmaker or punter placing or handling large bets
1950 *Australian Police Journal* Apr. 111: Big-note man Wealthy.
1956 J. T. Lang *I Remember* 115: When he was

not in Macquarie St, he was operating at Randwick. He became a 'big-note' man. At one stage he was a bookmaker's agent, laying-off bets for one of the leviathans of the day. At other times, he acted as a betting commissioner, placing bets for wealthy patrons.

big-note oneself, come the big-note   To attempt to inflate one's status or achievements
1953 Kylie Tennant *The Joyful Condemned* 23: 'Morton the bustman!' Rene sneered. 'Listen to him big-note himself. He's going to do a bust.'
1959 Dorothy Hewett *Bobbin Up* 137: 'You've made a career out of the Party. You don't give a bugger about the workers. You're just big-notin' yourself, carving out a slice of your own particular glory.'
1967 B. K. Burton *Teach Them No More* 127–8: Terry had often laughed with the other workers at the attempts of George to big-note himself, to make himself appear bigger in character and experience than he really was.
1970 Barry Oakley *A Salute to the Great McCarthy* 65: 'Don't come the big note with me, Fortune, your next sarcasm may be your last.'
1974 John Powers *The Last of the Knucklemen* 21: 'This gives him a chance to big-note himself.'
1981 *Sydney Morning Herald* 19 Feb. 7: David Hill, the 34-year-old chief executive of the State Rail Authority is reluctant to be interviewed. 'The public doesn't want someone trying to big-note himself', he said. 'It just wants the trains to run on time.'

Big Run, the   Victoria River Downs station, N.T.
1951 Ernestine Hill *The Territory* 231: Flanking the river on both sides for about three hundred miles is the biggest cattle run in the world, Victoria River Downs. With 13,150 square miles until this year, it had an area larger than Belgium, and a steady population of about eight white men as compared with Belgium's eight millions ... With a hundred and seventy thousand cattle, a hundred and fifty black stockmen, and six outcamps – some of them sixty miles from the homestead – the Big Run covers the maze of ranges and creeks in mid-river.
1970 Jock Makin *The Big Run* [book title]
1983 *Australian* 25 May 7: 'The Big Run' as it is known to Territorians, is one of the world's biggest properties; before its subdivision in the mid 1930s, it covered 43,000 sq km – about the size of Belgium. But even today, its size is mind-boggling: about 1.3 million hectares, or 12,000 sq km.

big smoke   see **smoke**

bike   A promiscuous woman, usually in such expressions as 'the town bike', 'the office bike' [f.

ride for the male role in intercourse]
1945 Baker 123: A willing girl is sometimes described as an *office bike*, *a town bike* etc.
1951 Dal Stivens *Jimmy Brockett* 178: 'I might have known you were the bloody town bike.'
1965 Leslie Haylen *Big Red* 186: Murgatroyd, whose wife now had openly become the 'village bike'.
1972 David Williamson *The Removalists* 36: 'Turned out the tart was the biggest bike in the district.'
1980 Barbara Pepworth *Early Marks* 164: Juicy Lucy is the school bike, everyone's ridden her.

bike, to get off one's   To appear to be losing control of oneself
1938 Xavier Herbert *Capricornia* 565: 'I tell you I saw no-one.' 'Don't get off your bike, son. I know you're tellin' lies.'
1952 Jon Cleary *The Sundowners* 237: 'I'm sorry, I didn't mean to get off me bike like that.'
1962 Alan Seymour *The One Day of the Year* 24: Alf (*yelling from kitchen*) Where the bloody hell are you? Mum (*yelling back*) Awright, don't get orf yr bike!
1963 Randolph Stow *Tourmaline* 115: 'You make me sick,' she cried again. 'Don't get off your bike,' he said.
1984 Marian Eldridge *Walking the Dog* 163: 'Don't get off your bike, Joe, I'll pick up your pump', soothes Mr Kneebone.

bike, gone for a ride on the padre's   see **padre's**

Bill and Jim   Typical outback Australians in the 1890s, and typical soldiers in World War I: *obs.*
1896 *Bulletin* 31 Oct. Red Page: The harrowing tale of the lost Bill or Jim in the Australian desert whose eyes are picked out by the crows almost before his death-struggle ceases.
1899 Henry Lawson 'Jack Cornstalk' *Prose* ii 44: And so out back, to the land of Bill and Jim, where we carried swags together.
1911 E. S. Sorenson *Life in the Australian Backblocks* 14: Bill and Jim have lapses at long intervals, they go on a roaring bender for a week or two weeks, after which they do not touch a drop of liquor for months.
1916 Joseph Furphy *Poems* 29: Better we were cold and still, with famous Jim and Bill, / Beneath the interdicted wattle-bough. / For the angels made our date five-and-twenty years too late, / And there is no Up the Country for us now.
1919 W. J. Denny *The Diggers* 171: The freedom with which 'Billjim' spends his pay not unnaturally adds to the warmth of his welcome.

billabong, on the   Out of work and camped on a waterhole: esp. N.T. and W.A. [f. Ab. *billabong*

33

waterhole]

1954 Tom Ronan *Vision Splendid* 16: 'The north has got better men than you, better men than me. When it gets a man it generally throws him on the Billabong and leaves him there.'

billabonger One of those 'on the billabong'

1883 John Farrell 'My Sundowner' *How He Died* (1913) 63: Sam, the Billabonger.

1954 Tom Ronan *Vision Splendid* 217: They dispensed tactfully casual invitations for lunch or tea to billabongers who hadn't eaten a really square meal for months.

billabong whaler see **whaler**

billet A post, job, appointment (at first including lodgings): *obsolescent* [f. *billet* order providing quarters for a soldier OED 1644]

1846 L. W. Miller *Notes of an Exile to Van Dieman's Land* 343: 'What in the name of common sense do you want to get into the *wash-house* for?' I asked. 'Oh, it is a *billet*. The work is light, and performed under cover; and the men get tobacco, and enough to eat into the bargain.'

1865 J. F. Mortlock *Experiences of a Convict* (1965) 101: Mr Jones used his influence to get me made clerk (being one of the best 'billets' for which I was eligible).

1879–80 Ned Kelly 'The Jerilderie Letter' in Max Brown *Australian Son* (1956) 281: What would people say ... to a policeman who for a lazy loafing cowardly bilit left the ash corner deserted the shamrock, the emblem of true wit and beauty to serve under a flag and nation that has destroyed massacred and murdered their fore-fathers.

1885 *The Australasian Printers' Keepsake* 64: Up-country billets oft are loss; / Work for tucker – trust the boss.

1890 *Bulletin* 4 Oct. 12: 'Why,' says the layman, 'you give all the best billets to men from Scotland [when appointing clergy] and think Australians only fit for the back bush blocks.'

1892 William Lane *The Workingman's Paradise* 14: 'I've got a pretty good billet. A pound a week and not much lost time.'

1902 Henry Lawson 'The Story of "Gentleman-Once"' *Prose* i 535: 'He got a billet in the Civil Service up-country ... He commenced to drink again, and went on till he lost his billet.'

1938 Xavier Herbert *Capricornia* 325: She had learnt that Steggles would be going to a Government billet in Singapore when his work in Capricornia was done.

1941 Baker 10: *Billet* A position or job.

1950 *Coast to Coast 1949–50* 191: 'H'm,' he says, 'You'll have to take care of your billet.'

bill-poster, busy as a one-armed ~ in a gale see **one-armed**

billy A cylindrical vessel with a wire handle, of various capacities, used in the outback for carrying water and boiling it to make tea, also as a cooking utensil; in suburban Australia mainly a container for milk, when it was delivered in bulk; often fitted with a lid [abbr. of *billycan*. Prob. f. *billy-pot* cooking utensil SND c. 1828: the derivation f. Ab. *billa* water is unlikely; although there is some evidence that *bouilli* tins were used as billies (see quot. 1911), the term itself was current earlier. NZ 1839 OED]

1855 William Howitt *Land, Labour and Gold* i 195: Edward came behind ... carrying in one hand a gun, in the other a tin kettle or billy, as the diggers call it.

1873 A. Trollope *Australia* ed. Edwards and Joyce (1967) 293: He carries also a pannikin and a 'billy'. The latter is an open pot in which he boils his water and makes his tea ... A bushman of any refinement has the pannikin for drinking; but the rough old chum will dispense with it as a useless luxury, and will drink his tea out of his billy.

1885 *The Australasian Printer's Keepsake* 16: Camp-fires were blazing in the open air, with pots and billies slung across, pannikins of tea were handed round.

1896 Henry Lawson *While the Billy Boils* [book title]

1903 Joseph Furphy *Such is Life* (1944) 78: I gave him my Shakespear as a keepsake, with a billy and pannikin, and a few days' rations.

1911 E. S. Sorenson *Life in the Australian Backblocks* 276: Billy is famous ... He seems to have originated on the Victorian goldfields. The early miners consumed great quantities of French tinned soup, called *bouilli*; and the empty bouilli-cans were used for the same purposes as are now the specially made 'billy-cans'.

1915 Vance Palmer *The World of Men* 4: Above the smouldering fire swung a huge billy of black tea.

1934 Thomas Wood *Cobbers* 77: We drank tea straight from the billy.

1969 D'Arcy Niland *Dead Men Running* 72: There was a fire nearby, a black billy singing in a cradle of flames.

1971 Colin Simpson *The New Australia* 483: We had boiled the billy hung from a hook on a tripod of steel rods that folded together – an invention of Dr Oxer's.

1981 *National Times* 10 May 49: Children still dawdle along country roads carrying billies of thick creamy milk.

billy boy

1969 Arthur Fadden *They called me Artie* 7: Another family friend made a job for me as 'billy boy' with his cane-cutting gang near the Pleystowe mill. My main job was to make their tea and, preceding the men, to thresh the cane before it was cut.

1981 *Sunday Mail* (Brisbane) 9 Aug. Color Mag. 7: The host for the evening was usually the 'billy-boy'. At just the right time he threw in handfuls of tea leaves, tapped the sides of the tins with a stick and then lifted them off to fill smaller billies and teapots.

Billy Barlow   see **Barlow**

billy, boil the   To make a cup of tea, not necessarily with a billycan; to stop for refreshments

1956 A. W. Upfield *The Battling Prophet* 5: 'Glad to meet you. Come on in and we'll boil the billy.' [an electric jug]

1958 H. D. Williamson *The Sunlit Plain* 5: Except for a break at noon to boil the billy, they had been on the move since dawn.

billycart   1   A type of dog-cart which might be drawn by a billygoat

1922 *Sun* (Sydney) 25 Jun. 'Us Fellers' comic strip in 'Sunbeams': illustration of billycart 1.

1923 *Sun* (Sydney) 14 Jan. 'Sunbeams' 3: Some young 'Beamers ride behind a goat in a billycart when they go out driving.

2   A platform on wheels, with the front axle on a swivel for steering, and sometimes a box-like structure at the rear: a home-made vehicle used by juveniles

1922 *Sun* (Sydney) 11 Jun. 'Us Fellers' comic strip in 'Sunbeams': illustration of billycart 2, there described as a 'racing cart'.

1959 Eleanor Dark *Lantana Lane* 253: It will be queer . . . when no kids trundle their billy-carts at leisure past our gates.

1961 Barbara Jefferis *Solo for Several Players* 96: If you want to steer her left, use left pedal. If you want to steer her right, right pedal. Just the same as a billycart.

1968 David Ireland *The Chantic Bird* 157: Billy-cart races, swimming in Hen and Chicken Bay, I remember it all.

1980 Clive James *Unreliable Memoirs* 38: Other children . . . constructed billycarts of advanced design, with skeletal hard-wood frames and steel-jacketed ball-race wheels that screamed on the concrete footpaths like a diving Stuka. The best I could manage was a sawn-off fruit box mounted on a fence-paling spine frame, with drearily silent rubber wheels taken off an old pram.

1980 *Mercury* (Hobart) 1 Jan. 7: Unwanted billy carts, tricycles and bicycles are desperately needed within a week by the Retarded Children's Welfare Association of Tasmania.

1982 *Sun-Herald* 17 Oct. 106: There's something about a billycart that brings out the boy in every man.

Billy, King   see **King Billy**

billy, swing the   see **swing**

billy tea   Tea made in a billy, i.e. outdoors

1897 David McKee Wright *Station Ballads* 17: The spuds and meat were nicely done, the billy tea was made, / With plates and bright tin pannikins the whisky-case was laid.

1943 Maurice Clough *We of the A.I.F.* 45: Men who have lived on billy tea / And damper.

1976 Helen Hodgman *Blue Skies* 7: They took their time, pausing at regular intervals to brew billy-tea, smoke and grin . . . through large mouthfuls of meat-pie.

1980 *Sydney Morning Herald* 6 Feb. 1: A new delicacy to join the ranks of damper, billy tea and meat pies? A City department store is now selling barbecued rabbits in its take-away food department.

bimbo   Term applied to a young tramp in the depression of the 1930s, usually with an implication of homosexuality [? f. It. *bambino*]

1966 Elwyn Wallace *Sydney and the Bush* 144: 'That "mate" as you call him is a queer,' Paddy explained. 'You know, a queen. I think they're called "Bimbos" on the track.'

1973 Frank Huelin *Keep Moving* 139–40: The older man claimed the younger as his nephew . . . but we concluded there was also a more intimate sexual relationship – that the younger was the older man's 'bimbo'.

bindi-eye   *Calotis cuneifolia*, a weed noted for its prickles or burrs [? Ab.]

1910 C. E. W. Bean *On the Wool Track* 226: Often the only sign that tells you he is a shearer at all is the scar made by binde-i or some other burr in the fleece on the back of his hand.

1937 Ernestine Hill *The Great Australian Loneliness* 304: Walking thirty or forty miles in the day, her feet impervious to the scalding sand or the torture of the bindi-eyes.

1959 C. V. Lawlor *All This Humbug* 62: The bindi-eye burrs had sent the little feet back to the comfort of the dust on the track.

1963 Bruce Beaver *The Hot Summer* 113: Continue on her way bare-footed, the blue-metal chips and bindy-eyes presenting less of a trial to her broad toughened feet.

1971 Rena Briand *White Man in a Hole* 32: Our shower clogs were a poor protection against burrs from small, brittle plants which grew profusely. 'Bindy-eye', the miners called them.

1981 *Sydney Morning Herald* 10 Jul. 14: Bindii is the curse of lawns during summer. The plants creep through the grass, often unnoticed until the seed-heads ripen and begin sticking painfully into bare feet. Bindii begins germinating from July, and it is worth spraying with a herbicide such as Weedoben M to control this unpleasant weed.

binghi *n.* & *a.* White term for an Aboriginal: *derogatory* [Ab. word for 'brother']
[1847 Alexander Harris *Settlers and Convicts* ed. C. M. H. Clark (1954) 173: 'Poor fellow you, binghi (brother).']
1902 A. B. Paterson 'Pearling Industry at Thursday Island' in *Song of the Pen* (1983) 83: Torres Straits Islanders ... have great contempt for the 'Binghies' or Australian Aboriginals.
1911 *Bulletin* 5 Jan. 7: Binghi, who left in all Australia not one single public work, is plainly one of the incapables. When a more advanced people comes along, the incapables pass out, either by disease, violence or invisible causes.
1920 *Sunraysia Daily* (Mildura) 16 Oct. 14: Binghi, Our Black Brother: Several Aspects of Aboriginal Life [heading]
1930 *Bulletin* 5 Feb. 23: Binghi was on his way to join the mob in a corroboree, having been summoned by smoke signals.
1936 H. Drake-Brockman *Sheba Lane* 167: 'And yer need ter be mighty careful not ter fall fer a binghi tart.'
1944 Lawson Glassop *We Were the Rats* 5: 'He stopped the abo in three last Saturdee. What a punch! It was a bloody beaut. I leaves me cart outside and sneaks in just in time to see Jerry knock Binghi as cold as a Polar bear's backside.'
1964 Mary Durack *The Rock and the Sand* 212: Before long every white family in Broome had acquired a mission educated 'binghi' couple.
see **boong, Jacky**

bingle A car crash, a 'prang' [? *bingle* a hit in baseball U.S. 1902 Mathews]
1953 Baker 169: *bingle* A skirmish. [as World War II slang]
1966 Baker 253: *bingle* a dent or fracture in a surfboard.
1966 Roger Carr *Surfie* 122: There was this clang of metal on metal and both cars lurched over the shoulder and we nearly went for a bingle.
1979 *NT News* (Darwin) 20 Sep. 7: The congestion wasn't helped by a three-car bingle on Bagot Rd near Nemarluk Drive.
1980 *Sydney Morning Herald* 29 Mar. 13: Cars flew, skidded, spun and rolled across dirt, grid, water and tar. There were bingles galore and cheers and shouts of 'Good one' as cars became airborne or skidded wildly.

bingy Belly [Ab.]
1832–4 Joseph Larmer 'Native Vocabulary 1832–4' (MS Mitchell Library) 24: 'Binje' in that neighbourhood is a word applied to the stomach.

1859 Henry Kingsley *Recollections of Geoffry Hamlyn* ii 94: 'Don't fret your bingy, boss.'
1887 *Tibb's Popular Songbook* 27: He's not much about the bingey, / But on legs he's standing high.
1889 Carl Lumholtz *Among Cannibals* 305: There are now a number of such words which are in vogue throughout the civilised part of the continent – for example, yarriman, horse; dillibag, basket; kabra, head; bingee, belly.
1908 *The Australian Magazine* 1 Nov. 1251: Two or three aboriginal words ... are now found in standard dictionaries ... but others have remained, and are likely to remain in the category of slang, such as bingy (bin jee), stomach.
1911 Steele Rudd *The Dashwoods* 111: Big-bingied, stiff-backed old fogies who did nothing all the week but smoke cigars.
1919 Edward Dyson *Hello, Soldier!* 31: Son pussied [crawled] on his bingie.
1924 *Truth* 27 Apr. 6: *Bingy* The stomach.
1931 William Hatfield *Sheepmates* 243: A well earned poke in the bingie.
1946 W. E. Harney *North of 23°* 188: He was lying on his back, or as the natives say in their quaint way 'Binji upwards', and as his belly rose and fell with his steady breathing, the lads stacked fifty-pound bags of flour upon him. He awoke at the eighth bag!

bird, a dead A certainty, esp. in horse-racing [see quot. 1898]
1889 *The Arrow* 20 Jul. 1: A school-teacher recently asked his class 'What is a moral?' and with one accord came the answer 'A dead bird, sir.'
1898 Morris: *Dead-bird* In Australia, a recent slang term, meaning 'a certainty'. The metaphor is from pigeon-shooting, where the bird being let loose in front of a good shot is as good as dead.
1941 Baker 22: *Dead Bird* A certainty.
1951 Dal Stivens *Jimmy Brockett* 47: It was betting on a dead bird. We had waited nearly a year for a killing like this.
1979 *Sun-Herald* 18 Nov. 63: 'I'm partial to a 'bird' (a betting certainty) on the racecourse, but I am even more keen on the real thing', he told me, pointing to a large aviary in his backyard.

bird, blue, bower see **bluebird, bowerbird**

birds, box of see **box**

birth stain The convict origins of Australia, so characterized by Lord Beauchamp on his arrival as Governor of New South Wales in 1899
1899 *Sydney Morning Herald* 11 May 5: Mr Corcoran, private secretary, handed the press [at Albany] the following message from Lord Beauchamp to the people of New South Wales. It is in

verse, being an adaptation of a verse of Rudyard Kipling's 'The Song of the Cities':

> Greeting, – Your birthstain have you turned to good,
> Forcing strong wills perverse to steadfastness,
> The first flush of the tropics in your blood,
> And at your feet success. – Beauchamp.

1903 Joseph Furphy *Such is Life* (1944) 65: This record transports you (saving reverence of our 'birth stain') something more than a hundred miles northward from the scene sketched in Chap. I.
1939 Herbert M. Moran *Viewless Winds* 69: An irate lady among the spectators had expressed herself picturesquely about those birth stains.

Biscay, Bay of ~ country Country with a very uneven surface for travelling; in S.A. unstable soil unsuited to building [f. reputation of the Bay of Biscay for rough seas]
1854 C. H. Spence *Clara Morison* (1971) 376: The jolting ... caused by a bad gully or an awkward piece of 'Bay of Biscay ground'.
1926 Alfred Giles *Exploring in the Seventies* 116: We proceeded five miles over Bay-o'-Biscay country which we found sticky as glue, and boggy.
1941 Charles Barrett *Coast of Adventure* 111: A low expanse of greyish sandstone, flaked and heaped fantastically; Bay of Biscay country, as easy to walk over as the ruins of a bombed stone building.
1951 Ernestine Hill *The Territory* 443: *Bay o'Biscay* Tumbled country, hills and hollows as of a rough sea.

bishing As for **bastardization** q.v. [? abbr. of rubbishing]
1983 *Newcastle Herald* 9 Apr. 7: The main difference between 1969 and 1983 is that bastardisation, in the college's lexicon of jargon, is now known as 'bishing'. Change comes slowly to Duntroon.

Bishop Barker see **Barker**

bite, put the ~ on To seek a loan, scrounge money or food [cf. *bite the ear* borrow OED 1879]
[**1859** Hotten 6: *Bite* to cheat, 'to be *bitten*', to be taken in or imposed upon.]
1919 W. H. Downing *Digger Dialects* 11: *Bite* (n. or v.) (1) A borrowing, to borrow. (2) an attempt to borrow.
1935 Kylie Tennant *Tiburon* 120: 'An' the perlice is only makin' themselves more work, see, puttin' chaps off the dole, so they 'ave t'bite people, see?' Ibid. 164: He watched the group stream down the road to 'bite' Tiburon and spread the tale of their hardships.
1949 Lawson Glassop *Lucky Palmer* 35: 'Can I bite you for a few quid, Lucky?'
1957 Ray Lawler *Summer of the Seventeenth Doll* 98: 'Your money's runnin' out, you know you can't put the bite on me any more, and so here's the new champion, all loaded and ready.'
1963 Alan Marshall *In Mine Own Heart* 164: 'Have you got any tucker with you or will we have to go in and bite the town?'
1969 Alan O'Toole *The Racing Game* 132: He pulled out a battered packet of cigarettes, bit the gentleman next to him for a light, and focussed his attention on the start.
1978 Richard Beilby *Gunner* 237: 'I'm putting the bite on you', Gunner explained gently. 'Putting the nips in, touching you for a loan.'

bite your bum Expression of refusal or rejection
1979 Kathy Lette and Gabrielle Carey *Puberty Blues* 30: 'Oh, Johnno, lend us ya ...' 'Bite ya bum.'
1979 *Weekend Australian* 24 Nov. 10: 'We were again able to tell the PJT, the Monopolies Commission and Trade Practices to go bite their bums.'
1982 *Weekend Australian* 6 Feb. 15: It was not immediately clear whether Australian favorites such as 'dingo' or 'bite yer bum' also get a mention.

bitser A mongrel dog
1941 Baker 10: *Bitser*: Anything made of bits and pieces; a mongrel animal.
1949 John Morrison *The Creeping City* 36–7: He called the dog Bitser because, as he candidly confessed to anyone who asked its breeding, it was 'just bits of this and bits of that'.
1958 A. W. Upfield *The Bachelors of Broken Hill* 212: 'Had one [dog] once, though. Black an' tan bitser.'
1968 *Australian* 4 Apr. 20: He lives with two bitser dogs that belonged to his mother.
1979 *Sun-Herald* 27 May 108: Don't rubbish the bitsa ... There are many crossbred sheepdogs in the bush who will work as well, if not better, than any purebred.
1980 *Sunday Telegraph* (Sydney) 13 Apr. 36: She took her dog, a small and amiable bitser aged about five.

bitumen, the 1 A tarred road
1953 Baker 137: *one for the bitumen*, a final round of drinks, i.e. 'one for the road'.
1972 W. A. Winter-Irving *Beyond the Bitumen* [book title]
1974 John Morrison *Australian by Choice* 118: It lay three miles off the bitumen, two miles of dirt road and one mile of winding track.
2 *The Bitumen* The highway between Darwin and Alice Springs
1949 H. E. Thonemann *Tell the White Man* 149: There were the workmen who made a beautiful road [during the war] now called the 'Bitumen'.

1959 Frank McCann *Medicine Man* 63: All the events I am about to describe occurred in those dim, distant days of the era now frequently referred to as 'B.B.' ('Before the Bitumen').

1965 *Australian* 28 Jan. 10: Maps may tell you the thousand miles long black ribbon linking Darwin with Alice Springs and the south is the Stuart Highway. But up here it is 'the Track' or 'the Bitumen'.

1969 Osmar White *Under the Iron Rainbow* 160: 'We used to get a lot of commercials there, travelling up and down the Bitumen.'* *The Bitumen: The sealed highway from Darwin to Alice Springs.

1981 *Weekend Australian* 16 May Mag. 14: I drove down the bitumen from Darwin.

bitumen blonde   Aboriginal girl

1943 Baker 10: *Bitumen blonde* An aboriginal girl or woman.

Black and Whites   The Swan Districts (W.A.) Australian Rules team [f. colours]

1980 *Daily News* (Perth) 14 Jul. 25: His main aim is to ensure the Black and Whites remain a force in league football for many seasons. 'Swans were a top club but nosedived because of bad administration,' Walker said.

1984 *Sunday Independent* (Perth) 29 Apr. 72: Swans' glory [heading] In the most dramatic finish one could ever hope to see the Black and Whites fell over the line.

Black Friday   13 January 1939, day of disastrous bushfires in Victoria when 71 lives were lost; applied to any other disastrous Friday

1969 Thomas Jenkins *We Came to Australia* 117: Neither of these fires was Australia's worst. That happened on Black Friday, January 13th, 1939, when 71 people died in bushfires in Victoria. The flames jumped seven miles at a time and tests ... recorded a temperature of 1,000 degrees.

1978 *Weekend Australian* 13 May 1: It was Black Friday in South Australia. Chrysler shut down its giant car plant, locked the workers out to avoid a mass sit-in protest, and started issuing security cards.

black hat   A newly arrived immigrant, inexperienced in the ways of the colony i.e. still wearing city clothes: *obs.*

1876 Rolf Boldrewood *A Colonial Reformer* (1890) 21: 'A "black hat" in Australian parlance means a new arrival.'

1881 Mrs Campbell Praed *Policy and Passion* 277: 'You remember that 'ere long chap from England as wur stopping here? Lord! if I were Mr Dyson Maddox I'd never let it be said that a *black hat* has cut me out sweetheartin'.'

Black Jack   1 Sir John McEwen (1900–80), leader of Federal Parliamentary Country Party 1958–71

1966 *The Wit of Sir Robert Menzies* ed. Ray Robinson 65: My colleague Jack McEwen has been nicknamed Black Jack. Now and again I address him as 'Black', and occasionally, when in highbrow mood, I call him '*Le Noir*'. That's only when I don't want other Country Party men to know what I'm talking about.

1984 *Australian* 23 Jul. 10: ALP policy goes 'back to Black Jack' [heading]

2 Sir Frederick Gallagher Galleghan (1897–1971), Commander of Changi Prison Camp 1944–5, promoted to Brigadier on return to Australia

black, living   see **living**

black prince   A variety of cicada [f. colour]

1951 Dymphna Cusack and Florence James *Come In Spinner* 106: 'Mine's a Floury Baker ... and mine's a Black Prince.' Young Jack and Andrew held up their fists for her to peep at frosted fawn body and tan-and-black.

1959 Anne von Bertouch *February Dark* 124: Through the shimmer of heat and the drilling song Helen saw the beautiful cicadas of childhood, the Black Prince, the Greengrocer, the Yellow Monday, held on a child's small hand.

1974 Ronald McKie *The Mango Tree* 18: He had talked to her about his first-puppy, a Black Prince and the Double Drummer he had caught in the garden.

1980 *Weekend Australian* 29 Mar. Mag. 12: If you find a Black Prince, you can trade it for 20 greengrocers, five yellow Mondays or three floury bakers.

black mist, the   Aboriginal expression for the fallout from the nuclear test at Maralinga, S.A., in 1956

1985 *Sydney Morning Herald* 27 Apr. 15: Wallatina station, about 40 km west of Marla, was the scene of the black mist – or 'puyu' – incident in 1956.

1985 *National Times* 3 May 9: That day's witnesses [at the Royal Commission on atomic tests] told of the Black Mist, an oily rolling incubus that overwhelmed the mulgas and camps and homesteads and left a greasy black residue, and a heritage in its witnesses of scaly skin, eye and stomach and bowel ailments down succeeding decades.

Black Saturday   10 December 1938, a day of severe bushfires in N.S.W.

Black Stump   1 An imaginary last post of civilization. There have been country properties so called, including one near Coolah N.S.W. dating from 1826, and another at Merriwagga N.S.W. (see *Sun-Herald* 22 Feb. 1970) but these names may have derived from the currency of the expression.

1954 Tom Ronan *Vision Splendid* 264: 'You're looking,' he boasted, 'at the best bloody station bookkeeper this side of the black stump.' [spoken in Adelaide]

1959 Eric Lambert *Glory Thrown In* 146: 'You're the greatest lurk-artist this side, or any bloody side of the black stump.'

1962 Criena Rohan *The Delinquents* 151: 'Good old, sweet old, wholesome, pure little Brisbane, best little town this or any side of the Black Stump.'

1971 Frank Hardy *The Outcasts of Foolgarah* 42: Moss was about the best bloody listener this side of the Black Stump.

1975 Xavier Herbert *Poor Fellow My Country* 1149: 'I've been played for the biggest mug this side o' the Black Stump.'

1984 Judge O'Dea *West Australian* (Perth) 8 Feb. 3: 'It may not be the greatest claim for compensation this side of the Black Stump. It is a simple broken jaw.'

2 The State Offices block in Sydney [f. appearance]

1970 Jon Cleary *Helga's Web* 263: His office was in the State Government block, a beautiful dark grey tower that the citizens, with the local talent for belittling anything that embarrassed them with its pretensions, had dubbed the Black Stump.

1981 *Sun-Herald* 28 Jun. 135: I gather that Nifty himself went around turning off a few lights in the Black Stump, setting an example to the troops.

Black Sunday 6 February 1938, the day of a record number of rescues by life-savers at Bondi beach, when five lives were lost

1982 *Sydney Morning Herald* 19 Jan. 23: One of his [Alf Vockler's] famous feats occurred on 'Black Sunday', February 6, 1938, when with 80 other members of Bondi Club he took part in the biggest surf rescue in Australian history. Time and again he went back into the water to help rescue nearly 300 people trapped in treacherous surf at Bondi. Five swimmers died in one of the country's worst beach tragedies.

black taxi A Commonwealth government car, providing free transport for politicians and public servants

1973 *Sun-Herald* 25 Nov. 112: Fred Daly ... has ordered a crackdown on official use of the 'black taxis'. He has warned MPs that the long black official limousines will not wait outside flats and hotels if those who ordered them aren't ready.

1975 *Sun-Herald* 3 Aug. 48: Commonwealth cars (flippantly known as 'black taxis' to those new to

power) were used to ferry junior aides to lunch.

Black Thursday 6 February 1851, a day of bush-fire devastation in Victoria

1855 William Howitt *Land, Labour and Gold* i 68–9: The great bush-fire of what is called Black Thursday, or Thursday the 6th February, 1851 ... raged fiercely in these parts.

1855 J. Jenkins *Diary of a Welsh Swagman* (1975) 139: This, the 6th of February, is the anniversary of 'Black Thursday' of 1851, when one half of the state of Victoria was on fire.

Black Tuesday 7 February 1967, day of severe bushfires in Tasmania, when 62 lives were lost

1981 *Australian* 4 Feb. 1: The blaze that swept through Zeehan [Tasmania] yesterday has brought nightmare memories of Black Tuesday – February 7 1967, when 62 people lost their lives in devastating bushfires.

black cockatoos fly over A portent of rain

1963 Hal Porter *The Watcher on the Cast-Iron Balcony* 153: I still believe ... that rain is on the way when swifts fly low, or black cockatoos fly northwards.

1979 Dorothy Hewett *The Man From Mukinupin* 101: 'Rain's comin' up. I heard the black cockatoos fly over.'

black velvet Aboriginal women, as sexual partners [listed by Partridge as English military slang in the nineteenth century]

1899 Henry Lawson 'The Ballad of the Rouseabout' *Verse* i 360: I known the track from Spencer's Gulf and north of Cooper's Creek – / Where falls the half-caste to the strong, 'black velvet' to the weak.

1929 K. S. Prichard *Coonardoo* 79: 'You're one of these god-damned young heroes. No 'black velvet' for you, I suppose?' I'm goin' to marry white and stick white,' Hugh said.

1938 Xavier Herbert *Capricornia* 24: He began to take an interest in native women, or Black Velvet as they were called collectively, affairs with whom seemed to be the chief diversion.

1958 Gavin Casey *Snowball* 17: 'Did you see the girls, when you were out there? ... The sort of black velvet that makes me sometimes wish I wasn't a policeman.'

blacks, they should give it back to the Expression of disgust at any inhospitable feature of Australia [? f. U.S. 'hand it back to the Indians']

1946 *Sunday Sun* (Sydney) 4 Aug. Suppl. 15: They reckon as he [Captain Cook] sailed away he gave one look back at the coast of Bananaland and said, 'Strewth, I'm glad to give that dump back to the blacks.'

1952 Jon Cleary *The Sundowners* 153: 'Give me the coast, and I'll give the rest of Australia back to the blackfellers.'

1969 Christopher Bray *Blossom Like a Rose* 75: 'They should give it back to the blacks'. 'What's that?' asked Jake. 'The bloody north,' said Tom.

1971 Colin Simpson *The New Australia* 213: Robin Boyd begins by saying that he often feels that Melbourne should be given back to the blacks.

blades, the The hand shears, used before the introduction of machine shearing

1905 *Old Bush Songs* ed. A. B. Paterson 26: I've shore at big Willandra and I've shore at Tilberoo, / And once I drew my blades, my boys, upon the famed Barcoo.

1910 C. E. W. Bean *On the Wool Track* 195: Most shearers told me the machines were a bit faster and easier than the 'blades'.

1964 H. P. Tritton *Time Means Tucker* 47: Conimbia was having its last season with the blades and was starting next day.

1973 Donald Stuart *Morning Star Evening Star* 20: I'd seen a double fleece or two shorn with the blades by a brokendown old bladeshearer.

Blake, Joe see **Joe Blake**

Blamey, a Lady See quots [wife of General Sir Thomas Blamey]

1945 Baker 157: *Lady Blamey* A beer bottle, from which the neck has been removed, used as a drinking vessel. [World War II slang]

1972 *Sydney Morning Herald* 28 Oct. 8: During this time she gave her name to the 'bottle' drinking glass used by thousands of Diggers. She taught them to slice an empty bottle cleanly in half with the aid of kerosene-soaked string. The string was wound round the bottle, and set alight. When the bottle was hot it was plunged into water and would break cleanly. The men used the lower part for drinking.

blanket (rug), Wagga see **Wagga**

blight, sandy see **sandy**

Blind Freddie see **Freddie**

Bliss, Johnny A piss [rhyming slang]

1973 Alexander Buzo *Rooted* 77: 'I couldn't bear to watch it, so I ducked out for a Johnny Bliss.'

blister A debt, bill [f. *blister* a summons OED 1903]

1888 E. Finn *Chronicles of Early Melbourne* ii 546: As far as the bushmen were concerned, they might certainly be styled 'blisters', for they burned their pockets while they had them. [The term 'blister' wrongly applied to 'shinplasters' q.v.]

1934 Vance Palmer *Sea and Spinifex* 14: 'Well, they need every quid they can rake together,' McVeagh defended. 'There's a blister on that boat that won't be worked off unless they strike a few good patches.'

1951 Ernestine Hill *The Territory* 431: [In the bush] never carry a 'blister', a bill or an account . . . A rider passing by was an honoured guest, and he couldn't be hounding a man down with bills.

block, do the To make a fashionable promenade, in Melbourne along Collins Street between Swanston and Elizabeth Streets, in Sydney in the area bounded by George, King and Pitt Streets: *obs.*

1869 Marcus Clarke *The Peripatetic Philosopher* 12: The 'doing the Block' is doubtless worthy of censure, 'Collins-street Folly' is foolish enough to be visited with the severest blame.

1887 Fergus Hume *The Mystery of a Hansom Cab* (1971) 58–9: It was Saturday morning and of course all fashionable Melbourne was doing the Block. With regards to its 'Block', Collins Street corresponds to New York's Broadway, London's Regent Street and Rotten Row, and to the Boulevards of Paris. It is on the Block that people show off their new dresses, bow to their friends, cut their enemies, and chatter small talk.

1892 Henry Lawson 'The Drover's Wife' *Prose* i 50: She takes as much care to make herself and the children look smart as she would if she were going to do the block in the city.

1902 Ambrose Pratt *The Great 'Push' Experiment* 278: I strolled down King Street to do the block.

1910 H. H. Richardson *The Getting of Wisdom* 134: They were going to 'do the block', Tilly explained, and would meet Bob there.

1945 Herbert M. Moran *Beyond the Hill Lies China* 131: Challis's mind slipped back to the days when, as a student, he 'did the block' on Saturday mornings. Down George Street and around the Post Office, up Pitt Street, past King Street, and through the Arcade, then back to George Street again.

block, do (lose) one's Of the various expressions in which 'block' is used as 'head' (OED 1635), such as 'knock your block off', the most 'Australian' seems to be 'do your block' i.e. lose rational control from rage, excitement, falling in love. The converse is to 'use your block' i.e. apply all shrewdness and judgement.

1907 Charles MacAlister *Old Pioneering Days in the Sunny South* 19: At this Mr Donovan 'lost his block' completely. 'Clear out of my sight, ye skunks,' he screamed.

1915 C. J. Dennis *The Songs of a Sentimental Bloke* 47: I done me block complete on this Doreen, / An' now me 'eart is broke, me life's a wreck!

1934 Thomas Wood *Cobbers* 159: 'When I've have five double whiskies I do me block[1], but when I've had six I'd tackle anything.' [1]lose my head.

1959 A. W. Upfield *Bony and the Mouse* 133: 'Not much of a bushman!' 'Good enough, if he uses his block, to get a long way.'

1963 Randolph Stow *Tourmaline* 63: 'Don't think you're the first bloke that ever did his block with Byrnie in this bar.'

1970 Patrick White *The Vivisector* 586: 'Orright! Don't do yer block! What else?'

1983 Bert Kelly *Bulletin* 26 Jul. 94: I became nervous that he was about to do his block so I said in my fatherly way: 'Don't get cross, Fred.'

blockee, blocker The owner of a block of land on which grapes are grown [listed by Baker as peculiar to S.A., but also encountered in Victoria]

1900 Let. of 4 Feb. in *Audrey Tennyson's Vice-Regal Days* ed. Alexandra Hasluck (1978) 85: The next day H. & I walked down to see some 'blockers' called Nott who we heard had been nearly burnt out.

1920 *Sunraysia Daily* (Mildura) 23 Dec. 1: A Blocker's Home in Karadoc Avenue, Mildura [heading]

1942 John Shaw Neilson *Autobiography* (1978) 131: I reported the matter to the blocker's wife & I think some measures were taken to help.

1945 Baker 197: *blocker* an owner of a vineyard, specifically, a block of land on which grapes are grown.

1948 *Coast to Coast 1947* 229: He stooped and straightened and thrust under the vines ... even when the blockie gave him a row to himself and kept the others working in pairs, he outstripped them.

1973 Frank Huelin *Keep Moving* 62: 'Th' blockees want us here t'r th' pickin' ... It's no good after the harvest. They couldn't care less then, but now that want us alive and fit to snatch their bloody grapes.'

1979 *Herald* (Melbourne) 8 Mar. 4: Of course there is work for grape-pickers ... A fortnight ago there were pickers everywhere and blockies were turning them away.

1980 *Weekend Australian* 26 Apr. Mag. 9: Several hundred million dollars are generated yearly by the dried fruit producers (blockies), orchardists, and from the processing and packaging industries in the area.

Bloke, the 1 The man in charge, the boss [f. naval slang for a ship's commander OED 1914]

1966 Tom Ronan *Once There Was a Bagman* 2: Kelly the Nip [imagined giving advice to Ronan, about to lunch on the royal yacht *Britannia*] 'See if you can work me in for a yarn with the Bloke. I'll

bite him if you won't.'

2 The hero of C. J. Dennis' *The Songs of a Sentimental Bloke* (1915)

1939 R. H. Croll *I Recall* 163: The Bloke has passed: Oh, dip the lid!

1967 R. D. FitzGerald *Southerly* 261: Remember too that when the one and only Bloke was presented with a son ... Dennis makes the Bloke say: 'Doreen she says 'e's got a poet's eyes; / But I ain't got no use for them soft guys.'

3 *The Old Bloke* God [outback slang]

1958 Russel Ward *The Australian Legend* 98: I was one of a party of four, driving an old truck through the Musgrave Ranges ... One of my companions gushed considerably over the beauty of the mountain sky-line, silhouetted against the sunset. An elderly stockman answered drily. 'Yes. The Old Bloke makes a good job of them up this way.'

blonde, bitumen see **bitumen**

blonde, bushfire see **bushfire**

bloodhouse A public house with a reputation for brawls, gambling

1938 Heard in conversation.

1953 Dymphna Cusack *Southern Steel* 138: 'Ought to have more sense than to go to the Seven Seas – nothing but a bloodhouse. Always blues there.'

1956 Tom Ronan *Moleskin Midas* 51: 'Try the bloodhouse – I mean, Silman's – next hotel down the street.'

1963 Frank Hardy *Legends from Benson's Valley* 104: He stopped to study the defences of the hotel – not such a bloodhouse as the Royal Oak, but nevertheless addicted to after-hours trading.

1971 Hal Porter *The Right Thing* 91: 'She toils in the Kilkenny blood-house, mother. Where father used to drink like a fish.'

1981 Peter Corris *White Meat* 10: We crossed the street and had a beer in the bloodhouse opposite.

Bloods The South Melbourne VFL club, later the Swans [f. team colours]

1979 *Herald* (Melbourne) 6 Apr. 26: Bloods are running hot [heading] South Melbourne will beat Richmond at South tomorrow.

Blood-stained Angels, the Former nickname of the South Melbourne VFL club

1984 Audrey Blake *A Proletarian Life* 6: We barracked devotedly for the 'Blood-stained Angels', the South Melbourne team. [recalling the 1920s]

bloody The 'great Australian adjective' q.v. is by no means distinctively Australian, but has always been conspicuous enough in the colloquial language to be seen as such by overseas visitors

1833 Trial before the Supreme Court, 9 and 10 December, in *True Patriots All* ed. G. C. Ingleton (1952) 149: John Larnack, being duly sworn, said; on the morning of the 5th November last, I went to the river to superintend sheep-washing; between 12 and 1 o'clock I heard a voice exclaiming – *'come out of the water every bloody one of you, or we'll blow your bloody brains out!';* on looking behind, I saw three men advancing towards me with guns.

1847 A. Marjoribanks *Travels in New South Wales* 57–8: The word bloody is a favourite oath in that country. One man will tell you that he married a bloody young wife, another, a bloody old one, and a bushranger will call out, 'Stop, or I'll blow your bloody brains out.'

1855 William Howitt *Land, Labour and Gold* ii 76: The language of the diggings is something inconceivable in its vileness, and every sentence almost is ornamented with the word bloody. That word they seem to think the perfection of phraseology; it is the keystone and topstone of all their eloquence, it occurs generally in every second or third sentence; and, when they get excited, they lard every sentence with it profusely ... Two diggers passing our tent one day, saw the thermometer hanging on the post: – 'What d – d, blasted, bloody thing is that now?' said one to the other. 'Why I'm blowed if it ain't a d – d, blasted, bloody old weather glass,' replied his mate.

1875 A. J. Boyd *Old Colonials* (1882) 107: I'll put my (adjective) fist where I (adjective) well please. I've a mind to knock yer (adjective) head off.'

1899 W. T. Goodge '—!' (The Great Australian Adjective!) in *Hits! Skits! and Jingles!* 115: The sunburnt—stockman stood, / And, in a dismal—mood, / Apostrophised his—cuddy; / 'The—nag's no—good, / He couldn't earn his—food – / A regular—brumby.

1942 C. Hartley Grattan *Introducing Australia* 193: When I asked an old 'cove' when he first arrived in Darwin, he replied, 'Young man, in nineteen bloody eight!'

1951 Dymphna Cusack and Florence James *Come in Spinner* 306: 'Got in a troop train ... after a fortnight comin' down from Broome across the Trans-contibloodynental.'

1969 Patsy Adam Smith *Folklore of the Australian Railwaymen* 218: One of the witnesses, a fettler, came into the inquiry room and tripped on a mat and said, 'What stupid bastard put that bloody mat there?' And he slung it out the door. 'Bull' Mitchell on the inquiry board said to him, 'None of your bloody swearing here, you just remember that you're at a bloody inquiry and bloody well behave yourself.'

1973 Mr C. Jones [Federal Minister for Transport] *Sydney Morning Herald* 18 Aug. 2: There is going to be some bloody mammoth changes – some mammoth changes which the Budget will disclose. Bloody mammoth changes, that is the only way you can describe them. I think Frank [Crean] has done a bloody good job to stand up to the pace. Bloody oath, he has done a marvellous job in standing up to the bloody pace.

1984 *Australian* 24 Sep. 18: As Bulldog captain Steve Mortimer said at the presentation: 'If you can beat a side as good as bloody Parramatta, then you're a bloody good side.' Bloody oath.

Bloody Sunday 4 May 1919, when a fight broke out in Fremantle between police and waterside workers. The president of the Fremantle Lumper's Union, Tom Edwards, later died from injuries received.

1984 *West Australian* (Perth) 12 Jan. 2: 'One elderly woman stopped me to tell me how her young brother had scaled one of the trees [in St John's Square, Fremantle] in 1919 to escape bullets being fired during an incident in Fremantle that became known as Bloody Sunday', Mr Turner said.

blot Anus, buttocks

1945 Baker 156: *blot* The posterior or anus. [World War II slang]

1965 William Dick *A Bunch of Ratbags* 262: He pushed me away and he gave me a kick up the blot.

1968 Frank Hardy *The Unlucky Australians* 67: As a parting gesture, sticks his fingers up the dog's blot.

1974 David Ireland *Burn* 146: Maybe he'll grab this last chance for some action after sitting on his blot all these years.

blow *v.* 1 'To boast, brag (chiefly dial.)' OED c. 1400–1873: *obsolescent*

1857 *Thatcher's Colonial Songster* 35: About your talents blow, / Mind, that's the regular caper.

1873 Rolf Boldrewood 'The Fencing of Wanderowna' *A Romance of Canvas Town* (1901) 31: 'Well, I thought he seemed a blowin' sort of fool.'

1879–80 Ned Kelly 'The Jerilderie Letter' in Max Brown *Australian Son* (1956) 279: He is the man that blowed before he left Violet Town if Ned Kelly was to be shot he was the man would shoot him.

1887 *Tibb's Popular Songbook* 24: The squatters blowed they'd cut the price / To seventeen and six.

1924 *Truth* 27 Apr. 6: *Blow* To boast.

1945 Gavin Casey *Downhill is Easier* 41: Ordinary rouseabout labourers don't get many chances to blow out their bags about what good men they are, unless they tell lies.

2 To lengthen in odds, the opposite to 'firm' (horse-racing)

1922 Arthur Wright *A Colt from the Country* 129: 'Ain't Lobitout fav'rit?' he gasped . . . 'No!' snapped the stranger. 'Got blown right out.'

1949 Lawson Glassop *Lucky Palmer* 63: 'I've got the commission for it this end of the ring, and I'm trying to blow the price out.'

1977 *Sun-Herald* 9 Jan. 47: The bookmakers blew Gold Spring's odds to 10–1, but the mud did not dull her speed.

1981 *Sydney Morning Herald* 9 Apr. 12: He opened an inquiry into the performance of a racehorse whose betting price 'blew' from 5–2 favourite to 20–1.

blower

1982 *National Times* 1 Aug. 14: Punters won't back 'blowers' (horses whose price lengthens significantly, indicating there is little backing for it).

blow *n.* 1 Bragging, boasting: *obsolescent* [f. *blow v.* 1]

1868 C. Wade Brown *Overlanding in Australia* 18: He seldom carries out his threats, it is more 'blow' (bounce) on his part than anything.

1885 *The Australasian Printers' Keepsake* 162: A European type, working in Sydney, was grievously galled by the 'blow' of the Cornstalks.

1893 Francis Adams *The Australians* 149: The drawling 'blow' (Anglice, boasting) of the competitive bushman borders on an anger which is so high-strung as to threaten insanity.

2 A stroke of the shears in shearing

1870 Rolf Boldrewood 'Shearing in Riverina' *In Bad Company* (1901) 309: Every 'blow' of the shears is agony to him, yet he disdains to give in.

1878 G. H. Gibson *Southerly Busters* 180: My tally's eighty-five a day – / A hundred I could go, / If coves would let me 'open out' / And take a bigger 'blow'.

1885–1914 'Click go the Shears' *Old Bush Songs* ed. Stewart and Keesing (1957) 254: The ringer looks around and is beaten by a blow, / And curses the old snagger with the blue-bellied 'joe'.

1911 E. S. Sorenson *Life in the Australian Backblocks* 233: The blades are pulled back and the knockers filed down, so the shears will take a bigger blow.

1964 *Sydney Morning Herald* 6 Apr. 2: The two men evolved a style which cuts out some fifteen blows (shearing strokes) a sheep and allows shearers to increase their tally.

1981 *Weekend Australian* 19 Dec. 5: The wider the comb, the more wool a shearer can remove with each 'blow'.

blow the froth off a glass of beer, couldn't see **couldn't**

Blow, Joe see **Joe**

blow, strike a To start or resume work

1974 Sir Robert Askin *Australian* 18 Dec. 9: 'I think it's bad that people can live on high interest rates, like 15 per cent, and can get enough money to live on them without striking a blow.'

blow through As for **shoot through**

blowie 1 A blowfly [abbr.]

1945 Gavin Casey *Downhill is Easier* 204: 'There was clouds o' blowies.'

1973 *Australian* 7 Jul. 16: I love this ripper country / Of funnel webs and sharks / With blowies big as eagles / Where your car gets booked by narks.

2 The blowfish, or toado

1983 T. A. G. Hungerford *Stories from Suburban Road* 74: You rubbed the blowies on the wooden planks of the jetty until they swelled up and then you stamped on them: if you did it right they went off with a bang like a penny cracker.

blow-in A casual arrival: *derogatory*

1937 Ernestine Hill *The Great Australian Loneliness* 32: They [the murals] had been painted by a 'blow-in', an Englishman named Malcolmsen, said to have been a crack steeplechase rider in his day.

1949 John K. Ewers *Harvest* 121: He didn't want dealings with blow-ins like them.

1953 T. A. G. Hungerford *Riverslake* 195: A couple of blow-ins from the Causeway, with loud-mouthed women.

1962 Dymphna Cusack *Picnic Races* 19: 'Lotta jumped-up blow-ins putting on more guyver than the Governor's wife.'

1973 Frank Huelin *Keep Moving* 91: They stared resentfully at blow-ins like ourselves, seeing in every work-seeker an additional threat to their chance of a job.

1983 *Sun-Herald* 9 Jan. 124: It's a bit like the characters who travel great distances to join the throng at Double Bay on Saturday mornings, only to learn that the locals all do their shopping during the week and that the crowd is made up of blow-ins.

blowtorch applied to the belly The test of political fortitude proposed by Mr Neville Wran (see quot. 1983)

1983 *Sydney Morning Herald* 16 Mar. 7: Asked recently what he thought of Greiner, Neville Wran said he obviously had ability 'but he hasn't had the blowtorch applied to his belly yet'.

1983 *Sydney Morning Herald* 23 Jul. 13: The Ivanov-Combe affair has presented the Hawke Government with a critical test early in its life. In the coming months Neville Wran's blowtorch will be applied to Hawke's belly. For the sake of the Government's survival, the Prime Minister had better have an asbestos belly-button.

1984 *Age* (Melbourne) 17 Mar. 11: The Premier will have four years in which, to borrow his own expression, to apply the blowtorch to the bellies of his detractors.

1984 *Sydney Morning Herald* 8 May 4: Yesterday the blowtorch was applied to the bellies of Clyde Holding and Stewart West.

bludge *n.*   A job requiring no exertion [f. *bludger* 2]

1943   Donald Friend *Gunner's Diary* 18: 'I've been three weeks in hospital with measles.' 'Ah – that's not a bad bludge.'

1949   Lawson Glassop *Lucky Palmer* 154: 'A man's got to earn a living and this is a good bludge.'

1962   Stuart Gore *Down the Golden Mile* 53: 'What a smart bludge he's on, eh? At six thousand a year or whatever it is he gets.'

1974   Desmond O'Grady *Deschooling Kevin Carew* 52: 'You don't like the course?' 'Oh it's all right. Plenty of time for fun and a good bludge.'

bludge *v.*   1   To live on the earnings of a prostitute

1947   Vance Palmer *Cyclone* 26: A secret shame was sapping his spirit. You oughtn't to take money from a woman; it was bludging.

2   To avoid effort and live by someone else's exertions; to acquire something without payment

1931   Vance Palmer *Separate Lives* 264: 'I've stood you too long already, loafing around here, and bludging on your mother.'

1957   Ray Lawler *Summer of the Seventeenth Doll* 37: 'I won't bludge. I'll get a job or somethin'.'

1964   Donald Horne *The Lucky Country* 26: Covering up for an incompetent mate is the usual thing as long as he is considered to be trying and not simply 'bludging'.

1975   Richard Cornish *The Woman Lilith* 25: We cleaned the house, painted the walls ... bludged some furniture.

bludge on the flag   To fail in one's duty; to exploit a patriotic cause

1919   W. H. Downing *Digger Dialects* 12: *Bludge on the flag* To fail to justify one's existence as a soldier.

1966   Elwyn Wallace *Sydney and the Bush* 72: Kate collected a war pension – 'bludging on the flag' Pete always called it.

bludger   1   Someone living on the earnings of a prostitute: *obs.* [f. *bludgeoner* OED 1842]

1898   *Bulletin* 17 Dec. Red Page: A *bludger* is about the lowest grade of human thing, and is a brothel bully.

1904   Henry Lawson 'The Women of the Town' *Verse* ii 54: And they profit from the brewer and

the smirking landlord down / To the bully and the bludger, on the women of the town.

1924   *Truth* 27 Apr. 6: *Bludger* A man who lives on the proceeds of prostitution.

1946   K. S. Prichard *The Roaring Nineties* 388: Bill led an attack on the French bludger who kept three or four Japanese women in miserable shacks at Kanowna.

1959   Dorothy Hewett *Bobbin Up* 115: 'But what about libel? "There's a name for a man who lives off women!" Can't you get pinched for callin' a man a bludger?'

1981   *Sydney Morning Herald* 7 May 1: Longley said members who lived off waterfront prostitution were known as 'bludgers'.

2   See quot. 1900–10

1900–10   O'Brien and Stephens: *Bludger* The word has come to be applied to any person who takes profit without risk or disability or without effort or work.

c. **1918**   'The Digger's London Leave' in *Australian Ballads* ed. Russel Ward (1964) 240: He went up to London and straightaway strode / To Army Headquarters in Horseferry Road, / To see all the bludgers who dodge all the strafe, / By getting soft jobs on the Headquarters staff.

1945   Gavin Casey *Downhill is Easier* 15: 'They don't put many on here, but they don't put many off either, unless they're dinkum bludgers.'

1958   H. D. Williamson *The Sunlit Plain* 21: 'You and your rotten, boozy cobbers! Think I don't see enough of 'em in this place to know what they are? Dirty, greasy mob of bludgers!'

1971   *Sydney Morning Herald* 6 Aug. 1: The only people who would benefit from full pay on workers' compensation would be 'genuine loafers, shirkers or bludgers', the Chief Secretary, Mr Willis, said in the Legislative Assembly yesterday.

1979   *Sydney Morning Herald* 25 Aug. 3: Auckland, Friday. – A man alleged to have called Princess Anne 'a bloody bludger' told a Magistrate yesterday he had spoken the truth. He said he had been making a political speech and the words were not insulting.

1983   James McQueen *Uphill Runner* 161: Never a bludger, he'd never been that. Thinking: I always paid my way, one way or another.

3   Affectionate, when addressed to friends, like *bastard* 3

1953   Dymphna Cusack *Southern Steel* 266: 'You bludger, ya!' Slap's voice was full of relief.

1965   William Dick *A Bunch of Ratbags* 216: 'Don't be scabs, yuh pack of bludgers, all youse ever think of is money,' Argles laughed.

bludger, dole   see **dole bludger**

blue   1   A summons, esp. for a traffic offence [f. colour of paper]

[1895 Cornelius Crowe *Australian Slang Diction-ary* 58: *Piece of blue paper* a summons.
1899 Henry Lawson 'Jack Cornstalk' *Prose* ii 50: He gets on the spree and into a row, and so into trouble that merits the serving on his person of what he calls 'a piece of blue paper'.]
1939 Kylie Tennant *Foveaux* 348: 'Take a look at these blues.' With a flourish he produced a wad of grey summonses which he shuffled like a pack of cards.
see **bluey** 3
2 A quarrel, brawl, particularly in expressions like 'bung (stack, turn) on a blue', 'pick a blue'
1943 *Khaki and Green* 105: The 'blue' started, and you knew you'd be going up. Not the whole reinforcement draft, first time.
1946 Rohan Rivett *Behind Bamboo* 395: *Blue* A row, trouble.
1957 Judah Waten *Shares in Murder* 58: 'Want to stack on a blue?' he said looking at her strangely.
1963 Jon Cleary *A Flight of Chariots* 178: 'That's one advantage to being a big bastard – people think twice about picking a blue with you.'
1974 David Ireland *Burn* 28: 'You tryin' to bung on a blue? I'll give you a smack in the chops in a minute.'
1981 *Sydney Morning Herald* 29 Jul. 7: Priest versus politician. It could be quite a blue.
3 A blunder, mistake [f. *bloomer*]
1941 Baker 11: *Blue* (2) An error or mistake; a loss.
1957 Randolph Stow *The Bystander* 187: 'I reckon you ought to tell your missus she made a bit of a blue.'
1969 D'Arcy Niland *Dead Men Running* 189: 'I still think they made a blue.'
1983 *Sun-Herald* 4 Dec. 168: Labor Party chappies were quick to ... score off Nick Greiner's tactical blue in saying the Opposition wasn't ready to govern yet.
4 Nickname for a red-headed person
1932 Leonard Mann *Flesh in Armour* 37: Blue McIntosh, No. 1, red in the head, a League foot-baller.
1950 Brian James *The Advancement of Spencer Button* 267: Two single ones ... became just Flora and Blue (she had red hair).
1961 Patrick White *Riders in the Chariot* 252–3: Hair – a red stubble, but red ... 'Blue is what he answers to.'
1976 Henry Gullett *Not as a Duty Only* 106: His mate was a red-haired man, called Blue of course, taller and slim.
1981 David Ireland *National Times* 25 Jan. 25: His name was Martin Dangerfield, but everyone called him Blue since his hair was red.

Bluebags, the In N.S.W., the Newtown Rugby League team [f. colours]
1976 *Sunday Telegraph* (Sydney) 6 Jun. 56: Hail the Bluebags! Gallant win over Tigers.
1983 *Sun-Herald* 24 Jul. 120: It'll be a big, emotional, memorable, nostalgic, sad night on Thursday when Newtown Leagues Club has its Bluebags' farewell dinner before selling up and moving to Campbelltown.

blue bird The police 'paddy-waggon' [f. colour]
1939 Kylie Tennant *Foveaux* 415: The two-up school on the corner took no notice of Bramley and Kingston. The only thing that really disturbed the streets was 'the blue-bird', the police car on its rounds.

blue duck Anything which does not come up to expectations; a dud, a 'write-off'
1895 Cornelius Crowe *The Australian Slang Dictionary* 10: *Blue Duck* No good; no money in it.
1902 Mrs Campbell Praed *My Australian Girl-hood* 21: 'One evening as he sits smoking outside the hut, without a moment's warning he finds a spear in his chest! Dam'd, but he would have been a blue duck if I hadn't ridden up at that very moment and scared the natives off.'
1911 Edward Dyson *Benno, and Some of the Push* 111: In the language of the flat Susie 'got nothing' for the next hour or two. As the pasters worked they exercised their ingenuity in reminding Miss Gannon of what she had lost ... 'Wot price th'opera 'n' the fam'ly jewels,' said Harrerbeller. 'They're a blue duck fer Susie.'
1917 A. B. Paterson *Three Elephant Power* 131: Time and again he had gone out to race when, to use William's own words, it was a blue duck for Bill's chance of keeping afloat, and every time did the gallant race pony pull his owner through.
1926 L. C. E. Gee *Bushtracks and Goldfields* 4–5: His sharp eyes could detect the smallest speck of gold in any of the stone given to him ... and his discards of 'blue ducks' saved much time in the examination of samples.
1949 John K. Ewers *Harvest* 142: Tolly would ask if there was any news, and Len would shake his head and say, 'No. Looks like a blue duck to me.'
1954 Tom Ronan *Vision Splendid* 252: 'If they'll step up my expense account to include a steno-grapher, the secretary's job is yours. Otherwise I'm afraid it's a blue duck.'
1978 Ronald McKie *Bitter Bread* 142: He had rung round the usual contacts. But this Saturday had, early, an unmistakable feeling of being a blue duck for news.

blue monge An improvised bush delicacy: N.T.
1951 Ernestine Hill *The Territory* 426: 'blue-monge' of cornflour and currants.

45

Blue Orchid A member of the R.A.A.F. in World War II, considered to have a more glamorous uniform than the other services: *obs*.

1943 George Johnston *New Guinea Diary* 76: In the hearing of a Port Moresby digger never call a R.A.A.F. pilot [giving much needed air support] 'Blue Orchid'!

1946 Rohan Rivett *Behind Bamboo* 395: *Blue Orchids*, Army chaffing for air force.

blue pointer See quot.

1983 *National Times* 11 Nov. 27: The Surfers Paradise lifesavers were standing in a tanned huddle near the water's edge, wearing their Speedos or 'blue pointers' as they are fondly called.

Blues, the 1 In N.S.W., the Newtown Rugby League team (see Bluebags) [f. colours]

1977 *Daily Telegraph* (Sydney) 25 Jan. 30: Newtown ... are ready to shake off their tag of the 'Battling Blues'.

2 The Carlton V.F.L. team

1975 *Sunday Telegraph* (Sydney) 6 Jul. 42: Blues win as Dons brawl.

3 A team representing N.S.W. in state competition

1976 *Sunday Telegraph* (Sydney) 21 Nov. 72: Red faces is order of the day for the Blues.

4 In Queensland, the Fortitude Valleys Rugby League team

1979 *Courier-Mail* (Brisbane) 20 Feb. 18: Dunn free to stay with Blues [heading] Bustling Rugby League centre Brian Dunn will definitely wear the royal blue of Fortitude Valleys again this season.

5 In S.A., the Sturt Australian Rules team

1979 *Advertiser* (Adelaide) 11 Jun. 16: It was the second time this season that Woodville had beaten the Blues ... and Sturt discard Larry Krieg had played a crucial role for Woodville.

Blues, the Two 1 In N.S.W., the Parramatta Rugby Union team [f. light and dark blue colours]

1979 *Australian* 30 Jul. 13: Melrose stars for Two Blues [heading] Star Australian rugby union five-eighth Tony Melrose ... steered Parramatta to a 15–12 win over Manly.

2 In Victoria, the Prahran V.F.A. team

1984 *Toorak Sunday* 10 Jun. 24: Prahran go to Frankston today ... The Two Blues have lost every match since the opening win over Dandenong and are not likely to do any better against the Dolphins.

blue-tongue A shed-hand, rouseabout, or other unskilled worker [f. (*blue-tongue*) *lizard*]

1943 Baker 12: *Blue tongue* A station rouseabout.

1968 L. Braden *Bullockies* 119; He did not have

an off-sider with him; he always drove by himself – they used to call off-siders Fridays or blue-tongues.

1975 Les Ryan *The Shearers* 124: 'Righto, you blue-tongues!' he bellowed out. 'Get stuck into it!'

bluey 1 A blanket [f. colour]

1891 Henry Lawson 'Harry Stephens' *Verse* i 409: Another bushman found him with his 'bluey' wrapped around him.

1918 Bernard Cronin *The Coastlanders* 181: We'd our blueys to cover us.

1924 *Truth* 27 Apr. 6: *Bluey* A blue blanket: a swag.

1936 Archer Russell *Gone Nomad* 61: I was ever ready to roll my bluey* and travel the roads again. *Blanket.

1941 Sarah Campion *Mo Burdekin* 209; To bed they went, wrapped as before in their blueys on the rain-loud verandah.

1958 *Coast to Coast 1957–8* 208: To the pack his wife held ready he added a piece of ground-sheet, a roll of newspaper, a bluey, and a heavy pullover.

2 The swag rolled in the blanket

1886 John Farrell 'My Sundowner' *How He Died* (1913) 60: His swag, the orthodox horse-collar 'bluey'.

1905 A. B. Paterson *The Old Bush Songs* 25n: To hump bluey is to carry one's swag, and the name bluey comes from the blue blankets.

1933 Acland: *Bluey* Swag.

3 As for **blue** 1

1965 Graham McInnes *The Road to Gundagai* 242: A uniformed John Hop with a tall patent leather helmet rang the bell and handed me the dreaded 'bluey', the summons for riding a bike without lights.

1974 *Sydney Morning Herald* 5 Nov. 1: After half a century the era of the 'bluey' is over. From now on, thanks to Dataprint, the Police Department's new $66,000 computerised traffic system, offending motorists will receive 'whiteys'. The blue summons paper has been replaced by white computer paper.

4 A cattle dog

1941 Baker 11: *Bluey* Colloquial name of a cattle-dog widely used in Australia.

5 Nickname for a red-headed person

1918 Harley Matthews *Saints and Soldiers* 48: Bluey's face went as red as his hair.

1944 Lawson Glassop *We Were the Rats* 277: I did not bother to ask which Bluey. Every fellow in the A.I.F. with ginger hair was called Bluey.

1965 Patrick White *Four Plays* 172–3: 'I don't like the red, freckly man!' 'Don't go much on the blueys meself.'

1975 Xavier Herbert *Poor Fellow My Country* 1120: They were calling her *Bluey*, from the copper curls popping out of her maroon cap.

6 See **Tasmanian bluey**

bluey, to hump To carry one's swag, take to the track [f. *bluey* 2]

1890 Henry Lawson 'Possum' *Verse* i 81: He 'umped his bluey ninety mile an' kum to Bungle-long.

1906 A. B. Paterson *An Outback Marriage* 147: 'I've got to hump my bluey out of this, and take to the road like any other broken-down old swagman.'

1911 E. M. Clowes *On the Wallaby through Victoria* 278: An expression used for what in England we call 'tramping' is 'going on the wallaby', otherwise, 'humping the swag', or 'the bluey', or 'sundowning'.

1919 W. K. Harris *Outback in Australia* 146: All the ... celebrities of the day were 'on the wallaby', 'humping bluey', and called at his particular station.

1934 Tom Clarke *Marriage at 6 a.m.* 46: *Hump your bluey* – pack up, move on.

see **drum, swag**

board The floor of the wool-shed on which the sheep are shorn [f. being constructed of smooth timber; other floors would be earthen]

1870 Rolf Boldrewood 'Shearing in Riverina' *Town and Country Journal* 5 Nov. 11: So unreasoning are they, that an act of simple justice is often the signal for a strike, which includes a third or a half of the men 'on the board', as the shearing floor is by them termed.

1873 Anthony Trollope *Australia* ed. P. D. Edwards and R. B. Joyce (1967) 156: The floor [of the wool-shed], on which the shearers absolutely work, is called 'the board'.

1893 Henry Lawson 'Stragglers' in *Prose* i 91: The 'board' is very uneven and must be bad for sweeping.

1908 W. H. Ogilvie *My Life in the Open* 36: A raised floor called 'the board', on which the shearers shear the sheep.

1911 E. S. Sorenson *Life in the Australian Backblocks* 249: On an ordinary single board there are two pickers-up, one to each half.

1933 Acland 363: *Board.* – The plank floor in a woolshed on which the sheep are actually shorn.

1966 D. E. Charlwood *An Afternoon of Time* 68: In the morning the engine started at seven-thirty and the shearers stooped on the board for the last day.

board, boss over the The man supervising the shearing, the contractor

1893 Henry Lawson 'Ladies in the Shed' in *Prose* i 105: The 'boss over the board' comes along to tell the men not to swear, 'there's ladies coming.'

1885–1914 'Click go the Shears' *Old Bush Songs*

ed. Stewart and Keesing (1957) 254: In the middle of the floor in his cane-bottomed chair / Is the boss of the board, with his eyes everywhere.

1910 C. E. W. Bean *On the Wool Track* 177: The wool-classer, the 'boss-of-the-board', and one of the 'experts' were strolling across to their cottage.

1964 H. P. Tritton *Time Means Tucker* 51: The boss of the board was a petty tyrant ... One day I mentioned that he had stood over me from bell to bell, but was howled down; each shearer claiming that he had been the exclusive subject of the boss's attention.

Bob, pig-iron see **pig-iron**

Bob, staggering A newly born calf, hence veal ('bobby veal' in N.Z.) [E. dial. *Staggering Bob* ... A calf just dropped, and unable to stand, killed for veal in Scotland Grose 1785]

1873 Charles de Boos *Congewoi Correspondence* 157: Well, there wasn't nothing handy afore I'd cooled down, and so master Staggerin Bob got orf that time, and I was saved from makin a fooler myself.

1877 Rolf Boldrewood *A Colonial Reformer* (1890) 343: 'I showed 'em how their cattle was falling off, and at last they offered the lot all round at eight and sixpence – no calves given in, except regular staggering Bobs.'

1908 Mrs Aeneas Gunn *We of the Never-Never* 173: 'The time I've had with them staggering bobs', he said, when we pitied the poor, weary, footsore little calves.

1917 A. B. Paterson *Three Elephant Power* 51: The very youngest calf, the merest staggering Bob two days old.

1959 Mary Durack *Kings in Grass Castles* 246: They had been forced to dispose of no less than thirteen hundred new born calves during the trip. It was a complete waste, for stockmen were oddly squeamish about eating veal or 'staggering Bob' as it was known in the cattle camps.

bob (two-bob) in, a See quot. 1931

1931 William Hatfield *Sheepmates* (1946) 172: A bob-in [referring to an episode described thus at 72–3: 'There's too big of a mob fer one man to shout the house on his pat at a zack a pop, so you shove in a deaner a nob and flip the rats an' mice, see? An' the winner clouts on the centre an' weighs in fer the shicker, then rams the bunce down south – that is to say, I forgot you were a new chum – in his kick.' Atherton wondered why someone couldn't have said – 'We subscribe a shilling each, dice for the pool, winner paying out of that for drinks.']

1964 Tom Ronan *Packhorse and Pearling Boat* 178: No one shouted the drinks. The poker dice and box were on the counter and it was 'two bob

in and the winner shouts for the mob'.
1969 Lyndall Hadow *Full Cycle* 232: After another bob-in, Buller and Nugget . . . went home.
1975 Les Ryan *The Shearers* 71: 'Well, what's it to be? . . . Two bob in?'
see **Tambaroora**

Bob, Yellowcake see **Yellowcake**

boco, boko A horse with one eye
1901 'Boko' *The Bulletin Reciter* 157: With his single eye to guide him, very few could live beside him.
1906 A. B. Paterson *An Outback Marriage* 243: 'I'm going to ride the boco.'*
*One-eyed horse.

bodger, bodgie *a.* Inferior, worthless, false, counterfeit [f. *bodge* to patch or mend clumsily OED 1552]
1945 Baker 156: *Bodger* Worthless, second-rate (this term is apparently related to English dialect in which *bodge* means to botch or work clumsily). [World War II slang]
1950 *Australian Police Journal* Apr. 111: *Bodger* Unreal, worthless, a fraud.
1951 Frank Hardy *Power Without Glory* 383: This involved the addition of as many more 'bodger' votes as possible.
1965 William Dick *A Bunch of Ratbags* 64: For having accepted the bodgie coin, he would be obliged to come good out of his pay at the end of the day.
1972 John de Hoog *Skid Row Dossier* 106: 'Oh, I gave a bodgy (false) name, and a bodgy last employer – the whole bloody form I filled out was a bodgy.'
1982 *Weekend Australian* 17 Apr. Mag. 7: Further counting had also revealed that 14 ballot papers for branch officer positions were also bodgy.

bodgie *n.* The Australian equivalent of the Teddy boy: see quots
1950 *Sunday Telegraph* 7 May 47: 'This youth frequents King's Cross milkbars with other young hoodlums and known prostitutes,' Vice Squad Constable Thompson said . . . [The accused] stood in the dock dressed in the bizarre uniform of the 'bodgey' – belted velvet cord jacket, bright blue sports shirt without a tie, brown trousers narrowed at the ankle, shaggy Cornel Wilde haircut.
1958 A. E. Manning *The Bodgie: A Study in Psychological Abnormality* [book title]
1966 Bruce Beaver *You Can't Come Back* 5: A would-be bodgie from Redfern, Sam. About five feet five of tight blue jeans, pea-jacket, long black side-levers, and a bit of the Presley look.
1970 Barry Oakley *A Salute to the Great McCarthy*

65: 'This clean-living country lad! I don't want him ruined by any of your pimply office bodgies, you understand.'
1984 Mike Carlton *Sydney Morning Herald* 29 Aug. 12: In his ACTU incarnation, Mr Hawke would slope into the studio like a retired bodgie, a riot of checks and stripes, sideburns and occasional beard a-go-go, hair slicked down to the rims of his horny spectacles.

bodyline Term applied to the type of bowling used against Australia by D. R. Jardine's team, especially Harold Larwood, in the 1932–33 test series: see quot. 1950
1933 18 Jan. cable from Australian Board of Control to MCC in *John Wisden's Cricketers' Almanack for 1934* 328: Body-line bowling has assumed such proportions as to menace the best interests of the game, making protection of the body by the batsmen the main consideration. This is causing intensely bitter feeling between the players as well as injury. In our opinion it is unsportsmanlike. Unless stopped at once it is likely to upset the friendly relations existing between Australia and England. [The Australian newspapers report 'body bowling' in the text of this cable, not 'body-line']
1933 J. C. Davis *The Referee* (Sydney) 1 Feb. 1: Australia has made her second move in the body-line game and sent it to the Marylebone C.C. at Lord's.
1950 Don Bradman *Farewell to Cricket* 66: Now what exactly was body-line bowling? It was really short-pitched fast bowling directed towards the batsman's body with a supporting leg-side field.

bog see **flybog**

bog a duck, wet enough to see **duck**

Bogan shower see **shower**

bogey, bogie *v.* To bathe, swim [Ab.]
1788 Daniel Southwell papers *HRNSW* ii 699: To dive *Bo-gie*. Ibid. 700: I have bathed, or have been bathing *Bogiè d'oway*. These were Colby's words on coming out of the water.
1830 Robert Dawson *The Present State of Australia* 166: I at length told him we must go, when he said 'Top bit, massa, bogy', (bathe) and he threw himself into the water, where he enjoyed himself as long as I could stay.
1907 Barbara Baynton *Human Toll* 72: 'Fanny', she gasped, 'naughty, wicked boys goin' to bogey [bathe] on Sunday are stealin' Aunt's peaches!'
1957 R. S. Porteous *Brigalow* 222: I called 'Bogie dogs. Bogie.' The waterhole was only fifty yards away.

bogey, bogie *n* A swim, bath, esp. in a river or waterhole

1847 Alexander Harris *Settlers and Convicts* ed. C. M. H. Clark (1954) 132: In the cool of the evening has a 'bogie' (bathe) in the river.

1894 G. N. Boothby *On the Wallaby* 246: Then an hour's sharp tennis ... prepared the body for the evening bathe, or bogie as it is usually called, after which comes dinner.

1901 Miles Franklin *My Brilliant Career* 142: In the late afternoon, as the weather got hot, we went for bogeys in a part of the river two miles distant.

1911 E. S. Sorenson *Life in the Australian Backblocks* 122: It is common to see the whole troop, blacks and whites, marching down to the river with towels for a 'bogey' after their day's ride.

1933 R. B. Plowman *The Man from Oodnadatta* 107: While the team went on the white men remained behind to have a bogey.

1973 Donald Stuart *Morning Star Evening Star* 60: Drinking tea, after a bogey and a good feed.

bogey hole A swimming-hole: the ocean rock-pool at Newcastle, N.S.W., is so named officially

1953 Dymphna Cusack *Southern Steel* 94: She and Arthur used to come along here in the mornings on their way to swim in the Bogey Hole.

1983 *Newcastle Herald* 10 Jan. 11: More than 200 people attended the Greek Orthodox Church's Blessing of the Waters service at Newcastle's Bogey Hole yesterday morning. The highlight of the service was when 30 men tried to retrieve the holy cross from the bottom of the old convict-built pool.

boggabri 'Fat hen' (*Chenopodium*) a kind of wild spinach valued as anti-scorbutic [see Morris under *Fat hen*]

1892 Henry Lawson 'The Bush Undertaker' *Prose* i 52: 'We'll get dinner,' he added, glancing at some pots on the fire; 'I can do a bit of doughboy, an' that theer boggabri'll eat like tater-marrer along of the salt meat.'

1910 Henry Lawson 'Native Fruit' *Verse* iii 323: The way to live away from home / That all Bush children know. / Cress, boggabri, sap of stringy bark, / And many a leaf and root.

1966 Patrick White *The Solid Mandala* 43: 'Boggabri or red-leg.'

bogghi, boggi The handpiece of the shears [? f. resemblance to shape of the *bogghi* lizard]

1952 *People* 13 Feb. 12: *Boggi* Handpiece of shears.

1957 D'Arcy Niland *Call Me When the Cross Turns Over* 47: A time in those summers past when a man could take a bogeye and shear two hundred a day.

1963 *Sydney Morning Herald* 17 Aug. 11: For the last ten years Darky's ... renunciation of the 'bogghi' (shearing handpiece) has become a stock joke among his shearing mates.

1975 Les Ryan *The Shearers* 45: 'A man needs a bloody axe, not a boggi.'

1983 *Daily Telegraph* (Sydney) 2 Apr. 70: On some bone-weary days he held more than 200 squirming sheep between his legs while the shearing piece, the bog-eye, fleeced them for their contribution to Australia's wealth.

bog in To start energetically on any task; to start to eat with a will ('Two, four, six, eight; Bog in, don't wait' is a mock 'grace')

1916 *The Anzac Book* 164: Vaulting the parapet and bogging into a dinkum bayonet charge.

1920 *Bulletin Book of Humorous Verses* 115: He'd say, 'Bog into Shakespeare, Syd; / He has the English style, no kid.'

1941 Baker 11: *Bog in, to* To eat (2) To take direct action, tackle a job with a will.

1941 Kylie Tennant *The Battlers* 88: 'There's plenty o' stoo', the Stray offered bountifully. 'Bog in for all you're worth.'

1951 Dymphna Cusack and Florence James *Come in Spinner* 360: He ... motioned them to the tray. 'Bog in, it's all on the house.'

1975 Les Ryan *The Shearers* 45: Clarrie stood nearby, munching a lamington, apparently disapproving of the two, four, six, eight, bog in don't wait, business going on.

boilover An unexpected result in racing, esp. from the favourite not winning

1878 Rolf Boldrewood *An Australian Squire* repr. as *Babes in the Bush* (1900) 175: How often is the favourite amiss or 'nobbled', the rider 'off his head', the certainty a 'boil over'!

c. 1882 *The Sydney Slang Dictionary* 1: *Boilover* Favourites not winning Bookmakers and sporting men out in their calculations.

1904 Nat Gould *In Low Water* 149: The members of Tattersall's has a wholesome dread of 'one of Hickin's hot pots', and were not as a rule inclined to deal speculatively in the hopes of a 'boil-over'.

1924 *Truth* 27 Apr. 4: One of the biggest boilovers in the rowing world was Queensland's meritorious win in the interstate eights for the King's Cup at Adelaide yesterday.

1965 Baker 237: *boilover*, a win by a long-priced entrant in a horse or greyhound race, a series of such wins at a race meeting.

1974 John Powers *The Last of the Knucklemen* 21: 'I've seen too many boil-overs to get sucked into mug bets any more.'

1975 *Sunday Telegraph* (Sydney) 8 Sep. 48: Roosters plucked in semi boilover.

1980 *Weekend News* (Perth) 11 Oct. 46: Young West Australian Chris Johnstone sprang a boilover by eliminating Syd Ball in the qualifying rounds.

boko   see **boco**

bolter   1   Runaway convict, bushranger
1844 Louisa Meredith *Notes and Sketches of New South Wales* 132: During our stay at Bathurst, a party of the mounted police went in search of a very daring gang of bush-rangers, or, as they are sometimes called, 'bolters'.
c. 1845 James Tucker *Ralph Rashleigh* (1952) 187: At length one of the bullock-drivers asked what the prisoners were charged with, and McCoy replied, 'Thay are *bolters* (runaway convicts). They belonged to that mob of Foxley the bush-ranger's.'
1865 J. F. Mortlock *Experiences of a Convict* (1965) 221: Three or four 'old hands' were pointed out to me as Tasmanian 'bolters', who had made their escape to England and been for another crime again transported.
2   An outsider (applied more recently to one who wins or succeeds)
1941 Baker 35: *Hasn't the bolter's* Used of a person or race-horse that has no chance at all in a contest or situation.
1973 *Sydney Morning Herald* 17 Sep. 1:   A South Coast publican who continually spurns the big money of Sydney Rugby League was the 'bolter' in the Australian team announced last night to tour France and England.
1975 *Sun-Herald* 14 Sep. 42: Books cheer as 'bolter' gets home.
1983 *Sydney Morning Herald* 26 Feb. 7: 'This could be a bolter – one of the most exciting New South Wales seats to watch in this election', Fred Daly said yesterday in Tamworth, the heart of National Party territory.
1984 *Age* (Melbourne) 6 Jun. 35: Pakenham bolter 'will win the Cup' [heading] The horse at the centre of this ambitious plan is Tasman, a 50/1 shot who returned from obscurity to take yesterday's Korean Horse Affairs Association Handicap.

bomb   1   An old or dilapidated motor-car
1950 *Australian Police Journal* Apr. 110: *Bomb, A* A dud – usually refers to second-hand motor vehicles in poor mechanical shape.
1958 Christopher Koch *The Boys in the Island* 69: 'Jake's gunna go out – taking his old bomb, so we'll get a free ride.'
1962 Gavin Casey *Amid the Plenty* 58: The car, they called it! Well, he never wanted to be seen in that old bomb, that was for sure.
1970 Patrick White *The Vivisector* 470: Italians from Temora who are here in a bomb they bought, they want to take us for a ride.
1980 *Mercury* (Hobart) 16 Apr. 6: If ever anyone

drove a 'bomb', it was the woman at the wheel of an early-model Holden station sedan spotted by a reader in the city yesterday.
2   In Rugby League football, a refinement of the 'up and under': a high kick at the end of the tackle count designed to land near or over the try line, esp. under the goal posts, so that a player catching it and going to ground will score
1977 *Sun* (Sydney) 23 Sep. 62: We haven't used many 'bombs'. Last year in the finals we put plenty up and scored from a lot of them.
1981 *Canberra Times* 9 Aug. 6: The 'bomb' has been the most significant tactical innovation in league for 20 years. It is significant because it is an adaptation of union's 'up-and-under', and because it is an attempt to use the kick as an effective try-scoring agent.

Bombay bloomers   Men's shorts, long and loose-fitting [? f. resemblance to those worn by the British in India]
1954 L. H. Evers *Pattern of Conquest* 80: The first drink he had of it put him in hospital for three weeks where he spent his time swatting green mosquitoes which he claimed wore yellow socks and Bombay bloomers.
1978 *Australian* 22 Nov. 2: Headline Harry [Jensen] they used to call him in his younger days when as Sydney's Lord Mayor he donned Bombay Bloomers in a vain attempt to persuade Australians to wear more suitable summer gear.
1981 Mike Fitzpatrick *Age* (Melbourne) 5 Oct. 11: The VFL issue [of shorts] this year is worse than last year's, which gave all the players a rash. These ones are Bombay bloomers, a reaction because last year the cheeks of one's behind kept peeping out from them.
1984 Mrs Andrew Peacock *Sydney Morning Herald* 23 Jan. 9: 'He [Mr Peacock] couldn't go to Parliament House wearing Bombay bloomers and an old sweat shirt and say "g'day mate, here I am"'.

bomber, brown   see **brown bomber**

bomber, grey   see **grey**

Bombers, the   The Essendon V.F.L. team [f. proximity to aerodrome]

bombo   Cheap wine [*bumbo*, a liquor composed of rum, sugar, water, and nutmeg OED 1748]
1941 Baker 12: *Bombo* whiskey.
1943 Baker 12: *Bombo* Cheap wine.
1948 Ruth Park *The Harp in the South* 255: 'Get back to yer bombo, yer old hag.'
1958 H. D. Williamson *The Sunlit Plain* 17: 'Feel crook,' he mumbled. 'Finished up on the bombo last night.'
1968 Stuart Gore *Holy Smoke* 26: 'He done in the

whole issue on sheilas and bombo.'

bombora   A submerged reef, esp. near the foot of a cliff [Ab.]
1933 *Bulletin* 24 May 27: 'Bombora' is an aboriginal word applied to the high-crested wave which breaks ... over submerged rocks near the coastline.
1945 Baker 224: *bomboora* ... a dangerous reef of rocks usually found at the foot of cliffs.
1975 *Sydney Morning Herald* 1 Dec. 2: Five men were tossed about in the darkness on a small liferaft for two hours yesterday after their yacht struck a reef and later sank. The mishap occurred about 3 a.m. when the yacht ... struck a bombora about a kilometre off Norah Head.
1983 *Sun* (Sydney) 16 Dec. 58: Kingfish are showing on the Toowoon Bay bombora.

bommy   A bombora [abbr.]
1979 *NT News* (Darwin) 7 Dec. 12: The waters there are clear and less turbulent than further south, with some very interesting bommies and reefs.
1983 *Sun* (Sydney) 16 Dec. 58: Outside fishing remains steady in this area with kingfish on the bommies south-west of Broughton Island.
1984 Don'o Kim *The Chinaman* 56: 'Bommie! Bommie on portside!' ... Vic spun the wheel furiously, away from the dark shadow of the submerged reef.

Bondi, to give someone   To beat someone up: *obs.* [f. a fracas between larrikins and the police at Bondi on Boxing Day 1884]
1890 *Truth* 19 Oct. 3: Suppose a live policeman is on the ground while the gay and festive members of a 'push' are 'giving him Bondi'. Ibid. 16 Nov. 7: The scribe ... accepted a hint to take his bloomin' hook. The hint was the picking up by one of the young gentlemen of an empty bottle, and the somewhat uncertain attitude of two or three others, who looked fully competent and perfectly willing to give him Bondi at a moment's notice.
1951 Dal Stivens *Jimmy Brockett* 67: Then Snowy got Maxie in a corner and began to give him Bondi.
1973 Ruth Park *The Companion Guide to Sydney* 415: 'Bondi' also means the heavy warrior's club, and the word was incorporated in a now-forgotten fragment of larrikins' cant – I'll give you Bondi!' meaning a severe bashing.

Bondi tram   The larva of the Cup Moth (*Doratifera vulnerans* Lewin)
1974 Bernard D'Abrera *Moths of Australia* 50: The best known species is of course *Doratifera vulnerans* Lewin a pest of ornamental shrubs, fruit trees and *Eucalyptus*. The larvae, brightly coloured, and known in N.S.W. as 'Bondi Trams'

possess spines which inflict a most painful sting. see **Chinese junk**

Bondi tram, to shoot through like a   To make a speedy departure [f. trams running from Sydney to Bondi beach, discontinued in 1961]
1951 Seaforth Mackenzie *Dead Men Rising* 53: He called the rolls ... looked up to check the inevitable comments from the ranks: 'Shot through like a Bondi tram.' 'Not 'ere today, Sar' Major.'
1956 Kylie Tennant *The Honey Flow* 151: 'We collected Mike from where he and Hertz was mixing it, and we went through like a Bondi tram.'
1962 John Morrison *Twenty-Three* 192: 'He shot through like a Bondi tram the minute the telegram arrived.'
1972 Geoff Morley *Jockey Rides Honest Race* 65: I punched him in the mouth and shot through like a Bondi tram.
1974 *Sunday Telegraph* (Sydney) 29 Sep. 11: The catch-phrase to 'shoot through like a Bondi tram' will have a fresh meaning when Sydney restores its city tramway system.
1982 *Sydney Morning Herald* 10 Apr. 25: Anyone not going to *Amadeus* seemed reluctant to leave this party. Unlike the Premier who shot through like a Bondi tram.

bone, to (point the bone)   1   In aboriginal 'magic', to will an enemy to die
2   Among whites, to place a 'jinx' or hoodoo on someone, single someone out with this purpose
1943 Donald Friend *Gunner's Diary* 21: The bone is pointed at myself and a few others. We are to be transferred to a draft battery.
1951 Dymphna Cusack and Florence James *Come In Spinner* 367: 'I just thought you been off the last coupla mornin's, you mightn't be too good like.' Guinea poked her in the ribs. 'Pointing the bone at me are you, you old witch?' [implying pregnancy]
1965 *Daily Telegraph* (Sydney) 27 Apr. 2: Harold Wilson has pointed the bone at the House of Lords. If they don't pull their heads in, he'll chop them off.
1970 Barry Oakley *A Salute to the Great McCarthy* 28: 'I am a bit older and I do understand. You're in no position to point the bone.'
1974 Morris West *Harlequin* 15: When you tell a banker that there are anomalies in his accounts, it is as if you point a bone at him or chant a mortal curse over his head.
1980 Bruce Grant *Cherry Bloom* 203: 'Nothing a lawyer could make stick. It just mentioned my name and my speciality – Vietnam – three times. It was what the great Australian culture – not yours – calls "pointing the bone".'

bonfire night   As for **cracker night** q.v.

1976 *Sydney Morning Herald* 12 Jun. 36: Police had warned against the misuse of firecrackers at traditional Queen's Birthday bonfire night celebrations tonight.

bong see **bung**

bontoger, bontosher, bonzarina (almost noncewords)
1904 *Bulletin* 14 Apr. 29: A bontosher is a real slasher . . . A bonsterina is a female bonster. Ibid. 5 May 29: 'Bonster' is a corruption of 'Bontojer' pronounced Bontodger, and 'Bontojer' is a corruption of the two French words *bon* and *toujours*.
1934 Thomas Wood *Cobbers* (1961) 212: 'She was a little bonzarina.'
see **boshter**

bonzer Excellent, deserving admiration: *obsolescent* [origin uncertain]
1904 *Bulletin* 14 Apr. 29: A bonser or bonster is comparatively superior to a bons.
1906 Edward Dyson *Fact'ry 'Ands* 246: 'He had er dull eye, 'n' er vacant face, 'n' no chin, his face jist slippin' off where his chin should iv come in, but 'e had er bonzer nose.'
1915 C. J. Dennis *The Songs of a Sentimental Bloke* 13: The air is like a long, cool swig o' beer, / The bonzer smell o' flow'rs is on the breeze.
1919 W. H. Downing *Digger Dialects* 12: *Bonzer* Good.
1925 Seymour Hicks *Hullo Australia* 88: 'Strange sayings the Australians have, sir, don't they? I asked Davis this evening what the weather would be like when we reached the other side and he said "Bonser".'
1934 Vance Palmer *Sea and Spinifex* 117: 'A bonza night!' she said with drowsy enthusiasm.
1947 John Morrison *Sailors Belong Ships* 72: 'I've got a bonzer little joint not ten minutes from the station.'
1969 Hal Porter *Southerly* 11: For me an anachronism mars all. An author should not have . . . 1957 Australian children saying, 'Bonzer!'
1979 *Age* (Melbourne) 21 Sep. 16: I do not have one friend, even acquaintance, who is anywhere near likely to say 'g'day cobber, like a cold tube? geez I like your sheila, no worries, bonzer sport . . .' etc. as most males do in television commercials.
1979 Dorothy Hewett *The Man from Mukinupin* 43: Hail, beauteous land, hail bonzer Western Australia, / Compared to ye all others are a failure.
1981 *Sydney Morning Herald* 24 Jan. 37: The first thing they'll ask you as you step off the plane is this, 'What do you think of Australia, mate?' And this is to be your reply, 'Bewdy, bottler, bonzer.'

boo-eye, the The remote rural areas: a New Zealandism, rarely encountered in Australia, equivalent to the Australian 'Woop Woop' or 'never never'
1955 D'Arcy Niland *The Shiralee* 67: Could have been worse. He could have been out there in the boo-eye, thrusting his body into the wind and rain, getting blown about like an old moll at a plonk party.

boofhead 1 A stupid person, a fathead [f. *bufflehead* A fool, blockhead, stupid fellow OED 1659]. The term was given further currency in Australia from a comic strip character with an elongated head invented by R. B. Clark in 1939 and introduced in the *Daily Mirror* in May 1941, running until Clark's death in 1970.
1941 Baker 12: *Boofhead*: A fool or simpleton.
1954 T. A. G. Hungerford *Sowers of the Wind* 117: 'Try taking your tweeds off, boof-head!'
1966 H. M. Barker *Droving Days* 81: Alf asked what he meant by B.C. 'Before the birth of Christ, you boof-head', was the answer he got.
1972 Geoff Morley *Jockey Rides Honest Race* 119: 'Haven't finished yet, Boofhead.'
1979 John Summons *Lamb of God* 40: 'I find it hard to believe that Jim would throw an apple at the statue on purpose. He wouldn't be that much of a boofhead.'
1983 *Australian* 23 Aug. 1: Mr Hayden . . . described the former ALP secretary [David Combe] as a 'boofhead'.
boofheadedness
1983 Mike Carlton *Sun-Herald* 18 Sep. 143: It is a scandal that they have been allowed to get away with this boofheadedness for so long.
2 Anyone with a big head (often with the implication 'fathead'); a horse with head out of proportion
1946 Rohan Rivett *Behind Bamboo* 395: *Boof head*, one with a big head.
1965 John Beede *They Hosed Them Out* 171: Tubby . . . asked, 'Who's that boofheaded old bastard, anyway?' It was an apt description and from then on . . . he was known as 'boofhead'. [referring (in 1944) to a colonel with an 'elongated and horselike' face, p. 168]
1981 *Alan Marshall's Australia* 132: 'What a boofhead of a foal,' he had thought – and so it was named. The foal did indeed have a large head, a hairy head, whiskered like a draught horse.
1984 Ron Quinton *Sydney Morning Herald* 19 Apr. 31: 'He [Mr Ambassador] is a big, clumsy, boofheaded type of horse.'

book A bookmaker [abbr.]
1898 A. B. Paterson 'A Disqualified Jockey's Story' *Singer of the Bush* (1983) 299: He said he reckoned he was stiff, / And all the books was

layin' six to four.
1907 *Lone Hand* May 86: The 'books' found themselves unable to lay any odds whatever against the majority of the starters.
1934 Thomas Wood *Cobbers* 97: Charles laid down his fork and said it was a skinner for the books.
1984 *Sun-Herald* 25 Nov. 152: A local rails book was abused by a professional punter.

Booligal Town in western N.S.W. given a place in folklore by A. B. Paterson's poem 'Hay and Hell and Booligal'
[**1787** Francis Grose *A Provincial Glossary* R₈v: From Hell, Hull and Halifax – deliver us. This was part of the vagrant's litany. At Hull all vagrants, found begging in the streets, were whipped and set in the stocks; and at Halifax persons taken in the act of stealing cloth, were instantly, and without any process, beheaded, with an engine called a maiden.]
1901 *The Bulletin Reciter* 193: Hot? Great Scott! / It was Hell, with some improvements, worse than Booligal a lot!
1902 A. B. Paterson *Rio Grande's Last Race* 40: 'Oh, send us to our just reward / In Hay or Hell, but, gracious Lord, / Deliver us from Booligal!'
[**1916**] Oliver Hogue *Trooper Bluegum at the Dardanelles* 58: It was generally thought that he had spent some time in hell, or Booligal, so familiarly did he speak of the infernal regions.
1953 *Caddie A Sydney Barmaid* 172: He told me he'd just come from Booligal, and asked me if I knew where it was . . . 'Surely you've heard of Hay, hell and Booligal?' I remembered then. It was a place of heat, dust and flies.
1955 John Morrison *Black Cargo* 11: We've cursed the Federation from Hell to Booligal for all the muck they've tossed out at us.

boomah, boomer 1 A very large kangaroo (*Macropus giganteus*) [f. *boomer* anything very large of its kind EDD]
1830 *Hobart Town Almanack* 110: We saw a huge kangaroo . . . What did we not feel when Juno [the hound] snapped the boomah's haunches and he turned round to offer battle.
1845 R. Howitt *Australia Felix* 273: A boomer, or large forester Kangaroo.
1981 A. B. Facey *A Fortunate Life* 81: The boomer had been hit through the chest and was dead when we ran to him.
2 Anything of exceptional size
1843 Charles Rowcroft *Tales of the Colonies* iii 97: 'There's one! and there's another! he's a regular boomah!' [describing a flea]
1896 Edward Dyson *Rhymes from the Mines* 102: It was said that a nugget – a boomer – / Had been found by the Chows in our shaft.

1926 'Alpha' *Reminiscences of the Goldfields* 21: 'What do you make of her?' said the skipper. 'Oh, sir, she is a boomer,' said I, 'she's 500 feet long.' [describing a whale]
1936 Miles Franklin *All That Swagger* 413: 'Old Robert's overdraft must be a boomer.'
1944 Stan Arneil *One Man's War* (1980) 167: I woke up with a boomer cold (almost my first in the tropics).
1956 Tom Ronan *Moleskin Midas* 114: 'Fights you're talking about! Well, I just seen a boomer!'
1974 *Sydney Morning Herald* 5 Jun. 17: The English Rugby League centre kicked several goals from the 25 metre mark on the sideline, and one boomer from right on the halfway mark.
1983 *Sun* (Sydney) 30 Dec. 41: 'I had three boomer seasons back home, including plenty of big race wins.'

boomalli To round up, corner in a dead-end, esp. cattle [? Ab.]
1890 Rolf Boldrewood *A Colonial Reformer* 210: 'Tonight yan longa camp; boomalli (shoot, slay) Hutkeeper'.
1945 Tom Ronan *Strangers on the Ophir* 99: A thousand head of bullocks, hungry and mostly thirsty, boomallied and knocked about as those had been, are hard to hold.
1981 Keith Garvey *Slowly Sweats the Gun* 177: 'I'll tell yer what yer spoilt, pampered little Guardsman [an unbroken horse] needs! A bloke with a good heavy whip to boom-alley him into a corner of the yard and flog the legs off him until he faces up and takes the bridle'.

boomerang To move like a boomerang; to recoil
1901 Henry Lawson 'The Mystery of Dave Regan' *Prose* i 327: He said that to the horse as it boomeranged off again and broke away through the scrub.
1945 Kylie Tennant *Ride on Stranger* 63: Money must boomerang back to his hand or it never left it in the first place.
1956 J. T. Lang *I Remember* 181: In the end bigotry boomeranged on its chief sponsor.
1982 *Age* (Melbourne) 1 Apr. 34: 'We don't want any action to boomerang against Australia', one African official said.

boomerangs, he could sell ~ to the blacks A persuasive personality
1974 Peter Kenna *A Hard God* 23: 'He's a first class con man. He could sell boomerangs to the blacks.'

boondy 1 A club: N.S.W. [Ab.]
1907 Charles MacAlister *Old Pioneering Days in the Sunny South* 88: The 'Knulla Knullas', or 'Boondies', were ironbark sticks, with a heavy nob

on the end, used in killing 'possums, etc., and sometimes in tribal warfare. Ibid. p. 124: They were mercilessly speared and 'boondied' (beaten to death with nullas) by the blacks.

1964 W. S. Ramson *The Currency of Aboriginal Words in Australian English* 15: In New South Wales, *boondee* or *bundy*, a throwing stick.

1978 *National Times* 2 Jan. 6: They had a boondi (a club the shape of a baseball bat carved usually from heavy myall or yarran).

2 A stone (of a suitable size for throwing): W.A. [Ab.]

1952 T. A. G. Hungerford *The Ridge and the River* 94: 'See that bastard, practising grenade-throwing with bits of boondies?'

1957 Randolph Stow *The Bystander* 132: 'He's chucking boondies on the roof!'

3 See quot. 1982

1982 Jack Davis *The Dreamers* 88: 'You got any *boondah*? Ibid. p. 141: *boondah*, money; literally, stone.

boong An Australian aboriginal; New Guinea native; any Asiatic: *derogatory* [Ab.]

1941 Kylie Tennant *The Battlers* 123: 'These boangs are all too matey,' Thirty-Bob grumbled. 'If a bit of trouble starts, it's a case of one in, all in.'

1943 George Johnston *New Guinea Diary* 186: The boys from the Middle East called them [the natives] 'wogs' at first, because it was their name for the Arabs. Soon they learnt the New Guinea army term, which is 'boong'. Before they have been there long they are calling them 'sport', which seems to be the second A.I.F.'s equivalent for 'digger'.

1946 Rohan Rivett *Behind Bamboo* 395: *Boong* Any Asiatic or coloured person. *Boongs with boots on* Japs.

1959 Xavier Herbert *Seven Emus* 58: 'He might have a lot of boong in him, but he's also got a lot of the white man.'

1966 Peter Mathers *Trap* 131: For several seconds she stared at him. Was it proper for her to serve a boong?

1976 Dorothy Hewett *Bon-bons and Roses for Dolly* 53: 'Give it back to the Boongs, me ol' Dad useta say.'

1980 *Australian* 8 Jul. 2: On the eve of National Aboriginal Week, the Victorian Aboriginal community is divided in its reaction to the Premier, Mr Hamer, referring to Aborigines as 'boongs' at a press conference last Friday.

1983 *Sydney Morning Herald* 7 Jul. 3: 'It [National Aborigines Week] is designed to appease the consciences of the whites. It's Pat a Boong on the Back Week ... what rubbish', said Mr Craigie, an Aboriginal Legal Service worker.

white boongs

1979 *Bulletin* 3 Jul. 57: Wingeing Poms are in a class of their own, but 'white boongs', as Kiwis are pejoratively, but not really maliciously, called by some Australians [at Bondi], are starting to be regarded as a race apart.

boot, chewy on see **chewy**

boot home To ride a horse to the winning post

1979 *Courier-Mail* (Brisbane) 1 Mar. 24: While Bill [Cook] was making his comeback to the Creek, son Peter booted home three winners at Canterbury.

1980 *Mercury* (Hobart) 2 May 19: Leading jockey Max Baker, who last weekend booted home seven winners, is expected to continue his winning run at Elswick tomorrow.

1983 *Sun-Herald* 10 Jul. 63: Brent Thomson ... booted Chez Nous to an easy win in the Headquarters Handicap at Flemington yesterday.

bootlace 1 See quot.

1933 Acland 363 *Boot Laces*. – Narrow strips of skin cut off by rough shearers, generally when opening up the neck.

2 Jerked meat (i.e. strips of meat cured by exposure to the sun)

1951 Ernestine Hill *The Territory* 107: Food in the pack-bags was flour, tea and four hundred pounds of jerked meat – 'bootlace'.

boot, put in the To kick an opponent when he is down; to be ruthless in pressing an advantage.

1915 C. J. Dennis *The Songs of a Sentimental Bloke* 42: 'It's me or you!' 'e 'owls, an' wiv a yell, / Plunks Tyball through the gizzard wiv 'is sword, / 'Ow I ongcored! / 'Put in the boot!' I sez. 'Put in the boot!'

1920 *Aussie* Apr. (Glossary): *Socked the boot into him* Took advantage of his misfortune.

1923 Steele Rudd *On Emu Creek* 174: They ... butted into him, played havoc with his clothes, threw him heavily every time he tried to rise, and put the boot into him.

1939 Kylie Tennant *Foveaux* 247: 'Give it to 'em! Put in the boot, boys!' the onlookers encouraged.

1946 Dal Stivens *The Courtship of Uncle Henry* 75: Anyone could see he was as mad as a cut snake about everything and wanting to put the boot in.

1950 Jon Cleary *Just Let Me Be* 67: He didn't want trouble, but he couldn't turn his back on savagery – a fight was anybody's business when someone started to put the boot in.

1962 Gavin Casey *Amid the Plenty* 79: 'You stand up to my old lady a bit, if you have to. If you let her get you down she'll put in the boot, don't you worry.'

1975 *Guardian* (London) 5 May 6: Anti-Marketeers put financial boot in.

1982 *Sun-Herald* 7 Mar. 15: After a good start this

year, Hawke like others, is eager to put in the boot.

boots and all   An all-out effort; 'no holds barred'
1953 Dymphna Cusack *Southern Steel* 260: 'When you do a thing you go into it boots and all.'
1968 *Australian* 4 Apr. 8: On this view, 1969 would see a rejuvenated LBJ in power and an American boots-and-all war in North Vietnam.
1974 John Power *The Last of the Knucklemen* 72: 'You lift your arse off that floor, mate, an' I'm gonna come wadin' into you – boots an' all!'
1975 *Sydney Morning Herald* 3 Jan. 6: His political opponents see him [Sir Robert Askin] as an old-style 'boots-and-all' political fighter, but his image with those who have worked under him . . . is of a tolerant boss.
1981 *National Times* 6 Dec. 1: The Left's drive for more power has been a 'boots and all' campaign.

boots under the bed   Evidence of a de facto relationship affecting a woman's eligibility for Social Security benefits
1983 Philippa Smith *Sun-Herald* 14 Aug. 119: Past practices of field officers inspecting homes and bedrooms – sometimes called the 'boot under the bed' inspections – were also criticised as an extreme intrusion of privacy.

booze bus   A police vehicle equipped for random breath-testing of motorists, introduced in N.S.W. 17 Dec. 1982
1982 *Sydney Morning Herald* 16 Dec. 2: Police 'booze buses' gear up for the start of random breath tests.
1984 *Sun-Herald* 5 Feb. 128: The booze bus era means that sensible drinkers get cabs home from parties, but what on earth do you do after a heavy day in the Hunter Valley?
1984 *Age* (Melbourne) 4 Oct. 1: About 1000 drivers will be tested each day by booze buses or normal police cars.

bo peep, have a   Take a look at
1944 Lawson Glassop *We Were the Rats* 79: 'Let's take a bo peep at what they got in the canteen.'
1979 *Herald* (Melbourne) 20 Mar. Heraldform 4: He ought to take a bo-peep at the lot I have to deal with at the pickle factory.
1983 *Sydney Morning Herald* 21 May 35: Sister prowled in regularly for a bo-peep at my progress.

borak, borack   Nonsense, gammon, humbug [Ab.]
1845 Thomas McCombie *Arabin, or, The Adventures of a Colonist* 273: *Borack*, Gammon, nonsense.
1885 *The Australian Printers' Keepsake* 124: Oh, we were bad – no borack, mind, boys.
1961 Tom Ronan *Only a Short Walk* 111: The chief steward was full of borack . . . He wasn't a

very good liar, this steward.

borack, to poke ~ at   To ridicule, make fun of
1885 *The Australian Printers' Keepsake* 75: On telling him my adventures, how Bob in my misery had 'poked borack' at me, he said – 'You were *had*.'
1893 J. A. Barry *Steve Brown's Bunyip* 21: They're always a-poking borack an' a-chiackin' o' me over in the hut.'
1915 Louis Stone *Betty Wayside* 268: 'If I catch anybody poking borack at my get-up, they'll hear some fancy English!'
1923 George S. Beeby *Concerning Ordinary People* 96: 'You'll be watched by the pickets, and them pokin' borack at you.'
1936 William Hatfield *Big Timber* 245: 'Poke borack at me, would you?' he snarled.
1947 Vance Palmer *Hail Tomorrow* 47: 'For God's sake, leave me alone, Jim. You're always poking borak at me!'
1962 Dymphna Cusack *Picnic Races* 22: 'Makes me ropeable that feller does, poking borak every time he gets a chance.'
1975 Xavier Herbert *Poor Fellow My Country* 349: 'The old boy had been poking borak at him about anthropology.'
see **mullock**

bore-casing   Macaroni: N.T.
1951 Ernestine Hill *The Territory* 426: 'Bore-casing', macaroni.

bored or punched, he doesn't know if he's   A state of stupidity or confusion [Australian version of English and Canadian 'he doesn't know if his arsehole's bored or punched': Partridge]
1952 T. A. G. Hungerford *The Ridge and the River* 120: 'They didn't know whether they were punched or bored, after that, until we got out again at the crossing, where you marked on the map.'
1959 Dorothy Hewett *Bobbin Up* 125: 'You're just a mad militant Snow. You wouldn't know if you was punched, bored or . . .'
1962 Stuart Gore *Down the Golden Mile* 301: 'The noise and the bloody flash . . . he won't know whether his stern's bored or countersunk!'

bore it up them   Equivalent to 'sock it to them' [Army slang from World War II]
1951 Eric Lambert *The Twenty Thousand Thieves* 178: 'A provost I got into a blue with in Tel Aviv was barkin' the orders. Christ! Did that bastard bore it up me?'
1952 T. A. G. Hungerford *The Ridge and the River* 198: 'Listen to that strafing. Bore it up 'em, you little beauties!'
1959 David Forrest, *The Last Blue Sea* 84: 'Into it!' he yelled at Three Platoon. 'Bore it into them!'
1963 Lawson Glassop *The Rats in New Guinea*

128: 'Stand fast, Aussies, and bore it up 'em.'
1971 Frank Hardy *The Outcasts of Foolgarah* 70: 'Good on you, Tich, bore it up 'em.'
1980 *Bulletin* 11 Nov. 155: Boring it up the bastards from the bush [heading]
1984 Rod Marsh *West Australian* (Perth) 21 Feb. 79: I handed out a lot of rockets as a captain but I also handed out a lot more praise than most captains. If players did badly I would bore it right up them and if they did well I would heap praise on them.

born in a tent   see **tent**

Borroloola sandwich   See quot.: *jocular* [f. place-name in N.T.]
1951 Ernestine Hill *The Territory* 426: A 'Borroloola sandwich' was a goanna between two sheets of bark.

boshter, bosker   Equivalent to bonzer, but never attaining the same currency: *obs.*
1906 Edward Dyson *Fact'ry 'Ands* 1: This was the fifth time Benno had declaimed on the 'boshter' qualities of the unknown.
1908 Henry Fletcher *Dads and Dan between Smokes* 50: Oh the North is a bosker country.
1915 C. J. Dennis *The Songs of a Sentimental Bloke* 14: The little birds is chirpin' in the nest, / The parks an' gardings is a bosker sight. Ibid. 13: Soft in the moon; such *boshter* eyes!
1916 *The Anzac Book* 36: 'A boshter* night for a walk', I remarked. *Bosker, boshter, bonzer – Australian slang for splendid.
1925 Arthur Wright *A Good Recovery* 52: 'What a bosker pair of earrings they'll make.'
1959 Gerard Hamilton *Summer Glare* 53: 'Gee, it's bosker, ain't it?' [set in 1920s]

boss, the   The headmaster of a school
1950 Brian James *The Advancement of Spencer Button* 61: There was variety in this little world, and no marked unity and solidarity, except, perhaps, in the matter of the Boss. It was the proper thing to slander and malign and hate the Boss – and to say so.
1978 *Quadrant* Dec. 65: The boss, as all the chalkies like to call their headmasters, had insisted on inspecting his class.
1984 Ned Manning *Us or Them* 25: 'The boss asked me to remind you about the shortage of duplicating paper.'

boss cocky   see **cocky**

boss over the board   see **board**

boss, pannikin   see **pannikin**

bot *n.*   A sponger, persistent borrower [? f. the bot-fly, which 'bites']
1919 W. H. Downing *Digger Dialects* 13: *Bott* (1) A cadger; (2) A useless person; (3) a hanger-on.
1924 *Truth* 27 Apr. 6: *Bott* Person who borrows.
1942 Leonard Mann *The Go-Getter* 124: 'Get out, you bot.' Chris ordered him [the beggar] and got up.
1960 A. W. Upfield *Bony and the Kelly Gang* 108–9: 'He says that only five per cent of first-class travellers going overseas pay their own fares. Says the other ninety-five per cent have their fares paid by the tax-payers. They're just bots. Politicians and top civil servants and marketing board people.'
1965 Eric Lambert *The Long White Night* 136: 'He had nothing left to buy schooners for bots like you.'
1978 Ronald McKie *Bitter Bread* 39: He was delighted to see the last of him. The bot had already cost him a small fortune.
1982 *Sydney Morning Herald* 12 Feb. 1: It might just have been possible to have chosen a happier name than Bot Australia Ltd for the new merchant bank launched this week.

bot *v.*   To borrow, sponge on
1934 *Bulletin* 7 Nov. 46: 'How many's that, sir?' he gazed rheumily into space, 'Six it is; that's three beers I owe y'. Settle up when I sell me next picture.' The notebook went back into his pocket and he sighed with relief. 'Well, that's settled. Never did like *botting* on a bloke.'
1944 Alan Marshall *These Are My People* 174: 'If you get plenty later I'll bot a cigarette off the lot of you.'
1951 Frank Hardy *Power Without Glory* 539: They would bot from you. They would accept your health and life in sacrifice, then dump you.
1962 Criena Rohan *The Delinquents* 105: Lola, she said, was a botting, bludging little bastard.
1978 Richard Beilby *Gunner* 232: Scruffy though he might be he wasn't going to have Eilie thinking he was botting on Whiteside.
on the bot
1965 John Beede *They Hosed Them Out* 156: To prove that she wasn't on the bot she bought me a drink.

Botany Bay   Name applied in the eighteenth and earlier nineteenth century to the penal settlement in Australia (actually Port Jackson), and to Australia as a whole [f. the landing place named by Cook in 1770]
c. 1790 'Botany Bay. A New Song' repr. in Hugh Anderson *Farewell to Old England* (1964) 35: Who live by fraud, cheating, vile tricks, and foul play, / Should all be sent over to Botany Bay.
1819 Barron Field *First Fruits of Australian*

Poetry (1941) 3: 'Botany-Bay Flowers' [poem title]
1859 John Lang *Botany Bay, or True Stories of the Early Days of Australia* [book title]
Botany Bay dozen
1792 George Thompson Jnl *HRNSW* ii 796: If guilty, he is taken to a cart-wheel to receive a Botany Bay dozen, which is twenty-five lashes.

bottle To hit over the head with a bottle
1962 Douglas McCallum *Australian Civilization* ed. P. Coleman 34: 'Bottling him' is a phrase which is still part of the Australian vernacular and an ugly use of beer glasses or bottles in fights is not of infrequent occurrence in bar-room brawls.
1968 David Ireland *The Chantic Bird* 29: Some of the fellows I know, you don't want to get drunk near them. They'd bottle you for two bob if they thought you were half shot.
1978 Kevin Gilbert *Living Black* 304: 'If he was too big to tackle, somebody bottled him.'

bottle, not full Not fully informed, not 'all there'
1969 Christopher Bray *Blossom Like a Rose* 223: 'Jake and Brody aren't full bottle on this so tell them what goes on, will yer?'
1981 *Sydney Morning Herald* 1 Aug. 16: I have sometimes wondered, during his trip to London [to cover the royal wedding], if Spike Milligan is still the full bottle.

bottle-oh An itinerant dealer in empty bottles [f. the cry]
1899 A. B. Paterson 'The "Bottle-oh" Man' in *Singer of the Bush* (1983) 332.
1902 Henry Fletcher *The Waybacks* 38: 'To get out of this smoke and noise, to get the door-bell off my nerves, and the bottle-oh out of my ears, to live truly rural under the lovely wattle trees – oh, it will be just lovely!'
1906 Edward Dyson *Fact'ry 'Ands* 217: Half-a-dozen of them would have died for the bibulous comp. despite the bottle-o's stock garnered in the trouser fringe at his boot heels.
1913 Henry Lawson 'Benno and his Old 'Uns' *Prose* i 803: Benno, a Sussex Street bottle-o . . . was an angry bottle-o that day.
1917 A. B. Paterson *Three Elephant Power* 138: Sometimes out in the back yard of their palatial mansion they hand the empty bottles, free of charge, to a poor broken-down bottle-O.
1935 Kylie Tennant *Tiburon* 7: Battered old motor-trucks, bottle-oh carts . . . paused here for the night.
1943 Margaret Trist *In the Sun* 99: A bottle-o followed him, crying cheerily, 'Bottles, bottles, any empty bottles, bottles, bottles, any kind of bottles.'
1962 Criena Rohan *The Delinquents* 278: They packed their clothes and sold the mattresses to the Bottle-oh who made his weekly round that after-

noon.
1970 Patrick White *The Vivisector* 39: Tommy Sullivan said that Hurt Duffield was the son of a no-hope pommy bottle-o down their street.
1983 Laurie Clancy *Perfect Love* 103: 'Did you get rid of those bottles?' she asked him. 'I got the bottle-oh out. He gave me six bob for them.'

bottler Someone outstanding in his class, for good qualities or bad [cf. the expression 'His blood's worth bottling']
1876 Rolf Boldrewood *A Colonial Reformer* (1890) 95: 'He's a bottler, that's what he [a horse] is, and if you ever go for to sell him, you'll be sorry for it.'
1952 T. A. G. Hungerford *The Ridge and the River* 122: 'The old bastard! The old hooer! What a bloody bottler!'
1969 Osmar White *Under the Iron Rainbow* 142: 'He's a little bottler astride a horse is that bloke,' he said, 'but he's a bloody poor manager.'
1972 Alexander Macdonald *The Ukelele Player under the Red Lamp* 33: The theatre rang with cries of 'Good on yer, Mo!' 'You little bottler!' and other endearments.
1975 Rodney Hall *A Place Among People* 109: 'I might get drowned in this weather.' 'Yes, it's brewing up for a real bottler.'
1984 *Sun-Herald* 5 Feb. 144: There's a bottler of a row between members and the committee at the Australian Golf Club at Kensington.
bottling
1919 W. H. Downing *Digger Dialects* 13: *Bottling* A phrase expressive of admiration.
1957 Ray Lawler *Summer of the Seventeenth Doll* 35: 'They made Dowdie ganger in his place, and what a bottling job he done.'

bottom In mining, to reach the level at which either gold will be found, or the mine will prove a failure; to succeed or fail in any enterprise
1853 John Sherer *The Gold Finder of Australia* 181: Having bottomed our hole (the bottom is generally pipe-clay), we pick up a good deal of gold – suppose four ounces – and return to our tent satisfied with our day's work.
1864 James Armour *The Diggings, the Bush and Melbourne* 8: We . . . arrived too late for anything better than an uphill claim, which we bottomed at about one third of the depth that gold might be expected at.
1880 Rolf Boldrewood *The Miner's Right* (1890) 55: 'Bottomed a duffer, by gum, not the colour itself, no mor'n on the palm o' my hand.'
1903 Joseph Furphy *Such is Life* (1944) 261: Bottoming on gold this time, she buried the old man within eighteen months, and paid probate duty on £25,000.
1942 Sarah Campion *Bonanza* 210: 'But there's

lots o' fellers as hasn't bottomed on payable dirt.'
1969 *Southerly* 61: Towards the end of his life he must have had the feeling that he had 'bottomed on mullock'.

bottom of the harbour   Name for tax avoidance schemes given currency by the McCabe-Lafranchi report to the Victorian parliament in 1982
1982 *Sydney Morning Herald* 5 Jun. 13: The 'bottom of the harbour' scheme was so named because a company once stripped of its assets, was dumped and, like a body in a cement suit, sank never to be seen again.

boudoir bandicoot   A promiscuous male
1983 *Sydney Morning Herald* 22 Sep. 14: Speaking in the Budget debate, Mr Hodgman said: 'The people of Australia are starting to wake up to this Prime Minister . . . I'm not much impressed by his public breast-beating about being a reformed alcoholic and a retired boudoir bandicoot'.
1984 Jack Hibberd *Squibs* 182: *Stiff* Why do you hate me? *Wheelie* Because you're a no-hoper . . . And a boudoir bandicoot.

bounce, the   The beginning of an Australian Rules game, equivalent to 'the kick-off' in other codes [because the umpire starts the game by bouncing the ball]
[**1906** Joseph Furphy *Rigby's Romance* ed. R. G. Howarth (1946) 249: Actual interest in the game was yet abeyant, and the organisms were collected in idle groups, pending the inaugural bouncing of the ball.]
1958 Barry Humphries *A Nice Night's Entertainment* (1981) 18: Had the usual trouble parking the vehicle . . . However, found a possie in the long run just when I was thinking I'd be late for the bounce.
1978 *Australian* 3 Apr. 15: Within two minutes of the opening bounce . . . Murray was reported by field umpire Glenn James.
1982 *Sun-Herald* 4 Apr. 87: Finally they got around to the bounce and the Sydney Swans were off and running.

Bourke, back of   Beyond the most remote town in north-west N.S.W.; in the remote and uncivilized regions generally
1898 W. H. Ogilvie *Fair Girls and Gray Horses* 161: 'At the Back o' Bourke' [poem title]
1919 R. J. Cassidy *The Gipsy Road* 88: 'I could dump you into the desert at the Back o' Bourke, and you'd be only a speck.'
1933 A. B. Paterson *The Animals Noah Forgot* (1970) 33: The Boastful Crow and the Laughing Jack / Were telling tales of the outer back: / I've just been travelling far and wide, / At the back of Bourke and the Queensland side.'

1959 Gerard Hamilton *Summer Glare* 89: I took the attitude that if girls didn't like to dance with me . . . they could go to Bourke or buggery.
1961 G. R. Turner *A Stranger and Afraid* 95: 'To you there is the City, and all else is back o' Bourke.'
1970 Alexander Buzo *The Front Room Boys* in Penguin *Plays* 38: 'I helped open up the bush, mate, I was out the back o' Bourke when you were a dirty look.'
1981 *Canberra Times* 21 Jun. 3: One of the customers whose accent was decidedly back o' Bourke complained that she had mixed up his order.

Bourke, no work at   see **Tallarook**
1968 David Ireland *The Chantic Bird* 43: I remember I was humming to myself, Things were crook at Tallarook and there was no work at Bourke.

Bourke Street, not to know whether it's Tuesday or   The Victorian equivalent of not knowing (in N.S.W.) whether it's Pitt Street or Christmas q.v.: a state of confusion or stupidity
1952 T. A. G. Hungerford *The Ridge and the River* 4: 'You waste too much time on the dope. He don't know whether it's Tuesday or Bourke Street.'
1971 Ivan Southall *Josh* 119: 'I told you he was dumb. He doesn't know whether it's Tuesday or Bourke Street.'

bovril   Euphemism for **bull**: *obs.* [f. trade name for a beef extract]
1937 *Bulletin of Australian English Association* July 2: A few years ago most young men here said Bovril! whenever they found anything unimpressive, and University students certainly made good use of a song. 'It all sounds like Bovril to me.'
1950 Brian James *The Advancement of Spencer Button* 273: 'Bovril, if you ask me,' said Mr O'Leary . . . 'Hooey!' said Mr Mooney complacently. 'Eyewash!' said Mr Sterling bitterly.

bower bird   A person with the habit of collecting and treasuring odds and ends [f. the bird's habits]
1941 Kylie Tennant *The Battlers* 233: George the Bower-bird . . . had the habit of searching camps for discarded trifles or bits of rubbish . . . old boots or clothes that the travellers threw away he gathered up as though they were priceless treasures.
1953 *Sydney Morning Herald* 3 Jan. 6: Those eccentric bower birds, the students of Australiana, are uttering shrill little chirrups of joy.
1955 Mary Durack *Kings in Grass Castles* 293: 'The Bowerbird', a quaint old kleptomaniac . . . who filched odds and ends from the miners' tents that would be tactfully retrieved when he was not

at home.
1966 Bruce Beaver *You Can't Come Back* 164: He put it back in his pocket, just like the old bower-bird he was.
1973 Patrick White *Southerly* 139: All my novels are an accumulation of detail. I'm a bit of a bower-bird.
1981 *Sunday Mail* (Brisbane) 14 Jun. 13: Brisbane State High School principal Mr Ray Fitz-Gerald admits to being a bit of a bower bird. Indicating his executive office he says: 'I don't know how I'm going to get this cleaned out by June 26.'

bower birding
1941 Kylie Tennant *The Battlers* 386: 'I don't want him bower-birding round this camp,' Mrs Tyrell complained.
1948 William Hatfield *Barrier Reef Days* 66: 'We couldn't put a thing down and turn our backs without somebody bower-birding it.'
1951 Ernestine Hill *The Territory* 443: *Bower-birdin'* Picking up unconsidered trifles for one's own use or camp.

bowl of cherries, a Something easily accomplished (cf. a piece of cake)
1983 *Sydney Morning Herald* 18 Jun. 32: He tried for 45 minutes fiddling with a wire, but couldn't get in. 'Normally it's a bowl of cherries,' he said, 'but you've got this fancy electronic locking.'

Bowral, the boy from Sir Donald Bradman [b. Cootamundra, but his cricketing career began in Bowral N.S.W.]
1930 Jack O'Hagan 'Our Don Bradman' in *The Barry Humphries Book of Innocent Austral Verse* 43: The boy from Bowral hits four after four.
1962 R. J. Hoare *The Boy from Bowral* [title of biography]
1983 *Sydney Morning Herald* 27 Aug. 60: The bat, used during the 1925–26 season, evoked almost as many memories for O'Reilly as it did for 'the boy from Bowral', who scored 985 runs with it.

bowyangs 1 A string tied round the trouser-leg below the knee [f. *bowy-yanks* leather leggings EDD]
1893 *Warracknabeal Herald* 22 Sep. 4: The two straps used to hitch the lower part of labourers' trousers are 'boyangs'.
1907 James Green *The Selector* 10: His moleskin trousers were tied below the knee with boyangs of string.
1924 *Truth* 27 Apr. 6: Bowyangs straps or string tied below the knee, outside the trousers, to give the leg freedom.
1939 Leonard Mann *Mountain Flat* 7: His pants were stiff moleskins caught in below the knee by bowyangs.

2 Applied derisively to anything rustic, clownish, out-of-date
1945 *Southerly* ii 14: The story is Romeo and Juliet in bowyangs, set in the Australian countryside.
1969 Don Whitington *The House Will Divide* ix: Menzies . . . was aided by the stubborn and intransigent attitudes of Labor leaders like Evatt, Ward and Calwell when it became obvious that Labor's bowyang days were past.
1972 A. A. Calwell *Be Just and Fear Not* 257: Anti-Labor parties have their troubles, too, but being composed of well-bred, middle-class, properly educated people who are concerned with the preservation of the status quo, they are better able to reconcile their personal and other difficulties than those possessing what conservatives have called 'bowyang' mentalities.
1983 Buzz Kennedy *Australian* 18 Feb. 11: I think it has to do with the increasing conservatism of the electorate and the disappearance of the true-blue, boots and bowyangs Labor man.

box see **glory box**

box *n.* 1 The female genitals [listed by Partridge as 'low English and Australian: C20']
1949 Alan Marshall *How Beautiful Are Thy Feet* 150: 'I believe Leila's running hot in the box,' said Sadie.
1972 Geoff Morley *Jockey Rides Honest Race* 38: 'Say, she's not real bad after all.' 'Nice big boobs.' 'Nice big box, too, I bet.'
1974 David Ireland *Burn* 60: 'Post Office? I know where she gets to and it's no post office. She's got the box and they all post with her.'
1976 *Australian Graffiti* ed. R. Ellis and I. Turner [32]: I've lost me virginity. Never mind long as you've got the box it came in!
1983 Robert Drewe *The Bodysurfers* 80: I've seen some great tits and some of the bushiest boxes you could imagine.

2 The protector worn by sportsmen, the 'rupture box'
1974 Keith Stackpole *Not Just for Openers* 45: Once, I was hit in the box during a one-day match; an agonizing blow that left me crook for four days. A supporter for the opposing team shouted, 'Weak Australian sod, get up.'

3 A mixing of flocks of sheep which should be kept separate; a blunder, esp. in the expression 'make a box of'
1870 Rolf Boldrewood 'Shearing in Riverina' *Town and Country Journal* 29 Oct. 10: This distinguished them from other sheep in the neighbourhood, in case of a 'box' or mixing of flocks, not always to be avoided where so many thousands and tens of thousands are on the march.
1941 Baker 13: *Box* A mistake or confusion, e.g.

'to make a box of something': to muddle.

box *v.* 1 To mix flocks of sheep which should be kept separate; to make a mess of something
1873 Rolf Boldrewood 'The Fencing of Wander-owna' repr. in *A Romance of Canvas Town* (1898) 69: Great was the bleating and apparent confusion – two flocks incontinently 'boxed', or mixed together.
1903 Joseph Furphy *Such is Life* (1944) 282: 'Tell him a lot o' his sheep was boxed with ours in the Boree Paddick.'
1905 *The Old Bush Songs* ed. A. B. Paterson 70: If the heavenly hosts get boxed now, / As mobs most always will, / Who'll cut 'em out like William, / Or draft on a camp like Bill?
1919 W. K. Harris *Outback in Australia* 154: The boundary rider must take heed to his fences . . . or trouble may result in the straying of sheep or the 'boxing' of flocks.
1934 Mary Gilmore *Old Days: Old Ways* (1963) 97: In the unfenced states of the newly settled country sheep boxed and then had to be sorted out.
1960 *Sydney Morning Herald* 19 Jul. 1: Thurber's moral is Those who live in grass houses shouldn't stow thrones. Emily boxed it.
2 To bet in a way which will cover two or more winning prospects or combinations, for a higher outlay; i.e. instead of taking a number of separate bets, the punter 'boxes' them together
1983 *Sydney Morning Herald* 25 Jun. 57: Footy TAB punters will be able to rake in a lucrative dividend this weekend if they 'box' two matches when they take their card. If form is any guide, it appears that there are five almost certain results this weekend . . . With an average payout of 135–1, it is worth boxing the two matches in doubt. It will cost a little more, but the end result will be worth it.

boxer The ringkeeper in two-up, who takes a percentage of winnings (his 'box'); sometimes an assistant to the ringkeeper who holds the stakes
1911 Louis Stone *Jonah* 216: The spinner threw down the kip, and took his winnings from the boxer – five pounds for himself and ten shillings for the boxer.
1935 H. R. Williams *Comrades of the Great Adventure* 184: So large were his wagers on each spin that it necessitated the help of two boxers, who saw that every bet was covered.
1949 Lawson Glassop *Lucky Palmer* 169: The man running a two-up game takes a percentage of the winnings of the spinner when there is a run of heads, but when tails are falling he depends on contributions from the tail backers. In response to the fat man's appeal for a 'Boxer', a few florins and shillings were tossed into the ring.

1950 *Australian Police Journal* Apr. 111: *Boxer* The ringkeeper at a two-up school.
1975 Les Ryan *The Shearers* 151: *boxer* one who holds the stakes being wagered at a game of two-up.

boxing kangaroo the Logo of the Australia II syndicate in the successful challenge for the America's Cup in 1983
1983 *Sun-Herald* 9 Oct. 71: As Australian as the boxing kangaroo [heading] . . . He was as Australian as gumtrees, koalas and blue-tongued lizards. I could have added Holden cars, but Phil was part and parcel of the bullock dray era.
1984 *West Australian* (Perth) 7 Jan. 20: Mr Jones pointed out that 'Australia II', '12 KA6' and the boxing kangaroo emblem were all syndicate property and copyright.
1984 *Sydney Morning Herald* 7 May 8: At the time of the America's Cup victory last year . . . Professor Horne distanced himself from the wave of ockerism that was sweeping the country: 'To the chant by the Benson and Hedges choir of our new national anthem, Come On, Aussie, Come On, our new national skipper, Alan Bond, will raise as our new national flag the green and gold boxing kangaroo.'

box of birds Equivalent to 'in good spirits': N.Z. rather than Australian
1951 Dal Stivens *Jimmy Brockett* 120: I was feeling as happy as a box of birds.
1955 D'Arcy Niland *The Shiralee* 122: 'I had a mate, but he got himself pinched. And just quietly, I been a box o' birds ever since.'
1966 G. W. Turner *The English Language in Australia and New Zealand* 136–7: A young English woman who had just arrived in New Zealand shared a cabin on an inter-island ferry with a woman whose conversation in the evening consisted only of the words, 'I feel a bit crook.' In the morning, asked how she was, the stranger replied, 'Oh, box of birds, now.'

box, out of the Exceptional, outstanding
1926 *Sun* (Sydney) 29 Jul. 1: Two out of the box. These Siamese cats are just looking at the world from the box in which they travelled on the Comorin. [caption to photograph]
1941 *Coast to Coast* 63: 'You talk about it as if 'aving kids is somethin' out of the box.'
1953 Dymphna Cusack *Southern Steel* 29: Come to think of it, both his brothers were something out of the box.
1975 *Sun-Herald* 9 Nov. 111: To be frank, the novel is nothing out of the box, and neither is the movie.
see **out of the bag**

box seat, in the   In the most favoured position (to succeed, control the situation) [f. the driver's seat on a coach]
   1949 Lawson Glassop *Lucky Palmer* 116: 'I jumped him away smartly and had him in the box seat all the way. Cantering just behind Lovely Rose and Murragum at the turn, he was.'
   1957 Judah Waten *Shares in Murder* 117: 'They'll do Fenton-Lobby favours now and again, and Fenton'll repay them when he's in the box seat.'
   1977 *Australian* 4 Jan. 6: With 15 overs and 56 runs required to win, Australia was in the box seat.

boy, the   The jockey, esp. an apprentice
   1881 A. C. Grant *Bush-Life in Queensland* ii 67: Now the boy is lifted on, and John leads his horse down the course a little.
   1888 A. B. Paterson 'Old Pardon, the Son of Reprieve' in *Singer of the Bush* (1983) 63: He showed 'em the method to travel – / The boy sat still as a stone.
   1923 Con Drew *Rogues & Ruses* 152: 'I wish the boy would make a move on the grey', he muttered. 'He's riding him like as if he wanted to lose.'
   1984 *Sydney Morning Herald* 18 Apr. 48: The crowd cheers when he mentions Theo Green, the trainer . . . claps again when he mentions 'the boy', Darren Beadman.
   1984 *Sun-Herald* 7 Oct. 67: TJ is renowned as a racing master from the old school, where trainers are always addressed as 'boss' and apprentices are the 'boys' employed about the stable to work long and hard.

boy from Bowral, the   see *Bowral*

boy, the old   see **old**

boy, you can take the ~ out of the bush, but you can't take the bush out of the boy   See quots [?Australian variations of an international catchphrase]
   1981 *Sunday Mail* (Brisbane) 20 Sep. 60: There's that old saying that you can take a boy out of the bush, but not the bush out of the boy.
   1982 Tom Krause *Australian* 31 Dec. 5: It goes back to an old line, which I remember from my youth: 'You can take the boy out of West Philly, but you can't take West Philly out of the boy.'
   1983 *Australian Literary Studies* May 75: Disavowing evaluative criticism, Docker's nomination of a new canon of neglected authors reintroduces evaluation in the allegedly more rigorous guise of a conceptually self-conscious criticism. It has been easier to take the boy out of Melbourne than to take Melbourne out of the boy.
   1983 Reg Livermore *National Times* 10 Jun. 29: 'After all, I am from the western suburbs, and like they say, you can take the boy out of Parramatta,

but you can't take Parramatta out of the boy.'

brass razoo, not a   see **razoo**

break it down   A plea to desist from or to moderate some action; an expression of disbelief or disagreement; i.e. 'Give over', 'Come off it'
   1944 Lawson Glassop *We Were the Rats* 193: 'There's no other bastard in the world can talk to me like that. For Christ's sake break it down or I'll lose me grip on meself. I'm tellin' ya now. Break it down, see.'
   1955 D'Arcy Niland *The Shiralee* 60: 'I'd have been just asking for more trouble and it would have been signing your death-warrant.' 'Ah, break it down,' Macauley said.
   1961 Hugh Atkinson *Low Company* 58: The barman was worried about the noise and kept saying uselessly, 'Now, now, blokes, break it down,' and 'Fair go there, fellars.'
   1966 Betty Collins *The Copper Crucible* 18: 'You're not going to refuse to talk to everyone who doesn't agree with your political beliefs?' 'Break it down, mate.'
   1979 *Advertiser* (Adelaide) 22 Apr. 25: Just the other day I heard a young man in North terrace say to his mate: 'Hey, break it down. What do you think this is, Bush Week?'

break out   Used of the discovery of a goldfield and the 'rush' following
   1856 Frederick Sinnett *The Fiction Fields of Australia* ed. C. H. Hadgraft (1966) 36–7: South Australia, at the time when the Victorian gold fields 'broke out', as the common phrase runs, presented a most remarkable social aspect.
   1882 A. J. Boyd *Old Colonials* 130: 'I was out prospectin' on the Palmer just after it broke out.'
   1901 Rolf Boldrewood *In Bad Company* 30: Labour was scarce, owing to the Coolgardie goldfield having broken out.

Breaker, the   Harry Morant (1865–1902): a pen-name derived from his skill as a horseman and horse-breaker

breeze, bat the   see **bat the breeze**

breezer   A fart (juvenile)
   1973 Patrick White *The Eye of the Storm* 380: 'And lets breezers, as if he didn't know there was anybody else in the room.'
   1974 Gerald Murname *Tamarisk Row* 91: Barry Launder has ordered every boy to write in his composition *at the picnic I let a breezer in my pants*, or else be bashed to smithereens after school.

brick   £10 Used most often in gambling, and esp.

in the expression 'London to a brick' q.v.

c. **1914** A. B. Paterson 'Races and Racing in Australia' in *The World of Banjo Paterson* ed. C. Semmler (1967) 324: 'Pop it down, gents, if yer don't put down a brick you can't pick up a castle.'

1949 Lawson Glassop *Lucky Palmer* 103: 'Tiger' ... slipped a ten pound note into his hand. 'Here's a brick,' he said in his lifeless voice.

1963 Frank Hardy *Legends from Benson's Valley* 151: Col took the ten bricks down to the Unemployed Workers headquarters and gave it to Tom Rogers before his thirst got the better of his principles.

1975 Les Ryan *The Shearers* 69: Moody flashed a roll of notes, peeled one off and handed it to Tricum. 'Put this brick on for me.'

brickfielder A wind carrying dust with it, originally from Brickfield Hill in Sydney. Confused by Morris with the 'southerly buster' or 'southerly' q.v.

1833 W. H. Breton *Excursions in New South Wales and Van Diemen's Land* 293: It sometimes happens [in Sydney] that a change takes place from a hot wind to a 'brickfielder', on which occasions the thermometer has been known to fall ... from above 100 degrees to 80 degrees! A brickfielder is a southerly wind, and takes its local name from the circumstances of its blowing over, and bringing into town the flames of a large brickfield. [Morris]

1839 W. H. Leigh *Reconnoitering Voyages, Travels, and Adventures in the new Colony of South Australia* 184: Whirlwinds of sand ... come rushing upon the traveller, half blinding and choking him ... The inhabitants [of Sydney] call these miseries 'Brickfielders', but why they do so I am unable to divine, probably, because they are in their utmost vigour on a certain hill here, where bricks are made. [Morris]

1843 John Hood *Australia and the East* 71: A sudden storm had arisen; we were quite unprepared and everybody [on board ship] was alarmed. It was one of the violent and dangerous squalls so frequent off this coast, which are called brickfielders, and came suddenly right off the land without warning. Ibid. 72: The sun this morning shines through a thick dust, which, as well as the wind which sets it in motion, is called a brickfielder.

1853 C. R. Read *What I Heard, Saw and Did at the Australian Goldfields* 38: The weather towards December, [on the Turon goldfields, N.S.W.] and for two or three months following was overpoweringly hot, and from the number of people travelling to and fro, together with the stuff thrown up from the holes caused one continual dust, and when the 'brickfielders'* came on, they could hardly be faced from the sharp quartz and gravel that was flying about nearly blinding you; this was generally followed by a tremendous thunderstorm, with a deluge of rain. *Heavy squalls.

1859 Frank Fowler *Southern Lights and Shadows* 87–8: The 'Southerly Buster', as this change is called, generally comes ... early in the evening. A cloud of dust – they call it, in Sydney, a 'brickfielder' – thicker than any London fog, heralds its approach ... In a minute the temperature will sink fifty or sixty degrees.

1861 H. W. Wheelwright *Bush Wanderings of a Naturalist* 231: In Melbourne a hot-wind day is called a 'brickfielder', on account of the dust, which darkens the sky.

1865 Henry Kendall 'A Death in the Bush' *Poetical Works* ed. T. T. Reed (1966) 85: So comes the Southern gale at evenfall / (The swift 'brickfielder' of the local folk) / About the streets of Sydney, when the dust / Lies burnt on glaring windows.

1891 Francis Adams *Fortnightly Review* Sep. 393: Sometimes the Antarctic gives Sydney, as it does Melbourne, its stormy 'change' – the dust-clouds of the 'brickfielder' ending in the tempestuous showers of the 'southerly buster'.

1935 H. H. Finlayson *The Red Centre* 21: A desert ... whose chief function is to provide material for the 'brickfielder' dust-storms which occasionally cloud the towns.

1962 Stuart Gore *Down the Golden Mile* 192: Behind him ... the sky looked forbidding, no longer pink but red, charged with a threat of dust straight from the desert heart. 'It's going to be a brick-fielder, Dad!'

bride's nightie, off like a Making a quick departure; acting promptly

1969 Christopher Bray *Blossom like a Rose* 26: 'Come on youse blokes!' he shouted. 'We're off like a bride's nightie!'

1972 Geoff Morley *Jockey Rides Honest Race* 148: At the furlong the jockey said 'Let's go', and Che Sera went off like a bride's nightie. In a flash she hit the front and won by several lengths.

1981 *Sydney Morning Herald* 24 Jan. 39: The first Australian who said that something came off 'like a bride's nightie' was a poet. The thousandth was just a parrot.

Bridle Track, the The Milky Way: N.T.

1951 Ernestine Hill *The Territory* 425: The Milky Way is the Bridle Track, or sometimes the Hopple Chain.

brim, the wider the ~, the smaller the property Formula for estimating the size of rural holdings

1962 Dymphna Cusack *Picnic Races* 189: 'There's a rule for it: "The smaller the property the wider the brim".'

1966 Craig McGregor *Profile of Australia* 162: 'The wider the brim the smaller the property', as the ironic saying goes.

bring back to the field   see **field**

brinny   A stone of the size thrown by children: *rare*
1943 Baker 14: *Brinny* A stone.
1977 Phil Motherwell *Mr Bastard* 43: I slowly crouch to pick up two brinnies from the ground.

Bris, Brizzie   Brisbane [abbr.]
1945 Cecil Mann *The River* 117: Up in Bris he gets himself shaved at the Barber's down the lower end of Queen Street.
1965 Patrick White *Four Plays* 149: 'Reckon I'll catch the evenin' train to Brizzy.'
1979 Thea Astley *Hunt the Wild Pineapple* 162: Mrs Wacker measured plane distances by noggins. 'It's two beers from Brissy to Townsville', she announced heartily, 'and then one more to the top.'
1981 *Sunday Mail* (Brisbane) 9 Aug. 2: We think that Tony Murphy, the top cop at Cairns, is coming back to Brissie as an assistant commissioner.

Brisbane, battle of   1   The Rugby League match between England and Australia on 19 June 1932
1979 *Sun-Herald* 17 Jun. 59: Memories of the famous 'Battle of Brisbane' Rugby League Test were far from the minds of the crowd of 18,000 as they started to file from the ground midway through the second half at Lang Park last night.
2   The Rugby Union match between England and Australia in 1975
1979 Steve Finnane *The game they play in heaven* 59: The Test was a good game and a great Australian victory but it will always be remembered for an incident that lasted just a few seconds and earned it the tag, 'Battle of Brisbane'. [Macdougall appearing to kick at Nelmes, on the ground]

Brisbane Line   Name given to a military plan to concentrate on the defence of vital areas of Australia, put to the Curtin government in February 1942, which led to claims that the abandonment of Australia north of Brisbane was contemplated (Paul Hasluck *The Government and the People 1942–1945* (1970) 711–17). The plan was attributed to the Menzies government by its political opponents.
1951 *The Calamitous Career of Dictator Bob* [Communist pamphlet] 4: Rather than wage a people's war against fascism Menzies devised the Brisbane Line to give Nth Australia to the Japs!
1951 Dymphna Cusack and Florence James *Come In Spinner* 307: 'All I got against the politicians and their flamin' Brisbane Line is that they didn't give the bloody place away.'
1965 Thomas Keneally *The Fear* 36: There were vacancies, the corset factories told her, but they were all above the Brisbane line, and if the country was invaded, the Government might aban-

don the North.
1967 R. G. Menzies *Afternoon Light* 20: This legend did not prevent the notorious 'Eddie' Ward from concocting a story, months later, that we had prepared plans to base Australia's defence against Japan on a so-called 'Brisbane Line' ... and that we were prepared to retreat ... to the extent of surrendering the northern part of Australia!
1984 *Weekend Australian* 2 Jun. Mag. 2: 'It's the old Brisbane Line mentality – everything in the north is dispensable.'

British to the boot heels   Statement by Sir Robert Menzies in 1963, subsequently interpreted out of its context
1963 Sir Robert Menzies *Commonwealth of Australia Parliamentary Debates*, House of Representatives, Vol. 40, 29 Oct. 2373: The deal made with the United States of America is probably the most favorable deal ever made by Australia with another country for something that is vital to Australia's defence. It is a very great mistake for anyone to think that this involves being pro-British or anti-British. As I have said before, I am British to the boot heels. I will not be told that I am hostile to what is done in Great Britain. But, like my honorable friend opposite, I have always esteemed my prime duty to be to my own country and to the safety of my own country. On that principle we have acted.
1963 *Sydney Morning Herald* 30 Oct. 4: Sir Robert Menzies said in the House of Representatives: 'As I have said before, I am British to the boot-heels. I am not going to be told that I am hostile to what is being done in Great Britain.'
1963 Sir Robert Menzies *Sydney Morning Herald* 2 Nov. 2: I am British to the boot-heels. [Sayings of the Week]
1964 Geoffrey Dutton 'Thoughts, Home From Abroad' *Overland* 29 14: But we, of course, are British to our arse-holes.
1981 *Australian Book Review* Nov. 42: No doubt new nationalism is better than being 'British to the bootstraps.'
1983 *Australian* 10 Aug. 3: Mr Hayden said Sir Robert Menzies had said in the 1960s that Australia was 'British to the bootlaces'. 'Well', he said, 'we are Australian to the backbone ... We don't want to go around boot-licking.'

Britt, Edgar   As for **Jimmies, Jimmy Britts** q.v.
1970 Alexander Buzo *The Front Room Boys* in Penguin *Plays* 22: 'Then he raced out to the john for an Edgar Britt.'
1983 Bruce Dawe *Over Here, Harv!* 101: 'Jeez', said Wooffer. 'You give me the Edgar Britts, sometimes.'

Broken Hill, the battle of   The attack by two Turks

on 1 January 1915 on a party of picknickers going by train from Broken Hill to Silverton, resulting in six deaths

bronze (bronza)   Backside
1953 Baker 105: *bronzo*, anus (a variation of *bronze*, used similarly).
1959 D'Arcy Niland *The Big Smoke* 164: He roared laughing and gave her a slap on the seat. 'The biggest bronza in the world – and just think, you're all mine.'
1968 Geoffrey Dutton *Andy* 262: 'Some bloody boomers, boy, be in it. But some hairy nosed dumpers as well. One of them set me right on my bronze on the bottom.'
1970 Barry Oakley *A Salute to the Great McCarthy* 75: 'Hear this: this is the last day you spend sitting on your bronzes in the sun.'
1975 Les Ryan *The Shearers* 104: 'Go and sit on your bronze while we give scabs your jobs.'
1982 *Australian* 25 Nov. 10: In the age of innocence [1953], we fell about at the lines: 'There's rust on me bust, and me bronze is all tarnished.'

bronzed   1   Applied to soldiers of the A.I.F. 8th Division in World War II (see quot. 1946); transferred to Australian servicemen generally
1946 Rohan Rivett *Behind Bamboo* 395: *Bronze gods* A.I.F. 8th Division. Term was used by a woman journalist visiting Malaya, and subsequently derisively. *Bronzie* member of the 8th Division. Used by officers to indicate other ranks, by British to indicate Australians.
1952 T. A. G. Hungerford *The Ridge and the River* 31: 'Oh, you big bronzed bastard, you! What you do in the war, daddy?' Ibid. 186: 'You big bronzed Anzac!' A bitter smile flickered at the corner of Malise's mouth.
1959 Eric Lambert *Glory Thrown In* 83: 'You can start getting yourself in the mood for the role of a drunken bronzed Anzac thirsting for sheilas and *alicante*.'
1960 John Iggulden *The Storms of Summer* 74: 'You won't be able to keep them out . . . you and all the other great bronzed Anzacs!'
2   The 'bronzed' Australian male (no military association)
1969 Thomas Jenkins *We Came to Australia* 174: These bronzed young gods take turns to watch from the top of a scaffolding tower for anyone in trouble in the sea. If they see a hand raised . . . they will swim to help, churning through the sea as if they were fitted with outboard motors.
1980 *Sunday Telegraph* (Sydney) 13 Apr. 160: We wonder what is happening to the big, bronzed Aussie male?
1982 *Sydney Morning Herald* 6 Nov. 34: March pasts symbolise the glory of Bondi's bronzed Aussies.

see **Anzac**

bronzewing   A half-caste aboriginal: N.T. and W.A. [f. colour of bronzewing pigeon]
1956 Tom Ronan *Moleskin Midas* 161: 'If there is a few bronzewings being born about my place, there's nearly as much chance of your being their daddy as me.'

brook, babbling   see **babbler**

broomie   A broom-hand in a shearing shed
1910 C. E. W. Bean *On the Wool Track* 203: There still remain the burry pieces which were skirted from the fleece at the wool-rolling tables and are lying on the floor. A boy, the 'broomy', sweeps them.
1933 Acland: *Broomie* A boy who keeps the board swept of locks, etc., at shearing.
1964 H. P. Tritton *Time Means Tucker* 64: Sam was expert, boss of the board, wool classer, tar boy and broomie, musterer and penner-up.
1975 Les Ryan *The Shearers* 142: 'That stupid broomie . . . oh, Gawd! . . . what a scream?'

brothel   Any untidy, crowded or disreputable place
[**1919** W. H. Downing *Digger Dialects* 31: *Knocking-shop*: An untidy or squalid place.]
1946 Rohan Rivett 331: *Brothel of a place*, poor place.
1953 T. A. G. Hungerford *Riverslake* 148: 'Always drunk. He does his work, in a way – enough to get by in a brothel like this. But in normal times he wouldn't be tolerated in a boong's kitchen.'

brothel, piano player in a   see **piano**

Brothers   The Christian Brothers Rugby Union team (Q.)
1979 *Courier-Mail* (Brisbane) 25 Jun. 16: Uni downs Brothers 16–11 [heading]

brown   A penny: *obs.* [f. *brown* a copper coin OED 1812; a halfpenny]
1865 *Queenslanders' New Colonial Camp Fire Song Book* 21: Most others are hard up for browns.
1871 Dogberry Dingo *Australian Rhymes and Jingles* 10: We think it sad to want a pound. / A shilling or a 'brown'.
1885 *The Australasian Printers' Keepsake* 24: We found no change in him – no, not a brown.
1895 Cornelius Crowe *The Australian Slang Dictionary* 12: *Brown* a copper.
1913 Henry Lawson 'The Kids' *Prose* i 806: But for the chartering of the aforesaid craft . . . there must be 'browns', or 'coppers'.
1946 *Sun* (Sydney) 20 Oct. Suppl. 25: Everybody's jumping about like a double-headed brown had

been found at a swy game.

brown bomber   In N.S.W., a parking policeman [f. colour of uniform]
1954 *Sun* 8 Jun. 1: New name for the Brown Bomber boys is Walkie-Chalkies.
1959 Baker 95: *brown bomber* A parking policeman in some cities.
1968 David Ireland *The Chantic Bird* 61: Next day a brown bomber – a parking cop – gave me a fright.
1970 Jon Cleary *Helga's Web* 160: He found a parking ticket on his car, put it in his pocket and swore at a parking policeman, one of the Brown Bombers in their khaki uniforms.
1975 *Sun-Herald* 23 Nov. 5: New uniform to boost new image for the Brown Bombers ... The long-standing, long-suffering brown is out. A new bluish-grey is 'in' for the city's parking squads.
1982 *NT News* (Darwin) 11 Jan. 7: A dedicated bomber was seen marking tyres at the Stuart Park shopping centre on Saturday afternoon.
see **grey ghost, grey meanie**

brown dog, fit to kill a   An adverse judgement on food, esp. as applied by Senator Ron Elstob in 1982 to the food at Parliament House
1982 *Sydney Morning Herald* 5 May 3: The much-published interjection that some meals in Parliament House would 'kill a brown dog' was finally laid to rest in the Senate yesterday. Senator Ron Elstob (Lab. SA) apologised 'unreservedly' for his remark.
1984 *Toorak Sunday* 10 Jun. 5: It was the sort of tucker which in the folklore of this great land of ours is reputed to be able to kill a brown dog at anything up to 15 paces.
1984 *Sydney Morning Herald* 19 Jul. 1: 'Brown dog' Nicol gets out of the kitchen [heading] ... James Nicol had fame thrust upon him when his cuisine was described as fit to 'kill a brown dog' The remark was made by the South Australian Senator, Ron Elstob, in 1982. It led to a strike by the catering staff at Parliament House and also to a large brown dog, sculpted in margarine which the large Scotsman solemnly carried into the Members' private dining room.

brownie   A bush cake made with currants and brown sugar
1883 J. E. Partington *Random Rot: A Journal of Three Years Wanderings* 312: It was an amusing sight to see the three of us, each with a huge hunch of 'browny' (bread sweetened with brown sugar and currants) in one hand.
1886 P. Clarke *The New Chum in Australia* 193: She makes 'browney', a sort of sweet currant cake for her customers.
1901 Henry Lawson 'Joe Wilson's Courtship' *Prose* i 541: 'Here's some tea and brownie' ... Jack

took a cup of tea and a piece of cake and sat down to enjoy it.
1903 Joseph Furphy *Such is Life* (1944) 80: In another hour ... I was having a drink of tea and a bit of brownie in the men's hut.
1919 W. K. Harris *Outback in Australia* 49: Damper, beef and tea sweetened with coarse brown sugar, was the usual fare, with an occasional 'brownie' cake to vary the menu.
1951 Ernestine Hill *The Territory* 443: *Brownie* A bush cake, damper with sugar and currants.

brown land, the wide   see **wide brown land**

brownout   A partial blackout in World War II
1942 A. G. Mitchell 'A Glossary of War Words' *Southerly* i 12: *Brownout* A partial blackout.
1946 Dal Stivens *The Courtship of Uncle Henry* 32: They pushed through the glass doors and went down the steps to George Street. The street was browned out and they couldn't see clearly for a minute.
1953 Dymphna Cusack *Southern Steel* 81: She hated the brown-out. It would have been better had they blacked-out the city, instead of this half-way business of restrictive light and deceptive shadow.
1961 *Sydney Morning Herald* 1 Jun. 1: Victoria Faces Brownout [report of electricity restrictions]
1970 Sumner Locke Elliott *Edens Lost* 115: She waited for the King's Cross tram in the brownout winter twilight. Cars went by sluggishly with their muffled headlights and overhead the filtered street lamps gave out a weak gingery light. [describing wartime Sydney]
1975 Hal Porter *The Extra* 207: The skylights, browned-out during World War II, are still painted over.
1980 Emery Barcs *Backyard of Mars* 186: I was walking down Pitt Street toward Attila's shop, thankful for the brownout.

Bruce   Name applied by the English to the typical Australian [f. the sketch in 'Monty Python Live at Drury Lane' 1975]
1981 *Bulletin* 6 Jan. 30: Aussie journalist Bruce Page – who confirms every pom's pugnacious conviction that all Australians are called Bruce – is currently under siege at the *New Statesman*.
1982 *Weekend Australian* 26 Jun. 13: Prince Bruce for Tech ... the son of Charles and Di could perhaps be given the opportunity to mix more with the masses by attending a good solid State school such as Brunswick East Tech ... It could also solve the problem of combing through the centuries for suitable names ... Bruce Windsor. Now there is a name that combines regal style with the grit and honor of the working person.
1984 Barry Humphries *Weekend Australian* 11

Feb. 4: Humphries' 50th Birthday – Hawke declares national holiday. Stories by Bruce Bain, Bruce Brown, Bruce Smith, Bruce Herbert, Bruce Small, Bruce Jones.

brumby 1 A wild horse [Ab. *booramby* wild Ramson 120]
1880 *Australasian* 4 Dec. 712: These our guide pronounced to be 'brumbies', the bush name here [Queensland] for wild horses. [Morris]
1892 Gilbert Parker *Round the Compass in Australia* 44: Six wild horses – warrigals or brombies, as they are called – have been driven down, corralled, and caught.
1899 Steele Rudd *On Our Selection* 40: Not that she had any brumby element in her – she would have been easier to yard if she had.
1915 Vance Palmer *The World of Men* 61: 'They used to go breaking together sometimes on the big stations in the North-west . . . turning young brumbies into ladies' hacks.'
1980 Rowan Hewison *Salt Pan* 24: The home-brew had the kick of a brumby.
1982 *Courier-Mail* (Brisbane) 26 Mar. 2: Two more brumbies have been found shot dead in scrub on Moreton Island.
2 A person with such attributes
1911 L. St Clare Grondona *Collar and Cuffs* 98: They were a brumbie lot of rotters, all swagmen, and to all appearances at least, considerably down on their uppers.
1936 Miles Franklin *All That Swagger* 444: 'I'm only a brumby compared with you.'
1940 K. S. Prichard *Brumby Innes* [play title]
1959 Frank McCann *Medicine Man* 167: Many of these youngsters were still in the half-tamed 'brumby' class.
1974 *Sydney Morning Herald* 16 Aug. 7: He [Dr Cairns] gave long allegiance to the Victorian Executive when it was the brumby of the ALP and the despair of ALP voters who wanted to see Labor back in power.

brush A woman; women collectively [Partridge suggests derivation from pubic hair]
1941 Baker 14: *Brush* A girl or young woman.
1965 William Dick *A Bunch of Ratbags* 226: We were all hanging out of windows, whistling up some of the bits of 'brush' (sheilas) that were walking along.
1967 Kylie Tennant *Tell Morning This* 16: 'Always be leary of the brush. There's many a man thought he was going to stand over some little lowie and now he's either looking through bars or else he's mowing the lawn for her.'
1975 Elizabeth Riley *All That False Instruction* 229: 'Beer first. Brush later.'
1983 T. A. G. Hungerford *Stories from Suburban Road* 87: We still called them 'the tarts', but he

called them 'brush' and 'swell kakas'.
1984 *Sun-Herald* 24 Jun. 82: He [was] intrigued by the younger men's comments about the beautiful 'brush' (women) eager to be entertained by visiting trainers.

brusher A small wallaby noted for its brisk movement; anyone with these characteristics [? f. *brush-kangaroo* an early name for the wallaby Morris 1802]
1882 *Freeman's Journal* 30 Sep. cit. *Australian Dictionary of Biography* iv 207: To 'Cassius' in the *Freeman's Journal*, 30 September 1882, he [W. J. Foster] was a 'fussy little brusher'.
1898 Morris: *Brusher* n. a Bushman's name, in certain parts, for a small wallaby which hops about in the bush or scrub with considerable speed.

brusher, to get To be rejected, 'brushed off'
1911 Edward Dyson *Benno, and Some of the Push* 33: Mr Dickson, mindful of the ignominy due to the man who gets 'brusher', thought he was combining airy indifference. . . .

brusher, give To abscond without paying one's debts, abandon a task: *obs.*
1898 T. E. Argles *The Pilgrim* 2nd Series No. 10, 5: He subsequently victimized Mr Weber, Post Office Hotel . . . indeed anywhere this penniless Hebrew obtained admission he never failed to give 'brusher' to the confiding boniface.
c. **1882** *The Sydney Slang Dictionary* 2: *Brusher (to give anyone)* To obtain or borrow something and not pay for it or return it.
1898 Morris: 'To give brusher' is a phrase . . . used in many parts, especially of the interior of Australia, and implies that a man has left without paying his debts. In reply to the question, 'Has so-and-so left the township?' the answer, 'Oh yes, he gave them brusher', would be well understood in the above sense.
1904 Henry Fletcher *Dads Wayback: His Work* 20: 'I s'pose I may as well give it brusher for ter-night,' replied Dan, as he wiped his scythe and walked with Dads to the house.
1914 Baker 14: *Brusher, give a* To go off without paying one's debts.

bubs, the Kindergarten [f. *bub* infant]
1962 Ross Campbell *Daddy, Are You Married?* 83: 'She's still in the bubs. The bubs are too little for me now', said Little Nell complacently.

buck, buckjump, buckjumper *v. & n.* See quots [U.S. 1869 Mathews]
1838 Stephen Black let. in Baker (1966) 65: I bought a colt . . . I was vain enough to think I could ride him, but in a week he convinced me of the

fallacy of this idea by sending me up in the air like a sky-rocket by buckjumping.

1848 H. W. Haygarth *Recollections of Bush Life in Australia* 78: Australian horses have a vicious habit known as 'buck-jumping', or as it is more familiarly called, 'bucking'.

1853 C. R. Read *What I Heard, Saw and Did on the Australian Goldfields* 120: My animal, having a peculiar dislike to spurs, commenced ... 'buck-jumping', I soon measured my length on the ground.

1867 J. R. Houlding *Australian Capers* 223: [He] would rather be crossing Bogie Plains on a buck-jumping horse.

1898 David Carnegie *Spinifex and Sand* 98: 'Wait till you make your evening feed off mulga scrub and bark – that'll take the buck out of you!'

1908 W. S. Ogilvie *My Life in the Open* 83: Some are old and noted buckjumpers, hopeless rogues whose names and reputations are known far beyond the station yards.

1926 K. S. Prichard *Working Bullocks* 47–8: Brumbies he had caught who bucked until they bucked their brands off.

1936 Ion L. Idriess *The Cattle King* 246: It was Albert who rode the notorious outlaw until it 'bucked its brands off'.

1981 *Sun-Herald* 10 May 87: It's like keeping a horse stabled up over the weekend. You watch them at the track on Monday morning and they're all bucking their brands off.

bucker   A horse that bucks

1856 G. Willmer *The Draper in Australia* 122: No sooner had we put the tackling on, than he unfortunately escaped from us, and being a first-rate 'bucker', as they term them in this country, it elicited many hearty laughs from all of us.

buckaroo   The one dollar coin, introduced in 1984 [f. *buck* dollar, and kangaroo design]

1984 *Sun-Herald* 0 Sep. 144: Banks are supposed to be short of dollar coins and to welcome the buckaroos.

bucket, drop a ~   See quots [f. bucket used as WC]

[**1950** *Australian Police Journal* Apr. 112: *Drop the bucket* Drop the responsibility on to someone else.]

1971 Alan Reid *The Gorton Experiment* 242: In Australian political argot to 'turn a bucket' means to attack someone on personal grounds, usually of a slightly scandalous nature.

1974 *Australian* 1 Apr. 6: While it might be valid to find Brisbane lacking in Adelaide's grace or Sydney's vigor or Melbourne's dignity, it is not valid to bucket it in total just because its authorities finger *Playboy* with distaste or fall into a faint at the sound of a fourlettered obscenity from the stage.

1977 *Weekend Australian* 26 Nov. Mag. 4: Tipping a bucket is now accepted parliamentary usage for releasing embarrassing information usually accompanied by personal insults, innuendo and allegations which, if made outside Parliament, would clearly be defamatory.

1979 *Australian* 11 May 4: MP claims he was bucketed on radio.

1981 *Sydney Morning Herald* 2 May 13: The spectacle of Mr Nixon effectively bucketing Mr Peacock brought home to a lot of Liberals where real power resides in the Cabinet.

1982 Buzz Kennedy *Australian* 28 Aug. Mag. 8: I have had enough of being expected to smile politely and resolve to mend my ways and the ways of my country simply because precious people from somewhere else flip in, flip out and bucket the place.

bucketing

1982 *NT News* (Darwin) 23 Jun. 4: Mr Whitlam copped a bucketing over his inclusion in a National Aboriginal Conference delegation leaving for Africa tomorrow.

buck, give it a   See quots: mainly N.Z.

1941 Baker 15: *Buck, give it a* Make an attempt at (something); to try.

1956 Ruth Park and D'Arcy Niland *The Drums Go Bang!* 103: 'Okay, pardner,' he said. 'We'll give it a buck.'

Buckley, who struck   See quot. 1873

[**1873** Hotten 99: 'Who struck Buckley?' a common phrase used to irritate Irishmen. The story is that an Englishman having struck an Irishman named Buckley, the latter made a great outcry, and one of his friends rushed forth screaming, 'Who struck Buckley?' 'I did' said the Englishman, preparing for the apparently inevitable combat. 'Then' said the ferocious Hibernian, after a careful investigation of the other's thews and sinews, 'then, sarve him right.']

1885 'The Broken-hearted Shearer' *Old Bush Songs* ed. Stewart and Keesing (1957) 266: She would turn and twist about, saying, 'That slews you, old chap'; / 'Sold again and got the money'; 'Who struck Buckley such a rap?'

1903 Joseph Furphy *Such is Life* (1944) 149: I found myself overflowing with the sunny self-reliance of the man that struck Buckley.

Buckley's chance (show, hope)   A forlorn hope, no chance at all [Origin obscure. Connections have been suggested with 'the wild white man' William Buckley, the convict who absconded from Port Phillip in 1803 and lived for thirty-two years with the natives. He gave himself up in 1835 and lived until 1856. Another suggested derivation is a pun on the name of the Melbourne firm of Buckley and

Nunn.]

1898 W. H. Ogilvie *Fair Girls and Gray Horses* 70: But we hadn't got a racehorse that was worth a dish of feed, / So didn't have a Buckley's show to take the boasters down.

1903 Joseph Furphy *Such is Life* (1944) 339: Brummy ... doesn't require to stoop at all – and *his* show is little better than Buckley's.

1908 E. G. Murphy *Jarrahland Jingles* 16: You've done the rattler in today, you ain't got Buckley's 'ope.

1915 C. J. Dennis *The Songs of a Sentimental Bloke* 20: I knoo / That any other bloke 'ad Buckley's 'oo / Tried fer to pick 'er up.

1936 H. Drake-Brockman *Sheba Lane* 164: 'We ain't got Buckley's chance of a deal, if that's the case,' he commented.

1944 Lawson Glassop *We Were the Rats* 44: 'I've got two chances,' I said. 'Mine and Buckley's.'

1953 T. A. G. Hungerford *Riverslake* 150: 'We've got two chances of making this immigration business work – our own and Buckley's.'

1963 John Cantwell *No Stranger to the Flame* 156: 'He won't stand Buckley's with that mob.'

1974 David Ireland *Burn* 18: 'You got two chances of cookin' this fish: your own and Buckley's. Git away before I knock yer block off.'

1983 *Australian* 11 Jan. 1: Miss Jenny May said civilians who worked at test sites had 'Buckley's chance' of getting compensation because their medical records were not held in one place.

bucks' party, night An all-male party, esp. before a wedding [cf. *stag* functions US 1843]

[**1907** Alfred Searcy *In Australian Tropics* 367: What grand 'buck sprees' we used to have there, to be sure; a lot of men together, pure fun and frolic.]

1942 Gavin Casey *It's Harder for Girls* 82: Bucks' Party [story title]

1957 Nino Culotta *They're a Weird Mob* 88: 'We're 'avin' a bucks' party fer Jimmy Fridy night. Cost yer 'alf a quid fer the grog an' the present.'

1962 David Forrest *The Hollow Woodheap* 54: 'Bucks' party, you understand. Quiet. The land-lady'll be away. Here's your chance to get out amongst men.'

1972 Geoff Morley *Jockey Rides Honest Race* 261: Ken organized my bucks night, because he was going to be my best man.

1980 *Sydney Morning Herald* 27 Dec. 24: My son has just had a bucks' party at which his friends totally encased him in wall plaster. We have tried soaking him in the bath to no avail. He is being married tomorrow. How do we get it off?

1982 *NT News* (Darwin) 15 Nov. 3: A weekend bucks party in Darwin ended in tragedy when one of the guests drowned in a backyard swimming pool.

1984 *Sun-Herald* 15 Jul. 125: It is hard to keep up with the demand [for Bollinger champagne], especially since word got around that the Prince and Princess of Wales had the RO '73 served at their wedding and Charles chose the '75 for his bucks' night.

Budgie, the Silver see **Silver**

Buffs, the The Darwin Australian Rules team [abbr. *buffalo*]

1979 *NT News* 19 Nov. 24: Buffs biffed [heading] Nightcliff gave Darwin a football lesson by creaming them in every aspect of the game.

bugger *n.* Like 'bastard' and 'bloody', bugger (noun, verb and extensions) is not distinctively Australian, but it is remarked upon by visitors as a feature of Australian speech. Intensive uses like 'bugger-all' and 'burnt to buggery' may be more characteristically Australian than the others. The noun is used as an equivalent to 'bastard' in all its senses; as an equivalent to 'damn' ('I don't give a bugger for that'); and in 'bugger all' as meaning 'nothing' [f. *bugger* 2b a coarse term of abuse or insult OED 1719]

1833 Trial before the Supreme Court 9 and 10 Dec. in *True Patriots All* ed. G. C. Ingleton (1952) 149: There was a general cry among the party coming down to me, of *'shoot the bugger.'*

1944 Lawson Glassop *We Were the Rats* 79: 'Wilson or Macduff. Who cares?' 'I don't give a bugger,' said Eddie.

1951 Dal Stivens *Jimmy Brockett* 294: I felt crook in the guts and miserable as buggery.

1952 Jon Cleary *The Sundowners* 153: 'Look at those plains, will you? Miles and miles of bugger all.'

1960 John Iggulden *The Storms of Summer* 121: 'You'd have bugger all chance of that!'

1964 Tom Ronan *Packhorse and Pearling Boat* 35: She had started life at Beagle Bay Mission and on the Bishop's arrival proudly informed him: 'Me properly bloody Catholic bugger, all the same you.'

1973 John O'Grady *Survival in the Doghouse* 63: 'An hour and a half to cook pork chops? They'll be burnt to buggery.'

1981 *Sydney Morning Herald* 29 Jul. 52: Asked how many [free tickets] had been given away, he replied: 'Bugger all, really.'

bugger *v.* 1 Used most often as an equivalent to 'damn'; also (with *up*) 'to make a mess of'; and (with *off*) 'to depart'

1942 C. Hartley Grattan *Introducing Australia* (1944) 171–2: The word bugger is used in numerous forms and contexts. 'Oh, bugger it all.' 'I'll be buggered.' 'Buggered if I will.' 'Bugger him.' 'Oh go to buggery,' 'The silly bugger.' 'I'm all buggered up.' And triumphantly combining all the favorite words, 'bugger the bloody bastard'. English people profess to find Australian men foul-mouthed.

1957 D'Arcy Niland *The Shiralee* 14: 'But one time I fell off the train and buggered my insides up.'

2 In the pidgin term 'bagarup'

1975 *Australian* 19 Sep. 1: Prince Charles broke into Pidgin at the end of his speech [in Papua New Guinea] saying 'Af de ren I bagarup mi nau arait' which meant 'Unfortunately rain caused me some inconvenience yesterday, but now everything is all right.'

Bugs Bunny   The U.S. war memorial in Canberra [f. resemblance to the rabbit in the cartoon]

1979 *Sun-Herald* 16 Dec. 152: A glance at the American War Memorial, or 'Bugs Bunny' as it is known with no particular affection.

1981 *Sun-Herald* 1 Nov. 148: There is a carillon donated by the Poms which plays Blue Belles of Scotland on alternate Sundays, and a war memorial donated by the Yanks which looks exactly like Bugs Bunny.

bulk   A lot of; on a large scale

1983 Tim & Debbie 'Bali Sketch' in *Brainspace Vol. II* [record]: I learnt bulk about Balinese art through their food.

1984 *Sydney Morning Herald* 18 Apr. 46: Bulk Dollars ... Yet to race beyond 1100 m but looks the one to beat.

1984 *Sydney Morning Herald* 19 Jun. 10: Now 34, she says she 'came into bulk parenthood quite late when we moved to Brisbane. You know, the talking to other parents at the barbecues about nappies and kindergartens and all of that.'

bull *n.*   1   A Torres Islander: *obs.*

1934 Vance Palmer *Sea and Spinifex* 29–30: The proffered notes were too much for Charlie, a tough little Torres Islander ..., 'Those bulls'll take on anything [McVeagh commented] if they're shown a few quid.'

2   A wharf labourer unfairly favoured for employment: see quots 1961, 1973

1957 Tom Nelson *The Hungry Mile* 80: The employers ... indulging in illegal trafficking of 'bulls' to suit their own ends. Ibid. 77: The battle to end the bull system is unsurpassed in the history of Australian unionism.

1961 *Sydney Morning Herald* 22 May 2: Under the 'bull' system, wharfies had to front the stevedore, and only the 'bulls' (company men or men who would sling to the foreman) could be sure of catching his eye.

1973 *Sydney Morning Herald* 2 Aug. 7: 'Bulls were tough, strong, hardworking men known to the bosses and, when the wharfies gathered outside the gate looking for work, the foreman would point his finger 'You, and you and you' – always to the 'bulls'. The old, the not so strong and the militants always got the dirtiest, most obnoxious jobs, or were ignored to trudge along the mile to the next gate.

3   Nonsense, pretence, deceit. 'Bull' in a sense close to this is recorded in the OED from 1630, and later in U.S. slang. It would be taken in Australia as an abbreviation of 'bullshit' q.v. and 'bull artist' and 'bull dust' q.v. would have the same implication.

[**1871** W. H. Cooper *Colonial Experience* (MS, Mitchell Library) ii 3: *Joe* Oh talk as much Bullock as you can. *Alfred* Bullock? *Joe* Yes, back yourself to ride anything that was ever foaled, tell any amount of crammers about Buckjumpers.]

1905–12 Joseph Furphy *The Buln-Buln and the Brolga* ed. R. G. Howarth (1948) [Title of a novella previously called 'The Lyre Bird and the Native Companion']

1917 Les Darcy let. 21 Apr. cit. Harry Gordon *An Eyewitness History of Australia* (1976) 212: This [U.S.A.] is a great country ... But they hand out a tremendous lot of bull – everything they have is a champion of the world or the best in the world.

1939 Kylie Tennant *Foveaux* 168: 'I never had any luck with the fair,' Mr True said sentimentally. 'They kid you along, and what does it all amount to, these blandishments? ... Bull, it's all bull.'

1941 Baker 14: *Bull* Nonsense, senseless chatter. cf. 'bullsh'

1951 Dal Stivens *Jimmy Brockett* 171: The old man was always talking about England and calling it the Mother Country and Home, but it sounded all bull to me.

1959 D'Arcy Niland *The Big Smoke* 56: 'I come here to get the truth out of you, and no bull. See?'

1969 William Dick *Naked Prodigal* 204: As I walked along the street I wondered if she really was in Heaven or whether it was just a lot of bull.

1973 Alexander Buzo *Rooted* 78: 'You might be an arty sort of bloke, but ... you don't bung on the bull like a lot of these blokes you see around the place these days.'

1983 *Weekend Australian* 26 Mar. Mag. 4: H. V. Jacques summed up the mood of many post-election correspondents:

> After the bull is over
> After the polling day
> After the members leaving
> Gone on their Canberra way
> Many a word that was spoken
> Proves to be fanciful
> And many a promise is broken
> After the bull.

see **confetti**

Bullamakanka   An imaginary place which is a byword for remoteness and backwardness, like

Woop Woop q.v.
1953 T. A. G. Hungerford *Riverslake* 230: 'Hitch out to Bullamakanka and live with the blacks.'
1965 Leslie Haylen *Big Red* 88: People rushing through the countryside by car would grin as they raced through Cooee. Here was the authentic bush town . . . Here was Bullamakanka.
1976 *Australian* 18 Dec. 22: Bullamakanka Premium Dry Red [mock wine label].
1977 *Southerly* 48: 'We've heard you say he lives in Bullamakanka because he likes being a big frog in a little puddle.'
1984 *Sydney Morning Herald* 7 May Guide 16: He zooms his voice up and down and round about, as the jocks used to do in Bullamakanka about a century ago.

bull artist   see **artist**

bull bag   See quot.
1980 *National Times* 16 Jun. 49: The bull bag was . . . the single most essential tool which we carried. It performs a similar function to a jack and consists of a large bag made of very heavy rubber connected by a nylon tube to the exhaust. Placed under the vehicle and filled with exhaust gases from the engine, it is capable of jacking both back or front wheels of a heavy vehicle a clear 18 in from the ground.

bull-bar   Protective grid on front of motor-car, truck etc.; or mustering device
1967 John Yeomans *The Scarce Australians* 97: Most beasts had been killed by one blow from the bull bars (the heavy horizontal steel tubing mounted as cattle guards) on the front of a road train.
1971 Colin Simpson *The New Australia* 360: Instead of bulldogging the wild steers from horseback, Land Rovers and Toyota vehicles are now used to knock them over with what is called a 'bull bar' mounted in front.
1980 *National Times* 27 Apr. 29: In front of the radiator is the bull-bar, a guard really designed for careless kangaroos.

bull, Barney's   A phrase suggesting clumsiness or incompetence [? f. *Barney's bull* a worthless person or thing OED 1908; influenced also by *bull* 3]
1930 Vance Palmer *The Passage* (1944) 59: 'By hell, we've got 'em. Trapped like Barney's bull!'
1957 Ray Lawler *Summer of the Seventeeth Doll* 17: 'What do they call him Barney for, anyway?' 'Barney's bull, I think. His right name's Arthur.'
all behind like Barney's bull   Delayed and confused; with outsize buttocks
1941 Baker 9: *Behind like Barney's bull, all* Late, backward, delayed.

bull, couldn't hit a ~ on the backside with a handful of wheat   Applied to someone with a bad aim
1954 L. H. Evers *The Pattern of Conquest* 81: 'Ah-h, you couldn't hit a bull in the behind with a bag full of wheat', said Honest John carelessly.
1970 Richard Beilby *No Medals for Aphrodite* 178: 'Her shoot! She couldn't hit a bull in the arse with a handful of rice!'
1981 *Sun-Herald* 3 May 92: 'When it comes to accuracy, he . . . couldn't hit a bull's bum with a handful of wheat.'

Bulldogs   1   In Victoria, the Footscray V.F.L. team
1974 *Sunday Telegraph* (Sydney) 11 Aug. 100: Bulldogs chase off the Blues.
2   In N.S.W., the Canterbury-Bankstown Rugby League team (formerly 'The Berries')
1978 *Sunday Telegraph* (Sydney) 19 Mar. 66: On paper, you would say the Bulldogs were in for only another average season.
3   In S.A., the Central District Australian Rules team
1979 *Advertiser* (Adelaide) 14 Apr. 12: Bulldogs select big name.
4   In W.A., the South Fremantle Australian Rules team
1983 *Sunday Independent* (Perth) 14 Aug. 35: There was plenty for . . . the South Fremantle supporters to get excited about. The Bulldogs ran away to a comfortable victory.
5   In Queensland, the Western Districts Australian Rules team
1979 *Courier-Mail* (Brisbane) 8 May 22: Powerplus play from Bulldogs.

bull dust   1   Fine sand or dust
1935 H. H. Finlayson *The Red Centre* 126: The loam proved unexpectedly heavy, having a rather spongy texture, like the intumescent clays of the Lake Eyre basin, known locally as 'bull dust'.
1945 George Johnston *Pacific Partner* 148: And there were vast areas of fine drift sand – the troops called it 'bull dust' – that would make other deserts look positively glacial.
1967 John Yeomans *The Scarce Australians* 122: Bulldust is the superfine red-grey dust which develops on the northern roads. Sometimes this lies in drifts, perhaps axle deep.
1971 Rena Briand *White Men in a Hole* 11: Deep holes filled with bulldust were booby traps for travellers unfamiliar with the road.
2   As for **bull, bullshit**
1946 W. E. Harney *North of 23°* 78: 'A chap called Darwin says if yer cut off a man's arm, then his sons and so on for generations, would be born without arms.' 'Bull dust', the Scrub replies.
1951 Ernestine Hill *The Territory* 443: *Bull dust* False promises, empty talk.

1953 T. A. G. Hungerford *Riverslake* 121: 'I suppose Bellairs told you that bit of bulldust about there being spies?'
1965 William Dick *A Bunch of Ratbags* 169–70: One bloke reckoned he dressed up as a bodgie and lived, ate, slept and ran with a pack of us for twelve months while he made notes. We reckoned it was a lot of bull-dust.
1966 H. F. Brinsmead *Beat of the City* 104: 'People are invariably happy,' said Uncle Stefan, 'when they are good.' 'Bulldust!' said Raylene.
1971 Frank Hardy *The Outcasts of Foolgarah* 23: No man is so gullible when it comes to a bit of bulldust sprinkled on the old national ethos than the Australian, who really believes the sun shines nowhere else except out of his arse and his beer is really the best.
1982 *Sydney Morning Herald* 10 Jul. 42: Terry Jackman says the idea is bulldust, that it won't happen, that it would establish a monopoly and would be bad for business.

bull jo   See **joe**

bullock   To toil as strenuously as a bullock
1875 Rolf Boldrewood *The Squatter's Dream* repr. as *Ups and Downs* (1878) 240: 'Let other fellows, if they're fools enough, do all that bullocking. Wise men buy their work afterwards and cheap enough too.'
1894 Henry Lawson 'The Lost Souls' Hotel' *Prose* i 155: Take a selector who has bullocked all his life to raise crops on dusty, stony patches in the scrubs.
1904 Steele Rudd *Sandy's Selection* 69: And talk about work! Sandy rarely rested. He would begin hard at daylight, and bullock till he couldn't see – bullock till the stars came out and blinked and blazed.
1911 E. M. Clowes *On the Wallaby through Victoria* 14: Carried apparently with so little exertion, and absolutely no bullocking.
1936 Miles Franklin *All That Swagger* 415: He would now have been in a comfortable school instead of having bullocked himself into an early grave.
1948 H. Drake-Brockman *Sydney or the Bush* 201: Now, what chance was there of giving Dick or Phil or Wally even half the things she'd bullocked for?
1983 *West Australian* (Perth) 7 Oct. 46: Set the reel drag so that a big fish can take line and don't try to bullock it to the shore or boat as though it was a herring or chopper tailor.

bullocky   1   A bullock-driver, teamster
1869 Marcus Clarke 'The Language of Bohemia' repr. in *A Colonial City* ed. L. T. Hergenhan (1972) 162: *bullocky* (a teamster).
1876 Henry Kendall 'Bill the Bullock Driver'

Poetical Works ed. T. T. Reed (1966) 167: Poor bullocky Bill! In the circles select / Of the scholars he hasn't a place.
1891 Henry Lawson 'Song of the Old Bullock-Driver' *Verse* i 162: The bullocks lay down 'neath the gum trees and rested – / The bullockies steered for the bar of the inn.
1905 Randolph Bedford *The Snare of Strength* 210: The bullocky went round the team and recovered the pole-pin.
1929 K. S. Prichard *Working Bullocks* 11: Red Burke was the youngest bullocky in the Karri to own his team, and one of the best drivers.
1941 Sarah Campion *Mo Burdekin* 143: The bullocky . . . stooped to yell at them as they drew level, cursing in the same breath all his plodding oxen.
2   The language of the bullock-driver
1916 *The Anzac Book* 103: Above it all we were certain we heard fragments of language, of the category known in Australia as 'bullocky'.*
*Bullocky – stands both for the bullock driver and for his chief gift.

bullocky's breakfast   see **bushman's breakfast**

bullocky's joy   Treacle
1933 Acland: *Bullocky's Joy* Golden syrup or treacle.
1934 Archer Russell *A Tramp-Royal in Wild Australia* 202: Luncheon and supper are much the same, except that damper and 'bullockys' joy' (treacle) take the place of porridge.
1951 Ernestine Hill *The Territory* 176: 1   case treacle, bullocky's joy.

Bulls   The Wide Bay (Q.) Rugby League club
1982 *Sunday Mail* (Brisbane) 21 Mar. 68: The Bulls Cop Blast! Wide Bay rugby league coach Gary Pearson has blasted his players on the eve of the Bulls' opening Winfield State League game against Wynnum-Manly in Maryborough today.

bull, scrub   see **scrub**

bullsh, bullshit *n.*   As for **bull** 3. Not an Australianism in origin, although very common in the colloquial language; the shortening to 'bullsh' is euphemistic
1919 W. H. Downing *Digger Dialects* 14: *Bullsh* 1) Insincerity; 2) an incorrect or insincere thing; 3) flattery; 4) praise.
1938 Xavier Herbert *Capricornia* 377: 'That's all bulsh about trouble if he takes on a coloured man.' Ibid. 395: 'This talk of invasion by the Japs is all plain bulsh.'
1951 Dal Stivens *Jimmy Brockett* 65: He'd kick up a bit of a shindy at first and talk a lot of bulsh about his reputation as a good and fair ref.
1959 D'Arcy Niland *The Big Smoke* 159: 'We

won't be able to get out for the bullsh in a minute,' jibed the lumberman. 'Look at it – it's up to me knees now.'

1965 Eric Lambert *The Long White Night* 23: 'It's an intangible thing, a sort of veneration for an idea for its own sake. It's hard to put into words. You'd probably call it bullshit.'

1974 John Powers *The Last of the Knucklemen* 96: 'I just want to see if all this "knuckleman" stuff's for real – or bullshit.'

bullshit *v.*   To talk 'bull', esp. in seeking to delude or impose

1965 John Beede *They Hosed Them Out* 196: 'Don't bullshit to me – I know how I look.'

1977 Helen Garner *Monkey Grip* 51: 'You're not bullshitting me, are you?'

bull's roar, within a   A measure of distance

1973 Patsy Adam Smith *The Barcoo Salute* 53: The sound of axes rang all the way down through Taroona, past places that hadn't been within a bull's roar of the fire.

1984 Mike Carlton *Sydney Morning Herald* 1 Feb. 10: La Humphrey at the opera is consumed by an onslaught of genteelism, a disease which afflicts so many of the Corporation's servants when they come within a bull's roar of Culture For The Masses.

bum to mum   See quots: Victorian sporting

1972 Ian Moffitt *The U-Jack Society* 146: Australian Rules, in Victoria, is, of course, a religion which divides man and wife ('Bum to mum' is the standard order for players forbidden intercourse before the big games).

1973 *Australian* 7 Apr. 17: Like the coach [in V.F.L.] who told his team on Fridays, 'well, it's bum to mum tonight boys', because they might wear themselves out in sexual activity.

bumper *n.*   A cigarette butt, esp. in the expression 'not worth a bumper'

1900–10 O'Brien and Stephens: *Bumper* a cigarette or cigar stump or butt.

1916 *The Anzac Book* 47: One mornin' early while we was standin' to arms 'e lights up a bumper.

1924 *Truth* 27 Apr. 6: *Bumper* butt of cigarette.

1947 Margaret Trist *Daddy* 164: 'My old man's not going to be worth a bumper that day.'

1960 Ron Tullipan *Follow the Sun* 90: 'By midday it won't be worth a bumper to you anyway.'

1974 David Ireland *Burn* 44: 'You're not worth a bumper,' Joy says. 'You couldn't fight your way out of a paper bag.'

1983 Ruth Park *National Times* 22 Apr. 27: An elderly neighbour kept all his butts in a jam jar and when out of tobacco would say complacently, 'Gonna peel me bumpers now.'

bundle, drop one's   To give up, lose one's nerve, surrender one's responsibilities

1900–10 O'Brien and Stephens: *Bundle* for a competitor to collapse or 'turn it up' is called dropping his bundle.

1906 Edward Dyson *Fact'ry 'Ands* 241: 'He gives er sad cry, 'n' drops his bundle, 'n' goes pluckin' at his 'air.'

1915 C. J. Dennis *The Songs of a Sentimental Bloke* 23: I carn't tell *wot* it is; all I know / I've dropped me bundle – an' I'm glad it's so.

1924 *Truth* 27 Apr. 6: *Bundle, to drop the* To show cowardice.

1936 H. Drake-Brockman *Sheba Lane* 279: Kent seemed to have come to the end of his tether. He'd dropped his bundle.

1942 Gavin Casey *It's Harder for Girls* 212: 'He dropped his bundle,' said Tom. 'No doubt about it, Sim was right. If they drop their bundles they're gone a million.'

1959 David Forrest *The Last Blue Sea* 96: 'Something happened to him there before the war. He just dropped his bundle. Properly.'

1972 Thomas Keneally *The Chant of Jimmie Blacksmith* 138: 'Panic?' Mort asked. 'Drop your bundle,' McCreadie explained.

1980 Shirley Hazzard *The Transit of Venus* 40: 'We could all give in', she said, when told that Miss Garside the librarian had completely dropped her bundle.

bundy   **1**   The 'clock' by which workers 'clock on' and 'clock off', esp. in the expression 'punch the bundy' [f. trade name]

1936 J. L. Ranken *Murder Pie* 73: 'I remember glancing at the bundy clock as I got in.'

1949 G. Farwell *Traveller's Tracks* 16: There are no bitumen roads back there, hardly an up-to-date picture show, no rush hours or bundies to turn life into a milling ant-heap.

1957 D'Arcy Niland *Call Me When the Cross Turns Over* 161: Thousands of men filing down a track ... to the ship-yards ... Through the gates. Punching the bundy.

1961 Mena Calthorpe *The Dyehouse* 140: 'I want you to make sure every man bundies off.'

1971 David Ireland *The Unknown Industrial Prisoner* 81: There had been another break at a State detention centre, one of those where men couldn't bundy out each day.

1974 *Bulletin* 3 Aug. 13: Relief for the Bundy punchers?

1983 *Sydney Morning Herald* 30 Apr. 33: After Bundying-on, the card was not to be replaced in its rack but droped into a box on the staff checker's desk.

2   Bundaberg rum, often in the expression 'bundy and coke'

1984 *National Times* 10 Mar. Colour Mag. 6: The

'spirit of the game' was overproof Bundy rum and all players entered freely into it.

bung-eye   Sandy blight or similar infection [cf. *bunged up* OED 1622]
1892 G. L. James *Shall I Try Australia?* 242: One pest of the bush and plains is 'Sandy blight' or inflammation of the eyes ... it is also known as 'bung-eye', because ... in the morning, the lids are tightly closed, and require no small amount of fomentation to get them open.
1903 Joseph Furphy *Such is Life* (1944) 353: 'Butler, he's laid up with the bung blight in both eyes.'
1934 Archer Russell *A Tramp-Royal in Wild Australia* 172: Bung-eyes, flysickness accompanied by severe vomiting, dysentery in its worst form, and Barcoo Rot ... become the lot of the human.
1946 E. L. Grant Watson *But to What Purpose?* 127: He mentioned a kind of ophthalmia, known locally as 'bung-eye', which was very common both amongst natives and whites.

bung (bong), to go   Originally to die, then to break down, go bankrupt, cease to function [Ab. *bong* dead]
[**1847** J. D. Lang *Cooksland* 430: A place called *Umpie Bung*, or the dead houses, where there had once been a Government Settlement, now long abandoned.]
1857 F. Cooper *Wild Adventures in Australia* 58: I asked him what had become of 'Solomons'? 'Boung!' said he, making use of the Cameleroi term for dead.
1875 A. J. Boyd *Old Colonials* (1882) 73: Sometimes you've got a horse as is good an' don't suit you, an' you sells him, but just afore you hands 'im over and gets the money, he goes bung* on you. *Dead.
1885 *The Australasian Printers' Keepsake* 40: He was importuned to desist, as his musical talent had 'gone bung', probably from over-indulgence.
1890 *Truth* 19 Oct. 1: The 'National' (?) Club appears to have gone bung. No wonder. It is the last retreat of the greedy, grasping bastard Toryism.
1901 Henry Lawson 'Telling Mrs Baker' *Prose* i 416: The world might wobble and all the banks go bung, but the cattle have to go through – that's the law of the stock-routes.
1911 Louis Stone *Jonah* 146: 'The firm's gone bung.'
1933 R. B. Plowman *The Man from Oodnadatta* 122: 'I heard that their well has gone bung, and their garden is completely ruined.'
1946 Dal Stivens *The Courtship of Uncle Henry* 109: 'The radio's gone bung again and I'm just fixing it.'
1951 Dymphna Cusack and Florence James *Come*

In Spinner 329: 'What's wrong with 'er? The bank gone bung?'
1982 *NT News* (Darwin) 15 Jul. 7: Downturn in the bauxite industry seems to be reflected in the choice of name for South Weipa's main street in NQ – Gonbung.

bung it on, to   To put on 'side'
1963 Alan Seymour *The One Day of the Year* 48: 'Well, she bungs it on a bit don't she? ... the young lady's too lah-dee-dah for us.'
1969 William Dick *Naked Prodigal* 187: These flash bastards ... give you the shits bunging on side like they do.
1973 Alexander Buzo *Rooted* 78: 'When I had my one and only exhibition in an art gallery, there was a whole lot of scientists there, bunging it on.'

bunji   See quots [Ab. W.A.]
1980 *Daily News* (Perth) 26 Sep. 11: James said that a 'bunji' man was a white man who patronised hotels like Cleo's in Fremantle, looking for sex with Aboriginal women.
1981 Archie Weller *The Day of the Dog* 64: They've been off with some bunji man grinding it into them for a few dollars. Ibid. 166: *bunji* 'to bunji around' is to go from person to person, conning them up and so forth. A bunji (man or woman) makes love to anyone.
1985 *National Times* 12 Apr. 20: They were Bunji men ... Today the term, widely used by the Aboriginal people around Perth, refers to the lonely, alcoholic old white men who wander the parks and back streets seeking 'black velvet' – sexual solace from Aboriginal women.

bunny   A 'muggins', dupe, person with no mind of his own; in cricket, a player who is no batsman [f. the timidity and helplessness of the rabbit]
1943 Baker 16: *Bunny* A simpleton or fool, an easy victim for exploitation.
1950 Jon Cleary *Just Let Me Be* 14: 'But you wait and see I'm not gunna be like all them bunnies over there for the rest of my life.'
1952 T. A. G. Hungerford *The Ridge and the River* 31: White often wondered why Shearwood had never got his commission when he could run rings round so many of the bunnies who had.
1959 Dorothy Hewett *Bobbin Up* 196: 'We're only the poor old unskilled mugs. The bunnies!'
1965 Wally Grout *My Country's Keeper* 41–2: Once again, at Johannesburg, in the fourth match of the tour, I was one of the 'bunnies'.

bunyip   Monster of Aboriginal legend, supposed to haunt water-holes; any freak or impostor [Ab.]
1848 W. Westgarth *Australia Felix* 391: Certain large fossil bones ... have been referred by the natives ... to a huge animal of extraordinary

appearance, called in some districts the Bunyup ... It is described as of amphibious character, inhabiting deep rivers, and permanent water-holes, having a round head, an elongated neck, with a body and tail resembling an ox.

1852 G. C. Mundy *Our Antipodes* ii 18–19: Did my reader ever hear of the Bunyip? (fearful name to the Aboriginal native!) a sort of half-horse, half-alligator, haunting the wide rushy swamps and lagoons of the interior ... a new and strong word was adopted into the Australian vocabulary. Bunyip became, and remains, a Sydney synonyme for *impostor, pretender, humbug,* and the like.

1903 Joseph Furphy *Such is Life* (1944) 244: 'He heard "Hen-ree! Hen-ree!" boomin' an' bellerin' back an' forrid across the bend in the dark, an' he thought the boody-man, an' the bunyip, an' the bashee, an' (sheol) knows what all, was after him.'

1930 J. S. Litchfield *Far-North Memories* 205: I had found the Territory a glorious country ... I found the 'awful climate' – a *bunyip*!

1956 A. D. Hope *Sydney Morning Herald* 16 Jun. 15: 'The Bunyip Stages a Comeback'. The bunyip of Australian literature is the mythical great Australian novel.

1975 *Bulletin* 9 Aug. 44: Literary gentlemen have tended to call the great Australian novel the bunyip, the monster that has never been revealed.

1984 *Sydney Morning Herald* 31 Mar. 34: Now the quest for national identity (our century-long pursuit of the bunyip) is on yet again.

bunyip aristocracy D. H. Deniehy's derisory description of W. C. Wentworth's plan for a colonial peerage in 1853; varied to apply to any similar attempt to imitate British institutions

1853 *Sydney Morning Herald* 16 Aug. in *Select Documents in Australian History* ed. C. M. H. Clark (1955) 342: [Report of speech by D. H. Deniehy on the proposal to establish a colonial peerage] Here they all knew the common water mole was transformed into the duck-billed platypus, and in some distant emulation of this degeneration, he supposed they were to be favoured with a bunyip aristocracy.

1960 *Sydney Morning Herald* 8 Aug. 3: The A.L.P. in N.S.W. is building up a bunyip peerage of his own [a class of hereditary legislators], even if the bunyips aren't titled, and sit in the Lower, not Upper, House.

1976 *Australian* 14 Jun. 7: The grafting of knighthoods on ... the Order of Australia is a laughable concession to bunyip snobbery.

1981 Max Harris *Weekend Australian* 21 Nov. Mag. 7: The bunyip aristocracy [The Old Families of Adelaide] were not as sure of themselves as their feeble imitation of their English betters made them seem.

1984 *Sydney Morning Herald* 5 Jan. 6: Hawke's 'de-politicising' of the office will, like his super-popularity, be transitory ... or we will move from a democracy to a bunyip monarchy.

1984 *Australian* 1 May 8: As one possible substitute [for The Last Post, Reveille etc.] what about We're Off To See The Wizard ... That song was hallowed by being sung by the Sixth Division of the Second AIF during the attack on Bardia in 1941, so it should conform to the current vogue of bunyip patriotism being promoted so vigorously by the Ausflag busybodies.

Burdekin duck See quots 1945, 1951 [f. river and district in Queensland]

1945 Tom Ronan *Strangers on the Ophir* 39: A meat fritter known in the Kimberleys as a 'Burdekin Duck', and on the Burdekin as a 'Kimberley Oyster'.

1951 Ernestine Hill *The Territory* 426: 'Burdekin duck', meat fritters.

1961 George Farwell *Vanishing Australians* 72: His damper, johnny-cakes, brownie and Burdekin duck were all evolved from simple materials.

Burdekin vomit See quot. [f. river and district in Queensland]

1918 C. Fetherstonhaugh *After Many Days* 272: What I called the Belyando Spue was a most trying ailment ... The Western fellows called it 'the Barcoo sickness', the Northern men the 'Burdekin vomit'.

burglar, gin see **gin burglar**

Burke and Wills, cover more ground than See quot. 1984 [f. the two explorers who crossed the continent from south to north and perished on the return journey]

1984 *Sunday Independent* (Perth) 18 Nov. 43: 'He's covered more ground than Burke and Wills' is the stock condemnation of a racehorse wandering all over the track.

1985 *Sydney Morning Herald* 4 Feb. Guide 1: Bert Bryant became the king of the extravagant image. Horses would ... 'cover more ground than Burke and Wills'.

burley see **berley**

burl, give it a To make a trial of, risk an attempt [f. *birl* a rapid twist or turn EDD 1892]

1924 *Truth* 27 Apr. 6: *Burl* To try anything.

1935 Kylie Tennant *Tiburon* 72: 'Come on,' Kahn murmured to Johnny as the crowd increased, 'give it a burl!'

1937 Vance Palmer *Legend for Sanderson* 79–80: 'Give it a burl, Leo,' Neil was pleading. 'You can't lose by it.'

1952 T. A. G. Hungerford *The Ridge and the River* 3: He pointed upwards to the threshing palm-fronds. 'Give it a burl?'
1964 George Johnston *My Brother Jack* 34: 'Even if you know you can't bloody win you still got to have a go. You'll always be pissin' into the wind, but that don't mean it isn't worth givin' it a burl.'

burn *v. & n.* To drive fast, esp. in an exhibitionist and competitive fashion [f. 'burning' tyres]
1963 Gunther Bahnemann *Hoodlum* 155: He parked his bike at the kerb and waited. Soon the others burned around the corner as if hunted by the devil in person.
1965 Colin Johnson *Wild Cat Falling* 109: 'What was the plan?' he asks. 'Pick up a car,' I say. 'Bust a store in this one horse town, then burn off out of the State.'
1966 Roger Carr *Surfie* 121: 'Come on', someone in her lot called, 'big burn on.'
1970 Jack Hibberd *White with Wire Wheels* in Penguin *Plays* 164: 'He . . . wants to know how the Valiant performs. I've promised to take him for a burn when I've driven it in.'

burn out See quot.
1979 *Herald* (Melbourne) 14 Apr. 5: A police spokesman said dieselene was used by street rodders when they were demonstrating a 'burn out'. The 'burn out' gives the effect of the car being on fire as large clouds of smoke billow from the squealing tyres as the car gains speed.

burn, Chinese see **Chinese**

burnt stick, better than a poke in the eye with a see **poke**

burst (bust) A spree, prolonged drinking bout, esp. in the phrase 'on the burst' [cf. *burst* an outburst of drinking EDD 1861; *bust* U.S. 1843 Mathews]
1852 *Select Committee on the Management of the Goldfields* 97: One-third of the miners are incorrigible drunkards . . . they frequently fall into good claims, and make large hauls in the course of the week, they then go 'upon the burst' as they call it, and drink until all their earnings are 'knocked down', and then go to work again.
1865 Henry Kingsley *The Hillyars and the Burtons* 146: Any corn-stalk cockatoo who might have treed his section on the burst, and come back to the shed.
1868 Marcus Clarke 'Night Scenes in Melbourne' repr. in *A Colonial City* ed. L. T. Hergenhan (1972) 102: Walking up the street, we meet a knot of station-men from the Murray with cattle. They have just put up their horses preparatory to 'goin' on the burst'.

1880 Rolf Boldrewood *The Miner's Right* (1890) 222: 'If your theory is right about his having a craving for drink, it will all come out the first time he has a "burst".' Ibid. 254: A note . . . that Mr Bulder had been 'on the burst' for several days, and that someone . . . ought to come down and look after him.
1899 W. T. Goodge *Hits! Skits! and Jingles!* 64: They'd long been chumps in fights and frays, / Together 'on the burst' for days.
1911 E. M. Clowes *On the Wallaby through Victoria* 106: Men still go 'on the bust', cheques are planked down, and 'shouting' – the Australian equivalent for 'treating' – indulged in till all the money is finished.
1932 Leonard Mann *Flesh in Armour* 140: 'The chap who looked as if he'd been on the bust?'
1942 Gavin Casey *It's Harder for Girls* 98: 'He was a real damn nuisance, allus in arguments an' stayin' on th' burst for as much as a fortnight at a time.'
2 A sudden spurt by a football player
1976 David Ireland *The Glass Canoe* 145: Danny's on the burst and swerves just before taking a pass from the half.

burster, buster see **southerly**

Bus, the Old see **Old**

bush *n.* The 'woods' or 'forest'; the unsettled or sparsely settled areas generally; the country as distinct from the towns [f. Dutch *bosch*]
1803 *Sydney Gazette* 17 Apr. 3: Upon perusing a paragraph in one of your Papers, which suggested the propriety of converting the Rocks into an Academy for *Tumblers*, I rather conceived that you might, with an equal promise of success, recommend some parts of the Bush for an improvement in the talent of *Dancing*, as there much instruction might be expected from the assistance of the accomplished *Kangaroo*.
1826 James Atkinson *An Account of the State of Agriculture and Grazing in New South Wales* 64: Very few of the stock owners have sufficient land to support the whole of their stock, and are therefore obliged to have recourse to the unoccupied tracts in the interior . . . they go into the interior, or *bush*, as it is termed, beyond the occupied parts of the country, usually procuring the assistance of some of the black Natives, as their guides.
1833 W. H. Breton *Excursions in New South Wales* 46: The only convenient way of travelling in the 'bush'* is on horseback. *Bush is the term commonly used for the country *per se*: 'he resides in the Bush', implies that a person does not reside in, or very near, a town. It also signifies a forest.
1848 H. W. Haygarth *Recollections of Bush Life in*

Australia 10: That hackneyed expression, 'the bush' ... the resident in Sydney would be apt to consider it any place beyond the suburbs of the town, the Hawkesbury or Illawarra farmer would place it between 30 and 100 miles from the capital; while the distant settler, the *bona fide* bushman, would smile at such fireside notions, and from his dwelling, 300 miles from Port Jackson, he still talks of 'going into the bush', which in his sense of the term implies his own lonely out-stations, or regions yet untrodden by the white man, in short any place beyond the boundaries of his own homestead, and 'on this side sundown'.
1853 S. Mossman and T. Banister *Australia, Visited and Revisited* 62: The term 'bush', as it is used in Australia, is indiscriminately applied to all descriptions of uncleared land, or to any spot away from a settlement, as a person in England would speak of the country when they are out of town.
1892 Henry Lawson 'The Bush Undertaker' *Prose* i 57: And the sun sank again on the grand Australian bush – the nurse and tutor of eccentric minds, the home of the weird, and of much that is different from things in other lands.
1950 Brian James *The Advancement of Spencer Button* 134: 'What's the good of your degree if they are going to send you to the bush?'

bush *v.* In the expression 'to bush it', to camp out in the bush; put up with the hardships of bush life
1827 W. J. Dumaresq in *Fourteen Journeys* ed. G. Mackaness (1950–1) 99: Not being provided for *bushing it*, in these early forests, we made up our minds to return. [OED Suppl.]
1838 T. Horton James *Six Months in South Australia* 157: A young man, not afraid of bushing it.
1845 D. Mackenzie *The Emigrant's Guide* 187–8: Were he [the innkeeper] to refuse cheques in payment of his bills, he would soon lose half his customers, who would in that case be obliged to 'bush it' every night.
1853 S. Mossman and T. Banister *Australia Visited and Revisited* 132: It was a matter of choice for us to 'bush it', and if we were travelling the same journey again, and well provided, we should often prefer it to putting up at some inns.

bush-bashing Driving through the bush (esp. with four-wheel drive vehicles, trail bikes) where there are no roads
1967 Len Beadell *Blast the Bush* ix: Short cuts through mulga scrub (known as 'bush-bashing') can be an interesting experience but is attended with real dangers.
1978 *Sydney Morning Herald* 8 Sep. 22: The days of laissez-faire bush-bashing are drawing to a close. There's a new perception of what must be done to preserve our natural heritage.
1982 *Age* (Melbourne) 18 May 26: Once you have

bashed a bit of bush there is not a lot to do in Alice.
bush-basher
1978 *Sydney Morning Herald* 22 Sep. 25: The 'bush-bashers' are alive and well, with various four-wheel drive organizations campaigning heavily against the establishment of national parks which they see as a threat to their activities.

bush, the bastard from the see **bastard**

bush bellows See quot. 1856
1856 G. Willmer *The Draper in Australia* 155: We had much trouble to light our fire, and but for our perseverance in puffing away with the bush bellows (our hats) for an hour, we should have been compelled to go without supper.

bush carpenter A rough and ready carpenter
1859 C. Calvert *Cowanda* 5: Every room boasted some three or four doors, beneath which – for bush-carpenters never manage to make things fit – the winter's winds whistled in chorus.
1882 Rolf Boldrewood *Robbery Under Arms* (World's Classics 1949) 10: It was a snug hut enough, for father was a good bush carpenter, and didn't turn his back to anyone for splitting and fencing, hut-building and shingle-splitting, he had had a year or two at sawing, too.
1942 John Shaw Neilson *Autobiography* (1978) 108: Frank had stayed behind ... doing some additions to my father's place. He is a pretty good bush carpenter.

bush dunny See **dunny, country dunny**
1983 Mike Carlton *Sun-Herald* 18 Sep. 143: Changi makes Sydney airport look like a bush dunny.

bushed Lost in the bush; having lost one's bearings generally
1844 *Georgiana's Journal* ed. Hugh McCrae (1966) 124: Even with the aid of his compass, Captain Reid thinks we ran the risk of being bushed for the night.
1845 C. Griffith *Present State of Port Phillip* 63: Some people never succeed in becoming good bushmen; and there have been instances of persons *being bushed* (that is, having to spend the night al fresco), within a mile of their own doors.
1849 Diary in L. Braden *Bullockies* (1968) 24: Very nearly bushed but we found our way at last and camped about 7 o'clock after a hard day's work over bad roads.
1855 William Howitt *Land, Labour and Gold* i. 79: The whole night passed, and he never found his way back; to a certainty he was bushed, as the phrase is, that is – lost!
1870 Marcus Clarke *His Natural Life* ed. S. Murray-Smith (1970) 620: It seemed that the

streets were endless, and that once entangled in that maze, he would be 'bushed' indeed.

1887 *All the Year Round* 30 Jul. 68: 'To be bushed', of course, simply meant at first to be lost in the bush, but now it is applied to a person in any mental or physical difficulty or muddle.

1907 Barbara Baynton *Human Toll* 42: Boshy paused, but his hearers were again bushed as to his drift.

1930 Vance Palmer *The Passage* 245: 'It wasn't her fault the youngster strayed off like that and got bushed.'

1941 Charles Barrett *Coast of Adventure* 83: You can easily get bushed there; missing the creek's way through the maze.

1965 Patrick White *Four Plays* 344: 'We reckoned on following the track down Hermit Valley ... but got a bit bushed.'

1980 Murray Bail *Homesickness* 228: 'I got bloody bushed in the subway on the way back.'

bushfire blonde   See quot.: World War II slang

1943 Baker 17: *Bushfire blonde* a red-haired girl.

1956 Ruth Park and D'Arcy Niland *The Drums Go Bang!* 121: The bushfire blonde is a mother now, / She has a little bub.

1984 Jack Hibberd *Squibs* 130: 'I love bushfire blondes.'

bushfire, get on like a   Applied to a rapidly developing friendship, or to any project that proceeds apace [variant of *like wildfire*]

1942 Sarah Campion *Bonanza* 184: They get on like the proverbial bushfire.

bush, to go   Used of an Aboriginal disappearing from his habitat, and so jocularly of anyone 'making himself scarce', with variants like 'head for the scrub', 'take to the mallee', 'take to the tall timber' qq.v.

1908 Mrs Aeneas Gunn *We of the Never-Never* 170: Maudie, discovering that the house was infested with debbil-debbils, had resigned and 'gone bush'.

1926 K. S. Prichard *Working Bullocks* 110: 'Duck Hayes told us you had gone bush. And that's the last we heard about you till a couple of months ago.'

1934 P. H. Richie *North of the Never Never* 157: He had not seen them since the cows and bull had gone bush eighteen years before.

1961 Patrick White *Riders in the Chariot* 383: Alf Dubbo now went bush, figuratively at least, as far as other human beings were concerned.

1984 *Sydney Morning Herald* 24 Mar. 6: A farmer 'went bush' for nine days after shooting a neighbour in a dispute over water supplies and boundary gates, the Central Criminal Court was told yesterday ... After the shooting Elford ran off and

lived for nine days in the bush, surviving on birds' eggs and sour lemons.

bush lawyer   See quot. 1926

1848 Let. cit. in W. S. Parkes *Village on the Wollombi* (?1968) 17: He has squandered by lawsuits and intemperance a considerable property ... and for some years past has solely subsisted ... acting the part of what is termed a Bush Lawyer ... writing of petitions, and whatever he can procure.

1868 C. Wade Brown *Overlanding in Australia* 68: He summoned us because he was put up to it by the old hand, who is a bit of a bush lawyer.

1926 James Vance Marshall *Timely Tips for New Australians: Bushlawyer* A man who gratuitously voices legal opinions although possessing no qualifications for doing so.

1934 F. E. Baume *Burnt Sugar* 179: 'You go off this ship at the Port. I'll have no bush lawyers here. I'll have no Red Feds on my ship.'

1955 Mary Durack *Keep Him My Country* 222: Bush lawyers appeared from all directions and a great deal of contradictory 'evidence' was advanced.

1967 Frank Hardy *Billy Borker Yarns Again* 135: In the old days in the bush, there were no registered lawyers, so some half-shrewd mug, usually a barber, would set himself up to advise all and sundry. So now anyone who throws around a lot of free advice is called a bush lawyer.

bush liar   A teller of tall stories

1893 Henry Lawson 'Stragglers' *Prose* i 93: Every true Australian bushman must try his best to tell a bigger outback lie than the last bush-liar.

1936 Archer Russell *Gone Nomad* 46: Probably the most dramatic Bush liar I met with on the tablelands ... was 'Longbow'—.

1957 R. S. Porteous *Brigalow* 83: As a yarn spinner and bush liar Wagga had no equal.

bushman, Piccadilly   see **Piccadilly**

Bushman's Bible   The *Bulletin* (pre-World War I)

1888 *Bulletin* 15 Dec. 5: 'The Bulletin is the Bushman's Bible.'

1903 P. F. Rowland *The New Nation* 204: A backblocks' shearer once told him that 'if he only had 6d left, he would buy the *Bulletin* with it.' Whatever may be thought of the anti-religious and separatist principles of this 'Bushman's Bible', it must be conceded to have done a very real service to Australia.

1908 C. H. S. Matthews *A Parson in the Australian Bush* 283: The *Sydney Bulletin*, the cleverest of Australian papers, and so widely read as sometimes to be called the 'Bushman's Bible', ceaselessly caricatures John Bull.

1958 Nancy Cato *All the Rivers Run* 67: He took the *Bulletin*, the bushman's Bible, and read all the hints for the man on the land.
1969 A. H. Chisholm *The Joy of the Earth* 314: Reading matter varying in quality and quantity, with Sydney's red-covered weekly *Bulletin* (then 'the bushman's bible') as first favourite.

bushman's breakfast Variously described as 'a drink of water and a good look around', 'a hitch in the belt and a good look around', 'a shave and a shit and a good look around': echoed in the title of the Phillip Theatre review of the 1960s, 'A cup of tea, a Bex and a good lie down'.
1945 Baker 81: *bullocky's breakfast*, a hitch in the belt and an attention to natural requirements.
1981 *Sydney Morning Herald* 18 Nov. 8: We must . . . applaud TCN 9's attempt to break new ground with the Sunday morning current affairs, and I was quite prepared to have a drink of water, a good look around, and settle to a two-hour bash.

bushman's cement See quot.
1977 Athol Thomas *Bulls and Boabs* 112: The stones were bonded together with a mortar made from antbed mixed with water – the bushman's cement.

bushman's clock The kookaburra, whose laugh is heard at dawn and sunset
1846 C. P. Hodgson *Reminiscences of Australia* 165: Laughing Jackass . . . is well and truly stiled the Bushman's clock.
1853 John Sherer *The Gold Finder of Australia* 102: With the first peep of dawn we were roused by the laugh of the jackass-bird – an extraordinary creature, which passes by the name of the Bushman's Clock, and which is rarely heard to give utterance to its merry note at any other hour of the day.
1861 H. W. Wheelwright *Bush Wanderings of a Naturalist* 128: The laughing jackass is the bushman's clock.
see **settler's clock**

bush medicine Reliance on the natural remedies provided by the bush
1982 *Weekend Australian* 6 Feb. 17: Interest in bush medicine has been revived by the publication by the Department of Health in Darwin of a dossier of indigenous plants in the Top End which have long been used by Aborigines to cure their ailments.

bush oysters See quot. 1971
1971 *Bulletin* 27 Nov. 48: Eating bull's testicles, or 'bush oysters' as they're known.

bush pickles See quot. 1962

1962 J. Marshall and R. Drysdale *Journey Among Men* 170: Bush pickles . . . are made by stirring a bottle of Worcester sauce into a large tin of plum jam.

bushranger 1 A man with some official task or responsibility in the bush (the English 'ranger')
[**1798** Matthew Flinders *Voyage to Terra Australis* (1814) cxxxv: This little bear-like quadruped is known in New South Wales, and called by the natives, *womat, wombat,* or *wombach,* according to the different dialects, or perhaps to the different rendering of the wood rangers who brought the information.]
1805 G. Caley to Sir Joseph Banks *Banks Papers* vol. 20 cit. Ramson 142: If the Bush rangers will always bring plants from the remote parts of their tours, I can form a good idea of what distance they have been.
2 A law-abiding citizen skilled in bush-craft, a bushman
1805 Gov. King *HRNSW* v 725: The whole of their story [of exploration] is so contradictory that I should not have inserted these particulars but to prove what little confidence can be put in this class of what is locally termed bushrangers.
1825 *Australian* 17 Feb. 1: We regret much that ever Mr Hume allowed such a person as Mr Hovell, who knows so little of the interior of the country, and possessed of such poor abilities as a bushranger, to be of his party.
1827 P. Cunningham *Two Years in New South Wales* ii 157: If pushing into a country at a distance from settlers, a pack-horse with provisions ought to accompany you. A steady white man who is a good bush-ranger, and a black native, complete your train.
1843 John Hood *Australia and the East* 176: I confess I was again induced to wish that my boys had remained at home in Britain instead of becoming bushrangers in New Holland.
3 A runaway convict trying to survive in the bush, not always by preying on others
1801 James Elder MS Journal cit. *Australian Literary Studies* Jun. 1966, 214: One of these Bushrangers [concerned in stealing a boat] was Williams.
1805 *Sydney Gazette* 17 Feb. 2: On Tuesday last a cart was stopped between this settlement and Hawkesbury, by three men whose appearance sanctioned the suspicion of their being bushrangers . . . they did not, however, take anything out of the cart . . . from whence it may be hoped they prefer the prospect of being restored to society to any monetary relief that might be obtained from acts of additional imprudence that could at best but render their condition hopeless.
1819 Let. in *True Patriots All* ed. G. C. Ingleton (1952) 82: Men at this settlement reduced to the

last stages of despair, frequently run into the woods and live upon what nature in her uncultivated state affords the wild productions of the forest ... A man of the name of Creig, actually asserts, that ... he beheld, leaning against a tree, a skeleton of a man, with a musket by his side, also against the tree, and which he supposes to be a *bushranger*, like himself. Many are compelled from hunger to give themselves up, and very frequently so starved that they can scarce crawl upon their hands and knees.
1823 *Godwin's Emigrant's Guide to Van Diemen's Land* 51: *Bush Rangers* are runaway convicts, who, absenting themselves from the settlements, resort to the woods, where there is plenty of game, which enables them to subsist, and renders them independent so long as they have a supply of ammunition. From 1808 to 1817 they increased in numbers, and were guilty of robberies, murders, and every species of atrocity.
1838 John Curtis *The Shipwreck of the Stirling Castle* 81: During his journey he fell in with a 'bush ranger' (that is a runaway convict) who had escaped from the penal settlement at Moreton Bay several years before, and had now united himself with a tribe of natives.
4 One who evades the law by keeping to the bush, and maintains himself by robbery (whether an escaped convict or not), usually a member of a gang: the commonest sense
1806 *Sydney Gazette* 16 Nov. 1: BUSHRANGERS. As the daring spirits of these desperate offenders occupies much serious attention at the present moment, we enter into the following particulars ... Five sheep have disappeared in the course of one night, notwithstanding every vigilant exertion of the stock keepers and guards ... Night and day they have been harassed by their daring visitors, their huts plundered as well as their flocks, & their provisions carried off.
1809 Gov. Bligh *HRNSW* vii 189: It is a momentous concern that a set of free booters (bushrangers as they are called) should be increasing in their numbers throughout the country. Report states, that about sixty, and some of them well armed, are now in the woods, and have a breed of good dogs with which they kill kangaroo.
1816 *Hobart Town Gazette* 23 Nov. 1: Soon after, the party were alarmed by the appearance of the Bush rangers, headed by *Michael Howe*, & his gang of 8 runaways.
1856 G. Willmer *The Draper in Australia* 107: I availed myself of the opportunity to deposit some gold, rather than carry it with me any longer, at the risk of being plundered of it by bush-rangers.
1867 J. R. Houlding *Australian Capers* 380: Bush-rangers who stopped them, then rifled the coach and passengers' pockets, and read all the letters in the mail bags that were interesting to them.

1880 J. C. Crawford *Travels in New Zealand and Australia* 6: About this time I had occasion to go to Yass, and on my return was, as they say, 'stuck up' by two bush-rangers.
1899 G. E. Boxall *The Story of the Australian Bushrangers* [book title]
5 A business enterprise exploiting the public
1951 Dymphna Cusack *Say No to Death* 52: 'Bush-rangers, aren't they? Ned Kelly was a gentleman compared with most of the landlords around here.'
1954 *Coast to Coast 1953–54* 160: When she overheard Sam [a junk dealer] described as a bushranger she spun round aggressively ready to do battle for her husband's honour.

bushranging
1822 James Dixon *Narrative of a Voyage to New South Wales* 45: Men rendered desperate retreat to the woods; or as it is termed, go a bushranging, and rob to supply their wants, and often commit worse crimes.
1823 *Godwin's Emigrant's Guide to Van Diemen's Land* 52: The Sydney Gazette, of October 4, 1817, contains the above particulars; but since that period little has been heard of Bush-ranging.
1827 P. Cunningham *Two Years in New South Wales* i 194–5: Some [convicts] disgusted with restraint and steady labour, will occasionally take to the woods, and subsist by plundering the settlers around, with whose convict-servants they are frequently leagued. This method of robbery is denominated 'bush-ranging'; it has been a severe scourge in Van Dieman's Land.
1939 Kylie Tennant *Foveaux* 425: Bud Pellager ... had taken to a mild and lucrative form of bushranging as owner of a garage on the Main Western Highway.

bush shower   A shower, originally improvised e.g. from a kerosene tin hung in a tree, later manufactured on similar principles
[**1937** Ernestine Hill *The Great Australian Loneliness* 97: 'You'll have to get up at piccaninny daylight for your bath', I had been told further south. 'It's a shower in a tree.' But ... the shower had been fenced in with roofless tin walls, and only a white cockatoo in the tree above bent an inquiring eye.]
1984 *Sunday Independent* (Perth) 22 Apr. 6: There'll be a billy tea and pork and beans and a bushman's shower slung from a tree.

bush, Sydney or the   see **Sydney**

bush, take the   1   To abscond (of convicts); jocularly 'to decamp'
1827 P. Cunningham *Two Years in New South Wales* ii 190–1: Indeed without the aid of that magic care-killer, the pipe, I believe the greater

portion of our 'pressed men' would 'take the bush' in a week after their arrival.

1834 Charles O'Hara Booth *Journal* 2 Jun. ed. Dora Heard (1981) 177: Mathews & Williams took to the Bush.

1847 Alexander Harris *Settlers and Convicts* ed. C. M. H. Clark (1954) 187: This luckless hutkeeper of Mr —'s was flogged in the five months I lived near the station no less than three times ... and but for my persuasion he would certainly have taken the bush.

1897 Thomas Archer *Recollections of a Rambling Life* 100: I jumped out of one of the back windows and 'took the bush', hiding behind a big gum tree.

1907 Charles MacAlister *Old Pioneering Days in the Sunny South* 118: A Strathaird convict – one Joe Green – had 'taken to the bush', as it was called, and it was reported that he was prowling in the vicinity of the 'Irishmen's Station'.

2 To become a bushranger

1844 Louisa Meredith *Notes and Sketches of New South Wales* 59: They do frequently evade the vigilance of their guards, and, 'taking the bush', that is, running away into the forests, they often become formidable in their attacks on travellers in the lonely roads up the country ... Several parties of bushrangers were out at the time of our journey.

1859 John Lang *Botany Bay* 156: The career of these men, who took to the bush ... was a very remarkable one. There was not a road in the colony ... upon which they had not stopped and robbed travellers.

1875 Rolf Boldrewood *The Squatter's Dream* repr. as *Ups and Downs* (1878) 165: 'Well, they say taking to the bush is a short life and a merry one,' grumbled out Redcap.

1899 G. E. Boxall *The Story of the Australian Bushrangers* 252: Before 'he took to the bush' he was known as a steady, industrious, kind-hearted young man.

bush telegraph   1   An informant alerting bushrangers to the movements of the police

1878 *Australian* i 507: The police are baffled by the false reports of the confederates and the number and activity of the bush telegraphs. [Morris]

1882 A. J. Boyd *Old Colonials* 175: In Queensland we have no bushrangers. There are no convict shepherds – no bush telegraphs – none of the thousand and one conveniences for securing the safety of these gentry.

1899 G. E. Boxall *The Story of the Australian Bushrangers* 238: The Press ... continued to urge the necessity for suppressing the 'bush telegraphs' and other sympathisers of the bushrangers.

2   The passing of information (not illicit) by unofficial channels e.g. word of mouth; any message so received

1895 Henry Lawson 'Black Joe' *Prose* i 255: The nearest squatter's wife ... arranged (by bush telegraph) to drive over next morning with her sister-in-law and two other white women in the vicinity, to see Mary decently buried.

1961 Patrick White *Riders in the Chariot* 381: She had acquired a numerous clientele, through her dealings in bottles, as well as by bush telegraph.

1981 *Sydney Morning Herald* 7 Aug. 16: Those seeking snapper off Broken Bay found them on the south marks. Those who were not linked to the bush telegraph went north and bombed out.

bush trifle   See quot. 1951

1951 Ernestine Hill *The Territory* 426: Dessert was 'bush trifle' – johnnie cakes, jam and condensed milk.

bush tucker   Food obtained from the bush environment, as distinct from rations or European food [**1827** P. Cunningham *Two Years in New South Wales* ii 158: Your muskets will furnish you with birds of various kinds; – and with a brace of good grayhounds you will never lack kangaroos and emus; so that your *bush*-fare is a true sportsman's feast.]

1935 Mary and Elizabeth Durack *All-About* 90: They come up to the homestead for their stock of supplies – beef, tea, sugar and flour. They can kill what 'bush tucker' they come upon, but this is a holiday and they need not go out of their way to hunt.

1962 Jock Marshall and Russell Drysdale *Journey Among Men* 169: The great majority have come to regard the eating of 'roo or other bush tucker as putting oneself on the subsistence level of tribal aborigines.

1978 H. C. Coombs *Kulinma* 228: Some communities found that their only cash income was that derived from old-age pensions and child endowment. Where the environment continued to provide generous supplies of 'bush tucker' this was sometimes enough to provide bare subsistence.

1982 *Sydney Morning Herald* 17 Jul. 1: 'Much of our food is bush tucker which we catch ourselves. Melville Bay ... is rich with barramundi and other fish, turtles and crabs. The bush behind has kangaroos and yams.'

bush week   1   In the expression 'What do you think this is, bush week?' as a protest or complaint: sometimes drawing the juvenile retort, 'Yes, and you're the sap'.

1945 Baker 76: The time honoured chant of derision, *What's this, bush week?*

1949 Lawson Glassop *Lucky Palmer* 37: 'I get smart alecks like you trying to put one over on me every minute of the day. What do you think this

is? Bush Week?'
1951 Seaforth MacKenzie *Dead Men Rising* 53: 'Fall in! Snap into it you lot of old women. Pull your fingers out, now! What do you think this is – bush week?'
1958 Tom Ronan *The Pearling Master* 309: 'What's the strong of pulling up in the middle of a block? What do you think this is? Bush week?'
1966 H. F. Brinsmead *Beat of the City* 26: 'You can just nail it back on again proper. What do you think this is, bush week?'
1975 Les Ryan *The Shearers* 74: 'What do you think this is – bush week?'
2   Name given to organized celebrations, esp. end-of-term student festivities at the Australian National University, Canberra.
1980 *Mercury* (Hobart) 4 Jan. 6: The Deddington Carnival to be held this weekend will turn into Bush Week if the organisers have their way. Part of the Tasmanian Fiesta celebrations, the carnival on Saturday may become a full week of bush activities. A major part of the carnival is the chopping events.
1981 *Canberra Times* 14 Aug. 8: Mr Dobson recalled that in past Bush Weeks a magistrate had been worth 100 points in the scavenger hunt.

bushwhacker   A backwoodsman; someone lacking in social graces or in acumen
1900 Henry Lawson 'Joe Wilson's Courtship' *Prose* i 544: He said I'd spoilt the thing altogether. He said that she'd got an idea that I was shy and poetic, and I'd only shown myself the usually sort of Bush-whacker.
1900–10 O'Brien and Stephens: *Bushwhackers* applied to uncouth, rawboned or unmannerly country people.
1903 Nat Gould *The Three Wagers* 271: 'You'll find it a trifle different riding against us . . . we are not a lot of bushwhackers down here, let me tell you.'
1915 Diary entry 11 Jun. cit. Bill Gammage *The Broken Years* (1974) 98: There are a lot of bush-whackers, copper-gougers etc. from the Cloncurry district . . . and I believe they are the finest of all soldiers, fearing nothing and as full of dash and endurance as man ever was.
1930 L. W. Lower *Here's Luck* 159: 'I wasn't goin' to have these city blokes pickin' me for a bush-whacker so I filled in a coupon for a complete rig-out from Sydney.'
1938 Xavier Herbert *Capricornia* 384: 'You've been readin' newspapers, which from start to finish are only fit for the purpose we bush-whackers use 'em for when we've read 'em.'
1951 Dymphna Cusack *Say No to Death* 170: He wasn't such a bushwhacker that he didn't know quality when he saw it.
1959 Gerard Hamilton *Summer Glare* 68: She was only sixteen, a real bushwhacker, short, buxom and stupid, with little or no education.
1967 K. S. Prichard *Subtle Flame* 38: 'Now, if you'd only grown a beard, you'd look a regular bushwhacker.'
1971 Rena Briand *White Man in a Hole* 17: 'It's the smallest dugout in Coober,' he said, 'but good enough for an old bushwhacker like me.'

bushwhacking   Living in the rough conditions of the bush
1935 H. H. Finlayson *The Red Centre* 24: To Giles the Englishman – after weeks of bush-whacking in the mulga farther north – these views appealed with special force.

bush work   See quot. 1882
1882 Rolf Boldrewood *Robbery Under Arms* (World's Classics 1949) 102: Fencing, dam-making, horse-breaking, stock-riding, from making hay to building a shed, all bushwork came easy enough to us.
1936 A. B. Paterson 'The Shearer's Colt' in *Song of the Pen* (1983) 678: 'I'm a bushman, I can do any sort of bush work.'
1940 Ion L. Idriess *Lightning Ridge* 73: 'Used to bush work?' 'Yes. Fencing, breaking-in, ringbark-ing, mustering, burr-cutting, crutching.'
bush worker
1911 E. S. Sorenson *Life in the Australian Back-blocks* 249: There are plenty of good classers among bush workers, who . . . take any other work offering between shearing, including boundary-riding, tank-sinking, and fencing.
1940 Ion L. Idriess *Lightning Ridge* 62: Bush workers often make a country town their base. They 'get known'.
1958 Russel Ward *The Australian Legend* 89: This deprivation of female companionship had very important effects on the behaviour and out-look of bush-workers.
1983 Arthur Cannon *Bullocks, Bullockies and Other Blokes* 174: He was a bush worker – one who could turn his hand to many jobs.

bushy, bushie (bush-head)   An uncomplicated bush-dweller, as distinct from a townsman
1887 *Tibb's Popular Song Book* 1: 'Bushy in Town'. Have you noticed in the city, / With the Sydney going push, / How they often stare and giggle, / At us chaps from down the Bush?
1900 Henry Lawson 'A Gentleman Sharper and Steelman Sharper' *Prose* i 226: 'We're two hard-working, innocent bushies, down for an innocent spree.'
c. **1914** A. B. Paterson 'Racehorses and Racing in Australia' in *The World of 'Banjo' Paterson* ed. C. Semmler (1967) 318: He saw a genuine bushman, bearded, cabbage-tree-hatted, sunburnt, and

silent. Bearing down on the old bushie he told him the old tale.

1949 John Morrison *The Creeping City* 241: 'I'm only a bush-head. I'm not supposed to have the intelligence to put two and two together.'
1955 Mary Durack *Keep Him My Country* 114: He never tried to swear the hardened bushies off the drink.
1973 Max Harris *The Angry Eye* 70: Warm-hearted, open-minded bushies are thin on the ground.
1980 *Sun-Herald* 1 Jun. 61: 4 Winners to 'Bushie' [heading] Former South Coast trainer, Paul Sutherland, yesterday won four races at Randwick in a feat seldom achieved by trainers much longer established in Sydney racing.

buster   See **southerly buster**
1911 Louis Stone *Jonah* 80: The air was still hot and breathless, but little gusts of wind began to rise, the first signs of a coming 'buster'.

busy as a one-armed bill-poster (milker)   see **one-armed**

but   Used with the force of 'however' or 'though' at the end of a sentence
1938 Eric Lowe *Salute to Freedom* 157: She had so few words to express her feelings. 'I love you – won't you kiss me, but!'
1957 Gerard Hamilton *Summer Glare* 112: 'Gee, they're lucky but, ain't they?'
1962 Stuart Gore *Down the Golden Mile* 218: 'I always seem to miss th' bastards ... I've given a couple of 'em a bloody good fright but.'
1969 Thomas Jenkins *They Came to Australia* 243: Adam has come back from a spin on his bicycle, saying: 'It's hot, but.'
1972 Turner 95: We congratulated him on the Sydney climate. He agreed it was good, then added 'We've got central heating, but.'
1977 Mary Gage *The New Life* 25: 'Two nuns took us. I'm not a Catholic or anything like that but.'

butcher   A measure of beer [see quot. 1898]
1898 Morris: *Butcher* n. South Australian slang for a long drink of beer, so-called (it is said) because the men of a certain butchery in Adelaide used this refreshment regularly.
1945 Baker 168: *Butcher* is Adelaide slang; in the early days it was used for a glass containing about two-thirds of a pint. In modern times the size has dropped to about half a pint.
1958 A. W. Upfield *The Bachelors of Broken Hill* 130: He ought to be in this pleasant saloon bar reading a paper and enjoying the best cigarettes with long 'butchers' of beer.
1971 Rena Briand *White Man in a Hole* 108: Johnny grinned and ordered three butchers.

1979 *Advertiser* (Adelaide) 6 Apr. 3: The Acting Prices Commissioner, Mr D. G. Selth, said yesterday the price of 170-millilitre (butcher) and 425-millilitre (pint) glasses and 370-millilitre Echo bottles would increase by 1c.
1980 *Sydney Morning Herald* 23 Feb. 12: Over a succession of 'butchers' – the traditional South Australian beer glass, small and quickly quaffed – he misses nothing.

butcher's, butcher's hook   Crook, in the senses 'angry' (go crook) or 'ill, out of sorts' [rhyming slang]
1918 *Kia Ora Coo-ee* 15 Aug. 5: A certain New Zealand Regiment, camped on the Jordan flats, recently came under the eagle eye of brother 'Jacko', who immediately went 'butcher's hook' or 'ram's horn'.
1941 Baker 16: *Butcher's, to be*: To be angry, annoyed (*about* something). Often 'go butcher's at' (i.e. 'go butcher's hook' or 'crook')
1951 Dal Stivens *Jimmy Brockett* 126: As soon as Sadie came in I went butcher's hook. 'What's this bloody nonsense about a studio, Sadie?' I said.
1980 *Sun-Herald* 2 Nov. 92: Those feeling a bit butcher's are advised to avoid this black comedy.
1981 Barry Humphries *A Nice Night's Entertainment* 186: Still feeling butcher's after your op, are ya?

buttinski   An inquisitive or interfering person: *obs.* [U.S. 1903 Mathews]
1924 *Truth* 27 Apr. 6: *Buttinski* An intruding person.
1926 J. Vance Marshall *Timely Tips for New Australians*: *Buttinski* A slang word frequently used to describe an inquisitive person.
1947 H. Drake-Brockman *The Fatal Days* 120: 'What you wanter speak t' young Ed for? You're a butinski.'
1966 Baker 222: *buttinski* a term used among telephone mechanics for the hand telephone used for cutting in on private phone calls.

buy into, to   To involve oneself, esp. in trouble or conflict
1951 Ernestine Hill *The Territory* 438: 'Can't you buy in on the conversation over there, Jack?'
1956 *Australian Signpost* ed. T. A. G. Hungerford 185: 'I don't think it woulda come to much if the mug Pongo hadn't bought in.' 'Private Smith', I told the major, 'thinks the situation was aggravated by the interference of an English soldier.'
1962 Alan Seymour *The One Day of the Year* 56: 'You fight your own battles. I'm not buyin' into any arguments. I get enough of 'em around here.'
1977 Kenneth Cook *The Man Underground* 122: 'As soon as we open the campaign we have Charlie on the air every day, buying in on everything that's

going on.'

buzznacking Moving about, esp. in an officious way [? f. *busk*, to cruise about, tack about OED 1665: nautical and dial.]
1865 Henry Kingsley *The Hillyars and the Burtons* 175: 'And I'll have it done, too, and not be kep' busnacking here in the rain.'
1903 Joseph Furphy *Such is Life* (1944) 353: 'Magomery, he's buzznackin' roun' the run as usual.'
1907 Barbara Baynton *Human Toll* 152: 'You a-bein' sich a sheep-dog a-busnackin', an' a-blatherin', an' a-barkin' roun' urdles day an' night.'

B Y O (G) Bring your own (grog): 1 Legend on informal invitations to a party, notice in restaurants without a liquor licence
1975 *National Times* 23 Jun. 5: B.Y.O. diplomat. The Australian Government last week paid for itself to be a 'guest' at a cocktail party given by the Japan-Australia Society . . . in Tokyo.

1982 *Townsville Daily Bulletin* 26 Mar. 4: The walk will begin at 10.30 a.m. from the Ranger's house. A midday BYO barbecue will follow.
2 Container for carrying liquor
1980 *Sun-Herald* 24 Feb. 29: The insulated B.Y.O. holds two bottles or four large drink cans. Looks smart and has a removable wine chiller, too. $12.99.
3 Type of restaurant
1981 *Sun-Herald* 24 May 132: Vive le BYO – it's a great way to dine.
4 Applied to things other than liquor
1980 *Weekend Australian* 16 Aug. 13: It is the problem of BYO toilet paper, to be brought in by some members to beat a ban imposed on the [S.A.] Parliament by the Australian Government Workers' Association.
1982 *Weekend Australian* 8 May 19: The coroner . . . censured the police for arming themselves with home-made or, as one lawyer sardonically described them, BYO weapons . . . It was commonplace for weapons, such as cut-down shovel handles to be available for use by police.

cab, first ~ off the rank   The first to take advantage of an opportunity

1977 *Australian* 19 Jul. 10: It is unlikely the Ranger partners will agree to new terms without concessions, such as being first cab off the rank if, as expected, the Government agrees to limited mining.

1979 *Australian* 29 Jun. 10: Telecom Australia will probably be first cab off the rank in testing the semi government loan market in the new 1978–79 financial year.

1982 *Sun-Herald* 15 Aug. 122: First cab off the rank this week was a luncheon fashion parade in Sydney Uni's Great Hall.

Cabbage Garden (Patch)   The colony or state of Victoria: *jocular* [f. size and crops]

1889 J. H. Zillman *Australian Life* 30: 'The cabbage garden', old cynical Sir John Robertson, of New South Wales, once called Victoria. [Morris]

1903 Joseph Furphy *Such is Life* (1944) 43: 'You are a native of the colonies, I presume?' 'Yes, I come from the Cabbage Garden.' Ibid. 124: I slid gently into the water, and paddled for the Cabbage Garden shore.

1916 Macmillan's *Modern Dictionary of the English Language* 776: *Cabbage Garden* the State of Victoria, in allusion to its small size, and also to its exportation of vegetables to Sydney.

1934 Thomas Wood *Cobbers* 144: People in other States call Victoria, rudely, the Cabbage Patch, and make a show of looking for it on the map with a magnifying glass. Victorians smile a stiff smile.

1939 R. H. Croll *I Recall* 153: The old New South Wales joke that Victoria was merely a 'cabbage garden'.

1970 *Australian* 31 Oct. 3: 'Cabbage patch history' was the way a leading historian yesterday described the Victorian Government's bicentenary awards – now the centre of a growing literary row.

cabbage-gardeners

1908 Henry Lawson 'His Coloured Country' *Prose* i 786: 'You can blanky well secesh and go in with the blanky Cabbage-gardeners.'

cabbage-tree mob   Precursors of the larrikin q.v. [f. *cabbage-tree hat*]

1852 G. C. Mundy *Our Antipodes* i 53–4: There are to be found round the doors of the Sydney theatre a sort of 'loafers', known as the Cabbage-tree mob ... These are an unruly set of young fellows, native born generally ... Dressed in a suit of fustian or colonial tweed, and the emblem of their order, the low-crowned cabbage-palm hat, the main object of their enmity seems to be the ordinary black headpiece worn by respectable persons, which is ruthlessly knocked over the eyes of the wearer as he passes or enters the theatre.

1894 James T. Ryan *Reminiscences* 223: Ned Sadler, bootmaker, of Sydney, was a wonder; he was a great politician, and belonged to the 'Cabbage Tree Mob', as they were then called.

1907 Charles MacAlister *Old Pioneering Days* 178: He earned the enmity of the 'Cabbage-tree Hat' mob on account of the part he took in securing the conviction of the Myall Creek (Aborigines) massacre in 1838.

cacker An undersized mudcrab (W.A.): phonetically the same as *kaka*, a young girl
1983 *Sunday Independent* (Perth) 21 Aug. 47: Cacker-catchers ... are generally recognisable by the size of their buckets, and their habit of indiscriminately slaughtering as many undersized fish and crustaceans as they can.

cactus, back to the To return to one's familiar haunts, usually away from the city: catch-phrase of the comedian 'Mo' (Roy Rene) in the McCackie Mansions series of the 1940s
1945 *Coast to Coast 1944* 174: He got in the car and started the engine. 'Well, it's back to the cactus,' he said.
1945 Roy Rene *Mo's Memoirs* 120: Mo is very nostalgic and dying for the end of his honeymoon: 'Oh to get back to the cactus. Just dying to get a saw in me hand.'
1980 *Sydney Morning Herald* 31 Dec. 7: We are today back to the cactus as our Antipodean friends would say.

Cairns, the battle of The forcible ejection of unemployed campers from the Parramatta Park showground, Cairns, on 17 July 1932

calabash A promissory note issued by bush-storekeepers and others: see quots. The name suggests that the calabash had the same brittleness as the 'shin plaster' q.v., as though inscribed on the shell of a gourd.
1917 R. D. Barton *Reminiscences of an Australian Pioneer* 159: Everyone was paid by orders, 'calabashes' we used to call them, drawn on himself by the person paying.
1938 *Smith's Weekly* 12 Nov. 6: Mention of 'shin-plasters' recently in 'Smith's Weekly' suggests a mention of 'Calabash'. This was a form of currency in the early days, and was originally an order for a small amount, drawn upon some agent of the drawer and payable at various dates after presentation. Finally a calabash became an IOU for sums under one pound.

call To broadcast a race description
1949 Lawson Glassop *Lucky Palmer* 247: 'There's no better race caller in Australia than "Lucky Palmer". When he was only fourteen he used to call the races from the verandah of a house.'
1977 *Sun-Herald* 9 Jan. 67: He's calling the dogs on 2UE on Fridays from Richmond and on Saturdays from Wentworth Park.

1979 *Sun-Herald* 24 Jun. 70: Sport? Cyril [Angles] called it all – the horses, dogs, trotters, boxing, wrestling, foot running, cycle racing. You name it and somewhere along the way Angles 'called' it.
caller
1980 Murray Bail *Homesickness* 78: They laughed at the leisurely race-callers. One would hardly know there was a race on.

Callan Park A psychiatric hospital in Sydney; used figuratively to represent any such institution
1904 Henry Fletcher *Dads Wayback: His Work* 35: 'No one out o' Callan Park, or who ought ter be there, ever does take it that way.'
1959 Dorothy Hewett *Bobbin Up* 163: 'Life's hard enough for everyone without puttin' up with a mad kid inter the bargain ... You feel as if you're orf to Callan Park yourself.'
1982 *Sydney Morning Herald* 10 Apr. 23: 'Why I'm not in Callan Park I'll never know.'

camp 1 To rest, lie down
1847 Alexander Harris *Settlers and Convicts* ed. C. M. H. Clark (1954) 130: A flock of sheep 'camping', as the shepherds call it, under the shade of a tree from the noontide heat.
1887 *All the Year Round* 30 Jul. 66: 'To go to camp', by a transference from its original meaning, now signifies, in the mouth of a dweller in houses, simply 'to lie down', 'to go to bed'.
1980 *Weekend Australian* 23 Aug. Mag. 1: Close to the road a small herd of prize-winning short-horns are 'camping' in the early morning sun under a tree.
have a camp
1899 Steele Rudd *On Our Selection* 127: Sometimes Dan used to forget to talk at all – he would be asleep – and Dad would wonder if he was unwell. Once he advised him to go up to the house and have a good camp.
1961 Noni Braham *The Interloper* 85: He took out the tarpaulin. 'You have a camp while I boil the billy.' Margaret stretched out gratefully.
1979 Bill Scott *Tough in the Old Days* 39: He stretched luxuriously on the grass as the sun warmed his bones. 'Think I'll have a camp', he said.
2 To die
1898 Henry Lawson 'Dust Thou Art' *Prose* i 325: 'I can imagine ... the chaps rubbing their hats off, and standing round looking as if it was their funeral instead of mine, and one of 'em saying, maybe, "Ah well, poor Jack, he's camped down at last!"'
1898 *Bulletin* 1 Oct. 14: When he's buried he has 'pitched his camp'.

Camp, (the) The original settlement at Sydney

Cove, or Hobart: *obs*.

1790 Daniel Southwell *let.* 20 Aug. *HRNSW* ii 724: He [Governor Phillip] treats us with more affability, and is all at once so polite as to beg of my only companion, Mr Harris, and self, whenever we come to camp, to let him have our co[mpany].

1827 P. Cunningham *Two Years in New South Wales* ii 70: It is the old resident – he who still calls Sydney with its population of twelve thousand bustling inhabitants *the camp* – that can appreciate these things: he who still recollects the few earth-huts and solitary tents scattered through the forest brush surrounding Sydney Cove (known properly then indeed by the name of 'The Camp').

1843 Charles Rowcroft *Tales of the Colonies* i 27: I met nothing between *camp*, as Hobart Town was then called, and New Town. Ibid. 172: A flour mill, which was much wanted, as there was no mill nearer than Camp, fifty miles off.

Campbell, Lady An alternative name for Paterson's Curse, q.v.

1983 *Weekend Australian* 25 Jun. 10: A certain Lady Campbell, during the construction of the Great Southern Railway through Western Australia in 1889 also helped by introducing it [*Echium plantagineum*] as a garden flower at her home not far from Broomehill. It then followed the construction of the line.

canary 1 A convict; his yellow clothing [f. *canary bird* a jailbird, or person kept in a cage OED 1673]

1827 P. Cunningham *Two Years in New South Wales* ii 117: Convicts of but recent migration are facetiously known by the name of *canaries*, by reason of the yellow plumage in which they are fledged at the period of landing.

1840 J. Pitts Johnson *Plain Truths* 56: Prisoners ... are commonly denominated 'the canary birds', so called from their dresses being yellow.

1843 Charles Rowcroft *Tales of the Colonies* ii 218: 'Your description of their dress,' said Mr Marsh, 'accounts for a jeering expression I have heard, and could not understand ... my bullock-driver called out to him [the prisoner] 'Going to be caged, my canary-bird?'

1870 Marcus Clarke *His Natural Life* ed. S. Murray-Smith (1970) 548: We can't bring him off ... in his canaries. He puts on these duds, d'ye see.'

1876 Rolf Boldrewood *A Colonial Reformer* (1891) 49: 'I goes up to the corporal, "I say, mate", says I, "can't you get your canaries off the track here for about a quarter of an hour, and let my mob of cattle pass?"'

2 A gold coin [f. *canary bird* guineas Grose 1785]

1853 Mrs C. Clacy *A Lady's Visit to the Gold Diggings of Australia in 1852–53* 91: For the sake of the uninitiated, I must explain that, in diggers' slang, a 'canary' and a half-sovereign are synonymous.

1895 Cornelius Crowe *The Australian Slang Dictionary* 14: *Canary Bird* a convict; a gold coin.

3 One hundred lashes

1859 John Lang *Botany Bay* 40: There were slang terms applied to these doses of the lash: twenty-five was called a 'tester'; fifty, a 'bob'; seventy-five, a 'bull'; and a hundred, a 'canary'.

canary, couldn't knock the dags off a sick see **couldn't**

captain See quots

1972 John de Hoog *Skid Row Dossier* 125: Stiffs have ... 'captains' (leaders of bottle parties).

1974 John Powers *The Last of the Knucklemen* 63: 'I'll be the captain for a round of beers'.

1977 Jim Ramsay *Cop It Sweet* 20: *Captain*: Person buying all the drinks.

1978 Kevin Gilbert *Living Black* 302: 'Have you seen 'em bludging up to a captain* who's just come onto the mission with money in his pocket?' *The reserve people's name for a white man who visits them to trade money or grog for sex.

carby The carburettor [abbr.]

1957 Nino Culotta *They're a Weird Mob* 47: 'Carburettor, matey,' said Joe. 'We'll start on the carby.'

1963 Gunther Bahnemann *Hoodlum* 187: 'Wait a minute, that carby's been flooding. It's dripping like a watering-can.'

1973 H. Williams *My Love Had a Black Speed Stripe* 71: 'He's been pumping the accelerator ... Flooding the carby.'

cardie A cardigan [abbr.]

1974 Patrick White *The Cockatoos* 169: She had torn her winter cardy on a nail.

1984 *Sydney Morning Herald* 26 May 42: The receptionist is a genteel North Shore matron of a certain age in spectacles and lemon hand knit cardie.

Cardinals The West Perth (W.A.) Australian Rules team [f. ecclesiastical red in the team colours]

1978 *Australian* 29 May 15: Cardinals favored to wear the mitre [heading]

1980 *Daily News* (Perth) 14 Jul. 26: East Perth coach Grant Dorrington denied the Royals took the field against West Perth with the intention of bashing the Cardinals off their game.

cark (it), to To break down, die [? f. *croak*, or the 'cark' of the crow]

1982 Nancy Keesing *Lily on the Dustbin* 50: A

'stiff dunny' is dead or, in other words 'has carked it'.

1983 Mike Carlton *Sydney Morning Herald* 4 May 8: If there was a bum camera shot or lighting effect that carked, it surely escaped me.

1984 Leo Schofield *Sydney Morning Herald* 17 Mar. 37: Meanwhile over in London they're flogging off the last of the D'Oyly Carte company's costumes. The tradition that we thought would die hard has carked completely.

see **kark**

carn Phonetic representation of 'Come on', esp. of an Australian Rules supporter ('Harry Carna' was the hero of a comic strip on Australian Rules by Peter Russell-Clarke which ran in the Melbourne *Herald and Weekly Times* from 25 March 1972)

1968 Bruce Dawe 'Life Cycle' *An Eye for a Tooth* 42: When children are born in Victoria / they are wrapped in the club-colours, laid in beribboned cots, / having already begun a lifetime's barracking. / Carn, they cry, Carn ... feebly at first.

1981 Ian Turner and Leonie Sandercock *Up Where, Cazaly?* 5: A deep-throated roar comes from the crowd: 'Carn the Tigers ... Carn the Blues'. The umpire blows his whistle, bounces the ball, and the game is on. At this moment, Melbourne comes to life.

1984 *Age* (Melbourne) 23 Mar. Weekender 11: Pick your spot and enjoy the passing parade, and the game. Carna Mighties!

carrion A term applied to bullocks, horses, most often collectively: *derogatory* [f. *carrion* poor, wretched or worthless beast OED 1634 *Obs*.]

1835 *Colonist* 22 Jan. 28: Passing the hut of a poor settler ... he heard the man's wife addressing an old scarecrow of a mare in some such terms as the following:– 'Bad luck to you, you old rottern carrion!'

1901 Henry Lawson 'The Little World Left Behind' *Prose* i 376: The same sunburned, masculine women went past to market twice a week in the same old carts and driving much the same quality of carrion.

1903 Joseph Furphy *Such is Life* (1944) 7: 'Where did you stop las' night? Your carrion's as full as ticks.' Ibid. 15: 'Now, chaps, round up yer carrion, an' shove 'em in.'

Carruthers, Go for your life, Lady A catch-phrase from the 'Gay Paree' sketch by Roy Rene ('Mo'); stock name for member of the English aristocracy

1970 Cynthia Nolan *A Bride for St Thomas* 29: I considered murmuring in her ear, 'Go for your life, Lady Carruthers, your days are numbered.'

1972 Alexander Macdonald *The Ukelele Player under the Red Lamp* 239: Mo asked Lady Carruthers how she herself was enjoying her stay in Gay

Paree. To which she replied, coyly. 'I've got something to confess, Mr McCackie – I've been here for a fortnight and I haven't once visited the Louvre.' ... Her next line was an exit-throwaway. 'But now I must go, I must go!' To which one night, with an expression of obscene sympathy, Mo added – 'Oh yes, go! Go! Go for your life, Lady Carruthers!'

caser Five shillings: *obs*. [f. Yiddish *kesef* silver: also English and U.S.]

1849 Alexander Harris *The Emigrant Family* (1967) 104: 'A caser (a dollar) if you give him a night of it; and four if he gets what'll make him quiet.'

1901 Henry Lawson 'Send Round the Hat' *Prose* i 471: He rolled the drunkard over, prospected his pockets till he made up five shillings (or a 'caser' in Bush language), and 'chucked' them into the hat.

1924 *Truth* 27 Apr. 6: *Caser* Five shillings.

1950 *Australian Police Journal* Apr. 112: *Caser* 5s.

cashed up Well supplied with money

1930 L. W. Lower *Here's Luck* 163: 'Straight from the Never-Never by the look of him. Is he cashed up?'

1959 D'Arcy Niland *The Big Smoke* 200: 'One of these days when I'm real cashed up like, I'm gonna get myself one of them trombones. They're great.'

1973 John Morrison *Australian by Choice* 127: I ... came back to Melbourne well cashed up, and for a few leisurely weeks lived well.

Casket, the The Golden Casket, the Queensland State Lottery

1934 Thomas Wood *Cobbers* 135: A was for Australia, B for Bradman, C for the Casket.[1] [1]The Golden Casket. A State lottery started by the Queensland Government; supported now nearly all over the Commonwealth.

1957 Vance Palmer *Seedtime* 117. 'Think I've been winning money in the Casket and have had one too many on the strength of it? No such luck.'

1962 David Forrest *The Hollow Woodheap* 8: 'Murder!' screamed the newsboy, 'Casket.'

1979 *Courier-Mail* (Brisbane) 2 Mar. 4: Don't you think it is time we returned the Casket money to the hospitals?

1981 *Sunday Mail* (Brisbane) 17 May 2: I've spent the last few days thanking my lucky stars. No, nothing like a Casket win. I drove through a radar trap without being pulled up.

Cassa A Casanova [abbr.]

1943 Baker 18: *Casa* A masher (R.A.N. slang)

1957 Ray Lawler *Summer of the Seventeenth Doll* 55: 'To listen to her you'd reckon I was the biggest Cassa in the North. It ain't as bad as that.'

1982 *National Times* 16 May 22: 'Every guy here is a real Cass'(anova), Camille, 23, a travel consultant warned me. 'They're right up themselves. Especially the first officers and pilots.'

cast, make a To make a sweep from a given point to pick up lost tracks; also used (mainly N.Z.) of a dog, so trained to muster sheep
1876 Rolf Boldrewood *A Colonial Reformer* (1890) 205: I wasted no time in the camp but made a cast around, to pick up the tracks of the fugitive. Mayboy, eager as a bloodhound, was soon on the trail.

castor A hat: *obs.* [f. *castor* a hat of beaver or rabbit fur OED 1640–1849; *castor* a hat Grose 1785]
1812 Vaux: *Castor* a hat.
1899 W. T. Goodge *Hits! Skits! and Jingles!* 151: When a 'castor' or a 'kady' / Is the name he gives his hat.

castor, on the castor Similar to 'jake', 'sweet': *rare* [? f. *castor sugar* hence 'sweet']
1945 Baker 156: *castor* Good, excellent. [as World War II slang]
1950 *Australian Police Journal* Apr. 111: *Castor* O.K.
1963 John Cantwell *No Stranger to the Flame* 103: 'How is he today?' 'Castor, now you've arrived,' Max said easily.
1967 Kylie Tennant *Tell Morning This* 283: 'Why am I on the castor with them?' 'Oh that.' Harold's face cleared. 'Soon's they knew you was in with Numismata, they all want to piss in your pocket.' Ibid. 438. 'We've got an eighteen foot stick,' Harold bragged ... 'She's castor.'
1980 Maj. Peter D. Rothwell *Sydney Morning Herald* 3 Jan. 6: In the action where 'Simmo' [Warrant Officer Ray Simpson] won his Victoria Cross [in Vietnam, May 1969], when the situation appeared hopeless, Ray crawled over to me amid the intense enemy fire, and said 'Don't worry, skipper, she will be castor', and it was.

cat 1 A beast without spirit, esp. a racehorse who lets the punters down
1877 Rolf Boldrewood *A Colonial Reformer* (1891) 386: 'They're not a very gay lot to look at now. But I shouldn't wonder to see you knocking ten pounds a head out of some of those cats of steers before this day two years.'
1982 *Sun-Herald* 14 Nov. 86: 'He went into the line sideways, so I told someone after the race that I thought Bernborough was "cat".'
1984 *Sun* (Sydney) 23 Mar. 91: 'Considering punters take 9/4 for some 'cats' at Warwick Farm midweeks, I think this is a great price for a horse like Bounty Hawk in the Canterbury Guineas', Beirne declared.
2 In sport, a player who cannot stand up to

punishment; any weak person
1978 *Sun-Herald* 1 Jul. 70: 'He's a cat. Bloody big cat. Can't cop it and the other forwards know it. They'll give him plenty' ... If you want to really condemn the player, call him 'a cat', the term in this game [Rugby League] which means coward.
1984 *Sydney Morning Herald* 15 May 2: 'It is very difficult to prove a rape in prison ... If you allow it to happen in jail you are identified as a cat – the weak person – and you become the subject of that sort of thing all the time. You're considered fair game.'
3 In prison slang, a homosexual
1958 Frank Hardy *The Four-legged Lottery* 117: Each cat [in prison] has her female name: Amber, Maude, Rosie ... Each has her favourite boy friends, who compete for her favours. They colour their hair with peroxide stolen from the hospital ... They borrow books from the library and use the red colour off the covers for rouge and lipstick.
1967 Brian K. Burton *Teach Them No More* 49: Terry was amazed to find that his friend was a homosexual, a cat.
1974 Robert Adamson and Bruce Hanford *Zimmer's Essay* 31: The big losers in the prison politik are the 'cats', who will not accept feminine status, but who are weak and so are raped, or coerced into cock-sucking. They do not receive the chivalry accorded queens.

Cats, the The Geelong V.F.L. team
1976 *Sunday Telegraph* (Sydney) 11 Apr. 74: Olsson has Cats on rampage.

cat, whip (flog) the To give way to feelings of chagrin, frustration, regret; to reproach oneself [OED records *whip (jerk, shoot) the cat* to vomit 1609–1830. This expression seems closer to 'kicking the dog' as a way of venting spleen.]
1847 Alexander Harris *Settlers and Convicts* ed. C. M. H. Clark (1954) 193: And now it was my turn to 'whip the cat'.
1878 G. H. Gibson *Southerly Busters* 68: Though William by the 'cat' was whipped, / He never 'whipped the cat'.* *To 'whip the cat' signifies, in native parlance, to weep or lament.
1901 Henry Lawson 'A Double Buggy at Lahey's Creek' *Prose* i 595: I 'whipped the cat' a bit, the first twenty miles or so, but then I thought, what did it matter?
1903 Joseph Furphy *Such is Life* (1944) 7: 'Evil-natured beggar, that,' he continued. 'He's floggin' the cat now, 'cos he laid us on to the selection in spite of his self.' Ibid. 20: 'Gosh, you had that bloke to rights. He's whippin' the cat now like fury.'
1919 W. H. Downing *Digger Dialects* 53: *Whip the cat* Experience chagrin.
1932 K. S. Prichard *Kiss on the Lips* 184: 'I been whippin' the cat, thinkin' I'd missed seein' the

mare do her gallop.'
1944 Alan Marshall *These Are My People* 137: 'I whipped the bloody cat all the way in the bus.'
1951 Dal Stivens *Jimmy Brockett* 255: Then I started whipping the cat for not having thought of it before.

catch and kill one's own   To rely on one's own resources in dealing with problems, without appealing to outside authority: a motto given prominence by the Federated Ship Painters and Dockers Union (see quot. 1975)
1973 Jim McNeil *The Old Familiar Juice* 69: 'It's all a caser catch 'n kill yer own in their joint . . . or else yer can attach yerself, like, ter someone who'll do all the battlin' and bring home the goodies ter yer.'
1975 T. B. Gordon, Federal secretary of the Federated Ship Painters and Dockers Union, in Transcript of the Royal Commission into Alleged Payments to Maritime Unions, 17 Feb. 2642–3, cit. in Royal Commission on the Activities of the Federated Ship Painters and Dockers Union *Discussion Paper: Media Bias and the Victorian Branch* (1982) 105: 'Mr St John': What about the thefts and fires, have there been any charges made in respect of those offences? —— No, we catch and kill our own. 'Is that a serious remark, Mr Gordon? —— Well, we look after our own end of the business always. We do not get much assistance from the authorities. They have not been able to track a herd of elephants through a field of snow up to date.

caught in a circular saw   see **circular saw**

Cazaly, up there   A cry of encouragement or congratulation, commemorating the V.F.L. player Roy Cazaly (1893–1963) noted for his high-marking
1943 Baker 85: *Up there, Cazaly!* Used as a cry of encouragement. (Cazaly was a noted South Melbourne footballer, whose specialty was high marking.)
1955 John Morrison *Black Cargo* 231: 'Up there, Cazaly!'
1957 Ray Lawler *Summer of the Seventeenth Doll* 30: 'Up there Cazaly, lots of love – Nance.'
1965 *Daily Telegraph* (Sydney) 18 Feb. 42: The other states and the Northern Territory play football – 'Up there, Cazaly'.
1969 A. H. Chisholm *The Joy of the Earth* 179: Roy Cazaly, whose high leaps promoted the Australian battle-cry 'Up there, Cazaly!' was in the same class as the players mentioned.
1973 Frank Huelin *Keep Moving* 97: The audience roared approval. Someone, evidently an ardent football fan from Melbourne, yelled 'Up there, Cazaly'.
1979 *Sun* (Sydney) 27 Jul. 57: Melbourne has

found a bestseller to match Come On Aussie, Come on. It's called Up There Cazaly, a song to promote VFL football. It sold 30,000 in one week.

cement, bushman's   see **bushman's**

Centre, the   Central Australia, sometimes the Red Centre
1901 F. J. Gillen *Diary* (1968) 149: She has a somewhat pleasant face of a type not common amongst the natives of the Centre.
1936 W. Hatfield *Australia through the Windscreen* 119: Throughout the whole of the Centre not a spot of rain fell between 1923 and 1930.
1974 *Australian* 18 Oct. 20: How red the Centre this summer?
Centralia
1930 *Bulletin* 8 Jan. 19: Some cattle on a Centralian station.
1944 Frank Clune *The Red Heart* 2: It needed a war to make tens and thousands of Australians realise that Centralia is one of the strangest and loveliest regions on the world.
1982 *NT News* (Darwin) 7 Jun. 12: Centralian beef is better. So goes the theme which will be used for Centralian cattle producers at this year's NT expo.

Centre, the Red   see **Red**

century, go for the   To try to shear 100 sheep in a day
1905 'Another Fall of Rain' *The Old Bush Songs* ed. A. B. Paterson 28: For some had got the century who'd never got it before.
1957 'The Backblock Shearer' *Old Bush Songs* ed. Stewart and Keesing 258: Tomorrow I go with a sardine blow / For a century or the sack.
1964 H. P. Tritton *Time Means Tucker* 92: Dutchy went for the 'century' and just failed. [recalling 1905–6]

certain grandeur, a   A phrase attached to E. G. Whitlam, Australian Prime Minister 1972–5
1974 C. J. Lloyd and G. S. Reid *Out of the Wilderness* 420: In the generally undistinguished, and often tawdry atmosphere of Australian national politics, it is impossible to deny the Whitlam Government a certain grandeur.
1977 Graham Freudenberg *A Certain Grandeur Gough Whitlam in Politics* [book title]
1983 Mike Carlton *National Times* 10 Jun. 33: How fortunate that H.E. The Hon E. G. Whitlam is alive and well and living in a certain grandeur at our Paris embassy.

chain, drag the   To lag behind: used first in shearing, but now most commonly of a drinker who does not keep up with his group at the bar

1933 Acland: *Drag the chain, to* To be the slowest shearer in a shed.
1941 Baker 25: *Drag the chain* To be slow, to be inferior, to 'tail' the field in any work or contest.
1954 Tom Ronan *Vision Splendid* 124: 'Pass the bottle, Top, you're draggin the chain.'
1961 Mena Calthorpe *The Dyehouse* 156: 'Maybe they could take it easy. Drag the chain just a little.'
1968 Geoffrey Dutton *Andy* 146: 'Rooster here's way behind; dragging the bloody chain. He's due to set 'em up.'

chair, to be in the   To be the one responsible for a round of drinks
1966 Baker 230: *to be in the chair* to be the person who pays for the next round of drinks (the pertinent question is often *Who's in the chair?*)
1972 Geoff Morley *Jockey Rides an Honest Race* 18: 'Just to show you what sort of a fellow I am, I'll go first in the chair.'
1974 John Powers *The Last of the Knucklmen* 78: 'Who's in the chair?' 'Me. My shout.'

chalkie   1   A schoolteacher
1941 Baker 17: *Chalk-and-talker* A school-teacher
1953 T. A. G. Hungerford *Riverslake* 29: 'I was a chalky before the war – just couldn't settle down to it again, after.'
1972 Richard Magoffin *Chops and Gravy* 46: Kev is a bushie too, although he's a chalkie. He teaches at a boarding school in Charters Towers.
1973 Max Harris *The Angry Eye* 229: The quiverful of clerical chalkies who instructed us in the subject.
1982 *NT News* (Darwin) 2 Jun. 16: Teachers union stunned [heading] Red 'chalkies' denied visas
chalk radio
1983 *Australian* 26 Jan. 25: After four years managing Sydney's 2SER-FM – one of the country's most successful educational radio stations – Keith Jackson ... reflects on the hopes and hazards of 'chalk' radio.
2   Post clerk in a stock exchange
1984 *West Australian* (Perth) 10 Jan. 44: Maureen Lang started at the [Melbourne] exchange 11 years ago as a 'chalky'. She remembers feeling quite self-conscious up on the catwalk posting buyers' bids and sellers' offers on the trading boards.

Challenge, Barcoo   see **Barcoo**

champagne, Northern Territory   see **Northern**

channel country   Area of south-west Queensland watered by three northern rivers, the Georgina, the Diamantina and Cooper's Creek
1947 Queensland Department of Public Lands

The Channel Country of South-West Queensland [title of Bulletin]
1976 Roland Robinson *The Shift of Sands* 38: We had entered the famous 'channel country', an area comprising 10,000,000 acres, watered and flooded by the three great rivers of the inland, the Cooper, the Diamantina and the Georgina. This was a region of high parallel sandridges, wide, smooth claypans, and dry river courses that had carved their way out in ravines and sudden waterholes, and areas of fine, grey flood silt.
1983 *Sydney Morning Herald* 8 Aug. Guide 14: The Channel Country is an area in south-west Queensland that fringes the Simpson Desert. It is a harsh, arid land where there is always either drought or flood – but mostly drought. It draws its name from the dozens of ephemeral channels that make up Coopers Creek, the main watercourse in the area.
1984 *Australian* 10 Apr. 9: Glengyle station has 2072 hectares of channel country, more than any other property in south-west Queensland.

charge like a wounded bull, the heavy brigade etc.   To charge high prices
1944 Randolph Bedford *Naught to Thirty-three* 177: Charles Troedel ... charged me like the Light Brigade, or a herd of wounded buffalo. But he was the best of all the printers I ever used.
1969 Osmar White *Under the Iron Rainbow* 37: The Americans have access to the duty-free and tax free stocks of the service canteens, while the Australians must do ... their drinking in a pub which is said in the local vernacular to 'charge like a wounded buffalo'.
1978 *Sydney Morning Herald* 10 Jun. 10: Australia Post may like to consider a change in the shape of postal pillar boxes. Why not use the shape of Ned Kelly's armour as a reminder of their bushranging postal rates? Or a wounded bull, since they charge like one? The ultimate – the piece de resistance – could be in the shape of Ned Kelly mounted on a wounded bull.
1978 *Weekend Australian* 11 Nov. Mag. 12: London restaurants, the better ones, charge like the heavy brigade.
1980 *Bulletin* 14 Oct. 96: Our light after-theatre supper cost a negligible $139.50. The Light Brigade has something to learn from *La Strada*.
1982 *Sun-Herald* 28 Feb. 144: Now we know why Telecom charges like a stuck boar.
1982 *Sun-Herald* 14 Nov. 172: I had to fight my way to a small counter for something to eat (and they charged like wounded bulls).

Charities   The government lottery set up in W.A. in 1932
1962 Stuart Gore *Down the Golden Mile* 166: 'After a turn-out like *that* I reckon you should have

–' 'A ticket in Charities', Joyce completed for her.

1972 G. C. Bolton *A Fine Country to Starve In* 244: Jack Scaddan ... was entrusted with the legislation setting up a government lottery, with 2s 6d tickets and a first prize of £3000. This was the famous Charities Consultation, which took its place beside Queensland's Golden Casket and Tasmania's 'Tatts' as the average Australian's dream of sudden wealth ... Before long it passed into common speech, and anyone wanting to give the strongest support to a debatable remark would say, 'I wish I were as sure of winning Charities.'

1983 T. A. G. Hungerford *Stories from Suburban Road* 6: 'You get down on your hunkers and ask him to let us win the Charities. Or we'll soon be in Queer Street.'

charity moll (dame)   An amateur prostitute who does not charge a professional rate; any woman who thus deprives the professional of trade

1953 Baker 125: An amateur harlot or one who undercuts regular professional prices, with little thought for the consequences of this deflationary activity, is called a *charity dame* or a *for-free*.

1962 Criena Rohan *The Delinquents* 104: 'Remember,' she warned, 'no charity moll capers with my men.'

charlie   A girl [f. rhyming slang *Charlie Wheeler* = *sheila*. Perhaps related to *charlies*, English slang for breasts.]

1949 Lawson Glassop *Lucky Palmer* 41: 'Charlie?' asked Eric. 'What do mean by Charlie?' 'Your Charlie,' repeated Max. 'Your canary.' 'Canary?' 'Ay, don't you speak English? Your sheila!'

1951 Dal Stivens *Jimmy Brockett* 102: The stocky little Charlie Wheeler said to me, 'I'm having a party soon and you must come along.'

1972 Geoff Morley *Jockey Rides an Honest Race* 61: There's plenty of charlies over here. The town is built for tourism and this has caused an influx of waitresses, barmaids, chambermaids, housemaids and other assorted frilly trillies.

1983 David Foster *Plumbum* 305: Some cunt'll steal your mags while you're chock-a-block up your charlie.

Charlie, Slippery (Circuitous)   Sir Charles Cowper (1807–75), Premier of N.S.W. on five occasions

1859 Frank Fowler *Southern Lights and Shadows* 71: Mr Charles Cowper, the Premier ... is commonly called 'Circuitous Charley', from Mr Lowe's saying of him, that if he saw the gate of heaven opened, he would not walk in straight, but would *wriggle* in like a worm.

1934 Hugh McCrae *Georgiana's Journal* 148: On dissolution of the old council, he was elected from Camden to the new, defeating 'Slippery Charlie' Cowper by a mere hatful of votes.

chase up a cow   see **cow**

cheerios   Cocktail frankfurts [Queensland and N.T.]

1982 *NT News* (Darwin) 15 Jun. 19: Cheerios $2.49 kg

cheque   The total sum received, esp. for work done by contract, or from the sale of some crop

1857 F. Cooper *Wild Adventures in Australia* 66: Drawing my 'cheque' from Wilder, I felt my exchequer sufficiently strong to allow of my embarking in another career, namely, that of an overlander.

1875 Rolf Boldrewood *The Squatter's Dream* repr. as *Ups and Downs* (1878) 93: The shepherd hands his cheque across the bar – and till every shilling, purchased by a year's work, abstinence and solitude, disappears, drinks – madly drinks.

1901 Henry Lawson 'His Brother's Keeper' *Prose* i 517: He was 'ringer' of the shed at Piora Station one season and made a decent cheque.

1922 Herbert Scanlon *Bon Jour Digger* 31: I myself was taking a trip on the results of my huge wool cheque.

1936 Archer Russell *Gone Nomad* 68: So was our mob delivered at last. The drover received the cheque that was due to him and Moleskin, Pilot and I were paid off.

1949 *Coast to Coast 1948* 162: 'If we make any sort of a cheque out of the crop this season you might make a trip to the States.'

1962 Tom Ronan *Deep of the Sky* 6: Calico Hat went for his private horses; at breakfast he asked for his cheque.

1975 *Sydney Morning Herald* 20 Dec. 19: Australia's wool cheque for the first half of the 1975–76 wool selling season is estimated at $367.2 million.

chequed up   Well supplied with funds in the form of a cheque

1940 Ion L. Idriess *Lightning Ridge* 126: They'd reappear again in six months time, 'chequed up' and smiling.

1966 Tom Ronan *Once There Was a Bagman* 84: 'You fellows should be well chequed up and if you don't speculate you won't accumulate.'
see **cashed up**

cherry   Virginity [listed by Partridge as the hymen; also U.S.]

1959 Dorothy Hewett *Bobbin Up* 158: 'And don't bank on your sailor boy comin' home to you ... I lost me cherry on the kitchen table to a sailor once. I was fifteen.'

1970 Germaine Greer *The Female Eunuch* 194: The Poison Maiden of *An American Dream* is called, appropriately enough, Cherry. She is pure, to all intents virgin as her name implies.

1974 Robert Adamson *Zimmer's Essay* 46: 'My tip is, do it easy. You have a good time in there. They'll have your cherry before you know it.'

1984 *National Times* 30 Nov. 17: 'Perhaps she has been seduced and because of conscience concludes in her own mind that the only way she can live with the fact that the cherry has been plucked is in the case where it has been taken against her will.'

Cherry nose   A type of cicada

1983 Densey Clyne *Sydney Morning Herald* 8 Dec. Life & Home 3: Around Sydney it's a jubilation of cicadas – Green and Yellow Mondays, Double Drummer and Cherry Nose, Red Eye and Floury Miller and Black Prince.

cherry picker scheme   A scheme by which an employer gains tax concessions on his contribution to an employee's superannuation, and also draws the benefits himself

1984 Maximilian Walsh *Age* (Melbourne) 26 Apr. 13: A cherry picker is a particularly nasty tax avoidance scheme against which the Government recently tried to legislate retrospectively ... The scheme involved a business setting up a superannuation fund into which it paid entitlements to employees – without their knowledge. The funds accumulated reserves on a tax-free basis as provided by the superannuation legislation. But when an employee approached retirement or eligibility for the proceeds, he or she was sacked or persuaded, in ignorance, to leave the firm prematurely. The principals of the business, who were also beneficiaries of the scheme, then became entitled to the proceeds and subsequently pocketed them ...

As Senator Peter Walsh, who presented the legislation to the Senate, explained: 'The cherries are ultimately picked by the managers of the fund, who are usually the owners of the company, the employers.'

1984 *Sunday Telegraph* (Sydney) 6 May 156: Senate debate ... dwelt on the so-called 'cherry-picker' scheme, in which it was alleged employees were deprived of their rightful superannuation benefits.

cherry-picking   See quot. 1971

1971 Len Beadell *Bush Bashers* 6: Eric's job of cherry-picking, or cleaning the finished dirt road free of hidden roots, stumps, and loose sticks was now about to resume.

Chesty Bond   Comic strip figure devised in 1938 by Ted Moloney, running in the *Sun* from March 1940, advertising the Bond's athletic singlet (marketed in 1926)

1953 Dymphna Cusack *Southern Steel* 328: Anne rolled over lazily and stared into his face. 'Hop in yourself, Chesty Bond.'

1971 Frank Hardy *The Outcasts of Foolgarah* 195: He swaggered down the hill, ... black hair bristling out of his chesty bond singlet.

1983 *Sydney Morning Herald* 7 May 38: Lennie Lower's humour can thus be viewed as the hole by which he let the sawdust out of Australia's stuffed shirts, stringed vests and Chesty Bonds.

1984 *Sydney Morning Herald* 30 Jan. Guide 9: 'What do you get when you match up Dolly Parton with James Bond? ... A chesty Bond, of course.'

chewy on your boot   See quots: Victorian sporting

1966 Baker 370: *Hope you have a chewie on your boot!* Used to express a wish that a football player kicking for goal misses because there is chewing gum on his boot.

1975 *Sydney Morning Herald* 8 Nov. 4: Mr Hawke puzzled the crowd when he described their reaction to the Khemlani disclosure as 'You were wrong, chewy on your boot.' He did not seem to realize that he had used an Australian Rules cat-call.

chiack, chiacking *n.*   Good-humoured banter; jeering, esp. collective

[**1859** Hotten: *Chi-ike*, a hurrah, a good word, or hearty praise; [added 1865] a term used by the *Costermongers* who assist the sale of each other's goods by a little friendly though noisy commendation.]

1853 C. R. Read *What I Heard, Saw and Did on the Australian Goldfields* 148: The 'skyhacking'* to which the police were subject when sent round to inspect people's licenses, was brought on principally by their own individual over-bearing conduct ... It no doubt was extremely vexing to be shouted after, but their own conduct and language rendered them obnoxious and encouraged people to shout. *Blackguarding

1869 Marcus Clarke 'The Language of Bohemia' in *A Colonial City* ed. L. T. Hergenhan (1972) 159: The hissing of gallery, or the gods, is called *chy-ike*.

1885 *The Australasian Printers' Keepsake* 154: One toff, who fancied himself, still kept poking borack, but Steve stopped his chyacking pretty quick, for he hauled off and let him have it.

1915 C. J. Dennis *The Songs of a Sentimental Bloke* 20: I felt as if I couldn't get that fur, / 'An start to sling off chiack like I used ... / *Not intrajuiced!*

1959 Gerard Hamilton *Summer Glare* 96: The boys made a few unhelpful suggestions and quite a bit of chyacking went on.

1962 Ross Campbell *Daddy, Are You Married?* 77: Another asset of Mrs Grunnett is her talent for chyacking. Butchers are fond of this ... When courses in butcher relations are given at girls'

finishing schools, as they should be, special attention must be paid to chyacking.
1979 David Ireland *A Woman of the Future* 260: If you wanted to find the ringleader of the chiacking on speech day . . . look no further.
1984 Marian Eldridge *Walking the Dog* 170: When their chiacking got too much I would go out and talk to the turkeys.

chiack *v.* To 'chaff', tease; to ridicule
1893 J. A. Barry *Steve Brown's Bunyip* 21: 'They're always a-poking borack an a-chiackin' o' me over in the hut!'
1896 Henry Lawson 'Across the Straits' *Prose* i 200: There were several pretty girls in the office, laughing and chiacking the counter clerks.
1908 Henry Fletcher *Dads and Dan between Smokes* 2: Don't walk about; it's tirin'; stand at street-corners and spit – besides, that's ther best place ter see life and chyack the girls.
1931 Vance Palmer *Separate Lives* 14: 'They've been chiacking me about my cold feet.'
1948 Ruth Park *Poor Man's Orange* 105: The milk-carters . . . sloshed the milk into the cans, chyacked Dolour about her goggles, and charged out again.
1967 K. S. Prichard *Subtle Flame* 105: The rowdy bodgie youths kept seats near this group, chiacking the buxom, brassy-haired waitress as she rushed around with a tray-load of dishes and lively back-chat.

Chinaman, I must have killed a Explanation of any bad luck
1898 George T. Bell *Tales of Australian Adventure* 12: 'By Jove, G.T., old man, you've got such hard luck. You must have killed a Chinaman.'
1923 Con Drew *Rogues & Ruses* 116: 'I've got a mocker hung on me.' Pinkey laughed. 'Been killin' a Chinaman?' he queried.
1940 Ion L. Idriess *Lightning Ridge* 115: 'We must have killed Chinamen, or looked cross-eyed at a black cat', growled Tom.
1967 Kylie Tennant *Tell Morning This* 201: 'I think maybe you musta killed a Chinaman, Dave . . . I thought you were a moral for a camp. But no – you're an escort, boy.'
1984 Don'o Kim *The Chinaman* 131: 'How's your fishing?' 'Not so good, mate.' 'Why, you didn't kill a Chinaman, did you?'

Chinese burn The burning sensation given by grasping someone's wrist in a two-handed grip and twisting the skin in opposite directions: *juvenile*
1937 Encountered in conversation
1980 Clive James *Unreliable Memoirs* 35: Mears's favourite means of persuasion was the Chinese Burn. Grasping your hand in one of his, he would twist your wrist with the other.

1983 *Sydney Morning Herald* 7 May 38: He [L. W. Lower] rabbit chops and Chinese-burns the language, reducing it to dreadful puns, playground non-sequiturs and crazy jokes.

Chinese junk The caterpillar of the Cup Moth (*Doratifera* spp.)
1979 John W. Wrigley *Australian Native Plants* 58: Children sometimes refer to these caterpillars as Chinese junks.

Chink, Chinkie A Chinaman: *derogatory*
1876 A. J. Boyd *Old Colonials* (1882) 233: Our colonialised 'Chinkie', as he is vulgarly termed (with the single variation 'Chow').
1887 *Tibb's Popular Songbook* 7: And educate a Chinkie / To import some thousands more.
1891 Henry Lawson 'The Cambaroora Star' *Verse* i 159: 'Get a move upon the Chinkies when you've got an hour to spare.'
1896 Edward Dyson *Rhymes from the Mines* 101: Here, I state that all Chinkies are vicious / And I hate them like fever and snakes.
1939 Kylie Tennant *Foveaux* 85: 'Went to a herbulist . . . He give me something that took it away. Wonderful them Chinks are.'
1951 Dal Stivens *Jimmy Brockett* 90: We've got the best country in the world and the best people, and we don't want any Chinks or other foreigners butting in on us.
1969 William Dick *Naked Prodigal* 5: He didn't seem a bad bloke for a chinky-chink.
see **Chow**

chip, dry as a Extremely dry [1631 Ben Jonson *The New Inn* iv.i.3–4: 'As dry as a chip! Good Jug, a cast o' thy name, / As well as thy office; two jugs!']
1889 Ernest Giles *Australia Twice Traversed* ii 30: Bunches of a thin and wiry kind of grass, though white and dry as a chip.
1957 Morris L. West *Kundu* 68: 'Drink your tea then. You're as dry as a chip.'
1984 John Hooker *The Bush Soldiers* 192: 'This place is as dry as a chip, I wonder what the buggers drink.'

chips, to spit see **spit chips**

Chloe, drunk as Very drunk
[1823 Jon Bee *Slang A Dictionary of the Turf, the Ring &c* 27: 'Drunk as Chloe'; she must have been an uproarious lass.]
1892 Barcroft Boake 'How Polly Paid for her Keep' *Bulletin* 6 Feb. 10, repr. in *Where the Dead Men Lie* (1897) 69: Drunk! with my loved ones on board, drunk as Chloe!
1941 Baker 17: *Chloe, drunk as* Exceedingly drunk.
1945 Cecil Mann *The River* 43: Drunk as Chloe on

the potent cognac of that green and pleasant isle.
1948 A. W. Upfield *An Author Bites the Dust* 140: 'I never seen a bloke stand up to it like he did. If you seen him coming like a parson to a funeral you could bet he was as drunk as Chloe.'
1950 Brian James *The Advancment of Spencer Button* 97: 'An old chap skittled – drunk as Chloe – walked right under it.'
1956 Kylie Tennant *The Honey Flow* 188: They would get as drunk as Chloe and probably end up in a fight somewhere.
1961 Noni Braham *The Interloper* 203: 'He's as drunk as Chloe', he told Margaret nonchalantly.
1979 Bobbie Hardy *The World Owes Me Nothing* 115: I'm out in the street then, drunk as Chloe, and abusing this constable.

chloroform factory The arbitration court (seen as an instrument of capitalism)
1918 George Dale *The Industrial History of Broken Hill* 94: Two days after Justice Cohen had opened his 'chloroform factory' we found ourselves without water.

chockablock See quots
1971 Frank Hardy *The Outcasts of Foolgarah* 80: 'They caught me at it once on the sofa in the living room, caught me right in the bloody act with a woman who came in to do the cleaning; chockerblock up her, I was, going for me life.'
1979 Robert Drewe *A Cry in the Jungle Bar* 146: It was as if he and Gigi had been the couple caught red-handed. On the job. Chocka – as the old schoolboy expression succinctly put it – chockablock.
1983 Clem Gorman *A Night in the Arms of Raeleen* 44: 'She come home early one night ... caught me scorin' ten from the usherette up the local pictures. Chock-a-block.'

choco 1 See quot. (World War I slang)
1919 W. H. Downing *Digger Dialects* 16: *Chocs* The 8th Brigade ('Tivey's Chocolate Soldiers'). Originally an abusive name; now an honourable appellation.
2 A member of the Militia, which did not serve outside Australia and its territories (World War II slang)
1942 *Salt* 14 Sep. 35: 'You labelled him a 'choco', because he did not fight / You thought he didn't have the guts to stick up for the right.'
1944 Lawson Glassop *We Were the Rats* 261: I told myself that I had misjudged the chocos.
1959 David Forrest *The Last Blue Sea* v: Militiamen (Chocolate Soldiers, Chokos) were mostly wartime conscripts, led by a mixture of pre-war militia officers and N.C.O.'s, and of A.I.F. officers with overseas battle experience during 1940–41.
1968 Geoffrey Dutton *Andy* 91: 'You are all

volunteers. Your country called you and you came. Not a chocko amongst you.'

Chocolate Soldiers The Penrith R.L. team, from team colours, and because they are supposed to melt when the heat is on
1983 *Australian* 11 Mar. 22: 'Even then [in 1976],' Brohman recalled yesterday, 'Penrith players were referred to as "chocolate soldiers". Let's face it – the club's record is not good.'

choke down 1 To subdue an unbroken horse
1882 Rolf Boldrewood *Robbery Under Arms* (World's Classics 1949) 6: Maybe it'll save some other unfortunate young chap from pulling back like a colt when he's first roped ... and choking himself down, as I've done.
1926 K. S. Prichard *Working Bullocks* 59: He [the brumby] threw himself down, the rope choking him, lay a moment, then scrambling to his feet tugged and pulled again until it looked as if he would break his neck. He choked himself down.
1962 Ron Tullipan *March into Morning* 6: He felt the rope burns caused by the fighting brumby old Riley and he had choked down and fitted with a bridle.
1975 Xavier Herbert *Poor Fellow My Country* 634: You choke down a calf or a micky-bull or some animal with a rope when he gets too tough.
2 To yield to the effects of alcohol
1945 Tom Ronan *Strangers on the Ophir* 131: Artesian Lake, for the first time on record, had, in the vernacular of the country, 'choked down'.

choko vine over a country dunny, couldn't train a see **couldn't**

choof To move; more often *choof off*, depart: *jocular* [echoic]
1965 Frank Hardy *The Yarns of Billy Borker* 61: So they choof to the travel agency and buy two one-way air tickets to Mexico.
1971 David Ireland *The Unknown Industrial Prisoner* 83: 'We were choofing along Highway One about forty-five or fifty.'
1975 Bruce Dawe *Just a Dugong at Twilight* 41: Come, choof out to the Reservoir, / Where the mini-farmers are!
1979 Bobbie Hardy *The World Owes Me Nothing* 156: 'If my presence is going to cause trouble ... I think I'll choof off.'

chook 1 A domestic fowl [f. *chook* a call to pigs, or occas. to poultry EDD]
1855 William Howitt *Land, Labour and Gold* ii 139–40: They overtook a huge and very fat hen ... they tied chucky up in a handkerchief, and rode on.
1882 Rolf Boldrewood *Robbery Under Arms*

(World's Classics 1949) 85: 'Ye'll mak' nae head of convairtin' thae young caterans any mair than ye'll change a Norroway falcon into a barn-door chuckie.'
1900 J. C. L. Fitzpatrick *The Good Old Days* 71: A game rooster that could massacre twenty of your neighbours' domestic chooks in as many minutes.
1907 Barbara Baynton *Human Toll* 49: 'You greedy chooks, not leave none fer poor liddle baby Lovey!'
1935 Kylie Tennant *Tiburon* 33: 'Chook! Chook! Chook!' she called to the fowls.
1951 Dal Stivens *Jimmy Brockett* 247: Miss Helen Bascombe was engaged to a cove called John Graham, who had no more go than a hypnotised chook.
1974 L. Oakes and D. Solomon *Grab for Power* 171: 'A lot of them [former Liberal ministers] wandered around like headless chooks for a long time, not having departmental heads to call on, and people to arrange their itineraries, and I think some of them had even forgotten how to use a telephone!'
1983 *Weekend Australian* 23 Apr. 13: One of the Premier's aides let slip one of Mr Bjelke-Petersen's stock phrases whenever approached by journalists or when attending a press conference: 'Here are my chooks – I'd better feed them.'
2 A woman (*jocular*)
1915 C. J. Dennis *The Songs of a Sentimental Bloke* 80: 'She's too young – too young to leave 'er muvver's nest!' / 'Orright, ole chook,' I nearly sez.
1959 D'Arcy Niland *The Big Smoke* 45: 'Funny old chook. I can get on all right with her, I think.'
3 Nickname of anyone called Fowler
1911 Louis Stone *Jonah* 126: 'Me name's Fowles – Arthur Fowles,' replied Chook.
1960 Nancy Cato *Green Grows the Vine* 180: The waiter's name was Feathers, and the other waiters called him Chook.
1967 Lon Beadell *Blast the Bush* 141: 'Chook' Fowler, driving the old D7, heaped up a barrier of dirt.
chookery, chookhouse, chook raffle, chookyard
1908 Henry Fletcher *Dads and Dan between Smokes* 129: 'I've seen quite a number o' coves start a chookery; some few battles along, far more comes a cropper.'
1982 *Sydney Morning Herald* 19 Jul. Guide 5: Describing the elation of a young jockey on his return to the scale after a winning ride, Mr Tapp said, 'I tell yer what, mate – he's got a smile on like a carpet snake in a chookhouse.'
1979 *Weekend Australian* 30 Jun. 11: Poor Dick Hamer, Premier of all Victoria – he started the week looking as if he couldn't run a chook raffle let alone a State budget.
1981 *Sunday Mail* (Brisbane) 8 Mar. 16: Another, who did not wish to be named, said 'The most exciting thing that happens here is the Friday night chook raffle.'
1984 *Sun-Herald* 22 Apr. 66: After a fund-raising chook raffle after yet another St Kilda loss, one disappointed supporter jibed: 'Why don't you raffle the players and play the chooks?'
1942 Gavin Casey *It's Harder for Girls* 126: 'I've seen one [willy-willy] take the roof off my front verandah an' land it in th' chookyard at the back.'
1983 Peter Corris *The Empty Beach* 7: With its gleaming chrome and tinted glass it was like a peacock in a chookyard.

chooks turn into emus and kick your dunny down   see **emus**

choom   An Englishman: *jocular* [f. dialectal pronunciation of 'chum' as a mode of address]
[**1916** *The Anzac Book* 31: 'Have you got any badges, choom?']
1919 W. H. Downing *Digger Dialects* 16: *Choom* An English soldier.
1946 *Sun* (Sydney) 18 Aug. Suppl. 15: That's how the Chooms came to send out Governor Macquarie.
1952 Jon Cleary *The Sundowners* 134: 'The Chooms have been telling us what's wrong with us ever since they came out here with the First Fleet.'
1962 Stuart Gore *Down the Golden Mile* 24: 'Me old pal the choom. And how would you be, Squire?'
1974 *Sun-Herald* 9 Jun. 17: Chooms make a few blues over Strine.

chop   Share, allocation, esp. in phrase 'get in for one's chop' [f. *chop* slice, cut OED 1640]
1919 W. H. Downing *Digger Dialects* 16: *Chop* Share. 'To hop in for one's chop' – to enter in, in order to secure a privilege or benefit.
1949 Lawson Glassop *Lucky Palmer* 104: 'Ginger's chop was twenty-six quid.'
1952 T. A. G. Hungerford *The Ridge and the River* 212: 'There's got to be leaders, so hop in for your chop. Think of the dough and the privileges.'
1966 D. H. Crick *Period of Adjustment* 21: 'Tell him his quid today'll be worth ten bob tomorrow, so he better get in for his chop.'

chop, no   No good [f. *first, second chop* OED 1823]
1864 J. F. Mortlock *Experiences of a Convict* (1965) 23: I was in Australasia, dragging a hand-cart (reckoned 'no chop') when informed of it.
1882 Rolf Boldrewood *Robbery Under Arms* (World's Classics 1949) 13: There's good and bad of every sort, and I've met plenty that were no chop of all churches.
1955 John Morrison *Black Cargo* 174: 'I've heard he's no chop, Rory.' 'No chop? – he's a bastard.'

chop, not much Unimpressive, inferior
1849 Alexander Harris *The Emigrant Family* (1967) 369: 'Oh, he's not much of a chop, I must say.'
1903 Joseph Furphy *Such is Life* (1944) 9: 'Mac's no great chop.'
1928 Miles Franklin *Up the Country* (1966) 13: 'That old parson is not much chop, I don't reckon,' he confided.
1944 Lawson Glassop *We Were the Rats* 180: 'We only had those three morning raids. None of 'em were much chop, apart from hitting H.Q.'
1957 Ray Lawler *Summer of the Seventeenth Doll* 125: 'What I'm offering is not much chop, but – I want to marry you, Ol.'
1962 J. Marshall and R. Drysdale *Journey Among Men* 146: 'How did you like the Big Smoke?' we asked ... 'She's orright, but she's not much chop for an 'oliday.'
1973 Alexander Buzo *Norm and Ahmed* 25: 'They've improved a lot, these clubs. Twenty years ago they weren't much chop, just a place to go when you wanted to get out on the grog.'

chop short of a barbecue, a   see **barbecue**

chopper   1 i.e. chopper tailor, fish not yet full size
1980 *Weekend News* (Perth) 8 Nov. 49: Most of the bigger tailor are being taken on mulies and lures, with the smaller choppers in the river falling victim to whitebait.
1981 *Sunday Mail* (Brisbane) 6 Dec. 91: Tailor fishermen on the North Coast beaches have been pleasantly surprised by the run of 'choppers' which has shown up on most of the surf areas.
1984 *West Australian* (Perth) 10 Feb. 40: Chopper tailor have been taken from Mosmans downstream and several reports have come in of bigger tailor to 1.5 kg being caught at Blackwall Beach.
2   A cow sold for pet food.
1984 James McQueen *Uphill Runner* 2: The barren ones [cows] had been sold as choppers at the end of the summer.
1985 *Newsletter* Nursing Mothers' Association of Australia March 22: Even dairy cows vary in the quantity of milk produced – from the champion blue ribbon milk producer to the 'chopper'.

Chow   A Chinaman: *derogatory* [f. *chow-chow* OED 1845]
1864 *Thatcher's Colonial Minstrel* 72: The China-man's Fate'. Chow Chow his hands with glee did rub.
1876 A. J. Boyd *Old Colonials* (1882) 233: Our colonialised 'Chinkie', as he is vulgarly termed (with the single variation 'Chow').
1880 Rolf Boldrewood *The Miner's Right* (1890) 196: 'Here's these cursed Chows working away

and rootin' out the gold like spuds.'
1908 Henry Fletcher *Dads and Dan between Smokes* 4: 'Give out yer washin' to a Chow.'
1921 K. S. Prichard *Black Opal* 59: 'Michael says he works like a chow.'
1945 Tom Ronan *Strangers on the Ophir* 115: The Chow would think the big fellow was sick and try to doctor him up with Chinese herbs.
1970 Patrick White *The Vivisector* 77: Like one of the Chinese beans the Chow had given them at Christmas.

Chrissy   Christmas [abbr.]
1972 Geoff Morley *Jockey Rides Honest Race* 229: Forgot to mention the Chrissy party at work.
1981 *Australian* 19 Jan. 9: 'Sorry, matey, but you can't expect us blokes to have a mechanic on duty on a Saturday arvo, just after Chrissie', the garage attendant said.

christening, like a moll (streetgirl, gin) at a   To be ill at ease, flustered, confused [variant of the English 'As demure as an old whore at a christening' Grose 1811]
1938 Eric Lowe *Salute to Freedom* 370: It was this, the thought of Carl's utter inaptitude, which made him laugh ... As useless as a whore at a christening!
1945 Robert S. Close *Love Me Sailor* 125: 'Get out of the rutting way ... You're like a moll at a christening!'
1954 Bant Singer *Have Patience, Delaney* 114: You got me floundering like a street-girl at a christening.
1962 Gavin Casey *Amid the Plenty* 124: 'I've had a very nice evening, Mr Mayhew.' 'No you haven't ... you been looking like a moll at a christening.'
1965 Thomas Keneally *The Fear* 192: 'Come on, Cec' the gunner roared to his mate. 'Talk about a gin at a bloody christening!'
1970 Richard Beilby *No Medals for Aphrodite* 31: 'Why don't you get going? You're mucking around like a moll at a christening.'

Christmas hold   See quots
1953 Baker 132: *Christmas hold* A hold applied by grabbing an opponent's testicles (a 'handful of nuts') [prison slang]
1956 Tom Ronan *Moleskin Midas* 115: 'I'll do my time willin' if I can get a Christmas hold on him for half a minute first.'
1964 Tom Ronan *Packhorse and Pearling Boat* 125–6: Joe came in low, looking for that grip which the west coast black fellow learned from that other clean fighter, the Jap: The Christmas hold (the handful of nuts).
1981 *Weekend Australian* 2 May Mag. 7: A woman in a dental surgery, lying on the dentist's couch, put the Christmas grip on the dentist. When the

dentist winced with pain, as anyone would wince if a Christmas grip were put upon him, she said, 'We are not going to hurt each other are we, Mr Dentist?'

Christmas, what else did you get for [also U.S.] Derisory retort to a motorist sounding his horn at another (as though playing with a new toy)
1962 David Forrest *The Hollow Woodheap* 102: The horn honked ... 'What else did you get for Christmas, Jack?' said Pudden sternly.
1981 *Daily News* (Perth) 19 Jan. 5: What *else* did you get for Christmas? Christmas is over – but for many the memory lingers on, as unsightly and unwanted weight. If you have a weight problem, the Weight Control Centre can help.

chromo A prostitute: *obs.* [? variant of *crow*]
1938 *Smith's Weekly* 31 Dec. 12: As Tilly remarked, 'Wot can you heckspect from a chromo, whose forefathers was never married.'
1944 Lawson Glassop *We Were the Rats* 103: 'No bad for chromos, are they?'
1949 Ruth Park *Poor Man's Orange* 200: The chromo next door got her money easy in dark doorways.
1953 Kylie Tennant *The Joyful Condemned* 166: 'He's one of those big he-men that go sneaking around the park waiting to snitch some chromo's handbag. Just a pie-eater.'
1959 D'Arcy Niland *The Big Smoke* 152: That old chromo from Campbell Street: the wrinkled face flaring with rouge and floury with powder.
1960 John Iggulden *The Storms of Summer* 297: 'Some rotten poxy bitch of a chromo dobbed them in.'
1975 *Bulletin* 4 Oct. 4: It is a pity the word 'chromo' is old Australian slang for prostitute (I never knew why). It would be an apt term for a colour television addict.

chuck Used in the sense of 'stage' or 'throw' (as in 'throw a fit') in a variety of expressions: **chuck a seven, chuck a doubler, chuck a heartie** (have a heart attack), **chuck a mental** (have a mental attack)
1908 see **seven, throw a**
1946 see **doubler, chuck a**
1980 Encountered in conversation ('He was out in the toilet chucking a heartie')
1985 Judy Johnson *Sun-Herald* 17 Feb. 163: Apart from chucking the occasional mental (as she [a teenage daughter] used to call it) I usually grinned and tried to make home a place you wanted to be.

chuck off As for **throw off** q.v.
1915 C. J. Dennis *The Songs of a Sentimental Bloke* 22: Me! that 'as barracked tarts ... 'An chucked orf at 'em like a phonergraft!

1922 Arthur Wright *A Colt from the Country* 140: 'What y' chuckin' off about?' he growled.
1958 A. E. Manning *The Bodgie* 76: Your friends 'chuck off' at you for being a 'goodie-goodie'.
1959 Dorothy Hewett *Bobbin Up* 150: She waddled away ... grinning at the good-humoured chucking off from the spinners and reelers.

chunder To vomit; a term given currency by the Barry McKenzie comic strip [variously explained as an abbreviation of 'watch under' (see quot. 1965) and as rhyming slang *Chunder Loo = spew* from Chunder Loo of Akin Foo, a cartoon figure in a long-running series of advertisements for Cobra bootpolish in the *Bulletin* from 8 Apr. 1909]
1950 Nevil Shute *A Town Like Alice* 76: 'The way these bloody Nips go on. Makes you want to chunda.'
1953 Baker 169: *chunder* To vomit, whence, *chundering*, vomiting; also *chunder*, a noun, vomit [World War II slang]
1965 Barry Humphries 'Barry McKenzie' *Times Literary Supplement* 16 Sep. 812: His favourite word to describe the act of involuntary regurgitation is the verb to chunder. This word is not in popular currency in Australia, but the writer recalls that ten years ago it was common in Victoria's more expensive public schools. It is now used by the Surfies, a repellent breed of sun-bronzed hedonists who actually hold chundering contests on the famed beaches of the Commonwealth. I understand ... that the word derives from a nautical expression 'watch under', an ominous courtesy shouted from the upper decks for the protection of those below.
1973 Alexander Buzo *Rooted* 91: She put a plate of rissoles down in front of me the other night and I chundered all over them.
1983 *Sun-Herald* 31 Jul. 48: I'm certainly not in favour of our Foreign Minister turning into a kind of diplomatic ocker, delivering verbal chunderings to sensitive Asian neighbours.

Churches, the City of   see **City**

chutty Chewing gum
1941 Baker 18: *Chutty*: Chewing gum.
1956 Ruth Park and D'Arcy Niland *The Drums Go Bang!* 9: 'Thought maybe you was just friends,' said the woman, taking out her chutty and parking it on the door-frame.

cigarette swag A very thin swag, indicating destitution
1943 Baker 20: *Cigarette swag* A small swag carried by a tramp when he comes to a city.
1955 Alan Marshall *I Can Jump Puddles* 158: 'He was humping a cigarette swag,' explained The Fiddler. 'We all dodge blokes with a swag like that.

They never have anything. They bot on you for the lot.'

1959 Donald Stuart *Yandy* 16: He had been camped in the river, with a cigarette swag* and almost no tucker. *A swag slim as a cigarette; a poverty swag.

1966 Tom Ronan *Once There Was a Bagman* 235: I was in my twenties and at least did have a couple of horses and some gear. Hughie was well in his sixties, with nothing but a cigarette swag.

1973 Frank Huelin *Keep Moving* 178: *Cigarette swag* One blanket, change of clothes and chaff bag.

circular saw, like being caught in a Metaphor for female promiscuity

1937 Ernestine Hill *The Great Australian Loneliness* 63: 'I understand you can give evidence regarding the paternity of this child', rapped out the magistrate. 'Oh, I wouldn't say that', said Con modestly; 'you see, it's this way. If you were injured by a circular saw, could you pick out the particular tooth that did the damage?'

1956 Tom Ronan *Moleskin Midas* 236: 'And gins never know properly who fathers their kids. It'd be like getting your hand caught in that circular saw . . . and saying what tooth it was that cut you.'

1962 J. Marshall and R. Drysdale *Journey Among Men* 136: 'Oh, Norah,' she said quietly, 'it's happened again. Who was it this time?' 'Mrs South,' replied Norah, 'if you'd been cut by a circular saw, would you know which tooth did the damage?'

circus Term applied to a team of professional sportsmen, not playing as official representatives of their country [f. the World Series Cricket competition begun by Kerry Packer in 1977, and references to the players as 'a troupe', 'Packer's circus', etc.]

1977 Rohan Rivett *Sydney Morning Herald* 5 Aug. 7: Since the Packer Circus plans were revealed I have talked to perhaps 50 or 60 cricket fans . . . Mr Packer has no chance of drawing a big audience for his 'Super Tests'.

1983 *Sydney Morning Herald* 31 May 26: Rugby circus 'will go on' . . . Mr David Lord, the Sydney sporting commentator who has thrown the Rugby Union world into turmoil with plans to set up a professional competition, said last night that the show would go on.

1983 *West Australian* (Perth) 29 Nov. 37: We've had Packer's cricket circus, we almost had David Lord's rugby circus and now we've got the world chess circus, with petty antics and temper tantrums of display.

City of Churches, the Adelaide, S.A.

1873 A. Trollope *Australia* ed. P. D. Edwards and R. B. Joyce (1967) 647: Adelaide has been called a city of churches.

1891 Edward Kinglake *The Australian at Home* 57: The capital of South Australia, Adelaide, is noted especially for the prevalence of the ecclesiastical element, it is often called the City of Churches.

1967 Sir Robert Menzies *Afternoon Light* 347: The genial 'barrackers' of Adelaide – the 'City of Churches' – raucously inquired whether he could 'do with a pint'.

1983 *Australian* 27 Jul. 7: Savage undercurrents in the City of Churches . . . Is Adelaide the Australian capital of bizarre sexual crime against the young?

clancy 1 An overflow [f. A. B. Paterson's poem 'Clancy of the Overflow']

1971 David Ireland *The Unknown Industrial Prisoner* 77: They'd had a clancy . . . He had dozed off with the water running, and there was water slopping everywhere.

2 An item in 'The Overflow Column' in the *National Times*, signed by 'Clancy'

1985 *National Times* 22 Feb. 7: It is a standard joke in the press gallery [in Canberra] that one story or another is 'worth a Clancy' in The National Times.

Claytons 'The drink I have when I'm not having a drink' (the commercial for Claytons, 'a full bodied non-alcoholic drink made from African kola nuts and citrus essences')

1982 *Sunday Telegraph* 28 Mar. 176: Who's the press secretary working out of the NSW parliament whose press-gallery nickname is Clayton . . . because he's the press secretary you're having when you're not having a press secretary?

1982 *Australian* 25 Aug. 1: The minimal public disruption prompted the Minister for Labor Relations . . . to dub the strike a 'Clayton's strike' – the general strike you have when you're not having a strike.

1983 *West Australian* (Perth) 24 Aug. 17: Senator Don Chipp said it was a Claytons budget – the sort of budget you have when you're not having a budget.

1984 *Sydney Morning Herald* 28 Jan. 3: The new Anzacs in The Sinai, with all the mordant wit of the old Anzacs, call it the 'Clayton's Gong' – the medal you're getting when you're not getting a medal. The medal they receive but are not allowed to wear is the MFO Medal awarded for service with the Multinational Force and Observers in the Sinai, monitoring troop movement under the 1979 peace treaty between Egypt and Israel.

1984 *Australian* 20 Feb. 1: The group [Centre-Left Labor] had been dubbed a Clayton's faction: the one you have when you don't have a faction.

cleanskin 1 An unbranded beast

1881 A. C. Grant *Bush-Life in Queensland* i 206: These clean-skins, as they are often called, to distinguish them from the branded cattle, are supposed to belong to the cattle-owner on whose run they emerge from their shelter.

1895 George Ranken *Windabyne* 42: The man who could run in a mob of clean skins, whip the brand on them by daylight and then be ready to swear anything in defence of his employer or his mate, that was the man in request.

1928 W. Robertson *Coo-ee Talks* 174: The sergeant of police declared that Jarvis's skill as a lifter of 'clean skins' (unbranded cattle) was only excelled by the cunning of his lubra.

1938 Xavier Herbert *Capricornia* 299: Oscar ... rode in looking for Clean Skins, or unbranded beasts.

1956 Tom Ronan *Moleskin Midas* 107: 'A man don't look for cleanskin cattle on a sheep station, or stand outside a church if he wants someone to buy him a drink.'

2   A person without a police record

1907 Alfred Searcy *In Australian Tropics* 112: The men I met with were good, honest, and hard working, although perhaps it might have been as well for a clean skin to fight shy of some of them.

1950 *Australian Police Journal* Apr. 111: *Cleanskin* A person without convictions – (One who, as it were, has been lucky.)

1957 Judah Waten *Shares in Murder* 56: 'They're careful spenders, boss', he said. 'All squareheads and cleanskins.'

1984 *Sun-Herald* 24 Jun. 11: Cameron's death was almost certainly ordered because the drug gang had no further use for the former 'clean skin' they had recruited and it was feared he would give evidence against them.

clinah, cliner   Girlfriend, sweetheart: *obs.* [? f. G. *kleine* little]

1895 *Bulletin* 9 Feb. 15: I'm ryebuck and the girl's okay. / Oh, she's a good iron, is my little clinah.

1899 W. T. Goodge *Hits! Skits! and Jingles!* 150: And his lady-love's his 'donah' / Or his 'clinah' or his 'tart'.

1913 Henry Lawson 'The Old Push and the New' *Verse* iii 82: They were faithful to a clinah, they were loyal to a pal.

1916 C. J. Dennis *The Moods of Ginger Mick* 72: Wiv me arm around me cliner, an' me notions far frum wrong.

1924 *Truth* 27 Apr. 6: *Cliner* A young girl.

1928 A. W. Upfield *The House of Cain* 79: 'I 'elped to get 'is clinah out of quod for what she and 'im did for me.'
see **kleiner**

clip, the   'The whole quantity of wool shorn in any place, or in one season' (OED 1825–67)

1840 T. P. MacQueen *Australia as she is and may be* 34: The clip will be from 1469 head at 3 lb each.

1850 B. C. Peck *Recollections of Sydney* 22: The clip this season, in New South Wales, falls very short of the average of many years past.

1925 C. E. W. Bean *On the Wool Track* 229: But every Australian State except Western Australia now has it own sales, and at which nearly the whole of the Australian clip is now disposed of.

1933 Acland: *Clip* The whole body of wool for the year (off a station, or belonging to a man).

1948 K. S. Prichard *Golden Miles* 32: She ... heard about the fine property Bill owned: how many sheep it ran and how well their clip had sold at the last wool sales.

1975 *Sydney Morning Herald* 20 Dec. 19: Australia's wool clip sells for $367.2m.

clock   To strike, hit in the face or head

1941 Baker 18: *Clock, to* To strike with the fist.

1956 F. B. Vickers *First Place to the Stranger* 135: 'Somebody will clock that bastard one day.'

1966 Bruce Beaver *You Can't Come Back* 7: 'You're no mate of mine. I very nearly clocked you back there, but I don't want to fight you or anyone else.'

1973 *Sun-Herald* 25 Mar. 108: Dick Woolcott, 46, the man whom Mr McMahon clocked with a squash racquet in America last year.

1982 *Age* (Melbourne) 29 Jun. 35: There's nothing dirty or underhand about what he does. If he's going to clock someone, he does it right out in the open.

clock, bushman's, settler's   see **bushman, settler**

clocker   Someone who times a racehorse with a stopwatch, esp. at training gallops [U.S. 1909 Mathews]

1895 Nat Gould *On and Off the Turf in Australia* 117: Ruses are resorted to at times to deceive or out-general the 'clocker' on the look-out for a good gallop.

1978 *Sun-Herald* 1 Oct. 62: His time of 2m 32½s clipped five seconds from the previous Randwick record and three and three-quarter seconds from the Flemington record. The 'clockers' couldn't believe their eyes.

1980 *Daily Mirror* (Sydney) 1 Apr. 111: She's an absolute flying machine and today made clockers look twice when she recorded 35 sec for her boom task.

close up   Almost [Pidgin]

1883 Edward M. Curr *Recollections of Squatting in Victoria* 349: All top ropes, of course; but were, as I heard, close up fly-blown [i.e. nearly penniless].

1908 Mrs Aeneas Gunn *We of the Never-Never*

305: He chuckled, 'Close up smash him Cognac all right.'

1929 K. S. Prichard *Coonardoo* 316: She was 'close up finish 'm', she knew, as the trooper had said.

1935 Mary and Elizabeth Durack *All-About* 97: 'I bin go mad and kill that Masha. Might 'im close up dead now.'

1946 W. E. Harney *North of 23°* 257: She is panting hard when she arrives, and complains about how she is 'close up been lose 'em wind.'

clucky Thinking of having a baby; indulging in sentimental feelings about parenthood; behaving in a maternally protective way

[**1839** Grose *Glossary of Provincial and Local Words* 32: *Cluckish*, said of a hen when inclined to sit. Kent.]

1941 Baker 18: *Clucky* Pregnant.

1980 David Williamson *Travelling North* 34: 'Moya Simpson's just had another one and it's made me clucky.'

1980 *Sun-Herald* 10 Feb. 17: The international tennis circuit's gone all clucky these days. Jimmy Connors and his wife demand a fridge in their hotel rooms so baby food can be stored at the right temperature, and another new dad, Brian Gottfried, insists on wife Windy and baby going wherever he goes.

1984 Paula Duncan *New Idea* 10 Mar. 5: 'I've always wanted a child. I've never been anything else but clucky.'

coach, who's robbing this Equivalent to 'Don't interrupt' or 'Don't interfere'

[Quot. 1971 refers to the anecdote that Ned Kelly held up a stage coach and announced that he would rob all the men and rape all the women. When a male passenger protested that he should take the money but leave the women alone, a female voice piped up 'Who's robbing this coach, you or Mr Kelly?' Ned Kelly held up no coaches, and the story is also told of Jesse James, who announced that he would rob all the women and rape all the men. When a passenger suggested that he'd got it wrong, a young man with a fluty voice interpolated 'Who's robbing this coach, you or Mr James?']

1945 Baker 250–1: Disapproval or disagreement is indicated by ... *who's robbing this coach?** *Reputed to be associated with bushranging days, this expression is equivalent to 'mind your own business!'

1951 Eric Lambert *The Twenty Thousand Thieves* 206: Chip's boom shattered the sudden tensity of feeling among them. 'Who's robbing this coach? Do you want to hear the news or not?'

1963 Hal Porter *The Watcher on the Cast-Iron Balcony* 108: 'Shut up, you great lazy beasts,' the aunts cry back to the uncles. 'Who's robbing this

coach, anyway?'

1971 Frank Hardy *The Outcasts of Foolgarah* 17: He carried on a dialogue with himself, his voice muffly-mimicky deep in the helmet. 'I'm going to rob all the men and fuck all the women': 'You can't do that, you dreadful man': 'Who's robbing this coach, you or Mister Kelly?'

1977 *Australian* 1 Dec. 8: Apart from raising the question as to which of Labor's four Treasurers-elect is robbing the coach, where does this leave Labor policy – except in tatters?

coach, coacher Docile cow or bullock used as decoy to attract wild cattle

1874 W. H. L. Ranken *Dominion of Australia* 110: To get them [the wild cattle] a party of stockmen take a small herd of quiet cattle, 'coaches'.

1898 Roland Graeme *From England to the Backblocks* 203: The inferior riders were left in charge of a lot of quiet cattle, or, as they are called, 'coachers'.

1906 A. B. Paterson *An Outback Marriage* 165: 'The way we get wild cattle hereabouts is to take out a mob of quiet cattle, what we call coaches, and let 'em feed in the moonlight alongside the scrub ... When the wild cattle come out, they run over to see the coaches, and we dash up and cut 'em off.'

1929 K. S. Prichard *Coonardoo* 71: 'Got the rest of the mob next evening,' Hugh drawled. 'Most of them, at any rate. But we had to turn in some coaches.'

1947 W. E. Harney *North of 23°* 28: We would find the small wild mobs, in mustering which, coachers – decoy cattle – would be used.

1967 John Yeomans *The Scarce Australians* 37: The docile cattle are called coaches, or coachers, because they coach the wild cattle in the right behaviour.

coat, on the 1 In disfavour, getting 'the cold shoulder'

1941 Baker 18: *Coat, on the* (of a man) To be sent to Coventry.

1949 Alan Marshall *How Beautiful Are Thy Feet* 219: 'Girls that are too easy are on the coat with me,' went on Ron.

1953 Kylie Tennant *The Joyful Condemned* 92: 'I happened to say something about that old hag Jess ... and she's had me on the coat ever since.'

1973 Fred Parsons *A Man Called Mo* 47: he stepped back a pace, and fingered his lapel. It was the 'He's on the coat' sign, a gesture of supreme contempt.

2 Used of a bet that is not genuine, made by arrangement to alter the odds

1949 Lawson Glassop *Lucky Palmer* 66: He held the lapel of his coat between his right thumb and forefinger and shook it. 'On the coat, them bets of mine, of course, Norm,' he said, making it clear they were not genuine.

coat, pull (tug) the 1 Not to make a genuine effort [f. *coat* 2]
1977 *Sunday Telegraph* (Sydney) 2 Jan. 45: Although there are many who believe he pulls the coat in Sheffield Shield, that's as far from the truth as you can get.
2 To act as an urger (horse-racing)
1977 Jim Ramsay *Cop it Sweet* 23: *Coat tugger*: Race-track urger.
1984 *Sydney Morning Herald* 19 Oct. 30: In racing parlance a 'coat puller' is someone who gives misleading advice at the track, stopping a punter backing his own selection which usually wins. Losing punters often take out their ire on their 'coat-pulling' mates.
3 To warn (criminal slang)
1975 *Bulletin* 26 Apr. 44: 'One of the old rorters up the Cross tugged me coat a week ago. His mail was that if I didn't weigh in soon I'd be gathered for sure.' Ibid. 46: The expression derives from the system of signals shoppies use in large stores; rather like the bookmakers' tick-tacking. One of these signals is tugging at the lapels of the signaller's coat, signifying danger.

Coathanger, the 1 The Sydney Harbour Bridge: *jocular*
1940 Dorothy Auchterlonie *Kaleidoscope* [7]: Twinkle, twinkle little stars / On a million motor-cars, / Along the Harbour Bridge so high, / Like a coat-hanger in the sky.
1946 *Sun* (Sydney) Suppl. 20 Oct. 15: The day the coathanger opens, Isaac Isaacs the G G polishes up his topper and bowls through the smoke to the bunfight with a big cavalry escort.
1957 Sydney Hart *Pommie Migrant* 51: 'Ah,' I countered, jestingly, 'that's what the Melbourne folk call the 'coathanger', isn't it?'
1975 *Sun-Herald* 5 Jul. 19: In one of the sketches Hogan returns to the Harbour Bridge, where he used to work as a rigger. This time he's not on the heights of the coat-hanger itself, but in a toll collector's booth.
1983 Kate Fitzpatrick *Sydney Morning Herald* 18 Jun. 31: I like it here [in Melbourne] but I'd give anything for a glimpse of the old coat-hanger.
2 A head-high tackle
1982 *NT News* (Darwin) 18 Aug. 36: Brothers Rugby League Club wants a Northern Suburbs player cited for a deliberate head-high tackle ... It claims the player delivered the coathanger tackle to the centre, Brian McSkimming, two minutes before half-time.

cobar A penny, a copper: *obs.* [f. name of copper-mining town]
1898 *Bulletin* 1 Oct. 14: A penny is a 'Cobar'.

1911 E. S. Sorenson *Life in the Australian Back-blocks* 36: When Jack makes anything for the pet creation, you can bet your bottom Cobar he will put all his ingenuity into it.

cobber Friend, mate: *obsolescent* [f. *cob* to take a liking to anyone EDD]
1895 *Bulletin* 9 Feb. 15: Oh she's a good iron, is my little clinah; / She's my cobber an' I'm 'er bloke.
1899 W. T. Goodge *Hits! Skits! and Jingles!* 150: And a bosom friend's a 'cobber'.
1900–10 O'Brien and Stephens: *Cobber* confidant, closest friend, mate or chum.
1910 Henry Lawson 'The Rising of the Court' *Prose* i 660: For the sake of a friend – of a 'pal' or a 'cobber'.
1916 *The Anzac Book* 151n: *Cobber* – Australian for a well tried and tested pal.
1933 F. E. Baume *Tragedy Track* 178: 'Can you imagine your old cobber on the talkies?'
1942 Gavin Casey *It's Harder for Girls* 15: It's only through the years, after a cobber or two has been unlucky ... that it begins to wear you down.
1965 Barry Humphries 'Barry McKenzie' *Times Literary Supplement* 16 Sep. 812: His vocabulary is borrowed from a diversity of national types, and words like 'cobber' and 'bonzer' still intrude as a sop to Pommy readers, though such words are seldom, if ever, used in present-day Australia.
cobber up
1923 Jack Moses *Beyond the City Gates* 29: 'Oh, fair,' said Jimmy, cobbering up in true Australian style.
1928 Arthur Wright *A Good Recovery* 21: 'I cobbered up there with another bloke what was on th' rocks.'
1938 Xavier Herbert *Capricornia* 397: 'What you cobberin' up with that yeller shisser for?'
1940 Ion L. Idriess *Lightning Ridge* 133: I'd cobbered up with a big yellow goanna that was constantly sneaking around the hut on the look-out for what he could pilfer.
1954 T. A. G. Hungerford *Sowers of the Wind* 51: I thought I might cobber up with them, but ... they don't even know that I'm alive.
1964 Tom Ronan *Packhorse and Pearling Boat* 213: On the trip down I tried to cobber up with the old fellow.

cobbera (cobra) Skull, head: *obs.* [Ab.]
1793 J. Hunter *An Historical Journal* ed. J. Bach (1968) 271: *Caberra*, The head.
1832 G. Tipsmill 'The Snake' *Old Bush Songs* ed. Stewart and Keesing (1957) 33: The helpless frogs must rin and quake / When they behold their foe, the snake; / They wish a stick effect would take / Upon your cobra.
1844 Louisa Meredith *Notes and Sketches of New*

South Wales 98: 'Good way up cobbra' means 'head high up'.

1867 J. R. Houlding *Australian Capers* 204: The savage cobbler, who, with a volley of oaths and slang, said he would crack Christopher's 'cobbera'.

1876 Rolf Boldrewood *A Colonial Reformer* (1891) 134: 'I should be cock-sure that having an empty cobbra, as the blacks say, was on the main track that led to the grog-camp.'

1881 A. C. Grant *Bush-life in Queensland* i 31: The black fellow who lives in the bush bestows but small attention on his 'cobra', as the head is usually called in the pigeon-English which they employ.

1899 George Boxall *The Story of Australian Bushrangers* 243: Gilbert dismounted, turned over Parry's body, and remarked coolly, 'He got it in the cobbera. It's all over with him.'

1904 Laura M. Palmer-Archer *A Bush Honeymoon* 348: *Cobra* Head (aboriginal term).

cobbler 1 The sheep left to the last in shearing, as the roughest to shear [f. pun on *cobbler's last,* ? and 'cobbled' appearance of the fleece]

1870 Rolf Boldrewood 'Shearing in Riverina' *In Bad Company* (1901) 315: The 'cobbler' (or last sheep) was seized.

1887 *Tibb's Popular Song Book* 11: But I struggled thro' Nekarboo, boys, / And saw the cobbler cut.

1910 C. E. W. Bean *On the Wool Track* 193: There is gradually left a bunch of animals with wrinkles stiffer than door mats. The stiffest, wrinkliest, is 'the cobbler', because he sticks to the last.

1961 George Farwell *Vanishing Australians* 96: Its name is The Cobbler – a term which, in sheep talk, means the sheep that is hardest to shear.

2 The cobbler-fish, *gymnapistes marmoratus*, with long rays like a cobbler's strings

1832 G. F. Moore *Diary of . . . an Early Settler in Western Australia* (1884) 136: There is another species, somewhat in the nature of an eel, with a sharp spine it can erect at pleasure; this is caught only in the fresh water, and is called a cobbler, a kind resembling it in salt water is named cat-fish.

1937 K. S. Prichard *Intimate Strangers* 154: When it was a cobbler, he called to the children to keep back until Prospero had hacked off the ugly brown head with its poisonous sting.

1969 Osmar White *Under the Iron Rainbow* 103: 'I always carry the kit here in the wheelhouse, . . . with a bottle of metho for cobbler stings.'

1978 Richard Beilby *Gunner* 66: Ted Morris was pouncing on something under a bush, bayoneting as if he was stabbing a cobbler, setting his boot down hard, withdrawing.

1983 *West Australian* (Perth) 19 Sep. 1: Cobblers forced the closure of Sorrento beach, north of Perth, yesterday.

cock it up Used of a woman offering herself sexually

1961 Xavier Herbert *Soldiers' Women* 202: 'He's waitin'' out there, and lookin' that nervous that if you cocked it up to him he'd put his hat over it and run.'

1963 Don Crick *Martin Place* 164: 'If they cock it up, what do they expect?'

1975 Richard Beilby *The Brown Land Crying* 210: 'You thought you had something on me, didn't you? You thought I'd cock it up to you.'

Cockaleechie, the Kid from The tennis-player John Fitzgerald, from Cockaleechie S.A.

1983 *Australian* 3 Oct. 1: John Fitzgerald, the Kid from Cockaleechie, became the toast of the nation yesterday when he put Australia into its first David Cup final in six years with an amazing victory over France's Yannick Noah at White City.

cockatoo n. 1 A sentinel or lookout, usually acting for those engaged in some illegal activity [f. belief that a flock of cockatoos when feeding posted a sentry to warn of approaching danger]

1828 P. Cunningham *Two Years in New South Wales* (2nd edn) ii 288: It being a common trick [among convict work gangs] to station a sentinel on a commanding eminence to give the alarm, while all the others divert themselves, or go to sleep. Such are known here by the name of 'cockatoo-gangs', from following the example of that wary bird.

1859 Henry Kingsley *Recollections of Geoffry Hamlyn* ii 141: Many a merry laugh went ringing through the woodland solitudes, sending the watchman cockatoo aloft to alarm the flock.

1949 Lawson Glassop *Lucky Palmer* 2: Snedden, the 'cockatoo', a little rat-faced unshaven man with stooped shoulders, whose job was to watch for the police.

1959 Dorothy Hewett *Bobbin Up* 159: The cockatoo kept watch outside the dirty house in Reservoir Street, where Thomos two-up school did a roaring, open trade.

1981 *Sun-Herald* 1 Nov. 152: Funny thing about the crackdown on casinos. All the big known gambling houses in the City area are closed, but cockatoos are still operating outside most of them.

2 A small farmer, usually with some overtone of disparagement, because of the cockatoo's inferiority to the squatter or because of his ingrained habits of thrift [see quots 1853, 1867, 1876]

1853 William Howitt, *Land, Labour and Gold* (1855) i 320: We were also very near being led into a dilemma by a mischievous cockatoo settler. Most agricultural settlers are thus styled by the squatters, because, I suppose, they look upon them, with their enclosures, as plunderers and encroachers on their wild woods, settling down upon them, as the cockatoos do on the ripening corn.

1865 Henry Kingsley *The Hillyars and the Burtons* 325: The small farmers, contemptuously called 'cockatoos', were the fathers of fire, the inventors of scab, the seducers of bush-hands for hay-making and harvesting, the interlopers on the wool-growers' grass.

1867 Lady Barker *Station Life in New Zealand* 110: These small farmers are called cockatoos in Australia by the squatters or sheep-farmers, who dislike them for buying up the best bits on their runs, and say that, like a cockatoo, the small free-holder alights on good ground, extracts all he can from it, and then flies away.

1873 A. Trollope *Australia* ed. P. D. Edwards and R. B. Joyce (1967) 647–8: The farmers of South Australia are usually called 'cockatoos' ... the name has been given as a reproach, and in truth it has been and is deserved. It signifies that the man does not really till his land, but only scratches it as the bird does.

1876 A. J. Boyd *Old Colonials* (1882) 32: Why cockatoos? . . . It might have originated with ticket-of-leave men from Cockatoo Island; or it may possibly have been a term of reproach applied to the industrious farmer, who settled or perched on the resumed portions of a squatter's run, so much to the latter's rage and disgust that he contemptuously likened the farmer to the white-coated, yellow-crested, screamer that settles or perches on the trees at the edge of his namesake's clearing.

1883 R. E. N. Twopeny *Town Life in Australia* 244: A 'cockatoo' is a selector who works his piece of land out in two or three years, and having done nothing to improve it, decamps to select in a new district.

1892 Henry Lawson 'The Ballad of Mabel Clare' *Verse* i 167: There dwelt a hard old cockatoo / On western hills far out.

1954 Miles Franklin *Cockatoos* 3: Both had fallen to the rating of cockatoos, or farmer-selectors, through inability to keep on the higher ledge of squattocracy.

3 A convict from Cockatoo Island (see *cockatoo n.* 2, quot. 1876): *obs.*

1870 J. L. Burke *The Adventures of Martin Cash* 123: He's the bravest man that could choose from Sydney men or Cockatoos*. *This name was applied to a body of desperate men, who were imprisoned on Cockatoo Island.

1888 J. C. F. Johnson *An Austral Christmas* 49: In the bush in those days, when so many old 'Derwenters' and 'Cockatoo Islanders' were to be met with.

see **cocky**

cockatoo *v.* 1 To act as a sentinel
1954 L. H. Evers *Pattern of Conquest* 216: 'You'd better stay down and cockatoo for us today.'

2 To take to the life of a cockatoo
1875 Rolf Boldrewood *The Squatter's Dream* repr. as *Ups and Downs* (1878) 245: A farm! Fancy three hundred acres in Oxfordshire, with a score or two of bullocks, and twice as many black-faced Down sheep. Regular cockatooing.

3 To perch on a fence
1876 Rolf Boldrewood *A Colonial Reformer* (1890) 224: The correct thing, on first arriving at a drafting yard, is to 'cockatoo', or sit on the rails, high above the tossing horn billows, and discuss the never-ending subject of hoof and horn. Ibid. 227: The cockatoo stockman . . . safely on the fence

1894 Ethel Turner *Seven Little Australians* 194: But everybody else had gone to 'cockatoo' – to sit on the top rail of the inclosure and look down at the maddened creatures: so at length he fastened his bridle to a tree and proceeded gingerly to follow their example.

cockatoo fence (improvised from crude materials), **cockatoo gate** (see quot. 1934), **cockatoo's weather** (ensuring the longest working hours) [f. **cockatoo** *n.* 2]

1867 Charles de Boos *Fifty Years Ago* 101–2: She . . . sheltered herself as well as she could under the rough logs of the cockatoo fence.

1884 Rolf Boldrewood *Old Melbourne Memories* 155: There would be roads and cockatoo fences . . . all the hostile emblems of agricultural settlement.

1899 Steele Rudd *On Our Selection* 15: A cockatoo-fence was round the barley, and wire-posts . . . round the grass-paddocks.

1934 Thomas Wood *Cobbers* 140: They [the cockies] work a few hundred acres apiece, and give their name to a gate made from two bits of stick and a length of barbed wire. A maddening structure. It falls down when you open it and will not stand up to be closed.

1933 Acland: *Cocatoo's weather* Fine by day and rain at night; or, sometimes, fine all the week and wet on Sunday.

Cockeyed Bob Sudden squall in N.W. Australia
1894 *The Age* 20 Jan. 13: On the approach of an ordinary thunderstorm or 'Cock-eyed Bob' they [the natives of the north-west of W.A.] clear off to the highest ground about.

1921 E. L. Grant Watson *The Mainland* 218: Often the silent heat of midday was disturbed by fierce gusts of wind known locally as 'Cock-eyed-Bobs'. These swifts and currents of air, not more than a yard or two in width, rush roaring across the levels, carrying a cloud of red dust with them and whirling along broken boughs.

1936 W. Hatfield *Australia through the Windscreen* 219: Only a few luggers were in [Broome] for the long 'lay-up' during the season of the treacherous 'willy willies' or 'Cock-eye Bobs' that come roaring out of a calm sea in those north-western waters anytime from December till March.

1947 Vance Palmer *Cyclone* 191: Nothing to the cock-eyed bobs they had encountered off Broome or the typhoons they had weathered in the China Sea.

1964 Tom Ronan *Packhorse and Pearling Boat* 36–7: One Sunday evening they were in residence when a 'Cock-eyed Bob' blew up. This is a sort of localized cyclone which comes from nowhere, without warning, rarely lasts more than a few minutes, and causes havoc.

1969 Osmar White *Under the Iron Rainbow* 157: 'Only wind. It blew my truck off the road the other side of Bustard Creek. It was the biggest Cock-eyed Bob I've ever been in.'

1973 Patsy Adam Smith *The Barcoo Salute* 151: Then the rain stopped as suddenly as it had begun. The air became deadly still and chilled. 'It's a cockeye-bob following up,' Paddy said. 'Cut into the house quick.'

1980 *Daily News* (Perth) 16 Jul. 2: A cockeyed-bob hit the small community yesterday afternoon, smashing windows, ripping roofs apart and sending tree branches flying.

cockrag   Loincloth worn by Aboriginals

1964 Tom Ronan *Packhorse and Pearling Boat* 46: Joe, clad in Malay style sarong, with a grey flannel shirt hanging down outside it ... at night put on the cockrag and joined the blacks in their corroboree.

1971 Keith Willey *Boss Drover* 144: 'Proper naked buggers – not even cock-rag.'

cocktail hour   See quot.

1964 *Sydney Morning Herald* 25 Apr. 11: Shearers, avid readers of the women's papers, refer ironically to their beer and rum sessions after work as the cocktail hour.

cocky   A cockatoo farmer, usually with an overtone of disparagement, from the sometimes wretched existence led by the cocky, from his reputation for exploiting hired help, from the contempt of the grazier or the stockman for those who scratch the earth [*cockatoo n.* 2]

1877 Rolf Boldrewood *A Colonial Reformer* (1890) 262: 'If it wasn't for these confounded cockies,' said Mr Windsor, 'that big flat would be a first-rate place to break 'em into.'

1887 *Tibb's Popular Songbook* 25: Says the cocky then to plough a bit / I think I'll stop at home.

1892 William Lane *The Workingman's Paradise* 165: 'Father a "cocky", going shearing to make both ends meet, and things always going wrong.'

1900 Henry Lawson 'An Incident at Stiffner's' *Prose* i 117: A tall, freckled native (son of a neighbouring 'cocky'), without a thought beyond the narrow horizon within which he lived.

1900–10 O'Brien and Stephens: *Cockatoo* or cockie, which form is mostly used – has become fixed as an epithet for small farmers. Among bushmen a 'cockie' is synonymous with everything poor and mean. A cockie's clip, in shearing, is equivalent to shaving a sheep ... Though 'cockie' practically covers every settler under the status of squatter, it more especially applies to the small selectors who hold from forty up to one hundred and fifty acres of land ... On many cockies' farms poultry, milk, butter and eggs are either unknown or positive luxuries.

1910 C. E. W. Bean *On the Wool Track* 64n: A 'cocky' is a small farmer. He usually selects himself a three-hundred or five-hundred acre holding, clears it, fences it, pays for it, ploughs it, sows wheat in it – and then goes to bed to wait for his crop. The next morning he gets up and finds the paddock white with cockatoos grubbing up his seed. He is there to plough and sow and reap – cockatoos. And that, they say, is how he got the name of a cockatoo farmer – a cocky.

1926 J. Vance Marshall *Timely Tips for New Australians: Cocky* A small agriculturalist employing labour apart from the members of his own family.

1936 William Hatfield *Australia through the Windscreen* 241: Up in the saddle a man conceives a lofty disdain for grubbing in the soil ... What? Get down and drive a plough? Be a miserable cocky? – Not on your life!

1957 Sydney Hart *Pommie Migrant* 163: He had been a 'Cocky' – which means he had owned a small farm in the open country.

1963 Frank Hardy *Legends from Benson's Valley* 15: He looked what he was: a taciturn recluse, the meanest of all the mean cockies in Bungaree.

1982 *Sydney Morning Herald* 3 Aug. 7: The image of the whingeing cocky, driving a Mercedes and worrying about missing his annual ski-trip ... is likely to be replaced ... as the drought is prolonged.

cane cocky, cow cocky, fruit cocky, spud cocky, tobacco cocky, wheat cocky   (referring to main source of income)

1973 Harold Lewis *Crow on a Barbed Wire Fence* 79: 'Dreaming of bein' a cane cocky still, Bluey?'

1914 Henry Lawson 'A Reconnoitre with Benno' *Prose* i 833: Cobb and Co's coaches ... ran from Mudgee to Wallerawang nearly as fast ... as the miserable cow-cocky train ... The district ... grows nothing now save cows and rabbits, and breeds nothing save increasingly hateful and well-to-do cow-cockyism.

1934 F. S. Hibble *Karangi* 37: The only difference

the Sabbath made ... on all surrounding cow cocky places, was that apart from the two milkings, calf and pig feeding, no other outside work was done.
1963 Hal Porter *The Watcher on the Cast-Iron Balcony* 131: A middle-aged cow-cocky's wife in a scarred and dirty Chevrolet.
1981 Dorothy Hewett *Susannah's Dreaming* 16: 'Cow cockies! All alike, always prayin' for rain.'
1941 Kylie Tennant *The Battlers* 351: 'Some of these fruit cockies down on the irrigation might come at it.'
1949 *Coast to Coast 1948* 161: For a fruit cockie, just nicely getting along, I should have been a very contented man.
1973 Frank Huelin *Keep Moving* 36: 'When we get among the spud cockies you can make a wagga from spud bags.'
1971 *Bulletin* 15 May 68: Australia's powerful tobacco cockies.
1941 Kylie Tennant *The Battlers* 7: 'My father was one of those half-starved wheat-cockies out from Temora.'

cockying Following the life of a cocky
1923 Jack Moses *Beyond the City Gates* 128: When you're cockyin' and battlin' and live on what you grow.
1942 Eve Langley *The Pea Pickers* 236: 'I'm cow-cockying now, Steve, and I don't get any days off.'
1947 Vance Palmer *Hail Tomorrow* 6: 'Cockying, eh? Kill a pumpkin every Saturday night to keep you and your family in food for next week.'
1973 Patsy Adam Smith *The Barcoo Salute* 140: I was cockying until then, but with the depression and the drought I went broke like lots more.

cocky, boss A person eminent among nonentities; someone enjoying the exercise of petty authority, usually with some element of assertiveness implied
[**1890** Tasma *A Sydney Sovereign* 129: The well-intentioned workers on the way to their selections, whose highest aim in life was probably to establish themselves on their 320 acres as 'boss cockatoos'.]
1900–10 O'Brien and Stephens: It is only the 'boss cockie' who is anything more than a wheat-grower.
1905 Joseph Furphy *Rigby's Romance* (1946) 49: A grazing paddock, consisting of frontage land, purchased or stolen by a squatter in the good old times, and now rented by a local boss-cockie.
1918 *Kia Ora Coo-ee* 15 Nov. 18: If ever I'm on my uppers in civvy life, I'll easy be able to hold down a job as boss cocky of a restaurant – one of those three-courses-for-a-tanner shows.
1920 Frank A. Russell *The Ashes of Achievement* 256: 'That's the boss cocky of all musical critics, isn't it? Hasn't he written reams exposing the ignorance of the whole profession?'
1926 J. Vance Marshall *Timely Tips for New Australians: Boss-cockie* A small farmer who works himself but also employs labour.
1945 Tom Ronan *Strangers on the Ophir* 138: 'The mob was with Nolan tonight. Why? Because I've been Boss Cocky too long.'
1965 Hal Porter *Stars of Australian Stage and Screen* 281: A country which has already driven out its most gifted actors and actresses, thus leaving English directors who were not good enough to make the grade in England to act boss-cocky to those Australians not good enough to make the grade in England.
1973 Max Harris *The Angry Eye* 131: Bob Hawke, the boss cocky of the ACTU, is a colourful force in the Australian social scene.

cocky on the biscuit tin, like the See quot. 1981
1981 *National Times* 1 Feb. 14: 'Left out like the cocky on the biscuit tin' ... dates from the pre-cellophane days when Arnott's biscuits were sold from a tin embellished with a parrot emblem. The cocky was on it and not in it; so the phrase describes a loser or someone left out.
1982 *Sydney Morning Herald* 24 Dec. 19: The expression *like the cocky on the biscuit tin*, applied to the non-participant, to someone in a merely decorative or even impotent role, may have been current for as long as the advertisement for Arnott's biscuits.
1983 *Australian* 14 Oct. 9: Russ Hinze recently said of Liberal MP Rosemary Kyburz that she was about as effective as a cockie in a biscuit tin.

Cocky Corner The National Country Party representation in the Federal parliament
1973 Alan Fitzgerald *Old Fitz's Unparliamentary Handbook* [30]: It was a change to listen to the quiet presentation of the honourable member for Berowra (Mr Edwards) which contrasted with the continual cacophony of cackling and caterwauling we have heard from the cockies' corner in recent weeks.
1984 Maximilian Walsh *Sydney Morning Herald* 17 Apr. 9: The approach of Messrs Page, Fadden and McEwen still guides the present occupants of Cocky Corner in the House of Representatives.

cocky's friend Fencing wire
1930 K. S. Prichard *Haxby's Circus* 239–40: Dan and the boys with hammer, nails and fencing wire, 'the cockie's friend', mended seats and fixed up stakes.

cocky's gate See quot. 1935
1935 R. B. Plowman *The Boundary Rider* 196: Some of these were what is known as 'cockies'' gates – the curse of all travellers. Instead of a pair

of wooden gates swung on hinges, these gates consist of several wires and a piece of wood. At one end the wires are fixed to a gate-post. At the other they are attached to an upright stick at intervals to correspond with those on the gate-post at the opposite end. In between are usually two sticks or droppers to keep the wires apart. The end stick, when the gate is closed, rests on the ground with its end inside a loop of wire attached to the second gate-post. Another such loop holds the top of the stick.
see **cockatoo gate**

cocky's joy   Golden syrup [see quot. 1911]
1910 C. E. W. Bean *On the Wool Track* 64: Cocky's joy is golden syrup in 2 lb tins, costing sevenpence – four times as cheap as jam and six times as portable.
1911 C. E. W. Bean *The 'Dreadnought' of the Darling* 293: Golden syrup goes by the name of 'cocky's joy' because it is cheaper than jam and is therefore supposed, not without reason, to be the delight of the cockatoo farmer.
1918 N. Campbell and L. Nelson *The Dinky-di Soldier* 28: And they'll do you well on cocky's joy, an' damper, an' the rest.
1952 *Sydney-Morning Herald* 12 Dec. 1: A customer asked for a tin of golden syrup. 'You know, Cocky's Joy'.
1965 Leslie Haylen *Big Red* 49: Cocky's joy or golden syrup was good on home-made bread smoking hot from the camp oven.

coconut black   See quot. 1983
1983 *Sydney Morning Herald* 14 Feb. 7: One word used in the north-west [of N.S.W.] is 'coconut blacks', Aborigines who, according to the radical blacks, are 'dark on the outside and white inside.'

coffee, hot   A state of anger or indignation: *obs.*
1885 *The Australasian Printers' Keepsake* 121: He was an Englishman – one of the worst sort – overbearing, ignorant, and impudent – and between him and me there was usually hot coffee.
1901 Rolf Boldrewood *In Bad Company* 13: 'Why, Bill what hot coffee you're a-gettin', all over a little joke.'

coit   see **quoit**

cold as a polar bear's behind   see **polar**

cold as mother-in-law's breath   see **mother-in-law's**

cold gold   A can of beer [f. 'Shake hands with a cold gold', the advertising slogan for Tooth's KB Lager from 1974]
1982 *Sun-Herald* 5 Dec. 87: Typical was one

mother's reaction as 'cold gold' in hand, she fiercely instructed her freckle-faced little monster to 'keep jumping up and down in front, so that nanna will see you on the telly.'
1985 *Bulletin* 14 May 32: They'd empty the joint quick as the first cold gold at the butchers' picnic.

coldie   A can or bottle of cold beer
1957 Nino Culotta *They're a Weird Mob* 126: 'Coupla coldies in the fridge', he said.
1978 John Hepworth *His Book* 127: Apart from the drunken lot that Harry brings home with him every night (leering and clutching coldies in their arms) the neighbours are always just dropping in at mealtimes.
1979 *Age* (Melbourne) 29 Sep. 19: The women are watching . . . not to mention all those ritually foul-mouthed macho chaps with coldies in their hands.
1981 *Sunday Mail* (Brisbane) 15 Feb. 18: There's nothing he would like more than to join his mate Lenny and share a few coldies in the dressing room later.

collar and cuffs   As for **cuffs and collars**
1901 Miles Franklin *My Brilliant Career* 28: The teacher, better known as old Harris, 'stood up' to the inspector. The latter was a precise, collar-and-cuffs sort of little man.

collar, soft   An easy job: *obs.*
1903 Joseph Furphy *Such is Life* (1944) 225: 'Soft collar we got here – ain't it?'

collect   To be hit by, collide with, 'cop'
1945 Roy Rene *Mo's Memoirs* 51: I can remember someone aiming half a brick at him. It just missed. You were liable to collect anything in those times.
1965 William Dick *A Bunch of Ratbags* 268: 'Yuh rotten mug', screamed Ritchie at the driver of an oncoming car who hadn't dipped his lights and practically collected us.
1971 Johnny Famechon *Fammo* 158: I was parked at the traffic lights . . . when a big truck hurtled around a corner and collected me on the passenger side, crumpling up the body work and giving me a terrible fright.
1984 *Age* (Melbourne) 25 Apr. 19: Quinlan said he had marked on Fitzroy's half-forward line, dummied around the player on the mark, had a bounce and was kicking the ball with his left foot when he was 'collected' . . . 'I didn't see him. He made contact with the right side of my body and I was knocked to the ground. It was a solid bump,' Quinlan said.

Collins St grazier, farmer   The Victorian equivalent of a **Pitt St farmer** q.v.
1971 Barbara Vernon *A Big Day at Bellbird* 114: 'Unfortunate farmers like Atkins forced off their

land so that Collins Street graziers can take over!'
1974 *Australian* 16 Jan. 10: Pitt and Collins Streets farmers are costing Australia between $10 and $15 million a year in lost tax, according to the Bureau of Agricultural Economics. What a surprise.
1983 Georgia Savage *Slate & Me and Blanche McBride* 156: The plane belonged to a Collins Street farmer who used a place in the hills as a tax dodge.

Collins, Tom   See quots
1895 Cornelius Crowe *The Australian Slang Dictionary* 86: *Tom Colins,* a fellow about town whom many sought to kill for touching them on 'sore points'; he was said to frequent the hotels, he always managed to vanish before his destroyer, as he was imaginary.
1903 [Joseph Furphy] *Such is Life Being Certain Extracts from the Diary of Tom Collins* [book title]
1951   R. G. Howarth *Southerly* 72: The pseudonym 'Tom Collins', which Furphy adopted as a contributor in the nineties to the Sydney *Bulletin* derives from a mythical bush character who was reputed to start all the idle rumours and taradiddles heard in the Riverina country.

colonial, a long   A long glass of beer of colonial brewing: *obs.*
1893   Henry Lawson 'The Darling River' *Prose* i 90: 'Wal, I reckon you can build me your national drink. I guess I'll try it.' A long colonial was drawn for him.

colonial boy, a wild   The bushranger of the ballad 'The Wild Colonial Boy' (*Old Bush Songs* ed. Stewart and Keesing (1957) 39); anyone sharing the same characteristics
1958 Russel Ward *The Australian Legend* 153: To the pastoral workers, to the free-selectors, to lower-class people in general, and usually to themselves, they [the bushrangers] appeared as 'wild colonial boys', Australians *par excellence*.
1959 A. W. Upfield *Bony and the Mouse* 108: 'A wild colonial boy, no woman was ever going to tame him. So he said a million times.'

colonial experiencer, colonial experience man   A young Englishman of good connections sent out to gain 'colonial experience', viewed with some cynicism by native Australians because he is an amateur in his work, and not really of their world
[**1862** Rachel Henning *Letters* ed. David Adams (1963) 111: He is up here 'to get colonial experience', though Biddulph pays him.
1867 John Morison *Australia As It Is* (1967) 216: That much vaunted 'colonial experience', extolled as the foundation of success.
1870 Rolf Boldrewood 'Shearing in Riverina' *In*

Bad Company (1901) 299: Young gentlemen acquiring a practical knowledge of sheep-farming, or, as it is generally phrased, 'colonial experience', a comprehensive expression enough.]
1876 Rolf Boldrewood *A Colonial Reformer* (1890) 95: 'You've really hired yourself to drive travelling sheep! Not but it's a sensible enough thing to do, still you're the first 'colonial experience' young fellow that it ever occurred to.'
1886 P. Clarke *The New Chum in Australia* 295: I remember on one occasion a planter put a new 'colonial experience'* man on to 'boss' a gang of black ladies. *Colonial experience is equivalent to apprenticeship of the new chum.
1893 J. A. Barry *Steve Brown's Bunyip* 208: 'I never did care much about these colonial experience fellows. They generally give a lot of trouble, especially when they're well connected.'
1903 Joseph Furphy *Such is Life* (1944) 347: The well-educated, well-nurtured and, above all, well-born, colonial experiencer, fresh from the English rectory.
1908 E. S. Sorenson *Quinton's Rouseabout* 93: Allan Banford's status on the squattage was summed up ... as a 'colonial experience fellow'. He was a city-bred young man, and blessed with a rich father who carried on business as a woolbroker in Sydney.
1938 Francis Ratcliffe *Flying Fox and Drifting Sand* 122: 'When I was in Bundaberg forty years ago there was a "colonial experience" named Thompson.'

colonial goose   See quots
1898 Morris 94: Colonial Goose, *n* a boned leg of mutton stuffed with sage and onions.
1953 *Sydney Morning Herald* 20 Jun. 7: Colonial Goose is another truly Australian national dish. It is boned leg of mutton stuffed with sage, onions and breadcrumbs, and baked.

colonial oath, my   Emphatic affirmation or agreement [euphemism for 'My bloody oath']
1859 Frank Fowler *Southern Lights and Shadows* 24: Your thorough-bred gum-sucker never speaks, without apostrophising his 'oath', and interlarding his diction with the crimsonest of adjectives.
1870 Marcus Clarke *His Natural Life* ed. S. Murray-Smith (1970) 413: 'There ain't a dodge going that he ain't fly to.' 'My colonial oath!' says Tom.
1882 Rolf Boldrewood *Robbery Under Arms* (World's Classics 1949) 381: 'My colonial oath, Dick, you're quite the gentleman.'
1893 Henry Lawson *Prose* i 78: 'His Colonial Oath' [story title]
1903 Joseph Furphy *Such is Life* (1944) 22: 'My (ensanguined) colonial!' assented Dixon and Bum, with one accord.

colour, the sc. of gold or opal: the indication of success to the miner

1859 W. Kelly *Life in Victoria* i 222: They had not, to use a current phrase, 'raised the colour'.

1882 A. J. Boyd *Old Colonials* 130: He could manage to get 'the colour', *i.e.*, small grains of gold, almost anywhere he tried, but only very rarely did he get anything approaching payable gold.

1897 Barcroft Boake 'The Digger's Song' *Where the Dead Men Lie* 66: Bah! there's not a colour in the bottom of the dish!

1944 Brian James *First Furrow* 44: The last shaft he'd sunk ... A rank duffer – not a colour in it.

1950 *Coast to Coast 1949–50* 137: I worked hard for three months, and I never saw a sight of colour.

1962 Dymphna Cusack *Picnic Races* 76: She considered likely-looking rocks that showed nothing she had learnt to recognize as 'colour'; not even a streak of pyrites that would give her a momentary thrill.

1979 Bill Scott *Tough in the Old Days* 40: We washed steadily and slowly for a couple of hours for no result except an occasional colour.

Colt from Kooyong, the Mr Andrew Peacock (who represents the federal electorate of Kooyong). The nickname is attributed to Senator Reginald Withers, applying it to Mr Peacock as a future Liberal leader.

1981 Russell Schneider *The Colt from Kooyong* [v]: As a colleague passed him in the Senate corridors on the day of his defeat [in the Liberal pre-selection for the post of President of the Senate on 17 Aug. 1981] Withers was asked about his future plans. 'I've got nothing much else to do,' he said. 'I think I'll start training.' 'Training what?' he was asked. 'The Colt from Kooyong,' he replied.

1982 *Australian* 12 Oct. 1: The colt from Kooyong has returned from his spell in the back paddock.

combo A white man co-habiting with an Aboriginal woman: N.T. and W.A.

1896 W. H. Willshire *The Land of the Dawning* 72: The *Sydney Bulletin* holds the proud sway over all Australian print productions. It not only reaches the combos and stockmen of Central Australia, but it reaches lepers on isolated islands, lighthouse keepers that are difficult to approach, and wild aboriginals have used its red cover as the salient point of their costume.

1905 Arthur Bayldon *The Western Track* 56: The combo sucked of soul and sense, a mooning hopeless wreck.

1926 K. S. Prichard *Working Bullocks* 47: 'Combo, I call him, gin shepherder ... combo's what they call a man tracks round with a gin in the nor'-west.'

1931 A. W. Upfield *The Sands of Windee* 99: The stockman ... in danger of becoming a 'combo', or a white man who is married – more or less – to a lubra.

1935 Mary and Elizabeth Durack *All-About* 68: He never had a lubra of his own, and was once known to have thrown a rug away because he was told a gin had slept in it. ('No b——Combo 'bout me').

1938 H. Drake-Brockman *Men Without Wives* (1955) 24: 'Some fellows simply don't seem to be able to help living with the gins. Going combo, we call it.'

1958 Gavin Casey *Snowball* 51: 'You know what combo means?' 'Joker that lives with black-gins, ain't it?'

1971 Keith Willey *Boss Drover* 46: The trouble was that the travelling combo was always on the lookout to snaffle somebody else's lubra.

come a gutser see **gutser**

come a stumer see **stumer**

come at 1 To take on, agree to, attempt (against obstacles)

1919 W. H. Downing *Digger Dialects* 17: *Come at* (vb.) Undertake.

1941 Kylie Tennant *The Battlers* (1965) 346: The Apostle, having failed in his tentative efforts to sell the truck, was persuaded to drive it to a bigger town and find a better market. 'Some of those fruit cockies down on the irrigation might come at it', Thirty-Bob advised. 'You leave it to me.'

1945 Cecil Mann *The River* 111: Without Skipper he'd have to come at some other work.

1957 D'Arcy Niland *Call Me When the Cross Turns Over* 92: 'No, Barbie, he wouldn't come at it. I know him.'

1965 Colin Johnson *Wild Cat Falling* 108: 'I said I'd never come at that again. Not after last time.'

2 To stomach, bear, tolerate

1962 Jock Marshall and Russell Drysdale *Journey Among Men* 169: 'My blackfellas eat it ... I just couldn't come at it, thanks all the same.'

1978 Margaret Tucker *If Everyone Cared* 38: Although I have not eaten these wriggling delicacies [witchetty grubs] since I was a child, I can say there is nothing to compare with them for taste. However, I could not come at it now.

1981 Patrick White *Flaws in the Glass* 67: It has always surprised me that Joyce with her nice wit could have come at any of that.

1984 Xavier Herbert *Age* (Melbourne) 18 Sep. 17: 'I went to Canberra deliberately to see him [Mr Hawke]. I spent a week there, but watching him at a distance I just couldn't come at it.'

3 To 'try on', presume

1961 Nene Gare *The Fringe Dwellers* 176: 'What's she comin at, sendin a baby off ta some mission?'

1969 D'Arcy Niland *Dead Men Running* 92: 'He wants to give me fourpence each for them ...

What's he coming at?'
1981 A. B. Facey *A Fortunate Life* 286: This made me see red. I said, 'What in the hell are you coming at? Are you trying to get cheap labour?'

come down   Flow in flood (of a river) [N.Z. 1863 OED]
1868 C. Wade Brown *Overlanding in Australia* 7: Whole plains are inundated with water almost instantaneously by the 'coming down' of the Darling.
1911 C. E. W. Bean *The 'Dreadnought' of the Darling* 22: The skipper knew the river was coming down on him, and he had been taking in his cargo the day before for all he was worth.
1932 Myrtle Rose White *No Roads Go By* 73: By flooded ground I mean a patch of land some twenty acres or so in extent which was inundated for a few hours by the overflow from Flood's Creek when it came down.
1969 Osmar White *Under the Iron Rainbow* 135: 'A big river, the Drysdale. Six hundred yards wide in the Wet.' 'Must be a ripper when it comes down.'

come down in the last shower, I didn't   see **shower**

come good   To turn out well (in a reversal of form) [cf. 'come to good', *come v.* 45g OED]
1952 T. A. G. Hungerford *The Ridge and the River* 50: If Wilder came good, it would be off his own bat – nothing that anyone else could say or do would make any difference.
1961 Myrtle Rose White *From That Day to This* 214: The others had to pump the water out of him, and brandy into him, before he came good.
1967 Kylie Tennant *Tell Morning This* 13: 'You're going to be all right, love. Don't you worry. From now on things are going to come good.'
1973 Harold Lewis *Crow on a Barbed Wire Fence* 72: 'He works for himself and one day his farm will come good, as they say out here.'

come in on the grouter   see **grouter**

come it   See quot. 1812
1812 Vaux 233: *Come it*: to divulge a secret; to tell anything of one party to another; they say of a thief who has turned evidence against his accomplices, that he is *coming* all he knows, or that he *comes it as strong as a horse*.
1882 Rolf Boldrewood *Robbery Under Arms* (World's Classics 1949) 171: 'The knockabouts and those other three chaps won't come it on us for their own sakes.' Ibid. 230: 'I wouldn't "come it", unless I could get that lovely horse of yours . . . I'd do anything in the world to have her.'
1893 James Demarr *Adventures In Australia* 175: After telling him the whole story he replied, that

someone had been "*coming it on me*" (informing of me).

see **guts, come one's**

come the raw prawn   see **prawn**

come to light with   To produce, as though from resources [N.Z. 1917 OED]
1956 Tom Ronan *Moleskin Midas* 260: 'He says if you don't come to light with a few quid soon he's goin' to summons you.'

comic cuts, comics   Guts [rhyming slang]
1951 Eric Lambert *The Twenty Thousand Thieves* 235: 'I want two quid in the guts! Gentlemen, I require two fiddleys in the old comic cuts!'
1955 F. B. Vickers *The Mirage* 58: 'Never drink this well water', he said. 'It makes you crook in the comics.'
1963 Frank Hardy *Legends from Benson's Valley* 26: 'What time would it be?' Arty asked. 'Be nearly midday – according to my comic cuts.'

commando, cut-lunch   see **cut-lunch**

commie   Someone living in a rural commune

compo   Worker's compensation: payment for time lost from an injury at work, or for a permanent disability so caused [abbr.]
1941 Kylie Tennant *The Battlers* 373: 'They've got nice rest-rooms for them who faints, and if you do slice your hand, they put you on compo . . . Compensation money while it heals.'
1969 William Dick *Naked Prodigal* 130: Brian had worked at the brick works once and had gotten burnt and was off on compo for a six week spell.
1974 *Australian* 26 Sep. 4: Compo plan changes will cost millions.

Condamine   1   The Condamine bell, with a distinctive note, used with stock [f. place of manufacture in Queensland]
1926 K. S. Prichard *Working Bullocks* 295: Duck Hayes tinkled the condamine he was carrying round to start events.
1955 Alan Marshall *I Can Jump Puddles* 173: 'The Condamine sends a horse deaf. It's too high a note. You bell a horse regular with a Condamine, he goes deaf.'
1962 Tom Ronan *Deep of the Sky* 109: A Condamine bell is one turned out of a cross-cut saw, which has a light but unmistakable note.
1975 *Australian* 9 Oct. 2: 'He is like the Condamine bell. He has a great tongue and a head full to nothingness.'
2   The drovers' name for Sirius: N.T. and W.A.
1951 Ernestine Hill *The Territory* 425: Sirius, ringing a steady note in the music of the spheres,

is the Condamine bell.

confetti, cowyard, farmyard, Flemington See
quot. 1941
1941 Baker 22: *Cowyard confetti* as for 'bullsh'.
Ibid. 31: *Flemington confetti:* Rubbish, piffle,
'bullsh'. [from the Flemington stockyards]
1951 Dal Stivens *Jimmy Brockett* 230: You could
pull the wool over his eyes if you talked enough
Flemington confetti about the woes of the working
class.
1973 *Sun-Herald* 30 Dec. 35: Lots of farmyard
confetti has been spoken and written about this
young man's selection.
1981 *Age* (Melbourne) 4 Aug. 16: 'Cowyard confetti' my long deceased great-uncle would have
called it when in polite company.

connie A tram conductor or conductress, esp. in
Melbourne
1943 Baker 21: *Connie:* A tram conductor (Melbourne slang).
1945 Roy Rene *Mo's Memoirs* 186: There's that
tram connie having a yike with a drunk.
1978 *Australian* 1 Sep. 1: The entire tramways
network in Melbourne could come to a halt by the
weekend because a conductress – or 'connie' –
refuses to join the union.
1984 *Age* (Melbourne) 4 May 1: Transport plan
sees the end of connies and guards [heading] The
Ministry of Transport is considering phasing out
all tram conductors and suburban train guards as
part of a long-term program to update and expand
Melbourne's public transport system.

Connolly, the luck of Eric A noted punter (d.
1944) and a byword for luck in betting
[**1949** Lawson Glassop *Lucky Palmer* 149:
'They're hard to pitch all right ... Eric Connolly
reckons he's known only one certainty in his life
and that got beaten.']
1958 Frank Hardy *The Four-legged Lottery* 134:
Jim Roberts announced his amazing win of
approaching two hundred pounds ... and Tom
Roberts said: 'Well, I'll be damned. We've got an
Eric Connolly in the house!'
1963 Frank Hardy *Legends from Benson's Valley*
73: 'They've had the luck of Eric Connolly all
night,' Darky said.

contract A difficult assignment
1953 T. A. G. Hungerford *Riverslake* 156: God,
what a contract –... Kerry's not going to appreciate being told what to do.
1954 Tom Ronan *Vision Splendid* 157: 'It would
be a contract to put bullocks up that hill with the
morning freshness on them. They'd never face it
to-night.'
1957 Vance Palmer *Seedtime* 174: 'Great woman,

your sister,' said Donovan emphatically. 'Not
many girls her age would have taken on a contract
like that.'

cooee, within In easy reach of; (negatively) nowhere near [f. *cooee* as an Aboriginal call to
someone at a distance]
1876 A. J. Boyd *Old Colonials* (1882) 284: 'When
you are starved, and are not within cooey of a
meat-safe or a bread-bin.'
1887 *All the Year Round* 30 Jul. 67: A common
mode of expression is to be 'within cooey' of a
place. Originally, no doubt, this meant to be within
the distance at which the well known 'cooey', or
bush cry, could be heard; now it simply means
within easy reach of a place.
1891 Henry Lawson 'The Shanty on the Rise'
Verse i 155: And I mind how weary teamsters
struggled on while it was light, / Just to camp
within a cooey of the Shanty for the night.
1908 Henry Fletcher *Dads and Dan between
Smokes* 43: But ef we's within cooee o' conquerin'
space an' distance, we's nigh handy to abolishin'
time.
1928 Arthur Wright *A Good Recovery* 63: Within
cooee of the house, covering a patch of cleared
country, stood the shearing shed.
1934 H. H. Richardson *The End of a Childhood*
72: No living thing but themselves moved on the
miles of desolate beach; not a neighbour was
within cooee.
1950 W. M. Hughes *Policies and Potentates* 43:
Darling Harbour – the goods depot within cooee
of the present Central Station.
1984 *Australian* 6 Jan. 1: Only a romantic 19th
century Irish stone farmhouse within cooee of
wild surf could qualify as the perfect honeymoon
hideaway for the leader of the Federal opposition,
Andrew Peacock, and his wife Margaret.

Cook, Captain See quot.
1984 *Sydney Morning Herald* 17 Nov. 37: The
white residents [of Redfern] discussed setting up a
tent embassy and drew up petitions to local council. But ... whenever they tried to explain their
plight they were 'Captain Cooked' by the Aborigines. 'We couldn't get past the attitude of "You've
been oppressing us for 200 years".'

Coolgardie A Coolgardie safe: see quot. [f. place-
name in W.A.]
1945 Elizabeth George *Two at Daly Waters* 32: To
keep food cool we had a home-made Coolgardie – a
frame covered with hessian, and with long strips
of flannel hanging over the sides and resting in
water to syphon and keep the hessian wet and
cool.
1973 Jack Hibberd *A Stretch of the Imagination* 8:
'Relax, pal, while I repair to the Coolgardie and

knock up a snack.'
1981 *Age* (Melbourne) 6 Aug. Green Guide 2: He also says things like 'If you're hungry I've got some meatloaf in the Coolgardie.'

coon   An Aborigine or other coloured person: mostly derogatory [f. *coon* for an American negro]
1921 *NSW Police News* 7 Dec. 22: 'We'd have to drop 'em [police overcoats] if we had to chase the coons, and then we'd have to explain to the Department if we couldn't find 'em.'
1952 T. A. G. Hungerford *The Ridge and the River* 208: 'You've got to know men, you've got to know the coons, you've got to know the country, you've got to know the Japs.' [in wartime New Guinea]
1954 Tom Ronan *Vision Splendid* 323: Carlson ... hit a mission-reared black fellow with a twelve-inch spanner for calling him a German bastard. The coon got a nasty gash on the scalp.
1969 D'Arcy Niland *Dead Men Running* 74: 'If that bloody coon was a white man,' he said, 'they'd shove up a monument to him.'
1981 *Sun-Herald* 4 Oct. 164: The Celtic Club of Melbourne has a large sign over the bar which says 'CHOGM – Coons Holidaying on Government Money'.
1982 Max Jessop *Weekend Australian* 6 Feb. 17: The average Queensland white is a racist bigot who calls Aborigines 'boongs' or 'coons' and wishes they would quickly disappear into the Never Never.

cop   A noun from the verb *cop*, meaning to be on the receiving end of something, and rarely encountered without a qualifying adjective e.g. 'a good cop' could be a piece of good fortune or a satisfactory job, 'a sure cop' would be a betting certainty
1898 A. B. Paterson 'A Disqualified Jockey's Story' *Singer of the Bush* (1983) 300: I know three certain winners at the Park– / Three certain cops as no one knows but me.
1915 C. J. Dennis *The Songs of a Sentimental Bloke* 67: An' then I tells 'er 'ow I got a job, / A storeman down at Jones' printin' joint, /A decent sorter cop at fifty bob.
1941 Baker 20: *Cop*: A good job obtained by shrewdness or luck; an agreeable proposition: a bit of luck.
1963 Hal Porter *The Watcher on the Cast-Iron Balcony* 99: The political fancy-men ... the confidence men on a soft cop.

cop it sweet   To accept a penalty without complaint
1965 Jack Dyer *'Captain Blood'* 115: The committee of the club copped it sweet, a sure sign that the old fire was gone.
1979 *Herald* (Melbourne) 17 May 48: Jockey Malcolm Johnston said he wasn't bitter over the

month suspension AJC stewards imposed on him ... 'It's just one of those things and you have to cop it sweet', Johnston said.
1979 *Sydney Morning Herald* 15 Sep. 1: Mr Hawke was philosophical about his defeat. 'I felt the position I put was a better one but obviously the delegates felt otherwise. You win some and you lose some. I cop it sweet.'
1984 *Sun-Herald* 29 Jul. 60: It was surprising that jockey Bruce Compton, rider of Missile runner-up Buena Gold, copped the flag start so sweet.

cop, silent   see **silent cop**

Cop this, young 'Arry   A catch-phrase of Roy Rene ('Mo') in the McCackie Mansions sketches, before giving Harry a clip under the ear. The original words were 'Young Harry, cop this!' The expression could now be used jocularly by someone passing a cup of tea.
1962 John O'Grady *Cop This Lot* 99: 'Cop that, young Harry,' Dennis said.
1976 *Australian* 15 Jan. 2: The script [for the Roy Rene revival] apparently is incomplete. Hence Spears' cheeky inscription on hand-bills advertising the Adelaide production: 'Cop this young Harry'.
1981 *National Times* 4 Jan. 29: It's vital for the future of quality TV to find out what it was about Bridge [*Water Under the Bridge*] that turns viewers off. Well, cop this, young 'Arry: *they never turned on.*

coppertail   The opposite to the **silvertail** q.v.
1890 A. J. Vogan *The Black Police* 116: The genus termed in Australian parlance 'silver-tailed', in distinction to the 'copper-tailed' democratic classes.
1898 Joshua Lake *Australasian Supplement* to *Webster's International Dictionary*: Copper-tail One belonging to the lower classes of society, as distinguished from *silver-tail*.
1905 Randolph Bedford *The Snare of Strength* 317: Charley Byers, being merely a clerk, danced at the Mechanics' Institute with the Coppertails.
1941 Baker 20: *Coppertail* A member of the proletariat, one of the hoi polloi.

cordie   A Duntroon cadet: see quot. 1984
1980 Christopher Lee *Bush Week* 2: Cordies were very regimental, and one day we were told they would make up the cream of Australia's new army. They would always open doors for women.
1982 *Sydney Morning Herald* 5 Jun. 34: Canberra life in the 60s was great for a 'Cordie', Canberra slang for a Duntroon cadet: 'Canberra mothers love a Cordie ... you know what they say, if you can't get a man, get a Cordie.'
1984 *Age* (Melbourne) 12 Apr. 11: Cadets are

nicknamed 'cordies' around Canberra because they have to rely on corduroy for casual wear, jeans being outlawed as unbecoming to an officer.

corduroy *n. v. a.*   To bed a road with logs to make it passable in wet weather; a road so constructed: *obsolescent* [f. the ribs in the fabric U.S. 1882 OED]
1860 Mrs A. McPherson *My Experiences in Australia* 292: The well-known though somewhat apocryphal tale of a traveller on a Canadian Corderoy road, whose right of treasure trove in a hat which he observed moving about on the surface of a bog by the roadside, was disputed by its submerged wearer.
1867 J. S. Borlase *The Night Fossickers* 159: They talk of *corduroy* roads in America, but I should like to show a Yankee a mile or two of the one we that day travelled over.
1880 J. C. Crawford *Recollections of Travels in New Zealand and Australia* 250: We passed Wallace-Town, and drove through a bad road cut through the bush to Invercargill. Part of this road was 'corduroy'.
1889 J. I. Hunt *Hunt's Book of Bonanzas* 71: The course of true love began to partake of the nature of a 'corduroy' road in the wet season.
1911 E. S. Sorenson *Life in the Australian Backblocks* 183: One teamster I remember 'corduroyed' a bog on the Tatham Road with smothered bullocks.
1938 Eric Lowe *Salute to Freedom* 359: Robin slowed the car down to take the corduroy crossing of Beni creek.
1943 Stan Arneil *One Man's War* (1980) 113: We arrived back in camp tonight at 11 p.m. after putting down a hundred yards of drained, corduroy road.
1957 Vance Palmer *Seedtime* 123: Donovan drove out over the corduroy road to the mills.
1968 L. Braden *Bullockies* 122: In those days we used to corduroy the roads (lay logs across the soggy spots) and sometimes the spars would wear through in places.
1980 *Australian* 31 Dec. 7: We walked along a corduroy track – logs laid across the track, and pushed together to form a bumpily firm footing – through the swampy bottom of a myrtle forest.

corn, on the   In prison [f. the hominy diet]
1949 Lawson Glassop *Lucky Palmer* 76: 'We look like doing three months on the corn.' 'The corn?' 'Yeah. The prison porridge.'

Corner, the (the Corner Country)   The area at the junction of the borders of N.S.W., Queensland and S.A.
1928 Arthur Upfield *The House of Cain* 84: 'It will be all of a fortnight before we strike "The Corner" of N.S.W.'

1932 William Hatfield *Ginger Murdoch* 1: Birdsville, Bedourie, and Betoota ... form a rough triangle and The Corner proper, and its border, unlike the arbitrary State divisions, is flexible and undefined, so that folk as far away as Goyder's Lagoon down in South Australia and even at Innamincka on Cooper's Creek may claim without dispute to belong to The Corner.
1949 Ion L. Idriess *One Wet Season* 147: 'The Corner', meaning the 'corner' country where the borders of south-west Queensland, north-west New South Wales, and the north-east of South Australia join.
1963 A. W. Upfield *The Body at Madman's Bend* 136: 'He was working out in Yandama, up in the Corner, when we won a pretty good prize in a lottery.'
1974 Ronald McKie *The Mango Tree* 115: Even men who had wandered from Cape York to the Corner could not recall such an event before.
1981 *Sydney Morning Herald* 5 Sep. 12: Today is Tibooburra's day, and best wishes to it from all of us. The faraway little capital of The Corner country, 425 km west of Bourke and near the junction of the NSW, South Australian and Queensland borders, is celebrating its centenary.

cornflakes packet   see **where did you get your licence?**

Cornstalk   1   A native-born Australian youth (as distinct from an emigrant) especially if tall and slender: *obs.*
1827 P. Cunningham *Two Years in New South Wales* ii 116: English and Colonial born, the latter bearing also the name of *corn stalks* (Indian corn), from the way in which they shoot up.
1834 George Bennett *Wanderings in New South Wales* i 341: The Australian ladies may compete for personal beauty and elegance with any European, although satirized as 'corn-stalks' from the slenderness of their forms.
1852 G. C. Mundy *Our Antipodes* (2nd edn) i 45: Cornstalk is the national nickname of the Australian white man.
2   Someone born in N.S.W., as distinct from the other states: *obsolescent*
1885 *The Australasian Printers' Keepsake* 162: A European type, working in Sydney, was grievously galled by the 'blow' of the Cornstalks.
1887 *All the Year Round* 30 Jul. 67: A native of New South Wales is known as a 'cornstalk', because the men generally grow tall and thin.
1897 Hume Nisbet *The Swampers* 179: They spent two days in Melbourne, going about and looking at everything with the prejudiced and disparaging feelings of all true-bred cornstalks towards things Victorian, and decided with gleesome alacrity that its days were over.

1899 Henry Lawson 'Jack Cornstalk' *Prose* ii 42: I regard the settled, or agricultural belt of New South Wales as the birth-place and home ... of Jack Cornstalk.

1903 Joseph Furphy *Such is Life* (1944) 44: 'When anybody calls him a Port Philliper ... he comes out straight: "You're a (adj.) liar," says he, "I'm a Cornstalk, born in New South Wales".'

1926 J. Vance Marshall *Timely Tips for New Australians: Cornstalk* A New South Welshman.

1957 Sydney Hart *Pommie Migrant* 51: 'Never say that to anyone in New South Wales, or you'll be laid out as flat as a pancake!' he warned me ... Couldn't the Cornstalks take a joke?

correct weight Announcement after a race that placings are confirmed and bets can be paid (as jockeys and placegetters have weighed in at the correct weight)

1949 Lawson Glassop *Lucky Palmer* 65: Before the correct weight signal was hoisted he managed to borrow forty pounds.

1982 *Australian* 21 Jan. 10: Stewards at Canterbury yesterday caused a flurry when they delayed a correct weight announcement to study a photofinish print.

1983 *Newcastle Herald* 1 Apr. 1: Mr Haigh told Mr Waterhouse that correct weight had been declared and the placing could not be changed.

corroboree A gathering or celebration: *jocular* [f. *corroboree* as Aboriginal dance]

1859 W. Kelly *Life in Victoria* ii 62: I derived a wicked enjoyment in the corrobborie [a colonial ball] as far as I was personally concerned.

1867 J. R. Houlding *Australian Capers* 134: A policeman danced a 'corroboree' in the roadway with his arms working.

1885 *The Australasian Printers' Keepsake* 98: There was a corroboree next day of bosses, clickers, and readers.

1926 J. Vance Marshall *Timely Tips for New Australians: Corroboree* An aboriginal dance. Commonly used in the colloquial to describe a noise or uproar.

1980 Thomas Keneally *The Cut-Rate Kingdom* 58: Each of them must have, during one or other of the Sunday afternoon corroborees at the Gaiety Theatre, seen herself as potentially John Mulhall's wife.

cossie A swimming costume [abbr.]

1926 J. Vance Marshall *Timely Tips for New Australians: Cossie* A sea-side term applied to a swimming costume.

1941 Baker 20: *Cossie* A swimming costume.

1959 Dorothy Hewett *Bobbin Up* 30: He imagined them lying on the dark sand behind the rocks at Bondi, undoing the straps of her cozzie, his hands full of her breasts.

1975 Les Ryan *The Shearers* 76: 'Oh!' she hesitated. 'Haven't got a cossie.'

see **bathers**

cot case Someone incapacitated, esp. by drink: *jocular* [f. hospital term for patient needing to be confined to bed]

1932 Leonard Mann *Flesh in Armour* 219: Sergeant Burke was boozing and often no better than a cot case.

1946 Kylie Tennant *Lost Haven* 196: Better soothe him, Cherry decided, or he'd be a cot-case.

1949 Ion L. Idriess *One Wet Season* 189: Before closing-up time they were cot cases.

1958 Vince Kelly *The Greedy Ones* 213: 'You're tougher than I thought ... I expected you to be a cot-case for quite a few hours.'

1961 Barry Humphries *A Nice Night's Entertainment* (1981) 54: To tell you the truth, Beryl was beginning to look very peaky and I thought, if this goes on much longer she'll be a cot-case.

couldn't blow the froth off a glass of beer, find a grand piano in a one-roomed house, knock the dags off a sick canary, knock the skin off a rice pudding, pick a seat at the pictures, pull the tail of a peewee, tell the time if the town hall clock fell on top of him, train a choko vine over a country dunny Various expressions for incompetence

1981 *Weekend Australian* 24 Oct. 17: 'They couldn't', Mr Wran said, referring to both Mr Dowd and Country Party Leader, Mr Leon Punch, 'blow the froth off a glass of beer.'

1981 *National Times* 25 Jan. 23: It sums up the inefficiency of the local copper at the time: 'He couldn't find a grand piano in a one-roomed house.'

1983 *Newcastle Herald* 28 Apr. 2: Mr Tickener told a meeting of graziers and shearers ... that graziers knew nothing about shearing and were not qualified to speak on the subject. 'Ninety per cent of cockies couldn't knock the dags off a sick canary', he told the meeting.

1984 *Sunday Independent* (Perth) 12 Aug. 48: The pilot, if you don't mind, is the geriatric Burgess Meredith who couldn't knock the skin off a rice puddin'.

1984 *Australian* 20 Aug. 18: Sydney rugby union coach Peter Fenton said yesterday the national selectors 'couldn't pick a seat at the pictures' after the shock omission of backrower Peter Lucas.

1983 *Sydney Morning Herald* 12 Nov. 35: The saying 'He couldn't pull the tail out of a peewee' has become very rare: it describes a man who 'can't fight', and belongs to a time when fighting ability was an important male skill.

1962 Gavin Casey *Amid the Plenty* 17: 'You wouldn't know what the time was if the Town Hall

clock fell on you'.
1981 *National Times* 29 Mar. 2: 'He [a football coach] couldn't train a choko vine over a country dunny.'
see also **homing pigeons, kick in a stampede, paper bag, revolving door**

couldn't head a duck   see **head**

country dunny   see **dunny**

country dunny, couldn't train a choko vine over a   see **couldn't**

Country, the Lucky   see **Lucky**

country, the sunburnt   see **sunburnt**

cow   1   Anything disagreeable or deserving vilification. The more intensive form is 'a fair cow' [? f. the English *cow* as an insult to a woman]
1864 *Thatcher's Colonial Minstrel* 14: Called each one of them [the bullocks] an old cow, / Whilst blows thick and fast he kept dealing.
1897 Hume Nisbet *The Swampers* 205: 'Police after him too ... Me know them, the blooming cows.'
1902 Henry Lawson 'Lord Douglas' *Prose* i 497: 'I vote we kick the cow out of the town!' snarled One-eyed Bogan.
1914 *Bulletin* 1 Jul. 47: Then he jerked his head back at the weather outside. ''S goin' to be cow of a day.'
1917 A. B. Paterson *Three Elephant Power* 51: In Australia the most opprobrious epithet one can apply to a man or other object is 'cow'. In the whole range of a bullock-driver's vocabulary there is no word that expresses his blistering scorn so well as 'cow'.
1925 E. S. Sorenson *Murty Brown* 143: 'He's a cow of a feller.'
1933 R. B. Plowman *The Man from Oodnadatta* 248: 'It's not so bad coming down the river ... But it's a fair cow going up.'
1939 Kylie Tennant *Foveaux* 236: 'And when I went back to get it,' he mourned indignantly, 'some cow had pinched it.'
1942 Gavin Casey *It's Harder for Girls* 13: The girls about the place were pretty uppish, and she must have had a cow of a time.
1956 Dorothy Hewett *Bobbin Up* 92: 'I starched your petticoat stiff as a board, and it was a cow to iron.'
1964 George Johnston *My Brother Jack* 121: 'How's the job with the baker?' 'It's a fair cow,' he said.
1965 Patrick White *Four Plays* 270: 'You're a cow of a goat at times.'
2   An object of compassion, as in the phrase 'the poor cow'
1933 Norman Lindsay *Saturdee* 164: Peter was sure the poor cow had never had a sit with girls in all his life.
1938 Francis Ratcliffe *Flying Fox and Drifting Sand* 194: 'Smith, our neighbour on the east, missed it [the rain] altogether, the poor cow.'
1945 *Coast to Coast 1944* 167: 'That poor cow's in a bad way.'
1947 Gavin Casey *The Wits are Out* 42: Sometimes, when misfortune overtook him ... people felt sorry for him, and decided he wasn't such a bad old cow, after all.
1948 K. S. Prichard *Golden Miles* 89: A bogger working near Dally on the Perseverance had been killed by a fall of earth. 'The poor silly cow,' he said tremulously.
1959 D'Arcy Niland *The Big Smoke* 164: 'Kind of the old cow,' Ocker said.

cow, hunt (chase) up a   To find a dry patch in the bush, usually with a sense of sexual opportunity
1957 John O'Grady *They're a Weird Mob* 144: 'Gunna be a bastard tryin' to find a dry spot.' 'Hunt up a cow.'
1959 Gerard Hamilton *Summer Glare* 80: We delighted in following couples at night when they went 'chasing up a cow', as courting was commonly called, for couples mostly began their night's love-making by wandering around looking for a sleeping cow that they could disturb to claim the warm patch of earth where it lay.

cow, Malley's   see **Malley's**

cowal   A lake, or a swampy depression supporting vegetation [Ab.]
1882 Charles Lyne *The Industries of New South Wales* 213: The homestead ... is not far from ... the shores of a lake which in this part of the Colony is called, in the language of the aborigines, a 'cowall', or 'cowell'.
1901 Rolf Boldrewood *In Bad Company* 19: Wading girth-deep through the subsidiary watercourses – billabongs, cowalls and such.
1910 C. E. W. Bean *On the Wool Track* 251: If one got bogged in a creek or cowal (which is a small tree-grown, swampy depression often met in the red country).
1934 Jean Devanny *Out of Such Fires* 220: They [the horses] could be trusted not to move far from the little shade afforded by the cowal.

cowboy   See quots
1933 Acland 371: *Cowboy.–* The boy who milks, etc. Not the romantic American horseman.
1961 Noni Braham *The Interloper* 46: Next to the natives, Margaret had discovered the cowboy was considered the lowest form of life on the station,

and was nevertheless one of the most essential. He was supposed to milk the cows, separate the milk, empty 'Tumbling Tommy' (the garbage-tin), feed the chooks, fill the stove, and do all the little lowly chores everyone else scorned.

cowyard confetti see **confetti**

crab-hole A hole supposedly burrowed or inhabited by a land-crab: mainly Victorian
1848 Let. in G. Goodman *The Church in Victoria* (1892) 72: Full of crab-holes, which are exceedingly dangerous for the horses. These are holes varying in depth from one to three feet, and the smallest of them wide enough to admit the foot of a horse ... These holes are formed by a small land-crab and then gradually enlarged by water draining into them. [Morris]
1855 William Howitt *Land, Labour and Gold* i 308: Crab-holes, or Frog-holes, as they are called in some districts from land crabs and frogs frequenting them when they hold water, are small pools or quagmires some few yards across.
1889 Ernest Giles *Australia Twice Traversed* i 256: Here we found a clay crab-hole. These holes are so-called in parts of Australia, usually near the coasts, where freshwater crabs and crayfish bury themselves in the bottoms of places where rain water often lodges; the holes these creatures make are tubes of two, three, or four feet deep, whose sides and bottom are cemented, and which hold water like a glass bottle.
1903 Joseph Furphy *Such is Life* (1944) 16: Price and Cooper, being cooks, had kindled an unobtrusive fire in a crab-hole, where three billies were soon boiling.
1944 Charles Fenner *Mostly Australian* 102: In central Victoria there are wide, treeless, basalt plains ... Such areas have a curious surface, consisting of shallow depressions with interven ing low ridges ... The depressions are miscalled 'crab-holes', a name which appears to have been commonly transferred from moist river flats, where crabs really did make holes.
1967 Len Beadell *Blast the Bush* 49: Having been there with the black-fellow and driven about the clearing, I knew it was free of crab holes or hidden ruts.
see **gilgie**

crabs, draw the To attract unwelcome attention, esp. enemy fire [? f. *crab* as abbr. of 'crab-louse', or *crab* to interfere (Vaux 1812)]
[**1919** W. H. Downing *Digger Dialects* 17: *Crabs* shells, shelling]
1932 Leonard Mann *Flesh in Armour* 144: 'The Tommies told us this was a quiet sector, but it's lively enough now, what with the Stokes chucking their muck and running, and leaving us to collect the crabs.' Ibid. 260: The Tommy captain lit a cigarette and I lit my pipe [in an air raid]. The young wench reckoned we would draw the crabs.
1942 *Salt* 25 May 8: *To bring the crabs around* To expose yourself to enemy fire. [reported as having come back 'with the AIF recently returned form the Middle East']
1959 Dorothy Hewett *Bobbin Up* 41: 'And we don't like 'em under age, draws the crabs'. [police]
1974 *Bulletin* 16 Mar. 17: When Prime Minister Whitlam last week told rural members of the Federal Parliamentary Labor Party that they should have expected the abolition of the superphosphate bounty because it was 'in the Coombs report', he really drew the crabs.

crack a fat see **fat**

crack hardy To put on a brave front in misfortune
1915 C. J. Dennis *The Songs of a Sentimental Bloke* 66: A fool 'oo tried / To just crack 'ardy, an' 'old gloom aside.
1919 Edward Dyson *Hello, Soldier!* 49: Always dressin' up the winder, crackin' hardy, though we felt / Fearful creepy in the whiskers, very cold beneath the belt.
1924 *Truth* 27 Apr. 6: *Crack hardy* To suppress feelings.
1935 R. B. Plowman *The Boundary Rider* 239–40: Old Bill was a great believer in 'cracking hardy'.
1946 K. S. Prichard *The Roaring Nineties* 147: Living from day to day in the heat and glare as if you were withering and drying up inside, but must crack hardy and joke about it to show your grit.
1961 *Australian Stories of Today* ed. C. Osborne 141: Our father stood there, wan and crackling hardy in his flannel and his cold despair.
1980 *Sydney Morning Herald* 6 Oct. 7: Mr Fraser had been cracking hardy about the results of the first two polls ... which showed a similar but less dramatic trend.

crack it To succeed in some enterprise, esp. sexual [f. 'cracking a safe', 'cracking a code', etc.]
1941 Baker 23: *Crack it* To record success in an amorous affair.
1948 Sumner Locke Elliott *Rusty Bugles* in *Khaki, Bush and Bigotry* ed. Eunice Hanger (1968) 61: 'Hello, Darky ... so you cracked it again I hear.'
1953 *Caddie A Sydney Barmaid* 255: 'Romped home with flying colours in his accountancy exams, but like me, he's never been able to crack it for a decent job.'
1963 Lawson Glassop *The Rats in New Guinea* 115: 'You wouldn't even crack it with a nymphomaniac.'
1973 Alexander Buzo *Rooted* 78: 'Keep on with your art, mate. You'll crack it one day, I'm sure of it.'

1975 Les Ryan *The Shearers* 75: 'What are you so bloody cocky about?' said Lofty . . . 'Cracked it, did yer?'
1982 *NT News* (Darwin) 12 Mar. 17: This pair have been round a while and never quite cracked it.

cracker   1   The tip of a stockwhip
1876 Rolf Boldrewood *A Colonial Reformer* (1891) 224: Pipes were lit, stockwhips greased and garnished with resplendent crackers, and all hands strolled in leisurely fashion towards the stockyard.
1905 Randolph Bedford *The Snare of Strength* 256: 'Ere's a cracker, Daven, for your whip; them spiders make the best crackers in the world.'
1908 W. H. Ogilvie *My Life in the Open* 6: Let the heavy stockwhip fall; fourteen feet from keeper to cracker it lies out along the sand.
2   A worn out horse, sheep, bullock
1950 *Sydney Morning Herald* 21 Jul. 1: A puzzled reader asks 'What is a cracker?' He sends a report of a cattle sale which says . . . 'stores from £7 to £10; crackers sold for less.' Well, this sort of cracker is a worn-out cow – bottoms in the cattle world.
1965 E. O. Schlunke *Stories of the Riverina* 63: 'Ever seen such a bunch of old crackers?' he said, laughing contemptuously [at the sheep]. 'Fit for nothing but the meat cannery.'
3   A brothel
1963 John Naish *That Men Should Fear* 143: My Aunt Helen worked in a cracker in Munro Street. Worked as a madam or a moll.

cracker, not worth a, haven't got a   No evidence has been found for Baker's identification of a 'cracker' with a one pound note (adopted in the OED Suppl.). The word 'cracker' is used for a worn-out cow, and for an attachment to the end of a stockwhip, but neither of these is a likely explanation. The U.S. 'cracker' (a biscuit) would have been unfamiliar to Australia until after World War II. As 'cracker' is found only in negative expressions – cf. 'skerrick' and 'razoo' – it may not refer to anything positive i.e. there is never a report of anyone who *does* have a cracker or *is* worth a cracker. Not to have a cracker is to be completely out of funds, not to be worth a cracker is to be worth nothing at all.
   Vaux records 'cracker' in 1812 as 'a small loaf, served to prisoners in jails, for their daily subsistence', but there is no other occurrence of the word in this sense in Australian English.
1934 W. S. Howard *You're Telling Me!* 300: 'What about money?' shade number two asked doubtfully. 'We haven't got a cracker.' [OED]
1942 Gavin Casey *It's Harder for Girls* 162: 'He's got guts, anyway,' said Sayers. 'I didn't think he was worth a cracker.'

1944 Lawson Glassop *We Were the Rats* 83: 'I walked into a country hotel in Queensland without a cracker but with my fur coat and black homberg on.'
1957 Judah Waten *Shares in Murder* 29: 'I've heard her husband didn't give her a cracker when he divorced her.'
1963 Randolph Stow *Tourmaline* 65: 'It doesn't matter a cracker to me.'
1973 Ward McNally *Man from Zero* 110: 'I better clear outa the Northern Territory now – my life won't be worth a cracker if I don't.'
1980 *Daily News* (Perth) 22 Dec. 40: 'The pub safe had been knocked off the night before. That left us stranded in Wiluna without a cracker.'

cracker night   The night of Empire Day (24 May) celebrated with a bonfire and fireworks; later transferred to Commonwealth Day and the Queen's Birthday, now the Saturday of the Queen's Birthday weekend
1953 Ruth Park *A Power of Roses* 184: 'Just twenty-seven years ago I met me missus on Cracker Night.'
1963 *Sydney Morning Herald* 17 Apr. 1: A state Government Committee will urge local councils and the general public to discourage public bonfires on 'cracker night' this year.
1976 *Sun-Herald* 30 May 38: Cracker night accidents were avoidable if fireworks users followed simple safety rules, an expert said this week.
1980 *Mercury* (Hobart) 3 Jun. 4: We don't usually run 'lost and founds' in this column, but a dog missing since 'cracker night' is an exception.
1982 *Weekend Australian* 12 Jun. 17: In a build-up to 'cracker night' (an orgy of fireworking that explodes every Queen's birthday weekend), tiny tots [in Canberra] are firing off penny bungers, rockets and catherine wheels in every street.

crash hot   Outstanding; in the forefront; up to the minute [? variant of *shit-hot*]
1956 Encountered in conversation
1973 Alexander Buzo *Rooted* 86: 'You'll like it here, Gary's a good bloke and his Mum cooks a crash hot rissole.'

crash through or crash   A principle advanced by E. G. Whitlam as Labor leader
1972 E. G. Whitlam TV interview with David Frost: 'When you are faced with an impasse you have got to crash through or you've got to crash' cit. Laurie Oakes *Whitlam PM* (1973), p. 122.
1983 Mr Justice Macken *Sydney Morning Herald* 6 Jul. 5: It is no small thing for a company as important as Comeng to decide unilaterally to make major variations en masse to the contract of employment of its workers and to hope by a policy of 'crash through or crash' to render due processes

ineffective.

1984 *Sydney Morning Herald* 29 Aug. 11: Mr Stone was the apostle of conflict and confrontation. Crash through or crash could have been his motto had that other great political success, Gough Whitlam, not bagged it first.

crawl To ingratiate oneself with those in authority: *derogatory*

1881 A. C. Grant *Bush-Life in Queensland* ii 45: He had crawled his way up in 'the foorce' to his present distinguished position from obscurity.

1908 Giles Seagram *Bushmen All* 31: He, being free from 'side' and from any suspicion of toadyism or 'crawling' was generally liked by the men.

1933 Frank Clune *Try Anything Once* 168: I was accused of 'crawling to the Pott's Pointers.'

1939 Kylie Tennant *Foveaux* 140: 'Not 'cause you're payin' me. I ain't ever crawled to anyone for that.'

1950 Brian James *The Advancement of Spencer Button* 155: Accusations of 'crawling to the boys' to get them to work.

1965 Eric Lambert *The Long White Night* 22: 'Trying to do a good job!' mimicked Clancy. 'He's crawling for his third [stripe], you mean.'

1969 William Dick *Naked Prodigal* 247: I didn't crawl to him ... I wouldn't crawl to no bastard for nothing.'

crawler 1 A sheep, cow or other animal that is laggard, weak or docile: *obs.*

1853 *Letters from Victorian Pioneers* ed. T. F. Bride (1898) 218: On this run, out of 1,500 head of cattle, all had been driven off but about 30 'crawlers'. It was many weeks before they were re-mustered.

1868 C. Wade Brown *Overlanding in Australia* 2: Many [sheep] die, particularly such as are old, or weak, technically termed out here the 'crawlers'.

1876 Rolf Boldrewood *A Colonial Reformer* (1890) 321: 'Well, they're a middling lot of quiet cattle for one thing, they're regular crawlers.' Ibid. 217: The well-bred station 'crawlers', as the stockmen term them for their peaceable and orderly habits.

1896 N. Bartley *Australian Pioneers and Reminiscences* 26: Mr Kirby came up and counted them (the sheep), and found them to be 9,924 ... with 6 crawlers left on the road.

1911 E. S. Sorenson *Life in the Australian Backblocks* 167: The stragglers or crawlers (as the weak ones, doddering miles behind, are called).

2 A shepherd, from the slowness of his activities, and from the contempt of those who worked on horseback: *obs.*

1853 S. Mossman and T. Banister *Australia Visited and Revisited* 64: As we approached him [the shepherd] at a walking pace, we could not but contemplate his peaceful occupation, so much in accordance with the stillness of the Australian wilderness ... you find him a long-bearded, bronze-featured 'crawler', as he is termed in the colony.

1857 F. Cooper *Wild Adventures in Australia* 50: Fit only for shepherding – the one employment despised by all classes in a country where the strongest reproach was to be a 'crawler'.

1867 John Morison *Australia As It Is* 221: The pastoral life, following flocks of sheep ... was much more agreeable ... to them than clearing land and working at farms under a scorching sun. They are now scattered all over the occupied interior, and are mostly debilitated old men, to whom the settlers gave the name of 'old crawlers'.

1875 Rolf Boldrewood *The Squatter's Dream* repr. as *Ups and Downs* (1878) 67: 'Do I look like a slouching, 'possum-eating, billy-carrying crawler of a shepherd? I've had a horse under me ever since I was big enough to know Jingaree mountain from a haystack, and a horse I'll have as long as I can carry a stock-whip.'

3 A 'slowcoach', loafer, shirker; also unspecific term of contempt: *obs.*

1837–8 *Report from the Select Committee on Transportation* ii 75: The clever knaves among the convicts very seldom fell into such an unfortunate predicament as these refuse of the convicts get into on road-parties. The cant name for these among the prisoners themselves was 'the crawlers'. They were scarcely able to work, people whom no settlers wished to employ.

1849 Alexander Harris *The Emigrant Family* (1967) 32: 'You'll have the pick of a score every day; shepherds, tradesmen, and men that never were men yet; good men and crawlers.'

1867 J. R. Houlding *Australian Capers* 186: These colonies are not good places for old folks to come to ... for few persons care to employ 'old crawlers' (as they are called by the natives) when there are lots of young men and women to be had.

1883 Rolf Boldrewood *Robbery Under Arms* (World's Classics 1949) 607: 'Haven't you served those drinks yet, Bob? ... I never saw such a slow-going crawler as you are.'

1901 Henry Lawson 'Telling Mrs Baker' *Prose* i 418: 'You're surely not crawler enough to desert a mate in a case like this?' Ibid. 548: 'You're a damned crawler, Romany!' I said.

1924 Rann Daly *The Outpost* 80: 'They're to protect the crawlers who come here to make easy money.'

1931 Miles Franklin *Back to Bool Bool* 265: 'Flaming crawlers!' he commented ... 'I don't know what to make of the young people to-day. They're born dead.'

4 Someone who toadies to the boss, or any superior

1892 William Lane *The Workingman's Paradise* 104: 'And you'd get more inclined to humour the boss every time you had to try again [for a job].' 'Naturally. That's how they get at us. No man's a crawler who's sure of a job.'
1902 Henry Lawson 'Lord Douglas' *Prose* i 494: 'As for turning blackleg – well, I suppose I've got a bit of the crawler in my composition (most of us have), and a man never knows what might happen to his principles.'
1934 J. M. Harcourt *Upsurge* 165: The head of her department said that he had no complaint to find with her – though he had recanted after he had seen his master, the bloody crawler.
1939 Miles Franklin and Dymphna Cusack *Pioneers on Parade* 140: Albert ... pondered on what a crawler love could make of a man, though he had never grovelled so with Lizzie.
1945 Kylie Tennant *Ride on Stranger* 22: 'A crawler ... Ready to do anything as long as he's a good fellow.'
1953 *Caddie A Sydney Barmaid* 135: 'I'm sick of working amongst that mangy lot of crawlers. I'm satisfied they've got legs on their bellies.'
1965 John Beede *They Hosed Them Out* 82: 'You've got to be a crawler to get the odd gongs that are going.'
1973 Roland Robinson *The Drift of Things* 92: 'Don't try to get in good with the boss. He knows what "crawlers" are.'

cray Crayfish, usually regarded as a delicacy
1916 C. J. Dennis *The Moods of Ginger Mick* 46: 'An we'll 'ave a cray fer supper when I comes marchin' 'ome.'
1920 Frank A. Russell *The Ashes of Achievement* 88: 'Who told you the old boy was fond of a cray?'
1941 Baker 21: *Cray* A crayfish.
1959 Dorothy Hewett *Bobbin Up* 13: 'Crays and a bottla beer. It's the drunks' special for Saturdee night.'
1972 David Williamson *The Removalists* 27: 'I can walk out of this station tonight, grab myself a cray and half a dozen tubes, get home, sit m'self down in front of the box and watch the wrestling.'
1980 *West Australian* (Perth) 11 Jun. 3: Warning to cray men on pot quotas [heading]

crayfish To sidle, move in a way calculated to avoid attention
1893 Henry Lawson 'The Mystery of Dave Regan' *Prose* i 328: 'All the other chaps crawfished up and flung themselves round the corner and sidled into the bar after Dave'.
1946 Dal Stivens *The Courtship of Uncle Henry* 39: He ... darts into the kitchen. In a minute he crayfishes out with a hot roast in a dish and bolts back to the log with me following.

creamie 1 A cream-coloured horse
1887 *Tibb's Popular Songbook* 28: He likes all lively hacks, / He's very partial to the creamies, / And he'll mate up with the blacks.
1902 Henry Fletcher *The Waybacks in Town and at Home* 105: 'Der yer mind Jack Clark comin' ter our place er ridin' er bag o' bones he called a creamy?'
1945 Baker 71: *creamy,* a white or cream-coloured horse.
2 A quarter-caste Aboriginal girl; any girl of apparently mixed blood (see quot. 1887 above)
1937 Ernestine Hill *The Great Australian Loneliness* 33: The belles of the village and a few 'creamies', as the half-castes and *multum in parvo* are affectionately called.
1943 Baker 23: *Creamy* A quarter-caste aboriginal.
1962 Criena Rohan *The Delinquents* 12–13: The other children called her the Creamy. She had come from Singapore with her mother early in '42.
1963 John Naish *That Men Should Fear* 87: 'Reckon a man's a mug to go chasin' a creamie?' [half-caste girl]
1975 Xavier Herbert *Poor Fellow My Country* 52: 'I'm using the term Black Velvet not simply to apply to full-blooded women, but any of obvious aboriginal strain, 'yeller girls', or 'creamy pieces', as they're called, half and quarter.'

Creek, the 1 The Albion Park Q. sand circuit, closed to gallopers 30 Dec. 1981
1956 *Sydney Morning Herald* 17 Jul. 52: Last week I visited Albion Park, known to racegoers as 'The Creek'.
1979 *Australian* 28 Feb. 21: Smith looks for more at Creek [heading] Jockey Kerry Smith, who rode three winners at Albion Park last Wednesday, has prospects of a double there today.
1981 *Sunday Mail* (Brisbane) 15 Feb. 5: 'Close the Creek? Fair dinkum?' Old Tom Harper couldn't believe his ears ... It took a minute or two to convince Tom the Albion Park racing will come to an end and the racecourse will be redeveloped as a trotting complex.
2 In N.T., Tennant Creek
1979 *NT News* (Darwin) 19 Sep. 3: Boring event at Creek [heading]

Creeker A horse able to perform well at Albion Park
1979 *Courier-Mail* (Brisbane) 21 Feb. 21: 'He looks a natural Creeker, but also goes well on the grass.'
1981 *Sydney Morning Herald* 7 Dec. 17: Auction, who won 19 races at Albion Park, is the most popular 'Creeker', but many old-timers are convinced that there were better performers at the track.

crim   A criminal [U.S. 1909 OED]
1953 Baker 124: *crim*, a criminal or, loosely, a member of the underworld.
1957 Judah Waten *Shares in Murder* 62: 'Nobs and crims often rub shoulders.'
1967 Kylie Tennant *Tell Morning This* 256: 'There's all these little crims in the swi-game and the S.P. betting.'
1974 Robert Adamson and Bruce Hanford *Zimmer's Essay* 31: Most crims and screws share a working-class morality.
1980 *Sun-Herald* 2 Nov. 5: Crims muscle in on gay bars [heading]

cringe, the cultural   The phrase invented by A. A. Phillips to describe the denigration by Australians of their own culture, and their attitude of subservience to the culture of overseas countries
1950 Arthur Phillips 'The Cultural Cringe' *Meanjin* 299: Above our writers – and other artists – looms the intimidating mass of Anglo-Saxon culture. Such a situation almost inevitably produces the characteristic Australian Cultural Cringe.
1971 *Australian* 14 Oct. 10: [editorial on the appointment of the Duke of Edinburgh as President of the Australian Conservation Foundation] The cause of Australian conservation deserves better than to be set back into the mould of the great Australian cultural cringe.
1973 *Sydney Morning Herald* 25 Aug. 10: The public will not suffer, tomorrow, the kind of cultural cringe it once felt when confronted by the home-created product.
1980 *National Times* 25 May 20: This cataloguing of our 'oddities' is no more that a revival of the cultural cringe which Mr Horne in earlier days has done much to discourage.
1984 *Sydney Morning Herald* 23 Mar. 20: Cultural cringe is alive and well in Melbourne.

cronk   Out of order, unsound, dishonest, fraudulent; also 'run cronk' (run a dishonest race), 'go cronk' (go wrong, break down): *obs.* [f. *crank* one that is sick or ill OED 1567; G. *krank* sick, ill]
1889 Rolf Boldrewood *Nevermore* (1892) 271: 'From the look of him . . . I shouldn't be surprised if there was something "cronk" about him, for all his gold-buying.'
1894 Henry Lawson *Letters* 57: Things went cronk shortly after my arrival in Sydney.
1903 Joseph Furphy *Such is Life* (1944) 129: 'When a girl's gone cronk, like you, she must expect to see white things darting about.' Ibid. 287: 'It paid us to give him two notes to run cronk.'
1934 F. E. Baume *Burnt Sugar* 58: 'It all sounds pretty cronk to me.'
1958 Jack Lindsay *Life Rarely Tells* 213: 'Not that I believe in doing anything cronk.'

crook   1   Ill, out of sorts, debilitated
1898 *Bulletin* 17 Dec. Red Page: *Krook* or *kronk* is bad.
1915 C. J. Dennis *The Songs of a Sentimental Bloke* 88: An' then, I sneaks to bed, an' feels dead crook.
1934 Thomas Wood *Cobbers* 19: 'Tell the Gov. I can't come today; I'm crook in the guts.'
1945 Roy Rene *Mo's Memoirs* 107: All through our tour to North Queensland I was feeling crook, but I certainly never realised just how crook I was.
1955 Patrick White *The Tree of Man* 185: 'Are the burns bad? We must dress them. Tell me,' she said, 'do they feel crook?'
1962 Jon Cleary *The Country of Marriage* 76–7: 'Are you feeling crook?' Crook: now there is a good Aussie term. It describes me perfectly: sick, hollow, head aching.
1969 William Dick *Naked Prodigal* 22: 'He's been drivin' her mad since he's been off with his crook back.'
1984 Marian Eldridge *Walking the Dog* 10: 'Colin dipped out on school today. Reckons he's got a crook throat.'
2   Defective, disagreeable, unattractive
1915 Let. in Bill Gammage *The Broken Years* (1974) 44: Sand in your tucker, in your ears, nose, everywhere, and anywhere, it was real crook.
1924 *Truth* 27 Apr. 6: *Crook spin* Run of bad luck.
1983 Leo Schofield *Sydney Morning Herald* 29 Jan. 27: Unlike Dame Joan's dress, which looked better on tele than it did in real life, those horrible banks of ill-assorted and appallingly arranged blooms looked crook on the box but worse in the hall.
see **Tallarook**

crook, go   To upbraid, abuse
1911 Louis Stone *Jonah* 190: 'Yer niver 'ad no cause ter go crook on me, but I ain't complainin',' cried Chook hoarsely.
1915 C. J. Dennis *The Songs of a Sentimental Bloke* 113: Goes crook on life, an' calls the world a cheat.
1919 W. H. Downing *Digger Dialects* 26: *Go crook* Become angry or abusive.
1929 Herbert Scanlon *Old Memories* 17: 'I wasn't going crook . . . I was only barraking you.'
1944 Lawson Glassop *We Were the Rats* 207: 'Then I thinks she'll go crook on me for speakin', seein' that we ain't been introduced.'
1965 Patrick White *Four Plays* 150: 'Dad says Mr Masson is liable. He went real crook.'

crooked maginnis   see **maginnis**

Crooked Mick   see **Mick**

crooked on   Hostile to, averse to

1949 Lawson Glassop *Lucky Palmer* 87: He shuddered when he said 'working'. 'That work,' he said. 'I'm crooked on that.'
1959 Xavier Herbert *Seven Emus* 101: 'It's no good talking religion to Bronco. He's dead crooked on it.'
1962 Alan Seymour *The One Day of the Year* 73: 'Now, if Alf was you he'd have a reason to be crooked on the world.'
1966 Elwyn Wallace *Sydney and the Bush* 52: 'The cops have . . . a whole lot more work with no extra money. That's why they're real crooked on dolies.'
1980 *NT News* (Darwin) 23 Feb. 7: The thing he was really crooked about was the standard of dress of some of the gamblers – shirts open to the waist and so on.

croppy 1 An Irish convict (from the rebels of 1798, who had their hair cut short in sympathy with the French Revolution)
1800 *HRA* I ii 581: That he hath often been in company with Holt when drinking inflammatory and seditious Toasts – 'Success to the Croppies' and other improper Expressions were made use of by Holt, that he had asked the Witness if there was a rising of the Irish if he would not join them . . . that Holt then said 'You are an Irishman, Kennedy, and we will all go home in one ship together.'
2 A convict; a runaway convict; a bushranger
1809 *HRNSW* vii 216: It is high time that some fresh Governor should have arrived here before this as such doings was never known – pardons to the worst of characters, Croppeys, and thieves.
1830 Robert Dawson *The Present State of Australia* 294: I said to the natives, as I often had done before, 'You look out, you know, and take care croppy (convict) no crammer (steal).' Ibid. 302–3: Not knowing the persons of the white men, the natives concluded that they were 'croppies,' who had run away from the penal settlement at Port Macquarie.
1883 W. H. Breton *Excursions in New South Wales* 234: The settlers are allowed to be present, but not the convicts, whom they call croppies, of course a word which they [the natives] have learnt from whites.
1848 H. W. Haygarth *Recollections of Bush Life in Australia* 9: Robbed of his horse, valise . . . by the well-known 'croppies' – 'Black Joe' or 'Irish Tom'.
1849 Alexander Harris *The Emigrant Family* (1967) 378: 'He says he'll shear off our hair – and make croppies of us.'

Cross, the 1 The Southern Cross
1931 Miles Franklin *Back to Bool Bool* 43: The Cross was twinkling southwards.
1939 Kenneth Slessor *Five Bells* 15: Night and water / Pour to one rip of darkness, the Harbour

floats / In air, the Cross hangs upside-down in water.
1968 Stuart Gore *Holy Smoke* 15: 'Look at the old Cross, shining away up there.'
2 King's Cross, Sydney
1946 Dal Stivens *The Courtship of Uncle Henry* 184: 'What a dump,' Jack said. 'The Cross will look good after this.'
1951 Dymphna Cusack and Florence James *Come In Spinner* 58: 'Us girls have got a flat together up at the Cross.'
1966 Elwyn Wallace *Sydney and the Bush* 138: People in Sydney . . . always say 'Down the 'Loo' or 'Up the Cross'.

Cross, when the ~ turns over When the Southern Cross has tilted from an eastern to a western orientation, indicating the end of a drover's watch (see *Southerly* 1975 33–7)
[**1881** A. C. Grant *Bush-Life in Queensland* i 217: 'Hadn't you better turn in?' suggests Sam. 'We've good three hours yet by the Southern Cross.']
1951 Ernestine Hill *The Territory* 425: 'Call me when the Cross turns over,' you will hear the drovers say, or 'when the Pointers are clear.'
1957 D'Arcy Niland *Call Me When the Cross Turns Over* 124: 'You know what the drovers say, Mrs Anderson – Call me when the Cross turns over, they say. The Cross turns over for everybody. It marks for some the end of a sleep, for some the beginning.'

crow 1 A woman who is old or ugly: *derogatory*
1925 H. H. Richardson *The Way Home* 84: Between ourselves it makes me feel a proper old crow.
1949 Lawson Glassop *Lucky Palmer* 60: She's no crow, he thought, A real good-looking filly, this one.
1953 T. A. G. Hungerford *Riverslake* 220: 'Those old crows in the office get high and mighty ideas about themselves. They want taking down a peg or two.'
1965 Hal Porter *The Cats of Venice* 112: Surprised at the old Pommy crow's interruption he spares a glance.
1970 Jon Cleary *Helga's Web* 21: She would have been quite a looker. 'Why do they kill the good-looking ones? There are plenty of crows around.'
1974 *Sunday Telegraph* (Sydney) 3 Nov. 9: Mrs Whitlam lashed out at some of the critics who blasted her show. 'I don't mind if they call me an old crow, but you naturally think they're unfair if they attack something you think went very well.'
2 A prostitute [The It. *cornacchia* means 'a loose woman', and there is a Fr. proverb of the seventeenth century comparing a whore to a crow]
1950 *Australian Police Journal* Apr. 111: Crow Prostitute.

1953 Kylie Tennant *The Joyful Condemned* 47: 'She's in with all the higher-ups. And what does she do? Slugs a guy like a cro on a beat.'
1965 Eric Lambert *The Long White Night* 80: 'That big café down on the waterfront. The Universal. The crows hang round it there in droves.'
1972 Dorothy Hewett *The Chapel Perilous* 76: 'Marry you, an amateur moll like you? Marry a crow who deserted her husband and kid!'
1979 *Herald* (Melbourne) 14 Apr. 9: 'There are some Broady [Broadmeadows, Vic.] girls out crowing (engaging in prostitution) in St Kilda now.'
1980 Bob Herbert *No Names . . . No Pack Drill* 77: 'What are you, anyway. A Kings Cross crow. Every Yank in town's been rootin' you.'
see **chromo**

crow, draw the   To come off worst in any allocation [f. the anecdote about sharing out the day's shooting, the bag containing a number of table-birds and one crow, so that someone would 'draw the crow' in his share]
1944 Lawson Glassop *We Were the Rats* 113: 'That poor bloke drew the crow.' Ibid. 207: 'I reckon with sheilas I always draw the crow.'
1952 T. A. G. Hungerford *The Ridge and the River* 75: 'Oh, all right.' Sweet's tone was resigned. 'I always cop the bloody crow.'
1970 Richard Beilby *No Medals for Aphrodite* 169: 'I knew we'd drawn the crow as soon as I seen this place!'
1975 Les Ryan *The Shearers* 44: 'What a bastard – period,' Sandy said . . . He had drawn the crow.

crow (eagle), when the ~ shits   Payday [also U.S.]
1974 *Southerly* 108: 'Ah well, the crow shits tomorrow . . . Pay day,' he explained, placing it with his lips, 'we get our dough tomorrow.'
1977 Jim Ramsay *Cop it Sweet* 33: *Eagle shits, when the* When the pay-master comes around; Pay day.

Croweater   A native of South Australia: *jocular, obsolescent*
1900–10 O'Brien and Stephens: *Croweater* An epithet applied to the natives or citizens of South Australia.
1903 Joseph Furphy *Such is Life* (1944) 123: The wire parted, and Pup and I were deck passengers, ong root for the land of the Crow-eater.
1919 W. K. Harris *Outback in Australia* 8: The one exception, a long, typical 'crow-eater' (as South Australians are called).
1934 Thomas Wood *Cobbers* 144: So let this mob of Cornstalks, Crow-eaters, Sandgropers, and Banana-landers[1] go on yapping, say Victorians.
[1]New South Welshmen, South Australians, Western Australians, and Queenslanders.
1973 Frank Huelin *Keep Moving* 29: 'South Aus.

is the worst State in th' country – bloody crow-eaters!'
1982 *NT News* (Darwin) 29 Nov. 7: Crow-eaters, we've long suspected, are a little different from normal folk.

crows, stone the   Expression of surprise, regret, or disgust. Sometimes 'stiffen the crows', or 'stone the crows and stiffen the lizards', occurring most frequently in comic-strip Australian [listed by Partridge as Cockney]
1918 Harley Matthews *Saints and Soldiers* 116: 'Starve the crows,' howled Bluey in that agonised screech of his.
1924 C. J. Dennis *Rose of Spadgers* 110: 'I'm sorry, sonny. Stone the crows! It's sad / To see yer face so orful cut about.'
1930 L. W. Lower *Here's Luck* 189: 'Stone the crows!' exclaimed Stanley indignantly.
1934 Vance Palmer *Sea and Spinifex* 155: 'Stone the crows, how can a man hit a crawler like that? He'd never get the stain off his hands.'
1942 Eve Langley *The Pea Pickers* 321: 'Stone the crows,' he said faintly. 'What is it?'
1952 T. A. G. Hungerford *The Ridge and the River* 24: 'Stiffen the crows! . . . One thing I don't like, it's mucking around in ambushes.'
1964 Jon Cleary *A Flight of Chariots* 72: 'Stone the bloody crows, you don't know what you've missed!'
1981 *Sun-Herald* 19 Jul. 159: The top honours must go to lanky Bryan Brown, the dinkum Aussie digger. How refreshing it was not to see some sort of ocker caricature blast on to the screen, all stone-the-crows and struth and beaudy.

crows, where the ~ fly backwards to keep the dust out of their eyes   One of the attributes of **Woop Woop** q.v. or any similar locality
1899 W. T. Goodge *Hits! Skits! and Jingles!* 6: 'The Oozlum Bird'. It's a curious bird, the Oozlum, / And a bird that's mighty wise, / For it always flies tail-first to / Keep the dust out of its eyes!
1936 Ion L. Idriess *The Cattle King* 153: 'I couldn't see the township', growled Bill, 'let alone a mob of cattle. No wonder they call this the place where the crows fly backwards to keep the dust out of their eyes.'
1971 Rena Briand *White Man in a Hole* 137: Posters covered the walls, and there was a sign proclaiming that, 'this isn't the Waldorf, therefore no complaints, please – even the crows fly backwards in these parts.'

cruel (the pitch)   To spoil someone's chances [f. *queer the pitch* thieves' slang]
1915 C. J. Dennis *The Songs of a Sentimental Bloke* 16: But wot's the use, when 'Eaven's crool'd 'is pitch?

1922 Edward Dyson *The Grey Goose Comedy Company* 69: 'If I said anythink lars night, I'd only have cruelled everythink. We must think out a plan.'

1928 Arthur Wright *A Good Recovery* 179: 'We found that two men were coming to town who were likely to cruel our chances with you girls.'

1938 Xavier Herbert *Capricornia* 374: 'Do you think the Southern graziers'll stand bein' taxed to bring down beasts to cruel the market for 'em?'

1941 Baker 21: *Cruel, to* To spoil or ruin (something), e.g. a person's chances of success.

1951 Dal Stivens *Jimmy Brockett* 142: Things were going well with Sadie and myself and I didn't want to cruel anything.

1971 David Ireland *The Unknown Industrial Prisoner* 83: He never made it. His eagerness for overtime and promotion cruelled him.

1980 Thomas Keneally in *Days of Wine and Rage* ed. Frank Moorhouse 262: In that second, Carey would later believe, the friendship was cruelled forever.

cruiser Name sometimes given to 20 oz. beer glass in N.S.W., as the size larger than the 'schooner'

crumpet, not worth a Utterly worthless

1944 Lawson Glassop *We Were the Rats* 153: 'He won't be worth a crumpet in action, not worth a bloody crumpet.'

1962 Alan Seymour *The One Day of the Year* 73: 'Ballyhoo. Photos in the papers. Famous. Not worth a crumpet.'

crusher See quots

1965 Frank Hardy *The Yarns of Billy Borker* 59: A crusher's a bloke who backs a horse at, say, five to one; then lays it in a bookmaker's bag, at say three to one. Has two points going to nothing.

1979 Bill Casey *Sun-Herald* 63: A crusher ... is a bloke who takes a price about a horse knowing it will shorten, and then when it does allows the bookie to back it with him [by laying off the bet]. He finishes with the horse running for him for a point or two to nothing.

1984 *Sun-Herald* 12 Feb. 144: The AJC deserves praise for – at long last – planning to do something about punting bookies who operate as crushers pushing odds down around the ring and reducing betting value to punters. They look like being curbed to laying off only enough to cover liabilities.

1985 Judge Alfred Goran *Sydney Morning Herald* 25 Jan. 1: A crusher really is not a racing man at all. His practice is to back a horse at longer odds, having received some sort of information that its price is likely to shrink during the betting, and then to sell his betting ticket to somebody at odds

which are lower than those shown on the ticket but which are still higher than those currently being offered in the ring.

crust, a A livelihood

1908 Henry Fletcher *Dads and Dan between Smokes* 116: 'Common labor, battlin' fer a crust, is willin' ter graft fer a crust.'

1910 Henry Lawson 'The Rising of the Court' *Prose* i 660: Police-court solicitors ... wrangling over some miserable case for a crust.

1918 Bernard Cronin *The Coastlanders* 115: 'I'll bet a new bridle he's earned his crust in the country some time or other.'

1924 *Truth* 27 Apr. 6: *Crust* Livelihood.

1939 Kylie Tennant *Foveaux* 312: 'What's y'r old man do for a crust?' Curly asked ... 'Driver a taxi.'

1946 K. S. Prichard *The Roaring Nineties* 211: 'He goes around cadging old clothes ... as if he were a poor boy willing to do anything for a crust.'

1962 Stuart Gore *Down the Golden Mile* 65: 'Still, a man has to earn a crust somehow.'

1974 Jack Hibberd *Dimboola* 39: 'What do you do for a crust?' 'I'm a reporter.'

1984 Ross Gittins *Sydney Morning Herald* 16 May 9: The [Egg] corporation would like us to believe that every time we pay too much for a dozen eggs we are making a 40 cent contribution towards the welfare of a dinkum Aussie battling to make a crust out of a few hundred birds.

cry poormouth see **poormouth**

cue, put one's ~ in the rack To retire [f. billiards]

1982 Neville Wran *Sydney Morning Herald* 20 Mar. 13: 'I wouldn't mind being in Federal politics before I put my cue in the rack.'

1982 Alex Buzo *Sun-Herald* 27 Jun. 51: The great moments in commentary, such as the question Rex Mossop asked of Mr Hughes, father of 23.7 percent of the Canterbury team: 'Are you gunna have any more or do you reckon it's time to stick the cue back in the rack?'

1983 *Sun-Herald* 7 Aug. 128: Two other Labor MLAs are seriously considering tossing in the towel ... They feel it's time to put the cue in the rack, and the longer they stay the more they'll lose on super benefits due to the new tax.

cue, to See quot. 1935

1935 R. B. Plowman *The Boundary Rider* 146: 'We have got to cue some of the bullocks in our team that have got tender footed.' ... Picking up a farrier's tool-box, he ... took from it a hammer and nails and a flat piece of steel – a cue. This was just large enough to cover one half of the horny part of the hoof from the cleft to the heel, and was about an inch and a quarter wide. On the outside it was fairly thick, but was thinned off to a

knife-edge on the inside. Taking the hammer and some shoeing nails, Harry fitted the cut [?cue] to one half of the foot, inserted the point of a nail into a hole, such as is found in a horseshoe, and tapped gently.
1951 Ernestine Hill *The Territory* 324: He cued his bullocks at Cueing Pen Spring.

cuffs and collars The insignia of those set apart from the manual workers, esp. in the bush; a jackeroo or 'dude'
1895 Henry Lawson 'The Grand Mistake' *Verse* i 405: You bushmen sneer in the old bush way at the new-chum jackeroo, / But 'cuffs-'n'-collers' was out that day and they stuck to their posts like glue.
1911 Leo St Clare Grondona *Collars and Cuffs, The Adventures of a Jackeroo* [book title]
1923 George S. Beeby *Concerning Ordinary People* 79: 'All you women are the same – always yearning for cuffs and collars.'
1935 Kylie Tennant *Tiburon* 66: 'I sees this young lady walkin' in an' I says, "There's one of the bourgeoisie, if y' like. One of the real middle-class cuff-an'-collar team." An' then she turns out to be a friend of Will ... who taught me all the finer points about workin' class politics.'
1983 *Journal* of Ship Painters and Dockers cit. *Sydney Morning Herald* 26 May 1: We who help keep the ships afloat / No matter the dirt, noise and stench / Are maligned by those in white collar and cuffs / From Parliament, media and Bench.

cultural cringe see **cringe**

Cumberland roll See quots
1979 *Bulletin* 7 Aug. 51: The 'Cumberland Roll' – when a player throws his opponent over his hip.
1979 Steve Finnane *The game they play in heaven* 43: Urquhart professed ... a deep interest in [Ray] Price's hip-throw tackling technique which had become known as the Cumberland Throw, after his club's home ground.
1983 *Sun-Herald* 6 Feb. 63: Ray Price was renowned for something called the Cumberland Throw ... 'It's like a half-judo throw using the hip. If you don't do it properly they trample all over you,' Ray said. 'It is becoming legal now and the Sorensons of Cronulla and I use it effectively. It can really hurt a big man. I did it to Artie Beetson and he never forgot it.'

cundy A stone [Ab.]
1941 Baker 21: *Cundy* a small stone.
1962 Stuart Gore *Down the Golden Mile* 113: 'Look, mine friendt, you are scouting roundt for some big coondies, stones, you know?'
see **boondy**

cunning as a shithouse (sewer) rat see **rat**

Cup of tea, a Bex, and a good lie down The title of a Phillip Theatre (Sydney) revue in the 1960s, perhaps echoing the **bushman's breakfast** (q.v.); a stereotype of Australian suburbia
1983 *Newcastle Herald* 4 Jun. 8: When the day was finally over, I collapsed with a Bex, a cup of tea and a good lie down.
1985 *National Times* 8 Feb. 39: In a few months time the Valium experience – like the now-quaint notion of the 'cuppa tea, a Bex and a good lie down' – will be old hat.

Cup, the The Melbourne Cup
1889 J. Jenkins *Diary of a Welsh Swagman* (1975) 177: This year the Cup was won by a horse named 'Bravo', and he started as third favourite.
1895 A. B. Paterson *The Man from Snowy River* 3: There was Harrison, who made his pile when Pardon won the Cup.
1896 Nat Gould *Town and Bush* 127: At Cup time Melbourne is not the most moral city on the face of the globe. There is an influx of undesirable citizens from all parts of the colonies.
1918 C. J. Dennis *Backblock Ballads* 115: 'I'll lay you ten to one in quids he'll say: 'Wot's won the Cup?'
1934 'Leslie Parker' *Trooper to the Southern Cross* (1966) 6: I came nearer crying then than I ever have since I put my money on the wrong horse for the Cup in nineteen twelve.
1942 John Shaw Neilson *Autobiography* (1978) 97: I hung on to it till Cup time, when half a dozen of us were put off as the owners were reducing hands.
1963 Brian James *Hopeton High* 37: 'Can we get the cricket news, and the Cup, and all that?'
1975 *Sun-Herald* 2 Nov. 1: Record $25m gamble hangs on the Cup

currency 1 The local money used in the colonies, as distinct from sterling (OED 1755)
1813 *Sydney Gazette* 27 Nov. 1: Whereas divers Victuallers, Publicans, and others ... altered the then subsisting Rate of Exchange between the Bills drawn for the Public Service, and the Promissory Notes issued by different Individuals, known by the Name of Currency, by means whereof great Confusion has been introduced into all Private Dealings and Transactions. Ibid. 2: The above [advertised commodities] to be had wholesale and retail, for sterling money, or negotiable currency bills.
1817 *HRA* ix 216: On the 30th of June, 1810, I [Governor Macquarie] issued a strong Proclamation ... prohibiting under severe penalties the further issue of Notes of Hand, other than such as expressed in specific terms, *payable in Sterling*

Money only, wherein our ... object was to check the destructive issue of what was termed *Currency* Notes, the nature of which was such that the depreciation of the relative Value, when in comparison with Sterling Money, actually became the Chief source of profit and advantage ... to the Issuers of these Notes.
1826 James Atkinson *An Account of the State of Agriculture and Grazing in New South Wales* 132: In the early periods of the Settlement ... every trader constituted himself a Banker, and issued his promissory notes, which were denominated *currency* of various values ... When it was required therefore to exchange the Colonial currency against sterling bills ... the former was always exchanged at a discount.
2 The native-born as distinct from the English immigrant, usually as 'currency lads' and 'currency lasses'
1824 *Sydney Gazette* 26 Feb. 2: Owing to this successful issue, the currency lads are in great glee.
1827 P. Cunningham *Two Years in New South Wales* i 54: Educating twenty of our young *currency* females in all the requisites necessary to constitute good servants. Ibid. ii 53: Our colonial born brethren are best known here by the name of *Currency*, in contradistinction to *Sterling*, or those born in the mother-country.
1832 *The Currency Lad* [title of newspaper running from 25 Aug. 1832 to 18 May 1833]
1845 Thomas McCombie *Arabin* 134: Nearly all of the species known as 'currency' are matter-of-fact men, with very few elements of originality in their composition, and ignorant of the pleasure to be derived from the fine arts.
1853 S. Mossman and T. Banister *Australia Visited and Revisited* 286: The 'currency-lads', we trust, are not all destined to be shepherds and gold-diggers, any more than that this embryo nation is to remain always dependent upon Great Britain for her supplies of merchandise.
1861 H. W. Wheelwright *Bush Wanderings of a Naturalist* 247: As for the young 'currency lads', they are more precocious than the youth at home.
1877 Rolf Boldrewood *A Colonial Reformer* (1890) 342: 'You're a regular Currency lass, Tottie,' laughed Mr Banks, 'always thinking about horses.'

Curry, the Cloncurry, Queensland
1934 F. E. Baume *Burnt Sugar* 234: 'Name's Bert Cross. Whaddayer like for Satdy? Come from the Curry.'
1946 W. E. Harney *North of 23°* 35: All round the Curry – short for Cloncurry – were the Selwyn Ranges.
1959 Mary Durack *Kings in Grass Castles* 237: From 'the Curry' the route ran over a deep crossing where the cattle were forced to swim.
1975 Robert Macklin *The Queenslander* 143: They had lost all their money in a pontoon game at the 'Curry's billiard saloon.
1984 *Weekend Australian* 16 Jun. Mag. 4: The Curry, still hot and tough, turns 100 [heading]

curry, to give someone To make it 'hot' for him, assault verbally or physically
1941 Baker 21: *Curry, to give someone* To abuse, reprove, express anger at a person.
1944 *Coast to Coast 1943* 124: She was trying to think up what she was going to say from the platform. 'I'm going to give those old tarts a bit of curry tonight, Ron.'
1951 Dal Stivens *Jimmy Brockett* 152: 'She had all those ideas once, but when most of the critics gave her curry over her exhibition, she woke up to herself.'
1960 Thea Astley *A Descant for Gossips* 175: 'You can't possibly blame yourself if the kids give her a bit of curry for a few days.'
1970 Alexander Buzo *The Front Room Boys* in Penguin *Plays* 53: 'Let's give the ratbags a bit of curry. Here, tip some rubbish on them.'
1977 Jeff Thomson *Sunday Telegraph* 30 Jan. 48: My old mate Lennie Pascoe gave the Bananalanders some curry yesterday ... he shattered the first four wickets for only 16 off seven overs.
1980 *Sun-Herald* 28 Sep. 149: Once upon a time, you could ask someone how they're going, and they'd reply, 'Oh, not bad. The old back's been giving me a bit of curry, but can't complain.'
1984 *National Times* 20 Apr. 16: He used to play football, until he was sent down for giving curry to the ref.

cut *n.* A stroke of the cane
1890 A. B. Paterson 'My Various Schools' in *Singer of the Bush* (1983) 117: All the others ... took two cuts of the cane on each hand as per usual.
1900 Henry Lawson 'The Master's Mistake' *Prose* i 252: 'Just a couple of cuts with the cane and it'll be all over.'
1902 Ambrose Pratt *The Great 'Push' Experiment* 12: 'Mr Collins frowned and administered six cuts on each of my hands.'
1933 Norman Lindsay *Saturdee* 144: 'Hold out!' Five apiece they got ... cuts which extinguished them in a purple mist of anguish.
1940 Ion L. Idriess *Lightning Ridge* 15: The teachers ... called me up for two, four, or six cuts as occasion required.
1959 Gerard Hamilton *Summer Glare* 51: He gave four 'cuts' to every kid who had played treasure – two hard wallops on each hand.
1965 William Dick *A Bunch of Ratbags* 142: He locked the door and got out his strap and gave me

four cuts of it.
1974 Gerald Murnane *Tamarisk Row* 91: She gives them each two stinging cuts and sends them back to their class.

cut *adj.*   Angry, resentful (teenage) [f. *cut up*]
1984 *National Times* 19 Oct. 23: 'Boys who have their flasks of spirits confiscated feel really "cut". They say "He took my bloody alcohol!" They feel humiliated.'

cut-lunch commandos   See quot. 1953
1944 Keith Attiwill *Cut-Lunch Commandos* [title of a novel on the public service]
1952 T. A. G. Hungerford *The Ridge and the River* 123: 'Come on! Think I got nothin' to do but wait for a bunch of cut-lunch commandos.'
1953 Baker 170: *cut-lunch commandos* Soldiers serving with a home base unit.
1978 Ray Lawler *The Doll Trilogy* 121: 'Talk about cut lunch commandos.'

cut out *v.*   1   To separate selected cattle from the herd
1844 *Georgiana's Journal* ed. Hugh McCrae (1966) 127: Mr Jamieson was able to identify some of his own bullocks . . . whereupon, he and Captain Reid, with much shouting and cracking of whips, proceeded to 'cut them out' from the mob.
1873 Anthony Trollope *Australia* ed. P. D. Edwards and R. B. Joyce (1967) 415–16: I went out one morning at four a.m. to see a lot drafted out of a herd for sale. 'Cutting out' is the proper name for this operation.
1876 Rolf Boldrewood *A Colonial Reformer* (1890) 222: Riding in pairs, and separating or 'cutting out', as the cattle station phrase is, divers excited animals . . . from the herd.
1897 Barcroft Boake 'Jack's Last Muster' *Where the Dead Men Lie* 7: Thrice Jack with a clout of his whip cut him out.
1918 Bernard Cronin *The Coastlanders* 66: 'He's the best hand at cutting out in a muster that I ever saw.'
1955 Mary Durack *Keep Him My Country* 350: *Cut out* To divide certain beasts from the main mob.
2   Used of the completion of a contract job, either

of the work coming to an end or of the worker finishing his labours
1882 Rolf Boldrewood *Robbery Under Arms* (World's Classics 1949) 28: 'You and George can take a turn at local preaching when you're cut out' [referring to a fencing contract] Ibid. 83: Jim and I stopped at Boree Shed till all the sheep were cut out.
1892 G. L. James *Shall I Try Australia?* 97: The day before we start to 'cut in' – which is the term for commencing to shear (when we have finished we are said to have 'cut out') – is a busy day.
1905 *The Old Bush Songs* ed. A. B. Paterson 24: Oh, we started down from Roto when the sheds had all cut out.
1919 W. K. Harris *Outback in Australia* 141: Last month, they were in full swing, to-day they will be 'cut-out'.
1936 Ion L. Idriess *The Cattle King* 52: The shearers and rouseabouts were there, freshly 'cut out' from Mount Gipps and Corona.
1941 Kylie Tennant *The Battlers* 364: In a little over a week the job [bag sewing] cut out and they went on again.
1958 H. D. Williamson *The Sunlit Plain* 24: He had rested a week since the fencing contract had cut out.
1960 Donald McLean *The Roaring Days* 124: Mansfield's Reward turned out to be only a small field . . . but a few fossickers stayed on for a year or two after it cut out – like they always do.
1973 Roland Robinson *The Drift of Things* 102: In those days a man who arrived in town after a long spell of bush work would throw his cheque down on the bar, and say to the publican 'Let me know when that's cut out'.

cut out *n.*   The completion of shearing, or other rural work
1911 E. J. Brady *River Rovers* 187: North Yanco shearing shed, where 53,000 sheep were destined to leave their wool before the 'cut out'.
1962 *Sydney Morning Herald* 24 Nov. 12: Later, after the cut out . . . the rep. admitted the sheep were as dry as a punctured water bag.

cut snake, mad as a   see **mad**

D, dee 1 A detective, or policeman in plain clothes. Also an abbr. for **demon** q.v.

1877 T. E. Argles *The Pilgrim* i 4: After my name and occupation had been entered in a ledger by the educated sergeant, I was searched. The pitiless 'D.' took all my property away.

c. **1882** *The Sydney Slang Dictionary* 3: *Dee* (D) A detective policeman. 'The D's are about, so look out!'

1894 *Bulletin* 18 Aug. 14: The inevitable result will be that each private 'D' will keep his own corroborator on the premises.

1924 C. J. Dennis *Rose of Spadgers* 77: ''E's bein' chased,' she sez, 'by Ds, I've 'eard.'

1930 L. W. Lower *Here's Luck* 152: 'These two gentlemen,' she repeated, 'are private detectives.' 'D's!' shouted Woggo.

1945 K. S. Prichard *Golden Miles* 23: Detective Sergeant Kavanagh and a staff of dees were sent up to investigate.

1965 William Dick *A Bunch of Ratbags* 210: 'Crikey, look at the coppers,' I said as I saw the police-sign up on the front of the Ford. 'They're Dees, too.'

1973 Ward McNally *Man from Zero* 109: 'Those bloody Dees were each over fourteen stone.'

2 A D-shaped loop or clip on a saddle [f. *dee* metal loop in harness OED 1794]

1888 W. S. S. Tyrwhitt *The New Chum in the Queensland Bush* 59: On the solitary occasion when it was my lot to swim a flooded creek, my horse did it so well that my lunch in a pouch hanging behind me from the D's of the saddle, was kept perfectly dry.

1911 E. S. Sorenson *Life in the Australian Backblocks* 207: Novices and others who lack proficiency use . . . a monkey (a strap looped between the D's for the right hand to grip).

1931 Miles Franklin *Back to Bool Bool* 280: Each saddle had a quart pot or something else on the dees, and tucker and oil-coats on the pommel.

1959 Desmond Martin *Australia Astride* 194: A leather strap or binding through the pommel D's.

dacca, dakker Drugs, esp. marijuana [f. S.Afr. *dagga* hemp, cannabis]

1977 *Sun-Herald* 16 Oct. 63: Some new words emerge [among the unemployed youth of the western suburbs] like 'dakker' for drugs.

Essay, boy 16: Why I like dakker. 'I like dakker because it makes me forget about all my troubles and hassles. As well it is relaxing and soothing.'

1982 *Sydney Morning Herald* 18 Sep. 1: At a teenage party you may be offered dacca or spot. Called marihuana by some, it's likely to send you off your face.

Dad and Dave Title of a radio serial of the 1930s and later, derived somewhat remotely from characters in Steele Rudd's *On Our Selection*: now a byword for a humorous version of unsophisticated rural Australia before World War II

1943 Manning Clark *Meanjin Papers* ii 340: What are we to do about Dad and Dave, about this ideal

... which embarrasses the élite and sustains the vulgar?

1943 Maurice Clough *We of the A.I.F.* 44: Like 'Dad and Dave' of 'hayseed' jokes.

1974 Geoffrey Blainey *Australian* 4 Oct. 8: On the farmlands the trees were ringbarked in their hundreds of thousands, and behind post-and-rail fences they often stood in their pale cemeteries for five or fifteen years before Dad and Dave burned them down.

1977 *Sydney Morning Herald* 14 Jan. 1: Javed Miandad, the Pakistani cricketer, pronounces his name Me-an'-dad. So what have the Australian test players nicknamed him? Dave, of course.

1980 *Australian* 6 Oct. 7: Flo Bjelke-Petersen is ... so adept at the unique Dad and Dave manners and graces of the bush that she consistently traps urbane interviewers.

1984 *Australian* 23 Feb. 11: If Dad and Dave and Mabel were still battling it out on their selection today the chances are the Australian taxpayer would be footing the bill.

see **Dave and Mabel, Snake Gully**

daddy The supreme instance, esp. in the phrase 'the daddy of them all' [also English and U.S. ? f. expressions like 'the father of a hiding']

1898 W. H. Ogilvie *Fair Girls and Gray Horses* 54: Though shaky in the shoulders, he's the daddy of them all; / He's the gamest bit of horseflesh from the Snowy to the Bree.

1902 Henry Lawson 'A Droving Yarn' *Prose* i 357: 'Billy was the daddy of the drovers.'

1923 Jack Moses *Beyond the City Gates* 105: There were many who wondered that night how Clinker, the daddy of all horsemen, would come out of the battle.

1932 Myrtle Rose White *No Roads Go By* 135: Then we came to the big sandhill, the 'Daddy of the lot'.

1942 Jean Devanny *The Killing of Jacqueline Love* 154: 'She was the daddy of all liars.'

1954 Bant Singer *Have Patience, Delaney* 77–8: I been in a lot of wild mix-ups in my time ... but this is sure the daddy of the whole flaming lot.

1961 Ion L. Idriess *Tracks of Destiny* 80: Of the Territory pioneer women perhaps the 'daddy' of the lot is Mrs Phoebe Farrar.

dag 1 'One of the locks of wool clotted with dirt about the hinder parts of a sheep' OED 1731

1878 G. H. Gibson *Southerly Busters* 179: I'm able for to shear 'em clean, / And level as a die; / But I prefer to 'tommy hawk', / And make the 'daggers' fly.

1899 W. T. Goodge *Hits! Skits! and Jingles!* 42: With leathery necks and dags galore, / A bad machine and a slippery floor, / And how could a shearer want for more?

1933 Acland: *Dag, dags* hard or soft dung hanging from the breech of a sheep. Cutting this off the sheep with an old pair of shears is called dagging.

1971 Frank Hardy *The Outcasts of Foolgarah* 2: Sir Percival Dagg, the sheep millionaire.

2 A would-be dashing and stylish fellow (the sense replaced by **lair** q.v.); a humorist, wag, eccentric

1916 *The Anzac Book* 47: Yes; 'Enessy was a dag if ever there was one!

1918 *Aussie* 18 Jan. 14: The Dag – on leave [cartoon of nattily turned out soldier with a self-satisfied expression]

1924 *Truth* 27 Apr. 6: *Dag* A funny fellow.

1932 Leonard Mann *Flesh in Armour* 57: Johnny Wright, a solicitor from a country town, now a bit of a dag, with the habit of going on a real bender now and then. Ibid. 299: They could imagine that whimsical grin. There he was, just the same old dag.

1937 Vance Palmer *Legend for Sanderson* 33: 'He was a dag, old Chris.'

1946 Kylie Tennant *Lost Haven* 351: He had to be the Alec who was 'a bit of a dag', who always had a joke.

1963 Hal Porter *The Watcher on the Cast-Iron Balcony* 110: Partly to give Uncle Y, the wit, the funny-man, the sad case, the dag, the trimmer, the one-never-lost-for-a-smart-come-back, a further opportunity to set them giggling and squealing.

1982 *NT News* (Darwin) 29 Oct. 7: The stories of his outrageous acts abound ... All in all, quite a wag, or perhaps a dag.

3 Someone untidy in dress or appearance [? f. *dag* 1]

1982 *Australian* 18 May 7: Mr Hay, who describes himself as a 'bit of a dag – perhaps the worst dressed superintendent in Australia', says he is a humanitarian.

1982 *Southerly* 310 20: The young man in question was stood self-consciously by her side, his new suit marginally too big for him, his hair greased and hurriedly combed back for the photograph ... 'He looks a bit of a dag.'

4 Someone conventional, bourgeois, 'square'

1975 *National Times* 13 Jan. 40: The surf has a glamour the ordinary boy lacks. 'They're dags,' says Colleen Field, of Kellyville, of ordinary boys. Despite the repulsive tag, dags are the sort of boy every mother would like her daughter to bring home. At least she knows, by the medium-long haircut, that he is a boy. His clothes are tidy, he wears shoes and is known to wear a tie.

1979 *NT News* (Darwin) 24 Nov. 14: *Dag*: a person who isn't 'with it', he's un-cool.

1981 *Sun-Herald* 29 Mar. 130: 'Just wait till you hear this ad!' she cried. '"Stand-in grannie required by working mother to look after two nice teenagers after school." Have you ever heard of

anything so wet? I wonder who're the dags who need the baby-sitter?'
1984 *National Times* 20 Apr. 29: Rather than using the sledgehammer tactics often characteristic of young performers, The Castanets maintain they are 'the dags who do good', with their motto of 'niceness instead of evil'.

daggy   [f. *dag* 1 and 3]
1981 *Australian* 26 Mar. 3: The Oz man has, by and large, the reputation of being a pretty daggy old dresser.
1983 *Sydney Morning Herald* 3 Dec. 43: If he [the dance partner] was daggy there was a moment's hesitation, but better him than sitting like a passenger on a disused platform.

daily double   See quot. [f. the racing term]
1983 *Sun-Herald* 9 Jan. 124: In some circles, having your wedding at St Mark's, Darling Point and the reception at the Royal Sydney Golf Club is known as the daily double. Another commentator ... suggested that 'trifecta' would be a good word to describe belonging to Royal Sydney and the Black and White Committee, as well as having a bungalow at our most prestigious beach suburb [Palm Beach].

Dame Nellie, doing a   see **Melba**
1984 Rod Marsh *Gloves, Sweat and Tears* 112: I didn't want to officially quit and then discover that I really wanted to play on after all ... I wasn't going to do a Dame Nellie.

damper   The form of bread best known to the workforce of outback Australia in the nineteenth century and later, hence used colloquially in phrases like 'worth your damper', 'earn your damper'. [f. *damper* A luncheon, or snap before dinner: so called from its damping, or allaying, the appetite Grose 1785]
1827 P. Cunningham *Two Years in New South Wales* ii 190: The farm-men usually bake their flour into flat cakes, which they call *dampers*, and cook these in the ashes.
1834 George Bennett *Wanderings in New South Wales* i 260: 'Damper' is merely a cake of flour and water, or milk, baked in the ashes; it is the usual mode of bread-making in the bush.
1848 J. C. Byrne *Twelve Years' Wanderings in the British Colonies 1835–1847* i 364: The traveller ... gathers some wood, kindles a fire, boils a pot of tea, and with a lump of damper*, and a cut of salt meat soon satisfies his appetite. *The word damper signifies bread unleavened, baked in the ashes, about a couple of inches thick.
1855 E. P. R. *A Romance of the Bush* 52: The next two days' stages were to the meanest of roadside houses and of accommodation, where beef and

damper* was all that could be procured. *Flat cakes of flour and water, without yeast, used as bread.
1867 J. S. Borlase *The Night Fossickers* 46: We ... lit a fire, made tea in our billies, baked some damper in the embers, and sat down to our supper.
1895 A. B. Paterson *The Man from Snowy River* 14: They wouldn't earn much of their damper / In a race like the President's Cup.
1903 Joseph Furphy *Such is Life* (1944) 327: 'You're not worth your damper at this work.'
1934 Brian Penton *Landtakers* 51: 'You wait till I get out. Your damper'll be dough.'
1961 Patrick White *Riders in the Chariot* 382: 'You are not worth your damper,' she said at once, 'layin' around!'

dark 'un   See quot. 1957: wharf slang
1957 Tom Nelson *The Hungry Mile* 81: Some 25 years back a gang of us refused an order of the Union Co. to come back after the breakfast break for four hours, after doing a 'dark-un' (24 hour shift).
1961 *Sydney Morning Herald* 22 May 2: One reason for rank-and-file militancy is that many of those who remember the bad days – the jostling for jobs and the 24-hour 'dark-'uns' – are still in the industry.
1977 *Sunday Telegraph* (Sydney) 6 Mar. 7: 'For 12 years as foreman I worked a weekly 'darkun' – a 24-hour shift. These shifts were inhuman'.
1982 Wendy Lowenstein and Tom Hills *Under the Hook* 17: 'We was on a darkie, a midnight shift.'

darky   An Australian Aborigine [f. application to American negro]
1882 Rolf Boldrewood *Robbery Under Arms* (World's Classics 1949) 168: 'Starlight's been took, and the darkey with him.'
1889 Ernest Giles *Australia Twice Traversed* ii 329: These young darkies seemed very good, and friendly fellows.
1907 Charles MacAlister *Old Pioneering Days in the Sunny South* 87: The 'darkies' were great believers in the natural remedy of 'bleeding' in many forms of illness, and were acquainted with the medicinal qualities of eucalypti leaves, and other plants and herbs.
1935 Mary and Elizabeth Durack *All-About* 25: Our darkies have none of the docile inferiority complex which makes such excellent servants of their brothers of other lands. They never bow and scrape to the white man.
1981 *Sun-Herald* 4 Oct. 11: 'I'd sell about 360 flagons a week to the darkies – it's a good line, they really knock it over.'

Darling Pea   *Swainsonia galegifolia*, a plant which

when eaten by cattle sends them mad [f. Darling river and districts]

1889 T. Quin *The Well Sinkers* 101: 'The man's mad!' he said ... 'No ... he's got a touch of what we call the Darling Pea.'

1904 Laura M. Palmer-Archer *A Bush Honeymoon* 349: Darling Pea Madness.

1918 N. Campbell and L. Nelson *The Dinky-Di Soldier* 29: When the Darlin' pea is drivin' men an' cattle off their chump.

see **pea**

Darling pie See quot.: N.T. and W.A.

1951 Ernestine Hill *The Territory* 426: 'Darling pie', baked rabbit and bindi-eyes with scurvy grass for greens if you were diabetic or dietetic.

Darling shower see **shower**

Darlo Darlinghurst, N.S.W. [abbr.]

1941 Baker 22: *Darlo* The district of Darlinghurst, Sydney.

1967 Donald Horne *Southern Exposure* 125: The surfies hang five at the beaches; the beats grow their hair long at Darlo.

1971 Craig McGregor *Don't Talk to Me about Love* 64: Those incorruptible eagle-eyed and pinioned defenders of the Majesty of the Law, the Darlo plainclothes squad.

1983 *Sydney Morning Herald* 1 Oct. 101: From Darlo to Vaucluse mortgages are much the same.

dart Some especially favoured object; a cherished plan or scheme: *obs.*

[**1859** W. Kelly *Life in Victoria* i 218: *Dart* [in gold-mining] is the designation of stuff worth washing, as contra-distinguished from that considered useless.]

c **1882** *The Sydney Slang Dictionary* 3: *Dart* Object of attraction, or enticing thing or event, or a set purpose.

1882 Rolf Boldrewood *Robbery Under Arms* (World's Classics 1949) 46: The great dart is to keep the young stock away from their mothers until they forget one another, and then most of the danger is past.

1893 Daniel Healey *The Cornstalk* 77: 'You see it's a blooming good dart. We hook on to a cove or a gal that has some friends with a little spons, and is somewhat inclined to be givey.'

1902 Ambrose Pratt *The Great 'Push' Experiment* 77: 'Then, ye see, when ye stand for member later on, you'll get respectable, all-round support as well as from the Push. See my blimey dart?'

1911 Louis Stone *Jonah* 60: 'Your dart is ter be King of the Push, an' knock about the streets.'

1924 C. J. Dennis *Rose of Spadgers* 84: 'Wot's yer dart?'

Dart, the old see **Old Dart**

Darwin stubby The beer bottle introduced in 1958 with the capacity of 80 fl. oz., changed to 2.25 l. in 1973, and to 2 l. in 1982

1977 *Australian* 4 Nov. 7: A Darwin Stubby, the mammoth 2.5-litre bottle.

date (dot) Backside, anus

1959 D'Arcy Niland *The Big Smoke* 41: He said, 'Shove it up your black dot,' and went down the stairs.

1961 Mena Calthorpe *The Dyehouse* 214: 'In your bloody date! What do you think we are?'

1973 *Snatches & Lays* 25: The Australian lady emu, when she wants to find a mate, / Wanders round the desert with a feather up her date.

date *v.* To 'goose' someone

1976 Dorothy Hewett *Bon-bons and Roses for Dolly* 52: 'I was up on a chair fixing the new curtains and he comes up behind and dates me. Large as life. Without a word of a lie. He dates me. Cheeky mug.'

Dave and Mabel Characters in the radio serial 'Dad and Dave' q.v., and hence a byword for unsophisticated rural Australians before World War II

1973 Frank Huelin *Keep Moving* 39: The boss's daughter – a girl in her early teens – who played Mabel to Stan's Dave.

1975 Hal Porter *The Extra* 212: Their table manners pass muster, their accents aren't affectedly Dave and Mabel.

see **Dad and Dave, Snake Gully**

dawn, piccaninny see **piccaninny**

day, that'll be the An ironical rejoinder meaning 'That would be worth waiting for' or 'That will never happen.' Accepted by Turner 134 as a New Zealand coinage, but often heard in American films.

1918 *Kia Ora Coo-ee* 15 Aug. 4: Just wait for leave to Aussie. Oh! that'll be the day.

1941 Sidney J. Baker *New Zealand Slang* 50: *That'll be the day!* used as a cant phrase expressing mild doubt following some boast or claim by a person.

1952 T. A. G. Hungerford *The Ridge and the River* 46: White's derisive laughter sounded through the gloom of the fox-hole. 'That'd be the day!'

1957 D'Arcy Niland *Call Me When the Cross Turns Over* 125–6: 'I've got a waiting list.' He smiled. 'Any time you want to go down at the top just say the word.' 'That'll be the day.'

1963 Anthony Coburn *The Bastard Country* 12: 'He reckons he's stayin' on. Says Dad'll let him.' 'That'll be the day.'

1977 Sumner Locke Elliott *Water Under the*

Bridge 82: Everythink she said was mean or sarcastic. *'That'll* be the day,' she warned if ever you said somethink hopeful. 'I'll believe *that* when I see it.'

de facto Someone cohabiting without being legally married [f. the legal term *de facto*, as distinct from *de jure*]
1962 Max Harris *Australian Civilization* ed. P. Coleman 61: Australians prefer to pick themselves up a *de facto*, rather than divorce and remarry.
1972 Dorothy Hewett *The Chapel Perilous* 76: 'You're not one of the great whores of history. You're a de facto, living in a pokey bed-sit in the suburbs.'
1979 *Bulletin* 12 Jun. 62: In New South Wales . . . unless a de facto is mentioned in the will, he or she has no rights, no matter how long the couple lived together.
1980 *Weekend News* (Perth) 27 Sep. 15: She said that no matter how long a woman had been living with a man as his de facto and the mother of his children, the law still discriminated against her.
1984 *Age* (Melbourne) 9 Jun. 1: De factos may get tax relief [heading] The Federal Government is considering giving the dependent spouse tax rebate to people in de facto relationships.

dead bird   see **bird**

dead finish, the   1   The 'last straw', 'the limit', the ultimate test of one's tolerance
1881 A. C. Grant *Bush-Life in Queensland* i 201: 'He's the dead-finish – go right through a man', rejoins Sam, rather sulkily. 'Blessed if he didn't —— near skiver my hoss!'
1902 J. H. M. Abbott *Tommy Cornstalk* 64: There are few colloquialisms more expressive of wearisome disgust, dissatisfaction and discontent than is 'Dead Finish'. It is almost synonymous with 'the Last Straw'.
1908 Mrs Aeneas Gunn *We of the Never-Never* 112: 'It's the dead finish', he said dejectedly; 'never struck anything like it before.'
1912 Arthur Wright *Rung In* 95: 'I know you won a thousand on Bushland, and I don't believe you've shouted y'self a pint out of it. You're the dead finish.'
1918 Cuthbert Fetherstonhaugh *After Many Days* 205: Another bit of slang that originated at Gayndah was 'the dead finish'. Now it is 'the limit' or 'above the odds'.
1980 Rod Ansell *To Fight the Wild* 110: If some do-gooder had come along and shoved the poor old buggers in a nice clean home, that would have been the dead finish of them.
2   A prickly shrub with yellow flowers
1885 Harold Finch-Hatton *Advance Australia!*

272: On the western slopes, rose-wood, myall, dead-finish.
1904 Laura M. Palmer Archer *A Bush Honeymoon* 348: *Dead finish* A kind of shrub.
1911 L. St Clare Grondona *Collar and Cuffs* 70: 'Wait-a-bit' . . . 'nevertire' . . . and 'dead finish' – Heaven knows why – are all desert shrubs, the last being, in reality, a prickly undergrowth.
1940 Ion L. Idriess *Lightning Ridge* 30: We'd be thirty miles out in the midst of sombre, rocky hills scantily clothed in Dead Finish, wattle and quandong.

Dead Heart   The interior of Australia, from J. W. Gregory's book of 1906
1906 J. W. Gregory *The Dead Heart of Australia* [book title]
1936 Archer Russell *Gone Nomad* 47: 'Dead Heart' though this region may be to some, it was never so to me. To know the gibber lands you must go and live amid their silence.
1961 Kenneth Cook *Wake in Fright* 6–7: Further out in the heat was the silent centre of Australia, the Dead Heart.
1974 David Ireland *Burn* 110: 'I'll tell you where the dead heart of Australia is. It's right back there in the cities. Not out in the sand and the mulga and the stones burning hot under the sun.'

dead horse, working (off) a   Working for a return that is immediately consumed in the payment of a debt, and thus for no personal benefit [OED 1638; To work for the dead horse; to work for wages already paid Grose 1785]
1798 David Collins *An Account of the English Colony in NSW* (1975) i 409: Settlers gave assignments on their coming crops of wheat for the different sums in which they were indebted . . . to use their own expression, they had now 'to work for a dead horse'.
1847 Alexander Harris *Settlers and Convicts* ed. C. M. H. Clark (1954) 181: Endeavour on the part of the labourer, after having largely overdrawn his account, to get rid of the debt; they call working out such a debt, *riding the dead horse*.
1863 Samuel Butler *A First Year on Canterbury Settlement* 146: They will come back possibly with a *dead horse to work off* – that is, a debt at the accommodation house – and will work hard for another year to have another drinking bout at the end of it.
1898 *Bulletin* 17 Dec. Red Page: *Working dead horse* is working to pay off a back debt; or, as a teamster would say, 'This trip has got to pay for a horse that I lost last trip; £20 to make up to pay for the new horse.'
1907 Alfred Searcy *In Australian Tropics* 21: Having incurred certain liabilities in forming the home at Croker Island, Robinson undertook to

work them off. This he did, and effectually buried the 'dead horse' at Port Essington.

1932 William Hatfield *Ginger Murdoch* 38: 'I'm hobbled here workin' orf a huge dead horse.'

1945 Tom Ronan *Strangers on the Ophir* 37: I've got a dead horse at McGarry's that is as big as an elephant.

deadhouse   Room attached to a hotel in which the drunks could sleep it off [f. *deadhouse* morgue]

1876 Rolf Boldrewood *A Colonial Reformer* (1890) 133: I remember coming to myself in the dead-house of a bush inn.

1888 E. Finn *Chronicles of Early Melbourne* ii 547: Another usage grew up with the old hotels ... the attaching of a littered room or deadhouse – not the dreary-looking ghostly morgue, where suicides or accidentally made corpses are laid in state, but a secure, unwindowed, comfortably strawed exterior apartment, into which the bodies of those who got dead-drunk by day or night were stowed away, and suffered to rest in peace and sleep off the debauch.

1900 T. Major *Leaves from a Squatter's Notebook* 131–2: [The shearer] might be seen for weeks or days ... swilling the fiery, poisonous stuff called 'real' Jamaica rum, until, unable to sit or stand, the shanty-keeper carried or dragged him to the 'dead-house' – a shed so named, built near the shanty – and there, on a bunk or on the ground, he slept the sleep of stupefaction.

1922 Arthur Wright *A Colt from the Country* 114: 'Another pint, as you say, and it'd be me f'r th' dead-house.'

1962 Alan Marshall *This is the Grass* 46: 'He has no money and when he goes out to it they toss him into the dead house beside the stable.'

dead marine   An empty bottle (of beer or spirits) [? f. *dead men* empty bottles OED 1700, Grose 1785]

1885 J. Brunton Stephens *Convict Once and Other Poems* 308: We had filled a dead marine, sir, at the fam'ly waterhole.

1892 Henry Lawson 'Jones's Alley' *Prose* i 41: A small bony horse, which, in its turn, dragged a rickety cart of the tray variety, such as is used in the dead marine trade.

1911 Louis Stone *Jonah* 74: Borrowing a dead marine from the heap of empty bottles, shuffled off to the hotel to get it filled.

1932 Myrtle Rose White *No Roads Go By* 202: All the dead marines from previous festivities were resurrected and a great bottle-washing competition entered into.

1948 K. S. Prichard *Golden Miles* 375: 'Wood-cartin's not the game it used to be, neither is collectin' dead marines.'

1952 *Coast to Coast 1951–1952* 193: Sitting at that bit of a table with a bottle, and bottles on the floor, dead marines.

1973 John Morrison *Australian by Choice* 128: Carry out the dead marines and stack them in the yard.

1983 Laurie Clancy *Perfect Love* 100: They were all indistinguishable dead marines to her, horrible brown objects that she hurled violently out into the backyard.

dead men's graves   See quots

1855 William Howitt *Land, Labour and Gold* i 309: Akin to these Crab-holes are Dead-men's Graves. They are oblong heaps of earth distributed over certain extents of these low, volcanic plains, which for all the world present the appearance of a graveyard.

1901 Rolf Boldrewood *In Bad Company* 482: I was walking the horses over a curious formation of small mounds, provincially known as dead men's graves.

dead pig   See quot. 1969

1969 Alan Reid *The Power Struggle* 183: Even though it would not stand up to close scrutiny it was a magnificent 'dead pig' to throw into the arena. [Note] 'To throw in a dead pig' in Australian political argot is to make a charge which though it has no firm basis is certain to cause trouble and confusion.

1982 Mungo MacCallum *Sun-Herald* 7 Mar. 141: The Laughing Doc has just thrown a dead pig into the ring.

dead set *adj.*   Absolute, utter

1965 Frank Hardy *The Yarns of Billy Borker* 119: 'I'm a real crusader against acid stomach, got a dead-set cure for it.'

1974 David Williamson *The Coming of Stork* 11: 'I bet there's some dead set nymphos around here, boy.'

1976 David Ireland *The Glass Canoe* 64: Ernie was a dead set prick – we all thought so – but he looked after his Mum's nineteen cats religiously.

1980 Rod Ansell *To Fight the Wild* 75: Everywhere, a dead-set pest. It's not exactly poisonous to stock, but it's not any good as feed either.

1981 *National Times* 21 Jun. 3: 'The man was a dead set unionist who tried to help his members and all he got out of it was character assassination.'

dead set *adv.*   Equivalent to 'fair dinkum'

1979 Kathy Lette and Gabrielle Carey *Puberty Blues* 36: 'Deadset Kim, Dave's stoked in you.'

1982 John Singleton *Sydney Morning Herald* 6 Feb. 40: 'I've worked bloody hard. Deadset, I was into work at three, four, five in the morning when I started, and I'd be the last to leave at night.'

1984 Billy Walker *Sunday Telegraph* (Sydney) 15 Apr. 60: 'Whenever I get the chance to watch Parramatta I'll go and see them just to watch Grothe. Dead set I'm in love with him.'

dead-un A horse not ridden to its full capacity, to ensure better odds when it next races [cf. U.S. and English *stiff 'un*]
1896 Nat Gould *Town and Bush* 225: He has a remarkable way of scenting a 'dead un', or of finding out a non-starter.
1933 Samuel Griffiths *A Rolling Stone on the Turf* 49: 'Well I'm damned!' he exclaimed ... 'Another bloody dead 'un has come home on me!'
1977 *Sun-Herald* 24 Jul. 57: No matter how you analyse the performance of a suspected dead-un there is really only one person who knows absolutely for sure – the man holding the reins.
1982 *National Times* 1 Aug. 14: 'You hear a lot about dead 'uns *after* the race,' said Beirne, 'but 99 per cent of it is sour grapes.'

Dean Maitland   see **Maitland**

deaner   see **deener**

death adders in one's pocket, to have   see **pocket**

death, packing   see **packing**

death seat   1   In trotting, the position outside the leader, from which it is difficult to win. The horse or reinsman is said to 'sit' in this position
1982 *Weekend Australian* 7 Aug. 44: Prince Jade sat behind a different leader (Rhonda's Al), with Local Honored in the 'death seat' – from where he faded while Prince Jade got a miracle rails run in the final stages to win.
1983 *Sydney Morning Herald* 5 Feb. 54: Popular Alm (9–2 on) had to produce one of the great runs of his career to beat Gammalite (12–1) by one and a half metres after being forced to sit in the death seat for most of the race.
1984 *Sunday Independent* (Perth) 17 Jun. 89: 'He was the first pacer to break 2 min on a country track in Australia ... I sat in the death seat with him and we cruised home.'
2   The seat next to the driver of a car (as the occupant is the one most liable to injury in an accident) [also U.S.]
1971 Craig McGregor *Don't Talk to Me About Love* 149: Paula, feet braced against the Mazda floor in case of a head-on smash, in which case she, being in the death-seat, would have the chance for neither mistakes nor regrets.

debbil debbil   see **devil-devil**

deckie A deckhand [abbr.]

1984 *Sunday Independent* (Perth) 18 Nov. 2: This season Judy is a deckie on Brian Bollard's 12.8m crayboat Aqua Lass, working equal halves of the deck with a male deckie.

dee   see **D**

Deek Robert de Castella, Australian marathon runner
1983 *Sun* (Sydney) 15 Aug. 1: They Got Deek's Name Wrong! Australian marathon hero Rob de Castella handed back his gold medal moments after the world title presentation today. Officials had spelt his name wrong.
1984 *Australian* 12 Oct. 20: Deek's pride and passion geared to reclaim top spot [heading]

deener Shilling [before the introduction of decimal currency in 1966) [OED 1839]
c. **1882** *The Sydney Slang Dictionary* 3: *Deaner* A shilling.
1901 Henry Lawson 'At Dead Dingo' *Prose* i 452: 'Stumped?' inquired Jim. 'Not a blanky, lurid deener!' drawled Bill.
1923 Con Drew *Rogues and Ruses* 22: 'We couldn't afford a deaner to see an earthquake.'
1937 A. W. Upfield *Mr Jelly's Business* 146: 'If I 'ad lorst a deaner I'd have got hell for a week.'
1942 Gavin Casey *It's Harder for Girls* 55: 'My dad's got plenty of money ... I can get a few deeners from him easy enough.'
1965 William Dick *A Bunch of Ratbags* 19: One thing about him, though, he knew how to make a deener on the side.

Deep North   see **North**

deep sinker A long glass of beer: *obs*.
1877 T. E. Argles *The Pilgrim* vi 64: These misguided mortals spend in 'deep sinkers' ... that money which their landladies are daily sighing for – and sighing for in vain.
1886 Frank Cowan *Australia: A Charcoal Sketch* 32: Long-sleever, Bishop Barker, and Deep-sinker, synonyms of the Yankee Schooner.
1898 Joshua Lake *Australasian Supplement* to *Webster's International Dictionary* 2021: *Deep sinker* A kind of tall drinking glass; also, the drink which it contains; so called from the fancied resemblance of the glass to the shaft of a deep mine.
1899 W. T. Goodge *Hits! Skits! and Jingles!* 162: 'Can't yer give us a deep-sinker? / Ain't yer got a cask o' beer behind the screen?'

defence, streaker's   see **streaker's**

deli A delicatessen [abbr.]
1973 Max Harris *The Angry Eye* 164: The deli

owner would have to employ a bloke with a pencil and paper classifying every sale.

1975 *Australian* 11 Oct. 25: It was the same with Dean's, a pacesetter in the delicatessen world, operating a 'deli' before anyone really had heard the term.

1982 Doreen Clarke *Roses in Due Season* 73: Listen love, could you nip down to the deli for some fags for me?

delo Delegate, in trade union parlance [abbr.]

1961 *Sydney Morning Herald* 20 May 2: The boys had been battling for gloves, so I went up to the foreman, I'd cut me fingers and that. The pano said 'See your delegate!' So the delo fronted him and said 'If we don't get gloves we'll walk off!'

demon A policeman, esp. in plain-clothes; a detective [? f. *dee*. The OED Suppl. derivation from Van Diemen's Land is unlikely]

1889 Barrère and Leland: *Demons* (Australian) prison slang for police.

1900–10 O'Brien and Stephens: *Demons* detectives, i.e. plainclothes generally (from D's).

1919 J. Vance Marshall *World of the Living Dead* 71: 'They say she's an open slather up there. Not a demon in the burg.'

1941 Kylie Tennant *The Battlers* 118: Adelaide had been triumphantly certain that the shearers were 'demons', or plain-clothes detectives.

1959 Dorothy Hewett *Bobbin Up* 124: Queueing up for your dole tickets and then out again at the crack of dawn, before the demons got on your tail.

1961 Tom Ronan *Only a Short Walk* 19: Some smart demon ... would start getting ideas. And those plain clothes men knew how to stick to a track once they got on to it.

Demons 1 The Melbourne V.F.L. team (previously the Red Demons, and the Redlegs) [f. team colours]

1973 Rev. Alan Walker, in Keith Dunstan *Sports* 230: 'Ladies and Gentlemen gathered here on this great occasion, whichever team we may support – the Saints or the Demons – we can surely agree that we are joined together as brothers in Jesus Christ.'

1975 *Sunday Telegraph* (Sydney) 13 Apr. 38: Demons Slam the Roos.

2 The Perth (W.A.) Australian Rules club

1980 *West Australian* (Perth) 25 Mar. 83: Be a Demon [heading] Join the Perth Football Club now.

3 The North Hobart (Tas.) Football Club

1980 *Mercury* (Hobart) 22 Mar. 54: Lift for Demons [heading] The Schweppes soft drink company will sponsor North Hobart Football Club for $7,000 this season.

Derby, Benghazi see **Benghazi**

dermo Dermatitis, in World War II army slang [abbr.]

1948 Sumner Locke Elliott *Rusty Bugles* in *Khaki, Bush and Bigotry* ed. Eunice Hanger (1968) 52: 'They send you south if you get dermo more than three times bad enough to put you in hospital.'

1972 'Darwin Interlude' *Comic Australian Verse* ed. Geoffrey Lehmann 165: My men are down with dermo and with every tropic curse.

dero A derelict, i.e. someone unemployed and destitute [abbr.]

1973 *Sun-Herald* 8 Apr. 9: 'And you bump into a lot of very strange people – druggies and deros.'

1975 Elizabeth Riley *All That False Instruction* 126: 'Dero came up to me in the city the other day, wanted twenty cents – and I knew why.'

1984 *Sunday Independent* (Perth) 5 Feb. 23: Perth's deros stagger through life and the courts [heading]

derry An alarm, police search; in the expression 'to have a derry on', an attitude of hostility, a 'down', a grudge against [? f. the refrain 'derry, derry down']

1882 Rolf Boldrewood *Robbery Under Arms* (World's Classics 1949) 68: 'Said he knew a squatter in Queensland he could pass him [the stolen stallion] on to; that they'd keep him there for a year and get a crop of foals by him, and when the 'derry' was off, he'd take him over himself.' Ibid. 171: 'We could take a long job at droving till the derry's off a bit.'

1892 Henry Lawson 'A Derry on a Cove' *Verse* i 173: 'It's cruel when the p'leece has got a derry on a bloke.'

1893 J. A. Barry *Steve Brown's Bunyip* 199: 'Them's the coves as we've got a derry on.'

1908 E. S. Sorenson *Quinton's Rouseabout* 24: Murphy had a derry on those people, and was determined to make an example of them.

1915 C. J. Dennis *The Songs of a Sentimental Bloke* 49: I took a derry on this stror-'at coot / First time I seen 'im dodgin' round Doreen.

1926 K. S. Prichard *Working Bullocks* 51: 'Anybody got a derry on you?'

1937 Vance Palmer *Legend for Sanderson* 226: 'More interested in his job and in giving his men a fair spin than in raking off big profits. That was why the other contractors had such a derry on him.'

1958 Vince Kelly *The Greedy Ones* 214: 'She's got a derry on Porkreth, too, because he shot up her boy friend.'

1974 Donald Stuart *Prince of My Country* 155: And warfare, that's another thing Peter has a derry on.

Derwenter An ex-convict [f. the convict settlement on the Derwent river in Tasmania]

1853 John Rochfort *Adventures of a Surveyor* 51: The proprietor of our tent (an old Derwenter) stationed himself at the door to receive payment as we departed.

1865 J. F. Mortlock *Experiences of a Convict* (1965) 220: Among the officials were no less than three old 'Derwenters'.

1888 J. C. F. Johnson *An Austral Christmas* 49: In the bush in those days, when so many old 'Derwenters' and 'Cockatoo Islanders' were to be met with, Craig's past record would not have greatly militated against him.

1899 George Boxall *The Story of the Australian Bushrangers* 139: It was popularly supposed that these bushrangers were all convicts from 'Van Diemen's Land', hence they were known as 'Van Demonians', 'Derwenters' from the River Derwent, and 'Tothersiders.'

deuce, deucer 1 To shear 200 sheep in a day: someone capable of this feat [f. *deuce* two]

1950 Jack Sorenson *Collected Poems* 32: I thought perhaps he may have chanced to hear / Of how I almost deuced them* at Murgoo. *'Deuce them' – To shear 200 sheep.

1953 Baker 69: *deucer*, a shearer who can shear 200 sheep or more a day.

2 A double shift

1953 Dymphna Cusack *Southern Steel* 138: 'He's doing a deucer,' Landy explained. 'The snipe on the 12 to 4's sick.'

1979 George Stewart *The Leveller* 56: If any of the firemen were sick or injured you were called upon to work a 'Deucer' (two hours of his watch each).

devil-devil An evil spirit, in Aboriginal belief [Pidgin]

1844 Louisa Meredith *Notes and Sketches of New South Wales* 95: I never could make out anything of their religious ideas, or even if they had a comprehension of a beneficent Supreme Being but they have an evil spirit, which causes them great terror, whom they call 'Yahoo' or 'Devil-devil' ... The name Devil-devil is of course borrowed from our vocabulary, and the doubling of the phrase denotes how terrible or intense a devil he is.

1881 A. C. Grant *Bush-Life in Queensland* ii 186: The man left, and after some time returned, saying the rest were unanimous that the 'devil-devil' had caused it [the darkness].

1905 Jeannie Gunn *The Little Black Princess* 6: She said that if you had on a red dress when there was a thunderstorm the Debbil-debbil who made the thunder would 'come on' and kill you 'dead-fellow'.

1938 Xavier Herbert *Capricornia* 72: A deserted house was a delightful playground, but an occu-

pied house a place to be avoided like a reputed lair of debil-debils.

1961 Noni Braham *The Interloper* 239: 'You listen to the blacks. They'll tell you all about the debble-debbles who live there.'

1971 Colin Simpson *The New Australia* 363: 'They believed that the light signified a debbil-debbil man, who, while they slept, cut them open and put a stone inside them.'

1983 G. E. P. Wellard *Bushlore* 120: The fire in the entrance [to a mia mia] is a must. Apart from being useful to cook on, it also prevents any debble debble coming in during the night.

devil-devil country Any hazardous terrain

1870 Edward B. Kennedy *Four Years in Queensland* 20: 'Devil devil' country ... is simply one formation of holes and hillocks, in some districts of great depth and size.

1907 Alfred Searcy *In Australian Tropics* 156: I had to work my way through a belt of mangroves, and then on my stomach crawling for some distance over 'devil-devil', or Bay of Biscay country.

1920 Louis Esson 'The Drovers' in *Dead Timber* 36: 'D' you remember ... the short cut through the devil-devil country, where the ground broke under your feet, and the ants would eat you alive?'

1946 Ion L. Idriess *In Crocodile Land* 46: We returned with Fred, an awful ride, jolting over devil-devil country all ploughed up from last wet by countless buffalo hoofs.

1955 Mary Durack *Keep Him My Country* 351: *Debil-debil country.* Black soil plains full of pitfalls hidden under long grass.

1963 Xavier Herbert *Larger than Life* 93: Before the fastest car could get anywhere near him travelling over the devil-devil country of the downs.

devils on the coals As for **beggars-on-the-coals** q.v.

1862 Arthur Polehampton *Kangaroo Land* 76: Instead of damper we occasionally made what are colonially known as 'devils on the coals', which I imagine are somewhat similar to Indian chupatties.

devil's number The score of 87 for an Australian cricketer (13 from 100), or any other score including those numbers

1984 *Weekend Australian* 17 Nov. Mag. 19: The dreaded Devil's Number for Australian batsmen, 87 runs.

Devine, Tilly see **Tilly**

devo A deviate [abbr.]

1982 *Sydney Morning Herald* 10 Jul. 32: 'They're the spiritual devos (deviates)', says one of the staff.

dice To reject, abandon [f. *dice* To lose or throw away by dicing OED 1618]

1944 Lawson Glassop *We Were the Rats* 50: 'I says, Mrs 'Aliburton, I haven't seen Snow since the day before yesterday. He hasn't diced me, has he?' 'Gee, Shirley,' she says, 'he musta got another girl friend.'

1953 T. A. G. Hungerford *Riverslake* 190: 'You want to make up your mind and dice whatever you don't want.'

1963 Frank Hardy *Legends from Benson's Valley* 213: 'No bastard puts my daughter in the family way then dices her . . . and gets away with it.'

dickhead A fool, idiot [f. *dick* penis]

1974 Barry Humphries *A Nice Night's Entertainment* (1981) 147: They'll stitch you up, stick it up you and take you for a dead-set dickhead.

1979 David Ireland *A Woman of the Future* 267: 'Where's he at, the dickhead?'

1980 *Bulletin* 28 Oct. 141: The senator also showed a thorough grasp of student parlance, referring variously to his opponents on the library lawn as 'dickheads, thick heads and wankers'.

1982 Max Harris *Weekend Australian* 6 Mar. Mag. 4: Food and wine buffs perforce have to be dickheads.

Dickless Tracy A policewoman [f. Dick Tracy, the cartoon figure]

1980 Bill Hornadge *The Australian Slanguage* 197: The only inventive feminine nickname I have come across is Dickless Tracey (a woman police officer).

1984 *Sydney Morning Herald* 4 Feb. 37: Mangan is one of 18 policewomen at Darlinghurst (out of 136 police) whom one sergeant calls Dickless Tracys.

dicken 1 An exclamation of disbelief or rejection: *obs.* [? f. *Dickens*]

1894 *Bulletin* 5 Apr. 13: *Witness:* Then he biffed me. *Chief Justice:* And did you stouch him back? *Witness:* No. *Chief Justice:* Dicken. *Witness:* Swelp me.

1911 Louis Stone *Jonah* 68: 'Dickon ter you,' said Mrs Yabsley, 'Yer needn't think they're got up ter kill ter please yous.'

1915 J. P. Bourke *Off the Bluebush* 190: If Life's waitresses say 'Dicken!' / When you reach out for the chicken, / Cop the broth.

1929 Hal Eyre *Hilarities* 46: 'Those were the days when . . . we said 'No flies on you,' 'Dickon to that,' and similar things. So you see it was some time ago.

1936 William Hatfield *Australia through the Windscreen* 293: 'There's a catch in this Light Horse business. You've got to tie your horse up, feed and water him, and *groom* the bastard before you get near a bit of picking for yourself. Dickon to that. The infantry'll do me.'

1949 Alan Marshall *How Beautiful Are Thy Feet* 91: He suddenly became playful and patted her leg above the knee. 'Some leg.' 'Don't paw like that.' 'Dicken you don't like being handled.'

2 In S.A., an expression of agreement, like 'you bet', 'too right'

1981 *Sydney Morning Herald* 24 Jan. 35: Mr Dutton remembers being laughed at as a boy at school in Melbourne when he used the term 'dicken!' as an expletive rather in the way in which 'my oath!' is usually employed. 'A common term in South Australia', he said, 'but no one in Victoria ever heard of it.'

didee Lavatory [*didy* diaper U.S. 1902 OED]

1965 Frank Hardy *The Yarns of Billy Borker* 56: 'Having the didee in the backyard isn't very convenient,' the wife says. 'How right you are,' he tells her, 'get the plumbers in and build the best toilet that money can buy, right inside the house.'

Diehards The Fortitude Valleys (Q.) R.L. team

1979 *Courier-Mail* (Brisbane) 24 Feb. 36: Valleys staged a typical Diehard finish to down Souths 12–10.

dig Abbreviation of *digger* 2, 4 and 5, qq.v.

1929 *Reveille* 31 Aug. 14: The first time I heard 'Digger' was in London, early in 1917, when an American soldier addressed me as 'Dig'.

1932 Leonard Mann *Flesh in Armour* 83: One of the Mth, seated on the ground, cried to Charl, 'Give us a smoke, for Gawd's sake, dig.'

1942 Gavin Casey *It's Harder for Girls* 156: 'You'll see all the water you want in the morning, Dig.'

1953 T. A. G. Hungerford *Riverslake* 50: 'What about you, dig?' the big man demanded, pushing his face so close.

1966 D. H. Crick *Period of Adjustment* 170: 'How are yer, dig?'

1972 Dorothy Hewett *The Chapel Perilous* 83: 'Haven't got the price of a drink on you, have you dig?'

1980 Emery Barcs *Backyard of Mars* 209: Frequently, someone in the place wanted to shout us a beer, and inquired whether one of us or both had been at Tobruk or on the Kokoda trail. They called me 'Dig' and I felt like a fraud.

dig, pull out ~, the dogs are pissing on your swag see **pull**

digger 1 An Australian gold-miner of the 1850s and later [? f. U.S.]

1852 Lord Robert Cecil *Goldfields Diary* (1935) 36: When the diggers address a policeman in uniform they always call him 'Sir', but they always address a fellow in a blue shirt with a carbine as 'Mate'.

1856 G. Willmer *The Draper in Australia* 67: We met with many diggers rambling from one gold-field to another.

1867 J. S. Borlase *The Night Fossickers* 2: I did not come, however, as a seeker of the yellow metal – I had no ambition to become a digger.

1914 Henry Lawson 'I'll Bide' *Prose* i 826: On the ferry I sat beside a man I took to be an old digger ... He'd been in Westralia, after Coolgardie, where I had been – also Papua, South Africa, Klondyke and South America.

diggeress, diggerdom

1855 William Howitt *Land, Labour and Gold* i 43: There were open carriages driving about, crowded with diggers and their diggeresses, at the rate of 1*l*. per hour. Diggerdom is gloriously in the ascendant here.

2   An Australian soldier in World War I, esp. an infantryman; an Australian soldier in any later war [Unexplained: returned soldiers writing in to *Reveille* for 31 July, 31 August, 30 September and 31 October 1929, including C. E. W. Bean, offer some twenty different accounts of the origin of the term.]

1917 Diary cit. Bill Gammage *The Broken Years* (1974) 241: Some Diggers were walking along the street [in England] when two Tommy officers approached and on coming close to the diggers prepared for a salute ... The diggers just walked past grinning from ear to ear.

1918 *Aussie* 18 Jan. 11: 'Digger' has taken the place of the time-honoured 'Cobber' in the parlance of the Australian soldier. Anyone know the origin of the new word?

1918 *Kia Ora Coo-ee* 15 Sep. 8: This term Digger is a very universal one in France; and it's fairly recent in origin. It has supplanted 'Billjim' and 'Billzac' as generic terms – and even 'Cobber', as a name by which you accost your friends, is quite out of it, 'Hullo, Digger', is the greeting now. It is a title very jealously guarded. Bean has celebrated the triumph of the *entente cordiale* between the Australians and the Americans, by declaring that, after the second German push, when they fought together, all Americans became technically classi-fied as Diggers. The origin of the term is a bit obscure. I don't think it connotes the habit of diggin-in, peculiar to the Infantryman. I rather think it began amongst the West Australian battalions, where the miner was so frequent. Anyhow, it's a very honourable appellation now.

1932 Leonard Mann *Flesh in Armour* 83: Mingled with the prisoners were Australian walking cases, Germans and Diggers possessed with the like anxiety that their luck might hold until they were out of it.

1945 Herbert M. Moran *Beyond the Hill Lies China* 142: A man in shabby uniform accosted Challis: 'Kin yer spare a deaner, Mister, for a digger down on his luck?'

1965 Patrick White *Four Plays* 105: A bit seedy, battered. Good features of the hatchet variety. The Digger type.

1971 *Australian* 25 Sep. 1: Diggers still being sent to Vietnam.

1984 *Weekend Australian* 28 Jan. 7: The mines buried in the [Sinai] desert during five wars are a dangerous legacy for today's Diggers and desert dwellers.

3   A private soldier, as distinct from one with any rank

1984 *National Times* 5 Oct. 22: 'You can go into the army as a digger and if you're lucky, 14 years later you might make it to a sergeant.'

4   An Australian who is not a soldier: used as a mode of address like 'mate'

1926 J. Vance Marshall *Timely Tips for New Australians: Digger* A familiar term of address such as 'friend' or comrade. Originally it was only applied to soldiers but now its use is universal.

1934 Thomas Wood *Cobbers* 173: 'What's up, digger?' asked the policeman.

1953 T. A. G. Hungerford *Riverslake* 159: 'Hey, digger, you got any dough?'

1983 Margaret Jones *Sydney Morning Herald* 5 Aug. 8: No wonder jokey Britons, introduced to an Australian, invariably say in what they believe to be Oz dialect: ''Ow are yer, mate, 'ow yer going, digger?'

5   Anyone thought of as showing typically Austra-lian characteristics

1978 *Nation Review* 9 Mar. 20: Don Chipp has chosen to sink the slipper into the image of the sunbronzed digger.

1985 *Sydney Morning Herald* 6 May 42: Allan Border's boys were 'diggers to the bone, slouching, gum-chewing Aussies who will bow the knee to no one, least of all an Englishman', he [Scyld Berry] wrote ... There had always been two types of Australians, Berry said. 'The Diggers, anti-English, anti-establishment, anti-everything ex-cept amber fluid; and the "Old Australians", Brits abroad, clean-shaven types like Kim Hughes and Terry Alderman'.

digger hat   The slouch hat first worn by Australian soldiers in the Boer War, known as the 'digger hat' after World War I

1955 John Morrison *Black Cargo* 114: A digger's hat hanging on a nail driven into the mantelpiece.

1958 Gavin Casey *Snowball* 74: His army days, through the years when a digger hat had made him the equal of all the young men who wore digger hats.

1960 Nancy Cato *Green Grows the Vine* 37: He

had been wearing, as usual, a battered old Digger's hat, its wide brim pulled down fore and aft.

1969 Osmar White *Under the Iron Rainbow* 125: He wore blue shorts, army boots without sides, and a drooping Digger hat bound with plaited rawhide.

1976 *Sydney Morning Herald* 18 Feb. 24: Monique Connolly, the French wife of the Liberal MP for Bradfield, was outstanding in a Dior outfit – an off-white, light wool dress, featuring big silver buttons, a multi-coloured scarf, and matching felt Digger hat with feather band.

Digger, the Little William Morris Hughes (1864–1952) Australian Prime Minister in World War I, and diminutive in size

1919 *Daily Telegraph* (Sydney) 15 Sep. 6: The Little Digger [heading] . . . There were wavings of hats and hands and handkerchiefs, and a wild burst of cheers for 'the Little Digger'.

1952 *Sydney Morning Herald* 20 Oct. 2: No title that he earned was so dear to Mr Hughes as that of 'The Little Digger', and today none will mourn his passing more deeply than the veterans of the first world war.

1956 J. T. Lang *I Remember* 242: It [the Country Party of 1922] didn't like Hughes and lost no opportunity to voice its opinions of the Little Digger.

1975 *Australian* 25 Jan. 16: The redoubtable Billy Hughes once observed that he trusted only two people – Jesus Christ and the Commonwealth Statistician (The 'Little Digger' incidentally added that he still wasn't too sure about the former).

dike (dyke) Urinal, lavatory, esp. for communal use, as in a school or army camp [f. *dike* ditch or trench OED 847]

[**1839** Grose *Glossary of Provincial and Local Words* 47: *Dike*, in Scotland, a bank; or even a wall, especially when it surmounts a ditch.]

1923 Manchon *Le Slang* 104: Dike, les cabinets. [OED]

1948 Sumner Locke Elliott *Rusty Bugles* in *Khaki, Bush and Bigotry* ed. Eunice Hanger (1968) 42: 'Make sure you do everything on the double . . . run to mess . . . run back . . . run to the dike.'

1954 Jon Cleary *The Climate of Courage* 179: He pointed to the men's toilet farther along the platform. 'We can wait in the dyke till they've gone.'

1969 D'Arcy Niland *Dead Men Running* 47: Anyway, the dyke would be occupied. He knew that from experience, he had always been the last to get there.

1971 George Johnston *A Cartload of Clay* 138: 'I mean, be orright for a dike, I suppose [the name *Merde Alors*] but funny for a house.'

1974 David Williamson *Three Plays* 121: 'Get your hands off me. I'm going to the dyke.'

1983 Georgia Savage *Slate & Me and Blanche McBride* 2: 'Can I go to the dyke?'

dill A simpleton, an incompetent [f. *dilly*]

1941 Baker 23: *Dil* A simpleton or fool (2) A trickster's victim.

1945 Gavin Casey *Downhill is Easier* 197: 'Them dills'll never find out who done him in.'

1957 Judah Waten *Shares in Murder* 50: 'You must think I'm a dill if you expect me to take any notice of it.'

1966 Patrick White *The Solid Mandala* 46: Waldo decided not to listen to any further dill's drivel.

1968 *The Barry Humphries Book of Innocent Austral Verse* 76: America is hard to gauge, / The way she backs and fills, / I often wonder, is she straight, / Or is she run by dills?

1975 *Bulletin* 28 Jun. 30: Queenslanders resent being looked on as a mob of dills.

1982 David McNicoll *Bulletin* 30 Nov. 60: Would I be going too far in saying that there must be some dills in Australia's diplomatic and military outposts?

dilly Foolish, silly, 'dopey-looking'; having lost one's presence of mind: *obs.* [*dilly* cranky, queer E. dial. OED 1873]

1906 Edward Dyson *Fact'ry 'Ands* 213–14: 'Who should come sprintin' upstairs but me nibs, pale's er blessed egg, hair on end – fair dilly.'

1912 R. S. Tait *Scotty Mac, Shearer* 71: 'I daresay you've seen a few puzzles in your time, and you have looked at them, and thought them over until you were likely to go dilly.'

1915 C. J. Dennis *The Songs of a Sentimental Bloke* 16: If this 'ere dilly feelin' doesn't stop / I'll lose me block an' stoush some flamin' cop!

1935 Kylie Tennant *Tiburon* 21: 'Bless you, lady, bless you,' he says, all dilly with joy, see, thinkin' he's on a good thing.

1949 John K. Ewers *Harvest* 204: 'Cripes, it'd drive a bloke dilly!'

1970 Kenneth Slessor *Bread and Wine* 31: One translation which he [C. J. Brennan, d. 1932] has pencilled after the Latin words *ocules languidum tuens* – 'with a dilly look in her eyes'.

dillybag Aboriginal word for a small bag or basket, applied to similar small bags made and used by whites

1876 A. J. Boyd *Old Colonials* (1882) 283: 'What is there in the dillybag?' 'About enough beef and flour for a day's feed, and a pound of tea.'

1881 Mrs Campbell Praed *Policy and Passion* 179: Lord Dolph . . . armed with a dilly-bag and a trowel, clambered up the precipice to search for roots.

1953 *Sydney Morning Herald* 16 May 5: Mrs

Eunice Woolcott Forbes said ... that her bank account was a 'joint dilly bag' for the transactions of her bankrupt husband ... and their children.

1959 Dorothy Hewett *Bobbin Up* 149: Jeanie was stuffing things into her dilly bag ... Behind the long line of rovers the women were packing up tote bags and baskets.

1975 Hal Porter *The Extra* 213: Into their dilly-bags go sugar, pepper, salt, bread rolls.

1980 Emery Barcs *Backyard of Mars* 185: After issuing each of us with three woollen blankets, mess-gear in a calico dilly bag, and a cheap safety razor in a metal box, he said amiably, 'Now you are ready for action.'

ding *n.* 1 An Italian or Greek; a foreigner generally: *derogatory*

1941 Baker 23: *Ding* An Italian.

1948 K. S. Prichard *Golden Miles* 100: Serbs, Bulgarians, Italians and Greeks, who worked on the mines, were gathering in excited groups ... over the latest news. The Dings, as the northern people were called, and the Dagoes, which included the southern European races, had never fraternised very much.

1957 Randolph Stow *The Bystander* 21: 'No speak-a too bad-a da English, eh?' 'She wouldn't talk like that, anyway,' Nakala said scornfully. 'She's not a Ding.' 'She says you're not a Greek,' Frank explained ... 'Or is it an Italian. I never remember which is a Ding and which is a Dago.'

1962 Stuart Gore *Down the Golden Mile* 30: 'He's a Ding for mine. He was born in Italy, wasn't he?'

1971 Rena Briand *White Man in a Hole* 11: 'And them Greeks ... if yer wanner leave them dirty dings they're gonna run yer outa town.'

1979 George Stewart *The Leveller* 24: This was the beginning of a savage fight involving miners and all foreigners. No matter what race, Slav, Greek, Italian, Maltese, they were all Dings.

1982 Tim Winton *An Open Swimmer* 103: 'Al the Ding. He runs the deli down the road.' [an Italian]

2 (also *dinger*) Backside, anus

1948 Sumner Locke Elliott *Rusty Bugles* in *Khaki, Bush and Bigotry* ed. Eunice Hanger (1968) 96: 'In your great dinger, you rotten crawling choco.'

1953 T. A. G. Hungerford *Riverslake* 161: 'Why *my* mate, particularly?' 'Hell he thinks the sun shines out of your dinger!'

1972 Geoff Morley *Jockey Rides Honest Race* 209: 'You can get fined or sent to gaol for kicking a cat in the ding, but it's okay if it's a three-month-old baby.'

1975 Les Ryan *The Shearers* 119: 'Ar, pigs to you!' 'In your dinger, too!'

1980 Bob Herbert *No Names ... No Pack Drill* 49: 'It's not only 'is MPs that's lookin' for 'im. Our wallopers are too ... An' they're right up 'is dinger.'

3 A party, celebration [f. *wingding*]

1956 *Sydney Morning Herald* 18 Oct. 1: In New Guinea a party is called a 'ding' and a house is a 'donga'. So if they have a party at home it's a ding in their donga.

1967 Frank Hardy *Billy Borker Yarns Again* 40: It appears that he had drunk fifteen of them there drinking horns of beer at a Commemoration Day ding.

1972 Alexander MacDonald *The Ukelele Player under the Red Lamp* 205: Only there was no beer. Just trayfuls of battery-fluid and cochineal ... that was the kind of ding it was, all very outer-space and quaint and inconceivably twee.

1974 *Australian* 20 Jun. 3: Seventy lonely women from all over Australia got together in Melbourne last night for a 'mid-winter ding' while several thousand miles away in the Antarctic their husbands and boyfriends prepared for a similar celebration.

1984 Max Harris *Weekend Australian* 16 Jun. Mag. 10: I'm in favour of stylishness ... But we musn't let the newspapers fool us. It has nothing to do with the latest social ding at the Sydney Opera House.

4 A dent, esp. in a surfboard

1963 *Pix* 28 Sep. 62: *Ding*: A hole in the fibreglass sheath of the board.

1964 *Quadrant* 30 16: He was demoted to working with Storky on dings, the repair of dents and damage.

1979 Kathy Lette and Gabrielle Carey *Puberty Blues* 32: They checked their boards for dings and stood over us as we waxed them.

1984 *Sydney Morning Herald* 23 Apr. 12: Pity about that speck of rust on the door. And that little ding in the front.

ding *v.* To throw away, abandon, give up, esp. in the expression 'to ding it': *obsolescent* [f. thieves' slang: see quot. 1812]

1812 Vaux: *Ding* to throw, or throw away ... To ding a person, is to drop his acquaintance totally, also to quit his company, or leave him for the time present.

1875 A. J. Boyd *Old Colonials* (1882) 68–9: 'If any man was to try and get along carryin' on the Northern road with only twelve horses, he'd very quickly find he'd have to ding it.'

1880 Rolf Boldrewood *The Miner's Right* (1890) 22: 'I say ding it this very night, and let's try for a show somewhere else.'

1896 Edward Dyson *Rhymes from the Mines* 74: Ding it? No. Where gold was getting I was on the job, and early.

1903 Joseph Furphy *Such is Life* (1944) 178: 'I'm as weak as a sanguinary cat. I must ding it.'

dingbat 1 An Army batman: World War I slang:

obs.

1919 W. H. Downing *Digger Dialects* 19: *Dingbat* See Batman. *Batman* An officer's servant.

1932 Leonard Mann *Flesh in Armour* 161: The lieutenant and his dingbat slid down into the trench.

2 Someone eccentric or deranged

1918 *Kia Ora Coo-ee* 15 May 5: There are men who will tell you that they like camels, and I reckon that they ought to be put in the Dingbat Home at Abbassia. There's something wrong with their brains.

1957 Nino Culotta *They're a Weird Mob* 29: 'Some ding bat after that job . . . He sounds a bit crackers to me.'

1977 Sumner Locke Elliott *Water Under the Bridge* 71: 'They ought to have him put away in Callan Park with the other dingbats.'

1984 *Weekend Australian* 21 Apr. Mag. 10: As surely as the sun sets in the west . . . *A Big Country* must run out of those wonderful dingbats and weirdos they have so lovingly presented throughout the years.

dingbats, to be, have the To have delirium tremens; to be in an irrational state [N.Z. 1918 OED]

1924 *Truth* 27 Apr. 6: *Dingbats* To be annoyed; D.T.'s.

1925 Arthur Wright *The Boy from Bullarah* 66: 'It's enough to give a fellow the dingbats. I suppose you've been soaking up this damned stuff till it's sent you ratty, eh?'

1932 Leonard Mann *Flesh in Armour* 103: 'I think that corporal who came up's getting the dingbats. Cobber's head blown off, or something.'

1943 Margaret Trist *In the Sun* 29: 'May as well take another job soon,' he said, 'a man would only get dingbats hanging around here too long.'

1955 H. Drake-Brockman *Men Without Wives and other Plays* 90: 'Well, if you want my opinion, the poor dope musta been dingbats if he wasn't poking borak.'

1972 Richard Magoffin *Chops and Gravy* 106: *dings* ding-bats, dee-tees, delirium tremens, the horrors.

dinger see **ding** 2

dingo *n.* 1 Aboriginal word for the native dog, a term of extreme contempt when applied to a man, because of the animal's reputation for cowardice and treachery

[**1855** William Howitt *Land, Labour and Gold* ii 168: The coward dingo of the bush.]

1908 Henry Fletcher *Dads and Dan between Smokes* 116: 'Them townies must be a fair lot o' dingoes.'

1923 Con Drew *Rogues and Ruses* 133: 'You're

not goin' to fight! . . . I always thought you were a flamin' dingo!'

1944 Randolph Bedford *Naught to Thirty-three* 79: Jock Robertson had a great and affectionate following, although some bushmen called him 'Dingo Jack'.

1951 Eric Lambert *The Twenty Thousand Thieves* 26: They've got the equipment, these Ities, but they're dingoes . . . as soon as it comes to the hand-to-hand stuff up go the hands and out they come yelling for mercy.'

1958 H. D. Williamson *The Sunlit Plain* 158: Any trick was good enough to put over that dingo.

1962 Tom Ronan *Deep of the Sky* 180: 'Jim Campbell was a different proposition. He was a bloody dingo.'

1973 *Australian* 21 Nov. 11: 'He has shown cowardly instincts by trying to restrain this action,' Mr Anthony said of Mr Whitlam. 'All I can say of him in the Australian language is that he is a dingo.'

2 See quot.

1984 *Sydney Morning Herald* 11 Aug. 34: Merchant bank BA Australia yesterday launched its second series of DINGOs – a new investment avenue in the form of zero coupon government bonds. Known as Discounted Investment in Negotiable Government Obligations, DINGOs are unique among financial securities in Australia in that no income is received until the securities mature.

dingo *v.* To behave like a dingo (also 'dingo out', 'turn dingo', 'act the dingo')

1935 *Bulletin* 29 May ii: In the second round he 'dingoed', letting us through repeatedly, much to his team-mates' disgust [OED Suppl.]

1941 Baker 23: *Dingo* A term of contempt. Also, 'to dingo on', to betray, let down, 'rat on' a person.

1945 Margaret Trist *Now That We're Laughing* 133: 'That's the kind she is. Turn dingo on her own sister if it suited her.'

1952 Eric Lambert *The Twenty Thousand Thieves* 335: 'Where is Allison?' 'He dingoed at the last minute.'

1963 T. A. G. Hungerford *Shake the Golden Bough* 217: 'Now you've dingoed, and I wonder just what the hell mates are for.'

dingoism

1983 *NT News* (Darwin) 17 Feb. 6: Stop this dingoism [heading] . . . the Northern Territory Government apparently believes that it is necessary for the Liquor Commission to send its officers on secret missions to tempt the innocent proprietor of a flower shop, of all things, into breaking the law . . . What it is allowing the Liquor Commission to do to decent people has only one word to describe it: Dingoism.

dingoes, did they forget to feed the Jocular greeting to an unexpected arrival

1968 Walter Gill *Petermann Journey* 13: He looked up, saw it was me, and barked, 'You again! Christ, ain't they fed the bloody dingoes lately?'

dingo's breakfast A variant of the **bushman's breakfast** q.v.

1983 Tim Vaughan *Sydney Morning Herald* 5 Apr. Good Living 1: My compatriot Pierre and I amused the fellow-travellers by starting the day with a dingo's breakfast, before we strolled to the bar for a more leisurely Spanish breakfast.

1984 *Age* (Melbourne) 16 Jun. Extra 11: A dingo's breakfast, a pee and a look around, is free, which I'm told is popular with tourists on buses.

dink *v.* To carry a passenger on the cross-bar of a bicycle, or on a pillion seat (originally from doubling-up on a horse: see **double-bank, double-dink**)

1941 Baker 23: *Dink, to*: See 'double dink'.

1959 Gerard Hamilton *Summer Glare* 111: When I was getting my bike out from under the veranda, she came up to me and said, 'How about dinking me home from school?' ... 'All right,' I said. 'Hop on'.

1976 Dorothy Hewett *This Old Man Comes Rolling Home* 50: 'Last time you carried me school case home and dinked me up Redfern hill past the clock, peddlin' against the wind'. Ibid. 101: *dink* to give a ride on the crossbar of a bicycle.

1979 Sally Morrison *Who's taking you to the Dance?* 49: 'Can you dink me down to the car?'

dink *n.* A ride taken by 'double-dinking'

1934 *Bulletin* 5 Sep. 20: The fortunate Melbourne school-kid with a bike ... is asked by his cobbers for a 'dink'.

1965 D. E. Charlwood *All the Green Year* 46: 'I'll give y' a dink'. He drew up with me on his new bike and I jumped on the bar.

1980 *Sydney Morning Herald* 13 Feb. 7: I rode a bicycle, which cramped my style a little. Girls only start to get interesting after they cease to accept 'dinks' on bikes.

1984 *Age* (Melbourne) 15 Dec. 11: Bowen used to dink Murphy home from school on his pushbike.

dinkum *n.* 1 Work, toil: *obs.* [E. dial. OED 1891]

1882 Rolf Boldrewood *Robbery Under Arms* (World's Classics 1949) 47: It took us an hour's hard dinkum to get near the peak. Sometimes it was awful rocky, as well as scrubby ... but there was no help for it.

2 An Australian soldier in World War I: *obs.*

1918 *Aussie* 18 Jan. 3: 'And how often do you get leave to Australia?' asked the inquisitive old lady.

'Once every war,' replied one of the dinkums, 'at the end of it.'

1919 W. H. Downing *Digger Dialects* 19: *Dinkums (The)* The 2nd Division. Also applied to the New Zealanders.

dinkum *a.* & *adv.* Authentic, genuine, esp. in the expression 'fair dinkum' ('on the level')

1894 *Bulletin* 5 May 13: *Chief Justice*: And did yer stouch him back? *Witness*: No. *Chief Justice*: Fair dinkum? *Witness*: Yes.

1906 Edward Dyson *Fact'ry 'Ands* 64: He pointed to the centre of his breasts and his eyes were round with inquiry. 'Fair dinkum', telegraphed Linda.

1911 Louis Stone *Jonah* 63: 'Garn, ye're only kiddin'!' she cried with an uneasy grin. 'Fair dinkum!' said Jonah.

1919 W. H. Downing *Digger Dialects* 19: *Dinkum* Genuine, reliable.

1920 Frank A. Russell *The Ashes of Achievement* 40: 'Fair dinkum?' asked the English boy in faultless Australian. 'Square dinkum,' replied the ally.

1922 Arthur Wright *A Colt from the Country* 78: 'It's like a story out of a book,' went on Bucks. 'But it's dinkum.'

1934 Vance Palmer *Sea and Spinifex* 285: 'Here we are, ladies and gentlemen: a dinkum love-offering.'

1945 Cecil Mann *The River* 19: 'It's a dinkum this time,' the Bombardier said.

1951 Ernestine Hill *The Territory* 433: If from the other side I can do anything for you, Paddy Murray or Bill Sheahan, I will, fair dinkum. Good luck, everybody. [from the will of a N.T. drover]

1965 William Dick *A Bunch of Ratbags* 237: 'I'm sorry, Cookie,' said Croker. 'I didn't know, fair dinkum I never.'

1973 *Australian* 15 Sep. 1: 'If we show we are dinkum [Mr Whitlam said], the trade union movement stands ready to show restraint in the interest of the whole people.'

1984 *Sydney Morning Herald* 3 Mar. 38: Fair dinkum. Last week I saw Don Dunstan wearing a tie.

dinkum oil see **oil**

dinky-di 1 An intensive form of 'dinkum', usually with nationalistic overtones

1918 N. Campbell and L. Nelson *The Dinky-Di Soldier and other Jingles* [book title]

1924 *Truth* 27 Apr. 6: *Dinky-di* Integrity: reputable.

1939 Miles Franklin and Dymphna Cusack *Pioneers on Parade* 41: 'You raise my hopes that there are some real Australians.' 'Yes, we have some,' smiled Prim ... 'My cousin is a dinki-di specimen.'

1973 *Australian* 19 Sep. 14: If one has the ability

to drink oneself into an alcoholic stupor without falling flat on one's face in front of one's mates, one apparently has then achieved the true blue hallmark of excellence of today's dinky-di Aussie. **1983** Claire Tedeschi *Sydney Morning Herald* 26 Aug. 10: Cutesy disco has turned into disco-funk and all of a sudden it's OK to dance. In fact, it's more than OK – it's a dinky-di trend.

2   Abbr. for 'dinky-di Australian'
1981 *Australian* 11 Mar. 2: Bob Ansett's a born-again dinky di now [heading] Bob Ansett, along with his American accent and trans-Pacific worldliness, is in Australia to stay, and to prove he means it got himself naturalised at the Opera House in Sydney yesterday.
1982 *Sydney Morning Herald* 4 Oct. Guide 2: Some of the skits go over the heads of us dinky dyes down under, distanced as we are from the personalities of British television, politics and business.

dinner, to be done like a   To be completely worsted
1847 Alexander Harris *Settlers and Convicts* ed. C. M. H. Clark (1959) 88: 'If we don't give the rain time to wash out the horse-tracks we shall be done like a dinner.'
1853 *Letters from Victorian Pioneers* ed. T. F. Bride (1898) 170: The driver . . . up to his neck in water, calling out to me 'he was done like a dinner'.
1892 Barcroft Boake 'Featherstonhaugh' *Bulletin* 11 Jun. 22 repr. in *Where the Dead Men Lie* (1897) 134: Already he heard a smothered roar – / 'They're done like a dinner!' quoth Featherstonhaugh.
1901 *Crip* 5 Doo. [1]: The Southern Rivers 'Done like a Dinner' [headline]
1965 William Dick *A Bunch of Ratbags* 236: 'Chassa came out from behind the counter and done him like a dinner and threw him out the door.'
1975 *Australian* 10 Feb. 1: Senator Wriedt last night confirmed that he was seeking the Senate leadership. 'I am never hopeful in those sort of things,' he said. 'I was done like a dinner last time. I could be done like a dinner again.'
1980 Blanche d'Alpuget *Monkeys in the Dark* 90: 'They went off half-cocked and got done like dinners.'

dinnyhayser   A knockout blow; anything of exceptional size or force [f. the boxer Dinny Hayes]
1907 Nathan Spielvogel *The Cocky Farmer* 14: 'Then I gets a dennyaiser in the eye, and sits down suddenly.'
1925 E. S. Sorenson *Murty Brown* 106: 'The Koponey slipped his anchor and made a dinnyaiser for his lake.' [a long and desperate trip]
1946 K. S. Prichard *The Roaring Nineties* 17: He

. . . got him dancing mad and blowing like a grampus before he let him have a dinnyazer that knocked him.
1949 Ion L. Idriess *One Wet Season* 141: Here, too, the teamsters have their 'last drink'. A dinnyhayser, at times.
1966 D. E. Charlwood *An Afternoon of Time* 80: 'Gunna be a dinnyheazer of a storm,' said Percy.

dip   A punch, thump, delivered to an opposing player in Australian Rules [f. cricketing slang *dip*, hit, slog]
1963 Lou Richards *Boots and All!* 88: Like most Brownlow Medallists, he was still no angel – I saw him have a bit of a dip on more than a few occasions.

dip one's lid, to   To raise one's hat to: (fig.) to salute
1915 C. J. Dennis *The Songs of a Sentimental Bloke* 21: 'This 'ere's Doreen,' 'e sez. 'This 'ere's the Kid.' / I dips me lid.
1930 Jack O'Hagan 'Our Don Bradman' in *The Barry Humphries Book of Innocent Austral Verse* (1968) 43: Don Bradman every Aussie dips his lid to you!
1963 D. H. Crick *Martin Place* 176: Paula swept off an imaginary hat. '"I dips me lid".'
1975 Rodney Hall *A Place Among People* 238: 'I'm here to say I was wrong, I dip me lid to a fellow like you. You're a man.'
1979 *Sun-Herald* 30 Dec. 15: If one thing above all others makes this a lucky country, it's people like this – the men and women who faced and fought the fires and now will start all over again. I dips me lid.
1984 *Sydney Morning Herald* 9 Jul. Guide 16: So now three journalists, White, Day and Thomson, own a radio station. Us ordinary journos dips our lids.

dip out (on)   To withdraw, renege; fall behind
1952 T. A. G. Hungerford *The Ridge and the River* 56: There wasn't a man in the section who would dip out on a patrol so long as he could drag one leg after the other.
1968 David Ireland *The Chantic Bird* 111: I reckon if I'd ever said things like that when I was a kid, my parents would have stayed alive instead of dipping out, just to hear more.
1979 *Weekend Australian* 6 Oct. Mag. 8: Agatha Christie dips out to Shakespeare [heading]
1983 *Sydney Morning Herald* 29 Oct. 1: The ABC's new managing director will be named probably on Monday – but it won't be Bruce Gyngell, who dipped out of the race yesterday.

dip your eye (in fat)   A retort expressing derision
1953 T. A. G. Hungerford *Riverslake* 163: 'Dip

your eye!' Randolph said with gutter coarseness, putting into the words as much as he could of his dislike of Condamine.
1959 Edward Lindall *No Place to Hide* 189: 'Dip your eye', I said.

dirt-tin, like a lily on a   see lily

Dirty Digger, the   See quots
1973 Mungo MacCallum *Nation Review* 8 Jun. 1041: Keith Rupert Murdoch, better known to his admirers as the Dirty Digger.
1981 *National Times* 3 May 4: For more than a decade, the Dirty Digger, as he is known on Fleet Street, has been by far the most successful of Britain's press proprietors.
1984 *Bulletin* 3 Jul. 165: Rupert Murdoch continues to be seen as a suitable case for biographical treatment. John Wilcock, a New York-based writer ... arrived in Australia late last week hoping to round up people willing to relate Dirty Digger yarns.

Dirty Half Acre   See quot.
1934 Thomas Wood *Cobbers* 107: There were seven hotels at the beginning of the Golden Mile, on a patch of ground called the Dirty Half Acre.

Dirty Half Mile   See quot. 1970
1934 F. E. Baume *Burnt Sugar* 338: Mario could ... mention Bondi and Coogee with detachment and grin knowingly when anyone spoke of the Dirty Half Mile.
1940 Arnold L. Haskell *Waltzing Matilda* 139: It [King's Cross] was once the centre of the red light district, 'the dirty half-mile'.
1951 Dymphna Cusack and Florence James *Come In Spinner* 189: 'Got above herself, she has. Stuck up in one of them flash joints round the Dirty Half Mile and for all I care, she can stay there and rot.'
1954 Peter Gladwin *The Long Beat Home* 11: The tram crawled up the last of the hill and swung into King's Cross and the conductor cried: 'All ashore for the Dirty Half-mile.'
1970 Kenneth Slessor *Bread and Wine* 18–19: Woolcott Street has become respectable and changed its name to King's Cross Road ... William Street itself ... has been transformed completely since the days when I walked its length coming back from the Stadium. Then it was less than half its present width, a narrow and somewhat sinister street lined on one side with frowsy terraces and dimly-lit shops. It was the original 'Dirty Half-Mile', a title afterwards transferred to Woolcott Street and now without a claimant.
1984 *Sydney Morning Herald* 2 Jul. Guide 16: The *Nightwatch* mike found a trio of buskers near the Dirty Half Mile.

dirty on, to be   To hold in disfavour
1965 Jack Dyer *'Captain Blood'* 153: I was a bit dirty on being beaten.
1972 Geoff Morley *Jockey Rides Honest Race* 230: There's Deena talking to her boyfriend. I know he's got a bird out in the car waiting for him. She's gonna get dirty if she finds out.
1976 David Ireland *The Glass Canoe* 73: 'They're dirty on me, but they have to agree.'
1984 *Age* (Melbourne) 29 Mar. 28: Even without losing money I get very dirty on a team for not winning when everything points to its certain success.
1984 *Sunday Telegraph* (Sydney) 15 Apr. 60: Walker, probably Canberra's best player yesterday, was a little dirty on coach Don Furner.

Dirty Reds   see **Reds**

dish, go for the big   To plan a large bet, gamble for a large amount
1949 Lawson Glassop *Lucky Palmer* 74: 'A quid?' he asked scornfully. 'A quid? Only a quid! Cripes, you're playing with their dough now. Go for the big dish.'

dish up   To defeat in a contest, worst completely [f. *dish* To 'do for', defeat completely OED 1798]
1916 *The Anzac Book* 101: He said to me: 'Corporal Wilson, / You've dished up the beggars in style.'
1919 J. Vance Marshall *The World of the Living Dead* 84: Me remish I lorst fer dishin' up a screw.

disperse   Euphemism for destroying the natives: *obs.*
1887 E. M. Curr *The Australian Race* iii 20: To an observer of languages, it is interesting to note the new signification of the verb *to disperse*: that when a Black girl of fifteen is shot down she is said to be *dispersed*.
1890 J. A. Barry *Steve Brown's Bunyip* 182: Earliest dawn heralded the pitiless swoop of the native troopers on the quiet camp. His tribe 'dispersed', baby Billy, the sole survivor, was brought to B——.
1918 C. Fetherstonhaugh *After Many Days* 232: One of the native police officers ... told me that on one occasion when they were 'dispersing' (that was what it was called) some blacks, he saw Jerry, one of his boys, with a little picaninny boy in his hand. He was swinging the little chap round preparatory to knocking out his brains against a tree.
1928 W. Robertson *Coo-ee Talks* 157: When the Queensland Parliamentary Commission investigated the charges made against the black police, one of the sub-inspectors was asked: 'What do you mean by dispersing the aborigines?' His reply was frank, and tersely told, in the words 'Firing at

them.'
1930 Frank Hives *Journal of a Jackaroo* 226: They were told that the band of raiders had been 'dispersed', and that nothing more need be feared from them ... They were well aware that 'dispersed' might have another meaning, and knew too well that the Websters were not the men to waste their time 'dispersing' savages leaving them free to return.

distance, tyranny of   see **tyranny**

Dix(er), Dorothy   A parliamentary question asked by a member of the Government party so that the Minister may make a prepared answer, to his own advantage [f. 'Dear Dorothy Dix' the newspaper feature consisting of answers to correspondents' problems]
1963 *Australian Financial Review* 31 Oct. 16: Queensland Senator Dame Annabelle Rankin may have been posing a 'Dorothy Dix' (political jargon for a planted question) to Senator Sir William Spooner.
1971 *Australian* 24 Apr. 5: Mr Barnard said Dr Forbes was reading from a prepared statement and obviously answering 'a question that is more commonly known in the House as a Dorothy Dixer'.
1981 *Sydney Morning Herald* 4 Jun. 14: He got his chance with a nice little Dorothy Dixer from the Government backbenches.

do   To expend or consume completely; lose or forfeit
1859 Frank Fowler *Southern Lights and Shadows* 181 A wealthy tavern keeper who came to England with us, used to boast of 'doing' his forty nobblers of brandy a day.
1908 E. G. Murphy *Jarrahland Jingles* 38: And it's all the same to me / How I gather in a crust / Doin' brass or goin' strong.
1921 *Aussie* 15 Mar. 54: 'Just done me last dollar up at the swi school.'
1928 Arthur Wright *A Good Recovery* 87: 'Got on th' shikker, done me money.'
1932 Leonard Mann *Flesh in Armour* 247: 'By Gawd,' said Darky softly, 'thirty-two good francs I've done.'
1948 Sumner Locke Elliott *Rusty Bugles* in *Khaki, Bush and Bigotry* ed. Eunice Hanger (1968) 34: 'Done the lot ... Done the flamin' lot. Yeah, done me thirty quid. How's a bloke's luck.'
1959 Dorothy Hewett *Bobbin Up* 117: 'What do you want me to do, do me job cold?'
1960 Donald McLean *The Roaring Days* 199: 'I want a few quid for th' school tonight ...' 'You'll get down there and do th' lot as usual.'
1974 David Ireland *Burn* 52: 'Don't bet on it, son. You might do your dough.'

do a bear up   see **bear up**

do the block   see **block**

do a bucket job   see **bucket**

doing a Dame Nellie   see **Dame Nellie**

do the lolly   see **lolly**

do a Melba   see **Melba**

do the messages   see **messages**

do over   1   To bash up, equivalent to U.S. 'work over'; attack and destroy (military)
1944 Lawson Glassop *We Were the Rats* 76: 'Do this galah over,' he whispered in my ear. 'He's a king hit merchant.'
1952 T. A. G. Hungerford *The Ridge and the River* 98: They could spend the night there and do the Jap camp over in the morning.
1965 William Dick *A Bunch of Ratbags* 177: Sometimes they'd eject some of the more rowdy ones of our mob and take them to the station and do them over.
1965 John Beede *They Hosed Them Out* 101–2: We had gone into France to do over some secret installations that the underground had pin-pointed.
1975 Les Ryan *The Shearers* 103: 'Get goin' before the mob does you over too.'
2   Applied to the male role in intercourse [f. *do with* have intercourse with OED 1175]
1952 T. A. G. Hungerford *The Ridge and the River* 172–3: 'Wait till you see a few of the girls in the villages in the hills, where they haven't been done over.'
1961 Mena Calthorpe *The Dyehouse* 101: 'You're not the first dame that's been done over, not by a long shot.'
1975 Richard Beilby *The Brown Land Crying* 110: 'Anyrate, 'e never done 'er over, if that's what ya worryin' about.'

do a perish   see **perish**

do a walk   see **walk**

dob in   1   To inform against, implicate, betray
1957 Judah Waten *Shares in Murder* 173: 'You said you'd go to the police and dob him in unless he coughed up ... That's the story isn't it?'
1966 H. F. Brinsmead *Beat of the City* 144: 'But you feel such a rat to tell on her. To dob her in.'
1975 Rodney Hall *A Place Among People* 240–1: 'He came back to squeeze more money from his mother and she dobbed him in.'
1982 *Weekend Australian* 11 Dec. 3: Victoria's

'dob in a druggie' campaign has been hailed as an outstanding success by the Police Commissioner, Mr Doug Miller.

dobber
1958 *Coast to Coast 1957–1958* 201: 'How's his flipping form? Dobber-in Number One?'
1968 David Ireland *The Chantic Bird* 149: Girls are great dobbers.
1974 John Powers *The Last of the Knucklemen* 95: 'Don't look at me, you bastards! I'm no bloody dobber!'
1975 Nancy Keesing *Garden Island People* 66: Henderson was known as a relentless 'dobber-in' of anyone who drank on the job.
1981 *National Times* 22 Nov. 12: It seems there is no shortage of 'little Aussie dobbers' anxious to have the authorities check on the status of their coloured or Asian neighbours.
2   To contribute (probably confused with 'dub in' as in 'dub up')
1954 Tom Ronan *Vision Splendid* 179: 'Very pleased to subscribe. Pity more of the staff aren't home. I'm sure they all dub in.'
1965 William Dick *A Bunch of Ratbags* 225: It was his birthday and we all dobbed in and bought him the latest black-and-white Italian-style bodgie jumper.
1968 Geoffrey Dutton *Andy* 197: 'The ground crew are dobbing in too,' said Rogerson, 'and there should be some other donations.'
1971 David Ireland *The Unknown Industrial Prisoner* 86: 'For the price of few cents a week, we can all have a ticket . . . Dob in, men!'

doco   A documentary
1981 *Sun-Herald* 9 Aug. 151: Mr Dunstan has made a series of dockoes on Australia Past, Present and Future.
1982 *Sydney Morning Herald* 2 Oct. 16: Too often a docco is a strung-together report full of sound and flickers but signifying little.

doctor   1   A bush cook, esp. for a number of men [a ship's cook U.S. 1821 OED]
1868 C. Wade Brown *Overlanding in Australia* 71: Grumbling is contagious in its nature, so for this reason alone a good cook, or 'doctor', as he is called, is a necessary individual in a camp.
1888 'Overlander' *Australian Sketcher* 1: 'Well, if some of you fellows will just take a look round the cattle, and the doctor (all bush cooks are called the doctor) will put another bucket of tea and a log on the fire.'
1900–10 O'Brien and Stephens: *Doctor* A nickname for the station cook.
1908 Giles Seagram *Bushmen All* 192: 'By the way, we've no Doctor. All hands take it in turns to cook.'
1933 Acland: *Doctor* Slang for cook.

1945 Robert S. Close *Love Me Sailor* 144: 'Hey doctor! What about something to eat?'
2   A refreshing sea-breeze, usu. named from a specific place (e.g. Albany, Fremantle q.v.)
1914 *World's Standard Dictionary* (Aust. Suppl.): *doctor* (in W.A.) a cool, healthy sea-breeze which blows *bet.* November and April (the summer months).
1976 Max Brown *The Black Eureka* 97: Perhaps on an evening when a Port Hedland Doctor blew in from the ocean they even knew what they sought.

doctor, go for the   To make an all out effort, esp. in horse-racing; bet all one's money
1949 Lawson Glassop *Lucky Palmer* 250: 'Passing the seven, Gelignite is only half a length in front of Laughing Water – Jim Minburry seems to be going for the doctor – closely followed by Harristine, Pirate Gold.' Ibid. 74: 'Go for the doctor, Slap a tenner on it.'
1951 Dal Stivens *Jimmy Brockett* 86: There were three of the bastards and they went for the doctor. But I had time to get on my guard.
1966 Tom Ronan *Strangers on the Ophir* 80–1: But a jackeroo . . . whose horsemanship was of no standard at all suddenly sat down and started to go for the doctor. With his whip going like a flail and his spurs like pistons he drove his cuddy to the lead.
1976 *Sydney Morning Herald* 20 Apr. 13: 'I decided to go for the doctor rather than let Taras Bulba fight for his head.'
1982 Joe Andersen *Winners Can Laugh* 153: There was only one thing to do – go for the doctor and make Knox chase him.

dodge   1   To move cattle or sheep, esp. along a droving track
1881 A. C. Grant *Bush-Life in Queensland* ii 134: Dodging Cows [chapter heading]
1911 E. S. Sorenson *Life in the Australian Backblocks* 167: Dodging the crawlers along is the most disheartening of all stock work.
1936 Archer Russell *Gone Nomad* 27: My cattle-camp and sheep-dodging* days. *Sheep mustering and droving.
2   To acquire dishonestly, as in 'poddy-dodging' q.v. [? f. *dodge* a dishonest stratagem]
1965 Tom Ronan *Moleskin Midas* 149: 'For every poddy that's up in the Coronet breakaways there's a dozen blokes trying to dodge it off.'
see **monkey dodger**

dodger   Bread, esp. in army, boarding school, etc.: *obsolescent* [cf. *dodge* a large irregular piece, a lump OED 1562]
1919 W. H. Downing *Digger Dialects* 19: *Dodger* Bread.

1924 *Truth* 27 Apr. 6: *Dodger* Bread.

1950 *Australian Police Journal* Apr. 112: *Dodger* Gaolbread.

1957 Nino Culotta *They're a Weird Mob* 51: Joe said to Jimmy, 'Smack us in the eye with another hunk o' dodger, matey.' Jimmy gave him some bread, but I was unable to see the connection between the request and the reply.

1964 Thomas Keneally *The Place at Whitton* 91: 'A couple of rounds of mouldy dodger and you'll be right.'

doer A 'character', an incorrigible, an eccentric. Often a **hard doer** q.v.

1919 W. H. Downing *Digger Dialects* 19: *Doer* A person unusually humorous, reckless, undisciplined, immoral or eccentric.

1924 *Truth* 27 Apr. 6: *Doer* Humorist.

1930 L. W. Lower *Here's Luck* 161: 'My crikeys!' he added. 'That young Stanley must be a bit of a doer!'

1958 Hal Porter *A Handful of Pennies* 95: 'A real doer . . . oh, a dag when you got to know him.'

dog 1 An informer; one who betrays his associates, often in the expression 'turn dog' [U.S. 1846 OED]

1864 J. F. Mortlock *Experiences of a Convict* (1965) 78–9: Men betraying their companions or accepting authority over them are often called 'dogs', and sometimes have their nose bitten off – the morsel being termed 'a mouthful of dog's nose'.

1882 Rolf Boldrewood *Robbery Under Arms* (World's Classics 1949) 56: 'Are you going to turn dog, now you know the way in?'

1895 Cornelius Crowe *The Australian Slang Dictionary* 24: *dog* 'to turn dog', to turn Queen's evidence.

1903 Joseph Furphy *Such is Life* (1944) 252: I'd be turnin' dog on the station if I took advantage o' your message, to go round warnin' the chaps that was workin' on the paddick.'

1911 Edward Dyson *Benno, and Some of the Push* 1: 'There isn't a bit o' common in treatin' women decent. If y' do, they'll dog on yer for a cert.'

1922 Arthur Wright *A Colt from the Country* 166: 'Never mind, Missus, I won't turn dog on the old boy. I'll see him through this.'

1937 *Best Australian One-Act Plays* 205: 'You don't expect me to turn dog on the union.'

1941 Kylie Tennant *The Battlers* 350: 'Old Sharkey turned dog on us, didn't he, Bet? Said he'd get me for abduction.'

1950 W. M. Hughes *Policies and Potentates* 226: It had been a neck and neck contest, and but for California's turning dog on the Chief Justice, President Wilson would have been defeated.

1962 Tom Ronan *Deep of the Sky* 30: Always someone would turn up who knew him as the man who had sent his mates to the gallows. No one, free immigrant, currency lad, or old lag, would eat, work or travel with Tully the Dog.

1979 Les Newcombe *Inside Out* 152: Kevin had come down to the cage the afternoon prior to the fight, and accused him of being a dog. As this is the worst insult you can throw at a crim, Gilbert had wanted to know who made the accusation.

1981 *National Times* 12 Jul. 11: She told me that the criminals consider most prostitutes 'dogs', which is to say, informers.

2 A dingo (the native dog)

1899 A. B. Paterson 'Father Riley's Horse' in *Singer of the Bush* (1983) 337: It was Hogan, the dog poisoner – an aged man and very wise.

1910 C. E. W. Bean *On the Wool Track* 52: Some forgotten shepherd penned his sheep night after night from the dogs and the natives.

1938 Francis Ratcliffe *Flying Fox and Drifting Sand* 235: I also learned a thing or two about dingoes. In the North-east, at least on those stations I had visited, dogs are no longer a serious pest; but there the story was different.

1944 Archer Russell *Bush Ways* 132: Strapped to his camel packs . . . were six hundred dog scalps, all of pure-bred dingo.

1969 Bobbie Hardy *West of the Darling* 231: Sidney Kidman had by 1914 already erected considerable lengths of dog-proof fencing to protect his Yandama and Corona holdings.

1979 *Advertiser* (Adelaide) 31 Jul. 14B: Dog fence review [heading] Protection and restoration of the 60-year-old dog fence was being treated as a matter of urgency, the Minister of Land and Environment, Dr Cornwall, said yesterday.

3 A horse or sheep difficult to manage

1945 Baker 175: A *dog* is a horse difficult to handle.

1965 Leslie Haylen *Big Red* 117: The Ape tried giving him 'dogs' to shear. That is, old, rough, wrinkled wethers, knobbly, burry, dusty, hard to shear.

4 Canned meat i.e. **tinned dog** q.v.

1977 F. B. Vickers *A Stranger No Longer* 25: 'I always keep a few tins of dog on hand, son. The bloody blowflies are so bad you can't keep anything fresh. So just in case the old corn goes green or bad, I've got the dog.'

Dog Act, the See quot. 1898

1898 A. B. Paterson *Bulletin* 31 Dec. 31: There is an Act compelling a publican to refuse drink to an habitual inebriate. This is locally known as the 'Dog Act' and to be brought under the Dog Act is a glorious distinction, a sort of V.C. of Northern Territory life.

1941 Baker 24: *Dog-list, on the* To be barred from drinking. Also, 'to be put on the dog-list', obliged to take out a prohibition order.

1965 Xavier Herbert *Larger than Life* 217: 'Let me hear of you drunk again, and I'll have you put under the Dog Act.'

1974 Robert Adamson and Bruce Hanford *Zimmer's Essay* 16: Helm was the sort of prisoner that it probably wouldn't hurt to classify insane, to treat for alcoholism under the Dog Act, or certify.

dog, all prick and ribs like a drover's (shearer's, swaggie's)   see all

dog and goanna rules   No rules at all (as in a fight between a dog and a goanna)

1971 *Sydney Morning Herald* 12 May 1: Says a Merimbula reader: A propos of the recent reference to Queensland politics now working under a 'dog and goanna franchise', as an octogenarian I can remember the good old days when Queensland cemeteries voted almost to a man.

1979 *Weekend Australian* 1 Dec. 13: When it comes to takeovers in the business world, Mr Bjelke Petersen wants a Marquis of Queensberry style conduct observed, not the dog and goanna rules and tactics so often displayed in his parliament.

dogbox   A compartment on a long-distance train, in a carriage with no corridor

1905 Nathan Spielvogel *A Gumsucker on the Tramp* 43–4: I found at last railway cars worse than the worst Australia possesses. The one I came down here in was a dog box. Under the seat was a collection of old wine bottles and broken lunch baskets, etc.

1941 Baker 24: *Dog-boxes* A contemptuous but adequately descriptive term for many passenger carriages on country railway services.

1958 E. O. Schlunke *The Village Hampden* 115: 'We had to get out of our sleepers into dog-boxes and found we still had over a hundred miles to go.'

1963 Bruce Beaver *The Hot Summer* 128: They found a dog-box all to themselves which meant an uninterrupted half hour between Mundulla and the first stop.

Dog Collar Act   The Transport Workers' Act (1928) and the Transport Workers' (Seamen) Regulations (providing for the licensing of seamen before they could work), so styled by the Seamen's Union in challenges of 1935–6 and later

1939 *The Seamen's Journal* 1 Sep.: Vicious Acts that we are now shackled with such as the *Crimes Act*, the *Transport Workers' Act* (Dog Collar).

1941 Baker 24: *Dog Collar Act* The Aust. Transport Workers' Act.

1953 Dymphna Cusack *Southern Steel* 255: 'The Government put the Dog-Collar Act on the wharfies when they refused to load shipments of pig-iron.'

1957 Tom Nelson *The Hungry Mile* 74: This decision was helped by threats of the Lyons Government to impose the 'Dog Collar Act'.

1982 Wendy Lowenstein and Tom Hills *Under the Hook* 62: The Dog Collar Act destroyed the WWF as an industrial power for more than twenty years, until it was repealed by the Curtin Labor Government in 1942.

dogger   1   A hunter of dingoes (native dogs)

1910 C. E. W. Bean *On the Wool Track* 55: He asked to be taken on as a dogger.

1934 Archer Russell *A Tramp-Royal in Wild Australia* 113: It is along the fences, most often, that the 'wild dogger' sets his traps, into which, more often than the wily dingo, steps the unsuspecting bustard.

1955 Douglas Stewart 'The Dogger' *Collected Poems* (1967) 137: Who'd be a dogger / Following where the dingoes follow / Sly shadows of water?

1967 Len Beadell *Blast the Bush* 109: Although the old bush professional government doggers had many tricks up their sleeves to catch their quarry, I'm sure this would have been something new to them.

1971 Colin Simpson *The New Australia* 489: As a dogger (dingo destroyer) Charlie had shot or trapped as many as 275 dingoes in one year, earning $60 a week plus $4 a 'scalp' (ears and tail).

1984 *West Australian* (Perth) 19 Jan. 45: The Minister for transport, Mr Julian Grill, is pressing for the reinstatement of a dogger for the Salmon Gums area after complaints of attacks by dingoes on sheep flocks.

2   A slaughterer of horses for pet food

1978 *Sun-Herald* 21 May 80: The despised horses being bought by the 'doggers' for the people who manufacture canned pet-food.

dogged, to be

1967 John Yeomans *The Scarce Australians* 23: 'Some of them horses have got so poor in this drought they'll have to be dogged ... You know – sold to one of them men that come up from Sydney buying horses to kill for dogmeat.'

dogging   Dingo-hunting

1910 C. E. W. Bean *On the Wool Track* 55: A man is generally kept dogging, and the boundary rider gets a few pounds out of occasional scalps.

1919 W. R. Harris *Outback in Australia* 88: The German had been doing casual station work but was then 'dogging'.

1928 Arthur Upfield *The House of Cain* 89: 'I bin dogging round Lake Frome.'

1932 William Hatfield *Ginger Murdoch* 167: 'Yes, dogging – dingo-stiffening, you know.'

1937 Ernestine Hill *The Great Australian Loneliness* 96: Men that have 'gone dogging' over the ranges.

1944 Archer Russell *Bush Ways* 132: The wild-dog trapper and camel-man ... had been slowly packing-in from one of his periodical 'dogging' trips into the Musgrave and Petermann Ranges.
1965 *Australian* 15 Feb. 8: Peter ... has been dogging for forty years. In ten years around the Alice they killed nearly 40,000 dogs.

dog, head like a robber's   see **head**

dogleg fence   See quots
1863 Rachel Henning *Letters* ed. David Adams (1963) 136: It is what is called a 'dog's-leg' fence, made of unbarked saplings, but crossways, and it looks quite pretty as it goes up and down the gullies.
1875 R. and F. Hill *What We Saw in Australia* 61: We made acquaintance with the 'dog's leg' fence. This is formed of bare branches of the gum-tree laid obliquely, several side by side, and the ends overlapping, so that they have somewhat the appearance that might be presented by the stretched-out legs of a crowd of dogs running at full speed. An upright stick at intervals, with a fork at the top, on which some of the cross-branches rest, adds strength to the structure. [Morris]
1882 Rolf Boldrewood *Robbery Under Arms* (World's Classics 1949) 112: We could see ... a longish wing of dog-leg fence, made light but well put together.
1901 Henry Lawson 'Water Them Geraniums' *Prose* i 577: The clearing was fenced in by a light 'dog-legged' fence (a fence of sapling poles resting on forks and x-shaped uprights).
1911 E. S. Sorenson *Life in the Australian Back-blocks* 25: Dog-leg fences were [among] the leading features of the old bush home, and still are in many places; but in settled districts ... two-rail and wire fences succeed the dog-leg.
1934 Steele Rudd *Green Grey Homestead* 75: Crossing your legs to steady yourself, and looking like a section in a dog-leg fence, your eyes will meet Josie's by accident.
1955 Alan Marshall *I Can Jump Puddles* 171: A decayed dog-leg fence, erected from trees felled along its line, encircled the paddock, in which saplings and scrub marked the return of the bush.

dog licence   Certificate exempting an Aborigine from the provisions of the Aborigines Protection Act 1909–13, esp. as allowing the holder to drink in a hotel (discontinued in 1967): *derogatory*
1955 F. B. Vickers *The Mirage* 257: 'Monty wants us to get the dog licence – that's the paper they give you ... If we had this paper, me and you could have walked into that pub and stood at the bar all day and none of 'em could have said a word to us.'
1962 Cynthia Nolan *Outback* 80: If Moonlight had been asked why he had not applied for a Certifi-cate his answer might possibly have been the same as that of the half-caste drover who replied furiously; 'If I've got to have a licence to be equal to a white man I'd rather stay as I am – it would be like taking out a dog licence.'
1978 Kevin Gilbert *Living Black* 297: Before the 1967 referendum, before citizenship, Aborigines could receive these exemption cards – dog certifi-cates – which enabled them to enter a hotel.
1979 *Sydney Morning Herald* 4 Aug. 18: In 1957, after years of this petty restriction, Mrs Simon was granted an exemption certificate, the infamous dog licence, as it was called.

dogman   A man who rides on the hook of a crane, and directs operations by signals [f. *dog* sb. 7a OED]
1962 Robert Clark *The Dogman and other Poems* 2: The dogman dangles from the clouds, / Astride a beam of swinging air, / Unrealized hero of the crowds, / Whose upturned faces dimly stare.
1965 *The Tracks We Travel* ed. L. Haylen 42: The shrill whistle of the dogman 150 feet above warns us that he is signalling the winding driver to lower away.
1966 Jan Smith *An Ornament of Grace* 123: The smell of concrete new-mixed, the sight of swaying dogmen.
1974 Geoffrey Lehmann *A Spring Day in Autumn* 171: 'I'm a dogman,' he replied. 'I work high up on office buildings.'
1981 *Australian* 14 Oct. 7: Dogmen, who 'rode the hook' (stood on loads being lifted by cranes to direct the driver) in high winds and on ever-higher buildings, were dying at the rate of a dozen a year in the 60's. Riding the hook was unnecessary if two dogmen were employed per crane.

dog, shoot your own   see **shoot**

dog's disease   Influenza
1919 W. H. Downing *Digger Dialects* 19: *Dog Fever* A mild form of influenza.
1932 Leonard Mann *Flesh in Armour* 218: Half the platoon had had dog's disease.
1953 Baker 166: *dog's disease* Malaria. [as World War II slang]

Dogs, the   1   The Footscray V.F.L. club [abbr. of Bulldogs]
1979 *Herald* (Melbourne) 7 Apr. 34: Dogs die! Melbourne survived fierce, relentless pressure from Footscray to snare a 12-point victory at the MCG this afternoon.
2   The Canterbury Bankstown Rugby League club
1979 *Australian* 1 Jun. 16: Top 'Dogs' return for Manly game [heading]

dogs are pissing on your swag   see **pull**

dog tied up See quots
1906 A. B. Paterson *An Outback Marriage* 178: 'Paddy's 'ad a dorg tied hup 'ere (ie. an account outstanding) this two years.'
1900–10 O'Brien and Stephens: *Mad dog* An unpaid score at a public house.
1944 Lawson Glassop *We Were the Rats* 83: 'He's left so many dogs tied up all over Australia it's a wonder there're enough of 'em left to hold tin-hare meetings.'
1962 John O'Grady *Gone Fishin'* 124: 'I says what about me three pound six, I haven't got a dog tied up here, have I?'

dog, tinned see **tinned dog**

dole-bludger Someone drawing unemployment benefits even though work is available
1977 *Bulletin* 22 Jan. 14: The last three Labor Ministers have all talked a lot about cracking down on 'dole bludgers' but there is little anyone at the top can do.
1982 *Australian* 18 Nov. 22: Federal parliamentary references to the unemployed have turned about. Some time ago the unemployed were dubbed 'dole bludgers', now they are the 'disemployed' and 'those with no opportunity for commencing employment'.

doley Someone on the dole, in the Depression of the 1930s
1943 Baker 27: *Doleys* Soldiers in employment platoons (Digger slang).
1953 *Caddie A Sydney Barmaid* 209: 'You needn't worry about 'im Caddie. 'E's a friend to all us doleys.'
1966 Elwyn Wallace *Sydney and the Bush* 108: 'You track dolies are more trouble than you're worth. Better bloody fed than I am.'
1982 *Sydney Morning Herald* 5 Apr. 6: How do the rest of you poor, frustrated, out-of-work 'dolies' feel?

Doll, the Ray Lawler's play *Summer of the Seventeenth Doll*, first performed in 1955, and taken as marking a renaissance in Australian drama
1963 *Sydney Morning Herald* 16 Mar. 12: 'The Doll' Hits Iceland!
1974 *Southerly* 215: Since *The Doll* naturalism has retained its force in Australian drama.

doll, knock over a To incur the consequences entailed in any activity [? f. the contest of throwing at dolls at a sideshow]
1954 T. A. G. Hungerford *Sowers of the Wind* 142: 'Surely to God he knows that if he throws the ball he's got a chance of knocking over the dolly!' [i.e. contracting venereal disease]
1959 Gerard Hamilton *Summer Glare* 95: 'Knock-

ing a doll' was an old belief among us youths. We had never believed the story of the stork or of the cabbage patch either. Years ago the big boys had told us a much better story. It was that inside all women there was a number of small babies sitting in a row, and when a man, or a boy big enough, knocked one over, it was born after nine months. Thus our saying 'to knock a doll'.

dollar The sum of five shillings (until the introduction of decimal currency in 1966) [f. equivalence of value with the U.S. dollar]
1911 Louis Stone *Jonah* 65: As she was rather suspicious of a wedding that cost nothing, she decided to give the parson a dollar to seal the bargain.
1924 *Truth* 27 Apr. 6: *Dollar* Five shillings.
1942 Gavin Casey *It's Harder for Girls* 55: 'I can get half a dollar from dad.'
1945 Herbert M. Moran *Beyond the Hill Lies China* 100: Bets of a 'dollar' on the favourite or a 'deaner' on the outsider.
1964 Tom Ronan *Packhorse and Pearling Boat* 119: With tobacco at twelve shillings per pound he found it hard to send more than a dollar a week up in smoke.

dollar, holey The 'ring' dollar authorized in 1813 by the striking of a circular piece (a **dump** q.v.) from the centre of a Spanish dollar
1849 J. P. Townshend *Rambles and Observations in New South Wales* 10–11: This place [Ulladulla] . . . is commonly called 'Holy Dollar'. The origin of the corruption of this native name is this; it used to be the practice to cut the centre out of a dollar, and the middle piece was called 'a dump' and the remainder of the original coin 'a holey dollar'.
1859 See **dump** 1
1984 *Sydney Morning Herald* 28 Jan. 7: A 170-year-old 'holey dollar' fetched $18,275 at a public auction in Melbourne yesterday. The coin was one of 40,000 Spanish coins punched with holes by order of Lachlan Macquarie in 1814. About 150 'holey dollars' are known to be left. They were used in lieu of a local currency and the centres were punched out to render them worthless outside Australia.

dollar, not the full As for **not the full quid** q.v.
1976 Robert Drewe *The Savage Crows* 8: Was he the full dollar these days?
1983 Peter Corris *The Empty Beach* 86: 'I hear that Freddy might not be the full dollar. He was in Changi, which wouldn't have done him any good.'

dolly's wax, full up to See quot. 1982
1945 See **pussy's bow**
1965 Barry Humphries *A Nice Night's Entertainment* (1981) 85: Everyone was full up to dolly's

wax and I was absolutely stonkered, so unfortunately it was hardly touched.

1982 Nancy Keesing *Lily on the Dustbin* 17: When my children were small a man, then in his eighties, sat back from our table after lunch and announced, 'I'm full up to dolly's wax!' It had to be explained that dolls once had delicate, modelled wax heads with a neck shaped so that it could be sewn to a stuffed rag body.

Dolphins, the   The Redcliffe (Q.) Rugby League club

1981 *Sunday Mail* (Brisbane) 20 Sep. 1: After joining Redcliffe from Roma in 1964, Beetson helped the Dolphins to their first and only premiership the following year.

don   1   Doyen [f. *don* a leader, first class man, an adept OED 1634–1853]

1898 W. H. Ogilvie *Fair Girls and Gray Horses* 55: He's the don at every muster and the king of every camp.

1901 Henry Lawson *Verse* ii 2: He's a don at peeling spuds.

2   *The Don* Sir Donald Bradman, the cricketer

1949 J. Fingleton *Brightly Fades the Don* [book title]

1965 Wally Grout *My Country's Keeper* 12: 'The Don' looked ageless behind the sticks, and his cover drive was still the most exciting thing in cricket.

dona, donah   Sweetheart, esp. in larrikin argot: *obs.* except for the saying 'Don't introduce your donah to a pal'. [f. Sp. *dona*, It. *donna* woman]

[**1859** Hotten. *Donna and Feeles* A woman and children.]

1874 *Melbourne Punch* 9 Jul. 276: [legend to a cartoon] *Cad* (yells to friend) 'Yar-icks – Nobby 'ere's Nixon with a new dona!' (Which being interpreted, meaneth that Nixon is paying his addresses to a fresh sweetheart).

1896 Nat Gould *Town and Bush* 103: When they dare not smash windows, they perform upon the faces and bodies of their female acquaintances, familiarly called 'donahs'.

1906 A. B. Paterson *An Outback Marriage* 23: To be discussed in this contemptuous way by a larrikin and his 'donah'.

1923 Jack Moses *Beyond the City Gates* 136: But at this moment Bill's donah became hysterical and fainted.

1945 Tom Ronan *Strangers on the Ophir* 123: 'This'll teach your donah who's the right bloke to go with,' jeered Luke.

done like a dinner   see **dinner**

dong *v.*   To strike, punch

1916 Let. in Bill Gammage *The Broken Years* (1974) 233: I feel that the Corporal would have failed his manhood had he not 'donged' him.

c. **1928** Louis Esson 'Vagabond Camp' in *Ballades of Old Bohemia* (1980) 160: 'You donged him, and you can't deny it.'

1939 A. W. Upfield *The Mystery of Swordfish Reef* 228: 'Stop that, Bob, or I'll dong you one.'

1946 Margaret Trist *What Else is There?* 90: 'Don't you reckon it's funny when them girls go off in a car with a fellow and then dong him for kissing them?'

1956 Kylie Tennant *The Honey Flow* 159: 'I kept after him down the road ... donging him with rocks every chance I got.'

1963 John Cantwell *No Stranger to the Flame* 19: 'Some murdering bastard of a kid must have donged it with this gibber and then shot through.'

1970 Patrick White *The Vivisector* 10: She came up and donged him one with her skinny hand.

1981 *Australian* 28 Apr. 3: England captain Ian Botham threatened to dong him [Henry Blofeld] at Bermuda airport.

dong *n.*   A blow

1932 L. W. Lower *Here's Another* 14: How would they like a dong in the gills with a golf ball?

1938 Francis Ratcliffe *Flying Fox and Drifting Sand* 167: I ... was just about to have a dong at him when the brute changed its mind and shot ahead.

donga   1   A natural depression or gully [f. S. African *donga* A channel or gully formed by the action of water OED 1874]

1937 Ernestine Hill *The Great Australian Loneliness* 330: *Donga* Depression in sandy country.

1945 Stan Arneil *One Man's War* (1980) 230: Working in the open, in hot, steamy dongas, with fields of tapioca around us, I revel in the simplicity and crudeness of the soil.

1978 *Sydney Morning Herald* 28 Oct. 11: He knows it well ... Where the bores are, and the dongas (hollow depressions), where salt bush changes to blue bush.

2   A makeshift shelter: see quot. 1972

1956 *Sydney Morning Herald* 18 Oct. 1: In New Guinea a party is called a 'ding' and a house a 'donga'. So if they have a party at home it's a ding in their donga.

1972 Turner 22: *Donga* 'a gully' was current among soldiers in the Second World War, expanding its meaning to include any kind of shelter, until now among the Europeans in New Guinea it is a local word for 'house'. Only *donga* among all these words seems likely to be traceable to the battlefields of the Boer War.

1975 *Overland* 62 7: Like many of the older houses [in Darwin] Bill's little donga has survived

in some form, though the roof's gone, and a wall.
1980 *NT News* (Darwin) 26 Jan. 5: The Territory's bush bard sits in his 'donga' at Gunn Pt. drinking, smoking interminable cigarettes and telling yarns about the Top End.
1983 *Australian* 7 Oct. 7: The single men call their steel prefab homes dongas – easily demountable for cartage to the next job site.

donkey-lick   To defeat easily, esp. in horse-racing
1890 A. B. Paterson 'Our New Horse' in *Singer of the Bush* (1983) 109: He sold for a hundred and thirty, / Because of a gallop he had / One morning with Bluefish and Bertie, / And donkey-licked both of 'em bad.
1902 Henry Fletcher *The Waybacks* 55: 'It's er put-up job! ... Goanna had 'em donkey licked!'
1907 Arthur Wright *Keane of Kalgoorlie* 50: 'What's more, he can donkey-lick a stable full of crocks like Yalgoo.'
1944 *Truth* 13 Feb. 4: Breasley saw Kintore donkey-lick a field of youngsters in the Federal Stakes.
1958 Frank Hardy *The Four-Legged Lottery* 42: 'Who won the footie?' 'Ah, Richmond got donkey-licked.'
1963 John Naish *That Men Should Fear* 126: It wasn't much of a sport, they felt, if one could be donkey-licked by a doddering old grandad of eighty.
1971 *Sunday Sun* (Brisbane) 17 Oct. 14: Only last week I donkey licked the local kindy kids at drop the hankie.
1981 *National Times* 5 Jul. 50: The Pommies ... threw in a quartet of speedsters that had been donkey-licked by every cricketing nation around the world.
1984 *Sun-Herald* 30 Sep. 65: Hawthorn donkey-walloped Essendon in last year's one-sided grand final by 83 points.

donkey vote   A vote recorded by simply numbering preferences down the ballot paper in the order in which the names appear
1963 *Sydney Morning Herald* 23 Mar. 2: The 'Donkey Vote' in Australia.
1979 *Advertiser* (Adelaide) 12 Mar. 1: Mr Corcoran said the by-election showed the Australian Democrats were a spent force. 'If you take the donkey vote away from them they would be down to about 4 p.c.' he said.
1984 *Sun-Herald* 11 Mar. 168: Remember Rev Fearless Fred Nile getting the number one spot on the Upper House ballot papers for his Call to Australia group at the last election? God's work, said Fred, to help him get the donkey vote.

Dons, the   The Essendon V.F.L. team (also the Bombers) [abbr.]

1975 *Sunday Telegraph* (Sydney) 29 Jun. 38: Dons' Rally Pays Off.

don't argue   The straight-arm warding off movement in Rugby football [f. illustration in the trademark of J. C. Hutton Pty Ltd: see quot. 1977]
1977 *Australian* 14 Apr. 18: Rugby football fans around the world know the straight-arm fend-off as a 'Don't argue', and its origins go back to the turn of the century. The creator of the symbol was Mel. B. Spurr, a pianist, singer, dancer, vaudevillian, monologist, cartoonist and story-teller. Mel Spurr starred in Melbourne's Tivoli, the Athenaeum Hall and the Town Hall in the golden days of vaudeville. Spurr invented the two man symbol and took it to Hutton's Melbourne manager. The 'Don't argue' slogan was quickly evolved, and in a short time became one of Australia's best-known trade-marks.
1982 *Sydney Morning Herald* 28 Aug. 30: 'The kid's got everything ... He has the size and strength to burst through tackles, a 'don't-argue' fend, and he loves scoring tries.'

Dooley, give someone Larry   To administer punishment, give a hiding [unexplained, although a connection has been claimed with the pugilist Larry Foley]
1946 Alan Marshall *Tell Us About the Turkey, Jo* 104: I had driven him [the bull] back a week before and that morning I gave him Larry Dooley.
1962 Stuart Gore *Down the Golden Mile* 52: 'Gives that Buick of his flamin' Larry Dooley, don't he?' observed Horrigan as they watched the car go lurching and bucketing through the saltbush.
1969 Patsy Adam Smith *The Folklore of the Australian Railwaymen* 118: I nodded towards the Governor's train. 'They'll [the mosquitoes] give his nibs larry-dooley tonight.'
1973 Chester Eagle *Who could love the Nightingale?* 3: 'How're the kids treating you? They'd give you a bit of larry dooley, wouldn't they?'

doorknock   A fundraising campaign for charity which is conducted by seeking donations from door to door [f. the Anti-Cancer Appeal Doorknock of 1958, organized by Don Chipp: see quot. 1978]
1973 *Bulletin* 16 Jun. 22: Winter: season of doorknocks, of middle-aged women smiling winningly on the porch and writing out receipts with cold fingers and blotty ball-points in the front hall.
1974 Patrick White *The Cockatoos* 259: He started trying to freshen up his patter ... 'the old door-knock for the Heart Foundation. Care to make a contribution?'
1978 Don Chipp in Tim Hewat and David Wilson *Don Chipp* 10: I gathered together a committee of bright young people and I invented the name Doorknock. On the day we had 55,000 volunteers;

we did hit every home in Melbourne; and that first Doorknock raised £350,000 ($700,000) in two hours.
1981 *National Times* 21 Jun. 9: Austcare, the charitable organisation with the dubious honour of having invented the doorknock, is to run its own Mr Australia competition next year.
1984 *Alice Springs Star* 8 Aug. 1: The appeal, launched by Chief Minister, Mr Paul Everingham last week culminates in a Territory-wide door-knock on Sunday.

Dorothy Dixer   see **Dix(er)**

dose of salts, go through like a   see **salts**

dot   As for **date** q.v.
1978 Ronald McKie *Bitter Bread* 104: She did not look or act like a real pro, although with so many amateurs around trailing their dots you could not always tell.
1984 John Hepworth *Toorak Sunday* 10 Jun. 5: Only one bird [in King's Cross] hawking the dot – and she had *pants* on.

dot, wine   see **wine**

double-bank   1   To yoke on a second team of bullocks to pull a load out of a bog, or to overcome some similar difficulty
1863 Rachel Henning *Letters* ed. David Adams (1963) 128: I should rather like to see them at the river or some of the bad creeks, where they 'double-bank the bullocks' as it is called: that is, put the whole team, thirty yokes perhaps, on to each dray to drag it over.
1877 Rolf Boldrewood *A Colonial Reformer* (1890) 323: 'But if you lose your team, and break your pole, and spoil your loading when you're on a long overland trip, how are you to help your mates or any other chap that's bogged, when they want you to double-bank? ... You've got to stand and look on, just like a broke loafer.'
1911 E. S. Sorenson *Life in the Australian Back-blocks* 158: When he had burst it [the log] along the top he double-banked the middle wedge, which caused another to drop into the crack.
1913 John Sadleir *Recollections of a Victorian Police Officer* 168: The teamsters did not travel alone, for there were many places where double-banking was a necessity, and six or more horses in single file might often be seen hauling one load over some bad pinch.
2   (also *double-dink*) To double a load; carry an extra person on a horse or bicycle
1876 A. J. Boyd *Old Colonials* (1882) 77: By-and-by, down goes the mare, dead beat ... so we unpacked her, and double-banked my other mail-horse, and the inspector got along on the first one.

1882 Rolf Boldrewood *Robbery Under Arms* (World's Classics 1949) 221: 'We must double-bank my horse,' whispers Jim ... He jumped up, and I mounted behind him.
1898 George T. Bell *Tales of Australian Adventure* 30: 'Jump up in the saddle and carry your luggage in front of you, and I'll get up behind. Old Balley's used to double-banking.'
1933 R. B. Plowman *The Man from Oodnadatta* 223: 'I have only one spare riding camel ... They could double-bank on him if they liked.'

double dink   As for **double-bank** 2
1941 Baker 25: *Double-dink*: To carry a second person on the top bar of a bicycle.
1942 Eve Langley *The Pea Pickers* 35: Kelly came down from Black Mountain every Sunday after that, and we went double dinking on his white mare. Ibid. 34: They ... pityingly offered to 'double dink' me. My shame had double damned me, and now, double dinked, I bent over the bar of Kelly's bike and off we went.
1943 Charles Shaw *Outback Occupations* 120: It was back in the days when the boys were little fellows, still going to school, double-dink on the old brown mare.
1959 Gerard Hamilton *Summer Glare* 105: Once or twice I had double-dinked her home from school on my bike.
see **double bank**

double dipping, double dip   See quots
1983 *Sydney Morning Herald* 22 Apr. 3: This review will take into account 'double dipping' by pensioners who take their superannuation in a lump sum form and then draw the age pension.
1983 Paul Keating *Australian* 27 May 10: 'A trend had emerged in Australia where people took their benefits in a lump sum, arranged their affairs to minimise income and then double-dipped the public purse by taking the age pension.'

double drummer   A variety of cicada [f. sound]
c. **1905** A. B. Paterson 'Done for the Double' in *Song of the Pen* (1983) 248: Certainly the locust was a 'double-drummer', and could deafen the German Band when shaken up judiciously; still, it was dear at the price of a sovereign.
1951 Dymphna Cusack and Florence James *Come In Spinner* 105: There came the piercing crackle of a cicada. 'He's a double drummer.'
1974 Ronald McKie *The Mango Tree* 18: He had talked to her about his first puppy, the Black Prince and the Double-drummer he had caught in the garden.

Double Pay   The Sydney suburb of Double Bay [f. shop prices]
1981 *Sydney Morning Herald* 20 Feb. 1: It's yet

another irritating example of Opera House tenants' unswerving devotion to Le Rippe Off, on the assumption that everybody who goes to the place is from Double Pay.
1984 *Sunday Telegraph* (Sydney) 25 Mar. 158: This one's not Double Pay [heading] Unbelievable food at realistic prices is what Tony's International restaurant at Double Bay has to offer.

doubler, chuck a   To 'have a fit'
1946 *Sun* (Sydney) 1 Sep. Suppl. 23: When he lamps Sydney he chucks a doubler.

doughboy   Name given to the colonial versions of the doughboy ('A boiled flour dumpling' OED 1865), most often cooked in fat
1834 Let. in Edward Shann *Cattle Chosen* (1926) 58: Dawson fried some pork, and Phoebe cooked some doughboys for dinner.
1846 G. F. Angas *Savage Life and Scenes in Australia and New Zealand* i 161: Our cook had not been idle: there were 'dampers', 'dough-boys', 'leather jackets', 'johnny-cakes', and 'beggars-in-the-pan.'
1855 William Howitt *Land, Labour and Gold* i 117–18: A suet pudding, called a dough-boy . . . put into the fat, and when ready, beef steaks or mutton chops are fried.
1881 A. C. Grant *Bush-Life in Queensland* ii 142: The cook has with difficulty boiled doughboys, which, although tough and indigestible, are nevertheless hot, and are washed down with pannikins of steaming tea.
1895 A. B. Paterson 'Johnson's Antidote' in *Singer of the Bush* (1983) 231: Where the station cook in terror, nearly every time he bakes, / Mixes up among the doughboys half a dozen poison snakes.
1904 Tom Petrie *Reminiscences of Early Queensland* 235: The prisoner made round things which passed as doughboys.
1933 Acland 374: *Doughboy.–* A dumpling made of flour, sugar and suet, boiled. It was a favourite dish out mustering.
1983 *West Australian*(Perth) 31 Dec. 15: 'We hadn't eaten all day and when we asked for a meal, tha farmer boiled us up some doughboys in a kerosene tin.'

doughnut (golden)   1   The vulva
1972 David Williamson *The Removalists* 53: 'We'll be in like Flynn there tomorrow night. We'll thread the eye of the old golden doughnut – no worries.'
1974 Barry Humphries *Barry McKenzie Holds His Own* 33: [Barry is watching an attractive girl] Ohh, I could hit that on the golden doughnut like a plate of porridge.
2   See quot.

1981 *Sydney Morning Herald* 20 Apr. 1: They started their usual entertainment of 'doughnuts'. This involves a motor cyclist spinning his machine in tight circles.

Douglas   An axe [f. brand name]
1945 Baker 78: *kelly* and *douglas*, an axe (from the names of makers).
1966 James Hackston *Father Clears Out* 160: Sometimes on a Sunday morning exhibitions of axemanship (theoretical) were given; right and wrong way to swing Douglas.

dover   A bush knife, esp. in the expression 'flash your dover' as an invitation to eat; also food [f. brand name]
1870 Marcus Clarke *His Natural Life* ed. S. Murray Smith (1970) 616: 'Hang up your moke, my young Ducrow, sit down, and flash your Dover.'[1] 1 *Flash your Dover* is essentially *Colonial* slang. The majority of clasp knives imported in to the Australian colonies twenty years ago were made by one 'Dover'. Hence 'flashing your Dover' is equivalent to 'drawing your Toledo'.
1873 J. C. F. Johnson *Christmas on Carringa* 16: Ses he there's mutton and damper / And on the fire there's tea / So flash your Dover* hearty / For there's heaps for you and me. *Flash your Dover, draw out your knife, so called from the maker's name, 'Dover', on the orthodox bush knife of 25 to 30 years ago.
1881 G. H. Gibson 'A Ballad of Queensland' *Bulletin* 26 Mar. 8 in *Australian Bush Ballads* ed. Stewart and Keesing (1955) 313: You were 'flashin' your dover' six short months ago / In a lambin' camp on the Paroo.
1885 *The Australasian Printers' Keepsake* 75: He . . . returned with half a loaf of bread, part of a shoulder of mutton, and some cold potatoes. He roared exultingly – 'Here's the sanguinary dover for yer – now let us have a blooming pint!'
1908 Giles Seagram *Bushmen All* 164: 'He was a loud, red-faced man who used his blooming dover like a shovel.'

down, have a ~ on   To have a grudge or prejudice against, to be hostile to [f. thieves' slang: see quot. 1812]
[**1812** Vaux: *A down* is a suspicion, alarm or discovery, which taking place, obliges yourself and *palls* to give up or desist from the business or depredation you were engaged in; to *put a down upon a man*, is to give information of any robbery or fraud he is about to perpetrate, so as to cause his failure or detection.]
1835 *Colonist* 10 Sep. 289: To use the colonial slang, Up comes Mr Cory himself . . . to Sydney, to have a *down* upon us, poor *misfortunate* Editor, for a libel!

1848 J. C. Byrne *Twelve Years' Wanderings in the British Colonies* i 266: His master had what is called a down upon him.

1849 Alexander Harris *The Emigrant Family* (1967) 90: Biddy, too, had 'a down' upon him, because it was well known that he had a 'down' on John Thomas.

1855 Raffaello Carboni *The Eureka Stockade* ed. G. Serle (1969) 14: I, a living witness, do assert that, from that day, there was a 'down' on the name of [Commissioner] Rede.

1863 R. Therry *Reminiscences of Thirty Years' Residence in New South Wales* 122: 'I am very sorry to tell your Grace that there's a great down upon the Romans in this country.'

1881 G. C. Evans *Stories told round the Campfire* 83: 'Now I know why he had such a down on me; he did not like to see us in possession of your father's property.'

1896 Henry Lawson 'Stiffner and Jim' *Prose* i 127: 'I had a down on Stiffner, and meant to pay him out.'

1907 Ambrose Pratt *The Remittance Man* 185: 'I can't see why you should have such 'a down' on him. How has he offended you?'

1917 A. B. Paterson *Three Elephant Power* 25: He ... had a desperate 'down' on canvassers generally.

Down Under Australia: rarely used by Australians themselves

1886 J. A. Froude *Oceana* 92: We were to bid adieu to the 'Australasian' ... She had carried us safely *down under*.

1916 *The Anzac Book* 145: He sat down to think, little dreaming that he was fulfilling Macaulay's prophecy concerning the man from 'down under' sitting on the ruins of London Bridge.

1951 Simon Hickey *Travelled Roads* 121: Because I came from 'Down Under', they gave me imposing statistics on petroleum, helium, sulphur, mercury, beef cattle.

1975 Ray Robinson *On Top Down Under: Australia's Cricket Captains* [book title]

1981 *Weekend Australian* 18 Apr. 12: Early on Tuesday morning, as the space shuttle Columbia zipped above Canberra tracking station, astronauts John Young and Bob Crippen announced: 'Now we have a little Slim Dusty and Waltzing Matilda for the Australians down under.'

drac(k) Unattractive, esp. as applied to women, in phrases like 'a drack sort' [? f. *Dracula's Daughter*]

1945 Baker 127: *Sope* is an old larrikin word ... the direct antithesis of *bonzer* ... *Drack* and *bodger* are modern equivalents.

1949 Ruth Park *Poor Man's Orange* 180: He was always stuck with drack types like Dolour Darcy.

1953 *A Sunburnt Country* ed. Ian Bevan 130: *Drack* (again especially of the female gender, in which case the ungallant phrase is 'a drack sack') means poor or unattractive. [Army slang]

1953 T. A. G. Hungerford *Riverslake* 94: 'Anyway, it's a football dance, not just one of those drac turns they slap on for the locals.'

1968 Geoffrey Dutton *Andy* 265: 'You blokes get on to some bloody drack subjects.'

1972 *Sydney Morning Herald* 26 Sep. 9: Mr Hardy said he would put aside his memories ... of meeting Raquel Welch ('A drac sort – not nearly as good looking in the flesh as you would expect').

drag A prison term of three months [thieves' slang: see quot. 1812]

1812 Vaux *Drag*: a cart. The *drag*, is the game of robbing carts, waggons, or carriages ... *Done for a drag*, signifies convicted for a robbery of the before-mentioned nature.

1877 T. E. Argles *The Pilgrim* i 6: He expected to receive at the hands of the magistrates a term of imprisonment which he designated as a 'drag' (three months).

1919 J. Vance Marshall *The World of the Living Dead* 87: *Drag* Sentence of three months.

1939 Kylie Tennant *Foveaux* 311: 'I got a drag,' he said not too regretfully. Three months was a good deal less than he had expected.

1950 *Australian Police Journal* Apr. 112: *Drag* 3 months' imprisonment.

drag the chain see **chain**

dragged screaming from the tart shop see **tart shop**

Dragons, the The St George (N.S.W.) Rugby League team (also the 'Saints') [f. club emblem]

1974 *Australian* 8 Aug. 20: Dragons will draw extra fire to beat Easts.

draw the crabs see **crabs**

draw the crow see **crow**

dreamtime, the The mythological past of the Aborigines, used colloquially to refer to anything remote, out of touch with the present

1953 T. A. G. Hungerford *Riverslake* 235: Slim and the kitchen and Riverslake seemed to have receded into a dream-time that had no tangible link with the present and the immensity of the revelation that had come over him.

1966 Roger Carr *Surfie* 118: 'Listen', I told her. 'Don't talk about her anymore. She's part of what was. Part of the dreamtime.'

1983 *Australian* 1 Jun. 16: The suggestion that all post-graduate awards should be taxed showed the 'dreamtime mentality' of many senior academics and administrators, according to the Council of Australian Postgraduate associations ... The report had failed to understand the realities of the needs of postgraduates.

1983 Keith Dunstan *Sydney Morning Herald* 12 Nov. 36: Back in the dreamtime when I first began newspaper work, everyone wore a hat.

drink a horse   see **horse**

drink with the flies   see **flies**

drongo   Someone who is stupid, clumsy, worthless [f. the racehorse described in quots 1946, 1958, 1977. The horse would presumably have been named (before it acquired this reputation) after the swift and alert *drongo* (family *Discruridae*), a bird resembling the starling]

1941 *Salt* 22 Dec. 36: An airforce recruit is a drongo, and this word, it is suggested, is taken from the name of a large clumsy flying bird found in the Cape York Peninsula.

1946 *Salt* 8 Apr. 22: Drongo a horse foaled in 1921 and retired in 1925 who failed to win a race, and after that anybody or anything slow or clumsy became a Drongo.

1948 Sumner Locke Elliott *Rusty Bugles* in *Khaki, Bush and Bigotry* ed. Eunice Hanger (1968) 33: 'Yeah ... a bloke 'ud have to go troppo in a hut full of drongoes like youse.'

1949 Ruth Park *Poor Man's Orange* 181: It wasn't his fault he was a drongo ... He didn't want to have pimples, or a thin neck, or that hair all snowflaked with dandruff.

1951 Dymphna Cusack *Southern Steel* 4: Free of the army for twenty-eight days at least! Rid of the drongos who got in your hair in the irritating friction of everyday contact over a long period.

1958 Tom Ronan *The Pearling Master* 181–2: His continued run of second placings, both in and out of the classroom, brought from a senior of some standing the comment that ... 'Weyland was another Drongo' ... They all knew about Drongo: the colt had been a popular fancy for the previous Derby at Flemington. After a careful preparation ... he had run second. Throughout Oliver's first year at school the horse continued running seconds. He dropped out of the quality races and competed in moderate class handicaps, but he never managed to have his number hoisted first by the judge ... Drongo, first synonymous with a capacity for always being narrowly beaten, gradually changed to be an epithet flung at anything or anybody too cow-hearted to try to win.

1963 Randolph Stow *Tourmaline* 63: 'Put your head back, drongo,' Kestrel said to Byrne.

1975 *Sydney Morning Herald* 5 Jul. 9: There's no doubt that Australia fields a very poor political team, that our orating drongoes pose a more serious threat to democracy than the falling dominoes of Asia.

1977 *Sunday Telegraph* (Sydney) 13 Feb. 120: The 1600 m Drongo Handicap – for apprentice jockeys and horses without a win for more than a year – is raced in memory of a horse who gave his name to the language ... running second in a VRC Derby and St Leger, third in an AJC St Leger and fifth in the 1924 Melbourne [*in error for* Sydney] Cup. The trouble was he couldn't win in 37 starts.

1982 *Sydney Morning Herald* 20 Nov. 29: 'In fact,' Tite told Senator Gareth Evans, who was at Magdalen in the 1960s, 'of all the colonial drongoes – that's the word, is it not? – that ever passed through my hands, Fraser was the greatest.'

droob   A 'sad sack', hopeless-looking person [? f. *droopy*]

1945 Baker 156: *drube* A term of contempt for a person. [Army slang]

1948 Ruth Park *Poor Man's Orange* 181: A sick feeling entered Dolour's heart when she saw Harry standing there, his hands thrust into his pockets like packages and a little, saliva-stained fag stuck on his lower lip. Of all the nice boys going to Luna Park ... she had to draw this droob.

drooby

1972 James Searle *The Lucky Streak* 50: 'You'll 'ave to wear something a bit decent ... you look pretty drooby in them.'

1981 *Sunday Mail* (Brisbane) 25 Oct. 18: The party was rotten – drooby creeps, spooks, twits, bores etc.

drop   A fall of wicket in cricket

1977 *Sunday Telegraph* (Sydney) 9 Jan. 62: A wicket-keeper who bats first drop, Tony is also skipper of the Nepean ... side.

drop a bucket   see **bucket**

drop one's bundle   see **bundle**

drover's dog   1   From Mr Hayden's statement on being replaced as Labor leader by Bob Hawke shortly before the Federal election in 1983: see quot.

1983 Bill Hayden *Australian* 4 Feb. 1: 'I believe a drover's dog could lead the Labor Party to victory the way the country is.'

1983 *Sydney Morning Herald* 14 May 1: Sir Kenneth's retirement, aged 70, came fortuitously for the Labor Party: it enabled the party, having decided at last that Dr Bert Evatt was no drover's dog, to find a soft landing for him as Chief Justice.

1983 Evan Whitton *Sydney Morning Herald* 4 Oct. 6: All things being equal, the legendary drover's dog would have a useful chance against the tiring and increasingly shrill Mrs Margaret Thatcher.

1984 *Sun-Herald* 2 Dec. 3: Mr Hayden said the election result was a 'dreadful' blow to the Government ... 'The drover's dog has won again but he's clapped out a bit this time.'

2 Mr Hayden himself

1983 *Australian* 28 Dec. 9: Bill Hayden: both nicknames, Bellyache Bill and Whingeing Willie, have been dropped. Now it is the Drover's Dog.

1984 Andrew Peacock *Sydney Morning Herald* 25 Feb. 12: The drover's dog and his pups are in Adelaide setting up a new faction.

1984 *Australian* 12 Jul. 1: Drover's dog becomes ALP's elder statesman [heading] When he resigned from the leadership of the Labor Party just before the last election, Bill Hayden remarked that a drover's dog could lead the ALP to victory. Mr Hayden, now the Minister for Foreign Affairs, has thus become known as the Drover's Dog.

drum *v.* To impart necessary and reliable information; to set someone straight [see *drum n.* 1]

1919 J. Vance Marshall *The World of the Living Dead* 30: Hurriedly he impressed upon me the exact location ... and proceeded to 'drum me up' with the message.

1948 Sumner Locke Elliott *Rusty Bugles* in *Khaki, Bush and Bigotry* ed. Eunice Hanger (1968) 32: 'You never get out of here, mate – I'm drumming you.'

1957 Ray Lawler *Summer of the Seventeenth Doll* 98: 'And I'm drummin' yer, you don't pull your socks up pretty quick, you're gunna find next season that our mob have got a new ganger for keeps.'

1960 Anthony Kimmins *Lugs O'Leary* 76: 'I'm drummin' you,' pleaded the little man, 'he's a moral.'

1969 D'Arcy Niland *Dead Men Running* 105: 'Don't bite me, son. I was only gonna drum you.'

drum *n.* 1 Information requisite to some particular situation; reliable information generally, esp. in the expression to 'give someone the drum'

[**1812** Vaux: *Drummond:* any scheme or project considered to be infallible, or any event which is deemed inevitably certain, is declared to be a *Drummond*; meaning, it is as sure as the credit of that respectable banking-house, Drummond and Co.]

1923 Con Drew *Rogues & Ruses* 88: 'But how do you know that Ding Dong won't be tryin'?' says the clerk ... 'Because I got the drum on the way out to the races,' says Cracker.

1937 K. S. Prichard *Intimate Strangers* 262: 'If I give my punter the drum from the field, you can't blame me, can you?'

1944 Lawson Glassop *We Were the Rats* 36: 'That was before I got the drum, as Spike would say, that Margaret might be going.'

1955 John Morrison *Black Cargo* 82: 'Why didn't you give us the drum then?'

1969 Thomas Keneally *The Survivor* 167: 'I was hoping for the drum on Antarctica, I was thinking you might cough up some Antarctic quintessence, something that can't be learnt from the journals.'

1971 George Johnston *A Cartload of Clay* 70: 'Listen, I'll give you the drum,' the big man was saying.

1980 *Bulletin* 18 Nov. 132: 'I've just had the drum,' he whispered, 'that Susan Sangster has bought herself a stunning new outfit on the grounds that she's going to lead the Cup winner in and wants to look her best.'

2 A swag, esp. in the expression 'hump one's drum' [? f. cylindrical shape]

1861 *Penguin Book of Australian Ballads* (1964) 87: No more through the bush we'll go humping the drum.

1868 T. Wade Brown *Overlanding in Australia* 64: He is 'humping his drum' (i.e. travelling) looking up a job.

1887 *All the Year Round* 30 Jul. 66: In Australia, the 'swag', also sometimes called a 'drum', is the bundle, generally consisting of a large blanket rolled up which contains the personal luggage of the man who carries, or 'humps' it.

1891 Henry Lawson 'On the Wallaby' *Verse* i 134: I am out on the wallaby humping my drum.

1905 'The Sheep-Workers' Lament' *The Old Bush Songs* ed. A. B. Paterson 55: But lonely now I hump my drum / In sunshine and in rain.

3 A brothel [f. thieves' slang: *Drum* a house, a lodging ... *Flash drum,* a house of ill fame Hotten 1860]

c. **1882** *The Sydney Slang Dictionary* 3: *Drum, or Crib* House of ill repute.

1894 *Bulletin* 18 Aug. 14: Grog scarce, 'drums' shut.

1900–10 O'Brien and Stephens: *Drum* A brothel.

1924 *Truth* 27 Apr. 6: *Drum* A brothel.

1944 Lawson Glassop *We Were the Rats* 103: 'There's another drum down here,' said Eddie.

1951 Dymphna Cusack and Florence James *Come In Spinner* 254: 'This place has the rep. for being one of the safest drums in the town.'

1963 T. A..G. Hungerford *Shake the Golden Bough* 91: 'A drum?' Leroy said, his forehead wrinkled. Charlie thought for a moment, and then said: 'A cathouse.'

1975 Hal Porter *The Extra* 50: 'What's a nice boy like you doing in a drum like this?'

drum, not to run a Fail to perform as tipped (turf slang)

1942 *Truth* 31 May 2: Ridden by McMenamin, Vanity Fair was always at an unprofitable quotation, more especially when she subsequently failed to 'run a drum'.

1945 Baker 174: A horse that *runs a drum* performs and wins as tipped.
1957 Nino Culotta *They're a Weird Mob* 72: 'Makes no difference. 'E never run a drum, anyway.'
1962 Stuart Gore *Down the Golden Mile* 261: 'Backed Sweet Friday for a spin ... But it never run a drum.'
1978 John Hepworth *His Book* 113: Warrego Willie went like a hairy goat – never even looked like running a drum.

drummer 1 A commercial traveller [U.S. 1827 OED]
1886 P. Clarke *The New Chum in Australia* 124: A 'drummer' – that is, a commercial traveller.
1907 Charles MacAlister *Old Pioneering Days in the Sunny South* 146: I witnessed a fierce brawl between an aggressive bagman and a tipsy shearer ... The 'drummer' got the worst of the fistic argument.
2 The slowest shearer, the one with the lowest tally in the shed.
1898 *Bulletin* 1 Oct. 14: 'To carry the drum' is to be last man in the shed.
1911 E. S. Sorenson *Life in the Australian Backblocks* 240: The drummer, or slowest shearer, is about the only man who doesn't seem to care when supper-time comes.
1933 Acland: *Drummer* The slowest shearer in a shed.
1964 H. P. Tritton *Time Means Tucker* 92: In his previous sheds he had been drummer all the time.
3 See **double drummer**

drunk as Chloe see **Chloe**

Dry, the The dry season of the year, the months without rain
1908 Mrs Aeneas Gunn *We of the Never-Never* 219: It was August, well on in the dry .
1930 J. S. Litchfield *Far-North Memories* 206: Football is played during the wet season (October to March), cricket during the dry (June to September).
1938 Xavier Herbert *Capricornia* 115: People scoffed at O'Cannon's cotton, saying at first that it would never see the Wet through, then that it would never live through the Dry.
1943 Charles Barrett *Up North* 8: The black soil plains, impassable in the wet season, are 'Bay of Biscay' country in the 'dry', when millions of ruts and cattle footprints have hardened into troughs and miniature craters.
1965 *The Tracks We Travel* ed. L. Haylen 78: On many such holdings, water has to be drawn from very great depths in the 'dry' in order to keep the cattle alive.

dry as a chip see **chip**

dry as a Pommy's towel (bath-mat) see **Pommy's**

dry-blow, dry-blower, dry-blowing 1 Gold-mining terms for the process of separating out the gold when water is unavailable for 'washing': hence any monotonous and unproductive activity
1894 *The Argus* 28 Mar. 5: When water is not available, as unfortunately is the case at Coolgardie, 'dry blowing' is resorted to. This is done by placing the pounded stuff in one dish, and pouring it slowly at a certain height into the other. If there is any wind blowing it will carry away the pounded stuff. [Morris]
1915 J. P. Bourke *Off the Bluebush* 103: 'Do you have any luck at the diggings,' I said / To a dryblower grizzled and grey.
1950 K. S. Prichard *Winged Seeds* 18: Dinny started dry-blowing his reminiscences as if Young Bill ... had never heard them before.
1967 Kylie Tennant *Tell Morning This* 50: Miss Montrose, who realised that she had struck pay-dirt at last after so much dry blowing at Grandma's conversation, clicked her tongue to express sympathy and interest.
2 See quot. 1979
1979 David Ireland *A Woman of the Future* 257: I didn't find out till later that some of them can mimic the spasms of ejaculation, and produce nothing. 'Dry-blowing', it's called.

dub A lavatory
1956 Ruth Park and D'Arcy Niland *The Drums Go Bang!* 170: 'A hot-water heater! and a hand basin. And look at that dub!'
1961 Nene Gare *The Fringe Dwellers* 25: 'If ya wanta use the dub it's round the side.'

dubbo Stupid; a stupid person (in N.S.W.)
1977 Jim Ramsay *Cop it Sweet* 32: *Dubbo*: pec. N.S.W. Yokel.
1979 Kathy Lette and Gabrielle Carey *Puberty Blues* 46: 'Sprung!' cried Jeff Basin, the local dubbo.* *Idiot/Bankie-type
1980 *Sun-Herald* 27 Jan. 66: In New South Wales, of course, a person wouldn't be yarra, he'd be dubbo.
1982 *Sydney Morning Herald* 10 Jul. 36: Dubbo is an Aboriginal word for 'red earth', which does not explain why, on the east coast, this word is used to describe those who are slightly thick.
1984 *Sydney Morning Herald* 15 Oct. Guide 15: Sylvester Stallone as Rocky ... he's shaken off his dubbo image.

duchess To treat anyone 'as a duchess', esp. applied to the courtesies extended by overseas governments to visiting Australian politicians, as

though imposing on their naivety
1969 Leslie Haylen *Twenty Years' Hard Labor* 134: Cables from London, telling us about the Labor delegation flashing through London in Rolls Royces, of being 'duchessed' in the Commons or on the lawns at the Palace, didn't exactly send the Labor benches into transports of delight.
1973 *Sydney Morning Herald* 30 Apr. 20: 'Did Mr Heath give you any encouragement? Did he, to use a word of Mr Chifley, duchess you?'
1976 *Sun-Herald* 27 Jun. 38: It cannot be said that Malcolm Fraser was 'duchessed' during his memorable stay in Peking. But the flattering, seductive treatment he received did resemble the softening up process thus named to which Australian political leaders visiting London used to be exposed.
1983 *Sun-Herald* 12 Jun. 21: All this – and the fact that Bob bounced Prince William on his knee – ... prompts the thought that Hawke has been duchessed by royalty.
1984 *National Times* 18 May 2: In times past, left-wingers liked to be seen as on their guard against being 'duchessed' at a vice-regal level. We're sure Ms McHugh [in dining with the Governor General] has withstood the danger in her case of being 'duked'.

duck, blue   see **blue duck**

duck, Burdekin, Hawkesbury   see **Burdekin, Hawkesbury**

duck, couldn't head a   see **head**

duckhouse, one up against your   A point scored in some way against an adversary: *obs.*
1933 Norman Lindsay *Saturdee* 7: 'You think you hid me cap, so that's one up agen your duckhouse.'
1941 Baker 26: *Duck-house, up against one's* A phrase used to describe some setback to a person's plans: e.g., 'that's one up against your duck house', that baffles you, that makes you think.
1968 Stuart Gore *Holy Smoke* 52: He says, 'That's one up against your duckhouse, Jonah!'
1981 Ross Campbell *Sydney Morning Herald* 21 Nov. 45: National Trust needed to preserve historic Australian idioms, e.g. 'Shove that up against your duckhouse'.

duck-shoving   Jockeying for position; manipulative action generally
1870 *Notes & Queries* 6 Aug. 111: Duck-shoving is the term used by our Melbourne cabmen to express the unprofessional trick of breaking the rank, in order to push past the cabman on the stand for the purpose of picking up a stray passenger or so. [Morris]
1944 Keith Attiwill *Cut-Lunch Commandos* 115:

The moral ... is that he who would trip abroad must learn to conjugate the verb 'to wangle' – I wangle; thou wanglest; he duckshoves; and so on.
1945 Robert S. Close *Love Me Sailor* 14: 'Well fercrysake,' I said. 'It sounds like a lot of funny duck-shoving somewhere to me.'
1972 Don Crick *A Different Drummer* 13: After a lot of duck-shoving, he finally got going.
1977 *Sun-Herald* 3 Apr. 15: The sensitive report has been shuffled off to a variety of Public Service committees for more study and evaluation, but all the Public Service duck-shoving will not change the basic arguments.
1982 *Sydney Morning Herald* 9 Aug. 1: Mr Wran said retrospective billing was totally unacceptable ... 'This sniping and duck shoving between county councils and the Electricity Commission should also cease,' he said.

duck, wet enough to bog a   Extremely wet
1879–80 Ned Kelly 'The Jerilderie Letter' in Max Brown *Australian Son* (1956) 272: The ground was that rotten it would bog a duck in places.
1920 *Bulletin Book of Humorous Verses* 9: And the ground was soft enough to bog a duck.
1934 Thomas Wood *Cobbers* 89: What about them tracks? ... Six inches of rain in three days would bog a duck.
1975 Ted Egan *Australian Voices* ed. Rosemary Dobson 89: The Six Mile is a blacksoil plain, where you'd bog a duck after an inch of rain.
1981 Garry Disher *Approaches* 12: 'This mud's soft enough to bog a duck.'

duff, up the   Pregnant [listed as Australian by Partridge, although used in England ? f. *the pudding club*]
1941 Baker 26: *Duff, up the* (of a woman) Pregnant.
1962 Gavin Casey *Amid the Plenty* 192. Good enough for the bastard, getting poor Freda up the duff, and taking her away.
1970 Alexander Buzo *The Front Room Boys* in Penguin *Plays* 49: 'They reckon she was up the duff not long ago, and blamed it on Donnie Dixon.'
1975 Xavier Herbert *Poor Fellow My Country* 57: 'Anyway, next thing she's up the duff. But to whom?'

duff, duffing   Stealing cattle, esp. by branding unbranded calves ('poddy-dodging' q.v.) or by altering brands; poaching grass [f. *duffer*]
1869 E. C. Booth *Another England* 138–9: There was a 'duffing paddock' somewhere on the Broken River, into which nobody but the owner had ever found an entrance, and out of which no cattle had ever found their way ... The man who owned the 'duffing paddock' was said to have a knack of altering cattle brands. [Morris]

1875 Rolf Boldrewood *The Squatter's Dream* repr. as *Ups and Downs* (1878) 162: 'I knew Redcap when he'd think more of duffing a red heifer than all the money in the country.'
1903 Joseph Furphy *Such is Life* (1944) 47: Such a sound at such a time is ominous to duffing bullock drivers.
1915 K. S. Prichard *The Pioneers* 222: 'Oh, why have you got yourself mixed up with duffing and crooked ways?'
1928 W. Robertson *Coo-ee Talks* 174: Jarvis was a past master in cattle-duffing.
1938 *Salute to Freedom* 28: 'It's silly to surround cattle duffing with a cloak of romance as many people do. It's straight out theft.'
1960 *Sydney Morning Herald* 2 Feb. 9: Spokesmen for the graziers in N.S.W. and Queensland yesterday called for urgent Government action to combat cattle-duffing ... The police had formed a special 'duffing' squad.
1964 H. P. Tritton *Time Means Tucker* 102: Never were we refused a bit of grass for our horses (I suppose they knew we would duff it if it was refused).
1984 *Age* (Melbourne) 30 Jun. 17: Cattle, sheep and horse duffing is alive, well and booming in Victoria.

duffer *n.* **1** Someone who steals cattle, esp. by counterfeiting the brands, or branding cleanskins [f. *duffer* One who sells trashy goods as valuables, upon false pretences 1756 OED]
1877 Rolf Boldrewood *A Colonial Reformer* (1891) 352: 'Your husband takes to idle ways and worse, and your children grow up duffers and planters, and perhaps end in sticking up people.'
1907 Charles MacAlister *Old Pioneering Days in the Sunny South* 252: The latter promptly pulled a burning stick from our camp fire and thrust it into the 'duffer's' face, singeing his red beard and making him howl with pain.
1937 Ernestine Hill *The Great Australian Loneliness* 83: O paralyse the duffer's hand, / When he lifts up his flaming brand.
1984 *Age* (Melbourne) 30 Jun. 17: Some time during the night of 7–8 May a group of duffers drove their truck on to Mr Wheelhouse's 50-hectare farm at Mooroopna, near Shepparton, and stole 28 Hereford steers worth about $13,000.
2 A mine that proves unproductive, esp. in expressions like 'sink a duffer', 'bottom a duffer'
1861 T. McCombie *Australian Sketches* 193: 'It was a terrible duffer anyhow, every ounce of gold got from it cost £20 I swear.' [Morris]
1873 A. Trollope *Australia* ed. Edwards and Joyce (1967) 298: Much useless labour has been expounded on 'duffers'. A shaft sunk without any produce from it is a duffer.
1880 Rolf Boldrewood *The Miner's Right* (1890)

55: 'Bottomed a duffer, by gum, not the colour itself, no mor'n on the palm o' my hand.'
1889 Henry Lawson 'The Sleeping Beauty' *Verse* i 58: He sunk a duffer on the Flat.
1905 Randolph Bedford *The Snare of Strength* 8: 'Then two or three duffer rushes; they put the Central country out of court.'
1936 A. B. Paterson 'The Shearer's Colt' in *Song of the Pen* (1983) 719: 'There's two thousand to be picked up in weight-for-age races and we'd laugh our heads off if we left a goldmine behind us and went away and bottomed on a duffer.'
1944 Brian James *First Furrow* 44: The last shaft he'd sunk ... A rank duffer.
1960 Donald McLean *The Roaring Days* 58: In the drought of '92 he'd sunk a shaft that turned out a duffer as far as silver was concerned.

duffer *v.*
1888 *Boomerang* 7 Apr. 11: That hall is going up this year – unless the whole Eidsvold 'duffers'.

dummy *n.*   One who acts under his own name on behalf of someone else, to gain an illegal advantage: orig. applied to those employed by the squatters, when their runs were opened to 'free selection', to take up the best areas and so forestall genuine selectors
1865 *Australasian* 23 Jun. 5: There were twenty-two *bona fide* applicants, no dummies, and no certificate holders.
1886 Frank Cowan *Australia: A Charcoal Sketch* 32: *The Dummy* man of straw in buying land.
1901 Henry Lawson 'Water Them Geraniums' *Prose* i 578: I had an idea that he wasn't a selector at all, only a 'dummy' for the squatter of the Cobborah run. You see, selectors were allowed to take up land on runs, or pastoral leases. The squatters kept them off as much as possible, by all manner of dodges and paltry persecution. The squatter would get as much freehold as he could afford, 'select' as much land as the law would allow him to take up, and then employ 'dummies' (dummy selectors) to take up bits of land that he fancied about his run, and hold them for him.
1953 *Caddie A Sydney Barmaid* 178: 'This pub's a goldmine and they own three others in the country as well.' ... 'But how do they get round the licences?' 'Aw, they get over that hurdle by putting in a dummy.'

dummy *v.* **dummying**   To act as a 'dummy'; the system so developed
1873 Anthony Trollope *Australia* ed. Edwards and Joyce (1967) 134: The ... system is generally called 'dummying' – putting up a non-existent free-selector – and is illegal.
1884 A. W. Stirling *The Never Never Land* 147: This 'dummying' consists of getting 'your sisters,

your cousins and your aunts', indeed even your very shepherds, to 'select' for you in their own names, with the implied intention of handing over the land to you as soon as the title is complete, you, meanwhile, paying all the charges.

1892 Gilbert Parker *Round the Compass in Australia* 75: He [the squatter] paid men to 'dummy' for him.

1903 Joseph Furphy *Such is Life* (1944) 35: 'Bob and Bat were dummying on the station at the time, and looking after the Skeleton paddock.'

1936 H. Drake-Brockman *Sheba Lane* 251: Begging the Government to take steps to suppress the dummying of luggers – the practice whereby a white man lent his name (at a price) to a coloured man, who was not allowed by law, to hold a pearling licence.

dump *n.* 1 Coin struck from the centre of a Spanish dollar in 1813, valued at 1s. 3d. [f. *dump* A term familiarly applied to various objects of 'dumpy' shape OED 1770; *Dumps* are also small pieces of lead, cast by schoolboys in the shape of money Grose 1811. (The term seems most often to be applied to the residue of some industrial process)]

1821 *Sydney Gazette* 5 May 2: A Number of BAD DOLLARS and DUMPS having been lately offered in Payment at the Bank of New South Wales, the Public, for their Information and Protection, are hereby apprised that the following Description of illegal Coin is much in circulation: – Dollars and Dumps that are not silver ...

1826 *Hobart Town Gazette* 29 Apr. 1: The Spanish Dollar will be received at Four Shillings and Four-pence, the Colonial Dollar at Three Shillings and Threepence, and the Dump at One Shilling and One Penny.

1826 James Atkinson *An Account of the State of Agriculture and Grazing in New South Wales* 132: A piece was struck out of the centre of each [dollar]; this centre piece was called a dump, and was put into circulation at fifteen-pence sterling value.

1859 Daniel Bunce *Travels with Dr Leichhardt in Australia* 59: Our first change for a pound consisted of two dumps, two holy dollars, one Spanish dollar, one French coin, one half-crown, one shilling, and one sixpence.

2 Small coins, contemptuously referred to; any trivial amount

1826 *Sydney Gazette* 22 Apr. 2: The offender, who had money in both pockets, very cheerfully paid the fine, observing, 'that was the way to spend dumps'.

1889 Ernest Giles *Australia Twice Traversed* i 281: He said, 'What's the use of only a nobbler or two? I wouldn't give a d——,' dump, I suppose he meant, 'for grog unless I could get drunk.'

1905 Randolph Bedford *The Snare of Strength* 294: 'I'm that thirsty I'd drink with Nosey Bob the

hangman. It doesn't matter a dump who pays.'

1915 J. P. Bourke *Off the Bluebush* 125: She hasn't been out for a flutter since then / And she don't care a dump for a dance.

1981 Bill O'Reilly *Sun-Herald* 13 Dec. 97: From now on you can have your three pronged Australian pace attack ... I wouldn't give you a tuppeny dump for it.

3 A marble

1959 Gerard Hamilton *Summer Glare* 76–7: 'If you an' me were playing dumps' ... 'I see,' he said. 'Dumps are marbles.'

dump *v.* 1 To press bales of wool

1872 C. H. Eden *My Wife and I in Queensland* 98: The great object of packing so close is to save carriage through the country, for however well you may do it, it is always repressed, or 'dumped' ... by hydraulic pressure on its arrival in port, the force being so great as to crush two bales into one. [Morris]

1884 A. W. Stirling *The Never Never Land* 155: Other men pick up the fleeces, fold them and put them in bales, when they are pressed and sometimes 'dumped' i.e. subjected to hydraulic pressure to make carriage easier.

1910 C. E. W. Bean *On the Wool Track* 265: To squash each bale into about two-thirds of its original size by 'dumping' (which means binding it round so tightly that what was formerly its length is squeezed into about the same dimension as its breadth).

2 (of a wave) To break and hurl a surfer down

1938 Jack Moses *Nine Miles from Gundagai* 88: W'en de breakers dumped / Me at Curl Curl.

dumper A large wave that breaks suddenly and hurls the surfer down, instead of carrying him in to shore

1920 A. H. Adams *The Australians* 185: A dumper is a badly behaved breaker, easily recognisable by the expert, that instead of carrying you on its crest gloriously right up to the beach till you ground on the sand; ignominiously breaks as it strikes the shallow water and deposits you, smack! in a flurry of sand and water, any side up. Dangerous, too; you might break your arm.

1924 *Truth* 27 Apr. 6: *Dumper* A curling breaker.

1942 Gavin Casey *It's Harder for Girls* 153: Most of our mob didn't know what to do when they got in front of a 'dumper', but I could still manage them.

1954 Peter Gladwin *The Long Beat Home* 193: 'Not that one,' he yelled. 'It's a 'dumper' ... He saw the wave's crest, instead of sliding, arch enormously and hang, and hurl her down and crash on her.

1965 Thomas Keneally *The Fear* 165: A dumper of a wave slammed down a confirmatory fist on the

159

beach.

Duncan   The rolled swag: *rare* [unexplained]
1905 Arthur Bayldon *The Western Track* 56: With tucker-bags and billy-cans and Duncan on their back / They trust to luck to pull them through, and face the Western Track.
1906 H. J. Tompkins *With Swag and Billy* 8: Choice may be said to lie between the knapsack, rucksack, and swag – good old Duncan or Matilda.

dungaree settler   See quot. 1826
1826 James Atkinson *An Account of the State of Agriculture and Grazing in New South Wales* 29: I beg here to be understood as only alluding to the early Settlers, and the lower order of the present – what are technically termed in the Colony *Dungaree Settlers*, from a coarse cotton manufacture of India which forms their usual clothing; a more improvident, worthless race of people, cannot well be imagined.
1840 *Sydney Gazette* 8 Feb. 3 repr. in *Old Bush Songs* ed. Stewart and Keesing (1957) 29: I'll tell them about delegates, cooks mates and victuallers, / And give them a letter on Dungaree settlers.
1847 Alexander Harris *Settlers and Convicts* ed. C. M. H. Clark (1954) 4: It is a common assertion, that the poor Australian settler (or, according to colonial phraseology, the Dungaree settler; so called from their frequently clothing themselves, their wives and children in that blue Indian manufacture of cotton known as Dungaree) sells his wheat crop from pure love of rum.
1880 Henry Kendall 'Christmas in the Splitters' Camp' *Poetical Works* ed. T. T. Reed (1966) 440: Byron's 'Address to the Ocean' / Would fall rather flat on these 'dungaree' chaps.

dunny   A privy, esp. outside [f. *dunnakin* a necessary OED 1790; *dunegan* A privy A water closet Grose 1811]
1947 *Coast to Coast 1946* 216: 'We gotta get some wood from somewhere, or we'll freeze' . . . 'We're buggered too – been burnin' the floor boards orf the dunny.'
1952 T. A. G. Hungerford *The Ridge and the River* 18: Right now there might be a Shinto under every bush, and me stuck out like a dunny in a desert.
1965 G. McInnes *Road to Gundagai* 38: In the far corner, tastefully screened by a trellis of wistaria, was the lavatory, or the 'dunny' as Dad used to call it.
1974 *Sunday Telegraph* (Sydney) 8 Sep. 9: Someone once said he [Paul Hogan] was as Australian as a slab off a dunny door.
1979 Bill Scott *Tough in the Old Days* 184: We went to the fancy dress ball at the Town Hall and the man at the door refused to admit the fellow who had built himself a costume of plywood and

come to the ball as a country dunny.
1982 *Australian* 25 Oct. 9: On Friday night and Saturday, November 12 and 13, Tongala will hold a Burn the Dunny Festival – to celebrate the town's connection to the sewerage.
dunny, bush see **bush**
dunny cart
1980 Clive James *Unreliable Memoirs* 50: I often watched the dunny cart from the front window. As it slowly made its noisome way down the street, the dunny men ran to and from it with awesome expertise.
dunny, country Used in figurative expressions of isolation or conspicuousness
1953 Baker 268: *Loneliness:* all by himself like a country dunny.
1976 *Australian* 22 Mar. 26: The influence is there, but it doesn't stick out like the proverbial Australian country dunny.
1982 *NT News* (Darwin) 12 Mar. 17: Two players stood out like the proverbial country dunny for Nightcliff last week.
1985 Sir Joh Bjelke-Petersen *Sydney Morning Herald* 2 Feb. 22: New Zealand is out on its own – like a country convenience.
dunny door, to bang like a
1981 Garry Disher *Approaches* 53: 'There used to be this bird from Mawson at St. Margaret's. Bang like a dunny door.'
dunny man
1962 Hal Porter *A Bachelor's Children* 280: Early in December, one found a card on the lavatory seat:
Enjoy Christmas as best you can,
And don't forget the dunny man.
1972 David Ireland *The Flesheaters* 5: The dunnyman in his heavy loaded truck looked tired as the motor ground up the hill.

dunny, kick your ~ down   see **emus**

dunny, useful as a glass door on a   see **useful**

durry   A cigarette [? f. Hindi *dhurri*, a cotton carpet of Indian manufacture]
1941 Baker 26: *Durry:* A cigarette butt.
1976 Sam Weller *Bastards I have met* 80: Crot slumped in the saddle, shirt out, feet out of the irons, reins on the horse's neck and a durry stuck to his lip.
1979 *NT News* (Darwin) 24 Nov. 14: *Darryls:* Another name for cigarettes (also Durries).
1982 *Sydney Morning Herald* 18 Sep. 1: Cigarettes, also known as durries, lungbusters and backnails are still smoked behind the toilet block after school.
1984 Ned Manning *Us or Them* 6: STEVE (*stubbing out his cigarette*) Waste of a good durry!

dust Flour, in bush parlance

1878 G. H. Gibson *Southerly Busters* 25: 'A pint o'dust' – that was his low / Expression meaning flour.

1903 Joseph Furphy *Such is Life* (1944) 256: The storekeeper measured me out a pannikin of dust into a newspaper.

1919 W. R. Harris *Outback in Australia* 146: The proverbial free pannikin of 'dust' (flour).

1924 *Truth* 27 Apr. 6: *Dust* Flour.

dust, bull-, heifer-   see **bull, heifer**

dyke   see **dike**

each way, two bob   see **two**

Eagles   1   The Manly-Warringah Rugby League team (N.S.W.): also the Sea Eagles [f. club emblem, and Manly as a seaside suburb]
1983 *Sun* (Sydney) 15 Aug. 27: Gutsy Eagles floor Bears [heading] Manly stunned North Sydney on Saturday with a 54–16 win.
2   In S.A., the West Torrens Australian Rules team
1979 *Advertiser* (Adelaide) 24 Mar. 20: Eagles sign full back [heading] West Torrens has gained the services of Richmond defender Barry Grinter.
3   In Queensland, the Windsor-Zillmere Australian Rules team
1979 *Courier-Mail* (Brisbane) 17 Apr. 23: The Eagles won the knocks five to two.

earbash   To talk unremittingly, harangue [World War II slang]
1944 Lawson Glassop *We Were the Rats* 205: 'Are you going to sit there ear bashing all night?'
1953 Kylie Tennant *The Joyful Condemned* 22: 'She was ear-bashing me all over tea how you came lairizing round at our place like you owned it.'
1960 *Sydney Morning Herald* 7 Sep. 1: You are in a pub knocking back a few after work and being earbashed by a mate.
1975 *Bulletin* 8 Nov. 33: A Canberra dentist whose wife ear-bashed him unmercifully about her good score – her best ever in her golfing career.
1981 *Sydney Morning Herald* 31 Jan. 16: Confer-ring awards on writers is usually a mistake. It encourages them to earbash instead of getting on with their writing.

earbasher   A persistent talker, a bore
1946 Rohan Rivett *Behind Bamboo* 396: *Ear basher,* one who talks too much.
1954 *Coast to Coast 1953–1954* 85: He was an ear-basher and a known liar.
1965 William Dick *A Bunch of Ratbags* 155: Ape was dumb ... and on top of this he was an ear-basher.
1975 *Sydney Morning Herald* 6 Sep. 12: Xavier Herbert is a cantankerous, outrageous old ear-basher.
1984 *Sunday Independent* (Perth) 26 Feb. 16: Now he's a middle-aged, overweight earbasher who drinks far too much.
earbashing
1953 Dymphna Cusack *Southern Steel* 260: 'I think we might as well shut up now and give Pop and Mum a chance. They must be just about sick to death of this ear-bashing.'
1964 Gavin Casey and Ted Mayman *The Mile that Midas Touched* 23: He didn't need a lot of ear-bashing from Bill.
1975 *Sunday Telegraph* (Sydney) 17 Aug. 69: The latest in earbashing. Pop music blaring from two loudspeakers has suddenly arrived at the Opera House Harbourside restaurant.

earlies, the   The early years of settlement in any

region: N.T. and W.A.

1933 Charles Fenner *Bunyips and Billabongs* 65: However, the interesting story of the wild adventurers who lived on this remote island in the 'earlies' is not our subject.

1936 Archer Russell *Gone Nomad* 8: In the space of a few hours I had accomplished what it would have cost me five days to do in the pre-train, stage-coach days of 'the Earlies'.

1941 Charles Barrett *Coast of Adventure* 140: 'He loved to talk about his wonderful life up here in the Earlies'.

1951 Ernestine Hill *The Territory* 428: 'In those trails of yours, especially in the earlies, I suppose you've often travelled where no white man has ever been before you?'

early opener   See quot. 1980

1972 John de Hoog *Skid Row Dossier* 10: We'd finished breakfast and gone for a drink, a quick one, to the Chamberlain Hotel, an early opener.

1980 *Bulletin* 28 Oct. 36: I refer to the early opener: one of those hotels licensed to open their doors at dawn, up to four hours before the rest of the country's pubs serve their first heart-starters of the day. There are 53 early openers in Sydney alone. The early-opening idea caught on in 1955 when 6 pm closing ended in New South Wales. Some licensees whose pubs depended for their custom on the wharves or food markets or other specific industries with early shifts applied for and were granted different trading hours from the general 10 am to 10 pm.

early shower, to take an   see **shower**

Eastern States, the   The states east of Western Australia (usu. excluding N.T.)

1963 Xavier Herbert *Larger Than Life* vii: I wrote my first short story at the age of thirteen. It . . . was published in an Eastern States school paper.

1984 Buzz Kennedy *Weekend Australian* 26 May Mag. 24: I was raised in the West Australian belief that everything evil, rapacious and sinful in Australia was in 'the Eastern States' – and you have to be a West Australian to be able to produce the tone of voice that conveys the loathing, suspicion, fear and frightfulness 'the Eastern States' phrase creates in the State of Excitement.

easy   Having no preference for one course of action over another, usually in the expression 'I'm easy' [listed by Partridge as 'R.A.F. coll.: since ca. 1938']

1942 Gavin Gasey *It's Harder for Girls* 229: 'We might as well all stop here now,' said Clara. 'We'd just have to go down and come almost straight back.' 'I'm easy,' said Tom.

1955 John Morrison *Black Cargo* 90: Clarrie looks at me and Bob Grainger. 'What about it?' 'I'm easy,' I tell him, 'but a seven o'clock finish would do me.'

1966 Tom Ronan *Once There Was a Bagman* 191: Ned now wanted me to go to the Depot instead of to Hall's Creek. I was easy.

easy, life wasn't meant to be   see **life**

Echuca, no lucre at   see **Tallarook**

Edgar Britt   see **Britt**

Eels, the   The Parramatta Rugby League team (N.S.W.) [one of the Ab. meanings of 'Parramatta' is 'place where the eels lie down']

1974 *Australian* 22 Jul. 18: South's drought against Eels ends.

eh   Supposedly used at the end of sentences in the speech of Queenslanders, not necessarily as an interrogative

1976 David Ireland *The Glass Canoe* 164: He was a Queenslander and though this is an interesting fact about any man, some get over it. Eh never did. Eh is pronounced 'ay' as in day. It was a question at the end of every sentence. That was the way up north Queensland . . . When the boys got tired of calling him Eh they called him Guy, to stir him.

1982 Nancy Keesing *Lily on the Dustbin* 52: In central Queensland 'eh' or 'ay' is substituted for 'but' [at the end of a sentence], and on a rising inflection.

1983 *Australian* 30 Sep. 7: The men wear broad hats, the toilet doors swing outwards and almost everyone ends each sentence with an 'ay' 'G'day Vince. Doing a bit of tripping round this week, ay', says the garage attendant as she fills our car with petrol at 53.9c a litre. Despite the inquisitive 'ay' and the upward inflection, it isn't a question. She had heard on the radio that Vince Lester would be in his electorate.

eight, ten, two and a quarter   See **ten, ten, two and a quarter**

1937 William Hatfield *I Find Australia* 34: Rations per man per week were eight pounds of flour, ten pounds of meat, two pounds of sugar and a quarter pound of tea. Eight-ten-two-and-quarter, it was known.

1978 Keith Garvey *Tales of My Uncle Harry* 72: 'In those days the squatters had all the money and men like Stevo and me had to exist on 8, 10, 2 and a $\frac{1}{4}$.'

eighteen   1   An eighteen-gallon keg of beer

1918 George Dale *The Industrial History of Broken Hill* 117: The procession proceeded to the goods station, loaded some foodstuffs and five

'eighteens' of beer, and started back to the mine.
1942 Gavin Casey *It's Harder for Girls* 218: 'We got an eighteen, and plenty o' bottles coming over.'
1971 Frank Hardy *The Outcasts of Foolgarah* 194: 'Two eighteens, twenty dozen hot dogs,' Molly counted to herself, a hostess to the finger tips.
1976 David Ireland *The Glass Canoe* 112: At his benefit we arranged a few kegs – eighteens – because we were all pretty sad.

2   An Australian Rules team
1966 D. E. Charlwood *An Afternoon of Time* 103: 'Melb'n first eighteen was after him last year an' Collingwood this year,' Percy confided.
1981 Leonie Sandercock and Ian Turner *Up Where, Cazaly?* 3: At 11.30, the two top Reserve Eighteens play out their Grand Final.

3   An eighteen-footer (i.e. 18-foot skiff)
1982 *Bulletin* 12 Jan. 79: Today, the eighteens are still part and parcel of a Sydney summer weekend out on the harbour.

eighteen-footer   An eighteen-foot skiff
1946 Eleanor Dark *Waterway* 99: On Saturdays and Sundays all the eighteen-footers were out; they came racing down the harbour, their white sails fat and straining with wind, their crews leaning out horizontally over the water while they turned round the buoy and went skimming back again.
1967 Kylie Tennant *Tell Morning This* 200: 'I used to sail in the eighteen-footers.'
1984 *Sydney Morning Herald* 25 Sep. 33: Seven new 18-footers, representing an investment of more than $350,000, will be launched this season – the greatest number of new boats in five years.

Ekka, the   Brisbane Exhibition Grounds; the annual Exhibition there
1979 *Courier-Mail* (Brisbane) 31 Jul. 22: How to see the Ekka – and survive [heading] An expected 810,000 people will forge optimistically through the Brisbane Exhibition turnstiles this year ... The Courier-Mail has prepared an Exhibition Survival Guide.
1980 *Sunday-Mail* (Brisbane) 17 Aug. 3: Maternity hospitals in Brisbane report an upsurge in premature births during the annual Ekka. It appears that the Super Loops, Pirate Ship and other similar thrill-seeking sideshows induced quite a few births.
1983 *Sydney Morning Herald* 18 Aug. 4: They discovered it was Ekka Day. Ekka is opening day for the Royal Brisbane Exhibition. It is also known as Family Day and is the most sacred public holiday in the Queensland calendar.

elephant, the   The Commonwealth Bank [f. logo used since 1965, in association with the slogan Get With the Strength, on money boxes etc.]

1973 Alexander Buzo *The Roy Murphy Show* in *Three Plays* 112: 'Now it's time for the Commonwealth Bank Passing Competition and you know the rules. Three passes at the target ... You get ten points for an Elephant's Eye and the Elephant's the symbol of the Commonwealth Bank and it's a pretty good idea to get with the strength.'
1984 *Sydney Morning Herald* 4 Apr. 1: As to whether the 'elephant' will eventually lose its monopoly right in NSW to the banking business of those budding business tycoons – the schoolchildren – Mr Christie conceded that the bank could indeed soon be having to face competition from the other banks in this area.

embassy, tent embassy   An encampment set up by Aborigines on the lawns of Parliament House on 26 January 1972, as a protest against government policies esp. on land rights; any similar demonstration
1972 *Sydney Morning Herald* 29 Jan. 2: Mr Howson ... attacked a protest on Aboriginal land rights being staged outside Parliament House by members of the Black Power movement. He said ... there was a disturbing undertone in the use by the protesters of a sign reading 'Aboriginal Embassy'.
1972 Ian Moffitt *The U-Jack Society* 157: Most of us averted our eyes from the Aboriginal 'Embassy' outside Parliament House when we first saw it ... while the odd racist drove by yelling 'Niggers!'
1983 *Sydney Morning Herald* 28 Jan. 3: Protests against 'embassy' arrests [heading] The NSW Council for Civil Liberties and the NSW Society of Labor Lawyers deplored the arrest of seven people by police preventing demonstrators setting up an Aboriginal tent 'embassy' opposite the Premier's Macquarie Street office.
1983 *Australian* 30 Aug. 3: Members of Sydney's gay community will set up a 'gay embassy' outside the Woollahra home of the NSW Premier, Mr Wran, after the arrest of 11 men at a homosexual club last weekend.

Emma Chisit   The Strine equivalent of 'How much is it?'
1964 *Sydney Morning Herald* 30 Nov. 1: Monica Dickens, busily autographing her books in a city store, signed one handed her by a woman shopper. Miss Dickens THOUGHT that the lady then said 'Emma Chisit'. 'Oh,' said Miss Dickens brightly. 'You'd like me to write your name in it?' And she scrawled, 'To Emma Chisit'. 'I asked,' the lady said crossly, 'HOW MUCH IS IT?'

Emmaville express, the   Debbie Wells, the sprinter, born in Emmaville (N.S.W.)
1978 *Australian* 5 Jun. 18: Debbie Wells, the Emmaville Express, rated Australia's most prom-

ising woman sprinter in years, is in danger of missing out on the Australian Commonwealth Games squad for Edmonton in August.
1984 *Weekend Australian* 25 Feb. 5: The Emmaville Express is back on the track [heading]

emu   See quot. 1966 [f. *emu-bobbing*]
1966 Baker 237: *emu*, a race-course lounger who picks up discarded betting and tote tickets in the hope of finding one which has not been cashed.
1983 *Sun-Herald* 23 Jan. 50: There was an epidemic of emus at Rosehill yesterday ... 'Perhaps it is a sign of the recession times but I have never seen so many emus picking up discarded tote tickets at a race track' ... Candrick said.
1984 *Age* (Melbourne) 20 Mar. 50: 'He picks up all the old betting tickets. They call them emus.'

emu-bobber   Someone employed to pick up after clearing or burning-off in the bush (emu-bobbing) [see quot. 1964]
1920 *Bulletin Book of Humorous Verses* 187: A score of 'emu-bobbers' came a tramping from the Bland.
1959 C. V. Lawlor *All This Humbug* 16: 'Emu bobbing' consisted of gathering up small timber and twigs.
1964 H. P. Tritton *Time Means Tucker* 87: We ... went to Wingadee to work for a contractor at burning-off. This work is also know as 'stick-picking' or 'emu-bobbing'. A group of men bending to pick up the fallen timber, with heads down and tails up, look very much like a flock of emus.
1973 Roland Robinson *The Drift of Things* 79: I was on 'emu-bobbin'' with him. Tom would axe, cut and stack the big logs ... I picked up the smaller timber and sticks and threw them on the stacks.

Emu Hilton, the   Term applied to a blacks' camp adjoining a white settlement (e.g. in Kununurra valley W.A.)
see **Jesus Hilton**

emu parade   In the army, a parade to clean up an area by 'emu-bobbing'
1941 T. Inglis Moore *Emu Parade* [book title]
1951 Eric Lambert *The Twenty Thousand Thieves* 315: 'Round up some men for an emu parade and parties to tidy up slit trenches and fix guy ropes.'
1982 *Weekend Australian* 8 Mar. 48: Gordon rugby union breakaway Greg Owen, after losing part of an ear in a match: 'Can we organise an emu parade to find the rest of my ear.'

emus, may your chooks turn into ~ and kick your dunny down   An expression of ill will
1974 Barry Humphries *Barry McKenzie Holds His Own* 48: Oh, I hope all yer chooks turn to Emus / Kick yer dunny down flat to the grass / I hope yer balls turn to bicycle wheels / And back-pedal up yer arse.
1975 Nev Hauritz *M7 Records MS055*: 'I Hope Your Chooks Turn into Emus and Peck Your Dunny Down' [song title]
1980 *Bulletin* 12 Aug. 48: The antipodean Candide would lash back with, 'I hope your chooks turn into emus and kick your dunny down.'
1982 *Sun-Herald* 28 Mar. 167: The Premier, Mr Never Wrong, lashed out angrily at five and a half million people in NSW, accusing them of using too much electricity in a bid to embarrass his government ... 'I hope your chooks turn into emus and kick your dunnies down.'
1983 *Weekend Australian* 15 Jan. Mag. 16: Then there was *I Hope Your Chooks Turn Into Emus and Peck Your Outhouse Down*, another Hauritz composition inspired, like a thousand others, by a chance remark in a pub.

end, to get one's ~ in   To succeed in having intercourse with a woman
1969 William Dick *Naked Prodigal* 243: 'Look, you go and get your end in. I'll be O.K. You take your bird home, orright?'
1972 David Williamson *The Removalists* 117: 'I knew a Marilyn once. Biggest knock in Footscray. Got your end in yet?'
1974 John Powers *The Last of the Knucklemen* 34: 'Well, twice a year, if you're lucky, you can put your end into a whore down in the town.'
1981 Garry Disher *Approaches* 53: 'Where's your moll, Rymers? Not getting your end in tonight?'

Enzed, Enzedder   A New Zealander [f. N.Z.]
1915 Ion L. Idriess *The Desert Column* (1965) 11: The Australians and En Zeds waited until the Turkish charge was within fifty yards and then every man blazed away.
1941 Baker 27: *Enzedder*, a New Zealander.
1943 *Khaki and Green* 28: There were a lot of prisoners there: Tommies, Enzeds, and ... South Africans.
1949 Lawson Glassop *Lucky Palmer* 83: Approaching the home turn, Reed let the Enzedder go and he shot away with a winning break before you could say 'Phar Lap'.
1952 *Bulletin* 31 Dec. 10: Two Enzedders, E. P. Hillary and G. Lowe, will be included in Colonel Hunt's British Everest expedition, which will have its shot at the hill in the new year.
1970 Richard Beilby *No Medals for Aphrodite* 166: 'The Aussies and Enzeders are into it again.'
1979 *Weekend Australian* 1 Jul. Mag. 12: New Zealand's budget may be hard on Enzeders, but for visiting Australians it means our dollar has five per cent greater spending power.
1983 David Foster *Plumbum* 202: You can buy

any Australian girl with that, and a fair percentage of En Zedders.
see **Kiwi**

E.S.   Eastern States, from standpoint of W.A.
1981 *Australian* 15 Sep. 16: Places like Victoria, NSW, and Queensland do not really exist in the Sandgroper's mind: instead they are lumped together and described collectively as the ES – or Eastern States.
1983 *West Australian* (Perth) 18 Aug. 19: E.S. lamb now a buyer's dream [heading] Len Tidy said that the influx of Eastern States lamb had allowed him to offer much more competitive prices than if he had been selling local lamb.

esky   Trade name of portable cooler for drinks, etc. [f. *eskimo* as previously used in trade name of an ice chest]
1971 Craig McGregor *Don't Talk to Me about Love* 152: George and Sonia with a transistor and an Esky beside them in the wilderness.
1976 *Sunday Telegraph* (Sydney) 25 Jan. 26: 'Look, Mate, I don't mind a tidal wave as long as it doesn't knock over my Esky.'
1984 *Sydney Morning Herald* 21 Jan. 1: 'We should have brought the esky to stand on,' one teenage girl remarked to a friend as they strained to catch a glimpse of the ceremony.

Essie Gee   Strine version of S.C.G., Sydney Cricket Ground
1978 *Sunday Telegraph* (Sydney) 26 Nov. 176: Oh woe is Essie Gee! A colleague noted last Monday that all around the edge of the famed cricket ground's lush green sward are the pale green stalks and deceptively pretty white flower of the dreaded onion weed.

ethnic   'designating a racial or other group within a larger system' OED: in Australia, any recognizable member of a non Anglo-Saxon community
1980 *Sydney Morning Herald* 4 Jun. 6: Bondi Beach not worth writing about! This jewel in the crown of Sydney, this meeting place of locals and 'ethnics' of all ages, this happy playground of a vibrant city.
1981 *Sydney Morning Herald* 20 Jun. 37: Spokesmen for the Melbourne communities claim that Sir Nicholas ... is a kind of 'token ethnic', or an ethnic person in name only (he was born in Coogee of Lebanese parents).
1981 *Age* (Melbourne) 11 Aug. 11: That ethnics suffer persecution in school is no more than what happens in society at large.

ethno   A migrant [f. *ethnic*]
1976 *Sydney Morning Herald* 18 Aug. 1: There's been a backlash against the widespread use of the word 'ethnic'. A social worker with the Department of Social Security tells us that school pupils are now calling migrants 'ethnos'.

euchred   Exhausted, destitute, at the end of one's resources [f. *euchre* outwit U.S. 1855 Mathews]
1946 K. S. Prichard *The Roaring Nineties* 34: 'I've got to get water for me horses at the next tank, or we're euchred.'
1952 T. A. G. Hungerford *The Ridge and the River* 143: 'We can't do much more of that.' He pointed down the slope. 'We'd be euchred.'
1959 Frank McCann *Medicine Man* 40: Although he himself had acted as midwife on the three previous occasions, now, he said, he was 'properly bloody well euchred'.
1973 John Morrison *Australian by Choice* 83: This man has worked hard in Australia for forty years, but he's euchred now.
euchre   To ruin, wreck
1974 *Australian* 12 Oct. 19: He sits in the mayoral car ('So many dials and buttons! I hope I don't euchre this thing').

Eugene   See quot. 1980
1980 *Sunday Mail* (Brisbane) 18 May 3: 'If anyone picked me up in a suit, I wouldn't go. Eugenes are jerks,' says 13-year-old Melinda McMahon. In translation, Melinda doesn't like boys who dress very conservatively and rather formally in ties, jackets and the rest.

Eulo Queen, the   Isabel Robinson, later Gray (d. 1929), mistress of the Royal Mail Hotel at Eulo in south-western Queensland in the 1890s
1892 Barcroft Boake 'Skeeta' *Bulletin* 17 Dec. repr. in *Where the Dead Men Lie* (1897) 90: 'On the Paroo I saw him; he'd been / In Eulo a fortnight then, drinking, and driving about with 'The Queen'.
1902 Harry Morant 'For Southern Markets' in F. M. Cutlack *'Breaker' Morant* (1962) 145: We came through Eulo township and camped to see 'the Queen' / (As every drover has done who has through Eulo been!).
1936 A. B. Paterson 'The Shearer's Colt' in *Song of the Pen* (1983) 688: 'Maggie'll be like the Opal Queen that used to keep the pub at Eulo, and get all the best opal from the gougers when they came in to knock down their cheques.'
1964 H. P. Tritton *Time Means Tucker* 113: Of all the pub-keepers concerned in the many stories told of 'lambing-down', two women were running equal for pride of place, Mrs Brown of Grawin, and Isobel Gray, 'The Eulo Queen'.

Excitement, State of   see **State**

expert, the   In a shearing-shed, the man in charge

of the machinery; anyone qualified to deal with farm machinery

1910 C. E. W. Bean *On the Wool Track* 195: The expert (the man in the engine-room).

1912 R. S. Tait *Scotty Mac, Shearer* 55: The expert was a fidgety German, and the alterations he had to make in his work gave rise to the suspicion that he was not as experienced in shearing machinery as he ought to have been.

1923 Steele Rudd *On Emu Creek* (1972) 168: Much time and 'language' would be wasted trying to locate the trouble and fix it [the reaper and binder] up, or waiting for an 'expert' to arrive to do it.

1938 Eric Lowe *Salute to Freedom* 113: 'It's the new shearing machines . . . Campbell's expert will be here in a couple of days.'

1964 H. P. Tritton *Time Means Tucker* 40: 'The expert' is another important man in the shed. He is responsible for the smooth running of the machinery and has to have a thorough knowledge of everything mechanical in the shed.

eyes, pick the ~ out To occupy the choice portions of a run, in order to make the rest of the territory unusable by another (a technique used in the conflict between squatter and selectors)

1865 *Australian* 23 Jun. 11: As the day advanced [at the land office], and sections were taken up, and the 'eye picked from the area'.

1881 *Adelaide Observer* 22 Oct. 44: His expression about the selectors being free to pick out Mr Gray's eyes was not really so savage as it sounded – only referring to what are called the 'eyes of the run', the watering places and choice blocks.

1892 Gilbert Parker *Round the Compass in Australia* 75: He [the squatter] paid men to 'dummy' for him, and . . . he made it pretty hot for the beggars who did pick the eyes out of his country.

1903 Joseph Furphy *Such is Life* (1944) 208–9: These people saw where the most eligible allotments were, and presently picked the eyes out of the run.

1934 Brian Penton *Landtakers* 138: 'Ay, like the rest of them – pick the eyes out of the country and leave it.'

1975 Xavier Herbert *Poor Fellow My Country* 786: 'The general idea is they'll pick the eyes out of the land, and that you're helpin' 'em.'

1981 Leonie Sandercock and Ian Turner *Up Where, Cazaly?* 213: There is much interstate resentment against Victoria's ability to 'pick the eyes' out of Australian football.

see **peacock**

faceless men Term applied (esp. in the 1963 election campaign) to the non-parliamentary members of the Labor Federal Executive, who held powcr ovcr the parliamentary representatives

1963 *Sydney Morning Herald* 3 Sep. 2: They will lay themselves open to the same charges they laid against the Opposition Leader, Mr Calwell, in accepting policy directions on North-West Cape from the 36 'faceless men' constituting the special A.L.P. Federal Conference.

1967 R. G. Menzies *Afternoon Light* 291: One of our great criticisms of the Labour Party was that every Labour Member of Parliament, from the leader down, was bound to accept the directions of the non-Parliamentary Federal Executive of the Labour Party; the 'thirty-six faceless men', as we were later to describe them with devastating effect.

1972 Don Whitington *Twelfth Man* 175: He [Mr Whitlam] destroyed the 'faceless men' myth that had dogged Labor like an albatross for years, and was used against every Labor leader whenever other ammunition was lacking.

1984 *Age* (Melbourne) 25 May 9: Mr Peacock yesterday revived the 'faceless men' jibe of the Menzies era to describe senior ACTU officials involved in tax-cut negotiations with the Federal Government ... 'The faceless men of the ACTU have been able to get behind Treasury doors and Cabinet doors to see Cabinet ministers to discuss taxation rates, the economy generally, and the framing of the Budget,' he said.

1984 *Sydney Morning Herald* 30 Jun. 13: Hawke is indeed fortunate not to be facing the '36 faceless men' meeting behind closed doors, as Mr Whitlam and earlier Labor leaders had to before his reforms.

factory (female) 1 Place of detention for women convicts

1819 W. C. Wentworth *Statistical ... Description of the Colony of New South Wales* 18: The public institutions [at Parramatta include] ... a factory, in which such of the female convicts as misconduct themselves, and those also who upon their arrival in the colony are not immediately assigned as servants to families, are employed in manufacturing coarse cloth.

1826 *Sydney Gazette* 18 Mar. 1: Wanted for the Use of the Female Factory at Parramatta, One Ton of Colonial Flax, scutched.

1827 P. Cunningham *Two Years in New South Wales* i 98: You come [in Parramatta] to the Female Factory, surrounded by a twelve-feet high wall, which, however, some of its liberty-loving inmates occasionally find no great difficulty in clambering over.

1832 'Australian Courtship' *Sydney Gazette* 14 Jul. 4 repr. in *Old Bush Songs* ed. Stewart and Keesing (1957) 20: But the lass I adore, the lass for me, / Is a lass in the Female Factory.

1844 Louisa Meredith *Notes and Sketches of New South Wales* 84: The second division of the township [of Bathurst] contains the gaol, police-office, female factory, barracks.

1855 John Lang *The Forger's Wife* 67: She was a convict who had absconded from the factory at Paramatta, some six years previously, and it was supposed she had perished in the bush.

1855 William Howitt *Land, Labour and Gold* ii 360: We paid a visit to what is called the Female Factory at Ross [in Tasmania], a neat village on the banks of the Macquarie river. This female factory is a depot of the female convicts who are not consigned to particular persons, or who are sent hither by an order from the magistrate for one cause or other. It is at once a house of asylum and correction.

1931 Miles Franklin *Back to Bool Bool* 200: 'Blanche would have been well placed in the Parramatta "Factory" stirring up the inmates.'

2 The Australian National Gallery, Canberra

1982 *National Times* 24 Jan. 23: Among Canberra's glitterati the aggressively shaped bulks of white concrete – relieved only by steel-framed skylights – of Colin Madigan's building have been pejoratively nicknamed The Factory.

fair crack of the whip   see **whip**

fair dinkum   see **dinkum**

fair go 1 The call in a two-up game indicating that all the rules have been satisfied and that the coins may be spun, and at the same time enjoining that there be no hindrance to the spinning

1911 Louis Stone *Jonah* 216–17: The seventh man threw down the kip, and Chook, as if obeying a signal, rose from his seat and walked into the centre of the ring. He handed five shillings to the boxer, and placed the pennies tail up on the kip. His stake was covered with another dollar, the betting being even money. 'Fair go!' cried the boxer. Chook jerked the coins upward with the skill of an old gaffer; they flew into the dome, and then dropping spinning. As they touched the canvas floor, a hundred voices cried 'Two heads!'

1925 Arthur Wright *The Boy from Bullarah* 17–18: For a few moments the spinner stood waiting, while the players noisily made their wagers, and then again the voice of the ring-keeper rang out. 'Fair go! Set a quid.' All eyes followed the spinning pennies as they rose in the air.

1949 Lawson Glassop *Lucky Palmer* 167: He handed the kip to the spinner ... placed two pennies, tails up, on it with infinite care and said 'Fair go'. He heard a rustling in a corner, strode over, picked up two ten shilling notes off the canvas, crushed them in his hand, threw them out of the ring over his head, and growled, 'Yous knows the rules. No bets after I say "Fair go". I'm runnin' this game and I'm runnin' it proper.'

2 Any situation or arrangement which meets the basic requirements of fairness, with neither favour nor prejudice being shown; the elementary fair treatment to which anyone must be entitled

1907 James Green *The Selector* 37: I'll buy her first, then ride her,' replied Woolham. 'It's a fair go,' Patrickson exclaimed.

1908 Henry Fletcher *Dads and Dan between Smokes* 31: One o' ther coves is fair, an' six foot; t' other dark, and five-foot somethin'. 'Tain't a fair go,' someone sez, 'the little 'un ain't got no chance.'

1919 W. H. Downing *Digger Dialects* 22: *Fair Go* Equitable treatment, a fair field and no favour.

1924 *Truth* 27 Apr. 6: *Fair-go* Just treatment.

1932 L. W. Lower *Here's Another* 84: All we ask is a fair go.

1945 Gavin Casey *Downhill is Easier* 146: 'He's given me a fair go, so far,' I stated.

1951 J. B. Chifley *The Light on the Hill* 56: I do not think the miners gave the Labor Government a fair go while it was in office.

1964 Donald Horne *The Lucky Country* 24: There is a whole set of Australian characteristics summed up in the phrase 'Fair go, mate'. This is what happened in Australia to the ideals of Liberty, Equality and Fraternity ... The general Australian belief is that it is the government's job to see that everyone gets a fair go – from old age pensioners to manufacturers.

1973 Dr J. Cairns *Sunday Telegraph* (Sydney) 7 Oct. 30: Australia is no longer the country of 'a fair go'; it is a country of 'get what you can'.

1981 *Sydney Morning Herald* 1 May 1: A poster now widely distributed by the National Parks and Wildlife Service carries the slogan: 'Give the poor bustard a fair go'. Bustards, the poster reminds us, are still in danger of extinction.

1983 Franca Arena *Weekend Australian* 23 Apr. 12: I hope *The Australian*, a newspaper that has often given indication of a timid republican leaning, will give the old Australian 'fair go' to the republicans of this country.

3 'Fair go!' as an exclamation may be a protest, a plea, a humorous disclaimer: always as though appealing to basic principles

1938 *Smith's Weekly* 31 Dec. 4: When the laugh had gone on long enough, he would silence it by his opening words, 'Fair go, mob'.

1957 Randolph Stow *The Bystander* 187: 'You didn't happen to give her a bit of cheek, I suppose!' 'Fair go, boss,' Fred begged. 'I wouldn't cheek *your* missus. You know me better than that.'

1958 H. D. Williamson *The Sunlit Plain* 192: 'Struth, fair go, mate! I'm not a bloody magician. I can't pull money out of the air.'

1962 Alan Seymour *The One Day of the Year* 32: *Alf.* Wack and me are old mates. At the war together. *Jan.* Which one? *Alf.* Fair go. Second.

1970 Jessica Anderson *The Last Man's Head* 133: 'I still think that was him, all right. No – fair go –

I think it *could* have been him.'
1983 *Sun-Herald* 14 Aug. 21: Daley, one of Sydney's best-known policemen because he worked in police public relations and presents Police File on Channel 10, is known as 'Fair Go' because of his common retort to persevering reporters.

Falcons The West Perth (W.A.) Australian Rules team, formerly the Cardinals
1983 *Sunday Independent* (Perth) 14 Aug. 37: Sharks Savage the Falcons [heading] East Fremantle ... took West Perth on and never gave them a chance after half time.

fall in To 'come a cropper', suffer a reverse (through miscalculation)
1894 A. B. Paterson 'How the Favourite Beat Us' *Singer of the Bush* (1983) 221: If I can't get a cropper, by Jingo, I'll stop her, / Let the public fall in, it will serve the brutes right.
1903 Joseph Furphy *Such is Life* (1944) 363: I wouldn't advise you to count upon the institution ... You might fall-in.
1920 Louis Esson 'The Woman Tamer' in *Dead Timber* 21: 'I fell in. Nine months I done. I was dead innocent.'
1923 Con Drew *Rogues & Ruses* 164: 'I've fell in meself before to-day and I know that it hurts real bad.'

fang *v.* To drive a car at high speed
1973 Alexander Buzo *Rooted* 36: 'Let's hop in the B and fang up to the beach.'
1979 *Sun-Herald* 30 Dec. 68: Then you could chuck a wheelie and fang off to the beer garden at lunchtime.
1981 *Bulletin* 10 Nov. 43: 'We pick up sheilas, get drunk, steal cars, fang 'em (drive them fast) ... anyfink!'
1984 *National Times* 14 Sep. 14: 'They've had half a dozen drinks and, you know, they want to impress the girls and their mates at how fast they can fang their car around the corner.'

fangs, put the ~ in To **bite** q.v.
1919 W. H. Downing *Digger Dialects* 22: Fangs 'To put in the fangs' – to demand money, etc.
1932 Leonard Mann *Flesh in Armour* 250: They were all short of cash ... 'I'll stick the fangs in him all right,' Tich averred.
1952 T. A. G. Hungerford *The Ridge and the River* 218: 'Give me a smoke,' Wallace suggested. 'If there's one thing I like, it's to sink the fangs into an officer.'
fang *v.*
1975 *Daily Telegraph* (Sydney) 10 Jul. 2: 'What if they'd fanged us for $8000 million?'
1979 *Herald* (Melbourne) 3 Mar. 41: He fanged me for a brick and next thing I know he's shot

through all the way to Darwin.

f.a.q. Fair average quality
1929 Sir Hal Colebatch *A Story of a Hundred Years* 249: There is considerable competition for the bagged wheat amongst the agents of the wheat merchants. It is purchased at bushel rates on what is known as the f.a.q. (fair average quality) basis.
1930 Edward Shann *An Economic History of Australia* 311: It is impossible to 'bear' a land boom by selling f.a.q. land for future delivery.
1963 Hal Porter *The Watcher on the Cast-Iron Balcony* 155: Mother has questioned me about his scholarship ... and has heard me answer that it is f.a.q. to mediocrity.
1971 Colin Simpson *The New Australia* 66: The food was f.a.q.-plus with fresh fish every day.
1982 *Sydney Morning Herald* 23 Jun. 8: The questions were faq – when did you first want to enter politics, how do you handle the pressure, how long can you last, what do other people think of you?

Farm, the 1 Australia, usually in the expression 'buying back the farm' (from overseas investors)
1973 *Australian* 10 Apr. 9: According to Mr Baume, 'buying back the farm' is partly government public relations.
1975 *Sun-Herald* 3 Aug. 7: The Minister for Minerals and Energy, Mr Connor, revealed this week his plans to 'buy back the farm' in less than three years.
1981 Maxwell Grant *Inherit the Sun* 350: 'The Government was getting touchy about selling off the farm as it was called, selling off the country to foreign interests.'
1983 *Sydney Morning Herald* 20 Jan. 13: Mr Coates said policyholders could be sure that AMP would do one or more big deals this year to follow up its 'buying back of the farm' policy of investing heavily in companies such as Comalco and MIM Holdings.
2 Monash University, Victoria, as distinct from 'the shop' (University of Melbourne)
1964 *Sydney Morning Herald* 28 Aug. 2: Third University for Melbourne. La Trobe joins 'the Shop' and 'the Farm'.
3 Warwick Farm racecourse, N.S.W.
1975 *Sydney Morning Herald* 7 Nov. 14: Two likely 'stars' on trial at Farm.
4 Eagle Farm racecourse, Queensland
1981 *Sun-Herald* 8 Feb. 62: Farm washout [heading] Stewards cancelled the last two races of the Eagle Farm race meeting in Brisbane yesterday.

farmer, Collins St, Pitt St see **Collins St, Pitt St**

farrago of facts, falsity and filth The description of a document before the Petrov Royal Commission, later known as Document J, by Mr W. J. V.

Windeyer, chief counsel assisting
1954 *Sydney Morning Herald* 19 May 4: Mr Windeyer said that the document appeared to be just a 'farrago of facts, falsity and filth'.
1984 Neville Wran *Sydney Morning Herald* 7 Apr. 2: On the basis of this farrago of facts, filth and falsity [the *Age* tapes] ... the whole integrity of two Labor Governments, one of the greatest judges in the history of the High Court of Australia and other reputations are to be impugned and dragged down.

fat, crack a   Achieve an erection
1941 Encountered in conversation
1968 Barry Humphries *The Wonderful World of Barry McKenzie* [56]: 'Pommy Sheilas? Aw, they're apples I s'pose – but the way I feel now I don't reckon [I] could crack a fat!'
1970 Jack Hibberd *White With Wire Wheels* in Penguin *Plays* 224: 'By Christ, if he races her off, it'll be the last fat he ever cracks.'
1976 Robert Drewe *The Savage Crows* 88: When he'd cracked a fat against her ... 'Hey Stiffy,' she'd whispered in his ear, and giggled.

fat cake   A variety of damper, fried in fat
1844 Louisa Meredith *Notes and Sketches of New South Wales* 163: His bread is 'damper', baked in the ashes, and varied occasionally by a 'fat cake' done in the fryingpan.
1847 Alexander Harris *Settlers and Convicts* ed. C. M. H. Clark (1954) 240: Whilst I put down at the wood-fire a couple of quart-pots for tea, my wife made some fat-cakes in the frying-pan.
1855 William Howitt *Land Labour and Gold* i 117: A fat-cake is the same thing as a leather-jacket, only fried in fat, and is not only much sooner done, but is really excellent.
1900–10 O'Brien and Stephens: *fat-cake* bread or cake made with the addition of fat in some form.

Father's Day, happy as a bastard on   see **bastard**

Father's Day massacre   Confrontation of two bikie gangs, the Bandidos and the Comancheros, in the car park of the Viking Tavern, Milperra, N.S.W. on 2 Sep. 1984, when seven were shot dead and twenty others injured
1984 *Australian* 3 Sep. 1: Seven die in Father's Day massacre [heading]
see **Milperra massacre**

fats   Fat cattle or sheep, intended for market
1902 Mrs Campbell Praed *An Australian Girlhood* 166: He often passed our way with 'stores' and 'fats'.
1903 Joseph Furphy *Such is Life* (1944) 228: 'I come with some fats as fur as Wilcannia; an' a drover took charge o' them there.'

1932 Myrtle Rose White *No Roads Go By* 106: A succession of mobs of 'fats' were mustered and started down to market.
1979 *Courier-Mail* (Brisbane) 16 Mar. 4: Twelve months ago good fattening-age store cattle sold for $80 each. Today, as fats, they are meeting increasing demand at $300 and $350 each.

Faugh-a-ballagh (Fog-a-bolla)   As an imperative, 'Be off!'; also used as a place-name: *obs.* [f. *Fag an Bealac* ('Clear the way') the regimental march of the 87th Foot, in late C19–20 the Royal Irish Fusiliers (Partridge)]
[**1855** William Howitt *Land, Labour and Gold* ii 41: A very prudent measure if they meant ... to escape what are called Bendigo Faugh-a-ballahs, the same class of mortals as M'Ivor Stickers-up and Balarat All-serenes – in plain English, thieves.]
1885 *The Australasian Printers' Keepsake* 124: 'Be off wid yees at wanst, for Ould Fusty's on the prowl. *Faugh-a-ballagh!*' I cleared, for I knew he referred to the overseer.
1899 A. B. Paterson 'Father Riley's Horse' in *Singer of the Bush* (1983) –37: He had called him Faugh-a-ballagh, which is French for 'clear the course'.
1903 Joseph Furphy *Such is Life* (1944) 294: He would fetch food and water at the Faugh-a-ballagh Tank. Ibid. 293: 'Which Jack? Old Jack, or Young Jack, or Jack the Shellback, or Fog-a-bolla Jack?'

favourite, head like a beaten   see **head**

feather duster, a rooster one day and a ~ the next   Catchphrase for the uncertainty of (political) success [? f. U.S. See quot. 1972]
1972 A. A. Calwell *Be Just and Fear Not* 266: Years ago I told the House of Representatives a basic truth that I had read in a United States publication. The writer said that a politician is 'a rooster one day and a feather duster the next.'
1973 Jim McNeil *The Old Familiar Juice* 83: 'To-day's rooster ... is to-morrow's feather-duster.'
1976 *Sun-Herald* 25 Apr. 34: After last Sunday's Balmain-Eastern Suburbs League match, Senator Jim McClelland was quoted as applying to an off-form Easts' star 'Fred Daly's dictum' on parliamentarians: 'Today a rooster, tomorrow a feather duster' ... Its author was the late Arthur Calwell.
1984 *Age* (Melbourne) 27 Apr. 13: From rooster to feather duster is a common enough story in politics, but reversing the process as Mr Young has done is very rare indeed.

feature with   To achieve sexual intercourse with [given currency by Barry McKenzie comic strip]
1965 Barry Humphries *Times Literary Supple-*

ment 16 Sep. 812: Barry's amorous aspirations are expressed in a desire to 'feature with a lass'.

Feds   Members of Federal parliament, as distinct from states; members of the Federal body of a political party, as distinct from state branches [parallel to U.S. usage]
1978 *Bulletin* 11 Apr. 14: At the moment they're leaving it all to Joh, whom they can trust to see that the Feds don't pull any swifties.
1980 *Sun-Herald* 24 Feb. 50: My impression is that purges are not on. The Queensland branch is very cocky. It has the cash, and the Feds (according to them) cannot get hold of it.
1980 *Sydney Morning Herald* 11 Dec. 6: Mr Hills has resorted to rule No. 2 in the State politicians' handbook to justify this situation. Rule No. 2 says: If you can't blame The Feds blame your predecessor.

feeding time at the zoo   see **zoo**

Fella, Big   see **Big**

fellow, the old   see **old**

female factory   see **factory**

fence, over the   Unconscionable, unreasonable [also U.S.]
1918 *Kia Ora Coo-ee* 15 May 4: 'It's over the blinking fence,' cried one chap, and he voiced the general opinion.
1930 K. S. Prichard *Haxby's Circus* 79: 'Bruiser's over the fence. He *makes* trouble.'
1941 Baker 28: *Fence, over the* Unreasonable, beyond the pale of commonsense or justice.
1943 Charles Shaw *Outback Occupations* 25: To fraternize with lolloping hares was a bit over the fence.
1964 *Sydney Morning Herald* 18 Sep. 11: Some publications which unduly emphasize sex were 'entirely over the fence', the Chief Secretary, Mr C. A. Kelly, said yesterday.

fencing wire, tough as   Very tough
1893 Henry Lawson 'Lake Eliza' *Verse* i 252: The grass is tough as fencing-wire, / And just as good for fodder.
1900 Henry Lawson 'Joe Wilson's Courtship' *Prose* i 542: 'She asked me if you were delicate, and I said no, you were as tough as fencing-wire.'
1930 Vance Palmer *The Passage* 103: 'He'll last the lot of us out. Tough as fencing wire the old boy's always been.'
1941 Baker 28: *Fencing wire, tough as*: A superlative degree of hardness.
1968 Stuart Gore *Holy Smoke* 9: Only a little bloke, picked before he was ripe, but game as Ned

Kelly and tough as fencing wire.

ferret   See quot.
1977 *Sun* (Sydney) 11 Nov. 60: Number 11 batsmen are sometimes scornfully referred to as ferrets (they go in after the rabbits).

fibro   Fibro-cement [abbr.]
1946 Margaret Trist *What Else is There?* 167: The house was a dishevelled structure of brick, weatherboard and fibro.
1957 Nino Culotta *They're a Weird Mob* 177: 'No matey. Not fibro. No matter 'ow you do ut, fibro looks like a shack.'
1972 David Ireland *The Flesheaters* 2–3: Brick additions had been made to the stone, timber extensions to the brick, fibrocement additions to the timber, and from fibro down to corrugated iron, hessian, and then chaff bags sewn together.
1981 *Sydney Morning Herald* 20 Jun. 1: When Wests play Manly at Brookvale tomorrow, will it be a class struggle as well as a Rugby League match? One could be excused for thinking so after hearing 2GB's advertisements yesterday ... 'The Western Suburbs fibro set takes on the Manly silvertails,' the station said.

fiddley   A one pound note [f. rhyming slang *fiddley did = quid*]
1941 Baker 28: *Fiddley* A £1 note.
1949 Lawson Glassop *Lucky Palmer* 175: 'Here's yer dough. Ninety fiddlies.'
1957 Ray Lawler *Summer of the Seventeenth Doll* 29: 'Two quid – two lousy fiddlies – a fortune!'
1963 *Sydney Morning Herald* 17 Aug. 11: I bet a thousand fiddlies to nothing old Dark is back again with us next year.
1975 Xavier Herbert *Poor Fellow My Country* 102: 'If I could only lay me hands on two hundred and fifty fiddleys.'

field, to bring (come) back to the   To disturb someone's pretensions or delusions, to restore a sense of reality to a situation [f. the distinction between the front runner and the main body in horseracing]
1944 Lawson Glassop *We Were the Rats* 82: 'Don't worry,' said Bert ... 'The poor bastard's hopeless. He'll come back to the field.'
1954 T. A. G. Hungerford *Sowers of the Wind* 4: 'Young Mark Flannery should come back to the field.'
1977 *Sydney Morning Herald* 21 May 29: Hookes and the steady Craig Serjeant brought a tearaway Somerset back to the field at the delightful recreation ground here.
1984 *Sun-Herald* 11 Mar. 96: Whenever a comparative newcomer enjoys quick success at some facets of racing, his seniors tag him as 'a lucky,

young upstart who will quickly come back to the field'.

fields, the   i.e. the goldfields, esp. W.A.
1942 Gavin Casey *It's Harder for Girls* 198: Up here on the fields he had plenty of sunshine and plenty of good food.
1950 K. S. Prichard *Winged Seeds* 124: Barb Reidy was one of the best bushmen on the fields.
1962 Stuart Gore *Down the Golden Mile* 20: 'He's been on the 'Fields over thirty years.'
1983 *West Australian* (Perth) 21 Nov. 64: Power line a key in Fields growth [heading] The new power line between Muja and Kalgoorlie is expected to be instrumental in bringing many gold prospects in the Goldfields into production.

fifty   1   A 50 lb. bag of flour (or other commodity)
1904 Henry Fletcher *Dads Wayback: His Work* 20: Dads had gone to Dan Robins' place for fifty of flour.
1914 Henry Lawson 'The Flour Bin' *Verse* iii 103: Though bakers' carts run out – / Still keeps a 'fifty' in it / Against a time of drought.
1959 Donald Stuart *Yandy* 98: 'D'you bring any flour? We're right out this last three days.' 'Yeah, we got two fifties for you.'
2   A glass of half 'old' and half 'new' beer (N.S.W.)
1971 Frank Hardy *The Outcasts of Foolgarah* 76: 'Five schooners of fifty, thanks love.'
1974 *Festival* ed. B. Buckley and J. Hamilton 55: He said he would have his usual middy of fifty.

Fiji uncle   An imaginary rich uncle overseas, backing some venture in which the unwary may be persuaded to invest: *obs.*
1902 Henry Fletcher *The Waybacks* 6: 'Ain't yer got an uncle in Fiji?' demanded Dads, with scorn. 'Ain't yer got two hundred quid to give to the honest man who will trust you to the same amount?'
1906 T. E. Spencer *How McDougall Topped the Score* 50: 'Coves with uncles in Fiji / Are frauds who are deceiving you.'
1914 Henry Lawson 'Mitchell on the Situation' *Prose* i 716: They were both spielers ... Their game was anything weaker or stupider than themselves that had cash or property, and when they were in Sydney their uncles lived in Fiji.
1928 Arthur Wright *A Good Recovery* 9: 'I'm beginning to think that rich uncle is like the one from Fiji, eh, Lance?'

financial   In possession of funds
1926 J. Vance Marshall *Timely Tips for New Australians* 11: In Australia, to describe a man as being 'financial' is to describe him as being possessed of means.
1941 Baker 28: *Financial, to be*: To be in funds, to

have ready money available.
1963 Lou Richards *Boots and All!* 197: A majority of them are now putting in licensed bars, which will mean that they are going to be pretty financial clubs [in S.A.] in the near future. Once they do become financial I would say that Victoria could be in trouble as far as their top-line players are concerned.

find a grand piano in a one-roomed house, couldn't   see **couldn't**

fine day for travelling   see **travelling**

fire   In sport, to play to one's full capacity [f. an engine firing]
1977 *Australian* 19 Jan. 22: With three fine quick bowlers you can rest assured one will be firing at any given stage of a Test.

fire low, and lay them out   The instruction relayed by Lieut.-Col. Tom Price to the Mounted Rifles on 31 Aug. 1890, the day of a mass meeting of unionists in Melbourne during the maritime strike
1890 *Truth* 19 Oct. 1: This is what Col. Price said to the Melbourne Mounted Rifles: ' ... fire low and lay them out, lay the disturbers of law and order out, so that the duty will have to be again performed.'
1892 Henry Lawson *Verse* i 184: 'The Lay-'em-out Brigade' [poem title]
1971 Frank Hardy *The Outcasts of Foolgarah* 229: Lt. Colonel Gravel, receiving the order to fire low and lay them out, took a rifle ... and fired the bullet shattering Moss's good leg.

firm   To shorten in odds, the opposite of 'blow' (horse-racing)
1977 *Sun-Herald* 9 Jan. 43: Cool Look opened second favourite at 5–4 yesterday, but under consistent support firmed to start a solid even money favourite.

Firm, the   J. C. Williamson Ltd, theatrical entrepreneurs
1938 *Life Digest* Oct. 97: In the early 'eighties the famous firm known as 'The Triumvirate' came into being. Its components were J. C. Williamson, Arthur Garner and George Musgrove. Later they were invariably termed 'The Firm' and finally, after Musgrove separated from Williamson and Garner dropped out, the firm was J. C. Williamson, as it is today.
1945 *Salt* 16 Jul. 25: As acknowledged rulers of the Australian professional stage, J. C. Williamson Ltd. – known as 'The Firm' and consisting of the four brothers Tait – has frequently been attacked on these grounds.
1965 Hal Porter *Stars of Australian Stage and*

Screen 279: The Firm's luke-warm, carbon-copy commercial successes which catch the social sheep, and the night-out-at-the-theatre-on-mum's-birthday celebrants.

1975 Robert Macklin *The Queenslanders* 291: Not to the Playhouse group this time but to 'The Firm', the biggest Australia had to offer.

first cab off the rank   see **cab**

First Fleeter   One who arrived in Australia with the First Fleet in 1788, usually a convict; a modern descendant of the arrivals on the First Fleet

1830 *HRA* xv 371: Of these, 5 came in the first Fleet. One of these first Fleeters died a few Years ago at the advanced Age of 104 years without having lost a Tooth.

1848 H. W. Haygarth *Recollections of Bush Life in Australia* 93: A man who by his own account, is of so long standing in the neighbourhood as to have been what is called in the colony a 'first fleeter'.

1849 Alexander Harris *The Emigrant Family* (1967) 339: Principles of penal discipline ... such as are now to be heard of only rarely and in the legends of 'first or second Fleeters'.

1870 Marcus Clarke *His Natural Life* ed. S. Murray-Smith (1970) 623: Mooney was one of the 'First Fleeters'.

1934 Mary Gilmore *Old Days – Old Ways* 267: In the days of the first fleeters ... the hills and shores of Sydney Cove were sheets of flowers.

1940 Arnold H. Haskell *Waltzing Matilda* 93: The original rabbit was a 'First Fleeter'.

1977 *Australian* 24 Jan. 2: The Fellowship of First Fleeters will hold its annual dinner to celebrate Australia Day in Sydney on Saturday night.

first Tuesday in November   Melbourne Cup day

1983 Donald Horne *National Times* 30 Sep. 4: It is no accident that Australia's two greatest national days are April 25 and the first Tuesday in November.

fit as a mallee bull   see **mallee**

fix someone up   To attend to his wants, pay him what is due [cf. *fix* 8b OED 1889]

1908 Mrs Aeneas Gunn *We of the Never-Never* 14: We heard that as Mac had 'only just arrived from Katherine, he couldn't leave his horses until they were fixed up'.

1939 Kylie Tennant *Foveaux* 121: 'Linnie will fix you up.'

1945 Cecil Mann *The River* 54: 'He must have his own sword, of course. I'm sure we'll be able to fix him up.'

1949 Lawson Glassop *Lucky Palmer* 117: 'If you can fix me up now I'll be able to get started' ... 'Here's the dough, Sam,' said 'Lucky', 'and here's a couple of quid for yourself.'

1962 Gavin Casey *Amid the Plenty* 151: 'You could get him fixed up [with a job], sooner or later, couldn't you?'

1970 Alexander Buzo *The Front Room Boys* in Penguin *Plays* 29: 'You'd better go and see him and he'll fix you up. Through that doorway and first to your left.'

fiz-gig   A police informer

1895 Cornelius Crowe *The Australian Slang Dictionary* 29: Fizgig a spy for a detective.

1924 *Truth* 27 Apr. 6: Fizgig Police informer.

1950 *Australian Police Journal* Apr. 112: Fizz-gig, or Fizzer A Police informant.

1957 Judah Waten *Shares in Murder* 14: He was known as the king of the fiz-gigs: no detective had more informers serving him.

1984 *Sun-Herald* 29 Jan. 47: We described him as a big crim and also a 'fiz gig' – an interesting Australian word that means a grass, an informer.

fizzer   Anything which disappoints expectations; a firework which fizzes but fails to explode [? f. *fizzle*]

[**1941** Baker 29: *Fizz out on*: To let down, fail in a promise.]

1977 Fred Daly *From Curtin to Kerr* 153: The Petrov episode proved to be a fizzer, but it ruined Evatt.

1978 *Sun-Herald* 25 Jun. 72: As a typical Test match it was a fizzer. There was no fire and the match was played at an even, gentle pace.

1983 *Newcastle Herald* 5 Feb. 4: Mr Hawke would either be a great Prime Minister or a great fizzer.

flaming fury   An outdoor latrine, periodically 'sanitised' by firing with oil or kerosene

1961 Jack Danvers *The Living Come First* 130: The lavatory was a 'flaming fury' behind the hut.

1982 *NT News* (Darwin) 13 Dec. 7: We have heard of a famous Territory dunny that was known far and wide in the post-war years as 'The Blue Room' ... For a 'flaming fury' it was something out of the ordinary.

flash as a rat with a gold tooth   Very flash

1978 Bill Peach *Sun-Herald* 27 Aug. 59: Eddie [Coogan] is the ultimate lurk-man ... as flash as a rat with a gold tooth. He patronises Ginger, heckles him, attempts at every turn to trip him up or do him down.

1981 *Bulletin* 25 Aug. 53: Most Press descriptions of Grassby over the years had seemed to focus rather unnecessarily on his clothing, implying snidely that he was as flash as a rat with a gold tooth.

1984 *Sunday Independent* (Perth) 3 Jun. 35: Reilly – Ace of Spies has suddenly become as flash as a rat with a gold tooth.

flash one's dover   see **dover**

flash jack   Someone swaggering in behaviour and possibly ostentatious in dress [f. *flash* dashing, ostentatious, swaggering, 'swell' OED 1785]
1901 Henry Lawson 'The Golden Graveyard' *Prose* i 343: Dave Regan – lanky, easy-going Bush native; Jim Bently – a bit of a 'Flash Jack'.
1905 *The Old Bush Songs* ed. A. B. Paterson 26: 'Flash Jack from Gundagai'. [poem title]
1934 Archer Russell *A Tramp-Royal in Wild Australia* 41: 'Leave that kind of talk to flash Jacks.'

flat as a tack   Very flat, esp. in mood
1965 Jack Dyer *'Captain Blood'* 39: We were as flat as a tack when we met South in the Grand Final and they romped away with the flag.
1976 David Ireland *The Glass Canoe* 60: His beer was still there, flat as a tack.
1983 *Sydney Morning Herald* 13 Jun. 25: 'I rode her in the Brisbane Cup and she went disgracefully', Quinton said. 'She was as flat as a tack after the hard run.'

flat out like a lizard drinking   see **lizard**

flax-stick   A New Zealander: *obs.* [f. New Zealand flaxbush]
1896 Henry Lawson 'His Country – After All' *Prose* i 201: 'I always thought Australia was a good country,' mused the driver – a flax-stick.

flea, so bare you could flog a ~ across it   Applied to land bare of vegetation
1866 Rolf Boldrewood 'A Kangaroo Drive' *Cornhill Magazine* xiv 740–1: The vast natural meadow was, as one of the stockmen feelingly observed, 'as bare of grass as the palm of your hand', while another gravely professed his belief 'that you could hunt a flea across it with a stock whip.'
1903 Joseph Furphy *Such is Life* (1944) 207: The famine was sore in the land. To use the expression of men deeply interested in the matter, you could flog a flea from the Murrumbidgee to the Darling.
1954 Tom Ronan *Vision Splendid* 61: He told of roads so bare 'you could flog a flea along them with a greenhide whip'.
1964 Bill Wannan *Fair Go Spinner* 79: 'You could flog a flea across the paddocks, go home to dinner, and come back and *still* find him.'
1972 *Sydney Morning Herald* 10 Apr. 6: I first heard the expression 50 years ago. It was used to describe land so denuded of grass and herbage by drought as to be quite bare and devoid of possible cover, even for a flea … 'So bare that you could flog a flea across it'.

flicker, let her   Usu. preceded by 'Okay', and giving the word to start some operation that has been prepared for [? f. starting a reel of film]
1945 Encounted in conversation
1953 T. A. G. Hungerford *Riverslake* 129: 'Right-oh, gents, let 'er flicker.'

flies, no ~ on   Applied to someone who is alert and astute [? f. habit of flies to settle on a sluggish beast: also U.S.]
1845 C. Griffith *The Present State of Port Phillip* 78: The person who excites their [the old hands'] greatest respect is the man who is alive to their attempts (or, as they express it themselves, *who drops down to their moves*) and the highest encomium they can pass on such a one is, *that there are no flies about him.*
1848 H. W. Haygarth *Recollections of Bush Life in Australia* 101: 'It's lucky we got them,' said Amos; 'there were "no flies" about that black bull.'
[1865 Hotten 135: *Flies* trickery, nonsense. 'There are no *flies* about me, sir.' Connected with *fly*, wide-awake &c.]
1932 Leonard Mann *Flesh in Armour* 305: They admitted, though, there were few flies on him.
1959 Eric Lambert *Glory Thrown In* 118: 'I bet Sophie knew what he was up to. There's no flies on *her.*'
1961 Hugh Atkinson *Low Company* 121: He was far from being a gawking hayseed … there were no flies on Byron.
1984 *Sun-Herald* 29 Jan. 136: No flies on officials at the SCG. That's why members now have coded plastic card keys which they must pop into the computer before turnstiles click open to them.

flies, drink with the   To drink by oneself in a pub, indicating an unsociable attitude, or the aversion of others
1925 Arthur Wright *The Boy from Bullarah* 114: 'A few days ago a common swaggie, drinking with the flies.'
1941 Baker 25: *Drink with the flies* A drink consumed without the company of others. Also, to drink alone.
1944 A. W. Upfield *No Footprints in the Bush* 90: He says he doesn't like drinking with the flies.
1957 R. S. Porteous *Brigalow* 212: 'I've got a bottle of O. P. rum with only two nips taken out of it. Didn't enjoy drinking with the flies.'

flip oneself off   To masturbate (of a man)

flipwreck   Someone presumed to have been debilitated by the practice

Flo hat   See quot.
1981 *Sydney Morning Herald* 16 May 2: The Flo hat joined the Joh hat yesterday in the great Bjelke-Petersen anti-skin cancer campaign. Senator Florence Bjelke-Petersen, wife of Queens-

land's Premier, launched the Flo hat by wearing it on a leisurely cruise down the Brisbane River. Her face protected by the hat's extra-wide brim, the senator nibbled contentedly on a pumpkin scone.

floater   1   A meat pie in a plate of peas or gravy: esp. S.A. [listed by Partridge as dumpling in gravy or sausages in mash]
1959 *Australian Letters* Dec. 13: She bought me a floater, meat pie in a plate of peas.
1969 Thomas Jenkins *We Came to Australia* 51: The Floater is, believe it or not, a meat pie floating in a plate of pea soup. It is mainly served from pie-stalls in the streets. The true floater aficionado, of course, douses his pie with ... tomato sauce.
1974 *Australian Women's Weekly* 11 Sep. 67: A floater consists of a meat pie submerged in a sea of pea soup, with a flavouring of tomato sauce or vinegar, depending on taste ... Floaters were first sold in Adelaide by James Gibbs, a pastrycook who migrated from the English county of Devonshire before the turn of the century. He set up a handcart at the corner of the two busiest streets, Rundle and King William.
1978 John Hepworth *His Book* 44: It was many a mortal year since he had been able to sink a fang into the soothing savory pie-and-pea-soup sog of the dreaded 'floaters' which are Adelaide's pride.
1981 *Sydney Morning Herald* 11 Jul. 39: Late at night celebrities and society couples still occasionally pull up in expensive cars on the Cowper Street roadway to eat a 'floater' (pie 'n' peas) and slum it with taxi drivers and sailors.
2   Loose opal-bearing or gold-bearing rock of low value [f. *float* loose rock brought down by the action of water U.S. 1814 OED]
1903 Joseph Furphy *Such is Life* (1944) 198: The surrounding country had been prospected for a few floaters ... and there was the jeweller's shop.
1937 Ernestine Hill *The Great Australian Loneliness* 232: It was a 'floater,' quite worthless, but an indication of the jewel in the country.
1948 K. S. Prichard *Golden Miles* 294: When they picked up a couple of floaters they thought they were on to something: loamed in every direction [for gold] until a small leader was located.
1962 Stuart Gore *Down the Golden Mile* 103: A detailed account of the finding of 'floaters' – little bits of gold-bearing rock that had broken away from the main body and worked – or 'floated' – downhill with the action of centuries of wind and weather.
1971 Colin Simpson *The New Australia* 153: Opal fields are usually indicated by stones found on the surface, 'floaters'.
3   On the wharves, men not attached to any gang
1955 John Morrison *Black Cargo* 35: Plenty of men available this morning. Over fifty gangs in, as well as hundreds of floaters. Floaters are the men not attached to gangs.
1982 Wendy Lowenstein and Tom Hills *Under the Hook* 107: 'Blokes that wouldn't join gangs – they just floated around ... If anyone was away, they'd send you a floater.'
4   See quot. 1979
1979 *Age* 24 Dec. 3: Among barristers they're known as 'floaters'. They're the defence briefs that pass from one barrister to another as cases are scheduled for hearing, postponed, rescheduled, postponed again and so on ... The record is said to be 13. Prosecution and defence witnesses were notified 13 times that the trial was set to begin on a certain date but on 12 occasions were told, usually late the day before, that it was not going ahead after all.

flock of homing pigeons, he couldn't lead a   see **homing**

flog the cat   see **cat**

flogger   A stick with streamers attached, for waving by supporters at Australian Rules matches
1982 *Age* (Melbourne) 25 May 34: The VFL may have to take further action against cheer squad members who wield floggers at League matches. Police have written to VFL chiefs making it clear that they believe the floggers to be dangerous and that they fear for the safety of players and umpires. In the early 1970s the League banned the use of floggers. However, in discussions with cheer squad officers, they made a concession and said smaller sticks decorated with streamers and the like could be used, provided they were only waved inside the fence. The mini floggers quaintly known as 'Patty Dukes' (they are short sticks adorned with colored pom-poms) have suddenly blossomed, and, in effect, are identical to the banned floggers.

flogging parson   see **parson**

floury baker   A variety of cicada [f. colouring]
1951 Dymphna Cusack and Florence James *Come In Spinner* 106: 'Mine's a Floury Baker ... and mine's a Black Prince!' Young Jack and Andrew hold up their fists for her to peep at frosted fawn body and tan-and-black.

floury miller   *Abricta curvicosta*, a cicada partly covered with white down, also called 'floury baker' [OED 1904]
1981 *Sydney Morning Herald* 19 Dec. 29: So we missed them – greengrocer, black prince, double drummer, floury miller – where had they gone?

flow on *n.* & *v.*   The process by which a wage

increase granted to workers in one union by the Arbitration Commission results in a similar increase for workers in a related union; a wage increase so gained

1974 *Australian* 12 Oct. 4: $9 metal award flow-on for building workers . . . A Deputy President of the Commission . . . decided that last month's $9 increase in the Metal Trades Award should flow on to the Carpenters and Joiners Award. The hearing for flow-ons to this award is regarded as a test-case for the whole building industry.

1984 *West Australian* (Perth) 14 Jan. 30: Farmers are worried that wage flow-ons for farm workers will push up shearing costs.

flute, have the   To talk incessantly: *obs.*

1896 T. W. Henry *The Girl at Birrell's* 23: 'You've got the flute properly tonight, Graham,' returned the other. 'You can gas for all hands.'

1908 E. S. Sorenson *Quinton's Rouseabout* 84: 'He never had much to say, though he'd chip in at times when Joe had the flute.'

fluter   An incessant talker

1898 *Bulletin* 17 Dec. Red Page: An incessant talker is a *skiter* or a *fluter*, and a request to him to *pass the flute* or the *kip* is to allow someone else to 'do a pitch'.

1959 D'Arcy Niland *The Big Smoke* 178: 'Where's Phil the Fluter now?'

fly, the Big Men   Phrase applied to Australian Rules football, referring to the high leap needed to take a mark

1963 Lou Richards *Boots and All!* 68: Dick stood about 5 ft. 11 in. in his socks, and on top of this he had very long arms, which gave him a decided advantage as a rover, because he could fly for marks against bigger men.

1969 Alan Hopgood *And the Big Men Fly* [play title]

1979 *Weekend Australian* 2 Jun. Mag. 1: Why the Big Men are flying north [heading]

1981 *Australian* 22 Dec. 1: The big men cry as club splits [heading] State representative footballer Stephen Wright broke down and cried when the South Melbourne Football Club crisis worsened last night.

1982 *NT News* (Darwin) 27 Sep. 13: The big words fly . . . Melbourne Age writer, Geoff Slattery, looks back on a typical week in Australia's football-mad capital.

see **aerial ping pong**

fly, give it a   To chance it, make a trial of, have a go

1919 W. H. Downing *Digger Dialects* 24: *Fly (to give it a)* To make an attempt.

1928 Arthur Wright *A Good Recovery* 119: 'I'm willing to give it a fly, but –.'

1934 Thomas Wood *Cobbers* 19: 'We're proud of

the Trots in Perth . . . They come in for miles, some of 'em, to give it a fly.'

1949 Lawson Glassop *Lucky Palmer* 75: 'We're playing with their dough . . . Might as well give it a fly.'

1976 *Sydney Morning Herald* 14 Sep. 2: 2SM's general manager, Mr G. Rutherford, said yesterday that the station was 'just having a fly at something.'

see **burl, go, lash**

flyblown   Penniless, destitute: *obsolescent* [? f. the condition of flyblown meat]

1853 C. R. Read *What I Heard, Saw and Did at the Australian Gold Fields* 51: His friend rushes into the billiard room to relate poor Newchum's misery to his fraternity, who deeply regret that it did not fall to their lot 'flyblowing him'.* *Being 'flyblown' is a Colonial term for being 'done up'.

1873 J. C. F. Johnson *Christmas at Carringa* 21: Just before we comes to a grog shanty on the road, he pulls up and ses – 'Look here, mate, you might as well do me a good turn, for I'm regular fly blowed.* *A rather unpleasant term used by the old school of bushmen to signify that they are penniless, usually after 'knocking down' their cheque at some bush public house.

c. **1882** *The Sydney Slang Dictionary* 4: *Fly-blown* To be thoroughly hard up.

1883 E. M. Curr *Recollections of Squatting in Victoria* 348: 'Six or eight of them, knocking down their cheques at Young's . . . as I heard, close up fly-blown (i.e. nearly penniless) the day before yesterday.'

1903 Joseph Furphy *Such is Life* (1944) 20: 'So he was flyblowed as usual in regard o' cash.' Ibid. 116: 'Well, after bin had like this, we went out on the Lachlan, clean fly-blowed.'

1931 William Hatfield *Sheepmates* 161: 'Sit in, some o' yous that aint flyblown – some o' yous that's got a month or two in, an' their IOU's is good, if there's no real Oscar about the joint.'

1966 Tom Ronan *Once There Was a Bagman* 25: 'They'd been on that Katherine railway job, living from pay to pay, and when it shut down they were flyblown.'

flybog   Jam: World War I slang, in World War II often shortened to 'bog'

1920 *Aussie* Apr. Glossary: *Flybog* Jam.

1941 Baker 29: *Flybog* Jam.

1944 Jean Devanny *By Tropic, Sea and Jungle* 214: Sometimes you take a tin of flybog (treacle) with you as a luxury.

1968 Stuart Gore *Holy Smoke* 27: 'I know them cockies! Not even a tin of fly-bog of a Sunday's tea.'

flyer   A swiftly moving kangaroo, usually female; a half-grown kangaroo

1826 James Atkinson *An Account of the State of Agriculture and Grazing in New South Wales* 24: The animals of this kind that are not quite full grown are termed flyers; they are exceedingly swift.

1834 George Bennett *Wanderings in New South Wales* i 287: The males of this species [kangaroo] are called by the colonists 'foresters', the females 'flyers.'

1838 Thomas Walker *A Month in the Bush of Australia* 33: Who has not experienced a feeling of repugnance to the sport of kangaroo hunting on observing the young female (termed flyers).

1844 *Georgiana's Journal* ed. Hugh McCrae (1966) 129: On our way back, Dr Barker and Mr McCrae put up a kangaroo-doe, or 'flier', as it is called, and soon had the dogs in full chase.

1861 H. W. Wheelright *Bush Wanderings of a Naturalist* 4: In bush parlance, the old male kangaroo is called an 'old man'; the young female a 'flying doe'.

1927 Steele Rudd *The Romance of Runnibede* 199: While the halfgrowns, or 'flyers', were swifter than greyhounds, many of the 'old men' were in difficulties.

flying biscuit-tin The RAAF Beaufighter in World War II [f. square appearance]

1943 George Johnston *New Guinea Diary* 251: 'The flying biscuit-tin' is his [Wing-Commander Bruce Walker's] name for the Beaufighter.

Flying Fornicator, the See quot. 1979

1979 *Sun-Herald* 1 Jul. 43: The last train back from Sydney [to Wollongong] on Sundays is packed with young people and known to some as the Flying Fornicator.

flying fox An overhead cableway from which buckets etc. are suspended, often as part of an elaborate system; an improvised cableway for conveying things across a gorge or river [f. the bat (*Pteropus*) so called]

1901 May Vivienne *Travels in Western Australia* 210: To convey the stone along the open cut to the mill there is a wonderful aerial tramway composed of wire cables, on which the trucks run high up in the air; it is a marvellous way of conveyance, but more peculiar still is what is here called the 'Flying Fox', which has an iron bucket on a single rope of twisted wire. Machinery on the top of the shaft and above the crushing mill conveys it to its destination; then the bucket empties as if by magic, and flies back to the bottom of the open cut, a quarter of a mile journey, to be again replenished.

1916 Henry Lawson 'The Passing Stranger at Burrinjuck' *Verse* iii 360: The 'flying foxes', / From the cable tower on the rocky height, / Seem to swerve with their swinging boxes, / Like damaged 'gents' who've been out all night.

1935 F. D. Davison and B. Nicholls *Blue Coast Caravan* 131: Then there was the 'flying fox', a contrivance of pulleys and wires, that enabled the banana bunches to be drawn up from hill-side plantations where the incline was too steep for them to be carried.

1945 Elisabeth George *Two at Daly Waters* 82: A flying-fox was erected, and when the creek was running a banker, I packed sandwiches and cookies in boxes and Jerry and Stumpy took them across on the flying-fox.

1953 Archer Russell *Murray Walkabout* 41: On the river bank I passed beneath an immense wooden tower, somewhat like the pit-head of a mine. On the opposite bank of the river arose a similar construction; and stretching between the two towers ran a long steel cable. This was the overhead cableway, or 'flying-fox' as it is perhaps more often termed, for the transmission of material from the bank to the point of construction.

1961 Noni Braham *The Interloper* 106: Margaret suddenly noticed wires strung overhead. 'What on earth are they for?' 'A "flying-fox",' Colin explained. 'During the wet, it's the only way they can get supplies.'

1982 *Sydney Morning Herald* 13 Mar. 6: In earlier years cabin owners constructed flying foxes from the escarpment to carry materials and supplies down to the beaches.

flying kangaroo, the The logo of Qantas

1981 *Sydney Morning Herald* 23 Feb. 1: The flying kangaroo has been seen in some odd places lately because of Qantas's union troubles. Passengers on QF1 to London last week found themselves high above the Greenland icecap.

1984 *Australian* 5 Jun. 1: Our flying kangaroo stays aloft [heading] Qantas will unveil a new look for its aircraft today, but despite rumours, the flying kangaroo symbol will not ... be replaced by a koala to appeal to the highly competitive US market where some tourists have mistaken the kangaroo for 'a big white rat'.

flying peanut Nickname of Joh Bjelke-Petersen, Premier of Queensland [because he is a peanut-farmer and flies in his own plane, piloted by Beryl Young]

1975 *Australian* 3 Dec. 6: Ignoring the 'go home Joh' and 'flying peanut' calls the Queensland Premier appealed to 'that great silent majority'.

1980 *Australian* 25 Apr. 2: The success of the Queensland Premier, Joh Bjelke-Petersen, has prompted a Kingaroy trotting trainer to name his best horse after him ... He said: 'I'm not sure how the Premier would have felt had I called our horse Joh, so instead I went for Flying Peanut. More than a few people seem to call the Premier by that name.'

Flying Pieman   William Francis King (d. 1874), noted for such feats as walking from Sydney to Parramatta and back (thirty-two miles) in six hours, for a wager
1847 *Heads of the People* 31 Jul. 124: Francis King, better known as the flying pieman, undertook last week, without any consideration, except as he states the pleasure of gratifying the ladies, to walk 50 miles in twelve hours, for six successive days.
1859 Henry Kingsley *Recollections of Geoffry Hamlyn* ii 95–6: A rather small, wiry, active man . . . in running superb, a pupil and *protégé* of the immortal 'flying pieman'.* *A great Australian pedestrian; now, I believe, gathered to his fathers.
1907 Charles MacAlister *Old Pioneering Days in the Sunny South* 54: That long-winded wonder, the 'Flying Pieman', whose running feats against the coaches I can vouch for from personal experience.

flying, sparrows (geese, peacocks, swallows) ~ out of one's backside   see **sparrows**

Flynn, in like   Seizing an opportunity offered, esp. sexual [see quot. 1973]
1963 T. A. G. Hungerford *Shake the Golden Bough* 219: 'You're in like Flynn, and there's no turning back.'
1972 David Williamson *The Removalists* 53: 'We'll be in like Flynn there to-morrow night. We'll thread the eye of the old golden doughnut – no worries.'
1973 Alexander Buzo *Rooted* 137: *Flynn, in like* (also *in like Errol*), refers to the athletic and sexual prowess of the late Australian-born Hollywood actor.
1975 David Niven *Bring on the Empty Horses* 119: Errol was acquitted [of charges of statutory rape on the *Sirocco* in 1942], but the stigma of rape was attached to him, he never shook it off, and for years he gritted his teeth when hailed with cries of 'In like Flynn!'

Fog-a-bolla   see **Faugh-a-ballagh**

forby, four by two   A Jew [rhyming slang]
1977 Jim Ramsay *Cop it Sweet* 37: *Forby* . . . See Four by Two. *Four by Two*: rhym. Jew.
1984 Sandy Gutman *National Times* 20 Jan. 4: 'Here I am, the full-on forby ('Four-by-two' = Jew) from Vaucluse working out at f——g Parramatta.'

forest devil   A stump-pulling device
1915 F. C. Spurr *Five Years under the Southern Cross* 184: Certain portable 'forest devils' have been invented by means of which one man can,

with the aid of a lever and a wheel-gear, draw from the ground the most stubborn stump of a tree. Agricultural dentistry – that is what it is!
1920 H. J. Rumsey *The Pommies* 127: With the help of a 'forest devil', which had been loaned to him, he pulled the trees over.
1942 John Shaw Neilson *Autobiography* (1978) 96: My next job was grubbing – I was working a forest devil.
1947 C. K. Thompson *Yes, Your Honour!* 103: This type of forest devil . . . is not the sort they sell you up on the Blue Mountains disguised as a doll or a pipe cleaner. It is a gadget for pulling stumps from the earth.
1951 Ernestine Hill *The Territory* 275: A traction engine and two forest devils trundled down to clear it, the first consequential machinery the north had ever seen.

forester   Name given rather indiscriminately to the larger types of kangaroo, but sometimes restricted to *Macropus giganteus*
1804 R. Knopwood *Journal* in *Historical Records of Port Phillip* ed. J. J. Shillinglaw (1972) 184: Killd a very large kangaroo – a forester.
1826 James Atkinson *An Account of the State of Agriculture and Grazing in New South Wales* 24: The forester is the largest of the common kinds [of kangaroo], frequently weighing 150 lbs. It is seldom found in an open country, delighting in forests that have occasional thickets of brush.
1832 J. Bischoff *Sketch of the History of Van Diemen's Land* ii 27: There are three or four varieties of kangaroos; those most common . . . are denominated the forester and brush kangaroo.
1843 Charles Rowcroft *Tales of the Colonies* iii 191: We saw five kangaroos – foresters – in the middle, and one prodigious fellow, whom the natives greeted with the title of boomah! boomah!
1859 John Lang *Botany Bay* 209: His kangaroo dogs . . . had killed a forrester (a large species of kangaroo).
1864 J. F. Mortlock *Experiences of a Convict* (1965) 85: Three or four species of kangaroo – of sizes from the 'Forrester', as heavy as a man, down to the Wallaby, not bigger than a large hare, are found in the 'bush' [of Tasmania].

fork, write with a   See quot.: *rare*
1951 Ernestine Hill *The Territory* 446: *Write account with a fork, to* To charge three times as much.

form   Expected mode of behaviour. To 'know someone's form' is to have summed him up, unfavourably: 'How's your rotten form?' is a jeering reproach, given currency in World War II slang [f. racing form]
1955 D'Arcy Niland *The Shiralee* 129: 'I know

your form. I just wanted you to know that I know it.'

1957 Ray Lawler *Summer of the Seventeenth Doll* 47: *Bubba* Come in and see us if you've got the time. Roo. I'm on the perfumes. *Roo* Yeh. That's about my form, ain't it?

1961 Russell Braddon *Naked Island* 13: 'How's his rotten form! Steals anything.'

1975 Les Ryan *The Shearers* 104: 'That's just like your dirty rotten form,' Fetlock said. 'Go on. Get the cops.'

1981 Barry Humphries *A Nice Night's Entertainment* 189: That van at the bottom of the drive could be a bunch of ASIO pricks. Just their form to come snooping around here.

forties Thieves, swindlers: *obsolescent* [f. 'Ali Baba and the Forty Thieves']

1879 T. E. Argles *The Pilgrim* i 12: A collection of shock-haired ruffians – the dregs of the 'forties' – i.e. forty thieves – of the city.

c. **1882** *The Sydney Slang Dictionary* 8: *The Forties* The worst types of 'the talent', who get up rows in a mob, often after midnight and sometimes assault and rob, either in bar-rooms or the streets. Name originated with a gang in Sydney under 'Dixon the dog hanger', 'King of the Forties'.

1893 J. A. Barry *Steve Brown's Bunyip* 21: 'You want to get away amongst the spielers and forties of the big smoke?'

1894 G. N. Boothby *On the Wallaby* 254: The racing code is lax, and over and over again, we met men who made it their sole business, from year's end to year's end, to tramp the bush with a likely animal, practically living on what he earned them, either by winning, or what's technically termed 'running stiff'. These men are called Forties, otherwise Spielers or Blacklegs.

1910 C. E. W. Bean *On the Wool Track* 226: A few sharpers with a slight knowledge of shearing often get into a big shed, and get a 'school' going – a nightly gamble. They are regularly called 'forties' – the forty thieves – and they sometimes make a pile out of young shearers.

1927 M. M. Bennett *Christison of Lammermoor* 194: Rowdies and 'forties' – gambling sharpers who travelled from shed to shed making five pounds by cheating for every five shillings they earned.

1966 Tom Ronan *Strangers on the Ophir* 76: The usual percentage of spielers and forties, rogues and vagabonds.

forty-foot pole   see **pole**

fortyniner   A member of Federal parliament first elected in the Liberal victory of 1949

1979 *Age* (Melbourne) 8 Dec. 13: The 1949 election was Australia's Restoration ... A political generation was formed, the fortyniners who were

to dominate national life for more than two decades.

fossick   To search out small quantities of gold, esp. in abandoned diggings; to search, rummage for something [f. *fossick* to 'ferret out' EDD]

1852 James Bonwick *Notes of a Gold-Digger* 8: Though most of these may be wrought out, a good living may be got ... by the newcomer, in a little tin-dish fossicking in deserted holes.

1853 C. R. Read *What I Heard, Saw and Did at the Australian Goldfields* 119: People used to be perfectly satisfied at 'fossicking'* or 'nuggetting'. *Picking the gold out of the crevices of rocks, &c.

1867 John Morrison *Australia As It Is* 151: 'Fosacking' is the term given to the employment of those who go about searching for gold thus exposed on the surface of the ground, and the tools of those persons consist merely of a pocket-knife and hammer.

1896 Henry Lawson 'The Man Who Forgot' *Prose* i 158: The swag had been prospected and fossicked for a clue, but yielded none.

1901 May Vivienne *Travels in Western Australia* 187: There are always a lot of men fossicking (looking for gold at the surface) about Bayley's.

1923 Jack Moses *Beyond the City Gates* 119: He started early ... in order to give himself full time to fossick among likely-looking country.

1934 Tom Clarke *Marriage at 6 a.m.* 46: *Fossick* – to dig or search, e.g. for gold.

1979 *Sydney Morning Herald* 17 Oct. 13: Those wishing to fossick on private land declared as a fossicking area must first obtain the landowner's permission. To fossick in a Crown fossicking area, they must obtain a licence from the Department of Mineral Resources and Development.

fossicker   One who fossicks

1867 J. S. Borlase *The Night Fossickers* 94: The 'night fossickers' – miscreants who watched for the richest holes during the day, marked them, and plundered them at night.

1911 E. S. Sorenson *Life in the Australian Backblocks* 256: Fossickers, who settle on what they term 'played-out fields', build more lasting homes.

1923 Jack Moses *Beyond the City Gates* 119: Luck was with the fossicker and they hit it thick and heavy.

1955 F. B. Vickers *The Mirage* 133: There were still fossickers on the Flat – old miners, on the pension now, but still panning off a few grains of alluvial gold, still hoping to strike it rich, as they had hoped all their lives.

1962 Alan Marshall *This is the Grass* 60: An old fossicker clumped into the bar with his heavy, hob-nail boots.

1979 *Weekend Australian* 15 Sep. Mag. 3: There is a certain technique in using metal detectors and in knowing likely spots. The gold rush has created a boom in their sale and most of the new fossickers discuss them and their relative merits in the same way that back in suburbia they would compare the relative performances of different makes of cars.

Four bob Robbo   see **Robbo**

fourpenny dark   A cheap wine [f. price and colour]
1966 Baker 226: The original *fourpenny dark* was served in a miniature mug with a handle and a saying went: *Around the world for fourpence!*
1967 Frank Hardy *Billy Borker Yarns Again* 5: A week on the fourpenny dark did nothing to make his hand any steadier.
1976 Dorothy Hewett *This Old Man Comes Rolling Home* 11: 'You better watch your step with that fourpenny dark. It'll get you before you know it.'
1981 *National Times* 7 Jun. 39: You could have a fourpenny dark, a small glass of sweet wine, usually muscat.

fourth-graders   Mr Paul Keating's term for backbench critics of the Government's handling of the MX missile controversy in February 1985
1985 Paul Keating *Weekend Australian* 9 Feb. 2: Every [Labor party] faction thinks they have got to have their viewpoint in the marketplace and a few of them would do well to just frankly shut up . . . I think that some of the fourth graders who are trying to crash into the act would do better to just keep their place in Caucus and hold their tongues.
1985 Gregory McMahon *Weekend Australian* 23 Feb. 14: Would the world's greatest Treasurer please explain to us, fourth graders, what is happening to the Australian dollar?
1985 *Sun-Herald* 3 Mar. 44: To borrow a quote from Mr Paul Keating, it would now be appropriate if those involved would stop behaving like fourth graders and shut up.
1985 *National Times* 17 May 7: Government members were quick to point out to Keating that whoever had leaked the information had to be closely involved with the Cabinet . . . John Scott interjected: 'You can't blame the fourth-graders this time'.

fourths   See quot. 1838
1834 Let. of 4 May in *The Tanner Letters* ed. Pamela Statham (1981) 80: He has put his sheep out on fourths.
1838 G. F. Moore *Diary of . . . an Early Settler in Western Australia* (1884) 366: I give him also 100 sheep to keep for three years on a fourth share of the increase; to the other man I let 4000 acres for five years, and I give him 200 sheep on fourths.
see **thirds**

fox   1   To pursue stealthily, to 'shadow'
1892 Henry Lawson 'Billy's "Square Affair"' *Verse* i 226: The 'gory' push had foxed the Streak,

they foxed her to the park.
1899 Henry Lawson 'Jack Cornstalk' *Prose* ii 47: I cannot say for certain that Jack has his own way of making love − never having been guilty of what he would call 'foxin'' him − a very dangerous proceeding, by the way.
1900–10 O'Brien and Stephens: *Fox* To stalk anyone without being observed (thieves).
1918 Bernard Cronin *The Coastlanders* 174: 'You've been foxing me and Red all the morning . . . I think it's about time you came out into the open.'
2   To chase and retrieve a cricket ball, etc. (*juvenile*)
1942 Leonard Mann *The Go-Getter* 3: The batsman said, 'You bowled it, you fox it!'
1943 Margaret Trist *In the Sun* 87: Then a ball came down near her and rolled away beyond her, 'Fox it, Eleanor', called someone, and Eleanor ran swiftly after it.

fox, flying   see **flying fox**

foxie   A fox-terrier [abbr.]

frame   An emaciated animal, esp. horse or bullock [U.S. 1880 OED]
1903 Joseph Furphy *Such is Life* (1944) 249: 'By-the-way, there's four of your frames left − out near those coolibahs.'
1946 A. J. Holt *Wheat Farms of Victoria* 327: 'You raise and kill a decent beast yourself and divide it with your neighbour. When it comes for his turn he picks out some rangy old frame with only hair on it.'
see **carrion**

franger   A condom
1979 Rae Desmond Jones *Walking the Line* 20: The little frangor & KY peddler.

freckle   The anus
1971 Barry Humphries *Bazza Pulls It Off!* [25]: 'Flop your freckle on the grass there.'
1979 *Australian* 30 Apr. 2: 'I'll punch your flaming teeth so far down your throat that you'll have to shove a toothbrush up your freckle to clean them.'
1983 *Sydney Morning Herald* 19 Mar. 37: It is not only a sailor who has *dooks* and *lugs*, a *belly-button* and a *freckle*.

Fred   The ordinary, unimaginative Australian; the average consumer [? a coinage of Max Harris]
1973 Max Harris *The Angry Eye* 21: Even down where the Freds are browsing in their nocturnal pastures, the herd heroes are largely wasted. The John Laws and Brian Hendersons of Fredsville could well be their own men, real individuals down in the jungle of the sub-culture. Ibid. 139:

I'm not sure whether they switch over from Homicide out in Fredland or not.
1975 *Sunday Telegraph* (Sydney) 20 Apr. 90: The Centura is aimed at what is loosely known as the average Fred market – the ordinary family motorist who wants basic transport for a price and who is not an imported car buff.
see **Alf, Ocker**

Freddie, blind   An imaginary figure representing the highest degree of disability or incompetence, and so used as a standard of comparison [derived by Baker (1953: 53n) from a blind hawker in Sydney in the 1920s]
1944 Dal Stivens *The Courtship of Uncle Henry* 188: 'He doesn't want to go on with tonight. Blind Freddy could see that.'
1959 Anne von Bertouch *February Dark* 203: 'Blind Freddy could've seen there would be prawns that night.'
1966 Betty Collins *The Copper Crucible* 56: 'I know there's a principle involved – blind Freddie could see that.'
1970 Richard Beilby *No Medals for Aphrodite* 49: 'Christ, Harry, Blind Freddie could have beaten the Ities with one hand tied behind his back!'
1975 Hal Porter *The Extra* 218: All the characters who've been around since Julius Caesar was a pup, and wouldn't fool blind Freddy.
1976 *Australian* 28 Dec. 6: Bill Hayden's reference to Mal and Phil as 'Blind Freddie and his dog' may have been aptly arch, but it was not accurate. The original Blind Freddie did not have a seeing-eye dog ... not even a white cane.
1983 *Sydney Morning Herald* 2 Jul. 3: 'Over the last year even blind Freddie could see the council has been split like the Grand Canyon. Why don't you get together for the good of Mudgee?'

Fremantle doctor   See quots
1941 Baker 30: *Fremantle doctor* A refreshing sea-breeze that blows into Fremantle and Perth after hot weather, esp. in the evening.
1972 G. C. Bolton *A Fine Country to Starve In* 2: The 'Fremantle doctor', the afternoon sea-breeze which so often tempered the more than Mediterranean heat of the city in January and February.
1974 *Sunday Telegraph* (Sydney) 22 Dec. 27: Just as the Fremantle 'doctor' (a sea breeze) arrived as a lifesaver to weary cricketers, so the season of Christmas comes like a breath of fresh air.
1982 *Australian* 2 Jun. 2: The Freo Doc is on the honker ... It and other westerly zephyrs stink to high heaven – because they are laden with the effluvium of live sheep loaded on ships for export to the Middle East.
see **Albany doctor**

frenchy   A condom [f. *French letter*]
1970 Patrick White *The Vivisector* 188: 'And never found nothun – but a used Frenchie!'
1975 Robert Macklin *The Queenslander* 33: He hadn't used a frenchy either.
1979 *National Times* 3 Nov. 26: They have a friend who works at a chemist and provides 'frenchies' on discount.

frog   A condom [f. *French letter*]
1952 T. A. G. Hungerford *The Ridge and the River* 23: Having a bath and a shave, getting into clean clothes, whacking a froggie into the kick, to lare up at the dance.
1970 Alexander Buzo *The Front Room Boys* in Penguin *Plays* 40: '"Jees I forgot the frog", he said ... I was disgusted. I put my pants back on and told him to take me home immediately.'
1983 Clem Gorman *A Night in the Arms of Raeleen* 45: 'Nine is gettin' yer length in, with a frog on, and both fully stripped, and ten is gettin' yer end in, with no frog, and both fully stripped.'

frog's eyes, eggs   Sago (or sometimes tapioca) pudding
1953 Baker 104: *frog's eyes*, boiled sago.
1983 *Sydney Morning Herald* 21 May 35: Sweets were mostly tapioca, watery junket and stodgy slabs of steamed pudding, labelled frog's eyes, white wobble and tombstone.

front   To appear before, 'front up'
1945 Kylie Tennant *Ride on Stranger* 67: Mr Litchin was ... making frantic signs to Beryl who fronted him much in the manner of a ruffled kitten.
1950 *Australian Police Journal* Apr. 112: *Front, To* To appear before. 'Front' the court.
1961 *Sydney Morning Herald* 20 May 2: So the delo fronted him and said 'If we don't get gloves we'll walk off!'
1969 Alan O'Toole *The Racing Game* 154: 'I say straight up into the Murray with this bloke the next time he fronts.'
1974 John Powers *The Last of the Knucklemen* 29: 'They reckon it's strange you don't front down there any more – not since that night.'

front, more ~ than Myers, Foy and Gibson's   An excessive 'hide', 'cheek', effrontery [f. facade of large departmental stores in Melbourne and Adelaide]
1958 Frank Hardy *The Four-Legged Lottery* 87: 'Must get back to the game. Some of these bastards have more front than Myers; might get their hand caught in the tin.'
1966 Baker 347: *more front than Foy and Gibson's*, said of a person who is extremely daring in his or her demands, or of a girl with large breasts.
1978 Barry Humphries *A Nice Night's Entertainment* (1981) 165: He's a cheeky beggar – always has been – more front on him than Myers.

1983 Clem Gorman *A Night in the Arms of Raeleen* 30: 'That guy's got more front than the National Bank.'

front page, to put sport back on the   see **sport**

frontage   'Land which abuts on a river or piece of water, or on a road' (OED 1622–1875). Not an Australian term, but much used in land settlement.
1838 T. L. Mitchell *Three Expeditions into the Interior of Eastern Australia* i 12: There might be found abundance of good soil unavailable for any purpose except grazing, only from the want of 'frontage' (as it is termed), on a river or chain of ponds.
1840 HRA xxi 114: The principal (though of course not the sole) circumstance, which gives to some pastoral lands a much higher value than to others, is the command of Water or 'Water frontage' as it is usually called in the Colony.
1863 R. Therry *Reminiscences of Thirty Years' Residence in New South Wales* 261–2: I took up a tract of country with thirty miles of frontage to the Murrumbidgee river.
1875 Rolf Boldrewood *The Squatter's Dream* repr. as *Ups and Downs* (1878) 22: The herd had spread by degrees over the wide plains of 'the back', as well as over the broad river flats and green reed-beds of 'the frontage'.
1908 Giles Seagram *Bushmen All* 262: Leaving the creek frontage to their kinsfolk, they contented themselves with the back country.
1942 Tip Kelaher *The Digger Hat* 22: The 'hoppers' who have lately found the need / To come in from the scrub to flog the 'frontage' of its feed.

froth off a glass of beer, couldn't blow the   see **couldn't**

fruit for the sideboard   Easy money, esp. from a gambling win [f. slogan of bookmaker Andy Kerr 1897–1955, in taking bets at long odds on outsiders]
1953 T. A. G. Hungerford *Riverslake* 128: He was not afraid that they would ever wake up to it ... not the poor dopes who came back week after week to buy the fruit for his sideboard.
1966 Baker 157: *fruit for the sideboard*, easy money. [as underworld cant]
1973 Alexander Buzo *Rooted* 8: 'Some of our blokes were easy picking for those bastards. Fruit on the sideboard. That's what they were.'
1980 *Sun-Herald* 2 Nov. 81: Grey Receiver ... was going to be the fruit on the sideboard the other day, but Voigt came along on Fantastic Planet to beat him in the closest of camera finishes.
1982 *Sydney Morning Herald* 6 Mar. 13: No political party in Australia, least of all the Liberals, has the courage to stop giving public money to people who do not need it. The political consequences of playing Robin Hood by depriving the most articu-

late political force in Australia of some fruit on the sideboard would be catastrophic.

frying pan   1   Applied to one brand superimposed dishonestly on another [f. appearance]
1857 F. Cooper *Wild Adventures in Australia* 104: 'This person was an "old hand" and had got into some trouble ... by using a "frying pan brand". He was stock-keeping in that quarter, and was rather given to "gulley raking". One fine day it appears he ran in three bullocks belonging to a neighbouring squatter, and clapt his brand on the top of the other so as to efface it.'
1941 Baker 30: *Frying pan brand:* A large brand used by cattle thieves to cover the rightful owner's brand.
1951 Ernestine Hill *The Territory* 444: *Frying-pan* A botched cattle brand.
2   Equivalent to 'small time' (cf. 'tea and sugar' burglar)
1864 J. F. Mortlock *Experiences of a Convict* (1965) 93: Some, unarmed, prowl about, watch the inmates of a dwelling away, and then pilfer. These are called 'frying-pan' bushrangers, being looked upon with much contempt.
1966 Tom Ronan *Strangers on the Ophir* 46: 'Oh, just a frying-pan fighting man who blew in from Coronet with a silver cheque.'

Fuchsias, the   Former nickname of the Melbourne VFL club [f. resemblance of red flowers of the fuchsia to team colours]
1981 Leonie Sandercock and Ian Turner *Up Where, Cazaly?* 148: By the end of the decade Melbourne (who were called the Fuschias [sic] until Checker Hughes changed their name in the 1930s to the Demons) had won another two premierships.

fucktruck   A panel van, esp. with fitted mattress
1979 Rae Desmond Jones *Walking the Line* 19: The boys wearing blue singlets in their striped fuck trucks yelled and pressed down on their horns but Fifi kept going.
1982 John Tranter *Meanjin* 395: How did you adapt / your fuck-truck style of driving to a foreign car?

fuckwit   An idiot
1972 David Williamson *The Removalists* 101: 'I've seen some cowardly fuckwits hiding behind their uniforms in my time but without a doubt you're the bottom of the bloody barrel.'
1975 Alex Buzo *Tom* 33: 'Yes sir, I'm very angry too. The man is patently a fuckwit.'
1980 Jessica Anderson *The Impersonators* 46: That morning a girl, a heroin addict of seventeen, had said to him, idly, 'Yes, but you're just a middle-class fuckwit, aren't you?'
1982 *National Times* 11 Jul. 13: It has often been

suggested that those who complain are 'hypochondriacs', 'hysterical neurotics', or, in the words of one academic expert in ventilation, simply 'f***wit women'.

1983 Rob George *Sandy Lee Live at Nui Dat* 64: 'Listen to me Anderson. You're a fuckwit.'

full Used in various comparisons to indicate drunkenness

1911 Louis Stone *Jonah* 226: ''Ard luck, to grudge a man a pint, with 'is own missis inside there gittin' as full as a tick.'

1941 Baker 30: *Full as an egg (goog, tick)* Completely drunk.

1951 Dymphna Cusack and Florence James *Come In Spinner* 367: 'She's been as full as a goog, ever since 'er boy friend went back.'

1955 D'Arcy Niland *The Shiralee* 86: 'The same old Lucky. Full as a boot and happy as Larry.'

1959 Hal Porter *A Bachelor's Children* 285: 'I'm going to get full as a State School ... blind sleeping drunk!

1961 Patrick White *Riders in the Chariot* 448: 'I bet that nephew of yours will be full as a piss-ant by eleven!'

1964 Lawson Glassop *The Rats in New Guinea* 151: 'We'll get as full as the family po.'

1983 *Daily Telegraph* (Sydney) 2 Apr. 3: The saying 'as full as a Bourke Street tram' is soon to take on a new meaning in Victoria, where alcohol may soon be served to passengers as the rails sing by.

full bottle, not the   see **bottle**

full dollar, not the   see **dollar**

full quid, not the   see **quid**

full up to dolly's wax   see **dolly's wax**

furphy   1   A water-cart made by Furphy of Shepparton, Victoria

1916 *The Anzac Book* 56n: Furphy was the name of the contractor which was written large upon the rubbish carts that he supplied to the Melbourne camps. The name was transferred to a certain class of news item, very common since the war, which flourished greatly upon all the beaches.

1955 E. O. Schlunke *The Man in the Silo* 208: The wood-and-water-Joey came trudging along with a load of water slopping out of the Furphy.

1959 C. V. Lawlor *All This Humbug* 95: Walter drove his own mare, Polly, in his 'Furphy' water cart. This was a nickname given to this particular type of water-cart which was considered to be the best type of all, and was patented by a Mr Furphy, of Shepparton, in Victoria. [referring to the 1930s]

1969 Patsy Adam Smith *The Folklore of the Australian Railwaymen* 25: Lying there in my bed [in the 1920s] I'd hear the rattle of kerosene tins, buckets, tin dishes, even the rumble of a horse-drawn furphy, the little iron tank on wheels.

2   A rumour thought to have arisen in gossip around the water-cart in World War I (a latrine rumour); any false report

1915 C. E. W. Bean Diary 7 Jun. in *Gallipoli Correspondent* (1983) 126: The place has been full of spy rumours these last few days ... Blamey has asked me if I can get out a 'Furfies Gazette', with these furfies so exaggerated as to laugh them out of court.

1916 C. J. Dennis *The Moods of Ginger Mick* 122: I know wot I wus born fer now, an' soljerin's me game, / That's no furphy.

1918 *Aussie The Australian Soldier's Magazine* 18 Jan. 3: A Tassie indignantly urges us to deny the Furphy that Tasmania is seeking a separate peace.

1919 W. J. Denny *The Diggers* 67: We were not quite certain of our destination and 'Furphies'* became rife. *This word is used by Australian soldiers to signify rumours without foundation. It originated in a Victorian camp from the name of the proprietor of the sanitary carts – Furphy.

1924 *Truth* 27 Apr. 6: *Furphy* Wild rumour.

1932 Leonard Mann *Flesh in Armour* 269: All this could portend only one thing. Each day lent truth to the furphies.

1946 Rohan Rivett *Behind Bamboo* 371: We sat around all the morning yarning, drawing rations, and hearing optimistic furphies which I was in no mood to believe.

1953 T. A. G. Hungerford *Riverslake* 147: 'Had you heard this furphy about Radinski?'

1963 Hal Porter *The Watcher on the Cast-Iron Balcony* 78: Anyway, we do not attempt to disbelieve the furphy.

1982 Dick Klugman *Bulletin* 10 Aug. 5: Please stop repeating the same furphy; it upsets my constituents and causes eager political correspondents for the afternoon papers to ring me at 6 am.

fuzzy-wuzzy   Term applied in World War II to natives of Papua New Guinea working as stretcher-bearers, etc. [Applied to Soudanese in 1892, from appearance of hair OED]

1952 T. A. G. Hungerford *The Ridge and the River* 205: They had already had their reward – a slushy poem written from the gratitude of a soldier's heart and dedicated to them, the fuzzy-wuzzy angels, the Christs with black faces.

1972 John Bailey *The Wire Classroom* 31: These are the Fuzzy-Wuzzy Angels, now known as coons, and of course refused membership or even entry to the club, except as servants.

G

Gabba, the The Queensland Cricket Association ground at Woollongabba, a suburb of Brisbane [abbr.]

1976 *Sydney Morning Herald* 26 Nov. 13: Test hopes on line at the Gabba.

1981 *Australian* 29 Jun. 1: VFL cracks Gabba record [heading] The Brisbane Cricket Ground attracted a record crowd yesterday when the Victorian Football League came to town.

gaff To gamble [f. English thieves' slang]

1812 Vaux 242: *Gaff* to gamble with cards, dice, &c., or to toss up.

1881 Rolf Boldrewood *Robbery Under Arms* (World's Classics 1949) 69: The youngsters, havin' so much idle time on their hands, take to gaffin' and flash talk.

1911 Arthur Wright *Gamblers' Gold* 58: 'Y'lie', screamed the woman, 'where'd y' git th' brass t' go t' th' gaffin' school last night?'

1918 George Dale *The Industrial History of Broken Hill* 95: The Doctor ... spent ... a few evenings at a toney 'gaffing school', where he is said to have got considerable cash.

galah An ass, nincompoop, sometimes in the expression 'mad as a gumtree full of galahs' [? f. the cockatoo so named]

[**1935** H. R. Williams *Comrades of the Great Adventure* 83: He busied himself lighting a fire, chattering like a treeful of galahs meanwhile.]

1944 Lawson Glassop *We Were the Rats* 142: 'When will these galahs wake up? It's a wonder there aren't no gum-trees around fer 'em ter nest in.'

1948 Sumner Locke Elliott *Rusty Bugles* in *Khaki, Bush and Bigotry* ed. Eunice Hanger (1968) 30: 'Bit of a galah yourself, aren't you?'

1957 D'Arcy Niland *Call Me When the Cross Turns Over* 39–40: Poor old Dummy, lying in a hospital bed in Port Augusta, pinching the nurses' bottoms and telling the doctors what a lot of galahs they were.

1962 Dymphna Cusack *Picnic Races* 97: 'Mad as a gum tree full of galahs,' McGarrity stormed. 'Why don't they pay cash?'

1969 Leslie Haylen *Twenty Years' Hard Labor* 201: One has only to listen to the speeches on Grievance Day to realize that the private member has been reduced to the status of a political galah.

1971 David Ireland *The Unknown Industrial Prisoner* 255: 'I hope when we ask for something we need in the way of safe working ... we won't be outvoted by office galahs that don't know what we're talking about.'

1975 Les Ryan *The Shearers* 45: 'Hey!' Sandy shouted. 'Some galah has hooked me mug!'

1981 'Stork' Hendry *Sydney Morning Herald* 3 Nov. 31: 'These bloody galahs going around now are bowling feet wide of the stumps and being hailed as good bowlers.'

galah session An interval on the Flying Doctor radio network when anyone may come on to the air, to exchange gossip [see quot. 1961]

1959 Jon Cleary *Back of Sunset* 111: 'You're just in time for the galah session. I never take that meself. Can't stand a bar of a lotta women magging their heads off.'

1961 Barbara Jefferis *Solo for Several Players* 30: 'They [galahs] make a noise like a bunch of women nattering. That's why they call it the galah session. There's this time every morning when they can get on their radios and have a good mag to each other.'

1967 John Yeomans *The Scarce Australians* 58: In the evenings, before short wave reception deteriorates too much, the air is thrown open for what is called the 'Galah Session', during which anybody can come on the air and call anybody else for a gossip, provided he or she can get a word into the hubbub of scores of other voices talking at once.

1971 Robin Miller *Flying Nurse* 103: During the gossip or 'galah' sessions, people can hear the cheerful voices of their 'next door neighbours' – who may be more than 100 miles away.

Galloping Greens   see **Greens**

gallows   A frame from which the carcass of a slaughtered beast could be suspended

1847 Alexander Harris *Settlers and Convicts* ed. C. M. H. Clark (1954) 159: Another convenience it [the stockyard] must contain is what is called 'the gallows' for hauling up a beast that has been slaughtered, to take the hide off.

1853 S. Mossman and T. Bannister *Australia Visited and Revisited* 83: He [the ox] was skinned and hoisted up to the gallows, where the meat was allowed to cool during the night.

1877 Rolf Boldrewood *A Colonial Reformer* (1890) 350: Close to the side of the house was a stockyard, comprising the 'gallows' of the colonists, a rough, rude contrivance consisting of two uprights and a crosspiece for elevating slaughtered cattle.

1900 Henry Lawson 'The Selector's Daughter' *Prose* i 62: Her father finished skinning, and drew the carcase up to a make-shift 'gallows'.

1906 A. B. Paterson *An Outback Marriage* 68: At the back were the stockyards and the killing pen, where a contrivance for raising dead cattle – called a gallows – waved its arms to the sky.

1955 Mary Durack *Keep Him My Country* 95: The butcher's gallows stood out eerily against the rising yellow moon.

galoot   An awkward and stupid fellow [U.S. 1869 OED]

1903 Joseph Furphy *Such is Life* (1944) 9: 'And that strapping red-headed galoot, riding the bag of bones beside him.'

1912 Henry Lawson 'Grandfather's Courtship' *Prose* i 879: 'You'd best see that big galoot safe out

the gate, Harriet, or he'll forgit to shut it.'

1924 C. J. Dennis *Rose of Spadgers* 112: That pie-faced galoot.

1930 *Bulletin* 16 Jul. 21: The big galoot spends 'arf 'is time a-'anging round my place.

1948 K. S. Prichard *Golden Miles* 325: O'Reilly accused him of being a silly old galoot to be acting soft about Frisco.

1960 Donald McLean *The Roaring Days* 215: 'I've just thought of something that will interest Ian. What a galoot I am not to think of it sooner.'

galvo   Galvanized iron [abbr.]

1973 Donald Stuart *Morning Star Evening Star* 97: A canoe that you'd made with your own hands from a sheet of galvo.

1977 *Sydney Morning Herald* 5 Mar. 11: Risk drowning yourselves in canoes made from sheets of galvo.

game as Ned Kelly, a pebble, a pissant   see **Ned Kelly, pebble, pissant**

game, the ~ they play in heaven   Rugby Union football

1979 Steve Finnane *The game they play in heaven* 168: It would be nice to think of a schoolboy in the year 2007 giving a rugby tourist a similar answer to the one John Lambie got from a Welsh lad in 1976. Lambie asked why rugby played such a special part in the lives of the Welsh. The sing-song reply came back as quick as a Gareth Evans pass: 'Why it's the game they play in Heaven, Mr Lambie.'

1982 *Weekend Australian* 3 Apr. 48: 'The game they play in heaven' is a label often attached to rugby union by its lilywhite fans.

1983 M. F. Unuk *Australian* 3 Aug. 6: An advertisement which recently appeared in your pages said 'Rugby – the game they play in heaven'. To whom was this information revealed, or has someone returned from heaven? Are there any other games played in heaven? What games do they play in hell?

game, the greatest ~ of all   Rugby League football

1973 Alexander Buzo *The Roy Murphy Show* in *Three Plays* 113: 'I must say, Sharon, you've added a touch of glamour to the greatest game of all.'

1982 *Sun-Herald* 28 Feb. 74: 'The greatest game of all', as its followers insist on calling it . . . seems for the moment to be secure from any serious takeover.

gangie   See quot.

1983 Wayne Pearce *Daily Mirror* 13 Sep. 55: Premiers Parramatta would be well advised to eliminate what they term the 'gang tackle' from their repertoire. For those not in the know, a 'gangie' is when three or four defenders converge on the ball-carrier and crash him to the ground, presumably to make him think twice the next time he handles.

gants Variant of **gonce** q.v.
1902 Ambrose Pratt *The Great 'Push' Experiment* 76: 'Luckily we have plenty of gants in hand; but this'll run to hundreds.'

Gap, the Cliff near South Head (Sydney) which has been the scene of suicide attempts: the offer of 'a one-way ticket to the Gap' is a sign of disfavour
1867 J. R. Houlding *Australian Capers* 223: They stood for a short time, and gazed into the Gap – that fatal chasm.
1925 Seymour Hicks *Hullo Australians* 251: The Gap is a jumping off place for all those who don't believe in the allotted span.
1934 Thomas Wood *Cobbers* 174: 'So they [the intending suicide and the policeman] had a talk about it first. Then they both went over the Gap.'
1945 Baker 196: *Over the Gap, to go* To commit suicide.
1959 Dorothy Hewett *Bobbin Up* 18: 'Reckon she'll throw 'erself over the Gap?'
1975 *Quadrant* Jul. 34: Do you want to be an editor? Yeah, like I want a one-way ticket to the Gap.
1984 *Sun Herald* 15 Jan. 120: Not that anyone's taking a one-way taxi trip to The Gap, but it was noticeable at Randwick on Wednesday that . . . five rails and several paddock men didn't field.

garbo A garbage-collector, dustman [abbr.]
1953 Baker 105. *garbo* a garbage man.
1973 *Sun-Herald* 8 Apr. 9: Being a 'garbo' has compensations, according to Joe.
1980 *Australian* 30 Jul. 1: 'I was sacked after 18 years in the game, first as a rank and file garbo, then as a foreman and latterly as a supervisor.'
1983 *Sunday Independent* (Perth) 14 Aug. 3: Garbos complain of victimisation [heading]

Garden, Cabbage see **Cabbage**

Garden State, the Victoria, in the language of tourist advertising, and in the legend on car registration plates
1978 *Sydney Morning Herald* 26 Jun. 1: Victoria, the self-styled Garden State, is definitely taking litter seriously.
1981 *National Times* 31 May 4: The Victorian Liberals gunned down Hamer – their successful standard bearer at three elections – while he was away flogging the Garden State to the Americans.
1982 *Bulletin* 21 Sep. 12: Victoria may be the Garden State . . . but we all know what you put on gardens.

gardie A garfish [abbr.]
1983 *West Australian* (Perth) 23 Sep. 38: There has been excellent gardie fishing at Red Bluff.

Gar's Mahal The High Court building in Canberra, constructed while Sir Garfield Barwick was Chief Justice [f. the Taj Mahal]
1979 *Australian* 1 Jun. 2: Sir Garfield had strong views about his place in legal history – he wanted a substantial monument to his stewardship. The building . . . had been dubbed 'Gar's Mahal'.
1981 *Bulletin* 22 Dec. 58: The monument by Lake Burley Griffin, dubbed Gar's Mahal, has become a gilded cage from which judges are not to fly.

Gateway, the The area at the centre of Circular Quay, Sydney, where Captain Phillip landed, to be preserved by a low building line between the AMP towers and Goldfields House, offering a 'gateway' to the city
1977 *Sydney Morning Herald* 24 Aug. 3: The State Government has taken control of the Circular Quay area from the City Council and imposed building height restrictions to protect the City 'gateway' concept. An interim development order gazetted by the Minister for Planning and Environment, Mr Landa, will prevent construction of a huge 650 ft tower block halfway along Alfred Street.
1983 Paul H. Johnson *Sydney Morning Herald* 25 Apr. 6: My committee has been actively opposing the erection of a highrise on the Gateway Site at Circular Quay. This area of land, partly reclaimed from the original Sydney Cove and Tank Stream, is the very place where Captain Arthur Phillip stepped ashore on January 26, 1788, to formally commence European settlement of Australia.
1985 *Sydney Morning Herald* 30 Jan. 20: The Gateway: a win for the few, a loss for many [heading] Developers have finally won approval to build an office tower on the historic Gateway site at Circular Quay.

gazebo A fool, 'mug': *rare* [see **gazob**]
1934 Brian Penton *Landtakers* 23: 'Aw, leave the old gazebo. He's drunk.'

Gazette, Bagman's, Hominy see **Bagman's, Hominy**

gazob A 'mug', fool: *obs.* [? f. *gazabo* a fellow, 'guy' U.S. 1896 OED]
1906 Edward Dyson *Fact'ry 'Ands* 162: 'But I thought barrer-pushin' was er game fer gazobs?'
1915 C. J. Dennis *The Songs of a Sentimental Bloke* 42: Ar! but 'e makes me sick! A fair gazob!
1924 *Truth* 27 Apr. 6: *Gazob* A foolish person.

geebung Derisive term for an uncultivated native-born Australian (cf. *stringy bark*); place-name for any remote and primitive locality [f. *geebung* the native plum (*Persoonia*) a small and tastless fruit]

1859 D. H. Deniehy *Southern Cross* 12 Nov. 2: Born and bred (the Geebung is always a native) where pecuniary success is with the majority ... the Geebung's first business is to make money. [The term is used idiosyncratically by Deniehy to denote the Australian equivalent of Arnold's 'philistine'.]

1874 Charles de Boos *The Congewoi Correspondence* 109: You know morer these things than I do, seein' as I'm only a poor old geebung, as ain't up to the ins and outser politics.

1895 A. B. Paterson 'The Geebung Polo Club' *The Man from Snowy River* 43: It was somewhere up the country, in a land of rock and scrub, / That they formed an institution called the Geebung Polo Club.

1900 Henry Lawson *Prose* i 21: 'Bogg of Geebung' [story title] Ibid. 295: 'He drank again, and no wonder – you don't know what it is to run a *Geebung Advocate* or *Mudgee Budgee Chronicle*, and live there.'

geek *v. & n.*   Look [? f. *geck* to toss the head OED 1724]

1919 W. H. Downing *Digger Dialects* 25: Geek (vb. or n.) Look.

1954 T. A. G. Hungerford *Sowers of the Wind* 190: 'There's a circus down by the dance-hall, a Jap show,' Waller volunteered. 'What about having a geek at that?'

1970 Jack Hibberd *White With Wire Wheels* in Penguin *Plays* 204: 'It's just a good solid reliable car. Just have a geek at the figures. It doesn't compare with the Valiant.'

1974 Robert Adamson *Zimmer's Essay* 20: 'Aw – give us a geek.'

see **gink**

geese flying out of one's backside   see **sparrows**

General, the   The imaginary presiding genius of General Motors-Holden's

1974 *Sunday Telegraph* (Sydney) 21 Apr. 74: The General knows the selling game and with his back to the wall in the Australian market he's not going to pull any punches.

1977 *National Times* 9 May 54: Why estimates of the General's profits can be so different. [heading]

1981 *Australian* 16 Jul. 36: Motor industry figures for June issued yesterday showed that Ford has pipped 'The General' in the sales battle for the second month running.

George   Female codeword for menstruation [listed by Partridge as meaning defecation]

1979 Sally Morrison *Who's taking you to the*

Dance? 43: 'I'm having a baby ... I haven't had George for two whole months.'

1982 Nancy Keesing *Lily on the Dustbin* 31: Kathy says to Mary 'You lot go on. Don't miss the bus, but I've just remembered I'm out of white bread, and George is calling tonight.' Mary understands that Kathy wants to dash into a chemist shop to buy sanitary napkins.

George Moore's whistle   The imaginary whistle the jockey George Moore was supposed to blow to clear the way for a winning run

1982 *Sun-Herald* 10 Oct. 77: 'You'll know that it is Ray Selkrig looking for an inside run, just as George Moore did when he blew his whistle.'

geri   A geriatric [abbr.]

1977 *Sydney Morning Herald* 5 Apr. 7: Geris (short for geriatrics) is applied by the young to anyone over 40, and has replaced 'oldies' in the Ocker vocabulary.

1984 *Sydney Morning Herald* 3 May 14: Enrol now in training schemes for the care of our growing legion of gerries.

get a bag   see **bag**

get a guernsey   see **guernsey**

get a load of   see **load**

get off one's bike   see **bike**

get on like a bushfire   see **bushfire**

get on one's quince   see **quince**

get one's end in   see **end**

get one's issue   see **issue**

get the arse   see **arse**

get the spear   see **spear**

get up   To win (of a horse; sometimes a sporting team)

1904 Henry Fletcher *Dads Wayback: His Work* 100: 'When ther public fancies yer nag's chance, an' puts ther beans on, ther books gives yer ther office, an' that prad don't quite get up that time; though he runs close.'

1949 Lawson Glassop *Lucky Palmer* 48: 'The way you bet you're up for a bundle if the favourite gets up.'

1958 Frank Hardy *The Four-Legged Lottery* 176: Snozzle Purtell timing his run, getting up in a punishing photo finish.

1974 *Australian* 6 Nov. 22: Rival owner sorry

Leilani didn't get up.
1983 Phillip Adams *Sun-Herald* 9 Oct. 9: 'I can't think of one confronting feature film that has criticised our society and got up.'

getting any?   sc. sex: Current in Services slang in World War II, with stock replies
1945 Baker 124: The jocular greeting between man and man, *gettin' any?*
1951 Dal Stivens *Jimmy Brockett* 125: 'Getting any, Jimmy?' he'd asked a couple of nights ago. 'You bet,' I told him. 'I have to put an extra man on.' Ibid. 174: 'Getting any, smacker?' I'd ask him. More often than not he'd come back at me, 'I've got to climb trees to get away from it.'
1963 John Naish *That Men Should Fear* 82: 'Hey there, Hans, gettin' any, kid?'
1973 Alexander Buzo *The Roy Murphy Show* in *Three Plays* 103: 'Morning, Col. Getting any? That's the stuff.'
1981 Garry Disher *Approaches* 51: 'So, you're not getting it these days?'
1984 *National Times* 6 Jul. 5: The Prime Minister's informal contact [on overseas trips] runs to occasional en-route card games lasting for hours with several press favorites ... and social banter of the 'are yer gettin' any' kind.

getting off at Redfern   see **Redfern**

Ghan, the   The train which from 1929 to 1980 ran on the narrow gauge track from Marree to Alice Springs (it had previously terminated at Oodnadatta). It connected with a broad gauge track from Adelaide to Port Pirie, and a standard gauge track from Port Pirie to Marree. It was replaced in 1980 by the new Ghan connecting Adelaide with Alice Springs via Tarcoola, on a standard gauge line. [See quot. 1969]
1933 F. E. Baume *Tragedy Track* 21: This train, once known as the Ghan, because it was largely patronised by Afghans going to the then railhead of Oodnadatta, to-day is making history.
1957 A. W. Upfield *Bony Buys a Woman* 31–2: I came down the Birdsville Track on the mail truck to Marree, caught 'The Ghan' to Coward Springs, where I contacted Constable Pierce.
1961 George Farwell *Vanishing Australians* 164: In the pre-diesel days, there were two 'Ghans'. In popular parlance there was the 'Flash Ghan', the passenger train that had sleeping berths and served meals on board; and the 'Dirty Ghan', a mixed train that had cattle trucks as well as carriages. On the Dirty Ghan you carried your own tucker, and at whistle-stops climbed down to boil your billy in the saltbush and spinifex.
1969 Patsy Adam Smith *Folklore of the Australian Railwaymen* 250: The Ghan, that now runs from Port Augusta to Alice Springs but was named back

when the line ran only as far as Oodnadatta. Railway literature gives two explanations for the name, one that it was named Ghan because of the many Afghan camel men using it, the other that it was because of the number of Afghans and their families living at Oodnadatta, the railhead.
1976 *Australian* 11 Feb. 1: Copter rescue for Ghan. Two RAAF helicopters and a light plane last night airlifted all 79 passengers and crew of the Ghan train, which is stranded by floods near Oodnadatta.
1982 *Sydney Morning Herald* 24 Dec. 17: After about an hour the Ghan was shunted down along the platform. It is a gleaming silver train of 16 cars, hauled by two Australian National diesels.
1984 *Australian* 16 Jan. 1: The Ghan, which operates between Adelaide and Alice Springs, has been cancelled until further notice.

ghost, grey   see **grey ghost**

gibber   1   A boulder: *obs.* [Ab. word for 'stone': Morris 1834]
1847 Alexander Harris *Settlers and Convicts* ed. C. M. H. Clark (1954) 87: He did not object to stow himself ... under the 'gibbers' (overhanging rocks) of the river.
1882 Rolf Boldrewood *Robbery Under Arms* (World's Classics 1949) 62: A kind of gully ... something like the one we came in by, but rougher, and full of gibbers (boulders).
1962 Cynthia Nolan *Outback* 21: Gibbers may either be the size of boulders or of pebbles; during the whole trip we did not tire of searching for interestingly shaped and coloured small ones.
2   A stone of the size thrown by children
1893 Dan Healey *The Cornstalk* 66: 'Now boys, get your gibbers, here's a man beating seventeen of us.'
1908 E. S. Sorenson *Quinton's Rouseabout* 146: They could all bowl, having practised in spare time with gibbers, using the hut for wicket.
1949 *Coast to Coast 1948* 34–5: He could also hurl goolies; gibbers, and plain bluemetal with devastating accuracy.
1963 John Cantwell *No Stranger to the Flame* 19: 'Some murdering bastard of a kid must have donged it with this gibber and then shot through.'
3   A wind-polished stone, esp. in the phrase 'gibber plain' [almost a technical term in geology, rather than a colloquialism]
1906 J. W. Gregory *The Dead Heart of Australia* 51: Our journey lay mainly over sand plains and 'gibber' plains; these last have a hard brown soil, littered with rough fragments of schist and quartzite.
1933 R. B. Plowman *The Man from Oodnadatta* 17: From the unfenced buildings of Blood's Creek Store, the gibber tablelands spread far and wide.

1938 Francis Ratcliffe *Flying Fox and Drifting Sand* 231: 'Gibbers' are the iron-stained, wind-polished stones that are strewn on the surface of so much of the arid Australian inland.
1959 David Forrest *The Last Blue Sea* 23: His eyes were not cheerful, but hard, hard as a gibber plain under a summer sun.
1971 Rena Briand *White Man in a Hole* 11: Where it passes through gibber* country it would be corrugated again within a month, he predicted. *Rockstrewn.

gibber gunyah   A rock cave
1847 Alexander Harris *Settlers and Convicts* ed. C. M. H. Clark (1954) 117: I coincided in his opinion that it would be best for us to camp for the night in one of the ghibber-gunyahs. These are the hollows under overhanging rocks, and afford a most welcome shelter where they are met with in wet weather.
1878 Rolf Boldrewood *An Australian Squire* repr. as *Babes in the Bush* (1900) 260: The 'gibber gunyahs', or rock caves, which the aboriginals and their canine friends had inhabited apparently from the most remote ages.

gidgee   A spear made from the wood of the gidgee (gidyea); any long spear
1878 *Catalogue of Objects of Ethno-typical Art in National Gallery, Melbourne* 46: Gid-jee. Hardwood spear, with fragments of quartz set in gum on two sides and grass-tree stem. Total length, 7 feet 8 inches.
1937 K. S. Prichard *Intimate Strangers* 154: He screwed the fish on the end of the gidgee and raked him, whirling and flapping, into the boat. Prospero seized and pulled the fish off the gidgee.
1979 Helen Wilson *The Skedule* 192: Mr Brent gidgied a section of bakewell tart which had bounced off his plate. Ibid. 184: I've seen him throw a gidgie spear quicker than any black.
1983 *West Australian* (Perth) 17 Dec. 3: A boy was rushed to hospital yesterday afternoon with the head of a three-pronged spear embedded in his stomach . . . he accidentally fell on a 'gidgee'.

gig *v.*   1   To look at [see *gig n.* 2]
1953 Ruth Park *A Power of Roses* 164: 'A girl don't want people giggin' her when she's just starting to branch out.'
1959 Baker 112: *To gig (at)* To stare.
1965 Kylie Tennant *Tell Morning This* 393: 'Let's have some light on it,' his host muttered. 'Can't waste our whole bloody life gigging out of windows.'
2   '? To befool, hoax' (OED 1795); to make fun of
1953 Baker 103: *gig* To tease.
1969 Wilda Moxham *The Apprentice* 149: He scowled. He didn't ever like being gigged.

1977 *Sydney Morning Herald* 17 Sep. 11: Should I win the Alfa Romeo the last thing that will worry me will be being gigged by my neighbours.

gig *n.*   1   'A queer-looking figure, an oddity; *dial.* a fool' (OED 1777–1856)
1945 *Salt* 13 Aug. 11: 'I'm not going to look like a gig for the sake of a few principles.'
1953 T. A. G. Hungerford *Riverslake* 19: He knew that, behind their bland glances, they were saying to themselves, 'Who's this gig?'
1960 Ron Tullipan *Follow the Sun* 97: 'Man's a gig to take that kind of risk!'
1971 Johnny Famechon *Fammo* 72: They were terrible, those early interviews, and my friends used to rubbish me when I made such a gig of myself.
1982 *NT News* (Darwin) 4 Aug. 7: Ever feel a real gig when you misplace your car key?
2   A look, glance [? variant of *geek, gink*]
1924 C. J. Dennis *Rose of Spadgers* 65: 'Is this 'ere coot,' I arsts, 'well knowed to you? / The parson takes another gig. 'Why, yes.'
1949 John Morrison *The Creeping City* 8: 'You pay sixpence to go in and have a gig at his fern-gully and fishponds.'
1973 Frank Huelin *Keep Moving* 145: 'I scarpered like a scalded cat – didn't even get a good gig at her.'
3   A fiz-gig (q.v.), a police informer
1984 *Bulletin* 19 Jun. 69: Fifty per cent of the Drug Squad's arrests are based on information received and woe betide a user, supplier or anyone else who becomes a dog, a gig.

giggle-house   A mental asylum
1919 W. H. Downing *Digger Dialects* 26: Giggle-house Lunatic asylum.
1935 H. R. Williams *Comrades of the Great Adventure* 53: 'As silly as the "giggle-house" on a moonlight night.'
1957 D'Arcy Niland *Call Me When the Cross Turns Over* 116: 'Your own brother is half in the rats with worry and anxiety. Unless something's done he'll end up in the giggle-house.'
1973 Frank Huelin *Keep Moving* 169: The 'Giggle-house', a large, barrack-like building once used as a mental home.
1982 Max Harris *Weekend Australian* 27 Nov. Mag. 14: The classic story of . . . John Clare, who had himself locked up in the giggle-house for nearly a quarter of a century.

gilgai, gilgie   1   'A saucer-shaped depression in the ground which forms a natural reservoir for rain-water. *Ghilgais* vary from 20 to 100 yards in diameter, and are from five to ten feet deep.' (Morris) [Ab.]
1903 Joseph Furphy *Such is Life* (1944) 68: Veri-

fying the tracks of the thirsty bullocks so near the gilgie that it seemed a wonder they hadn't walked into it.
1931 Vance Palmer *Separate Lives* 231: Their horses feeding on Denison's grass and drinking from his gilgais.
1938 Eric Lowe *Salute to Freedom* 301: She was almost running ... sometimes disappearing altogether as she stumbled into the dip of a gilgi hole.
1964 Tom Ronan *Packhorse and Pearling Boat* 157: It was just dark when the old packhorse floundered into a gilgai (small billabong).
2   A freshwater crayfish
1944 *Coast to Coast 1943* 174: Watching a gilgie hole he saw after a time the waving antennae and the cautious claws, then the black head and part of the body come out. He threw a bit of bark at the water and the gilgie jerked back into the hole.
1965 Colin Johnson *Wild Cat Falling* 12: 'What say we catch gilgies?'
1982 Jack Davis *The Dreamers* 142: *gilgy*, known as yabbies in the Eastern states; a small, freshwater crustacean. A corruption of *tjilki*.

gin at a christening, like a   see **christening**

gin burglar   A white man who has casual sexual relations with Aboriginal women
1947 W. E. Harney *North of 23°* 77: We had the eternal clash of 'gin burglar' versus 'gin shepherd'.
1971 Keith Willey *Boss Drover* 46: The manager would refer to 'combos' and 'gin burglars' as though they were social outcasts. But let his wife go away for a while ... and he would be down to the blacks' camp in no time.

gin burglary
1965 *Australian* 5 Feb. 10: In Hall's Creek gin burglary is the local hobby. What chance could who have, however advanced, in an area where the station ringers divide girls into three classes, 'albinos' (white), 'creamies' (half-castes) and 'studs' (black) – and treat them accordingly.

gin jockey   As for **gin burglar**
1955 D'Arcy Niland *The Shiralee* 121: He hated the ignominy of capitulating to a harlot, and a black one at that. Macauley, the gin-jockey, they could say. The black velvet for Macauley.
1963 Randolph Stow *Tourmaline* 84: 'Anything out of the camp'd do for Kes' ... 'Ah, he's a gin-jockey too, is he?'
1968 Frank Hardy *The Unlucky Australians* 13: 'The only whites who drink in the Bull Ring are nigger-lovers and gin jockeys.'
1975 Xavier Herbert *Poor Fellow My Country* 54: 'They only have to see you treating an Aboriginal woman like a human being to raise the cry *Gin Jockey*.'

1982 Brian Syron *Australian* 30 Aug. 9: 'I'm the product of a gin jockey. They [the whites] see the sins of their forefathers in my face.'

gin shepherd   1   A white man who cohabits with Aboriginal women: *rare*
1929 K. S. Prichard *Coonardoo* 54: Sam Geary had been known as 'a gin shepherder' for some time and a family of half-castes swarmed about his verandas.
2   Someone seeking to protect Aboriginal women from white men: *derogatory*
1947 W. E. Harney *North of 23°* 75: The age old instinct to protect his herd was strong in Joe. 'A gin shepherd' the bagmen called him, but Joe only smiled when they called him that, as he knew that here was one who had been unsuccessful in the hunt.
1954 Tom Ronan *Vision Splendid* 58: She had a self-imposed, utterly sincere mission to save the lubras from the lust of the white men. She failed in her endeavour, earned herself the name of the 'greatest gin shepherd in the country', and was eventually responsible for her husband losing his job because he couldn't keep men.
1971 Keith Willey *Boss Drover* 46: The practice of separating the women from the combos was known as 'gin shepherding'.

gin's piss, weak as   Very weak
1951 Seaforth Mackenzie *Dead Men Rising* 243: 'Whisky is nothing – what you call gin's water, is it?' 'Gin's —'. Poole stopped himself.
1983 *Weekend Australian* 5 Feb. Mag. 1: A new brand of white wine ... can be purchased in Tennant Creek and Alice Springs by tourists who want a really different souvenir. It costs $8 a flagon and bears the label 'Gin's Piss and Yakka Gum'. Maker and bottler unstated.

ging   A catapult (*juvenile*)
1933 Norman Lindsay *Saturdee* 152: Peter took out his ging to make a show of catapulting a stone at a non-existent bird.
1965 Colin Johnson *Wild Cat Falling* 13: I put a stone in the ging and let fly.
1968 Geoffrey Dutton *Andy* 93: A ging, you know, a dirty great catapult, a real beaut.
1983 T. A. G. Hungerford *Stories from Suburban Road* 20: 'Help me cut the rubbers for my ging, Tommy.'

ginger   See quot. 1945
1945 Baker 139: A prostitute who robs a man by taking money from his clothes is known as a *gingerer*. She usually works with an accomplice. To *ginger* and *gingering* are associated terms.
1953 Kylie Tennant *The Joyful Condemned* 5: 'I've just gingered the copper. Give him his pants back

when he gets too noisy' . . . 'Gingering', or robbing prospective clients, was considered low taste, but after all the man was a copper.
1961 Xavier Herbert *Soldiers' Women* 306: 'Call the cops and prove it for yourself. They'd like to do business with the gal who gingered Plug for his roll.'

Gingerbeer   An army engineer
1941 Baker 31: *Gingerbeers* The Aust. Engineer Corps.
1951 Eric Lambert *The Twenty Thousand Thieves* 149: 'And minefields! The Ginger Beers have laid so many mines they've lost trace of some of 'em.'
1970 Richard Beilby *No Medals for Aphrodite* 83: 'Who are these people, sergeant?' 'Couple of Gingerbeers, sir. Picked 'em up along the track.'

gink   1   A fellow, 'guy', interchangeable with *gig*: derogatory [U.S. 1910 OED ? f. *geck, geke* a fool, simpleton 1515]
1924 *Truth* 27 Apr. 6: *Gink* A peculiar fellow.
1939 Miles Franklin and Dymphna Cusack *Pioneers on Parade* 35: 'Quick! Look at that gink over there. Isn't he a cut!'
1946 Rohan Rivett *Behind Bamboo* 396: *Gink* term of abuse.
1954 Bant Singer *Have Patience Delaney* 16: Up front the gink in the blue suit . . . stands up and peers after the ambulance.
1966 H. F. Brinsmead *Beat of the City* 18: 'They're bossed around by an old gink who's some crazy sort of parson.'
1971 Barbara Vernon *A Big Day at Bellbird* 185: He understood that long gink with her was her fiancé.
2   A look (? variant of *geck*)
1945 Robert S. Close *Love Me Sailor* 227: I kept staring so that he could get a gink at me wide awake.
1961 Robert S. Close *Hooves of Brass* 121: 'And get a gink at that chin, mates!'
1962 Stuart Gore *Down the Golden Mile* 205: 'Come up to my camp on the way home in the morning and have a gink at it then.'

give away   Abandon, give up, cease operations [? f. *give it best*]
[**1892** Henry Lawson 'Cross the Border' *Verse* i 179: Workmen struggle, and are beaten, and they give it best and go.]
1948 Sumner Locke Elliott *Rusty Bugles* in *Khaki, Bush and Bigotry* ed. Eunice Hanger (1968) 98: *Andy:* How's the garden going, Ot? *Ot:* Give it away.
1949 Lawson Glassop *Lucky Palmer* 195: 'I don't mind ordinary competition, but if I've got to compete with a horse I think it's about time I gave the game away.'

1955 John Morrison *Black Cargo* 14: 'If it was me I'd give it away,' I say to Tiny. 'He's got Buckley's chance.'
1961 Patrick White *Riders in the Chariot* 408: 'What's wrong with your job, Alf? You haven't given it away?'
1971 Colin Simpson *The New Australia* 157: 'Well, I gave the city away. Best thing I ever did, and my wife agrees.'

give curry   see **curry**

give it the herbs   see **herbs**

give it to a Jap on Anzac Day, you wouldn't   see **Jap**

give the lizard a run   see **lizard** 4

give them heaps   see **heaps**

glad, gladdie   A gladiolus
1968 Barry Humphries *A Nice Night's Entertainment* (1981) 110: Most other invalids get glads or carnies so Beryl said Valda must have really put her thinking cap on.
1972 Ian Moffitt *The U-Jack Society* 154: The breakfast gong has not summoned the tourists yet to the hotel dining-room (vases of gladdies in a funeral pink glow).

Glad, Our   Miss Gladys Moncrieff (1892–1976), singer who took leading roles in *Maid of the Mountains* (1921, 1942), *Rio Rita* (1926) and in Gilbert and Sullivan productions
1939 *Life Digest* Mar. 99: A very vital and kind-hearted woman is Gladys; everyone's friend, she is known to countless Australians simply as 'Our Gladys'.
1974 *Australian* 20 Nov. 3: Our Glad ill. Gladys Moncrieff has been admitted to a Gold Coast private hospital suffering from a virus complaint.
1984 *Sydney Morning Herald* 15 Oct. Guide 14: It's Livvy – Australia's 'Our Glad' of the eighties – in another cornucopia of song and dance that can only be described as lavishly dazzling.

glass door on a dunny, useful as a   see **useful**

glass of beer, couldn't blow the froth off a   see **couldn't**

glassy, just the   Superlative; the one who excels, is most admired: *obsolescent* [f. the 'glassy' as the most prized marble]
1906 Edward Dyson *Fact'ry 'Ands* 166: 'They're all right, ain't they?' asked the man, and he dusted them [the trousers] carefully. 'Oh, they're jist ther glassy.'

1911 Steele Rudd *The Dashwoods* 25: 'I said it would be just the glassy marble – the sort of thing I'd like to be at.'
1915 C. J. Dennis *The Songs of a Sentimental Bloke* 42: 'E's jist the glarsey on the soulful sob, / 'E'll sigh and spruik, an' 'owl a love-sick vow.'
1920 *Aussie* 15 May 34: 'Old Bill was the oil – the glassy – oh Hell!'
1951 Dymphna Cusack and Florence James *Come In Spinner* 300: 'Low profits and quick turnover, and this is the glassy marble.'

Gloria Soame   The 'Strine' formulation of 'a glorious home'
1965 *Sydney Morning Herald* 6 Jan. 1: The first advertisement in pure Strine reached our 'classified' department yesterday. It advertised a 'gloria soame' of 14 squares, with amenities.
1971 Frank Hardy *The Outcasts of Foolgarah* 11: But Gloria Soames all and dominating the scene atop the hill.
1983 *Australian* 28 Jun. 7: Keating ... recently bought a four-storey Victorian terrace for $225,000 in the smart apartment precinct of Elizabeth Bay. At the moment this 'gloria soame' is divided into 10 flatettes, grossing about $31,000 a year.

glory box   A box kept by young women for storing clothes etc. in preparation for marriage: *obsolescent* (U.S. *hope chest*)
1915 Louis Stone *Betty Wayside* 244: It was her glory box, containing all her treasures that she had gathered together against such a day as this.
1934 F. S. Hibble *Karangi* 110: They came to gossip and rave over the glory box, being frank in their envy.
1947 H. Drake-Brockman *The Fatal Days* 299: 'Remember that glory-chest you admired down the furniture store?'
1959 Dorothy Hewett *Bobbin Up* 167: Johnny had ... broken all her glory-box utility set.
1966 Bruce Beaver *You Can't Come Back* 118: 'That's my glory-box ... I'm saving up things so I can get married and get away from here.'
1975 Rodney Hall *A Place Among People* 149–50: 'She has been buying quite good quality things for her glory box.'
1981 Dorothy Hewett *The Golden Oldies* 40: 'He jilted my Ellie, her glory box ready, doilies and supper cloths, embroidered shams.'

gluepot   A depression in which a cart or wagon becomes bogged
1885 *The Australasian Printers' Keepsake* 84: Bullocks to make one more effort to extricate the dray from a 'glue-pot'.
1903 Joseph Furphy *Such is Life* (1944) 55: 'Hello! where's Damper?' 'Stuck in a gluepot, just

in front o' the (adj.) hut,' replied Mosey.
1906 Mrs Harrison Lee *One of Australia's Daughters* 145: 'What about riding ... over roads that have earnt the names of glue-pots?'
1949 George Farwell *Traveller's Tracks* 74: It was only just under water, but underneath was red mud – a real gluepot.
2   A muddy race track
1984 *Sun-Herald* 13 May 63: 'Gluepot' going a hazard [heading]

gnamma   see **namma**

go bung   see **bung**

go bush   see **bush**

go for one's quoits   see **quoits**

go for a century   see **century**

go for the doctor   see **doctor**

go for your life, Lady Carruthers   see **Carruthers**

go, give it a   As for **give it a burl** q.v.
1924 *Truth* 27 Apr. 6: *Give it a go* To make an attempt.
1934 Thomas Wood *Cobbers* 10: 'Besides, we want people from the other side to see our State. Give it a go!'
1946 Kylie Tennant *Lost Haven* 114: 'Going to give it a go tomorrow?'
1950 Gavin Casey *City of Men* 288: With Joe he would be giving himself a chance – the only chance he would ever be likely to get. 'I'll give it a go,' he announced suddenly.
1964 Donald Horne *The Lucky Country* 39: Impelled to action, Australians 'give it a go'. They try something to see if it works, pretty sure that it will.
1971 Robin Miller *Flying Nurse* 172: Damascus airport was closed by fog, but ... I was prepared to give it a go.

go nap on   see **nap**

go off   1   To be raided by the police, when engaged in something illegal
1941 Baker 31: *Go off* When an hotel or club is raided by the police for permitting gambling or after-hours drinking, it is said to 'go off'.
1949 Lawson Glassop *Lucky Palmer* 5: 'Clarrie, he ain't gone off in six months. Must sling to the cops. Wonder how much he pays 'em'.
1967 Kylie Tennant *Tell Morning This* 10: 'The nice thing about this place ... is that it's never raided. Number Eighteen went off last week, and the Vice Squad are always in and out of the place

two doors down – but us – we never seem to have them.'
1977 Jim Ramsay *Cop it Sweet* 41: *Go off* The raiding of premises taking part in illegal activities.
1982 *NT News* (Darwin) 3 Apr. 33: Among those who 'went off' that night was one Harry David, who had a fruit and veg. business in Tennant Creek.
1984 *Bulletin* 10 Jul. 49: Mona last went off in December 1983 when she was charged under her real name, Lucy Domingo, and fined $200 for having been the keeper of a brothel.
2   See quot. 1941
1941 Baker 31: *Go off* When a horse is expected or 'fixed' to win a race it is said to 'go off'.
1949 Lawson Glassop *Lucky Palmer* 176: 'A bloke who's got a mare like Laughin' Water is extra welcome. Let's know when she's goin' off.'
1976 Sam Weller *Bastards I have met* 104: They had a real hot-pot ready to go off and they played it very cagey.
3   To be stolen
1953 T. A. G. Hungerford *Riverslake* 151: 'I wondered if you'd mind my wireless while I'm in Sydney? If I leave it in my room it'll go off.'
1963 Frank Hardy *Legends from Benson's Valley* 44: 'There's been a lot of wood goin' off from yards round the town lately.'

go over the hill   see **hill**

go the knuckle   see **knuckle**

go through   To abscond, make a swift departure, esp. to avoid some obligation (interchangeable with 'shoot through')
1943 Baker 34: *Go through* To desert from a northern base to the south. War slang.
1949 Lawson Glassop *Lucky Palmer* 79: 'When will you fellows wake to it? Here it is twenty to twelve and you blokes are still believing he'll be here. Can't you see he's gone through?'
1951 Eric Lambert *The Twenty Thousand Thieves* 222: He shrugged. 'I'll probably have to go through meself again.' He said it as though going A.W.L. was as casual a thing as shaving.
1973 Frank Huelin *Keep Moving* 179: *Gone through* Left town.

go through like a dose of salts   see **salts**

go to market   see **market**

go to the pack   see **pack**

go to town   see **town**

go under someone's neck   see **neck**

goanna, sand   see **sand**

goat, a hairy   A racehorse which performs badly
1941 Baker 34: *Hairy goat, run like a* (used esp. of horses) To perform badly in a race.
1951 Dymphna Cusack and Florence James *Come In Spinner* 40: 'The last one you gave me [as a racing tip] ran like a hairy goat.'
1956 J. T. Lang *I Remember* 150: They told him it was a 'hairy goat', but Smithy decided it would be better to ride the 'hairy goat' than not have a mount. [recalling 1904]
1965 John Beede *They Hosed Them Out* 192: Our skipper, from the time we got near the enemy coasts, flew like a hairy goat.
1969 Osmar White *Under the Iron Rainbow* 110–11: If there'd been a few hairy goats galloping around and a couple of bookies standing on whisky cases it'd have looked like the bloody Roebourne races.
1978 John Hepworth *His Book* 113: When the barrier flew up Warrego Willie went like a hairy goat – never even looked like running a drum.

goburra   The kookaburra: *obs.* [Ab.]
1834 George Bennett *Wanderings in New South Wales* i 222: The natives at Yas call the bird 'Gogera' or Gogobera', probably from its peculiar note, which has some resemblance to the sound of the word.
1843–63 Charles Harpur 'The Kangaroo Hunt' in *Poetical Works* ed. Elizabeth Perkins (1984) 495: Gooburra is an aboriginal name of the large kind of king-fisher which is commonly known by the tasteful and poetic sobriquet of the Laughing Jackass.
1873 Anthony Trollope *Australia* ed. P. D. Edwards and R. B. Joyce (1967) 210: It is also called the settler's clock; – and by the aboriginals gogobera, that being to the black man's ear the sound of the animal's voice.
1894 *Bulletin* 18 Aug. 22: A goburra in native trim – / The settlers' gum-tree clock of yore.
1902 Henry Fletcher *The Waybacks* 38: 'How delicious it will be to picnic under the wide spreading shade of the gum trees and listen to the sweet notes of the goburra as he merrily pipes his lay.'
1905 *Old Bush Songs* ed. A. B. Paterson 114: Until they chime in the rude rough rhyme of the wild goburra's song.

Godzone   Australia [f. the use of this heading (for 'God's own country') in a series of articles in *Meanjin Quarterly*]
1966 *Meanjin Quarterly* 133: Godzone (1) The Retreat from Reason [Note:] This is the first of a new series of commentaries on the reality of present-day life and living in God's Own Country.

1976 *Australian* 15 May 21: Godzone's richest acres. A fine-focus on the best addresses in Australia.
1981 Buzz Kennedy *Australian* 14 Dec. 2: The ennui of the jet-setter. I don't know how the beautiful people stand up to it. But cripes – it was bonzer to get back to Godzone.

goer A project, proposal likely to be put into effect or to succeed
1977 *Bulletin* 29 Jan. 29: The film is now finally a goer. Hellwig's money is in and the rest will come from private investment ... and film commissions.
1980 *Mercury* (Hobart) 31 Mar. 30: 'I've said it before and I'll say it again – without the public's support, this competition can never be a goer.'
1982 *NT News* (Darwin) 15 Jun. 2: Barge service a goer [heading] A monthly barge service from Darwin to Singapore ... will go ahead despite union opposition.

gogobera see **goburra**

golden doughnut see **doughnut**

golden girl An Australian woman athlete who has won an Olympic gold medal; any outstanding Australian sportswoman [f. the 1956 Olympics, when Australia won the women's relay, and Betty Cuthbert three gold medals]
1956 *Sunday Telegraph* (Sydney) 2 Dec. 3: Golden Girls Triumph in Relay. Ibid. 9 Dec. 1: Australia's four 'golden girls' led the parade of athletes in a moving closing ceremony at the main Olympic stadium today.
1973 *Sydney Morning Herald* 11 Jan. 15: Golden girls set new swim times.
1974 *Australian* 7 Aug. 21: Whatever happened to Evonne Goolagong – our golden girl who won this year's Australian tennis title.
1982 *NT News* (Darwin) 9 Sep. 37: Reviving memories of the 'Golden Girls' [heading] With the Commonwealth Games starting in three weeks, Australia's female athletes ... are reviving memories of the 'Golden Girls', Marjorie Jackson, Betty Cuthbert and Shirley Strickland.

golden hole A very rich mining claim
1855 Raffaello Carboni *The Eureka Stockade* ed. Geoffrey Serle (1969) 176: Below at a depth of 140 feet in a ... hundred pounds weight Golden Hole.
1861 Horace Earle *Ups and Downs* 290: 'Here's luck, Tom!' ... 'A golden hole to you, Tom!' sounded from every quarter.
1880 Rolf Boldrewood *The Miner's Right* (1890) 32: The adjacent lot to the highly satisfactory 'golden-hole claim', as the miners phrased it, was to be had for the pegging-out first.

1896 Henry Lawson 'An Old Mate of Your Father's' *Prose* i 67: Poor Martin Ratcliffe – who was killed in his golden hole.
1950 K. S. Prichard *Winged Seeds* 22: 'Everywhere they tapped the reef, she was lousy with gold. They thought they'd struck a golden hole.'

Golden Mile, the 1 See quot. 1971
1901 May Vivienne *Travels in Western Australia* 210: From this place one has a glorious view of the other great mines on the Golden Mile, so-called on account of the marvellous quantity of gold that has been and still is being extracted from its depths – Lake View, Great Boulder, Ivanhoe, Boulder Perseverance, and Golden Horsehoe.
1908 E. G. Murphy *Jarrahland Jingles* 120: He has toiled along the Golden Mile among the cyanide.
1971 Colin Simpson *The New Australia* 557: The Golden Mile lies between Kalgoorlie and Boulder and is an extra-ordinarily rich auriferous reef area that is actually about two miles long and a third of a mile wide and has been mined to thousands of feet.
2 See quot. 1983
1982 *Sydney Morning Herald* 10 Jul. 35: Behind all this activity run constant rumours about a mass move of the gay establishments from this golden mile of Oxford Street.
1983 *Daily Telegraph* (Sydney) 5 Feb. 21: A trip along that section of Oxford Street that runs from Darlinghurst to Paddington which the gays call 'The Golden Mile'. It starts at the western, city, end at Patchs disco and is generally considered to run out at the Apollo restaurant, Paddington.

golden roo The dollar coin, bronze in colour with a kangaroo motif on the back, introduced in 1984
1984 *Australian* 14 Jun. 5: 'Golden 'roo coin' a headache for retailers [heading] The $1 coin is one month old today and despite gradually increasing community acceptance the 'Golden 'Roo' is still causing headaches for retailers, pensioners, hotel staff and the public transport system. Confusion between the coin and the 10c piece ... is causing problems for customers and shop-keepers alike.

Goldfields scavenger As for **willy-willy**: *rare*
1929 Jules Raeside *Golden Days* 341: Goldfields residents also knew of the 'Willy-willy', or, as it was sometimes called 'the Goldfields Scavenger'.

goldfish Tinned herrings, as issued to the Services in World War II
1942 *Salt* 25 May 8: *Goldfish* Herrings.
1944 Lawson Glassop *We Were the Rats* 224: 'Termorrer', said Eddie, 'we oughter have some goldfish'. Goldfish were herrings.
1952 T. A. G. Hungerford *The Ridge and the River*

189: 'Flaming pigeon-pie every day instead of bullamacow and goldfish!'
1962 Jock Marshall and Russell Drysdale *Journey Among Men* 104: 'Tell us about your part in that rather disagreeable goldfish business during the war' . . . 'It was not goldfish', said Dom quietly. 'The fish is *Nematalosa erebi*, a so-called bony bream. It is, in fact, a true herring – one of the soft-rayed clupeoid fishes.'
1970 Richard Beilby *No Medals for Aphrodite* 44: The monotony of bully and biscuits, rice and prunes, and the hated issue 'goldfish'.

golfer   A woman's cardigan, esp. in Queensland
1975 Hal Porter *The Extra* 178: Some delightful young Queensland maiden . . . who wears golfers, eats cracknels, and says, 'Oh scissors!'

golly *v. & n.*   To spit (*juvenile*)
1938 Encountered in conversation.
1941 Baker 32: *Gollion* A gob of phlegm.
1975 Les Ryan *The Shearers* 153: *Gobber* Ejaculation of saliva; a golly.
1978 Donald Hutley *The Swan* 48: He drew back from the nose and brought up from the chest and gollied out into the rain.

gonce   Money: *obsolescent* [? Yiddish]
1899 W. T. Goodge *Hits! Skits! and Jingles!* 159: 'The nearest guess will get the gonce as sure as you are there!'
1901 *Bulletin Reciter* 183: Yes, I'm doin' pretty middlin', / And I'm layin' up de gonce. Ibid. 194: And the nearest guess will get the gonce.
1916 Joseph Furphy *Poems* 17: Gonce to men of enterprise.
1918 Bernard Cronin *The Coastlanders* 114: 'They know how to treat a gent in them places, provided he has the gonze.'
1930 J. S. Litchfield *Far-North Memories* 8: 'Old dad can't spare any time for frills; but he's got the gonce all right. He's worth more than most of the first-class travellers on this boat.'
1941 Baker 32: *Gons* Money.

gone a million   see **million**

gone for a ride on the padre's bike   see **padre's**

gone to Gowings   see **Gowings**

gone to Moscow   see **Moscow**

Gong, the   1   Wollongong N.S.W.
1979 *Sun-Herald* 1 Jul. 42: The 'Gong: . . . a city brave or sad.
1980 *Sunday Telegraph* (Sydney) 13 Apr. 36: I don't know why a lady professor from the Gong launched her book in Melbourne.

1982 *Bulletin* 14 Dec. 52: Down in the 'Gong we're all on the dole / Looking for a job's like climbing a greasy pole.
2   Nickname of Evonne Cawley, née Goolagong
1982 *Sydney Morning Herald* 29 Nov. 22: 'It's good to have you back, Gong', Martina Navratilova told Evonne Cawley as they shook hands over the White City centre court net.

good iron   see **iron**

good-oh   Expression of agreement of approval; a state of well-being
1918 *Kia Ora Coo-ee* 15 Aug. 5: 'Fish for dinner to-day, Jack?' 'Good O! What sort?'
1923 Jack Moses *Beyond the City Gates* 166: 'You are to come and help . . . in the eating of the big fat turkey, the sucking pig and the plum pudding. Isn't that good oh!'
1924 *Truth* 27 Apr. 6: *Goodo* All right.
1925 Seymour Hicks *Hullo Australians* 225: I never say 'Thank you' now – I simply says 'Good-Oh!'
1934 Thomas Wood *Cobbers* 174: 'I've got to ask questions about you for the Census.' 'Good-o. Ask away.'
1940 Arnold Haskell *Waltzing Matilda* 36: If your companion says 'good oh' you know that he understands and approves.
1948 *Coast to Coast 1948* 122: 'Gee, you look good-o.'
1958 Frank Hardy *The Four-Legged Lottery* 36: 'Gee it must be good-oh at the races, Dad.' 'It's good-oh, all right.'
1963 Arthur Upfield *The Body at Madman's Bend* 69: 'Happen to see a tall bloke?' 'Yes, he just passed me.' . . . 'Goodoh!'
1970 Cynthia Nolan *A Bride for St Thomas* 57: 'Good-oh', I said, over-loudly, trying to get closer to the retreating wall, 'Right-oh, bonzer.'

good oil   see **oil**

good on you   Expression of approval, congratulation, goodwill
1908 Giles Seagram *Bushmen All* 84: One man said, 'Good on yer, Mac.'
1922 Arthur Wright *The Colt from the Country* 171: 'Good on you, mate,' he said. 'We'll have a go.'
1935 Kylie Tennant *Tiburon* 273: 'Good on her,' Polly said cheerfully. 'May be the best thing she's ever done.'
1942 Gavin Casey *It's Harder for Girls* 166: 'Good on you, dad,' said Williams over the side. 'Aw, go t' hell!' chattered the old man.
1954 *Sydney Morning Herald* 10 Feb. 4: More than 10,000 people at Newcastle Sportsground today clapped and shouted, 'Good on you, Philip', when the Duke of Edinburgh quickly opened up an

umbrella to shield the Queen from the rain. Ibid. 19 Feb. 6: Shouts of 'Good on you, Liz' and 'Good on you, Phil'.

1964 William Dick *A Bunch of Ratbags* 242: 'Good on yuh, Charlie. Good on yuh, Terry,' they said as they patted us on the back.

1974 L. Oakes and D. Solomon *Grab for Power* 486: 'We want Gough! We want Gough!' chanted the crowd. When he entered the Picador they sang 'Advance Australia Fair'. 'Good on yer, Gough baby!' they shouted. 'Good on yer, mate!'

1981 *Weekend Australian* 22 Aug. Mag. 8: Of course Lady Diana was a virgin bride – and good on her.

good, to come   see **come**

goofy, goofy-footer   See quots
1963 *Pix* 28 Sep. 62: *Goofy Foot*: Surfing with the right foot forward.

1964 Bruce Beaver *The Hot Sands* 10: The most remarkable feature of Lou's skill and finesse was his unconventional stance on the board. He was a 'Goofy Footer' – a right foot forward boy.

1983 *National Times* 7 Oct. 51: The 'goofy' tag simply means that he is the pedal version of a molly-dooker or a cacky-hander, or that when he stands on a surfboard, he puts his wrong (right) foot forward.

gooley   A stone of a suitable size for throwing (*juvenile*) [? f. Hindustani *goli* a bullet, ball]
1924 *Truth* 27 Apr. 6: *Gooley* A stone.

1941 Baker 32: *Gooly* A stone or pebble.

1949 Ruth Park *The Harp in the South* 47: 'Someone's been bunging goolies through her window.'

1963 John Cantwell *No Stranger to the Flame* 20: 'I lobbed it with a gooley and knocked it cold.'

1974 David Ireland *Burn* 18: 'Garn, get out of it,' Gunner says, 'before I let fly with a goolie.'

goom   Methylated spirits, In Aboriginal parlance
1977 Jim Ramsay *Cop it Sweet* 41: *Goom* Methylated spirits.

1982 *Meanjin* 453: Goom! What a name for methylated spirits.

goomee A metho drinker
1977 Kevin Gilbert *Living Black* 93: 'My uncle was a goomee and when he died it really broke me up.'

1982 *Sydney Morning Herald* 3 Jul. 29: Musgrave Park [in Brisbane] is also the home of the drones, or the goomies, a word used by the Aborigines themselves for a homeless black, and by the whites in a derogatory sense for a metho-drinker.

goon   A flagon of wine [urban Ab.]
1982 *Sydney Morning Herald* 13 Nov. 30: Tim Stanford started off drinking with 'the goon'. It's a

flagon of moselle or riesling.

1983 *Sydney Morning Herald* 23 Nov. 1: Three flagons of port (known as goons) have been consumed noisily [in Brewarrina] by about 8.30.

Gordon, in more trouble than Speed   Beset with extraordinary difficulties [f. the character in the comic strip]
1971 Alan Reid *The Gorton Experiment* 381: Scott, a pathetic figure in some ways, who had been in more trouble than Speed Gordon while Customs Minister, went quietly.

1974 John Powers *The Last of the Knucklemen* 14: We might just find ourselves in more trouble than Flash Gordon.

1980 *Daily Telegraph* (Sydney) 12 Mar. 48: Les Boyd has found himself in more trouble than Speed Gordon since his switch to Manly.

Gordon, went through like Speed   Jocular reply to request for someone's whereabouts
1948 Sumner Locke Elliott *Rusty Bugles* in *Khaki, Bush and Bigotry* ed. Eunice Hanger (1968) 31: 'Andy Edwards ... Andy Edwards there?' 'Went mad and they shot him.' 'Went through like Speed Gordon.'
see **shot through on the padre's bike, went for a crap and the sniper got him**

Gorillas, the   1   In Queensland, the Wilston-Grange Australian Rules team
1979 *Courier-Mail* (Brisbane) 28 May 18: Centre half forward Gary Maddison turned in another brilliant performance for the Gorillas.
2   Former nickname of the Fitzroy V.F.L. club
1984 Lou Richards *Sun* (Melbourne) 9 Mar. 31: To give the team a psychological lift and a bit of bite they changed their name to the Gorillas ... The idea was great – some of the players were built like Tarzan, but unfortunately for Fitzroy they played like Jane.

Government house   The residence of the owner or the manager on a sheep or cattle station, as distinct from the 'barracks' and the 'hut' qq.v., more often just 'the house'
1887 Simpson Newland *The Far North Country* 12: The 'Government House', as the operator's residence is called [at Charlotte Waters Telegraph Station], is the principal building, chiefly remarkable for ugliness and heat.

1896 Henry Lawson 'Stragglers' *Prose* i 91: 'Government House' is a mile away [from the wool shed], and is nothing better than a bush hut: this station belongs to a company.

1919 W. K. Harris *Outback in Australia* 2: 'Government House' (the owner's or manager's residence) on a big sheep station.

1936 A. W. Upfield *Wings Above the Diamantina*

77: Heading this class trilogy on the average station is the owner or manager, and his family. They reside in what is termed 'government house', the main residence on the property and centre from which it is directed.

1951 Ernestine Hill *The Territory* 444: *Government House* The homestead of a head station.

Government man A convict

1802 David Collins *An Account of the English Colony in New South Wales* ed. B. Fletcher (1975) ii 19: The following prices of labour were now established ... A government man allowed to officers or settlers in their own time 10d.

1820 *The Evidence of the Bigge Reports* ed. J. Ritchie (1971) i 85: Mr. Cox has allowed me to have a Government man in consequence of my marriage.

1835 *Colonist* 30 Apr. 140: He there meets with ... somebody's government man or convict-servant, who is desirous, of course, to treat him to some rum.

1843 Charles Rowcroft *Tales of the Colonies* ii 235: 'I must warn you, that we never speak of the convicts in this country by that term; we always call them "government men", or on some occasions, prisoners; but we never use the word "convict", which is considered by them as an insulting term.'

1854 W. Shaw *The Land of Promise* 49: The asperity of the word *convict* shocks their ears, so the more mollifying term of 'government man' has been substituted.

1864 James Armour *The Diggings, the Bush, and Melbourne* 16: From the talk that followed I learnt that nearly all the company had been 'Government men', as convicts style themselves.

1874 Charles de Boos *The Congewoi Correspondence* 148: As to bandicoots, they're like Government men, they never turn out in wet weather, but keep theirselves snug at home.

1882 Rolf Boldrewood *Robbery Under Arms* (World's Classics 1949) 8: Like a lot more of the Government men, as the convicts were always called round our part, he saved some money as soon as he had done his time.

1891 Edward Kinglake *The Australian at Home* 144: It is not their fault that their grandfather, perhaps, was seventy years ago a 'government man'.

Government stroke The indolent working style of government employee, originally on road work

1855 C. R. Thatcher 'The Bond Street Swell' cit. R. Ward *The Australian Legend* (1958) 117: And then he went upon the roads, / As many a young swell must ... / You may see him do the Gov'ment stroke / At eight bob every day.

1873 A. Trollope *Australia* ed. Edwards and Joyce

(1967) 190: In colonial parlance the government stroke is that light and easy mode of labour – perhaps that semblance of labour – which no other master will endure, though government is forced to put up with it.

1876 Rolf Boldrewood *A Colonial Reformer* (1890) 236: 'As long as they have their grub and their wages they'll hang it out ... regular Government stroke, as we say in this country.'

1903 Ada Cambridge *Thirty Years in Australia* 216: The labourer naturally prefers the Government stroke, and can be tempted away from that easy and pleasant way of passing his time only by an increased rate of wages.

1916 Macmillan's *Modern Dictionary of the English Language* 781: *government stroke* a half-hearted way of doing work, supposed to be characteristic of some government employees.

1933 Leslie Haylen *The Game Darrells* 172: The awful exhibition of the government stroke in the building of this line.

1949 George Farwell *Traveller's Tracks* 93: Why should the white fellow have a monopoly of the government stroke?

1969 Osmar White *Under the Iron Rainbow* 108: 'Once them New Australians get the idea of the Government stroke and union rules they leave the Aussies for dead when it comes to bludging.'

1979 Bill Scott *Tough in the Old Days* 74: The uninitiated, watching a gang of navvies at work, will speak scornfully of the 'Government stroke', and think they are watching lazy men.

Gowings, gone to Advertising slogan used in series of cartoons from the 1940s showing scenes vacated in a hurry by those seeking bargains [f. Sydney retail store]

1945 *Sun* (Sydney) 4 Jan. 2: Gone to Gowings [advertisement showing note left by bridegroom, with bride and congregation waiting in the church]

1979 *Sun-Herald* 4 Nov. 29: 111 years and they're still going to Gowing's [heading]

graft *n.* Work, esp. manual labour [? f. *grave* to dig c. 1000 OED; *graft* work of any description EDD 1891]

1853 John Rochfort *Adventures of a Surveyor* 47: Afterwards I could have obtained an engagement in my own profession at 300 l. a year, but, finding that I could make more money by 'hard graft', as they call labour in the colonies, I would not take it.

1892 William Lane *The Workingman's Paradise* 104: 'I've been out of graft for months and haven't got any money.'

1896 Edward Dyson *Rhymes from the Mines* 23: Not a man of us is weary, though the graft is pretty rough.

1935 Kylie Tennant *Tiburon* 199: He was tired of being an agrarian organiser in this west that

regarded hard graft and bad food and hard times as just as inevitable as a dust storm.
1957 Sydney Hart *Pommie Migrant* 81: 'What a mug ya are to come 12,000 miles to do this kind of graft for a living.'

graft *v.*   To work; to work hard
[**1859** Hotten: *Graft* to go to work]
1892 Harry Morant 'Paddy Magee' *Bulletin* 20 Feb. 14: What are you doing now, Paddy Magee? / Grafting, or spelling now, Paddy Magee?
1900 Henry Lawson 'Drought-stricken' *Prose* ii 96: They were very poor – often lived and grafted on damper, tea, and sugar.
1910 C. E. W. Bean *On the Wool Track* 129: 'He can't ride. He can graft a bit; but he's not much intelligence, oh no. He's an Englishman.'
c. **1919** Herbert Scanlon *Much in Little* 29: He informed me that he was grafting in the quarries.
1941 Kylie Tennant *The Battlers* 7: 'He grafted like a team of bullocks, and ... had me out ploughing and clearing and fencing.'

grafter   A hard worker
1901 F. J. Gillen *Diary* (1968) 277: Stephen like his brother John is an old friend of mine and a great grafter.
1918 C. J. Dennis *Backblock Ballads* 29: And though still a steady grafter, he grew restless ever after.
1953 *Caddie A Sydney Barmaid* 12: He was a grafter* and worked out in the bush six days a week. *In Australia a grafter is a very hard worker.

grand piano in a one-roomed house, couldn't find a   see couldn't

grandfather's pudding   An improvised bush delicacy: see quot.
1951 Ernestine Hill *The Territory* 426: 'grandfather's puddin' – stale damper soaked in black tea and sprinkled with sugar.

Grannies   Variant of **apples** q.v. [f. the Granny Smith apple]
1963 Bruce Beaver *The Hot Summer* 115: 'She'll be Grannies', cackled the ragged informant.

Granny   *The Sydney Morning Herald* (founded 1831 as *The Sydney Herald*) [see quot. 1931]
1851 *The Press* 23 Apr. 189: In the same number of 'My Grannie O', (which we beg to submit as a very good cognomen for the *Herald* and its antiquated and obsolete notions on the subject of government), there is a letter from the honorable member for Northumberland.
1901 Henry Lawson *Prose* ii 125: Even some London Conservative dailies come wonderfully refreshing to me after the *Sydney Morning Herald* ('Grannie').
1931 *A Century of Journalism* 239: The *Herald* has long been affectionately – and sometimes contemptuously – known as 'Granny'. The nickname being supposed to refer to its age, its allegedly conservative methods and the untiring energy with which it has always dealt out advice, comment, and criticism.
1940 Arnold L. Haskell *Waltzing Matilda* 176: The dean of papers is the *Sydney Morning Herald*, 'Grannie', an organ of conservative views and amazing respectability.
1950 Jon Cleary *Just Let Me Be* 241: 'You're beginning to talk like some old spinster,' Harry said. 'You'll be writing letters to Granny Herald next.'

grape on the business, a   Someone whose presence spoils things for others; an odd man out [? variant of *gooseberry*]
1941 Baker 32: *Grape on the Business, A* (of a person) One who is a blue stocking, a wallflower or a drag on cheery company.
1944 Lawson Glassop *We Were the Rats* 9: 'I've got nobody to go with. All the girls'll be going with their boy friends and I don't want to be a grape on the business.'
1946 Alan Marshall *Tell us about the Turkey, Jo* 62: She hasn't got a bloke. She is a grape on the business.

grass castles, kings in   1   See quot. 1878
1878 Patrick Durack in Mary Durack *Kings in Grass Castles* (1959) title page: 'Cattle Kings' ye call us, then we are Kings in grass castles that may be blown away upon a puff of wind.
1984 *Age* (Melbourne) 21 Mar. 11. When the kings in grass castles divided the land among themselves, Aborigines were needed to work the cattle and their dependants were tolerated.
2   The mansions built in Griffith N.S.W. from supposed profits from growing marijuana
1980 Alfred W. McCoy *Drug Traffic* 291: The Grass Castles of Griffith [subheading]
1984 *Sydney Morning Herald* 17 Oct. 15: The murder ... of Donald Mackay, who had been campaigning against the 'kings in grass castles' of the Griffith marijuana trade, was probably the biggest mistake ever made by organised crime in Australia.

grasshopper, knee-high to a   Used to express diminutive size, or extreme youth [listed by Partridge as Canadian]
1941 Kylie Tennant *The Battlers* 7: 'When I wasn't knee-high to a grasshopper he had me out ploughing and clearing and fencing.'
1951 Dal Stivens *Jimmy Brockett* 161: Ever since I'd been knee-high to a grasshopper I'd loved the

fight game.
1961 Tom Ronan *Only a Short Walk* 135: Only a little thing – knee-high to a grasshopper, you could say.

grasshoppers   Visitors to Canberra, esp. in tourist groups, as distinct from the permanent residents
1965 *Sydney Morning Herald* 3 Jul. 5: A full bus-load of 'grass-hoppers' (the Canberra term for tourists – 'they eat everything in sight and never have a drink').
1969 Leslie Haylen *Twenty Years' Hard Labor* 204: The private member has, however, his visitors from the electorate. Now ... they arrive in such numbers that they have come to be called 'the grasshoppers'. They come in a cloud, eat everything about the place.
1972 *Sydney Morning Herald* 3 Nov. 6: At last the politicians are gone from Parliament and have dispersed to their electorates ... King's Hall ... has been taken over by 'grasshoppers' – an old Canberra nickname for tourists.

greasy   1   An outback cook; any cook for a collection of men [f. grease on clothes]
1873 J. C. F. Johnson *Christmas on Carringa* 1: Bill, who himself was our *chef d' cuisine* ... in the vernacular, cook or 'greasy', had on this occasion quite excelled his usual excellence.
1919 W. H. Downing *Digger Dialects* 27: *Greasy* A cook.
1938 *Smith's Weekly* 19 Nov. 22: 'Greasy' was the officers' mess cook, but sad to relate, he was not an expert.
1953 T. A. G. Hungerford *Riverslake* 148: 'God, cooks aren't people!' Carmichael retorted ... 'I'm going to write a book about greasies one day!'
2   A shearer
1956 F. B. Vickers *First Place to the Stranger* 134: 'When those five greasies get moving they'll shear a lot of sheep.'
1963 *Sydney Morning Herald* 17 Aug. 11: A lot of greasies (shearers) get hen trouble. Some shearers' wives reckon we shearer blokes are either too tired, too drunk or too far away.
1975 Les Ryan *The Shearers* 123: 'The greasies have hung up. Why can't we?'

greasy pig, a   In two-up, a throw of tails after a succession of heads
1949 Lawson Glassop *Lucky Palmer* 174: 'Come on, gents, he's done 'em four times. Here's a chance for a greasy pig!'

Great Adventure, the   Australian participation in World War I, esp. the Gallipoli expedition
1918 *Kia Ora Coo-ee* 15 Mar. 1: The Great Adventure [heading] April 25th., 1915. What a host of memories the date conjures up.

1935 H. R. Williams *Comrades of the Great Adventure* [book title]

great Australian adjective, novel   see **Australian**

Great Divide, the   The Great Dividing Range
1907 Charles MacAlister *Old Pioneering Days in the Sunny South* 1: John Hamilton Hume ... first bore the white man's burden across the Great Divide.
1914 A. B. Paterson 'Song of the Wheat' in *Song of the Pen* (1983) 364: It's west by south of the Great Divide / The grim grey plains run out.
1983 *Sydney Morning Herald* 30 Apr. 29: City folk ... may forget that there is life beyond the Great Divide. The CWA does not.

Great White Shark   The fair-haired golfer Greg Norman
1984 *Weekend Australian* 23 Jun. Mag. 3: In the 1981 US Masters he finished fourth, but gained considerable attention with his 'shark hunting' stories, and thus became known as The Great White Shark ... 'Actually, I never went out hunting sharks at all. I only shot at some when I became irritated that they were eating the fish I was catching. And I only did that a few times.'

Greek's, the   The local milk bar, café, etc. (often run by Greeks)
1946 Margaret Trist *What Else is There?* 144: She caught up with Mamie and Teddy outside the Greek's. 'How about an ice-cream?' asked Teddy.
1953 T. A. G. Hungerford *Riverslake* 234: 'Sometimes they eat at the Greek's, down at the Kingston shops.'
1968 Geoffrey Dutton *Andy* 176: Steak and eggs and a cup of ghastly coffee at the Greek's.
1977 Ted Roberts *Lindsay's Boy* in *Five Plays* ed. Alrene Sykes 234: 'Should be out celebrating. What about a feed at the Greeks?'

green and gold   Australia's sporting colours in international competition (unofficial until 1984)
1981 *Sydney Morning Herald* 18 May 28: Their lack of heart and fight must have been nauseating to the great players who have worn the green and gold in the past.
1984 *Bulletin* 15 May 124: Prime Minister Hawke's announcement that Australia's official colours were to be green and gold has caused some consternation at the Australian Bicentennial Authority, which has formally colored itself blue and gold.

green cart   The van supposed to take people to the mental asylum
1959 Dorothy Hewett *Bobbin Up* 109–10: 'You're mad, that what's up with you. They'll come for you

in the green cart one of these days me lady and not before time.'
1975 *Overland 62* 27: The green cart will come for me, and I'll disappear into Callan Park, and that will be some kind of solution.

Green Rats, the Warringah (N.S.W.) Rugby Union club [f. Rats of Tobruk, battling against odds]
1982 *Sun-Herald* 1 Aug. 77: Year of the green rats is coming [heading] For the first time, Warringah look like they could win the Rugby premiership.

Green Season See quot. 1979
1979 *NT News* (Darwin) 3 Nov. 12: It's official! There's no more wet season as far as the tourist people in the Top End are concerned . . . As from last month and until March Top Enders will be going through the Green Season. And that's how the tourist people are promoting the old wet season.
1983 *Sydney Morning Herald* 15 Jan. 26: 'The Green' is the Territory's new name for the wet and it's supposed to keep the tourists coming.

greengrocer A variety of cicada [f. colouring]
1951 Dymphna Cusack and Florence James *Come In Spinner* 106: 'Mine's a Greengrocer – look!' Durras opened his hand carefully, showing a cicada with iridescent wings folded back on a body of delicate green.
1959 Anne von Bertouch *February Dark* 124: Through the shimmer of heat and the drilling song Helen saw the beautiful cicadas of childhood, the Black Prince, the Greengrocer, the Yellow Monday, held on a child's small hand.
1976 Douglas Stewart *Southerly* 177: Yellow Monday and Greengrocer / High and far and shrill and closer / In the trees begin their din.

greenie A supporter of the 'green bans' imposed by the Builders Labourers Federation in 1973 on demolition and development projects considered contrary to principles of 'conservation'; a trendy conservationist
1973 *Nation Review* 28 Sep. 1572: The local greenies have despaired of stopping the dreaded post office tower by indirect means, and have started on a little direct action.
1973 *Australian* 1 Oct. 7: The middle class 'greenies' have an unusual stake in the elections.
1981 *Age* (Melbourne) 5 Oct. 10: Her father, a retired professor, is leading a battle by greenies to save from 'development' the inner-suburban street in which he lives.
1983 *Sun-Herald* 13 Feb. 24: Organisation for Tasmanian Development posters are chilling: 'Fertilise the SW – bulldoze a greenie.'

Greens, the Galloping The Randwick (N.S.W.)

Rugby Union team (also the Wicks) [f. team colours]
1974 *Australian* 26 Sep. 20: Eels to knock gloss off the Greens.

Gregory's *Gregory's Sydney Street Directory*, first published by Cecil Albert Gregory in 1934
1983 Peter Corris *The Empty Beach* 93: My *Gregorys* showed Mark Lane to be a little trickle of a thoroughfare in Clovelly near the boundary with Randwick.

grey In two-up, a double-headed penny, or a penny with two tails [f. English thieves' slang OED 1812–68]
[**1812** Vaux: *Gray*: a half-penny, or other coin, having two heads or two tails, and fabricated for the use of gamblers, who, by such a deception, frequently win large sums.]
1898 *Bulletin* 3 Sep. 32: He'd simply smashed the two-up school / (Assisted by a 'grey'!)
1943 Baker 35: *Gray* A double-tailed penny.
1946 K. S. Prichard *The Roaring Nineties* 387: A spieler had been caught ringing in the grey, a two-headed penny, and the boys were giving him a rough time. Ibid. 125: 'The grey', a penny with two tails.
1975 Les Ryan *The Shearers* 153: *Greys* Double tail pennies.

grey bomber As for **grey ghost** q.v.
1983 *Newcastle Herald* 8 Feb. 3: Six parking officers, or grey bombers as they are better known, are being trained in Newcastle.

grey ghost A N.S.W. parking policeman, successor to the **brown bomber** q.v. [f. colour of uniform]
1976 *Sydney Morning Herald* 10 Jul. 1: Don't think you can park just anywhere in the City during the national strike – the police will get the Grey Ghosts on the job.
1979 *West Australian* (Perth) 5 Dec. 8: Sometimes derisively and sometimes jocularly referred to as 'grey ghosts', Perth's parking inspectors must rank as one of the most maligned groups in the city.
1983 *Sun-Herald* 11 Dec. 37: About 18 grey ghosts are rostered on weekend nights because of heavily increased parking in popular areas.

grey meanie A parking policeman in Victoria [f. colour of uniform]
1971 *Sunday Australian* 1 Aug. 3: Mr McMahon walked into the hotel's lounge and took tea. Meanwhile one of Melbourne's famous 'grey meanies' slapped the ticket on the Prime Minister's car.
1984 *Age* (Melbourne) 3 Apr. 17: Grey meanies, and how to beat them [heading]

greys, Hexham see **Hexham**

grid (iron)   A bicycle: *obsolescent*
  1941 Baker 32: *Grid (iron)* A bicycle.
  1942 Gavin Casey *It's Harder for Girls* 125: 'Here, you go on, on my grid, an' I'll do the walking.'
  1955 F. B. Vickers *The Mirage* 114: 'You'll see him wheelin' the grid along the Ninety Mile Beach.'
  1962 Stuart Gore *Down the Golden Mile* 128: Riding his father's ramshackle old grid; wobbling, with a leg thrust under the top bar to reach the offside pedal.

grog   General term for alcoholic drink, usually beer [f. *grog* as rum (and water) OED 1770]
  1833 George Fletcher Moore *Diary of Ten Years* (1884) 185: With you 'grog' means a mixture of spirits and water, in the ratio of one to three, or one to four − no such thing here − it means unmixed ardent spirits.
  1938 Xavier Herbert *Capricornia* 256: 'Sorry − I've knocked your grog over. Let's buy another . . . What are you drinking?' 'Double whiskey.'
  1949 Lawson Glassop *Lucky Palmer* 8: 'Likes his beer, does Darky.' Clarrie groaned. 'The grog,' he said. 'He can't beat the grog.'
  1953 *The Sunburnt Country* ed. Ian Bevan 126: Grog is beer: and beer, to the A.I.F. is sacred. The first sound heard from any Australian convoy arriving in any foreign port will always be the cry 'How's the beer?'
  1964 George Johnston *My Brother Jack* 379: 'We could go up to the Royal Empire and have a grog.'
  1973 Alexander Buzo *Rooted* 44: 'Hammo had been on the grog and he didn't give way to his right and this bloke smashed into him.'
  grog on   To continue steady drinking
  1965 John Beede *They Hosed Them Out* 185: We grogged on till closing time; it was evident we all had one thing in common − a liking for the amber liquid.
  1979 Bobbie Hardy *The World Owes Me Nothing* 146: The pubs were full of shearers grogging on and waiting for a break in the weather.
  grog-up   As for **beer-up** q.v.
  1962 Alan Seymour *The One Day of the Year* 77: 'We're sick of all the muck that's talked about this day . . . It's just one long grog-up.
  see **sly-grog**

Groper   As for **Sandgroper** q.v.
  1908 E. G. Murphy *Jarrahland Jingles* 29: 'Give me the goblet of good ruddy wine!' / Cried a Groperland Poet who gropes.
  1926 J. Vance Marshall *Timely Tips for New Australians: Groper* A West Australian.
  1929 Jules Raeside *Golden Days* 125: Many of the 'Gropers' (early settlers) of the West.

Grouper   A member of one of the 'Industrial Groups' set up in the Labor Party in 1945–6 to counter Communist influence in the trade unions
  1955 *Sydney Morning Herald* 27 Apr. 1: Last year the groupers altered the rules to give two delegates for every 250 members from a State electoral council.
  1956 *Daily Telegraph* (Sydney) 11 Apr. 3: Supporters of the industrial groups have laid charges against non-groupers.
  1959 Dorothy Hewett *Bobbin Up* 128: 'That Grouper Short stopped my Frank sellin' 'is *Tribs* outside the Trade Union Club.'
  1964 *Australian* 22 Jul. 8: They tend to see themselves as upholders of the pure faith of anti-Grouperism.
  1985 *Sydney Morning Herald* 24 Apr. 5: He [Fred Daly] said that the activities of the 'groupers' meant that he and his mates spent the best years of their political lives in the wilderness.

groupie   A participant in the Group Settlement scheme in Western Australia in the 1920s, under which hundred-acre allotments were made to English emigrants in the backward south-west
  1972 M. L. Skinner *The Fifth Sparrow* 119: Few of the 'groupies' knew anything about farming at all and the raw land daunted and frustrated them.
  1979 Justina Williams *White River* 11: I had to milk three of the cows . . . My mother milked three, my father four, so caring for the total that the authorities provided for each groupie, as they were called.
  1983 John K. Ewers *Long Enough for a Joke* 111: The Collie miners were earning good money; the groupies were earning only sustenance.

grouse   Excellent, outstanding: *obsolescent* [origin unknown]
  1924 *Truth* 27 Apr. 6: *Grouse* something good.
  1944 Lawson Glassop *We Were the Rats* 5: 'You know them two grouse sheilas we've got the meet on with tomorrer night?'
  1953 T. A. G. Hungerford *Riverslake* 74: 'Seven o'clock, O.K.?' 'Yeah, that'll be grouse.'
  1959 Eric Lambert *Glory Thrown In* 72: 'That was grouse!' he said . . . 'You should have been in it.'
  1963 John Cantwell *No Stranger to the Flame* 81: 'Same when we were kids − always getting between me and the grouse things.'
  1974 Jim McNeil *How Does Your Garden Grow* 111: 'And then there's the advertising in the papers . . . usually with a grouse sheila in the picture all ready to get her gear off if yer use whatever stuff they're trying to sell yer.'
  1982 Ford Ray *Bulletin* 12 Jan. 10: My recollection is that 'grouse' was used in three forms. 1. Grouse, as in 'What a grouse lookin' sheila.' 2. Extra grouse, as in 'That was extra grouse tucker, Mrs Dutton', and finally, the superlative degree 3.

THE grouse, as in 'I reckon a cold beer on a scorcher like this would be the grouse!'
1983 *Sun-Herald* 24 Jul. 71: In three words it's grouse Shakespeare, mate.

grouter, come in on the   To seek benefit from a situation not of one's own making, esp. in two-up by withholding any bet until a run of heads or tails indicates that a change must soon occur (hence a 'grouter bet')
1918 *Kia Ora Coo-ee* 15 Oct. 14: The pudding had gone and someone had got in on a grouter.
1919 W. H. Downing *Digger Dialects* 27: *Grouter* An unfair advantage. 'Come on the grouter' – gain an unfair advantage.
1941 Baker 36: *Grouter* one who takes advantage of others. (2) An unfair advantage. Whence 'on the grouter', on the lookout for something for nothing.
1944 Lawson Glassop *We Were the Rats* 113: 'I reckon you Seventh Div. jokers have come in on the grouter.' I felt ashamed. 'Our turn'll come,' I said. 'We've got to do some more training yet.' Ibid. 129: 'Looks as if you blokes are going to come in on the grouter.'
1946 K. S. Prichard *The Roaring Nineties* 125: Sometimes a successful bettor twisted, after backing heads, and backed tails: 'Catching the grouter,' that was called. But a grouter bettor could only have one or two bets a night.
1949 Lawson Glassop *Lucky Palmer* 174: 'A real grouter bet, gents,' he said. 'Any tailie who missed out on that run of heads can come in on the grouter now.'
1954 Tom Ronan *Vision Splendid* 230: 'Bloke here headed 'em eight times. Good chance for a grouter.'
1965 Wally Grout *My Country's 'Keeper* 90: I saw a cove who had been watching me play the machine step up to it, whip in a few coins, and crack the jackpot. A nice easy way to earn a living. We call that 'coming in on the grouter.'
1970 Richard Beilby *No Medals for Aphrodite* 239: Turk was an inveterate tail-better while Squeaker liked to 'come in on the grouter', when the odds against the spinner had considerably lengthened.

grubber   Hospital [listed by Partridge as 'A casual ward: tramps' c. (–1932)']
1973 Frank Huelin *Keep Moving* 90: 'How'd ya feel, mate?' he asked. 'Ya'll have ter go ta th' grubber.'

grunter   A promiscuous woman [f. *pig* prostitute]
1973 Alexander Buzo *Rooted* 70: 'I'll line up a bird for you, too. I know a couple of grunters.'

gub, gubbah   Aboriginal term for a white
1972 *Sydney Morning Herald* 2 Nov. 12: Mr Gub

is ... the white man. The word is the diminutive of garbage.
1973 *Australian* 12 Dec. 14: He [Kevin Gilbert] sat in a coffee shop in Redfern with his present European wife Cora (his 'favourite gubbah').
1981 Peter Corris *White Meat* 41: 'You were too late gubb, someone else got him first.' Ibid. 100: 'We don't like gubbs who hang around bull-shitting us.'
1982 *Sydney Morning Herald* 14 Feb. 7: A young Aboriginal woman described last month how she walked into a hotel [in Moree] to find a black man drinking alone with whites. She told him sneeringly that he was a 'gubber lover'.

Gucci Kid, Mr Gucci   Mr Andrew Peacock [f. the joke by the actress Shirley MacLaine that he used a Gucci toothbrush]
[**1981** Russell Schneider *The Colt from Kooyong* 133: MacLaine helped fuel the rumours with her remark to a Sydney nightclub audience that Peacock was the only man she knew who kept a Gucci toothbrush in his bathroom.]
1982 *Townsville Daily Bulletin* 26 Mar. 4: He is known as the Suntan Kid – or, because of his taste in toothbrush and tie, the Gucci Kid.
1982 *National Times* 5 Sep. 7: Former ministerial star Andrew Peacock is known as 'the Sunlamp Kid' or 'Gucci'.

guernsey, get a   To gain recognition or approval; succeed [f. selection in a sporting team]
1918 Let. in Bill Gammage *The Broken Years* (1974) 218: In 1918 troops chosen for an attack 'got their guernseys.'
1964 George Johnston *My Brother Jack* 298: 'As long as you're going to get a guernsey, that's the main thing.'
1974 Senator J. McClelland *Australian Humanist* No. 31 7: This extra channel ... will give us ... programmes for ethnic groups, art, technology, all the things that are never going to get a guernsey in the present setup.
1976 *Sydney Morning Herald* 30 Apr. 1: Sydney gets a guernsey in the book, *The 300 Best Hotels in the World,* just published by Thomas Cook.
1981 *Sunday Mail* (Brisbane) 27 Sep. 2: Two well known Brisbane racing scribes were delighted recently to score a guernsey for last Wednesday's plush Horse of the Year bash in Melbourne.

guiver, gyver   Flattering pretence; loquacity; general 'carry-on': *obsolescent* [? Yiddish]
1864 *Thatcher's Colonial Ministrel* 13: 'I'll give you the sack pretty quick, / If my wife you offend with your guiver.'
1899 Barrère and Leland 436: *Guiver* (theatrical) flattery, artfulness.
1899 W. T. Goodge *Hits! Skits! and Jingles!* 18: I

ain't got the style and guiver/ Of them bank clerks and students and sich.
1901 *The Bulletin Reciter* 16: And you should have seen his guiver when he scalped the bullock-driver.
1902 Henry Fletcher *The Waybacks in Town and at Home* 22: 'But yous er bloke as knows ther inside runnin' o' things; tell me, straight, what's this Federation guiver all amount ter?'
1915 C. J. Dennis *The Songs of a Sentimental Bloke* 79: I s'pose the wimmin git some sorter fun / Wiv all this guyver.
1924 *Truth* 27 Apr. 6: *Guyver* pretence.
1947 Vance Palmer *Cyclone* 68: 'Chuck that cheap guyver, Con. It doesn't suit you. Leave it to the girls in Finnegan's bar.'
1951 Dal Stivens *Jimmy Brockett* 102: Helen didn't put on as much guiver as the others.
1962 Dymphna Cusack *Picnic Races* 19: 'Lotta jumped-up blow-ins putting on more guyver than the Governor's wife.'

Gulf country The country near the Gulf of Carpentaria in Queensland
1872 *Punch Staff Papers* 62: Talk of the Gulf country, and the Great Australian Bight – they are fertile paradise compared to the district between Albany and Perth.
1892 Barcroft Boake 'Skeeta' *Bulletin* 17 Dec. 14 repr. in *Where the Dead Men Lie* (1897) 87: And gave Harry Parker the order to go to 'the Gulf' for the mob.
1901 Henry Lawson 'Telling Mrs Baker' *Prose* i 416: He was going North to new country round by the Gulf of Carpentaria ... I and my mate Andy M'Culloch, engaged to go with him. We wanted to have a look at the Gulf Country.
1906 A. B. Paterson *An Outback Marriage* 4: He was out in the Gulf-country in the early days.
1911 C. E. W. Bean *The 'Dreadnought' of the Darling* 96: You find the cattle to this day farther out – in the country which is still unfenced up by 'the Gulf'. n. The Gulf of Carpentaria is known by Australians as 'the Gulf'.
1938 Eric Lowe *Salute to Freedom* 570: 'Up in the Gulf country some of the boys used to send stories to Brisbane and Sydney papers. They got a few bob out of it.'
1957 R. S. Porteous *Brigalow* 10–11: 'I put in two years jackerooing in the Gulf Country.'

gully-raker 1 One of those engaged in **gully-raking** q.v.
[**1865** Hotten 148: *Gully-rakers* cattle thieves in Australia, the cattle being stolen out of almost inaccessible valleys, there termed *gullies*.]
1869 E. C. Booth *Another England* 138: The old fellow had lost his team, and had been seeking them ever since. Hearing that the 'gully-rakers'

about were not very particular, he had travelled down the river as far as Shepperton.
2 A long whip
1881 A. C. Grant *Bush-Life in Queensland* i 40: Following up his admonition by a sweeping cut of his 'gully-raker', and a report like a musket-shot.
1919 W. K. Harris *Outback in Australia* 85: Long whips with short handles, and short whips with long handles, eight strands and upwards, from the redoubtable old 'gully-rakers' to the exaggerated thong affixed to a hunting crop.

gully-raking The rounding up of unbranded cattle by searching the gullies and other places where they may have been overlooked; illegally appropriating cattle by this practice [*gully* in Australian usage is not limited to a channel made by a watercourse]
[**1855** William Howitt *Land, Labour and Gold* ii 225: Our way from Bendigo was through a rather fine country, with ever-succeeding swells and glades, or gullies, as they call them here; though a gully, to my mind, is a deep, narrow ravine torn out by a watercourse. But here the broadest and smoothest valleys, or any dimple amongst the hills, is a gully.]
1847 Alexander Harris *Settlers and Convicts* ed. C. M. H. Clark (1954) 140: If he could find an unbranded beast in the bush, had no qualms about making it his own by clapping his brand on it. In this way, by a process technically called 'gully-raking', he had quadrupled the little herd his father gave him.
1857 F. Cooper *Wild Adventures in Australia* 104: 'He was stock-keeping in that quarter, and was rather given to "gulley raking". One fine day it appears he ran in three bullocks belonging to a neighbouring squatter, and clapt his brand on top of the other so as to efface it.'
1875 Rolf Boldrewood *The Squatter's Dream* repr. as *Ups and Downs* (1878) 236: A long-legged, brown-faced, long-haired son of the soil, of the worst type of pound-haunting, gully-raking bush native, returned without the horses.

gumleaves, the smell of Symbol of what is authentically Australian, perhaps from the influence of Lawson's short story 'His Country – After All'
1894 Henry Lawson 'His Country – After All' *Prose* i 203: 'The smell of them gum leaves set me thinking'. And he thought some more.... 'What do you Britishers know about Australia? She's as good as England, anyway'.
1947 Margaret Trist *Daddy* 126: She went abroad. Now she's come back a sort of success woman ... Once you get rid of the smell of gum-leaves you can cash in on anything.
1982 Bill O'Reilly *Sydney Morning Herald* 23 Oct. 56: As soon as he [Brett Henschell] took his stance

and played his first shot past point I detected an almost overpowering smell of gumleaves ... The vigorous manner in which he belts his side-on shots through the off, the purposeful way in which he chances his arm by smacking straight into the pitch of on-side deliveries, all acknowledge that he comes from the wide open spaces.

gumsucker A native of Victoria; a native-born Australian [? f. *gumtree*: see quot. 1885]
1855 William Howitt *Land, Labour and Gold* i 24: Bitten twice by the over 'cute 'gum-suckers' as the native Victorians are called.
1859 Frank Fowler *Southern Lights and Shadows* 24: Your thorough-bred gumsucker never speaks, without apostrophising his 'oath', and interlarding his diction with the crimsonest of adjectives.
1865 J. F. Mortlock *Experiences of a Convict* (1965) 230: Both Sydney and Melbourne boast of establishments dignified by the term University; being on a par with English public schools. The attempt to educate, as at Cambridge or Oxford, young 'gumsuckers' savours of the absurd.
1885 *The Australasian Printers' Keepsake* 20: Our Colonial lads showed their right to the appellation of 'Gumsucker', by chewing transparent lumps that appended from the silver-wattle.
1903 Joseph Furphy *Such is Life* (1944) 44: When anybody calls him a Port Philliper, or a Vic., or a 'Sucker, he comes out straight ... 'I'm a Cornstalk, born in New South Wales.'
1914 Nathan Spielvogel *The Gumsucker at Home* 9: I hoped to wander all around Victoria, spending a few weeks in each place, and so in the course of four of five years to know all about the land of the Gumsucker.

gumtree, up a In great difficulties, in a state of confusion (like an animal which has been treed) [? US song 'possum up a gumtree' Mathews 1831]
[**1888** W. S. S. Tyrwhitt *The New Chum in the Queensland Bush* 150: The opossum, more generally known as the possum, as a rule occupies his proverbial position in a gum tree.]
1941 Baker 33: *Gumtree, up a* In trouble, in a quandary.
1945 Gavin Casey *Downhill is Easier* 87: They wanted to known whether or not we'd been kidded up a gum-tree, and they shouted and roared a lot about it.
1958 Douglas Stewart *Four Plays* 163: 'He's up a gum-tree. Bushed, I tell you, near Greta. / He's running round in circles.'
1973 *Sun-Herald* 25 Mar. 108: Up a gumtree [heading] During the Yugoslav Premier's visit, energetic policemen went along the shores of Lake Burley Griffin shaking young gum trees. Security cars in the motorcade were marked with special markings on the roofs, so they could be spotted by

police sharp-shooters overhead.
1982 *National Times* 15 Aug. 12: 'It was not until the analyst sent back his magnificent document ... that we realised we were up the original gum tree.'

gun *n. & a.* A shearer with a high tally; anyone pre-eminent in some activity [f. *big gun, great gun* OED 1815]
1898 'Whaler's Rhyme' *Bulletin* 9 Jul. Red Page repr. in *Old Bush Songs* ed. Stewart and Keesing (1957) 250: There's brand-new-chums and cockies' sons, / They fancy that they are great guns.
1933 Acland: *Gun, big gun* A really fast shearer, one who could ring most sheds.
1940 Ion L. Idriess *Lightning Ridge* 152: The 'gun shearer' there was a two hundred-a-day man, the tally of the lowest was over a hundred a day.
1957 D'Arcy Niland *Call Me When the Cross Turns Over* 131: He was a champion at other things too. He was a gun potato-digger and pea-picker.
1961 George Farwell *Vanishing Australians* 51: You heard tales of 'gun' drovers still in the saddle, of famous ones now passed away.
1971 *Sydney Morning Herald* 29 Oct. 14: He [John Benaud] was N.S.W.'s gun batsman last summer with 782 runs with an average of 55.86.
1982 *Sydney Morning Herald* 12 Aug. 1: The NSW secretary of the AWU ... says only a few gun shearers are left. 'They've got out because the pay's no good.'

gundy An Aboriginal hut
1876 Rolf Boldrewood *A Colonial Reformer* (1891) 204: There were a dozen 'goondies' to be visited, and their inmates started to their work.
1908 Mrs Aeneas Gunn *We of the Never-Never* 186: The camp-fires were all around us: dozens of them, grouped in and out among the gundies.
1956 Tom Ronan *Moleskin Midas* 158: 'Men I've known ... Not miserable rats waiting outside a blackfellow's gundy for the buck to send out the gin when he's done with her himself.'

Gundy, no good to Applied to something adverse: *obsolescent* [origin unknown]
1919 W. H. Downing *Digger Dialects* 35: *No good to gundy* Of no advantage.
1922 E. O'Ferrall *Bodger and the Boarders* 46: One of them scrawled 'I don't want none of youre dam sympathy. Out 'ere it's 107 in shade and all that there talk about comin and settin be fires made me sweat like an orse. No good to Gundy.'
1923 Jack Moses *Beyond the City Gates* 128: 'Taint no good to Gundy to see the fluid go, / When you're cockyin' and battlin' and live on what you grow.
1937 *Best Australian One-Act Plays* 204: 'That's

not the point. Privately's no good to Gundy. The shilling's neither here nor there.'
1968 Stuart Gore *Holy Smoke* 35: 'This is no good to gundy, they say.'

gungible See quot. [urban Ab.]
1983 *Sydney Morning Herald* 7 Dec. 11: A white person could be mistaken as a gungible (police officer).

gunyah An Aboriginal hut (Morris, 1798), but applied colloquially to shelters improvised by whites
1841 *A Mother's Offering to Her Children* 150: They only went two miles that afternoon; and then encamped: making a snug hut, or gunyah, with boughs.
1853 S. Mossman and T. Banister *Australia Visited and Revisited* 53: He [the gold-digger] would be as much at home lying down in his dirty clothes for weeks together, in a tent or bark gunya, as he was at home on his straw pallet in his mud cabin.
1859 Let. in M. H. Walker *Come Wind, Come Weather* (1971) 96: Our gunyah was between two young trees being placed from one to the other about four feet from the ground. Against this sheets of bark were reared overlapping one another, on these heavy branches were laid to keep them in place and at each end boughs were put to keep out the wind.
1882 Rolf Boldrewood *Robbery Under Arms* (World's Classics 1949) 112: As we rode up we could see a gunya made out of boughs, and a longish wing of a dog-leg fence.
1903 William Craig *My Adventures on the Australian Goldfields* 113: Other shelter and accommodation had, however, to be obtained, and the following day we procured from Spring Creek the necessary calico for a 'gunyah'.
1919 E. S. Sorenson *Chips and Splinters* 12: The sawyers, whose home was a bark gunyah nearby, were tradesmen whose work was important to them.

guts, come (give) one's To inform to the police, or other authority
[c. **1882** *The Sydney Slang Dictionary* 2: *Come it* To inform.]
1945 Tom Ronan *Strangers on the Ophir* 172: 'He'll give away all his guts to try and save his worthless hide.'
1953 Kylie Tennant *The Joyful Condemned* 295: The sullen, big oaf, baited and jeered at by everyone, a man who had 'come his guts to the coppers', was almost driven desperate.
1959 Dorothy Hewett *Bobbin Up* 135: 'She's in the manager's office half the day, with her legs crossed so you can see everythin' she's got, givin'

him all our guts.'
1961 Xavier Herbert *Soldiers' Women* 272: 'You gotta be careful not to give ya guts. Every word you say's writ down and goes to the beak.'
1966 Elwyn Wallace *Sydney and the Bush* 141: 'Me? Come me guts? A top-off?'

guts, in the In two-up, referring to bets placed 'in the ring' as distinct from 'on the side'
1948 Sumner Locke Elliott *Rusty Bugles* in *Khaki, Bush and Bigotry* ed. Eunice Hanger (1968) 30: 'I'll spin 'em for a quid ... Get set in the guts ... Another two bob for the guts.'
1951 Eric Lambert *The Twenty Thousand Thieves* 235: 'Heads it is! I want two quid in the guts! Gentlemen, I require two fiddleys in the old comic cuts!'
1965 Leslie Haylen *Big Red* 101: Outside he could hear the gamblers: 'Come on, I want a dollar in the guts.'
1975 Les Ryan *The Shearers* 96: 'Money up or shut up!' Lofty called out. 'Four quid wanted in the guts.'

guts, rough as Extremely rough or uncouth
1966 Bruce Beaver *You Can't Come Back* 118: 'I'm shy all right, but I'm not smooth ... I'm rough as guts.'
1968 Frank Hardy *Unlucky Australians* 11: 'The old Territorian is a good bloke, rough as guts but his heart's in the right place.'
1978 Helen Hodgman *Jack and Jill* 89: She was getting rough as guts – just like her Dad.

guts, the good Reliable information (mainly Services slang)
1919 W. H. Downing *Digger Dialects* 27: *Guts* The substance or essential part of a matter, information.
1946 Rohan Rivett *Behind Bamboo* 396: *Good guts* news, information, secret radio news.
1948 Sumner Locke Elliott *Rusty Bugles* in *Khaki, Bush and Bigotry* ed. Eunice Hanger (1968) 33: 'Got any good guts on replacements?' Ibid. 57: 'Heard the late good guts on the leave?'
1952 Jon Cleary *The Sundowners* 154: 'Wireless is going to be a bloody big thing one of these days, and I'm studying to get the good guts on it.'
1965 William Dick *A Bunch of Ratbags* 196: 'What about Sharon?' asked Joey. 'How much does she charge, Elaine? Give us the good guts on her.'
1975 Les Ryan *The Shearers* 83: 'We'll get the good guts soon.'

gutser, come a To 'come a cropper' (used both literally and figuratively)
1918 *Aussie* 18 Jan. 3: 'It's stoo,' said the pugnacious looking cook, emphatically, 'and if anyone says it aint stoo he can come outside.' 'I say

it aint stoo,' said Private Kummagutzer.

1919 W. H. Downing *Digger Dialects* 27: *Gutzer* A disappointment; a misfortune. 'To come a gutzer' – suffer a reverse of fortune.

1933 Norman Lindsay *Saturdee* 215: Snowey . . . stood upright on the top rail of the fence, and saying scornfully to Peter, 'Bet yer can't do this', threw himself recklessly off it and landed such a gutser that he knocked all the wind out of himself and lay there crowing and gasping.

1936 Miles Franklin *All That Swagger* 381: 'The banks will fetch old Robert a gutser one of these days.'

1945 Gavin Casey *Downhill is Easier* 127: 'They've come a gutzer once, an' they won't try again for a while.'

1953 Dymphna Cusack *Southern Steel* 385: He'd come a terrible gutser if anything ever went wrong; but nothing would ever go wrong with Anne.

1963 Jon Cleary *A Flight of Chariots* 179: 'They thought we'd knuckle under, but they came a gutser.' 'A gutser?' 'Came a thud. Made a mistake.'

1973 Patrick White *The Eye of the Storm* 493: He stumbled into a pothole: could have come a gutser.

1983 Ron Mulock *Sydney Morning Herald* 20 Oct. Life & Home 3: 'My pride got hurt when I came a gutser, and I made sure that next time round I made up for the failure.'

gutter   In goldmining, the channel of an old watercourse, now auriferous

1855 William Howitt *Land, Labour and Gold* ii 275: The gold here runs in veins, or gutters as they call them, – that is, it appears to lie in the channels of the ancient watercourses, which now are buried from 80 to 160 feet in clay.

1857 *Thatcher's Colonial Songster* 8: The gutter at home, and the gutter our here, / Are things widely different, to all is quite clear.

1880 Rolf Boldrewood *The Miner's Right* (1890) 81: If we happened to drop right down on the 'gutter', or main course of the lead, we were all right.

1899 W. T. Goodge *Hits! Skits! and Jingles!* 49: The chaps that struck the gutter and the boys that whipped the cat; / We were like a band of brothers, there was no mistaking that.

1903 Joseph Furphy *Such is Life* (1944) 64: I shall pick out of each consecutive month the 9th day for amplification and comment . . . This will prospect the gutter of Life (gutter is good) at different points.

gutter-gripper   A motorist who drives with one arm out of the car window gripping the 'gutter' on the roof

guzinter   A schoolteacher: *obsolescent* [see quot. 1945]

1945 Baker 133: A schoolteacher is called variously a *chalk-and-talker, guzinter* (i.e. one 'guzinter' two, two 'guzinter' four, etc.)

1951 Dal Stivens *Jimmy Brockett* 52: I wanted to ask the old guzinter where all his bright boys were today, but I let it pass.

gym   Small quantities of gold, esp. if pilfered from the mines [see quot.]

1941 K. S. Prichard *The Roaring Nineties* 209: The miners used him to get rid of a bit of gym, which was what they called the gold they got out of a mine with the Gympie hammer. It was easy to get away with in their crib bags or billies. Ibid. 379: 'It's no use objectin' to the boys gettin' away with a bit of gym.'

gympie   1   A hammer [f. place name]

1945 Baker 94n: The single-hand or *Gympie hammer* was also called a *Massey hammer*.

1979 Donald R. Stuart *Crank Back on Roller* 182: He would be . . . good on a windlass or swinging a gympie.

2   A steel drill

1964 H. P. Tritton *Time Means Tucker* 75: hammer and drills (tap and gympie).

1979 Bill Scott *Tough in the Old Days* 129: The four of us were given two fourteen pound sledge hammers and a handful of steel drills, 'gads' or 'gympies' were the colloquial names for these drills.

3   A nettle-tree [Ab.]

1895 Archibald Meston *Geographic History of Queensland* 55: GYMPIE [place name]. The Mary River blacks' name for the stinging tree.

1938 Francis Ratcliffe *Flying Fox and Drifting Sand* 68: The 'Gympie nettle' of South Queensland, *Laportea gigas*, is replaced in the northern scrubs by a closely allied species, *Laportea moroides*. The chief difference between them seemed to be that the latter possessed an even more terrible touch than its southern cousin.

1959 Eleanor Dark *Lantana Lane* 249: There was a big rock beside a Gympie tree.

gyver   see **guiver**

ha ha pigeon A kookaburra (the laughing jackass): *rare*
  1941 Baker 34: *Ha-ha Pigeon*: A kooka-burra.
  1962 Jock Marshall and Russell Drysdale *Journey Among Men* 169: Italian migrants have begun to put themselves on the wrong side of the law by eating willy wagtails, jacky winters, kookaburras ('ha ha pigeons') and, in fact, almost everything in feathers.

hairy goat see **goat**

hall, bachelors' see **bachelors' hall**

hammer, to be on someone's To pursue, to maintain pressure upon [explained by Baker (1945:286n) as rhyming slang: *hammer and tack = track*]
  1942 *Truth* 31 May 12: Someone 'drums' me there's two 'Jacks' on me 'hammer'.
  1944 Lawson Glassop *We Were the Rats* 140: 'We can't stop. The Jerries might be right on our hammers for all we know.'
  1955 D'Arcy Niland *The Shiralee* 37: The child was on his hammer from the moment he woke. She pestered him impatiently.
  1956 Kylie Tennant *The Honey Flow* 157: 'The only way to get the best out of a dope like Mongo is to keep on his hammer all the time.'
  1962 Ron Tullipan *March into Morning* 96: 'We have such a small force and the Japs are right on our hammer.'

1975 Les Ryan *The Shearers* 5: 'The shearing committee will be on your hammer later on.'

hand, old see **old**

handbrake on a Holden, useful as a see **useful**

Handicap, Benghazi see **Benghazi**

handle A glass of beer, esp. in N.T. (and New Zealand) [f. tankard style glass]
  1943 *Bulletin* 14 Apr. 27: The chap who leaves his work or office at 5 p.m. and wants his two or three handles before going home often has to fight his way into a saloon or front bar and stand and wait in a queue, because all lounges and such places are full of females.
  1982 *NT News* (Darwin) 2 Mar. 1: Beer prices will rise by up to 10 cents a handle following major wage increases to Territory hotel workers . . . The price of a 285 ml handle will jump to an average of 80 cents.

hang up 1 To tether (a horse) [U.S. 1835 OED]
  1859 Henry Kingsley *Recollections of Geoffry Hamlyn* i 124: 'Come down off the bridge, my love, and let us talk together while I hang up the horse.'
  1887 W. S. S. Tyrwhitt *The New Chum in the Queensland Bush* 128: The three quiet horses are led out of the yard and hung up by the bridle outside.
  1900 Henry Lawson 'Bill, the Ventriloquial Roos-

208

ter' *Prose* i 143: The fellows from round about began to ride in and hang up their horses round the place.
1917 A. B. Paterson *Three Elephant Power* 117: Here some two hundred people had assembled, and hung up their horses and vehicles to the fence without the slightest concealment.
1930 Vance Palmer *The Passage* 281: He hung up his mare at the fence and stumbled over the uncropped grass.
1962 Alan Marshall *This is the Grass* 60: 'Why didn't you hang up your horse outside?'
2   To hang up the shears i.e. stop work
1962 *Sydney Morning Herald* 24 Nov. 12: A shearer putting in a wet ticket, after a majority dry vote, can 'hang up', and go to the huts without dismissal.
1974 Les Ryan *The Shearers* 123: 'The greasies have hung up. Why can't we?'

hanging state, the   Victoria, before the abolition of capital punishment in 1975

Hanrahan   The persona of John O'Brien's [the Rev. Father P. J. Hartigan's] poem 'Said Hanrahan', whose prophecy was 'We'll all be rooned', whatever the circumstances
1921 P. J. Hartigan 'Said Hanrahan' *Around the Boree Log* 77: 'We'll all be rooned', said Hanrahan, / In accents most forlorn . . . 'We'll all be rooned', said Hanrahan, / 'Before the year is out.'
1980 *National Times* 20 Apr. 16: Nixon immediately took what is known in the Prime Minister's Department as 'the Hanrahan option', after the bush ballad which includes the recurring line: 'We'll all be ruined said Hanrahan'. He would not want anyone to think that farmers were well off.
1982 Les Murray *Meanjin* I 122: The tunes or contours of whingeing, the rhetoric of the dying fall or the depressive ululation, the Hanrahan note.

happy as a bastard on Father's Day   see **bastard**

happy as Larry   see **Larry**

Harbour, our   Sydney Harbour, as referred to by the local residents
1883 R. E. N. Twopeny *Town Life in Australia* 19: I suppose that nearly everyone has heard of the beauties of Sydney Harbour – 'our harbour', as the Sydneyites fondly call it.
1892 Francis Adams *Australian Life* 194: When he got to Sydney . . . he set to taking stock of 'their harbour', their town and their people.
1914 Nathan Spielvogel *The Gumsucker at Home* 111: Sydney folk ask your opinion about 'our 'Arbour', Ballarat folk about 'our lake', and Warrnambool folk about 'our breakwater'.

1925 Seymour Hicks *Hullo Australians* 242: 'Our 'arbour' as its owners humorously and lovingly call it is indeed a veritable marvel.
1933 Leslie Haylen *The Game Darrells* 186: If a resident . . . asked her what she though of 'our 'arbour', even then she did not give herself away.
1940 Arnold L. Haskell *Waltzing Matilda* 136: Sydney . . . is dominated by the Harbour, 'our harbour' as it is so proudly called.
1965 Graham McInnes *The Road to Gundagai* 71: 'Our 'Arbour, Our Bridge and Our Bradman' was the Melbourne jibe at Sydney.

hard doer   A stronger version of a **doer** q.v.
1926 K. S. Prichard *Working Bullocks* 168: Terrible Tommy's patter and jokes . . . had been on the road as long as he had, but never failed to make the country people laugh – if it was only good humouredly – to see such old hard-doers again.
1932 Leonard Mann *Flesh in Armour* 242: He tried to reassure himself that, after all, it had been merely a youth's brag, the commonest sort – the brag of being a hard-doer with the girls.
1934 Thomas Wood *Cobbers* 19: 'They come in for miles, some of 'em, to give it a fly. Real hard do-ers, y' know.'
1947 Gavin Casey *The Wits are Out* 55: Everybody looked at him with amusement and admiration, and laughed. 'He's a hard doer,' someone said, chuckling.

hard-hitter   A bowler hat
1895 J. Roberts *Diary* 7/2: I had long ere this put on my own clothes . . . of the 'masher' type – white shirt, hard-hitter, tight trousers, etc. [OED]
1901 Henry Lawson 'Buckolts' Gate' *Prose* i 440: Jim sat in his shirt-sleeves, with his flat-brimmed, wire-bound, 'hard-hitter' hat on, slanting over his weaker eye.
1910 C. E. W. Bean *On the Wool Track* 160: The helmet in which he chose to explore the centre of Australia was a 'hard-hitter'.
1926 J. Vance Marshall *Timely Tips for New Australians: Hard-hitter* A slang term denoting a bowler hat.
1951 Dal Stivens *Jimmy Brockett* 51: He had his Sunday clobber on, wore a hard-hitter and carried a stick.
1969 Alec. H. Chisholm *The Joy of the Earth* 143: As our manly dignity increased, we graduated from felt hats to bowlers in winter. (Why we became attached to those formidable 'hard-hitters' is a nice puzzle.)
1982 Joe Andersen *Winners Can Laugh* 19: In his frock coat and black 'hard hitter' his was an overwhelming presence.

hard word, put the ~ on   Used most often of a man seeking sex (outside marriage) and as the expres-

209

sion for bringing matters to a point, but applied also to other requests that approach an ultimatum [cf. *put the acid on*]

1919 W. H. Downing *Digger Dialects* 28: *Hard word* An outrageous demand. (Put the hard word on)

1926 J. Vance Marshall *Timely Tips for New Australians*: To '*put the hard word on*' To make a request.

1936 H. Drake-Brockman *Sheba Lane* 192: 'I loved him, and I found out I wasn't any better than the others when he started to put the hard word on me.'

1939 Kylie Tennant *Foveaux* 359: The landlord tried to make love to her, or, as she termed it, 'put the hard word on her.'

1945 Gavin Casey *Downhill is Easier* 16: 'We should have put the hard word on that office bloke for a few bob.'

1951 Dal Stivens *Jimmy Brockett* 117: If I'd slung a diamond bracelet her way before I'd put the hard word on her, it'd have been a very different story.

1963 Jon Cleary *A Flight of Chariots* 178: 'I like my bit of fun, but I'm not a bastard. I don't go around putting the hard word on lonely wives.'

1972 *Sydney Morning Herald* 9 Mar. 'Look' 2: She [Lady Hasluck] deplored the absence of a museum devoted exclusively to historic Australian costumes, and added 'Is it one we should put the hard word on the Government for?'

1981 Angelo Loukakis *For the Patriarch* 32: 'What did they say?' I ask Bill. 'Ah, stupid here put the hard word on 'em too early,' he says, pointing at Con.

hat, black   see **black**

hatful of arseholes, ugly as   Very ugly

1972 Geoff Morley *Jockey Rides Honest Race* 62: The floor as filthy as a hatful of arseholes and sheilas sitting down against the wall.

1982 Let. in Nancy Keesing *Lily on the Dustbin* 25: If you had no claim to great beauty you were 'as ugly as a hatful of arseholes.'

hat, Joh, Flo   see **Joh, Flo**

hat, to throw one's ~ in first   To test the likely reception beforehand

1953 *Caddie A Sydney Barmaid* 248: As he walked in through the back door I said: 'Hadn't you better throw your hat in first?'

1960 Ron Tullipan *Follow the Sun* 53: 'There is, I suppose, a need to throw my hat in where you're concerned, Julie?'

1975 Xavier Herbert *Poor Fellow My Country* 343: It was Fay McFee again, declaring in her brassy contralto that she supposed she ought to throw her hat in first, but didn't have one.

1981 *Weekend Australian* 25 Apr. Mag. 18: The builder returned with a big smile: 'Should I throw my hat in first?' he asked, as his only concession.

hatter   A bushworker who lives and works alone; a bush eccentric [? f. *mad as a hatter* OED 1849]

1853 John Rochfort *Adventures of a Surveyor* 66: The Bendigo diggings are suitable for persons working singly … Such persons are humorously called 'hatters'. They live alone, in a tent often not more than six feet long, three feet high, and three feet wide.

1865 *The Australian Journal* 9 Dec. 226–7: Nobody cared about him for a mate, and, indeed, he never looked after one himself, but went and worked as a hatter at some surfacing which had just been struck on the side of Ironbark Gully.

1873 Rolf Boldrewood 'The Fencing of Wanderowna' *A Romance of Canvas Town* (1898) 36: I always hated the 'hatter' or solitary shepherd system.

1883 George Darrell *The Sunny South* (1975) 34: 'Grump is a digger who fossicks and digs along without mates, and that's what we call a hatter.'

1900 Henry Lawson 'No Place for a Woman' *Prose* i 398: I was surprised to hear of a wife, for I thought he was a hatter.

1911 C. E. W. Bean *The 'Dreadnought' of the Darling* 99: The life [of the boundary rider] was the most solitary in Australia, and men were apt to turn into 'hatters', as they call them, strange silent fellows who from sheer disuse of human society have almost become unable to endure living amongst other men.

1928 Vance Palmer *The Man Hamilton* 196: 'I know what's the matter with you, Conlon: you're getting bush-shy, like some of these old hatters.'

1935 R. B. Plowman *The Boundary Rider* 82: Among the many station-hands were one or two old hatters. In the kitchen they felt at ease, but for no consideration would they have entered the station sitting-room.

1946 K. S. Prichard *The Roaring Nineties* 27: Ford was a regular hatter … surly and uncommunicative.

hatting

1902 Henry Lawson 'That Pretty Girl in the Army' *Prose* i 488: When a man drops mateship altogether and takes to 'hatting' in the Bush, it's a step towards a convenient tree and a couple of saddle-straps buckled together.

have on, to   See quot. 1941

1941 Baker 34: *Have (someone) on*: To be prepared to fight a person: to accept a challenge to a contest or fight.

1962 Stuart Gore *Down the Golden Mile* 137: 'I'm as good as some o' you young jokers. I'll have any one of yer on – old and all as I am.'

1979 *Sun-Herald* 30 Dec. 4: 'If I had another 50 rounds I would really have these bastards on.'
1980 *Sun-Herald* 6 Apr. 24: 'I never picked fights, but if someone picked one with me, I'd have them on.'

Hawkesbury duck   See quot.: *obs.*
1845 James Tucker *The Adventures of Ralph Rashleigh* (1952) 96: He had been roasting a *Hawkesbury duck* – which was the colonial phrase for a cob of parched maize.

Hawkesbury rivers   The shivers [rhyming slang]
1941 Baker 35: *Hawkesbury rivers* The shivers (rhyming slang).
1951 Dal Stivens *Jimmy Brockett* 72: I had the Hawkesbury Rivers every time I thought of what could happen if the press boys got on to it.

Hawkespeak   Term applied in various ways to the utterances of R. J. Hawke, Prime Minister 1983– [f. analogy with Newspeak, etc.]
1   With an implication of 'doublespeak', esp. by political opponents, but often reflecting a careful choice of words which may mislead the unwary
1983 Andrew Peacock *Parliamentary Debates House of Representatives* 26 May 1015: It [the imposition of taxes on lump sum superannuation payments] is the re-emergence of our old bogey, Hawkespeak: the Prime Minister says one thing but really means the opposite ... Not one but several newspapers reported on 16 April that the Prime Minister had stated that there would be no increase in tax on lump sum superannuation. Yesterday the Prime Minister told the House that these reports were without substance. Later in the day, he described these reports as 'speculation'. [See comment by Mike Steketee *Sydney Morning Herald* 26 May 1:

On April 15, Mr Hawke was asked at a news conference about the speculation over taxing lump sum superannuation. He replied: 'Because there has been speculation, a number of my ministers have spoken with me and I can say on the basis of the conversations I have had, without pre-empting the decision that will have to be made in the Cabinet procedures, that I think you will find that there has been no basis for the speculation.'
The Sydney Morning Herald and other newspapers interpreted the Prime Minister's remarks as ruling out a tax increase for superannuation. The previous day, the Herald and other newspapers reported that Mr Hawke had made the same promise to the ACTU executive.
There was no attempt by the Government to deny the reports, although a close reading of Mr Hawke's comments show that he left himself a way out.]

1984 Andrew Peacock *Age* (Melbourne) 2 Jun. 16: In his statement, the Prime Minister poured scorn on 'the pursuit of narrow individual self-interest'. That's Hawkespeak for working hard, and saving to get ahead.
2   To denote the excessive use of 'in respect of', 'consideration', 'position' etc.
1983 Mike Steketee *Sydney Morning Herald* 25 Jun. 30: It is a strong Hawke-speak day [in the U.S.]. Al Haig as Secretary of State had a particular talent for turning nouns into verbs, as in 'I want to caveat my response'. Hawke's forte is turning nouns into adverbs, as in: 'Let me say foundationally ...' On the 11-hour flight back to Canberra, journalists amuse themselves with Hawke-speak renditions, delivered in suitably nasal accents, such as: 'In respect of, foundationally-speaking, our position down the track, the viability of the kangaroo is in place'.
1983 *Sydney Morning Herald* 22 Jul. 1: In respect of Mr Hawke's press conference in Canberra yesterday, the vocabulary of Hawkespeak was fully respected by the P.M. The word 'respect' occurred 26 times.
3   To refer to the use of involved and discursive sentences
1983 David Dale *Sydney Morning Herald* 13 May 12: In the course of explaining why he hadn't told David Combe about allegations made by ASIO, Mr Hawke said: 'Now quite clearly you are in a delicate situation there in respect of what happened in respect of the Soviets and what their action was, which made it absolutely imperative, if you were going to take into account the consideration of national security, that there be no exposition in any way, to any one, of what had transpired and since I had to make a decision and my colleagues had to make a decision with me as to what you could possibly do in those circumstances which discharged your obligation in national security terms and did as much as you could do to protect the civil liberties of David Combe.' That's 109 words, which is the score to beat.
1984 *National Times* 14 Dec. 2: If you don't know by now what Hawkespeak is then here is a verbatim excerpt – from the official transcript – of what our Great Communicator drops off-the-cuff as communication:
Journalist: Prime Minister, yesterday in a statement, the Left of the Party said the poor result of the election was caused to some extent by traditional Labor voters being disenchanted, specifically young people.
Hawke: Let me say that I am not commenting upon, if I can be this juxtaposition 'the right of the left', on the basis of results, to talk about the electoral perception of positions. That is for others to do. It is an interesting exercise. But I really want to say this – that I can understand that in that interregnum that a group wanted to express its view. Let me say this, that I expect into the future that the discussion about these matters will be conducted within the Party, within the framework of the Party, and I believe the attitude that was exhibited in the Caucus today was one of

acceptance of that position that we have, from myself speaking on behalf of the Ministry, indicated in good faith, that we will be consulting fully with the Caucus, with all sections of the Party . . .
Hawkespeaker
1985 Mike Carlton *Sydney Morning Herald* 22 May 12: Mr Peter Shack, Liberal, Western Australia, is a closet Hawkespeaker . . . In an interview with Max Walsh on Monday night I distinctly heard him drop the phrase 'in respect of'. He will go far.

Hawks, the   1   The Hawthorn V.F.L. team
1950 *Melbourne Sun* 8 Apr. 3: It was Cazaly who changed Hawthorn's nickname from the 'Mayblooms' to the 'Hawks'.
1975 *Sun-Herald* 27 Jul. 60: Hawks battle home by four points.
2   In Queensland, the Sandgate Australian Rules team
1979 *Courier-Mail* (Brisbane) 8 May 22: The Hawks stretched their lead to nine points at half-time.

hay   Money (modifying the U.S. sense of a trivial amount of money as in 'that ain't hay')
1962 Gavin Casey *Amid the Plenty* 130: 'We're on the way to get the hay.'
1983 *Sun-Herald* 4 Dec. 168: When all the work ends soon to rejuvenate Randwick racetrack and complete the all-weather training track, $1 million will have been spent in the past six months. Seems a lot of hay.

head a duck, couldn't   A disparaging comment on a racehorse
1902 A. B. Paterson 'Sitting in Judgment' in *Song of the Pen* (1983) 81: 'Homeward Bound!' says the fat man. 'Why, the pace he went wouldn't head a duck.'
1925 Arthur Wright *The Boy from Bullarah* 81: 'They raced his legs off after that at all sorts of meetings, but he didn't seem able to head a duck.'

heading them   Playing two-up [f. throwing 'heads']
1890 A. G. Hales *Wanderings of a Simple Child* 10: I saw a large crowd of the genus digger, engaged in the refined pastime known to the elite of the back blocks as 'heading 'em'.
1897 Henry Lawson 'The Boss's Boots' *Verse* i 320: Just keep away from 'headin' 'em', and keep away from pubs.
1907 Charles MacAlister *Old Pioneering Days in the Sunny South* 191: My prospective buyer was so intent on 'heading 'em' that it was sometime before he condescended to look at the horse.
1915 C. J. Dennis *The Songs of a Sentimental Bloke* 15: Wiv Ginger Mick, / Jist 'eadin' 'em, an' doin' in me gilt.

1930 Frank Hives *The Journal of a Jackaroo* 8: On Sunday mornings there would be a 'school' in the backyard of the hotel, when the game of 'heading them' would be indulged in for high stakes.
1959 Anne von Bertouch *February Dark* 69: 'We might just as well take up heading 'em for a living', said Peter. 'Heading 'em?' said Helen. 'Two-up,' said Max.
1964 *Sydney Morning Herald* 25 Apr. 11: A mob of ringers (station hands) in for a sublimating grog-up and full of beer and nostalgia start 'heading 'em' in the bar.

head like a beaten favourite, a robber's dog, a twisted sandshoe   Ill-favoured
1961 Frank Hardy *The Hard Way* 249: 'Have a look at him!' I advised the audience. 'Have a good look at the head on him like a robber's dog.'
1981 *National Times* 25 Jan. 23: A face like a twisted sandshoe.
1982 *Sydney Morning Herald* 27 Nov. 28: When he captures the real Australia in expressions like 'She's got a head like a beaten favourite', McKellar is at his timeless best.

head over turkey   see **turkey**

head, pull your ~ in   Equivalent to 'shut up' or 'come off it' (in schoolboy parlance in the 1940s, 'Pull your head in, they'll think it's a cattle truck', addressed to a passing train, etc.)
1944 Lawson Glassop *We Were the Rats* 111: 'It's no use sayin', "Put ya head in, they'll think it's a cattle truck". It bloody well is a cattle truck!'
1953 T. A. G. Hungerford *Riverslake* 20: 'Pull your head in,' Charlesworth advised him, 'or get it knocked off.'
1963 John Cantwell *No Stranger to the Flame* 20: 'I know you, Max Sinclair. So pull your silly skull in.'
1974 *Australian* 4 Jan. 1: When reporters continued questions, the Minister for Minerals, Mr Connor became angry and said: 'Give us a bloody chance to work it out. Come off this, pull your bloody head in.'
1981 *Age* (Melbourne) 11 Jul. 3: He said Mr Grassby should 'pull his head in' and that Mr Kennett should 'grow up'.

heads, the   1   In N.S.W., the North and South Heads of Sydney Harbour
1802 Matthew Flinders *Voyage to Terra Australis* (1814) 9 May i 226: At one o'clock we gained the heads, a pilot came on board, and soon after three the Investigator was anchored in Sydney Cove.
1867 J. R. Houlding *Australian Capers* 216: 'Catch me in a fishing-boat outside the Heads again, if you can'.
1939 Kylie Tennant *Foveaux* 497: The Saturday

afternoon procession of ships passed at slow intervals from the Heads.

1951 Dymphna Cusack and Florence James *Come In Spinner* 86: 'She was born in Manly, and never been outside the heads except on a Saturday afternoon cruise.'

1984 *Sun-Herald* 18 Nov. 152: The cop who took him in had a grin as wide as The Heads.

2 Those in authority [listed by Partridge as 'more gen. Colonial than English; very common in the A.I.F.']

1916 C. J. Dennis *The Moods of Ginger Mick* x: If I was up among the 'eads, wiv right to judge the game, / I'd look around fer chance to praise, an' sling the flamin' blame. Ibid. 145: *'Eads (Heads)* The authorities; inner council.

1919 W. H. Downing *Digger Dialects* 28: *Head* a person of rank or standing.

1935 H. R. Williams *Comrades of the Great Adventure* 184: General Birdwood interrupted our game. Two-up was not encouraged by the 'heads'.

1969 Patsy Adam Smith *Folklore of the Australian Railwaymen* 105: What is expected of you is to get the job done safely and well, and in between that, as far as the 'heads' go, what they never know will never hurt them.

1975 Donald Stuart *Walk, Trot, Canter and Die* 48: 'Seen too many blokes get miner's complaint, cough their bloody lungs out . . . an' who gets all the profits? The heads, that's who. Big fat bastards with nuggets o' gold on their watchchains . . .'

1978 Kevin Gilbert *Living Black* 62: 'My brother's a big head at Canberra but I just turned out a drunk.'

health hazard A phrase, with variants, given currency by the requirement of the Broadcasting and Television Act in 1972 that each advertisement for cigarettes (or cigarette tobacco) broadcast or televised should be followed by the statement 'Medical authorities warn that smoking is a health hazard'.

1972 *Parliamentary Debates House of Representatives* 18 May 2828: [Mr D. J. Hamer moved an amendment] In the proposed section 100A.–(1) omit 'The National Health and Medical Research Council warns that cigarette smoking is dangerous to health'; insert 'Medical authorities warn that smoking is a health hazard'.

1978 *Weekend Australian* 16 Sep. 10: Too many doctors a health hazard [heading]

1979 *Advertiser* (Adelaide) 28 Feb. 3: Kissing may be a tooth hazard [heading] Kissing may transmit tooth decay, a SA doctor says.

1979 *Sydney Morning Herald* 17 Aug. 14: The latest tarted-up models are about $4,000, still no wealth hazard.

1984 *Sun-Herald* 7 Oct. 107: I have heard that jeans can be a health hazard.

heaps, to give them To contest strenuously, deal severely with an opponent

1978 *Sydney Morning Herald* 26 Sep. 2: Good Luck Kangaroos (and give 'em heaps) Tooths KB is proud to sponsor the 1978/79 Kangaroo tour of Great Britain and France. And wish players and officials good luck in their quest to keep the Ashes.

1979 *Bulletin* 9 Oct. 6: Keep up the great work, Max Harris. Give 'em heaps. Stuff it up their pinched and arid little nostrils. Hold the banner high and fight the good fight against the burgeoning growth of mindless Australian mediocrity.

1982 *Sunday Mail* (Brisbane) 5 Sep. 80: Punters give Malcolm heaps [heading] Malcolm Johnston was booed after champion galloper Kingston Town was beaten into fourth place . . . at Randwick yesterday.

Heart, Dead see **Dead**

Heart, the Red see **Red**

heaven, the game they play in see **game**

heifer dust A variant of **bulldust** 2 [OED 1927]

1941 Baker 35: *Heifer dust* Nonsense, 'bullsh'.

1951 Dal Stivens *Jimmy Brockett* 52: If Jimmy Brockett had any say, kids would not have to clutter up their brains with a lot of the heifer dust that is pushed up to them.

1955 D'Arcy Niland *The Shiralee* 96: 'All they could do was take his money and string him a line of heifer dust as long as your arm.'

heifer paddock A girls' boarding school: *obs.*

1885 Mrs Campbell Praed *Australian Life* 50: 'Next year I shall look over a heifer-paddock in Sydney and take my pick.' N.B. Heifer-paddock in Australian slang means a ladies' school.

1897 Mark Twain *Following the Equator* 221: heifer-paddock – young ladies' seminary.

hen's teeth, scarce as Very scarce [listed by Partridge as 'mostly Australian']

1965 John Beede *They Hosed Them Out* 203: 'You'll find they're as scarce as hen's teeth on this squadron.'

1966 Elwyn Wallace *Sydney and the Bush* 133: Work was scarcer than hens' teeth.

1976 *Bulletin* 16 Oct. 53: 'I'd really like to be in PR or travel, but those jobs are scarce as hen's teeth.'

1980 *Weekend Australian* 27 Sep. 40: VFL grand final tickets are as scarce as hen's teeth and fans will try anything to obtain one.

herbs, give it the To give extra power (esp. applied to accelerating a car) [? f. extra taste given by the addition of herbs]

1957 Randolph Stow *The Bystander* 116: 'Go on, give him the herbs. Bet he doesn't even notice you're there.'
1960 Barry Humphries *A Nice Night's Entertainment* (1981) 42: It's pretty hot on herbs, but that bus of his is certainly a phenomenal little performer.
1961 *Age* 20 May Lit. Suppl. 17: One teaser I want explained . . . is 'herbs' for a car's horse power.
1975 Don Townshend *Gland Time* 140: 'Them glands have given him more herbs than a tractor.'

Hexham greys Mosquitoes of exceptional size [f. place-name in N.S.W.]
1895 A. B. Paterson *The Man from Snowy River* 170: They breed 'em at Hexham, it's risky to vex 'em, / They suck a man dry at a sitting, no doubt.
1964 H. P. Tritton *Time Means Tucker* 12: The Hexham swamps are the home of the famous 'Hexham Greys', the biggest and hungriest mosquitoes in Australia, or maybe in the world. And it is no exaggeration to say there were millions of them.
1983 *Newcastle Herald* 21 Mar. 3: Our friend the Hexham Grey mosquito doesn't deserve his bad reputation. It isn't the grey that puts the bite on unsuspecting gardeners; it's the salt-marsh mosquito. Hexham Greys do bite but the black salt-marsh mosquito is much more common and more vicious.

hide See quot.
1979 Donald R. Stuart *Crank Back on Roller* 138: South Australians used 'hide' as a slightly derogatory form of 'bloke' or 'feller'. Ibid. 159: 'You bloody hides, sleepin' in daylight, anyone'd think you were still in rompers.'

Highlanders, the The Gordon (N.S.W.) Rugby Union team [f. the regiment so named]
1979 *Sunday Telegraph* (Sydney) 20 May 107: Highlanders' fling not good enough [heading] Gordon scored two tries to one, had a feast of possession, but still lost 15–11 to Randwick.

Hill, the The uncovered area in front of the scoreboard at Sydney Cricket Ground
1925 Seymour Hicks *Hullo Australians* 246: A place they call the Hill is occupied by thousands of barrackers . . . who are sure they understand cricket better than the umpires.
1979 *Weekend Australian* 2 Jun. Mag. 1: It's enough to . . . cause a cricket connoisseur on The Hill to exclaim 'Oh, well blocked, Boycott!'
1981 *Daily News* (Perth) 19 Jan. 28: The most astonishing discovery of the season was that the mob on Sydney's notorious Hill, in spite of their beery belligerence, are a thin-skinned, sensitive lot who were deeply offended when Richard Hadlee described them as the worst-mannered cricket crowd in the world.
Hillite
1933 *The Referee* 11 Jan. 12: His action was obviously a gesture to the noisy Hillites.
1983 *Sydney Morning Herald* 4 Jan. 22: Few people at the cricket are lost for words, whether they are Hillites or sitting in the members' stands.

hill, go over the Abscond, clear out (Army slang)
1966 Don Crick *Period of Adjustment* 35: 'If you don't want to be in it, get out,' Jim said. 'Go over the hill.'

hill, the light on the see **light**

Hills, the Surry Hills, a suburb of Sydney, N.S.W.
1966 Elwyn Wallace *Sydney and the Bush* 2: Molly was one of the few who always had plenty of money and to the Hillites she was a good sport with a heart as big as The Hills itself.

Hilton, Emu see **Emu**

Hilton, the Jesus see **Jesus**

hip pocket in a singlet, useful as a see **useful**

hold a bull (elephant) out to pee, strong enough to
1955 D'Arcy Niland *The Shiralee* 122: 'He'd eat me, you know. Big enough to hold an elephant out, he was.'
1981 *National Times* 25 Jan. 23: The occasional bushman is still to be found who is 'strong enough to hold a bull out to pee.'

Holden, useful as a handbrake on a see **useful**

holding In funds
1924 *Truth* 27 Apr. 6: *Holdin'* Possessing money.
1932 William Hatfield *Ginger Murdoch* 29: 'If you want a few bob, I'm holdin' sweet.'
1949 Ion L. Idriess *One Wet Season* 189: Sir Perceval was holding and insisted on doing the lordly.
1959 Tom Ronan *Moleskin Midas* 165: 'Well, it's like this, matey. We ain't holding too well just now.'
1963 Alan Marshall *In Mine Own Heart* 166: 'How're ya holding?' Darkie asked me, looking intently at me with hard, suspicious eyes. 'I've got thirty bob,' I said.
1979 George Stewart *The Leveller* 120: Barney asked us how we were 'holding' (did we have any money).
1980 Jessica Anderson *The Impersonators* 93: His message was: HOW ARE YOU HOLDING? . . . 'Oh,' she said . . . 'how am I holding for money? I'm quite all right.'

holey dollar   see **dollar**

Holiday Isle, the   Tasmania, in the language of tourism
  1980 *Sydney Morning Herald* 14 Nov. 1: Column 8 takes exception to the trite slogans appearing on new number plates ... Who needs to be told that Tasmania is the Holiday Isle?
  1983 *Weekend Australian* 30 Jul. 11: Comments this week from prominent Tasmanian business-man, Sir Donald Trescowthick, on the economic direction needed in the State could not have been more timely ... In part Sir Donald said: 'We call ourselves the Holiday Isle. What a load of rubbish.'

hollow log   1   See quot. 1983
  1982 *National Times* 31 Oct. 15: Was he planning to do a Wran, keeping all charges steady while he emptied the hollow logs?
  1983 *Bulletin* 12 Jul. 27: They all had good reason for remembering this 'heated' meeting [in August 1977]: it was the first confrontation between the Treasury officials and Wran's advisers over the idea of drawing funds from the State's 'hollow logs' – a process which saw some $230 million scooped from the cash reserves of statutory authorities to support the State's capital works program.
  2   A dog, esp. racing [rhyming slang]
  1979 *Sun-Herald* 29 Apr. 74: Greyhounds are dills. I reckon they must be the least intelligent of all breeds of hollow logs.

holts, in   At grips with; in dispute, quarrelling or fighting [f. *holt* U.S. 1823 OED]
  1935 R. B. Plowman *The Boundary Rider* 123: 'Hefty looking brute. Wouldn't like to get into holts with him.'
  1947 Norman Lindsay *Halfway to Anywhere* 215: 'You'll mull the part properly unless you get to holts with her like you was really doing a bear-up.'
  1952 T. A. G. Hungerford *The Ridge and the River* 83: 'I noticed you and him in holts a couple of times today!'
  1966 D. H. Crick *Period of Adjustment* 162: Had I come to holts with him over it, I might have said that I couldn't think of Jim Campion as being part of Furnley's machinery.

home   Great Britain, from a colonial standpoint: *obsolescent*
  1791 George Barrington Let. of 1 Jul. *HRNSW* ii 784: There are in the bay with us two ships ... which afford us an excellent opportunity of writing home. But, why should I say *home*? What is England, or Ireland, or Scotland to me now?
  1834 Charles O'Hara Booth *Journal* 25 Dec. ed. Dora Heard (1981) 189: Enjoyed ourselves – but still the thoughts of Home would come to mind and

cause a gloom.
  1855 William Howitt *Land, Labour and Gold* i 56: The people in too great a hurry to make fortunes, with the favourite and universal idea of 'going home'.
  1864 'The Rising Generation' *Thatcher's Colonial Songster* 102: At home of course you're well aware / A child is sent to school / To learn to cipher, read, and write, / That he mayn't grow up a fool: / ... But over here those horn contrivances / Don't trouble the kids at all
  1898 Beatrice Webb *The Webbs' Australian Diary* ed. A. G. Austin (1965) 33: He was extremely bitter at the whole tone of Society: its aspiration to go 'Home' and belong to the Prince of Wales' racing set.
  1981 *Sun-Herald* 19 Jul. 54: Like it or not, Australia is still linked intimately to Great Britain, the United Kingdom. Many Australians have family links with what used to be called 'home'. Many have professional or philosophical links.

home and dried, home and hosed, home with a rug on   Used of successfully completing some enterprise with a margin to spare [f. horseracing]
  1918 *Kia Ora Coo-ee* 15 Oct. 14: All being home and dried, 'Shorty' went over to the 'Q. Emma's' to borrow a bit of 'buckshee' sugar.
  1920 Frank A. Russell *The Ashes of Achievement* 48: 'We're home and dried.'
  1922 Arthur Wright *A Colt from the Country* 37: 'If my prayers can help him,' laughed Sadie, 'he's home and dried, as Tommy would say.'
  1934 Thomas Wood *Cobbers* 96: Charles would make a book ... and he would lay two to one port-wine jelly, five to two apple pie. Nine times out of ten he was, in his own phrase, home in the stall with a rug on.
  1951 Dal Stivens *Jimmy Brockett* 219: I was home and dried.
  1959 Eric Lambert *Glory Thrown In* 219: 'Look!' he yelled to Christy. 'A and C Companies home and hosed!'
  1967 Frank Hardy *Billy Borker Yarns Again* 18: 'Don't tell a soul: number six, Hairy Legs, is home and hosed.'
  1972 *Bulletin* 26 Aug. 11: The government is home and hosed and can thank the budget.
  1981 *Sunday Mail* (Brisbane) 9 Aug. 57: Ideal Planet, having the second start of his career, was 'home and hosed' until Black Shoes came with her unbeatable challenge.

home, kick   see **kick**

Home of the America's Cup   See quot.
  1983 *West Australian* (Perth) 5 Oct. 2: Australia II's success has prompted the WA Government to adopt a new slogan for its vehicle licence plates –

'WA – Home of the America's Cup' – plus an outline of the cup itself.

homer   See quot. 1945 (World War II slang)
1945 Baker 156: *homer.* A wound sufficiently serious to cause a man to be sent home.
1952 T. A. G. Hungerford *The Ridge and the River* 173: 'He'll get a homer out of it – perhaps Australia.'
1978 Richard Beilby *Gunner* 87: 'Ya got a homer, mate, you arsey bastard.'

homestead   Used in a special sense like **house** q.v. for the residence of the owner or manager on a station, significantly set apart from the barracks and the men's hut [N.Z. 1849 OED]
1903 Joseph Furphy *Such is Life* (1944) 66: I had drawn up to Goolumbulla homestead with six tons of wire. The manager, Mr Spanker . . .
1935 R. B. Plowman *The Boundary Rider* 70: 'Government House' – as the owner's residence is called in the back country. Solidly built of stone and with a broad sweep of veranda across its front, it looked the part of homestead to the largest station in that part of South Australia.
1952 Jon Cleary *The Sundowners* 221: Halstead was a good bloke, better than most bosses; but the homestead was an enemy camp and no worker worth his salt ever stepped across the boundary.
1965 Graham McInnes *The Road to Gundagai* 248: Everyone knew that J. M. Molesworth was the boss, that he lived in an enormous homestead, and that he was worth a hundred pounds or so.
1979 *Sydney Morning Herald* 3 Mar. 12: The homestead is seldom a tin-roofed building sitting in a fenced-off garden wilting in the sun. It is more likely to be a large, modern ranch-style building set in flourishing lawns with a swimming pool and entertainment area.

homing pigeons, he couldn't lead a flock of   Comment on R. G. Menzies attributed to W. M. Hughes
1977 Fred Daly *From Curtin to Kerr* 116: Menzies tolerated him [W. M. Hughes]. Probably never forgot the time Billy said Menzies could not lead a flock of homing pigeons.
1980 Alan Reid *Bulletin* 29 Jan. 365: Hughes stabbed a finger in the direction of Menzies' office. 'Him', he said, derisively. 'Him. Couldn't lead a flock of homing pigeons'. Then he stamped off.

hominy   Prison food, used in expressions like 'hominy bus', 'hominy gazette' (gaol rumours)
1895 Cornelius Crowe *Australian Slang Dictionary* 36: *Hominey* prison fare.
1953 Baker 129: The jail tram that runs between Darlinghurst Police Station and Long Bay Gaol is called the *hominy bus*.

1919 J. Vance Marshall *The World of the Living Dead* 85: O, no more I'll quiz The Hominy Gazette for shearin' news / Or'll use the Holy Bible fer me fags.

honey bag   As for **sugar bag** q.v.
1931 Vance Palmer *Separate Lives* 65: He imitated the old king cutting out a honey-bag with the bees around him.

honkoe   Vague term of abuse: *rare* [cf. U.S. *honkie* abusive term directed towards whites by blacks]
1953 Baker 106: *honk*, a bad smell.
1965 William Dick *A Bunch of Ratbags* 42: 'I don't care about them honkoes over at the Mont, they're only wackers.'

Hong Kong Tiger   Sir Frank Duval (d. 1981, aged 71) 'Tiger' from his fearless punting, 'Hong Kong' from his business interests in the east (actually in Tokyo)
1983 *Bulletin* 26 Jul. 98: The late Sir Frank Duval was an extraordinary man . . . Dubbed 'the Hong Kong Tiger' by racing scribes, he was a mammoth punter.

hooer   Possibly a variant of 'whore', but applied to men in a generally derogatory way, like 'bastard.'
1952 T. A. G. Hungerford *The Ridge and the River* 31: Cranky old hooer! White thought, with a wry smile. Always on the bloody job.
1962 Stuart Gore *Down the Golden Mile* 152: 'What the hell's those two silly hooers tryin' to *do* – kill their bloody selves!'
1975 Les Ryan *The Shearers* 63: 'Ar, go to blazes, you drunken hooer.'

hook up   To 'pull' a racehorse, deliberately prevent it from winning
1949 Lawson Glassop *Lucky Palmer* 245: 'Owners always want favourites hooked up. I know it all.'

hooks, put the hooks into   As for **put the nips into**

hoon   1   A procurer of prostitutes; general term of insult
1938 Xavier Herbert *Capricornia* 338: 'You flash hoon,' he went on.
1953 Baker 124: *hoon* or (by rhyme) *silver spoon*, a procurer of prostitutes.
1973 Jim McNeil *The Chocolate Frog* 48: 'A hoon! A weak mug that bludges beer money off weak molls!'
1976 *Cleo* Aug. 33: Hoon is a nebulous sort of word. It means someone living off the girls. He is not a pimp for them, he can be a standover man. It is an insult to be called a hoon . . . something worse than a bludger.
1982 *Sunday Mail* (Brisbane) 20 Jun. 45: They

fear bashings and wrecking of their homes by prostitutes and their hoons if they speak out.

2 Anyone given to loutish behaviour

1979 *Herald* (Melbourne) 18 Jun. 4: The hoons have taken over, and somehow we let it happen. In every walk of life the hoons have succeeded, some may be better educated than others, come from better addresses, but they are hoons nevertheless. In some cases they are called the underprivileged; in some cases, the over indulged.

1981 *Sunday Telegraph* (Sydney) 8 Feb. 106: No doubt the crowds attracted to this travesty of a game will be of the same calibre as the average British soccer fan or the can-chucking hoons of the Sydney Hill.

1981 *Sunday Mail* (Brisbane) 8 Feb. 2: A father, taking his son to his new high school after the holidays, couldn't figure out what the untidy and badly dressed group was doing in the grounds. The shock came when he discovered they were members of the staff – teachers and teachers' aides. 'I thought they were hoons', he said.

1982 *NT News* (Darwin) 15 Sep. 7: The prize hoon who has been shooting at dogs with an airgun at Stuart Park had better lay off in future.

hoon around

1984 *Sydney Morning Herald* 27 Jan. Metro 1: For $15 you can hoon around the city with a group of 60 people, all wearing Groucho Marx masks, making unannounced and disruptive visits on restaurants, clubs and shops, while Quantock delivers a comic commentary.

hoop A jockey [f. hooped colours]

1941 Baker 36: *Hoop* A jockey.

1949 Lawson Glassop *Lucky Palmer* 245: 'It'll be a soda for a hoop like you. It won't be hard to get her beaten.'

1951 Dal Stivens *Jimmy Brockett* 100: We dropped hints to various hoops, owners and trainers we'd done favours for that we didn't want their horses to win.

1956 *Australian Signpost* ed. T. A. G. Hungerford 184: 'Lofty has a sister in Sydney and she tracks square with a hoop.'

1969 Alan O'Toole *The Racing Game* 79: 'We'll see if this hoop of yours has turned up.'

1975 *Bulletin* 28 Jun. 66: He was very fast at writing large-type headlines for the page one – like ... Star Weds Top Hoop.

1982 *Sunday Mail* (Brisbane) 27 Jun. 74: Brisbane jockey Gary Palmer replaced Kiwi hoop Michael Mein who became ill after wasting.

Hooray, Hooroo Equivalent to 'Cheerio' as a farewell

1917 F. J. Mills *Dinkum Oil* 73: There was a vast deal of ... 'Goodbye Auntie, toolraloo Bill ... hooray Dick', and so forth.

1931 William Hatfield *Sheepmates* 238: 'Well, hooroo!' And he was gone in the direction where the fire glowed like a dropped cigarette butt.

1939 Kylie Tennant *Foveaux* 278: 'Well, hoo-ray, I'll be seeing you.'

1942 Leonard Mann *The Go-Getter* 221: 'So long, Chris.' 'Hooray, boy.'

1951 Dymphna Cusack and Florence James *Come In Spinner* 396: Lofty thrust his head through the window and waved 'Hoorroo!'

1959 Anne von Bertouch *February Dark* 193: 'We'll see you later. Hooray.'

1969 Patsy Adam Smith *Folklore of the Australian Railwaymen* 175: Then he said 'Hooroo' and I left to take the seven camels back the 350 miles by myself.

hoot Money [N.Z. 1879: see quot. 1896]

1881 G. C. Evans *Stories Told Round the Campfire* 265: Why the very stuff you are now drinking has been bought with 'hoot' obtained from stolen goods.

1896 *Truth* 12 Jan. 4: There are several specimens of bush language transplanted from the Maori language. 'Hoot' is a very frequent synonym for money or wage ... The Maori equivalent for money is *utu* pronounced ... with the last syllable clipped.

1898 Joshua Lake *Australasian Supplement* to *Webster's International Dictionary* 2024: *Hoot* (Maori *utu* vengeance) Payment; reward; recompense; rate of wages (Slang, N.Z.)

1938 Xavier Herbert *Capricornia* 301: 'On the construction you could make a pot of hoot in no time.'

1942 Sarah Campion *Bonanza* 154: 'Carn't raise the hoot, ole Mick carn't!' they said.

1962 Hal Porter *A Bachelor's Children* 185: 'He's got plenty of hoot; has shares in everything from here to Perth.'

1977 *Sun-Herald* 24 Jul. 111: 'It's about a Q.C. and his wife, who live in Point Piper and obviously have lots of hoot.'

hop into As for **slip into** q.v.

1945 Robert S. Close *Love Me Sailor* 160: 'Did you see young Ernie hopping into Christenson?'

1958 Gavin Casey *Snowball* 207: 'All right, kid, hop into your tucker,' Plugger ordered briskly.

horror budget The 1951 budget of the Menzies government, introduced by Arthur Fadden as Treasurer: so styled by its political opponents

1951 Arthur Calwell *Commonwealth of Australia Parliamentary Debates, House of Representatives*, Vol. 214, 3 Oct. 286: The Prime Minister sees virtue in his budget, but only a month ago he said it would be a 'horror budget'. [Mr Menzies had predicted severe budgetary action after the 12*s.*

basic wage increase on 18 July, and at the end of the Economic Crisis Conference on 31 July.]

1969 Arthur Fadden *They called me Artie* 121: As soon as the referendum was over I introduced my 1951–52 Budget, dubbed 'The Horror Budget' by my political opponents.

1978 *Sydney Morning Herald* 21 Jun. 21: The Government looks to be locked in on an increased deficit for next year ... That is unless it wishes to bring down a horror budget in August.

1981 *Australian* 4 Dec. 13: Britain's Chancellor of the Exchequer, Sir Geoffrey Howe, has brought down a horror mini-Budget which expounds the theme 'pay up for the sake of Britain'.

horse, jump a ~ over the bar, eat or drink a ~ To sell a horse for liquor or supplies

1900–10 O'Brien and Stephens: *Jumping your horse over the bar* to sell his horse or mortgage it to the publican so as to prolong his spree.

1904 Laura M. Palmer-Archer *A Bush Honeymoon* 349: *Jumped over the bar* Paid away for liquor.

1919 E. S. Sorenson *Chips and Splinters* 34: It had been ... given to a rabbit-poisoner known as 'Billy-the-Rooster' for a skewbald packhorse which Billy had 'jumped over the bar'.

1957 'The Poor Bushman' in *Old Bush Songs* ed. Stewart and Keesing 229: My horses all sold – they'd jumped over the bar – / And I got the dirty kick-out.

1962 Tom Ronan *Deep of the Sky* 101: When his rations were exhausted he 'ate a horse' – that is, sold one for what he could get and converted the proceeds into supplies.

horse, to sell a See quots

1939 R. H. Croll *I Recall* 54: You 'sell a horse' by putting in a shilling apiece, one member writes a number down privately, then all count as in a kiddies' game. The person who calls the hidden number scoops the pool and buys the drinks.

1964 Tom Ronan *Packhorse and Pearling Boat* 234: 'Selling a horse' ... a very simple substitute for the cards and dice and, when there are fourteen in the party, much quicker. The barman collects the two bobs and, on a scrap of paper, writes down a number between fifty and a hundred. Then the party forms up in a group, someone starts counting at any number between one and ten, and whoever calls the figure the barman has written down scoops the pool.

horse, working off a dead see **dead horse**

hosed, home and see **home**

hostie An air hostess [abbr.]

1975 *Australian* 26 Mar. 10: For poor old West-ern Australia, already isolated by flooded railway lines and impassable roads, the final separation caused by the hosties' strike is the last straw.

1982 *Sun-Herald* 25 Apr. 151: Hosties these days are called flight attendants ... but there is still a cause to be made out for a good-looking bird to flog the coffee and biscuits.

hostile An 'educated' word used colloquially, like *strife*

1941 Baker 36: *Hostile* Angry, annoyed. Also, 'go hostile at', express annoyance (towards someone).

1951 Seaforth Mackenzie *Dead Men Rising* 85: 'Dammit, that'll mean sleeping in for me. The wife will be hostile about it.'

1958 H. D. Williamson *The Sunlit Plain* 175: 'All right', Duveen protested in high, aggrieved tones. 'All right, mate. There's no need to get hostile.'

1962 Dymphna Cusack *Picnic Races* 176: 'Nobody really blames her but they go pretty hostile on the bloke.'

1973 Frank Huelin *Keep Moving* 83: 'We don't want to get hostile about it. Yous got your ideas and I've got mine. Let it go at that.'

hottie A hotwater bottle [abbr.]

1958 Barry Humphries *A Nice Night's Entertainment* (1981) 17: We'd had a run of late nights and we were pretty fagged so round about ten I filled the hottie and Beryl and I went to bed.

house, the On a station, the residence of the owner or manager, and so distinct from the accommodation for the station hands (the men's hut), for the jackeroos (the barracks) and others

1869 Marcus Clarke *The Peripatetic Philosopher* 41: At the station where I worked for some time ... three cooks were kept during the 'wallaby' season – one of the house, one for the men, and one for the travellers.

1876 A. J. Boyd *Old Colonials* (1882) 81: 'The squatters know well enough when a man is fit for the house or the kitchen, and they consider a gentleman's a gentleman, no matter what he's employed at.'

1893 J. A. Barry *Steve Brown's Bunyip* 202: The dealer, having pretty well cleaned out 'the hut', determined to try his luck at 'the House'.

1901 Rolf Boldrewood *In Bad Company* 285: After the changes which turned the homesteads of the larger stations into small villages, the 'big house', as it came to be called, was no longer expected to accommodate the proprietor, the overseer, and the young gentlemen learning Colonial experience, in addition to every wanderer that turned up. The overseer generally had a commodious if, perhaps, plainly-furnished cottage alloted to him. This came to be known as the 'barracks', and to be used as a convenient abode for strangers and pilgrims, as well as for the storekeeper, the working overseers, and the young gentlemen.

1921 M. E. Fullerton *Bark House Days* 117: I was a favourite with the men, being even then a reader of the newspapers, I constituted myself the medium by which the huts were supplied with the weeklies as soon as the house was finished with them.

1936 William Hatfield *Australia through the Windscreen* 64: It is pitiful to see the perturbation on the face of a manager when a presentably dressed traveller pulls up at a station where he must be given accommodation, trying to guess correctly whether the stranger is a 'house' or a 'hut' man.

1954 Tom Ronan *Vision Splendid* 76: He would leave the Big House as soon as it was politely permissible and stroll down for a yarn with the men.

1973 John Morrison *Australian by Choice* 116: Across the garden I had got a glimpse of the long verandah of the House; coloured lights, moving figures: the Boss and his wife, the Overseer, one of the jackeroos, guests from a neighbouring station.

Howe, Jacky Sleeveless flannel shirt [f. shearer (1855–1922) so named]

1930 *Bulletin* 9 Apr. 19: Long Jim was telling us how . . . it took nine bars of soap to wash his 'Jacky Howe' flannel.

1933 Acland: *Jacky Howe* Sleeveless singlet, cut nearly to the waist under the arms.

1940 Ion L. Idriess *Lightning Ridge* 97: He was clad only in loose pants and a Jacky Howe flannel.

1949 Ruth Park *Poor Man's Orange* 122: He had finished his tea and was sitting in his Jackie Howe, which is a singlet with the sleeves out of it, and called after a famous shearer, of the blade days.

1979 Dorothy Hewett *The Man from Mukinupin* 51: Harry Tuesday re-enters . . . dressed in tight-fitting moleskin trousers and a black Jackie Howe singlet.

1981 *Australian* 30 Sep. 3: At payment rates of 80c a head that means quite a good income for any girl prepared to invest in a Jacky Howe wardrobe and study the gentle art of holding down a sheep.

hoy Bingo or housie: Queensland [? f. shout]

1975 Bruce Dawe *Just a Dugong at Twilight* 30: The State Crown Law Office, Queensland, was called upon to decide whether the game known as 'Hoy' was illegal or not.

Hoyt's, the man outside The commissionaire outside Hoyt's Theatre in Melbourne in the 1930s, so elaborately dressed as to seem a person of consequence, and jocularly referred to as the authority for various reports

1953 Baker 133: *Hoyts, the man outside* A mythical person who starts all false rumours; the source of stolen property which an innocent(!) receiver is found to have in his possession.

1961 Frank Hardy *The Hard Way* 85: 'Struth, it's funny enough for a fat bludger dressed up like the man outside Hoyt's[1] to come into a prison cell in the middle of the night.' [1]Uniformed announcer outside Hoyt's Theatre in Melbourne who wears a most elaborate uniform.

1966 Hal Porter *The Paper Chase* 64: The Regent, the State, the Capitol, the Plaza, Hoyt's de Luxe (where the commissionaire, hoarsely and non-stop, brays himself into fame and the Australian vernacular as The Man Outside Hoyt's) – are, at the height of the Depression, at the height of their magnificence.

1975 *Sydney Morning Herald* 5 Jul. 9: We might be better off to abandon pre-selections and elections, and choose our politicians by having the Governor (or the man outside Hoyts) stick pins into the telephone book.

Hughie Name given to God in the outback, esp. in the expression 'Send 'er down, Hughie' used when it is raining hard; also to the deity of the surf [Partridge lists 'Send her down, David']

1918 L. J. Villiers *The Changing Year* 12: Down Hughie* pours *Hughie = the rain.

[**1919** W. H. Downing *Digger Dialects* 44: *Send her down, Steve!* Let it rain on.]

1922 *Bulletin* 26 Jan. 22: The missionary tackled him [the aboriginal boy] with 'Who made this country, Peter?' 'Dunno' – says Peter – 'was here when I came.' 'Well,' says Parson, 'who is it makes the rain?' Peter knew that all right. 'Ole Hughie,' he answered promptly.

1946 K. S. Prichard *The Roaring Nineties* 30: Miners and prospectors would turn out and yell to a dull, dirty sky clouded with red dust. 'Send her down! Send her down, Hughie!'

1951 Seaforth Mackenzie *Dead Men Rising* 210: 'All you want to do is get married and have kids,' he said. 'Don't worry about the money. Hughie looks after that, my boy.' The Corporal was diverted. 'Who's this Hughie?' he said . . . 'Ah,' Gell said, affecting a gravity which was not altogether false. 'You don't say "God", you see, because nobody believes in God but everybody believes in Hughie. I dunno – it's just a thing you hear the boys say.' Ibid. 207: 'Hughie's throwing it down all right.'

1964 H. P. Tritton *Time Means Tucker* 92: With only a couple of thousand to go 'Hughie' answered the prayers of the loppies with a fairly heavy shower. Ibid. 42: To the best of my belief, it was at Charlton [in 1905] that 'Hughie' as the chief deity in the job of controlling the weather came into being.

1969 Osmar White *Under the Iron Rainbow* 163: The clouds burst. 'Send her down, Huey!' cried the man in the wheelchair, raising clenched fists and flinging back his head.

1975 Robert Macklin *The Queenslander* 30: He threw his head back and laughed as the rain splashed on his face. 'Send her down, Hughie.'

1980 *Sun-Herald* 21 Sep. 60: Hughie (who is presumably a Liberal) immediately started to send it down, and this Canberra version of the ALP's perpetual floating barbecue showed every sign of becoming well and truly afloat.

1981 *National Times* 20 Dec. 26: Incoming waves may be assessed, and sometimes the ancient cry will rise during a lull: 'Send 'em up, Huey!' Meaning: push some waves in. Some surf scholars believe Huey to be a corruption of Jupiter Pluvius.

1984 *Sydney Morning Herald* 31 Jan. 31: During the award ceremony [for a malibu board-riding contest], an organiser said: 'I want to thank Hughie upstairs (Hughie's the surfie's name for God) for the waves (between 6 ft and 8 ft) and the good weather.'

hum *n.* A cadger, sponger: *derogatory*

1915 J. P. Bourke *Off the Bluebush* 190: If you cannot be a spendthrift, be a hum.

1919 J. Vance Marshall *The World of the Living Dead* 70: Almost beneath the bottom rung of the social ladder there is ... the 'hum', the unskilled derelict or derelict-to-be who stands upon the 'pub' corner kerb, 'bites' all and sundry, and, at regular intervals succeeds in getting lumbered for 'vag'.

1937 *Best Australian One-Act Plays* 163: 'Generally winds up with ... one of 'em nipping you for a couple of bob ... Perfect hums some of 'em.'

1953 *Caddie A Sydney Barmaid* 183: In a class of his own is the hum. Some of these are casuals, temporarily out of cash, but with an unquenchable thirst. But it's the professional who merits recognition, for he has developed the technique of the bite until it is almost one of arts.

1957 D'Arcy Niland *Call Me When the Cross Turns Over* 136: 'Rigby's a twister. He's a hum and a liar.'

hum *v.* To borrow, scrounge (not used in such a pejorative sense as the noun)

1915 J. P. Bourke *Off the Bluebush* 77: Got no coin to treat a pal! Got no face to hum!

1919 W. H. Downing *Digger Dialects* 29: *Humm* To cadge.

1919 W. R. Harris *Outback in Australia* 47: 'What'll happen to *us* if you townies start on the 'humming' game?'

1937 Xavier Herbert *Capricornia* 257: 'You're only humming for a drink. Nick off home.'

humbug Used not only to imply sham and deception, but also to suggest nuisance, fuss and bother, trouble: *rare* [? Pidgin]

1845 Thomas McCombie *Arabin* 232: Vexation seems to be my lot. I never was so humbugged in all my born days.

1937 Xavier Herbert *Capricornia* 275: 'Do you like the job?' 'No-more!' she cried, wrinkling a pretty nose. 'All dem sister proper humbug.' 'How's that?' 'All time roustin'. All time tink we go out wid boys.'

1946 W. E. Harney *North of 23°* 158–9: The greatest problem on station, mission or government compound is the dogs ... Should you become desperate and destroy a number of these dogs, the natives might be annoyed at first, but afterwards they would tell you that 'it more better, as dog too much humbug'.

1959 C. V. Lawlor *All This Humbug* 21: 'How came it [Humbug Creek] by that name?' 'Well, they tell me that a man named John Regan discovered it, and because it was such a nuisance when it was in flood, and hard to find in his exploring trips from the Bland, he called it a Humbug.'

1983 Paddy Rae *gularabulu* 95: 'humbug' means 'cause a nuisance'.

hump bluey, the drum, the swag To follow the life of the swagman, carrying one's belongings on one's back

1855 William Howitt *Land, Labour and Gold* i 226: He 'humped his swag', in diggers' phrase that is, shouldered his pack, and disappeared in the woods.

1861 *Penguin Book of Australian Ballads* (1964) 87: No more through the bush we'll go humping the drum.

1883 R. E. N. Twopeny *Town Life in Australia* 244–5: He 'humps his drum', or 'swag', and 'starts on the wallaby track', i.e. shoulders the bundle containing his worldly belongings, and goes out pleasuring.

1892 Henry Lawson 'Jack Dunn of Nevertire', *Verse* i 222: He humped his bluey by the name of 'Dunn of Nevertire'.

1895 A. B. Paterson *The Man from Snowy River* 84: The lonely swagman through the dark / Must hump his swag past Chandos Park.

1898 David W. Carnegie *Spinifex and Sand* 156: He had saved enough money to pay his passage to Perth; and from there he 'humped his bluey' to Coolgardie, and took a job as a miner.

1911 E. M. Clowes *On the Wallaby Through Victoria* 278: An expression used for what in England we call 'tramping' is 'humping the swag' or 'the bluey'.

1934 Tom Clarke *Marriage at 6 a.m.* 46: *Hump your bluey* pack up, move on.

1943 Maurice Clough *We of the A.I.F.* 45: Men

who have lived on billy tea / And damper, humping their 'bluey'.
1961 George Farwell *Vanishing Australians* 44: 'When I first set eyes on him, he was humping his drum, hoofing it down the road from Tilpa.'

humpy An Aboriginal bark hut (Morris, 1846), but also applied to any rude shelter or hut constructed by a white
1881 A. C. Grant *Bush Life in Queensland* i 133: To dwell in the familiar old bark 'humpy', so full of happy memories. The roof was covered with sheets of bark held down by large wooden riders pegged in the form of a square to one another. [Morris]
1896 Henry Lawson 'In A Dry Season' *Prose* i 79–80: The only town I saw that differed much from the above consisted of a box-bark humpy with a clay chimney, and a woman standing at the door throwing out the wash-up water.
1919 Edward Dyson *The Escapades of Ann* 91: Ryan was an unmitigated nuisance, his old humpy was an eyesore in a neighbourhood that was beginning rather to fancy itself.
1924 *Truth* 27 Apr. 6: *Humpy* bush hut.
1931 Vance Palmer *Separate Lives* 12: His humpy was on the edge of the settlement, a ragged lean-to made of slabs and old iron that he had built in his spare time out of such scraps as his neighbours discarded.
1949 Ion L. Idriess *One Wet Season* 83: A fair-sized bush humpy, built of cypress-pine, cool and roomy, roofed with paperbark, walled by corrugated iron, hobstone floor.
1959 Dorothy Hewett *Bobbin Up* 19: Looking round the three-roomed humpy, sunken sideways with damp and age.
1961 Nene Gare *The Fringe Dwellers* 27: The humpy was ... a ramshackle arrangement of tarpaulins and scrap-iron nailed to bush timber.
1981 *Weekend Australian* 18 Apr. 3: 'In some cases school buildings are non-existent – they are just humpies', said Mr Lloyd.

hungry Grasping, stingy, often as part of a nickname: *derogatory*
1855 William Howitt *Land, Labour and Gold* ii 294: At one station I asked two men who were resting with their cart by the road-side whose station that was? 'Hungry Scott's' was the reply.
1891 Rolf Boldrewood *A Sydney Side Saxon* 166: 'I was never to say stingy about a trifle of rations like 'hungry Jackson'.
1895 A. B. Paterson 'Saltbush Bill' *Collected Poems* 27: And he knew where the hungry owners were that hurried his sheep ahead.
1902 Henry Lawson 'Two Sundowners' *Prose* i 99: They came to a notoriously 'hungry' station, where there was a Scottish manager and storekeeper.
1936 Miles Franklin *All That Swagger* 320–1: If Danny had been known as Hungry Delacy instead of Honest Danny he might have transmitted a strain to make his sons financial nabobs.
1948 K. S. Prichard *Golden Miles* 74: 'There's some hungry bastards,' the men said, 'making big money on their ore, and never give the poor bugger boggin' for 'em a sling back.'
1959 Dorothy Hewett *Bobbin Up* 198: 'She works two jobs in two mills and she's hungry ... She's real bonus-happy.'
1962 J. Marshall and R. Drysdale *Journey Among Men* 153: The old story of the 'hungry' sheep-farmer who ... runs as many sheep as possible on unimproved pastures.
1975 Les Ryan *The Shearers* 51: 'There are some hungry bastards in the game.'
1981 *Sydney Morning Herald* 27 May 24: One glance at the price of Dom Perignon – $75 – confirms just how hungry Mischa is.

Hungry Mile, the The part of Sussex Street, Sydney, fringing the waterfront, with the office of the Waterside Workers Federation
1930 Ernest Antony *The Hungry Mile* 5: To see Sydney wharfies tramping down the hungry mile.
1957 Tom Nelson *The Hungry Mile* 75: The stretch along Sussex Street was called the 'Hungry Mile' by the wharfies ... a very apt title indeed.
1960 Ron Tullipan *Follow the Sun* 173: 'I'm going to the Hungry Mile to be a wharfie.'
1973 *Sydney Morning Herald* 2 Aug. 7: When I was much younger the 'Hungry Mile' of Sydney waterfront was an area of glamour.

hunt To drive away, dismiss
1870 Rolf Boldrewood 'Shearing in Riverina' *In Bad Company* (1901) He ... makes a calculation as to who are unreasonably bad, and who, therefore, will have to be 'hunted'.
1928 Arthur Wright *A Good Recovery* 69: 'Walk!' she repeated. 'My horse – ' 'I've hunted Boora. You're coming with me, or walking home.'
1941 Kylie Tennant *The Battlers* 235: 'Thanks for looking after the kid.' 'I couldn't do no less,' the woman answered loudly. 'I'm not one to hunt kids.'
1953 T. A. G. Hungerford *Riverslake* 24: 'The grog's got him. He'll get hunted soon.'
1975 Xavier Herbert *Poor Fellow My Country* 1132: 'What'll I do ... hunt him?'
1983 T. A. G. Hungerford *Stories from Suburban Road* 118: I'd heard them saying she'd been got into some sort of trouble by Mr Floyd, and that her parents had hunted her.

hunt up a cow see **cow**

hut, the (men's) On a station, the accommodation

provided for the station-hands, usually a large structure, but distinct from 'the house' and 'the barracks' qq.v.

1843 Charles Rowcroft *Tales of the Colonies* ii 258: 'Mr Clover came into the hut, the men's hut ... John Buttress did not go on being ordered out: Mr Clover then took him by the collar, and shoved him out of the hut.'

1869 Marcus Clarke *The Peripatetic Philosopher* 41: I have seen as many as twenty able bodied hungry men come up to a home-station with the stereotyped inquiry, 'Want any hands, sir?' and receiving a reply in the negative ... go merrily down to the 'men's hut' and, having smoked, eat some two pounds of 'fat wether' per man.

1873 A. Trollope *Australia* ed. Edwards and Joyce (1967) 138: The labouring man ... is sent to the 'hut'. There is a hut at every station, fitted up with bunks, in which the workmen sleep. Here the wanderer is allowed to stretch his blanket for the night – and on all such occasions two meals are allowed him.

1893 J. A. Barry *Steve Brown's Bunyip* 202: The dealer, having pretty well cleared out 'the Hut', determined to try his luck at 'the House'.

1901 Rolf Boldrewood *In Bad Company* 11: The 'men's hut' came first into view – a substantial dwelling, with horizontal sawn slabs and shingled roof, a stone chimney and a dining-room.

1911 E. M. Clowes *On the Wallaby Through Victoria* 103: The shearers live – that is, sleep and eat – in what is known as 'the hut', a long narrow structure with bunks at either side, in two tiers, each bunk just long enough to hold a man.

1931 William Hatfield *Sheepmates* 76: 'Rough diamond, you know, used to be in the Hut – stockman, horse-breaker and all that you know, though I say you can't hold it against a man because he came from the Hut.'

hut, upside-down   see **upside-down**

hydraulic (jack)   Nickname for anyone with the habit of 'lifting' things, i.e. a thief, esp. on the waterfront

1977 *Sunday Telegraph* (Sydney) 24 Apr. 136: 'They call him Hydraulic – he'll lift anything that isn't nailed down'.

iceberg Someone who regularly takes an early morning swim throughout the winter, esp. as a member of a club; anyone who braves the water on a cold morning

1932 L. W. Lower *Here's Another* 12: 'One of the toughest surfs I've experienced this winter. All the Icebergs agreed.'

1952 A. G. Mitchell Suppl. to Chambers' *Shorter English Dictionary* 796: *Iceberg* one who surfs regularly throughout the winter.

1964 Tom Ronan *Packhorse and Pearling Boat* 79–80: I admit that I did not join the icebergs who favoured cold showers even on the bitterest winter mornings.

1974 Geoffrey Lehmann *A Spring Day in Autumn* 174: 'I'm a regular swimmer myself, right in the middle of winter. They reckon I'm the oldest iceberg in Sydney.'

1981 *Sydney Morning Herald* 21 Sep. 1: The Bondi Icebergs, under the veteran swimmer Alf Vockler, keep getting tougher. Once they merely leaped into their pool and splashed among the icebergs. Yesterday they had 30 competitors running along the beach for 4km before diving into freezing water for a 400 metres freestyle race.

identity (old) A resident of long standing in a particular place [N.Z.: see quot. 1874]

1862 *Thatcher's Dunedin Songster* 2: 'The Old Identity' [song title]

1874 Alexander Bathgate *Colonial Experiences* 26: The term 'old identities' took its origin from an expression in a speech made by one of the members of the Provincial Council, Mr E. B. Cargill, who in speaking of the new arrivals, said that the early settlers should endeavour to preserve their old identity. The strangers, who were inclined to laugh at the aboriginals as a set of old stagers, caught up the phrase, and dubbed them 'old identities'. A comic singer helped to perpetuate the name by writing a song.

1880 Rolf Boldrewood *The Miner's Right* (1890) 213: Some of the old identities still survived.

1885 *The Australasian Printers' Keepsake* 15: The 'old identities' of Stawell become quite garrulous concerning this most famous street of tents.

1890 Edward Dyson *Rhymes from the Mines* 42: 'Twas old Flynn, the identity, told us / That the creek always ran pretty high.

1901 F. J. Gillen *Diary* (1968) 11: Met Harry Pannell an old identity of the interior who has been a teamster on three inhospitable roads since the days of the construction of the line.

1915 J. P. Bourke *Off the Bluebush* 94: 'Dan the Hatter An Old North Country Identity' [poem title]

1929 Jules Raeside *Golden Days* 42: Volumes could be written about many of the identities of those days.

1937 A. W. Upfield *Mr Jelly's Business* 77: 'Several of the old identities swear that he must be nearer ninety than eighty.'

1973 Alexander Buzo *Rooted* 77: 'I was in the pub having a quiet beer with a few Werris Creek identities, when this bloke came up and started picking a blue with Simmo.'

if it was raining   see **raining**

if it's a fair question   see **question**

igloo, the   The Academy of Science building, Canberra [f. shape]
1984 *Sydney Morning Herald* 11: Oct 9: The igloo – also known as the Academy of Science, perhaps Canberra's most architecturally successful building, blending simplicity and compatibility with the low hills of the capital and rounded contours of the Brindabellas in the distance.

ignore, to treat with   To deliberately ignore someone's presence or request
1938 *Bulletin* 6 Jul. 26: The habit of 'treating with ignore' our own industrial experience is quite wrong.
1943 Baker 83: *Treat with ignore, to* To overrule (Digger slang).
1946 Alan Marshall *Tell us about the Turkey, Jo* 202: At first he treats me with ignore, then he answers me back, then he just looks at me.
1963 John O'Grady *The Things They Do to You* 110: I saw her a couple of times, and attempted to discuss the work and the weather ... But, as we used to say in those days [in the war], she 'treated me with ignore'.
1975 *Sydney Morning Herald* 1 Jul. 7: With gathering speed downhill, the train treated Wollstonecraft with ignore.
1983 *Sydney Morning Herald* 27 May Metro 3: When you ask politely for room to pass, you can be treated with cold ignore.

illywhacker   A professional trickster, esp. operating at country shows [derived by Baker (1945:138) from *spieler*]
1941 Kylie Tennant *The Battlers* 183–4: An illywacker is someone who is putting a confidence trick over, selling imitation diamond tie-pins, new-style patent razors or infallible 'tonics' ... 'living on the cockies' by such devices, and following the shows because money always flows freest at show time. A man who 'wacks the illy' can be almost anything, but two of these particular illy-wackers were equipped with a dart game.
1943 Baker 40: *Illywacker* A trickster or spieler.
1975 Hal Porter *The Extra* 15: Social climber, moron, peter-tickler, eeler-spee, illy-wacker.

imbo   An imbecile; a criminal's victim [prison slang]
1953 Baker 125: Australia's under-worldsters have commemorated the services of their victims by calling them any of these assorted terms: ... *imbo.*

1974 Jim McNeil *How Does Your Garden Grow* 141: *Imbo* (colloquial abbreviation) imbecile.

improve, on the   Improving
1959 Baker 119: *improve, on the*: Improving in health or proficiency.
1965 Hal Porter *The Cats of Venice* 144: Had a bout of Bronchitis but on the improve.
1978 John Pringle *Sydney Morning Herald* 18 Sep. 7: I am moved to protest against the increasing tendency to use the appalling phrase 'on the improve' instead of 'improving'. This is particularly popular with one of the ABC's weather announcers, who regularly tells us, sometimes mistakenly, that 'Sydney's weather is on the improve.'
1982 *Weekend Australian* 17 Apr. 44: Channel 10 said 'Canberra is on the improve, and could prove too good.'
1984 *West Australian* (Perth) 4 Jan. 92: Regal Martin on the improve [heading] Three-year-old Regal Martin showed improvement with a smart trial over 800m on the wood fibre track at Ascot yesterday morning.

in it, to be   To participate, join in a planned action (in the imperative, usually an appeal to group loyalty)
[1823 Jon Bee *Slang. A Dictionary of the Turf, the Ring &c.* 105: *In it* – concerned or making part of a gang, or lot.]
1928 Arthur Wright *A Good Recovery* 37: 'It's a queer business,' ventured Trilet, 'and if I'm to be in it, I want to know the strength of it.'
1945 Gavin Casey *Downhill is Easier* 149: 'We're goin' for a couple o' days shootin' in the mornin',' South said to me. 'You'd better be in it.'
1951 Frank Hardy *Power Without Glory* 520: Just then an enthusiastic marcher called out. 'Be in it mate', and the man dragged the woman after him. 'Come on, Liz. We gotta march with 'em.'
1957 John O'Grady *They're a Weird Mob* 88: 'Are you on?' 'Am I on?' 'Yeah, will yer be in ut?' 'Thank you, Joe. I will be in it'. 'Good-o. Bring yer gear out Saturdy.'
1962 Alan Seymour *The One Day of the Year* 68: 'It's too sweet, that stuff. I won't have any.' 'Go on, be in it.'
1965 William Dick *A Bunch of Ratbags* 198: Elaine continued to try to coax me to come into her place to sleep with her, but I wouldn't be in it.

in like Flynn   see **Flynn**

in more trouble than Speed Gordon   see **Gordon**

Indons   Indonesians
1973 Jack Hibberd *A Stretch of the Imagination* (1981) 37: 'The Indon and Kanaka we will civilize.'
1982 *Age* (Melbourne) 30 Jun. 10: End Indon

arms aid, inquiry told [heading]
1983 *National Times* 13 May 2: Intriguing is the request recently made by the Indonesian Government to the Department of Foreign Affairs in Canberra. The Indons want to know the sleeve measurement of the Prime Minister, Bob Hawke.

inked   Drunk, incapacitated
1898 *Bulletin* 1 Oct. 14: To get drunk is to get 'inked'.
1919 W. H. Downing *Digger Dialects* 29: *Inked* Drunk.
1924 *Truth* 27 Apr. 6: *Inked* To be drunk.
1951 A. W. Upfield *The New Shoe* 94: 'What is he like when properly inked?' 'Quiet as Mary's lamb,' was the surprising answer. 'Ten beers and he goes to sleep.'
1969 Patsy Adam-Smith *Folklore of the Australian Railwaymen* 85: Driver found well and truly inked and lying down to it.

inland, the   The sparsely settled interior of Australia (often with a capital letter, esp. after the formation of the Australian Inland Mission in 1912)
1890 A. B. Paterson "Those Names" in *Singer of the Bush* (1983) 126: There were men from the inland stations where the skies like a furnace glow.
1911 E. S. Sorenson *Life in the Australian Backblocks* 282: The majority of inland youngsters have to go through that mill.
1932 Ion L. Idriess *Flynn of the Inland* [book title]
1935 R. B. Plowman *The Boundary Rider* 60: The station folk of the Inland know how to dispense hospitality.
1944 Frank Clune *The Red Heart* 78: Andrew ... departed from Sydney once again on the inland trail.
1954 Vance Palmer *The Legend of the Nineties* 146: Most of them had been born in the inland and their work of shearing, droving, kangaroo-shooting had given them a certain independence of outlook.

inlander   An inhabitant of the inland
1911 E. S. Sorenson *Life in the Australian Backblocks* 282: There is one thing about the inlander that favourably impresses itself upon those who have to look after a city's water supply, and that is his careful use of the liquid.
1913 John Flynn (ed.) *The Inlander* [journal title]
1944 Archer Russell *Bush Ways* 132: He was a typical inlander, quite, reliable, an experienced and hardened desert-rider.
1962 Cynthia Nolan *Outback* 33: Interference from outsiders is resented by these inlanders.

Innisfail, in jail at   see **Tallarook**

inside   Within the more settled areas of Australia (in the nineteenth century), the opposite of **outside** q.v.
1864 Rachel Henning *Letters* ed. David Adams (1963) 171: When Biddulph first took up Exmoor it was a very outside run northwards, and when he dissolved partnership with the Tuckers a year after it was valued at £4,000. Now it is quite an inside station, every bit of country is taken up for several hundred miles round it, and just before he went to Sydney Biddulph refused £25,000 for it.
1889 Barcroft Boake Let. in *Poems* ed. A. G. Stephens (1897) 190: I often wonder if a day will come ... when the wealthy man, perhaps renowned inside for his benevolence, shall see pass before him a band of men – all of whom died in his service, and whose unhallowed graves dot his run.
1910 C. E. W. Bean *On the Wool Track* 27: Whilst the 'inside' stations may grow [sheep] for meat if they care, the 'outside' stations grow for wool.
1919 W. K. Harris *Outback in Australia* 48: While the 'Inside' man has enjoyed almost uninterupted prosperity, the 'Outback' pioneers have had many ups and downs.
1949 George Farwell *Traveller's Tracks* 17: Such conditions have eased considerably on the Inside. But on the Outside track they are still the norm, and the bushman remains the sardonic and resourceful character of Australian legend.
1984 *Sydney Morning Herald* 20 Oct. Colour Mag. 24: The Charnleys think they have been out west long enough and next year they will take their two children 'down inside', somewhere east of Bourke.

I.P.   1   Intending purchaser
1876 Rolf Boldrewood *A Colonial Reformer* (1890) 187: I hope the I.P. (intending purchaser) is a good plucked one.
2   Irate parent (visiting a school)

iron *v.*   To 'flatten'
1953 Baker 104: *To iron,* to attack or fight (a person) i.e. *to flatten* him.
1965 William Dick *A Bunch of Ratbags* 228: Argles was ready behind the big bloke to king-hit him and iron him out.
1970 Barry Oakley *A Salute to the Great McCarthy* 37: 'You see their bruiser over there? Leave him to me. First, I iron him out, that's the signal. Then we run all over them.'
1974 Jim McNeil *How Does Your Garden Grow* 126: 'How many [pills] yer take?' 'Told yer. Half a dozen.' 'Oh well, that'll iron yer right out.'
1984 *Sunday Independent* (Perth) 9 Sep. 86: He was absolutely ironed out ... with a shirt-front bump you could feel in the press box.

iron   Corrugated iron
1877 Let. in *Letters from Grenfell*, ed. G. J. But-

land (1971) 74: Many of the towns in the interior of this colony were born of the enterprise of the gold miner and in their infancy are built of calico or bark or iron.
1946 W. E. Harney *North of 23°* 35: Women lived in these places and reared their children in humpies with bag sides and iron roof.
1958 Patrick White *Australian Letters* I iii 39: Even the ugliness, the bags and iron of Australian life, acquired a meaning.
1960 Nancy Cato *Green Grows the Vine* 8: The low iron roof of the house, painted a faded red, stood out against a clump of shapely gum trees.
1983 *Sydney Morning Herald* 30 Apr. 32: His modest fibro and iron home in the township was bought on an eight-year term with repayments of $245 a month.

iron, good   Expression of approval or agreement: *obsolescent* [see quot. 1908: Partridge lists *bad iron* a failure, a mishap, bad luck]
1894 Ethel Turner *Seven Little Australians* 46: 'Good iron!' Pip whistled softly, while he revolved the thing in his mind.
1895 *Bulletin* 9 Feb. 15: Oh, she's a good iron, is my little clinah.
1898 *Bulletin* 17 Dec. Red Page: Good-iron, synonymous with 'Bravo!'
1908 *Australian Magazine* 1 Nov. 1250: 'Good iron', a very Australian approbatory ejaculation, comes from quoits, the players in the old days being wont to call the phrase after the manner of 'good ball' of the cricketers.
1936 Miles Franklin *All That Swagger* 100: 'Good iron! I don't rob little boys.'
1941 Baker 32: *Good iron* (something) good, pleasant, desired.

iron lung, he wouldn't work in an   The ultimate standard of laziness [f. the artificial respirator which did the patient's breathing for him]
1948 Encountered in conversation.
1971 Frank Hardy *The Outcasts of Foolgarah* 79: Silver Tails who wouldn't work in an iron lung.
1974 Barry Humphries *Barry McKenzie Holds His Own* 27: 'Work! Brits couldn't even spell it. Bloody Poms couldn't work in an iron lung.'
1980 Nicholas Hasluck *The Blue Guitar* 86: 'Some of us have to work for a crust. Remember?' 'Bullshit. You wouldn't work in an iron lung.'
1984 Russ Hinze *Bulletin* 17 Apr. 125: I never

recall anybody being able to convince me that he has ever worked in his life, this bloke. I don't think he would work in an iron lung.

ironclad   Tinned food
1937 Ernestine Hill *The Great Australian Loneliness* 151: Living on damper and ironclads, with native tucker to follow when it gives out ... a policeman's lot is not a happy one.

Isa, the   Mount Isa, Queensland
1979 Bill Scott *Tough in the Old Days* 76: 'The Isa' was a town of goats and dogs and red dust, divided down the centre by the railway line and the mine smelters.

Island, the   Cockatoo Island Gaol (until 1919)
1910 Henry Lawson 'The Rising of the Court' *Prose* i 664: The Sergeant seems anxious to let Mrs Johnson off lightly. It means anything from twenty-four hours or five shillings to three months on the Island for her.

Isle, the Apple   see **Apple**

Isle, the Holiday   see **Holiday**

issue, get one's   To be killed
1919 W. H. Downing *Digger Dialects* 29: *Issue* (1) A portion; (2) 'to get one's issue' – to be killed.
1932 Leonard Mann *Flesh in Armour* 77: 'Jack Martin's got his issue.'

issue, that's the   Equivalent to 'That's the lot' [Services slang]
1919 W. H. Downing *Digger Dialects* 29: *Issue* (1) A portion; (2) 'to get one's issue' – to be killed.
1930 Fredric Manning *Her Privates We* 351: 'What are you talkin' about?' ... 'The whole bloody issue,' said Bourne, comprehensively. 'Officers, and other ranks.'
1941 Baker 38: *Issue* All, everything, the lot.
1962 Alan Seymour *The One Day of the Year* 73: 'Y' got no family, a room in a boardin' 'ouse – and us. And that's the issue.'
1968 Stuart Gore *Holy Smoke* 26: 'He done in the whole issue on sheilas and bombo.'

it's moments like these you need Minties   see **Minties**

J

jack 1 The anus, backside
[1896 J. S. Farmer and W. E. Henley *Slang and its Analogues* iv 33: *Jacksy-pardy*, the posteriors]
1951 Seaforth Mackenzie *Dead Men Rising* 196: 'He thinks the feller had it [the concealed cord] up his jack ... It's so thin it'd easily go into the rectum.'

2 *The jack* Venereal disease
1954 T. A. G. Hungerford *Sowers of the Wind* 3 'Pencillin'll take care of that. They reckon they just pump you full of it, and bingo! No more jack!'
1958 Hal Porter *A Handful of Pennies* 23: 'Jack is the euphemism,' said the Major, 'for venereal disease.'
1962 Alan Marshall *This is the Grass* 164: 'I tell you I was crook. I wanted to get to town. It's no good, a man with jack on the job.'
1971 David Ireland *The Unknown Industrial Prisoner* 37: 'You bastards tell me if he pisses in there with us. I don't want the jack.'
1975 Alex Buzo *Tom* 39: 'I should hop down to the Clinic if I were you. You want to watch out for the jack. Wait on, don't move, I might have some Condy's crystals and a plunger. Didn't they teach you hygiene at Abbotsleigh?'

jacked up Infected
1962 Alan Marshall *This is the Grass* 164: 'I got a dose from a sheila I went out with ... she was jacked up and I was the mug.'

jack of, to be To be fed up with something, to the point of rejecting or abandoning it

1896 Edward Dyson *Rhymes from the Mines* 98: No, you can't count me in, boys; I'm off it – / I'm jack of them practical jokes.
1908 E. G. Murphy *Jarrahland Jingles* 58: And Brim's in London on his 'ace', / Of Andrew Barr a trifle 'jack'.
1944 Jean Devanny *By Tropic, Sea and Jungle* 155: I used to like to get out on my pat for a week – prospecting you know – but not for more than a week. Too much of it makes you jack of it quick.
1965 William Dick *A Bunch of Ratbags* 69: 'There ain't nothin' much to do, is there? I'm getting jack of those holidays.'
1970 Jessica Anderson *The Last Man's Head* 201: 'You know my feelings about it, I made them clear the other day. I'm jack of it.'

jack up v. 1 To give in, collapse [*To jack up* To give up suddenly or promptly OED 1873]
1903 Joseph Furphy *Such is Life* (1944) 178: 'I ain't a man to jack-up while I got a sanguinary leg to stan' on; but I'm gone on the inside, some road.'

2 To reject, abandon [*To jack up* to throw up, give up, abandon OED 1873]
1880 Henry Kendall 'Jim the Splitter' *Poetical Works* ed. T. T. Reed (1966) 159: The nymph in green valleys of Thessaly dim / Would never 'jack up' her old lover for him.
1880 Rolf Boldrewood *The Miner's Right* (1890) 35: Having that morning decided to 'jack up' or thoroughly abandon work at our present claim.
1895 Cornelius Crowe *The Australian Slang*

Dictionary 39: *Jacked Up* (or chucked up), suddenly leaving off doing work.

3 To refuse orders, esp. as a collective action (Services slang); to refuse or abandon a task assigned, as though going on a protest strike

1898 Rolf Boldrewood *A Romance of Canvas Town* 253: The half-used plates and dishes were to me as things loathsome. They operated prejudicially upon my dinners in prospect even, as well as upon those which had 'gone before'. So, as a man, a gentleman, and a squatter, I 'jacked up' at the cookery.

1936 Miles Franklin *All That Swagger* 470: 'Grandfather always took Grandma with him everywhere until she jacked up.'

1951 Eric Lambert *The Twenty Thousand Thieves* 277: The night parade was fixed for seven. When the time arrived, only the N.C.O.s remained in the company lines ... B Company had 'jacked-up'!

1959 David Forrest *The Last Blue Sea* 38: 'They'll jack-up like they did on the Townsville wharf.'

1984 *Sunday Telegraph* (Sydney) 1 Apr. 58: Higgs was the easiest touch I've met. I reckon anyone could get a minimum of three 'accounts' with him before he jacked up.

jack up *n.* The action of refusing orders, esp. if collective

1948 Sumner Locke Elliott *Rusty Bugles* in *Khaki, Bush and Bigotry* ed. Eunice Hanger (1968) 94: 'By gee, if I'm not on the next draft I'm telling you there's going to be the biggest jack-up you ever saw.'

1953 *The Sunburnt Country* ed. Ian Bevan 125: This jacking up is a procedure which no army but the Australian could tolerate. It is not mutiny ... It consists simply of selecting some minor regimental parade or order and boycotting it, to a man, as a public expression of a legitimate grievance.

1959 *Daily Telegraph* (Sydney) 16 Sep. 19: Askin backs 'Jack-Up' of Bus Drivers.

jackaroo (jackeroo) A young man of good connections working on a station as a cadet to gain experience of station management

1873 Rolf Boldrewood 'The Fencing of Wanderowna' *A Romance of Canvas Town* (1898) 70: 'It's very hard on the poor man ... You won't want no hands from shearing to shearing except two or three Jackaroos.'

1878 G. H. Gibson *Southerly Busters* 19n: Young gentlemen getting their 'colonial experience' in the bush are called 'jackeroos' by the station-hands.

1887 *Tibb's Popular Songbook:* With crawlers two and a Jackeroo / You make a noble start.

1896 Henry Lawson 'She Wouldn't Speak' *Prose* i 114: There was a lot of jackeroo swells [in the pub dining-room], that had been on a visit to the

squatter, or something, and they were sitting down at dinner; and they seemed to think by their looks that we ought to have stayed outside and waited till they was done – we was only two rough shearers, you know.

1917 A. B. Paterson *Three Elephant Power* 49: For assistants, he [the manager] had half a dozen of us – jackeroos and colonial experiencers – who got nothing a year, and earned it. We had, in most instances, paid premiums to learn the noble art of squatting.

1934 Tom Clarke *Marriage at 6 a.m.* 46: Jackeroo an apprentice on a station.

1973 Patrick White *Southerly* 136: While I was a jackeroo I used to shut myself up at night with a kerosene lamp and write.

1981 *Sunday Mail* (Brisbane) 22 Nov. 76: At 17 he shipped out to Australia on an assisted passage to become a jackaroo on a station near Dubbo.

jackaroo *v.* To work as a jackaroo

1875 Rolf Boldrewood *The Squatter's Dream* repr. as *Ups and Downs* (1878) 239: 'A year or two more of Jackerooing would only mean the consumption of so many more figs of negrohead, in my case.'

1890 Tasma *In Her Earliest Youth* 152: 'They knock down all their money at first go-off, and then there's nothing for them to do but to go and jackaroo up in Queensland.'

1938 Eric Lowe *Salute to Freedom* 71: Boyd Freeman had gone to the University, and six months earlier John Morgan had left and was now jackerooing on a station in Queensland.

1957 R. S. Porteous *Brigalow* 10–11: 'I put in two years jackerooing in the Gulf Country and finally tossed it in to do the overland trip.'

1980 *Weekend Australian* 23 Feb. Mag.: A year after he ran away from home to go jackerooing in the Queensland bush the then 14-year-old Jim Killen fell off a horse.

jackass, the laughing The kookaburra, *Dacelo gigas* (Morris 1798)

1827 P. Cunningham *Two Years in New South Wales* i 232: The loud and discordant noise of the *laughing jackass.*

1834 George Bennett *Wanderings in New South Wales* i 138: The peculiar noise of the laughing or feathered jackass (*Dacelo gigantea*), which increases from a low to a loud thrilling gurgling laugh, was often heard.

1847 Alexander Harris *Settlers and Convicts* ed. C. M. H. Clark (1954) 67: Every night when the 'laughing jackass', the settler's clock, a common bush bird, calls him home from the field.

1859 Henry Kingsley *Recollections of Geoffry Hamlyn* ii 4: Below us, in the valley, a mob of jackasses were shouting and laughing uproariously.

228

1902 Henry Lawson 'Lord Douglas' *Prose* i 494: Barcoo-Rot, who took Mitchell seriously (and would have taken a laughing jackass seriously).

Jack the Painter A coarse green tea used in the bush, apt to colour the utensil or the mouth: *obs.*
1852 G. C. Mundy *Our Antipodes* i 329: Another notorious ration tea of the bush is called 'Jack the painter'. This is a *very* green tea indeed, its viridity evidently produced by a discreet use of copper drying pans in its manufacture.
1855 William Howitt *Land, Labour and Gold* i 240: Till I saw and tasted them, I had no idea that commodities so vile could be procured in any part of the world ... Jack-the-painter tea, that is, a green preparation of leaves of some kind, which taste like a mixture of copperas and verdigris, and leave a green scum on the infusion.
1877 Rolf Boldrewood *A Colonial Reformer* (1890) 413: He drank his 'Jack the Painter' tea milkless, most probably, and flavoured with blackest sugar.
1918 C. Fetherstonhaugh *After Many Days* 30: The Colonial tea had two names, 'Jack the Painter', that was the green tea, and it had a whiff of paint.
1924 *Truth* 27 Apr. 6: *Jack the Painter* strong bush tea.

Jackey, Jackie Generic name for the Australian Aboriginal
1885 *The Australasian Printers' Keepsake* 26: All the valleys where ... Jacky Jacky hurled his boomerang.
1898 D. W. Carnegie *Spinifex and Sand* 154: Handed him a plate of scraps for his dinner, calling out, 'Hi, Jacky-Jacky, this one your tucker', to which Jim replied with stern dignity, 'Who the h– are you calling Jacky-Jacky? Do you think I'm a – blackfellow?'
1916 Joseph Furphy *Poems* 12: And Jacky in his native scrub, / On bandicoot and yam.
1930 *Bulletin* 6 Aug. 20: Jacky lets himself be caught because he regards the calaboose as a convenient camping place, where he can enjoy plenty white-pfeller tucker.
1944 *Salt* 31 Jan. 6: 'Here's the Good Oil about Jackie' [title of review of W. E. Harney's *Taboo*]
1954 Tom Ronan *Vision Splendid* 216: 'Now a Jacky with new clothes every two months and five sticks of tobacco a week can look down on us and he's going to keep doing so.'
1965 Frank Hardy *The Yarns of Billy Borker* 113: 'Just like calling an American negro Sambo, or an Australian aboriginal Jacky. The white man who says it means well, but it's patronising, if you get what I mean.'
1972 Basil Fuller *West of the Bight* 152: 'We'll fetch a Jackie and let him try.' When the native came more time passed while he combed the country afresh.
1978 *Sydney Morning Herald* 8 Apr. 13: 'I have been treated like a jacky', he [Senator Neville Bonner] said.

Jackey, to sit up like To sit up straight, 'as large as life', almost cheekily
1941 Baker 38: *Jacky, sit up like* To behave, sit up straight.
1948 H. Drake-Brockman *Sydney or the Bush* 176: Cripes, the way they sat there, stiff as Jacky, not saying a word.
1958 Peter Cowan *The Unploughed Land* 182: 'Arriving in state today,' he said. 'Sitting up here in the front like Jacky.'
1969 Pasty Adam Smith *Folklore of the Australian Railwaymen* 180: As we were rattling along north to Darwin I happened to look back out of the guard's van and there they [the hoboes] were – sitting up like Jacky in the commissioner's car behind us.
1975 Hal Porter *The Extra* 139: He's telling Edinburgh, and those writers sitting up like jacky in tiers behind him, about the construction of his next book.

Jacko Generic name for the Turkish soldier in the Gallipoli and Palestine campaigns in World War I
1918 Let. in Bill Gammage *The Broken Years* (1974) 136: Our position is serious as Jacko is giving us chaps a bad time further back & we are pretty well cut off & cant get rations.
1935 H. R. Williams *Comrades of the Great Adventure* 23–4: The impetuosity of the Anzacs was too much for 'Jacko', who steadily gave ground before the vehemence of the onslaught.

jake All right, in good order, 'apples' [U.S. 1921 Mathews]
1919 W. H. Downing *Digger Dialects* 29: *Jake* Correct
1924 *Truth* 27 Apr. 6: *Jake* All right, in order.
1932 Leonard Mann *Flesh in Armour* 266: 'I think she was jake.'
1944 *Coast to Coast 1943* 192: Everything was O.K. he told himself. Everything jake.
1957 Vance Palmer *Seedtime* 184: 'Easy to believe the ship's come home to port at last and everything's jake.'
1965 William Dick *A Bunch of Ratbags* 242: 'We're all right mate; she's jake.'
1980 Dudley McCarthy *The Fate of O'Loughlin* 236: Jimmy had finished what he had to do on the engine and said 'She's jake now, mate, as good as new!'
jakerloo
1919 W. H. Downing *Digger Dialects* 29: *Jakealoo*: See *jake*.
1938 Xavier Herbert *Capricornia* 189: 'Not

wounded, are you?' . . . 'I'm jakerloo.'

jackshay, jackshea A quart-pot
1881 A. C. Grant *Bush-Life in Queensland* i 209: The party, therefore, carry with them a light blanket apiece, stowed away in the folds of which is each man's supper and breakfast. Hobbles and Jack Shays[1] hang from the saddle-dees. 1 A tin quart-pot, used for boiling water for tea, and contrived so as to hold within it a tin pint-pot.
1885 'The Broken-hearted Shearer' *Old Bush Songs* ed. Stewart and Keesing (1957) 267: I've some tea, and some tobacco, and a half a bar of soap, / Some flour and some matches, a billy, and jackshay.
1892 Barcroft Boake 'Down the River' *Bulletin* 6 Feb. 15 repr. in *Where the Dead Men Lie* (1897) 114: The sunlight glances, / Silver-gilding the bright 'Jack Shay'.
1911 E. S. Sorenson *Life in the Australian Back-blocks* 276: Empty boulli-cans were used for the same purposes as are now the specially made 'billy cans'. Quart pots, jackshays, pannikins, and other relatives followed as a matter of course.
1932 Ion L. Idriess *The Desert Column* 119: Before daylight, we warily returned to the oasis and boiled our jackshays.

Jacky Howe see **Howe**

jam, to put on To adopt an affected speech or manner
c. **1882** *The Sydney Slang Dictionary* 5: *Jam (Putting on)* Assuming false airs of importance.
1888 E. Finn *Chronicles of Early Melbourne* ii 780: 'Putting on jam', a phrase of modern slang, and increasing in popularity.
1901 Miles Franklin *My Brilliant Career* 219: People who knew how to conduct themselves properly, and who paid one every attention without a bit of fear of being twitted with 'laying the jam on'.
1951 Dal Stivens *Jimmy Brockett* 30: Sadie put on a bit of jam when she talked, but not too much.
jammy
1911 Alfred Searcy *By Flood and Field* 219: A new chum fellow with notions of city decorum, and not a little 'jammy', ran over from the store.

Jap on Anzac Day, you wouldn't give it to a The ultimate degree of the unacceptable
1973 Jim McNeil *The Chocolate Frog* 36: *Shirker* Our mate 'ere seems ter *like* people . . . *Tosser Like* 'em! I *reckon* he does! He'd kiss a Jap on Anzac Day . . . red 'ot poof, fer mine.
1981 *National Times* 1 Mar. 2: The booze here is so crook you wouldn't give it to a Jap on Anzac Day.

Jaycee Member of a Jaycee club (of the Junior Chamber of Commerce) [U.S. 1946 OED]
1976 *Sydney Morning Herald* 12 Jun. 23: Jaycees work to relieve the sufferings of others. Members of Jaycee clubs in NSW have raised more than $6,000 . . . to improve public awareness of cystic fibrosis.

jerran Afraid [Ab.]
1798 David Collins *An Account of the English Colony in New South Wales* ed. B. H. Fletcher (1975) i 455: A man who would not stand to have a spear thrown at him, but ran away, was a coward, jee-run.
1827 P. Cunningham *Two Years in New South Wales* ii 59: The native word *jirrand* (afraid) has become in some measure an adopted child, and may probably puzzle our future Johnsons with its *unde derivatur*.
1841 *A Mother's Offering to Her Children* 213: The black man looked dreadfully shocked; and exclaimed 'Too much *gerun* me': (meaning frightened).
1847 Alexander Harris *Settlers and Convicts* ed. C. M. H. Clark (1954) 122: I began to feel rather 'jerran', as the blacks say (*i.e.* timorous).

jerry to, to To become 'wise' to [U.S. 1908 Mathews]
1911 Arthur Wright *Gamblers' Gold* 111: 'I always thought I'd seen yer somewhere, but I on'y jerried ter yer when yer was dealin' it out.'
1919 W. H. Downing *Digger Dialects* 30: *Jerry* To understand suddenly.
c. **1928** Louis Esson 'Vagabond Camp' in *Ballades of Old Bohemia* (1980) 163: 'I didn't jerry to to it before.'
1938 Xavier Herbert *Capricornia* 232: 'Use y' bit o' brains,' he says, 'an take a jerry to y' self.'
1945 Cecil Mann *The River* 26: 'I've just taken a jerry to y'. Never struck me before. You got your woman here.'
1950 *Australian Police Journal* Apr. 116: *Jerry* To be awake to.
1975 *Bulletin* 26 Apr. 44: I should've jerried when the guy gave me a tug.

jersey, get a As for **get a guernsey** q.v.

Jessie, more hide (arse, cheek) than An excess of effrontery [f. the elephant at Taronga Park Zoo, d. 1939 aet. 67]
1951 Dal Stivens *Jimmy Brockett* 130: 'You've got more cheek than Jessie the elephant!' I said.
1962 Stuart Gore *Down the Golden Mile* 21: 'More arse than Jessie,' the barman gloomily informed the bar at large, as the swing door flipped shut behind them.
1965 Eric Lambert *The Long White Night* 81:

'You've got more arse than Jessie,' I told him.
1968 Rodney Milgate *A Refined Look at Existence* 59: 'I knew that was coming. More hide than Jessie the ...'
1975 Les Ryan *The Shearers* 143: 'The bastard's got more hide than Jessie,' he said.
1982 *Sun-Herald* 24 Jan. 150: So Bill McMahon gets the old age pension ... It tells you all you need to know about Australia, about the kind of man we put ourselves up to run it, about noblesse oblige Australian style, about the hide of Jessie.

Jesus Hilton, the St Vincent's Private Hospital, Sydney
1984 *Bulletin* 10 Apr. 55: William McMahon: on top again after a stay in the Jesus Hilton [caption to photograph]

Jets, the Newtown (N.S.W.) Rugby League team (also the 'Blues')
1974 *Sydney Morning Herald* 15 Jul. 13: Manly ground Jets.

jeweller's shop In mining, a pocket or patch glistening with gold; a rich claim
1855 Raffaello Carboni *The Eureka Stockade* ed. G. Serle (1969) 10: The jewellers shops, which threatened to exhaust themselves in Canadian Gully were again the talk of the day.
1861 Horace Earle *Ups and Downs* 328: The produce was so vast that the holes there ... were known throughout the entire field as jewellers' shops.
1870 Marcus Clarke *His Natural Life* ed. S. Murray-Smith (1970) 801: 'Bottomed a jeweller's shop, eh?'
1880 Rolf Boldrewood *The Miner's Right* (1890) 133–4: This was the famous 'jeweller's shop', where the very earth seemed composed of gold dust, with gold gravel for a variety.
1903 William Craig *My Adventures on the Australian Goldfields* 218: They sank over a 'pocket' at the foot of the reef ... and dropped upon a veritable 'jeweller's shop'.
1950 Gavin Casey *City of Men* 57: 'We're on leaders now that are going to take us right into the jeweller's shop.'
1960 Donald McLean *The Roaring Days* 62: 'A jeweller's shop might be under your feet, or it might be a duffer.'

jewy A jewfish [abbr.]
1945 Cecil Mann *The River* 107: The jewy he got that night on the Back Beach tipped the beam at 120 lb.
1983 *West Australian* (Perth) 23 Sep. 38: The biggest fish was Charlie Young's magnificent 19kg jewie.

jig To play truant
1977 Jim Ramsay *Cop it Sweet* 50: *Jig* Run away, play truant.
1979 *National Times* 3 Nov. 25: A group from Leichhardt High 'jig' school at the shops, taking care to avoid the police ... If you can't nick off sometimes you can find a place to hide, and jig it in the toilets or the change rooms.
1983 *Sydney Morning Herald* 26 Jul. 1: 'I used to jig school almost every day because I just hated the place, and did not like the teachers very much either', Sarah said yesterday.

jigger 1 A radio set improvised in gaol
1953 Kylie Tennant *The Joyful Condemned* 212: Jake Fletcher ... was not making large sums selling 'jiggers', tiny wireless sets, at five pounds each.
1967 Brian K. Burton *Teach Them No More* 190: 'I'm aware that other fellows in here have jiggers, but that's not good enough for us.'
2 Any device for illegally stimulating a racehorse
1958 Frank Hardy *The Four-Legged Lottery* 172: A jigger is a battery. It is not used in the actual race. A horse is 'hit with it' on the training tracks.
1982 Joe Anderson *Winners Can Laugh* 99: Hand held devices were designed just to make a sound similar to that made by the painful jigger used only in track gallops. When the horse heard the sound during a race it anticipated a coming shock and accelerated in order to avoid it.
3 Anyone 'jigging it', or playing truant
1983 *Sydney Morning Herald* 26 Jul. 1: Sarah was sent to Ormond where she and the 39 other school children there have one thing in common: they are chronic 'jiggers', or truants.

jillaroo Female counterpart of the **jackaroo** q.v.
1943 Baker 42: *Jillaroo*: A Land Girl (War slang.)
1945 Baker 62: The past few years have given us a variant in *jillaroo*, a female station-hand (the play is on Jack and Jill), especially used during World War No. 2 for a Land Girl.
1969 Osmar White *Under the Iron Rainbow* 100: 'Everybody knows Patsy. She's our little jilleroo.' 'Jilleroo?' 'We call her that. Our little black stock girl.'
1978 R. A. Nicholls *Almost Like Talking* 44: 'She'd been a station cook and a jillaroo, and she was the best horsewoman I've ever seen.'
1984 *Bulletin* 3 Apr. 48: She [Greta Scacchi] worked as a jilleroo before returning to England for three years of drama school.
jillarooing
1984 *Age* (Melbourne) 2 Jun. 2: She reckoned she learnt it while jillarooing in the outback.

jim The sum of £1: *obs.* [see quot. 1945]
1906 Edward Dyson *Fact'ry 'Ands* 214: He was

tearin' ratty t' raise another jim ... 'Twas only fer a day, he said, cause he was goin' under er operation yes'day ter recover ther lost goblin.

1911 Arthur Wright *Gambler's Gold* 76: It was the loud-voiced winner speaking with a mouthful of saveloy and peas. 'Here's 'arf a jim for y'.'

1915 J. P. Bourke *Off the Bluebush* 61: For many, many years ago / You cost a modest 'jim'.

1936 H. Drake-Brockman *Sheba Lane* 158: 'But we've got a choice little mob, three hundred-odd at twenty jims a head.'

1945 Baker 109: £1 – *jim* (from the old English slang *jimmy o' goblin*, a sovereign).

Jimmies, Jimmy Brits A fit of nerves; a state of anger [rhyming slang for 'shits', f. the boxer Jimmy Britt, who toured Australia in World War I]

1941 Baker 13: *Brits up, have the* To be afraid, alarmed.

1952 T. A. G. Hungerford *The Ridge and the River* 116: 'I'm sorry, Clem,' he said ... 'Must be a touch of the Jim-brits.'

1955 F. B. Vickers *The Mirage* 127: 'There's hardly a bloke breathin' that aint got the jimmies over some other bloke ... Wars is caused because one country's got the jimmies over what the other might do.'

1957 D'Arcy Niland *Call Me When the Cross Turns Over* 48: 'Thirsty weather, this. Gives you the jimmy brits.'

1961 Patrick White *Riders in the Chariot* 415: She was not accustomed to see the grey light sprawling on an empty bed; it gave her the jimmies.

1972 Don Crick *A Different Drummer* 37: He gave me a touch of the Jimmy Brits.

1975 Les Ryan *The Shearers* 120: 'Gees!' Sandy exclaimed in awe. 'Has he got the jimmy brits!' 'We're for it,' Lofty said.

see **Britt, Edgar**

Jimmies, Jimmy Grants Immigrants: *obs.* [rhyming slang]

1845 E. J. Wakefield *Adventures in New Zealand* ii 180: Knots of whalers, who had come on a cruise to the new settlement, were loitering about ... curiously divided between contempt for the in-experience of the 'jimmy-grants,' as they call the emigrants, and surprise at the general industry and bustle prevailing.

1850 J. D. Mereweather *Diary* in *Settlers* ed. John Hale (1950) 184: A young person at table, speaking contemptuously of some newly-arrived immigrants ('Jimmy Grants', I think, was the slang term she applied to them) I asked her how long she had been out herself?

1859 Henry Kingsley *Recollections of Geoffry Hamlyn* ii 154: 'What are these men that we are going to see?' 'Why, one,' said Lee, 'is a young Jimmy (I beg your pardon, sir, an emigrant), the

other two are old prisoners.'

1878 Rolf Boldrewood *An Australian Squire* repr. as *Babes in the Bush* (1900) 270: 'The country was worth living in, not like it is now, overstocked with 'jimmies' – a lot of useless trash.'

1895 James Kirby *Old Times in the Bush of Australia* 144: As soon as he got to camp, he unyokes, and we found out from him that he was a 'Jimmy-grant' (emigrant), and was loaded with stuff for a station.

1924 *Truth* 27 Apr. 6: *Jimmy* An immigrant. Word now obsolete.

1963 Xavier Herbert *Disturbing Element* 91: When we kids saw people on the street dressed like that we would yell at them: 'Jimmygrants, Pommygranates, Pommies!'

Jimmy Woodser see **Woodser**

job To punch, clout [f. *job* to peck, dab, stab, prod, punch; in pugilistic language, to strike with a sharp or cutting stroke OED 1537]

1890 A. B. Paterson 'More Reminiscences' in *Singer of the Bush* (1983) 119: Some other choice youths ... advised our man to 'hold him up and job him', which he did and so won the fight.

1900 Henry Lawson 'Andy Page's Rival' *Prose* i 362: 'I'll find out for you, Andy. And, what's more, I'll job him for you if I catch him!'

1915 C. J. Dennis *The Songs of a Sentimental Bloke* 121: *Job, to* To smite.

1920 Louis Esson 'The Woman Tamer' in *Dead Timber* 19: 'I don't job women.'

1924 *Truth* 27 Apr. 6: *Job, to* To attack: to strike.

1950 Brian James *The Advancement of Spencer Button* 123: 'I'll job you. Sawkins, if you say I boned two bags of lollies.'

1961 Mena Calthorpe *The Dyehouse* 77: 'He jobbed him,' Larcombe said ... 'Laid him out cold.'

1974 David Williamson *Three Plays* 57: 'If you lay a hand on me, I'll fucking well job you. Right?'

1982 Nicholas Enright *On the Wallaby* 27: A man comes up to me, cap in hand, and says, 'Help me sir, I haven't had a job in weeks.' So I jobbed him.

jockey Someone travelling with the driver of a taxi who can claim to have already hired it if the destination of an intending passenger would mean an unprofitable trip; anyone riding with the driver by arrangement

[**1900–10** O'Brien and Stephens: *Brewer's jocky* Melbourne – a man who rides about with the driver of a brewer's waggon helping him load and unload on the chance of a share of the drinks which fall to the lot of a brewer's man.]

1945 Baker 140: A *jockey* is a taxi-driver's accomplice who pretends to be a passenger in order to encourage legitimate travellers to pay extortionate fares to secure the taxi.

1974 John Powers *The Last of the Knucklemen* 58: 'One of the cattle stations used a helicopter for spottin' stray cattle. I jockeyed for the pilot.'

jockey, gin   see **gin jockey**

joe   An ant, usu. in combinations like *bulljoe, redjoe*
1944 Brian James *First Furrow* 16: A great worker, but with a weakness for ants. Davie always had a pickle bottle for staging heroic contests between red-joes and black-joes – or either of these against twice their number of road ants.
1946 Margaret Trist *What Else is There?* 134: 'I don't want to be bitten by bulljoeys neither.'
1965 Leslie Haylen *Big Red* 164: 'You'd have written your poetry on an ant bed with your arse bitten off by the bull joes.'

Joe   On the Victorian goldfields, a trooper enforcing the regulations of Governor C. Joseph La Trobe; a warning cry of the approach of a trooper
1854 Raffaello Carboni *The Eureka Stockade* ed. G. Serle (1969) 48: From my tent, I soon heard the distant cries of 'Joe!' increasing in vehemence at each second. The poor soldiers were pelted with mud, stones, old stumps, and broken bottles.
1855 William Howitt *Land, Labour and Gold* i 400: Hermsprong rode away followed by his men, and by the execrations of the whole diggings in that quarter, expressed in the well-known cry of 'Joe! Joe!' – a cry which means one of the myrmidons of Charley Joe, as they familiarly style Mr La Trobe, – a cry which on all the diggings resounds on all sides on the appearance of any of the hated officials.
1864 *Thatcher's Colonial Minstrel* 22: The crowd were very peaceable, / The traps rode to and fro, / The license-hunting days are past, / So no one sang out *'Joe'*.
1870 Marcus Clarke *His Natural Life* ed. S. Murray-Smith (1970) 722: The flat instantly bristled with waving arms. 'Run, mate, run! Joe! Joe! Joe!' and at the sound of the dreaded watchword, a dozen un-licensed ones abandon tub and cradle, making, like rabbits, for the deeper burrows.
1919 W. H. Downing *Digger Dialects* 30: *Joey* A military policeman.
c. **1926** 'Alpha' *Reminiscences of the Goldfields* 75: The signal adopted announcing the arrival of the police was 'Joe, Joe, Joe'.
1953 *Caddie A Sydney Barmaid* 140: A whistled Joey from a barmaid was the danger signal [of the proprietor's approach].
joeing, being joed
1854 Raffaello Carboni *The Eureka Stockade* ed. G. Serle (1969) 21: A mob soon collected round the hole: we were respectful, and there was no 'joeing'.
1857 *Thatcher's Colonial Songster* 7: But if he were to ride down the Ballarat-road, / I rather think he would be jolly well 'joed'.
1882 A. J. Boyd *Old Colonials* 160: No one wears a coat – if a bank manager even wore a coat he would be 'joed'.* *'Joed', i.e. hooted.
1903 William Craig *My Adventures on the Australian Goldfields* 255: No more amusing sight could be witnessed than the retreat of the miners up the precipitous sides of the ranges, where in security they 'Joe'd' and jeered the police to their hearts' content.

Joe Blake   1   A snake [rhyming slang]
1941 Baker 39: *Joe Blake* A snake.
1951 Ernestine Hill *The Territory* 446: There is little rhyming slang in the Territory. A snake is always 'Joe Blake'.
1958 Peter Cowan *The Unploughed Land* 40: It should make a nice camp. Might be a few Joe Blakes; still, they're anywhere.
1964 H. P. Tritton *Time Means Tucker* 88: A snake can look remarkably like a slender branch and several times a day you would see men jump back with a string of curses after almost picking up a 'Joe Blake'.
2   *the Joe Blakes*: see quot. 1969
1944 Alan Marshall *These Are My People* 155: 'You feel nothin' when you're on a bender ... You get the Joe Blakes bad after a few weeks.'
1969 Osmar White *Under the Iron Rainbow* 153: It's the electricity in the air that gives a man the joe-blakes* just before the Wet. *Rhyming slang: Delirium – Seeing Snakes – Joe Blakes.

Joe Blow   A nondescript; the average man; the man in the street [also U.S.]
1966 Peter Mathers *Trap* 73: You couldn't tell him from Joe Blow.
1971 *Sydney Morning Herald* 1 Oct 11: The union hoped that this did not mean the introduction of direction of labour. It asked: 'Is the "dole" to be withheld if Joe Blow will not leave home, wife and children at Albury, to live in a labour camp for eleven months of the year?'
1978 Hal Porter *Overland* 71 25: It's more than probable that such symbolic and vocal *bêtises*, outrageous to me, aren't even dimly apparent to Mr and Mrs Joe Blow.

joes, the   A fit of depression
1915 C. J. Dennis *The Songs of a Sentimental Bloke* 41: It gimme Joes to sit an' watch them two!
1920 Louis Esson 'The Woman Tamer' in *Dead Timber* 18: 'You give a man the joes.'
1937 *Best Australian One-Act Plays* 181: 'This place gives me the joes.'

233

1942 Leonard Mann *The Go-Getter* 97: The weather's bad enough to give a man the joes.
1955 Mary Durack *Keep Him My Country* 182: 'Soothing!' Millington exclaimed. 'It fair give me the joes.'

joey 1 A baby kangaroo, carried in the mother's pouch [Morris 1839]
2 A baby, an infant
1887 *All the Year Round* 30 Jul. 67: 'Joey' is a familiar name for anything young or small, and is applied indifferently to a puppy, or a kitten, or a child.
1898 Morris: *Joey* n. (2) Also slang used for a baby or little child, or even a young animal.
1948 K. S. Prichard *Golden Miles* 75: 'A girl never knows when she'll be bringin' home a joey if she goes with you.'
1955 D'Arcy Niland *The Shiralee* 27: 'Got a joey with yer, have yer? And what's your name, young 'un?'
1968 Stuart Gore *Holy Smoke* 42: 'Along comes young Daniel, not much more'n a joey at the time, but pretty shrewd for his age.'

joey, wood and water   see **wood and water**

Joh hat   A broad-brimmed Queensland hat sponsored by Mr Joh Bjelke-Petersen in 1979 as part of a campaign against skin cancer
1979 *Australian* 18 Jan. 2: The Queensland Premier, Joh Bjelke-Petersen, yesterday launched the new Queensland Hat – which he described as a big hat for a big sun in a big state ... Yesterday's launching of the $6 polypropylene broad-brimmed Queensland Hat was to highlight a campaign by the Queensland Cancer Fund and the State Government. The campaign is to alert people to the danger of skin cancer, which affects one in three Queenslanders – the highest skin-cancer rate in the world ... The Queensland Cancer Fund will receive a royalty of 10c for each hat sold.
1982 *Sunday Mail* (Brisbane) 13 Jun. 2: They'll probably take that opportunity to test the market for such typical Queensland exports as peanuts and Joh hats.
see **Flo hat**

John, John Hop   A cop [? f. *gendarme* and rhyming slang]
1909 Edward Dyson *Fact'ry 'Ands* 99: 'He had er John in tow ... ther policeman was fer me.'
1915 C. J. Dennis *The Songs of a Sentimental Bloke* 15: Me, that 'as done me stretch fer stoushin' Johns.
1918 Harley Matthews *Saints and Soldiers* 73: The Nipper had an idea they were policemen – 'John Hops'.
1923 D. H. Lawrence *Kangaroo* 356: 'Police!'

snarled Jack. 'Bloody John Hops!'
1935 Kylie Tennant *Tiburon* 278: 'No Johns ain't goin' to the bother of shiftin' us,' Stainer Rod declared.
1946 Dal Stivens *The Courtship of Uncle Henry* 76: Next morning when I turn up at the shop there are two John Hops there.
1958 H. D. Williamson *The Sunlit Plain* 25: 'I hope she hasn't got that dirty, greasy john hop with her.'
1966 Bruce Beaver *You Can't Come Back* 63: 'No brothers or sisters?' I asked her, just like a john, getting the drum on her.
1975 Xavier Herbert *Poor Fellow My Country* 1151: Brumby Toohey ... had the Provosts after him now, instead of the Johns as of old.

Johnny Bliss   see **Bliss**

johnny-cake   Similar to damper, but closer in size to a scone: made basically of flour and water, and cooked in the ashes or in a pan [f. the name of a flat cake of corn bread U.S. 1739 Mathews]
1846 G. F. Angas *Savage Life and Scenes in Australia and New Zealand* i 161: Our cook had not been idle: there were 'dampers', 'dough-boys', 'leather-jackets', 'johnny-cakes', and 'beggars-in-the-pan.'
1862 Rachel Henning *Letters* ed. D. Adams (1963) 102: Tom lit a great fire and made some beautiful 'johnny-cakes' – thin soda cakes which are baked in about ten minutes and are the best bread you ever ate.
1889 Ernest Giles *Australia Twice Traversed* i 308: We now found we had nothing to eat, at least nothing cooked, and we had to sacrifice a drop of our stock of water to make a Johnny-cake.
1893 Henry Lawson *Letters* 53: No work and very little to eat: we lived mostly on Johnny cakes and cadged a bit of meat here and there.
1905 'The Old Bullock Dray' *Old Bush Songs* ed. A. B. Paterson 6: We'll have leather jacks, johnny cakes, / And fritters in the pan.
1954 Tom Ronan *Vision Splendid* 76: 'When he got back I was living on Johnny cakes and lizards.'
1962 J. Marshall and R. Drysdale *Journey Among Men* 165–6: Take some flour and water and mix them together into a paste. This is worked into a thin, stiff, saucer-shaped wafer which must be dropped flat on the glowing embers of a raked over or dying fire. When the dough is cooked crisp, you have a johnny-cake. (Some bush cooks mix a bit of fat with the flour.)
1964 H. P. Tritton *Time Means Tucker* 121: 'Yair', he said, 'I'd be flatter than a Johnny cake.'

Johnny Raw   A new chum, novice, new recruit [colonial application of *Johnny Raw* nickname for an inexperienced youngster OED 1813]

1845 Thomas McCombie *Arabin* 248: 'I think,' said Arabin, 'you have managed to get very cleverly out of a scrape.' 'Yes, I am no Johnny Raw,' replied the other.

c. **1845** *Ralph Rashleigh* (1952) 30: These ... were a sort of *pariahs* among the prisoners, chiefly *Johnny Raws*, or country chaps, apprentices, or others, who had no acquaintances to assist them while in gaol.

1888 E. Finn *Chronicles of Early Melbourne* ii 905: The 'Expirees' regarded the others with a feeling of pitying contempt, a species of simpletons who should have stayed at home. They called them 'Johnny Raws' and 'New Chums'.

1908 *Australian Magazine* 1 Nov. 1251: A 'jackeroo' (a new chum on a station out for colonial experience) is supposed to be 'Jacky Raw' with a kangaroo's tail as it were.

1941 Baker 39: *Johnny Raw* A 'new chum'.

Johnny Warder   see **Warder**

joker   A fellow, chap [N.Z. 1868 OED]
1900 Henry Lawson 'Meeting Old Mates' *Prose* i 165: 'I haven't seen him for more than three years. Where's the old joker hanging out at all?'
1908 E. S. Sorenson *Quinton's Rouseabout* 205: 'So yer didn't get that joker?' said Tracey.
1929 Herbert Scanlon *Old Memories* 13: 'If it wasn't for me, you two jokers would never have got a spot.'
1942 Gavin Casey *It's Harder for Girls* 218: 'What're you jokers doing tonight?' asked Winch. 'Like to come to a party?'
1951 Dal Stivens *Jimmy Brockett* 84: 'I heard a couple of jokers are out to get you.'
1965 Eric Lambert *The Long White Night* 88: 'Don't you recognize this joker?' 'Why should I? Who is he?'

jonic, jonnick   Genuine, fair, reliable: *obsolescent* [E. dial. *jannock* fair, straight-forward OED 1828]
1874 Charles de Boos *The Congewoi Correspondence* 173: 'I don't think as he acted jonick.'
1923 Jack Moses *Beyond the City Gates* 112: I'm camping down in Logan's, at the old pub in the Glen, / Where the fluid's always jonick.
1935 H. R. Williams *Comrades of the Great Adventure* 163: 'You don't say so!' said Elliott feigning surprise. 'Yes, it's jonick,' continued Peter.
1953 T. A. G. Hungerford *Riverslake* 166: 'Got the knife right into him.' 'Jonic?' 'Jonic!'
1968 Stuart Gore *Holy Smoke* 65: 'That's jonnick, ain't it?' 'Yes. Ridgey-the-didge, mate.'

journo   A journalist [abbr.]
1971 *Southerly* 271: Many who met Slessor in his more formal and conservative moments would have regarded him as the most journo of journos.
1974 David Williamson *Three Plays* 157: 'Didn't I hear you were living with someone? ... A young journo or something.'
1981 *Sunday Mail* (Brisbane) 27 Sep. 2: Junkets for Journos are not all they are cracked up to be.

joy, bullocky's   see **bullocky's joy**

joy, cocky's   see **cocky's joy**

judge, salute the   see **salute**

jug handle   see **monkey** 2

Julia Creek, things are weak at   see **Tallarook**

July fog   See quots
1893 Francis Adams *The Australians* 167: The shearer ... crawling up to the shed with his 'mate' after the dispersal of the 'July fog' (the dead season when no shearing is done).
1945 Baker 90: *the July fog*, the dead season when no shearing is done.

jumbuck   A sheep [Ab. or Pidgin]
1824 Let. 26 Jan. cit. W. S. Ramson *Australian English* (1966) 107: They smacked their lips and stroked their breasts, 'boodjerry patta! murry boodjerry! – fat as jimbuck!!' i.e. good food, very good, fat as mutton.
1843–63 Charles Harpur 'The Kangaroo Hunt' in *Poetical Works* ed. Elizabeth Perkins (1984) 510: Jimbuc is an aboriginal name of a little shag-haired species of kangaroo which is peculiar to mountain copses. It may be called the mountain wallaby ... The Blacks of the Hunter call the sheep jimbuc, no doubt from a resemblance, however remote, arising out of the hairy shagginess of the one and the woolliness of the other.
1849 Alexander Harris *The Emigrant Family* ed. W. S. Ramson (1967) 224: 'That jumbuc (sheep) too much drink up all bardo (water).'
1895 A. B. Paterson 'Waltzing Matilda' in *Singer of the Bush* (1983) 250: Up came the jumbuck to drink at the waterhole, / Up jumped the swagman and grabbed him in glee.
1902 Henry Lawson 'The Shearer's Dream' *Verse* ii 3: Our pay was wool on the jumbuck's backs, so we shore till all was blue – / The sheep was washed afore they was shore (and the rams was scented too).
1918 *Kia Ora Coo-ee* 15 Apr. 2: 'When the job was finished, dashed if he didn't stick half the jumbuck under his arm and proceed on his way.'
1934 Brian Penton *Landtakers* 26: 'What's a thousand of them poor jumbucks to me?'
1941 Sarah Campion *Mo Burdekin* 240: 'There wasn't a jumbuck in sight nor one around fer

miles, but he maintained I was a-upsettin' of his bleedin' sheep.'

1983 *Sydney Morning Herald* 13 Sep. 15: The idea is to promote lamb by controlling production and processing from the time of lambing until the chops, roasts, lamburgers and spare ribs hit the plate in the Big Jumbuck restaurant chain.

jump a horse over the bar   see **horse**

jump, take a running ~ at yourself   Equivalent to 'get lost', 'go to blazes'

1941 Baker 75: *Take a run at yourself* Run away! Go to the devil!

1977 *Sunday Telegraph* (Sydney) 22 May 59: We can only hope that when this unlikely Pommie lot get here they manage to take a series of running jumps at themselves.

jump up   A sudden steep rise in a road: mainly N.T. and W.A.

[**1844** Louisa Meredith *Notes and Sketches of New South Wales* 70: The main portion of the road is *bad* beyond an English comprehension; sometimes it consists of natural step-like rocks protruding from the dust or sand one, two, or three feet above each other, in huge slabs the width of the track, and over these 'jumpers', as they are pleasantly termed, we had to jolt and bump along.]

1894 G. N. Boothby *On the Wallaby* 189: A little later the line crossed the Burdekin River, by means of what seemed to us a most dangerous bridge, technically termed a 'jump up' ... The descent on one side and the ascent on the other are very steep.

1948 H. Drake-Brockman *Sydney or the Bush* 230: Buncker turned the wheel sharply to avoid a jump-up in the track.

1964 Tom Ronan *Packhorse and Pearling Boat* 151: On the first stage out from Hodgson we climbed a jump-up: not a cliff, nor an escarpment, nor a bluff, but in the magnificently adequate basic English of the cattle country, a jump-up.

jump up whitefellow   An expression reflecting an Aboriginal belief that those with white skins are reincarnations of dead blacks

1830 Robert Dawson *The Present State of Australia* 158: 'When he makes blackfellow die,' I said,

'what becomes of him afterward?' 'Go away Englat (England),' he answered, 'den come back white pellow.' This idea is so strongly impressed upon their minds, that when they discover any likeness between a white man and any one of their deceased friends, they exclaim immediately, 'Dat black pellow good while ago jump up white pellow, den came back again.'

1841 *A Mother's Offering to Her Children* 213: The black man looked dreadfully shocked; and exclaimed 'Too much *gerun* me? (meaning frightened) 'jump up white fellow long time ago.'

1860 Mrs Alan MacPherson *My Experiences of Australia* 227: Their notions regarding a future state appear to be very vague and unformed ... but some enunciate the somewhat startling theory 'Me jump up whitefellow'. I have heard an anecdote of some poor creature who was to expiate on the gallows a murder he had committed, and his last words previous to execution were 'Very good, me jump up whitefellow; plenty sixpence then.'

1875 Rolf Boldrewood *The Squatter's Dream* repr. as *Ups and Downs* (1878) 224: 'Me die fast enough ... I believe to-morrow. You think I jump up white fellow?'

1882 A. J. Boyd *Old Colonials* 198: The trooper had a suspicion that if shot, his deceased relative would not 'jump up whitefellow'.

1927 M. M. Bennett *Christison of Lammermoor* 109: One old gin wanted to claim Munggra [Christison] as a defunct brother who had 'jumped up white fellow'.

jungle juice   See quot. 1945

1945 Baker 157: *jungle juice* Any alcoholic beverage concocted by servicemen in the tropics.

1948 Sumner Locke Elliott *Rusty Bugles* in *Khaki, Bush and Bigotry* ed. Eunice Hanger (1968) 75: 'He hasn't half been on the jungle juice.'

1958 Randolph Stow *To the Islands* 19: 'In the war, the cartoons I could never understand about going troppo and drinking jungle juice.'

1968 Geoffrey Dutton *Andy* 268: The Americans had two bottles of bourbon and one of jungle juice made from fermented coconut milk and surgical alcohol.

see **snake juice**

just quietly   see **quietly**

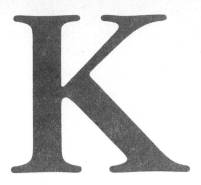

kadoova, off one's   Deranged, off one's head: *rare* [? f. *cady, kadi* hat]
1941 Baker 50: *Off one's kadoova* To be silly, cranky, stupid.
1946 Dal Stivens *The Courtship of Uncle Henry* 72: I reckoned then Thompson was a bit off his kadoova.

kaka   A girl (in juvenile slang, W.A.)
1978 T. A. G. Hungerford in *Memories of Child-hood* ed. Lee White 44: We were hanging thirstily on his startling disclosures about the parts and purposes of what we still called 'the tarts' but which he referred to as 'the brush' or the 'swell kakas'.

kanga   1   Money [? f. rhyming slang *kangaroo = screw*]
1969 Alan O'Toole *The Racing Game* 6: 'On account of you being a mighty bloke, and sending Ape that kanga without asking any questions, we're all agreed on one thing. You're getting the biggest share.'
1978 Eunice Hanger *2D and Other Plays* 44: 'Your daughter's got a bit of kanga, but, hasn't she?' 'Kanga?' 'Cash. That's what they say in the bush.'
2   A jackhammer [? f. 'hopping' motion, also brand name]
1975 *Sun-Herald* 20 Jul. 13: A bone-shaking ride on a 'kanga' – a jackhammer, to the uninitiated.

kangas   see **Kangaroos**

kangaroo   1   To move jerkily (used of a car when the engine is warming up)
1964 *Sydney Morning Herald* 14 Sep. 1: Be on the lookout for a grey car kangarooing through the Manly area. Mrs – has just received her driver's licence.
1971 Craig McGregor *Don't Talk to Me about Love* 187: The car . . . jerked and kangarooed off into the night.
2   To defecate in a kangaroo-like posture
1955 D'Arcy Niland *The Shiralee* 115: It ended up with the injunction in snaggled capitals: Kanga rooing it Not Allowed. And in smaller letters: Remember others have to sit where you shat.

Kangaroos, the   1   The Rugby League team repre-senting Australia internationally
1933 *Sydney Morning Herald* 14 Sep. 12: The Australian Rugby team, the 'Kangaroos' beat York-shire today by 13 points to nil.
1949 *Sydney Morning Herald* 25 Sep. 17: Kanga-roos had it easy.
2   The North Melbourne V.F.L. team
1975 *Sunday Telegraph* (Sydney) 10 Aug. 55: Roos catch the Tigers in hectic scramble.
Also **the kangas**
1979 *Herald* (Melbourne) 21 Apr. 36: Kangas bounce back.
3   The touring Australian Rules team
1984 *Weekend Australian* 28 Jul. 56: The National Football League executive gets no points for its move earlier this week of declaring the national

Australian football team to tour Ireland in October the 'Kangaroos'. The Kangaroo tag has been worn by our national rugby league team overseas with distinction since 1908.

kangaroos in one's top paddock, to have See quots
1908 *Australian Magazine* 1 Nov. 1250: If you show signs of mental weakness you are either balmy, dotty, ratty or cracked, or you may even have white ants in your attic or kangaroos in your top paddock.
1941 Baker 40: *Kangaroos in one's top paddock, to have* To be silly, crazy.
1946 Dal Stivens *The Courtship of Uncle Henry* 70: Talked like a toff himself, he did, but he had kangaroos in the top paddock, as you'll see.
1968 Stuart Gore *Holy Smoke* 59: 'Kangaroos in the top paddock, by the seem of it.'
1981 *Sydney Morning Herald* 7 Nov. 44: None of the patients appears to have any more kangaroos in the top paddock than the people one meets at work or in the pub.

Kanowana chutney An improvised bush delicacy: N.T. [f. place-name]
1951 Ernestine Hill *The Territory* 425: 'Kanowana chutney' – which is a bottle of Worcestershire sauce stirred into a tin of plum jam.

kark (it), to As for **cark it**
1982 *Sydney Morning Herald* 18 Dec. 24: We talked parties, weddings, people karking it and the attendant floral arrangements.
1983 Mike Carlton *Sydney Morning Herald* 2 Mar. 8: The Nightly Technical Trouble reared its ugly head again in the ABC's telecast of the Australian Swimming Championships in Hobart at 11 pm last Sunday. Cameras karked, the videotape screeched to a halt many times, chaos reigned supreme and, for all the ABC could tell us, it is possible that some competitors are still swimming.
1984 *Sydney Morning Herald* 7 Mar. 47: 'She's finally karked it!' [a truck breaking down]. 'C'mon ... We'll have to hoof the rest!'
1984 *Sunday Independent* (Perth) 17 Jun. 48: His friend and co-explorer stopped a shovel-nosed spear in the midriff and karked it.

Kath, Kathleen Mavourneen An indefinite period (from the refrain of the song, 'It may be for years, it may be forever'): applied to a gaol sentence, and by transfer to an habitual criminal [listed by Partridge as 'An indefinitely long term of imprisonment' (N.Z. 1914), and 'The hire purchase system' (Anglo-Irish 1932)]
1903 Joseph Furphy *Such is Life* (1944) 201: Heaven grant that that parting may be a Kathleen Mavourneen one.

1920 Louis Esson 'The Woman Tamer' in *Dead Timber* 25: 'It's a Kathleen Mavourneen, you know. It may be for years, or it may be for ever. You'd better watch yourself.'
1941 Baker 40: *Kath* An indeterminate gaol sentence, *Kathleen Mavourneen* ... An habitual criminal.
1950 *Australian Police Journal* Apr. 116: *Kathleen Mavourneen* Declared an habitual criminal. ('It may be for years ...')
1951 Simon Hickey *Travelled Roads* 38: One hawker owed £75 to his supplier ... and called to tell him that he was on a Kathleen Mavourneen (it may be for years, it may be forever) trip to Beirut.
1983 *Sydney Morning Herald* 20 May 16: Only two on a lengthening list of the Bowen Basin's 'Kathleen Mavourneen' mines whose development could be for years or could be forever.

keep nit see **nit**

keep yow see **yow**

Kelly 1 An axe [brand name]
1941 Baker 40: *Kelly* An axe.
1968 Stuart Gore *Holy Smoke* 94: 'A man'd better be reckoning on a bit of shut-eye, if he's going to be any good on the kelly in the morning.'
1982 *NT News* (Darwin) 15 Jun. 7: Our anthropologists, many with a large 'Kelly' to grind, would have us believe the Aborigine to be Superman, Tarzan and JC in one package.
2 Nickname for a crow
1935 Henry G. Lamond *An Aviary on the Plains* 51: As we leave the camp Kelly the Crow, being the sanitary contractor of the bird world ... floats down to inspect the small litter we've left.
1959 Ian Mudie *The Blue Crane* 37: 'Kellys of Despair' [poem title] ... and all day the crows *kaark-kaark* / with a professorial tilt of the head, / a lecturer-like eye cocked at the corpses of culture, / and a most distinguished and academic accent.
1980 *Mercury* (Hobart) 28 Jun. 6: Replies to a questionnaire sent to all pasture protection boards in the State [of N.S.W.] indicated firm support for the economic value of the crow and advocated its protection as an important force for control of grass grubs ... 'Kelly' the crow was a good bird to have about.
3 See quot. 1953
1953 Baker 142: *kelly*, a tram or omnibus inspector.
1980 Clive James *Unreliable Memoirs* 155: The inspectors [on the buses] were called Kellies, after Ned Kelly, and were likely to swoop at any time.

Kelly, Ned see **Ned Kelly**

238

Kenso 1 Kensington, a suburb of Sydney, N.S.W.

1949 Lawson Glassop *Lucky Palmer* 24: 'Might be Kenso or Victoria Park or even Moorefield or Warwick Farm.'

2 The University of New South Wales (at Kensington)

1972 Geoff Morley *Jockey Rides Honest Race* 10: You enrol at Kenso High School (in-joke) and pay your fees. You go to Uni five nights a week and work here five days a week.

kero Kerosene (paraffin) [abbr.]

1938 Xavier Herbert *Capricornia* 148: 'Take it and buy some tucker and kero.'

1965 *The Tracks We Travel* ed. L. Haylen 43: I could hear the old clock ticking away behind the kero tin where I had thrown it.

1969 Osmar White *Under the Iron Rainbow* 76: These times with kero refrigerators and bottled gas it was different.

1973 Frank Huelin *Keep Moving* 171: A shallow wash dish made from another cut-down kero-tin.

1979 *Weekend Australian* 17 Mar. Mag. 16: Did you know that kero is an excellent laxative, and operates for DAYS afterwards?

kick To accelerate (of a racehorse); usu. in the expressions 'kick away', 'kick clear'

1980 *Sun-Herald* 8 Jun. 57: Winter's Dance made the home turn awkwardly and appeared to get on the wrong leg. Her supporters had given up hope as the leaders kicked away.

1983 Phillip Smith *Sun-Herald* 17 Apr. 65: 'I was confident that we had Veloso covered but it was the opposite – he just kicked clear and won easily.'

kick, he couldn't get a ~ in a stampede (stable) Reproach to an inadequate Australian Rules player

1981 *National Times* 25 Jan. 23: The Australian Rules footballer who 'couldn't get a kick in a stampede'.

1984 *Sunday Independent* (Perth) 1 Apr. 72: They couldn't win a kick in a stable.

kick home As for **boot home** q.v.

1979 *Australian* 9 Jan. 16: Last week he kicked home a dozen winners on four race-tracks.

1983 *Sun* (Sydney) 25 Aug. 51: Before returning home for his wedding on Monday, Johnston was kicking home plenty of winners in Singapore.

kick on To carry on, with just enough funds for the purpose

1949 Lawson Glassop *Lucky Palmer* 153: 'I knew him when I used to slip ten bob out of the till ... so he could kick on with it.' 'You can often kick on with ten bob,' said Lucky judicially.

1957 Ray Lawler *Summer of the Seventeenth Doll*

50: 'What about all those times when you've carried me – every year when I've run dry down here you've kicked me on?'

kick the tin To make a contribution [? f. rattling of collection box]

1966 Baker 230: Such suggestions as *kick the tin* ... to the person who is due to buy drinks.

1969 Leslie Haylen *Twenty Years' Hard Labor* 36–7: He [Mr Chifley] gave me £50 for my campaign funds out of his own pocket and said, rather unnecessarily I thought, 'I'm kicking the tin for a few others as well so you needn't mention this.'

1976 *Sunday Telegraph* (Sydney) 30 May 34: When A.L.P. president Bob Hawke was appealing for money to help pay the Federal election campaign debt of $300,000, the NSW Labor Party was claiming it could not afford to 'kick the tin'.

1978 Barry Humphries *A Nice Night's Entertainment* (1981) 174: He reckoned the Department would kick the tin on this trip.

1982 *Australian* 11 Aug. 9: The Tasmanian Premier would do all (except, presumably, kick the tin) that the Victorian Premier would not do.

kid from Cockaleechie see **Cockaleechie**

Kidman's delight Golden syrup or **cocky's joy** q.v. [f. Sir Sidney Kidman (1857–1935), a famous cattleman]

1935 R. B. Plowman *The Boundary Rider* 187: The better class employer added [to the station rations] a tin of jam per week, or its equivalent in 'Bullocky's Joy' (treacle) or what was later known as 'Kidman's Delight' (golden syrup).

1943 Baker 44: *Kidman's blood mixture* Treacle.

kidstakes Pretence, nonsense; as an exclamation, equivalent to 'Fiddlesticks': *obs.* [f. *kid* to hoax, humbug OED 1811]

1916 C. J. Dennis *The Moods of Ginger Mick* 88: Mick reads the boys them ringin' words o' praise; / But they jist grins a bit an' sez 'Kid stakes!'

1919 W. H. Downing *Digger Dialects* 30: *Kidstakes* Insincere flattery; inveiglement; a wheedling or deceitful speech or action.

1922 Arthur Wright *A Colt from the Country* 201: 'It was no kid stakes,' declared Bucks. 'The old man had the roll ready.'

1938 Xavier Herbert *Capricornia* 567: 'I didn't see him, I tell you.' 'You told his Ma you did.' 'That was only kidstakes.'

1945 Gavin Casey *Downhill is Easier* 138: All his kidstakes during the afternoon had probably been caused by his jealousy of Peter South.

killer A bullock or sheep to be killed for meat

1897 I. Scott *How I Stole over 10,000 Sheep in Australia and N.Z.* 9: 'You know the killers, don't you?' ... i.e. the sheep the boss used for his own mutton at the house. [OED]

1929 K. S. Prichard *Coonardoo* 112: Warieda had gone out after a killer, cut up the beast and given everybody in the uloo his or her share.

1931 Vance Palmer *Separate Lives* 124: He had put it [the bullock] among the herd of killers in the home paddock in the hope that the new overseer might use it for beef in mistake.

1949 *Coast to Coast 1948* 149: 'The killers are in the paddock behind the pen. You can leave the meat hanging.'

1957 R. S. Porteous *Brigalow* 232: 'We'll have to get a killer in tomorrow. We're just about out of meat.'

1966 Tom Ronan *Once There Was a Bagman* 36: Most of my time seemed to be spent chasing killers ... In between meat-chasing trips I was supposed just to find myself something to do.

kill our own, we catch and see **catch**

Kimberley cool Applied to beer drunk at the temperature of the atmosphere [f. the early days of the Ord scheme, when beer was drunk by construction workers from the drums in which they kept it]

Kimberley Formal A dress style for men requiring shirt and shorts, shoes and socks

Kimberley mutton, oyster, walkabout See quots [place-name in N.W. Australia]

1945 Tom Ronan *Strangers on the Ophir* 39: A meat fritter known in the Kimberleys as a 'Burdekin Duck', and on the Burdekin as a 'Kimberley Oyster'.

1959 Jon Cleary *Back of Sunset* 167: The roast goat, Kimberley mutton, as it was called.

1971 Keith Willey *Boss Drover* 72: Horses ... would die in hundreds from what we called the Kimberley walkabout. This was a disease which set a horse walking, round and round and up and down, knocking into trees and rocks and never stopping to eat, until in a few hours or days he would literally have walked himself to death.

1976 Roland Robinson *The Shift of Sands* 348: 'They [the donkeys and mules] don't get the Kimberley walkabout disease that kills off the horses. The C.S.I.R.O. reckon it's caused by a plant called 'Croatalaria'. We call it rattle-pod.'

Kinchela, putting ~ on them See quots: *obs.*

1897 *Bulletin* 25 Sep. Red Page: 'Putting Kinchela on 'em' is evidently inspired by the fact that one Kinchela, some years ago, wrote and published a pamphlet on the art of sharpening and 'keeping' shears. The expression was at first confined exclusively to shear-sharpening but in time came to have a wider application.

1911 E. S. Sorenson *Life in the Australian Backblocks* 233: The blades are pulled back and the knockers filed down, so the shears will take a bigger blow. This is called 'putting kinchler on them', from the fact that it was first adopted by John Kinsella, who died in Armidale about August 1902.

kinder Kindergarten, esp. pre-school (Victoria)

1978 *Herald* (Melbourne) 5 Sep. 9: A Kinder Group Wants to Expand [heading] The International Montessori Association wants to expand its educational program in Australia. The association ... has six kindergartens and two primary schools in Melbourne suburbs.

1981 *Age* (Melbourne) 25 Sep. 16: No one has to choose between home and kinder because it is possible to enjoy both. The pre-school year is a transition between the years at home with mum and the years ahead at school (all 13 of them).

1983 Morris Lurie *Seven Books for Grossman* 100: Little Norbert and little Hermione and little all the rest of them, are all tucked nicely away in their kinders and creches and day-care centres.

kindy Kindergarten, esp. pre-school [abbr.]

1969 Lyndall Hadow *Full Cycle* 189: The house was vapid when he was at work, the children at school, Philip at morning kindie.

1979 *Australian* 11 Oct. 20: Kindy teacher canes weary squad [heading] The bone-weary Australians ... made their way to a nearby school but had no sooner started warming up than the teacher ordered them off the field.

1980 *Daily News* (Perth) 17 Oct. 44: Lorrelle Holman (5), of Mt Pleasant, is learning pots about the animal kingdom, thanks to her local kindy. Her proud dad Ken says the kids were issued with tadpoles last week.

1984 *Sun-Herald* 17 Jun. 154: 'Same thing with my kids', I said. 'I told them almost from kindie that they had to be *dying* before they didn't go to school cos I was working.'

king In combinations like 'cattle king', 'shepherd king', 'squatter king', 'wool king'

1908 W. H. Ogilvie *My Life in the Open* 25: Tyson, the Queensland cattle king, who died a few years ago.

1936 Ion L. Idriess *The Cattle King: The Story of Sir Sidney Kidman* [book title]

1951 Ernestine Hill *The Territory* 306: Then he had been a cattle king. Now, with a swag for home, he made up his mind for a last camp.

1962 Tom Ronan *Deep of the Sky* 30: The only survivor of those who had worked for the two great Australian Cattle Kings, Tyson and Kidman.

1875 Rolf Boldrewood *The Squatter's Dream* repr. as *Ups and Downs* (1878) 277: Entering the parlour in a suit of rough tweed, he felt much more like a shepherd king of the future than the death-doomed pioneer . . . of the preceding few days.

1921 William Baylebridge *An Anzac Muster* 26: 'I am settling portions of my holding with embryonic sheep-kings – those ambitious trouble-hunters I spoke of.'

1945 Elizabeth George *Two at Daly Waters* 15: Bill had been working for Sir Samuel McCaughey, the sheep king of New South Wales, on his Riverina stations.

1891 Francis Adams *Fortnightly Review* Oct. 542: All the old profuse hospitality, the hunts and dances and four-in-hands of the squatter kings, live now but as a dim tradition.

1869 *Australian Journal* Jul. 685: *Wool King* A squatter.

1900 Henry Lawson 'Middleton's Peter' *Prose* i 257: The Australian squatter is not always the mighty wool king that English and American authors and other uninformed people imagine him to be!

1911 E. J. Brady *River Rovers* 46: This splendid territory, embracing millions of acres of irrigable land . . . cannot remain forever in the possession of a few dozen wool kings and foreign investors.

1947 Vance Palmer *Hail Tomorrow* 18: 'The man who . . . found this country grovelling at the feet of a few fat-bellied wool-kings and gave it a backbone and a soul.'

king *v.* Abbr. of **king-hit** q.v.

1959 Gerard Hamilton *Summer Glare* 97: 'Ken kinged him.'

1962 Alan Marshall *This is the Grass* 144: 'If a bloke comes at you buttoning up his coat you always king him when he's on the last button. It's just common sense.'

1975 *Bulletin* 26 Apr. 45: 'He kinged a floor-walker.'

King Billy The imaginary patriarch of the Aboriginal race; nickname for any Aboriginal singled out from the rest.

[**1841** *A Mother's Offering to Her Children* 205: Billy the black man killed one of his little babies.]

1898 D. W. Carnegie *Spinifex and Sand* 190: Finding the water that King Billy (for so had we named the Buck) eventually took us to.

1902 Henry Lawson 'A Bush Publican's Lament' *Prose* i 467: An' supposin' Old King Billy an' his ole black gin comes round at holiday time and squats on the verander.

1920 E. S. Sorenson *Sunraysia Daily* (Mildura) 16 Oct. 14: It is a libel on the race to take the degenerate King Billy, who loafs about the towns, as a criterion, embodying as he does the results of rum, opium, tobacco and other vices of the white man.

1921 M. E. Fullerton *Bark House Days* 52: It was a great blessing that the old creek had cut its course through that valley. Even before King Billy's traditions began it had wormed itself there between the hills.

1975 Richard Beilby *The Brown Land Crying* 35: 'You'll see Captain Cook coming ashore from the South Perth ferry . . . And I suppose there'll be a few Aborigines, King Billy with his nulla-nullas and spears.'

king-hit *n.* A knockout punch; a surprise punch, probably unfair

1924 *Truth* 27 Apr. 6: *King-hit* The winning blow in a fight.

1935 H. R. Williams *Comrades of the Great Adventure* 192: Swung with terrific force, the unusual weapon scored a 'king-hit' which spread-eagled the second 'Jack'.

1944 Lawson Glassop *We Were the Rats* 76: 'Do this galah over,' he whispered in my ear. 'He's a king-hit merchant.'

1960 Ron Tullipan *Follow the Sun* 128: 'He's a king-hit merchant, always has been, and when he misses the surprise shot, he doesn't get a second free one with a bloke like me.'

1969 Don Whitington *The House Will Divide* xiii: Where Menzies might have used subtle ju-jitsu pressure on a nerve and Holt would have favoured a cunning ankle trap, Gorton employed a king hit that everyone, including the umpire, could see and deplore.

1975 *Sydney Morning Herald* 9 Aug. 3: Judge censures 'cowardly king hit' by policeman.

1984 *Sun* (Melbourne) 16 Jul. 3: The reported player had been bashed in the face by a 'king hit' which started the brawl.

king-hit *v.* To deliver a knockout punch, or a surprise punch, probably unfair

1962 Stuart Gore *Down the Golden Mile* 277: 'King-hit me, the bastard,' he muttered. 'With me own gun!'

1965 William Dick *A Bunch of Ratbags* 88: I was learning the art of street-fighting: how to king-hit and how to rabbit-chop, how to gouge their eyes.

1972 John Bailey *The Wire Classroom* 140: The previous cop at Wendi who had been known to king-hit a native who had spat on the pavement near his wife.

1980 *Daily News* (Perth) 25 Sep. 39: Ruck-rover Wayne Cormack was 'king hit' behind the play early in the third term.

king-pin The leading figure, most important person [U.S. 1867 OED ? f. *king-bolt* a main or large bolt in a mechanical structure OED 1825]

1907 Charles MacAlister *Old Pioneering Days in the Sunny South* 262: The notorious Frank

Gardiner – the King-pin of Australian bushrangers – so began his stirring career.

1915 C. J. Dennis *The Songs of a Sentimental Bloke* 102: But 'struth! 'E is king-pin! The 'ead serang!

1926 K. S. Prichard *Working Bullocks* 258: 'My!' Mary Ann gasped incredulously, 'and you was the king pin last week, Mark.'

1938 H. Drake-Brockman *Men Without Wives* 78: 'Andy, where is old man Lovatt?' 'Out on the run. For the moment I'm king-pin.'

1957 Judah Waten *Shares in Murder* 99: 'Then he must be the biggest fence of the lot. The kingpin. The daddy of all fences.'

kings in grass castles see **grass castles**

kip The small flat piece of board from which the coins are tossed in two-up [cf. *kep* to catch EDD 1781; *keper* a flat piece of wood secured in the mouth of a horse to prevent his eating the corn EDD 1897]

1898 *Bulletin* 17 Dec. Red Page: The kip is the piece of wood used in 'two-up'.

1904 Henry Fletcher *Dads Wayback: His Work* 12: An' most everyone, high an' low, rich an' poor, plays up ther coin, an' heads 'em off the kip.

1911 Louis Stone *Jonah* 215: The spinner placed the two pennies face down on the kip, and then, with a turn of the wrist, the coins flew twenty feet into the air.

1916 C. J. Dennis *The Moods of Ginger Mick* 108: 'It's like two-up: I'm 'eadin' 'em this trip; / But lookin', day be day, to pass the kip.'

1949 Lawson Glassop *Lucky Palmer* 167: He handed the kip to the spinner ... placed two pennies, tails up, on it with infinite care and said 'Fair go.'

kipper An Englishman (Services slang in World War II) [f. the prominence of kippers in English diet. See also quots 1946, 1962]

1946 *Daily Telegraph* (Sydney) 22 Jan. 11: Hansen told Mr Goldie, S. M. that the girls called them 'Pommies' and 'kippers'. 'I understand that in Australia "kipper" means two-faced and gutless,' Hansen added.

1954 T. A. G. Hungerford *Sowers of the Wind* 204: 'The kippers have got orders not to go about alone now.'

1962 J. Marshall and R. Drysdale *Journey Among Men* 190: This unlovable trait has led to the application of the expression *Kipper* to a certain type of Englishman. A kipper, by virtue of its processing, has become two-faced with no guts.

1975 *Bulletin* 30 Aug. 63: The Australian naval slang term for a Pommy matelot is – or was – 'bloody kipper'. Retrospective lower-deck etymology gives the derivation as 'A two-faced bastard with no guts.'

kiss-and-ride See quot.

1975 *Sydney Morning Herald* 16 Jan. 6: The kiss-and-ride system – the wife drops her husband off at the station or terminal, keeps the car for her own use during the day, and picks him up at night.

1982 *Sun-Herald* 18 Apr. 23: Parking areas, kiss'n'ride facilities and bus/ferry interchanges would be the responsibility of local councils.

kitchen tea A pre-wedding party to which the guests bring some item of kitchen equipment as a gift

1934 Tom Clarke *Marriage at 6 a.m.* 17: Tom Rawlings led me off to see the bride at a 'kitchen tea' ... it was so called because each guest brought a kitchen utensil as a wedding-gift.

1943 Kylie Tennant *Time Enough Later* 200: 'I beg of you, restrain them from any idea of visitings and junketings and gruesomeness in the form of kitchen teas.'

1980 *NT News* (Darwin) 9 Jan. 19: A Traditional Kitchen Tea was held for last Saturday's bride Sue Jennings ... Guests took along gifts for the bride's future home which will be in Darwin.

Kiwi *n. & a.* A New Zealander [f. the bird unique to New Zealand OED 1918]

1935 H. R. Williams *Comrades of the Great Adventure* 210: 'We're darned lucky we are not all beaten up like your Kiwi friend.'

1965 *Daily Telegraph* (Sydney) 13 Apr. 64: We never had less than 150 Aussie and Kiwi girls on our own temporary staff.

1976 *Australian* 11 Feb. 19: Testing time looms for promising Kiwi colt.

1982 *Sydney Morning Herald* 18 Mar. 6: There is a view that New Zealand has made a significant contribution to the number of drag queens at the Cross. 'Kiwi fruits' is the term used, I'm told.

Kiwi Valley

1979 *Bulletin* 3 Jul. 57: This invasion, which is turning Bondi into a 'Kiwi Valley' similar to Kangaroo Valley in London's Earl's Court, is beginning to breed local resentment.

kleiner As for **clinah** q.v.

1899 W. T. Goodge *Hits! Skits! and Jingles!* 17: Well, spare me days, kleiner, I love yer!

knobtwister Bookmaker [f. the knobs for controlling the betting board]

1984 *Sun-Herald* 25 Nov. 152: At Canterbury on Wednesday two rails knobtwisters were reprimanded for not betting each-way when they should have.

knock *n.* An act of intercourse; a promiscuous

woman [f. *knock v.* 1]
1965 William Dick *A Bunch of Ratbags* 199: I had caused him to miss out on a knock many weeks ago with Elaine, and he had never forgiven me. Ibid. 158: To tell your best mate that one of his family was a knock was unethical and uncalled for.
1972 David Williamson *The Removalists* 117: 'Never turn down a knock, Russy boy. Tomorrow you might get run over by a tram.'

knock *v.* 1 To copulate with [OED 1598], in Australia more common in expressions like 'knock off', or 'do a knock with' (to strike up an acquaintance, seeking favours)
1933 Norman Lindsay *Saturdee* 138: 'Supposin' I was to do a knock with girls, what 'ud I say to them?'
1969 William Dick *Naked Prodigal* 112: 'She all right? Does she look like she knocks?'
1971 Frank Hardy *The Outcasts of Foolgarah* 15: 'Well, he's not knocking orf my sister-in-law and that's for sure.'
2 To disparage, criticize, find fault with [U.S. 1896 Mathews]
1892 William Lane *The Workingman's Paradise* 85: 'Admit it's a business concern and that everybody growls at it, it's the only paper that dares knock things.'
1903 Joseph Furphy *Such is Life* (1944) 32: 'Hold on, hold on,' interrupted Mosey. 'Don't go no furder, for Gossake. Yer knockin' yerself bad, an' you don't know it.'
1920 *Sunraysia Daily* (Mildura) 6 Nov. 7: Don't knock too hard, Mick ... for the love of Australia don't deny the existence of story-writers at least as capable ... as those of other English-speaking countries.
1936 H. Drake-Brockman *Sheba Lane* 128: 'I hate "Knocking" you – why the hell you and dad didn't get into partnership beats me.'
1958 E. O. Schlunke *The Village Hampden* 233: 'She seemed to be so nice and friendly, I wasn't going to knock my good luck.'
1975 *Sun-Herald* 15 Jun. 4: Mr Whitlam last night lashed out at critics within the Labor movement who were 'knocking' his Government's efforts.
1981 *Australian* 17 Oct. Mag. 2: Knocking – like sunshine, fresh air and punting – is as Australian as lamingtons.

knocked, knocked out Killed or wounded in action (Services slang)
1917 Diary cit. Patsy Adam-Smith *The Anzacs* (1978) 215: We just go into the line again and again until we get knocked.
1918 Let. in Bill Gammage *The Broken Years* (1974) 220: Am leaving now to go over to the attack. If you receive this, I shall have been knocked out.

1918 Harley Matthews *Saints and Soldiers* 73: Then the machine-gun corporal got knocked out.
1932 Leonard Mann *Flesh in Armour* 312: 'Corporal Jeffreys knocked, sir,' he said.
1944 Lawson Glassop *We Were the Rats* 128: 'If a section leader got knocked, somebody ... would just take over and the rest would follow without question.'
1951 Eric Lambert *The Twenty Thousand Thieves* 230: 'It's a pity he couldn't have been knocked!'

knock back *v.* 1 To reject
1918 *Kia Ora Coo-ee* 15 Jul. 12: Have you ever got arrangements completed for your holidays to commence on a Monday at home, and then about six of your fellow workers got sick on the Saturday, and you have been knocked back?
1935 Kylie Tennant *Tiburon* 27: A number ... failed to make any application on the grounds that they weren't 'going to give old Ma Claufield the satisfaction of knocking them back'.
1938 Eric Lowe *Salute to Freedom* 267: 'It's just that I don't want you to feel disappointed if you get knocked back.'
1944 Lawson Glassop *We Were the Rats* 104: 'Ya still goin' ter be true to Margaret? Still goin' to keep knockin' back the sheilas?'
1966 Tom Ronan *Strangers on the Ophir* 46: 'I knocked him back for credit and put him to sleep with a special drink.'
2 To drink, consume [OED 1931]
1962 J. Marshall and R. Drysdale *Journey Among Men* 164: He took the top off one [bottle] and poured himself a glassful. He knocked this back in one hit.
1973 H. Williams *My Love Had a Black Speed Stripe* 110: He kept knocking back the whisky I kept slipping into his glass.
1975 Don Townshend *Gland Time* 231: He was knocking back the grogs at an alarming rate.

knock bandy see **bandy**

knock down *v.* To spend (esp. a cheque) until funds are exhausted, generally on liquor
1853 C. R. Read *What I Heard, Saw and Did on the Australian Goldfields* 98: A volume might almost be written on the ridiculous manner in which this class of people squander away their money; many, I have heard boasting at the diggings, as to the shortness of time in which they could 'knock down' a thousand or two pounds, and return to the diggings, without sufficient to buy a pickaxe.
1867 J. R. Houlding *Australian Capers* 386: A jolly shepherd 'knocking down' a year's wages.
1873 A. Trollope *Australia* ed. Edwards and Joyce (1967) 203: The labourer who can live and save his money, who can refrain from knocking down his cheque, may no doubt in Queensland become

the real lord of all around him and dwell on his own land in actual independence.

1883 E. M. Curr *Recollections of Squatting in Victoria* 348: 'All I've heard of was a Devil's River lot, six or eight of them, knocking down their cheques at Young's.'

1891 Henry Lawson *Verse* i 135: For the bushman gets bushed in the streets of a town, / Where he loses his friends when his cheque is knocked down.

1905 'On the Road to Gundagai' *The Old Bush Songs* ed. A. B. Paterson 25: In a week the spree was over and the cheque was all knocked down, / So we shouldered our 'Matildas', and we turned our backs on town.

1919 W. K. Harris *Outback in Australia* 74: 'Knocking down a cheque' is not a common occurrence in the Bush nowadays, but there are still some Outback townships which look forward to the periodical visit of hands from some of the 'further out' stations.

1946 Ion L. Idriess *In Crocodile Land* 209: 'A bushie had blown in that day and started to knock down his cheque.'

knock out To earn [N.Z. 1871 OED]
1881 A. C. Grant *Bush-Life in Queensland* i 31: These were part of the Ipswich tribe, and knocked out a precarious living by hunting in the bush and begging in the town.

1896 Edward Dyson *Rhymes from the Mines* 93: Yet Jo contrived to knock out bread and butter, / And something for a dead-broke mate.

1941 Baker 42: *Knock out, to* To earn (a certain sum of money).

1975 *Bulletin* 30 Aug. 16: What about the schoolteacher, the young computer programmer or plumber knocking out about $200 a week.

knock over a doll see **doll**

knock the dags off a sick canary, couldn't see **couldn't**

knock the skin off a rice pudding, couldn't see **couldn't**

knockabout man A station-hand doing odd jobs; a rouseabout
1868 Marcus Clarke 'Swagmen' repr. in *The Peripatetic Philosopher* (1869) 41: At the station where I worked for some time (as 'knock-about man').

1880 Rolf Boldrewood *The Miner's Right* (1890) 60: 'If we don't make a rise before that time, we shall have become wages men, bush-rangers, or knock-about-men on a station – farm-labourers.'

1916 Macmillan's *Modern Dictionary of the English Language* 785: *knockabout man* (bush term) a general labourer, employed about a

squatter's homestead, or on a sheep- or cattle-run; a man who makes himself generally useful in the shearing-sheds, etc.

knockback *n.* A refusal; rejection of an overture, often sexual [E. dial. 1902 OED]
1919 W. H. Downing *Digger Dialects* 31: *Knockback* A refusal.

1933 Frank Clune *Try Anything Once* 25: There was no need for any further hands about the place. This was rather a blow, but already I was getting used to knock-backs and I felt that something or other would turn up.

1941 Kylie Tennant *The Battlers* 181: The busker, always ready to save money, and realising from several 'knockbacks' that he had little hope of lodging in the town, immediately pre-empted the vacant sleeping-place.

1957 Ray Lawler *Summer of the Seventeenth Doll* 101: 'Yeh – you, the great lover that's never had a knock back.'

1963 Frank Hardy *Legends from Benson's Valley* 11: 'I get a lot of knock backs but I get a lot of naughties.'

1975 Les Ryan *The Shearers* 76: 'Please yourself,' he said, looking like Humphrey Bogart after a knock-back. 'I'll be around.'

knockdown, the An introduction [U.S. 1865 OED]
1916 C. J. Dennis *The Moods of Ginger Mick* 149: *Knock-down* A ceremony insisted upon by ladies who decline to be 'picked up'; a formal introduction.

1924 *Truth* 27 Apr. 6: *Knock down* An introduction.

1938 *Bulletin* 6 Jul. 48: 'Another bloke gave me a knockdown to 'im.'

1950 Jon Cleary *Just Let Me Be* 9: 'She'll never give you a knock-down while you're just a milkman. You'll have to go up in the world.'

1969 Osmar White *Under the Iron Rainbow* 75: There'd be a lot of fellers who knew Don. One of them might give me a knockdown to him.

1981 *Sun-Herald* 1 Mar. 97: 'Crikey, that's a grouse-looking little sheila over there, Sal. Any chance of a knockdown to her later on?'

knocker 1 Common sense: *obs.*
1900 Henry Lawson 'Two Larrikins' *Prose* i 231: 'The old woman might have had the knocker to keep away from the lush while I was in quod.'
2 Someone addicted to fault-finding, disparagement of what others praise [f. *knock* v. 2]
1923 Jack Moses *Beyond the City Gates* 154: The 'knocker' of his home town is, on this line of deduction, a 'knocker' of his Empire; a destroyer of thought, labour, and enterprise.

1961 *Meanjin* 399: 'For one terrible moment I thought you were going to be a knocker. In

Merulga there's no place for knockers.'

1962 Max Harris *Australian Civilization* ed. P. Coleman 57: It is said that Australians are 'knockers'; that is, they gain pleasure from seeing superiority in talent, intellect or energy reduced to the scale of average mediocrity.

1972 Keith Dunstan *Knockers [book title]*

1982 *Age* (Melbourne) 1 Jul. 12: Fellow Melburnians, how much longer are we going to honor our reputation for being the world's greatest 'knockers'?

knockerette

1980 *Weekend Australian* 16 Aug. 12: Geraldine Pascall demonstrates in her article ... that she is the latest 'knockerette'.

knocker, on the   Promptly, on demand, esp. in the expression 'cash on the knocker' [listed by Partridge as English slang for 'on credit']

1962 Jon Cleary *The Country of Marriage* 297: Sid was a man who wanted cash on the knocker.

1967 Frank Hardy *Billy Borker Yarns Again* 71: 'Settle our monthly bills dead on the knocker.'

1972 Richard Magoffin *Chops and Gravy* 106: *Cash on the knocker* immediate cash payment.

1975 *Australian* 12 Aug. 9: 'He has to pay cash on the knocker for everything he buys, but he has to wait two or three months for payment from the big firms.'

knot in bluey, put a   To prepare to travel, prepare for action

1945 Tom Ronan *Strangers on the Ophir* 144: 'And put a knot in your bluey yourself, Joe, I've got a job for you.'

1966 Baker 108: The expression *to put* (or *tie*) *a knot in* (a swag strap) means to quit a job.

know more than one's prayers   see **prayers**

knuckle, go the   To punch, fight

1944 John Devanny *By Tropic, Sea and Jungle* 160: I always got on well with the blacks, because I never went the knuckle on them, and never interfered with their women.

1959 D'Arcy Niland *The Big Smoke* 15: 'He reckoned you could go the knuckle a bit.'

1962 Stuart Gore *Down the Golden Mile* 26: Then he said: 'Want to watch out for them quiet snoozers. Sometimes they can go the knuckle a bit themselves.'

1975 Richard Beilby *The Brown Land Crying* 156: 'Old Sam goin' the knuckle. Well, whaddya know.'

knuckle sandwich   A punch in the mouth

1973 Alexander Buzo *Norm and Ahmed* 2: 'He tried to hang one on me at Leichhardt Oval once, so I administered a knuckle sandwich to him.'

koala   1   The $200 gold coin issued in 1980 [f. koala in design]

1980 *Sydney Morning Herald* 3 Sep. 14: In November 1977 the then Federal Treasurer, Mr Lynch, told Parliament that the Government would issue a gold coin. Almost three years later we have the $200 coin, which will probably acquire the nickname 'koala' because of its design.

1984 *Australian* 27 Jul. 9: Readers win five $200 gold koalas [heading]

2   Nickname for an unappreciative male [cf. *root v.* 1]

1976 David Ireland *The Glass Canoe* 31: She christened the Koala Bear, who eats roots and leaves.

see **wombat** 2

koala bear   A member of the militia in World War II, who originally could not serve outside Australia: *derogatory*

1943 Baker 45: *Koala bear*: A Militiaman. (War slang.)

1945 Baker 152: An attempt was made in October 1942 to pin the name *koala bears* on the militia, 'because you can't shoot at 'em and you can't export 'em,' but the term has small currency.

1984 *Sydney Morning Herald* 30 Jun. 13: Conscripts or 'chocos' or 'koalas' as they were called (chocos because they were supposed to be chocolate soldiers and koalas because they were not expected to be exported or shot at) were part of the militia force which met, stopped and drove back the Japanese landing at Milne Bay.

kooka   Kookaburra [abbr.]

1923 Jack Moses *Beyond the City Gates* 18: The carolling of the magpie and the laughter of the kookas heralded dawn.

1968 David Ireland *The Chantic Bird* 123: A kooka was on the verandah sill, his cocked head very still.

1980 *West Australian* (Perth) 3 Mar. 6: The dear old 'kooka' should be removed from the protected list and then removed from Western Australia to give the small fry a chance in their own habitat.

koori   An Aborigine (a term applied by Aborigines to themselves)

1834 L. E. Threlkeld *Australian Grammar* 87: Ko-re, Man, mankind.

1894 Ethel Turner *Seven Little Australians* 207: 'A tall young Koree who was coming that way saw the wipparoo, and with one blow from his strong nulla-nulla, which, being interpreted, meaneth a club, cut its head from its body.'

1955 F. B. Vickers *The Mirage* 167: 'Plenty longa camp Meekatharra. I get you kurri! Young fella gin!'

1978 Kevin Gilbert *Living Black* 40: 'He was one

gub man, I reckon he was the best I ever struck in my life . . . He'd give a Koori a go.'
1978 Robert J. Merritt *The Cake Man* 12: 'See'n I'm a Kuri. The Australian Aborigine, that's who I am and what I am.'
1981 *Australian* 31 Mar. 7: At one inner-city primary school, where nearly half the students are black . . . the gubbers (whites) pick up words from the koories (blacks).
1982 Jack Davis *Kullark* 34: 'He a *Nyoongah*?' 'Nah, 'e's a *Koori*, black fella from the Eastern States.'
1983 *Sydney Morning Herald* 7 Dec. 1: 'If a Koorie (Aboriginal) gets off a train at Central, he can come to Eveleigh Street and see someone he knows', explained one prominent Aboriginal.

1985 Billy Marshall-Stoneking *Weekend Australian* 2 Feb. Mag. 15: The word 'koori' comes from an Aboriginal dialect of the central coast of NSW and means, literally, 'people'. [review of James Miller, *Koori*]

Kremlin, the   See quot. 1981
1981 *Australian* 3 Nov. 7: Broken Hill takes its orders from the Kremlin . . . Otherwise known as the Trades Hall, it is headquarters for the Barrier Industrial Council.

k's   Kilometres
1984 Robert Caswell *Scales of Justice* 31: 'The cars could have driven twenty or thirty k's.'

LA   Low alcohol [abbr.]
1979 *Sydney Morning Herald* 17 Dec. 1: It will be Sydney's first LA (low alcohol) Christmas. How will it go?

La Stupenda   see **Stupenda**

lady, white   see **white**

lady's waist   A 5 or 7 oz glass of beer [f. shape]
1941 Baker 42: *Lady's waist* A gracefully shaped glass in which beer is served (2) Whence, the drink served.
1954 *Sydney Morning Herald* 8 Nov. 2: Calling for an appropriately named Sydney 'lady's waist' in Adelaide would probably result in being hauled off to gaol.
1978 Ronald McKie *Bitter Bread* 85: He could not even afford a lady's waist, and that was the smallest glass you could buy.

lag *n.*   **1**   A convict or ex-convict, esp. if transported
1812 Vaux 249: *Lag*: a convict under sentence of transportation. Ibid. 255: *Old lag*: a man or woman who has been transported, is so called on returning home, by those who are acquainted with the secret.
1845 Charles Griffith *The Present State and Prospects of the Port Phillip District* 76: The old hands are men, who, having been formerly convicts, (or lags as they are generally termed) have become free by the expiration of their sentences.
1855 William Howitt *Land, Labour and Gold* i 20: The old lags, another name for convicts, are flocking over from Sydney and Van Diemen's Land.
1873 A. Trollope *Australia* ed. P. D. Edwards and R. B. Joyce (1967) 587: It is perhaps something of a disgrace to Western Australia that the other colonies will not receive a stranger from her shores without a certificate that the visitor has not been a 'lag'.
1882 A. J. Boyd *Old Colonials* 19: I believe he was originally a confinee during Her Majesty's pleasure; in other words, he was strongly suspected of being a 'lag'.
1907 Charles MacAlister *Old Pioneering Days in the Sunny South* 106: It is hardly remarkable ... that many of the old 'lags' should have no friendship for such services when fifty lashes was the penalty for sneezing in church.
1934 Brian Penton *Landtakers* 18: 'Comes home suddenly and finds his old woman locked up in the store-room with one of the lags. He flogs them both half to death with a stockwhip.'
1964 H. P. Tritton *Time Means Tucker* 66: In my schooldays I had known an old 'lag' known as 'Bill the Juicer' ... When he was drunk, he would pull off his shirt to show what a flogger could do.

2   **lagger**   A police informer
1974 Robert Adamson and Bruce Hanford *Zimmer's Essay* 31: Maitland also houses the cretins, and the laggers who would be killed if they

were left in cells among crims they had lagged upon.
1975 *Sydney Morning Herald* 3 Jul. 11: A lagger is someone who puts people in to the police.

lag, be lagged *v.* **1** To be transported as a convict; to be arrested and convicted
1812 Vaux 249: *Lag*: to transport for seven years or upwards.
1847 Alexander Harris *Settlers and Convicts* ed. C. M. H. Clark (1953) 18: My fellow-traveller had a brother living, whose lagging (transportation) having occurred some years before his own, he was now free. Ibid. 127: He was a great low-lived looking ruffian, not long 'lagged' (transported).
1873 A. Trollope *Australia* ed. P. D. Edwards and R. B. Joyce (1967) 505: Now and then goodnatured reference is made in regard to some lady or gentleman to the fact that her or his father was 'lagged'.
1879–80 Ned Kelly 'The Jerilderie Letter' in Max Brown *Australian Son* (1956) 283: It only aids the police to procure false witnesses and go whacks with men to steal horses and lag innocent men.
2 To inform on someone
1847 Alexander Harris *Settlers and Convicts* ed. C. M. H. Clark (1953) 187: 'I thought it was — (the overseer), and if it had been, I would have knocked him on the head and put him into a hollow log before he should have *lagged* (transported) me'. [The speaker had already been transported: the interpolated explanation is probably a misunderstanding.]
1973 Jim McNeil *The Chocolate Frog* 34: 'You won't never alter the fact that yer lagged yer mate! Be as sorry as yer like ... but yer lagged 'im.'

lair A showoff; a flashily dressed person; a term of general contempt (esp. 'mug lair') [see *lairy*]
1935 Kylie Tennant *Tiburon* 106: He was also considered something of a lare among the girls.
1944 *Coast to Coast 1943* 51: He saw a mug-lare with a yellow tie ogle the girl.
1958 Gavin Casey *Snowball* 208: He didn't want to dress like a lair, and he rejected the brilliant blazer and the too-pale grey slacks he'd bought ... three months earlier.
1962 Ron Tullipan *March into Morning* 28: 'A lot of young lairs get flash on motor-bikes.'
1974 John Powers *The Last of the Knucklemen* 30: 'I don't get hustled into punch-ups with two-bob lairs.'
1979 *Sunday Telegraph* (Sydney) 25 Mar. 9: Prince Charles flew out of Perth for Canberra yesterday leaving behind a shaken co-driver. 'I'd reckon he'd be a lair on the road', grinned Danny Tenardi, who rode with the prince in a huge iron ore truck.
1983 T. A. G. Hungerford *Stories from Suburban*

Road 117: He used to wear gold cuff-links in the coat sleeves of his blue serge suit: I suppose he was what we used to call a lair.

lair around, lair up To behave like a lair, dress like a lair
1952 T. A. G. Hungerford *The Ridge and the River* 23: Having a bath and a shave, getting into clean clothes ... to lare up at the dance.
1955 H. Drake-Brockman *Men Without Wives and Other Plays* 83: 'He's a trimmer. Always laring around. No good to girls.'
1962 Stuart Gore *Down the Golden Mile* 64: 'He climbs out of the cockpit, all laired up in this red rig-out and whiskers.'
1975 Xavier Herbert *Poor Fellow My Country* 397: 'Better go and wash yo'self.' Sure,' said Nobby. 'Think I'm goin' leave the lairin' up all to you?'

lairize To behave like a lair
1953 Kylie Tennant *The Joyful Condemned* 22: 'She was ear-bashing me all over tea how you came lairizing round at our place like you owned it.'
1965 Wally Grout *My Country's 'Keeper* 139: Most people thought I did it 'lairising' – being a show-off, as we say at home. It seemed to them I had caught the ball and spilled it only when throwing it in the air, a favourite flourish of 'keepers.
1970 Jessica Anderson *The Last Man's Head* 116–17: 'I pretty soon lost my taste for that part of it, the lairising part.' Ibid. 171: Alec tended to mistrust and stigmatise as lairising all such devised gaiety and charm.
1981 *Bulletin* 19 May 65: The crew raced for stretchers, first aid kits, splints. The mountain men looked on impassively. 'He was lairising', they said.

lairy Flashily dressed; (of colours) bright and showy: *obsolescent* [? f. *leery* wideawake, knowing, 'fly' OED 1796]
[**1859** Hotten 58: *Leary* flash, or knowing. *Leary bloak* a person who dresses showily.]
1906 Edward Dyson *Fact'ry 'Ands* 160: Minnie piped something to the effect that she would disdain to be 'found drownded with a bloke what done-up 'is 'air dead leary', next morning the elaborate festoons had disappeared from Chiller's brow, and his hair was parted with the oily precision characteristic of Sunday-school superintendents and reputable young barbers.
1915 C. J. Dennis *The Songs of a Sentimental Bloke* 35: Fer 'er sweet sake I've gone and chucked it clean: / The pubs and schools an' all that leery game. Ibid. 122: *Leery* Vulgar; low.
1932 Leonard Mann *Flesh in Armour* 291: 'Who've we got?' 'Lairey Ridley.' They laughed ... Captain Ridley had been a recognized hard-doer.

His helmet was tilted rakishly over his left ear and his tunic and light coat were of the ultra fashionable style.

1949 Lawson Glassop *Lucky Palmer* 142: 'You ought to see the rug I got for Bunny. All done in my colours, red, green, and gold. Classy, eh? Some of the boys reckon it's too lairy, but I reckon it's a beaut.'

1964 David Ireland *Image in the Clay* 47: 'There was the travelling rodeo at the next town. All the boys lairy in big hats and check shirts.'

1975 Rodney Hall *A Place Among People* 13: Chick nodded in the direction of a newcomer heading for the bar, 'That's a lairy rig-out isn't it?'

lamb down   To defraud a 'chequed up' bushman by keeping him drunk until his funds are supposedly exhausted [f. helping a ewe to give birth]

1869 Marcus Clarke *A Colonial City* ed. L. T. Hergenhan (1972) 162: *To lamb-down* – that is, to make drunk and incapable – of course originated with some shepherd.

1878 G. H. Gibson *Southerly Busters* 24: He got upon the spree, / And publicans was awful cheats / For soon lamm'd down was he.

1888 E. Finn *Chronicles of Early Melbourne* ii 546: The publican's harvest consisted chiefly in fleecing (or 'lambing down', as it was technically termed) the stockmen, bullock-drivers, shepherds and shearers who made periodical trips to Melbourne for a 'spree' or to 'knock down their money'.

1902 Henry Lawson 'A Bush Publican's Lament' *Prose* i 469: 'Someone's sure to say he was lambed down an' cleaned out an' poisoned with bad Bush liquor at my place.'

1908 C. H. S. Matthews *A Parson in the Australian Bush* 242–3: Podgy belongs to the old order of bush publicans ... whose one aim in life seems to be to 'lamb down' the shearers and any other cheque-possessing Bush toilers who are unfortunate enough to fall into their hands.

1945 Tom Ronan *Strangers on the Ophir* 27: 'How the hell is the publican going to make a crust if the travellers won't let themselves be lambed down?'

lambing down   The process or experience of being 'lambed down'

1873 J. B. Stephens *Black Gin* 51: It is the Bushman come to town ... / Come to spend his cheque in town, / Come to do his 'lambing down'.

1885 'The Broken-hearted Shearer' *Bulletin* 31 Oct. 5 in *Old Bush Songs* ed. Stewart and Keesing (1957) 267: But it's nothing when you're used to it to do a lambing down.

1903 Joseph Furphy *Such is Life* (1944) 328: The lambing down of two stalwart fencers by a pimply old shanty-keeper.

1910 C. E. W. Bean *On the Wool Track* 215: When sheep are lambing men are sent into the paddocks to see that everything goes smoothly. The process is called 'lambing down'. By a gentle metaphor the words have been tranferred to the assistance which in the old days it was customary for publicans to give to men who came in to get rid of a cheque.

land, man on the   see **man**

landing, the   The landing at Gallipoli on 25 April 1915

1916 *The Anzac Book* 1: 'The landing' By a Man of the Tenth [heading]

1945 Herbert M. Moran *Beyond the Hill Lies China* 125: A mere boy from Heggity's Lane won a high decoration for his conduct at 'The Landing'.

1983 T. A. G. Hungerford *Stories from Suburban Road* 99: He'd been Wounded at the Landing, and we all called him Soldier Tom.

larrikin   1   A young street rowdy [*larrikin* a mischievous or frolicsome youth EDD Suppl.]

1870 Marcus Clarke *A Colonial City* ed. L. T. Hergenhan (1972) 78–9: The larrikin has been a little noisy lately. The daily press records his doings with unction. For instance, on Sunday morning last, at about 3 o'clock, a respectable young man, who was a carpenter, 'strolls' into that pleasant lounge, Wright's Gin Palace, and in a jovial manner 'shouts' for some dozen ... Feeling a strange hand in his pocket, he remonstrates, whereupon he is mobbed, kicked, struck and hustled into the street. The constables, after a protracted search and a severe struggle, arrested three of the gang.

1877 T. E. Argles *The Pilgrim* 1 viii 5: Here, packed like sardines, are a motley crew of that hideous excrescence of blind-alleys and right-of-ways – the Sydney Larrikin – and the female companion he so much affects.

1883 R. E. N. Twopeny *Town Life in Australia* 98: The 'larrikins', as they are called ... roughs of the worst description, insulting and often robbing people in Melbourne itself, and moving about in gangs with whose united force the police is powerless to cope ... In a younger stage they content themselves with frightening helpless women, and kicking every Chinaman they meet.

1888 J. A. Froude *Oceana* 138: There is an idle set at the lower end of the scale: noisy, riotous scamps, who are impertinent to peaceful passengers, and make rows at theatres, a coarse-type version of the old Mohawks – they call them *Larrikins*.

1896 Henry Lawson 'A Visit of Condolence' *Prose* i 32: 'How dare you talk to me like that, you young larrikin? Be off! or I'll send for a policeman.'

1911 Louis Stone *Jonah* 67–8: They were dressed

in the height of larrikin fashion – tight-fitting suits of dark cloth, soft black felt hats, and soft white shirts with new black mufflers round their neck in place of collars – for the larrikin taste in dress runs to a surprising neatness. But their boots were remarkable, fitting like a glove, with high heels and a wonderful ornament of perforated toe-caps and brass eyelet holes in the uppers.
1924 *Truth* 27 Apr. 6: *Larrikin* A rowdy, ill-mannered youth.
1980 *West Australian* (Perth) 14 Jan. 3: After recent reports of larrikins and drunkenness at Rottnest, it was relatively quiet on the island this weekend, with no problems at the hotel.

larrikiness, larrikinism
1892 William Lane *The Workingman's Paradise* 43: As they stood in George-street, waiting for their bus, a high-heeled, tightly-corsetted, gaily-hatted larrikiness flounced out of the side door of a hotel near by.
1870 *The Australian* 10 Sep. 3: A slight attempt at 'larrikinism' was manifested. [Morris]
1875 A. J. Boyd *Old Colonials* (1882) 52: Let the state take cognizance of 'larrikinism' as an offence against the law.
2   In a more favourable sense, as though referring to authentically 'Australian' characteristics of non-conformism, irreverence, impudence (projected on to the larrikin as romanticized by Lawson and C. J. Dennis)
1973 Donald Horne *Australian* 12 Apr. 8: The Australian style swings back and forth between the larrikin and the suburbanite ... Evatt was the larrikin type, Hasluck the suburbanite. The way Connor is handling the Minerals and Energy ministry, announcing things without any inquiry, I'd describe him as the larrikin type.
1974 *Sydney Morning Herald* 29 Jun. 11: The heroine with a larrikin streak [article on Joan Sutherland]
1983 *Bulletin* 30 Aug. 28: Certainly, Hinze's larrikin public image leaves a lot to be desired.

Larry Dooley   see **Dooley**

Larry, happy as Completely happy [origin obscure]
1905 Joseph Furphy *Rigby's Romance* ed. R. G. Howarth (1946) 62: 'But now that the adventure was drawing to an end, I found a peace of mind that all the old fogies on the river couldn't disturb. I was as happy as Larry.'
1910 Henry Lawson *Prose* ii 216: And Frank Myers – 'As happy as Larry in Castlebarry.'
1915 Louis Stone *Betty Wayside* 254: 'If it hadn't been for that busybody we'd have been happy as Larry, and nobody any the wiser.'
1922 Arthur Wright *A Colt from the Country* 88: 'The old boy is as happy as Larry.'

1934 Thomas Wood *Cobbers* 25: He said he was as happy as Larry to see a fresh face.
1946 K. S. Prichard *The Roaring Nineties* 369: 'I'm as happy as Larry to be on the job again,' Alf exclaimed eagerly.
1957 Ray Lawler *Summer of the Seventeenth Doll* 15: She wanted a doll on a walking-stick too, she said ... and in the end that's what they had to bring her back. Well, she was as happy as Larry; off she went to bed, one in each hand.
1966 Hal Porter *The Paper Chase* 125: Here I am solitary, happy as Larry, singing to myself, and busy as a weaver.
1983 Georgia Savage *Slate & Me and Blanche McBride* 128: He dumped me in the main street and went off as happy as Larry because he'd got it all off his chest.

lash, have a   To take part in something, make an attempt at
1941 Baker 42: *Lash at, have a* To make an attempt at (something).
1948 Ruth Park *Poor Man's Orange* 222: The blithe pipings of old men who safe [from the fight] up on their balconies, leaned over rails and exhorted everyone to 'ave a lash.
1952 T. A. G. Hungerford *The Ridge and the River* 16: 'Don't buy any trouble unless you're forced into it – we don't want to stir the bastards up until we're better settled in here, just in case they decide to have a lash.'
1965 Eric Lambert *The Long White Night* 151: 'Let someone also have a lash at Rommel and his bloody Nazi Youth.'
1970 Jack Hibberd *Who?* in Penguin *Plays* 146: 'We might even have a lash at some juicies ourselves.'

last shower, didn't come down in   see **shower**

later, see you   An expression of farewell (not a proposal for a later meeting)
1942 Gavin Casey *It's Harder for Girls* 75: 'Well,' I said, 'I'd better get along.' 'Yes,' said Phil. 'I gotter pick up some packages. See you later.'
1948 William Beard *'Neath Austral Skies* 177: ''Ooray,' returned the drover, shaking Ralph's hand. 'See you later!'
1965 Patrick White *Four Plays* 346: (*Hikers move off*). *First Hiker* See you later then!
1984 *Sydney Morning Herald* 4 Apr. 1: Canon Jim Glennon, of St Andrew's Cathedral, was driving over the Harbour Bridge after church last Sunday when he was stopped by an RBT unit. With him were the Primate of Australia, the Most Rev Sir John Grindrod, and the Dean of Sydney, the Very Rev Lance Shilton, both wearing in clerical collars. The Dean tells us that, after testing Canon Glennon, the policeman waved him on, saying 'see

you later.' 'The policeman didn't seem to realise what great portent that phrase had for all of us,' the Dean said.

laughing jackass see **jackass**

Laura Norda Strine equivalent of 'law and order'
1981 *Canberra Times* 4 Jun. 12: Mr Newman ... went on to conclude, to rapturous applause from the lauranorda aficionados on the government benches, that he would like to 'commend the police' for being 'most considerate'.

law, two kilometre see **two**

lay-by n. & v. **1** To secure an item for sale by making a deposit and paying instalments until the full price is paid, without interest charges, the goods being taken only when payment is complete
1930 *Sydney Morning Herald* 16 Oct 4: Avail yourself of our Lay-by service. [Hordern's advertisement]
1932 *Sydney Morning Herald* 5 Dec. 1: A New Service! / 'Lay-By' at Farmer's / Lay-Away-a-Gift Plan! / Farmer's now assist with a practical, worryless 'Lay-By'.
Begin tomorrow and lay a gift away each day until your list is completed. Farmer's grant you ample time in which to pay the balance without any hardship on your purse. When your thoughts, in future, turn to 'Lay-By', think of Farmer's quality stocks now easily within your reach.
1978 *Sydney Morning Herald* 9 Jan. 1: The widespread acceptance of credit cards is marking the demise of laybys, which have dropped from 6 per cent of total sales to about 1 per cent.
1984 *Age* (Melbourne) 30 Jun. Extra 7: In our circle, the line was drawn at the lay-by (always 'the lay-by'), a sort of half-way house of credit in which you were given the thrill of purchase but denied the pleasure of consumption. Women of this era were forever putting twin-sets on the lay-by.

LBII Abbreviation of **Life Be In It** q.v.
1979 *Australian* 30 Apr. 13: Clearprint holds the trade mark and business registration name for LBII products on behalf of the Victorian Government.
1984 *Age* (Melbourne) 20 Mar. 2: During his speech Mr Adams made a few acerbic comments about Norm's sedentary nature, which he claimed included a complete lack of sexual interest or arousal. This, however, cannot also be said about the reaction of the invited guests to the next stage of the proceedings – an aerobics dance display by two young women in pink costumes who stretched and bounced in time to a LBII jingle with a disco beat.

lead a flock of homing pigeons see **homing**

leaping Lena Nickname of the train running from Birdum to Darwin
1940 Ernestine Hill *The Great Australian Loneliness* 124: There is a train a week in the Territory ... They call it Leaping Lena. One terminus is Birdum, three shacks in the bush, and the other the first breaker of the Indian Ocean ... The Sentinel – Leaping Lena's official name – is a string of scarcely glorified cattle trucks.
1945 G. H. Johnston *Pacific Partner* 149: When Australia declared war, Leaping Lena had to be entrusted overnight with vital military movements. In fact, she became the only troop train in the Northern Territory.
1962 J. Marshall and R. Drysdale *Journey Among Men* 44: Jouncing from side to side in this machine, which he informed us was known as Leaping Lena or the Abortion Express.

leatherjacket A kind of pancake, made from dough and fried in fat
1846 G. H. Haydon *Five Years in Australia Felix* 151: A plentiful supply of 'leatherjackets' (dough fried in a pan).
1853 S. Mossman and T. Banister *Australia Visited and Revisited* 126: 'Leatherjackets' – An Australian bush term for a thin cake made of dough, and put into a pan to bake with some fat. The term is a very appropriate one, for tougher things cannot well be eaten.
1855 William Howitt *Land, Labour and Gold* i 117: The leather-jacket is a cake of mere flour and water, raised with tartaric acid and carbonate of soda instead of yeast, and baked in the frying-pan; and is equal to any muffin you can buy in the London shops.
1894 Henry Lawson *Prose* i 52: 'I wish I had just enough fat to make the pan siss; I'd treat myself to a leather-jacket; but it took three weeks' skimmin' to get enough for them theer dough-boys.'

leatherneck A rouseabout in a shearing shed, etc.: *obsolescent*
1898 *Bulletin* 1 Oct. 14: The rouseabouts [are] 'leathernecks'.
1941 Baker 43: *Leather-neck* A station 'rouseabout'.

leghorn, white see **white leghorn**

leg-opener Alcohol, esp. wine or spirits, thought of as making women more vulnerable sexually
1959 Dorothy Hewett *Bobbin Up* 93: 'Gotta bit of leg opener in the back seat of the heap.'
1965 Leslie Haylen *Big Red* 133: There was a bottle of wine or two there for a birthday party or for the women at Christmas time. Shearers had

been known to buy a bottle of Charlie's 'leg opener' to knock off a sheila.

1968 Geoffrey Dutton *Andy* 154: The bottle of sparkling burgundy (a disgusting drink, apart from its legendary powers as leg-opener).

1975 Les Ryan *The Shearers* 108: 'Leg opener?' Sandy asked. Baldo said 'A bottle of each mate. Gin, and lemon.'

1979 Helen Garner *Age* (Melbourne) 23 Nov. 20: My mother had told me that Pimms No. 1 cup was 'what they called a leg-opener'. I only dimly visualised what this could mean.

lemons, to go in   To do something with a will: *obs.*

1903 Joseph Furphy *Such is Life* (1944) 17: 'Grass up over yer boots, an' the carrion goin' into it lemons.'

1904 Laura M. Palmer-Archer *A Bush Honeymoon* 350: *Going in lemons* Enthusiastically.

lemony   Annoyed, peeved [? f. sourness]

1941 Baker 31: *Go lemony at* To become angry, express anger towards someone.

1944 Dal Stivens *The Courtship of Uncle Henry* 75: He's as lemony as hell when he opens the door and doesn't say a word to me.

1968 Stuart Gore *Holy Smoke* 35: 'They went real lemony on 'im!'

lesbo   Variant of **leso** q.v.

1961 Xavier Herbert *Soldiers' Women* 235: 'She's a lesbo, I think. She took a shine to me right away.'

leso   A lesbian [abbr.]

1976 Dorothy Hewett *The Tatty Hollow Story* 118: 'What's up with you? Are you a leso or something?'

1978 *Weekend Australian* 24–5 Jun. Mag. 12: It all ends in the great united cry of 'Up the Lesos', shouted with beer cans held aloft in militant Les-Power salute.

1983 *National Times* 22 Jul. 37: 'And *Gay*! What an insult to the poofs and lezzos who made this country what it is today!'

let her flicker   see **flicker**

licence, where did you get your   see **where**

lid, to dip one's   see **dip**

Life. Be In It   Slogan of a fitness campaign launched in November 1975 by Brian Dixon, Victorian Minister for Youth, Sport and Recreation, with a series of television commercials conceived by Phillip Adams and featuring the cartoon character 'Norm' (q.v.), becoming a national campaign on 1 November 1977

1975 *Age* (Melbourne) 24 Nov. 2: The Minister for Youth, Sport and Recreation, Mr Dixon, yesterday launched a five year plan to make healthier Victorians ... The Life – Be In It campaign with a budget of $200,000 for the first stage up to June next year, is the first attempt in Australia to use modern marketing and advertising techniques to sell fitness ... Advertisements, pamphlets, posters, stickers and iron-on transfers all bearing the Life – Be In It logo will go throughout the State from today.

1979 *Australian* 30 Apr. 13: The likelihood that Norm and friends of Life Be In It fame are to be adopted by a U.S. recreational association means the opening of promising revenue avenue for the Federal Government. The Government, which is already reaping the benefits of the franchising of the program locally, expects to take about 7 per cent of sales of Life Be In It products in the U.S.

1980 *Daily News* (Perth) 16 Dec. 44: A festive card has turned up for the Life. Be In It organisers ... Norm and his pals are shown with haloes, under the message, 'Hark the herald angels sing, Life. Be In It and do your thing.'

1984 *Sydney Morning Herald* 30 Jun. 1: The Life. Be In It campaign will soon have a new star, a 'trendy, zany, young' woman, who will act as sister and foil to the slothful, pot-bellied Norm. Thirty per cent of people voted in a national poll to name her Libby. The runner-up names include Norma, Doreen and Narelle, followed by Maureen and Sheila.

Life – Be Out Of It

1979 *National Times* 3 Nov. 26: The girls were wearing marihuana-leaf carvings and the guys had Bong On Aussie and Life – Be Out of It! badges.

1981 *Sun-Herald* 22 Nov. 160: Rex Jackson ... couldn't help breaking into a grin last week while inspecting the inside of Parramatta Jail. A lifer had on a T-shirt which said, 'Life, be out of it.'

life, go for your   An expression of encouragement, as though guaranteeing no interference

1928 Arthur Wright *A Good Recovery* 128: 'I'll get plenty of witnesses from the west as soon as ever they're wanted. Go for your life, cobber; I'll be ready.'

1939 Kylie Tennant *Foveaux* 362: 'He'd go for his life, if we asked him.'

1947 Gavin Casey *The Wits are Out* 27: 'I'd just as soon have sherry,' Myra said. 'Then get a bottle and go for your life,' Bill said.

1949 John Morrison *The Creeping City* 63: 'Then go for your bloody life!' Bob got up and waved his hand as if the whole matter were already disposed of. 'I ain't standing in your way.'

1959 Anne von Bertouch *February Dark* 248: 'D' you mind if I take your hurricane lamp and run up to the house?' 'No. Go for your life.'

lifesaver Officially a member of a Life Saving Club; more colloquially one of the stereotypes of the Australian male

1969 Thomas Jenkins *We Came to Australia* 174: You can see the Lifesavers sitting up in their tower. All volunteers, these bronzed young gods take turns to watch from the top of a scaffolding tower for anyone in trouble in the sea. If they see a hand raised ... they will swim to help, churning through the sea as if they were fitted with outboard motors.

1972 Geoff Morley *Jockey Rides Honest Race* 170: I could feel the soft fleshiness of you when my strong Australian life-saver arms held you, and it was strangely erotic.

1981 *Sydney Morning Herald* 18 Mar. 3: That bronzed, muscular Aussie life-saving image painted in the minds of millions of foreigners is one of the classic myths of our time. Australians are, in fact, a sedentary race which takes its physical well-being entirely for granted.

1984 *West Australian* (Perth) 13 Jan. 23: Not all surf lifesavers are 6-foot, macho men with broad shoulders, bulging biceps and sun bleached hair. The WA beaches are also serviced by slim, lithe, athletic women.

life wasn't meant to be easy A saying associated with Malcolm Fraser, Australian Prime Minister (1975–83) [cf. the proverb 'Life is not all beer and skittles'; Longfellow, 'Life is real! Life is earnest' ('A Psalm of Life'); G. B. Shaw *Back to Methuselah* (World's Classics 1945) 263: 'Life is not meant to be easy, my child; but take courage: it can be delightful']

1970 *Australian* 1 Apr. 11: As a farmer in Victoria's Western District he [Mr Fraser] felt life was too easy. 'I don't believe life is meant to be easy.'

1971 J. M. Fraser *Toward 2000: Challenge to Australia* The Fifth Alfred Deakin Lecture 20 July 1971 p. 2: Arnold Toynbee once wrote twelve volumes to demonstrate and analyse the cause of the rise and fall of nations. His thesis can be condensed to a sentence, and is simply stated: That through history nations are confronted by a series of challenges and whether they survive or whether they fall to the wayside, depends on the manner and character of their response. Simple, and perhaps one of the few things that is self-evident. It involves a conclusion about the past that life has not been easy for people or for nations, and an assumption for the future that that condition will not alter. There is within me some part of the metaphysic, and thus I would add that life is not meant to be easy.

1977 *Australian* 3 May 3: The Prime Minister, in an address to the A.C.T. Liberal Party last night, lamented that he should have taken out a copyright on his now famous statement 'Life wasn't meant to be easy.'

1979 *Sun-Herald* 11 Nov. 69: True intimacy is hard to achieve. People have to work hard at it. Romantic love rarely lasts. True love wasn't meant to be easy.

1981 *Times* (London) 16 Mar. 6: Perhaps he [Mr Fraser] has gained his most notorious reputation for either his obsession with the horror of Russian expansionism or for having once allegedly said 'life wasn't meant to be easy', which had been requoted hundreds of times. Did he actually say it? The Prime Minister smiled reflectively and said: 'I said something very like it. It's from *Back to Methuselah* by Bernard Shaw. Look, I can remember as clearly as anything that a friend who I was visiting in hospital asked me why I didn't give up politics and return to the good life at "Nareen". I said life wasn't meant to be like that. That would be too easy. So that's what it grew from. I wouldn't mind a cent for every time it's been quoted or misquoted. It's the best thing I ever said.'

light on Sparsely supplied, of short weight [? abbr. of *light on the ground*]

1944 Lawson Glassop *We Were the Rats* 122: 'You're a bit light on too, aren't you?' 'Purely a temporary state of poverty, Reynolds old boy.'

1954 Tom Ronan *Vision Splendid* 76: 'A month later our rations were starting to get a bit light on.'

1960 Nancy Cato *Green Grows the Vine* 17: 'He's not a bad foreman ... never goes crook at yer if your tins is a bit light-on.'

1973 Frank Huelin *Keep Moving* 133: 'Yous blokes waitin' f'r a feed?' the cook asked, thrusting his head out of the galley. 'Might be a bit light on.'

1975 *Overland* 62 25: The heroines were a bit light on the ground, but there was always La Passionara.

1980 *Daily News* (Perth) 16 Jul. 30: 'We have an abundance of depth in half forwards, rucks, and wingers but we are light-on for back-up rovers.'

1984 *Age* (Melbourne) 22 Aug. 5: It is largely because Canberra is light-on for events, certainly anything on the scale of the Grand Final and the Melbourne Cup, that it makes such a fuss about Budget day.

light on the hill, the The symbol of the socialist objective of the Australian Labor Party

1949 J. B. Chifley policy speech *Sydney Morning Herald* 15 Nov. 4: We do say that it is the duty and responsibility of the community, and particularly those more fortunately placed, to see that our less fortunate fellow citizens are protected from those shafts of fate which leave them helpless and without hope. This is the objective for which we are striving. It is, as I have said before, the beacon,

the light on the hill, to which our eyes are always turned, and to which our efforts are always directed.
1967 R. G. Menzies *Afternoon Light* 129: The Socialist objective, his 'light on the hill', must not be blotted out or obscured in this way.
1974 *Australian* 26 Apr. 8: In 1971 and 1972 the left wing became quiescent ... Where there had existed a wild passion to get to the socialist 'light on the hill', quieter, more disingenuous instincts were mobilized. The changes proved profitable.
1984 *Australian* 13 Apr. 6: Coalition fails to put a light on the hill [heading].

like   Used to suggest approximation, tentativeness in any statement
1945 Robert S. Close *Love Me Sailor* 129: 'That cask looks as if it might have gone bad like, sir,' said the cook.
1949 Lawson Glassop *Lucky Palmer* 153: 'That's the lastest new-fangled subject they teach 'em at school – Sarcasm, a branch of English like.' Ibid. 212: 'He's all right, I s'pose. Not my type like.'
1979 Patrick White *The Twyborn Affair* 201: 'She could talk about their homes, their clothes – their divorces, by the hour. It was her religion like.'
1980 *Sydney Morning Herald* 9 May 15: 'I realised like, if you are renting it at 7/6 a week you are not getting anything, but if you are going to purchase at 7/6 a week well, it was a good thing to me.'

lily on a dirt-tin, like a   See quot. 1970
1970 Partridge 1391: *shag on a rock, standing out – occ. sitting – like a*; or ... *like a lily on a dirt-tin*; or, rarely, ... *like a beer bottle on the Coliseum*. These picturesque Australian similes, dating from, resp., ca. 1930, 1935, 1945, bear three distinct senses: Lonely, as in 'He shot through and left me sitting like a shag on a rock'; conspicuous, as in 'It stood out like a lily on a dirt-tin'; incongruous, as in 'He was as out of place as a beer bottle on the Coliseum.'
1982 Nancy Keesing *Lily on the Dustbin Slang of Australian Women and Families* [book title]

limpy   A male homosexual [f. *limp-wristed*]
1984 *Sunday Telegraph* (Sydney) 22 Apr. 17: 'I think he was a limpy, actually.' (This is polite Inner Sydney argot for chaps of a gaily different persuasion, used by those of us who nostalgically recall when gay meant carefree.)

line   1   A line of patter, a 'technique', esp. in such expressions as 'doing a line', 'selling a line' for a male approach to women [also U.S.]
1933 Norman Lindsay *Saturdee* 242: 'I suppose you're going with Elsie Coote, aren't you?' 'Oh, yes, I'm doin' a line with her', said Peter.
1941 Kylie Tennant *The Battlers* 101: 'A man

might do a line with her, dippy or not.'
1946 Dal Stivens *The Courtship of Uncle Henry* 71: I ambled over to her and started selling her a line.
1951 Dymphna Cusack and Florence James *Come In Spinner* 364: 'My dear, he's a wow. And what a line! He calls me his little dream-dust and kisses me as though I was made of glass.'
1961 Nene Gare *The Fringe Dwellers* 286: 'I'm gunna do a line with the little gel that wants to go to Perth with me.'
1966 Roger Carr *Surfie* 51: Femmies are pretty good at handing out a line of rubbish when they want.
2   A girl or woman, as an amorous prospect
1944 Lawson Glassop *We Were the Rats* 5: 'You seen that new blonde barmaid at the Royal? A real good line.'
1954 T. A. G. Hungerford *Sowers of the Wind* 74: 'You looking for a sheila, sarge? ... I can put you on to some, only it'll cost you yen. They're good lines, though.'

Line, Brisbane   see **Brisbane**

Lions, the   The Fitzroy V.F.L. team (from 1957)
1976 *Sunday Telegraph* (Sydney) 18 Apr. 55: The Lions led by eight points by half-time.
2   The Subiaco (W.A.) Australian Rules team.
1980 *West Australian* (Perth) 19 May 59: Lions find their roar ... Subiaco played with courage, confidence, and a fierce desire to win.
3   The Brisbane soccer team
1978 *Sunday Telegraph* (Sydney) 30 Apr. 94: Penalty miss lets Lions in.

lippie   Lipstick [abbr.]
1940 Encountered in conversation.
1965 Hal Porter *The Cats of Venice* 139: 'Is there any lippy on the snowy tats?' And she bares her brilliant teeth at Mum like a poster Polynesian.
1983 *Sydney Morning Herald* 30 Apr. 31: If at many local league clubs the home team isn't putting on a little lippy for a lark and prancing round the stage, they can be found among the audience at ... any of a number of ... popular drag cabarets.
1983 *Sydney Morning Herald* 19 Dec. Guide 1: On radio, Miss Buttrose sounds as though she is wearing a sunfrock, bit of lippie and a pair of orthopaedic sandals.

Lithgow flash, the   Miss Marjorie Jackson (b. 1932), of Lithgow N.S.W., winner of Gold Medals for the 100 and 200 metres sprint at the Olympic Games in 1952.
1952 *Sydney Morning Herald* 10 Aug. 1: A pennant with the words 'Lithgow Flash' flew from the bonnet. At the rear was a banner with the

words 'Hail, Marjorie Jackson'.
1979 *NT News* (Darwin) 22 Sep. 3: 'She was trying to get away', he said. 'But with her weight and size, no one could compare her to the Lithgow Flash.'
1981 *Canberra Times* 3 Oct. 40: Marjorie Jackson, the 'Lithgow Flash', made a return to international athletics yesterday when she was appointed as manageress for the 1982 Australian Commonwealth Games team.

little Aussie battler, the   Anyone (preferably not tall) seen in the role of underdog, while exhibiting genuine Australian characteristics
1979 *Sun-Herald* 12 Aug. 54: I do not think one could seriously quarrel with Mr Murdoch's 'Australianism', even though I do find his 'little Aussie battler' act a bit rich.
1981 *National Times* 10 May 8: Little Aussie battler Tasmanian Liberal backbencher Bruce Goodluck came to the defence of his Tassie colleague . . . Hodgman last week.
1982 Blanche d'Alpuget *Robert J. Hawke* 285: His [Hawke's] very ordinariness – his flashy suits, flat voice, friendly manner and vulgar humour – had been among his greatest advantages with crowds, because he appeared so like everyone else, only more so: the quintessential Australian, the little Aussie battler.
1983 *Australian* 30 Aug. 7: The little Aussie battler who's got them running terrified [heading] . . . no one is ever going to forget Ben Lexcen and America's Cup of '83.
1984 H. G. Kippax *Sydney Morning Herald* 11 May 10: Melba – fascinating as a careerist, if you are interested in psychology – is here reduced to the Little Aussie Battler, unflappable amid the alien corn.
1984 *Sunday Times* (Perth) 5 Aug. 96: Jon Sieben, 'the little Aussie battler' from Brisbane who was on the dole before the Olympics, beat the world yesterday in one of the greatest rags to riches upsets in Olympic swimming history.

Little Digger, the   see **Digger**

little mate, my   see **my**

live on the smell of an oil-rag, to   see **oil-rag**

liver, shit on the   see **shit**

living black   Following the Aboriginal way of life
1937 Ernestine Hill *The Great Australian Loneliness* 244: I stumbled upon . . . Mrs. Jackie Forbes, otherwise Witchetty, the only authentic case to date of a white woman 'living black' with the tribes.
1949 John K. Ewers *Harvest* 194: 'It's all right for a white boss in peace-time', he said. 'But our boys

[in New Guinea] are living black. They're not used to it.'
1977 Kevin Gilbert *Living Black* [book title]

lizard   1   A shepherd; a man maintaining boundary fences (and so crawling along or stretching out in the sun)
1908 Giles Seagram *Bushmen All* 127: The term 'lizard' was one rather contemptuously applied to the shepherds by the horsemen. Ibid. 240: 'This blessed lizarding is bad enough, but wood and water joey is worse.'
1931 W. Hatfield *Sheepmates* 120–1: 'You're goin' in the camp, aren't you? – Not goin' lizardin'?' . . . 'Yes,' said Hallett, 'you'd be better out in the camp with me than crawlin' around a fence like a fly-catcher lizard.'
1937 Arthur Upfield *Winds of Evil* 174–5: 'What bloke wouldn't be depressed at coming down to a fence lizard! . . . Come down to fencin' and you want to know why a bloke's depressed.'
2   The handpiece of the shears [f. resemblance to a lizard]
1979 Keith Garvey *Tales of My Uncle Harry* 37: 'The sheep was dead in no time, and the young fellow panicked. He pulled the lizard out of gear, and rushes down the board.'
see **bogghi**
3   A flathead [f. resemblance]
1980 *Weekend News* (Perth) 27 Dec. 44: Some great flathead have been landed during the week. Touching the scales at well over a kilo the old lizard is one of the best table fish around.
4   The penis
1979 Steve Finnane *The game they play in heaven* 86: Most conversations are about women. A country voice cuts across the others: 'Did you give the lizard a run, mate?'

lizard, flat out as a ~ drinking   Working 'flat out', without a moment to spare
1944 Jean Devanny *By Tropic, Sea and Jungle* 227: The mother [kangaroo-rat] went one way and the young one another . . . It ran straight, as flat out as a lizard drinking.
1951 Dal Stivens *Jimmy Brockett* 70: The Wednesday of that week I was flat out like a lizard drinking when the phone rang.
1952 Jon Cleary *The Sundowners* 183: 'You've been flat out like a lizard drinking, but this cove is right with you all the time.'
1970 Max Harris *Australian* 10 Jan. 14: Have you ever copped the way those girls serve the community at the Sydney Telephone Exchange? Flat out like lizards drinking, all day long.
1984 *Age* (Melbourne) 25 Apr. 3: Myers, Coles and McDonald's stores all reported very brisk trading. One McDonald's franchise-holder said he had been 'as flat out as a lizard drinking water'.

lizards, stiffen (starve) the An exclamation of astonishment, protest, disbelief: sometimes 'Stone the crows and stiffen the lizards' (comic strip Australian)
1944 Lawson Glassop *We Were the Rats* 204: 'God starve the lizards,' said Eddie, 'another dud. Reckon half their bloody shells are duds.'
1965 Eric Lambert *The Long White Night* 89: 'Starve the bloody lizards!' breathed Clancy. 'Now I've seen the lot!'

load of, get a Take notice of, get an 'eyeful' of [U.S. 1929 OED]
1941 Baker 44: *Load of, get a* To take notice of, understand.
1952 John Cleary *The Sundowners* 133: Bluey looked at Sean and jerked a thumb at Venneker. 'Get a load of who's talking?'
1959 Dorothy Hewett *Bobbin Up* 178: 'Get a load of that, when she bends over!'.
1965 Frank Hardy *The Yarns of Billy Borker* 147: 'Get a load of this outfit. Look at me flamin' hat.'
1975 Les Ryan *The Shearers* 14: 'Hey Lofty! Get a load of that!' he said, as a blonde salesgirl in white uniform entered.

lob (in) To arrive, turn up
1915 C. J. Dennis *The Songs of a Sentimental Bloke* 56: 'Twas at a beano where I lobs along / To drown them memories o' fancied wrong.
1918 *Kia Ora Coo-ee* 15 May 7: ''Member when we uster lob inter camp, covered in dust and dry as bones? Why, we was happy as Larry.'
1924 E. J. Brady *Land of the Sun* 89: A man who would insist on telling things lobbed in.
1931 Vance Palmer *Separate Lives* 220–1: 'When I lob home,' said Chook, 'd'you know the first thing I'll do?'
1950 K. S. Prichard *Winged Seeds* 24: 'You never knew who'd lob into the camp.'
1973 John Morrison *Australian by Choice* 187–8: She was the first woman Sam spoke to when he lobbed in the town.
1983 *Weekend Australian* 9 Jul. Mag. 20: Ken Myer is nuts about all things Asian and will be interested in finding a place for Clive when he lobs back in the next month or so.

Lochinvar An abductor of lubras: N.T. [f. the poem by Sir Walter Scott]
1951 Ernestine Hill *The Territory* 311: Lochinvars sold the women to the drovers and the stations at £10 a head, but they didn't have it all their own way. A good many were speared.

lock on with, to To fight (*juvenile*)
1959 Gerard Hamilton *Summer Glare* 107: When I looked around they were fighting – 'locked on' as we called it. Ibid. 108: 'Why did you lock on with

Nancy this arvo?' I said.

logs, the Gaol: *obs.* [f. timber used in construction]
[**1802** David Collins *An Account of the English Colony in NSW* ed. Brian Fletcher (1975) ii 1: The governor ... resolved on constructing a strong and capacious Log Prison at each of the towns of Sydney and Parramatta ... he called upon every officer, settler and housekeeper within the above-mentioned districts, to furnish a certain number of logs for this purpose.]
1870 Marcus Clarke *His Natural Life* ed. S. Murray-Smith (1970) 784: 'Tomorrow morning – Mac, we'll have all these fellows comfortably in the logs.'
1873 Rolf Boldrewood 'The Fencing of Wanderowna' *A Romance of Canvas Town* (1898) 119: The aforesaid lock-up, popularly known as 'The Logs' from the preponderating quantity of these massive timbers displayed in the floor, the wall, and indeed the ceiling of the edifice.
1903 Joseph Furphy *Such is Life* (1944) 369: 'It seems sort a' hard lines when a man's shoved in the logs for the best three months in the year for a thing he never done.'

lolly A sweet, esp. coloured [abbr. of *lollipop*]
1854 Catherine Spence *Clara Morison* (1971) 278: Fanny ran away to the nearest lolly shop, and all her brothers and sisters followed her.
1859 Oliné Keese *The Broad Arrow* i 324: 'She wouldn't give me any more lollies.'
1883 R. E. N. Twopeny *Town Life in Australia* 54: You will see babies without number left in the blazing sun, some hanging half-way out of their perambulators, others sucking large painted 'lollies' or green apples.
1900 Henry Lawson 'The Songs They Used to Sing' *Prose* i 37: We got lollies (those hard old red-and-white 'fish lollies' that grocers sent home with parcels of groceries).
1911 Louis Stone *Jonah* 93: The trays heaped with sweets coloured like the rainbow, pleased his eye, and, remembering Ada's childish taste for lollies ...
1931 Vance Palmer *Separate Lives* 64: Coloured lollies in bottles that made the mouth water.

lollyboy The vendor of a tray of sweets and ice cream at the cinema
1951 Frank Hardy *Power Without Glory* 460: Above the mumble of five thousand voices could be heard the calls of the drink and lolly boys with their trays.
1971 G. Johnston *A Cartload of Clay* 45: The lights came on for interval and the lolly boys were shuffling raucous with their trays.
1981 *Sydney Morning Herald* 28 Nov. 40: The

advertising man Bani McSpedden wore white. A white jacket with vanilla coloured revers, the kind lolly boys used to wear at Saturday matinees, white pants and white Gucci sneakers.

lolly, do the   To lose one's temper, presence of mind
[1859 Hotten 60: *Lolly* the head.]
1959 Dorothy Hewett *Bobbin Up* 178: 'Keep an eye on me machine will you Jeanie. S'pose we'll haveta keep it goin' now Dick's doin' his lolly.'
1962 Criena Rohan *The Delinquents* 132: 'Don't start talking to me as though you were a plain-clothes cop,' said Lola, 'or I'm liable to do the lolly.'
1964 Thomas Keneally *The Place at Whitton* 18: 'I didn't want to antagonize them, and the first one I meet, I do my lolly with him.'
1971 Frank Hardy *The Outcasts of Foolgarah* 116: A strong debater even if prone to do the lolly on the Red issue.
1983 *Weekend Australian* 26 Mar. Mag. 16: 'In Britain they had seen Richard Carleton's *Nationwide* interview with Hawke in which Hawke did his lolly.'

lollywater   Soft drink, esp. if coloured
1945 Baker 231: *lolly-water* soft drink. [as an example of derivation from pidgin]
1948 Sumner Locke Elliott *Rusty Bugles* in *Khaki, Bush and Bigotry* ed. Eunice Hanger (1968) 56: 'Only one bottle of lolly water per man.'
1953 *The Sunburnt Country* ed. Ian Bevan 127: The greatest indignity that ever befell the hapless defenders of Darwin was not the Japanese air-raids ... [but] that its garrison was issued not with beer, but with bottled cordial. This they christened, contemptuously, 'lolly water': and weed killer could not have been more detested.
1958 Gavin Casey *Snowball* 155: 'That gingah ale, it blows a man up.' 'It does that, Tiger. They'll understand that a man in trainin' can't sit around guzzlin' lolly-water too long.'
1966 Hal Porter *The Paper Chase* 300: 'Soda-water please. And you can ask the bar-boy for a bottle of lolly-water for yourself.'
1968 Thomas Keneally *Three Cheers for the Paraclete* 5: Under Brendan's sporadic directions, the car left the lolly-water ambience of the big streets and found its way among terraces.
1973 John Morrison *Australian by Choice* 114: Christmas dinner was distinguised by plum pudding ... and some bottles of soft drink sent down from the house. The pudding was appreciated, not the lolly-water.
1984 *Age* (Melbourne) 9 Jun. 11: The nearby sandwich shop sold only lolly water and Big M, neither of which I would be caught dead with.

London to a brick on   A statement of betting odds

(a brick = £10) popularized by the racing commentator Ken Howard (1914–76)
1965 Frank Hardy *The Yarns of Billy Borker* 108: 'Close: but Magger by a head,' the course announcer Ken Howard says, 'London to a brick on Magger.'
1974 *Sydney Morning Herald* 1 Jan. 2: A Howard trademark was his confident prediction of the winner in a tight finish – 'It's London to a brick on.' ... Where did the expression 'London to a brick on' come from? 'I don't know, but I probably picked it up in the billiards halls when I was younger,' he said. 'I used to meet a lot of Damon Runyon characters, listen to their talk and pick up some of their expressions.'
1983 *Australian* 11 May 15: A senior Customs official told the spirit industry recently that higher taxes were 'London to a brick on' unless a miracle happened.

long oats   see **oats**

long colonial, a   see **colonial**

long paddock, the   The stock route, as opposed to the stockowner's holding
1933 Acland 386: *Long paddock, the.* – Slang for the road. People turn stock out on it, or travel them on it, to get cheap grazing.
1941 Baker 44: *Long paddock, the*: The open road.
1979 *Age* (Melbourne) 8 Nov. 3: 'From here [Queensland] to Victoria is the "long paddock". You put your cattle on the road for 180 days from Queensland to Echuca, and by the time they get there, they're nice and fat.'
1980 *Sydney Morning Herald* 17 May 14: Some farmers deliberately graze their stock on the reserves and the road (known as the 'long paddock'), thereby conserving their own land and destroying the feed for legitimate drovers.
1982 *Australian* 21 Sep. 9: They've put their stock in the long paddock – the old stock routes and the open road.

long sleever   A tall glass of beer: *obsolescent* [f. *sleever* measure of 13 fluid ounces OED 1896]
1877 T. E. Argles *The Pilgrim* viii 18: I should blow the froth from off the festive 'long sleever.'
1887 *All the Year Round* 30 Jul. 67: A frequent invitation is to take a 'long sleeved 'un', that is, a drink from a long pint glass.
1890 A. G. Hales *Wanderings of a Simple Child* 98: 'If you like to stand another long sleever, I'll give you some more'.
1905 Joseph Furphy *Rigby's Romance* ed. R. G. Howarth (1946) 26: The old gentleman, of course, took a long sleever, looking with ostentatious pity at the Doctor's sarsaparilla.
1908 Henry Fletcher *Dads and Dan between*

Smokes 126: Yous can get a bloke with a long sleeve hat, frock coat, an' made ter order pants.
1931 *Henry Lawson* by his Mates 126: Forty years ago there were many hospitable places between Hay Street and the Town Hall where one could procure 'long sleevers' of colonial beer for three-pence.
1975 Xavier Herbert *Poor Fellow My Country* 1144: Sims had a long-sleever.

long streak of pelican shit   see **pelican**

Loo, the   Woolloomooloo, a Sydney suburb
1893 Daniel Healey *The Cornstalk* 39: Tim Bunyip was of Austral birth, / Born at the classic 'Loo.
1908 *Evening News* 7 Jul. 7: The camphor trees ... will in a day or so become the centre of attraction to the rising generation of the 'Loo' on the warpath for cheap firewood.
1924 *Truth* 27 Apr. 6: 'Loo Woolloomooloo, suburb of Sydney.
1930 *Bulletin* 24 Dec. 42: 'I'm off back home to me job and the 'Loo.'
1959 Dorothy Hewett *Bobbin Up* 15: The shabby, genteel poverty of bed sits and bed and breakfast, running downhill into the slummy rabbit warrens of Paddo and the Loo.

look, take a ~ at   A wry injunction intended to draw attention to the realities of a situation
1943 Dymphna Cusack *Morning Sacrifice* 27: 'Take a look at me, cherub, and remember that nothing comes to the woman who waits.'
1957 Ray Lawler *Summer of the Seventeenth Doll* 78: 'Glamorous nights! I mean – look at us.'
1959 Eleanor Dark *Lantana Lane* 21: 'By golly!' they will snort bitterly. 'Just take a look at us, and then take a look at the graziers! They have it all taped.'
1971 Frank Hardy *The Outcasts of Foolgarah* 57: Take a look at the no-hopers sitting up like jackey at a football match, Call-me-Jack said to himself, no wonder the council was considering sacking the lot and employing contract labour.

loop, the   The City Circle Loop Service of the Melbourne underground, linking Flinders St, Spencer St, Flagstaff, Museum and Parliament
1981 *Australian* 30 Apr. 9: Tedium-racked tourists have been known to ride the Paris Metro in the hope of exhilarating encounters with muggers or rapists. But what is that to the daily adventures offered by the Melbourne loop? Boarding it is an odyssey into the unknown, a grand roulette in which destination and arrival time is decided by a quirk of fate. The colourful cries of commuters making their third successive and non-stop circuit of the city have to be heard to be fully appreciated.

loppy   A rouseabout
1898 *Bulletin* 1 Oct. 14: The rouseabouts [are] 'leathernecks', 'spoonbills', 'loppies', or 'Jacks'.
1911 L. St Clare Grondona *Collar and Cuffs* 85: 'Loopy' as the rouseabout is called.
1964 H. P. Tritton *Time Means Tucker* 92: With only a couple of thousand to go 'Hughie' answered the prayers of the loppies with a fairly heavy shower.

Louie   A fly, from 'Louie the Fly' in the Mortein commercials of the 1960s and later
1967 *Billy Borker Yarns Again* 2: 'Who's Louis the Fly?' 'The ringkeeper at Tommo's Two-up School; had buck teeth like the fly in the T.V. commercials. His mates used to say to him: 'I hate Mortein. Louis hates Mortein.'
1979 *Age* (Melbourne) 17 Oct. 3: Louie the fly is making a comeback. The 'bad, mean and mighty unclean' little blowie will be back on the box within a fortnight. Samuel Taylor Pty Ltd has decided – after what it says is a 15-year absence – that it's time to engage Louie to sell Mortein again.
1980 Peter Luck *This Fabulous Century* 347: The 'Louies' we see in television commercials are actually raised in science laboratories.

lower than a snake's belly   see **snake**

low heel   A prostitute; a woman of easy morals
1939 Kylie Tennant *Foveaux* 311: In this crowd of low heels, quandongs and ripperty men, she looked at her ease and yet not of them.
1941 Baker 44: *Lowheel*: a prostitute.
1951 Dal Stivens *Jimmy Brockett* 56: Sheilas generally get round in pairs. If you do see a sort on her own it's an even chance she's a pro or a lowheel.
1965 John Beede *They Hosed Them Out* 193: My well-bred low-heel declared it was the first time she'd been done on the floor and voted it an exceedingly diverting experience.
lowie
1967 Kylie Tennant *Tell Morning This* 16: 'There's many a man thought he was going to stand over some little lowie and now he's either looking through bars or else he's mowing the lawn for her.'
1979 *Sydney Morning Herald* 3 Mar. 13: A group of bikies ... stagger in and out, beer cans in hand, chatting up the 'loweys' who hang about beside the entrance waiting to be picked up.

luck of Eric Connolly   see **Connolly**

Lucky Country, the   The Australia of the 1960s, from a book of that title (1964) by Donald Horne
1969 *Australian* 13 Sep. 11 C: Illegitimacy in the Lucky Country.
1970 Donald Horne *The Next Australia* 19: When

I invented the phrase 'The Lucky Country' it was quickly misunderstood as it quickly caught on ... So a phrase that was intended as an ironic rebuke became a phrase of self-congratulation.
1970 Jon Cleary *Helga's Web* 140: Suddenly she hated all Australians, the whole lucky country as they called themselves.
1974 *Sun-Herald* 29 Dec. 15: In two years of power, the Whitlam Government has turned 'the lucky country' upside down and achieved none of its aims.

Lucky Shop, the   The TAB, in Victoria
1979 *Age* (Melbourne) 19 Dec. 24: He was intrigued by the number of people at the so-called 'Lucky Shop' frittering away all kinds of money on undisciplined quadrella betting.
1982 *Sun-Herald* 7 Mar. 144: Victoria's TAB (quaintly called lucky shops).

lucky, strike me   A catch-phrase of the comedian Roy Rene ('Mo') and the title of a film in which he starred in 1935
[**1859** Hotten *Strike me lucky!* a simple form of an oath common amongst the lower orders when making a bargain, and appealing to their honour.]

lumber   To arrest, imprison
1812 Vaux 251: A man apprehended, and sent to gaol, is said to be *lumbered*, or be *in lumber*, or to be in *Lombard street*.
1882 *Sydney Slang Dictionary* 6: *Lumber* To take or carry away to the lock-up.
1896 Edward Dyson *Rhymes from the Mines* 77: This job, I think, just saved me being lumbered on the vag.
1951 Dal Stivens *Jimmy Brockett* 94: Every time I see a bloke being lumbered, I want to pitch in and help him. I've never had much time for cops.
1956 Ruth Park and D'Arcy Niland *The Drums Go Bang!* 14: 'We'd all have been lumbered for disturbing the peace.'
1968 Stuart Gore *Holy Smoke* 58: 'That's about the strong of 'em ... cunnin' as sewer rats when

they're trying to lumber someone under the Act.'
1977 Jim Ramsay *Cop it Sweet* 56: *Lumbered*: Arrested.

lurk   1   A dodge, a scheme, stratagem
[**1859** Hotten 61: *Lurk* a sham, swindle, or representation of feigned distress.]
1945 Tom Ronan *Strangers on the Ophir* 37: 'There was a good lurk picking up horses inside and working them through here and up to Camooweal.'
1951 Dal Stivens *Jimmy Brockett* 113: It might be a good lurk to float it into a company and get out while the going was good.
1961 George Farwell *Vanishing Australians* 76: It [lambing down] denoted a lurk used by some publicans.
1972 Basil Fuller *West of the Bight* 31: 'He knew all the lurks, o' course.'
1975 *Australian* 15 Sep. 7: 'There are a lot of lurks down in Canberra,' he said ... 'They pay senators $37 a day while in Canberra – that's too much. And you can take a relative down four times a year.'
1980 *Mercury* (Hobart) 11 Apr. 5: Greedy medicos discover a new lurk.
lurk-man
1980 Clive James *Unreliable Memoirs* 97: He was something of a lurk-man, but he had the additional quality of humour.
2   A job, occupation (close in implication to 1)
1915 C. J. Dennis *The Songs of a Sentimental Bloke* 20: I found 'er lurk / Was pastin' labels in a pickle joint.
1953 T. A. G. Hungerford *Riverslake* 189: 'I dunno why you don't take up teaching again. That's your lurk.'
1959 Vance Palmer *The Big Fellow* 269: Whenever he passed a spread of furrows and a man behind a plough he felt something wake in his blood. But a farm was no longer his lurk.
1962 Alan Marshall *This is the Grass* 159: 'What's your lurk, anyway?' 'I just knock around,' I said ... I added, 'I'm a clerk.'

mad as a cut snake   Out of one's mind; extremely annoyed
1920 Louis Esson 'The Drovers' in *Dead Timber* 34: 'The Boss is as mad as a snake – he was flourishing his greenhide and cursing like thunder and lightning till we got 'em together again.'
1932 William Hatfield *Ginger Murdoch* 30: 'But you're mad!' said Mick, 'mad as a cut snake!'
1946 Dal Stivens *The Courtship of Uncle Henry* 75: He was mad as a cut snake about everything and wanting to put the boot in.
1951 Seaforth Mackenzie *Dead Men Rising* 203: 'Mad as a cut snake,' Johnson said admiringly, 'and there's not a better feller in the whole camp.'
1964 Dan Reidy *The Road to Tabuggeree* (1967) 33: 'That's Noisy Joyner's; he's as mad as a snake on a chain.'
1975 Don Townshend *Gland Time* 148: 'Never seen anythin' like it. Mad as a cut snake she was.'
1982 Tim Winton *An Open Swimmer* 23: 'He's as mad as a cut snake.'
see **silly as a two-bob watch**

mad as a meat-axe   As for **mad as a cut snake**
1934 'Leslie Parker' *Trooper to the Southern Cross* (1966) 78: I was as wild as a meat-axe.
1946 *Coast to Coast 1945* 252: 'The cow's mad – mad as a meat-axe!' Jack said with conviction.
1974 David Ireland *Burn* 97: 'Struth, love, you're mad as a meat-axe.'
1984 Max Harris *Weekend Australian* 28 Jul. Mag. 4: John McArthur is ruled out. He was monomaniac, if not as mad as the proverbial meat-axe.

mad, he went ~ and they shot him   Jocular reply to a request for anyone's whereabouts (World War II slang)
1944 Lawson Glassop *We Were the Rats* 47: 'I just came in for a yarn with Happy. Where is he?' 'If ya referrin' ter Mr Simpson he went mad and they shot him.'
1948 Sumner Locke Elliott *Rusty Bugles* in *Khaki, Bush and Bigotry* ed. Eunice Hanger (1968) 31: 'Andy Edwards ... Andy Edwards there?' 'Went mad and they shot him.'
1953 *The Sunburnt Country* ed. Ian Bevan 129: *'He went mad and they shot him'* is the routine answer to any superior seeking the whereabouts of a subordinate.
1975 *Woman's World* 8 Oct. 71: Father was unusually late home, having been held up in a traffic jam. Five-year-old son, tired of waiting for Dad, announced, 'Perhaps he went mad and they shot him.'
see **went through like Speed Gordon, gone for a ride on the padre's bike, went for a crap and the sniper got him**

mad mick   see **mick**

madwoman's custard (knitting, lunch-box), all over the place like a   In complete disarray
1953 T. A. G. Hungerford *Riverslake* 18: 'What a

joint! All over the place like a mad woman's knitting.'

1957 D'Arcy Niland *Call Me When the Cross Turns Over* 199: 'In the end he was blood from head to hocks and all over the place like a mad woman's custard.'

1973 Alexander Buzo *Norm and Ahmed* in *Three Plays* 10: 'I floored this bloody Kraut. Really laid him out. He was all over the place like a mad woman's lunch box.'

1983 Robert Drewe *The Bodysurfers* 88: When I first got out I was all over the place like a mad woman's lunchbox.

mag *v.* To talk: *derogatory* [1778–1885 OED]
1906 Edward Dyson *Fact'ry 'Ands* 232: 'Yeh never did, Goudy! Don't mag to me, yeh never did'.
1915 C. J. Dennis *The Songs of a Sentimental Bloke* 122: *Mag* To scold or talk noisily.
1924 *Truth* 27 Apr. 6: *Mag* To talk; scold.
1941 Sarah Campion *Mo Burdekin* 35: 'Sure, they all mag – men 'n wimmen alike'.
1957 Nino Culotta *They're a Weird Mob* 19: 'I can't stand 'ere maggin' ter you all day.'
1967 Kylie Tennant *Tell Morning This* 207: He was told . . . to get going and stop magging.
1973 Alexander Buzo *Norm and Ahmed* in *Three Plays* 23: 'Just to talk to someone, that's all I want. And when I do find someone to talk to, I just mag away like an old woman and ruin everything.'

mag *n.*
1913 C. J. Dennis *Backblock Ballads* 198: *Mag*, vulgar raillery.
1914 Edward Dyson *Spats' Fact'ry* 39: Another lay that's popular with lads what don't want their girls t' cherish mad idears is the mag about marriage bein' barred by the great hinstitution what pays 'em thirty bob a week fer their hinvaluablo services
1919 W. H. Downing *Digger Dialects* 33: Mag (vb. or n.) Chatter.
1934 Brian Penton *Landtakers* 382: 'I thought it was your mag I was hearin', she said.
1953 Kylie Tennant *The Joyful Condemned* 343: 'Hey, Jimmy . . . c'mon over here. I want a bit of a mag with you.'
1961 Barbara Jefferis *Solo for Single Players* 30: 'There's this time every morning when they can get on their radios and have a good mag to each other.'

maginnis, a crooked A hold (as in wrestling) that puts an opponent at a complete disadvantage: *obs.* [derived by Baker (1966: 126) from a wrestler called McGinnis]
1900–10 O'Brien and Stephens: *putting the McGinnis on* To put an opponent or combatant hors-de-combat. A grip or hold that cannot be unlocked or resisted.
1903 Joseph Furphy *Such is Life* (1944) 15: 'You see, Tom,' he remarked to me, 'this fixter'll put the crooked maginnis on any fence from 'ere to 'ell.'
1905 Joseph Furphy *Rigby's Romance* ed. R. G. Howarth (1946) 66–7: 'I could see my way to Agnes in a more manly, off-hand way than depending on the sort of crooked maginnis I had on her.'

maggot, dead as a Inert, incapacitated, quite dead
1954 Tom Ronan *Vision Splendid* 93: 'As dead as a maggot', he commented.
1965 William Dick *A Bunch of Ratbags* 73: 'He's dead orright, dead as a maggot'.
1976 David Ireland *The Glass Canoe* 15: Someone hit one of Danny's mates with an iron bar. Dropped him cold as a maggot.

maggoty Angry, bad-tempered [*maggoty* freakish, whimsical OED 1678–1864]
1919 W. H. Downing *Digger Dialects* 33: *Maggotty* Angry.
1941 Baker 45: *Maggoty* Angry, irritable, 'snooty'.
1951 Dal Stivens *Jimmy Brockett* 31: I didn't need to, but I shaved every day and my old man made me maggotty by asking me one day, 'Do you shave up or down?'
1959 David Forrest *The Last Blue Sea* 74: 'He's down there in the R.A.P. going maggotty about doctors and Japs and boongs.'

magnoon Crazy, mad: Services slang in World War I and II [f. Arabic]
1918 *Kia Ora Coo-ee* 15 Mar. 9: A 'magnoon' Waler is next to ride with every chance of a fall.
1919 W. H. Downing *Digger Dialects* 32: *Macnoon* (Arab.) Mad.
1944 Lawson Glassop *We Were the Rats* 191: 'They're *magnoon* blokes who think it's an honour to die for their Fuehrer'.
1970 Richard Beilby *No Medals for Aphrodite* 140: 'She could be a bit magnoon in the head. Women are funny like that.'

magnune Variant spelling of *magnoon*
1918 *Kia Ora Coo-ee* 15 Jul. 17: The Bombologist is known by the sobriquet of 'Magnune Mick'.

magpie A halfcaste [urban Ab.]
1982 Brian Syron *Australian* 30 Aug. 9: 'It's difficult if you're a "magpie". You cop it from both sides.'

Magpies, the 1 in N.S.W., the Western Suburbs Rugby League team [f. black and white colours]
1976 *Sunday Telegraph* (Sydney) 11 Apr. 58: Magpies breakfast on the Berries.
2 In Victoria, the Collingwood V.F.L. team
1963 Lou Richards *Boots and All!* 12: I was born

into a Magpie family and reared in the Magpie nest, kicking tin cans and paper footballs around the streets of Collingwood and Abbotsford.
1974 *Sunday Telegraph* (Sydney) 8 Sep. 84: Magpies get home easily.
3 In S.A., the Port Adelaide Australian Rules club
1978 *Sunday Telegraph* (Sydney) 17 Sep. 103: Port Get Up in Late Burst [heading] The Magpies were 28 points down going into the last quarter, but stormed home.
4 In Queensland, the Southern Suburbs Rugby League club
1979 *Courier-Mail* (Brisbane) 16 Apr. 17: Young Magpie centre Mal Meninga calmly booted a goal to give Souths a 9–7 win.
5 In N.T., the North Darwin Australian Rules club
1979 *NT News* (Darwin) 19 Nov. 23: Magpies flutter to earth ... North's slogan for the season 'Fly high with the Magpies' looks to be degenerating into a sick joke.
6 In Tasmania, the Glenorchy Australian Rules club
1980 *Mercury* (Hobart) 25 Jan. 23: New secretary for Magpies [heading] Mr Stan Walker is the new secretary of the Glenorchy Football Club.

mail   Rumour, report, esp. a racing tip
1966 Baker 77: Along with the variations *mulga mail* (or *wire*), it can mean a source of rumour.
1975 *Bulletin* 26 Apr. 44: 'His mail was that if I didn't weigh in soon I'd be gathered for sure.'
1977 Jim Ramsay *Cop it Sweet* 57: *Mail* Information.
1983 *Sun-Herald* 27 Mar. 66: The mail is the Minister for Sport, Mike Cleary, is wary of new betting introductions following footie flop.
1984 *Age* (Melbourne) 19 Sep. 38: 'I had never heard of the horse [Fine Cotton] before. I didn't receive any special "mail" on it, but I've gone to races all my life – money speaks all languages.'

Mainland, the   Australia, from a Tasmanian standpoint
1934 Thomas Wood *Cobbers* 164: They are tied to Australia – 'the mainland', they call it ... 'the mainland' is an object of suspicion, envy, and dislike.
1958 Christopher Koch *The Boys in the Island* 15: He lived in an island. At six years old he knew about that. He heard it at school, and knew about it from Uncle Charlie's talk about the Mainland, Australia.
1968 Geoffrey Dutton *Andy* 200: 'Soon as I blew from the book, I headed down for the Old Tassy ... I'll get over on the Mainland soon, or up the islands.'
1975 Don Townshend *Gland Time* 33: The mainland was foreign to him and always would be foreign. On Monday morning he flew back to Tasmania.

maintain the rage   see **rage**

Maitland, Dean   A silent person [f. the film *The Silence of Dean Maitland*, 1914 and 1934, based on the novel by Maxwell Grey]
1948 Sumner Locke Elliott *Rusty Bugles* in *Khaki, Bush and Bigotry* ed. Eunice Hanger (1968) 88: *Ot:* Poor old Dean Maitland ... *Vic.* There must have been a lot on his mind. I never saw him speak the whole time he was here.
1969 R. S. Whitington *The Quiet Australian* 98: The twenty-two players were far too tense to talk during the twenty-minute break. Twenty-two 'Dean Maitlands' sipped their tea in silence.

Major's line, the   The route followed by Major Thomas Mitchell in his expedition of 1836, opening up Victoria for pastoral settlement
1853 *Letters from Victorian Pioneers* ed. T. F. Bride (1898) 52: We followed the track of those before us ... and in a short distance came on the Major's line, which was easily recognized at this time.
1855 William Howitt *Land, Labour and Gold* ii 99: Well might Sir Thomas Mitchell, in his route across this colony at this season of the year, describe it as a splendidly grassed country. We crossed his track, still called the Major's Line, a short time ago.
1883 E. M. Curr *Recollections of Squatting in Victoria* 22: Being again in Melbourne in January 1841, he purchased a sheep station which was situated on the Major's line*, about seventy miles from Melbourne, and five miles south-west from where the town of Heathcote now stands. *The 'Major's line' is a term signifying the track, or line of road, formed by the drays of Major (afterwards Sir Thomas) Mitchell in his explorations. In some localities the track or road which his drays left behind is called 'the Major' to this day.

makings, the   Tobacco and cigarette papers [N. Amer. 1905 OED]
1938 Eric Lowe *Salute to Freedom* 420: He pulled the inevitable 'makings' from his tunic pocket and started to roll a cigarette.
1947 Vance Palmer *Cyclone* 6: He took the makings from a tin beside him and began rolling them in his palm.
1958 H. D. Williamson *The Sunlit Plain* 17: 'Got the makings on you?' Eddie ... handed over a tin of tobacco and papers.
1969 Christopher Bray *Blossom Like a Rose* 7: He reached deep into the pocket of his jeans and drew out the makings. It was the last scatter of tobacco and the last paper.
1981 Maxwell Grant *Inherit the Sun* 327: He put

his firearm down and took the makings from his shorts pocket.

Mal, Big Mr Malcolm Fraser, Australian Prime Minister 1975–83 [f. height]
1976 *Sydney Morning Herald* 30 Aug. 1: Big Mal has urged us to spend up, and his latest support comes from the Champagne Information Centre.
1983 *Sun-Herald* 6 Feb. 61: Thanks to the cricket rebels and the Australian Government's strong stand on apartheid, visas are as hard to get as a smile on Big Mal's face.
1984 *Age* (Melbourne) 12 Sep. 2: The number of visitors [to Parliament House] last year was almost 13,000 fewer than during 1982–83 – Big Mal's final days. So much for charisma.

mallee, the Equivalent to 'the scrub' in expressions like 'take to the mallee' [f. the mallee scrub in Victoria]
1958 E. O. Schlunke *The Village Hampden* 127: 'They're going to lynch you, Rogerson,' Harry told him, grinning. 'You'd better take to the mallee before they come for you.'

Mallee bull, fit as a Extremely fit; Victorian [see quot. 1974]
1962 John Morrison *Twenty-three* 163: 'How's Bubby?' 'Fit as a Mallee bull! Got another tooth . . .'
1969 William Dick *Naked Prodigal* 257: 'You're orright, are yuh?' 'Fit as a mallee bull and twice as dangerous.'
1974 Jim McNeil *How Does Your Garden Grow* 45: *Mick*: Ha! (*Posing*) Fit as a mallee bull! Ibid. 141: *A mallee bull* is thus a beast toughened by spartan living conditions.
1976 *Australian* 31 May 8: 'There's a fairly high degree of male homosexuality among male [ballet] dancers but they seem to range from one extreme to the other, where some guys can do absolutely astonishing things – the proverbial Mallee Bulls, if you like. Their bodies are so finely tuned and dance is such a physical thing.'
1981 *Sun-Herald* 14 Jun. 151: He looked as fit as a Mallee bull.

Mallee gate See quot.
1966 *Coast to Coast 1965–1966* 150: 'D' you know what a Mallee gate is, Bob?' 'Yes, it's a short loose panel, just droppers and wires.'

mallee root A prostitute [rhyming slang]
1941 Baker 45: *Mallee root* A prostitute.

Malley's cow See quot.: N.T.
1951 Ernestine Hill *The Territory* 441: 'By the look o' the sun I better get a move on, missus. I'm Malley's Cow. I'm a goner!' Ibid. 445: *Malley's*

*Cow** A person gone away. *Back in Monaro folklore one Malley in a mustering-camp was told to hold a particular cow. When the boss came back and asked for it, Malley grinned. 'She's a goner,' he said.

Maluka, the The chief, the boss [Ab.]
1905 Jeannie Gunn *The Little Black Princess* 3: I was 'the Missus' from the homestead, and with the Boss, or 'Maluka' (as the blacks always called him), was 'out bush', camping near the river.
1928 Martin Boyd *The Montforts* 238: 'You'd better come and see the Maluka.' 'What's that?' ventured Raoul. 'It's aboriginal for headmaster.'
1946 W. E. Harney *North of 23°* 257: Then 'tucker ready, Mulaka', I hear Topsy call, so we go and have a feed.
1956 Tom Ronan *Moleskin Midas* 340: The Yates's Place blacks were in, all wanting to see their 'properly Old Man Maluka'.
1971 Keith Willey *Boss Drover* 140: An aboriginal with me said: 'Pickum grass, Maluka.'
1983 *NT News* (Darwin) 1 Jan. 6: Anthony Thomas is a quiet, self-effacing man. And that is probably the reason the Chief Minister overlooked him in the realignment of responsibilities. A source close to the Maluka told me he was unaware of the fact that Anthony is a vet.

man in white   see **white**

man, the old   see **old**

man on the land, the A rural producer (other than an employee on wages). The phrase is emotionally toned, allowing both the implication that he is the possessor of staunch qualities, and that he may be acquisitive of subsidies and given to whingeing. The Man on the Land was the heading to a column in the *Bulletin* for many years.
1929 Jack Moses *Beyond the City Gates* 23: The 'man on the land', in pursuit of his daily vocation, has much to contend with, hardships to encounter that would break the spirit of the average man.
1940 Ion L. Idriess *Lightning Ridge* 128: Every drover knows that the most suspicious man in the world is the Man on the Land – when travelling stock are about.
1984 *Bulletin* 13 Mar. 102: We heard a lot of eloquence from farmers about the many fine qualities of the 'man on the land', how he was morally superior to city slickers and how dedicated he was to the production of export income – not for his but for the country's good.
1984 *Sydney Morning Herald* 17 Apr. 9: Sir Arthur Fadden . . . reported with pride in his autobiography how he realised that subsidies for rural producers were politically sensitive and that the same effect could be achieved by establishing

tax deductions designed to help the man on the land.

manatj   As for **monarch, monaych** q.v.
1982 Jack Davis *The Dreamers* 143: *Manatj*, police, literally 'black cockatoo'. The dark peak-cap uniforms of the early police caused them to be compared to this bird.

manchester   Used as *n.* and *adj.* to apply to Manchester goods (i.e. cotton materials) from at least the 1920s
1969 Thomas Jenkins *We Came to Australia* 124: Light bulbs were called globes and the linen department the manchester department.
1981 *Weekend Australian* 8 Aug. Mag. 7: The newly located DJ's Manchester (towels, sheets etc) department on the sixth floor.
1983 Max Harris *Bulletin* 29 Nov. 90: My wife experienced an episode of some confusion, if not embarrassment, in the John Lewis department store in London recently. She had just concluded a transaction and was asked if she would take her purchase with her. 'No,' she said, 'just hold it. I have to go to manchester but I'll be back in a while.' A baffled sales assistant informed madam that it was quite a long way to Manchester. My wife insisted that it was merely on the second floor. The assistant looked as if he should be calling in some nice men with white coats to take her away.

mangle   A bicycle (juvenile) *obs.* [? f. humorous resemblance]
1941 Baker 45: *Mangle* A bicycle.
1965 Graham McInnes *The Road to Gundagai* 122: 'Where's the grid?' My bike!' 'Yeah, the old mangle; isn't this where we left it?' [recalling the 1920s]

Mankad, to   To run out a batsman at the non-striker's end, for moving up the wicket before the ball has been bowled (Vinoo Mankad dismissed W. A. Brown in this way in the 1947/8 test series)
1982 *Australian* 17 Nov. 22: In the 1978–79 Perth Test against Pakistan, Sikander Bakht backed up too far and was 'Mankaded' by Alan Hurst.
1983 *Australian* 1 Oct. 44: When Devlin again left his crease, Pascoe twisted and threatened to 'Mankad' the batsman.

mantle of safety   The Rev. John Flynn's phrase for the protection given to outback Australia by the Flying Doctor service.
1927 *The Inlander* (ed. John Flynn) Oct. 70: To all who have battled for this 'Mantle of Safety' to spread over isolated pioneers we tender our sincerest gratitude.
1947 Ernestine Hill *Flying Doctor Calling* 146:

This should add a very sympathetic touch to the 'Mantle of Safety' already provided by the presence of the doctor and the transceiver sets.
1961 Noni Braham *The Interloper* 2: 'The Flying Doctor spreads a mantle of safety over the whole area.'
1971 Colin Simpson *The New Australia* 80: The Flying Doctor Service of Australia ... began spreading its 'mantle of safety' over the outback when, on 2nd August 1927, the first flying doctor trip was made from Cloncurry.
1983 *Australian* 20 Sep. 6: Next Friday will be the 60th anniversary since the Birdsville Hospital was opened and another link formed in Rev Dr John Flynn's vision of a 'Mantle of Safety' for the folk of the inland.

Maoriland   New Zealand [f. Maoris as the original inhabitants]
1884 *Maoriland An Illustrated Handbook to New Zealand* [book title] (Morris)
1896 Henry Lawson 'Steelman's Pupil' *Prose* i 209: They battled round together in the North Island of Maoriland for a couple of years.
1905 *Bulletin* 12 Jan. Red Page: A certain poet went down from Tasmania to Maoriland, and fell among words, which stripped him of his simplicity and stunned him, and never departed leaving him half dead.
1930 *Bulletin* 2 Jul. 11: Everyone had contributed at least one good lie except the man from Maoriland.

Maorilander
1902 J. H. M. Abbott *Tommy Cornstalk* 220: Of all the troops engaged in this arduous war, none were quite so good as the 'Maorilanders'.
1905 *The Old Bush Songs* ed. A. B. Paterson 51: Once more the Maorilander and the Tassey will be seen / Cooking johnny cakes and jimmies on the plains of Riverine.
1942 Eve Langley *The Pea Pickers* 411: In the corner of his paddock, on the site of the Maorilander's tent, stood another's.

map, throw a   See quot. 1945
1945 Baker 135: *throw a map, to* To be sick.
1978 *Weekend Australian* 25 Mar. Mag. 5: I failed to find 'throw a map', a term much in use in the 'fifties. Persistent map-throwers were known as cartographers.

marble, to make one's ~ good   To make the grade, confirm or improve one's status or prospects (cf. *alley*) [N.Z. 1926 OED]
1950 Brian James *The Advancement of Spencer Button* 162: 'He's trying to make his marble good, all right.'
1963 Don Crick *Martin Place* 223: 'Take my tip, if you wanter make your marble good: say nothing.'

264

marble, to pass in one's To give up, die

1908 *Australian Magazine* 1 Nov. 1250: Instead of dying you can 'chuck a seven', 'pass in your marble', or 'peg out'.

1916 Diary 31 Oct. cit. Bill Gammage *The Broken Years* (1974) 173: I absolutely threw my marble in and if it wasn't for the thought that I was on active service I think I would have wasted a cartridge on myself.

1918 Arthur Wright *Over the Odds* 102: 'I suppose the old pot knew y' old man before he passed in his marble,' ventured Dick.

1924 *Truth* 27 Apr. 6: *Throw in the marble* To relinquish.

1951 Dal Stivens *Jimmy Brockett* 304: 'I'm not going to pass in my marble just yet.'

1961 George Farwell *Vanishing Australians* 77: He ... went into a coma, and it was some time before the coves he was shouting woke up that he'd really passed in his marble.

1973 Jack Hibberd *A Stretch of the Imagination* 24: 'What if I pass in my marble like this?'

see **alley** 2

Marble Bar, till it rains in Indefinitely [f. W.A. town of low rainfall]

1943 Douglas Stewart *Ned Kelly* in *Four Plays* (1956) 172: 'And we'd have held this country against the troopers / Till it rains in Marble Bar!'

March, the The march of ex-servicemen on Anzac Day

1945 Cecil Mann *The River* 136: Clarkey is not in the March this year.

1962 Alan Seymour *The One Day of the Year* 79: 'We started at a pub in King Street straight after the march.'

Mardi Gras A carnival held at any time of the year [f. *Mardi Gras* (Shrove Tuesday) as a festival]

1977 *Sunday Telegraph* (Sydney) 16 Jan. 76: A closing highlight of the Festival of Sydney will be a huge Mardi Gras at the Haymarket on the night of Saturday, January 29.

1984 *Australian* 3 Feb. 7: The Rev. Troy D. Perry author of *The Lord is my Shepherd and He Knows I'm Gay*, will be special guest at Sydney's Mardi Gras ... All the Mardi Gras needs now is a gay ayatollah.

marines, dead see **dead marines**

mark, marking Abbr. of 'earmark', generalized to cover the whole process of ear-marking, docking and castrating lambs; also a euphemism for 'castrate'

1826 Let. in *Mortmain* ed. E. FitzSymonds (1977) 125–6: Some of the stolen sheep newly ear marked returned to the flock and claimed their mothers ... For the sheep delivered to Lindsey and Jenkins your Memorialist received cattle from the Herd of their Master Mr. Lord, and was to have had some more after the cutting and marking had finished.

1883 Edward M. Curr *Recollections of Squatting in Victoria* 153: Shortly after taking charge I marked two thousand lambs.

1898 Alfred Joyce *A Homestead History* ed. G. F. James (1969) 82–3: It was usual ... to give them a bonus of a shilling a head for all lambs marked over a certain percentage, generally eighty-five per cent ... A few weeks after the completion of the lambing, the work of emasculation, tail-docking and ear-marking would be gone through.

1905 *The Old Bush Songs* ed. A. B. Paterson 49: Then at the lamb-marking a boss they'll make of you. / Now that's the way to get on, Jimmy Sago, Jackaroo.

1911 E. S. Sorenson *Life in the Australian Back-blocks* 143: When the pens are full there is a blessed respite while the lambs are marked ... The markers are ranged on the outside of the pen, and operate on the lambs as they are dumped on the rail by the catchers, who hold a foreleg and a hindleg in each hand. Knives and teeth are used alternately by the operators.

1933 Acland: *Mark* To ear-mark. Now a frequent euphemism for *cut and tail*. *Cutting and tailing* was the old name for earmarking, castrating and taking the tails off lambs, all of which operations are performed together. *C. and t.* is the general name mostly used by shepherds, but (owing to more ladies living up country, I suppose) is being replaced by *tailing* or *marking*.

1946 Dal Stivens *The Courtship of Uncle Henry* 140: 'There are a few lambs want marking, but I was thinking of ' said the boss, and before he could finish the bloke was running to the paddock and pulling out his Jno. Baker knife.

1982 *Sydney Morning Herald* 8 May 13: As he signed the last departmental file yesterday ... Killen remembered the blessed relief he felt long ago at the end of a long, hot morning marking (castrating) a couple of thousand lambs the old way (dragging them out with your teeth).

market, go to To behave in a violent or angry way (superseded by 'go to town')

1870 Rolf Boldrewood 'Shearing in Riverina' *Town and Country Journal* 12 Nov. 13: He slackens the rein, and saying, 'Go to market now old fellow,' sits the wild plunge of the colt like a Mexican vaquero.

1881 A. C. Grant *Bush-Life in Queensland* i 130: 'Well', said one, 'that fellow went to market like a bird.' 'Yes', echoed another. 'Bucked a blessed hurricane'.

1898 *Bulletin* 17 Dec. Red Page: To *get narked* is to lose your temper; also expressed by *getting dead wet* or *going to market*.

1908 W. H. Ogilvie *My Life in the Open* 83: Playful or vicious, according to their breeding and temperament, almost all of them [the horses] 'prop' or 'go to market' in some form or other.

1918 *Kia Ora Coo-ee* 15 Jul. 4: Later on, in the mess, a brother officer was 'going to market' because he had been rebuked for his failure to name men whose names the General sought.

1926 K. S. Prichard *Working Bullocks* 64: 'If we'd time I'd break him without learnin' him to buck. But as it is I reck'n he'll go to market a bit.'

1941 Baker 46: *Market, go to* To become angry, complain bitterly (about something).

1948 K. S. Prichard *Golden Miles* 29: 'She goes to market when I get shickered,' Bill admitted.

1951 Frank Hardy *Power Without Glory* 35: 'I have me instructions, so it's no use going to market on me.'

Marmaduke   Nickname of Neville Wran, premier of New South Wales

1984 *Sydney Morning Herald* 2 Aug. 1: The Premier, Mr Wran, said yesterday that the name 'Neville' appeared in the report by the Chief Stipendiary Magistrate, Mr Clarrie Briese, about alleged attempts to influence the outcome of a court case. But he denied this could refer to him ... He said he was thinking of changing his name to Marmaduke 'because that is a very distinctive name and if Marmaduke was mentioned in the same context then it is a good chance that it would be me.'

1984 *Age* (Melbourne) 12 Sep. 17: Mr Howard referred to Mr Keating as 'junior Marmaduke', a crack at NSW Premier Neville Wran's current nickname.

1985 *Sydney Morning Herald* 9 Mar. 1: The founder and captain of the Marmadukes, the State Parliamentary press gallery cricket team, is leaving to report on the Federal political sphere ... The Premier, after whom the team was named, signed Stanley's farewell card.

Maroons, the   1   A sporting team representing the state of Queensland, esp. in Rugby League football [f. team colours]

1973 *Sydney Morning Herald* 12 Jul. 13: A Blue Day for the Maroons.

1983 *Sun-Herald* 17 Jul. 78: Bosly grew up in Roma and there is still a healthy dash of the maroon in his make-up.

2   Former nickname of the Fitzroy V.F.L. club

1984 Lou Richards *Sun* (Melbourne) 9 Mar. 31: When I first played against them they were known as the Maroons.

Marvellous Melbourne   Melbourne as described by G. A. Sala (see quot. 1885)

1885 George Augustus Sala 'The Land Of The Golden Fleece' VII *The Argus* 8 Aug. 5: Life is a perpetual perhaps. Yet I am enabled to be tolerably well assured that it was on the 17th March in the present year of grace, 1885, that I made my first entrance, shortly before high noon, into Marvellous Melbourne.

1891 Edward Kinglake *The Australian at Home* 145: Marvellous Melbourne, but fifty years old, grown to be bigger than its sister Sydney which is twice its age, is justly entitled to take a place among the cities of the world of first rank and importance.

1896 Nat Gould *Town and Bush* 118: Marvellous Melbourne is a term often applied to the Victorian capital, and the city is not unworthy of it.

1910 *Marvellous Melbourne – Queen City of the South* [title of film screened at Spencer's Modern Picture Theatre, Melbourne, 22 Nov.]

1984 *Age* (Melbourne) 10 Apr. 23: Somewhat tensely clutching his SR45 emergency life-support system, our columnist Garrie Hutchinson begins his historic hike along Marvellous Melbourne's south-eastern trunk sewer.

mary   A girl or woman [Pidgin]

1876 A. J. Boyd *Old Colonials* (1882) 234: They [the natives] fail to comprehend how it is that a Chinaman who is 'baal white fellow' can get a white woman for a wife. They say, 'Chinaman got'im white Mary; blackfellow get'im white Mary.'

1885 Mrs Campbell Praed *Australian Life* 74: He asked what the Blacks wanted, and Boney replied, 'Altogether numkull; altogether marra white Maries.' [To kill every one; and to take away the white women.']

1902 A. B. Paterson 'Voyage of the Pilgrims' in *Song of the Pen* (1983) 106: A lot of 'boys' and perhaps a 'Mary' or two went on board a recruiting vessel to hear a musical box play.

1919 W. H. Downing *Digger Dialects* 56: *Mary* Woman [under heading Papua (Pidgin English)]

1931 Vance Palmer *Separate Lives* 68: 'White mary no walk about all day. She belonga one boss, sit down longa one house.'

1956 Tom Ronan *Moleskin Midas* 326: 'Harness up the buggy and take this Mary back to town.'

Mary Lou, on the   On credit: *rare* [rhyming slang *Mary Lou* = *blue* (credit, while 'red' is debit)]

1949 Lawson Glassop *Lucky Palmer* 248: He was betting on credit – 'Lucky' called it betting 'on the blue', 'on the Mary Lou', or 'on the nod'.

massacre, Father's Day, Milperra   see **Father's Day, Milperra**

mate   1   A working partner; an habitual companion; a fellow-participant in some corporate activity (always a man)

[1859 Hotten 62: *Mates* the term a coster or low person applies to a friend, partner or companion. 'Me and my mate' did so and so, is a common phrase with a low Londoner.]

1845 C. Griffith *The Present State ... of Port Phillip* 79: Two [bushworkers] generally travel together, who are called mates; they are partners, and divide all their earnings.

1847 Alexander Harris *Settlers and Convicts* ed. C. M. H. Clark (1954) 176: It is quite surprising what exertions bushmen of new countries, especially mates, will make for one another, beyond people of the old countries. I suppose ... difficulties prevailing make them more social and mutually helpful.

1855 William Howitt *Land, Labour and Gold* i 86: These gentlemen were themselves very soon obliged to get rid of their free and easy *mates*, to use the colonial phrase, who ... persisted in using our names at the squatting stations.

1864 James Armour *The Diggings, the Bush and Melbourne* 23: After much talk about the perfidy of former mates, he said that ... he would take me for a partner.

1880 Rolf Boldrewood *The Miner's Right* (1890) 136: 'We have been firm friends and true mates all this time.'

1899 Henry Lawson 'Crime in the Bush' *Prose* ii 35: Then there is the unprovoked, unpremeditated, passionless, and almost inexplicable bush murder, when two mates have lived together in the bush for years, until they can pass days and weeks without exchanging a word.

1915 Let. in Bill Gammage *The Broken Years* (1974) 59: Where are the rest of my 13 mates? ... myself I consider lucky getting away from the acres of dead men.

1947 John Morrison *Sailors Belong Ships* 20: Poor old Joe! Too much courage and too little brain ... A grand mate, though.

1953 *The Sunburnt Country* ed. Ian Bevan 126: No cry rings louder in the A.I.F. than this ... 'Don't bludge on your mates.'

1960 Donald McLean *The Roaring Days* 1: 'My mate' is always a man. A female may be my sheila, my bird, my charley, my good sort, my hot-drop, my judy or my wife, but she is never 'my mate'.

1983 *Sydney Morning Herald* 13 Jun. 12: Mr Hayden observed that the word 'mate' is 'an expression of deep loyal male friendship', but in NSW 'it's like the mafia presenting you with a bunch of flowers.'

2   As a mode of address, indicating equality and friendliness

1852 Lord Robert Cecil *Goldfields Diary* (1935) 36: When the diggers address a policeman in uniform they always call him 'Sir', but they always address a fellow in a blue shirt with a carbine as 'Mate'. 'Mate' is the ordinary popular form of allocution in these colonies.

1862 Arthur Polehampton *Kangaroo Land* 99: A man, who greeted me after the fashion of the Bush, with a 'Good day, mate'.

1981 *Age* (Melbourne) 20 Jul. 9: Lear, disgusted with the nature of man, cries out: 'Let copulation thrive'. From the back stalls came a shout of 'Too bloody right mate' and the audience went wild.

3   As a neutral or hostile mode of address, to someone not an acquaintance

1855 Raffaello Carboni *The Eureka Stockade* ed. Geoffrey Serle (1969) 5: 'Your licence, mate', was the peremptory question from a six-foot fellow in a blue shirt, thick boots, the face of a ruffian armed with a carabine and fixed bayonet.

1944 Lawson Glassop *We Were the Rats* 75: 'I'm not looking for trouble.' 'Yer may not be bloody well lookin' fer it, mate, but yer'll bloody well get it.'

1953 T. A. G. Hungerford *Riverslake* 50: 'I'll remember you, mate. You'll keep!'

1974 *Sydney Morning Herald* 14 Feb. 7: At 8.26 that evening a train arrived at Gosford. The destination sign on the platform was not shown. I asked a station attendant (attired in a dirty open-necked shirt and trousers, recognizable only by a dirty cap) if the train was the North-West Mail. 'I wouldn't have a clue, mate,' was the reply.

mate, my little   see **my**

mates with, to be   To have as a *mate* 1 [N.Z. 1880 OED]

1900 See **rush**

1945 Cecil Mann *The River* 23: Odd little bloke; funny being mates with him.

1976 Henry Gullett *Not as a Duty Only* 8: Our truck driver, Brockley, usually marched with this section when he was not driving because he was mates with Vic Maloney and Joe.

mateship   The fellowship implied in *mate* 1, and given currency by Henry Lawson: not really a colloquialism [OED 1593]

1894 Henry Lawson 'The Cant and Dirt of Labor Literature' *Prose* ii 27: When our ideal of 'mateship' is realised, the monopolists will not be able to hold the land from us.

1910 *Australian Magazine* Aug. 610: With such eloquence did he preach the gospel of communistic 'mateship' that he soon had even hundreds of men selling all they had, and following him to the social El Dorado in far-off Paraguay.

1932 Ion L. Idriess *Flynn of the Inland* 262: The preacher appealed to his hearers to stand up to the claims of mateship, to help all hands as well as their mates, just as does the Great Mate to whom all men are mates.

1945 Cecil Mann *The River* 62: At the war he belonged to a unit ... There was fellowship, mateship.

1959 Dorothy Hewett *Bobbin Up* 124: There was mateship, sharing a billy of bitter-black tea, a smoke and a yarn.

1973 Max Harris *The Angry Eye* 77: Historians have come to accept fairly calmly the notion that the Australian national philosophy of 'mateship' emerged from what was perhaps the world's only homosexual social ordering of things.

1983 *Sydney Morning Herald* 13 Apr. 26: In his summit launching speech, he [Mr Hawke] said, 'Our problems call for the application of those qualities of innovation, initiative, independence, tolerance – and, need I say, mateship – the qualities which we like to think are distinctly Australian.'

Matilda   A swag [f. woman's name: origin otherwise obscure. See Richard Magoffin *Fair Dinkum Matilda* (1973)]

1893 Henry Lawson 'Some Popular Australian Mistakes' *Prose* ii 24: A swag is not generally referred to as a 'bluey' or 'Matilda' – it is *called* a 'swag'.

1899 W. T. Goodge *Hits! Skits! and Jingles!* 159: In the morning came a swaggie with 'Matilda' across the flat.

1910 John X. Cameron *The Spell of the Bush* 55: 'I sling Matilda on my back and steer whichever way she slews me.' 'Matilda!' repeated O'Carroll. 'Bluey.'

1915 J. P. Bourke *Off the Bluebush* 62: But, ah! a wintry wind / Awakes Matilda's charms: / I calmly spread the old girl out / And snuggle in her arms.

1924 *Truth* 27 Apr. 6: *Matilda* Aussie term for swag.

1939 R. H. Croll *I Recall* 81: Mostly to me that has meant tramping the bush; often it has implied carrying Matilda, the swag.

1962 J. Marshall and R. Drysdale *Journey Among Men* 116: It was good to stretch out in the arms of Matilda at the end of the day, and slowly smoke a cigarette. Ibid. 146: We unrolled our Matildas between the dunes.

Matilda, waltzing   Carrying the swag, an expression given currency by A. B. Paterson's poem with this title, composed in 1895 and published in *Saltbush Bill J.P.* (1917), since achieving the status of an unofficial national anthem

1893 Henry Lawson 'Some Popular Australian Mistakes' *Prose* ii 24: No bushman thinks of going on the wallaby' or 'walking Matilda', or 'padding the hoof'; he goes on the track – when forced to it.

1902 Henry Lawson 'The Romance of the Swag' *Prose* i 501: Travelling with the swag in Australia

is variously and picturesquely described as 'humping bluey', 'walking Matilda', 'humping Matilda', 'humping your drum', 'being on the wallaby'.

1917 A. B. Paterson *Saltbush Bill J. P.* 23: Who'll come a-waltzing Matilda with me?

1934 Brian Penton *Landtakers* 387: 'Didn't we waltz Matilda together, work a claim together, and sweat our guts out together?'

1944 M. J. O'Reilly *Bowyangs and Boomerangs* 45: There was a vast difference between those swaggies of the early goldfields and the professionals found 'Waltzing Matilda' along the banks of the Darling, Murray or Murrumbidgee.

matinee   Sex in the day time

1971 Frank Hardy *The Outcasts of Foolgarah* 3: 'Lately I'd just as soon have a cold beer and a hot matinee with old Florrie while the kids are at Sunday school.'

1977 *Weekend Australian* 31 Dec. Mag. 6: *Matinee*: love in the afternoon.

1980 Bob Herbert *No Names ... No Pack Drill* 63: JOYCIE: You 'aven't made your bed. KATHY: I know. JOYCIE: (*giggling*) Have a matinee, did you?

Mavournee, Kathleen   see **Kath**

Mayblooms, the   Former nickname of the Hawthorn V.F.L. club

1950 *Sun* (Melbourne) 8 Apr. 3: It was Cazaly who changed Hawthorn's nickname from the 'Mayblooms' to the 'Hawks'.

McEwen's bank   The Australian Industry Development Corporation, set up in May 1970 [see quot. 1971]

1971 *Sydney Morning Herald* 22 Sep. The establishment of the corporation – sometimes called the McEwen Bank – was one of the last achievements of the former Trade Minister, Sir John McEwen.

1983 *Bulletin* 23 Aug. 98: How Labor will use Jack McEwen's Bank [heading] With its finances and credibility restored, the Australian Industry Development Corporation is poised to expand its operations vastly under Labor.

mean, so ~ he wouldn't give you a light for your pipe at a bushfire, wouldn't give a dog a drink at his mirage, wouldn't shout if a shark bit him, wouldn't give you a wave if he owned the ocean, wouldn't give you a fright if he was a ghost, wouldn't give you a shock if he owned the powerhouse, wouldn't give a rat a railway pie; still has his lunch money from school; with short arms and long pockets

1919 A. B. Paterson 'The Cook's Dog' in *Song of the Pen* (1983) 404: 'They reckon he's that mean he wouldn't give you a light for your pipe at a bushfire.'

1936 A. B. Paterson 'The Shearer's Colt' in *Song of the Pen* (1983) 707: 'He's that mean he wouldn't give a dog a drink at his mirage.'

1976 Sam Weller *Bastards I have met* 2: If he owned the ocean, he wouldn't give you a wave.

1981 *Daily Mirror* (Sydney) 23 Jan. 36: Albert wouldn't shout if a shark bit him.

1981 *National Times* 25 Jan. 23: 'He'd be too mean to give you a fright if he was a ghost'.

1981 *National Times* 25 Jan. 23: The skinflint . . . who still has his lunch money from school.

1983 *Sun-Herald* 23 Oct. 82: Australians don't usually rate railway tucker highly. 'He's so mean he wouldn't give a rat a railway pie', is a popular way of saying someone is parsimonious.

1984 *Toorak Sunday* 1 Jul. 24: My lunch was $10, and I forgot to tip the waiter. It's not true, as the waiter probably thinks, that I have short arms and long pockets in my Mike Treloar tailor-made suits.

meanie, grey   see **grey meanie**

meat-axe, mad as a   see **mad**

meat pie, as Australian as a   Unmistakably Australian [f. prominence of meat pie in Australian diet]

1972 *Sunday Australian* 16 Apr. 4: Apart from his name and his forebears, Barassi with his wide grin and fierce desire to win is as Australian as a meat pie.

1972 *Bulletin* 13 May 41: I am drawn back to 'Lane End' each week to see Meillon, his face as genuinely Australian as a meat pie, give his performance.

1981 Vivian Smith *Oxford History of Australian Literature* 420: In some poems he uses a dramatic voice which is Australian as a meat pie.

1984 *Sun-Herald* 4 Mar. 15: The days of the Holden being as Australian as meat pies or koalas are finished.

Medifraud   Fraud and over-servicing in the Federal health system [f. *Medibank* and *Medicare*]

1982 *Sydney Morning Herald* 18 Sep. 3: Medifraud task force planned [heading]

1984 *Age* (Melbourne) 28 Mar. 4: Medifraud is on the rise, researchers claim [heading]

Mediterranean back   See quot. 1981

1981 *Australian* 20 Apr. 7: For afflictions such as vertebrate disease – known by many as 'Greek back' or 'Mediterranean back' – Greeks are 15 times more likely to be disabled compared with Australians.

1982 Nancy Keesing *Lily on the Dustbin* 51: There are racist overtones to the . . . 'Mediterranean back' which denotes derisive suspicion about a back-ache.

1983 *Australian* 9 Dec. 9: A report by the Human Rights Commission published yesterday dwells on complaints which can be an incitement to racial hatred. 'Mediterranean back', 'ethnic jokes' (especially Irish ones) and the use of the word 'Pom' receive special mention.

meet   A sports meeting, esp. a swimming or athletics competition [applied to huntsmen and hounds in England 1831 OED]

1985 *Weekend Australian* 12 Jan. 56: AIS plans super swim meet [heading]

Melba, to do a   To make a habit of returning from retirement, in a number of 'farewell' performances [f. Dame Nellie Melba 1861–1931]

[**1933** Samuel Griffiths *A Rolling Stone on the Turf* 97: Crozier has become as noted as a certain famous singer for the number of his 'final' appearances.]

1971 *Australian* 20 Feb. 22: The later years were marked by a seemingly endless round of farewell performances. 'Doing a Melba', they call it.

1976 *Sydney Morning Herald* 28 Apr. 23: 'There will be no Nellie Melbas for me . . . I have retired and I will not play again,' a sad Langlands told me.

1981 *Sunday Mail* (Brisbane) 20 Sep. 60: Scamp has been known to do a 'Melba' before. In fact he has announced his retirement four times, and yesterday's exclusive to the Sunday Mail was his fifth retirement.

Melbourne, Marvellous   see **Marvellous**

merchant   Used similarly to 'artist', in combinations like 'stand over merchant', 'king-hit merchant', usually with some derogatory suggestion

1944 Lawson Glassop *We Were the Rats* 133: 'Just a top-off merchant, that's all he is.'

1951 Dymphna Cusack and Florence James *Come In Spinner* 253: 'He was nothing but a bloody stoush merchant any way.'

1954 T. A. G. Hungerford *Sowers of the Wind* 9: 'I'm no lurk merchant, Mark,' Craigie said placidly.

1965 *The Tracks We Travel* ed. L. Haylen 122: 'If these panic-merchants only knew when to leave alone!'

merino, pure   An early colonist priding himself on his freedom from the convict taint; a member of the most affluent and socially prominent class [f. breed of sheep]

1827 *Monitor* 13 Jan. 2: A round-about story has come to us . . . which, as it operates greatly to the credit of the pure Merino Bank, for which we have such an ardent regard . . . we shall here detail for the amusement of our readers.

1827 P. Cunningham *Two Years in New South Wales* ii 116: Next, we have … such as have legal reasons for visiting this colony; and … such as are free from that stigma. The *pure Merinos* are a variety of the latter species, who pride themselves on being of the *purest blood* in the colony.

1863 R. Therry *Reminiscences of Thirty Years' Residence in New South Wales* 58: The term *pure merino*, a designation given to sheep where there is no cross-blood in the flocks, was applied to mark a class who were not only free and unconvicted, but who could boast of having no collateral relationship or distant affinity with those in whose escutcheon there was a blot. These *pure merinos* formed the topmost round in the social ladder.

1893 Francis Adams *The Australians* 56–7: It was in the interests of this narrow-minded and insignificant horde, reinforced by their allies, the 'pure merinos' (the big squatters), that a university was built up on the played-out model of the old Oxford. Ibid. 63: His early manhood found him [Henry Parkes] a counter-jumper in a Sydney toy-shop, eager to show his parts by impassioned and turbid 'spouting' against 'the pure merinos' – the squattocracy and officialism of the hour.

1936 Miles Franklin *All That Swagger* 262: Norah was consulted, being married and of the pure merino squattocracy.

1954 Tom Ronan *Vision Splendid* 113: 'Old Mentmore … is one of your pure merino sportsmen: member of all the big racing clubs down south.'

mermaid A weighbridge inspector (road hauliers' slang)
1976 *Sun* (Sydney) 28 May 7: Department of Main Roads weighbridge inspectors … are called 'mermaids' … because they have scales.

messages, do the To do minor household shopping [f. *message*, a mission, an errand OED 1290]
1907 Barbara Baynton *Human Toll* 109: 'You're to go a message', said her aunt … handing her the list.
1938 Nettie Palmer *Letters* (1977) 159: I must get up: type some radio talk … do some messages.
1946 Margaret Trist *What Else is There?* 76: 'Hullo, Emmy', said Mrs Henderson. 'You come for your mother's messages?'
1961 Ruth Park *The Good Looking Women* 50: Dette … came home for lunch, or, more honestly, to do the messages.
1977 Robert Close *Of Salt and Earth* 6: I had been at school a year or so when my mother started to send me to do the household shopping … I began to dread being sent on messages.
1983 Laurie Clancy *Perfect Love* 159: Nora sent the two girls down to the local milk bar for what she always called messages.

Messiah, the Nickname of Mr R. J. Hawke, as Prime Minister 1983–
1983 Craig McGregor *Sydney Morning Herald* 30 Mar 7: In the Canberra press gallery they have begun to refer to Hawke, somewhat sardonically, as The Messiah.
1983 Jack Mundey *National Times* 30 Sep. 45: Gough was thought to be somewhat vain, but compared to this PM, his performance was shy, even modest. When are the respective ministers going to assert themselves and show us that the Messiah hasn't got to do everything Himself.
1984 Paul Kelly *Sydney Morning Herald* 16 Mar. 9: The notion of Bob Hawke as a Labor traditionalist has been denied publication and it is a shame, surely, to conceal this facet of the messiah.

metho Methylated spirits [abbr.]
1935 Kylie Tennant *Tiburon* 23: The two metho-drinkers were escorted out firmly.
1949 Judith Wright *Woman to Man* 35: 'Metho Drinker' [poem title]
1950 Brian James *The Advancement of Spencer Button* 168: A drinking party … had taken a supply of spirits – mostly 'metho' – to a cave on the foreshores.
1955 Alan Marshall *I Can Jump Puddles* 159: 'He'd been on the metho for a couple of days, they say. He rolled into the fire in the night.'
1973 Alexander Buzo *Rooted* 96: 'He died of alcoholism … Went on the metho, slept in the park, fell apart at the seams.'
1983 *Australian* 19 Apr. 9: Shopkeepers near the park defend the sale of metho to Aborigines.

Mexican A Victorian (viewed from N.S.W.); someone from N.S.W. or Victoria (viewed from Queensland) [f. south of the border]
1980 *Sydney Morning Herald* 21 Apr. 3: Victorians – whom South Coasters affectionately call Mexicans – used to use the Hume [Highway] as the quickest route to holiday spots such as Surfers Paradise and the Sunshine Coast.
1982 *Sydney Morning Herald* 10 Mar. 7: The people in Albury call people from south of the border Mexicans.
1984 *Sydney Morning Herald* 6 Mar. Good Living 1: Just over two years ago the Gold Coast went into shock. Mexicans (patois for people south of the border) had stopped crossing the Tweed River armed with retirement money. There was a depression.

mia mia An Aboriginal bough or bark hut [Morris 1845] but used of any rude shelter constructed by a white
1855 William Howitt *Land, Labour and Gold* i 252: Then there are huts of mingled boughs and sheets of bark, and here and there simple mimies,

in imitation of the mimi of the natives, that is, just a few boughs leaned against a pole, supported on a couple of forked sticks, and a quantity of gum-tree leaves for a bed.
1883 Edward M. Curr *Recollections of Squatting in Victoria* 72: My companion had made the mia-mia with forked sticks, some pieces of bark stripped from a fallen tree, and our saddle-cloths.
1898 Alfred Joyce *A Homestead History* ed. G. F. James (1969) 60: The meal as ground was carried well up the bank into a rough bark mia-mia, and safely protected till all was through, when it was carted up to the store for sifting as required.
1911 E. S. Sorenson *Life in the Australian Back-blocks* 100: Between the tent and the average dwelling-house there is a long list of humpies and hovels, gunyahs, mi-mies, canvas and galvanised-iron habitations, and bark huts.

see **humpy**

mick A Roman Catholic: *derogatory* [f. 'Mick' for an Irishman]
1934 'Leslie Parker' *Trooper to the Southern Cross* (1966) 89: We used to have a song at school:
  Catholic dogs
  Jump like frogs
which we always yelled at the Micks.
1939 Patrick White *Happy Valley* 25: Protestants called him a Micky, but he didn't mind.
1951 Dal Stivens *Jimmy Brockett* 231: Only a few revolutionaries, dingoes, loafers and a mob of Micks don't want to get into the war.
1964 George Johnston *My Brother Jack* 159: 'I don't care whether she's a mick or a Protestant or a holy roller.'
1972 David Williamson *The Removalists* 26: 'Five kids in seven years. Bastard's a mick.'
1975 Nancy Keesing *Garden Island People* 62: He maintained with supporting evidence which was plainly true at least for Garden Island, that the public service was 'given over to the micks', but did not hold this against Roman Catholics.

Mick, Crooked A mythical figure of N.T. and N. Queensland credited with prodigious feats
1945 Tom Ronan *Strangers on the Ophir* 234: Chris Christian, reared on legends of his ancestors, agreed ... that Thor, god of the thunders, rode high. The irreverent votaries of a newer and more humorous folklore commented 'Crooked Mick was kicking the billy-cans about.'
1966 Bill Wannan *Crooked Mick of the Speewah* [book title]

mick, mad A pick [rhyming slang]
1924 *Truth* 27 Apr. 6: *Mad mick* a pick.
1941 Baker 45: *Mad mick* A pick.
1946 Rohan Rivett *Behind Bamboo* 397: *Mad mick* pick.

1953 T. A. G. Hungerford *Riverslake* 224: 'I swung a mad-mick there for eighteen months during the depression.'
1973 Frank Huelin *Keep Moving* 78: 'Well, I won't buy drinks for any bloody gangers, just for a chance to swing a mad mick.'

mickey The vulva
1970 Alexander Buzo *The Front Room Boys* in Penguin *Plays* 49: 'Barry Anderson reckons he got her in the locker room the other day. Mucked around, played with mickey, she didn't mind.'
1975 Don Townshend *Gland Time* 238: 'Can't blame her for it, 'cause her mickey was probably throbbin' for it.'

micks, a pair of The call of 'tails' in two-up. At first erroneously explained as 'heads' (see quots 1919, 1941), an explanation as yet unsupported by any evidence. Quot. 1938 is to be interpreted in the light of the tradition that the spinner backs heads. [Origin obscure: the 'tail' of the pennies used in two-up represents Britannia and her trident]
1919 W. H. Downing *Digger Dialects* 33: *Mick* (1) The Queen's head on a coin (e.g. 'Micks are right', when two heads have turned up in a game of 'two-up'); (2) a queen in a pack of cards.
1938 John Robertson *With the Cameliers in Palestine* 198: The New Zealanders are very religious men. Their priests lead them out to a quiet spot where they can pray. The priest spreads out a holy mat with marks on it which means something they have great faith in. He kneels down beside the mat, then a row of worshippers kneel all round him, with another row bending over them, and another row standing behind them. The worshippers throw their offerings on to the holy mat, and the priest places two coins on a short piece of polished wood which he calls a kip, and raising his eyes to the sky, he throws up the coins as an offering to Allah. All the worshippers raise their eyes also to the sky, and then bow solemnly over the mat, and say together, 'God Almighty', and the priest answers, 'A pair of Micks', which means that the offerings are not accepted, or he may say, 'Oh Lord, he has done 'em again,' and the joyful cries of some of the worshippers show that Allah is pleased, and so they, too, are glad.
1941 Baker 46: *Mick* The 'head' of a penny.
1953 T. A. G. Hungerford *Riverslake* 126: 'I got ten bob to say he tails 'em – ten bob the micks!'
1966 Baker 242: If a spinner throws two 'tails' he is said to *mick them* or throw *two micks*.

micky A bull calf, usually unbranded
1876 Rolf Boldrewood *A Colonial Reformer* in *A Town and Country Journal* 9 Dec. 942: The wary and still more dangerously sudden 'Michie', a two-year-old-bull (so called after an eminent Aust-

ralian barrister famous for bringing his 'charges' to a successful issue). [1890 edition, ii 98, reads 'micky' and omits the derivation]

1881 A. C. Grant *Bush-Life in Queensland* i 227-8: Straining, roaring, jumping, dashing violently against the rails, a yellow brindled Micky is dragged up ... Red-hot brands are now brought from the fire.

1893 Harry Morant 'Since the Country Carried Sheep' *Bulletin* 4 Mar. 19: The 'mickies' that we've branded there! The colts we used to ride!

1924 *Truth* 27 Apr. 6: *Micky* An unbranded, uncastrated calf approximating a year in age.

1933 R. B. Plowman *The Man from Oodnadatta* 63: Taking up the headrope the boss lassoed a big micky (bull calf).

1945 Tom Ronan *Strangers on the Ophir* 82: Some battler earmarks a mangy mickey.

1951 Ernestine Hill *The Territory* 445: *Mickey* A half-grown bull calf, unbranded.

1961 George Farwell *Vanishing Australians* 68: Bill is also enthusiastic about the cod of a mickey (young bull) roasted over the coals at branding time.

1980 Rod Ansell *To Fight the Wild* 50: We were started off on small heifers, then cows and small mickeys (young bulls, not fully grown).

micky, chuck a   To throw a fit, panic

1952 T. A. G. Hungerford *The Ridge and the River* 22: 'And he don't chuck a micky every time something goes off behind him!'

middy   A measure of beer: in N.S.W., 10 oz.; in W.A., 7 oz.

1945 Baker 169: The *middy*, a beer glass containing nine ounces, is a measure used only in N.S.W. hotels.

1953 Baker 138: The nearest approximation to the Queensland *pot* is the N.S.W. *middy*, which holds 10 oz. of beer. At the time of writing my previous book, the size of the *middy* was fixed at nine ounces.

1972 John O'Grady *It's Your Shout, Mate!* 15: 'A glass is five ounces [in Western Australia], a middy is seven ounces, an' a pot's ten. Got it?' Ibid. 67: 'Now I've been down in Sydney [from Queensland], see. Why do they call a pot a middy?' ... 'Because it's midway between nothing and a pint.'

1976 David Ireland *The Glass Canoe* 150: Poor Liz ... She didn't have the same old bounce, and she went down from schooners to middies.

mike   A cup of tea: *rare*

1949 Ruth Park *Poor Man's Orange* 101: ''Ere's yer mike,' said his host, shoving over a pannikin of stewed and boiling tea.

Mile, the Golden   see **Golden**

Mile, the Hungry   see **Hungry**

milfissed the balfastards   see **balfastards**

milker, busy as a one-armed ~ on a dairy farm   see **one-armed**

milko   A milkman [abbr. or from cry]

[**1865** J. F. Mortlock *Experiences of a Convict* (1965) 120: He proposed that I should carry his pails round the town and shout out 'Milk O!' at the customers' doors.]

1969 Mena Calthorpe *The Defectors* 180: The milko hesitated, then he ran along the street rattling the crates and bottles.

1976 *Australian* 14 Feb. 40: One loyal disciple rings up each week from Melbourne, just for the milko's tips.

1983 *Newcastle Herald* 19 Mar. 3: No one misses the milko on the Cessnock East run. The milko sounds his truck's horn as he delivers. But the horn doesn't 'beep', it 'moos'.

milkshake, the singing   see **singing**

million, gone a   In a hopeless state; utterly disadvantaged or defeated [see quot. 1969]

1916 C. J. Dennis 'The Battle of the Wazzir' in A. H. Chisholm *The Making of a Sentimental Bloke* (1946) 131: Fer young Bill was gone a million, an' 'e never guessed the game.

1917 F. J. Mills *Dinkum Oil* 84: 'What's Sydney?' Carl would say with a contemptuous gesture. 'Take away your harbour and you're gone a million.'

1919 J. Vance Marshall *The World of the Living Dead* 128: 'Times are mighty hard too. You've gotter keep up appearances or else you're gonner million.'

1922 Arthur Wright *A Colt from the Country* 142: 'What hope would you have when that came out? You'd be gone a million.'

1924 Steele Rudd *Me an' th' Son* 129: 'Let him ... reckon th' horse is going to buck to the right when ud bucks to th' left, an' he's gone a million.'

1930 K. S. Prichard *Haxby's Circus* 187: 'If it weren't for you. I'd be gone a million on the minx.'

1942 Gavin Casey *It's Harder for Girls* 212: 'If they drop their bundles they're gone a million.'

1951 Dal Stivens *Jimmy Brockett* 232: 'If Pat Regan gets hold of her before we do, we're gone a million.'

1969 Sir Paul Hasluck *Sun-Herald* 24 Aug. 48: When I was a boy in Western Australia ... there was a Premier, John Scaddan (1911–16) who was usually referred to among our friends as 'Gone a Million, Jack' ... Scaddan increased spending from loan funds, which in those days meant State public borrowing, to a level with which the State was quite unfamiliar and, in answering criticism, made some such remark as 'What's a million?' and gained a nickname that was intended to brand him as a careless person.

1973 Frank Huelin *Keep Moving* 107: 'What evidence would we have to prove it wasn't us? We'd be gone a million!'

1976 *Australian* 1 Mar. 1: 'Gough's gone a million.' It's the end for Whitlam. We have the votes, say party rivals.

1982 Blanche d'Alpuget *Robert J. Hawke* 297: Hawke, in conveying the common belief of the officers that Whitlam would not survive as Leader, remarked, 'Gough's gone a million.'

Milperra massacre See **Fathers' Day massacre**

1984 *Sydney Morning Herald* 3 Sep. 1: The Milperra massacre: police quiz hundreds [heading]

Ming Nickname of R. G. Menzies (1894–1978), Australian Prime Minister 1939–41, 1949–66 [f. pronunciation of Menzies as 'Mingis', and Ming the Merciless in the Speed Gordon comic strip]

c. 1954 Communist Party of Australia *'Our Bob': Further Misadventures of Ming (the Merciless) Menzies* [pamphlet title]

1975 *Australian* 4 Jul. 8: The swinging vote, which ended the Ming Dynasty after 23 years, has swung back to whence it came.

1978 *Australian* 16 May 1: The shy man behind Ming the Merciless [heading]

Ming Wing, the The Robert Menzies School of Humanities, Monash University, Victoria

mint 1 Deficient in some ingredient (i.e. not used)

1979 Kathy Lette and Gabrielle Carey *Puberty Blues* 19: 'Oh, mint of the margarine. Check out how much they give ya'. She displayed two measly dabs of margarine inside the slobbery yellow bun.

2 First-class (in mint condition)

1984 *West Australian* (Perth) 7 Jan. 33: 'The kids also love Monty Python – they think it's "mint".'

Minties, it's moments like these you need Slogan used in advertising cartoons (from 1927) for the sweet launched by James Stedman-Henderson in 1922: applied to anyone in extremities

1963 Frank Hardy *Legends from Benson's Valley* 162: It's Moments Like These ... [story title]

1978 *Sydney Morning Herald* 9 Jun. 1: In a Sydney court yesterday a solicitor representing Life Savers Ltd was told by a Sydney magistrate that his clients' case could not be heard because it was not listed. 'It's moments like these,' the magistrate added, 'you need Minties.'

1980 *National Times* 14 Dec. 29: This was an unexpected presentation and James was deeply

moved. Then they asked him to sign the honoured guests book, make a comment too. Still a bit misty eyed he wrote 'It's moments like these you need Minties' in a carefully rounded hand.

1983 *Sun-Herald* 5 Jun. 113: At moments like these, it isn't Minties I need, it's a pantry shelf and freezer stocked with instant or almost instant foods.

miserable Close-fisted, stingy, mean [OED 1484; E. dial. 1816–59]

1903 Joseph Furphy *Such is Life* (1944) 17: 'The more swellisher a man is, the more miserabler he is about a bite o' grass for a team, or a feed for a traveller.'

1941 Baker 46: *Miserable* Mean-spirited, miserly.

1958 Frank Hardy *The Four-Legged Lottery* 183: 'Not all bookies are miserable; some of them are happy-go-lucky, generous blokes. They make money easily and spend it easily, give to charity and so forth. Pittson is miserable.'

1976 *Australian* 20 May 6: A 'lousy dollar a day!' Could any government be more miserable?

missus, the The wife of the owner or manager on a station, from the standpoint of the employees [f. *missus* as wife, and (esp. in U.S.A.) as employer of negroes]

1901 Miles Franklin *My Brilliant Career* (1965) 76: 'Oh, the missus might catch me'.

1908 Mrs Aeneas Gunn *We of the Never-Never* xi: We – are just some of the bush-folk of the Never-Never ... The Maluka, The Little Missus, The Sanguine Scot ...

1958 Nancy Cato *All the Rivers Run* 216: Annie ... tacked a piece of bright oil-baize that the missus had given her over the slabtable.

1967 John Yeomans *The Scarce Australians* 39: In the Australian outback, where the manager or owner of a station has the standard title of Boss among those who do not call him by his first name, his wife has the standard title of Missus.

1981 Maxwell Grant *Inherit the Sun* 366: 'I suppose with your father away you are the Missus?'

Mo The comedian Roy Rene, b. Harry van der Sluice (1892–1954)

mob 'A large number, the Australian noun of multitude, and not implying anything low or noisy' (Morris): used almost as a technical term of cattle, etc., but more colloquially of people, as of a group with common interests

1838 Thomas Walker *A Month in the Bush of Australia* 8: I beheld a level plain, as even as a bowling green, not a rise nor a tree nor an object of any kind to interrupt the view, with the exception of 'mobs' of cattle scattered over the surface.

1852 G. C. Mundy *Our Antipodes* i 53: There are to be found round the doors of the Sydney theatre a sort of 'loafers', known as the Cabbage-tree mob . . . an unruly set of young fellows, native-born generally.

1853 S. Mossman and T. Banister *Australia Visited and Revisited* 82: This was a mixed herd of cattle, or as the squatters call them, a 'mob' of two hundred head.

1857 *Thatcher's Colonial Songster* 22: She said in return she'd just landed, as one / Of Missis Chisholm's mob.

1878 Rolf Boldrewood *An Australian Squire* repr. as *Babes in the Bush* (1900) 248: Ardmillan, Forbes and Neil Barrington, with all the 'Benmohr mob', as they were somewhat disrespectfully [1900 familiarly] called, were in the vanguard.

1918 Harley Matthews *Saints and Soldiers* 148: Big Snowy and his mob were back in camp behind the line.

1959 Anne von Bertouch *February Dark* 66: 'You can't get out of line with this mob, they don't miss a trick.'

1962 Alan Seymour *The One Day of the Year* 16–17: 'I'm sick of elegant young men talking of tapered shoes and Jags and MGs, in fact I'm sick of everybody in our mob, everybody.'

1973 H. Williams *My Love Had a Black Speed Stripe* 27: It's bad enough having McMahon and Whitlam and that lot without worrying about Tito and his mob.

1980 Rod Ansell *To Fight the Wild* 55: I just pulled up a big mob of dry grass to make a good thick padding.

1983 *NT News* (Darwin) 10 Mar. 6: Darwin City Council is heading for mobs of trouble over the swimming pool fencing by-law, set for introduction in 11 days.

mock (mockers), to put the ~ on To frustrate someone's plans; to place a hoodoo on someone, destroy his luck [see *moz*]

1911 Edward Dyson *Benno, and Some of the Push* 33: 'All toms is 'erlike t'me,' he said . . . 'but, all the same, it's up t'me t'put a mock on that tripester.'

1923 Con Drew *Rogues and Ruses* 115: 'They'll have to race without me tomorrow. I've got a mocker hung on me.'

1938 Xavier Herbert *Capricornia* 473: 'Comin' here to put the mocks on us,' said Kit. 'Might be there's a reward.'

1941 Lawson Glassop *Lucky Palmer* 62: 'It's that sheila,' he said. 'She's put the mocker on us . . . We'll never have a good trot until you get rid of her.'

1965 Wally Grout *My Country's 'Keeper* 206: I hope I am not 'putting the mock' on Norm because my feelings are the same as the rest of the Australian Test players: when O'Neill is a doubt-

ful Test starter the job always looks grimmer.

1974 David Ireland *Burn* 21: 'You tryin' to put the mockers on me?'

1983 *Bulletin* 2 Aug. 34: The double loss put the mockers on everything.

mocker Clothes [Partridge lists *mockered up* dressed in one's best: low: late C.19–20]

1953 Baker 106: *mocker*, clothes in general.

1961 Frank Hardy *The Hard Way* 77: 'They're fulla new mocker, see. Good clothes I got from mugs in Pentridge.'

1976 David Ireland *The Glass Canoe* 55: 'Now who's got good mocha on?' he says, looking round . . . Danny's gone mad for the occasion and has his grey suit on that he wears to weddings, funerals and smokos.

1979 Donald R. Stuart *Crank Back on Roller* 214: 'We've got good mocker, good boots, the lot.'

mockered up

1953 *Caddie A Sydney Barmaid* 223: 'I won't be likely ter be gettin' mokkered up before Saturday, so I'll pop me clobber termorrer ter raise the wind.'

mole A girl or woman: *derogatory* [? variant pronunciation of *moll*]

1965 William Dick *A Bunch of Ratbags* 270: 'Just because you've got yourself some rich bloke's mole of a bloody daughter, don't come telling me and the boys what to bloody do.'

1979 Rae Desmond Jones *Walking the Line* 19: Give us a hand you lazy mole!

1983 *Sun-Herald* 15 May 51: 'If a girl does it all the time then she's a mole. Moles are scum, worse than dirt.' . . . 'I know one girl who goes out with someone for one night and hops into bed with them – I'd call her a mole.'

moll at a christening see **christening**

molly-dooked, molly-dooker Left-handed; a left-handed person [? f. *mauly* fist OED 1780]

[**1926** J. Vance Marshall *Timely Tips for New Australians: Mauldy* Left-handed.]

1941 Baker 47: *Mollydooker* A left-handed person. Whence, 'molly dook' (adj.) left-handed.

1969 Hal Porter *Southerly* 8: Someone molly-duked, atheist, over-educated, young leftist, Queensland-nurtured.

1975 *Sydney Morning Herald* 30 Aug. 11: A word of good cheer to all molly-dookers.

monarch, monaych Aboriginal term for the police: W.A. [see *manatj*]

1961 Nene Gare *The Fringe Dwellers* 35: 'Skippy gets off. An ya know the first thing e says ta them monarch? E turns round on em an yelps, "An now ya can just gimme back that bottle."'

1975 Richard Beilby *The Brown Land Crying* 10: Myra was terrified. The coppers! Monaych! The native word contained a history of oppression: the Men with Chains!

1979 Kirk Weller *The Dwarf* ed. Noni Braham 28: When I'm broke I'm just Tommy Caylun, the boong, shuffling down the street, with an eye out for the monaych – coppers.

1981 Archie Weller *The Day of the Dog* 91: 'Let's clear off out of this before the monaych come.'

Monday, yellow see **yellow Monday**

mong 1 A dog of mixed breed [abbr. of mongrel]
1923 Jack Moses *Beyond the City Gates* 152: 'What does it matter? He was only a mong!'
1944 Jean Devanny *By Tropic, Sea and Jungle* 227: It takes a good mong dog to catch a rat-kangaroo in the bush.
2 Any dog
1957 R. S. Porteous *Brigalow* 16: An irritable voice called, 'Go and lie down, you rotten mong.'
1982 *National Times* 21 Feb. 29: The only victim I can recall is a mong. A redback sank its fangs into an Australian fox terrier.
3 A human being: *derogatory*
1933 *Bulletin* 16 Aug. 39: 'Most likely he just felt faint, same as you get on *any* job, and went out to it for a minute. And the mong fired him!'
1967 *Southerly* 199: The bludging, dirty mong to whom she had . . . entrusted heart and hand.

monkey 1 A sheep
1881 A. C. Grant *Bush-Life in Queensland* i 88: Sheep lost on Saturday imperatively constrained every one on the head station to look for them . . . and no one felt better pleased than he did to see the last lot of 'monkeys', as the shearers usually denominated sheep, leave the head-station.
1893 Francis Adams *The Australians* 137: A 'mob' of the wild, timid, yet inquisitive 'monkeys' (sheep).
1905 'The Wallaby Brigade' in *The Old Bush Songs* ed. A. B. Paterson 126 and note: You've only to sport your dover and knock a monkey over – / There's cheap mutton for the Wallaby Brigade. To knock a monkey over is to kill a sheep, monkey being slang for sheep in many parts of the bush.
1924 *Truth* 27 Apr. 6: *Monkies* A bush term for sheep.
1934 Brian Penton *Landtakers* 414: 'You'd have the stock, you say. Thirty or forty thousand monkeys all told, not reckoning cattle and horses.'
1942 Sarah Campion *Bonanza* 161: 'If only a man could breed sheep with fifty ribs apiece instead of – well, however many ribs the bleeding monkeys *do* have – he'd make his fortune!'
monkey-dodger A shepherd
1912 R. S. Tait *Scotty Mac, Shearer* 138: 'Behold

in me chief serang, head monkey dodger to the high and holy Hungry Harris.'
2 See quot. 1959 [cf. *monkey-rope* U.S. 1851 OED]
1911 E. S. Sorenson *Life in the Australian Backblocks* 207: Novices and others who lack proficiency use . . . a monkey (a strap looped between the D's for the right hand to grip).
1959 Desmond Martin *Australia Astride* 194: *Monkey*. Also known as a Wagga grip or jug handle. It is used by weak riders to mount, or to try and ride buckjumpers.
3 The vulva
1970 Patrick White *The Vivisector* 111: 'Too much dirty water. That's what's wrong with Spargo. 'E'd carry 'is bed any time a woman up an' showed 'im 'er monkey.'

monte, monty A certainty, 'a sure thing' [f. card game U.S. 1841 Mathews]
1894 Henry Lawson *Verse* i 269: 'I've got a vote for Hughie – but it ain't no monte yet.'
1901 *The Bulletin Reciter* 182: 'It's the biggest bloomin' monte / Dat 'as ever come our way.'
1908 E. S. Sorenson *The Squatter's Ward* 122: 'It's a monty the little squib would let out a yell jest as I was gettin' clear.'
1930 K. S. Prichard *Haxby's Circus* 41: 'She's the chance of a life-time,' he yelled. 'The biggest bloomin' monty ever started on a racecourse.'
1945 Cecil Mann *The River* 52: As they're rushing up the straight, old toothless Past: He's a monty? We always were lucky.
1950 Brian James *The Advancement of Spencer Button* 230: 'You make a monty of that mark, and get to Sydney.'

Monts The Claremont (W.A.) Australian Rules football team (also the Tigers) [abbr.]
1978 *Australian* 4 May 17: 'Every match is now a tough one for Monts as every team in the League tries to stop us winning.'

moogie See quot. 1983
1983 *National Times* 8 Apr. 14: The Aboriginal slang word around Cunnamulla for a male homosexual is 'moogie' and it's common usage around the town as the ultimate insult.

moosh Gaol porridge [variant of *mush*]
1945 Baker 141: Jail food is *moosh*.
1950 *The Australian Police Journal* Apr. 116: *Moosh* Gaol porridge.
1967 B. K. Burton *Teach Them No More* 17: Moline took his plate back to his cell, where he pushed his unwilling spoon into glutinous material. The food resisted the spoon's assault. 'What's this muck?' 'That's mush,' Ted explained. 'I knew an old lagger once. He was quite famous.

He made little statues out of his mush.'
1973 Jim McNeil *The Chocolate Frog* 117: Mush pronounced to rhyme with push, prison porridge.

mopoke A dreary or stupid fellow [see quot. 1845]
1845 Richard Howitt *Impressions of Australia Felix* 233: 'A more-pork kind of fellow' is a man of cut-and-dry phrases; a person remarkable for nothing new in common conversation. This, by some, is thought very expressive; the more-pork being a kind of Australian owl, notorious for its wearying nightly iteration, 'More pork, more pork.'
1876 Rolf Boldrewood *A Colonial Reformer* (1891) 125: 'What a regular more-pork I was to be sure, to go and run my neck agin' a roping-pole, and all for a false jade, who'd have come to see me hanged.'
c. **1905** Joseph Furphy *The Buln-Buln and the Brolga* ed. R. G. Howarth (1948) 124: 'Plop them in the tub, an' let them soak in minit, you more-poke,' I replied.
1910 H. H. Richardson *The Getting of Wisdom* 205: At the idea of shutting herself up wholly with such mopokes, of cutting herself off from her present vital interests, Laura hastily reconsidered her decision.

moral A 'moral certainty' (OED 1646) i.e. certain to win, esp. in horseracing
[**1847** Alexander Harris *The Emigrant Family* ed. W. S. Ramson (1966) 279: It was a moral certainty that the three white cattle were from the same stock.]
1878 Rolf Boldrewood *An Australian Squire* repr. as *Babes in the Bush* (1900) 175: It was understood that he was entered on the chance of the two cracks destroying each others chances, in one of the numerous accidents to which such races are liable, in which case Bargo would be a 'moral'.
1889 *The Arrow* 20 Jul. 1: A school-teacher recently asked his class 'What is a moral?' And with one accord came the answer 'A dead bird, sir.'
1916 C. J. Dennis *The Moods of Ginger Mick* 40: 'E 'as struck it fer a moral. Ginger's found 'is game at last.
1944 Lawson Glassop *We Were the Rats* 16: 'Think Tiger will win?' he asked. 'He's a moral,' I said. 'A lay-down misere. I might have two quid on him.'
1952 T. A. G. Hungerford *The Ridge and the River* 14: 'They're a moral to lamp your footprints where you came into the road from the track.'
1965 John Beede *They Hosed Them Out* 121: Clarkey, given enough grog, we felt, was a moral to talk.
1970 Richard Beilby *No Medals for Aphrodite*

253: 'They're a moral to be after those guns. We'd better get out!'
1975 Les Ryan *The Shearers* 79: 'Andy Burns rang last night . . . reckons Dallas is a moral in the first.'
1980 Jessica Anderson *The Impersonators* 139: 'I don't know about television. It depends on what else they have. But it's a moral for the evening papers.'

more front than Myers see **front**

more hide (arse, cheek) than Jessie see **Jessie**

Moreton Bay A fiz-gig or gig, i.e. police informer [rhyming slang for 'Moreton Bay fig']
1953 Baker 134: *Morton Bay (fig).* Any witness who lays an information, anyone who unwarrantably attends to or meddles in the affairs of others; by rhyme on *gig*, which is used similarly, and which may be a contraction of *fizgig*, an informer.
1975 *Bulletin* 26 Apr. 46: If there were Mortons nearby (Morton Bay Figs; gigs, meaning busybodies).
1984 *Bulletin* 19 Jun. 69: Fifty per cent of the Drug Squad's arrests are based on information received and woe betide a user, a supplier or anyone else who becomes a dog, a gig, or as the police term it, a Moreton Bay.

Moreton Bay rot See quot. [place-name]
1918 C. Fetherstonhaugh *After Many Days* 207: All the ills that flesh is heir to in a new and tropical country, to harass us, such as fever and ague, Moreton Bay rot (skin scurvy), Belyando Spue (pyrosis or water brash), sandy blight.

morning glory See quots [f. the flower so called, and the occurrence of an erection on awaking]
1977 Jim Ramsay *Cop it Sweet* 60: *Morning glory*: Fornication before noon.
1979 *Sydney Morning Herald* 6 Oct. 2: The dam's second unusual feature is a 'morning glory', or trumpet-shaped tower spill-way built to handle flood discharge.
1984 Bill Reed *Crooks* 185: It makes Stein's morning glory of an erection pull its woolly head in quick smart.

Moscow Corner See quot. 1985
1985 *Sydney Morning Herald* 16 May 4: When they [a delegation of Russian officials] were welcomed to Question Time by the Acting Speaker, Joan Child, an uproar broke out as Opposition members suggested they should be sitting in 'Moscow Corner' – a pet name for the back corner of the Government benches occupied by the left wing.

Moscow, gone to, in In pawn

[c. **1882** *Sydney Slang Dictionary* 6: *Moskeener* To pawn with a view to obtaining more than the actual value of an article.]
1941 Baker 47: *Moscow* A pawnshop.
1953 *Caddie A Sydney Barmaid* 217: 'Me clobber's already in Moscow, an' so is me tan shoes.'

mossie   A mosquito [abbr.]
1941 Baker 47: *Mossie, mozzie* A mosquito.
1959 Dorothy Hewett *Bobbin Up* 76–7: They sat in the cool on the back verandah, slapping at the mozzies.
1966 Elwyn Wallace *Sydney and the Bush* 60: 'A cowdung fire does the trick, you know. The mossies can't stand it.'
1981 *National Times* 19 Apr. 52: The couple had become experimental in their lovemaking over the years; after watching Don's Party on television recently, they made love in the backyard for the first time. 'But we got bitten by mozzies', she said.

mote   To move fast [f. *mote*, to drive, or ride in, a motor car OED 1892]
1937 *Bulletin of Australian English Association* Jul. 2: To *mote* is defined by Mr Partridge as 'to drive or ride in a motor car', but for many years now Australian schoolboys have been using it in the more general sense of 'move quickly', so that often they say in praise of an athlete, 'There is no doubt he can mote.'
1941 Baker 47: *Mote* To move quickly (used of a vehicle or athlete).
1949 Ruth Park *Poor Man's Orange* 181: The pair of them surely would look tricks moting around together.
1983 *Sydney Morning Herald* 5 Apr. 22: 'He [Strawberry Road] motored into the bit when I gave him a kick on the home turn, then went so fast you would have sworn he was on dry ground', Dittman said.

mother-in-law's breath, cold as   Very cold
1956 Encountered in conversation.
1979 *Sunday Telegraph* (Sydney) 13 May 168: It's refreshing to hear an old Australian phrase amid all the government and advertising jargon. A taxi wound down a window on a freezing night this week. 'Out there, mate,' said the driver, 'it's as cold as a step-mother's breath.'
1983 Buzz Kennedy *Australian* 9 Feb. 14: Then there are the family kisses – not only of the sort labelled 'as cold as a mother-in-law's kiss' but of the affectionate variety.

motherless   Used as an intensive, esp. in the phrase 'motherless broke'
1898 *Bulletin* 17 Dec. Red Page: To these are prefixed the adjectives *motherless* and *dead*, thus *dead motherless broke.*

1916 Arthur Wright *Under a Cloud* 35: 'I'm stone motherless meself an' I could do with that hundred Booth is offerin'.'
1925 E. S. Sorenson *Murty Brown* 135: 'That leaves me stony, motherless broke again.'
1945 Gavin Casey *Downhill is Easier* 20: I'd only known Reg when we were both stone motherless broke.
1956 F. B. Vickers *First Place to the Stranger* 231: 'I had to stick it. You've got no option when you're motherless broke.'
1961 George Farwell *Vanishing Australians* 67: The fact that he would be stone motherless broke was hardly worth mentioning.
1972 Alexander Macdonald *The Ukelele Player under the Red Lamp* 247: Happy, full as a boot, and stone motherless broke.

motorbike, useful as an ashtray on   see **useful**

motser, motza   A large gambling win; a 'certainty' that would ensure such a win [? f. Yiddish *matzo*, bread]
1936 A. B. Paterson 'The Shearer's Colt' in *Song of the Pen* (1983) 739: 'It's a motzer. It's a schnitzler. We'll have to pack 'em in on the roof of the grand-stand'.
1943 Baker 51: *Motser, motza* A large sum of money.
1950 *Australian Police Journal* Apr. 116: *Motza* A lot of money.
1970 Richard Beilby *No Medals for Aphrodite* 214: 'The Stuka'll be a motsa to have a go at him.'
1977 *Bulletin* 24 Dec. 46: The lady on my left, blonde, beautiful and making a motza out of retailing.
1983 *Weekend Australian* 19 Feb. 5: 'Win a motza on the footy' is the slogan for the new game [Footy TAB] which will be launched tomorrow.

mousetraps in one's pocket, to have   see **pocket**

Movement, the   The Catholic Social Study Movement established in 1945 as 'a loose national alliance of Catholic actionists, particularly unionists, with the object of fighting communism in the union movement' (Patrick O'Farrell *The Catholic Church in Australia* (1968) 264)
1951 Frank Hardy *Power Without Glory* 634: 'I have here the most recent report of 'The Movement' which, as you know, is the arm of Catholic Action in the Trade Unions'. .... 'In each diocese or suburb we have set about establishing cells of The Movement and in many factories and Trade Unions we have similar groups.'
1974 Desmond O'Grady *Deschooling Kevin Carew* 13: He was exasperated that they accepted church involvement in politics through 'the Movement', which was an off-shoot of Catholic Action

designed to fight Communist influence.

1977 Fred Daly *From Curtin to Kerr* 120: B. A. Santamaria ... since the late 1930s had been a powerful figure in the National Secretariat of Catholic Action and later the Catholic Social Studies Movement fighting Communist power in the trade union movement. From these two bodies Santamaria developed an extreme right-wing group called 'The Movement' which, through the Catholic Church, sought to encourage Catholic trade union members to attend meetings and work and vote for the defeat of Communists.

1980 B. A. Santamaria *Australian* 26 Dec. 7: In October 1954, Dr Evatt made his celebrated, if fictitious, 'discovery' that the leaders of the ALP industrial groups and of the Movement (National Civic Council), whose support Evatt had sedulously cultivated for three years, were engaged in a conspiracy against the Labor Party and himself.

see **grouper**

moves, if it ~ , shoot it; if it doesn't, chop it down   Reputedly an Australian national motto

1963 Alan Ross *Australia 63* 202: The country had still to be conquered. The general attitude was: 'If it moves, shoot it. If it stands still, chop it down.'

1964 *Sydney Morning Herald* 4 May 2: 'If it moves, shoot it; if it doesn't; chop it down.' So goes the old Australian saying, and according to our foresters it has been the motto of this country for too long.

1971 George Johnston *A Cartload of Clay* 77: 'Remember the old rule we had about coming to grips with this country, when we were trying to settle it? If it grows chop it down, if it moves, shoot it.'

1971 Bill Hornadge *A Squint Down Under* 24: If it moves, shoot it. / If it doesn't, chop it down. Australian Motto.

mozz   As for **put the mozz on**

1941 Baker 47: *Moz* To interrupt, hinder.

1965 Frank Hardy *The Yarns of Billy Borker* 107: 'Don't mozz a man,' I tells him. 'You're well named, I'll say that for you, Calamity.'

1974 John Powers *The Last of the Knucklemen* 49: 'Don't let him mozz you, Monk.'

mozz, to put the ~ on   To prejudice someone's chances, place a 'jinx' on something [f. *mozzle*]

1924 C. J. Dennis *Rose of Spadgers* 75: 'Too much soul-ferritin'' might put the moz / On this 'ere expedition.'

1941 Baker 47: *Put the moz on someone* To inconvenience a person.

1956 Alan Marshall *How's Andy Going?* 200: 'Looking ahead like that never does any bloody good to any man,' observed Pat. 'It puts the moz on him.'

1963 Hal Porter *The Watcher on the Cast-Iron Balcony* 81: Mother is wishing Miss Brewer some female ill, is putting the mozz on her.

1974 Keith Stackpole *Not Just for Openers* 32: She felt she put the moz on him ... She couldn't bear to go in case she was a jinx.

mozzie   see **mossie**

mozzle   Luck, bad luck [f. Heb. *mazzal* luck]

1898 *Bulletin* 17 Dec. Red Page: *Mozzle* is luck ... *Good mozzle* = good luck; *Kronk mozzle* = bad luck.

1903 Joseph Furphy *Such is Life* (1944) 280: 'And how much do you stand to lose, if your mozzle is out?' I asked.

1919 Edward Dyson *Hello, Soldier!* 32: 'Twas rotten mozzle, Neddo. We had blown out every clip.

muck, Sing 'em   Supposed advice of Nellie Melba to Clara Butt on undertaking a tour of Australia

1928 W. H. Ponder *Clara Butt: Her Life Story* 138: 'So you're going to Australia!' she [Melba] said. 'Well, I made twenty thousand pounds on my tour there, but of course *that* will never be done again. Still, it's a wonderful country, and you'll have a good time. What are you going to sing? All I can say is – sing 'em muck! It's all they can understand!'

1934 Vance Palmer *The Swayne Family* 170: 'Show you're higher organism by adapting yourself. Appeal to sense of fun. Turn dark cloud inside out. Sing 'em muck.'

1949 *Sydney Morning Herald* 1 Oct. 8: We can imagine the scene at the publishing house when the unprofitable author calls in for his royalty cheque. 'No, sir,' says Mr Chapman, shaking a forlorn head and pointing to the shelves of unsold copies ... 'If you were only to do something like 'Sun and Shade' by the author of 'Ursula's Wooing', we might strike a winner, and everyone would be happy. Give 'em muck, sir! Give 'em muck!'

1977 Sumner Locke Elliott *Water Under the Bridge* 295: 'I want to hear all you girls in the balcony "There's a *track* winding *back* to an oh-*old*-fashioned *shack* ..." Sing 'em muck', he often told Maggie.

1983 B. A. Santamaria *Australian* 8 Feb. 11: The media presentation of the forthcoming election as a macho contest between Messrs Fraser and Hawke underlines the wordly wisdom of the late Dame Nellie Melba's celebrated aphorism 'sing 'em muck'.

muck up day   The last day at school before the final examinations, marked by an absence of restraint, practical jokes etc.

1979 *Sun-Herald* 4 Nov. 123: Performers wrapped each other up in alfoil, like a large cut-lunch, and coated themselves in shaving cream (they'd obviously never got over their sixth-form muck-up day).
1980 Barbara Pepworth *Early Marks* 272: Muck-up Day is here at last . . . My form races around in a frenzy. They're celebrating our last day at school before the exams start . . . hurling eggs and rotten tomatoes at one another, sifting flour bombs, releasing pent-up nervous energy.
1982 *Sydney Morning Herald* 19 May 23: With Mr Fraser out of the country, the boys in the Senate decided it was muck-up day and began saying all the silly things they normally wouldn't get away with.

muddie   A Queensland mudcrab
1977 *Australian* 8 Jan. 1: Each year the people of N.S.W. eat 200,000 of the prize Queensland muddies, which is all right except that they are eating mud crabs that Queenslanders are not allowed to eat.
1980 *Sun* (Sydney) 22 Feb. 21: According to Queenslanders, 'muddies' are the seventh wonder of the world – the eighth is Joh.
1982 *NT News* (Darwin) 27 Jul. 10: Muddies will be ropable [heading] One of Darwin's unique tourist attractions – the mudcrab tying contest – will be staged at Lim's Hotel on August 4.

Muddy, Little   The river Yarra, Victoria [f. colour of water. *Big Muddy* is the Missouri]
1965 *Nation* 3 Apr. 10: Few people could draw the breath of conscience and describe the Yarra as a proud river sweeping southward to the sea, Little Muddy nevertheless commands great local affection, whatever is said about it in another place.

mudlark   See quot 1941 [variant of *mudrunner*]
1914 A. B. Paterson 'Racehorses and Racing' in *Song of the Pen* (1983) 312: Some horses revel in mud . . . The mudlark contingent are generally horses with good loin power, that keep their legs under them while racing.
1941 Baker 47: *Mudlark* A racehorse that runs well on a muddy course. Also footballers who play on a sodden field.
1951 Dymphna Cusack and Florence James *Come In Spinner* 40: 'Could yer blame 'im?' Elvira asked reproachfully. 'Raining like it was last Saturdee? 'E's no mudlark.'
1975 *Sunday Telegraph* (Sydney) 6 Apr. 48: Born Star a Mudlark [heading]. Born Star, a two-year-old yesterday outclassed the field at Sandown in his first start on a rain-affected track.
1984 *Sun* (Sydney) 27 Jan. 68: If the track is rain-affected it will suit Rustglow even better as

he is a real mudlark.

mud map   A sketch drawn by a bushman on the ground, to give directions
1919 E. S. Sorenson *Chips and Splinters* 14: The mud maps that Phineas draws on the road with a stick when directing some unfortunate wanderer.
1936 Ion L. Idriess *The Cattle King* 102: He built up the fire, then sat back on his heels, and with a stick scraped the ground clear. 'I'll make you a mud map.'
1956 Tom Ronan *Moleskin Midas* 171: 'I want a fresh horse and some tucker and a mud map for getting to town without hitting too many roads.'
1962 J. Marshall and R. Drysdale *Journey Among Men* 37: 'I'll draw yer a mud map the way they went.'

mulga   A species of acacia: colloquially 'the mulga' may refer to uninhabited or inhospitable regions generally
1928 Vance Palmer *The Man Hamilton* 26: Manager of this isolated place in the mulga, a hundred miles away from anywhere.
1934 Jean Devanny *Out of Such Fires* 277: 'Why don't you come with us? You belong in the mulga.'
1946 Rohan Rivett *Behind Bamboo* 397: *Mulga*, the surrounding jungle.
1952 Jon Cleary *The Sundowners* 198: 'You've heard what they call 'em down in the city. Bush-wackers. The mugs from the mulga.'
1968 Stuart Gore *Holy Smoke* 58: 'Man ought to get his head seen to', he said moodily. 'Stuck up here in the mulga, when he could be earning good money down in the city.'
1973 Alexander Buzo *Rooted* 87: 'Gary's gone away for the weekend, cavorting in the mulga with the Werris Creek push.'
1983 Peter Bowers *Sydney Morning Herald* 5 Nov. 13: The mulga mafia [the National Party in Queensland] has come out of the sticks to the extent that it has broadened its electoral appeal to embrace city votes.

mulga wire   As for **bush telegraph** 2
1899 T. Quinn *The Well Sinkers* 100: 'How do you hear it, Micky?' 'Mulga wires, missus, mulga wires.'
1908 E. S. Sorenson *Quinton's Rouseabout* 186: 'They'll be that delighted to find it was only a mulga that they'd toast you as "a jolly good fellow".'
1913 Henry Lawson 'Triangles of Life' *Prose* i 658: Tom had been out early, or had got what we call a bush telegraphy or mulga wire.
1933 R. B. Plowman *The Man from Oodnadatta* 21: The padre was not surprised to find that Stan was aware of his coming. Throughout the Inland news travels far and fast by means of the 'mulga

wire'.

1937 Ernestine Hill *The Great Australian Loneliness* 207: Warned by mulga wires of the approach of a white woman . . . there were some of them who 'went bush' rather than meet me.

1950 K. S. Prichard *Winged Seeds* 297: 'The troops 've had it all by mulga.'

mullet, like a stunned   Dazed, so unaware as to be almost unconscious

1953 Baker 267: *Dullness* (looking) like a stunned mullet.

1963 John O'Grady *The things they do to you* 147: I returned and lay on the bed like a stunned mullet.

1974 Jack Hibberd *Dimboola* 46: 'Just look at him! Just look at him. Looks like a stunned mullet.'

1977 *Australian* 16 May 1: Mr Hawke said yesterday the Federal Government had responded like a stunned mullet to his acceptance of the proposed Industrial Relations Bureau.

1980 *Daily Mirror* (Sydney) 22 Apr. 34: The storyline is impossibly interwoven, the actors wander around like a group of stunned mullets and even that old pro Glenn Ford looks bewildered.

mullock, to poke   To mock, ridicule [f. *mullock* the rubbish heaped at the top of a mineshaft]

1916 C. J. Dennis *The Moods of Ginger Mick* 74: I own me eyes git brighter / When I see 'em pokin' mullock at the everlastin' sea.

1924 *Truth* 27 Apr. 6: *Mullock, to poke* To deride.

1931 Vance Palmer *Separate Lives* 210: 'D'you think I'm going to sit in that galley with Curran and the other blokes all poking mullock at me?'

1942 Gavin Casey *It's Harder for Girls* 153: The chaps poked mullock at me, but it wasn't that that hurt.

1957 Ray Lawler *Summer of the Seventeenth Doll* 71: 'Oh, so that's what you got me in for, is it – to poke mullock?

1962 John Morrison *Twenty-Three* 86: 'I heard what you said when you grabbed that rope. Poking mullock at us because we won't go out over an empty hatch.'

see **borak**

munga (mungaree, mungareer)   1   Food (Army slang) [f. Fr. *manger*, adapted into Arabic as *manjaria*, with poss. influence of English dialect *mung*]

[**1787** Francis Grose *A Provincial Glossary: Mung.* Food for chickens.

1859 Hotten 65: *Mungarly* bread, food. *Mungarly cassey* a baker's shop.]

1919 W. H. Downing *Digger Dialects* 34: *Mungaree* (Arab.) – Bread. *Mungy* (Fr., Manger) – Food; a meal.

1944 G. H. Fearnside *Sojourn in Tobruk* 74: 'The mungaree has arrived', he said. 'The Ration Party is to report to Company Headquarters and pick it up.'

1944 Lawson Glassop *We Were the Rats* 114: 'They're lining up for mess,' said Harry. 'Any starters for the Mungareer[1] Stakes?' [1]Food.

1963 Lawson Glassop *The Rats in New Guinea* 149: 'Sit down and have some *munga,* John,' I said.

1965 Patrick White *Four Plays* 123: 'Okay, Nola! Shan't keep anyone waiting when the *mungareer's* on the table!'

1969 Osmar White *Under the Iron Rainbow* 96: 'You don't mean to tell me you'd eat kangaroo unless you were starving, do you? That's blackfellow's munga!'

1970 Richard Beilby *No Medals for Aphrodite* 37: 'It tastes better when it's fried, but it's not bad munga' . . . 'What does that word mean, please?' 'Food.' Turk explained the soldier-Arabic 'mungaree', shortened Australian-wise to 'munga'.

1982 Leo Schofield *Sydney Morning Herald* 27 Nov. 28: There were odd complaints about the food . . . from mouths that nonetheless wrapped themselves gleefully around the free munga and booze.

2   See quot.

1946 W. E. Harney *North of 23°* 93: Maybe the fare would be 'munga', a Malay pidgin word for that staple food the nargweami or nuts of the Cycad palm, which are pounded, soaked in water to take away the poison, and then cooked. It kept one alive, although the smell was high. 'He who ate of the munga palm was surely a son of the soil.'

murder, to cry bloody   To make a hullabaloo, like The Man from Ironbark when the city barber, for a joke, slashed the back of a red hot razor across his throat [cf. the English 'cry blue murder']

1895 A. B. Paterson *The Man From Snowy River* 67: And all the while his throat he held to save his vital spark, / And 'Murder! Bloody Murder!' yelled the man from Ironbark.

Murphy's law   A U.S. expression ('If anything can go wrong, it will') given currency in Australia when Senator Lionel Murphy was Attorney General

1977 *Sydney Morning Herald* 31 Dec. 23: Murphy's Law – 'if something can go wrong, it will' – is all too familiar to oilmen.

1978 *National Times* 27 May 26: It was one device of the Attorney-General's in those days that didn't attract the sanction of Murphy's law. Everything went smoothly.

1983 *Weekend Australian* 23 Apr. 11: The RAAF's handling of orders to photograph work on the Franklin dam site had turned into a classic application of Murphy's law, the Attorney-General, Senator Evans, told the Senate yesterday. (Murphy's law states that if anything can go wrong, it will.)

Murray cod, on the On the nod, i.e. on credit [rhyming slang]
1977 *Weekend Australian* 23 Jul. Magazine 1: A punter, well known in Sydney, who bets on 'the murray cod' (the nod) walked into City Tattersalls on Monday settling day carrying $240,000 cash.

murree, murri An Aborigine (often applied by Aborigines to themselves)
1911 E. S. Sorenson *Life in the Australian Backblocks* 160: They [the drovers] are hemmed in on all sides, and where once only King Murri was concerned about their movements they are now closely watched by boundary riders, mounted troopers, and stock inspectors.
1963 Xavier Herbert *Larger Than Life* 82: Half the crowd were 'murris', people of aboriginal stock.
1978 *Sydney Morning Herald* 8 Apr. 13: 'Murree doesn't eat one mango, Murree eats seven', Senator Bonner tells me. 'Murree' is the word for Aboriginal in these parts, and 'Dughi' for white.
1983 *Sydney Morning Herald* 14 Feb. 7: There are two Aboriginal words for the races in Moree. One is 'murri', an Aboriginal word for themselves, which is quite acceptable. The other, for whites, is 'gubber', which is derogatory.

Murrumbidgee whaler A swagman camping in the bends of the Murrumbidgee or any other river, and a byword for indolence [see *whaler*]
1873 J. C. F. Johnson *Christmas on Carringa* 16: Men when on the tramp through the Riverina country often carry a piece of twine and a hook to catch cod or blackfish. This is termed Murrumbidgee Whaling.
1878 G. H. Gibson *Southerly Busters* 177: Murrumbidgee whalers are a class of loafers who work for about six months in the year – i.e., during shearing and harvest, and camp the rest of the time in bends of rivers, and live by fishing and begging.
1885 *The Australasian Printers' Keepsake* 72: [He] eyed Bob very suspiciously, muttering 'spieler' and 'Murrumbidgee whaler'.
1906 H. J. Tompkins *With Swag and Billy* ix: Such a proceeding is common enough in the country where it is considered undignified to walk, since it savours too much of the Murrumbidgee whaler. To have admitted having walked from daylight until dark is to give yourself away as a downright vagrant sundowner.
1911 Edward S. Sorenson *Life in the Australian Backblocks* 70: There was a well-known Murrumbidgee whaler in the Wagga district, who had been doing the one circuit – embracing Gundagai, Hay, and Wagga – for thirty odd years, and during the whole of that time had never done a tap of work.

1953 Archer Russell *Murray Walkabout* 147: He was a 'Murrumbidgee whaler', the river prototype of the tramping sundowner.

mush see **moosh**

muscle, a ball of see **ball**

mushie A mushroom [abbr.]

muster, bangtail, Tambaroora, tarpaulin see **bangtail, Tambaroora, tarpaulin**

Muswellbrook, thing are crook at see **Tallarook**

mutton, underground see **underground mutton**

Myers, more front than see **front**

my little mate Phrase given currency by the allegation in 1983–4 that Mr Justice Lionel Murphy, in a telephone conversation with the NSW Chief Stipendiary Magistrate, Mr C. R. Briese in 1982, sought to influence a court case involving the Sydney solicitor, Mr Morgan Ryan, in the remark 'Now what about my little mate?'
1984 *National Times* 27 Jul. 3: Briese said that he had enlisted Murphy's support in his attempts to have the Government grant independence to NSW magistrates, who were then, and still are, public servants. According to Briese's statement, on one occasion Murphy rang him and told him the Government would support the independence proposition. Murphy then said, 'Now what about my little mate?' Briese says that Murphy had referred to Ryan as his 'little mate' in an earlier conversation. Briese claims he did not respond to these alleged attempts to intervene in the case against Ryan.
1984 Ross Gittins *Sydney Morning Herald* 12 Sep. 9: Spare a thought for my little mate John Howard.
1984 *National Times* 5 Oct. 2: After a few words from these luminaries, the author [Ron Tandberg] ascended the podium. 'Thank you, my mate Creighton, and thank you, my mate Bob', the cartoonist said graciously. 'I won't call either of you "my little mate", since I know you're both sensitive about your height'.

my troubles, worries see **troubles, worries**

my word Used for agreement or emphasis (given extra currency in Australia from occurring in Pidgin)
1865 Henry Kingsley *The Hillyars and the Burtons* 68: Some of the young ladies said: Their word – they were surprised.
1881 A. C. Grant *Bush-Life in Queensland* i 239: 'Black fellow, cawbawn patter, my word.'[11]Literally ... 'Black fellow plenty eat, my word.'

1887 *All the Year Round* 30 Jul. 68: 'My word' is an exclamation in constant and universal use.
1903 Joseph Furphy *Such is Life* (1944) 229: 'That's just the sort o' thing would put a hump on me. Sort o' off-sider for a gang o' Chinks! My word!'
1904 Let. in Harry A. Spurr *Mel. B. Spurr* (nd) 76: 'Did I tell you what Colonialisms they indulge in over here? One oft-recurring phrase is 'Not so bad!' They often say 'My word!' and 'My oath!' just as we would say 'By jove!''
1934 Vance Palmer *Sea and Spinifex* 213: 'Big sea running there outside t' reef. My word!'
1950 Nevil Shute *A Town Like Alice* 90: 'It's hot', he said. 'Oh my word, it can be hot when it tries.'
1981 *Sun-Herald* 13 Dec. 192: There are lots of Pakistani shopkeepers in London, oh my very word.

myall 1 An Aborigine who has had little or no contact with whites [Ab. The relationship between senses 1 and 3 is uncertain]
1798 David Collins *An Account of the English Colony in New South Wales* ed. B. H. Fletcher (1975) i 507: Mi-yal§ A stranger §This word has reference to sight; Mi, the eye.
1838 T. L. Mitchell *Three Expeditions into the Interior of Eastern Australia* i 20: Those who still remain in a savage state ... are named *'myalls'* by their half civilized brethren.
1849 Alexander Harris *The Emigrant Family* ed. W. S. Ramson (1967) 213: 'They're a regular myal (savage) mob. There's not above half of 'em can speak any English. The rest stand and stare at you like a lot of wild cattle.'
1864 Rachel Henning *Letters* ed. David Adams (1963) 185: They were myalls (i.e. wild blacks).
1881 A. C. Grant *Bush-Life in Queensland* ii 121: They would be certain to come in contact with *myalls*. [Note] Wild, uncivilized aboriginals – *jangalis*.
1902 Henry Lawson 'A Bush Publican's Lament' in *Prose* i 468: 'He's been on the roads this forty year, till he's as thin as a rat, and as poor as a myall black.'
1905 Jeannie Gunn *The Little Black Princess* 90: Bittertwine was a wild little nigger boy or 'myall', and terrified of white men.
1920 Louis Esson 'The Drovers' in *Dead Timber* 36: 'Only three of us and a Myall nigger!'
1954 Tom Ronan *Vision Splendid* 48: 'There's just as much work to be done in the kitchen on Sunday as any other time and I'm expected to get through it with one fat, lazy, useless, half-myall gin instead of the six I should have.'
1969 W. E. H. Stanner *After the Dreaming* 12: On the outskirts of the settlement there were a few groups of 'myalls' (bush natives) who were as wild as hawks, timid and daring by turns, with scarcely a word of English.

1983 Bob Dixon *Searching for Aboriginal Languages* 49: Willie was the most myall of all, and if anyone knew any language it would be him.
2 Any 'untamed' creature
1934 Vance Palmer *Sea and Spinifex* 222: 'Eight hundred bloody head. Scary brutes that hadn't seen a white man all their days – nothing by myalls and buffaloes.'
1938 Xavier Herbert *Capricornia* 72: Anna chased him through mud and mangroves and brought him home thrice before it occurred to her that he was what she called a Myall, a wild creature.
1941 Sarah Campion *Mo Burdekin* 203: In truth she was appalled, this myall who was at her happiest in bush.
3 Varieties of acacia, esp. *A. pendula*
1845 Edward John Eyre *Journals* i 47: Late in the afternoon we reached a watercourse, which I had previously named 'Myall Ponds', from the many and beautiful Acacia pendula trees that grew upon its banks.
1859 Daniel Bunce *Travels with Dr Leichhardt* 91: In places which were slightly elevated, many species of *Acacia* made their appearance, including the celebrated Weeping Myall (*A. pendula*), with an erect-growing species, known as Coxen's Myall.
1882 A. J. Boyd *Old Colonials* 2: It is a magnificent stockwhip ... to its elaborately carved handle of scented myall.
1901 Rolf Boldrewood *In Bad Company* 450: The glaucous-foliaged myall, 'intense and soulful-eyed', with its swaying arms and drooping habit, looks like a tree out of its mind. It boasts with its more sturdy cousin, the yarran, a strangely-powerful violet perfume.
1938 Francis Ratcliffe *Flying Fox and Drifting Sand* 229: We ran first through red bluebush country with scattered myalls (one of the endless regiment of Acacias).
1964 H. P. Tritton *Time Means Tucker* 27: The timber was different, coolibah, pine, myall and yarran.

myxo Myxomatosis, disease used to exterminate rabbits [abbr.]
1953 *Daily Telegraph* (Sydney) 22 Jan. 6: Trappers said tonight that the incidence of 'myxo' was waning, and the rabbit population was increasing.
1966 *Coast to Coast 1965–1966* 135: 'The myxo'll look after the rabbits ... Them C.S.I.R.O. blokes did a good job there.'
1971 David Ireland *The Unknown Industrial Prisoner* 294: 'There's a poor devil of a rabbit out there in the mangroves. Got a dose of myxo?'
1982 Max Harris *Weekend Australian* 6 Mar. Mag. 4: Restaurant critics are spreading like myxo.

N

naga, narga Waistcloth worn by an Aborigine, esp. in North-West Australia [? f. Macassarese]

1907 Alfred Searcy *In Australian Tropics* 81: I . . . paid them with tobacco and rice, and Turkey-red for the women for nargers (waist cloths).

1930 J. S. Litchfield *Far-North Memories* 46: 'Might be you got it naga (loin-cloth) you give it longa me?'

1938 Xavier Herbert *Capricornia* 90: Oscar looked and saw a blackfellow in a red naga toiling up the flood-bank.

1945 Elizabeth George *Two at Daly Waters* 100: I am reminded of the time, in our very early storekeeping days, when a myall, clad simply in a naga (length of cloth wound about him from the waist), came up to the verandah with silver in his hand, burning to buy something.

1961 Noni Braham *The Interloper* 123: A toddler, a brilliant red narga tied about her merry face, caught with one hand at her mother's flying skirts.

nailrod A coarse dark tobacco: *obs.*

1890 A. J. Vogan *The Black Police* 200: He hands our black friend a piece of 'nailrod' with which to charge his evening pipe.

1891 C. J. Brennan *Southerly* (1963) 171: Pleasant incense of Long Cut and Nailrod commingled.

1896 Henry Lawson 'Drifted Back' *Prose* i 235: 'You can give me half-a-pound of nailrod,' he said.

1967 Julian Stuart *Part of the Glory* 157: I could smoke or leave it alone, and as the jail weed was 'nail rod' or 'sheep dip' I left it severely alone.

namma hole See quots [Ab.]

1842 G. F. Moore *A Descriptive Vocabulary of . . . the Aborigines of Western Australia* 2: Amar, subst. A hole or pool of water in a rock. Ibid. 167: Water, standing in a rock – Gnamar.

1893 *Australasian* 5 Aug. 252: The route all the way from York to Coolgardie is amply watered, either 'namma holes' (native wells) or Government wells being plentiful on the road. [Morris]

1901 May Vivienne *Travels In Western Australia* 339: Native wells as 'nammaholes' have saved many a prospector from death by thirst.

1916 Macmillan's *Modern Dictionary of the English Language* 790. namma hole serving as a natural well, or storage place for rainwater.

1929 K. S. Prichard *Coonardoo* 52: His eyes, namma holes in viscid orbits, glittered at her, as he swung his naked feet.

1946 W. E. Harney *North of 23°* 69: Handed on by tradition is the secret of the namma wells . . . These are the secret watering places of the desert blacks.

nan nan A straw hat; a young man affecting this as part of a mode of dress; a 'lair': *obs.* [origin obscure: cf. *nana*]

1899 Henry Lawson 'If I Could Paint' *Prose* ii 38: A boarding-house keeper, with two or three grown-up white-shirted, stand-up-and-turn-down collared (mother does all their linen herself), straw-hatted, cigarette-smoking sons . . . I'd like to paint her and the children – and the 'nan-nan' sons.

1899 W. T. Goodge *Hits! Skits! and Jingles!* 39: One little maid with a bashful smile / Given for a salutation; / Two little dudes of the nan-nan style / Bent on captivation.

1900–10 O'Brien and Stephens: *Nan-nan* A straw hat for men's wear.

nana 1 The head, in such expressions as 'off one's nana', 'do one's nana' [? f. *banana*]

1894 A. B. Paterson 'Hughey's Dog' in *The World of Banjo Paterson* ed. C. Semmler (1967) 29: 'Off his nanny again,' thought the boss, 'the sooner he goes the better.'

1968 *Coast to Coast 1967–1968* 9: 'Arright, Mister Mighty Boss. Don't do your narna.'

1975 *Australian* 8 Feb. 13: 'We've all learned to laugh at ourselves and our predicament,' Trevor England said. 'If we hadn't we'd all be off our nanas.'

1983 Phillip Adams *Weekend Australian* 3 Dec. Mag. 2: Samson does his 'nana' and kills Abimilech.

2 A fool, an ass [listed by Partridge as English, a *softy* f. soft fruit]

1965 Graham McInnes *The Road to Gundagai* 148: Although he was obviously a gent, he was not a 'tonk' or a 'nana' . . . he was all right.

3 Applied to haircut [? f. resemblance to banana shape]

1941 Baker 48: *Nana (hair) cut:* A utilitarian haircut in which the back of the head is closely shaved.

1966 *Coast to Coast 1965–1966* 35: If you used a brush-back, wore the hair long, or horror of horrors, had a *nana* haircut.

nanto A horse: *obsolescent* [? Ab. see quot. 1957]

1889 *The Arrow* 20 Jul. 2: And then the cove looks at our / 'Nantos' and says he, 'Well, I'm your man.'

1904 A. W. Howitt *The Native Tribes of South-East Australia* 299: He [the Aboriginal] walked with me for some miles on our next day's journey round Lake Hope, and was much amused at my remark, when the horse I was leading suddenly terrified him by neighing close to his ear, – 'Wotta yappali yenni, nanto yattana,' that is, 'Do not fear; the horse is talking.' [recalling a period before 1889]

1907 Alfred Searcy *In Australian Tropics* 116: While at the 'Bar' we saw a Myall nigger who, if he had never seen nanto (horse) before, at any rate had never mounted one.

1911 Sydney Partrige *Rocky Section* 12: 'Take old Vagabond and run him on the section, and you'll always have a second nanto if anything happens to the other.'

1924 *Observer* (Adelaide) 14 Jun. 17: He [an old Aborigine] would go on to tell how some of the tribe lower down south had seen these strange people . . . and the wonderful nantoes (horses).

1935 H. H. Finlayson *The Red Centre* 98: The house boys knew 'nantos' from A to Z and were good trackers, keen on the job.

1946 W. E. Harney *North of 23°* 257: They call a horse 'nandoo', which means in some other tribes 'ears'.

1957 W. E. Harney *Life Among the Aborigines* 12: They saw many . . . with their strange 'nantus' (a word in reference to the distended nose of a horse after it has been ridden hard).

nap Blankets, bedding etc. [f. *nap* the pile on a fabric OED c. 1440)

1892 Barcroft Boake 'A Song from a Sandhill' *Bulletin* 2 Apr. 13 repr. in *Where the Dead Men Lie* (1897) 59: Drip, drip, drip! and one's 'nap' is far from dry.

1918 C. Fetherstonhaugh *After Many Days* 279: That night he could not catch the donkey, and he had to camp without any 'nap' (blankets).

1926 L. C. E. Gee *Bushtrackers and Goldfields* 41: The quarts were boiled and an after-dinner supply of coffee made, the 'nap' spread out on soft sandy spots, the two travellers reclined with pipes.

1933 R. B. Plowman *The Man from Oodnadatta* 2: The blackboy's nap (blankets, waterproof sheet, etc) filled in the rear compartment.

1968 Walter Gill *Petermann Journey* 24: I knew where to put my 'nap', the Territory word for a 'swag'.

nap, go ~ on In Australia, most often used negatively, meaning 'not to be keen on', not to favour, not to care for [f. card game: *to go nap* to stake all one can, to speculate heavily OED 1884]

1918 *Kia Ora Coo-ee* 15 Dec. 3: Talking of souvenirs, I don't go nap on any of the ordinary kind which lose their interest after they have been looked at once or twice.

1923 Con Drew *Rogues & Ruses* 164: 'My trainer goes nap on Sunshine, but I'm wanting Bright Gleam to win.'

1932 William Hatfield *Christmastown* 43: Didn't go nap on wine himself. A drop of whisky, now –.

1939 Miles Franklin and Dymphna Cusack *Pioneers on Parade* 105: 'She knows I don't go nap on him, and I have to be careful not to seem prejudiced.'

1955 Patrick White *The Tree of Man* 80: 'I never went nap on the priest meself.'

1957 D'Arcy Niland *Call Me When the Cross Turns Over* 184: But he never went nap on the city, he said, and now he had done with it for good.

1961 A. W. Upfield *Bony and the White Savage* 59: 'The woman who runs the bookshop knows we don't go nap on the sexy stuff.'

Napoleon   Nickname of R. J. Hawke, Prime Minister 1983– [f. Mr John Stone's Edward Shann Memorial Lecture, 27 August 1984, referring to Napoleon in George Orwell's *Animal Farm*]
1984 John Stone *Australian* 28 Aug. 1: 'They [businessmen reading *Animal Farm*] might thereby be reminded of the fate of all those other good-hearted and well-meaning animals – such as the old horse Boxer – who in a spirit of trust and, one might even say, "consensus" allowed the pigs under their charismatic leader Napoleon to lead them forward through their "advisory councils" and the like to their ultimately bitter end.'
1984 *Age* (Melbourne) 30 Aug. 2: It sounded like a potent drop and, as we all know, 'Napoleon' drinks mineral water these days.

narangy   Joseph Furphy's term for those whose status on stations entitled them to be quartered in the **barracks** q.v.; hence a subaltern on a station, someone with authority lower than that of the manager [Ab.]
[**1793** J. Hunter *Historical Journal* ed. J. Bach (1968) 273: *Narrong*, Any thing small.]
1855 John Lang *The Forger's Wife* 121: He had mixed a good deal with the blacks ... when he used the word 'narang' (small) but 'bidgee' (good), the groom did not quite comprehend the gentleman's praise of his horse.]
1903 Joseph Furphy *Such is Life* (1944) 254: Being a little too exalted for the men's hut, and a great deal too vile for the boss's house, I was quartered in the narangies' barracks. Ibid. 65: Jack Ward, the senior narangy, made some remark the two junior narangies supported Ward. Ibid. 270: The four narangies ... went to the veranda of the boss's house for their day's orders.
1941 Baker 48: *Narangy* As for 'silvertail'.
1947 *Bulletin* 6 Aug. 4: Miles Franklin, who has made a close study of *Such is Life* and written a book about the author, believes that 'narangy' is synonymous with 'jackeroo': probably a blackfellow's word. She knows it only in *Such is Life*, where it is always used for the jackeroos, otherwise 'gentleman apprentices', on a station and others who were entitled to eat with them. They ate in the barracks on big places like Runnymede and with the family on small stations such as she grew up on.

narga   see **naga**

nark *n.*   A spoilsport [f. *nark* a police informer OED 1865]
[**1859** Hotten 57: *Knark* a hard hearted and savage person.]
1898 *Bulletin* 17 Dec. Red Page: An informer or mar-plot is a *nark* or a *Jonah*.
1908 *Australian Magazine* 1 Nov. 1251: *nark*, a

spoil-sport.
1919 W. H. Downing *Digger Dialects* 35: *Nark* A malevolent or bad-tempered person; a spoil-sport.
1928 Vance Palmer *The Man Hamilton* 94: 'Oh, don't be a nark, Miss Byrne,' he coaxed her.
1933 Frank Clune *Try Anything Once* 81: Lieutenant Hennessy fulfilled the most exacting requirements of what a 'nark' should be.
1946 Kylie Tennant *Lost Haven* 369: Here he was spoiling things for two kids, like a crabby old nark.
1959 Dorothy Hewett *Bobbin Up* 33: 'You're turnin' into a real nark,' Hazel said sulkily.
1961 Patrick White *Riders in the Chariot* 347: Others still, suspected him of being some kind of nark or perv, and cursed him as he lifted them out of their own vomit.
nark *v.*   To annoy, thwart [f. *nark* to annoy, vex, irritate, exasperate EDD 1888]
1975 Richard Beilby *The Brown Land Crying* 200: 'Ya'd do anything to nark me, anything to put me down, wouldn't ya?'

narked   Peeved, angry
1896 Henry Lawson 'The Shearing of Cook's Dog' *Prose* i 96: The cook usually forgot all about it in an hour ... But this time he didn't; he was 'narked' for three days.
1898 *Bulletin* 17 Dec. Red Page: To *get narked* is to lose your temper.
1903 Joseph Furphy *Such is Life* (1944) 21: 'I noticed the other feller was a bit narked when he seen me on the horse to-day.'
1911 Louis Stone *Jonah* 9: 'Orl right, wot are yer narked about?'
1946 Margaret Trist *What Else is There?* 135: 'Gee, Mum's going to be narked,' said Billy. 'You'll have to stick up for me, Ruby.'
1958 *Coast to Coast 1957–1958* 104: 'Most of 'em are after wives for their boys. They're real narked now.'
1963 A. W. Upfield *The Body at Madman's Bend* 180: 'She raised it to half the wages this morning, Then looked narked 'cos we went slow.'

Nar Nar Goon   Byword for any remote locality [f. place name]
1918 *Kia Ora Coo-ee* 15 Sep. 18: Jimmy was thinking of home, how his mother would be feeling, what his father would say about him, and how things in general were at Nar Nar Goon. Yes, dear, old, sleepy Nar Nar Goon.
1963 Lou Richards *Boots and All!* 176: They've had some shockers, too, players who would have struggled for a game with the South Nar Nar Goon fifths!
1981 *Age* (Melbourne) 8 Jun. 2: Television football commentaries generally tend to be about as rewarding as a night game at Nar Nar Goon football ground in a power strike.

Nasho Compulsory military training (abolished in 1972); a youth undergoing such training [abbr. of *National Service*]

1962 Criena Rohan *The Delinquents* 52: 'I'm not keen on Nashos,' she said. 'I prefer bodgies.'

1966 Bruce Beaver *You Can't Come Back* 5: Sam, the new one, was just eighteen and due for his Nasho training.

1975 David Malouf *Johnno* 70: Now the Grand Central was the drinking place of 'Nashos'.

1980 *Sunday Mail* (Brisbane) 10 Feb. 5: Joh wants 'Nasho' back [heading] The Premier, Mr Bjelke-Petersen, yesterday suggested renewed national service to help boost the defence of northern Australia.

national game, Australia's 1 Two-up

1930 L. W. Lower *Here's Luck* 70: He had a small piece of wood in his hand, on which were balanced two pennies. The national game was in progress.

1944 Stan Arneil *One Man's War* (1980) 188: 'Two-up', our national game is severely frowned upon in the camp and all efforts are made to suppress it.

1963 Frank Hardy *Legends from Benson's Valley* 108: The demise of the bookmakers increased attendance at the Sunday sessions of Australia's national game. The two-up school operated on the plateau above the valley.

1976 *Bulletin* 10 Jan. 45: There's no greater humiliation than being a failure at the national game.

1983 *Sun-Herald* 23 Jan. 35: 'You can't wipe out two-up; it's our national game.'

2 Australian Rules Football

1889 Arthur Streeton *The National Game* [painting in Art Gallery of N.S.W.]

native A native plant

1977 Rodney Pybus *Times Literary Supplement* 14 Oct. 1213: A notice by the gate will stop / the stranger short: 'Australian natives', it says, / 'one dollar each'.

1979 *National Times* 4 Aug. 39: Although a wide variety of Australian natives has become available to gardeners in recent years, there is still comparatively little use made of native climbers.

naughty Sexual intercourse [f. *go naughty, do the naughty* OED 1869]

1959 Eric Lambert *Glory Thrown In* 106: 'Until I met Thelma, I always thought that sheilas had to be talked into a bit of a naughty.'

1963 Frank Hardy *Legends from Benson's Valley* 11: He put his arm around her, patting her buttock. I smiled, remembering his oft-repeated remark: 'I get a lot of knock backs but I get a lot of naughties.'

1972 Geoff Morley *Jockey Rides Honest Race* 71:

'These sheilas fascinate me ... I want them to invite me in for a good old-fashioned naughty.'

1975 Xavier Herbert *Poor Fellow My Country* 439: 'I'll give you a new dress ... and we'll 'ave a bit of a party, and then another naughty, eh?'

1983 *Sun-Herald* 27 Mar. 29: Colin Chapman, of the ABC radio program Midday, scooped the sensation-peddling international press with his comment on Charles and Diana's giving the news-hounds the slip at Alice Springs. 'My goodness, where were they off to?' asked Chapman. 'A nice cold beer and a naughty?'

neck, go under someone's To forestall an action contemplated by another, usurp someone else's prerogative [? f. horse racing]

1953 T. A. G. Hungerford *Riverslake* 61: 'I wouldn't want to go under your neck,' Randolph said sarcastically. Ibid. 220: 'Why jack up? ... You just race in the mob from the office and go under our necks.'

1961 Mena Calthorpe *The Dyehouse* 120: 'She knew she was going under Patty What's-her-name's neck. We can't shed tears of blood over these dames.'

1965 John Beede *They Hosed Them Out* 188: WAG was so egotistical and self-opinioned I could easily go under his neck. His mode of operation was to sit with his chest out and chin in and expect the girls to fall for him.

1977 *Sunday Telegraph* (Sydney) 6 Feb. 128: Is Queensland Premier Joh Bjelke-Petersen getting under Neville Wran's neck? Joh is touring the north-west of Western Australia with mining magnate Lang Hancock.

1982 *NT Times* (Darwin) 7 Dec. 7: Bob-a-job Boy Scouts in England have got under the neck of the Pommie Post Office by starting a cheap Christmas card delivery service.

neck-to-knees An old-fashioned bathing costume

1910 *Daily Telegraph* (Sydney) 20 Jun. 17: Neck to knee costumes have been for some time past insisted on at all popular resorts.

Ned Kelly 1 A name applied to anyone with 'bushranging' attributes [f. the famous bushranger (more strictly, bank-robber) hanged in 1880]

1941 Baker 41: *Kelly, Ned* Any person of buccaneering business habits.

1953 *The Sunburnt Country* ed. Ian Bevan 129: Phrases such as 'do a Ned Kelly' ... lend so much verve and colour to the Australian serviceman's vocabulary.

1956 Tom Ronan *Moleskin Midas* 307: 'Tell that Commissioner of Taxation that Ned Kelly was a jackeroo alongside him.'

2 The belly: *rare* [rhyming slang]

1951 Dal Stivens *Jimmy Brockett* 86: I got his arm

and rammed a right into his Ned Kelly.

1969 Alec H. Chisholm *The Joy of the Earth* 302: Those lads who customarily referred to ... the belly as 'the Ned Kelly', to boots as 'daisy roots', to a snake as a 'Joe Blake', and so on.

Ned Kelly, game as   Extremely plucky and insouciant

1945 Roy Rene *Mo's Memoirs* 24: He was game as Ned Kelly, and he'd ride anything.

1953 Dymphna Cusack *Southern Steel* 41: 'Is that kid game? Game as Ned Kelly.'

1958 H. D. Williamson *The Sunlit Plain* 90: In fact, to pay him his due compliment, he was as game as Ned Kelly.

1966 Don Crick *Period of Adjustment* 66: 'Are you game?' 'As Ned Kelly.'

neddy   A horse; in plural, usually race horse [f. *neddy* a donkey OED 1790]

1887 *Tibb's Popular Songbook* 9: So they saddled up their Neddys / And like loafers sneaked away.

1895 Cornelius Crowe *The Australian Slang Dictionary* 52: *Neddy* a horse.

1901 Rolf Boldrewood *In Bad Company* 217: 'Just as we was a-saddlin' up – some of us had one neddy, some two – a mob of horses comes by.'

1918 Bernard Cronin *The Coastlanders* 74: A hot cinder lit on my neddie's rump.

1965 William Dick *A Bunch of Ratbags* 40: My old man was backing the neddies as usual.

1975 Les Ryan *The Shearers* 69: 'Joe Clement's neddy – Wingay. Station hands reckon he's home and hosed.'

ned, red   see **red**

neg driving   The offence of driving negligently [abbr.]

1973 Alexander Buzo *Rooted* 41: 'Remember the time ... when Hammo had a prang in his B and got dobbed in for neg driving?'

Never-Never, the   The regions remote from civilization, and as yet unsettled or unexplored, at first referring to north-western Queensland or northern Australia, generally. The term was given currency by Mrs Aeneas Gunn's classic *We of the Never-Never* (1908) [see quot. 1857]

1857 F. Cooper *Wild Adventures in Australia* 68: I had the cattle mustered, and the draft destined for the Nievah vahs* ready for the road. *Nievah vahs, sometimes incorrectly pronounced never nevers, a Cameleroi term signifying unoccupied land.

1875 Rolf Boldrewood *A Colonial Reformer* (1890) 174: 'But here is seems to be the Never-Never country, and no mistake.'

1882 A. J. Boyd *Old Colonials* 202: My soliloquy ends with the inquiry, 'What on earth is to be done in this wretched Never-never* country?' *Never-never* is the far outside country beyond the centres of civilization.

1893 Francis Adams *The Australians* 11: Beyond this [the pastoral land west of the Dividing Range] lie vast realms of 'scrub' – more or less occupied for another four or five hundred miles westward, till the outskirts of the great central desert are reached, and we pass into no man's land, or 'the never-never.'

1899 W. T. Goodge *Hits! Skits! and Jingles!* 89: It was on the Never-Never where the Jackeroos endeavour / To be very, very, clever with the strangers imbecile.

1901 Henry Lawson 'Shall We Gather at the River' *Prose* i 509: He was known from Riverina down South in New South Wales to away up through the Never-Never Country in Western Queensland.

1906 Joseph Furphy *Rigby's Romance* ed. R. G. Howarth (1846) 228–9: My undercurrent of thought was persistently dwelling upon that glimpse into the Never-never of my companion's soul.

1917 A. B. Paterson *Three Elephant Power* 41: The typical Australian bullock ... is bred away out in Queensland, on remote stations in the Never Never land, where men live on damper and beef, and occasionally eat a whole bottle of hot pickles at a sitting.

1959 Dorothy Hewett *Bobbin Up* 21: 'I can remember when Bondi was just a heapa sand hills and scrub, goin' dirt-cheap. Nobody'd buy it then. We thought it was out in the never-never. An look at it now.'

1979 *Weekend Australian* 29 Sep. Mag. 1: The new Never Never [heading] The most burning issue in the Northern Territory today is that of Aboriginal land rights.

new chum   1   A newly arrived prisoner in a gaol or hulk [English thieves' slang]

1812 Vaux: *Chum*: a fellow prisoner in a jail, hulk, &c; so there are *new chums* and *old chums*, as they happen to have been a short or a long time in confinement.

1830–1 Henry Savery *Quintus Servinton* (1962) 287: 'There's near a thousand chaps here [in the hulk] ... 'twont do to draw no distinctions like, with new chums.'

c. 1845 James Tucker *Ralph Rashleigh* (1952) 51: As Ralph and his associates in punishment marched past these dens [in the hulk], they were saluted by obstreperous shouts of 'New chums! New chums!' from both sides.

2   Any new arrival, inexperienced in the conditions into which he has come

1838 T. L. Mitchell *Three Expeditions* i 99: He was also what they termed a 'new chum', or one newly arrived.

1849 Alexander Harris *The Emigrant Family* (1967) 141: Indeed, no one but a 'new chum' could have missed the course from the feeding ground to the hut.

1859 Frank Fowler *Southern Lights and Shadows* 26: I have already said that the young Australian is systematically insolent to the new-chum ... A new-chum is fair game for anyone.

1869 Marcus Clarke *The Peripatetic Philosopher* 3: 'New Chums' [essay title]

1873 A. Trollope *Australia* ed. Edwards and Joyce (1967) 413: The idea that Englishmen, – that is, newchums, or Englishmen just come from home, – are made of paste, whereas the Australian, native or thoroughly acclimatized, is steel all through, I found to be universal.

1886 Percy Clarke *The New Chum in Australia* [book title]

1901 Henry Lawson 'Send Round the Hat' *Prose* i 474: A new-chum parson, who wanted a subscription to build or enlarge a chapel, or something, sought the assistance of the Giraffe's influence with his mates.

1929 Jules Raeside *Golden Days* 50: We were all new chums, and very indifferent bushmen, but our enthusiasm over-ruled our ignorance.

1935 F. D. Davidson and B. Nicholls *Blue Coast Caravan* 21: He was taking his craft through channels marked only in his memory. 'This is no place for a new chum to fool about,' he remarked as we came to the narrows.

1957 Sydney Hart *Pommie Migrant* 159: 'You a new chum?' he asked. It was the first time I'd heard the expression.

1971 Rena Briand *White Man in a Hole* 132: Newchums at opal mining, they were soon involved talking 'shop' with Johnny while I set the billy on the fire.

Newk The tennis player John Newcombe

1980 *Sun-Herald* 13 Jan. 48: The undoubted winner in the Sports War has been the viewer, who's been able to alternate from Test match to tennis tournament with a flick of the dial. Bewdy Newk, good one Lillee.

New South, sunny An affectionate or jocular way of referring to New South Wales: *obsolescent*

1905 *The Old Bush Songs* ed. A. B. Paterson 61: Sunny New South Wales [ballad title]

1922 Arthur Wright *A Colt from the Country* 83: 'With that finished ... we can kiss good-bye to sunny New South for a spell.'

nick To move smartly, to decamp [cf. E. dial. *nip* to move rapidly or nimbly OED 1825; *nit* to depart hurriedly]

1894 Ethel Turner *Seven Little Australians* 141:

'Meg could talk to father,' Bunby said, 'and Pip could keep teasing the General till Esther would be frightened to leave the room, and then me and Judy would nick down and have a run, and get back before you let them go.'

1901 Miles Franklin *My Brilliant Career* (1965) 189: If you go to a picnic, just when the fun commences you have to nick off home and milk.

1938 Xavier Herbert *Capricornia* 257: 'You're only humming for a drink. Nick off home.'

1939 Kylie Tennant *Foveaux* 177: 'If Curly hadn't nicked round that screen ...'

1946 K. S. Prichard *The Roaring Nineties* 94: 'Guess you're dying for a cup of tea ... I'll nick over to the camp and put on the billy.'

1957 Ray Lawler *Summer of the Seventeenth Doll* 124: 'Is it the boys he's nicking off with on Monday?'

1969 Osmar White *Under the Iron Rainbow* 105: 'You haven't got to nick off on my account.'

1978 Wendy Lowenstein *Weevils in the Flour* 308: The man would come and post this notice up outside the house. We'd watch through the windows, then we'd nick out and grab it.

1981 *Sydney Morning Herald* 11 Apr. 13: There is no lavatory so the Labor candidate ... and his helpers nick across the road to use Ansett's.

Nifty Nev. Mr Neville Wran, N.S.W. Premier 1976– [see quots]

1977 *Bulletin* 20 Aug. 35: Nifty Nev gave a farewell party for Diamond Jim at the Wrans' Woollahra pad.

1979 *Sun-Herald* 25 Mar. 176: Nifty trip [heading] And how did he get that nickname 'Nifty'? According to the Premier it happened when the young Neville Wran lived in Balmain and his mother gave him two pennies each day to catch a tram into the city and back. He regularly returned home with a penny in his pocket – that's nifty.

1983 *Sun-Herald* 18 Dec. 20: He [Wran] worked as a junior to Lionel Murphy who was then often briefed by Sydney solicitor Morgan Ryan. It was Ryan who gave Wran the nickname 'Nifty'.

nigger 1 An Australian Aborigine: now derogatory [f. application to the American negro]

1881 A. C. Grant *Bush-Life in Queensland* ii 171: A few of the more brutal spirits thought as little of 'knocking over a nigger' at sight as they would have done of shooting a kangaroo.

1905 Jeannie Gunn *The Little Black Princess* 7: Bett-Bett believed all these tales, for she was a little nigger, every bit of her.

1917 F. J. Mills *Dinkum Oil* 30: 'I was kangarooin', and was camped with about a dozen niggers who was 'elpin' me.'

1930 J. S. Litchfield *Far-North Memories* 110: We usually bought any dead bodies from the niggers,

paying them a bag of flour for the 'dear departed'. We used to bury the corpse in an ant-hill, and when all the flesh had been eaten from the bones, we sent the skeletons to museums, and received up to ten pounds each for them.
1959 Lyndon Rose *Country of the Dead* 41: 'I'll get that damn' nigger yet!' he told himself savagely. 'I'll have to, to show the other natives who's master.'
1982 *National Times* 28 Feb. 29: We ... met a young white girl who warned us not to camp along the river because 'the gins and niggers get ferocious at night.'

2   Luderick, or black bream
1981 *Sunday Mail* (Brisbane) 12 Jul. 55: If you have never tried black bream or 'nigger' fishing and would like to try them the next few months will provide an excellent opportunity.
1981 *Weekend Australian* 12 Sep. 1: When Mr Somare explained what sort of fish would be caught in PNG waters Mr Jones said: 'Oh well, where I come from in Newcastle we catch a lot of blackfish – we call them niggers of course.'
1983 *Sun* (Sydney) 30 Sep. 28: Brisbane Water has been best of the estuaries, with bream, niggers and mullet.

night   A nightgown [abbr.]
1969 Thomas Jenkins *We Came to Australia* 124: Waltz nights were not evenings with Strauss, but short nighties.
1979 *Sydney Morning Herald* 26 Dec. 14: Waltz or long nights $4 & $8 Pure cotton waltz length floral print nights, sizes 12 18, $4.
1983 *NT News* (Darwin) 4 Apr. 19: Ladies Nights 6.48 Short nights with lace trim and shirt tail hem in sizes 12–20.

night's a pup   see **pup**

niner   A nine-gallon keg of beer
1951 Dal Stivens *Jimmy Brockett* 304: I had a belly now like a niner.
1964 George Johnston *My Brother Jack* 111: 'Does he know how to breach a niner and get the bung in, that's the point?' He waved at the nine-gallon keg of beer, which had been propped up on the sofa.
1973 Alexander Buzo *Rooted* 77: 'He backed five winners at the picnic races, floored three locals in a brawl, demolished a niner, and torpedoed the minister's daughter.'

ning nong   see **nong**

nips, to put in the   As for **bite** q.v.
1919 W. H. Downing *Digger Dialects* 35: *Nip* To cadge (or 'Put in the nips').
1937 *Best Australian One-Act Plays* 398: 'He came

along to put the nips in, so I gave him a couple of bob.'
1949 Lawson Glassop *Lucky Palmer* 230: 'You can't put the nips into old Alf. He's got death adders in his pockets.'
1955 D'Arcy Niland *The Shiralee* 41: 'He was here yesterday, too. Put the nips into me for tea and sugar and tobacco in his usual style. The biggest bludger in the country.'
1973 Frank Huelin *Keep Moving* 48: Parsons, priests, doctors, lawyers and professional people generally were legitimate prey, and we had no scruples about 'putting the nips' into them.

nit   A cry to warn of the approach of some authority; (as a verb) to decamp hurriedly
[**1864** Hotten: *Nix!* The signal word of schoolboys to each other that the master, or other person in authority, is approaching]
1882 *The Sydney Slang Dictionary* 10: *Nit* Get away (usually from a foe), make tracks.
1899 Henry Lawson 'If I Could Paint' *Prose* ii 38: I'd call it 'Nit! There's Mother'.
1911 Louis Stone *Jonah* 8: Suddenly there was a cry of 'Nit! 'Ere's a cop!' and the Push bolted like rabbits.

nit, to keep   To act as sentinel (or **cockatoo** q.v.) esp. for someone engaged in some illegal activity
1940 Ion L. Idriess *Lightning Ridge* 20: Bill kept nit for his elder brother who was courting a girl, and earned a shilling.
1952 T. A. G. Hungerford *The Ridge and the River* 10: 'Send two men a couple of hundred yards up and down the track to keep nit.'
1957 Ray Lawler *Summer of the Seventeenth Doll* 44: 'Keepin' nit for the S.P. bookies, eh.'
1963 Gunther Bahnemann *Hoodlum* 79: Jerry, the lookout man stayed there, to keep nit.
1971 David Ireland *The Unknown Industrial Prisoner* 77: They had transgressed the unwritten law that you didn't let yourself go to sleep while you were keeping nit for your mates.
1983 *Sun-Herald* 25 Sep. 77: Johnny's a nice bloke ... But confront him with a bookie and his thinking sinks to such depths that Ned Kelly would refuse to keep nit for him.

nitkeeper   One who 'keeps nit'
1935 *Bulletin* 22 May 21: That outlaw the sulphur-crested cockatoo is not the only bird to post a 'nit-keeper' when transgressing against society.
1943 *Khaki and Green* 101: Outside a window an abo was acting in a mysterious manner, reminiscent of a nit keeper in the days of S.P. bookies.
1963 Frank Hardy *Legends from Benson's Valley* 108: An elaborate network of nitkeepers on all sides frustrated the new policeman for three

weeks.

1971 David Ireland *The Unknown Industrial Prisoner* 77: The Great White Father called in at the wharf at six one morning, just the time the nit-keepers should have wakened those who were down.

1981 Maxwell Grant *Inherit the Sun* 183: Red knew there would be a nit-keeper, a man keeping watch who could slip out for the police if there was trouble.

Noah A shark [f. rhyming slang *Noah's Ark*]

1952 A. G. Mitchell Suppl. to *Chamber's Shorter English Dictionary* 800: *Noah's Ark*, *n*. (*slang*) a shark.

1966 Roger Carr *Surfie* 116: I've seen a four-gallon tin squashed in by the force of the water when a big Noah got caught and dragged it down. But mostly a four-gallon drum will drown any shark.

1978 John Hepworth *His Book* 82: The sun-bronzed ones refused to dunk their pinkies in the surf while the Noah's Ark was also in it.

1982 *Bulletin* 13 Jul. 65: 'I'll tell you what's worse than the Noahs', said Edgar. 'What about those bloody dragon-flies?'

nobbler A glass of liquor, usually spirits and water [origin obscure]

1851 *Illustrated Australian Magazine* Nov. 248: The public houses are crowded with friends taking their last nobbler.

1853 John Sherer *The Gold-Finder of Australia* 177: I have only had two noblers* (as they are called) since I came to the place, and paid 1s. 6d. per nobler. *Noblers are tumblers of spirits and water, which, with the gambling propensities of the colonists, threaten to swamp the prosperity of the country.

1854 C. H. Spence *Clara Morison* 171: 'A nobbler is half a glass of spirits, generally brandy, and when it is taken neat, it means that it is undiluted.'

1867 J. R. Holding *Australian Capers* 132: 'Regular bars ... where any men can go and call for a 'nobbler'.

1873 A. Trollope *Australia* ed. Edwards and Joyce (1967) 660: A nobbler is the proper colonial phrase for a drink at a public-house.

1885 Mrs Campbell Praed *Australian Life* 103: Having accepted at my hands the customary 'nobbler', he would sit down for half-an-hour, talking.

1905 'The Shepherd' *The Old Bush Songs* ed. A. B. Paterson 116: He was going a pace, / Shouting nobbler after nobbler, with a smile upon his face.

nobblerize

1857 *Thatcher's Colonial Songster* 23: And she'd sit in the tent, while to work he went, / And all day nobblerise.

1883 R. E. N. Twopeny *Town Life in Australia* 70: But there are two other liquids – whisky and brandy – which play an important part in nobblerising.

no-hoper A horse with no prospect of winning; a man of whom nothing can be expected; a general term of contempt

1943 Baker 53: *No-hoper* An outsider (Racing slang).

1945 Tom Ronan *Strangers on the Ophir* 121: There were actually eight runners in it: the three favourites; three no hopers hardly up to hack-race standard.

1957 Ray Lawler *Summer of the Seventeenth Doll* 53: 'There's no excuse for that sort of thing, you're just a no-hoper.'

1966 Patrick White *The Solid Mandala* 18: 'A couple of no-hopers with ideas about 'emselves', he would grumble, and then regurgitate: 'The Brothers Bloody Brown!'

1970 Jon Cleary *Helga's Web* 8: His mother had prayed that he might become a priest, but God in his wisdom had recognised a religious no-hoper when he saw one.

nong Someone stupid or ineffectual: *derogatory* [? f. E. dial. *nigmenog* a very silly fellow OED 1700: see also quot. 1865]

[**1865** Hotten: *Ning-nang* horse-coupers' term for a worthless thorough-bred.]

1953 Baker 171: *nong* A simpleton or fool. [as World War II slang from New Guinea and the islands]

1958 Hal Porter *A Handful of Pennies* 30: 'Old or not old, he's one of them: he's only a nong'. [i.e. one of the Japanese during the Occupation]

1959 Dorothy Hewett *Bobbin Up* 127: Stan had never carried a bunch of flowers in his life before, and said he felt like a nong-nong.

1962 J. Marshall and R. Drysdale *Journey Among Men* 143: The traveller who ... has mislaid his letter of credit, is not necessarily a crook but merely a bit of a *nong* who should be put in funds and told gently to try not to do it again.

1969 Leslie Haylen *Twenty Years Hard Labor* 210–11: The continuance of compulsory voting means that the 'nongs', the indifferent and the plain bloody stupid, will continue to dominate the voting in the Commonwealth and the States for years to come.

1974 Sir Charles Cutler *Sydney Morning Herald* 26 Sep. 8: Personally, I think the people of Australia have been betrayed by the most divided, disorganized group of academic nongs that have ever been in charge of this country.

1982 Mike Carlton *Sydney Morning Herald* 21 Jul. 8: If The Price is Right has one small virtue, it is that the show quite happily and honestly appeals to nongs, without in any way trying to disguise the fact.

noodle, noodling   To prospect for opal in mullock heaps
1902 *Queensland Department of Mines Geological Survey* No. 177 cit. J. S. Gunn *An Opal Terminology* (1971) 30: Some splendid opal is found ... by turning over and searching the old heaps and mullock – 'noodling'.
1921 K. S. Prichard *Black Opal* 73: They went noodling together, or gathering wild flowers. Ibid. 157: Potch gave him some scraps of sun-flash, and colour and potch to noodle, and he sat and snipped them contentedly.
1948 E. F. Murphy *They Struck Opal* 128–9: New industries began cropping up – such as that called 'lousing the dumps'. This was carried out by a small army of women and children, who picked over the opal dirt on the dumps, looking for any loose opals that the miners may have missed ... The Queensland and Lightning Ridge name for this practice – noodling – seems a more logical one. It originated from the discovery of small egg-shaped opals. ... A visiting geologist tabbed these 'nodules' ... The miners soon altered the name to 'noodles'.
1956 Ruth Park and D'Arcy Niland *The Drums Go Bang!* 97: Tiger began to noodle. Down on her knees with the sun behind her, she was pecking away with a little hand pick like a kiwi's beak. The face of the mound crumbled away and showed gravel, clods of red earth, white kopi dirt.
1971 Rena Briand *White Man in a Hole* 27: 'Why don't you have a go at noodling*?' he suggested. *Local term for scraping the rubble heaps in search of opal.
1976 Morris West *Bulletin* 20 Mar. 40: 'It takes two months for a novel to germinate with me. One fiddles with it, noodles it and then the day comes when I'm ready to go.'
noodler
1940 Ion L. Idriess *Lightning Ridge* 104: The industrious noodlers were every day like ants scratching at the dumps of the lucky gougers.
1975 Nino Culotta *Gone gougin'* 131: 'I'll show them to those noodlers over there. You never know your luck.'
1982 *Sun-Herald* 31 Jan. 100: Thousands of noodlers will have been there before you, but the chances of digging a cuttable opal from the dumps are good provided you work at it.

norks   A woman's breasts [origin uncertain: the wrapping on Norco butter shows a cow's udder]
1962 Criena Rohan *The Delinquents* 157: 'Hello, honey, that sweater – one deep breath and your norks will be in my soup.'
1966 Baker 215: *nork*, a female breast, usually in plural. (Ex Norco Co-operative Ltd., a butter manufacturer in N.S.W.)
1970 Barry Oakley *Let's Hear it for Prendergast* 71: 'Wow, she's peeled right off. What norks!'
1973 Patrick White *The Eye of the Storm* 593: Hits herself in the eye with an independent nork it isn't any laughing matter.
1980 Thomas Keneally in *Days of Wine and Rage* ed. Frank Moorhouse 252: 'All Maureen's got to do is trail one of her big lovely norks at him and the bugger dashes off another one of his press releases.'

Norm   1   The cartoon figure in the *Life Be In It* (q.v.) commercials conceived by Phillip Adams: see quot. 1975
1975 *Australian* 24 Nov. 2: Brian Dixon, Victoria's Minister for Youth, Sport and Recreation, has commissioned a new ocker character to help him in his latest campaign to get people off their backsides and into fitness activity. His name's NORM and he appeared for the first time last night on TV. Norm's idea of activity is sitting in front of his own set with a beer watching other people wear themselves out. 'Being your normal Australian, I'm a sportsman,' says Norm. 'Any sort of sport – I'll be in it 'cos I'm an all-round sportsman. There's not many of us left though. I rang the mates this arvo, warmed the set and cooled the tinnies. No takers. Tommo said he was taking his dog for a walk. Fred said he was going to mow the lawn. George said he was going for a walk down the park. Davo said he was taking the family out flying kites. I dunno. Us all-round sportsmen are a dying race.'
1979 *Sydney Morning Herald* 23 Nov. 3: Norm, the overweight lazy television character who has spent the past two years trying to budge Australians from their lounge chairs into the outdoors, appears to be getting his message through. A national survey completed last month, in which more that 1,000 people were questioned, has shown that Australians believe they are slowly becoming more active.
1983 *Australian* 18 Nov. 9: Norm of 'Life. Be in it', the pot-bellied slouch who has spent eight years clutching tinnies and viewing the telly as a warning to lazy Australians, was yesterday dropped by Federal and Victorian Governments. Creator of the campaign, Phillip Adams, farewelled his brainchild who has found many millions of admirers in the US. More than 40 States have used the 'Life' campaign to prompt Americans to use their leisure time more actively. The President and his wife, Nancy, 'often toss an Australian frisbee around the Oval Office' ... 'And the US Marines' recent invasion of Grenada was a 'Life. Be in it' recreational activity,' claimed Adams.

Norma
1979 *Age* (Melbourne) 17 Oct. 5: The life of Norm, the nation's favourite slob, will never be the same again. His shop assistant wife, Norma, is pushing for a promotion at the local aupermarket and has left him to cook dinner for the family while she goes to a union meeting ... Norma is a creation of the Shop Distributive and Allied Employees' Association, which is urging its 100,000 women members to take a more assertive role at work, in the union and at home.
1982 Max Harris *Weekend Australian* 20 Mar. Mag. 4: These programs were being shown on a channel which specialises in servicing the ockers, the simplest minds, the worthy mass of Norms and Normas.
2   Generic term for any inactive Australian male
1980 *Sun-Herald* 7 Sep. 53: Sports World was in full swing on Channel 7. Aah Rugby League. Decided to do a 'Norm', open a tinny and perhaps learn something about the game from Rex Mossop before lunch.
1981 *Australian* 26 Oct. 3: For most 'Norms' it [daylight saving] means an extra hour in the pub.
1982 *Weekend Australian* 6 Feb. Mag. 3: Despite the urgings of every Norm in Australia, Laird missed out on his first century.
1984 *Sydney Morning Herald* 26 Apr. 6: Mr Windschuttle argues that being a 'Norm', watching sport rather than playing it, isn't so bad.

Normanton cocktail   See quot. [f. place-name]
1963 John Cantwell *No Stranger to the Flame* 38: 'Give us a Normanton cocktail, darl – a gin and two blankets,' one of the cutters said.

North, the Deep   Queensland: *derogatory* [f. the 'Deep South' and its associations of intolerance in U.S.A.]
1974 Peter Porter *Australian* 5 Oct. 13: I learned that things have changed but not enough to placate the southerners, for whom Queensland in general and Brisbane in particular are sources of scorn and contempt. 'The Deep North' is the phrase used in Sydney.
1980 *Sunday Mail* (Brisbane) 12 Oct. 3: The forthcoming elections will take the smile off the faces of those southerners who laugh at our so called 'deep north' politics.

northern myth, the   The belief in north Australia as having vast potentialities awaiting exploitation, attacked by B. R. Davidson in *The Northern Myth* (1965)
1969 Osmar White *Under the Iron Rainbow* 50: Kununurra ... is the focal point of hope for all those whose faith in the northern myth remains unshaken by the repeated failure of large agricultural projects in the Australian tropics.

Northern Territory champagne   See quots
1973 *Sunday Telegraph* (Sydney) 26 Aug. 112: Evidence was given that many Aboriginals drink 'Northern Territory champagne' – methylated spirits mixed with health salts.
1979 *Weekend Australian* 1 Dec. 13: When the recipe for Territory champagne is 'metho and Sal Vital', it is hardly surprising our spirit consumption almost trebles the national average.

nose, have a ~ on   To hold in disfavour [cf. *snout*]
1903 Joseph Furphy *Such is Life* (1944) 17: 'I don't blame ole Martin to have a bit of a nose on me,' continued Mosey laughingly.

nose, on the   Ill-smelling; offensive, viewed with disfavour (popularized as World War II slang)
1941 Baker 49: *Nose, on the* (Said of things) disliked, offensive.
1944 Lawson Glassop *We Were the Rats* 273: 'One of them base wallopers ... He's on the nose.'
1946 Rohan Rivett *Behind Bamboo* 398: *On the nose*, ill-smelling, unsavoury, suggestive of dishonesty.
1953 Dymphna Cusack *Southern Steel* 138: 'The beer's on the nose and the plonk'd make a willy-wagtail fight an emu.'
1959 Dorothy Hewett *Bobbin Up* 42: 'It's on the nose alright. Stinks of bugs.' Ibid. 29: 'Gawd your language is on the nose Dawnie.'
1960 Nancy Cato *Green Grows the Vine* 46: 'You know, pongs. It means something's on the nose.'
1973 Frank Huelin *Keep Moving* 20: He removed his boots and the narrow strips of rag wrapped round his feet. 'By cripes! They're a bit on the nose,' said my mate, wrinkling his nose.
1974 *Australian* 12 Dec. 13: Australian singer Helen Reddy has become a naturalised U.S. citizen. In a small ceremony in a Los Angeles Federal court building this week, she renounced her Australian citizenship and swore everlasting loyalty to the Stars and Stripes. A bit on the nose, we think.
1982 David Combe *Bulletin* 5 Jan. 25: The swing against us in Bass was about 17 per cent ... We were on the nose, electorally speaking.
1983 *NT Times* (Darwin) 3 Feb. 7: Ever noticed how some of Darwin's street bins are a bit on the nose first thing in the morning when they should be empty?

note   A £1 note
1867 J. R. Houlding *Australian Capers* 131: 'Mr Buckles had not half a dozen notes (pounds) when he landed here three years ago.'
1885 *The Australasian Printers' Keepsake* 95: 'You'll easily pick up five notes a week.'
1899 George Boxall *The Story of the Australian Bushrangers* 191: Then the traveller would say that he was willing to pay 'a note' for their

recovery.
1923 Con Drew *Rogues & Ruses* 129: 'Where's the cow who's shook my 'alf-note?' he demanded.
1934 F. E. Baume *Burnt Sugar* 353: He took one look at the cheque and dashed for the 'phone. 'A hundred notes, Maise. A hundred notes.'
1942 Gavin Casey *It's Harder for Girls* 18: I gave mum a score of notes, and she bought a new outfit and went down for the wedding.

novel, the great Australian   see **Australian**

nuddy, in the   In the nude
1953 Baker 104: *nuddy,* nude, especially in the phrase *in the nuddy.*
1959 Dorothy Hewett *Bobbin Up* 42: 'Take your bloody clothes and quit standin' there half in the nuddy.'
1963 John Cantwell *No Stranger to the Flame* 15: 'Been swimming – in the nuddy and on me pat.'
1975 Xavier Herbert *Poor Fellow My Country* 116: 'You're not shocked by my bathing in the nuddy, are you?'

nugget *n.*   1   A lump of gold [f.*nug* a lump, a block; *nugget* a lump of anything EDD 1853]
1852 G. C. Mundy *Our Antipodes* iii 322: Gold was not so plentiful as was anticipated, – not to be picked up on the hill-sides in an afternoon's stroll; nor were nuggets* to be dug up, like potatoes, by the bushel. *The word nugget among farmers signifies a small compact beast – a runt; among goldminers a lump, in contradistinction to the scale or dust gold.
2   An unbranded calf
1882 Rolf Boldrewood *Robbery Under Arms* (World's Classics 1949) 21: So, as Jim had lighted the fire, we branded the little red heifer calf first – a fine fat six-month-old nugget she was   and then three bull calves.

nugget *v.*   1   To pick out nuggets of gold
1852 Lord Robert Cecil *Goldfields Diary* (1935) 31: He himself was snugly 'nuggeting' (picking out nuggets with a pen-knife or oyster knife) on his own behalf.
1857 F. Cooper *Wild Adventures in Australia* 103: The speaker ... had been there, nuggetted from the surface-rocks three ounces of the pure metal in two days.
2   To appropriate unbranded calves
1881 Mrs Campbell Praed *Policy and Passion* 25: 'It is said that she has an eye to business, and does not disdain nuggeting*.' *To *nugget*: in Australian slang, to appropriate your neighbours' unbranded calves. Ibid. 182: 'If he does steal a calf now and then, I know several squatters who are given to "nuggeting".'

nuggety   Stocky, thickset
1874 Charles de Boos *The Congewoi Correspondence* 141: He's just oner them short, square-built, nuggetty kinder fellers.
1887 *All the Year Round* 30 Jul. 67: A native of New South Wales is known as a 'cornstalk', because the men generally grow tall and thin. The opposite kind of build, short and thickset, is called 'nuggetty'.
1901 Henry Lawson 'Poisonous Jimmy Gets Left' *Prose* i 354: He was a short, nuggety man, and could use his hands, they said.
1924 Gavin Casey *It's Harder for Girls* 16: Molly was tall and dark ... The chap she got hold of was just the opposite, a nuggety, fair little bloke.
1969 Osmar White *Under the Iron Rainbow* 107: He was a nuggety little bloke and moved as if he could handle himself in a blue.

Nullarbor nymph   A semi-naked woman reported near Eucla in 1972
1972 *Sun-Herald* 2 Jan. 7: An Adelaide railway worker said today he thought the elusive 'Nullarbor Nymph' reported to have been seen hand-feeding giant kangaroos near Eucla, was his missing 27-year-old daughter ... She matched the description of the half-naked blonde reported to have been seen several times.
1973 *Australian* 31 Jan. 1: 'If,' he [Prince Charles] said at an Australia Day dinner, 'I've put my foot in it, I should probably be given a compulsory exit visa to the Antipodes and there find my name linked romantically (in the best traditions) with the naughty Nullarbor Nymph.'
1980 *Sydney Morning Herald* 31 Mar. 1: Sightings of the Nullarbor Nymph, a blonde girl who ran wild with the kangaroo, were reported widely here and overseas until the township of Eucla owned up to the publicity stunt.

numbers are up, when the   When the results of a horse race are declared, hence when some issue is resolved
1890 Tasma *In Her Earliest Youth* 349: 'Yes, we've got two', said George meditatively; 'and as for the family, it's the same as with everything else – you never can tell till the numbers are up.'
1920 Frank A. Russell *The Ashes of Achievement* 199: 'My guess is as good as his, before the numbers go up.'
1969 Mena Calthorpe *The Defectors* 181: 'You can expect a few sharp counter moves ... You'll be hard at it until the numbers go up.'
1982 Joe Andersen *Winners Can Laugh!* 123: The numbers were up and that's what the bookies pay on.

Nyoongar   A West Australian Aborigine (see quot. R. M. Berndt 1982); sometimes applied to those

293

who are not full blood

1845 E. J. Eyre *Journal* ii 396: Men or people Yoon-gar [Western Australia]

1959 K. S. Prichard *N'Goola* 24: *Nyoongar*: Black people.

1965 Colin Johnson *Wild Cat Falling* 10: Mum's always at me about this Noongar mob ... A few of them are as light coloured as herself [a half caste], some even as near white as me but most of them are pretty dark skinned. None of them are real aboriginal, though sometimes a full blood relative will drift in.

1969 Lyndall Hadow *Full Cycle* 157: 'Us all N-Yoongars.'[1] [1]Aborigine of south-west Australia.

1982 Jack Davis *Westerly* Dec. 114: A lot of my family is white, you know; I've got white grandchildren with blue eyes and fair skin and they call themselves 'Nyoongar', which means 'black'.

1982 R. M. Berndt in Jack Davis *Kullark* xv: At first European settlement there were probably at least 6,000 Nyungar people ... They occupied, roughly, all the inland and coastal country of the south-west of Western Australia, from a line drawn diagonally from Mullewa to the north toward Kellerberrin and south-east to a little beyond Esperance. The whole area was divided among about thirteen dialectal/language territorial units, later consolidated under the general label of *nyungar*, meaning 'man' or 'person'.

1984 *ANU Reporter* (Canberra) 27 Apr. 3: Archie [Weller] describes himself as an 'octoroon', being one-eighth Aborigine. But in conversation he uses the Aboriginal word 'Nyoongah', meaning 'people' or 'man', when referring to his mates and himself. He says this is considered more appropriate than the European title of 'part-Aborigine'.

oats, long   See quots

1964 H. P. Tritton *Time Means Tucker* 111: 'Long oats', as part of the bush vernacular, went out with the horse. If you went to a pub or a dance and left your horse tied up to a fence all night, you were said to be feeding him on long oats. Ibid. 110: 'I never let a mate's horse chew long oats, so I put 'em in the stable and feed 'em.'

Ocean Hell, the   Norfolk Island, as a place of secondary punishment in the convict system

1855 William Howitt *Land, Labour and Gold* ii 8: They are the vilest of the vile, the incorrigible, the refuse of the mass of convict scoundrelism, who are sent thither from Sydney or Van Diemen's Land to work in chains, whence Norfolk Island is styled the Ocean Hell.
1864 J. F. Mortlock *Experiences of a Convict* (1965) 67: The commandants preceding him [Maconochie] ... ruled with such injudicious severity, as to make the place well deserving its Australian name, 'The Ocean Hell'.

ocker   The uncultivated Australian, a term superseding **Alf** q.v.; the nickname of anyone called Stevens [A colloquial form of names like Oscar, made a generic term by a character called Ocker played in a series of T.V. sketches by Ron Frazer (see quot. 1975)]

1927 *Sun* (Sydney) 1 May 'Us Fellers' [comic strip in 'Sunbeams'] 1: 'And you know what I did to 'Ocker' Stevens at school on Wednesday don't you?'
1939 Kylie Tennant *Foveaux* 122: 'Will you get out of this, Okker,' Miss Montague requested irritably ... Oscar responded in brotherly fashion.
1948 Sumner Locke Elliott *Rusty Bugles* in *Khaki, Bush and Bigotry* ed. Eunice Hanger (1968) 60: 'I've been talking to some of the RSD blokes and Occa Stevens is going to be in it.'
1959 D'Arcy Niland *The Big Smoke* 185: 'Ocker White lost more than I did. Ocker White, he's got a lot to remember and a lot to forget.'
1971 George Johnston *A Cartload of Clay* 71: The big man would be a good player, a vigorous clubman, a hearty participant in the companionship of the club bar. He was a type Julian had sometimes talked to him about, what the boy called an 'Ocker'.
1974 *Sydney Morning Herald* 24 Apr. 6: That image, of the RSL itself as a sabre-rattling élitist organisation with an over-privileged influence on governments, and of RSL members themselves as beer-swilling, 'pokey-playing' Ockers, has, executives believe, faded if not totally evaporated.
1975 Ron Frazer *Sun* (Sydney) 20 Aug. 37: 'Back in the Ocker days, guys would come up to me in their thongs and shorts and with a can in their hand and say, 'Y'know, mate, I know a guy just like that Ocker character.'
1980 *Australian* 4 Sep. 14: There was a cheerful Ocker parading in front of the Pavilion [at the end of the Centenary Test] and shouting to the England team: 'We'll be back in another hundred years

mate – so look out.'
1982 *NT News* (Darwin) 25 Aug. 7: Traveller, arriving late at the airport to find the flight fully booked, was told by the cheerful airline worker: 'Sorry, ocker, the Fokker's chocker'.

ockerdom, ockerette, ockerina, ockerish, ockerism
1975 Max Harris *Australian* 18 Jan. 18: The resurgence of an aggressive Australian ockerdom was coincident with the first election of the Whitlam Government and the discovery of a 'new nationalism'.
1984 *Sun-Herald* 25 Nov. 7: Jeanne Little, the strident ockerette of Mike Walsh Show fame, has made it into the top people's handbook, Debrett's.
1975 *Sunday Telegraph* (Sydney) 27 Jul. 96: Ockerina of the week was surely the woman on the Eastern Suburbs bus, studying a race guide while slurping down a meat pie.
1979 *Sun-Herald* 24 Jun. 91: How typically ockerish. Next we'd be eating meat-pies.
1974 Peter Porter *Australian* 5 Oct. 13: The new Australian boorishness is known as Ockerism, from a slob-like character called Ocker in a television series – the embodiment of oafish, blinkered self-satisfaction.
1979 *Age* (Melbourne) 10 Jul. 2: Bull-necked and bullish, Jim Houghton has a wisecrack or natural ockerism for every occasion. Arriving late for our interview, my apologies were spurned by Mr Speaker: 'Aw, I know, ya been out chasin' them young birds.'

off like a bride's nightie   see **bride**

off one's kadoova, pannikin see **kadoova, pannikin**

off shears   see **shears**

office bike, the   see **bike**

offside   To act as an **offsider** q.v.
1883 Let. in Mary Durack *Kings in Grass Castles* (1959) 272: I have put up a yard on Galway since Uncle Jerry left. Pumpkin and Kangaroo offsiding.
1917 R. D. Barton *Reminiscences of an Australian Pioneer* 93: I met a black-fellow who was offsiding for the horse-driver, and was called Archie.
1920 Louis Esson 'The Woman Tamer' in *Dead Timber* 16: 'You couldn't get a job roasting peanuts. You couldn't offside in a fourpenny fish-joint.'
1954 Tom Ronan *Vision Splendid* 284: He could always offside for Block and Carlson on Big House renovations if there was nothing to do in the store or the office.
1960 A. W. Upfield *Bony and the Kelly Gang* 167:

Bony was asked to offside for Joe Flanagan, the settlement's electrician.

offsider   The assistant to a bullock-driver, walking on the offside of the team; a helper of any kind, in a subordinate position; an understudy
1880 Henry Kendall 'Jim the Splitter' *Poetical Works* ed. T. T. Reed (1966) 159: And, as to a team, over gully and hill, / He can travel with twelve on the breadth of a quill, / And boss the unlucky 'offsider'.
1903 Joseph Furphy *Such is Life* (1944) 229: 'That's jist the sort o' thing would put a hump on me. Sort o' off-sider for a gang o' Chinks! My word!'
1905 'The Old Bullock Dray' *The Old Bush Songs* ed. A. B. Paterson 6 and 8 note: They say there's no delay / To get an off-sider / For the old bullock dray. An offsider is a bullock-driver's assistant – one who walks on the off-side of the team and flogs the bullocks on that side when occasion arises. The work afterwards came to mean an assistant of any kind.
1910 C. E. W. Bean *On the Wool Track* 168: An 'offsider' ... is a gentleman who is learning bullock-driving, and who is allowed to try his apprentice tongue on the offside of the bullock team. The term is transferred to the assistant whom the cook must engage at a big shed.
1919 E. S. Sorenson *Chips and Splinters* 14: He was able to ride after bullocks and act as offsider at pinches for his father.
1920 Louis Esson 'The Drovers' in *Dead Timber* 39: 'They're going to give me a blanky Chow for an offsider.'
1930 Vance Palmer *The Passage* 262: 'My little spree's come to an end, Mick, so you'll have to pick up another offsider.'
1953 *Caddie A Sydney Barmaid* 211: 'I'll get me offsider. He's outside in the cart.' He trotted outside, returning with a lad of about fourteen.
1962 Gavin Casey *Amid the Plenty* 196: 'They want a storeman ... Not a boss storeman to run it, just an offsider.'
1983 Arthur Cannon *Bullocks, Bullockies and Other Blokes* 120: When the team got stuck, or was crossing difficult country which demanded an extra pull, the offsider would go around and drive the bullocks from the offside. This, of course, was opposite to the bullocky, who would be on the nearside of the team, hence the name: 'offsider'.

oil   Reliable information, esp. in expressions like 'the dinkum oil', and 'the good oil'
1916 C. J. Dennis *The Moods of Ginger Mick* 87: Now that's the dinkum oil from Ginger Mick.
1919 W. H. Downing *Digger Dialects* 36: *Oil* News; information.
1922 Arthur Wright *A Colt from the Country* 126: 'That's Dreamy Dan's owner,' remarked Knocker;

'we'll get the oil in a minute.'

1934 F. E. Baume *Burnt Sugar* 346: 'You're O.K. That's why I'm giving you the right oil.'

1937 A. W. Upfield *Mr Jelly's Business* 145: 'You oughta 'ave come with me acrost to the pub when I gave you the oil.'

1946 *Coast to Coast 1945* 33: 'You better play a hand or two,' he said shortly, 'and get the oil about the place.'

1953 *Caddie A Sydney Barmaid* 179: Ivy gave me the oil about him. 'Better look out for the old ram, he walks in his sleep.'

1970 Richard Beilby *No Medals for Aphrodite* 279: 'I told ya, son. We're goin' to Crete. I got the good oil.'

1982 *NT News* (Darwin) 4 Jun. 7: We've got the good oil . . . that Humpty Doo school fete tomorrow is going to be even better than the first one.

oil rag, to live on the smell of an   Metaphor for the ability to survive on minimum food or income [listed as a characteristic Irish expression in P. W. Joyce *English as We Speak it in Ireland* (1910) 129] [**1893** Simpson Newland *Paving the Way* 228: 'I'd rather live on the smell of a greasy rag here than make millions in a climate like that.']

1900 Let. 28 Oct. in *Audrey Tennyson's Vice-Regal Days* ed. Alexandra Hasluck (1978) 125: The Germans are universally acknowledged to be the best colonists, they live on nothing – the saying is 'they live on an oiled rag', hardworking and so thrifty and keep a good deal to themselves.

1903 Joseph Furphy *Such is Life* (1944) 39: It is easier . . . to recognise the various costly vintages than to live contentedly on the smell of an oil rag.

1911 E. S. Sorenson *Life in the Australian Backblocks* 267: 'There was Bill Brown . . . livin' on the smell of an oil rag for years.'

1951 Dymphna Cusack and Florence James *Come In Spinner* 140: 'Oh, Bridie always could live on the smell of an oil rag.'

1963 O. Bonutto *A Migrant's Story* 13: An argument against the admission of Italians into Australia, was that they would undermine the Australian standard of living because of their frugality and ability to live on 'the smell of an oil rag.'

1977 Colleen Klein *The Heart in the Casket* 36: She would live on the smell of an oil-rag, she vowed to herself, smiling to remember the words that her father had used to describe a miserly acquaintance.

1983 Laurie Clancy *Perfect Love* 258: 'How are you going to support her? . . . She can't live off the smell of an oil rag, you know.'

Old Barn, the   see **barn**

old boiler   An air hostess (now a 'flight attendant') [f. Sir Reginald Ansett's description of air hostesses

on strike in 1975; and application of terms like 'chook' to women]

1975 *Courier-Mail* (Brisbane) 3 Apr. 5: Sir Reginald Ansett: 'A batch of old boilers. We can do without them' [heading]. It wasn't so much Sir Reginald's crack about hostesses being 'old boilers' that needled the girls, but his suggestion that they were 'glorified waitresses'.

1981 *Sunday Mail* (Brisbane) 5 Jul. 2: Those 'old boilers' stay as trim as ever . . . Any woman who has ever been an air hostess seems to have that special something about her. As if she's been to a very good finishing school.

1984 *Sydney Morning Herald* 9 Feb. 8: Does he call them 'old boilers', as Reg Ansett once described some of his air hostesses?

old boy, the   The penis

1972 Geoff Morley *Jockey Rides Honest Race* 172: 'Well what is it, your old boy fall off?'

1982 *Bulletin* 9 Mar. 96: I'll never forget the look on guests' faces in a Manchester hotel one night, when they arrived back to find a well known Australian player draped on a chaise-longue in the public lounge, having what is commonly referred to as his 'old boy' autographed by a member of the opposite sex.

see **old fellow**

Old Bus, the   Sir Charles Kingsford-Smith's name for his aircraft *The Southern Cross*

1934 *The Old Bus* [title of film directed by Jack Percival, screened at the Liberty Theatre, Sydney, Aug. 1934]

1980 *Australian* 20 Feb. 9: Construction will begin in a few weeks on a full-scale replica of Sir Charles Kingsford-Smith's most famous aircraft – the original Southern Cross – the 'Old Bus' in which he made most of his historic first flights.

old chum   The converse of **new chum** q.v. (quot. 1812)

1846 C. P. Hodgson *Reminiscences of Australia* 22: Remember it may soon be your turn to act the same part, and give an asylum and 'Bush' education to the 'New Chum'*. *'New Chum' in opposition to 'Old Chum'. The former 'cognomen' peculiarizing the newly arrived emigrant, the latter as a mark of respect attached to the more experienced Colonist.

1855 Raffaello Carboni *The Eureka Stockade* ed. G. Serle (1969) 13: I frequently saw horrid scenes of blood; but I was now an old chum and therefore knew what was what in colonial life.

1905 'The Squatter of the Olden Time' *The Old Bush Songs* ed. A. B. Paterson 108: And quaffs his cup of hysonskin, the beverage old chums choose.

1924 *Truth* 27 Apr. 6: *Old chum* Experienced person.

Old Dart, the   England [origin obscure]
1832 Pierce Egan *Book of Sports* cit. G. C. Ingleton *True Patriots All* (1952) 119: News has been received from London, of this extraordinary match, which excited exceeding interest amongst the sporting fraternity in the *Old Dart*.
1908 E. S. Sorenson *Quinton's Rouseabout* 206: Murty unexpectedly came in for something like £800 by the death of a distant and almost forgotten relative in the old dart.
1923 Jack Moses *Beyond the City Gates* 170: Bring it to the notice of those chaps with a bit of cash in the 'Old Dart'.
1941 Sarah Campion *Mo Burdekin* 89: 'Still as green,' interjected Dad, 'as a pommy straight from th' "Old Dart"!'
1953 *Caddie A Sydney Barmaid* 26: When he came out to Australia he decided to forget his relatives in the 'Old Dart'*, so he changed his name by deed-poll. *Slang term for England.
1962 Stuart Gore *Down the Golden Mile* 261: 'Gettin' too much of the good Aussie beer into you, instead of that warmed-up bilge water they sell in the Old Dart.'
1975 Xavier Herbert *Poor Fellow My Country* 1234: 'Even those you know have some degree of radicalism are identifying themselves with the Old Dart.'
1981 *Australian* 29: Sep. 20: Christie's . . . opened up down under back in 1969, a mere 203 years after it started its operations in the Old Dart.

old fellow, the   The penis
[**1957** D'Arcy Niland *Call Me When the Cross Turns Over* 110: 'The day you're defenceless, sister, he said, that's the day me and the big feller are waiting for.]
1972 Dorothy Hewett *The Chapel Perilous* 61: 'When she takes off her clothes it'll make the ol' feller stand up.'
1983 Max Harris *Weekend Australian* 31 Jul. Mag. 14: Even if you flashed the old fellow, your trained Italian waiter would remain as unseeing as blind Samson.
1983 Clem Gorman *A Night in the Arms of Raeleen* 44: 'Chock-a-block. Old feller was in there, right up to the maker's name.'
see **old boy**

old hand   **1**   An ex-convict
1837 James Mudie *The Felonry of New South Wales* 180: The more knowing ones, – that is, the very worst characters amongst the convicts, – seldom undergo any real punishment at all . . . they bring out with them letters to some of the 'old hands' in the colony, so as to ensure their being applied for as assigned servants by persons of the *right sort*.
1845 C. Griffith *The Present State . . . of Port*

Phillip 76: The old hands are men, who, having been formerly convicts (or lags as they are generally termed) have become free by the expiration of their sentences.
1852 G. C. Mundy *Our Antipodes* i 93: A convict, *eo nomine*, is seldom mentioned in N.S.W. He is 'a prisoner of the Crown', an 'old hand', a 'government man'.
1865 Henry Kingsley *The Hillyars and the Burtons* 57: Now and then you will find a jail-bird who will, in appearance, pass muster among honest men; but in this case the word 'Old hand' was too plainly written on the face to be mistaken.
1901 Henry Lawson 'The Golden Graveyard' *Prose* i 324: Mother Middleton was an awful woman, an 'old hand' (transported convict) some said.
1934 Brian Penton *Landtakers* 17: Like many others in the room, he was an Old Hand, had done time for sheep-stealing.

2   Someone long established in a particular place or mode of living; a person of particular experience (quots 1843, 1848 could include ex-convicts, but would not be confined to them)
1843 John Hood *Australia and the East* 215: The *amor patriae* is strong among the 'old hands', as the fathers of the colony are called; but then it shows itself merely in the wish to sell their share of it for an enormous price!
1846 C. P. Hodgson *Reminiscences of Australia* 25: Having allowed your friend as the older 'hand', and therefore better skilled in bush eccentricities. n. 'Hand' synonymous with Chum; not elegant appellations, but very significant.
1848 H. W. Haygarth *Recollections of Bush Life in Australia* 26: Upon hearing a party of what are called 'old hands' in the country talking together . . . a stranger might not unreasonably suppose that he was listening to a race of people who had forgotten their mother tongue, and adopted that of the devil in its stead.
1862 Arthur Polehampton *Kangaroo Land* 60: It was and is a constant source of ambition among 'new chums', especially the younger ones, to be taken for 'old hands' in the colony.
1916 Let. in Bill Gammage *The Broken Years* (1974) 116: My new men are all frightfully keen and anxious to get into a scrap – and I will admit that many of us 'old hands' are beginning to hanker after powder again.
1937 Ernestine Hill *Ports of Sunset* 41: Who will tell stories like that when the old hands are gone? Not the neat bank-clerks and motor salesmen of to-day I fancy.
1959 Dorothy Hewett *Bobbin Up* 149: Alice and Lil, both old hands, were all tidied up, waiting for the signal to switch off.
1963 Gunther Bahnemann *Hoodlum* 11: Warder Frankston was an old hand in houses of detention,

reformatories, and jails.

1978 Ronald McKie *Bitter Bread* 96: Some were old hands ... They knew how to dig a trench and square it to the eye, or how to handle a lathe or make harness.

old handism

1859 Frank Fowler *Southern Lights and Shadows* 15: The battle of 'old-handism' against 'new chumism' is not everlastingly waging in Victoria as it is in New South Wales.

oldie A member of the older generation [OED 1874]

1960 A. W. Upfield *Bony and the Kelly Gang* 168: 'The oldees can natter and gossip and tell tales.'

1972 Geoff Morley *Jockey Rides Honest Race* 210: 'Things are getting better, but it's a slow process. You've got to give us oldies a chance.'

1971 David Ireland *The Unknown Industrial Prisoner* 196: It was no joke to be forty-five with fifty not far away and them looking to get rid of the oldies.

old man Of exceptional size (from the term applied to the fully grown kangaroo)

1834 George Bennett *Wanderings in New South Wales* i 286: Many persons when alone are afraid to face a large 'old man' kangaroo.

1845 R. Howitt *Impressions of Australia Felix* 233: I stared at a man one day for saying that a certain allotment of land was 'an old-man allotment': he meant a large allotment – the old-man kangaroo being the largest kangaroo.

1861 H. W. Wheelwright *Bush Wanderings of a Naturalist* 4: In bush parlance, the old male kangaroo is called 'an old man'.

1903 Joseph Furphy *Such is Life* (1944) 122: A picaninny alternative, that, you say? I tell you, it proved an old-man alternative before it ran itself out.

1934 Archer Russell *A Tramp Royal in Wild Australia* 190: Central Australia was experiencing ... its usual climatic respite from days of blistering heat in an 'Old Man' sand storm.

old man, the The penis

1969 D'Arcy Niland *Dead Men Running* 284: He told her that just the look of her at times made the old man stand up like a brick chimney, and he hoped it would be the only thing ever to come between them.

see **old boy, old fellow**

Old People, the The Aborigines, esp. in a tribal state

1938 Xavier Herbert *Capricornia* 364: The elegant half caste nephew and heir had gone on walkabout with the Old People.

1959 Lyndon Rose *Country of the Dead* 94: He knew that he would never go back to live with the People.

1974 Donald Stuart *Prince of My Country* 4: Beyond the woolshed ... there are the humpies of the Old People, his mother's people.

Old Tin Shed, the see **Tin Shed**

Old Viceroy, the see **Viceroy**

on In agreement, willing to take part, often in the expression 'Are you on?' 'You're on' denotes the acceptance of a bet [cf. *on* adv. 13c OED 1812: having a wager on something]

1877 Rolf Boldrewood *A Colonial Reformer* (1891) 368: 'Anyhow, the odds are right. I'm on!'

1883 George Darrell *The Sunny South* (1975) 29: 'What do you say if we throw them into the fish pond?' 'I'm on!' 'So am I!'

1903 Joseph Furphy *Such is Life* (1944) 128: 'If each of you gives me a kiss, of her own good will, I'll promise not to tell. Are you on?' Ibid. 281: 'Failing the fulfilment of either double, the wager is off?' 'That's it. Are you on?'

1900–10 O'Brien and Stephens: *On* I am on, I am willing, I am game.

1916 Let. in Bill Gammage *The Broken Years* (1974) 160: We heard a wounded chap crying out, he was in 'No Man's Land' ... I said 'I'm on' so over the parapet we crawled.

1939 Kylie Tennant *Foveaux* 350: 'Are you on?' Herb asked impatiently as he began to remove his coat. 'I'll give it a go.'

1949 Lawson Glassop *Lucky Palmer* 89: 'I'll have a pony on it.' 'You're on,' said Lucky, turning to him with a beaming smile.

on one's ace see **ace**

on the castor see **castor**

on the grass See quot. 1941

1941 Baker 51: *On the grass* Free, at large. A criminal is 'on the grass again' after being released from gaol.

1962 Alan Marshall *This is the Grass* [book title]

on the grouter see **grouter**

on the improve see **improve**

on it sc. the liquor

1938 Eric Lowe *Salute to Freedom* 38: He knew how drink affected Brand, and he muttered to his wife, 'He's on it proper to day, mother.'

1945 H. M. Moran *Beyond the Hill Lies China* 105: For days, while he was 'on it' he did everything horrible except beat his wife.

1956 Patrick White *The Tree of Man* 141: 'It is him,' she said finally. 'It is that bastard. He is on it again.'

1968 *Coast to Coast 1967–1968* 157: 'You've got the shakes,' he said. 'Been on it, have you?'

on, it was ~ (for young and old) An expression for an outbreak of disorder, any general absence of restraint

1951 Eric Lambert *The Twenty Thousand Thieves* 258: Peter Dimmock bounded between the tents leaping into the air at every few paces and whooping: 'It's on! It's on for young and old!'

1955 John Morrison *Black Cargo* 77: 'A day come when some of our blokes in Sydney just put their coats on and walked off the job. It was on then for young and old.'

1969 William Dick *Naked Prodigal* 49–50: Just before closing time a brawl started when some bloke walking by spilt beer on Ackie so Ackie's young brother king hit him and the bloke's mate stepped in so Archie hit *him* – and then it was on.

1971 David Martin *Hughie* 106: He almost forgot about it until the evening of Sunday when the party was due and when, in Harry's words, it was on for young and old.

1979 *Bulletin* 10 Apr. 60: He picked up a bottle, and hurled it back into the crowd – and it was on again for young and old.

1984 *Sunday Independent* (Perth) 19 Feb. 63: As always seems to happen someone in the lineup just 'can't wait' and takes off before everyone else . . . and then it's on for young and old.

on your pat see **pat**

on a promise see **promise**

on tap see **tap**

on thirds see **thirds**

on the track see **wallaby track**

oncer See quot.

1976 *Sun-Herald* 12 Dec. 15: A 'oncer' is the term coined by politicians for those elected in a land-slide and can only expect to serve one term in Parliament.

one-armed bill-poster (milker), busy as a Extremely busy or harassed ['As busy as the devil in a high wind' Grose 1811]

1951 Dal Stivens *Jimmy Brockett* 214: I was as busy nowadays as a one-armed bill-sticker in a gale.

1971 Frank Hardy *The Outcasts of Foolgarah* 216: 'I'm in more trouble then a one-armed bill-poster in a high wind.'

1983 *NT News* (Darwin) 29 Jan. 21: Ask her if she's busy and likely she will reply: 'As busy as a one-armed milker on a dairy farm.'

one day of the year, the Anzac Day (25 April) commemorated as a public holiday

1945 Cecil Mann *The River* 149: 'As you all heard the Padre and Premier both say at the service, it is the one day in the year which we, with very great pride, can call our *own* Day.'

1962 Alan Seymour *The One Day of the Year* [play title]

1971 Frank Hardy *The Outcasts of Foolgarah* 211: A retired officer of high rank . . . out late celebrating the One Day of the Year.

1974 David Ireland *Burn* 115: I never went to a march on Anzac Day. I can always remember the kids that died up there in the slush . . . I don't have to wait for one day of the year.

one-roomed house, couldn't find a grand piano in a see **couldn't**

one them, to In two-up, to throw a head and a tail

1949 Lawson Glassop *Lucky Palmer* 168: The pennies hit the canvas. One jumped in the air, landed and lay flat. It was a tail. 'And he's – ' began the fat man. The other penny ran a few feet and stopped. It was a head. ' – one'd 'em!' finished the fat man.

ones, two The cry in two-up when the spinner throws a head and a tail

1911 Louis Stone *Jonah* 217: He set two pounds of his winnings, and tossed the coins. 'Two ones!' cried the gamblers, with a roar.

1925 Arthur Wright *The Boy from Bullarah* 17: Ronter possessed himself of the kip, and, placing the pennies upon it, spun them high into the air. 'Two ones.'

1951 Frank Hardy *Power Without Glory* 324: 'Two ones!' Rand said as the two pennies thudded down, one head and one tail showing.

1979 *Bulletin* 14 Aug. 36: If one head and one tail showed, then it was 'ones', meaning that the spinner must continue spinning until two sides showed together.

onion See quot. 1969

1969 *Sydney Morning Herald* 16 Jul. 13: When he had passed the circle of men, he knew an 'onion was going on' . . . The Court was told on Monday that the expression 'onion' meant a girl was available for sexual intercourse with two or more men.

1984 Brian Singleton *National Times* 30 Nov. 17: 'If the girl alleges the traditional on-i-on or onion as it is sometimes incorrectly pronounced, by a group of motor bike riders in a disused gravel pit after several hours of riotous drinking I suppose the spinsters will do [as jury members].'

onka 1 Finger: *rare* [rhyming slang Onkaparinga (place-name) = *finger*]
1975 *Bulletin* 26 Apr. 46: onka (short for Onkaparinga; finger).
1979 *Sun-Herald* 27 May 78: The tote clerk heard the bell ring for closing time, and slammed the window on his 'onkaparinga'.
2 An Onkaparinga brand blanket
1984 *Age* (Melbourne) 23 Mar. Weekender 10: You will need to have tested the thermos for leaks ... and shaken the summer's sand from the Onka.

onkus Disordered, out of action, gone wrong
1924 *Truth* 27 Apr. 6: *Onkus* Unpleasant; absurd.
1941 Baker 51: *Onkus* All wrong, incorrect; (of machinery) out of order.
1947 Norman Lindsay *Halfway to Anywhere* 84: He took a pull at it, adding: 'A bit onkus, but drinkable. Have a swig.'

Oodnagalahbi Imaginary place which is a byword for backwardness and remoteness, given currency in the Mavis Bramston show [? f. *Oodnadatta* and *galah*]
1969 *Sydney Morning Herald* 1 Dec. 6: Last night the show [Hard Day's Week] was firmly bogged down in Oodnagalahbi (may it be eaten by grasshoppers) and Dad and Dave and Mabel wore felt hats pulled down on their foreheads and cracked jokes about carpet snakes in the dunny.
1972 Geoff Morley *Jockey Rides Honest Race* 93: 'Fifty per cent of the Australian population only buy their newspaper to see if Nancy and Sluggo finally get married. The other fifty per cent want to find out who won the third race at Oodnagallabi.'
1981 *Canberra Times* 30 Jul. 15: Canberra was chosen for the premiere season of 'Centrespread' in an effort to qualify the film for this year's Australian Film Institute awards. It would have been better to have opened it in Oodnagalahbie, where it could have sunk without trace as it deserves.

open slather see **slather**

open, they were sc. the pubs (when times of business are prescribed by law)
1942 Sarah Campion *Bonanza* 19: It was eleven – 'they' were open.

Orchid, Blue see **Blue**

oscar Cash: *obsolescent* [rhyming slang from Oscar Asche (1871–1936) the Australian actor]
1919 W. H. Downing *Digger Dialects* 36: Oscar

Money.
1931 William Hatfield *Sheepmates* 161: 'Sit in, some o' yous that aint flyblown ... an' their I.O.U.'s is good, if there's no real Oscar about the joint.'
1942 Leonard Mann *The Go-Getter* 16: 'Get the oscar off Tom soon's I see him. He's honest.'
1959 D'Arcy Niland *The Big Smoke* 21: 'If you'd been fighting all those blokes in the ring you'd have more oscar in your kick now than the Prime Minister himself.'

O.T., the The Overland Telegraph line from Adelaide to Darwin
1898 A. B. Paterson *Bulletin* 31 Dec. 31: The Overland Telegraph ends at Palmerston and employs a large staff known as the O.T. men.
1933 F. E. Baume *Tragedy Track* 36: A telephone system as far north as Ryan's Well, 78 miles along the O.T.
1942 Charles Barrett *From a Bush Hut* 38: I followed the O.T. (overland Telegraph) down to the Alice, where I hopped the rattler.

Our Glad, Harbour see **Glad, Harbour**

out of the box see **box**

outback *adv.* Out in or to the regions remote from the settled districts of Australia
1875 Rolf Boldrewood *The Squatter's Dream* repr. as *Ups and Downs* (1878) 31: The whole party ... rode silently along the indistinct trail which led 'out back'.
1892 Henry Lawson 'In a Dry Season' *Prose* i 80: Somebody said to me, 'Yer wanter go outback, young man, if yer wanter see the country. Yer wanter get away from the line.' I don't wanter; I've been there. You could go to the brink of eternity as far as Australia is concerned and yet meet an animated mummy of a swagman who will talk of going 'out back'. Out upon the out-back fiend!
1898 W. H. Ogilvie *Fair Girls and Gray Horses* 125: I was travelling, weak and footsore, on a river road Out Back.
1930 Edward Shann *An Economic History of Australia* 125: They fenced paddocks which grew larger and larger as the carrying capacity grew lighter 'out-back' – where paddocks of 20 or 40 thousand acres are not rare.
1972 Ian Moffitt *The U-Jack Society* 122: 'His dream was to get some land outback.'

outback *adj.* Pertaining to the regions remote from the settled districts
1893 Henry Lawson 'Some Popular Australian Mistakes' *Prose* ii 25: We wish to Heaven that Australian writers would leave off trying to make a paradise out of the Out Back Hell.

1911 C. E. W. Bean *The 'Dreadnought' of the Darling* 99: Boundary riders on the out-back runs are seldom permanent hands – not because they are not wanted to stay, but more because the life is such that they are always ready for a change.
1935 R. B. Plowman *The Boundary Rider* 71: It was a peculiarly Australian outback community at Wooltana in its dependence and interdependence.
1943 Charles Shaw *Outback Occupations* [book title]
1958 Russel Ward *The Australian Legend* 95: Whatever the prime cause of outback drunkenness, there is no doubt that a traditional pattern of behaviour ... grew up very early among up-country workmen.
1962 Cynthia Nolan *Outback* 92: A quite erroneous opinion, generally held in the cities, is that wives on these outback stations are eager to have a visit from another white woman.
1984 *Australian* 4 Oct. 1: The plan, which is seen as a major electoral carrot for remote areas, will give regional television stations a say in the content of outback programs.

outback *n.*   The regions remote from the settled districts
1897 Henry Lawson 'The Bush and the Ideal' *Prose* ii 31: No one who has not been there can realise the awful desolation of Out Back in the ordinary seasons; few even of those who have tramped there can realise it.
1913 W. K. Harris *Outback in Australia* 1: There is no limit to the hospitality of the far Outback.
1932 Myrtle Rose White *No Roads Go By* 73: There are some very fine specimens scattered over that vast expanse known as the 'far outback'.
1944 C. Hartley Grattan *Introducing Australia* 57: Only in the far outback where cattle are chiefly run, do you get into unfenced country.
1958 Russel Ward *The Australian Legend* 68: There is substance ... in the traditional belief that the 'true' or 'typical' Australians were the men of the outback.
1966 Craig McGregor *Profile of Australia* 160: In the outback Australians have had to wrestle with some of the harshest physical conditions in the world.
1981 *Age* (Melbourne) 11 Jul. 13: While Australian doctors queue for highly-paid jobs in the Middle East, long-standing vacancies remain for medical staff at Aboriginal health centres in the outback.
outbacker
1913 W. K. Harris *Outback in Australia* 3: Another feature in the character of the Outbacker and the Bush-dweller generally, and closely associated with his hospitality, is his honesty.

outbackery   The conscious cultivation of 'outback'

values
1966 Tom Ronan *Once There Was a Bagman* 124: The phase of life, now sneered at by our pharisaical, suburban, scholarship-nurtured intelligentsia – 'Outbackery' they call it – has its intervals of excellence.
1971 *Bulletin* 14 Aug. 49: 'No violence, no sex, no self-conscious outbackery; the only complaint, the book is too short. [book review]
1984 *Bulletin* 17 Apr. 63: Studio B was filled with bales of straw, outbackery, bird noises and large photos of Hogan abseiling.

outer, on the   Not favoured to win, not given a chance; disliked, ostracized [? f. the outside track or the outer ground in racing]
1924 *Truth* 27 Apr. 6: *Outer, on the* to be poor; to be outside.
1926 J. Vance Marshall *Timely Tips for New Australians: To be 'on the outer'* To be penniless.
1928 Arthur Wright *A Good Recovery* 157: 'You told me yourself that you were the cause of my being on the outer.'
1944 Jean Devanny *By Tropic, Sea and Jungle* 97: He had been thrown on the 'outer' at the completion of a job for Cinesound Studios, Sydney, and with his few remaining pounds he had made his way north.
1953 T. A. G. Hungerford *Riverslake* 174: 'And you're on the outer for sticking up for him?'
1958 Thea Astley *Girl with a Monkey* 44: 'I'm already on the outer with this bunch. I can't afford to make a mistake.'
1966 Don Crick *Period of Adjustment* 77: 'Harold was engaged to another girl and I think his father took a dim view of him breaking it off. Puts me a bit on the outer at the moment.'
1970 Ivan Southall *Bread and Honey* 54: Warren had always been on the outer, like a stray dog, always getting pushed.

outside   Relating to the interior of Australia, beyond the settled regions near the coast (the **inside** country, q.v.)
1864 See **inside**.
1884 A. W. Stirling *The Never Never Land* 123: One talks of ... the wretched hut in which the manager of an outside station lives, as the 'house'.
1895 George Ranken *Windabyne* 216: We had not found it easy to learn much about the outside country, but the nearer we got to the actual frontier we found that information was the more difficult to get.
1901 Rolf Boldrewood *In Bad Company* 271: 'Why don't you go outside? ... I mean *real outside country*, beyond the settled districts, in Queensland, Western Australia, Kimberley – anywhere.'
1910 C. E. W. Bean *On the Wool Track* 47: The men who owned 'outside' runs before the drought,

and who own the same runs still, may almost be counted on the fingers.

1934 Brian Penton *Landtakers* 313: The valley, recently wasteland, is now only on the fringe of the vast 'outside', that ever-shifting, unknown, unconquered Never-Never.

over the fence   see **fence**

overland *v.* **overlanding** *n.*   To drove cattle long distances

1871 Marcus Clarke *Old Tales of a Young Country* 163: 'Overlanding' was a profitable and, withal, romantic occupation. Young men of spirit, wearied of the capital, and prompted by love of gain and adventure, purchased cattle and sheep in New South Wales, and drove them 'overland' to the 'New Orleans' of Colonel Torrens.

1923 Jack Moses *Beyond the City Gates* 119: When I met him first he was in charge of a mob, overlanding from the Gulf to Vic.

1971 Keith Willey *Boss Drover* 48: The big road trains have taken the work away from the drover nowadays but at one time overlanding cattle paid big money, provided you knew your job.

overlander   A man droving cattle over long distances, and so one of the more dashing of the bushworkers

1841 George Grey *Journals of Two Expeditions of Discovery* ii 183: The Overlanders are nearly all men in the pride of youth, whose occupation is to convey large herds of stock from market to market and from colony to colony.

1848 H. W. Haygarth *Recollections of Bush Life in Australia* 120n: An overlander is one who makes long expeditions from one colony to another with stock, either for the purpose of finding new pasture land on which to establish himself, or to take advantage of a favourable market.

1857 F. Cooper *Wild Adventures in Australia* 66:

The overlanders are the pioneers ... in taking large herds of cattle beyond the boundaries far into the bush, and finding a 'run' or tract of land, sufficiently well grassed and watered for their purpose ... and protect the cattle from the aggressions of the natives until other 'squatters', following in their tracks muster in sufficient numbers ... when the overlanders relinquish their charge, and with another herd repeat the process.

1863 Rachel Henning *Letters* ed. D. Adams (1962) 136: Two atrocious young 'overlanders', first-rate specimens of the free-and-easy Australia. They ... came up and shook hands patronizingly with Biddulph, who had never seen them before in his life, and ... turned out their horses ... so that they might make themselves comfortable here for some days.

1865 'The Overlander' in *The Queenslanders' New Colonial Camp Fire Song Book* 11: We steer up to the girls, that rig themselves with grandeur, / And while they sweat our cheques – they swear, they love the Overlander.

1907 Alfred Searcy *In Australian Tropics* 125: If a crowd of overlanders and backblockers happened to be present, things would be made lively.

1915 Vance Palmer *The World of Men* 39: An overlander who was travelling to some far river in the South to take charge of a mob of cattle.

1933 F. E. Baume *Tragedy Track* 85: The grave ... stands mutely to remind the overlander of the tragedy.

oyster, Kimberley   see **Kimberley**

Oz   Australia [abbr. of *Aussie*]

1981 Buzz Kennedy *Australian* 14 Dec. 2: They can say what they like about The Overseas ... but the Old Oz will do me.

1983 Leo Schofield *Sydney Morning Herald* 3 Sep. 31: Computer Customs check-in and plane spraying are unique to Oz.

P

pack, go to the The lapse into a lower state; deteriorate, fall into disrepute [listed by Partridge as a New Zealandism]

1915 C. J. Dennis *The Songs of a Sentimental Bloke* 94: I've sent the leery bloke that bore me name / Clean to the pack wivout one pearly tear. [? in error for 'sent packing']

1919 W. H. Downing *Digger Dialects* 26: *Go to the pack* Deteriorate.

1924 *Truth* 27 Apr. 6: *Pack, go to the* To fall away; to collapse.

1938 Francis Ratcliffe *Flying Fox and Drifting Sand* 245: I learned of areas which had gone completely to the pack, where man had given nature best, and the holdings had been abandoned one by one.

1948 Patrick White *The Aunt's Story* 267: 'I was devoted to 'is kids, Lilian and little 'Enry, though 'Enry went to the pack.'

1958 Gavin Casey *Snowball* 118: 'You wait till he gets a bit older. Them abos always go t' the pack.'

1963 Don Crick *Martin Place* 196: 'Things are goin' to the pack. If they get any shorter of work, they'll close down.'

1984 Ian Leslie *National Times* 20 Apr. 4: Susan Peacock was extremely attractive, she shone and had great appeal. But now she looks matronly, frumpish, she's gone to the pack a bit.

packapoo ticket see **pakapoo**

packing them, packing death Scared i.e. holding back nervous diarrhoea (Services slang in World War II)

1951 Eric Lambert *The Twenty Thousand Thieves* 132: 'He's packing them badly. He's quite useless.'

1959 David Forrest *The Last Blue Sea* 69: You know something, thought Ron Fisher, you're no good. You're packing them.

1961 Russell Braddon *Naked Island* 44: 'Who's panicking?' 'You are, son. Fair packing 'em, y' are.'

1971 David Ireland *The Unknown Industrial Prisoner* 132: 'They were packing the shits when he went off his head in the control room last time.'

1975 Les Ryan *The Shearers* 6: 'That bloke will be packing 'em all the way to the border.'

1982 *Sydney Morning Herald* 10 Jul. 12: Of course, girls would be 'packin' it', going down an aisle in front of about thirteen hundred people, including photographers and TV cameras, which would be a very nerve-wracking experience for any 17-year-old girl.

1983 *Sun-Herald* 24 Jul. 118: Some banks, long scared of competition, have been Westpacking death.

pad A track trodden by bullocks, horses etc.

1903 Joseph Furphy *Such is Life* (1944) 170: I found myself following a pad, and noticed the fresh tracks of the bullocks, mile after mile.

1910 C. E. W. Bean *On the Wool Track* 101: The pads he [the rabbit] makes going down to drink in the Darling River are in places two feet deep.

1935 R. B. Plowman *The Boundary Rider* 238: A

pad ran off the main track and branched to the right. The big horse followed it.
1942 Gavin Casey *It's Harder for Girls* 155: 'I was through a dozen times when the track was just a camel-pad'.
1959 Peter Ryan *Fear Drive My Feet* 187: We would go over a little-known and little-used pad straight across the mountains.
1964 Tom Ronan *Packhorse and Pearling Boat* 158: A main horse pad (bridle path, to you) led from the far end of this swamp.
1983 Arthur Cannon *Bullocks, Bullockies and Other Blokes* 104: Cattle have an inclination to follow a marked line, whether it be a rutted road, a plough furrow, or just a cattle-pad.

Paddington Bear affair Incident arising from the failure of Mr Mick Young to declare to Customs some items in his unaccompanied baggage in 1984, including a Paddington Bear toy
1984 *Sydney Morning Herald* 24 Jul. 1: With the so-called Paddington Bear affair (after one of the gifts in the luggage) coming on top of his leaking last year of a Cabinet decision on the expulsion of the Soviet diplomat, Mr Valery Ivanov, Mr Young will carry some lead in his political saddlebags in future.
1984 *Australian* 19 Oct. 8: The review of customs baggage declaration forms was still in progress in the wake of the 'Paddington bear affair', the Government's Senate leader, Senator Button, said yesterday.

Paddo Paddington, the Sydney suburb
1945 *Coast to Coast 1944* 163: 'Just down the road a piece I live, down in Paddo.'
1959 Dorothy Hewett *Bobbin Up* 15: Running downhill into the slummy rabbit warrens of Paddo and the Loo.
1964 Arthur Staples *Paddo* [book title]
1974 *Australian* 14 Aug. 3: Paddo gets a National Trust rating.
1982 *Sydney Morning Herald* 24 Feb. 13: Slice of Paddo history for sale ... The gatekeeper's lodge, once part of Juniper Hall at Paddington, one of Sydney's earliest grand mansions, is to be auctioned on March 5.

paddock Playing field
1978 *Australian* 3 Jul. 17: 'Hage is open season. Sure he's vigorous. The general opinion is to get him off the paddock and the game will be all right,' Glossop said.
1981 *Canberra Times* 24 Jul. 16: 'My doctor is a beaut and he is giving me great confidence in myself', he [Len Pascoe] said. 'I'm sticking to his guidelines and he promises me I'll be back on the paddock ready to go if I work along with him.'
1984 *Daily Mirror* (Sydney) 6 Apr. 85: Young set

the example for the team when it mattered most in the centre of the paddock.

paddock, heifer see **heifer**

paddock, the long see **long**

paddock, saddling see **saddling paddock**

paddock, wouldn't be seen (dead) with someone in a (forty-acre) An expression of extreme dislike [Australian version of 'not being seen dead in a ten-acre field']
1900 Henry Lawson 'Andy Page's Rival' *Prose* i 362: 'You needn't think you're goin' to cotton on with me any more after this! I wouldn't be seen in a paddock with yer.'

padre's bike, gone for a ride on the Jocular reply to any request for someone's whereabouts (World War II slang)
1953 *The Sunburnt Country* ed. Ian Bevan 129: 'He went mad and they shot him' is the routine answer to any superior seeking the whereabouts of a subordinate. An alternative version is that he has 'gone for a ride on the padre's bike.'
1968 Stuart Gore *Holy Smoke* 80: 'Shot through on the Padre's bike', she says to the rozzers when they show up.
1979 *Sydney Morning Herald* 16 Jul. 6: A popular phrase in the Services at that time [1944] was 'to shoot through on the padre's bike', meaning to go Absent Without Leave.
see **went through like Speed Gordon, went for a crap and the sniper got him**

Painter, Jack the see **Jack the Painter**

pakapoo ticket, like a Untidy, disordered: *obsolescent* [f. the difficulty in deciphering a Chinese betting slip]
[**1911** Louis Stone *Jonah* 92: He had come down early to mark a pak-ah-pu ticket at the Chinaman's in Hay Street.]
1951 Eric Lambert *The Twenty Thousand Thieves* 144: Henry opened Dooley's pay-book, the pages of which showed liberal sprinklings of the red ink in which fines and convictions were entered. 'What a pay-book!' he sighed. Dooley grinned. 'Like a pak-a-poo ticket,' he agreed.
1968 Stuart Gore *Holy Smoke* 86: 'You wouldn't have a clue where to start once you got a pen in your hand – your paper'd be marked like a paka-poo ticket!'
1972 Alexander Macdonald *The Ukelele Player under the Red Lamp* 227: His bi-weekly betting lists made an average pakapoo ticket look like a model of stark simplicity.
1975 *Bulletin* 29 Nov. 17: Senate elections,

because of the complexity of the system . . . are more in the nature of a pack-a-poo ticket.

1983 *Sydney Morning Herald* 3 Jan. 6: Pakapoo ticket to register a car [heading] The Department of Motor Transport's Application for Renewal of Registration of Motor Car would have to be the worst form designed by a bureaucracy. The numerous boxes, underlinings, bold printing, shaded areas and arrows do not really assist . . .

pan out   To 'turn out', yield results [f. the pan used in washing alluvial gold U.S. 1868 Mathews]

1898 D. W. Carnegie *Spinifex and Sand* 70: Plans so simple on paper do not always 'pan out' as confidently expected.

1908 *Australian Magazine* 1 Nov. 1250: 'Pan out' obviously comes from the old alluvial worker.

1911 Alfred Searcy *By Flood and Field* 78: The sun was low in the west as we wended our way back to camp, all hands being satisfied that the crabbing expedition had 'panned out' in rare style.

1928 Vance Palmer *The Man Hamilton* 146: 'If you don't worry about it, it's got a knack of panning out right.'

1959 D'Arcy Niland *The Big Smoke* 11: It doesn't pan out the way you've built it up for yourself.

pannikin boss   Someone with minor authority over his fellow-workers: *derogatory*

1898 Morris: *Pannikin-boss*, or *Pannikin-overseer*, n. The term is applied colloquially to a man on a station, whose position is above that of the ordinary station-hand, but who has no definite position of authority, or is only a 'boss' or overseer in a small way.

1907 Charles MacAlister *Old Pioneering Days in the Sunny South* 27: The cause of that rib-cracking journey was my sister's marriage to Sergeant Doyle, before mentioned, and I went along as a kind of country page, or 'pannikin overseer', on the journey.

1918 George Dale *The Industrial History of Broken Hill* 74: Some miles from Grassmere they met a pannikin overseer, who by some means conveyed the news of their approach to the station.

1926 J. Vance Marshall *Timely Tips for New Australians: Pannikin boss* A shift boss. A man in charge of a small gang of workmen.

1950 Gavin Casey *City of Men* 170: What a hell of a life, anyway, with a pannican boss standing over you all day.

1959 Dorothy Hewett *Bobbin Up* 72: All their unshakable distrust of the pannikin boss, the boss's man . . . the lowest of the low in a world where dog ate dog.

1969 D'Arcy Niland *Dead Men Running* 121: Father Vaughan seemed to project himself as no more than the mouthpiece of a pannikin boss of a

God who sounded like a brutal and violent pirate.

1983 Arthur Cannon *Bullocks, Bullockies and Other Blokes* 100: The owner was away and a foreman, or 'pannikin-boss', was in charge.

pannikin snob

1953 *Caddie A Sydney Barmaid* 41: My mother-in-law was a pannikin snob as my father would have said.

pannikin, off one's   Out of one's mind [variant of 'off his head', the pannikin being a familiar utensil to the bush-worker]

1895 Cornelius Crowe *Australian Slang Dictionary* 56: Off his pannikin, silly.

1899 Steele Rudd *On Our Selection* 107: 'I seen 'im just now up in your paddick, an' he's clean off he's pannikin.'

1904 Henry Fletcher *Dads Wayback: His Work* 13: 'Gamblin' takes 'em clean off their pannikins.'

1916 C. J. Dennis *The Moods of Ginger Mick* 126: 'Per'aps I'm orf me pannikin wiv' sittin' in the sun.

1934 Brian Penton *Landtakers* 383: 'He's gone raving off his pannikin in Sydney with the guts half crushed out of him.'

see **kadoova**

panno   Abbr. for **pannikin boss**: *derogatory*

1957 Tom Nelson *The Hungry Mile* 50: So we decided to follow the 'panno' and tracked her to the Australian Stevedoring Industry Board Office.

1960 Ron Tullipan *Follow the Sun* 31: 'I thought he might have been a panno. Perhaps it's only the panno blood makes him choose his drinking mates with such care.'

1965 Frank Hardy *The Yarns of Billy Borker* 24: Within a week [of having won the lottery], he jobbed the panno, snatched his time and bought an air ticket to gay Paree.

Panthers, the   1   The Penrith, N.S.W., Rugby League team [f. club emblem]

1976 *Sun-Herald* 9 May 68: Manly try blitz tames the Panthers.

2   The South Adelaide Australian Rules team

1979 *Advertiser* (Adelaide) 7 May 18: Panthers leap to the lead.

3   Wests, Q., Rugby League team

1979 *Courier-Mail* (Brisbane) 25 Jun. 15: Panthers on top [heading] A mighty defensive effort . . . took Wests to an upset 24–12 win over Rugby League premier Easts at Purtell Park yesterday.

4   Morningside, Q., Australian Rules team

1979 *Courier-Mail* (Brisbane) 2 Jul. 14: Panthers in upset win over premiers [heading] Morningside had a shock three-point win over Australian Rules premiers Western Districts at Hawthorn Park yesterday.

paper bag, couldn't fight one's way out of a   To

lack strength, fighting skill [also U.S.]
1918 N. Campbell and L. Nelson *The Dinky-di Soldier* 5: W'y, you can't fight yer way thro' a brown paper bag!
1936 A. B. Paterson 'The Shearer's Colt' in *Song of the Pen* (1983) 676: 'He can't hit hard enough to punch his way out of a paper bag.'
1941 Baker 28: *Fight one's way out of a paper bag, couldn't* To be a weakling.
1955 Alan Marshall *I Can Jump Puddles* 136: 'Skeeter couldn't fight his way out of a paper bag,' Joe asserted.
1963 A. W. Upfield *The Body at Madman's Bend* 62: 'Feller named Grogan wants to fight and he can't fight his way out of a paper bag, and everyone knows it.'
1974 David Ireland *Burn* 44: 'Billy, you're not worth a bumper,' Joe says. 'You couldn't fight your way out of a paper bag.'
1978 *Sunday Telegraph* (Sydney) 9 Jul. 128: Millions of women might fancy actor Robert Redford, but not Colleen McCullough. She greeted reports that Redford would play Father Ralph in the movie of The Thorn Birds with: 'I don't think Robert Redford can act his way out of a paper bag.'
1980 *West Australian* (Perth) 2 Apr. 7: 'You couldn't fight your way out of a wet paper bag ya fairy.'

paper yabber   see **yabber**

para   See quots [abbr.]
1967 John Yeomans *The Scarce Australians* 56: 'I used to be in pretty good condition for a para, you know, but I've gone to the pack now.'
1979 David Ireland *A Woman of the Future* 55: 'Hey, para!' Para was the word for paraplegic. Kids shouted it at football matches if someone missed the ball, or just for the sound of it.

paradise, the working man's   see **working man's**

parcel post   Epithet applied to the newly arrived and inexperienced, esp N.T. [see quot. 1946]
1931 William Hatfield *Sheepmates* 118: Hallett took charge of the three 'parcel post' men and showed them a bunk where they could deposit their belongings.
1946 W. E. Harney *North of 23°* 23: Young lads bursting with romance and itching to be out in the wide open spaces, would sign on in the cities to work on far inland stations. 'Parcel post men' they called them; that is, they were labelled and addressed to a certain place, and travelled as a parcel does in the mail.
1951 Ernestine Hill *The Territory* 431: 'Parcel post' was influence – a station manager, or a jackeroo from the cities, who might be the boss's nephew or going to marry his daughter ... 'He

come up by parcel post', they still say. 'He don't know nothin'.'
1974 *Australian* 28 Dec. 14: 'In the old days, no fences at all. You just went from one place to another, mustering. But everyone got lazy. All parcel post boys, new chums from the city.'
parcel-poster
1935 R. B. Plowman *The Boundary Rider* 151: 'A parcel-poster! What does that mean?' 'Up one mail an' down the next. The comp'ny what 'e's goin' up to work for gives blokes like 'im a job w'en they gets off the boat; and sends them up to work on one of their stations. Poor cows don't know w'at they're goin' to. A few sticks it out; but most of 'em don't. They gets off the train at Farina, goes up on the mail, finds out w'at the job's like, and comes down on the next mail a fortnight after. That's w'y they're called parcel-posters.'

Parra   See quots
1979 *NT News* (Darwin) 24 Nov. 14: *Parra*: A term to describe people from the western suburbs (derived from Parramatta).
1981 *Sydney Morning Herald* 19 Dec. 26: Western Suburbs foreigners are as loathed as a disease [at Palm Beach]: 'They should clean up the Parras, shoot them or something.'

Parramatta   1   A cloth originally manufactured in the gaol factory at Parramatta, N.S.W.
1826 James Atkinson *An Account of the State of Agriculture and Grazing in New South Wales* 131: The coarse woollens are known in the Colony by the appellation of Parramatta cloth, having been first made there.
1827 P. Cunningham *Two Years in New South Wales* i 46: The government gangs of convicts ... and the solitary ones straggling here and there, with their white woollen Paramatta frocks and trowsers.
1840 J. Pitts Johnson *Plain Truths* 54: There is at Botany Bay a very coarse cloth manufactory, it is termed Parramatta cloth, and is solely used for convicts' clothing, it is manufactured by Mr Simeon Lord, and is very cheap.
1843 John Hood *Australia and the East* 345: A fabric, called Paramatta cloth, much used in the clothing of convicts, is also made.
1846 C. P. Hodgson *Reminiscences of Australia* 30: Not in shirt and trowsers, but in polished boots and 'paramatta'* coat. *'Paramatta' a peculiar tweed, made in the colony and chiefly at Paramatta.
2   Parramatta gaol
1941 Kylie Tennant *The Battlers* 7: 'I went to Parramatta. I was in an' out up to the time I was eighteen.'
1951 Dymphna Cusack and Florence James *Come In Spinner* 269: 'Whether you done it for love or

for cash, you'll end up in Parramatta just the same.' ... 'If they stick me back in Parra, I swear I'll beat it again.'

1973 Jim McNeil *The Chocolate Frog* 10: In the midst of life we are in Parramatta. That is to say, in prison.

Parramatta wall A line of players running in feints and obscuring the flight of the ball, esp. as developed by Jack Gibson as coach of Parramatta Rugby League team

1983 *Sun-Herald* 21 Aug. 76: It happened again this week with claims of obstruction for a number of moves that involve the Parramatta Wall. The wall has been around for a number of years. Jack Gibson uses it at tap moves and with good variation.

parson, the flogging Rev. Samuel Marsden (1764–1838), noted for his severity as a magistrate

1983 *Sydney Morning Herald* 13 May 1: Justice Hope is a descendant of the redoubtable 'flogging parson' of Parramatta, the Rev Samuel Marsden.

pass in one's marble see **marble**

passage, saloon see **saloon**

pat, on one's Alone [rhyming slang for 'Pat Malone']

1908 *The Australian Magazine* 1 Nov. 1251: 'On my own' (by myself) became 'on my Pat Malone' and subsequently 'on my Pat' a very general expression nowadays.

1908 Mrs Aeneas Gunn *We of the Never-Never* 146: He travels day after day and month after month, practically alone – 'on me Pat Malone', as he calls it.

1916 C. J. Dennis *The Moods of Ginger Mick* 110: But torkin' straight, the Janes 'av done their bit, / I'd like to 'ug the lot, orl on me pat!

1920 Louis Esson 'The Woman Tamer' in *Dead Timber* 29: 'I can't live without you. It's lonely on your pat.'

1938 Xavier Herbert *Capricornia* 132: 'Who's paying?' asked Oscar. 'Abo Department?' 'Oh no,' said Lace lightly. 'I'm doing it on my pat.'

1959 D'Arcy Niland *The Big Smoke* 146: 'On the way he's got to make a bit of a call, so he leaves you on your pat in the car.'

1966 Don Crick *Period of Adjustment* 68: I asked him what was he doing now? 'Out on the Pat Malone. Second hand cars and spares.'

1981 *Australian* 7 Oct. 18: Was John Snow the most ferocious bowler he faced? ... 'I had probably as much trouble as anyone against him when we lost the Ashes in 1970–71, but I was not on my Pat Malone', he [Doug Walters] said.

Patch, Cabbage see **cabbage**

Paterson's Curse *Echium plantagineum* or *echium vulgare* (viper's bugloss), a spreading, blue-flowered weed [f. the Patersons said to have introduced it as a garden flower at Cumberoona, near Albury, c. 1880]

1905 J. H. Maiden *Agricultural Gazette of New South Wales* xvi 268: That 'Paterson's Curse' produces some feed is undoubted, but it is a smothering, rough, coarse plant ... the vernacular name 'Curse' shows what many people think of it.

1918 P. G. Gilder *The Farmers' Handbook* 795: Weeds proclaimed Noxious within Municipalities and Shires in the State of New South Wales up to May, 1917 ... *Echium plantagineum* (Paterson's Curse, or Purple Bugloss, or Blue Weed).

1978 *Sun-Herald* 10 Sep. 176: Grazing interests have been lobbying the Federal Government to wipe out Paterson's Curse, which they consider a threat. Now the honey industry has described it as a valuable honey and pollen source.

1982 Max Harris *Weekend Australian* 6 Mar. Mag. 4: What ... I don't understand is how, after rabbits, grasshoppers, Paterson's curse, and mice, this nation has come to be plagued by restaurant critics.

see **Lady Campbell, Salvation Jane**

patriotic six, the The six independent members of the Legislative Council of Van Diemen's Land (Charles Swanston, Michael Fenton, John Kerr, William Kermode, Thomas Gregson, Richard Dry) who in 1845 resigned their seats in protest against the Appropriation Bill, and were in 1848 reinstated by the Queen

1852 John West *The History of Tasmania* i 252: The cause of 'the patriotic six', as they were called, was eagerly espoused by the colony.

Patty Duke see **flogger**

pav Pavlova [abbr.]

1980 *Sydney Morning Herald* 4 Oct. 4: The big breakthrough from the board [the NSW Egg Marketing Board] is a never-fail pavlova mix. You open a packet, add water and whip like blazes. The technologists at the board assure me it's so easy that even a kid of six could get a perfect 'pav' every time.

1983 *Weekend Australian* 9 Jul. Mag. 20: The food ... included the best pav I've had in years (although the topping of kiwi fruit somehow departed from the WA theme).

payback Retaliatory action taken according to a tribal code, esp. in Papua New Guinea and among Australian Aborigines; the imitation of this in white society [Pidgin]

1929 Patrol report in Penelope Hope *Long Ago is Far Away* (1979) 103: The Ferimi natives had killed one of the Niai natives some time ago and the Niai people are waiting to pay back.

1978 *Weekend Australian* 28 Oct. Mag. 3: The threat is that all tribal injuries and deaths [in PNG] must be avenged; the Bible called it an eye for an eye; more prosaically, the tribesmen call it 'payback' ... This payback could take years and even decades to occur. For example, last year some tribal leaders have paid over 100 cassowaries, 70 cattle and about 1000 pigs to some tribes who suffered many dead on their behalf in a fight before the old tribal leaders were born.

1980 *Sun-Herald* 26 Oct. 11: Someone rang the police and the mob think it was me. The bricks – and the rest – are a payback.

1982 *NT News* (Darwin) 12 Mar. 4: Wilson, in evidence, said their lives had been threatened after they had interfered with a payback at the prison.

1984 *Age* (Melbourne) 19 Sep. 11: It is simply asking too much of human nature for people not to see Mr Wran's advertising switch as pay-back to Fairfax.

pay dirt, to strike (bottom on) To reach the object of one's search, achieve success [f. goldmining U.S. 1856 Mathews]

1892 Henry Lawson 'The Bush Undertaker' *Prose* i 53: He set to work to dig it [the grave] up, and sure enough, in about half-an-hour he bottomed on payable dirt.

1946 Kylie Tennant *Lost Haven* 331: Mr Cassell's party was the only one that approached anything like payable dirt.

1965 David Martin *The Hero of Too* 79: Neither ... [was] in a position to further his research. It was a pity, but not unexpected; a man did not strike pay-dirt at the first attempt.

1976 *Sydney Morning Herald* 15 Nov. 55: West Indies batsmen struck pay dirt aplenty at the SCG yesterday.

1982 *Sun-Herald* 1 Aug. 67: Bart's boy hits pay-dirt ... Anthony Cummings said he could not recall a better day for the stable since they switched operations from Melbourne.

pea, the The one likely to emerge as the winner in a competition; the person in a favoured position; the person in a position of authority [Partridge lists *pea* The favourite; one's choice: low: 1888]

1911 Edward Dyson *Benno, and Some of the Push* 206: Mr Dickson ... ran his eye down the card and chanced it. 'Dandy's the P,' he said. 'Put yer whole week's wash on Dandy, 'n' hold me responsible if the goods ain't delivered.'

1953 Baker 118: Other expressions used by racing fans include *pea*, a horse that is being ridden to win, especially when there is doubt about the genuineness of other runners.

1958 Frank Hardy *The Four-Legged Lottery* 190: 'I've got the tip about it. Old Dapper Dan earwigged at the track. Swordsman is the pea.'

1969 Mena Calthorpe *The Defectors* 17: 'For the time being, I'm satisfied.' 'You're the pea,' Mick said.

1973 Alexander Buzo *Rooted* 92: 'He's had his eye on her for some time, you know, but I'm the pea, she said.'

1974 *Sun-Herald* 1 Sep. 15: The usual assumption has been that the Social Security Minister, Mr Hayden, 41, would move into the Treasury ... Recent events have cast some doubts on that. The Deputy Prime Minister and Overseas Trade Minister, Dr Cairns, now seems the 'pea' for any change at the Treasury.

1982 *Sunday Mail* (Brisbane) 31 Jan. 2: We still think Eddie Kornhauser and Sir Leslie Thiess are the peas for the casino licences.

pea, on the Deranged (like cattle driven mad by eating the Darling pea q.v.)

[**1864** Rachel Henning *Letters* ed. David Adams (1963) 180: Biddulph showed him the poison plant that grows in the desert between here and the Flinders and which killed so many of our sheep ... The sheep went quite mad after eating it. It is a pretty shrub with whitish leaves and a crimson pea-shaped blossom.]

1903 Joseph Furphy *Such is Life* (1944) 288: 'Ill-natured, cranky beggar, Alf is – been on the pea – but there's no end of grass in his paddock.'

1908 Giles Seagram *Bushmen All* 224: 'He's got the Darling Pea right enough. Mad as a hatter.'

1932 'Bushman's Farewell to Queensland' *Old Bush Songs* ed. Stewart and Keesing (1957) 200: There's poison grass and Darling peas / Which drive the cattle raving mad.

peastruck

1981 Eric Rolls *A Million Wild Acres* 111: It [Darling Pea] is not only poisonous but addictive and does not provide enough nourishment to support life. Pea-struck animals eat nothing else. They lose condition rapidly. Their gait changes to a high-stepping stagger and their expressions to a fixed stare.

peacock 'To peacock a piece of country means to pick out the eyes of the land by selecting or buying up the choice pieces and water frontages, so that the adjoining territory is practically useless to anyone else.' (Morris 1898)

1916 Macmillan's *Modern Dictionary of the English Language* 793: *peacocking* The selection and purchase of the best and most conveniently situated lands in a district, *esp.* those which give access to a stream, the object of this land-grabbing process being to render the other areas of little or no value.

1930 Edward Shann *An Economic History of Australia* 194: The pre-emptive right ... certainly gave effective power to buy the 'eyes of the land' – to 'peacock' the country as this was called.

1938 *Smith's Weekly* 3 Apr. 1: The story of Italian infiltration into Queensland and the 'peacocking' of the rich irrigation lands of the Murrumbidgee (N.S.W.) by Mussolini's colonists has been revealed by *Smith's Weekly* as it has happened.

1982 Humphrey McQueen in *A Bunyip Close Behind Me* by Eugénie McNeil v: It would be possible to produce a sparkling review by peacocking all the best anecdotes.

peacocks flying out of one's backside see **sparrows**

peanut, the flying see **flying**

pea soup, if it was raining see **raining**

pebble An indomitable or incorrigible man or beast: *obsolescent*

1842 *The Hobart Town Courier and Van Diemen's Land Gazette* 4 Feb. 3: 'I say, Bill,' began a mysterious and surly-looking fellow, '*he* died game, and no mistake!' 'Yes, Jim,' returned the other, on whose brow the propensity for destructiveness was strongly indicated, though perhaps deficient on his cranium, 'now *didn't* he die a pebble!'

1870 Marcus Clarke *His Natural Life* ed. S. Murray-Smith (1970) 627: 'You're not such a pebble as folks seem to think,' grinned Frere.

1876 Rolf Boldrewood *A Colonial Reformer* (1890) 49: We had an old blue half-bred buffalo cow and her son, a four-year-old black bullock ... He was a regular pebble.

1916 C. J. Dennis *The Moods of Ginger Mick* 114: They wus pebs, they wus narks, they wus real naughty boys.

1941 Baker 53: *Pebble* A person (occasionally an animal) hard to control. (2) A larrikin, a street tough.

pebble, game as a Courageous, with staying-power (often of horses): *obsolescent*

1893 K. MacKay *Outback* 188: Cabbage Tree Ned is as game as a pebble, and may try to dash through in spite of us.

1895 A. B. Paterson 'The Open Steeplechase' *The Man from Snowy River* 72: But they both were game as pebbles – neither one would show the feather.

1906 K. S. Prichard *The New Idea* 6 Jul. 45: He's firm and upright on his old grey nag, and game as a pebble.

1918 C. Fetherstonhaugh *After Many Days* 223: Traveller was game as a pebble, and he just passed Quadrant on the post and no more.

1974 Donald Stuart *Prince of My Country* 166: 'He was hard as nails and as game as a pebble.'

Peckers The Woodville (S.A.) Australian Rules team [abbr. of *Woodpecker*]

1979 *Advertiser* (Adelaide) 4 Apr. 26: Pecker coach likely to play [heading] Coach Barry Goodingham is likely to lead Woodville on Saturday.

pee in the same pot, to Feminine equivalent of 'to piss in each other's pockets' q.v.: to be on terms of great familiarity

peewee, couldn't pull the tail out of a see **couldn't**

pelican shit, a long streak of Applied to anyone exceptionally tall; an expression given currency from occurring in the film *Gallipoli* (1981) scripted by David Williamson

1973 Alexander Buzo *Norm and Ahmed* in *Three Plays* 12: 'Tall bloke, he was. A long thin streak of pelican shit.'

1982 *Sydney City Monthly* Jun. 30: One of his [Alex Buzo's] favourites was overheard in a pub: *He's like a long streak of pelican shit.*

1984 *Sydney Morning Herald* 16 May 10: 'Logie lips', [Graham] Kennedy called him [Ross Symonds], 'a long, tall streak of Pelican ... er ... deliciousness.'

People, the Old see **Old**

perenty A large goanna, *Varanus giganteus* [Ab.]

1889 Ernest Giles *Australia Twice Traversed* ii 8: We saw ... one of those very large iguanas which exist in this part of the country. We had heard tales of their size and ferocity from the natives near the Peake (Telegraph Station). I believe they call them Parenties. The specimen we saw today was nearly black, and from head to tail over five feet long. I should very much have liked to catch him; he would make two or three good meals for both of us.

1946 W. E. Harney *North of 23°* 80: I listened wide-eyed to his tales of 'parintis', giant monitor lizards, that would attack a man.

1951 Ernestine Hill *The Territory* 27: The Territory is a land of lizards, from the friendly gecko ... to eight-foot *prenti* of the g.w. spaces, galloping like a brumby, nearly a Komodo dragon.

1959 Lyndon Rose *Country of the Dead* 27: Unda was stalking Cranky Jimmy, just as he might have stalked an emu or a perentie.

1978 Osmar White *Silent Reach* 203: Mary Dalziel walked out of the stringbark scrub ... dragging a dead perenty lizard.

1983 G. E. P. Wellard *Bushlore* 114: This particular bungarra was what is known as a perenty. They can grow about eight feet long ... they have very sharp, long, claws and a good set of teeth and know how to use both.

Peril, the Yellow see **Yellow**

perish (perisher), to do a To come near to death, esp. from lack of water or food; to suffer any kind of deprivation or ordeal
[**1882** Rolf Boldrewood *Robbery Under Arms* (World's Classics 1949) 499: He was as sober as a judge between one burst and another ... Then he most times went in an awful perisher – took a month to it, and was never sober day or night the whole time.]
1894 *The Argus* 28 Mar. 5: When a man or party has nearly died through want of water, he is said to have 'done a perish.' [Morris]
1899 Henry Lawson 'Pursuing Literature' in Australia' *Prose* ii 113: Did a three-months' unemployed 'perish', and then went with a mate to a sawmill in the Hutt Valley.
1910 Henry Lawson 'A Tale with Horns' *Prose* i 714: 'It was cold 'n' I did a perish because I'd come without me big coat.'
1929 K. S. Prichard *Coonardoo* 60: 'We near done a perish for water.'
1934 Archer Russell *A Tramp-Royal in Wild Australia* 223: 'You'd a done a perisher ... but for him.'
1955 Mary Durack *Keep Him My Country* 281: 'A man could do a perish before anyone would know. I'd like a quid for all the blokes I buried on that track.'
1961 George Farwell *Vanishing Australians* 160: Wells lost consciousness and had to be nursed along to camp. On a second sortie, Bejah, in his turn, nearly did a perish.
1979 Dorothy Hewett *The Man from Mukinupin* 45: 'He hasn't been right since he did that perish in the desert.'

permanents, the The Permanent Building Societies
1972 *Sydney Morning Herald* 11 Aug. 12: An analysis of the record of the 'permanents' show that in June 1971, already one in every 14 people in NSW had an account with a society.

perv *n.* **1** A pervert [abbr.]
1949 Ruth Park *Poor Man's Orange* 38: 'That dirty old cow, always making up to kids ... Merv, Merv, the rotten old perv.'
1959 Eric Lambert *Glory Thrown In* 18: 'He was a perv. Special attention given to small boys.'
1961 Patrick White *Riders in the Chariot* 399: 'Hannah ... took an intelligent interest in the private life of any perv. The old whore would

nearly pee herself watching a drag act in some of her own clothes.
1967 B. K. Burton *Teach Them No More* 139: 'Stand up, you two bloody pervs,' he was saying, pointing at Terry and his friend.
1976 Gwen Kelly *The Middle-Aged Maidens* 48: 'Such lovely masculine Arab-type men. I'm a real perv. about Arab-type men.'
1980 Murray Bail *Homesickness* 161: 'Should always lock the door ... You can get any perv coming in.'
2 Someone given to 'perving'; the act of 'perving'
1963 John Cantwell *No Stranger to the Flame* 15: 'Never even saw him. Might have been a spook.' She did up the top button on the green blouse. 'Even spooks like a bit of a perv.'
1974 Keith Stackpole *Not Just for Openers* 38: After the next ball had been bowled, the blokes' heads would turn around unobtrusively so they could have a 'perv' at a bird in a mini-skirt walking down the aisle.
1980 Patrick White *Sydney Morning Herald* 20 Sep. 11: I remember hearing Sydney ladies who had gone to ingenious trouble and considerable expense to smuggle Nabokov's classic satire into Australia – to enjoy a perv – afterwards protesting with disgust: 'It's so boring you can't read it.'

perve *n.* To act as voyeur; to observe and relish the female form or the intimacies of others
1944 Lawson Glassop *We Were the Rats* 183: 'Doing a bit of perving again?' I asked, looking at the gallery of nudes he had gathered from all sorts of magazines.
1962 David Forrest *The Hollow Woodheap* 153: He had ... sunglasses on, through which he was making a careful inventory of every bikini-clad female ... 'Well,' said Paddy reasonably, 'if you're going to perv, you might as well be honest about it.'
1970 Patrick White *The Vivisector* 233: 'You're a kind of perv perving on people even on bloody rocks!'

peter **1** A till, cash register (thieves' slang) [f. *peter* a portmanteau or trunk OED 1668]
[**1812** Vaux: *Peter* a parcel or bundle, whether large or small; but most properly it signifies a trunk or box.]
1895 Cornelius Crowe *The Australian Slang Dictionary* 57: Peter a till.
1924 *Truth* 27 Apr. 6: *Peter* Cash box.
1944 Randolph Bedford *Naught to Thirty-three* 171: 'Looking Glass Fred', whose speciality was 'Peter touching'; which is the vulgate for robbing tills.
1950 *Australian Police Journal* Apr. 119: *Tickle the peter* To embezzle or steal funds, usually by the servant of an employer.
1957 Judah Waten *Shares in Murder* 100: He

simply did not like investigating rich men, respectable citizens ... even bank clerks who had obviously 'tickled the peter' as the saying went.
1964 Tom Ronan *Packhorse and Pearling Boat* 93: 'His sentence wasn't much more than would be handed out to some bloke on the bottle, who tickled the Peter in somebody's store.'
1983 James McQueen *Uphill Runner* 68: 'I've been tickling the peter, and I'm into my trust funds for about sixty thousand.'
2   The witness box
1895 Cornelius Crowe *The Australian Slang Dictionary* 56: *Peater* the witness box.
1958 Vince Kelly *The Greedy Ones* 14: 'Mounting the peter. Going into the witness box.'

phantom broadcast, meeting   Simulation of an 'actuality' broadcast, with studio effects, like the 'synthetic' broadcasts of Test cricket in England by the A.B.C. in 1934; other sporting fixtures conducted on similar principles
1975 *Sun-Herald* 26 Jan. 58: Many people will remember the 'phantom' fight description of 1946 when Vic Patrick and Tommy Sands were contesting the welter-weight championship at Sydney Stadium. Permission to broadcast the fight direct was refused, and ... from a small cottage near the stadium, Clif Carey staged his amazing 'phantom' broadcast. Inside the stadium, Bill Delaney made punch-by-punch notes, which were rushed to Garth Carey, Allan Toohey and others to Clif at the cottage ... Sound effects were fed in from the studio.
1983 *NT News* (Darwin) 4 Jan. 23: Yesterday, the first of nine phantom meetings to be held by the Darwin Turf Club during the current racing season was a qualified success ... Admission was free with all services operating including seven bookmakers who reported satisfactory holdings in the circumstances [i.e. betting on races interstate, in the absence of any actual races on the course.]

Phar Lap   An improvised bush delicacy: N.T. [name of race horse]
1951 Ernestine Hill *The Territory* 426: They specialized in 'Phar Laps', wild dog with the hair burnt off, trussed and cooked in the ashes.

piano player in a brothel   Someone implicated in an activity, but accepting no moral responsibility for it [also U.S.]
1972 *Hansard* 21 Sep. 1741: Mr Bury: Have the trade union leaders paid any more than lip service to decrying violence? Have they taken any effective action, or have they adopted the general, traditional attitude of the man playing the piano on the ground floor of the brothel and affecting neither to know nor care what goes on upstairs?
1977 Fred Daly *From Curtin to Kerr* 90: 'Well',

replied Wentworth, 'if you don't know what is happening in Victoria you are like a pianist in a brothel, you do not know what is happening upstairs.'
1981 *Weekend Australian* 4 Apr. Mag. 20: Robert Hughes, art critic for *Time* magazine, who's been back on homeground for a month promoting his book on modern art, *The Shock of the New*: 'I'm just the piano player in the whorehouse of art.'

Piccadilly bushman   See quots
1941 Baker 53: *Piccadilly bushman* A wealthy Australian who lives (or lived) in the West End of London.
1961 Ray Lawler *The Piccadilly Bushman* [play title]

piccaninny   Tiny, little [a West Indian term for a child (OED 1657) applied to Australian Aboriginals]
1833 G. F. Moore *Diary of ... an Early Settler in Western Australia* (1884) 203: He at once understood me, and said 'piccany cow? yes! yes! yes!' and seemed quite satisfied.
1844 Let. 6 Nov. cit. *No Place for a Nervous Lady* ed. Lucy Frost (1984) 167: The blacks still say as they said the last flood, 'this is only piccaninny – big one coming.'
1870 W. M. Finn *Glimpses of North-Eastern Victoria* 29: If any of the Coburglars or Merrivillains from Pentridge Stockade ever escape to Rutherglen, I would not give much for the safety of this 'Piccaninny Bank.'
c. **1905** Joseph Furphy *The Buln-Buln and the Brolga* ed. R. G. Howarth (1948) 107: 'Blackfellers mostly goes in for a piccaninny fire – jist three sticks, with the ends kep' together.'
1975 *Sydney Morning Herald* 15 Sep. 1: 'Nambawan pikinini b'long Misis Kwin' is the pidgin English term for his [Prince Charles'] position as first son of the Queen and heir apparent to the throne.

piccaninny dawn (light)   The approach of dawn, first light
1848 W. Westgarth *Australia Felix* 104: Great numbers were mustering from the surrounding country, and ... the hut would be attacked before 'piccininni sun'.* *About daylight in the morning.
1903 Randolph Bedford *True Eyes and the Whirlwind* 321: By pickaninny daylight, the mounted men were in motion, and Quinn and his camel went with them.
1933 R. B. Plowman *The Man from Oodnadatta* 9: 'Picaninny daylight, Dick!' ... While the stars paled before the approaching dawn, the white man lit the fire and prepared breakfast.
1945 Tom Ronan *Strangers on the Ophir* 12: That first pale flush of dawn which the bushman calls

'Piccaninny daylight' showed in the eastern sky.
1958 Gavin Casey *Snowball* 125: He was up before the piccaninny dawn, and in the first gentle glow of it he slid out of the house on his bare feet.
1970 Richard Beilby *No Medals for Aphrodite* 219: It was almost dawn, the 'piccaninny daylight' of the Big Country back home.
1983 *Weekend Australian* 30 Jul. Mag. 3: After a while there is a slight paling of the eastern sky. 'Piccaninny dawn', R.M. says.

pick the eyes out   see **eyes**

pick a seat at the pictures, couldn't   see **couldn't**

pick handle   As for **axe handle** q.v.
1979 *Sun-Herald* 11 Mar. 93: He was just over six feet tall, about three pick handles across the shoulders and had muscles on the muscles in his arm.

picker-up   A shed-hand, lower in the hierarchy than the shearer, who gathers the fleece after it has been shorn
1870 Rolf Boldrewood 'Shearing in Riverina' *Town and Country Journal* 12 Nov. 13: The wool-press-men – the fleece-rollers – the pickers-up – the yarders – the washers' cooks – the hut cooks ... paid off.
1892 G. L. James *Shall I Try Australia?* 99: The 'picker-up' stands over the filmy looking rug which lies in a heap on the floor, gathers it up deftly, and bearing it to the table, flings it neatly out full length, with the cut side downwards.
1901 Rolf Boldrewood *In Bad Company* 454: the shearers proper are all white men. The pickers-up and sorters of the fleece are a trifle mixed, the former being chiefly aboriginal blacks, some of the latter Chinamen.
1910 C. E. W. Bean *On the Wool Track* 166: The rouseabouts, the pickers-up, and sweepers, and tarboys, and the rest are paid by the day ... the shearers ... are not being paid when not shearing.
1964 H. P. Tritton *Time Means Tucker* 40: Pickers-up took the fleece as it fell on the 'board' (shearing floor) and spread it skin-side down on the wool table.

picnic   A troublesome experience [f. *picnic* used ironically]
1898 Morris *Picnic*, n. Besides the ordinary meaning of this word, there is a slang Australian use denoting an awkward adventure, an unpleasant experience, a troublesome job.
1906 A. J. Tompkins *With Swag and Billy* 69: Decent grassland is scarce where this sort of country is pressed into service, and what a picnic it must be to muster.
1945 Baker 263: We call a wild confusion or a particularly difficult task a *picnic*.
1952 A. G. Mitchell Supplement to Chambers' *Shorter English Dictionary* 801: *picnic* an awkward situation: a troublesome happening or accident: a to-do, hullabaloo, mess-up.
1955 D'Arcy Niland *The Shiralee* 38: 'All I know is I'm going to have one helluva picnic if she doesn't find it.'
1959 Nancy Cato *Time, Flow Softly* 122: 'She's going to be a picnic, this trip. You'll be seeing the river just about at its worst.'

picnic races   Race meetings held in country areas, and regarded as a social occasion
1896 Nat Gould *Town and Bush* 224-5: Picnic race-meetings are got up in various parts of the country. These meetings are for amateur riders only ... The owners of the horses running at picnic races are generally men of means.
1911 C. E. W. Bean *The 'Dreadnought' of the Darling* 294: Up country they seem to judge their towns by two infallible criteria. If a town has picnic races or a polo week, it is 'alive'. If it has not, it is 'dead'. The population for many miles around spends these weeks in town – generally there are several dances as well.
1939 Miles Franklin *All That Swagger* 470: She was ... familiar to the public through the pictures of her ... leading-in her father's winners at picnic races.
1941 Kylie Tennant *The Battlers* 149: The hotel was crowded with the *élite* who had come into town for the week of the picnic races.
1962 Dymphna Cusack *Picnic Races* [novel title]
1972 *Sunday Telegraph* (Sydney) 15 Oct. 132: And what is the big event? Why everyone, but everyone, is getting ready for the Bong Bong Picnic Races next Saturday. Mr Richmond assures us it's 'a very, very toney' event. 'We get our young socialites stalking around with woolly terriers,' he said.

pie-eater (biter)   Someone who is 'small-time', of little account (? living on meat pies instead of proper meals): *derogatory*
1911 Edward Dyson *Benno, and Some of the Push* 144: 'Little Benny's frenzy when the game got goin' would freeze yer blood. He was that angry with the South pie-biters, he didn't care what 'appened to 'em, 'n' the way he screamed at the doomed wretches...'
[**1922** Arthur Wright *A Colt from the Country* 122: 'They're meat-pie bookies, all right,' he exclaimed displaying a bunch of tickets. 'Had to make four bets of it.']
1949 Lawson Glassop *Lucky Palmer* 96: 'The trouble is, Mr Hughes, you're too good for the pie-eating bookmakers round these parts. You bet too well for them, Mr Hughes.'

1953 Baker 134: *pie-eater* (or *cruncher*) A small-time crook. [in prison slang]

1953 Kylie Tennant *The Joyful Condemned* 166: 'He's one of those big he-men that go sneaking around the park waiting to switch some chromo's hand bag. Just a pie-eater.'

1958 Frank Hardy *The Four-Legged Lottery* 176: 'Look at 'em. Here, out on the Flat, on the Hill, even in the members' enclosure. Pie and tomato sauce. Gravy running down one side of the sleeve, sauce down the other. Leaning forward away from the wind . . . A nation of bloody pie-eaters.'

1975 Keith Miller *Sun* (Sydney) 10 Jan. 52: A bunch of pie-eaters. Excuse me if I find an expression from my old mate, the late Siddie Barnes, but that's what the English team has turned out to be.

1980 *Sydney Morning Herald* 5 Sep. 2: 'Some of the goods are not the best quality. If you are a connoisseur you know the difference. If you are what we call a pie eater, then you don't.'

pie-face   See quot. 1985

1985 *National Times* 26 Apr. 26: It was not enough to stop him shouting 'There's pie-face in the audience!' when he spotted an Asian sitting in the front row . . . Jackson told The National Times later that pie-face was a nickname for Asians, because pies had little marks in the top of them like 'slant eyes'.

Pies   1   The Collingwood V.F.L. team [abbr. of Magpies]

1979 *Herald* (Melbourne) 7 Apr. 34: Lions Devour Pies [heading]

2   In Tasmania, the Glenorchy Australian Rules club

1980 *Mercury* (Hobart) 21 Jun. 56: Pies to send Roos up river [heading] Glenorchy will beat Clarence in a reply of last year's TFL grand final at Bellerive today.

pigeon, ha ha   see **ha ha**

pigeons, he couldn't lead a flock of homing   see **homing**

pig-iron Bob   Nickname given to 1   Mr R. G. Menzies, Attorney-General in the Lyons Government, after he invoked the Transport Workers Act in 1935 when watersiders refused to load the *Dalfram* with iron for Japan

1965 Thomas Keneally *The Fear* 127: The Japanese and Pig-Iron Bob Menzies ('Thank God he's finished with politics for good,' said the priest. 'I'd prayed for that.')

1975 *Australian* 1 Nov. 21: Remember the days when 'Pig Iron Bob' decorated every railway siding?

2   Bob Hawke, Australian Prime Minister 1983– ,

from his negotiations with the steel industry in China

1984 *Sydney Morning Herald* 10 Feb. 7: Pig Iron Bob makes a deal with the future [heading] As a result of talks yesterday between Mr Hawke and Premier Zhao Australia and China have agreed to establish a working party to investigate the possibility of Australian exports of crude steel to the world's potentially biggest market.

1984 *Toorak Sunday* 10 Jun. 24: Bring Malcolm Fraser back, and save us from the Socialist Ratbags of Bodgie Bob-Yellowcake-Pigiron Hawke.

pigs   Expression of disagreement or derision [abbr. of 'in a pig's eye (arse)', listed by Partridge as U.S.]

1919 W. H. Downing *Digger Dialects* 38: *Pig's ear* A contemptuous ejaculation.

1933 Norman Lindsay *Saturdee* 124: 'Pigs to you, yer old man's got the stringholt.' Ibid. 165: Peter had to cover his confusion by saying 'Pigs to you' as he went out kicking the door.

1951 Eric Lambert *The Twenty Thousand Thieves* 322: 'Pig's arse to that!' another voice cried. 'A jack-up – that's the shot.' [In 1963 edn, 198, 'Pig's to that!']

1957 Ray Lawler *Summer of the Seventeenth Doll* 76: 'Get yourself a job somewhere.' 'Like in a paint factory? Pigs I will!'

1965 John Beede *They Hosed Them Out* 192: I said defensively, 'The wheel slipped off the runway.' 'Pig's bum,' he replied.

1969 George Johnston *Clean Straw for Nothing* 307: 'That's because she won't face realities.' 'Pig's arse. And anyway who are you to talk?'

1975 Les Ryan *The Shearers* 119: 'Ar, pigs to you!' 'In your dinger, too!'

piker   A wild bullock [? f. *piker* a vagrant OED 1838]

1887 *All the Year Round* 30 Jul. 67: 'Pikers' are wild cattle.

1898 W. H. Ogilvie *Fair Girls and Gray Horses* 55: He's the lad to stop the pikers when they take you on the rush.

1904 Laura M. Palmer-Archer *A Bush Honeymoon* 347: *Piker* Wild bullock.

1936 Ion L. Idriess *The Cattle King* 62: The boy bought a teamster's cast-off bullock for two pounds. It was an old piker, worked to the very bone.

1955 Mary Durack *Keep Him My Country* 352: *Piker* A troublesome beast to muster.

pimp   *n.*   A sneak, tell-tale (mainly juvenile); an informer to the police or other authority: *derogatory* [f. *pimp* pander OED 1607]

1938 Xavier Herbert *Capricornia* 567: 'I'm not a pimp'. 'What you mean pimp?' 'I'm not a police-

informer.'
1939 Kylie Tennant *Foveaux* 399: 'A very nice, beautiful, lovely day', Mrs. Metting answered sourly, 'for any landlord's pimps that can go sneakin' about'.
1941 Gavin Casey *It's Harder for Girls* 51: 'I just say I'm not a pimp', Brownie insisted, beginning to blubber.
1958 Frank Hardy *The Four-Legged Lottery* 182: 'Don't worry, I've drummed him. We have ways of dealing with pimps and squealers.'
1963 Alan Marshall *In Mine Own Heart* 205: 'I'm a wake-up to pimps.'

pimp *v.* To act as a pimp
1938 Xavier Herbert *Capricornia* 524: 'He reckons I pimped on him – and that's how the jonns went out and grabbed 'em both.'
1945 Gavin Casey *Downhill is Easier* 109: 'This dago bastard pimped on him to Hayes, an' lost him his job'.
1948 K. S. Prichard *Golden Miles* 28: 'There was a man pimping for the boss, a while ago. Fell down a winze on the two hundred foot level. Nasty accident it was.'
1957 Judah Waten *Shares in Murder* 155: 'You made up to me so you could get me to pimp on Charlie for you.'

pineapple, the rough end of the Hostile or unfair treatment
1961 Ray Lawler *The Piccadilly Bushman* 37: 'He'll know what I mean when I talk of getting the wrong end of the pineapple.'
1976 *Sydney Morning Herald* 23 Oct. 9: Waffling witnesses, even those of lofty social standing, were given short shift, if not the rough end of the pineapple.
1979 David Williamson *Age* (Melbourne) 29 Sep. 19: Despite the club's glorious past, your modern Collingwood supporter has, to be absolutely frank, had the rough end of the pineapple. I got home from Denmark and the buggers lost again.
1983 *Sydney Morning Herald* 6 Jun. Guide 16: Back in World War II, we sent bundles to Britain. Now, as repayment, their producers are sending back jolly World War II thrillers, such as Danger UXB, The Fourth Arm and Tenko. I think we got the rough end of the pineapple.

ping pong, aerial   see **aerial**

pink To shear closely so that the colour of the skin shows through
1899 W. T. Goodge *Hits! Skits! and Jingles!* 113: The leathery necks he pinked 'em too, / Did Gentleman Jack of Jamberoo.
1905 'Flash Jack from Gundagai' *The Old Bush Songs* ed. A. B. Paterson 27 and note: I've pinked

'em with the Wolseleys and I've rushed with B-bows, too. 'Pinking' means that he had shorn the sheep so closely that the pink skin showed through.

pink-hi, pinkeye A 'walkabout': holiday celebration [Pidgin]
1929 K. S. Prichard *Coonardoo* 34: Every year at midsummer, for as long as Coonardoo could remember, the tribes for a hundred miles about had gathered for pink-eye on Wytaliba.
1936 H. Drake-Brockman *Sheba Lane* 131: He found his natives in good tucker and clothes and gave the faithful Jimmy – most wonderful gift – a horse and cart for the yearly pink hi, when he visited his tribe.
1937 Ernestine Hill *The Great Australian Loneliness* 329: Pink-hi Holiday, walkabout.
1955 F. B. Vickers *The Mirage* 256: 'He reckoned we'd been havin' a pink-eye – layin' up on the grog.'
1962 J. Marshall and R. Drysdale *Journey Among Men* 89: We talked with a party of aborigines camped in the river bed. They had quit their station jobs, as they are prone to do, and had gone on a hunting walkabout and a 'pink-eye'.
1969 Osmar White *Under the Iron Rainbow* 139: This year Nolan's Ford Picnic Races and Rodeo – One Thousand Dollars in prizes, Bar-B-Que, Grand Ball, Red Donovan and his Combo – was obviously going to be a successful pink-eye.
1976 Max Brown *Black Eureka* 87: When pinkeye came – six weeks holiday over the hot time – he was handed a half-bag of flour.

pinkic Cheap wine [? f. colour]
1935 Kylie Tennant *Tiburon* 93: Staines, nodding his fat, puffy face into his cup of pinkie ... hadn't a very good head for the cheap raw wine he was drinking.
1941 *Coast to Coast* 23: 'Better put that bottle away ... If the trooper comes round somebody'll be getting into trouble for selling Charley pinkeye again.'
1959 Dorothy Hewett *Bobbin Up* 69: He'd drink anything they reckoned, plonk, pinkie, straight metho.
1966 Elwyn Wallace *Sydney and the Bush* 125: 'Only a bullocky's hut and a "pinkie bar" right out there alone in the wilds.'

pinnies Pinball machines [abbr.]
1979 *Sun* (Sydney) 5 Nov. 17: 'Lost all me money on the pinnies, so I pinched some lunch.'
1981 *Sun-Herald* 27 Sep. 15: 'The only job I ever think about is how great it would be to work in a pinball parlour, looking after the pinnies.'

pipe In the early years of the Australian colonies, a lampoon on someone in authority, rolled into a cylinder and left in public places

1816 Wentworth Papers (Mitchell Library): 'Lampoon or pipe, directed against George Molle, March 1816' [heading to set of verses]
1852 John West *History of Tasmania* i 107: Malice, or humour, in the early days, expressed itself in what were called *pipes* – a ditty, either taught by repetition or circulated on scraps of paper: the offences of official men were thus hitched into rhymes.

piss in someone's pocket, to To ingratiate oneself, be on very familiar terms with [*Pissing down anyone's back* Flattering him Grose 1811]
1967 Kylie Tennant *Tell Morning This* 283: 'Soon's they knew you was in with Numismata, they all want to piss in your pocket.'
1969 Christopher Bray *Blossom Like a Rose* 165: 'I don't mean to piss in yer pockets, but youse blokes are all right.'
1971 Frank Hardy *The Outcasts of Foolgarah* 77–8: 'I appeared before him many a time when I worked for the Union. If we piss in his pocket, he's just as apt to come our way.'
1975 Xavier Herbert *Poor Fellow My Country* 90: 'Not only do you let him piss in your pocket, but import the stuff for him to piss with.'
1983 Rob George *Sandy Lee Live at Nui Dat* 45: 'That's right, a word in the right ear, piss in the right pocket, that's how the world operates.'
see **pee in the same pot**

pissant around To mess about
1945 Baker 87: Someone is *pissanting around* when he is messing about.
1951 Dymphna Cusack and Florence James *Come In Spinner* 307: 'I been pissantin' round the Northern Territory most of the time.'
1959 Gerard Hamilton *Summer Glare* 138: 'Struth, you pissant around like a rooster that's too old.'

pissant, game as a Very brave or angry
[**1934** Archer Russell *A Tramp-Royal in Wild Australia* 115: 'Must be nearly eighty ... Straight as a gun-barrel an' game as an ant.']
1945 Baker 87: *game as a piss ant.*
1962 Ron Tullipan *March into Morning* 59: 'The old white lady [q.v.] makes you as game as a pissant.'
1975 Richard Beilby *The Brown Land Crying* 82: 'Ho! Real piss-ant, ain't 'e,' Bamma jeered. 'I like ya, boy. Ya got guts.'

pissing on your swag, the dogs are see **pull out**

Pitt Street or Christmas (Palm Sunday), not to know whether it's To be in a state of confusion
1951 Dymphna Cusack and Florence James *Come*

In Spinner 330: 'She's that pie-eyed, she don't know whether it's Pitt Street or Christmas.'
see **Tuesday or Bourke Street, Thursday or Anthony Horderns**

Pitt Street farmer See quots [f. Pitt St as one of the main streets of Sydney's business life]
1945 Baker 198: In Sydney a business man with minor farming interests is called a *Pitt Street farmer.*
1971 *Sunday Australian* 6 Jun. 8: Australia's 9000 Pitt Street farmers – the businessmen, stockbrokers, doctors, barristers and solicitors who make a tidy profit on the side by owning or sharing a farm. Most earn at least $16,000 a year from the venture, although few visit their properties.
1974 *Australian* 16 Jan. 10: Pitt and Collins Street farmers are costing Australia between $10 and $15 million a year in lost tax, according to the Bureau of Agricultural Economics. What a surprise.
1983 *Sun-Herald* 27 Mar. 3: The Hawke Government is planning a tougher crackdown on 'Pitt Street farmers'.
see **Collins Street farmers**

Pivotonians Former nickname of the Geelong V.F.L. club [see quot. 1859]
[**1859** W. Kelly *Life in Victoria* 160: The Pivot City is a sobriquet invented by the citizens of Geelong to symbolise it as the point on which the fortunes of the colony would culminate and revolve.]
1981 Jack Hibberd *National Times* 26 Apr. 64: Geoffrey Blainey, a supporter of the Pivotonians (Geelong).

place for a village, the see **village**

plant *n.* 1 'A hoard of stolen goods; also the place where they are hidden' (OED 1796)
[**1812** Vaux: The place of concealment is sometimes called *the plant* ... To *spring a plant*, is to find any thing that has been concealed by another.]
1853 John Sherer *The Gold-Finder of Australia* 166: He informed me that he had a 'plant', which he would make over to me, as it might be 'sprung' whilst he was in gaol.
1882 Rolf Boldrewood *Robbery Under Arms* (World's Classics 1949) 55: 'So take care and don't act foolishly, or you'll lose a plant that may save your life, as well as keep you in cash for many a year to come.'
2 The portable equipment of a drover, bullock-driver or other bushworker [f. *plant* The fixtures, implements, machinery and apparatus used in carrying on any industrial process OED *sb.* 6, 1789]
1903 Joseph Furphy *Such is Life* (1944) 311: 'Stewart has bought his plant, and engaged him

permanently.'
1917 R. D. Barton *Reminiscences of an Australian Pioneer* 179: I had to buy a plant-dray and three horses.
1945 Tom Ronan *Strangers on the Ophir* (1966) 16: At sundown he drove a plant of horses to the soak.
1951 Ernestine Hill *The Territory* 445: *Plant* A station or drover's outfit – horses, drays, cars, saddles.
1969 Osmar White *Under the Iron Rainbow* 126: 'Bring her over to the plant,' he [the dogger] said. 'I'll boil up a billy.'
1983 Arthur Cannon *Bullocks, Bullockies and Other Blokes* 181: Fencers took contracts to build new station fences, or repair old ones. They always had a plant, which consisted of tools of trade, their living requirements and a horse and wagonette, or a motor vehicle.

plant *v.* To conceal, secrete, usually with illegal intent [f. English thieves' slang OED 1610; recorded earlier in *Twelfth Night* II.ii.162]
1798 David Collins *An Account of the English Colony in NSW*, ed. Brian Fletcher (1975) i 331: These [stolen articles] must have been planted (to use the thief's phrase) a considerable time; for every mark or trace which could lead to the discovery of the owner was entirely effaced.
1812 Vaux: *Plant* To hide, or conceal any person or thing, is termed *planting* him, or it.
1827 P. Cunningham *Two Years in New South Wales* ii 59–60: An acquaintance in Van Dieman's land, who had ordered his eldest boy to give up a plaything to a younger ... was puzzled to make out the meaning of the latter, on its afterwards running in to him and calling out, 'Pa! Bill has *planted* it' (hid it).
1838 Thomas Walker *A Month in the Bush of Australia* 15: I doubt not the fellows have had our horses planted.
1848 Charles Cozens *Adventures of a Guardsman* 142: The practice ... of *planting* the bullocks of the various teams on the road and so keeping them until their owners are induced to offer a reward for finding them.
1875 Rolf Boldrewood *The Squatter's Dream* repr. as *Ups and Downs* (1878) 235: If not stolen, the horses had been 'planted' or concealed until a reward ... was forthcoming.
1882 A. J. Boyd *Old Colonials* 74: He loads up a keg of rum, and to make sure it wouldn't be touched he plants* it in a barrel of sugar. *To *plant* in bush parlance is *to hide*.
1907 Barbara Baynton *Human Toll* 105: 'Andree, Andree!' she screamed ... 'Plant me, plant me! God's after me; He's after me! Plant me in the brick oven!'
1936 Dal Stivens *The Tramp and other stories*

143: 'Of course she'll hang around you ... she knows you've got that money planted ... don't be a bloody fool.'
1958 H. D. Williamson *The Sunlit Plain* 234: 'That's why I planted these bottles in this here tent – so I'd have somewhere for a quiet gargle.'
1959 Dorothy Hewett *Bobbin Up* 20: He waddled out ... to fumble and curse under the stairs, where he planted his home brew.
1973 Frank Huelin *Keep Moving* 15: 'We'll plant our swags and have a look at this other joint.'
1983 Georgia Savage *The Tournament* 9: I nicked around the house and planted myself behind the mile-high pile of fruit cases standing there.

plaster As for **poultice** 2 q.v.
1932 Leonard Mann *Flesh in Armour* 248: 'The books must have got a plaster.'

plate A plate of sandwiches etc. brought by each person attending a social gathering as a way of catering for it
1962 Stuart Gore *Down the Golden Mile* 110: 'We might start by having some sort of social. Nothing elaborate, you know. Just perhaps all the ladies could bring a plate.'
1984 Ned Manning *Us or Them* 25: 'Bring your own if you drink anything sophisticated, otherwise we'll hit you for a couple of bucks for beer and wine, and ladies bring a plate.'

pleuro Pleuropneumonia (as a disease of cattle)
1874 Rolf Boldrewood *My Run Home* (1897) 176: 'Do you ever have any pleuro among your cattle?' said I, 'I heard something about it in England.'
1885 Mrs Campbell Praed *Australian Life* 244: 'Pleuro is very bad our way. I don't believe much in inoculation – do you?'
1892 Henry Lawson 'The City Bushman' *Verse* i 214: Did you fight the drought and pleuro when the 'seasons' were asleep?
1917 A. B. Paterson *Three Elephant Power* 42: Providence sends the pleuro, and big strong beasts slink away by themselves, and stand under trees glaring savagely till death comes.
1964 Tom Ronan *Packhorse and Pearling Boat* 68: 'I'd say that war is like pleuro in cattle: whenever you think it's eradicated it breaks out in a fresh place.'

plod *n.* The piece of ground on which a miner is working; the work card relating to this: W.A.
1941 Baker 55: *Pitching the plod* 'The exchange of words' between miners 'on the state of the ground when coming on or going off shifts.'
1948 K. S. Prichard *Golden Miles* 72: He had to go to the office for his plod – the card on which he filled in particulars of the work he was doing, its position in the mine, and the hours he was work-

ing. Ibid. 74: He held an 'unofficial' plod, because he was bogging for a machine man.

2 A yarn, a 'spiel' (see quot. 1941 above) [f. *plod* a short or dull story; a lying tale EDD]

1945 Gavin Casey *Downhill is Easier* 136: 'I suppose he told you the whole plod?' I sneered. Ibid. 162: He bought pots for the three of us, and started off on his plod.

1954 T. A. G. Hungerford *Sowers of the Wind* 241: 'That's the plod he put up, anyway.'

1970 Richard Beilby *No Medals for Aphrodite* 158: 'What sort of a plod are you going to put up about her?'

1975 Xavier Herbert *Poor Fellow My Country* 1126: 'Put in a plod for me, mate.'

plonk Cheap wine, or any improvised alcoholic drink; wine, from the standpoint of the beer drinker [Franklyn records *plink plonk = vin blanc*]

1938 Francis Ratcliffe *Flying Fox and Drifting Sand* 217: His drink at the bar had been 'plonk', and not the beer of his companions.

1941 Kylie Tennant *The Battlers* 128: 'Keep off the plonk,' Thirty-Bob said in an undertone to the Stray. 'They just spilt some on my boot and it burnt a hole.'

1946 Dal Stivens *The Courtship of Uncle Henry* 72: 'Jessie's been on the plonk again ... Goes round the wine bars at the Cross.'

1952 Jon Cleary *The Sundowners* 228: 'I'd finish up in the gutter, a plonk fiend, maybe even drinking metho.'

1960 John O'Grady *Cop This Lot* 210: 'Wot's better than beer?' Pat asked. 'Vino rosso. Vin rouge. Rotwein. The civilised and incomparable juice of the grapes.' 'Gees,' Pat said. 'Yer don' mean bloody plonk, do yer?'

1962 Alan Marshall *This is the Grass* 130: 'Round-the-world-for thruppence' they called the plonk that brought them their shielding stupor.

1975 Don Townshend *Gland Time* 15: When Butch looked into his red-flushed face and his rose-coloured murky eyes he knew he had been on the plonk again.

1980 Craig McGregor *The Australian People* 143: In the last few years the really astonishing growth has been in the consumption of wine, which used to be dismissed as 'plonk', but is now one of the nation's fastest-growing industries.

plonko A plonk-addict

1963 Alan Marshall *In Mine Own Heart* 187: 'You end up a plonko with bells ringing in your head.'

1965 William Dick *A Bunch of Ratbags* 69: 'We could go and see if there's any plonkos under Martin's Bridge and chuck rocks at 'em.'

see **pinkie**

plurry Pidgin version of 'bloody'

1907 Charles MacAlister *Old Pioneering Days in the Sunny South* 236: The blackfellow stipulated that I should 'go longa pound, and gib it money to Missus, too, or the Boss plurry well beat 'em both.'

1934 Tom Clarke *Marriage at 6 a.m.* 46: *Plurry good* – adjectively good.

1984 Bert Kelly *Bulletin* 3 Apr. 106: When Ginger was asked whether he preferred the infantry or the cavalry, he thought for a while and then voted for the infantry. Asked why, he replied, 'One day, the retreat will be sounded and then I don't want to be hindered by no plurry horse!'

pocket, to have death adders (mousetraps, scorpions) in one's To be a reluctant spender

1944 Lawson Glassop *We Were the Rats* 118: 'Why doancher buy a drink? Get them death adders outa ya pockets.'

1951 Dal Stivens *Jimmy Brockett* 277: Fuller was meaner than Dargan, if that was possible. He had death adders in his pocket.

1968 Stuart Gore *Holy Smoke* 99: *death adders in one's purse, to have*: To keep it closed; hold on to one's money!

1977 Colleen Klein *The Heart in the Casket* 139: 'He bought me some pink carnations ... He must be really keen, he's usually got a scorpion in his pocket.'

1978 *Sydney Morning Herald* 21 Oct. 18: 'Your old man would shout even when it wasn't his turn. No mousetraps in *his* pocket!'

1982 *Sun-Herald* 21 Feb. 65: Bookies reckon there's no shortage of punters with death adders in their pockets.

pocket, to piss in someone's see **piss**

pocket, useful as a hip ~ in a singlet see **useful**

poddy (calf) A hand-fed calf; any creature at an early stage of growth

1879–80 Ned Kelly 'The Jerilderie Letter' in Max Brown *Australian Son* (1956) 275: If a poor man happened to leave his horse or a bit of a poddy calf outside his paddock they would be impounded.

1897 Henry Lawson 'The Australian Cinematograph' in *Prose* i 460: She lifts a heavy oil-drum full of skimmed milk, destined to keep alive several wronged and wretched-looking poddy calves in the pen.

1901 Miles Franklin *My Brilliant Career* 24: It was my duty to 'rare the poddies'.

1904 Henry Fletcher *Dads Wayback: His Work* 118: She had brought up all these cows with almost the watchfulness a mother gives to a child; she knew their every trick of temper since they were poddies.

1913 C. J. Dennis *Backblock Ballads and Other Verses* 198: *Poddy*, a calf reared by hand.

1934 Brian Penton *Landtakers* 479: 'I'll soon have

him nursed up as fat as a poddy calf.'
1951 Ernestine Hill *The Territory* 307: Mustering cows and cleanskin calves just old enough to wean – the 'poddies' – they headed them up into the ranges.
1956 Brian James *The Bunyip of Barney's Elbow* 154: Taking the milk in and bringing back the skim for pigs and poddies.
1982 *Sun-Herald* 7 Mar. 141: The use of poddy mullet is illegal in NSW because they are less than legal size.

poddy *v.* See quot.
1892 Henry Lawson 'A Day on a Selection' in *Prose* i 45: Then he 'poddies' – hand feeds – the calves which have been weaned too early. He ... seizes a calf by the nape of the neck with his left hand, inserts the dirty fore-finger of his right into its mouth, and shoves its head down into the milk. The calf sucks, thinking it has a teat.

poddy-dodger A cattle-duffer who appropriates unbranded calves [f. *poddy* a hand-fed calf]
1937 Ernestine Hill *The Great Australian Loneliness* 83: Keep poddy-dodgers from the glen, / For Jesus Christ's sake, Amen.
1946 W. E. Harney *North of 23°* 93: Some of the small struggling 'poddy dodgers' would now and then bring in a few bullocks and sell them to the butcher, who would give them a credit at the store.
poddy-dodging
1945 Tom Ronan *Strangers on the Ophir* 9: 'He'll be a doctor or a lawyer or a banker with no need to go poddy-dodging for a living like his old jail-bird of a Dad.'
1957 R. S. Porteous *Brigalow* 61: Mick did a bit of poddy-dodging when things were slack ... He might lift a few head of cleanskins now and then.
1961 Noni Braham *The Interloper* 57: He didn't object to a bit of poddy-dodging
1975 Donald Stuart *Walk, Trot, Canter and Die* 136: He'd spend a day with Spadger ... if the old feller wasn't out with his blackfellers and his dogs poddy-dodging along his neighbours' boundary country.

point the bone see **bone**

pointer Someone who 'works points', takes an unfair advantage
1941 Baker 55: *Point, to*: To take an unfair advantage of a person, to loaf, impose on, to malinger. Whence, 'pointer': one who does these things.
1954 Tom Ronan *Vision Splendid* 164: There was no nark or pointer in the camp.

poisoner A cook, esp. for a collection of men
1905 E. C. Buley *Australian Life in Town and Country* 23: The shearers' cook is always a compe-

tent man and supplies his clients with the best fare obtainable, utterly 'belying' the name of 'poisoner', usually bestowed upon him.
1936 Archer Russell *Gone Nomad* 14: I had to take my turn at butchering the ration sheep and as 'slushy' to 'Dough-boy' Terry, the cook – 'camp poisoner', as we affectionately called him.
1969 Lyndall Hadow *Full Cycle* 208: 'I'm not much good at cooking but I'll try.' 'Never you mind about that. Up north we've got the best poisoners in the country.'
see **doctor**

poke borak, mullock see **borak, mullock**

poke in the eye with a burnt stick, better than a An expression of qualified pleasure, usually a retort
[**1852** George Eliot *Letters* ed. G. S. Haight (1954) ii 70–1: 'Then', he [John Chapman] said, in rather an affected, 'proper' drawl, looking pious, 'there are these "Letters from Ireland" which I hope will be something rather better than a *poke in the eye*'.
1928 Sidney S. Lenz *More Lenz on Bridge* ii 135: A penalty of three hundred is always better than a poke in the eye with a rusty nail.]
1974 *Bulletin* 6 Jul. 44: An Australian way of expressing ecstasy is to say: 'It's better than a poke in the eye with a burnt stick.'
1978 *Bulletin* 3 Oct. 39: The astonishing Miss M[idler] ... has sold 20,800 tickets in Sydney alone; which, at $13 a seat, is rather better than a poke in the eye with a burnt stick. For the vicariously avaricious, it's $270,400 better.
1981 *Bulletin* 5 May 46: Carter is close to finding a buyer for his Plains peanut warehouse business. A sale would be better than a poke in the eye with a burnt stick: the business is worth $1.45 million.

poke a stick at, more than one could see **stick**

pokies, the Poker-machines [abbr.]
1967 Donald Horne *Southern Exposure* 44: In the clubs of Sydney the poker machines ('the pokies') stand up in dozens and more beer flows than in a hotel.
1975 *Bulletin* 9 Aug. 23: Bingo is rapidly assuming the place in the Queensland lifestyle that is held by the pokies in New South Wales.

polar bear's behind, as cold as Very cold
1944 Randolph Bedford *Naught to Thirty three* 187: I knew [in the 1890s] ... Billy Evans, the newspaper man who wrote a ribald definition of cold, while freezing in the press gallery of the South Australian Parliament. It began 'cold as the Esquimaux, gloomy and glum ...'
1944 Lawson Glassop *We Were the Rats* 5: 'I ... sneaks in just in time to see Jerry knock Binghi as

cold as a Polar bear's backside.'

1951 Dal Stivens *Jimmy Brockett* 227: I'd only seen her about three times in the last four or five years. Mostly, she was cold as a polar bear's behind.

1957 Judah Waten *Shares in Murder* 55: For a man who was supposed to be as cold as a polar bear's paw he had plenty of hot blood in his veins.

1971 John O'Grady *Aussie Etiket* 85: In the words of an anonymous poet of genius, 'Cold as an iceberg, gloomy and glum, / Cold as the hair on a polar bear's bum.'

pole on   To impose, sponge on someone [? f. *poll* practise extortion OED 1521–1613]

1906 Edward Dyson *Fact'ry 'Ands* 66: 'What rot, girls, why don't yer get a shift on?' cried Feathers virtuously . . . 'polin' on the firm like this.'

1919 W. H. Downing *Digger Dialects* 38: *Poll* to take advantage of another's good nature.

1938 Xavier Herbert *Capricornia* 529: 'Call me a wastrel, would ya? You – why you're poling on Jesus Christ!'

1947 Vance Palmer *Hail Tomorrow* 10: 'I asked him why he should come up north and pole on men who were trying to win decent conditions for themselves, but he said he wanted a holiday.'

1953 *Caddie A Sydney Barmaid* 220: 'And while there's anything in the Sutton cupboard, Caddie,' he assured me when I said I couldn't stay and pole on them, 'it's yours.'

pole, up the   In error, in disorder, confused [cf. *up the pole* in the wrong, tipsy OED 1896, 1904]

1906 Edward Dyson *Fact'ry 'Ands* 188: Then, as a bright afterthought, she added, 'Yer fair up the pole!'

1915 C. J. Dennis *The Songs of a Sentimental Bloke* 47: The dreams I dreamed, the dilly thorts I thunk / Is up the pole, an' joy 'as done a bunk.

1950 Jon Cleary *Just Let Me Be* 108: 'If I go and see 'em now, tell 'em what I done and why I done it, I'd be well and truly up the pole.'

1965 William Dick *A Bunch of Ratbags* 92: 'Right,' said Curly, agreeing with Ronnie's logic for once. He generally thought Ronnie was all up the pole when giving advice to someone.

1970 Richard Beilby *No Medals for Aphrodite* 244: 'We'd a' been up the pole without him, that's why we didn't send him on his way.'

pole, wouldn't touch it with a forty-foot   An expression of extreme aversion or complete rejection [? variant of the English 'wouldn't touch it with a barge pole']

1903 Joseph Furphy *Such is Life* (1944) 27: 'The young feller he used to come sometimes an' just shake hands with her, but otherways he wouldn't touch her with a forty-foot pole.'

1937 *Best Australian One-Act Plays* 248: 'I wouldn't have touched those girls, myself, with a forty-foot pole!'

1941 *Coast to Coast* 167: 'Me take the harness off him!' my mother said, surprised. 'Why, I wouldn't touch that mad thing with a forty-foot pole.'

1958 E. O. Schlunke *The Village Hampden* 26: Business of the more or less shady sort that our reputable men wouldn't touch with a forty-foot pole.

1965 Graham McInnes *The Road to Gundagai* 180: 'I wouldn't touch it with a forty foot pole!' he gulped.

poler   1   The horse or bullock harnessed alongside the pole of the wagon

1863 Samuel Butler *A First Year in Canterbury Settlement* ed. R. A. Streatfield (1914) 95: The leaders . . . slewed sharply round, and tied themselves into an inextricable knot with the polars, while the body bullocks . . . slipped the yoke.

1870 Marcus Clarke *His Natural Life* ed. S. Murray-Smith (1970) 617: The huge waggons, the white body of a camping 'poler', and the three ragged figures round the glowing logs.

1919 W. K. Harris *Outback in Australia* 18: We had to blindfold that poler before we could put him in the 'body-lead'.

2   Someone given to 'poling on' others

1938 Xavier Herbert *Capricornia* 528: 'You long-jawed poler,' Norman roared. 'Living on the fat of the land, while your poor damn flock feeds on soup and coconuts and what they can root out of the bush.'

1952 A. G. Mitchell Supplement to Chambers' *Shorter English Dictionary* 801: *poler* one who sponges on another, or avoids his fair share of work.

policeman   See quot.

1983 *Australian* 3 Jun. 1: Mr Lewer said he had become 'suspicious' and had 'wondered what was going on' after Mr Farquhar had told him the magistrate he had allocated to the case, Mr Keith Hammond, was a 'policeman' (legal jargon implying the magistrate was more likely than some others to commit defendants) and to 'get him (Mr Hammond) off it.'

pollies   Politicians [abbr.]

1973 H. Williams *My Love Had a Black Speed Stripe* 28: I reckon they should keep argument out of politics altogether, but the pollies would never wear it.

1974 *Bulletin* 12 Oct. 12: Pollies peel off the tax perks.

1981 *Weekend Australian* 4 Jul. Mag. 4: Overseas pollies are just as bad.

1982 *Sunday Mail* (Brisbane) 29 Aug. 2: Our good

State pollies have been given an extra phone with a silent number for their electorate offices.

Pom Abbr. of **Pommy** q.v.
1919 W. H. Downing *Digger Dialects* 38: *Pom* – See Pommy.
1941 Baker 56: *Pom* An Englishman.
1956 F. B. Vickers *First Place to the Stranger* 133: 'Move over, Pom. D'you want all the bloody fire?'
1962 Alan Seymour *The One Day of the Year* 8: 'The place is full of 'em. Poms and I-ties.'
1973 Prince Charles [at an Australia Day dinner in London] *Sydney Morning Herald* 3 Feb. 2: All the faces here this evening seem to be bloody Poms.
1974 *Bulletin* 15 Jul. 38: Then there's the joke about the board that's supposed to be outside every Australian lion park: 'Cars $1; cars with senior citizens, 50 cents; Poms on bicycles, free.' Then the story goes on. A Pom did ride his bike into one of the lion parks. The lions rejected the Pom but ate the bicycle.
1980 *West Australian* (Perth) 29 Jan. 6: What has 100 years of playing cricket against the Poms brought about? We hate them and we have T-shirts with such friendly goodwill messages as 'Keep Australia beautiful – shoot a Pom.'
1984 *Sydney Morning Herald* 25 Apr. 12: Apparently some naughty person has been calling English people poms. A British migrant in South Australia complained about the use of the word by an ABC commentator during the departure of the British warship, the Invincible to the Acting Minister for Ethnic Affairs there, Mr Greg Crafter. Mr Geoffrey Whitehead, who we must point out was born in the mother country, the managing director of the ABC, has written back to Mr Crafter, and a copy has been sent to all Department Heads. 'While I believe that this word (pom) is used more often with affectionate familiarity than in a pejorative sense, I have already given instructions that no ethnic description which could be interpreted as a bias, by the ABC, against any minority group, should be used,' the letter said.

Pommification
1984 Derryn Hinch *Sun-Herald* 26 Aug. 150: The pommification of the ABC continues. They even considered giving the job of Radio Australia chief to an applicant flown out from England. Lucky for us he declined.

Pommy An English immigrant; an English national: *derogatory* [see quot. 1920]
1913 *Pommy Arrives in Australia* or *Pommy the Funny Little New Chum* [title of film directed by Raymond Longford and screened at Snowden Theatre, Melbourne, 13 Sep.]
1915 Let. in Bill Gammage *The Broken Years*

(1974) 86: We call the Regulars – Indians and Australians – 'British' – but Pommies are nondescript. Ibid. 240 (1916): They're only a b— lot of Pommie Jackeroos and just as hopeless. All they think of is their dress and their mess.
1916 *The Anzac Book* 31: 'A Pommy* can't go wrong out there if he isn't too lazy to work.' *Pommy – short for pomegranate, and used as a nickname for immigrants.
1920 H. J. Rumsey *The Pommies, or New Chums in Australia* (Introduction): Few people seem to know the origin of the word, but I can well remember its introduction in the early seventies ... Thousands of immigrants were arriving by the old clipper ships, and the colonial boys and girls, like all schoolchildren, ready to find a nickname, were fond of rhyming 'Immigrant', 'Jimmygrant', 'Pommegrant' and called it after the new chum children. The name stuck and became abbreviated to 'pommy' later on.
1922 Henry Lawson 'Gentlemen All' *Prose* i 920: There was the good and grateful pommy who had a fair start in life; the pommy rotter, known on every immigrant ship, with such slings off as 'Just like the Australians', etc.
1926 K. S. Prichard *Working Bullocks* 76: 'Kitty married Gaze's brother ... the pommy cocky who's got Drakes' old place.'
1931 William Hatfield *Sheepmates* 271: 'Not a bad sort of a poor coot, either, for a Pommy.' (The odious word had just drifted out [c. 1912] from the wharves and the railway construction camps.)
1952 Jon Cleary *The Sundowners* 49: 'A stuck-up bastard, ain't he? ... Must be a mate of your Pommy cobber.'
1963 Xavier Herbert *Disturbing Element* 90–1: He still wore the heavy clumsy British type of clothing of the day. When we kids saw people on the street dressed like that [before 1914] we would yell at them: 'Jimmygrants, Pommygranates, Pommies!'
1982 Steve Finnane *Bulletin* 4 May 96: 'Let me kick a Pommy and don't feed me for a month', is one sentiment I have heard expressed by a grizzly-faced ex-member of the AIF.
1983 L. Johnston *Sydney Morning Herald* 15 Aug. 8: In 1911, 1912, and 1913, I attended Granville Public School. In those three years, 200,000 migrants entered Australia, virtually all from Britain. Granville was expanding with industrial development and it seemed almost daily that migrant children appeared at the school, many of them with the rosy cheeks of their English complexions, which suggested the pink glow of the pomegranate, then not uncommon. Children have always chanted at one another and the native-born and earlier arrivals imitated the accents of the newcomers and chanted at them. The chant was simple and spontaneous: 'Immigranate, pome-

321

granate, pomegranate, immigranate.' From this the natural abbreviation was 'Pommy'.

Pommy bastard

1951 Dal Stivens *Jimmy Brockett* 214: Like most of these pommy bastards, he had funny ways but he wasn't a bad old bloke at heart.

1968 George Mikes *Boomerang* 66: It is always the Pommy Bastards who, instead of being grateful, keep on complaining.

1975 *Sunday Telegraph* (Sydney) 9 Feb. 96: A Sydney man will appear before the Royal Commission into Human Relationships later this month and allege that the fashionable T-shirts emblazoned with the words Pommie Bastards are libellous and discriminatory.

Pommyland

1957 Randolph Stow *The Bystander* 21: 'I'm a Pommy. And going back to Pommy-land, after twenty-four years.'

1967 Frank Hardy *Billy Borker Yarns Again* 61: Sir Robert himself wanted to be a whiskey-taster at the Melbourne Show, but ended up as some kind of wharfie over in Pommy Land.

1984 *Weekend Australian* 21 Apr. Mag. 20: Pommieland has just been hit by a new magazine called the *Royal Magazine* which informs a breathlessly waiting public that 'Princess Anne's favorite ploy at parties is to dress up as charlady and go about dusting chairs and tables.'

Pommy shop steward
A phrase given currency by the apparent prominence of English migrants in trade unions

1982 *National Times* 4 Apr. 16: The perennial, but unproven, 'pommy shops stewards' charge whenever strikes threaten to cripple the country.

Pommy's towel (bath-mat), dry as a
Very dry

1981 *National Times* 4 Jan. 5: Humphries had McKenzie downing his first beer and exclaiming he had been 'as dry as a Pommie's towel'.

1982 *Sydney Morning Herald* 13 Mar. 47: It was dry as a Pommy's bathmat in Adelaide last week.

1983 *Sun-Herald* 20 Mar. 143: The saying 'as dry as a Pommy's towel' has become part of the language.

Pommy, whingeing

1962 J. Marshall and R. Drysdale *Journey Among Men* 189: The British national pastime of 'grousing' . . . has given rise in Australia to the derisive expression *wingeing pommy*.

1972 Thomas Keneally *The Chant of Jimmie Blacksmith* 17: 'Pass a law to give every single wingeing bloody Pommie his fare home to England. Back to the smoke and the sun shining ten days a year and shit in the streets. Yer can

have it.'

1974 *Sunday Telegraph* (Sydney) 3 Aug. 110: His derogatory remark about whingeing Poms and the decline of the British Empire.

1982 *Australian* 2 Nov. 2: 'Whingeing Poms' are purely mythical, according to a survey by the Australia-Britain Society and the NSW Department of Immigration. It revealed that only 4 per cent of British migrants in the Sydney region were dissatisfied with their adopted lifestyle, compared with 58 per cent who claimed they were more than satisfied with their new home.

1984 *Sydney Morning Herald* 3 Feb. 8: What happened to the 'whingeing Pom' school of thought, and jokes like 'Grow your own dope – plant a Pom'?

Pompey, to dodge
To steal grass; to work on a sheep station [cf. *to dodge Pompey* to avoid work (Naval slang f. *Pompey* as the establishment at Portsmouth)]

1868 C. Wade Brown *Overlanding in Australia* 53: As for grass he must get what he can. He is necessitated to do a little trespassing on the quiet, which he calls 'dodging Pompey' thereby getting his sheep better fed.

1908 Giles Seagram *Bushmen All* 234: 'Yer don't s'pose that Dick the Devil an' Black Jim are just dodgin' Pompey at Bulla-bullina waiting for the traps to come and fetch 'em'.

see **dodge, monkey-dodger, poddy dodger**

Pong
A Chinese: *rare* [f. frequency of Chinese names like Wong]

1938 Xavier Herbert *Capricornia* 339: 'Your grandmother was a lubra and your grandfather was a Pong.'

1941 Baker 56: *Pong* A Chinese.

1957 Dal Stivens *The Scholarly Mouse* 65: We saw he was too tall to be a Pong or an Eyetoe, though there was something about him that made us think of both.

pongo
An infantryman in World War I; an Englishman [? f. *pong* smell]

1919 W. H. Downing *Digger Dialects* 38: *Pongo* A soldier; one of the rank and file.

1920 *Aussie* Glossary: *Pongo* Infantryman.

1945 Baker 160: *pongo* An Englishman [as Air Force slang in World War II].

1956 *Australian Signpost* ed. T. A. G. Hungerford 185: 'I don't think it woulda come to much if the mug Pongo hadn't bought in.' 'Private Smith', I told the major, 'thinks the situation was aggravated by the interference of an English soldier.'

1972 Turner 109: Like Australians, New Zealanders call the English *pommies*, but also have a variant *pongo* which seems rather less tolerant in its tone.

322

1982 *Weekend Australian* 30 Jan. Mag. 6: It came from somebody in the British Legion (the pongo equivalent of the RSL).

pony 1 The sum of £25 [OED 1797]
1895 Cornelius Crowe *The Australian Slang Dictionary* 60: *Pony* £25.
1922 Arthur Wright *A Colt from the Country* 121–2. 'Are you prepared to go a pony with me?' 'Let me see,' hesitated Yalty. 'Er – pony – er –.' 'Twenty-five quid,' said Knocker.
1950 *Australian Police Journal* Apr. 117: *Pony* £25.
1975 Les Ryan *the Shearers* 69: 'I have a pony to say he can win.'
2 A small glass of beer: in N.S.W., 7 oz.; in Victoria and W.A., 4 oz. [U.S. 1849 Mathews]
1895 Cornelius Crowe *The Australian Slang Dictionary* 60: *Pony* a small glass of beer.
1953 *Caddie A Sydney Barmaid* 87: He . . . leaned on the counter, and ordered a pony of lager.
1959 Gerard Hamilton *Summer Glare* 155: Os pulled a beer each for me and Tommy and a pony for himself. He always drank small beers.
1965 Graham McInnes *The Road to Gundagai* 222: Mr Watson . . . poured himself a tiny glass of beer. 'Just a pony,' he said.

poofter The commonest term for a male homosexual, or man of effeminate appearance: *derogatory* [Partridge lists *puff* a sodomist c. 1870]
1900–10 O'Brien and Stephens: *Pouf* or *poufter* a sodomite or effeminate man.
1941 Baker 56: *Poofter* A homosexual.
1953 T. A. G. Hungerford *Riverslake* 49: He hawked disgustingly and spat on the floor between his feet. 'They want men in the unions, not poofters.'
1965 Hal Porter *Stars of Australian Stage and Screen* 280: During the last ten years or more, there have been imported a coterie of *untalented* English homosexuals, English tonks unheard of outside their home country, to dominate sections of the Australian theatrical scene. If one cannot protest against the employment of the Pommy poofter instead of the Aussie poofter, one can record dismay at the employment of fifth raters who got nowhere near even spear-holding in Drury Lane.
1969 William Dick *Naked Prodigal* 12: I turned and exploded. 'You poofter bastards!' I yelled . . . 'I'll kill him. The bastard's a poofter. He touched me up.'
1973 Keith Dunstan *Sports* 232: The Tigers were five goals down but pulling up fast. Professor Turner heard a thirtyish, beer-gutted supporter scream: 'You bloody Commo, poofter, mongrel bastard.' This, he said, brilliantly released racial, political, sexual and male chauvinist prejudices.

1982 *Sydney Morning Herald* 21 Jul. 20: He [Senator Reg Withers] said that he had known Andrew Peacock for 20 years and in his time had encountered some silly images of him. 'I once said to one of my colleagues: "You know, I am supposed to be reasonably right wing and if you think I'd have a left-wing poofter for a mate you've got another think coming."'
poofteroo, poofy
1966 Partick White *The Solid Mandala* 18: 'You ought to move in with that pair of poofteroos across the road.'
1983 *Sydney Morning Herald* 8 Feb. 1: There's a new rule for newspaper photographers when snapping Bob Hawke – don't take shots while he's having his face wiped. 'It makes him look poofy', said longtime Labor Party ad man Malcolm Macfie.

poofter bashing An alleged Australian pastime
1978 *Weekend Australian* 4 Mar. Mag. 5: Poofter-bashing in Australia is an ancient and honorable sport, and quite a few men have died of it.
1981 Roger Raftery *The Pink Triangle* 29: 'Haven't you ever heard of poofter bashing? It's our national sport.'
1982 *Bulletin* 4 May 44: 'When I arrived in Sydney I was suffering from jet lag', he said, 'so when I saw the sign saying Australian Customs, I sang out 'cooee', played a Slim Dusty medley on a gum leaf and bashed a nearby poofter.'

pooh, in the Euphemism for 'in the shit'
1961 Jack Danvers *The Living Come First* 177: 'I guess it's my fault if you're rather in the pooh with the Adelaide police.'
1970 Richard Beilby *No Medals for Aphrodite* 229: 'If they catch you with her, then you're really in the pooh.'
1975 Xavier Herbert *Poor Fellow My Country* 873: 'She'll put you in the poo if she writes anything 'bout you.'

pool To inform upon, incriminate; to involve someone against his will [cf. *put in*]
1919 W. H. Downing *Digger Dialects* 39: *Pool* To involve; cast blame or a burden on.
1928 Arthur Wright *A Good Recovery* 117: 'Leave the sheilas alone; they're sure to pool a man sooner or later.'
1932 William Hatfield *Ginger Murdoch* 282: To rig that evidence against him – pool him.
1942 Leonard Mann *The Go-Getter* 313: 'I got pooled into it,' he explained.
1967 Kylie Tennant *Tell Morning This* 85: 'A man thought he'd do the decent thing and tide a girl over a patch of trouble, and she pools him every time. You can't prove it isn't your kid.'

pool of unemployment Phrase given currency by Labor party advertisements in the Federal election of 1949 that the Liberals supported the concept of a 'pool of unemployment' as allegedly advocated by Professor T. Hytten ('You'll be cool in Professor Hytten's pool')

1949 *Sydney Morning Herald* 25 Nov. 4: the Vice-Chancellor of the University of Tasmania, Professor T. Hytten, may take action to stop the publication of some Labour Party election advertisements. These advertisements suggest that Professor Hytten advocated a '6 per cent. pool of unemployment' in a paper he read to the Science Congress in Hobart in January. On Tuesday, Professor Hytten denied that he had ever advocated an unemployment pool.

1983 *Sydney Morning Herald* 21 Apr. 7: It casts considerable doubt on the old 'pool of unemployed' approach.

poon Equivalent to 'nong', but less commonly used [? f. *poind* (*poon*) a silly, useless, inactive person; one easily imposed on EDD]

1941 Baker 56: *Poon* A lonely, somewhat crazy dweller in the Outer Beyond (2) A simpleton or fool.

1972 Geoff Morley *Jockey Rides Honest Race* 73: 'They don't look for the guts of a lecture; just the mistakes. Then they can get up and shoot their mouths off and everybody else nods wisely and tries to pick up the mistakes of the poon that's just said his piece.'

1974 David Williamson *Jugglers Three* 69: 'What possessed Keren to shack up with a poon like you?'

1984 Jack Hibberd *Squibs* 134: 'Consorting with a toff. The kind of poon that gets out of the war his father is trying to promote!'

pooned up Flashily dressed

1943 Baker 60: *Poon up* To dress up, especially in flashy fashion.

1951 Dal Stivens *Jimmy Brockett* 48: Some of 'em were young lairs, all pooned up to kill.

1972 Arthur Chipper *The Aussie Swearer's Guide* 48: *Pooned up* Dressed to impress, often with sexual success in view.

poor fellow my country An Aboriginal lament

1946 W. E. Harney *North of 23°* 79: Next to go on watch would be the 'blackboy', a native stockman droving in strange parts. He sings his tribal songs – those plaintive themes that tell about the greatness of his race, murmuring every now and then: 'Poor fellow my country, poor fellow my country!'

1975 Xavier Herbert *Poor Fellow My Country* [book title]

1984 Jean Black *Sydney Morning Herald* 6 Dec. 10: I am concerned that Aboriginal issues were ignored during the whole election campaign . . . No doubt the future will bring the same paternalistic platitudes as before. Poor fella my country.

poormouth, to cry To claim to be in need, usu. with some element of pretence

1930 J. S. Litchfield *Far-North Memories* 141: Making poor mouths, they went the rounds of the camps, begging from all and sundry, so that they should not be asked to share their own food.

1959 Dorothy Hewett *Bobbin Up* 61: Lil liked to be independent. She'd never cried poor mouth in her life, and she was too old to start now.

1965 Leslie Haylen *Big Red* X 176: 'There's a drought on – the graziers will pull a poor mouth.'

1979 *Weekend Australian* 24 Feb. 32: The board turned its back on half a million dollars a year and now it is crying poormouth. If the board had accepted the offer it would have had plenty of money to pay its players.

1982 *NT News* (Darwin) 6 Aug. 6: It is incongruous for the major Aboriginal organisations to be crying poor-mouth.

1983 Greg Hartley *Sun* (Sydney) 25 Aug. 50: It's pointless Wests constantly crying poormouth, for, after all, they started the big spending in the 50s.

popping up, how are you How are you getting on?: *obs.*

1894 Henry Lawson 'The Mystery of Dave Regan' *Prose* i 328: 'How are yer?' 'Oh! I'm all right!' he says. 'How are yer poppin' up?'

1900–10 O'Brien and Stephens: *Popping up* getting on.

1907 Nathan Spielvogel *The Cocky Farmer* 16: 'Whatto, Joe. How are you popping up?'

1933 Norman Lindsay *Saturdee* 10: 'What-oh, Stinker, how you poppin' up?'

1942 Sarah Campion *Bonanza* 207: 'Howya poppin', cobber?'

poppy, tall 1 A person with a high income: given currency by J. T. Lang in N.S.W. in the 1930s by his policy of 'taxing the tall poppies' (see quot. 1970) [? f. Tarquin's decapitation of the tallest poppies at Gabii]

1931 *N.S.W. Parliamentary Debates* 30 Jul. 4840: The Premier cannot truthfully say that a measure which deals with a certain section of the community which he refers to as the privileged class and as 'tall poppies' is in accord with the Melbourne agreement.

1931 *Sydney Morning Herald* 6 Aug. 8: 'I'll put it on the shoulders of those able to bear it,' he [Mr Lang] shouted when it was pointed out to him by the Opposition that 'lopping the tall poppies' meant in some cases 80 or 90 per cent.

1961 Mena Calthorpe *The Dyehouse* 143: 'We've got more useless ornaments on the payroll than we can carry as it is. Too many tall poppies waiting to be cut down.'

1970 J. T. Lang *The Turbulent Years* 147: The next [step] was the introduction of the bill to reduce all government salaries to a maximum of £10 a week. I referred to those being paid more than that amount [in 1931] as the 'tall poppies'.

1973 *Sydney Morning Herald* 7 Aug. 1: Mr Cameron said the Public Service Board had developed a 'compulsive urge' to lavish public funds on the 'tall poppies' of the Public Service.

1984 *Sydney Morning Herald* 2 Jun. 12: The Government has not only found the Gruen Panel's 'tall poppies' test too hard, it has even rejected the panel's fall-back position, the 'modified tall poppies' test, under which the value of homes would be included only to the extent that it exceeded $150,000. What it settled on is a modified modified tall poppies test.

2 Anyone eminent in any way

1967 John Yeomans *The Scarce Australians* 85: The average city Australian is a complete conformist. If there is one place where the genuine eccentric is crushed, the tall poppy lopped and the penetrating discussion stifled, it is Australia.

1973 Patrick White *The Eye of the Storm* 465: Things were what they used to be, the tall poppies bowing mock apologies to those who held them guilty of the worst.

1976 *Bulletin* 28 Feb. 25: In local slang he [Mr Whitlam] is a 'tall poppy', someone egregious in stature and therefore vulnerable to the scythe.

1976 *Sydney Morning Herald* 26 Apr. 17: Auburn, playing a man short for most of the second half, lopped their second tall Soccer poppy in a week yesterday. Auburn ... held Western Suburbs to a scoreless draw.

1984 Les Murray *Sun-Herald* 25 Mar. 17: 'They call me a tall poppy – with secateurs behind their backs – only to find I have a wire stem'.

pork and bean A queen i.e. homosexual [rhyming slang]

1970 Richard Beilby *No Medals for Aphrodite* 189: 'I never been happy about this bloke. Looks a bit of a pork-an'-bean to me. That why ya shepherding 'im? Mates, eh?'

1977 Jim Ramsay *Cop it Sweet* 72: *Pork and bean* Quean, female homosexual.

port Portmanteau [abbr.]

1908 E. G. Murphy *Jarrahland Jingles* 82: Silently they packed their 'ports' and flitted to the West.

1915 J. P. Bourke *Off the Bluebush* 122: They see a young chap with a 'port' on his back.

1942 Eve Langley *The Pea-Pickers* 100: 'If they got their hands on my portmanteau that'd be the last of it. I got things in that port that might interest them.'

1944 Dal Stivens *The Courtship of Uncle Henry* 53: 'You take your port up and come back to the car.'

1954 Tom Ronan *Vision Splendid* 262: He dragged his ports up to the tram stop and took them to the railway cloakroom.

1962 David Forrest *The Hollow Woodheap* 159: Earl Douglas Lucas carried her port to the bottom of the front steps.

1972 Richard Magoffin *Chops and Gravy* 46: Roly grabbed his port ... charged towards the bus.

1983 Patrick White *Signal Driver* 7: He carries a large port with his left hand, and with his right an unwieldy wooden chest with a handle to it. The chest appears much heavier than the port. [stage direction]

possie (pozzy) A chosen position (given currency by the Gallipoli campaign) [abbr.]

1915 Tom Skeyhill *Soldier Songs from Anzac* 16: But 'e [the sniper] never shows 'is pozzy.

1916 *The Anzac Book* 10: The new sniper's pozzy* down at the creek. *Pozzy or possie – Australian warrior's short for 'position', or lair.

1925 Arthur Wright *The Boy from Bullarah* 99: 'Quick, get a pozzy with the machine.'

1932 Myrtle Rose White *No Roads Go By* 160: Dogs lay in wet hollowed-out holes, digging themselves possies wherever they could find a damp, shady spot.

1942 Gavin Casey *It's Harder for Girls* 217: We started on a short course of heavy drinking, hanging on to our possies at the bar and letting the mob push about and roar for drinks behind us.

1959 D'Arcy Niland *The Big Smoke* 213: They've all got their drinking places, and even their drinking possies, their special barmaids, their individual codes.

1970 Patrick White *The Vivisector* 620: 'Should have got here early – got us a good pozzy. Never be in the picture now.'

1981 *Weekend Australian* 26 Sep. Mag. 1: Thousands camped out from Thursday night to make sure of a good possie when the turnstiles opened.

possum, stir the To liven things up, create a disturbance; raise issues that others wish left dormant [? f. *playing possum* U.S. 1822 Mathews and song *Possum up a Gumtree* 1831]

1907 Charles MacAlister *Old Pioneering Days in the Sunny South* 51: Sometimes a strong sailor-man, just off a six months' cruise, would favour us with 'Nancy Lee' or other jolly sea-songs, or an ambitious carrier or drover would 'rouse the 'possum' by giving some long-winded ditty of the time.

1908 E. S. Sorenson *The Squatter's Ward* 144: 'I mean to stir the 'possum in Sultan Susman from this out. I'm a different woman now.'

1949 Ruth Park *Poor Man's Orange* 9: A mission was like a tonic. It stirred the 'possum in the people, and for months afterwards they could still feel the enthusiasm.

1972 *Sydney Morning Herald* 31 Oct. 3: Senate seat offer to stop 'stirring'. 'I could be sitting in Parliament now without any great cost provided I forgot this idea of stirring the possum,' he [Mr Gordon Barton] said.

1981 *Age* (Melbourne) 18 Jul. 15: Treasury secretary John Stone has a grand way of stirring the possum.

post-and-rail tea   A bush tea in which the floating particles resemble a post-and-rail fence

1851 *The Australasian* 298: *Hysonskin* and *post-and-rail* tea have been superseded by Mocha, claret, and cognac.

1852 G. C. Mundy *Our Antipodes* i 329: A hot beverage in a tin pot which richly deserved the epithet of 'post and rails' tea; it might well have been a decoction of 'split stuff' or 'iron bark shingles'.

1887 *All the Year Round* 30 Jul. 66: The tea so made [in a billy] is naturally of rather a rough and ready description, and when the stalks and coarse particles of the fragrant leaf float thickly thereon, it is sometimes graphically styled 'post-and-rails' tea.

1899 W. T. Goodge *Hits! Skits! and Jingles!* 75: There is 'post and rails' and 'brownie' / For yer breakfast now, yer know.

1904 Tom Petrie *Reminiscences of Early Queensland* 243: The tea then was all green tea, and very coarse, like bits of stick – indeed it was christened 'posts and rails'.

1936 Archer Russell *Gone Nomad* 24: Flour, 'post and rail' tea (the cheapest kind), black sugar, salt and meat, were the only rations provided.

posted, to be   To be 'stood up'

1975 *Bulletin* 26 Apr. 46: Limp wouldn't brass or post you (leave you for dead).

1977 Jim Ramsay *Cop it Sweet* 73: *Posted* Be left waiting.

1979 *Sydney Morning Herald* 30 Apr. 24: Not once was Beetson left 'posted' with no one to get the ball to.

postholes, a load of   An unloaded truck (in road hauliers' slang)

1976 *Sun* (Sydney) 28 May 7: *Postholes* (a load of) An empty load.

postie   A postman [abbr.]

1957 D'Arcy Niland *Call Me When the Cross Turns Over* 99: 'Don't forget to watch for the postie,' she called.

1970 Patrick White *The Vivisector* 202: 'He was a postie. The kind that turns scraggy later . . . always hurryin' ter reach the next box.'

1981 *Sydney Morning Herald* 29 Jan. 10: Australia Post is testing packs with aluminium frames to try to take some of the weight from posties' shoulders.

post, parcel   see **parcel**

pot   A measure of beer: in Victoria and Queensland 10 oz.; in W.A. various sizes

1918 N. Campbell and L. Nelson *The Dinky-Di Soldier* 12: I'd buy them a pot or a shandy, / (An' they'd always allow me to pay.)

1946 Dal Stivens *The Courtship of Uncle Henry* 76: Three pots had never made me see things before. It got me worried.

1962 John Morrison *Twenty-Three* 196: 'She'll be crooked on you coming in late with a few pots under the belt, won't she?'

1974 S. H. Courtier *Listen to the Mocking Bird* 76: Across from the Flinders Street entrance to the station, I entered the bar of a pub and ordered a pot of beer.

1984 *Age* (Melbourne) 4 May 5: Beer prices will rise by at least two cents a 200ml glass and three cents a 285ml pot.

pot, put someone's ~ on   To inform upon; destroy someone's prospects [? f. *pot* to outdo, outwit, deceive OED 1562]

[**1868** 'The Song of the Sundowner' *Sydney Punch* 14 Nov. 195 repr. in *Old Bush Songs* ed. Stewart and Keesing (1957) 231: To refuse us tucker, our game they'll kill, / And no doubt at last will 'pot us'.]

1879–80 Ned Kelly 'The Jerilderie Letter' in Max Brown *Australian Son* (1956) 274: Hall has been tried several times for perjury but got clear as this is no crime in the Police force it is a credit to a Policeman to convict an innocent man but any mutt can pot a guilty one.

1911 Arthur Wright *Gamblers' Gold* 138: 'Why should I pot the bloke? He done me a good turn, an' th' police is no good to me.'

1919 W. H. Downing *Digger Dialects* 40: *Put his pot on* Report him.

c. **1928** Louis Esson 'Vagabond Camp' in *Ballades of Old Bohemia* 160: 'I'll put your pot on yet, you cowardly swine. I'll see the plain-clothes man.'

1935 F. D. Davison and B. Nicholls *Blue Coast Caravan* 178: He saw some blacks with whom he was familiar standing on the platform under guard of a policeman. 'Hullo, what's up?' One of them replied, 'Aw, somebody's been putting our pot on.'

1949 Ruth Park *Poor Man's Orange* 190: 'If she opens her big mouth I'll tell the world she was right in there with the rest of them. I'll put her pot on, the bitch, thinking she's so holy.'

1957 Vance Palmer *Seedtime* 119: 'There's an

election coming on, and there's a chance I'll be dumped ... This afternoon's work has probably put my pot on.'
1978 Ray Lawler *The Doll Trilogy* 29: 'Oh ... looks like then I've put their pot on.'

potato, not the clean Of bad repute (sometimes with reference to a convict background) [? negative of the English expression *the potato* the (very, real or proper) thing, what is correct or excellent OED 1822–80]
1877 Rolf Boldrewood *A Colonial Reformer* (1890) 384: 'Well,' said Mr Cottonbush, smiling and wincing slightly, 'it ain't quite the clean potato, of course [to travel one's sheep and steal a neighbour's grass]; but if your sheep's dying at home, what can you do?'
1881 G. H. Gibson 'A Ballad of Queensland' *Bulletin* 26 Mar. 8 repr. in *Australian Bush Ballads* ed. Stewart and Keesing (1962) 313: You weren't quite the cleanly potato, Sam Holt, / And you hadn't the cleanest of fins.
1908 Giles Seagram *Bushmen All* 318: 'He's an awful fool, and – and not exactly the clean potato.'
1921 K. S. Prichard *The Black Opal* 148: 'I ain't always been what you might call the clean potato.'
1931 Miles Franklin *Back to Bool Bool* 233: She was only the great-grand-daughter of old Larry Healey of Little River, none so clean a potato, if rumour was correct.
1962 Tom Ronan *Deep of the Sky* 42: Some of the grand old pioneers and land-takers of history were not quite the clean potato.

poultice **1** A mortgage
1932 K. S. Prichard *Kiss on the Lips* 184: Mick Mallano ... sayin' if the bank wanted his farm, poultice or no poultice, it'd have to go out and take it from him, and he'd be waitin' for 'm with his gun loaded.
1934 Thomas Wood *Cobbers* 134: Men talked about their blister, or their poultice, which means a mortgage, with complacency.
1958 *Coast to Coast 1957–1958* 137: When the farm was free of its 'poultice' her father had promised to hand over to Sam ... But droughts and a fall in the price of wheat kept him battling to pay even interest on the mortgage.
2 A large sum of money
1951 Eric Lambert *The Twenty Thousand Thieves* 235: 'It's only two days to pay day and I've got a poultice in that pay-book of mine.'
1957 D'Arcy Niland *Call Me When the Cross Turns Over* 33: Like another time I got paid off, and it was a whacking big poultice, and I went into Pirie.
1979 *Sun-Herald* 24 Jun. 143: Singleton and Laws have another crony in their bid for a whack of television control, a bloke who made a poultice in

recent weeks when he sold Rupert a quarter of a million Channel Ten shares.
1983 *Sydney Morning Herald* 29 Oct. 16: Marshal Ky drives a Cadillac and is making a poultice in the liquor and insurance business, which must be some sort of definitive comment on the Vietnam war.
see **plaster**

Poverty Point Corner of Park and Pitt Streets, Sydney, as the meeting-place of out-of-work theatricals
1889 *Bulletin* 15 Jun. 7: At Poverty Point [heading to theatrical column]
1974 *Sydney Morning Herald* 5 Jun. 1: The northeast corner of Park and George Streets was the gathering place of out-of-work theatricals who met to gossip and discuss local productions at the turn of the century. The memory of 'Poverty Point', as it was known, is to be perpetuated. On Monday night, Sydney City Council will set aside $120 for a bronze footpath plaque to mark the site.
1979 Dorothy Murphy *Sun-Herald* 21 Oct. 190: How many are aware that another piece of Australian history has sadly been lost by the removal of a plaque that was at the base of a shop wall on the corner of Park and Pitt Streets? This was possibly the last of various places known at different times within the theatrical profession as Poverty Point. It was a place where performing artists met while temporarily 'resting', and where managers sometimes engaged actors.
1982 *Australian* 18 Aug. 10: Miller took his turn down at Poverty Point with all the other entertainers and managed to get work as a singer and violin player on the Tivoli circuit.

pox doctor's clerk, dressed up like a Dressed nattily, but in bad taste
[**1954** T. A. G. Hungerford *Sowers of the Wind* 263: 'What were you before you joined up? A pox-doctor's clerk?']
1957 Nino Culotta *They're a Weird Mob* 106: Joe said, 'Gees, Nino, yer done up like a pox doctor's clerk. Yer don' need no coat an' a coller an' tie. Too hot, mate. Take 'em orf.'
1965 Eric Lambert *The Long White Night* 136: 'They was all dressed like they was at Buckingham Palace and Foran was done up like a pox doctor's clerk.'
1971 Frank Hardy *The Outcasts of Foolgarah* 191: The Tiger of Bengal himself, dressed up like a pox doctor's clerk, wearing more medals than an American general.
1973 *Nation Review* 8–14 Jun. 1064: Good money was laid among the better class workingmen that he [Mr Don Dunstan] would, on this auspicious occasion, come up with an outfit to be the envy of every poxdoctor's clerk in the land.

1974 Barry Humphries [as Barry McKenzie] *Bulletin* 19 Jan. 13: If Al Grassby wants to convert me or any other clean-living Australians into getting dressed up like Lord Muck and getting round kitted up like a flamin' pox doctor's clerk, old Grazza's going to have his time cut out.

1983 Mike Carlton *Sydney Morning Herald* 2 Nov. 11: Young Simon Thing was togged out as a pox-doctor's clerk for his wedding to Vicki Thing on Seven's A Country Practice.

pozzy   see **possie**

prawn, come the raw   To try to impose on someone (Services slang in World War II)

1942 *Salt* 25 May 8: *Don't come the raw prawn* Don't try to put one over me.

1946 Rohan Rivett *Behind Bamboo* 398: *Raw prawn* something far-fetched, difficult to swallow, absurd.

1948 Sumner Locke Elliott *Rusty Bugles* in *Khaki, Bush and Bigotry* ed. Eunice Hanger (1968) 36: 'The filthy rotten Crab, he'd better not come the raw prawn on us.'

1959 Eric Lambert *Glory Thrown In* 41–2: 'Don't ever come the raw prawn with Doc, mate. He knows all the lurks.'

1968 Rodney Milgate *A Refined Look at Existence* 28: 'Don't come the raw prawn ... you know there's no such thing. Things don't happen just like that.'

1975 Les Ryan *The Shearers* 85: 'What do you think I am, a drongo? I take hundreds of bets, and we get blokes here who try to come the raw prawn.'

1984 *Sun-Herald* 11 Mar. 168: Some unions are threatening to come the raw prawn when Nick Greiner delivers his election opener at the Opera House tomorrow, by indicating every member of his commercial film crew will have to prove union membership.

prayers, to know more than one's   Not to be as innocent as one may seem

1934 F. S. Hibble *Karangi* 167: 'Claudie knows more than her prayers.'

1951 Frank Hardy *Power Without Glory* 512: Poor kid had been isolated from life; she was innocent and emotional, and young fellows to-day knew more than their prayers.

1957 Ray Lawler *Summer of the Seventeenth Doll* 12: 'She's a good kid, that.' 'Yeh. I'd say she knows more than her prayers, just the same.'

1976 Glen Tomasetti *Thoroughly Decent People* 116: 'She may be plain but she knows more than her prayers'.

prego   Pregnant [abbr.]

1951 Dymphna Cusack and Florence James *Come*

In Spinner 226: Guinea's face lighted with unholy glee. 'A Parker prego? Did I hear right?'

1965 Patrick White *Four Plays* 94: 'Can't resist the bananas.' 'Yeah. They say you go for them like one thing when you're preggo.'

1975 Valerie Elliston *The Tides of Spring* (1977) 218: 'I can't very well leave you if I'm preggo, can I?' Josie said.

premier state, the   N.S.W., from the legend on vehicle registration plates

1980 *Sydney Morning Herald* 17 Apr. 1: NSW – The Premier State, will soon be adorning vehicle number plates in NSW.

1980 *Australian* 13 Aug. 3: NSW the premier State for successful jail-breaks [heading]

1980 *Sydney Morning Herald* 8 Oct. 1: Reflectorised number plates bearing the slogan NSW – The Premier State were introduced for all newly-registered vehicles yesterday.

1981 *Weekend Australian* 31 Oct. 19: All pith and wind in premier State [heading]

1984 *Australian* 22 Mar. 6: He's [Mr Greiner's] denigrating in the worst sense this great State of ours, this Premier State, that all NSW people are proud to live and work in.

Presbo   A Presbyterian [abbr.]

1965 Leslie Haylen *Big Red* 78: Methos were Methodists, Presbos were Presbyterian.

1978 *Bulletin* 28 Nov. 35: My sympathies are with the 'continuing' [as distinct from 'uniting'] Presbos, who decided they weren't going to have any truck with the Methos, and the Congros and so on.

1982 *Bulletin* 14 Dec. 60: These very active Presbos have outlaid nearly a million on erecting buildings at a variety of centres ranging from Bega in the south to Forster to the north of Sydney.

prezzie   A present [abbr.]

1961 Jon Rose *At the Cross* 141: 'I bought you quite a lot of prezzies.'

1975 *Australian* 24 Apr. 13: From ... endeavours yesterday to discover what presents the Whitlams were taking overseas with them, we can inform you of the following piece of government policy: From this day forth no public announcements will be made about the nature of prime ministerial pressies.

1978 Patrick White *Big Toys* 18: 'Darling, I brought you a prezzie from the Other City.'

1983 Barry Humphries [as Edna Everage] *Australian Women's Weekly* Dec. 261: Even though I'm a fanatical Republican, the royal family always send me gorgeous prezzies, but as you can imagine *they're* terribly hard to buy for.

prick and ribs, all ~ like a drover's dog   see **all**

pricker, to have the   To be in an angry state: *rare* [variant of *get the needle*]
1945 Baker 121: A man in a temper is said ... *to have ... the pricker.*
1955 D'Arcy Niland *The Shiralee* 102: 'You've got the pricker properly, eh? You'll knock him into next week, will ya?'

Prince Albert, Alfred   see **Albert, Alfred**

Professor, the   1   The jockey Roy Higgins
1979 *Herald* (Melbourne) 25 Apr. 36: 'Professor' was hit at dinner [heading] Victoria's top jockey Roy Higgins was honoured by Tattersalls Club in Sydney last week by being asked to be the guest speaker at its inaugural Sydney Cup dinner.
2   The jockey Jack Thompson
1981 *Australian* 26 Jan. 2: Veteran Jockey Jack Thompson's four decades on the track have been recognised with an Order of Australia. Thompson, 58, know as 'the professor' among the racing fraternity, still gets his share of rides and has no plan for retirement.

promise, on a   Given a guarantee of having sex (used of males only)
1971 Frank Hardy *The Outcasts of Foolgarah* 3: 'If you were to believe Florrie, I'm on a promise at every second house.'
1983 David Foster *Plumbum* 123: The glance indicates to Jason that Pete's on a promise tonight.

prop   To pull up unexpectedly (originally of a horse)
1844 *Georgiana's Journal* ed. Hugh McCrae (1966) 127: Suddenly my pony propped, and I just had time to disengage my limb from the pommel before he started to roll himself on the beach.
1876 Rolf Boldrewood *A Colonial Reformer* (1890) 7–8: The colt ... stopped with deathlike suddenness; his rider was shot on to the crown of his head with startling force ... 'My word, sir,' was his single remark, 'I didn't think he'd ha' propped like that.'
1908 W. H. Ogilvie *My Life in the Open* 83: Playful or vicious ... almost all of them 'prop' or 'go to market' in some form or other.
1929 K. S. Prichard *Coonardoo* 67: 'The horse shied, propped and shot Ted fair over his head.'
1959 Dorothy Hewett *Bobbin Up* 121: They stuck out their jaws, and propped, and fought.
1969 Thomas Keneally *The Survivor* 70: Seconds later a university sedan, driven by George the university guard, wheeled fast through the gate and propped at the front of the house.
1970 Patrick White *The Vivisector* 602: The present mob might have trampled Rhoda underfoot if it hadn't suddenly realized she was something beyond its experience, so it propped, and divided.

1981 *Sydney Morning Herald* 31 Oct. 16: The inability to go in or out of any room without propping, like a sheep at a gate, and then perhaps lolling for a bit on the frame may be a feature of one school of method acting, but in my view is best used sparingly.
prop *n.*   The action of propping
1881 A. C. Grant *Bush-Life in Queensland* i 201: A sudden fierce prop, and Roaney has shot behind Sam's horse.

property, the smaller the ~, the wider the brim   see **brim**

public   A public (i.e. government) school, as distinct from a Catholic one; a child attending such a school
1956 Brian James *The Bunyip of Barney's Elbow* 140: People spoke of keeping their children at home, or ... 'putting them to the convent', or 'the public', as the case might be.
1959 Dorothy Hewett *Bobbin Up* 56: Frank was a Forbes boy, youngest son of a local cockie. He and Beryl had gone to the 'public' together, partnered each other at the local 'hop'.
1972 Philip Hickie introduction to Peter Kenna *The Slaughter of St. Teresa's Day* 7: They [the Irish and Italians of Paddington in the 1950s] were even further isolated by the Roman Catholicism into which they were born. The world was divided into Catholics and 'Publics'.
1984 Gabrielle Lord *National Times* 20 Apr. 13: These were known as the Publics. They went to public school, they ran about in the streets, they didn't believe in the Pope, and they went to something called Sunday school instead of Mass.

pufterlooner   A kind of scone made of dough and fried in fat [f. the way it rises during cooking]
1853 S. Mossman and T. Banister *Australia, Visited and Revisited* 126: 'Leatherjackets' – an Australian bush term for a thin cake made of dough, and put into a pan to bake with some fat ... The Americans indulge in this kind of bread, giving them the name of 'Puff ballooners', the only difference being that they place the cake upon the bare coals.
1870 Marcus Clarke *His Natural Life* ed. S. Murray-Smith (1970) 577: 'Have a pufterlooner, Master Dick,' suggests Derwent Jack, 'or a bit o' sweetcake.'
1906 A. B. Paterson *An Outback Marriage* 149: A tin plate of light, delicately browned cakes of the sort known as 'puftalooners'.
1935 F. D. Davidson and B. Nicholls *Blue Coast Caravan* 186: There was bush honey and a great platter of puff-de-loonies, all warm and crisp and golden brown.
1940 Ion L. Idriess *Lightning Ridge* 82: Pufta-

loons are tasty though; fry them in fat, then smother them with treacle and swallow 'em while greasy.

1964 Tom Ronan *Packhorse and Pearling Boat* 140: A camp oven full of 'puff de loons' (fried scones to the uninitiated).

1970 Patrick White *The Vivisector* 10: Mumma started telling all she had heard next door, with the kids stuffing on Mrs Burt's cold puftaloons.

1975 *The Commonsense Cookery Book* 181: Puftaloons (Fried Scones) [recipe]

pull the coat   see **coat**

pull your head in   see **head**

Pull out dig, the dogs are pissing on your swag   Advice to someone to abandon the tack he is on, as though by calling attention to some circumstance he has overlooked [f. message passed by Alan MacDonald to Eric Harrison in Parliament in the days of the Chifley government: see quot. 1977]

1977 Howard Beale *This Inch of Time* 39: One night Harrison, a good fighting speaker, was denouncing the government about something or other. When his speech – a little heavy-handed – had gone on for some time, I saw Alan MacDonald, the opposition whip who sat next to me, scribble something on a piece of paper and bustle down the aisle and hand it to Harrison in full cry at the table. It was usual to give a colleague a helping hand by passing him a note on some point which he might have forgotten, and so Harrison took the paper gratefully and read it. Then he threw it down on the table, completed his speech in one sentence, and sat down abruptly. What MacDonald had written was, 'Pull out digger, the dogs are pissing on your swag.'

pull the tail out of a peewee, couldn't   see **couldn't**

punched, bored or   see **bored or punched**

pup, the night's a   It's early yet

1915 Henry Lawson 'A Foggy Night in Antwerp' *Prose* i 913: The night was not even a pup yet – it was broad daylight, being Northern summer.

1921 K. S. Prichard *The Black Opal* 103–4: 'You're not taking her away yet, Michael? The night's a pup!'

1934 Vance Palmer *Sea and Spinifex* 165: 'What about coming out on the water for awhile? Night's still a pup.'

1949 Lawson Glassop *Lucky Palmer* 73: 'We'll get him in. The day's only a pup yet.'

1957 Judah Waten *Shares in Murder* 171: 'You still have time to take the young lady out ... The night's a pup.'

1968 Geoffrey Dutton *Andy* 198: 'Are you thinking of driving out to Hanging-stone to-night?' 'It's only forty miles and the night is a pup.'

1975 Hal Porter *The Extra* 99: The night's the sort of pup we don't usually abandon, but abandon it abruptly we do.

1983 *Newcastle Herald* 26 Apr. 2: So far the national shearers' strike is only a pup. Four weeks may be a long time without work in most industries, but in shearers' terms it is nothing.

pure merino   see **merino**

purler   Something exceptional in its class [f. *purl* To turn upside down OED 1856]

1935 R. B. Plowman *The Boundary Rider* 149: 'My face was covered in blood and I had a pearla of a headache.'

1941 Baker 57: *Purl, purler*: Something excellent, outstandingly good.

1980 *Weekend Australian* 16 Aug. 13: Flo's 35-minute speech was a pearler.

1980 *Mercury* (Hobart) 12 May 22: Shane Gifford ... climbed high over the pack to pull down a pearler.

1981 *Sunday Mail* (Brisbane) 1 Nov. 6: He came up with a pearler recently whilst we were discussing the movie Gallipoli. 'I want to join the army when I grown up,' he stated, 'and I'll quit when war breaks out.'

1984 *Age* (Melbourne) 12 Jun. 40: Michael Egan played a pearler in the back pocket for Footscray.

push   A crowd; a band of larrikins; an intellectual and cultural clique or others with some bond of association (see quot. 1896) [f. English thieves' slang]

1812 Vaux: *Push* a crowd or concourse of people, either in the streets, or at any public place of amusement &c., when any particular scene of crowding is alluded to, they say, *the push*, as *the push*, at the *spell* doors; *the push* at the *stooping-match*, &c.

1890 *The Argus* 26 Jul. 4: 'Doolan's push' were a party of larrikins working ... in a potato paddock nearby. [Morris]

1892 Henry Lawson 'The Captain of the Push' *Verse* i 186: As the night was falling slowly down on city, town and bush, / From a slum in Jones's Alley sloped the Captain of the Push.

1896 Henry Lawson 'For Auld Lang Syne' *Prose* i 267: He was the first of the old push to go – we use the word push in its general sense, and we called ourselves the Mountain Push because we had worked in the tourist towns a good deal ... We were plasterers, bricklayers, painters, a carpenter, a labourer and a plumber.

1911 Edward Dyson *Benno, and Some of the Push* [book title]

1917 A. B. Paterson *Three Elephant Power* 31: He had originally been quartered at Sydney, and had fought many bitter battles with the notorious 'pushes' of Bondi, Surry Hills and The Rocks.
1924 *Truth* 27 Apr. 6: *Push* A crowd of larrikins.
1939 Kylie Tennant *Foveaux* 263: 'If I did join anything, it wouldn't be your push.'
1942 Tip Kelaher *The Digger Hat* 25: I've spent it on the beaches with all the surf-club 'push'.
1963 John Cantwell *No Stranger to the Flame* 74: 'My mother and uncle and brother are well up in the holy Roman circles of this town. You one of their push?'
1963 *Sunday Telegraph* (Sydney) 20 Jan. 2: The Royal George Hotel, at the corner of King and Sussex Streets ... has for some years been the headquarters of members and ex-members of the Sydney University Libertarian Society known simply as 'The Push'.
1973 Alexander Buzo *Rooted* 87: 'Gary's gone away for the weekend, cavorting in the mulga with the Werris Creek Push.'
1981 Barry Humphries *A Nice Night's Entertainment* 209: *Push, the,* a forlorn and excruciatingly feeble group of punters and toss-pots who masqueraded as Sydney's Bohemia in the 1950s. Recent attempts to mythologise the push have been impeded since its artistic and literary legacy was nil.

pussy's bow, up to   See quot. 1945
1945 Baker 207: Among nursery expressions which have acquired a fairly stabilized currency in this country are ... *up to pussy's bow and dolly's wax,* to denote a surfeit, especially of food.
1983 T. A. G. Hungerford *Stories from Suburban Road* 58: I got swamped up to pussy's bow with their troubles.

put the bite on   see **bite**

put in the boot   see **boot**

put one's cue in the rack   see **cue**

put the fangs in   see **fangs**

put the hard word on   see **hard word**

put the mock (mockers) on   see **mock**

put in the slipper   see **slipper**

put someone in   To inform against, implicate
1922 Arthur Wright *A Colt from the Country* 153: 'I might have a chance with the girl again.' 'After what you did to put her in?' laughed the detective. 'I like your hide.'
1951 Seaforth Mackenzie *Dead Men Rising* 52: 'Nothing would give me greater pleasure than to put you in, only that's about the one thing I've never done in my life.'
1959 Dorothy Hewett *Bobbin Up* 71: 'Why doncha put her in to the foreman?'
1966 Peter Cowan *Seed* 106: 'I suppose when they make you a prefect you'll put us in.'
1975 *Sydney Morning Herald* 3 Jul. 11: A lagger is someone who puts people in to the police.
see **dob in, pool, pot**

put someone's pot on   see **pot**

put sport on the front page   see **sport**

putty, up to   Worthless, useless (sometimes abbr. to **upter** q.v.)
1919 W. H. Downing *Digger Dialects* 52: *Up to putty* Bad; useless; ineffectual.
1924 C. J. Dennis *Rose of Spadgers* 119: Once let 'em tangle, an' you take the blame / You're up to putty, an' yeh've lost the game.
1941 Baker 58: *Putty, up to* Worthless, of no importance.

pyjama cricket   One-day cricket [f. coloured uniforms worn by players, and because it is sometimes played at night]
1982 *Sun-Herald* 31 Jan. 35: He [Ernie Cosgrove, Australian Cricket Board official scorer for visiting teams] feels indulgent to 'pyjama' cricket, the name he gives to the one-day variety, but prefers the challenge that Test cricket poses.
1983 *Sun-Herald* 9 Jan. 5: The very mention of 'pyjama' cricket – a name born of the players' multi-coloured uniforms – makes veteran observers like former Test bowler, Bill O'Reilly, cringe.

quack A doctor, without the implication that he is unqualified

1918 George Dale *The Industrial History of Broken Hill* 76: The 'quack' in charge at the time of the Wilcannia Hospital mounted the witness stand.

1919 W. H. Downing *Digger Dialects* 40: *Quack* A medical officer.

1938 Xavier Herbert *Capricornia* 144: 'That noo quack says he's got a crook heart.'

1946 Dal Stivens *The Courtship of Uncle Henry* 150: 'The nearest quack was in Myralie, twenty miles away.'

1953 *Caddie A Sydney Barmaid* 223: 'Well,' said Bill, 'wot did the quack 'ave ter say?'

1960 John Iggulden *The Storms of Summer* 169: 'I'll get the quack at the Bush Hospital to have a look at it in the morning.'

1976 David Ireland *The Glass Canoe* 136: 'I go along to this quack and he says Get back to the surf and get some green vegetables into you.'

quaddy The quadrella [abbr.]

1979 *Age* (Melbourne) 19 Dec. 24: Cracking the quaddy as easy as 1234.

1982 *Age* (Melbourne) 28 May 26: Quaddie switch rattles TAB [heading]

quandong Someone disreputable, living by his or her wits [? because the quandong grows as a parasite]

1939 Kylie Tennant *Foveaux* 311: In this crowd of low heels, quandongs and ripperty men, she looked at her ease and yet not of them.

1973 Frank Huelin *Keep Moving* 178: *Quandong* Hobo who bludges or imposes on another.

1977 Jim Ramsay *Cop it Sweet* 75: *Quandong* Female who makes a practice of remaining virtuous after being wined and dined.

1980 *Sun-Herald* 27 Jan. 66: The way my luck is I'd finish up with a quandong . . . A beer and food bandit.

quanger A quince (*juvenile*)

1977 *Sydney Morning Herald* 5 Mar. 11: We had an abandoned quince orchard where we used to wage the most fantastic quanger wars.

Queensland Hat see **Joh hat**

Queensland salute A variant of the **Australian salute** q.v.

1981 *Sunday Mail* (Brisbane) 30 Aug. 2: The flies stick to you, and you suddenly realise what they mean when they talk about the Queensland salute.

Queensland sores See quot.

1892 G. L. James *Shall I Try Australia?* 242: 'Queensland Sores', or 'Barcoo rot' are, I believe, generally attributed to excessive thinness and poverty of the blood, caused by the great heat and absence of vegetable diet.

question, if it's a fair An apparent apology for

curiosity [also Irish, in Joyce's *A Portrait of the Artist as a Young Man* ch. 4]

1902 Henry Fletcher *The Waybacks* 90: 'So here's another taken down. How much, if it's a fair question?'

1903 Joseph Furphy *Such is Life* (1944) 30: 'Who's this Mother Bodysark – if it's a fair question?' asked Cooper.

1955 D'Arcy Niland *The Shiralee* 86: 'I don't want to be quizzy, Mac, but, if it's a fair question what's the drum?'

quid, not the full   Not 'all there', deficient [f. *quid* pound]

1953 Baker 132: *full quid* In full possession of one's faculties; a person who is said to be *ten bob* or *ten deaners* or even *tuppence* in the *quid*, is held to be a few shingles short.

1968 Geoffrey Dutton *Andy* 93: 'Yer mad. I don't think yer got a full quid.' commented the sailor.

1972 Ian Moffitt *The U-Jack Society* 227: We avoid individuality as firmly as we suspect joy ('You're not the full quid!').

1975 *Sydney Morning Herald* 5 Jul. 9: It's perfectly clear that not all members of our community are the full quid.

1982 Ian Moffitt *The Retreat of Radiance* 59: 'Best to stay clear of him. I'm beginning to think he's not the full quid.'

Quiet Achiever, the   Advertising slogan of BP Australia, given other applications

1982 *National Times* 30 May 41: Clutha is a wholly owned subsidiary of the oil company, BP Australia, whose latest advertising slogan for its mining operations in this country is 'The Quiet Achiever'.

1982 *Age* (Melbourne) 11 Sep. 30: Jeans – coaching's quiet achiever.

1984 *Sydney Morning Herald* 6 Sep. 14: It was his 40th birthday. He [Senator Gareth Evans] managed to find a few moments during the afternoon to cut a cake in his office, and to make a wish, which a staff member later revealed was 'to be a quiet achiever'.

quietly, just   Confidentially, between ourselves

1938 Xavier Herbert *Capricornia* 145: 'He'd love to see you 'fore you goes. Thinks a lot of you, just quietly.'

1941 Baker 40: *Just quietly* Between you and I.

1951 Eric Lambert *The Twenty Thousand Thieves* 161: 'Just quietly, he's up for a decoration.'

1972 Turner 109: *Just quietly* in Australia means 'between you and me' but tends to become a frequent and meaningless tag in New Zealand, just quietly.

1979 *NT News* (Darwin) 17 Oct. 6: Apparently the team has nothing to do with houses and just quietly, doesn't agree with the present policy.

quilt   To clout with the fist [E. dial. 'to beat, thrash, flog' OED 1832]

1945 Baker 120: *quilt* and *stoush* a person. [as fighting terms]

1973 Donald Stuart *Morning Star Evening Star* 111: More than one bloke I've seen Joe quilt good and proper for trying to make a joke of it.

quince, get on one's   To irritate, exasperate [unexplained]

1941 Baker 58: *Quince, get on one's* To annoy or aggravate deeply.

1959 Gerard Hamilton *Summer Glare* 45: 'That kid gets on my quince.'

1974 Desmond O'Grady *Deschooling Kevin Carew* 95: In an unguarded moment, he told Bull Moynihan 'This joint is getting on my quince.'

1979 Ron Barassi *Bulletin* 11 Sep. 72: 'There are times I get on the players' quince. A coach isn't there to be liked.'

Quist, to be Adrian   To be pissed i.e. drunk [rhyming slang on name of tennis player]

1978 *Australian* 31 May 9: I'm on the turps again – got Adrian Quist somethin' terrible the other night.

quoit   Buttocks [Partridge: 'ex roundness']

1941 Baker 58: *Quoit* The buttocks.

1951 Eric Lambert *The Twenty Thousand Thieves* 165: 'See those jokers sitting on their quoits over there?'

1954 T. A. G. Hungerford *Sowers of the Wind* 176: 'He blew the tripes outa me for nothing at all, and then he kicks a Nip in the coit.'

1972 John Bailey *The Wire Classroom* 82: 'I think he needs a good kick up the coit,' says Cromwell.

1984 J. B. Paul *Sydney Morning Herald* 20 Apr. 6: This 'anthem' [Advance Australia Fair] remains a horrid blend of words and music: execrable doggerel set to a banal strain. Such an undistinguished dirge is not calculated to sweep this sedentary citizen off his quoit.

quoits, go for one's   See quots [unexplained]

1941 Baker 58: *Quoits, go for one's* To travel quickly, go for one's life.

1952 Jon Cleary *The Sundowners* 34: 'Going for the lick of his coit up the street.'

1968 Stuart Gore *Holy Smoke* 80: 'Away they go for their quoits – flat out like a lizard drinking.'

R

rabbit-killer A blow to the back of the neck, like a karate chop [f. *rabbit punch* from the way a game-keeper puts a rabbit out of pain OED 1915]

1942 Gavin Casey *It's Harder for Girls* 23: I took a rush and gave him a rabbit-killer that must have nearly broken his neck.

1951 Dal Stivens *Jimmy Brockett* 99: 'He told me he was going to use a rabbit-killer punch on Hill.' 'If he does, I'll disqualify him.'

1963 Criena Rohan *Down by the Dockside* 255: He . . . had accounted for a couple more before he collected the rabbit killer that finally put him out of action.

1969 George Johnston *Clean Straw for Nothing* 282: The maddened Italian . . . kneed his host in the crotch and, as he doubled up in pain, felled him with a cruel rabbit-killer.

1981 *Alan Marshall's Australia* 39: 'His cobber barges in and Ted downs him with a rabbit-killer.'

rabbit-oh A hawker of rabbits for eating [f. the cry]

1904 A. B. Paterson 'Humours of a Horse Bazaar' in *Song of the Pen* (1983) 223: Dealers who know where they can place purchases at a profit – possibly with rabbit-oh vendors.

1911 Arthur Wright *Gambler's Gold* 75: Engaged in the hopeless task of trying to win the Rabbit-O man's money.

1943 Kylie Tennant *Time Enough Later* 181: Mrs Drew knew all about her neighbours from the butcher and the grocer and the rabbito.

1953 *Caddie A Sydney Barmaid* 199: I turned the corner of my street to see the rabbito's* horse and cart standing outside my gate. *An itinerant street seller of rabbits.

1975 *Sydney Morning Herald* 9 Apr. 1: Now 65, he is probably the last rabbit-oh in Sydney. 'I started helping my dad when I was just a boy,' he recalled. 'There were more rabbit-ohs then, but they've all died, or got old and given it away. Same as I'm going to do.' And he went on his way, shouting 'Rabbit-ohs!'

1983 Ruth Park *National Times* 22 Apr. 27: The 'rabbit-oh' was also a godsend [during the war], as rabbits were off the ration. You always bought a rabbit with the pelt on, as otherwise you might get a cat.

Rabbit-ohs, the The South Sydney Rugby League team ['The nickname has its origins in the 1930's Depression when club officials raised money for the players by raffling and hawking rabbits' *National Times* 4 Aug. 1975 36]

1975 *Australian* 21 Jul. 16: Rabbitohs hit rock bottom.

rabbit-proof fence A fence marking the borders between certain Australian states, therefore used as a point of reference

1957 Randolph Stow *The Bystander* 29: God! he thought. That's the coldest little bitch this side of the rabbit-proof fence.

1962 John O'Grady *Gone Fishin'* 24: 'You

wouldn't find a politer bloke this side of the rabbit-proof fence.'

1965 *The Tracks We Travel* ed. L. Haylen 75: A little, bow-legged, gappy-toothed ex-shearer from the other side of the rabbit-proof fence, chipped in.

1976 Dorothy Hewett *Bon-bons and Roses for Dolly* 28: 'Best little ticket takers this side of the rabbit-proof. Oh! We were a great team.'

race, not in the   Given no chance at all

1945 Margaret Trist *Now That We're Laughing* 73: 'With you and Daffy dressed up, none of us others will be in the race,' said Maureen.

1953 T. A. G. Hungerford *Riverslake* 227: 'See that bloke?' He pointed down the road after the vanished car. 'A few years ago he wouldn't have been in the race to own a car like that.'

1956 J. T. Lang *I Remember* 34: The trade unions realised that if the Chinese could get away with long hours and low pay they would not be in the race to get better conditions.

1984 *Sydney Morning Herald* 10 May 18: 'How could three men fight 50? They were not in the race.'

race off   To seduce; whisk away with a view to seduction

1965 William Dick *A Bunch of Ratbags* 185: Three of Knuckles's boys had raced Sharon off to the park to see if they could do any good for themselves.

1969 Wilda Moxham *The Apprentice* 87: 'That's one bird you won't race off,' Rufe said. 'I know her, and the bloke she's with.'

1970 Jack Hibberd *White with Wire Wheels* in *Penguin Plays* 224: 'By Christ, if he races her off, it'll be the last fat he ever cracks.'

1971 Rena Briand *White Man in a Hole* 30: 'If I don't race a sheila orf at night, I start thinkin' and can't sleep.'

1984 *Sydney Morning Herald* 3 Dec. 5. On Saturday night, in a huge crush outside the Southern Cross Hotel, she [Mrs Peacock] started for the party rally holding Andrew's hand, then found she was attached to the hand of a minder from Liberal Headquarters. 'I could have been raced off', she grins.

rack, to put one's cue back in the   see **cue**

rack off   To go missing; as an imperative, 'Get lost' [? variant of *nick off, fuck off, piss off*]

[**1786** William Beckford *Vathek* 70: Vathek ... was still employed [i.e. urinating], not having quite racked off his wine.]

1975 *Sun-Herald* 29 Jun. 83: 'Rak Off Normie' [title in list of pop records]

1976 *Australian* 3 Sep. 4: Rack orf Jack – we ain't

allowed to serve minors no more. [cartoon caption]

1981 Angelo Loukakis *For the Patriarch* 32: 'What'll we do now?' asks Bill. 'Let's rack off for a while', I say.

Rafferty (Rafferty's) rules   No rules at all [? *reffatory* refractory EDD]

1928 *Bulletin* 5 Jan. 37: M.Q. (and Rafferty) Rules [title of paragraph on a boxing match]

1935 *Sydney Morning Herald* 28 Dec. 11: Rafferty rules may suit Mr Keenan and the Communist party, but they are repugnant to the trade union movement.

1941 Baker 58: *Rafferty rules* No rules at all, applied to any system, organization or contest run in slipshod fashion.

1956 Miles Franklin *Laughter, Not for a Cage* 34: Dr Mulhaus ... being no English gentleman, follows Rafferty's rules with exhilarating results.

1964 H. P. Tritton *Time Means Tucker* 34: The Show adjourned at noon for the races. They seemed to be run on the 'Rafferty Rules' principle, but I heard no complaints.

1974 *Bulletin* 18 May 63: Rafferty's rules predominate.

1984 *Australian* 7 Feb. 16: Marylebone Cricket Club rules could become 'Rafferty's rules' if a cricket umpire's decision was not obeyed, a Queen's Counsel told the Supreme Court in Perth yesterday.

raffia mafia   See **basket-weaving**

1984 *Weekend Australian* 7 Jul. Mag. 20: Mr Hayden's office has not responded to my request ... why he should be seeking Victorian grandeur in Sydney's inner suburbs, which according to his colleague Paul Keating, are inhabited largely by basket weavers and what others are pleased to call the 'raffia Mafia'.

rage, maintain the   Mr E. G. Whitlam's advice to the crowd on the steps of Parliament House on 11 November 1975 after the reading of the proclamation dissolving Parliament

1976 Frank Moorhouse *Conference-Ville* 64: I thought to myself that it was those at the heart of the Labor Party who had not been able to 'maintain the rage'. They seemed to have been the most damaged in spirit by it all.

1979 Gough Whitlam *The Truth of the Matter* 119: I concluded: 'Maintain your rage and your enthusiasm through the campaign for the election now to be held and until polling day'.

1982 *Australian* 5 Aug. 9: Professor [Russel] Ward is one of those Australians who has 'maintained the rage' over the sacking of the Whitlam Labor Government.

1983 *Sun-Herald* 14 Aug. 11: The Queensland Liberals, led by Terry White, are finding, as Gough

Whitlam did in 1975, that it is very difficult to maintain the rage. Tomorrow the Liberals will have lost their seven ministries and revert to a team of 20 backbenchers.

rager 'An old and fierce bullock or cow, that always begins to rage in the stockyard' (Morris)
1876 Rolf Boldrewood *A Colonial Reformer* (1890) 225: The 'ragers' observing this movement [into the receiving yard] keep wildly and excitedly 'ringing'.

rah rahs Players and supporters of Rugby Union football [f. *rah rah*, 'characteristic of the spirit or feeling of college students, esp. in respect to sporting and social activities' U.S. 1914 Wentworth and Flexner]
1980 *Sydney Morning Herald* 3 May 66: Barry Stumbles has introduced an interesting feature to St George Rugby Union Club's training – torture ... The rah-rahs do things in style. They have called in the army.
1980 *Sunday Mail* (Brisbane) 29 Jun. 3: The 'rah rah' rugger boys of Ballymore really turned it on at yesterday's Test.
1983 Mungo MacCallum *Sun-Herald* 5 Jun. 72: Your basic Rugby Rah Rah in his tweed jacket with the leather patches on the elbows and the red setter as his constant companion may snort into his hip flask in disgust, but in this world all things change. Even Rugger.
1983 *Sydney Morning Herald* 20 Aug. 31: Do the people at the Rugby Union Test in Sydney today really deserve to be called a rah-rah crowd? The term is derisive. It suggests that Rugby followers, by and large, are sporting snobs. Australians use it in the belief, apparently, that it originated at Twickenham or some similar place where, as they imagine it, the Rugby gentry shout 'rah rah' for their team. (In fact, rah-rah attached itself to Rugby for a different reason. According to one dictionary, rah-rah-rah rounds off a certain Maori war cry which New Zealand Rugby players adopted as long ago as the late 1800s. Somehow it came to denote the character of the game itself and the type of people who followed it.)

Raiders, the The Canberra Raiders Rugby League club
1982 *Sun-Herald* 7 Feb. 73: Raiders make great start [heading] Canberra Raiders marked their entry into the Sydney Rugby League competition with a sound display last night.

rainbow See quots
1919 W. H. Downing *Digger Dialects* 40: *Rainbow* A reinforcement, or member of non-combatant corps, who joined a fighting unit after the Armistice. (Rainbow after the storm).

1935 H. R. Williams *Comrades of the Great Adventure* 174: 'Rainbow' was the nickname given to fellows who came to France after the 'storm' was over.
1938 Eric Lowe *Salute to Freedom* 433: 'Were you at Mesalaba?' he asked. 'No', Robin said, and added rather bitterly, 'I'm a rainbow – came over after the storm.'
1944 Lawson Glassop *We Were the Rats* 153: We remembered, too, how, when we had passed them [the Sixth Division] on the way up, they had called us the 'long thinkers' and 'rainbows'. 'Rainbows?' we had asked. 'Yeah,' they replied, 'you're rainbows all right. You always see a rainbow after a storm.'
1947 Vance Palmer *Cyclone* 181: 'Rainbow, eh? Mighty good, Clive always was, at showing up after the storm was over!'

raining, if it was ~ pea soup, I'd get hit on the head by a fork An expression (with many variants) of habitual ill luck [f. proverb 'If it should rain porridge, he would want [lack] his dish' OED 1670]
1944 Randolph Bedford *Naught to Thirty-three* 110: 'I'm that unlucky that if it rained soup, everybody else would have a spoon and I'd be left with a fork.'
1950 K. S. Prichard *Winged Seeds* 29: 'Unluckiest man I ever knew. If it was raining pea soup, he'd only have a fork.'
1954 T. A. G. Hungerford *Sowers of the Wind* 69: 'If it was rainin' palaces I'd get hit on the head with the handle of the dunny door.'
1967 Frank Hardy *Billy Borker Yarns Again* 88: He was so unlucky that when it was raining Paris night clubs he got hit on the head with a Woolloomooloo plonk shop.
1970 Richard Beilby *No Medals for Aphrodite* 169: 'Gawd, we're an unlucky battalion, we are. If it was rainin' virgins we'd be washed away with a poofta, dinkum!'

ram *n. & v.* A trickster employed to 'set up' victims for another [*ramp* to rob or swindle OED 1812]
[**1812** Vaux: *Ramp* to rob any person or place by open violence or suddenly snatching at something and running off with it.]
1941 Baker 59: *Ram* A trickster's confederate.
1952 *Coast to Coast 1951–1952* 199: Siddy might have been ramming for you, but what you didn't know, my lad, was that he was helping me to hook you. You were a goner from the start.
1964 H. P. Tritton *Time Means Tucker* 33: A gentleman with an umbrella, three thimbles and a pea was demonstrating how 'the quickness of the hand deceives the eye' and was raking in the money at a great rate. When business slackened, another gentleman would pick up the pea with surprising regularity. This would bring the crowd

back to try their luck again. No one seemed to wake up to the fact that the second gentleman was 'ramming' for the first gentleman.
see **amster**

rammies   Trousers: *rare* [? f. Malay *rami* a fibre or garment woven from it]
1919 W. H. Downing *Digger Dialects* 41: *Rammies* Breeches.
1943 Baker 63: *Rammies* Trousers.
1953 T. A. G. Hungerford *Riverslake* 42: 'Elastic for the old girl's rammies.'

rap   A 'boost', a commendation (interchangeable with **wrap** q.v.)
1939 Kylie Tennant *Foveaux* 176: 'Everyone wants to be seen with a high-up feller. When I pass the time of day to a cove he feels that's a rap for him, see?'
1959 D'Arcy Niland *The Big Smoke* 12: 'His old man give him a rap, and that's all I know.'
1963 Football coach reported in Keith Dunstan *Sports* (1973) 229: 'And if someone does something good, takes a good mark, give him a rap. Tell him.'
1974 *Sun* (Sydney) 19 Feb. 12: A few raps in the right places and I was chosen for City first against Country and then for NSW against Queensland.
1982 *Sun-Herald* 1 Aug. 77: 'Give Tony a rap. He was so cool under pressure', said Gordon coach Geoff Caban.

rap up   To speak highly of, 'boost' (interchangeable with **wrap up** q.v.)
1957 D'Arcy Niland *Call Me When the Cross Turns Over* 138: 'You dream and feel hopeless, I don't.' 'Rapping yourself up a bit, aren't you?' Ibid. 174: 'They couldn't rap him up enough then.'

rapt   Overjoyed, carried away (interchangeable with **wrapped** q.v.)
1974 Keith Stackpole *Not Just for Openers* 114. Poor O'Keefe wasn't so rapt; he took none for 121. Ibid. 122: Travelling in the bus back to the Waldorf that evening, everyone was rapt.
1976 *Australian* 21 Jan. 1: Thommo tops the PM with $63,000 a year. 'All I can say is I'm rapt.'

rat *v.*   To act as a sneak thief, esp. from a mining claim, swag
1919 W. H. Downing *Digger Dialects* 59: *Rat, to*: To steal: ferret through someone's belongings (2) to take property from a dead body.
1921 K. S. Prichard *The Black Opal* 69: If claims are ratted it is said there are strangers about, and the miners deal with rats according to their own ideas of justice.
1940 Ion L. Idriess *Lightning Ridge* 109: Two claims had been ratted in the night.

1964 David Ireland *Image in the Clay* 65: 'Soon as my back's turned, you've ratted my bags!'

rat, cunning as a (sewer) shithouse   Extremely cunning
1894 Henry Lawson 'Stiffner and Jim (Thirdly, Bill)' *Prose* i 124: He was meaner than a gold-field Chinaman, and sharper than a sewer rat.
1962 Criena Rohan *The Delinquents* 36: Mrs Hansen called Lola a dirty little half-bred, over-sexed slut, no better than the bloody blacks and cunning as a shithouse rat.
1971 George Johnston *A Cartload of Clay* 158: 'Real bastard. Doesn't do a tap. Cunning as a shithouse rat, too.'
1981 *Sunday Mail* (Brisbane) 25 Oct. 19: He was as cunning as the well known Australian dunny rat.

rat up a drainpipe, like a   Quick to seize an opportunity, esp. sexual
1959 Eric Lambert *Glory Thrown In* 104: 'First time we spoke she turned it on – I was like a rat up a rope!'
1962 Criena Rohan *The Delinquents* 76: 'He'd be up you like a rat up a drain-pipe, given the chance.'
1972 Geoff Morley *Jockey Rides Honest Race* 98: 'How'd you go?' 'Like a rat up a drainpipe.'
1978 Ronald McKie *Bitter Bread* 158: 'I figured that when I told the demons about 'em they'd be down 'ere like rats up a drain.'
1983 Clem Gorman *A Night in the Arms of Raeleen* 40: 'I used to get up them sheilas down there like a rat up a drainpipe!'

rat with a gold tooth   see **flash**

ratbag   An eccentric or stupid person [see *rats*]
1937 William Hatfield *I Find Australia* 138: 'You brought one rat-bag *in*,' said Ewens to me, 'so now do me a favour by taking one off my hands.'
1945 Roy Rene *Mo's Memoirs* 102. I don't want to give you the idea that we were nothing but a lot of ratbags, because we weren't.
1959 Gerard Hamilton *Summer Glare* 129: I told myself I had been a bloody ratbag for letting myself get worked up over Dookie.
1962 R. D. FitzGerald *Southmost Twelve* 31: I will go out and hear the strain / of rat-bag orators at large.
1965 Patrick White *Four Plays* 185: 'It's that Miss Docker.' 'That old rat-bag!'
1975 Don Townshend *Gland Time* 134: 'She's a bloody ratbag.'
1981 *Age* (Melbourne) 1 Oct. 2: His first 'Piggy' act of the day was to hang up on radio person Derryn Hinch because 'I don't talk to ratbags.'
ratbaggery
1984 *Age* (Melbourne) 23 Jan. Extra 16: 'Hey,

Hey' is exhausting, daring, often very funny rat-baggery.

rathouse   The lunatic asylum [see *rats*]
1922 Arthur Wright *A Colt from the Country* 83: 'He'll be the long-lost boy, instead of the guy that's missed and landed in the rat-house.'
1943 Margaret Trist *In the Sun* 44: 'Livin' so much alone's no good to anyone. It'll drive you to the rat house.'
1953 T. A. G. Hungerford *Riverslake* 190: 'You'll end up in the rat-house.'
1963 Brian James *Hopeton High* 174: 'This place is growing more like a circus or a rat-house every day', stormed Mr Rudder.
1971 Frank Hardy *The Outcasts of Foolgarah* 108: Poor devil, she ended up in the rathouse eventually.

ratpower   Derisive measure of a bowler's speed [cf. *horsepower*]
1974 Keith Stackpole *Not Just for Openers* 93: 'You've got nothing to grumble about. If you were quick, you might have, but you are only half rat-power.'
1983 *Weekend Australian* 12 Feb. 15: Some may see Geoff Lawson and Rodney Hogg bowling at what fellow players quaintly call 'half-rat power' as a sign of adapting successfully to the limited-over game.

rats, to have (be); ratty   To be odd, eccentric, irresponsible [? f. *ratty*, wretched, mean, miserable OED 1885]
1894 Henry Lawson *Prose* i 57: 'Rats' [story title]
1902 Henry Lawson 'Gettin' Back on Dave Regan' *Prose* i 367: 'I can't make it out at all. I believe she's gone ratty.'
1908 Henry Fletcher *Dads and Dan between Smokes* 65: In a town a whole population gets rats together, an' though they's all clean daft at times, yet, 'cause they all thinks alike, they don't doubt they's sane.
1922 Arthur Wright *A Colt from the Country* 86: 'There was a rough-up in a pub; he got a knock, had a fit, and went real ratty, and that was the end of him.'
1942 Sarah Campion *Bonanza* 17: Mo had watched all this ... imagining what it must be like to be mad. Not raving, dangerous, mad but simple rats, like Bogy.

Rats, the Green   see **Green**

ratshit   General term of opprobrium
1974 David Williamson *Three Plays* 153: 'In all fairness she used to have some sort of spark; but the word around the industry is that she's gone ratshit.'

1977 David Foster *Escape to Reality* 41: 'The money's ratshit. You don't work there for the money.'
1980 Rod Ansell *To Fight the Wild* 105: Some days I felt ratshit, depressed about getting weaker, worried ... and lonely.
1984 *Sun-Herald* 29 Jan. 9: Just the other day London asked if he [Bryan Brown] was interested in playing the lead in Guys and Dolls and what was his voice like? He said yes to the first question and 'ratshit' to the second.

rattle the pan   To 'kick the bucket', die
1948 A. W. Upfield *An Author Bites the Dust* 140: 'The last time he forgot was just before he rattled the pan.'

raw prawn, come the   see **prawn**

razoo, not a (brass)   No money at all. The expression is always negative (no one is ever mentioned as *having* a razoo, and no coin of the name exists) [? f. *not a sou*]
1931 William Hatfield *Sheepmates* 268: 'Richards never has a rahzoo.'
1939 Leonard Mann *Mountain Flat* 120: 'I wouldn't give you a razoo.'
1947 John Morrison *Sailors Belong Ships* 187: 'I wouldn't give you a razhoo for anything between there and Charmian Road.'
1957 Ray Lawler *Summer of the Seventeenth Doll* 35: 'I picked him up in Brisbane a week ago. By then he hardly had a razoo.'
1964 Jon Cleary *A Flight of Chariots* 361: 'Poor bastard,' he heard one of the men nearby say. 'I wouldn't give a brass razoo for his chances out there.'
1975 Jessica Anderson *The Commandant* 155: The pile had been stolen. Every penny. Every last brass razoo.
1981 *Australian* 13 Feb. 7: In fact had Expo gone ahead, by the end of the project it would have cost the taxpayers of NSW not a brass razoo.

Razor Gang   Committee for Review of Commonwealth Functions chaired by Sir Phillip Lynch 1981; any similar body, esp. the Expenditure Review Committee of the Hawke cabinet
1981 *National Times* 9 Aug. 17: The Public Service Board says there have been extensive redeployments as a result of the Razor Gang report, but is unable to give the exact figures.
1983 *National Times* 29 Apr. 6: The committee – Hawke's razor gang – held its first full-scale meeting in Adelaide this week.
1984 *Age* (Melbourne) 23 Jul. 4: Labor's razor gang gets the strop out [heading]

RBT   Random breath testing, introduced in N.S.W.

on 17 Dec. 1982

1983 *Sydney Morning Herald* 23 Dec. 6: RBT is not all that it seems [heading]

1984 *Sydney Morning Herald* 30 Jun. 3: RBTs up 80 pc, but charges only 25 pc [heading] A big increase in the level of random breath testing in NSW during the first five months of this year has failed to result in an equivalent rise in the numbers of motorists charged with drink driving.

read, you wouldn't ~ about it Expression of mingled incredulity and disgust

1950 Jon Cleary *Just Let Me Be* 135: 'Everything I backed ran like a no-hoper. Four certs I had, and the bludgers were so far back the ambulance nearly had to bring 'em home. You wouldn't read about it.'

1962 Dymphna Cusack *Picnic Races* 249: He drew a deep breath. 'You wouldn't read about it.'

1973 H. Williams *My Love Had a Black Speed Stripe* 69: You wouldn't read about it. A bloke his missus reckoned was a doctor of philosophy, whatever that was, and just about the biggest dill you could meet.

red blanket See quot.

1926 Alfred Giles *Exploring in the Seventies* 127: Tinned meat in 6 lb tins ('red blanket' we called it). The tins were painted red without labels or description of contents.

Red Centre, the Central Australia [f. the iron oxide colouring the soil]

1936 H. H. Finlayson *The Red Centre: Man and Beast in the Heart of Australia* [book title]

1981 *Weekend Australian* 18 Jul. Mag. 7: From life in the cities, a trip to the Red Centre is a battery-recharging exercise.

1982 *Age* (Melbourne) 28 Jun. 14: Camel trek in the red Centre [heading]

Redfern, getting off at *Coitus Interruptus* [f. Redfern as the station immediately before Sydney Central; see quot. 1970]

1956 Heard in conversation.

1970 *Times Literary Supplement* 4 Dec. 1422: *To get off at Redfern* ... is dull and unoriginal. Since the nineteenth century, natives of Newcastle upon Tyne have described the procedure alliteratively as *getting out at Gateshead*. [A correspondent commenting on a review of Partridge]

1976 Jack Beasley in foreword to Dorothy Hewett *This Old Man Comes Rolling Home* vii: 'Getting off at Redfern', the penultimate rail stop, was a euphemism for *coitus interruptus*.

Red Heart, the Central Australia [f. the presence of iron oxide in the soil]

1931 Miles Franklin *Back to Bool Bool* 45: The dawn was murky. Particles of the red heart of Australia had reached the pampered city, staining the arum lilies and irritating the housewives.

1932 Myrtle Rose White *No Roads Go By* 83: After climbing over the lake's rim we were faced with the flat sandy country again – the red heart of Australia!

1944 Frank Clune *The Red Heart: Sagas of Centralia* [book title]

1956 Ion L. Idriess *Flynn of the Inland* (1965) 184: He sleeps now in the harsh Red Heart of Australia.

1984 *Australian* 8 Oct. 3: It starts in the Waltzing Matilda country where the song was written ... It ends in the red heart. The proposed Outback Highway is now a corrugated track.

red hot Extreme, unreasonable, 'over the odds'

1896 Henry Lawson 'Jones's Alley' *Prose* i 38: When ... she paused for breath, he drew a long one, gave a short whistle, and said: 'Well, it's red-hot!'

1907 Arthur Wright *Keane of Kalgoorlie* 107: 'It's red hot,' put in Dave, 'th' way these owners makes 'er pore man give 'em a lump in th' sweep.'

1920 Louis Esson 'The Woman Tamer' in *Dead Timber* 24: 'That's red hot. You can't book me for the Vag.'

1924 *Truth* 27 Apr. 6: *Red 'ot* Unfair; extreme.

1941 Baker 59: *Red Hot* Unreasonable, unfair, e.g. 'a red hot price'.

1980 *Sun* (Sydney) 22 Feb. 21: Tomato prices are red hot.

red hots The trots [rhyming slang]

1979 *Herald* (Melbourne) 24 Feb. 35: It's not often I'd consider giving the red hots a miss on Saturday night – especially when I've got a couple of certainties.

1983 *Sydney Morning Herald* 22 Apr. 27: The reason for the press conference was to defend trotting and lay to rest the 'red hots' stigma. It is an unjustified tag which has remained with the industry since the late 1920s and early 1930s when, Judge Goran pointed out, someone with a penchant for rhyming slang coined the term.

Redlegs, the 1 The Melbourne V.F.L. team, in 1930; since the Red Demons, then the Demons [f. team colours]

2 In South Australia, the Norwood Australian Rules team

1979 *Advertiser* (Adelaide) 9 Mar. 20: Barton joins Redlegs [heading] Sturt rover Robert Barton has joined Norwood.

3 In Queensland, the Kedron Australian Rules team

1979 *Courier-Mail* (Brisbane) 17 Apr. 23: The Redlegs lifted their game in the second term.

4   In Tasmania, the City-South T.F.L. team
1980 *Mercury* (Hobart) 14 Apr. 18: Redlegs' hopes crash [heading] City-South's hopes of making the Winfield Cup finals took a nosedive . . . at Devonport Oval on Saturday.

red ned   Cheap red wine
1953 T. A. G. Hungerford *Riverslake* 35: 'There's a bottle of Red Ned in my room – slip down and hit it. You need a kick!'
1966 Hal Porter *The Paper Chase* 41: Plonk, steam, bombo, Red Ned, or Red Nell are among the derogatory names for wine. [in the 1930s]
1978 John Hepworth *His Book* 156: We got rid of them all – and made enough for a feed and a bottle of red ned.
1983 *Australian* 29 Jun. 9: Research indicates red wine may help control – and even prevent – that social inhibitor, herpes simplex II. It seems the specific ingredient that tackles the virus is tannin, 'the astringent mouth-puckering compound' found in abundance in Red Ned.

Reds, the (Dirty)   The Drummoyne, N.S.W., Rugby Union team [f. team colours]
1974 *Sunday-Telegraph* (Sydney) 8 Sep. 87: The complete lack of flair in the whole Drummoyne outfit raises doubts that the Dirty Reds could have done anything if given more chances.
1983 *Sun-Herald* 29 May 72: 'The spirit of the Dirty Reds is alive . . . Drummoyne High School, our nursery, has dropped from 800 to 400 boys, but at the same time five high schools in the area have switched from League to Union.'

red steer (bull), the   A bushfire
1930 *Bulletin* 21 May 20: There had been a number of grass fires in the district, and suspicion falling on 'Monkey' Brown . . . he was accused of loosing the 'red bull' on the community.
1941 Baker 59: *Red Steer, the* Fire, esp. a bushfire. (Bush slang.)
1963 John Cantwell *No Stranger to the Flame* 12: The cane-cutter, made negro by sun and by soot from fires (Red Steers, they called them).
1971 Frank Hardy *The Outcasts of Foolgarah* 118: Like the bushfires: hadn't he patented the special extinguisher to end the blight of the red steer for all time?

Reef, the   The Great Barrier Reef
1934 Thomas Wood *Cobbers* 219: It is not *a* Reef, a long breakwater tastefully coloured pink . . . It is *the* Reef.
1948 William Hatfield *Barrier Reef Days* 31: 'Never, *never* go in swimming anywhere on the reef or paddling or wading *without shoes*'.
1977 Judith Wright *The Coral Battleground* 1: My qualification for writing this book is that I was

privileged to be one of the people who fought the battle for the Reef itself.
1979 *Courier-Mail* (Brisbane) 12 May 2: Foreign labor fears may bring ban on Reef drilling [heading]

reffo   A European refugee: *derogatory* [abbr.]
1941 Baker 59: *Reffo* A refugee from Europe.
1951 Dymphna Cusack and Florence James *Come In Spinner* 278: 'The woman's a Viennese.' 'Oh, a reffo?'
1961 Patrick White *Riders in the Chariot* 221: He was, in any case, a blasted foreigner, and bloody reffo, and should have been glad he was allowed to exist at all.
1968 Geoffrey Dutton *Andy* 98: 'Those bloody reffos always pitch that yarn.'
1970 Jon Cleary *Helga's Web* 33–4: Reffo was a term that had been out of date for years; he wondered where the Italian had picked it up.
1981 Frank Devine *Sydney Morning Herald* 10 Jan. 16: I half suspect Channel 0 of being both a mean Australian practical joke on the reffos and yet another example of the Government's tight fistedness.

Reg Grundys, reginalds   Undies [rhyming slang]
1981 *National Times* 1 Feb. 14: Reg Grundies (undies).
1984 *Sydney Morning Herald* 7 Aug. Good Living 1: The masseuse, Debbie, said nonchalantly: 'Just pop all your clothes off and I'll be right back'. I should have known she meant everything, even the reginalds.

rego   Motor vehicle registration [abbr.]
1975 *Sydney Morning Herald* 15 Nov. 67: Austin 1800, 8 mths rego. Gd tyres, radio. Heater. Goes well. $450 o.n.o.
1983 David Foster *Plumbum* 309: Jason gave his car to a certain notorious character, even paid to transfer the rego.

rels, rellies, rellos   Relatives [abbr.]
1981 *Sydney Morning Herald* 18 Apr. 32: Physician to both mob and swells, / He loved his wife but not her rels.
1981 *Bulletin* 22 Dec. 208: Dreaded rellies are not so easily disposed of.
1982 *Sydney Morning Herald* 16 Dec. 6: It is very easy for dinkum Aussies to assert that we can't afford at present to let migrants bring out all their rellos.
1984 Damien Broderick *Transmitters* 77: I don't imagine Lanie's rellies would object to one more stray.

remittance man   Someone sent out to the colonies by his family, and sustained there by funds remitted at regular intervals; 'one who derives the means of an inglorious and frequently dissolute existence from the periodical receipt of money sent out to him from Europe' (Morris)

1897 Mark Twain *Following the Equator* 33: He was a 'remittance man', the first one I had ever seen or heard of ... dissipated ne'er-do-weels belonging to important families in England and Canada were not cast off by their people while there was any hope of reforming them, but when that last hope perished at last, the ne'er-do-weel was sent abroad to get him out of the way ... When he reached his destined port he would find a remittance awaiting him there. Not a large one, but just enough to keep him a month. A similar remittance would come monthly thereafter.

1901 Henry Lawson 'The Story of "Gentleman-Once"' *Prose* i 533: 'The remittance system is an insult to any manhood that may be left in the black sheep, and an insult to the land he is sent to. The cursed quarterly allowance is a stone round his neck which will drag him down deeper in a new land than he would have fallen at home. You know that remittance men are regarded with such contempt in the Bush that a man seldom admits he is one, save when he's drunk and reckless and wants money or credit.'

1905 Joseph Furphy *Rigby's Romance* ed. R. G. Howarth (1946) 81: 'You uncivilized animal; you're just about fit to associate with remittance men.'

1907 Ambrose Pratt *The Remittance Man* 27: 'A remittance man. He hasn't sixpence in the world, beyond a pittance he receives quarterly, through my father's bank from England – about £10 I think. His relatives allow him that to keep him away from home.'

1937 *Best Australian One-Act Plays* 61: 'These fellows are all the same – a ne'er-do-well – a remittance man.'

1946 Judith Wright *The Moving Image* 17: 'Remittance Man' [poem title]

1972 Alexander Macdonald *The Ukelele Player under the Red Lamp* 180: For then, as now, the A.B.C. never failed to cater for its homesick English listeners, including remittance men, out-of-work actors and retired plumbers from Wapping.

1980 Thomas Keneally *The Cut-Rate Kingdom* 92: Among other parliamentarians he looked like an English remittance man wandered into the house without warning and given second-class seating on the back benches of the proletarian party, among people with whom he had nothing in common.

reo A reinforcement: Services slang in World War II

1944 Lawson Glassop *We Were the Rats* 224: 'Where's our reos?' asked Eddie.

1952 T. A. G. Hungerford *The Ridge and the River* 22: 'He's on'y a kid, ain't he? I wonder if he's a reo for us, or something?'

1959 Eric Lambert *Glory Thrown In* 207: Doc was talking to the 'reos' in his platoon.

rep Representative, esp. a union representative [abbr.]

1899 Henry Lawson 'A Rough Shed' *Prose* i 465: The shearers' rep. requests both apostles to shut up or leave.

1907 Charles MacAlister *Old Pioneering Days in the Sunny South* 357: While fortunes are made from wool ... so long will the shearer be worthy of his hire; and so long, we believe, will the A.W.U. and the shed 'Rep.' be absolute necessities of the shearer's 'plan of campaign' for his just rights.

1919 A. B. Paterson *The Cook's Dog* in *Song of the Pen* (1983) 411: The shearers then drew apart and held a ballot for a 'rep' i.e., shearers' representative, whose duty it would be to bring forward any grievances, see that union rules were observed, and union dues collected from all hands in the shed.

1956 F. B. Vickers *First Place to the Stranger* 235: Curly our Union rep, had gathered up all our returns and sent them into Cranston as evidence.

1965 Leslie Haylen *Big Red* 5: To the rural worker in the nineteen-thirties the initials A.W.U. were the alphabetical abbreviation of a way of life in the country. The 'rep' was its vicar, its apostle, its propagandist, its dues collector.

Repat Repatriation, the government department concerned with the welfare of ex-servicemen and women [abbr.]

1951 *Argus* (Melbourne) 9 Aug. 6: Repat. Wards Wanted for Mothers [heading]

1959 Vance Palmer *The Big Fellow* 15: 'Repat would see me through.'

1968 Barry Humphries *A Nice Night's Entertainment* (1981) 109: The good people here at the Repat [hospital] have been particularly decent to me for the duration of my stay here.

1971 Frank Hardy *The Outcasts of Foolgarah* 42: He had come to the Repat. Hospital to take Moss away.

1983 David Foster *Plumbum* 367: Gonna join a dole queue, gonna ease my tension with a repat pension.

1984 Germaine Greer *Sydney Morning Herald* 9 Feb. 4: My father was listed as totally disabled by the Repat when he came back from the war.

Reps, the The House of Representatives [abbr.]

1982 *Bulletin* 19 Oct. 70: A private member's Bill on industrial democracy passed through the Senate. It will be considered soon in the Reps.

retread 1 A World War I soldier re-enlisting in World War II
1941 *Salt* 22 Dec. 36: *retread* a 1914–18 soldier enlisted a second time.
2 A retired schoolteacher returning to a temporary appointment
1950 Brian James *The Advancement of Spencer Button* 267: There were three 'retreads' among the men.
1953 Baker 142: *retread*, a school-teachers' word for a teacher who has been recalled to duty from retirement.
1984 *Sydney Morning Herald* 9 Jul. 3: Mr Culgin did work with some retired teachers for brief periods and they were referred to as 'retreads'.

returned man A returned serviceman
1935 H. R. Williams *Comrades of the Great Adventure* 305: Civilian life has failed to furnish many returned men with all they deserve.
1943 Herbert M. Moran *Beyond the Hill Lies China* 145: The Returned Soldiers' vote had, at the beginning, been an important factor at every Election. But soon their brief solidarity weakened and Returned Men voted on the old party lines.
1974 Barry Humphries *A Nice Night's Entertainment* (1981) 141: I'm reminded of a very dear old friend of ours, Pat Hennessy, a Returned man.
1979 George Stewart *The Leveller* 21: Another group with a certain comradeship were the returned men, ex-soldiers and sailors from World War One.
1981 A. B. Facey *A Fortunate Life* 289: He said that if I wasn't a returned soldier he would have had to fail me but they could not reject a returned man on war injuries.

rev head See quot. 1979
1979 *Sydney Morning Herald* 3 Mar. 13: Harkins points out the 'rev heads' (fast driving teenage yobos) and the 'loweys' (equally fast young girls) he knows lolling about outside the Commercial Hotel.
1982 *Sydney Morning Herald* 18 Sep. 1: Worriers are stressheads and fast drivers are revheads.
1984 *The Open Road* (Sydney) Apr./May 4: I still insist that being booked for speeding didn't force me to make the momentous decision to stop driving like a teenage revvy.

revolving door, couldn't go two rounds with a Vince Gair's opinion of Billy Snedden
1974 *Australian* 3 Apr. 5: Mr Daly said Senator Gair had described Mr Snedden as a man who 'could not go two rounds with a revolving door.'
1977 Fred Daly *From Curtin to Kerr* 148: Billy Snedden, as Leader of the Opposition, was very upset when Gair described him as 'a lightweight who couldn't go two rounds with a revolving door'.

1982 *Australian* 24 Feb. 9: He [Russ Hinze] told Senator Bonner on national television: 'You couldn't go two rounds with a revolving door'.
1984 *Sydney Morning Herald* 3 May 15: The famous quote of the late Mr Vince Gair about Sir Billy Snedden in 1974, that 'Billy Snedden couldn't go two rounds with a revolving door', is hardly likely to conjure up the image of the tough, fast moving man of property.

revvy see **revhead**

ribs, all prick and ~, like a drover's dog see **all**

ribuck see **ryebuck**

Rice, a roll Jack ~ couldn't jump over See quot. 1945
1945 Baker 107: A man well supplied with cash . . . may even be fortunate enough to have *a roll Jack Rice couldn't jump over*. Jack Rice was a racehorse noted for his performances over hurdles.
1954 Tom Ronan *Vision Splendid* 119: 'I've got a roll Jack Rice couldn't jump over.' Marty produced one of those wads of currency Mr Toppingham had seen only in the cruder American films and started peeling off ten-pound notes.
1960 John O'Grady *Cop This Lot* 82: 'Man walks around with a roll in 'is kick Jack Rice couldn't jump over, an' 'e's not worth a zac.'
1970 Jon Cleary *Helga's Web* 267: 'I never seen twenty thousand in cash before. Somehow you'd think it'd amount to a pile Jack Rice couldn't jump over.' Helidon wondered who Jack Rice was, then remembered it was a famous hurdle horse with a prodigious leap.
1982 Joe Andersen *Winners Can Laugh* 136: He called himself Jack Rice, but . . . the name was probably a tribute to the prince of hurdlers whose exploits gave rise to the expression, 'so big that Jack Rice couldn't jump it'. As proof of his success, he invariably carried a roll of notes of such dimensions.

rice pudding, couldn't knock the skin off a see **couldn't**

ridge (ridgie-didge) Genuine, 'on the level' [f. *ridge* gold OED 1665 (thieves' slang)]
[**1812** Vaux: *Ridge* gold, whether in coin or any other shape]
1945 Baker 126: We also describe something especially good as . . . *ridge*.
1950 *Australian Police Journal* Apr. 117: *Ridge (or reet)* Right; or O.K.
1953 *The Sunburnt Country* ed. Ian Bevan 130: *Ridgy Didge* (derived from 'rigid digger', in its turn meaning a straight-up soldier, and hence implying

integrity) means 'the truth'. The phrase is used invariably either as a simple question 'Ridgy Didge?' or as an unequivocal assurance: 'Ridgy Didge!'

1953 Kylie Tennant *The Joyful Condemned* 294: 'He'll tell you himself I'm ridgey-dite. I worked for him.'

1963 Lawson Glassop *The Rats in New Guinea* 153: 'It's ridgie-didge,' said Eddie. 'Spit me death.'

1971 David Ireland *The Unknown Industrial Prisoner* 130: 'I convinced her the whole thing was ridge! She went away thinking up recipes, how to get some variety into roast sparrow.'

1983 Bruce Dawe *Over Here, Harv!* 101: 'Go on', she said ... 'Ridgie-didge!' I said. 'We went to two-up school together.'

Ridge, the   Lightning Ridge

1940 Ion L. Idriess *Lightning Ridge* 157: I arrived back at the Ridge full of beans.

1978 *Australian* 4 Oct. 7: Opal Fever Rush Hits The Ridge [heading]

right, she'll be   An expression of general reassurance

1958 H. D. Williamson *The Sunlit Plain* 77: Eddie West smiled faintly at Deborah Tindall and whispered, 'She'll be right.'

1968 *Coast to Coast 1967–1968* 125: 'She'll be right, mate,' the man consoled him.

1971 Henry Williams *Australia – What is it?* 114: If the madmen triumph and the button is pressed and this earth is reduced to a smouldering radioactive cinder, maybe, out on the old Barcoo or somewhere out west, there will be a survivor, a lone battler to emerge from his timber-and-corrugated shack, look out across the ruined planet, roll up his sleeves and roll himself a smoke, and say, 'She'll be right, mate.'

1974 *Sunday Telegraph* (Sydney) 6 Oct. 63: Mundine's confidence of success is expressed with a 'She'll be right, mate' – and he has most of the Spanish-speaking hotel staff using the Strine phrase. Each time they see him the porters, bell boys and desk clerks greet Mundine with 'She'll be right, mate.'

1975 *Australian* 15 Nov. 20: Ten years ago all was beer and sport, good on yer, mate and she'll be right. Any sort of intellectual achievement was knocked and if you wanted to do your own thing the only place to do it was abroad.

ring *n.*   The buttocks, anus [f. shape]

1952 T. A. G. Hungerford *The Ridge and the River* 130: 'I'd get shot in the ring, that's what I'd get,' said Wallace.

1965 Randolph Stow *The Merry-go-Round in the Sea* 174: 'I bet I would have booted him in the ring if he hadn't run.'

1968 Thomas Keneally *Three Cheers for the Paraclete* 152: He said softly, 'It is your *episcopal* ring that I am supposed to kiss, My Lord.'

1974 Jack Hibberd *Dimboola* 9: 'Where do I sit?' 'On your ring.'

1982 *Sydney Morning Herald* 10 Jul. 16: The answer ... explains, in a nutshell, why the critics will never kiss their rings.

ring *v.*   **1**   Used of cattle forming themselves into a mass, with those on the outside circling the herd; used of horsemen riding about such a herd

1868 C. Wade Brown *Overlanding in Australia* 77: After an hour's amusement of this sort, they stop of their own accord. This evolution is termed 'ringing'. It is a food sign rather than otherwise.

1876 Rolf Boldrewood *A Colonial Reformer* (1890) 225: A desultory entry into the receiving yard then takes place ... The 'ragers' observing this movement keep wildly and excitedly 'ringing', like a first-class Maelstrom.

1906 A. B. Paterson *An Outback Marriage* 169: By degrees, as the horses went round them, the cattle began to 'ring', forming themselves into a compact mass, those on the outside running round and round.

2   To prove oneself the fastest shearer in the shed [f. *ringer* 1]

1895 A. B. Paterson *The Man from Snowy River* 88: They had rung the sheds of the east and west, / Had beaten the cracks of the Walgett side.

1905 'Flash Jack from Gundagai' in *The Old Bush Songs* ed. A. B. Paterson 27: And once I rung Cudjungie shed, and blued it in a week. [note] i.e. he was the ringer or fastest shearer of the shed, and he dissipated the earnings in a single week's drunkenness.

1923 Jack Moses *Beyond the City Gates* 47: In his third year of shearing, Gray 'rung' Wetherina, out west.

3   To **ringbark** q.v.

1853 S. Mossman and T. Banister *Australia, Visited and Revisited* 197: He destroyed the trees by 'ringing' them; that is, cutting off a strip of bark round the butt of the tree, which prevents the sap ascending, and thereby kills them.

1860 Mrs Alan MacPherson *My Experiences of Australia* 121: Formerly it was well wooded, but from the grass becoming valuable for pasture, all the trees have been ringed, that is a ring of bark a foot or so in depth has been cut out all round the trunks, and the trees have in consequence perished.

1885 Mrs Campbell Praed *Australian Life* 34–5: [Blacks] were only pressed into service when shepherds were scarce, or 'rung' trees (that is, gums which had been barked and allowed to wither) required felling.

ringbark   To kill a tree by cutting off a strip of bark around the trunk [f. *bark v.*[2] 3 To strip off the bark from (a tree); to cut off a complete circle of bark from it, so as to kill it 1545 OED]

1877 Rolf Boldrewood *An Australian Squire* repr. as *Babes in the Bush* (1900) 50: 'Dead – every one of 'em, Miss,' explained their ruthless conductor. 'They've been ringbarked, more's the pity.'

1887 W. S. S. Tyrwhitt *The New Chum in the Queensland Bush* 29: The quality of the grass of course is much injured by the existence of so many trees, and especially by trees that suck the moisture out of the ground as gums do, it is therefore the practice to have all freehold land . . . 'ringbarked'. On some runs large numbers of men are employed for months together in nothing else but killing all the trees by cutting a ring round them with an axe.

1890 Henry Lawson 'Skeleton Flat' *Verse* i 64: When the squatter's men came with the death-dealing axe, / And ringbark'd the Skeleton Flat.

1930 *Bulletin* 8 Jan. 20: Two new hands . . . were ringbarking on Blade's selection.

1957 R. S. Porteous *Brigalow* 150–1: 'The bullock paddock is nearly all ringbarked and there's still a bit of nourishment in the grass.'

1970 Germaine Greer *The Female Eunuch* 287: Mother went out the next day and ringbarked it, so it definitely died, and had to be felled after all.

1981 *Age* (Melbourne) 15 Jan. 16: Each tree [on Rottnest Island] has to be fenced for five years, otherwise the quokkas will ringbark them.

ringer   1   The fastest shearer in a shed; the outstanding man in any activity [f. *ringer* anything superlatively good EDD 1896]

1870 Rolf Boldrewood 'Shearing in Riverina' *In Bad Company* (1901) 313: The 'Ringer', or fastest shearer of the whole shed ['assembly' in 1901].

1886 John Farrell 'My Sundowner' *How He Died* (1913) 77: Flash Dick, the Ringer / From Wilson's shed, where they had just cut out.

1892 Henry Lawson 'At the Tug-of-War' *Verse* i 114: 'Twas in a tug-of-war where I – the guvnor's hope and pride – Stepped proudly on the platform as the ringer of my side.

1901 Rolf Boldrewood *In Bad Company* 432: I also hear that the 'ringer' in the pick and shovel brigade is a Hawkesbury man.

1910 C. E. W. Bean *On the Wool Track* 196: The man who shears most sheep is the 'ringer'.

2   A stockman, drover, general station hand [f. *ring v.* 1]

1910 John X. Cameron *The Spell of the Bush* 48: Dam-sinkers, fencers, scrub-cutters, ringers, and other men doing contract work in the vicinity.

1937 Ernestine Hill *The Great Australian Loneliness* 330: *Ringers* Drovers' men, wheeling round the cattle day and night on the road.

1964 *Sydney Morning Herald* 25 Apr. 11: If a mob of ringers (station hands) . . . start 'heading 'em' in the bar.

1983 *Sydney Morning Herald* 8 Oct. 37: There are young cowboys (called ringers) and a bunch of old-timers settling in.

ringie   The ringkeeper in two-up [abbr.]

1941 Baker 60: *Ringie* The keeper of a two-up school.

1951 Frank Hardy *Power Without Glory* 323: Red Ted was 'Ringie.' He supervised the game in the ring itself, seeing that the pennies were spun fairly, and calling the results.

1978 Richard Beilby *Gunner* 298: With the centre set the ringie called for the side bets.

ringtail   1   A ringtail possum
2   A 'ring in' in horseracing

1945 Tom Ronan *Strangers on the Ophir* 88: Blue Bonnet was a ring-tail. A flea-bitten gray, grandson of Snowdon, he had won hurdle races in Melbourne under another name.

1982 Joe Andersen *Winners Can Laugh* 175: Ringing in occurred regularly at local ARC meetings. In fact, it was said that the 'ringtails' there would outnumber the combined total to be found in the zoos of Australia.

ring the tin   See quot.

1972 *Sydney Morning Herald* 24 Feb. 12: A foreman at the mine is the subject of a 'ring the tin' ruling by members of the Workers' Industrial Union of Australia, the city's [Broken Hill] largest union with 2,500 members. . . . According to union officials, 'ring the tin' ruling means that the foreman will not be spoken to by WIU men who work under him. The ban will apply 24 hours a day on and off the mine lease.

rip you, wouldn't it   see **wouldn't it**

ripper   As for **beaut** [OED 1851]
[**1859** Hotten 82: *Ripper* a first-rate man or article *Som.*]

1951 Eric Lambert *The Twenty Thousand Thieves* 182: 'Good letter, Chips?' A gurgle. 'It's a ripper!'

1969 Alan O'Toole *The Racing Game* 200: 'Not a bad run,' I observed . . . 'A ripper,' Badger agreed.

1973 *Australian* 7 Jul. 16: I love this ripper country / Of funnel webs and sharks / With blowies big as eagles / Where your car gets booked by narks.

1975 *Bulletin* 15 Feb. (cover): Ripper party at Terrigal. Back to the slog in Canberra this week.

1981 *Australian* 15 Dec. 14: 'Jeez, what a night. What a ripper bloody night', they shouted at each other in parting.

rise, make a   To achieve some kind of prosperity: *obs.*
1876 Rolf Boldrewood *A Colonial Reformer* (1890) 183: 'I haven't seen my poor old mother for five years good, and I must go, if I was never to make a rise again.'
1902 Henry Lawson 'The Bulletin Hotel' *Verse* ii 7: But he'll pack up in a hurry and he'll seek a cooler clime, / If I make a rise in England and I get out there in time.
1903 Joseph Furphy *Such is Life* (1944) 114–15: 'Not much chance of a man makin' a rise the way things is now.'
1916 C. J. Dennis *The Moods of Ginger Mick* 18: Ginger Mick's bin at the races, an' 'e'd made a little rise.
1940 Ion L. Idriess *Lightning Ridge* 99: Andy sank five hundred shafts, toiled for years and years, and never made a rise.

rivers, Hawkesbury   see **Hawkesbury**

river, the only ~ in the world that flows upside down   see **upside**

Riverina Bluebell   An alternative name for Paterson's Curse q.v.
1979 *Sydney Morning Herald* 21 Jul. 10: Its loss [the loss of Paterson's Curse] will be a great blow to bee-keepers as it is a late winter flowering plant. It is also sold in flower markets under the name of Riverina Bluebell.
1980 *Australian* 25 Apr. 3: The war on Paterson's Curse, also known as Riverina Bluebell and Salvation Jane, was ordered by the Australian Agricultural Council and has caused a furore in the local honey industry.

roaring days, the   The period of the gold discoveries, romantically viewed
1897 Henry Lawson 'The Lights of Cobb and Co.' *Verse* i 339: But these seem dull and slow to me compared with Roaring Days.
1907 Charles MacAlister *Old Pioneering Days in the Sunny South* 197: It is well over half a century since I washed my first rich dish at Spring Creek, but it seems only yesterday, so strongly have the glorious annals of those 'roaring days' burned themselves on the camera of memory.
1918 *Kia Ora Coo-ee* 15 Dec. 5: In the Roaring Days in the lands of the Southern Cross a 'Digger' was one who, regardless of all dangers and hardships, pushed out beyond the marge of civilisation in quest of gold.
1921 M. E. Fullerton *Bark House Days* 116: We loved the stories of the 'roaring fifties'.
1936 William Hatfield *Australia Through the Windscreen* 53: In its roaring days 'The Duchess' was better than many a goldmine.

roar up   To rebuke, upbraid
1919 W. H. Downing *Digger Dialects* 42: *Roar up* Upbraid; abuse.
1920 *Aussie* Apr. (glossary): *Roar us up* Loudly abuse.
1934 'Leslie Parker' *Trooper to the Southern Cross* (1966) 100: I roared Catchpole up, but he said it wasn't his fault.
1947 Norman Lindsay *Halfway to Anywhere* 69: Bill was able to roar him up, anyway, for having the blinkin' cheek to come shoving his nose into Bill's affairs.
1958 H. D. Williamson *The Sunlit Plain* 191: 'I'll tear the tripe out of that bank manager. I'll give him such a roaring-up that he won't know whether he's coming or going.'

robber's dog, head like a   see **head**

Robbo, four bob   See quots
1897 *Bulletin* 23 Jan. 11: 'Four Bob Robbo' – four shillings Robinson, who lived in the classic suburb of Waterloo, Sydney . . . came into a bit of money and bought a horse and trap. The money was spent, and Robinson tired of the horse, which got poor; so he then sometimes let out the horse and trap (both somewhat worse of wear) for 4s. per half-day. There was a run on the cheap hire, and Rob. bought two other horses and traps, which he let out at same price. A neighbouring livery-stable keeper and his employés resented Rob's cutting-down prices and, when any of the rival's equipages passed, used to cry out, in derision, 'Four Bob Robbo!' The cry was taken up by the kids, and has now become a Waterloo classic. It has already cost one person £2 and costs, the magistrate ruling that 'Four Bob Robbo!' shouted after the original in the street, constituted insulting language calculated to create a breach of the peace.
1900–10 O'Brien and Stephens: Robinson, familiarly known as 'Robbo' – a Sydney dealer, i.e. costermonger, having accumulated money, set up as a dealer's liveryman in '94. Previous to his going into the business the usual rate per day for a dealer's horse and cart was six shillings, but Robbo cut the rates and let out a horse and cart at four shillings per day. These turnouts were called by the opposition livery men and hirers 'Robbos, / four bobs / shillings'. Robbo extended his livery business and let out buggies and hansom cabs at four shillings per day all of which came to be known as 'four bob robbos' and then by abbreviation 'robbos' . . . The term spread, and any horse and trap was called by street boys a robbo . . . Robbo has come to be applied to anything inferior, or a take-down or swindle.
1906 A. J. Tompkins *With Swag and Billy* 51: Right out of the haunts of the motor, the bike and the Robbo.

1939 Kylie Tennant *Foveaux* 430: 'Ever 'eard of Bert Robinson? . . . 'E kept a livery stable down at the Foot. I s'pose you've 'eard of the Four-bob Robbos, then? The chaps used to go an' hire a cart for four bob and take it round loaded with vegetables. The kids used to call after 'em, "Four Bob Robbo, Four Bob Robbo".'

robe A wardrobe [abbr.]
1969 Thomas Jenkins *They Came to Australia* 138: I had had an unsublimated ambition to possess a huge built-in wardrobe – or as the advertisement said, 'enormous floor-to-ceiling robes'.
1980 *Daily News* (Perth) 27 Sep. 29: The big master bedroom has a three-door built-in robe with a deep shelf.

Rock, the Ayers Rock
1979 *Sun-Herald* 28 Oct. 31: $32m project to save the Rock [heading] More than $32 million of public money and private money will be spent to save tourist-blighted Ayers Rock from environmental ruin.

rock-ape 1 Derogatory term for an Aboriginal
1983 *Weekend Australian* 5 Feb. Mag. 1: 'Coons, spiks, boongs, rock-apes, sunshines, I can't stand them', he said. 'Namatjira's in the right place, six feet under.'
1985 Xavier Herbert *National Times* 25 Jan. 22: 'To be a Territorian, you've got to talk about rock apes and black bastards, things like that.'
2 Anyone else viewed with disfavour, esp. a teenager
1984 Marian Eldridge *Walking the Dog* 217: 'Who's walking you home, not those rockapes, I trust?'
1985 *Sun-Herald* 27 Jan. 18: Up North Palm Beach way they call them the 'rock apes' – the nude sunbathers who hide among the rocks and the sand hills so as not to offend the affluent family set a few hundred metres away on Palm Beach proper.

rockchopper A Roman Catholic (sometimes abbreviated, as an adjective, to *chopper* e.g. 'He went to a chopper College'): *derogatory*
1982 Alan Gill *Sydney Morning Herald* 27 Aug. 7: A rock chopper is a Roman Catholic. It is a slang word used privately in some Protestant circles in the 1940s and 1950s. Its origin remains uncertain, but it may refer to the convict beginnings of Catholicism in Australia.
1982 Edmund Campion *Rockchoppers Growing up Catholic in Australia* 2: A symbol of such unfriendliness was the nickname 'rockchoppers'. Unknown to most Catholics, the word was used privately by ascendant Protestants to express

their dislike of the Irish-Australians whose proletarian roots went back to the convict rockchoppers . . . the *Macquarie Dictionary* gave it an entry, guessing (wrongly, in my view) that its origins lay in the initials RC.
1985 *Weekend Australian* 11 May Mag. 20: In the humid north the rock choppers have always had a tight grip on matters affecting both the law and racing.

Rocket The tennis player Rod Laver (b. Rockhampton, Queensland)
1976 *Australian* 21 Apr. 21: Rodney George Laver, alias the Rockhampton Rocket, has been the most prolific winner of major tournaments in the history of tennis.

rockhopper See quot. 1959
1959 Baker 140: *rock-hopper*: A person who fishes from rocks on a sea coast.
1978 *Sydney Morning Herald* 29 Dec. 16: Fishermen who assume that the sea will be placid all day can get a rude shock if they have broken the first rule of rock-fishing. That rule is that somebody in the party must be looking seaward. Alert rockhoppers seldom come to grief.
1983 *Sun* (Sydney) 30 Sep. 28: A moderate swell early this week kept rockhoppers away from deepwater locations on the northside.

rocking-horse manure, as scarce as Very scarce
1944 G. H. Fearnside *Sojourn in Tobruk* 33: Australian cigarettes were as rare as rocking-horse manure hereabouts.
1954 Tom Ronan *Vision Splendid* 41: 'Tailor-made smokes are as rare as rocking-horse manure around here.'
1981 Max Harris *Bulletin* 16 Jun. 81: The price in Australia, allowing freight and costs, is nearly par with the sterling price. And that, these days, is as rare as rocking horse manure.

rock, shag on a see **shag**

roley-poley See quots 1859, 1911
1859 Daniel Bunce *Travels with Dr. Leichhardt* 167–8: Very common to these plains, was a large-growing *salsolaceous* plant, belonging to the *Chenopodeaceae*, of Jussieu. These weeds grow in the form of a large ball, to the height of five or six feet, and, being annuals, die away in the autumn, and, as they do not speedily decay, lie loose on the surface . . . No sooner were a few of these balls (or, as we were in the habit of calling them, 'rolly-poleys') taken up with the current of air, than the mules begin to kick and buck.
1911 Edward S. Sorenson *Life in the Australian Backblocks* 112: The simple-looking roley-poley, a huge white ball of burrs and grass. It is met with

346

everywhere in the north-west, and rolls for miles across the plains, banking up against fences and filling up the corrals. ... Horses are often frightened by the roley-poleys, which come spinning towards them, or suddenly roll across the track under their noses. They are weird-looking things in the moonlight, hundreds of them rolling along like scurrying sheep, bounding over the banked fences, and gambolling on again.

1935 R. B. Plowman *The Boundary Rider* 252: In the meantime we had made a roaring fire, mainly of dry roley-poley – there was not much in the way of firewood on those sandhills.

1946 W. E. Harney *North of 23°* 262: I have just skipped here and there, like a roly-poly gathering a little, but leaving a lot behind.

1958 H. D. Williamson *The Sunlit Plain* 149: He was glad to hear about the belt of pines, which would also fence out the roly-polies.

1962 Jock Marshall and Russell Drysdale *Journey Among Men* 114: Often we saw the twisting dust columns of willy-willies moving across the land. Sometimes they rolled in their wake the odd roly-poly, a prickly ball of dry vegetation, occasionally a yard in diameter.

1974 Donald Stuart *Prince of My Country* 11: Across the river they go, and up the steep bank where the dry roley-poley crackles as the horses plough through it.

1984 *Sydney Morning Herald* 27 Jan. 2: I find the fields full of prickly saltwort, commonly known as rolly-polly because it breaks off in the wind and rolls across country.

roll up A mass meeting of workers to deal with some issue of common concern; any assembly of people

1861 *Sydney Morning Herald* 20 Jul. 8: On Sunday, the 30th June, the residents of Tipperary Gully were aroused by cries of 'Roll up', and in the course of a very short time upwards of a thousand men, armed with bludgeons and pickhandles, no firearms as yet appearing, were assembled around the 'No Chinese' standard.

1870 Rolf Boldrewood 'Shearing in Riverina' *Town and Country Journal* 12 Nov. 13: The bell sounded, but instead of the usual cheerful dash at the sheep, each man stood silent and unmoved in his place. Someone uttered the words 'roll up!' and slowly, but with one impulse, the sixty men converged and began to walk towards the end of the shed.

1880 Rolf Boldrewood *The Miner's Right* (1890) 308: 'Can't we have a few words without your ... making as much noise as if you'd hired the bellman for a roll-up?'

1898 D. W. Carnegie *Spinifex and Sand* 120: A 'roll-up' would be called, and those who cared to put themselves forward, would form judge, jury, police and all. The general verdict was notice to quit within so many hours – an order that few would dare to neglect.

1929 Jules Raeside *Golden Days* 139: In cases of any misdemeanour on the part of a digger, the usual course adopted was to sound the tocsin of the tin dish, and summon a 'roll-up', which consisted of a congregation of all miners, who constituted themselves for the nonce into a court of justice.

1937 Miles Franklin *Back to Bool Bool* 248: 'We are all making for the grand roll-up at Bool Bool.'

1956 Tom Ronan *Moleskin Midas* 201: Although the old-time Christmas races and sports had fallen through, there was a big roll-up that Christmas Eve.

1962 Alan Seymour *The One Day of the Year* 65: 'They still get a good rollup.'

1982 *Sydney Morning Herald* 12 Aug. 1: He expects a roll-up of about 1,000 pastoral workers at Dubbo Civic Centre.

1984 Janise Beaumont *Sun-Herald* 15 Jul. 120: Per usual, the roll-up included a fair share of ladies who occasionally still wear silk scarves on their heads and shoes with little chains on the front. It has been said that the polo set need the scarves to keep their mouths from falling open.

roll Jack Rice couldn't jump over see **Rice**

roo, golden see **golden**

Rookwood, crook as Very crook [f. Rookwood cemetery and crematorium N.S.W.]

1985 *Australian* 15 Mar. 3: Mr Wran had to admit that ... donations [to N.S.W. political parties] could probably be channelled through Queensland to disguise their real origin. 'I'm sure they would be welcome in Queensland, because they are as crook as Rookwood up there', he said. 'Everyone knows the price of a knighthood and you can't open up a new business unless there are donations'.

1985 Janise Beaumont *Sun-Herald* 5 May 174: By Wednesday night the Big Wet had me feeling as crook as Rookwood and it took a very small but special party to get the sparks going again.

Roos see **Kangaroos**

Rooshians see **Russians**

rooster one day and a feather duster the next see **feather duster**

Roosters, the 1 The Eastern Suburbs (N.S.W.) Rugby League team (also the Tricolours) [club emblem]

1974 *Sunday Telegraph* (Sydney) 15 Sep. 96:

Roosters flying high.

2   In S.A., the North Adelaide Australian Rules team

1979 *Advertiser* (Adelaide) 23 Apr. 13: Roosters' full back cages Tigers [heading]

root *n.*   1   An act of intercourse, esp. from the male point of view [? f. *rut*. Not included in the OED, although implied in the word-play in *The Merry Wives of Windsor* IV.i.42–6 cf. *root* male member]

1938 Encountered in conversation.

1958 Sir Roderic Chamberlain *The Stuart Affair* (1973) 111: He heard Moir ask Stuart, 'Did you have a root?' and Stuart reply, 'I had a tight one.'

1961 Frank Hardy *The Hard Way* 77: One shabby criminal struck a match revealing ... a sign scrawled on the wall: 'Best American root – ring such and such a number.'

1973 Alexander Buzo *Rooted* 43: 'Hey, do you remember the time he got pissed out of his mind and fronted up to this old duck and asked her for a root?'

1974 Peter Kenna *A Hard God* 33: 'Have you ever gone all the way with a girl? ... You know what I mean. Have you ever had a real root?'

2   A partner in intercourse

1971 Frank Hardy *The Outcasts of Foolgarah* 196: 'You're not only the best root in Foolgarah but good-natured as well.'

1973 Alexander Buzo *Rooted* 139: *weekend root* a casual partner.

1974 Barry Humphries *Barry McKenzie Holds his Own* 4: 'Going back to Oz, mate? What route are you taking?' 'No one, sport. I'm travelling with me Aunty Edna.'

1976 David Ireland *The Glass Canoe* 147: Johnny Bickel ... thought she'd be an easy root and began to take notice of her.

root *v.*   1   To copulate with, esp. from the male standpoint [see *root n.*]

1958 Sir Roderic Chamberlain *The Stuart Affair* (1973) 12: I took her bathers off. Then I raped her. She was hard to root.

1966 Patrick White *The Solid Mandala* 185: 'We'll root together so good you'll shoot out the other side of Christmas.'

1969 William Dick *Naked Prodigal* 118: 'The fat one, Leslie, roots like a rattlesnake.'

1974 David Williamson *Three Plays* 14: 'Country tarts would root a wombat if they thought he was going to be a doctor one day.' Ibid. 15: 'Bloody stunning. Almost too beautiful to root. Worries me a bit.'

1976 Dorothy Hewett *The Tatty Hollow Story* 108: 'I'm going to root the arse off you, and give you a bun in the oven.'

1981 Ken Linnett *Sequences from the Seventies*

17: We'll go into the lounge, get a couple of women, take them home, and root them silly. Just like old times.

rootable, rooter

1974 David Williamson *What if You Died Tomorrow?* 156: 'I had a gorgeous young dancer lined up. Quite stupid – apologies to you two feminists – but very rootable.'

1965 John Beede *They Hosed Them Out* 149: It was at one of these unscheduled bludging periods that the Rooters' Club was born. Its function was for a closer and more intimate relation with all females.

1984 Bill Reed *Crooks* 159: Club Finese is still for the higher class naughty little rooter.

get rooted   Insulting advice, like 'get stuffed'

1961 Mena Calthrope *The Dyehouse* 186: 'He can get rooted, for all I care,' Collins said bitterly.

1974 David Ireland *Burn* 29: 'I can tell anyone in the world to go and get rooted.'

2   To cause an upheaval, consternation esp. in the expression 'Wouldn't it root you!' (World War II slang) abbr. to 'Wouldn't it!' q.v.

1945 Baker 152n: The authentic digger form is *Wouldn't it root you!* A regimental paper 'Wiry' (1941) took its name from the first letters of the words in this phrase.

1964 George Johnston *My Brother Jack* 306: 'You know, and how they always wanted me to join 'em? Well – this'll root you – I bloody *have*, sport.'

3   To worst, disable, put out of commission esp. in the p.pl. *rooted*

1951 Dal Stivens *Jimmy Brockett* 244: 'It looks as though we're rooted, smacker,' I told Herb.

1973 *Sydney Morning Herald* 16 Nov. 17: Mr Snedden said to Mr Whitlam across the house table; 'You are gutless'. Mr Whitlam replied; 'It is what he (Dr Forbes) puts in his guts that has rooted him!' Dr Forbes ... said: 'I want these words to go on record so the people will know what an arrogant, foul-mouthed individual this man is.'

1974 John Powers *The Last of the Knucklemen* 93: 'The Hun's rooted ... Done like a dinner.'

1975 Xavier Herbert *Poor Fellow My Country* 970: 'They're all right chasin' burglars and molls, them blokes ... but put 'em in the bush, they're rooted.'

1981 *Weekend Australian* 21 Feb. Mag. 19: A roadside sign near Sunningdale, Berkshire. 'Rooted Xmas trees, £4.' Apparently better ones cost £8.

root, mallee   see **mallee**

ropeable   Enraged (i.e. needing to be tied up, put under restraint)

[**1910** P. W. Joyce *English as We Speak it in Ireland* 125: 'I was fit to be tied.' A common

348

expression among us to express great indignation.]

1874 Charles de Boos *The Congewoi Correspondence* 195: I don't know a nastier smell than the smeller new togs just fresh from the tailor's goose, and the thoughter that amost made me ropeable.

1898 Rolf Boldrewood *A Romance of Canvas Town* 322: 'Your aunt would be ropeable?' 'I believe you,' answered his companion. 'Blew me up sky high.'

1905 Joseph Furphy *Rigby's Romance* ed. R. G. Howarth (1946) 44: 'Up comes Moses, ropeable – and what d' you think he done?'

1919 Henry Lawson 'The Row at Ryan's Pub' *Verse* iii 385: 'Don't get ropable, or moony – and, above all, don't get spoony.'

1945 Kylie Tennant *Ride on Stranger* 122: 'When I think of that rat, it makes me just *ropeable!*'

1956 Patrick White *The Tree of Man* 278: 'I often remember how you broke that washstand at Yuruga. Mother was ropeable.'

1963 John Cantwell *No Stranger to the Flame* 125: 'She was going to have my kid, but she dropped it when another bloke put the acid on. I got ropeable and did her.'

1981 *National Times* 9 Aug. 51: Having Malcolm back in town unexpectedly means half the permanent heads have had to rearrange their golf games, and they tell me that some of the chaps from Treasury were absolutely ropeable.

Rorke's Drift R.L. test match at Sydney Cricket Ground 4 July 1914, won by England with only 10 men in the second half [f. Rorke's Drift in the Zulu wars, where the English force was so outnumbered by the Zulus]

1982 *Sun-Herald* 27 Jun. 53: England eventually won the [1914 R.L. test] series on the eve of World War I at the Showground in what has become known in League history as 'Rorke's Drift' because of England's gallant battle through injuries.

rort 1 A rowdy party; a 'stunt' (World War II slang) [f. *rorty* fine, splendid, jolly OED 1864]

[**1941** Baker 61: *Rort* (2) A crowd]

1952 T. A. G. Hungerford *The Ridge and the River* 81: 'Out we go on another bloody rort, so what's the use of saving a day?'

1963 John Cantwell *No Stranger to the Flame* 31: Life at the pub was one long post-operational rort, a perpetual celebration of imagined kills.

1969 George Johnston *Clean Straw for Nothing* 78: I am not, strictly, a true devotee of the wild Australian 'rort' and always remorseful in my hangovers.

1973 Alexander Buzo *Rooted* 93: 'We're holding a birthday party for Simmo . . . We'll need the whole house. It's going to be a real rort.'

1982 Thea Astley *An Item from the Late News* 71:

I can see a bunch of cattlehands who have driven in for a Friday night rort sitting up at the far end of the curved counter.

2 A deception, racket, dodge

1936 Jean Devanny *Sugar Heaven* 20: 'The cockies are supposed to pay this retention money into the bank . . . but normally they don't pay it in. They keep the use of it through the season and we draw the bare amount at the end of the cut. It's the greatest rort ever.'

1941 Baker 61: *Rort* A dodge, scheme or racket.

1954 T. A. G. Hungerford *Sowers of the Wind* 141: 'He could take lessons from old Craigie – he's well in on all the rorts?'

1975 *Sun-Herald* 12 Oct. 15: It didn't matter about the VIP plane or car 'rorts'. These matters were 'sensationalised' by the press, they said.

1980 *Sydney Morning Herald* 29 Aug. 10: The ACTU president, Mr Hawke, said in Melbourne last night that the move by Mr Colbung was a 'blatant rort'.

rorting

1981 *Sydney Morning Herald* 10 Jun. 6: Both sides blamed the other for massive 'rorting' in party branches. Rorting, in Labor jargon, is a charmingly flexible term to cover such practices as stacking branch membership, rigging elections, cooking branch records and, as a last resort, losing all branch records to frustrate a head office inquiry.

rorter 1 See quot. 1941

1941 Baker 61: *Rorter* A professional sharper: a hawker of worthless goods: one who practises sly dodges to obtain money.

1962 Alan Marshall *This is the Grass* 64: 'He's a small-time rorter. I know him.' Ibid. 150: Rorters like Flogger prepared to fleece any man who stood staring around him.

1973 Frank Huelin *Keep Moving* 178: *Rorter* Hobo who makes and sells articles such as clothes-pegs, toasting forks, and various pieces of wire work. [in the Depression]

1975 *Bulletin* 26 Apr. 44: rorters (petty con men).

2 A perpetrator of rorts in politics, trade unions etc.

1971 Frank Hardy *The Outcasts of Foolgarah* 56: None other than Call-me-Jack Wrorter himself.

1981 *National Times* 6 Dec. 18: On balance the Right – because they have much more experience and also happen to run the party's head office – are more accomplished rorters.

rosella 1 A sheep losing its wool, and therefore easy to shear (The pink skin showing through could recall the plumage of the parakeet so called.)

1910 C. E. W. Bean *On the Wool Track* 193: If there is an old ewe in the pen, a 'rosella' as they call her, with most of the lower wool worn off, she goes the first.

1933 Acland 392: *Rosella* A sheep that has cast most of his wool before shearing, so is very easy to shear.

1952 Jon Cleary *The Sundowners* 182: He had grabbed an old ewe, a 'rosella', with most of the wool along her belly worn off, and he had just that much start on Cooper.

1964 H. P. Tritton *Times Means Tucker* 119: Among the sheep were three 'rosellas'. These are sheep with the wool falling off, and are very popular with shearers. In fact, a shearer's idea of Paradise is a shed full of 'rosellas'.

2   See quot.

1898 Morris: 'In Northern Australia, it is a slang name for a European who works bared to the waist ... The scorching of the skin by the sun produces a colour which probably suggested a comparison with the bright scarlet of the parrakeet so named.'

rosiner   A stiff drink; any enlivening influence [f. *rosin* to supply with liquor; to make drunk OED 1729 (from the resin applied to violin strings)]

[**1865** Hotten: *Rosin* beer or other drink given to musicians at a dancing party.]

1945 Baker 170: *rozner* is a stiff pick-me-up.

1947 H. Drake-Brockman *The Fatal Days* 114: 'I've not had a solitary spot since four. I need a rosiner.'

1954 Tom Ronan *Vision Splendid* 345: Two nips that old Block had and the one I poured into Peter. They were rozeners I'll admit, but still the three I've had out of this second bottle haven't been exactly small.

1973 Donald Stuart *Morning Star Evening Star* 53: There's no harm in a bit of a rosiner after a hard day's travel, just once in a while.

rotate you, wouldn't it   see **wouldn't it**

rotten   Drunk [f. *rotten* as 'over-ripe', 'saturated with']

[**1910** P. W. Joyce *English as We Speak it in Ireland* 126: A person considered very rich: That man is rotten with money.]

1941 Baker 61: *Rotten, to get* To become exceedingly drunk.

1953 T. A. G. Hungerford *Riverslake* 135: 'Monday to-morrow – blasted work again. God, could I get rotten!'

1966 Roger Carr *Surfie* 128: All this because I'd got rotten.

1971 Johnny Famechon *Fammo* 145: A reporter from one of the Sydney papers – he was the last to leave, rotten.

1975 Xavier Herbert *Poor Fellow My Country* 1028: 'That's the actual catharsis of drinking for me ... not just getting rotten.'

Rotto   Rottnest Island, W.A. [abbr.]

1981 *Daily News* (Perth) 26 Jan. 2: 7 charged from Rotto [heading] Seven people were charged in Fremantle Court today over alleged incidents at Rottnest.

1984 *West Australian* (Perth) 28 Jan. 154: Some people are already convinced that the old, shabby, endearing Rotto is about to be forced out of thongs and into a dinner jacket.

rough as bags, guts   see **bags, guts**

rough end of the pineapple   see **pineapple**

roughie   1   Something 'hard to take', unfair

[**1907** Nathan Spielvogel *The Cocky Farmer* 51–2: 'Don't we have to stiffen the sinews when we are up to it with a roughie to shear?']

1939 Kylie Tennant *Foveaux* 122: 'Kelly put a roughie over Charlie to-day.'

1970 Richard Beilby *No Medals for Aphrodite* 269: 'I bluffed him, put a roughie over him.'

2   A horse at long odds, an outsider that wins

1934 Steele Rudd *Green Grey Homestead* 155: Those who had lost a wager or two will turn to Bell and say: 'You knew something about the roughie!'

1951 Dymphna Cusack and Florence James *Come In Spinner* 40: 'He's a roughie so 'e'll go out at long odds.'

1958 Frank Hardy *The Four-Legged Lottery* 14: 'I might just have a shilling on a roughie.'

1975 *Sun-Herald* 10 Aug. 57: Smith Roughie Upsets Crowd. Punters demonstrated after trainer Tom Smith won the Second Tennyson Graduation with 20–1 outsider Alterego at Rosehill yesterday.

1984 *Sunday Independent* (Perth) 4 Mar. 72: Diamond won by roughie [heading] Sydney two-year-old Street Cafe turned in the biggest reversal of form in the history of the Blue Diamond Stakes when he won ... at Caulfield today.

rouse (roust) on, to   To upbraid, berate [? *roust* to shout, roar OED 1513]

1900–10 O'Brien and Stephens: *Rouse* abuse or vilify.

1904 Henry Fletcher *Dads Wayback: His Work* 20: Dads was always 'rousing' at Mums because, just as certain as the roads were very bad from rain, or the teams were all wanted in the field, she would spring a sudden demand for flour or sugar.

1911 Louis Stone *Jonah* 126: ''E niver rouses on me. W'en 'e gits shirty, I just laugh, an' 'e can't keep it up.'

1915 C. J. Dennis *The Songs of a Sentimental Bloke* 88: If she 'ad only roused I might 'a smiled. / She jist seems 'urt an' crushed; not even riled.

1924 *Truth* 27 Apr. 6: *Rouse* To upbraid.

1934 Vance Palmer *Sea and Spinifex* 182: 'Combo's one of those sulky devils that forget

nothing . . . Can't take a bit of rousing as part of the day's work.'
1941 Sarah Campion *Mo Burdekin* 139: 'And 'avin im roust hell outa me for it.'
1951 Dymphna Cusack *Say No to Death* 30: 'Auntie used to rouse on me frightfully because I spent so much time on the beach.'
1961 Ray Lawler *The Piccadilly Bushman* 31: 'Don't rouse at me, Alec.'
1970 Patrick White *The Vivisector* 10–11: He hung around Mumma, waiting for her to settle, and she didn't roust on him.
1984 Marian Eldridge *Walking the Dog* 145: 'The silly bitch can't even keep the fire going without I have to rouse on her.'

rouseabout (roustabout)   An unskilled labourer in a shearing shed or on a station; any general employee of low status; a worker on an oilfield [*rouseabout* a restless creature never easy at home OED 1778; *roustabout* a wharf labourer or deckhand U.S. 1868 OED]
1881 *Chambers' Journal* 5 Mar 157: During shearing . . . there are thirty-six hands employed on Greenwood, together with about the same number of 'Rouseabouts'; these being men and boys who pen the sheep, pick up the fleeces as they are shorn, and sort and pack the wool, &c.
1887 *All the Year Round* 30 Jul. 66–7: A man who does odd jobs about a station and who can be put to any kind of work, is called a 'roustabout'.
1892 G. L. James *Shall I Try Australia?* 97: The 'roustabout' or 'rouseabout' implies a general utility man or boy in a shearing shed, the term is used frequently to denote all hands besides the shearers.
1902 Henry Lawson 'Two Sundowners' *Prose* i 100: They struck West-o'-Sunday station, and the boss happened to want a rouseabout to pick up wool and sweep the floor for the shearers.
1919 E. S. Sorenson *Chips and Splinters* 73: The boss was soon down, and the spread at once caught his eye. Barwon purposely mistook him for a rouseabout.
1933 F. E. Baume *Tragedy Track* 40: She knows how to deal with the wildest men of the North, and woe betide any drover or rouseabout who presents her with a cheque that is doubtful.
1951 Dymphna Cusack and Florence James *Come In Spinner* 39: 'They'll probably stick you in as rouseabouts in a lunatic asylum, seeing the experience you've 'ad 'ere.
1971 Colin Simpson *The New Australia* 518: The average young oilfield worker, called a 'roustabout', needed to have more than muscles. Technical competence was also called for and most, I was told, had had five years of secondary education.
1984 *Sydney Morning Herald* 13 Mar. 3: Mr McInerney claimed that the Western District

manager of Grazcos . . . had made statements about the town that he will not get local shearers into the sheds and will employ New Zealanders with their Maori girlfriends as rouseabouts.
rouser [abbr.]
1896 Henry Lawson 'Stragglers' *Prose* i 92: They are all shearers, or at least they say they are. Some might be only 'rousers'.

Roy   The 'trendy' Australian, opposite to **Alf** q.v.
1960 Murray Sayle *Encounter* May 28: The Australian business-man or big land-owner, the button-down shirt, lightweight suit type of smoothie from the North Shore Line in Sydney or Toorak Road in Melbourne, with his spurious 'taste' and 'culture' . . . In current Australian terminology, this is the 'Roy' type.
1965 *Nation* 27 Nov. 21: Middle-class 'Roys' in sports cars and yachting jackets.
1971 Frank Hardy *The Outcasts of Foolgarah* 143: The young executives, the in-people, call them what you like, the Roys, the jet set, the status seekers from Perisher Valley to Palm Beach, and none of them worth a pinch of shit if it comes to doing an honest day's work.

Royal Alfred   see **Alfred**

Royals   The East Perth (W.A.) Australian Rules football team [f. royal blue colours]
1980 *West Australian* 26 May 68: Royals oust tired Tigers [heading] An effervescent East Perth ran the legs off a match-weary Claremont side at Perth Oval on Saturday.

Roys, the   The Fitzroy V.F.L. team [abbr.]
1916 C. J. Dennis *The Moods of Ginger Mick* 33: Wot time the footer brings the clicks great joy, / An' Saints er Carlton roughs it up wiv 'Roy.
1979 *Age* (Melbourne) 7 Jul. 40: Roys to run on [heading] Fitzroy's long winning sequence will end soon . . . But they are hoping it lasts for at least two more matches.

RS   Ratshit q.v. [abbr.]
1976 David Ireland *The Glass Canoe* 46: 'Who wants to be old', he'd say. 'You're RS these days if you're old. You've gotta be young.' RS means ratshit.
1982 *Sun-Herald* 5 Sep. 133: 'If you don't get it [the HSC], you're RS. You need it to get a job – unless you know someone.'

RSL, the   The Returned Services League: the abbreviation is used colloquially to apply to the licensed clubs
1958 Barry Humphries *A Nice Night's Entertainment* (1981) 16: I went to the R.S.L. the other night and had a very nice night's entertainment.

1972 Ian Moffitt *The U-Jack Society* 217: Ron's got a second job as a steward at the RSL.
1973 Alexander Buzo *Norm and Ahmed* in *Three Plays* 16: 'It's the good times I miss, Ahmed, those magic moments that make life seem worthwhile. Like the time we danced all night at the Bronte R.S.L.'

rubbery Imprecise, uncertain (from Mr Phillip Lynch's account of 1977 budget estimates) later used as equivalent to unreliable, 'shonky'
1977 Phillip Lynch (addressing National Press Club on 17 August on the 1977 budget, and answering a question on the projected cost of certain tax changes in 1978–9): If you look into 1978–9, well of course the figures, whatever they have put down in whatever document, must be, if I use my own term, somewhat rubbery, for the simple reason that they must depend necessarily on a series of assumptions made during the course of 1978–79 as to things like growth, inflation, et al. [transcript in Australian National Library]
1982 *National Times* 5 Sep. 7: 'Rubbery' Phil is another affectionate epithet stemming from his description of the figures in one of the Budgets he presented as Treasurer.
1982 *Australian* 19 Aug. 8: The business community and labor leaders have labelled the figures in this year's Budget as 'rubbery' and the uncertainty of economic forecasts could soon return to haunt this Government.
1984 *Age* (Melbourne) 5 Oct. 3: Professor Blainey suggested that official figures on immigrants in the population were 'rubbery'.

rubbish To disparage, dispose of contemptuously
1953 T. A. G. Hungerford *Riverslake* 20: 'If Verity was going to tramp you for burning the tucker ... he would have rubbished you long before this.'
1969 Alan O'Toole *The Racing Game* 120: Andrew Killburn rubbished the very notion.
1971 David Ireland *The Unknown Industrial Prisoner* 352: They rubbished him every chance they got, why should he always go back for more?

rubbity A pub [rhyming slang *rubbity-dub*]
[**1898** *Bulletin* 17 Dec. Red Page: *Drum* – derived from the kettle-drums (evening parties) of the days of the Georges – was a high-class word, but it fell. The cockney turned it into *rub-a-dum-dum*; the Australian now calls the same thing a *rubadey*.]
1941 Baker 62: *Rubberdy, Rubbity, Rubby*: A public house. Rhyming slang on 'rub-a-dub-dub' for 'pub'.
1957 D'Arcy Niland *Call Me When the Cross Turns Over* 101: 'How about a gargle? Down to the rubberdy, come on.'
1962 David Forrest *The Hollow Woodheap* 11: 'Where ... is The Eagle on the Hill?' 'A rubbedy

in South Australia.'
1973 Alexander Buzo *Rooted* 63: 'Been down the rubbity lately?' 'No, I haven't hit the hops for a couple of weeks.'
1983 *Daily Telegraph* (Sydney) 2 Apr. 8: They are hopeful the prince (if not the princess) will grace them with a royal presence around the bar of one of the local 'rubbidies' over Easter.

rubby As for **rubbity**
1911 E. S. Sorenson *Life in the Australian Back-blocks* 81: Others swamp their earnings at the wayside rubby, and have themselves to blame that they are every year humping bluey.

Rules As for **Aussie Rules** q.v.
1946 Dal Stivens *The Courtship of Uncle Henry* 18: In those days ... they played Rules in long pants that reached below the knee.
1976 *Sydney Morning Herald* 27 May 22: Rules penalty upsets Saints.

Rules, Rafferty's see **Rafferty's**

Rum Rebellion The deposition of Governor Bligh in 1809 by officers of the N.S.W. Corps, noted for their trafficking in rum
1855 William Howitt *Land, Labour and Gold* ii 118: From the date of this 'rum rebellion', and the forcible deposition of poor Bligh ... the system of political grants went on swimmingly.
1871 Marcus Clarke *Old Tales of a Young Country* 38: The Rum-Puncheon Revolution [chapter title]
1938 H. V. Evatt *Rum Rebellion* [book title]

run 1 A tract of land for grazing; a sheep or cattle station; the station as distinct from the homestead
1804 *Sydney Gazette* 5 Feb. [4]: A Commodious DWELLING-HOUSE, with a fine Garden containing two Acres and a half of excellent Land, and a number of capital Fruit-trees of various kinds, the whole fenced in with seven-foot paling; a good run for stock, and plentifully supplied with water; eligibly and delightfully situate on the Brickfield Hill.
1826 James Atkinson *An Account of the State of Agriculture and Grazing in New South Wales* 66: A tract of land, or grazing *run*, as it is termed in the Colony.
1846 C. P. Hodgson *Reminiscences of Australia* 43: A peculiar scent and dusty soil, at length announce your proximity to one of the 'runs'. [Note] 'Runs', land claimed by the Squatter as sheep-walks, open, as nature left them, without any improvement from the Squatter.
1883 R. E. N. Twopeny *Town Life in Australia* 244: A 'run' is the least improved kind of land used for sheep, but the word is used almost alternatively with 'station', which denotes an improved

run. The run may be a mere sheep-walk, but a station is bound to have a house attached to it, and fenced 'paddocks' or fields.

1901 Miles Franklin *My Brilliant Career* 10: I felt cramped on our new run. It was only three miles wide at its broadest point.

1935 R. B. Plowman *The Boundary Rider* 109: Out on the run, or among a crowd of men, Alec Wilson ... was a somewhat rough, happy-go-lucky, daredevil sort of fellow.

1954 Tom Ronan *Vision Splendid* 270: 'Things aren't so good on the run, so I'll have to keep moving for a while. I'm turning the homestead end over to you'.

1970 Jock Makin *The Big Run The Story of Victoria River Downs Station* [book title]

2 In shearing, the uninterrupted stretch of work between meal breaks

1911 E. S. Sorenson *Life in the Australian Back blocks* 241: A run is anything from seventy-five to ninety minutes, when the bell rings for smoke-o, lunch, afternoon tea, or knock off.

1966 Ronald Anderson *On the Sheep's Back* 89: The day is divided into two-hour 'runs' and the rests are treasured.

1975 Les Ryan *The Shearers* 154: A day consists of 4 'runs' each of two hours' duration, with a half-hour 'smoko' morning and afternoon, and an hour for lunch. Work starts at 7.30 a.m., and finishes at 5.30 p.m.

1980 *West Australian* 24 Mar. 62: She sheared 43 sheep in the first day, 53 the second day and 23 in one run on the third day.

run a drum see **drum**

run over the bastards see **bastards**

rush The sudden migration of people to a gold discovery

1855 William Howitt *Land, Labour and Gold* i 174: Very little, if any, gold will be got out of the whole of this rush ... Indeed, it seems to be a general opinion that the rush was planned by the people ... who saw that they were watched, and resolved to mislead their watchers.

1861 T. McCombie *Australian Sketches* 2nd Series 78: An excellent opportunity presented itself to me of seeing the first great 'rushes' to the Australian goldfields.

1900 Henry Lawson 'The Story of the Oracle' *Prose* i 279: 'My Uncle Bob was mates with him on one of those 'rushes' along there – the 'Pipeclay', I think it was, or the 'Log Paddock'.

1915 K. S. Prichard *The Pioneers* 152: 'Hear Pat

and Tom Kearney have cleared out to the new rush? Eaglehawk, isn't it?'

Russians (Rooshians) Wild cattle [? f. *rush*]

1845 D. Mackenzie *The Emigrant's Guide* 118: These wild Russians, as they are here called, will ... clear at the first leap a stockyard six feet in height.

1849 Alexander Harris *The Emigrant Family* (1967) 53: 'Are there any "Rooshans" in the mountains?' he inquired.

1861 H. W. Wheelwright *Bush Wanderings of a Naturalist* 58: I always looked out on the plains, and whenever I saw a bullock standing sulking by itself, I always gave it a wide berth; such a one is generally a 'Roosian.'

1876 Rolf Boldrewood *A Colonial Reformer* (1890) 222: The head stockman there covenanting ... to give the Rainbar folks a turn, and draft their 'Roosians' for them.

rustbucket A car in a dangerously rusted condition [f. application to ships]

1965 *Daily Telegraph* (Sydney) 23 Apr. 20: It was a rust-bucket. That means a very badly rusted car.

1972 Ian Moffitt *The U-Jack Society* 121: 'They look beautiful, but underneath they're rust-buckets.'

1983 *Bulletin* 2 Aug. 34: It is not the classiest of limousines – in fact, it is an old rust bucket – but it worked in its own rather eccentric way.

ryebuck (ribuck) Possessing some degree of excellence; genuine; as a retort, an expression of full agreement: *obs.*

1895 *Bulletin* 9 Feb. 15: I'm ryebuck and the girl's okay.

1898 *Bulletin* 17 Dec. Red Page: *Ryebuck* (all right) is no doubt an abbreviation of 'all right, my buck'

1911 Louis Stone *Jonah* 11: 'Oh, I don't suppose you'll be missed,' replied Chook graciously. 'Rye buck!' cried Jonah.

1915 C. J. Dennis *The Songs of a Sentimental Bloke* 72: 'E'n in the days when she's no longer fair / She's still yer wife', 'e sez. 'Ribuck', sez I.

1916 C. J. Dennis *The Moods of Ginger Mick* 42: But the reel, ribuck Australia's 'ere, among the fightin' men.

1924 *Truth* 27 Apr. 6: *Ribuck* Expression of assent.

1943 Charles Shaw *Outback Occupations* 17: 'Ribuck, boss,' he says; 'but y're wastin' y'r time.'

1957 *Old Bush Songs* ed. Stewart and Keesing 267: 'The Ryebuck Shearer' [ballad title]

S

saddling paddock   The bar in the Theatre Royal, Melbourne, known in the nineteenth century as a resort of prostitutes; any known place of rendez-vous [f. *ride* for the male role in intercourse]

1868 Marcus Clarke 'Melbourne Streets at Mid-night' *Argus* 28 Feb. repr. in *A Colonial City* ed. L. T. Hergenhan (1972) 102: That door leads to the 'ladies refreshment-room', but is known to its fast frequenters by another name.

1876 Julian Thomas 'The Theatre Vestibules' *Argus* 1 Jul. 4 repr. in *The Vagabond Papers* ed. Michael Cannon (1969) 232: The stranger, stroll-ing out during an entr' acte [at the Royal], would be still more surprised at Melbourne manners and customs, as witnessed in the Vestibule. This is generally crowded with men and larrikins, smok-ing and chaffing the loose women who pass in and out . . . The stranger sees that the women, possibly picking up a male companion, all enter the com-partment which was previously closed, and which is now guarded by swing doors. Curiosity will doubtless prompt him to enter, and he will find himself in the far-famed 'saddling paddock' of the Royal. It is a small bar, presided over by a man – the proceedings here are too unpleasant for a barmaid to witness. Here the most notorious women of Melbourne nightly throng, and run in the companions they have caught in the stalls or in the vestibules.

c. **1880** T. E. Argles *The Pilgrim* i 6: At the Royal, however, the machinery of pimping, of 'saddling' is carried on openly; and the entrance lobby of the theatre set apart as a haven for scores of flaunting members of the demi-monde.

1955 D'Arcy Niland *The Shiralee* 66: The first . . . screamed for help when the game got real. The second, they were so often in the saddling paddock it wasn't natural.

1958 Gavin Casey *Snowball* 29: The ribald, popu-lar name of the enclosure round the Government Dam was 'the saddling paddock'.

1958 Jack Lindsay *Life Rarely Tells* 213: After a while he smoothed his hair . . . 'Back to the good old saddling-paddock' – by which he meant Maisie's bedroom.

safety, mantle of   see **mantle**

Saints, the   1   In N.S.W., the St George Rugby League team (also the Dragons)

1974 *Sydney Morning Herald* 3 Aug. 63: Exit of a great Saint.

2   In Victoria, the St Kilda V.F.L. team

1916 C. J. Dennis *The Moods of Ginger Mick* 33: Wot time the footer brings the clicks great joy, / An' Saints er Carlton roughs it up wiv 'Roy.

1976 *Sunday Telegraph* (Sydney) 30 May 54: Demons too good for the Saints.

3   In N.T., the St Mary's Australian Rules team

1979 *NT News* (Darwin) 8 Dec. 32: Saints above [heading] Tigers tipped to lose.

saloon passage   1   An unimpeded run on the race track

1981 *Sun-Herald* 4 Oct. 78: 'I got up on the fence with a saloon passage, but got squashed at the 1200m. and then only got clear in the last 200m.'

1982 *Australian* 5 Nov. 24: Dittman's saloon passage along the rails prompted ... Bart Cummings to observe: 'Only once in 50 years do you see a run like that in the Melbourne Cup.'

2 An easy win in sport

1981 *Australian* 21 Apr. 12: It was impossible to single out best players in such a free flowing saloon passage to the Balmain goal-line, in which a Canterbury try was scored on average about every seven minutes.

1983 *Sun-Herald* 4 Sep. 70: Manly earned themselves a saloon passage through to the grand final.

salts, go through like a dose (packet) of To move very quickly, demolish opposition [f. Epsom salts as an aperient]

1941 Baker 25: *Dose of salts, go through (something, someone) like a* To accomplish a task very rapidly: to deal drastically with a person.

1968 Geoffrey Dutton *Andy* 92–3: 'In the Army you can go through the world like a packet of salts.'

1971 R. F. Brissenden *Winter Matins* 26: Goes through the homestead like a dose of salts, / Clears out the bludgers.

1974 David Ireland *Burn* 10: He'd go through this town like a packet of salts.

1982 Ian Moffitt *The Retreat of Radiance* 59: 'The Communists aren't mucking around. They'll go through China like a packet of salts.'

salty A salt-water crocodile in the N.T.

1982 *Bulletin* 5 Oct. 31: I used to imagine that all the sharks up here had been eaten by the crocs ('salties', as they are known to the locals).

salute the judge To win a horse race

1979 *Herald* (Melbourne) 8 Jun. Heraldform 8: Toroa has not saluted the judge in his seven runs since August, but showed something like his true form last start.

1983 *Sun-Herald* 10 Jul. 67: 'Killing' for secret punter as Scarlet Major salutes judge [heading]

Salute, Australian, Barcoo, Queensland see Australian, Barcoo, Queensland

Salvation Jane Alternative name for Paterson's curse (q.v.) esp. in S.A. [f. resemblance of flower to Salvation Army bonnet, or for providing fodder when vegetation is scarce]

1935 Francis Birtles *Battle Fronts of Outback* 211: Every waterhole, creek and billabong ... was fringed with the bright heliotrope of Salvation Jane – a desert wild flower.

1962 Jock Marshall and Russell Drysdale *Journey Among Men* 193: The great growth of a flowering weed, Salvation Jane, covered the hillsides with a startling purple and green.

1979 *Sydney Morning Herald* 21 Jul. 10: The name Salvation Jane was given to this plant by sheep owners who greatly valued it in hard times as valuable fodder.

1980 *Sydney Morning Herald* 8 Aug. 12: Apiarists have been battling recently to prevent the release of biological control for Paterson's curse, the beekeeper's Salvation Jane (Echium plantagineum), which is a rich source of honey as well as being poisonous to stock.

1981 *Sydney Morning Herald* 24 Jan. 35: If you hear anyone refer to that brilliant purple weed known in NSW as Paterson's Curse as Salvation Jane, you should know instantly that you are listening to a South Australian.

Salvo (Sally) A member of the Salvation Army

1896 *Bulletin* 31 Oct. 27: The Salvo's Error [story title]

1908 C. H. S. Matthews *A Parson in the Australian Bush* 256: 'Well, I was rared a Carthlick, but I haven't followed it up much. To tell ye the truth, I class 'em all alike – priests, parsons, "salvos", and all the lot of 'em.'

1911 Louis Stone *Jonah* 271: 'I've 'eard old women at the Salvos' meetings talk like this, tellin' of the wonderful things they found out w'en they got converted.'

1936 Ion L. Idriess *The Cattle King* 189: The surest place to find Sid Kidman, when in town on a Saturday night, was among the crowd around the 'Sallies'.

1951 Dal Stivens *Jimmy Brockett* 249: He gasped like the Salvo bloke the time I put a fiver in his collection plate at Central Railway.

1959 Dorothy Hewett *Bobbin Up* 55: She had already been saved by the Salvoes, baptized into the Plymouth Brethren ... changed her Sabbath for the Seventh Day Adventists.

1965 Graham McInnes *The Road to Gundagai* 239: Those who suffered most were the Salvation Army, or the Salvoes as they were known to us.

1979 *Australian* 3 Jul. 3: Salvo appeal gets lift [heading] One thousand red and white helium-filled balloons sailed skywards yesterday to mark the start of the Salvation Army's 1979 Red Shield appeal in Sydney.

1984 *Alice Springs Star* 8 Aug. 1: When the Salvos call on Sunday morning, dig deep and remember some of the services they provide.

sand goanna See quot.

1981 *Sun-Herald* 4 Oct. 11: 'There are lots of whites here I call sand goannas. When they're talking to your face they aren't racist, but when you walk away it's different – they change colour.'

sandgroper A native of Western Australia [see quot. 1963]

1896 Henry Lawson *Letters* (1970) 62: W.A. is a fraud. The curse of the country is gold . . . The old Sand-gropers are the best to work for or have dealings with. The Tothersiders are cutting each others' throats.

1902 J. H. M. Abbott *Tommy Cornstalk* 2: In delicate reference to the nature of their country the West Australians are 'Sandgropers'.

1926 J. Vance Marshall *Timely Tips for New Australians: Groper* A West Australian.

1934 Thomas Wood *Cobbers* 14: If there had been no sand in Western Australia to goad people into reprisals, everybody there might have been tempted to lie on his back and bask in the sunshine. As it is, inhabitants of other States talk of 'Sand-gropers', slightingly; but groping has paid. W.A. can afford to smile.

1946 K. S. Prichard *The Roaring Nineties* 214: 'I'm a sand-groper,' she snapped . . . 'Don't know anything about London or Paris.'

1963 Xavier Herbert *Disturbing Element* 2: The name Sand Groper measured the contempt of the easterners for the comparative infertility of the West and the social backwardness of its first settlers.

1974 *Sunday Telegraph* (Sydney) 30 Jun. 36: Mining millionaire Lang Hancock has a sizeable number of sandgropers prepared to support his view that Western Australia should be detached from the rest of the nation.

1981 *Australian* 22 Jun. 1: It was a big match for sandgropers. In a devastating display of fast bowling . . . West Australians Dennis Lillee and Terry Alderman each claimed three English victims.

sandshoe, head like a twisted see **head**

sandy blight Name given to trachoma or any kind of conjunctivitis, when the eyes smart as though filled with sand

[**1834** George Bennett *Wanderings in New South Wales* i 302–3: There is an affection of the eye . . . called by the colonists the 'blight' . . . The integuments surrounding the orbit were puffed up so much, as totally to close the eye, which was found much inflamed, as in acute ophthalmia, and attended with symptoms, in some degree similar, with severe itching and pricking pain, as if sand had been lodged in it, with a profuse flow of tears.]

1846 *Georgiana's Journal* ed. Hugh McCrae (1966) 228: Cuts, splinter wounds, boils, and sand-blight, have been successfully treated.

1853 C. R. Read *What I Heard, Saw, and Did at the Australian Goldfields* 43: The most disagreeable and painful complaint, was a kind of ophthalmia, called sandy blight . . . The pain is most excruciating, being as if the eyes were filled with broken glass and sand, causing a great discharge.

1870 W. M. Finn *Glimpses of North-Eastern Victoria* (1971) 35: The day I called [at the school] the 'sandy blight' was so prevalent that many children were absent.

1892 G. L. James *Shall I Try Australia?* 242: One pest of the bush and plains is 'Sandy Blight' or inflammation of the eyes – it is, I believe, called 'sandy' owing to the pain being exactly similar to that which grains of sand upon the eyeball could cause.

1964 Tom Ronan *Packhorse and Pearling Boat* 7: In the time we lived in Derby I had sandy blight three times.

1982 Thea Astley *An Item from the Late News* 71: One eye is bunged up with sandy-blight.

sangar A dugout

1941 Diary 20 Apr. cit. *Sunday Mail* (Brisbane) 9 Nov. 1980 Mag. 4: We live in the ground here and the boys have become first class at repairing and rebuilding their cubby houses, called sangars, here [Tobruk]. First a hole is dug into the ground until one meets rock, at about 6 in., then sandbags and stones are used to build up the sides.

sanger A sandwich

1974 Jim McNeil *How Does Your Garden Grow* 26: 'Nothing like the old cheese sanger for a man on the go.'

1980 *Sunday Mail* (Brisbane) 24 Aug. 3: A colleague went to order a chicken 'sanger' and decided to ask the serving lady why they seemed 'a little thin of late'.

sav Saveloy [abbr.]

1968 Geoffrey Dutton *Andy* 229: 'Broughtcher buncher savs', he shouted, and held out his arms so that each pair of dancers could stop and dip their saveloys in sauce.

1970 Patrick White *The Vivisector* 216: 'I bought a few savs I thought we'd do for supper.'

1979 *Weekend Australian* 17 Feb. Mag. 16: Perhaps his organisation can also do something for the plight of the 'Battered Savs' which one frequently encounters in Snack Bars. I have long felt that something should be done to stop this particularly brutal practice.

1983 *Sydney Morning Herald* 30 Aug. 14: Scoffed down plates of pies, jellies, cream buns, battered savs, lollies and chocs.

save, have a saver See quot. 1882 [f. *To make saver*: to insure against or compensate for a loss OED 1613 *obs.*]

c. **1882** *The Sydney Slang Dictionary* 7: *Save* To give part of one bet for part of another. A and B have backed different horses, and they agree that in the event of either one winning he shall give the other, say 5. This is called 'saving a fiver', and generally is done when scratchings and knockings-out have left the field so that one of the two speculators must be a winner. Form of hedging.

1891 Nat Gould *The Double Event* 123: 'Wells says Perfection will win,' said Lady Mayfield to Jack Marston, 'but I've put a saver on Caloola.'

1917 A. B. Paterson *Three Elephant Power* 17: 'I had a quid on,' he says. 'And,' (here he nerves himself to smile) 'I had a saver on the second, too.'

1933 Samuel Griffiths *A Rolling Stone on the Turf* 55: I earnestly advised him to have a saver on Buzz, but he would not consider the idea.

1958 Gavin Casey *Snowball* 168: A lot of people who had bet on Benny – and made sure of a saver on the Negro – put on a few shillings more at the ringside.

1983 *Sydney Morning Herald* 12 Mar. 13: The electorate clearly has had 'a saver' on the Democrats and the Senate. While giving the Labor Party a clear mandate to govern in the House of Representatives, voters have left 'the minders' in control of the Senate, just in case the Government should get out of line.

scale To practise some kind of fraud, obtain something without paying: now used most often of travelling on public transport without paying a fare [? f. *scale* to split off scales or flakes from (coin) for purposes of fraud OED 1576]

1916 Arthur Wright *Under a Cloud* 32: 'How'd that happen,' asks Bill Odzon. 'Didn't think anyone could scale you.'

1933 Colin Wills *Rhymes of Sydney* 13: See the shoppers, toppers, tabs / Scalers by the score / Hopping off / Dropping off / Darting into shore

1941 Baker 63: *Scale, to* To ride on a train, tram or bus without paying a fare: esp. to ride a tram footboard in this way ... (2) To steal: to rob someone (3) To swindle a person, to take him down: to deceive. Whence, 'Scale 'em Corner', a George Street corner, near Central Station, Sydney, 'where appointments are made when one had no intention of keeping them.'

1950 Brian James *The Advancement of Spencer Button* 64: Boys who lived mostly on the streets, scaling on trams ... selling papers, running messages.

1953 Dymphna Cusack *Southern Steel* 3: Bumping in on the back of the old steam trams, too often scaling on the footboards because he hadn't the money to pay the penny fare.

1975 *Sydney Morning Herald* 18 Oct. 18: Excitements not mentioned at home were scaling on trams and fighting with rival gangs.

1984 *Sydney Morning Herald* 7 Jan. 31: The tram guards ... were generally much admired by little boys, even though we did our best to outwit them by 'scaling' a ride, crouching unseen on the foot-board on the other side of the tram.

scaler

1924 *Truth* 27 Apr. 6: *Scaler* A fraud.

1956 Ruth Park and D'Arcy Niland *The Drums Go Bang!* 28–9: We were caught riding first-class on a second-class ticket and an inspector ... intended to report the scaler to the Grand Firebox.

scarce as hen's teeth   see **hen's teeth**

scarce as rocking-horse manure   see **rocking-horse**

school   A two-up school, or any company of gamblers; a group of drinkers
[**1812** Vaux: *School* a party of persons met together for the purpose of gambling.]

1890 A. G. Hales *Wanderings of a Simple Child* 10: As I pushed my way through the throng, I at once perceived that 'school' was in.

1910 C. E. W. Bean *On the Wool Track* 226: A few sharpers with a slight knowledge of shearing often get into a big shed, and get a 'school' going – a nightly gamble.

1915 C. J. Dennis *The Songs of a Sentimental Bloke* 87: 'Come 'round an' try yer luck at Steeny's school.'

1929 Jules Raeside *Golden Days* 145: Among such a variety of men the gambling spirit was of course strong, and regularly organised 'schools' were arranged.

1935 H. R. Williams *Comrades of the Great Adventure* 184: We had just been paid, and the 'school' was a large one. Gathered around the ring were several hundred men, all deeply interested in the game.

1944 Alan Marshall *These are My People* 82: 'If I got into a school with some of these mugs round here they'd be penniless in two hours.'

1960 Donald McLean *The Roaring Days* 199: 'I want a few quid for th' school tonight, so don't be a bastard.'

1965 John Beede *They Hosed Them Out* 91: Lesser schools contented themselves with minor games of slippery sam, pontoon or black jack.

1980 Emery Barcs *Backyard of Mars* 185: 'He is in school', continued Freedman with a meaningful grin. Then to make it quite clear, he murmured, 'Poker school, of course.'

schoolie   1   A schoolteacher

1907 Nathan Spielvogel *The Cocky Farmer* 33: The prettiest of all the girls was the schoolie, and didn't she lead the lads a dance.

1958 Gavin Casey *Snowball* 17: 'Tough type for a schoolie, he is.'

1966 Hal Porter *The Paper Chase* 118: The Tretheways are the only ones poor enough ... to accept a boarder. The schoolie always stays with them.

1974 Thea Astley *A Kindness Cup* 5: His cutaway donned for the occasion – running the bejesus out of a back-town schoolie – stank in the heat.

2 Fish not yet full size, esp. jewfish, shark

1979 *Courier-Mail* (Brisbane) 1 Jun. 21: Several catches of 'schoolies' to 10 kg were taken during the week.

1984 *Sun* (Sydney) 23 Mar. 17: The best months for prawns are November and February, but the schoolies are running late this year and should be plentiful for Anzac Day reunions.

see **soapie**

schooner   A 15 oz. glass of beer in N.S.W., a 9 oz. glass in S.A. [f. *schooner* a tall glass of beer U.S. 1877 Mathews]

1939 Kylie Tennant *Foveaux* 52: The cries of 'Two of half and half', 'Schooner of new', 'Pint of old'.

1954 *Sydney Morning Herald* 8 Nov. 2: 'In Adelaide we call that a schooner' ... I expressed sympathy at such extreme myopia. 'A schooner, my friends, is a large glass,' I told him.

1967 B. K. Burton *Teach Them No More* 107: 'Just think of it – schooners of beer again, with white froth on the top, and cold all the way down your throat.'

1981 *Sun* (Sydney) 16 Jul. 43: He loves a drop of the amber fluid and his beefy right hand is curled around a schooner more often than a middy.

1983 *West Australian* (Perth) 31 Dec. 1: Other recommended new prices are: 140ml (pony) 48c (up 1c). 285ml (middy) 95c (up 3c). 1125ml (schooner) $1.30 (up 5c).

scone hot   See quot. 1941

1938 Xavier Herbert *Capricornia* 530: Halfcaste Shillingsworth goes Copra Co scone-hot!

1941 Baker 63: *Scone-hot* An intensive to describe great vigour of attack, scolding or speed. e.g., 'Go for someone scone-hot', to reprimand severely. (2) Exorbitant, unreasonable. (3) Expert, proficient, e.g. 'He's scone-hot at shearing.'

1944 *Coast to Coast 1943* 116: 'I don't want Reg going me scone hot because his wife's not capable of looking after herself.'

1957 R. S. Porteous *Brigalow* 223: 'Look out fer 'im,' Mick yelled. "E'll go ya, scone 'ot.'

1967 Kylie Tennant *Tell Morning This* 139: 'When my big brother Jim come home from work, he went Dad scone hot.'

1974 David Ireland *Burn* 136: 'When he finds out he'll go me scone-hot.'

scoot, on the   On a spree [? f. *scoot* to go away hurriedly]

1924 *Truth* 27 Apr. 6: *Scoot* To clear out; also continued bout of drunkenness.

1936 Ion L. Idriess *The Cattle King* 131: 'I'm sorry

to hear Eureka is on the scoot.' 'He's not. They don't go on the scoot out there. They drink dynamite and bust.'

1946 Dal Stivens *The Courtship of Uncle Henry* 74: 'Doesn't he like her getting on the scoot?'

1962 Stuart Gore *Down the Golden Mile* 120: 'Make mine a glass this time, seein' I have to go on the scoot with you booze artists to-night.'

1975 Xavier Herbert *Poor Fellow My Country* 1019: 'We could've ... gone on a proper scoot.'

score between the posts   Have intercourse with a woman [f. football]

1973 Alexander Buzo *Rooted* 89: 'Oh I get it, you're setting up for a naughty to-night, are you? ... Gunna score between the posts, are you?'

scorpions in one's pocket, to have   see **pocket**

scrammy   Nickname for a man with a defective hand or arm [f. E. dial. *scram* (*skram*) awkward; stiff, as if benumbed OED 1825]

1822 *HRA* x 776: A Man, who goes by the name of Scrummy Jack. [described by another deponent p. 775: 'he was a little Man, and has a dun or withered Arm']

1902 Barbara Baynton *Bush Studies* 44: Scrammy 'And [story title]

1906 A. B. Paterson *An Outback Marriage* 33: Scrammy Doyle (meaning Doyle with the injured arm).

1912 'Goorianawa' *Lone Hand* 1 Oct. 30 repr. in *Old Bush Songs* ed. Stewart and Keesing (1957) 273: And the sprees I've had with Scrammy Jack are more than I can count.

scrape *n. & v.*   To copulate with

1959 Donald Stuart *Yandy* 4: Like Jessie, Larrian was ready to scrape with the whitefellers.

1969 Osmar White *Under the Iron Rainbow* 64: She said she didn't mind lying down for white men at three dollars a time ... All the girls got scraped by someone ... She'd give the old sergeant a scrape for free and he'd make things easy for her while she was in the lockup.

1975 Robert Macklin *The Queenslander* 43: 'We rolled her over on the beach and started scraping.'

scratch, be scratching   To be struggling, in difficulty

1930 Vance Palmer *The Passage* (1944) 65: He and Bob had to scratch for a living the best way they could. Ibid. 160: 'We'll have to scratch for another year or two to pay off the new boat.'

1939 Kylie Tennant *Foveaux* 235: A preliminary boxer for a time, but now, as he said, 'scratching for a living.'

1953 T. A. G. Hungerford *Riverslake* 202: 'If his mob gets in next election they'll whip up a nice old depression, just like they did the last time, and we'll all be scratching for jobs again. The only difference is that there'll be a million or so of these bludgers scratching with us.'

1962 Alan Marshall *This is the Grass* 202: 'Not that I read much. I've been too busy scratching for a crust.'

screamer   In Australian Rules football, an exceptionally high mark ['A very powerful shot in a game' 1896 OED]

[**1859** Hotten 87: *Screaming* first rate, splendid. *Theat.*, but now applied generally.]

1963 Lou Richards *Boots and All!* 175: The only thing he did all day was to take a screaming mark.

1984 Les Carlyon *Age* (Melbourne) 30 May 39: The Melbourne Cricket Ground, citadel of Aussie Rules, the very place where international figures with names like *Jezza* take things called screamers.

screamer, two-pot   Someone very susceptible to alcohol

1959 Dorothy Hewett *Bobbin Up* 21: 'Look at Lou. She's a two-pot screamer, always 'as been.'

1972 John de Hoog *Skid Row Dossier* 95: 'It says experienced and sober, ya bloody two-pot screamer.'

1981 George Hutchinson *No Room for Dreamers* 10: And there's no need for poofters or two-pot screamers / And there's no room for bludgers – and no room for dreamers.

scrub, the   Anywhere remote from civilization, or in expressions like 'head for the scrub', 'out in the scrub', any place to which one might abscond, or avoid contact with one's fellows [f. *scrub* as a wooded but inhospitable region: see quot. 1834]

[**1834** J. D. Lang *A Historical and Statistical Account of New South Wales* i 354: In sterile regions, however, on rocky mountain-tracts, or on sandy plains, the forest degenerates into a miserable scrub, as the colonists term it; the trees are stunted in their growth and of most forbidding aspect.]

1956 Kylie Tennant *The Honey Flow* 270: If Col had won the toss and proposed first, I don't think it would have made any difference, except that Elsie might have taken to the scrub.

1959 David Forrest *The Last Blue Sea* 31: 'You see that bloke with the blue-an'-white arm-band comin', you 'ead f'r the scrub.'

1962 John Morrison *Twenty-Three* 194: 'You just get up in the morning, pack whatever you can lay hands on, and head for the scrub.'

1972 Peter Kenna *The Slaughter of St. Teresa's Day* 48: 'I'd arranged to ride in from the scrub and join Marty and the girls there.'

1976 *Australian* 9 Oct. 25: I have just spent a few relaxing weeks in the scrub – no offence meant – and have to report that Queensland offers a couple of items we could well do with down here, which is NSW.

see **mallee, mulga, tall timber**

scrub aristocracy   People with social pretensions in 'the scrub'

1900 Henry Lawson 'The Hero of Redclay' *Prose* i 296: 'The banker, the storekeeper, one of the publicans, the butcher ... the postmaster, and his toady, the lightning squirter, were the scrub-aristocracy.

scrub-bashing   Driving a road through the scrub

1967 Len Beadell *Blast the Bush* 151: I was not surprised at the end of forty miles of scrub-bashing that there was still no evidence of the other road.

1982 *NT News* (Darwin) 5 Aug. 7: The drongo club ... went scrub-bashing in their four-wheel drives.

scrub bull   A 'loner' (see quot. 1967) [cf. *scrubber*]

1959 Vance Palmer *The Big Fellow* 268: What she had roused in him then had kept him from being quite the tough scrub-bull that he might have been.

1966 Baker 82: Another synonym for *hatter* is *scrub bull*.

1967 Barry Oakley *A Wild Ass of a Man* 68: 'I'm different from the herd, and at that school they don't like the wanderers, the scrub bulls who forage for their nourishment in their own way, alone.'

1975 Xavier Herbert *Poor Fellow My Country* 702: The Scrub Bull, of all people, getting interested in settling the country.

scrubber   1   A term for cattle that have run wild, or never been branded [f. *scrub*]

1859 Henry Kingsley *Recollections of Geoffry Hamlyn* ii 125: 'It's lucky you've got them [the cattle] cheap, for the half of them are off the ranges.' 'Scrubbers, eh?' said the Major.

1878 Rolf Boldrewood *An Australian Squire* repr. as *Babes in the Bush* (1900) 268: 'May the devil take ye for a cross-grained contrary brindle-hided straggling bastard of a scrubber'. [addressed to a heifer]

1881 A. C. Grant *Bush-Life in Queensland* i 206: When the market price of ordinary quiet stock is low, the scrubbers have little or no value; but should a demand arise, every cattle-owner makes desperate exertions to capture them.

1898 W. H. Ogilvie *Fair Girls and Gray Horses* 55: And he loves the merry rattle of the stockwhip and the tramp / Of the cockhorned mulga scrubbers when they're breaking in the brush.

359

1907 Charles MacAlister *Old Pioneering Days in the Sunny South* 237: Little weeds of 'scrubbers' that couldn't be given away for boiling down in New South Wales were shipped and sold to the Maories at prices ranging from £5 to £50.
1911 E. S. Sorenson *Life in the Australian Backblocks* 126: A few quiet cattle are pastured in the open, near where the scrubbers water, to act as decoys. The scrubbers come out at night.
1934 Vance Palmer *Sea and Spinifex* 220: 'The worst bloody scrubbers along the Gulf ... Horns as long as your arms, and the pace of kangaroo-dogs.'
1955 Mary Durack *Keep Him My Country* 167: As the younger stockmen closed in around the scrubbers Benjamin took his place.
1961 George Farwell *Vanishing Australians* 29: 'Remember those wild-looking scrubbers we moonlighted?'
1982 Thea Astley *An Item from the Late News* 88: A chopper that went over running out scrubbers on the property west of him.
2   A horse racing on country tracks, or considered suitable only for the bush
1958 Frank Hardy *The Four-Legged Lottery* 177: 'Got a few scrubbers. Picks up a race in the bush occasionally. Likes to run his horses in the city.'
1982 Joe Andersen *Winners Can Laugh!* 176:. Their previous suspicions were now confirmed. This was no scrubber from the bush.
1984 *Sun-Herald* 11 Mar. 73: Here's a tip for those punters who cannot resist a favourite – stick to the Saturday meetings and forget the scrubbers at the midweek events! Figures ... show the percentage of successful favourites at Saturday meetings in Sydney since January 1 is a whopping 42 per cent. The midweek rate is about 33 per cent.
1984 *Sunday Independent* (Perth) 1 Apr. 73: Punters don't deserve to lose their money because 'scrubbers' and unfit horses ruin the chances of fancied runners when they drop back through the field after galloping for a couple of furlongs.
3   Any hardy individual, outside the conventional code
1984 Laurie Lawrence *Sunday Times* (Perth) 5 Aug. 96: He's [Jon Sieben] been a scrubber all his life, a hard boy to handle but one of the most mentally tough swimmers I've ever come across.

scrum   Threepence: *obs.*
1902 Henry Lawson 'Send Round the Hat' *Prose* i 472: The crown was worn as thin as paper by the quids, half-quids, casers, bobs and tanners or sprats – to say nothing of the scrums – that had been chucked into it.
1904 Henry Fletcher *Dads Wayback: His Work* 51: 'Yous can get er revolver fer three half-crowns, an' cartridges is only a bob-an'-a-scrum a hun-

dred.'
1941 Baker 64: *Scrum* A 3d piece.

scungies   Bikini-style swimming trunks, or 'vees' [f. *scungy*]
1979 Kathy Lette and Gabrielle Carey *Puberty Blues* 3: The art of changing in and out of board-shorts at the beach was always done behind a towel or when your girlfriend was at the shop. The ultimate disgrace for a surfie was to be seen in his scungies. They were too much like underpants. The boys didn't want us checking out the size of their dicks.
1979 *Sun-Herald* 21 Oct. 119: The studs strut around the pool in brief scungies.

scungy   Unattractive, disreputable in appearance [f. *scunge* To prowl around looking for food 1843 OED]
1963 Barbara Jefferis *The Wild Grapes* 64: 'He's much more sensitive than all the other Russels. He couldn't live with anyone who was skungey looking.'
1972 Geoff Morley *Jockey Rides Honest Race* 69: These painted women standing on the doorsteps of scungy little lovenests bore a strange fascination for me.
1980 Rod Ansell *To Fight the Wild* 56: The dressing on her leg was getting very scungy but I wasn't game to touch it until the bone had had time to begin setting.
1982 *Age* (Melbourne) 21 Jun. 14: It does perhaps have some documentary value as a record of a particular group, the self-consciously scungy middle class that invaded Carlton, at a particular time.

Sea Eagles, the   As for **Eagles** q.v.
1975 *Bulletin* 9 Aug. 21: 'What would you do,' asked the notice [on a Manly church], 'if Jesus Christ came to Manly?' To which some Sea Eagle-fancier had replied: 'Play him in the centre alongside Fulton and move Branighan out to the wing.'

seagull   A casual wharf labourer [f. the bird's habit of waiting for and swooping on scraps]
1965 Frank Hardy *The Yarns of Billy Borker* 115: 'He was a casual wharfie at the time I'm telling you about ... and they call casuals 'seagulls'.

Seagulls   1   In Queensland, the Wynnum-Manly R.L. club
1979 *Courier-Mail* (Brisbane) 5 Mar. 14: Seagulls in fighting comeback [heading] Wynnum-Manly's team of country youngsters staged a determined comeback to power their way to a 13–9 win over Valleys at Neumann Oval yesterday.
2   In Tasmania, Sandy Bay Australian Rules club
1980 *Mercury* (Hobart) 21 Apr. 22: Gulls saw it

slip away [heading]

seat at the pictures, couldn't pick a   see **couldn't**

secko   A sex pervert [abbr.]
1949 Ruth Park *Poor Man's Orange* 38: 'Just look at that dirty ole secko, will you?' he said disgustedly.
1961 Peter Mathers *Australian Letters* Jun. 48: It'll be like the city next. Seckoes everywhere.
1961 Frank Hardy *The Hard Way* 75: 'A secco', the Bush Lawyer whispered. 'Been flashing it . . .'
1969 William Dick *Naked Prodigal* 13: 'You look like you'd be the sorta bloke who'd take little kids down a lane and give 'em two bob, yeh bloody secko.'
1974 *Bulletin* 6 Apr. 45: 'I noticed Australians use a lot of diminutives, like Chrissie, pressie and journo.' 'In jails sex offenders are called seckos,' I told him.
1984 *Bulletin* 20 Mar. 47: A risk of being identified with a 'sekko' (sex offender).

see you later   see **later**

sein   Ten shillings *obs.* [? f. German *zehn*, ten]
1939 Kylie Tennant *Foveaux* 310: 'If someone did a night with you and threw you a sein, you'd snatch it with both hands.'
1945 Baker 109: *10s. sane* or *sein* (from the German *zehn*, ten).

semi   1   A semi-detached house
1959 Dorothy Hewett *Bobbin Up* 5: Always fighting a losing battle with life in the grey, warped, weatherboard semi in Maddox Lane.
1980 Natalie Scott *Wherever We Step the Land is Mined* 22: Semi, comprising two-and-a half bedrooms, kitchen, bath, inside W.C., rear access, very handy position.
2   A semi-trailer
1959 Dorothy Hewett *Bobbin Up* 2: A big shiny car had forced them over, to sideswipe an oncoming semi.
1979 *Advertiser* (Adelaide) 3 May 3: Tourists stranded by semi accident.
3   A semi-final
1979 *Sun-Herald* 24 Jun. 63: Bulldogs stay in semi race [heading]
4   A semi government authority, loan etc.
1979 *Australian* 29 May 10: Acid test for semi market [heading] Two leading semi-government bodies are about to provide an important test of the market's ability to fund the 1979–80 borrowing requirements of the authorities.

send her down, Hughie   see **Hughie**

septic   A Yank [f. rhyming slang *septic tank* = *Yank*]
1976 *Cleo* Aug. 33: Even before R and R, Americans [at King's Cross] were septics (septic tanks – yanks). Septic is now general usage.
1983 Clem Gorman *A Night in the Arms of Raeleen* 73: 'Some compliment, eh, comin' from a Septic Tank on Fifth Avenue?'

serve   An adverse criticism, reprimand [? f. tennis, or serving a summons]
[1812 Vaux: To *serve* a man, also sometimes signifies to maim, wound, or do him some bodily hurt, and to *serve* him *out and out*, is to kill him.]
1974 Keith Stackpole *Not Just for Openers* 104: I continued to give Snow a bit of a serve. He was foolish to bowl short on such a good wicket. Ibid. 54: Having seen only one player dismissed by it [Connolly's 'knuckle' ball], I had always wanted to give it a serve. I unleashed an almighty swing.
1977 *Australian* 1 Jun. 3: He [John Osborne] did manage to convey that he had a fairly miserable time in Australia, but he was glad to be leaving and he would be giving the country a serve in an unnamed English newspaper if it was willing to pay enough for his views.
1977 *Bulletin* 25 Jun. 3: He gives the ockers a big serve on Page 50.
1981 *Age* (Melbourne) 1 Oct. 2: He gave the Commonwealth Secretary-General, Mr Ramphal, a serve over their differences in interpreting the Gleneagles Agreement.
1983 *Sydney Morning Herald* 24 Nov. 3: 'One gets fed up to the neck of hearing spokesmen, and spokeswomen too, for that matter, who speak in the proudest of Pommy accents roasting Australia and giving Australians a serve.'

session   A period of steady drinking, in a group
1949 Lawson Glassop *Lucky Palmer* 215: 'I'll join you in a beer later, but I don't want to get into a session.'
1955 D'Arcy Niland *The Shiralee* 51: 'I don't want to make a session of it. I had a helluva night.'
1969 Christopher Bray *Blossom Like a Rose* 8: 'The pub's bin open five minutes! The session's begun!'
1973 H. Williams *My Love Had a Black Speed Stripe* 47: Back to work for the mugs and back to the Trades Hall and another grog session for Walters.
1983 Laurie Clancy *Perfect Love* 102: He had missed out on his session but he could at least bring some bottles home.

settler's cake   See quot.
1843 Charles Rowcroft *Tales of the Colonies* iii 93: 'There's a real settler's cake for you, gentlemen, made nice and light, like a pancake, only it wants eggs and milk.'

settler's clock   The kookaburra, or laughing jack-ass [see quot. 1827]

1827 P. Cunningham *Two Years in New South Wales* i 232: The loud and discordant noise of the *laughing jackass* (or *settler's clock*, as he is called), as he takes up his roost on the withered bough of one of our tallest trees, acquaints us that the sun has just dipped behind the hills . . . Again the loud laughter of the *jackass* summons us to *turn out*, and take a peep at the appearance of the morning.

1847 L. Leichhardt *Journal of an Overland Expedition* 234: I usually rise when I hear the merry laugh of the laughing-jackass *(Dacelo gigantea)*, which, from its regularity, has not been unaptly named the settler's clock.

1856 G. Willmer *The Draper in Australia* 224: The settlers prize this bird very much and do not destroy it, as it not only kills snakes, but rouses the inmates of the huts at day-break, while at night it is heard just as it is getting dark. From these circumstances it is called the settler's clock.

1873 A. Trollope *Australia* ed. Edwards and Joyce (1967) 210: The laughing jack-ass . . . is also called the settler's clock.

1894 Ethel Turner *Seven Little Australians* 205: 'Well, you might hear a worse story than about the jackass, or kukuburra, or goburra, or settler's clock – whichever it may please you to call it,' Mr Gillet said.

1919 E. S. Sorenson *Chips and Splinters* 82: 'The Settlers' Clock', as the settlers know, / Was only a kookaburra.

1943 *The Swagman's Note-book* ed. Charles Barrett 14: 'Settler's clock' may have been used in the early days, it has long been obsolete as a name for our laughing cavalier in feathers.

1966 D. E. Charlwood *An Afternoon of Time* 50: I heard kookaburras laugh a long way off, then remembered that old name of theirs – 'the settler's clock'.

settler's friend   Stringy bark and greenhide

1856 G. Willmer *The Draper in Australia* 216–17: The bark is fibrous, and being very tough, it was a few years ago looked upon as the settler's friend; even now it is much used for tying purposes, and in the absence of rope it certainly is still a capital substitute. It is no uncommon thing still to hear men in the bush speak of this bark and the green hide (the latter is used for halters) as the settler's friend.

settler's matches   See quot.

1891 Henry Lawson 'The Shanty on the Rise' *Verse* i 156: And we walked so very silent – being lost in reverie – / That we heard the 'settlers matches'* gently rustle on the tree. *The thin loose outer bark hanging on the trunks of white box, ash, and other smooth-barks.

seven   A 7 oz. glass of beer

1976 David Ireland *The Glass Canoe* 151: She went down . . . to middies, then to sevens, and finally got so low they moved her to hospital.

1977 David Foster *Escape to Reality* 136: 'I've seen you drink. Three sevens finish you for the night.'

seven, throw a   To die; to faint; to have a vomiting attack [f. *six* as the maximum score marked on dice]

1894 Henry Lawson 'Martin Farrell' *Verse* i 269: 'I am pretty crook and shaky – too far gone for hell or heaven, / An' the chances are I'm goin' – to "do the seven".'

1898 *Bulletin* 17 Dec. Red Page: If anyone dies it is known as *throwing the seven*.

1908 *The Australian Magazine* 1 Nov. 1250: Instead of dying you can 'chuck a seven'.

1919 W. H. Downing *Digger Dialects* 49: *Throw a seven* Die (Probably arose from dicing. It is impossible to throw a seven-spot.)

1926 L. C. E. Gee *Bushtracks and Goldfields* 32: They all reckoned that it was touch and go with me, that I was a 'goner', that I was bound to 'throw a seven'.

1932 A. W. Upfield *A Royal Abduction* 201: 'If she sees the thing she won't scream and throw a seven [faint]. She'll shoot.'

1958 Vince Kelly *The Greedy Ones* 104: 'Throwing a seven?' 'Collapsing – having a fit – fainting.'

1966 Tom Ronan *Once There Was a Bagman* 217: The partially digested fruit must have swollen inside me, for before long I was chucking sevens around the flat as I had done a few years before when I had that touch of ptomaine poisoning.

shag on a rock, like a   Isolated, deserted, exposed [OED records *wet as a shag* 1835]

1845 R. Howitt *Impressions of Australia Felix* 233: 'Poor as a bandicoot', 'miserable as a shag on a rock' &c.; these and others I very frequently heard them make use of.

1929 Jules Raeside *Golden Days* 16: The flood waters did not subside, and we were there like three shags on a rock.

1942 Gavin Casey *It's Harder for Girls* 216: There are plenty of people in the street, but it's no good roosting in the gutter like a shag on a rock.

1952 T. A. G. Hungerford *The Ridge and the River* 53: 'I got no time to be standin' here like a flamin' shag on a rock!'

1960 John Iggulden *The Storms of Summer* 100: 'We're stuck here like a shag on a rock until we get the net up, aren't we?'

1971 David Ireland *The Unknown Industrial Prisoner* 275: 'It's easy enough to curse England. Leaving us out here like a shag on a rock, but I don't apologize for being British.'

1979 Dorothy Hewett *The Man from Mukinupin*

60: 'Exiled here like shags on rocks.'
1982 Bill O'Reilly *Sydney Morning Herald* 28 Jan. 28: Perhaps it was a sympathetic reaction to one who was made to look like an old shag sitting on his proverbial rock that rallied my friends about me.

shake   To steal [f. *shake out* to rob OED c. 1412] [1812 Vaux: *Shake* to steal, or rob.]
1854 W. Shaw *The Land of Promise* 33: There commenced a torrent of interrogation, mostly in slang, 'what's he shook?' 'has he sloped?' and other flash phrases.
1855 William Howitt *Land, Labour and Gold* i 174: As for these diggings, they appear quiet and orderly; and people leave their tents all day, and seldom have them 'shook', as the phrase is, or robbed in plain English.
1869 *The Australian Journal* Jul. 685: *To shake* To steal. *Shook* Stole.
1889 Rolf Boldrewood *Nevermore* (1892) 77: 'What the blazes has a chap like that any call to shake a horse for?'
1906 Joseph Furphy *Rigby's Romance* ed. R. G. Howarth (1946) 251: 'What's come o' them two black horses o' yours?' 'Gone.' 'Sold?' 'Shook.'
1924 *Truth* 27 Apr. 6: *Shook* Stolen.
1935 Kylie Tennant *Tiburon* 198: 'I shook a tin o' petrol from Pearson's garage last night,' he said under his breath.
1965 Patrick White *Four Plays* 105: 'You don't think I'd shake anything off Ern? 'E's my mate!'
1979 Ted Schurmann *The Showie* 107: 'You're not going to take his pliers!' 'Heck, I'm only borrowing them, not shaking them.'

shake a stick at, more than one could   see **stick**

shanghai   A catapult [f. *shangan (shangie)* A stick cleft at one end for putting on a dog's tail EDD]
1863 *The Leader* 24 Oct. 17: Turn, turn thy shangay dread aside, / Nor touch that little bird. [Morris]
1900–10 O'Brien and Stephens: *Shanghai* boy's catapult.
1910 H. H. Richardson *The Getting of Wisdom* 205: Home was, alas! no longer the snug nest, in which she was safe from the slings and shanghais of the world.
1934 Vance Palmer *Sea and Spinifex* 94: 'No you don't want to trouble about the likes of them. Unless it's to go after them with a shanghai.'
1941 Sarah Campion *Mo Burdekin* 292: *Shanghai* Catapult.
1957 R. S. Porteous *Brigalow* 204: He gave a guilty start rather like a small boy stretching his shanghai for a trial shot at the family cat!
1965 William Dick *A Bunch of Ratbags* 130: I went back to making my new shanghai.

1982 *Sun-Herald* 17 Oct. 18: School holidays were spent 'down the bush', swimming all day or shooting a shanghai at whatever innocent wildlife crossed the track.

shanty   A public house, esp. unlicensed; a 'sly-grog shop' [OED] [f. the structure so called]
1864 J. Rogers *New Rush* 52: The Keepers of the stores and shanties grieve.
1875 A. J. Boyd *Old Colonials* (1882) 103: The Grog Shanty [chapter title]
1880 Rolf Boldrewood *The Miner's Right* (1890) 64: Any attempt to limit the licensing produced such a crop of 'shanties' or sly-grogshops.
1894 Henry Lawson 'The Spooks of Long Gully' *Prose* i 249: The son did die that night in the 'horrors' in a shanty.

Shark, the Great White   see **Great**

sharkbait(er)   Someone who swims further out than the other surfers, as though tempting the sharks
1912 Arthur Wright *Rung In* 34–5: It might be only some foolhardy 'shark baiter' as he heard the more venturesome of the bathers termed.
1920 A. H. Adams *The Australians* 177: Farther out in the deep water swam the venturous line of experts, technically known as 'shark-bait'.
1930 *Bulletin* 13 Aug. 45: By swimming past the first line of breakers Alma had declared herself to be that disquieting disturber of peace, a shark-baiter.
1941 Baker 65: *Sharkbait* A swimmer, esp. one who swims out beyond the breakers.
1951 Dymphna Cusack and Florence James *Come In Spinner* 221: 'Why didn't you come out with me?' 'Not me. I've given up shark-baiting. Mug's game.'
1959 Vance Palmer *The Big Fellow* 6: 'Hullo, Sharkbait,' he called down to her. 'How was the water?'
1967 K. S. Prichard *Subtle Flame* 99: 'I'm no good at shark baiting!'

Sharks, the   1   The Cronulla-Sutherland Rugby League team, N.S.W. [f. club emblem, and proximity of Cronulla to the sea]
1975 *Sydney Morning Herald* 21 Jul. 13: Rogers kicks Sharks home.
2   The East Fremantle (W.A.) Australian Rules team
1983 *Sunday Independent* (Perth) 14 Aug. 37: Sharks savage the Falcons [heading] East Fremantle . . . did it again yesterday.

sharp, so ~ as to cut oneself   A reproof of over-cleverness
1903 Joseph Furphy *Such is Life* (1944) 278:

'Gosh! You've been on the turkey; you'll be cutting yourself some of these times.'
1910 H. H. Richardson *The Getting of Wisdom* 142: 'If you're so sharp you'll cut yourself!'
1957 Randolph Stow *The Bystander* 123: 'You'll cut yourself one day, you're so sharp.'

sharpie   Member of a teenage cult with 'short back and sides' haircut, the counterpart of the English 'skinhead'
1965 William Dick *A Bunch of Ratbags* 202: The more a sharpie protested he was not a bodgie, the more they [the police] laughed and belted him.
1972 *Sydney Morning Herald* 20 Jan. 2: It was alleged in evidence that Still died during an incident involving 'sharpies' and 'long-hairs' outside Greystanes Progress Hall.
1975 *Sun-Herald* 13 Apr. 7: A sharpie is usually aged between 14 and 19 years. The boys wear their hair cropped short on the top and sides and longer at the back. The girls often wear 'dolly' makeup and have their ears pierced. Tattoos are often worn by both sexes. The sharpies wear blue jeans or high-waisted slacks supported by old-fashioned braces, matched with a tee shirt and sometimes a woollen cardigan ... They usually keep well clear of the beachside suburbs, the home of their arch enemies, the surfies.

she's apples, jake, sweet   see **apples, jake, sweet**

shearer's dog, all prick and ribs like a   see **all**

shears, off (the)   Used of sheep just shorn
1896 Thomas W. Heney *The Girl at Birrell's* 69: Now and again a buyer visited the stations to get cheap sheep 'off shears'.
1903 Joseph Furphy *Such is Life* (1944) 64: I camped with a party of six ... bound for Deniliquin, with 3,000 Boolka wethers off the shears.
1964 Tom Ronan *Packhorse and Pearling Boat* 147: It [the shearing shed] had never been used. The sheep had arrived off-shears and had been promptly annihilated by the depredations of meat-hungry aboriginals.
1983 Arthur Cannon *Bullocks, Bullockies and Other Blokes* 127: Stations usually sold sheep 'off shears' – that is, after shearing.

shed   A shearing shed
1857 F. Cooper *Wild Adventures in Australia* 105: 'He was bound for the shearing through New England. By this time, most likely, he has set in at some of the sheds on the Namoi.'
1902 Henry Lawson 'Two Sundowners' *Prose* i 96: The number of men employed is according to the size of the shed – from three to five men in the little bough-covered shed of the small 'cockatoo', up to a hundred and fifty or two hundred hands all

told in the big corrugated iron machine shed of a pastoral company.
1908 E. S. Sorenson *Quinton's Rouseabout* 24: Towards the end of winter crowds of men passed through on their way to the early sheds.
1919 W. K. Harris *Outback in Australia* 153: Shearing has to be stopped for two or three days, and instructions must be promptly forwarded to the men in charge of the sheep on their way to the 'shed' to camp temporarily.
1934 F. E. Baume *Burnt Sugar* 249: 'You might be a shed hand or just a hobo.'

sheila   A girl or woman. Not derogatory, although no woman would refer to herself as a 'sheila' [f. *Sheela* as generic name for an Irish girl, counterpart of *Paddy* for a man]
[**1828** *Monitor* 22 Mar. 1053: Many a piteous Shela stood wiping the gory locks of her Paddy, until released from that duty by the officious interference of the knight of the *baton*.
1859 Hotten 90: *Shaler* a girl.
1910 P. W. Joyce *English as We Speak it in Ireland* 320: *Sheela* a female Christian name ... Used in the South as a reproachful name for a boy or man inclined to do work or interest himself in affairs properly belonging to women.]
1895 Cornelius Crowe *The Australian Slang Dictionary* 72: *Shaler* a girl.
1885–1914 'The Spider by the Gwydir' *Australian Ballads* ed. Russel Ward (1964) 122: And he bit that rookin' sheila on the stern. / Then the sheila raced off squealin', / And her clothes she was un-peelin': / To hear her yells would make you feel forlorn.
1919 W. H. Downing *Digger Dialects* 44: *Sheila* A girl.
1928 Arthur Wright *A Good Recovery* 117: 'Leave the sheilas alone, they're sure to pool a man sooner or later.'
1931 Vance Palmer *Separate Lives* 220: 'There was a sheelah back in Salisbury who did her block on me,' Chook was saying.
1949 Lawson Glassop *Lucky Palmer* 28: 'Not married yet, eh?' Lucky laughed. 'Do I look like a mug?' he asked ... 'Sheilas don't interest me. They're not worth a bumper.'
1958 Christopher Koch *The Boys in the Island* 69: 'Should get on to some sheilas out there too. You want to come?'
1965 Patrick White *Four Plays* 111: 'We used to lie and talk about what we was goin' ter eat. An' the sheilas we was goin' ter do.'
1973 H. Williams *My Love Had a Black Speed Stripe* 17: Beats me how any bloke can enjoy himself talking with women. Sheila talk has always driven me up the wall.
1975 *Australian* 22 Sep. 1: Fat, lazy and going to seed ... That's yer spoilt Ocker sheila.

1984 Margaret Jones *Sydney Morning Herald* 4 May 8: My other vote for the most bannable word in the Australian vocabulary would be 'sheila', admittedly not much used by the young, but still surprisingly persistent among the adult male population and encapsulating perfectly and regrettably the speakers' attitudes to women.

shelf *n. & v.* An informer; to inform upon [? to put away on a shelf]
[**1859** Hotten 70: *On the shelf* to be transported.]
1926 J. Vance Marshall *Timely Tips for New Australians: Shelf* A slang word denoting an informer.
1947 C. K. Thompson *Yes, Your Honour!* 142: 'What is a top-off?' ... 'An informer, a pimp, a shelf, and so on', replied the police prosecutor.
1953 T. A. G. Hungerford *Riverslake* 20: 'If you spoil this one I damn well will shelf you.'
1958 Vince Kelly *The Greedy Ones* 104: 'We were mates in this affair and you don't shelf your mates. And anyone who does shelf a mate has got to take what's coming to him.'
1967 Kylie Tennant *Tell Morning This* 91: 'Who told you I shelfed you, who told you that?'
1984 *Sun-Herald* 9 Sep. 63: For all the pre-planning and agreements not to 'shelf' one another by being seen to start a rush to back Fine Cotton, several of those in the know could not contain their greed.

shelleys, a A function at which only soft drinks are served [f. Shelleys, the soft drink firm]
1983 Encountered in conversation.

shells, bag of Something easily accomplished [cf. a piece of cake]
1978 Ray Lawler *The Doll Trilogy* 125: JOSEF: That would be kind. NANCY: A bag of shells.

she-oak Colonial beer: *obs.* [? f. the native oak, a species of casuarina, and *oak* = cask]
1873 J. C. F. Johnson *Christmas on Carringa* 1: Able to put away at a sitting a larger quantity of colonial 'sheoak' than any man of his inches.
1881 G. C. Evans *Stories told round the Campfire* 17: 'Perhaps so,' he remarked, 'but when a man expects a drink of brandy, it is a great sell to find it is only sheoak.'
1893 J. A. Barry *Steve Brown's Bunyip* 282: Hastily finishing his pint of 'sheoak'.
1899 W. T. Goodge *Hits! Skits! and Jingles!* 125: We scorned the foreign yolk, / And much preferred she-oak, / And stuck to beer.

shepherd To hold a mining claim without working it, in order to deny others; (sporting) to ward off a player tackling a member of one's own team.
1855 William Howitt *Land, Labour and Gold* i

172: It is common practice for them to mark out one or more claims in each new rush ... But only one claim at a time is legal and tenable. This practice is called shepherding.
1895 Nat Gould *On and Off the Turf in Australia* 122–3: 'I got jammed in', said Martin, with a smile. 'One horse kept me in all down the straight; in fact, this horse was 'shepherding' me all through the race.'
1965 Frank Hardy *The Yarns of Billy Borker* 21: 'Did the players in the other team run across and stop him?' 'No fear, his team mates shepherded them off.'
1981 *Weekend Australian* 9 May 2: It is more difficult to contact the Premier during working hours. He has surrounded himself with personal staff who shepherd him flagrantly.
1982 *Sun-Herald* 4 Apr. 87: The bloke beside me yelled out: 'Didn't you see the shepherd? Where'd you get a ticket, ref, out of a cornflakes packet?'

shepherd's companion The willy wagtail
1870 E. B. Kennedy *Four Years in Queensland* 117: The 'shepherd's companion' is a species of water wagtail exceedingly tame, and frequenting the most desolate parts of the bush.
1908 W. H. Ogilvie *My Life in the Open* 5: Round and round your horse's feet flutters the black wagtail, the 'shepherd's companion' of the Bush, flying on ahead, then waiting or fluttering back.

sherbet Beer: *jocular*
1917 Henry Lawson 'Romani' *Verse* iii 214: And beer that we called 'sherbet'.
1965 John Beede *They Hosed Them Out* 204: At mid day I hit myself with a few sherbets.
1973 Fred Archer *The Treasure House* 18: He had a strident voice and with a few sherbets under his belt you knew he was about.
1981 *Bulletin* 5 May 52: Hayden's only chance of hanging on to the leadership would be for Hawke to slip back on to the sherbet.

shicer A mining claim that proves unproductive; a swindler (shyster) [G. *scheisser* and English (see quot. 1859) and U.S. slang (*shyster* 1846 Mathews)]
[**1859** Hotten *Shice*, nothing; 'to do anything for *shice*', to get no payment. The term was first used by the Jews in the last century ... *Shicer*, a mean man, a humbug, a 'duffer', – a worthless person, one who will not work.]
1855 Raffaello Carboni *The Eureka Stockade* ed. G. Serle (1969) 8: The whole flat turned out an imperial shicer. Ibid. 14: A hole was bottomed down the gully, and proved a scheisser.
1858 Thatcher's *Colonial Songster* 66: T'other day a German friend of ours, / His name is Mister Kaiser, / Blushed like a girl of sixteen, / When I mentioned the word '*shicer*'.

1867 J. R. Houlding *Australian Capers* 127: The hole was no good, or what they called a 'shicer'.
1885 *The Australasian Printers' Keepsake* 64: 'In the opening once or twice, sir, / You'll be reckon'd as a shycer.' Ibid. 71: 'He was full up of such a shicin' practice.'
1898 Morris: *Shicer* (2) A man who does not pay his debts of honour.
1958 Jack Lindsay *Life Rarely Tells* 213: 'There's nothing I hate more'n a shicer.'

shick, shickered, shickery   Drunk [Yiddish]
[**1859** Hotten: *Shickery*, shabby, badly]
1878 Rolf Boldrewood *An Australian Squire* repr. as *Babes in the Bush* (1900) 121: 'I'm always that fresh after a good night's sleep, when I've had a bit of a spree that I could begin again quite flippant. Old Tom had a goodish cheque this time, and was at it a week afore I came in. He was rayther shickerry.'
1898 *Bulletin* 17 Dec. Red Page: *shiker* drunk.
1911 Louis Stone *Jonah* 124: 'Whose cart is it?' inquired Pinkey. 'Jack Ryan's,' answered Chook, ''e's bin shickered since last We'n'sday, an' I'm takin' it round fer 'is missis 'an the kids.'
1915 C. J. Dennis *The Songs of a Sentimental Bloke* 81: ''E'd 'ad a couple, but 'e wasn't shick.
1922 Arthur Wright *A Colt from the Country* 44: 'He's half dead, anyhow,' declared Farvall, 'and he's shikkered as well.'
1945 Gavin Casey *Downhill is Easier* 9: They sat outside the pub in the sun every day, and most of them got a bit shickered on pension day.
1961 Patrick White *Riders in the Chariot* 261: 'I'm gunna get out of this!' he announced at last. 'I'm gunna get shickered stiff!'
1973 *Sydney Morning Herald* 25 Oct. 2: A back-bench senator referred today to the Jackson Pollock painting, 'Blue Poles' bought by Australia for $1.3 million as 'shicker art' ... Later outside the Senate he said that by 'shicker art' he meant paintings done by people who were shickered, or drunk.

shicker *v.*   To drink, get drunk
1913 Henry Lawson 'Benno and his Old 'Uns' *Prose* i 805: Her Old 'Un 'shickered' till he got 'mucked' every pay day.
1924 *Truth* 27 Apr. 6: *Shicker* To drink.
1951 Dymphna Cusack and Florence James *Come In Spinner* 33: 'He'd gamble his shirt off on any demn thing that's got a leg to run on, but he doesn't shicker.'
1980 *Bulletin* 27 May 50: Don made a speech ... in which he said that he really LIKED the team at *Pol* (that state of affairs will continue until the first night they all get shickered together in the local pub).

shicker *n.*   Liquor
1916 C. J. Dennis *The Moods of Ginger Mick* 154: *Shicker* Intoxicating liquor.
1928 Arthur Wright *A Good Recovery* 85: 'Yes, I've been on the shikker,' he answered huskily.
1945 Roy Rene *Mo's Memoirs* 49: One night the magician had been on the shicker, and with a fine disregard for life and limb he let the lion out.
1958 H. D. Williamson *The Sunlit Plain* 58: 'He was on the shicker when I was there last week.'
1980 *Weekend Australian* 20 Dec. Mag. 13: Ruth goes to Dennis's aid after he has had a few days on the shicker.

shilling in, a   As for **a bob in** q.v.
1942 Gavin Casey *It's Harder for Girls* 83: We had another shilling in, and bought some bottles to take to the restaurant.

Shinboners   Former nickname of the North Melbourne V.F.L. club [f. aggressive style of play: see also quot. 1981]
1981 Leonie Sandercock and Ian Turner *Up Where, Cazaly?* 51: The 'shin-boners', as they were then [1896] known (from the practice of local butchers decorating their shop-windows on football Saturdays with shin-bones of cattle tied around with blue and white ribbons), had an established reputation. Ibid. 191: Under Aylett and Barassi North lost the old shinboner image and became the most professional team in the League.
1984 *Australian* 17 Apr. 18: North Melbourne had a collective nickname – 'The Shinboners', a wonderfully inventive description of a group of players who went straight for the jugular if they couldn't break your legs.

shiner   Someone who seeks the limelight but avoids the hard work, esp. in sport
1939 Herbert M. Moran *Viewless Winds* 53: How well we got to know the shiner who was brilliant when all was going well and easy, but who was missing – hanging out on the outskirts of the ruck – when our horny-handed opponents were 'putting it in'.
1941 Baker 65: *Shine, to* To show off, play to the gallery. Also, 'shiner': an exhibitionist, a 'show off'.
1983 *Sun-Herald* 10 Apr. 69: He is not a fashionable player, he is not a shiner in the open. He is simply a player who will do his job.

shingle short, a   Weak in the head [variant of the English 'a tile loose']
1852 G. C. Mundy *Our Antipodes* iii 17: The climate is productive ... of chronic diseases rather than acute ones. Let no man having, in colonial phrase, 'a shingle short' try this country.

He will pass his days in Tarban Creek Asylum.

1869 *Australian Journal* Jul. 685: *A shingle short* The colonial rendering of the English phrase, 'A tile loose'.

1876 Rolf Boldrewood *A Colonial Reformer* (1891) 90: The overseer rode off, puzzled as to whether the new hand was laughing at him or was 'a shingle short'.

1881 Mrs Campbell Praed *Policy and Passion* 173: 'I have heard Lady Dolph say that I have "a shingle loose".'

1895 Henry Lawson 'The Fate of the Fat Man's Son' *Verse* i 280: The Fat Man's son was an Anarchist, a couple of shingles short.

1908 Henry Fletcher *Dads and Dan between Smokes* 65: So ther balmy cove takes to solitude an' ther bush quite natural. That 'counts fer some o' them, ther extra special shingle-shorters.

1928 Miles Franklin *Up the Country* 9: 'The only time I ever saw her, she seemed a shingle short.'

1941 Charles Barrett *Coast of Adventure* 15: 'A shingle short? Not much.'

1966 Patrick White *The Solid Mandala* 82: He accepted Arthur his twin brother, who was, as they put it, a shingle short.

shinplaster A promissory note issued by bush storekeepers and others, and used as a kind of currency. The name 'shinplaster' was often associated with the brittleness of the paper, which meant that the notes would disintegrate before they were cashed [U.S. 1824 Mathews]

1852 G. C. Mundy *Our Antipodes* i 163: Paper, for the most trifling sums, is current in the provinces, like 'shin plasters' in America. A great many more of these flimsy representatives of bullion than are really requisite are issued. It is averred ... that certain large proprietors make a practice of paying wages by orders, written purposely on small and thin scraps of paper, and that they pocket many hundreds a year by the loss or destruction of these frail liabilities in the hands of rough, careless and unsober characters.

1888 E. Finn *Chronicles of Early Melbourne* ii 546: These orders came to be known as 'Sticking Plasters', but I never could see the applicability of the phrase ... The landlord no sooner clutched the 'plaster' then he had it changed for cash.

1919 E. S. Sorenson *Chips and Splinters* 33: In that part the common mediums of exchange were cheques and shinplasters. Bank notes were rare, and a sovereign was a novelty.

1929 Sir Hal Colebatch *A Story of a Hundred Years* 458: A practice very generally in vogue up to the early nineties, when an order on Monger of York or Throssell of Northam was accepted with greater alacrity than a sovereign; a practice that still maintains throughout the Kimberleys, where there is no bank north of Broome, land where the 'shin-plasters' of Connor, Doherty, and Durack, and of many hotel and storekeepers, form the regularly accepted currency.

1937 Ernestine Hill *The Great Australian Loneliness* 329: *Shin-plaster* Bush currency, credit chits issued by an outpost storekeeper.

1956 Tom Ronan *Moleskin Midas* 264: He baked all his shin-plasters in the oven so that half of them would fall to pieces before they were cashed.

1974 *Australian* 27 Dec. 7: He pulls out an old shinplaster he picked up on a trip through Hall's Creek. It was a sort of personal printed postal note storekeepers and the like used to give when there was a shortage of coins and notes of the realm. This one was dated November 1, 1936, and signed Robert R. Smith.

shiralee A swag: rare until used as a title of novel by D'Arcy Niland

1892 Gilbert Parker *Round the Compass in Australia* 49: 'Let him down easy and slow ... Drop in his shirallee and water-bag by him.'

1898 Morris: *Shirallee* slang term for a swag or bundle of blankets.

1941 Baker: *Shiralee* A bluey or swag.

1955 D'Arcy Niland *The Shiralee* [book title]

shirl A female counterpart of an ocker

1973 *Australian* 20 Apr. 6: If the Okkers and Shirls in the back seat [of the taxi] launch forth on a dreary and interminable discussion ... they can quickly and effectively be silenced by a couple of extra decibels from the radio.

1978 *Airways Inflight* Sep.–Oct. 36: Though the ladies (or 'shirls' as they were called) were quite as sporting in the tug-of-war, for the men it was a much more serious affair.

shirt-and-sock night A formal occasion in Alice Springs, N T

1983 *Sydney Morning Herald* 18 Jun. 32: At shirt-and-sock night [in Alice Springs], where local customs would be demonstrated to city slickers, a sort of strobe lighting effect was provided by red and blue light bulbs with a loose connection.

shirt front In Australian Rules football, the tackling of an opponent whose chest is unprotected, esp. by a shoulder charge

1965 Jack Dyer 'Captain Blood' 87: He collected me with the perfect shirt-front, the knee coming up, the shoulder driving into my chest and the punch to the jaw on the follow-through. It was a real Victorian job.

1979 *Bulletin* 7 Aug. 59: The debate on whether Jesaulenko had been 'shirt-fronted' by a legitimate head-on collision or 'elbowed' with an illegal forearm jolt seemed nearly as long and as bitter as those on the Vietnam War.

1980 *Mercury* (Hobart) 24 Apr. 28: Cut out the shirtfront! [heading]
1984 *Sunday Independent* (Perth) 9 Sep. 86: In a series of classic shirt-front situations, the Sharks players established who was boss.
see **shoulder**

shirtlifter   A male homosexual
1966 Baker 216: *shirt lifter* a sodomite.
1974 Barry Humphries *Bulletin* 19 Jan. 13: When I first seen them photos of him in his 'Riverina Rig' I took him for an out-of-work ballet dancer or some kind of shirtlifter.
1981 *Australian* 17 Oct. Mag. 2: It is inadvisable ... to use age-old terms like poof, queer, faggot, fairy, shirt or shirtlifter, dyke or butch sheilah in company.

shithouse   General term of opprobrium
1972 Geoff Morley *Jockey Rides Honest Race* 173: 'You're probably right on all counts Ken, but I still feel shithouse about it.'
1974 David Williamson *Three Plays* 57: West How's your job? *Stork* Shithouse.
1979 *Age* (Melbourne) 26 Sep. 22: 'I love the people who say I'm good and I hate the people who say I'm shithouse.'
1983 *Sunday Independent* (Perth) 14 Aug. 23: At his first appearance before the Perth Press Club some years back, Bob Hawke was asked what he thought of Australia's foreign policy. 'Shithouse,' he said.

shit on the liver   A presumed cause of bad temper [cf. *liverish*]
[**1935** H. R. Williams *Comrades of the Great Adventure* 147: 'What's up with you, you bit stiff. Got hobnails on your liver?']
1944 Lawson Glassop *We Were the Rats* 197: 'Them Jerries oughta hunk a few lumps of — off their livers,' said Eddie.
1951 Seaforth Mackenzie *Dead Men Rising* 14: 'And how is Captain Hyacinth? I trust the Captain has no more'n 'is usual amount of s—t on the liver this morning?'
1959 Gerard Hamilton *Summer Glare* 219: My liver had dirt on it now. I felt I wanted to tear someone apart.
1961 Mena Calthorpe *The Dyehouse* 119: 'Got a bit on the liver,' Joe said. 'Gypped by that pert piece from the Dyehouse.'
1978 Richard Beilby *Gunner* 92: 'I wish he hadn't written such a lousy recipe for me. He had shit on the liver the day he wrote mine.'
1981 Archie Weller *The Day of the Dog* 81: 'Judge must of 'ad shit on 'is liver that day, unna?'
see **S.O.L.**

shivoo   A party, celebration, esp. if noisy [cf.

shivoo (shebo) a disturbance, 'row', shindy EDD]
[**1823** Jon Bee *Slang. A Dictionary of the Turf, the Ring &c.* 49: *Chevaux* Dinner, wine, song, and uproar, constitute a *chevaux*.]
1849 Alexander Harris *The Emigrant Family* (1967) 62: A 'Shiveau' at the Hut.
1889 John I. Hunt *Hunt's Book of Bonanzas* 82: 'Y'see, Jones had been to a lodge night shivoo, and he and the boys had a gay old time, you bet.'
1896 Thomas W. Heney *The Girl at Birrell's* 150: 'I wan' to know 'ow many's to be 'ere at the shivoo.'
1908 Henry Fletcher *Dads and Dan between Smokes* 56: A real tip-top Rookwood shivoo is worth a terrace o' houses to ther undertakers.
1919 W. H. Downing *Digger Dialects* 16: *Chivoo* A celebration.
1926 K. S. Prichard *Working Bullocks* 14: 'There's a shivoo at Marritown,' he cried teasingly, 'Me and Red's thinkin' of going on in.'
1939 Miles Franklin and Dymphna Cusack *Pioneers on Parade* 84: 'Do you think you'll be fit for another shivoo to-morrow?'
1959 Xavier Herbert *Seven Emus* 13: One of those bush shivoos where a great deal of energy is stamped out in bucolic frolic and as much poured back in the form of alcohol.
1970 Patrick White *The Vivisector* 625: On the morning after the big shivoo at the State Gallery.
1982 *Sun-Herald* 14 Nov. 176: The TAB boys will give him a farewell shivoo on November 19.

shonky   Deceptive, unreliable, unsound [? f. Yiddish *shoniker*, a petty trader or pedlar, or *shoddy + wonky*]
1970 Richard Beilby *No Medals for Aphrodite* 116: 'You shonkie sod!'
1978 *Sun-Herald* 9 Jul. 49: With the growing ground-swell of anti-communist feeling – and some fairly shonky electioneering from the Nixon camp – Richard M., then nicknamed 'Tricky Dicky', stormed in against the hapless Mrs Douglas.
1981 *National Times* 24 May 55: It was ridiculous, he claimed, for the State Government to squander resources tracking down shonky real estate deals.
1983 Peter Robinson *Sun-Herald* 7 Aug. 40: It used to be common practice for shonky company promoters to assault freedom of speech with a volley of legal writs, but it has not until now been the normal custom of Australian governments.

shook on, to be   To be enthusiastic about, infatuated with
1882 Rolf Boldrewood *Robbery Under Arms* (World's Classics 1949) 87: 'I'm regular shook on this old moke.' Ibid. 602: When he saw how handy I was in the yard he got quite shook on me.
1901 Henry Lawson 'Joe Wilson's Courtship'

Prose i 546–7: He was supposed to be shook after Mary too.
1916 C. J. Dennis *The Moods of Ginger Mick* 154: *Shook on* Infatuated.
1926 K. S. Prichard *Working Bullocks* 301: 'What's took Deb?' Mrs Pennyfather exclaimed . . . 'Didn't know she was so shook on Mark Smith.'
1957 Ray Lawler *Summer of the Seventeenth Doll* 31: 'She's not too shook on the whole thing.'
1965 Patrick White *Four Plays* 117: 'She got shook on these vitamins they write about in the magazines.'
1975 *Sunday Telegraph* (Sydney) 29 Jun. 49: Like Chappell, I'm not all that shook on cocktail parties myself.

shoot it, if it moves   see **moves**

shoot through   As for **go through** q.v.
1951 Seaforth Mackenzie *Dead Men Rising* 37: 'I'm shooting through – my woman's sick and I've waited longer than I should have.'
1957 Randolph Stow *The Bystander* 191: 'Just shoot through, son, and leave us to settle this.'
1962 John Morrison *Twenty-Three* 181: 'And – let us have it in plain Australian – while he was taking the call you shot through.'
1970 Richard Beilby *No Medals for Aphrodite* 233: 'You can shoot through on your own if you like, but I'm going to get her to Athens somehow.'
see **Bondi tram**

shoot your own dog, you   See quot.
1983 *Sydney Morning Herald* 23 Dec. 1: 'There's an old saying in the bush: "You always shoot your own dog"', Lin Gordon, Minister for Local Government and Lands, said yesterday [on a report that Mr Wran would be asking for his resignation] . . . 'It's not a very good way to go when you get the information in the paper as to how you are going to be asked to drop out', he said. 'I have been about for a long time and if I have any bad news to give anyone I have always done it myself.'

shop steward, Pommy   see **Pommy**

Shop, the   The University of Melbourne
1889–90 *Centennial Magazine* ii 218: It related how 'a medical student came up to the Shop' as a freshman, and 'thought through his exams. he would speedily pop.'
1902 Louis Esson let. to A. G. Stephens (Mitchell Library MS A1926): In certain quarters, not so very far distant from the University Wilson Hall, you are decidedly unpopular. I have had many an argument at the 'Shop', regarding the R. Page.
1918 Geoffrey Wall *Letters of an Airman* 15: I would be quite glad to get the Shop exam. results. They are generally published in a big list in 'The

Argus' about January.
1941 Baker 66: *Shop, the* Melbourne University, Student's slang.
1964 George Johnston *My Brother Jack* 260: 'The years at the Shop gave me nothing except a worthless B.A. and the privilege of being thrown into the University lake.'
1974 Desmond O'Grady *Deschooling Kevin Carew* 105: 'You've bought the Pommy idea of culture at the Shop', said Moynihan.

Shop, the Lucky   see **Lucky**

short of a sheet of bark   see **bark**

short, a shingle   see **shingle**

shot   At the end of one's tether [? f. shooting one's bolt]
1945 Gavin Casey *Downhill is Easier* 183: It was eight miles along the track to the Bordertown road, and late at night you could easily walk the twelve miles along that to Bordertown without seeing a vehicle. I realized I was shot.

shot, have a shot at   To try to 'get at' or 'take a rise' out of someone [f. *shot* a remark aimed at someone, esp. in order to wound OED 1841]
1915 K. S. Prichard *The Pioneers* 150: He was working for a shot at Donald Cameron through Young Davey.
1945 John Morrison *Sailors Belong Ships* 38: Mick, standing in the square, can't resist a shot at Beck. 'You were a long time making up your mind about this!' he yells.
1952 T. A. G. Hungerford *The Ridge and the River* 31: He was a sour bastard at times, and closed like a clam if he suspected that a man was having a shot at him.
1969 William Dick *Naked Prodigal* 46: 'You should know, Kenny. Yuh ain't worked much this year,' said Raincoat, having a shot at me.
1971 Keith Willey *Boss Drover* 28: We all knew him as Alec. If you called him 'Sir Alexander' he would reckon you were having a shot at him.
1975 Xavier Herbert *Poor Fellow My Country* 1103: It was typical of Jeremy to have that shot at Finnucane. Still, it was done with a grin.
1982 *Sydney Morning Herald* 18 Sep. 28: You could not have a friendly shot at Australian Rules anywhere in Victoria and expect to get a laugh.

shot, that's the   Expression of approval
1953 T. A. G. Hungerford *Riverslake* 143: 'That's the shot – buy a bit of land, and grow things.'
1963 Jon Cleary *A Flight of Chariots* 370: 'I think a good strong cuppa brew would be the shot.'
1970 Jessica Anderson *The Last Man's Head* 201: 'That's the shot,' said Stock with intimate approba-

tion. 'You're doing a good job. Keep it up.'

1976 David Ireland *The Glass Canoe* 227: 'That's the shot,' said Mick. 'Stick around and guard the place.'

1982 *NT Times* (Darwin) 5 Aug. 7: Blaring stereo, foul language and much boozing made it just the shot for a quiet weekend for everyone.

shoulder (drop a ~ on) In Australian Rules football, the tackle delivered as a shoulder charge

1965 Jack Dyer '*Captain Blood*' 106: I caught him straight down the middle with a perfect shoulder.

1981 *Age* (Melbourne) 11 Aug. 34: Irrepressible Brent Crosswell yesterday came out strongly in support of the inactive VFL umpires and dropped a shoulder on the VFL for its handling of the dispute.

see **shirt front**

shouse A lavatory [abbr. of *shithouse*]

1941 Baker 66: *Shouse* A privy.

1951 Dal Stivens *Jimmy Brockett* 214: I seen that now as plain as a country shouse although I didn't like it when she told me so.

1963 Hal Porter *The Watcher on the Cast-Iron Balcony* 56: The weatherboard dunny for which the modish names of the period include such as Aunt Mary, Houses of Parliament, the Little House, Down-the-back, Lavvy and Shouse.

1968 Thomas Keneally *Three Cheers for the Paraclete* 84: 'I'd like some trees on it, pines, and gums, so you don't have to see your neighbour's shouse first thing each morning.'

1971 David Ireland *The Unknown Industrial Prisoner* 82: 'Anyone seen Terrazzo?' 'Probably in the shouse.'

1975 Les Ryan *The Shearers* 98: Dewlap, who had been standing at the back of the ring, all alone like a country s'house, now sidled up.

shout *v.* To buy drinks for others, or to stand any similar 'treat' [f. *to stand shot* to meet the expenses, pay the bill (for all) OED 1821; *shot* the charge, reckoning OED 1475]

1855 Raffaello Carboni *The Eureka Stockade* ed. G. Serle (1969) 92: 'You shouted nobblers round for all hands – that's all right; it's no more than fair and square now for the boys to shout for you.'

1864 *Thatcher's Colonial Minstrel* 104: At ten o'clock we'd then toss up to see who was to shout.

1876 A. J. Boyd *Old Colonials* (1882) 268–9: This 'shouting', as 'treating' is termed in the colonies, is the curse of the Northern goldfields. If you buy a horse you must shout, the vendor must shout, and the bystanders who have been shouted to must shout in their turn.

1899 Henry Lawson 'The Stranger's Friend' *Verse* i 369: For he'd shout the stranger a suit of clothes, and he'd pay for the stranger's board.

1917 A. B. Paterson '"Shouting" for a Camel' *Saltbush Bill* 48: And there's plenty human camels who, before they'll see you waste it, / Will drink up all you pay for if you're fool enough to shout.

1924 *Truth* 27 Apr. 6: *Shout* To buy a drink.

1939 Kylie Tennant *Foveaux* 140: Any time Tommy tried to shout the family to the picture show there was a unanimous firm refusal.

1958 H. D. Williamson *The Sunlit Plain* 11: 'You'd better cash a cheque for me, Mick. I'd like to shout for the mob, too. This one's on me, you blokes.'

1969 William Dick *Naked Prodigal* 75: 'Like to come and have a beer with me? I'll shout.'

1981 *Daily News* (Perth) 23 Jan. 36: Bill has declared that Albert wouldn't shout if a shark bit.

shout *n.* 1 A free drink, or free round of drinks

[1853] *Letters from Victorian Pioneers* ed. T. F. Bride (1898) 127: On regaining his senses ... he applies to the landlord, who tells him that he is in debt; that the £60 is expended. On asking how – 'How?' repeats the host, 'do you forget the shout you stood – the shout for all hands?'

1860 Charles Thatcher *The Victorian Songster* Part 5 149: For they did me brown for half-a-crown, / The price of that 'ere shout.

1877 Rolf Boldrewood *A Colonial Reformer* (1890) 421: I threw my money about – must have a round of drinks for luck. I never saw a publican yet that could refuse to serve a 'shout'.

1890 Henry Lawson 'The Glass on the Bar' *Verse* i 69: 'We owe him a shout – leave the glass on the bar.'

2 One's turn to buy drinks; in the expression 'my shout', the acceptance of this or any similar expense

1902 Henry Lawson 'Send Round the Hat' *Prose* i 472: He was almost a teetotaller, but he stood his shout in reason.

1911 Louis Stone *Jonah* 101: Chook cried out, ''Ere, 'arf a mo' – this is my shout!' They were near the ice-cream stall, where trade was brisk.

1923 Jack Moses *Beyond the City Gates* 100: 'Have a drink?' 'No,' said Jones, 'it's my shout.'

1946 Dal Stivens *The Courtship of Uncle Henry* 197: We all drank together and ordered again. It was my shout.

1954 Seaforth Mackenzie *The Refuge* 16: 'Come up and have a cup of coffee – my shout.'

1974 John Powers *The Last of the Knucklemen* 22: 'I'll drink to that. Whose shout?'

show 1 '(Now only U.S. and Austral.) An opportunity for displaying or exerting oneself; a chance, "opening". Phr. *to give* (a person) *a show*; *to have* or *stand a* (or no) *show*' (OED): *obsolescent*

1876 Rolf Boldrewood *A Colonial Reformer* (1890) 183: As he's a gentleman, he's bound to give you a show.

1893 Henry Lawson *Letters* 54: I could not get a show in Auckland, so I spent my last pound to come down here.
1901 *The Bulletin Reciter* 97: But he still thought they'd a kind of show if only the food would last.
1906 Joseph Furphy *Rigby's Romance* ed. R. G. Howarth (1946) 258: 'I stand a good show, if there's a vacancy.
2 A mining claim, esp. if worked by an individual
1946 W. E. Harney *North of 23°* 205: Far and wide over the West Arm field the little men worked at their shows, exploiting the aboriginals and being exploited by them in turn.
1950 K. S. Prichard *Winged Seeds* 363: 'When the dees went out to have a look at Percy's show, they found he'd been treatin' ore not sands.'
1962 Stuart Gore *Down the Golden Mile* 263: The car that passed them that day on the way to Dutch George's show.

shower A dust-storm, in such expressions as 'Bedourie shower', 'Darling shower', 'Wilcannia shower' [f. place-names]
1898 Morris: *Darling Shower* A local name in the interior of Australia, and especially on the River Darling, for a dust storm, caused by cyclonic winds.
1903 Joseph Furphy *Such is Life* (1944) 331: The steady intensity of the shower augmented as I went on . . . the air was thick with skipping crumbs of hard dirt, which rattled on my skull like hail; in fact, everything not anchored to the ground was at racing speed, and all in the same direction. Ibid. 361: Here was the true key to the Wilcannia shower.
1924 *Truth* 27 Apr. 6: *Darling shower* – A dust-storm in Riverina.
1933 A. B. Paterson *The Animals Noah Forgot* (1970) 38: Nature visits the settlers' sins / With the Bogan shower, that is mostly dust.
1936 Ion. L. Idriess *The Cattle King* 195: 'That Bedourie shower yesterday was a beauty. There must have been thousands of tons of dust flying through the air.'
1961 George Farwell *Vanishing Australians* 174: A Darling dust storm – a 'Wilcannia shower', as they used to be called.
1964 H. P. Tritton *Time Means Tucker* 85: The air was filled with dust, bindii, spinifex and fine debris. We took full force of the wind and it was impossible to stand against it, so we lay flat on the ground with arms over our heads . . . The wind dropped, a few drops of rain fell, and the 'Darling shower' was over.

shower (rain), I didn't come down in the last A claim to a larger share of experience and shrewd-ness than one is being credited with
1906 Joseph Furphy *Rigby's Romance* ed. R. G.

Howarth (1946) 256: 'He didn't come down with the las' rain. Pity that sort o' bloke ever dies.'
1944 Lawson Glassop *We Were the Rats* 51: 'Listen, Mr Wilkerson,' I says, 'I'm awake-up, I am. Ya doan need ter come that stuff with me. I didden come down in the last shower.'
1951 Frank Hardy *Power Without Glory* 259: 'It's no use lying to me, Arty,' John West said. 'I didn't come down in the last shower.'
1962 Alan Seymour *The One Day of the Year* 56: 'How did you know?' 'I didn't come down in the last shower.'
1971 Barbara Vernon *A Big Day at Bellbird* 135: 'I didn't come down in the last shower, and neither did you.'
1981 Archie Weller *The Day of the Dog* 102: 'I've been beaten up before, ya know. I never come down in yesterday's rain.'
1984 *Weekend Australian* 30 Jun. Mag. 12: An irate theatregoer says it's about time they stopped treating patrons as though they had come down in the last shower, especially when they are being charged $25 for the privilege. This week he went to hear Shirley Bassey and had to spend the first hour listening to a ventriloquist.

shower, to take an early To be sent off in a football match
1980 *Sydney Morning Herald* 11 Nov. 28: I have often seen Rugby League referees point to the dressing room for some errant player to take an early shower.
1981 *Sun-Herald* 29 Mar. 61: Referee John Gocher . . . gave Giteau an early shower.
1982 *NT News* (Darwin) 10 Sep. 27: If he had thrown a couple of haymakers the Australians were certain the referee would have waved him to an early shower.

shrapnel Small change [f. appearance]
1919 W. H. Downing *Digger Dialects* 44: *Shrapnel* (1) Pork and beans; (2) Tattered French bank notes of small denominations.
1977 *Camera and Ciné* Nov. 24: 'I don't suppose you'd have a bit of shrapnel . . . ?' I shook fifty cents out of my purse and handed it to him.

shrewdie A shrewd person [abbr. of *shrewd head*]
[**1915** C. J. Dennis *The Songs of a Sentimental Bloke* 43: Now, this 'ere gorspil bloke's a fair shrewd 'ead.]
1916 Arthur Wright *Under a Cloud* 35: 'Look here, Wilson, you're not such a shrewdie as you imagine.'
1919 W. H. Downing *Digger Dialects* 45: *Shrewdy* See *shrewd head. Shrewd head* A cunning person.
1945 *Coast to Coast 1944* 85: He nudged Sam. 'A shrewdie, this bloke, eh? You can tell by his dial.'
1958 Gavin Casey *Snowball* 19: The young

shrewdies sometimes seemed to have an uncanny knack of summing certain things up.
1969 Sir Arthur Fadden *They Called Me Artie* 13: A syndicate of Mackay shrewdies figured in another picturesque incident.
1975 Xavier Herbert *Poor Fellow My Country* 365–6: Shrewdies, that they were ... they joined forces after years of enmity.

shypoo   Liquor of poor quality; a public house of low reputation [? f. Chinese for 'water-shop']
1901 *The Bulletin Reciter* 30: Paddy Grady's 'Hessian Palace' was a scene of wild delight, / And we drank the shypoo deeply, till the lateness of the night.
1908 E. G. Murphy *Jarrahland Jingles* 108: ... and the swell exclusive club, / Have swept the shypoo shanty from its lair amid the scrub.
1936 H. Drake-Brockman *Sheba Lane* 237: 'How about managing that shipoo for me?'
1944 Randolph Bedford *Naught to Thirty-three* 218: 'Shypoo' Jones – called 'Shypoo' because though half wages-miner, half prospector, he had for a season held a colonial-beer licence at Golden Valley.
1962 Tom Ronan *Deep of the Sky* 218: A hostelry ... restricted to the sale of beer and wine. Locally this was known as the 'Shypoo Shop'. I'm not sure of the derivation of 'Shypoo'. I think it is bastard Chinese for soft drink. To the sturdy second wave of pioneers of West Kimberley, beer and wine were soft drinks.

sick canary, couldn't knock the dags off a   see **couldn't**

sickie   A day's sick leave, taken whether one is sick or not
1953 T. A. G. Hungerford *Riverslake* 11: Now and then there would be one or more off on a sickie – they changed their jobs so frequently that they never let their sick leave accumulate.
1959 Dorothy Hewett *Bobbin Up* 81: She wished she could take a sickie tomorrer, but it was payday.
1969 Osmar White *Under the Iron Rainbow* 109: 'Put the bludger on a sickie, boss,' he says to me.
1972 *Sun-Herald* 16 Apr. 136: 'Sickies' last year cost Australian industry more than a million dollars in lost man-hours, according to the latest report on industrial absenteeism.
1984 *Age* (Melbourne) 25 Apr. 3: Has the flexi-time rendered the sickie obsolete?

silent cop   See quot. 1934
1934 Thomas Wood *Cobbers* 122: A circle in the middle of cross-roads ... round which all traffic changing direction must swing; a round yellow blob, known here as the Silent Cop, or the Poached

Egg.
1959 Dorothy Hewett *Bobbin Up* 2: This was the corner, by the silent cop, where she and Roy had come to grief.
1980 Barbara Pepworth *Early Marks* 10: I'm in the middle of the busy highway that runs outside the flats. I perch on a silent cop and pretend I'm one.

silly as a two-bob watch, as a wheel   see **watch, wheel**

Silver Budgie, the   R. J. Hawke, Prime Minister 1983– [? f. hair-styling]
1983 *Australian* 23 May 11: ACTU executive members focussed on the 2.2 per cent figure, saying that was well within the 3 to 4 per cent guideline set by the Prime Minister, Mr Hawke, who has become known as the Silver Budgie.
1983 *Australian* 28 Dec. 9: Bob Hawke: the Messiah. Lately, the Silver Bodgie or sometimes, mistakenly, the Silver Budgie.
1984 *Sunday Times* (Perth) 5 Aug. 67: Ripping into the Federal Government over its uranium policy, he [Patrick White] spoke of 'Hawkie, screaming from under his cockatoo hairdo the platitudes he has got by heart' ... It is not the first time that Mr Hawke's carefully tended hair-style has produced comparisons with birds. One of his nicknames around Parliament House is 'the silver budgie'. His detractors often alter this to 'the silver bodgie'.

Silver City, the   Broken Hill, N.S.W. [f. mining of silver]
1910 *The Silver City Cup* [title of newsreel screened by Lyceum Pictures, Adelaide in Jul. 1910]
1911 E. S. Sorenson *Life in the Australian Backblocks* 33–4: In and around Broken Hill many people live in houses built on wheels ... Removing in the Silver City means taking the house with you.
1919 W. K. Harris *Outback in Australia* 16: Broken Hill (the famous silver-field in New South Wales) is a great centre for the camels, and ... on the north side of the Silver City the teams may be seen starting off.
1933 Samuel Griffiths *A Rolling Stone on the Turf* 33: The latter experience I had at Broken Hill while on a visit to the 'Silver City' to act as stipendiary steward at the annual Cup meetings.
1956 Ion L. Idriess *The Silver City* [book title]
1961 Myrtle Rose White *From That Day to This* 88: On the third day of Tommy's sojourn in the Silver City the Boss received a telegram asking for a further £10.
1974 *Australian* 12 Oct. 19: Landslide in Seedy Silver City.
1981 *Canberra Times* 2 Jul. 2: The Silver City is a

harsh place, a frontier of civilised life, a man's town in the crude, last century 'western' sense.

Silver Slug The morning train from Wollongong to Sydney
1980 *Sun-Herald* 10 Feb. 101: Gave the Silver Slug a miss. Caught the next train from Austinmer at 8.17 a m and got a seat, but ... the train was 45 minutes late.

silvertail Someone affluent and socially prominent: *derogatory*
1890 A. J. Vogan *The Black Police* 116: A select circle of long-limbed members of those upper circles who belong to the genus termed in Australian parlance 'silver-tailed', in distinction to the 'copper-tailed' democratic classes.
1908 E. G. Murphy *Jarrahland Jingles* 116: And when they're playing billiards in their flannel tennis suits, / We feel like heaving something at these silver-tail galoots.
1929 K. S. Prichard *Coonardoo* 63: 'Mrs Bessie knew what she was doin' when she asked that damned young silver-tail to spend a winter on Wytaliba.'
1939 Kylie Tennant *Foveaux* 430: 'Even now you got no idea the real bang-up people who come from Foveaux, doctors and sirs and silvertails of all sorts.'
1947 Gavin Casey *The Wits are Out* 125: 'Mr Fleming doesn't build for basic-wage earners,' Bill said nastily. 'He hangs around waiting his chance to build for the silvertails.'
1951 Dal Stivens *Jimmy Brockett* 87: The Bascombes were silvertails. They were dirty with money
1963 Frank Hardy *Legends from Benson's Valley* 71: Duncan he hated twice: impersonally as a silver tail and the biggest employer in the town; and personally as the man who had sacked him for insubordination.
1970 Patrick White *The Vivisector* 127: 'Come on down, fuckun little silvertail! We'll put a frill around yer!'
1981 *Weekend Australian* 30 May 17: There is no room in this State [N.S.W.] for political silvertails who look as if they belong more in the chintzy tea houses of Toorak than on the hill at the SCG.

sing 'em muck see **muck**

singing milkshake, the Olivia Newton John
1983 *Sydney Morning Herald* 26 Oct. 24: *Grease* ... The film in which Our Olivia earned her unenviable reputation as 'The Singing Milkshake'.

singlet, useful as a hip pocket in a see **useful**

sit down 'To establish oneself in some position or place; to settle, take up one's abode' OED 1535–1817 (see quot. 1798) Obsolete in this sense in England, but preserved in Australia because adopted into Pidgin
1798 David Collins *An Account of the English Colony in New South Wales* ed. Brian Fletcher (1975) i 406: There was indeed a woman, one Ann Smith, who ran away a few days after our sitting down in this place, and whose fate was not exactly ascertained.
1849 Alexander Harris *The Emigrant Family* ed. W. S. Ramson (1967) 225: 'How many black fellow sit down along a camp?' said Beck.
1875 Rolf Boldrewood *The Squatter's Dream* (1878) 249: 'Better fattening country no man ever see. Pity you gentlemen don't sit down handy and be neighbours for us.'
1908 Mrs Aeneas Gunn *We of the Never-Never* 130: 'Me sit down? Eh, boss', he asked ... 'Please yourself!', the Maluka laughed.
1935 R. B. Plowman *The Boundary Rider* 78: 'Plenty rabbit sit down longa Deep Well paddock?'
1937 Ernestine Hill *The Great Australian Loneliness* 192: That paper-bark tree became the Mecca of a thousand thirsty men, who 'sat down' on the banks of the pretty river for a while, and then went on.
1956 Tom Ronan *Moleskin Midas* 221: Mon Tack, who had lost his wages in one night playing fantan with his uncle at George's Yard, was quite happy to sit down at the station.

sit down money Unemployment or pension benefits to Aborigines
1978 H. C. Coombs *Kulinma* 202: Community advisers became active in some communities in assisting Aborigines to apply for unemployment benefit ... generally Aborigines have been content to accept the 'sit-down' money without working. Ibid. 228: Aborigines found that they would receive in unemployment benefit ('sitting-down money' as it was called in some communities) more than it had been possible for them previously to earn for work on their community projects.
1981 *Weekend Australian* 31 Oct. 19: Mr Tuxworth said these companies should pay the out-of-work miners sit-down money to keep them in the territory for when the uranium boom begins.
1984 *Bulletin* 10 Jul. 77: On every second Wednesday when the social security cheques – 'sit-down money' – are collected, the queues [for liquor] are much longer.

six-bob-a-day tourist An Australian soldier on active service in World War I: *jocular* [f. the daily rate of pay, the highest to a private in any army at the time]
1916 Tom Skeyhill *Soldier Songs from Anzac* 28:

But 'e called me a chocolate soldier, / A six-bob-a-day tourist too.
1918 Let. in Bill Gammage *The Broken Years* (1974) 265–6: Its na poo war now barring a few minor little affairs . . . but I don't fancy us 6/- a day tourists will be required to do any of it.

six o'clock swill   see **swill**

skerrick   A fragment, esp. in negative expression ('not a skerrick', etc.) [*skerrick* a particle, morsel, scrap, atom EDD 1863]
1931 Ion L. Idriess *Lasseter's Last Ride* 205: Half a goanna's tail, the long thin end with not a skerrick of meat on it.
1937 Vance Palmer *Legend for Sanderson* 72: 'He didn't leave you any money, eh?' 'Not a skerrick,' Neil told him.
1947 H. Drake-Brockman *The Fatal Days* 116: Eddie had rushed off without leaving a skerrick of kindling; he often did.
1961 Patrick White *Riders in the Chariot* 226: 'There ain't no 22-gauge, Harry,' the gentleman announced. 'Not a bloody skerrick of it.'
1975 Hal Porter *The Extra* 215: There isn't a skerrick of liquid.

skillion (skilling) *n.*   A lean-to attached to another building, esp. with a sloping roof [*skilling* a shed or outhouse, esp. a lean-to OED 1389]
[**1799** Rev. Richard Johnson Let. 26 Aug. *Evangelical Magazine* (1800) 299: Making further search in the house, blood was discovered in different parts, particularly in a small skilling, where, as afterwards appeared, my friend was dragged.
1826 James Atkinson *An Account of the State of Agriculture and Grazing in New South Wales* 100: The barn may be built with lean-to's or skillings all round.]
1843 Charles Rowcroft *Tales of the Colonies* i 120: House . . . to be divided into one large room, twenty feet long; a passage ten feet wide; and on the other side of the passage four rooms . . . At the back of the long room of twenty feet, a skillion, to serve as a kitchen, &c.
1846 C. P. Hodgson *Reminiscences of Australia* 39: Skillions formed by a sloping verandah to receive the sheep in from the fold as required.
1877 Rolf Boldrewood *A Colonial Reformer* (1890) 351: At the back a skillion, a lower roofed portion of the building, contained several smaller rooms.
1893 Henry Lawson 'The Selector's Daughter' *Prose* i 62: She went to her bedroom – a small, low, slab skillion, built on to the end of the house.
1905 Randolph Bedford *The Snare of Strength* 25: Forby told them in a harsh voice to take the milk into the skillion.
1919 E. S. Sorenson *Chips and Splinters* 60: The fireplace was as wide as a skillion, and deep.

1959 Vance Palmer *The Big Fellow* 177: The heat beating down on the tin-roofed skillion in which she and her mother had bustled about serving up food.

skillion *a.*   In the phrase 'skillion roof' (as distinct from a 'gable' roof) referring to the sloping type of roof on a skillion
1911 James Nangle *Australian Building Practice* 171: *Lean-to Roof* This kind (sometimes called a Skillion Roof) . . . is generally used only in rear buildings, or verandahs where no ceilings are required.
1966 *Coast to Coast 1965–66* 136: It was little more than a skillion-roofed shack.

skin beginning to crack   A sign of extreme thirst: *jocular*
[**1930** L. W. Lower *Here's Luck* 266: 'I'm so dry I'm beginning to break out in little cracks.']
1957 R. S. Porteous *Brigalow* 96: 'Come on . . . You know bloody well yer skin's crackin'.' We drank quite a few beers that afternoon.
1961 George Farwell *Vanishing Australians* 80: It took him some hours to yoke up his bullocks; then his skin began to crack – as the bush saying puts it – for want of a drink.
1964 H. P. Tritton *Time Means Tucker* 101: 'Right now my flaming skin is cracking I'm so dry.'
1983 John K. Ewers *Long Enough for a Joke* 94: 'You can always tell when George's holidays are due. His hide begins to crack!'

skinner   A horse which wins at long odds; a betting coup so brought about (a *skinner for the books* is when the bookmakers do not have to pay out on a heavily backed favourite) [f. English thieves' slang: see quot. 1812]
[**1812** Vaux: *Skin* to strip a man of all his money at play, is termed *skinning* him.
1865 Hotten: *Skin-the-lamb* When a non-favourite wins a race, 'bookmakers' are said to 'skin the lamb', under the supposition that they win all their bets, no person having backed the winner.]
1895 Cornelius Crowe *The Australian Slang Dictionary* 74: *Skinner*, a term in racing, signifying that a horse not backed wins the race, thereby giving the book-makers a skinner.
1907 Arthur Wright *Keane of Kalgoorlie* 66: Although he had gone up in the weights considerably, his owner decreed that he should win the Rosehill handicap, and give the 'shop' another 'skinner'.
c. **1914** A. B. Paterson 'Racehorses and Racing in Australia' in *The World of 'Banjo' Paterson* ed. C. Semmler (1967) 323: No matter what wins the bookmaker cannot lose anything, while they will skin the lamb to some tune should an outsider get home. Ibid. 324: The bookmakers who bet while the race is being run offer ten to one but won't lay

it to much money. They don't want to spoil a real good 'skinner', by laying a lot of money in running.
1918 *Kia Ora Coo-ee* 15 Apr. 15: They'd never heard of 'Onward', so they gave him ten to one, / But Murphy had them thinking, at the setting of the sun. / For 'Onward' proved a winner, / For the books it was a skinner; / Pat had whisky with his dinner, sure, the world was made for fun.
1934 Thomas Wood *Cobbers* 97: Charles laid down his fork and said it was a skinner for the books.
1949 Lawson Glassop *Lucky Palmer* 88: 'Didn't you hear the bookies cheer? It was a skinner.'
1958 Frank Hardy *The Four-Legged Lottery* 175: This percentage varies from, say, 12½ per cent if a well-backed horse wins to 100 per cent if a rank outsider gives a 'skinner'.
1974 *Sydney Morning Herald* 8 Oct. 17: Skinner for bookmakers.

skin off a rice pudding, couldn't knock the see **couldn't**

skite *v.* To boast or brag [f. Scottish *bletherskate* a noisy, talkative fellow OED c. 1650; U.S. 1848]
1857 *Thatcher's Colonial Songster* 18: If ever you get into a fight, / Of course you'll not forget to skite.
1881 A. C. Grant *Bush-Life in Queensland* ii 78: 'Bosh! – you're always skyting about what you'll do.'
1899 Henry Lawson 'The Stranger's Friend' *Verse* i 369: The worst of it was that he'd skite all night on the edge of the stranger's bunk.
1907 Nathan Spielvogel *The Cocky Farmer* 12: 'I says that you are always skiting about what you are going to do.'
1916 C. J. Dennis *The Moods of Ginger Mick* 43: We've slung the swank fer good an' all, it don't fit in our plan; / To skite of birth an' boodle is a crime.
1932 Leonard Mann *Flesh in Armour* 34: In such an atmosphere, it was not hard even for Frank Jeffreys to skite a bit, though he was outdone easily by Charles.
1945 Gavin Casey *Downhill is Easier* 69: I managed to do it without actually telling lies, or skiting too much.
1957 Ray Lawler *Summer of the Seventeenth Doll* 113: 'Lyin' comes as natural to him as skiting.'
1963 John Cantwell *No Stranger to the Flame* 75: 'And spoil my big moment? I feel like skiting – first time I had anything much to skite about.'

skite *n.* 1 Boastful talk; showing off
1860 Charles Thatcher *The Victoria Songster* Part 5 160: You don't often see a chap given to 'skite, / Can do very much when it comes to a fight.
1910 E. W. Hornung *The Boss of Tarooomba* 180: 'Then none o' your skite, mate,' said Bill, knocking out a clay pipe against his heel.
1916 *The Anzac Book* 99: If there's one thing I hate, it is skiting.* *Skiting – Australian for 'swanking' in speech. 'Skite' – blatherskite.
1918 C. J. Dennis *Digger Smith* 53: P'r'aps we 'ave 'ad some skite knocked out, an p'r'aps we see more clear.
1918 Geoffrey Wall *Letters of an Airman* 85: This notepaper is a part of it, quite unnecessary skite. I thought you might like a sample of it, though.
1933 Norman Lindsay *Saturdee* 115: 'Ponk's the bloke to take the skite outer him.'
1947 H. Drake-Brockman *The Fatal Days* 295: 'We call that skiting.' 'What's that?' 'Boasting.'
2 (*skiter*) Someone given to skiting; a boaster
1898 *Bulletin* 17 Dec. Red Page: An incessant talker is a *skiter*.
1906 Joseph Furphy *Rigby's Romance* ed. R. G. Howarth (1946) 222: 'In spite of Rigby's very complimentary insinuation that I'm a skite and a liar, the wagon was gone.'
1916 C. J. Dennis *The Moods of Ginger Mick* 155: *Skiter* A boaster.
1933 Norman Lindsay *Saturdee* 181: Taunts began to hurtle . . . 'Who's a stinkin' skite?'
1958 Gavin Casey *Snowball* 84: Benny despised the skites, because he could make his own boasts and know they were not hollow ones.
1962 Alan Marshall *This is the Grass* 47: 'He'd take a rise out of any skite he met.'
1969 *Australian* 23 Sep. 2: Australians should not see themselves as boastful, arrogant skites, the Governor-General, Sir Paul Hasluck, said yesterday.

skulls As for **heads** q.v.
1964 George Johnston *My Brother Jack* 326: 'You knowing all the brass-hats and the skulls down at the Barracks . . . I don't suppose you could pull some strings for me?'
1978 Richard Beilby *Gunner* 135–6: The little man nodded towards Whiteside and the captain . . . 'Them skulls with you?'

sky pilot A clergyman
1892 Karl Lentzner *Dictionary of the Slang-English of Australia* 106: *Sky-pilot* (Australian), a parson.
1907 Charles MacAlister *Old Pioneering Days in the Sunny South* 189: All old Turon men will remember the famous Dr. Lang was one of the earliest 'sky-pilots' on the Turon.
1918 *Kia Ora Coo-ee* 15 Jun. 18: We've seen no milk and 'oney that sky pilots preach about.
1934 Brian Penton *Landtakers* 443: 'Naturally it'll be all over the place when the sky-pilot comes up.'
1968 Stuart Gore *Holy Smoke* 109: *sky-pilot* A clergyman.
1974 Barry Humphries *Barry McKenzie Holds*

His Own 19: 'Jeez, Baz, a brother who's a sky pilot! No wonder you never let on about him.'

slag   To spit
[1882 F. W. P. Jago *The Ancient Language, and the Dialect of Cornwall* 266: *Slag*. Misty rain, sleet.]
1965 William Dick *A Bunch of Ratbags* 238: He cleared his throat and spat on the car grille. 'Hell,' muttered Ritchie, 'he's slaggin' on me car!'

slanter (schlanter, slinter)   A trick: *rare* [? f. Du. *slenter*]
1915 C. J. Dennis *The Songs of a Sentimental Bloke* 55: The slanter game I'd played wiv my Doreen ... I seen what made me feel fair rotten mean.
1919 W. H. Downing *Digger Dialects* 45: *Slanter* (*or Schlanter*) A trick. 'To run a schlanter' – to make no genuine effort to win a game.
1925 Arthur Wright *The Boy from Bullarah* 133: 'A shlanter' he bellowed.
1944 Randolph Bedford *Naught to Thirty-three* 295: 'It was just up to him to have men go schlenter on his rag boarding-house'. Ibid. 297: 'The dhirty schlenterers, that gimme the go by for theyar boarrd.'
1965 Frank Hardy *The Yarns of Billy Borker* 70: The Greatest Slanter in the History of the Racing Game [story title]

slather, an open   A situation in which there is no hindrance to what one wishes to do
1919 J. Vance Marshall *The World of the Living Dead* 71: 'Try the races up Dingo Creek way ... They say she's an open slather up there. Not a demon in the burg.'
1949 John Morrison *The Creeping City* 227: 'You're asking to be allowed an open slather at an essential public service without being challenged.'
1955 D'Arcy Niland *The Shiralee* 209: 'You mean that would give her open slather?'
1975 Hal Porter *The Extra* 197: Let other writers gang up like metal-workers for an open slather.
1981 *Sun Herald* 10 May 87: Just about everything is to become 'self-regulating', which is a free-enterprise term meaning open slather.
1984 *Age* (Melbourne) 11 Jul. 1: In a tortured, tortoise-like manner, the ALP has taken another step towards an eventual open slather uranium mining policy.

sledging   In cricket, the taunting of a batsman by members of the opposing team in order to undermine his confidence
1975 *Sun-Herald* 21 Dec. 49: But 'sledging' ... or the gentle art of talking a player out ... has no place in women's cricket.
1977 *Australian* 1 Dec. 18: 'I haven't heard any sledging or deliberate baiting of batsmen this

season', he [Bob Simpson] said.
1982 *Sydney Morning Herald* 4 Nov. 10: The court has been told by Ian Chappell that the expression 'sledging' first came into vogue among cricketers in 1963–64. It came from the expression 'subtle as a sledgehammer' at a time when a man called Percy Sledge had a song on the English hit parade. It meant using words to exploit an opponent's weaknesses and put him off his game.
1984 *Weekend Australian* 8 Sep. 52: One area in which the women [tennis players] lead the men a merry dance is in 'sledging' of opponents at post-match press conferences.

sleever, long   see **long sleever**

sling   To pay a bribe or gratuity, esp. as a percentage of wages or winnings
1875 Rolf Boldrewood *The Squatter's Dream* repr. as *Ups and Downs* (1878) 250: 'I dare say he'll sling me a tenner if it turns out all right.'
1923 Con Drew *Rogues & Ruses* 139: 'How do they sling?' 'Fair', answered Paints; 'they slung me a fiver on a job I brought them in the other day.'
1939 Kylie Tennant *Foveaux* 172: 'I'm slinging it to Hamp,' Bardy said sullenly.
1949 Lawson Glassop *Lucky Palmer* 5: 'Clarrie, he ain't gone off in six months. Must sling to the cops. Wonder how much he pays 'em.' Ibid. 21: 'Here's a fiver for you ... Don't say I didn't sling.'
1953 T. A. G. Hungerford *Riverslake* 130: 'Sling, Stefan!' When the Pole looked at him uncomprehendingly Murdoch whipped a ten-pound note out of the bundle and handed it to the ring-keeper. 'He don't know,' he explained. 'It's the first time he's played.'
1971 Frank Hardy *The Outcasts of Foolgarah* 56: On first name terms with every shire President so long as they didn't forget to sling when backhanders came in.
1975 Les Ryan *The Shearers* 155: *Sling* Tip for services rendered.
sling (back)   Any payment so made
1948 K. S. Prichard *Golden Miles* 74: 'There's some hungry bastards,' the men said, 'making big money on their ore, never give the poor bugger toggin' for 'em a sling back.' The sling back might be ten bob on pay-day, or no more than a few pots of beer, but was always appreciated. Ibid. 82: Sling backs to the shift boss got some men their jobs.
1971 Frank Hardy *The Outcasts of Foolgarah* 34: The Garbo's margin for skill was only two bucks above the basic, but you had to take bottles into account and the sling from cafes who wanted extra tins emptied.
1981 *Sun* (Sydney) 16 Jul. 4: The bookie hadn't settled, so he missed his sling.

sling off (at)   To deride, ridicule, abuse [variant of

throw off q.v.]
1911 Steele Rudd *The Dashwoods* 24: 'I heard yer both slingin' off.'
1921 K. S. Prichard *Black Opal* 112: The rest of the men continued to 'sling off', as they said, at Bully and Roy O'Mara as they saw fit.
1942 Gavin Casey *It's Harder for Girls* 236: 'It was just some chaps'd been slinging off at him,' I said.
1951 Dal Stivens *Jimmy Brockett* 250: Until he came to work for me I'd always slung off at book learning.
1963 John Cantwell *No Stranger to the Flame* 86: 'Stop it,' Barry said, flushing. 'Stop slinging off.'
1975 Mary Rose Liverani *The Winter Sparrows* 232: She glowered at the driver suspiciously. Was he slinging off at her?

slip into   To attack
[**1860** Hotten 218: *Slip*, or *let slip* 'to *slip* into a man', to give him a sound beating, 'to *let slip* at a cove', to rush violently upon him, and assault with vigour.]
1973 Jim McNeil *The Old Familiar Juice* 66: 'I'll slip inter you inner minute!'
1974 Keith Stackpole *Not Just for Openers* 83: He turned to the grandstand and expressed his feelings. The Press slipped into him over that.
1979 *Weekend Australian* 1 Jul. Mag. 5: Howard is now refreshingly honest and quick to slip into anyone trying to ask a cute question.

slipper, put in the   Variant of **put in the boot**, q.v.
1982 *Australian* 9 Mar. 12: It's time the do-gooders stopped putting the slipper into the league violence.
1982 *National Times* 12 Sep. 2: Victoria's new Governor, Rear-Admiral Sir Brian Murray, sometimes lapses from God-like impartiality to sink the slipper into such sectors of the community as union officials and other assorted types

Slipper, the   The Golden Slipper Stakes, a race for two-year-olds inaugurated in 1957; in 1979 the prize-money of $250,000 (increased to $400,000 in 1984) made it the richest Australian race at that time
1979 *Courier-Mail* (Brisbane) 4 Apr. 26: How the Slipper was born [heading]
1980 *Sun-Herald* 27 Apr. 99: I've never gone off my food since, even when Blazing Saddles was beaten in the Slipper.

Slippery Charlie   see **Charlie**

slops   Beer
1947 Gavin Casey *The Wits Are Out* 55: 'He goes the slops too heavy, though' ... They agreed that it was a pity Ray drank so much.

1949 Lawson Glassop *Lucky Palmer* 5: 'Keep your shirt on. There's no harm in having a jug of slops, now is there?'
1953 T. A. G. Hungerford *Riverslake* 197: 'His wife and both of his kids got burned to death when his house went up ... they reckon that's what sent him onto the slops in the first place.'
1969 Osmar White *Under the Iron Rainbow* 33: 'What else is there to do in this godforsaken country except work and go on the slops?'

slot   See quots
1953 Baker 129: *slot* or *peter*, a prison cell.
1976 *Cleo* Aug. 33: Some of the old heads are in the slot, he says. The slot is jail.

slug *n.* & *v.*   (To make) a heavy charge or demand [? analogous to *sock, sting*]
1941 Baker 68: *Slug* A heavy bill. Also, 'get slugged': to be charged excessively.
1946 K. S. Prichard *The Roaring Nineties* 326: Alf knew the mine-owners were slugging the prospectors and alluvial diggers.
1970 Alexander Buzo *The Front Room Boys* in Penguin *Plays* 39: 'Ar jecs, another slug at the wallet.'
1977 *Sun-Herald* 9 Jan. 3: Gold Coast beats death tax slug.
1984 *Sun* (Sydney) 27 Jan. 3: New slug on petrol, beer and smokes [heading]

Slug, Silver   see **Silver**

slushy   Unskilled assistant to a bush cook; any unskilled kitchen help [f. *slush* refuse fat or grease obtained from meat boiled on board ship OED 1756]
[**1859** Hotten: *Slushy* a ship's cook.]
1899 Henry Lawson 'A Rough Shed' *Prose* i 465: 'We hate the boss-of-the-board as the shearers' "slushy" hates the shearers' cook.'
1907 A. Searcy *In Australian Tropics* 295: We shot two or three kangaroo and a few birds just for immediate use. I volunteered as 'slushy', so as soon as I had skinned and cleaned one of the kangaroos, I put some of the meat on the coals.
1919 W. H. Downing *Digger Dialects* 46: *Slushey* A mess orderly.
1924 *Truth* 27 Apr. 6: *Slushy* A kitchen hand.
1936 Archer Russell *Gone Nomad* 14: I had to take my turn at butchering the ration sheep and as 'slushy' to 'Dough-boy' Terry, the cook.
1946 K. S. Prichard *The Roaring Nineties* 64: Cursing and sweating over the cooking, and rousing hell out of Bill to find a slushy to help in the kitchen.
1953 *Caddie A Sydney Barmaid* 25: Nellie, a wisp of a girl who was slushie at Mrs Murphy's boarding-house. Slushie was the name given to anyone

who worked at a camp boarding-house.

sly grog (shop) Liquor sold without a licence; a place where it is sold
[1812 Vaux: *Sly* Any business transacted, or intimation given, privately, or under the rose, is said to be *done upon the sly*.]
1829 H. Widowson *The Present State of Van Diemen's Land* 24: There are ... upwards of thirty licenced public houses in the town ... to these ... I may safely add a like number of 'sly grog shops', as they are called.
1840 T. P. MacQueen *Australia as she is and as she may be* 23: Increased powers ought to be given the magistrates and police to prevent the nuisances usually termed sly grog shops.
1855 William Howitt *Land, Labour and Gold* i 339: She is well known as a sly grog-seller, and has been fined some dozen times or more.
1861 T. McCombie *Australian Sketches* 62: Before a start could be made in pursuit they were far beyond reach, most likely secure in some of the sly grog tents which everywhere abounded.
1880 Rolf Boldrewood *The Miner's Right* (1890) 64: Any attempt to limit the licensing produced such a crop of 'shanties' or sly-grogshops.
1901 Henry Lawson 'The Babies in the Bush' *Prose* i 415: I was beastly drunk in an out-of-the-way shanty in the Bush – a sly grog shop.
1957 Ray Lawler *Summer of the Seventeenth Doll* 44: 'Keepin' nit for the S.P. bookies, eh – drummin' up trade for the sly grogs.'
1969 William Dick *Naked Prodigal* 64: We were on our way to the sly grog joint to buy a dozen bottles.

smaller the property, the wider the brim   see **brim**

smartarse An offensively clever person
1937 Heard in conversation.
1962 Alan Seymour *The One Day of the Year* 49: 'Going round with smart-arsed little sheilas from the North Shore. It's all wrong, son.'
1965 William Dick *A Bunch of Ratbags* 245: 'Anyhow, where else could we go, do you know, smartarse?'
1970 Barry Oakley *A Salute to the Great McCarthy* 28: 'That smart arse from the city.'

smell of an oil-rag, live on the   see **oil-rag**

Smells, City of Melbourne: *obs.*
[1890 A. J. Vogan *The Black Police* 380: My trip to Melbourne, – Smelbourne, as the *Bulletin* calls it rightly.]
1897 *Bulletin* 18 Dec. 11: What a pious howl went through the City of Smells quite recently when Mrs Sutherland hinted that some of the Melbourne goody goody owned 'bad' houses.

Smithy Sir Charles Kingsford Smith (1897–1935), the Australian aviator
1936 *Daily Telegraph* (Sydney) 14 Aug. 7: 'It would provide a real tribute to "Smithy" because he did not favor statues and would ... have preferred something of a utilitarian character.'
1965 *Daily Telegraph* (Sydney) 13 Apr. 66: Jet flight on 'Smithy' route.
1975 *Sydney Morning Herald* 24 Apr. 3: 'Smithy's' relics coming home ... The collection, which includes logbooks and maps from 'Smithy's' greatest flights, will be brought from America in June.
1984 *Sydney Morning Herald* 5 Jun. 13: Smithy mini-series [heading] The story of the pioneer Australian aviator Sir Charles Kingsford Smith will be made into a television mini-series.

smoke To decamp hurriedly, 'vamoose' [cf. *like smoke* very quickly, rapidly OED 1833]
1893 *Sydney Morning Herald* 26 Jun. 8: 'Smoke' ... is the slang for the 'push' to get away as fast as possible. [Morris]
1896 Henry Lawson 'Stiffner and Jim' *Prose* i 124: 'Smoke be damned,' I snarled, losing my temper. 'You know dashed well that our swags are in the bar, and we can't smoke without them.'
1923 Con Drew *Rogues & Ruses* 178: 'Mind me havin' a look at your race book?' I says. 'I lent mine to a friend awhile ago, and he smoked with it.'
1941 Baker 68: *Smoke, to* To decamp, make oneself scarce.
1961 Patrick White *Riders in the Chariot* 415: Dubbo had gone all right. Had taken his tin box, it seemed, and smoked off.

in smoke In hiding
1924 C. J. Dennis *Rose of Spadgers* 72: 'Jist now,' says Brannigan, 'Spike Wegg's in smoke. / Oh, jist concerns a cove 'e tried to croak.'
1928 A. W. Upfield *The House of Cain* 76: 'When the lady comes out of smoke ... give it her with my compliments.'
1938 *Smith's Weekly* 31 Dec. 12: A cove beckoned me and said: 'Your mate's in smoke and can't show up.'
1945 Kylie Tennant *Ride on Stranger* 203: The New Zealand delegate returned anonymously, slipped ashore and 'went into smoke' like some famous criminal.
1951 Simon Hickey *Travelled Roads* 128: They are not sure whether you are the present President or the one before, come out of 'smoke' again.
1967 K. S. Prichard *Subtle Flame* 252: 'Meanwhile Tony's got to be kept in smoke?'

smoke, the big The city [f. *smoke* as the mark of a metropolis: applied to London (see quot. 1864) although the Australian use – almost invariably the 'big smoke' – is recorded earlier]

[1864 Hotten: *Smoke* London. Country-people when going to the metropolis frequently say, they are on their way to the Smoke, and Londoners when leaving for the country say, they are going out of the Smoke.]

1848 H. W. Haygarth *Recollections of Bush Life in Australia* 6: At first he has some power of choice in fixing on a resting-place for the night; but, as he gradually leaves behind him the 'big smoke' (as the aborigines picturesquely call the town), the accommodations become more and more scanty.

1893 J. A. Barry *Steve Brown's Bunyip* 21: 'You want to get away amongst the spielers and forties of the big smoke?'

1901 Rolf Boldrewood *In Bad Company* 214: 'Goin' to the big smoke to blue our cheques.'

1918 Bernard Cronin *The Coastlanders* 114: 'I'd clear fer the big smoke,' he says, 'and hit the high places.'

1946 *Coast to Coast 1945* 32: 'He says he's going to the big smoke to die.'

1959 D'Arcy Niland *The Big Smoke* [book title]

1964 David Ireland *Image in the Clay* 81: 'Fresh from the big smoke, too. Learn anything in the city?'

1970 Barry Oakley *A Salute to the Great McCarthy* 2: 'It kind of proves a point about them cities – keep away from the big smoke, see what happened to McCarthy?'

1982 Max Harris *Weekend Australian* 27 Mar. Mag. 4: He [Doug Anthony] is over-equipped with the decencies of the boy from the bush dealing with endless bastards from the big smoke.

smoko 1 A break from work for smoking and refreshment; the food and drink then taken

[1855 R. Caldwell *The Gold Era of Victoria* 129: A curious practice exists in the Colony of taking a 'smoking time' in the forenoon for a quarter of an hour, and again in the afternoon for a quarter of an hour. All the men leave off work and deliberately sit down and smoke.]

1881 *Adelaide Observer* 31 Dec. 46: 'I must go to "smoke O".'

1890 *The Worker* Mar. 14: Smoke Ho! [heading of column of miscellaneous news items]

1899 Henry Lawson 'A Rough Shed' *Prose* i 464: 'We go through the day of eight hours in runs of about an hour and twenty minutes between smoke-ho's . . . I've worked from six to six with no smoke-ho's for half the wages.'

1919 W. K. Harris *Outback in Australia* 152: The men were having five minutes' 'Smoke-oh!' and were overhauling their machines preparatory to beginning on the final batch of ewes for the day.

1930 Vance Palmer *The Passage* 247: At smoke, when they took a spell in the middle of loading the boat.

1947 John Morrison *Sailors Belong Ships* 50: Half-past three. Smoko. We get thirty minutes . . . Many stevedores don't leave the hold during smoko; they just curl up on the softest bit of cargo they can find and go to sleep.

1954 Tom Ronan *Vision Splendid* 179: 'If you blokes aren't coming down for your smoko I'll throw it away.'

1959 D'Arcy Niland *The Big Smoke* 114: 'I'll make you a bit of smoko.'

1961 *Sydney Morning Herald* 22 May 2: The job committee meets whenever necessary during smoko.

1971 Frank Hardy *the Outcasts of Foolgarah* 12: The camera crew better take a smoko and come back after lunch.

2 An informal social gathering, concert etc.

1918 G. A. Taylor *Those Were the Days* 30: The State Governor was present, and it was a rare incident for that distinguished party to grace an Art Society 'Smoko'.

1923 Jack Moses *Beyond the City Gates* 71: The 'Smoko' held annually in connection with the Wattle Flat Exhibition, is invariably described, year in and year out, as the great social gathering of the season.

1939 E. H. Lane *Dawn to Dusk* 89: I well remember a smoko of the Meat Industry Union held in the old Centennial Hall, Adelaide Street. There was an attendance of several hundred members and, of course, the beer flowed freely.

1976 *Australian* 24 Apr. 18: The Leader of the Opposition, Mr Whitlam, worked in his Sydney office and attended a 'smoko' at Wentworthville RSL club last night.

smoodge (smooge) To ingratiate oneself, make a display of affection [? f. *smudge* to kiss (cf. smouch); to covet, long for; to sidle up to; to beg in a sneaking way EDD 1839]

1908 E. G. Murphy *Jarrahland Jingles* 111: Amid the pop of the champagne cork, / The smoodgeful speech and cheers.

1910 C. E. W. Bean *On the Wool Track* 170: 'We reckon 'e smoogged [smoodged in later editions] for a bit after that. But it wasn't any good.'

1915 C. J. Dennis *The Songs of a Sentimental Bloke* 39: 'Lady, be yonder moon I swear!' sez 'e. / An' then 'e climbs up on the balkiney; / An' there they smoodge a treat.

1939 Kylie Tennant *Foveaux* 49: He patiently disentangled himself from her embrace and set about cutting the sandwiches. 'Don't smooge to me.'

1942 Gavin Casey *It's Harder for Girls* 9: A rug was reckoned to provide privacy enough for a bit of smoodging.

1955 D'Arcy Niland *The Shiralee* 122: 'He'd go round to the kitchen for a hand-out, and if there

was no blokes about, he'd come the smoodge to the women for a bit of a love-up.'
1973 Patrick White *The Eye of the Storm* 480: She came smoodging up at her father and he answered, but gently . . . and kissed her.
smoodger Someone given to 'smoodging'
1910 Edward Dyson *The Missing Link* 5: 'Kidder' a term that had gone out recently in favour of 'smoodger', and which implies a quality of sauve and ingratiating cunning backed by ulterior motives.
1924 *Truth* 27 Apr. 6: *Smooger* One who fawns.
1934 Vance Palmer *Sea and Spinifex* 229: 'Better hunt him home, Sid, home to his mother . . . yes, show him how we treat smoodgers.'
1961 Noni Braham *The Interloper* 91: 'I'd sooner co-operate with a tiger snake – a real smooger.'
smoodgingly
1969 D'Arcy Niland *Dead Men Running* 209: 'I wish you wouldn't see her, Joey,' she said smoodgingly.

snack Something easy to accomplish, 'a piece of cake'
1941 Baker 68: *Snack* A certainty.
1952 T. A. G. Hungerford *The Ridge and the River* 138: There was nothing to it . . . It was a snack.
1961 Mena Calthorpe *The Dyehouse* 150: 'In Hughie's day he'd make this a snack.'
1970 Richard Beilby *No Medals for Aphrodite* 274: 'How could I do that, Harry?' 'Easy. It'll be a snack.'

snag A bush cook: *rare*
1911 E. S. Sorenson *Life in the Australian Backblocks* 91: Concerning fighting cooks the tales are legion. I remember one snag . . . who cooked abominably, but rendered his position tenable by punching the ringer.

snagger 1 A rough shearer [see quot. 1969]
1887 *Tibb's Popular Songbook* 11: I found a lot a snaggers / Not a shearer in the mob, / At Mumba signed for seventeen / With a bonus of three bob.
1885–1914 'Click Go the Shears' *Australian Ballads* ed. Russel Ward (1964) 120: The ringer looks round and is beaten by a blow, / And curses the old snagger with the bare-bellied yeo.
1956 F. B. Vickers *First Place to the Stranger* 240: 'You've had the run of the good sheep up North. But I'm just a snagger. I don't get the long runs.'
1969 Bobbie Hardy *West of the Darling* 106: Since they were slow, inexpert, and rough in their performances, the poorest shearers in the shed were nick-named 'snaggers'.
2 A sausage, esp. in W.A. (elsewhere **snags** q.v.)
1953 T. A. G. Hungerford *Riverslake* 199: 'Give him a hand to open up some more snaggers, Randy.'

1955 F. B. Vickers *The Mirage* 69: 'What'll you have, son? Steak and kidney or snaggers?'
1983 *West Australian* (Perth) 23 Dec. 20: Come the day after Boxing Day, the left-over Christmas fare will have lost its appeal, and the humble snagger will come into its own.

snags Sausages (rarely used in the singular)
1941 Baker 68: *Snags* Sausages.
1949 Ruth Park *Poor Man's Orange* 33: 'I know. Let's have sausages.' The tension in Mumma's housewifely heart disappeared. Good old snags. They were always there to be fallen back on.
1968 A. Clifford *Send her down, Hughie!* 169: Sausages are 'snags' (a highly important part of the Australian diet).
1975 *Australian* 13 Nov. 2: Snags and mash at Burton bash.
1982 *Sydney City Monthly* Jun. 32: Someone of less-than-perfect mental facilities is *a few snags short of a barbie*.
1982 *Sun-Herald* 5 Dec. 98: Summer is here again – the bindy-eyes bloom while the roses shrivel and the drone of cicadas almost drowns out the sound of barbecuing snags.
see **snagger** 2, **snarler** 2

snake A sergeant, esp. in the term 'snake pit' for sergeants' mess
1943 Baker 73: *Snake pit* A sergeants' mess (War slang)
1948 Sumner Locke Elliott *Rusty Bugles* in *Khaki, Bush and Bigotry* ed. Eunice Hanger (1968) 91: 'Andy Edwards has been promoted and moved up to the snake pit with you and the other snakes.'
1951 Eric Lambert *The Twenty Thousand Thieves* 314: 'Baxter reckoned the officers and snakes are pinching our beer.'
1954 T. A. G. Hungerford *Sowers of the Wind* 222: 'Pity your big mate over at the snakes'-pit couldn't see you now!'

snake charmer A fettler
1937 A. W. Upfield *Mr. Jelly's Business* 16: 'And what are the Snake Charmers?' They are the permanent-way men.'
1969 Patsy Adam Smith *Folklore of the Australian Railwaymen* 279: Fettlers are invariably referred to as 'snake charmers'.

Snake Gully The locale of the radio serial 'Dad and Dave' q.v.
1945 Baker 198: *Woop Woop* and *Snake Gully*, as fictitious names for a remote outback settlement, the home of the most rustic of rustics.
1965 Leslie Haylen *Big Red* 88: People rushing through the countryside by car would grin as they raced through Cooee. Here was the authentic bush town. Here was Snake Gully.

1976 *Nation Review* 16 Jan. 338: South Australia is the quintessential utopia of enlightenment compared with which Valhalla would be thought to resemble Snake Gully.
1984 *Australian* 16 Feb. 7: This bucolic jollity in the rain was accompanied by a commentary from one Keith Lines, a man whose accent was pure Snake Gully and whose humor was as worn and salty as a cowlick.

snake juice Any improvised alcoholic drink; strong liquor generally
1903 Joseph Furphy *Such is Life* (1944) 108: Illicit snake-juice for them, and golden top for the other fellow.
1904 E. S. Emerson *A Shanty Entertainment* 70: Then he started them on snake-juice, known as Boot and Blacking Rum.
1916 C. J. Dennis *The Moods of Ginger Mick* 26: 'I've arf a mind to give cold tea a go. / It's no game pourin' snake-juice in yer face.'
1924 *Truth* 27 Apr. 6: *Snake juice* Strong drink.
1973 Roland Robinson *The Drift of Things* 290: Broke into Eric's hut, threw the 'pickled' specimens out of the jars, and drank the methylated spirits. That must have been the real 'Snake-Juice'. This is a name for the various kinds of beverages some of the alcoholics in the various camps used to concoct.

snake, mad as a cut see **mad**

snake's belly, lower than a Despicable
1932 Leonard Mann *Flesh in Armour* 290: 'It was a dirty trick. He knew about me and her.' 'Dirty! Lower than a snake's belly.'
1951 Dymphna Cusack *Say No to Death* 20: He'd only have to take one look at Jan to be convinced in his honest old heart that his son was lower than a snake's belly.
1967 D'Arcy Niland *Call Me When the Cross Turns Over* 181: My opinion of you is lower than a snake's belly.
1965 John Beede *They Hosed Them Out* 175: I thought, 'if I have to crawl to this illegitimate I'll get lower than a snake's belly.'
1979 *Australian* 2 Mar. 1: Mrs Fraser reacted to the allegation last night by saying that anyone criticising her father, Mr Sandford Beggs, over rural loans was 'lower than a snake's duodenum'.

snakey Bad-tempered, irritable
1919 W. H. Downing *Digger Dialects* 46: *Snaky* (adj.) (1) Angry (e.g., to turn snaky); (2) Irritable.
1941 Kylie Tennant *The Battlers* 86: 'Don't go snaky on the kid.'
1951 Dymphna Cusack and Florence James *Come In Spinner* 245: 'Snaky?' she asked, looking at him judicially, 'or just gone troppo?'

1974 David Williamson *Three Plays* 34: 'What are you snaky about this time?'

snarler 1 'Services no longer required': applied to a serviceman sent back as a failure from a theatre of war
1943 Baker 73: *Snarler* A soldier or flier sent back home from overseas service because of some misdemeanour.
1952 T. A. G. Hungerford *The Ridge and the River* 49: If he just couldn't make the grade, then Lovatt would bundle him back south for a Snarler.
1979 George Stewart *The Leveller* 45: I was rejected by the Army, Navy and Air Force: the Army because I was declared a snarler for ironing out a sergeant.
1983 *Sun-Herald* 17 Jul. 57: In the Navy's Weekly Postings he receives an official 'snarler' which is nautical slang for 'services no longer required' notification.
2 A sausage
1982 *Sydney Morning Herald* 18 Sep. 28: At the end of the dispensing line little chaps from the Boys' Brigade ejaculated a blob of rich red Fountain Tomato Sauce on top of each snarler.

snatch it, snatch one's time To demand the wages due and leave the job
[**1934** J. M. Harcourt *Upsurge* 258: 'Load that barrow or go and take your time. Any man here who doesn't care to load his barrow can take his time.']
1944 Alan Marshall *These Are My People* 158: 'I suppose you struck some bad bosses in your time?' 'If they're bad, I snatch it.'
1945 Gavin Casey *Downhill is Easier* 106: There was nothing to do but put up with it, unless I snatched my time and left.
1962 Tom Ronan *Deep of the Sky* 55: 'What's more, when we pass Silverton I'm snatching my time.'
1973 Frank Huelin *Keep Moving* 83: 'What are yous goin' to do? Snatch it or stay?'
1983 *Bulletin* 26 Jul. 41: About 12 months ago, Slattery (a) got sick and tired of newspapers (b) got married and (c) snatched his time.

snip To 'bite', exact a loan
1977 Jim Ramsay *Cop It Sweet* 83: *Snip*: Borrow money.
1984 *Sunday Telegraph* (Sydney) 1 Apr. 58: The battlers used to line up to 'snip' him [Roy Higgins] after the last. He would simply smile and hand over, and have his hand in his pocket for the next 'snip'.

snipe An election poster [? f. the bird's long bill]
[**1860** Hotten 220: *snipe* a long bill; also a term for attorneys – a race remarkable for their

propensity to long bills.]
1966 Baker 355: *snipe*, a political election poster, the size of which is limited to 10 in. by 6 in.
1977 Fred Daly *From Curtin to Kerr* 75: He posted snipes on nearly every post and on the day had his booths well manned.

sniper   A non-unionist on the wharves, 'sniping' the jobs of unionists
1945 Baker 248: A waterfront term of fairly recent origin is *sniper*, a non-union labourer.
1955 John Morrison *Black Cargo* 14: Plenty of Federation men also know him by sight, and it will need only one shout of 'Sniper!' and Lamond will be lucky to get out without being knocked down.
1957 Tom Nelson *The Hungry Mile* 72: The W.W.F. had preference of work, wharf by wharf. The outsiders (snipers) would stand back at the gate until the W.W.F. men were all used.

sniper, went for a crap and the ~ got him   Jocular reply to request for anyone's whereabouts
1965 Eric Lambert *The Long White Night* 94: I looked around me at the dark figures in the dusk and called Clancy's name. From behind the top of a lighted cigarette an anonymous voice told me: 'He went for a shit and the sniper got him.'
1971 David Ireland *The Unknown Industrial Prisoner* 90: 'Where's he gone?' 'Went for a crap and a sniper got him.'
see **he went mad and they shot him, shot through on the padre's bike, went through like Speed Gordon**

snob   The 'cobbler', the sheep left to the last as the most difficult to shear [see quot. 1945]
1945 C. E. W. Bean *On the Wool Track* The sheep most difficult to shear, which naturally is left last in the pen, is also called the 'snob'. As early as in Elizabethan times 'snob' was slang for cobbler (Shakespeare had 'snip and snob' for tailor and cobbler). The terms have persisted in old-fashioned English, and 'snob' has added to its several meanings this peculiarly Australian one.
1975 Les Ryan *The Shearers* 49: 'Get on to this wrinkled bludger!' he said. It was the last sheep in the pen ... 'Real snob ain't it?'

snodger   First rate, excellent, 'nifty': *obsolescent*
1919 W. H. Downing *Digger Dialects* 46: *Snodger* (adj.) Excellent.
1924 C. J. Dennis *Rose of Spadgers* 40: It was a snodger day! ... The apple trees / Was white with bloom. All things seemed good to me.
1946 *Sun* (Sydney) 11 Aug. Suppl. 15: There they find the con-ships fitted up snodger with bulk-heads studded with nails.
1950 *Australian Police Journal* Apr. 119: If something is snodger it is 'mighty' in Queensland, it is

'colossal' in NSW, and just 'very nice' everywhere else.
1965 Xavier Herbert *Larger than Life* 152: 'They got good stuff. Shirts, pants, some snodgin' stockwhips, watches.'

snoozer   Codger, chap, 'joker': *obsolescent*
1916 *Anzac Book* 99: The chaps of the 16th Battalion / Are not easy snoozers to beat.
1929 K. S. Prichard *Coonardoo* 261: 'Oh, I suppose I'm a cantankerous old snoozer, Bob,' Hugh said.
1932 William Hatfield *Christmastown* 42: Decent sort of snoozer, Allison – no girl stuff about him.
1946 *Sun* (Sydney) 20 Oct. Suppl. 15: They'd have lamped a snoozer rigged up as an army skipper clop-clopping along on a nag just behind them.
1962 Stuart Gore *Down the Golden Mile* 26: 'Want to watch out for them quiet snoozers. Sometimes they can go the knuckle a bit themselves.'
1964 *Herald* (Melbourne) 12 Dec. 34: Mr Bolte's mates in the local pub near his farm affectionately describe him as a 'real rough old snoozer'. They mean that down on the farm Mr Bolte is just one of the boys.

snork   A baby: *rare* [derived by Partridge from *stork*]
1941 Baker 68: *Snork* A baby (2) A sausage.
1944 Lawson Glassop *We Were the Rats* 273: 'Got a scar on his hand, but probably he's had it since he was a little snork.'
1973 Frank Huelin *Keep Moving* 178: *Snork/ Bimbo* Young hoboes from 14 to 18 years of age.

snout, have a ~ on   As for **have a nose on** q.v.
1916 C. J. Dennis *The Moods of Ginger Mick* 155: *Snout* To bear a grudge.
1949 Lawson Glassop *Lucky Palmer* 212: 'He's got a snout on the Kid for something.'
1957 Ray Lawler *Summer of the Seventeenth Doll* 50: 'You got a snout on that kid the first day you saw him working.'
1966 Tom Ronan *Once There Was a Bagman* 39: 'The reason you blokes have such a snout on him,' I argued, 'is that he's forgotten more Law than you've ever learned.'
1982 *Bulletin* 20 Jul. 17: I enjoy Semmler's occasional contributions to *The Bulletin* but I have a feeling that he has a 'snout' on Aunty and takes every opportunity to criticise her.

snouted   Rebuffed, in disfavour; annoyed with
1919 W. H. Downing *Digger Dialects* 46: *Snouted* Under disfavor.
1924 C. J. Dennis *Rose of Spadgers* 117: Don't mind my sulks ... But gittin' snouted ain't wot I expeck.
1943 Margaret Trist *In the Sun* 104: Some of the

juniors had him snouted because of it.

1944 Alan Marshall *These Are My People* 155: 'I was sore as a snouted sheila for weeks.'

1959 Vance Palmer *The Big Fellow* 152: 'He seems to have got me snouted.'

1960 John Iggulden *The Storms of Summer* 122: 'They're getting a bit snouted on fellers from the Inlet around here.'

1970 Richard Beilby *No Medals for Aphrodite* 149: 'That officer happened to have me snouted because I got you across the river, against his orders.'

Snowy, the 1 The Snowy River

c. **1834** John Lhotsky MS in *A Journey from Sydney to the Australian Alps* (1979) 192: 3 miles farther Cromwell falls into the Snowy, the junction takes place at a very obtuse angle.

1882 Rolf Boldrewood *Robbery Under Arms* (World's Classics 1949) 148: 'Then fish in all the creeks, besides the old Snowy'.

1911 C. E. W. Bean *The 'Dreadnought' of the Darling* 251: Plenty of blackfellows camped in the valleys of the Snowy.

1944 Archer Russell *Bush Ways* 67: We make our camp by the swift-rushing waters of the Snowy.

2 The region of the Snowy Mountains and Snowy River in S.E. N.S.W. used as a ski and fishing resort, officially the Kosciusko National Park

1967 Barbara Mullins *Kosciusko National Park* 17: Though camping is not encouraged in the higher altitudes ... facilities are provided in many areas of the lower Snowy.

1975 Alex Buzo *Tom* 2: 'Where did you go fishing? The Snowy?'

3 The Snowy River hydro-electric scheme

1953 T. A. G. Hungerford *Riverslake* 2: He had been working up on the Snowy River scheme, and ... he remembered what the chef at the Snowy had said.

1982 *Sydney Morning Herald* 3 Aug. 10: More trouble on the Snowy ... A spokesman for the Snowy Mountains Authority (SMA) said last night that power generation was down by about 400 megawatts.

soak, soakage See quots [f. *soak* a percolation of water; water which has oozed through or out of the ground, strata etc. OED 1707]

1895 *Australasian* 7 Sep. 461: The term soak in Western Australia ... signifies a depression holding moisture after rain. It is also given to damp or swampy spots round the base of granite rocks. [Morris]

1898 D. W. Carnegie *Spinifex and Sand* 80: Round the granite base a belt of grass of no great extent may be found, for the most part dry and yellow, but in places green and fresh. It is in such spots as these that one may hope to tap an underground reservoir in the rock. To these shallow wells has been given the name of 'Soaks'. They seldom exceed fifteen feet in depth.

1931 Vance Palmer *Separate Lives* 189: They had stayed out too long at a time when a bad spell had struck the spinifex, and soaks were drying up.

1937 Ernestine Hill *The Great Australian Loneliness* 330: *Soak* Water beneath the surface of the sand.

1981 A. B. Facey *A Fortunate Life* 70: This was what they called a soak. Water would sometimes seep up like this through a crack or thin spot in the layer of clay and make the surface damp. By digging down through the clay to let the water come up, a soak was formed.

soap A dupe, a 'square' [? f. *soft soap*]

1941 Baker 69: *Soapy* (adj.): (Of a person) stupid, silly, effeminate.

1953 Baker 125: Australia's underworldsters have commemorated the services of their victims by calling them ... *soap, gig, touch* and *bite*.

1981 *Bulletin* 10 Nov. 46: Short trousers (ankle freezers), odd-colored or school socks, ties or cheap sandshoes, label you as being 'poxy' or worse still, a 'soap'.

soap, not to know someone from a bar of To be completely unacquainted with someone

1938 *Smith's Weekly* 26 Nov. 23: [cartoon caption] 'I don't know you from a bar of soap.'

1945 Kylie Tennant *Ride on Stranger* 309: 'Why doesn't she marry the child's father?' ... 'It's my belief she doesn't know him from a bar of soap.'

1947 Gavin Casey *The Wits Are Out* 184: 'We can't do that, when we don't know them from a bar of soap.'

1970 Jon Cleary *Helga's Web* 130: 'I've never met any of his – interests. Certainly not this girl. I dunno her from a bar of soap.'

soapie Fish not yet full size, esp. jewfish ('soapies' are smaller than 'schoolies', q.v.)

1978 *Sydney Morning Herald* 27 Oct. 23: Small 'soapie' jewfish are plentiful but most anglers are not rigging heavily enough to land big jewfish.

1983 *Sun-Herald* 20 Nov. 74: Mulloway grow to a weight of more than 50 kg, but ... fishermen are happy when their scales register 5 kg or 10 kg, while the smaller 'soapie' of 2 kg or 3 kg is the norm. The term 'soapie' is used to describe the flavour of the smaller mulloway's flesh. It's unwarranted because such a fish is quite good eating if properly prepared.

Socceroos Members of a team representing Australia internationally at soccer (by analogy with the Kangaroos, the representatives in Rugby League)

1973 *Sydney Morning Herald* 15 Nov. 1: Now that

the Australian Soccer team is basking in honour and glory after its World Cup victory over South Korea it can surely do without the name 'Socceroos' which is being increasingly applied to it.
1976 *Australian* 3 Jun. 20: Socceroos turn the tide.

sod   A damper that has not risen [f. *sod* ill-raised bread OED 1836]
1900–10 O'Brien and Stephens: *Sod* badly cooked damper.
1941 Baker 69: *Sod* A damper, esp. a badly-cooked one.
1957 R. S. Porteous *Brigalow* 206: His dampers were leaden sods.
1975 Xavier Herbert *Poor Fellow My Country* 838: 'I want to cook our own damper, too . . . I don't want one of their sods.'

soda   Something easily done, a 'pushover' [? f. card game U.S. 1843 Mathews]
[**1895** Cornelius Crowe *The Australian Slang Dictionary* 98: *Zodiac*, or *Soda* the top card in the box in faro.]
1930 Vance Palmer *The Passage* 83: 'They're getting ready for the long dive now, and it ought to be a soda for you.'
1943 G. H. Johnston *New Guinea Diary* 151: 'The Middle East was a soda beside this,' one of them told me.
1955 Alan Marshall *I Can Jump Puddles* 108: 'Swipe him on the knuckles if you can. If he's like his old man he's a soda.'
1966 Hal Porter *The Paper Chase* 74: The job, for which I have no really specialized training, is nevertheless a soda.
1981 *Sun-Herald* 12 Apr. 65: Once politicians trembled at the thought of facing Mike Willesee on television. These days they must think it's a soda.

S.O.L.   Abbreviation for **shit on the liver** q.v.
1951 Dal Stivens *Jimmy Brockett* 137: 'I had a bit of S.O.L. the other day.'
1954 Jon Cleary *The Climate of Courage* 222: 'Sorry, chum. I've got a touch of S.O.L., I think.'
1978 Ronald McKie *Bitter Bread* 119: This was the first human sign for hours. Blue must be improving, getting rid of his s.o.l.

solid   Severe, excessive, unreasonable
1916 C. J. Dennis *The Moods of Ginger Mick* 155: *Solid* Severe; severely.
1917 Let. of 6 Dec. cit. Bill Gammage *The Broken Years* (1974) 215: Just before the poor fellow got killed he said to me that it was a bit solid and the sooner it finished the better.
1948 Ruth Park *The Harp in the South* 62: 'After all, Auntie Josie's got all them kids to look after. It

must be pretty solid for her with Grandma as well.'
1951 Frank Hardy *Power Without Glory* 41: 'I got fined fifty quid, Joe twenty-five.' 'Bit solid, wasn't it?'
1959 Eric Lambert *Glory Thrown In* 66: 'They'll be solid on him for that, won't they?'

sollicker   Something very big, a 'whopper' [cf. *sollock* impetus, force (He fell down with such a sollock) EDD]
1898 Roland Graeme *From England to the Backblocks* 82: 'Who was it I heard that in cutting-out some cattle on one of the Methvin plains, did come down a soliker and broke his horse's knees?'
1908 *Australian Magazine* 1 Nov. 1251: *sollicker*, very big.
1939 Miles Franklin and Dymphna Cusack *Pioneers on Parade* 168: 'She gave me a sollicker of a dose out of a blue bottle.'
1946 Kylie Tennant *Lost Haven* 155: 'It was a great big sollicking stitch if ever there was one.'
1956 Patrick White *The Tree of Man* 91: 'You can jump down, can't you? You're quite big, you know.' 'Of course he can . . . he's a sollicker.'
1982 *Sydney Morning Herald* 4 Sep. 32: Someone at the back of the room yelled 'She's a sollicker!' (This is an old traditional Irish-Australian word, meaning 'strapping young female person'. You don't often hear it these days.)

sook   **1**   A timorous person, a 'softie', a crybaby (juvenile) [? f. *suck* a 'muff'; a 'duffer'; a stupid fellow EDD]
1941 Baker 69: *Sook* A coward, a timid person.
1950 Brian James *The Advancement of Spencer Button* 9: If he nervously declares he can't fight, and shows that he doesn't want to fight, then he is a 'sook' or a 'sissy'.
1970 Patrick White *The Vivisector* 11: He wasn't a sook. He could run, shout, play, fight, had scabs on his knees, and twice split Billy Abrams's lip, who was two years older.
1980 *Bulletin* 11 Nov. 55: Hibberd was quoted as saying that Williamson went to Sydney because he liked the warmer weather, 'which makes him a bit of a sook'.
1984 Allan Caton *Age* (Melbourne) 22 Sep. 12: Who wants a sook for PM? I do not. If the heat gets too much for blubbing Bob, he should get out of the kitchen.
2   A timid horse
1980 *Sydney Morning Herald* 2 Aug. 59: White, answering charges that Panamint is unsound, described the horse as a 'big sook' . . . 'Invariably when he is taken in and out of the box he is timid.'
1983 *West Australian* (Perth) 17 Dec. 184: 'He is a real sook unless there is another horse with him . . . If there is not another horse alongside him, he starts to weave and get a bit uptight.'

1984 *Age* (Melbourne) 16 Apr. 28: According to Smith, the horse lost his confidence and became a dreadful 'sook'.

sooky

1953 Dymphna Cusack *Southern Steel* 328: 'Get along with you: you're getting real sookey.'

1977 Amy Witting *The Visit* 82: 'I used to do it when I was a sooky schoolgirl talking to my sister.'

1983 *Newcastle Herald* 5 Apr. 14: Newcastle United, alas, did not thrive as expected. It became a sickly sookie in fact.

sool   To incite someone to a course of action, from the command 'Sool him' to a dog to attack or harass some quarry [f. *sowl* to pull roughly . . . In later use esp. of dogs OED 1607]

1849 Alexander Harris *The Emigrant Family* (1967) 135: 'Hey! hey! sowl her boys!' roared Morgan: and on went the whole pack, seizing the poor beast by the ears, nose, and even eyelids.

1903 Joseph Furphy *Such is Life* (1944) 130: 'Soolim, Pup!' I hissed.

1907 Nathan Spielvogel *The Cocky Farmer* 68: 'Here, Spot. Sool him, s-o-o l him.' Joe's dog came with a bark, and Bill had to run for it.

1911 Louis Stone *Jonah* 31: The Push gathered round, grinning from ear to ear, sooling the women on as if they were dogs.

1920 Frank A. Russell *The Ashes of Achievement* 116: 'The author'll sool a lawyer on you first thing you know.'

1932 L. W. Lower *Here's Another* 89: It followed us to school one day . . . and we sooled it on to the teacher.

1942 Gavin Casey *It's Harder for Girls* 52: 'Sool the dogs after him,' someone called out.

1951 Dal Stivens *Jimmy Brockett* 84: 'I heard McGrath has sooled them on to you. That's all I know.'

1961 Mena Calthorpe *The Dyehouse* 83: Oliver Henery had sooled the Unions on to Renshaw over the loads that the girls were humping about.

1971 Germaine Greer *The Female Eunuch* 190: The hero may either have her on his side and like a lion-tamer sool her on to his enemies, or he may have to battle for his life at her hands.

sooler

1935 H. R. Williams *Comrades of the Great Adventure* 35: Here, as chief 'sooler', he was urging the passing soldiers to patronize the eating-house.

1963 Xavier Herbert *Disturbing Element* 141: She had been sending white feathers round . . . She had become what her former comrades of the I.W.W. called a Sooler.

1982 Anthony Splivalo *The Home Fires* 49: A few residents on the goldfields . . . resented the coercion of young men into military ranks. They referred to the coercers as 'soolers', which is the

Australian slang for persons who incite others to actions against their will.

sooner   1   An idler, a shirker (who would sooner loaf than work, fight, etc.): *obs*.

1892 Karl Lentzner *Dictionary of the Slang-English of Australia* 117: *Sooner* a weak idler, a lazy good-for-nothing.

1919 Edward Dyson *Hello, Soldier!* 31: He slugged a tubby Hun, / Then choked a Fritzie with his dukes, 'n' pinched the sooner's gun!

1931 Vance Palmer *Separate Lives* 17: 'The dirty sooners – they've done me down!'

2   'A jibbing horse (one that would sooner go backward than forward) 1939 NZ.' (Partridge)

1969 Patsy Adam Smith *Folklore of the Australian Railwaymen* 117: This was an old sooner of an engine. She'd had it. On a stiff climb in a tunnel she began to slip.

sore toe (finger), done up like a   1   Dressed up, and looking uncomfortable

1919 W. H. Downing *Digger Dialects* 46: *Sore finger* An overdressed person (e.g. 'dolled' up like a sore finger).

1939 Kylie Tennant *Foveaux* 430: 'You ought to a seen us in the ole days when we 'ad a procession every year – done up like a sore toe with banners and floats.'

1945 Margaret Trist *Now That We're Laughing* 125: 'Done up like a sore toe, she was, too.'

1958 H. D. Williamson *The Sunlit Plain* 10: 'Get an eyeful of him! Done up like a sore toe.'

1963 Hal Porter *The Watcher on the Cast-Iron Balcony* 81: 'Dressed up like a sore toe, but hasn't had a bath for weeks.'

1965 Patrick White *Four Plays* 168: 'I'm gunna get out of this suit. Dressed up like a sore finger.'

2   Looking conspicuous

1966 Elwyn Wallace *Sydney and the Bush* 69: One young man named Dave whose clean pressed shirt stood out like a sore thumb spoke up at this point.

sorry, you'll be   Jocular greeting to new army recruits in World War II

1944 Lawson Glassop *We Were the Rats* 66: Every soldier we passed on the road yelled, 'You'll be sorry.' Every soldier we encountered in camp until we got our issue clothes said, 'You'll be sorry.'

1951 Dymphna Cusack and Florence James *Come In Spinner* 185: A voice called derisively 'You'll be sorry!' Crooked smiles split the soldiers' faces.

1965 Eric Lambert *The Long White Night* 12: Still wearing his civilian clothes, and running the gamut of 'veterans', who had joined camp the day before and achieved uniforms, thereby feeling entitled to call out: 'You'll be sorry!'

sort   A girl or woman (at the same level of usage

as 'sheila'); applied rarely to men also: *obsolescent*

1933 Frank Clune *Try Anything Once* 93: 'Look here, George,' I said. 'Lend me a suit of civvies. I've got to meet a great little sort, and her father has a dead nark on soldiers.'

1941 Kylie Tennant *The Battlers* 276: 'Hey, Bob!' Dick Tyrell gave a low whistle. 'Take a look at that good sort.'

1949 Ruth Park *Poor Man's Orange* 180: Harry Drummy waited for her, draped mournfully over the rails in the peculiarly filleted manner of his kind, and eyeing off all the good sorts who were pushing and screaming their way on to the Luna Park ferry.

1953 T. A. G. Hungerford *Riverslake* 144: 'Felix came in after tea and said that his sort could come.'

1968 Kit Denton *A Walk Around My Cluttered Mind* 137: They'd told me, 'Don't worry about bringing anything except a bottle. The sorts are laid on.' Even after only ten months I understood this to mean that there would be feminine company.

1983 Janise Beaumont *Sun-Herald* 23 Oct. 128: Others included that divine Nick Shehadie (I've always thought he was the best sort in town).

see **drac**

soul-case, belt (worry, work) the ~ out of To subject to extreme hardship or punishment

1901 F. J. Gillen *Diary* (1968) 34: Fliers were celebrating some festival all night and worried the very soul cases out of us.

1937 K. S. Prichard *Intimate Strangers* 288: 'Eviction was what I got after clearing two thousand acres of virgin land: sweating my soul case out to grow wheat.'

1945 Gavin Casey *Downhill is Easier* 146: 'He used t' belt the soulcase out o' her till I come along.'

1951 Dymphna Cusack and Florence James *Come In Spinner* 152: 'If you've been going in for any of them beach girl competitions, Peggy my girl, I'll belt the soul case out of you.'

1962 Ron Tullipan *March into Morning* 13: 'Then he got the bright idea of bringin' in orphan kids and working the soulcase off them until they turn eighteen and have to be paid more money.'

south, the The Australian states south of Queensland, or of N.T.

1908 Mrs Aeneas Gunn *We of the Never-Never* 3: The Maluka spoke from experience, having been himself an interested onlooker 'down South', when it had been suggested there that the wife should be left behind.

1979 *Weekend Australian* 1 Dec. Mag. 4: It [the letter] contains, as well as the list of 61 large Queensland companies swallowed by the south, a

draft of proposed legislation which would ensure 'a southern takeover would not be detrimental to the economy of Queensland, or lead to reduced employment opportunities.'

1980 *Sunday Mail* (Brisbane) 28 Sep. 2: People are coming up from the south in droves to settle here. Not for the beauty of the City of Brisbane, but for the superbness of the quality of life that surrounds it.

1984 Ron McAuliffe *Sun-Herald* 13 May 67: I could have done more damage with a felt hat. I didn't think I'd live to see the day the Sydney blokes would turn into a team of squealers. The way some of them are going on down south, they'll end up wanting to play us in touch football . . . It's hard to be humble if you're a Queenslander.

southerner

1982 Thomas Shapcott *Sydney Morning Herald* 30 Jan. 38: Queenslanders are known to be sullen about southerners; the state encourages this.

southerly (buster) The cool, gusty wind that springs up at the end of a hot day, sometimes bringing a shower of rain (originally in Sydney)

1850 B. C. Peck *Recollections of Sydney* 132: It is almost a corollary, that the evening of a hot-wind day brings up a 'southerly buster', as we have heard the vulgar call it, very chill indeed . . . as the wind comes from the southerly region of the Australian Alps.

1859 Frank Fowler *Southern Lights and Shadows* 87–8: The 'Southerly Buster', as this change is called, generally comes . . . early in the evening. A cloud of dust – they call it, in Sydney, a 'brick-fielder' – . . . heralds its approach. In a minute the temperature will sink fifty or sixty degrees.

1867 J. R. Houlding *Australian Capers* 137: He left the place as much discomposed as . . . a fashionable belle who had lost her bonnet in a 'southerly burster'.

1880 J. C. Crawford *Travels in New Zealand and Australia* 300: The wind was from the northward when we left Wollongong, but a southerly 'burster' overtook us off Botany Bay.

1896 Nat Gould *Town and Bush* 96: The southerly buster is well named. The wind comes in bursts and whirls the dust about . . . The buster, however, makes up for the inconvenience it causes by clearing the heated atmosphere, and is generally followed by a refreshing shower of rain.

1926 J. Vance Marshall *Timely Tips for New Australians: Southerly buster* A strong, gusty wind peculiar to a section of the East coast of New South Wales.

1935 Kylie Tennant *Tiburon* 229: Complaints from parishioners he blew aside as a southerly wind would blow the washing on the line.

1949 Ruth Park *Poor Man's Orange* 146: After the unbearably hot day, the old men on the balconies were sniffing the air and saying, 'Here she comes!' The southerly buster, the genie of Sydney, flapped its coarse blusterous wing over the city ... The women undid the fronts of their frocks, and the little children lifted up their shirts and let it blow on their sweaty bottoms.

1956 Patrick White *The Tree of Man* 105: 'They say there'll be a southerly buster later in the afternoon. But no rain.'

1965 Graham McInnes *The Road to Gundagai* 63: The Southerly Buster had blown into town [Melbourne], whooshing up from the high latitudes near Antarctica and covering the suffocating city with a blanket of cool.

see **brickfielder**

souvenir To purloin [listed by Partridge as military slang (1915)]

1918 *Aussie* 18: Jan. 11: *Souvenir* – Is generally used in the same sense as salvage, but of small, easily portable articles. *Salvage* – To rescue unused property and make use of it.

1919 W. H. Downing *Digger Dialects* 46: *Souvenir* To steal, find, capture, etc.

1932 Leonard Mann *Flesh in Armour* 85: Artie Fethers bent down and souvenired the officer's pistol.

1951 Dymphna Cusack and Florence James *Come In Spinner* 395: Val stared at the cases. 'How on earth did you get those?' 'Souvenired 'em,' said Lofty with a broad wink.

1955 Mary Durack *Keep Him My Country* 298: 'The hides are no good but you might like to souvenir the heads.'

1970 Cynthia Nolan *A Bride for St Thomas* 95: I was just in time to prevent Sister Seymour's brass inkstand being souvenired.

spag An Italian: *derogatory* [abbr. of *spaghetti*]

1966 Baker 344: *spaggie,* an Italian. [as Victorian slang]

1974 *Bulletin* 1 Jun. 39–40: 'And [Al Grassby] brought in all those migrants ... y'know, those coons and spags.'

1982 *Sydney Morning Herald* 6 Aug. 10: 'Basically, we've got the wog problem under control ... we are aware of what these wogs, spags and dagoes want.'

sparrows (geese, peacocks, swallows) flying out of one's backside An expression for the male orgasm

1959 Gerard Hamilton *Summer Glare* 94: 'What's it like? ... You just wait, son. You'll think a flock of geese are flyin' out yer backside.'

1972 Geoff Morley *Jockey Rides Honest Race* 204: I exploded with feeling and a million sparrows flew out of my backside.

1977 Robert Close *Of Salt and Earth* 38: I clutched the girl passionately and jammed her against the truck. Then it seemed my navel sprang unscrewed, and a thousand peacocks flew backwards out of my arsehole.

1979 David Ireland *A Woman of the Future* 258: 'They said that when it happened I'd feel as if swallows were flying out of my arsehole.'

spaso See quot.

1979 David Ireland *A Woman of the Future* 55: The other word like para [q.v.] was spaso, short for spastic.

spear, get the To be sacked from a job [variant of the English 'get the bullet']

1912 'Goorianawa' *The Lone Hand* 1 Oct. 27 repr. in *Old Bush Songs* ed. Stewart and Keesing (1957) 273: I've been many years a shearer and I fancied I could shear, / I've shore for Rouse of Guntawang and always missed the spear.

spear To dismiss

1911 Steele Rudd *The Dashwoods* 13: 'If I was the boss here I would. I'd spear him without warnin'.'

spear tackle See quot. 1978

1978 *Sydney Morning Herald* 16 Mar. 7: There is nothing edifying about the spear tackle in Rugby League football – the player with the ball is inverted and goes down head first.

1983 *Sydney Morning Herald* 21 Apr. 28: There was one case a few years ago in which the victim was spear-tackled in a Rugby League Match in the country and became a paraplegic.

special A convict who is educated or well connected, and who is therefore given special treatment

1843 James Backhouse *A Narrative of a Visit to the Australian Colonies* 406: Port Macquarie ... still is a depot for that description of educated prisoners, denominated 'specials'.

1851 John Henderson *Excursions and Adventures in New South Wales* i 111: Port Macquarie, ever since it ceased to be exclusively a penal settlement, has been used as a *dépôt* for what are called 'specials'; that is, special, or *gentlemen* – convicts.

1867 John Morrison *Australia As It Is* 213–14: A laudable consideration was shown by the Government to a class of convicts belonging to what are usually styled 'the upper classes of society', and who were known by the name 'specials'. A settlement was set apart for them, and they were exempted from severe manual labour. One of them made himself very useful ... by teaching in families.

speck To search for gold in small quantities near the surface

1888 Henry Lawson 'His Father's Mate' *Prose* i 4:

A pick and shovel, and a gold dish ... with which he used to go 'a-speckin'' and 'fossickin'' amongst the old mullock heaps.
1901 May Vivienne *Travels in Western Australia* 171: Almost everyone in the camp went out for an afternoon's specking (looking on the ground for nuggets).
1932 K. S. Prichard *Kiss on the Lips* 219: Charley Beck and his old woman had specked a thirty-ounce slug.
1936 Ion L. Idriess *The Cattle King* 166: Next morning they picked up gold. In trembling excitement they 'specked' piece after piece.
1969 Alec H. Chisholm *The Joy of the Earth* 62: We even 'specked', in a certain street of the town following rain, on the way to school, and each of us carried a small round matchbox containing tiny 'specks' and tinier 'colours' of gold, which (in discreet moments) we displayed to each other in class. And, at times, we extended our specking activities to the scarred gullies beyond the town.
1978 *Australian* 4 Oct. 7: Now and then he reaches down for a piece of shale, spits on it, rubs it then casts it aside. He's specking [for opal].

Speck, the Tasmania [f. size in relation to mainland Australia]
1930 *Bulletin* 11 Jun. 21: N.S.W., V., Q., S.A., W.A. and the Speck.

speedo The odometer (mileage indicator) in a car
1969 Mena Calthorpe *The Defectors* 140: He glanced at the speedo ... He'd driven almost five miles.
1970 Richard Beilby *No Medals for Aphrodite* 33: We've done just on forty [miles] so far ... I'm not a complete dill! I can read a speedo!'
1978 *Bulletin* 3 Oct. 108: Winding back the speedo remains an Australian car sharp's practice, according to the latest Trade Practices Commission Report.

Speewa A legendary station used as the locale for tall tales of the outback
1944 Alan Marshall *These Are My People* 144: He suddenly grinned. 'I cooked on Speewa.' I had heard of Speewa, that mythical station used as a setting for all the lies put over on new-chums. I knew many of the tales, so I answered him: 'It's a big place. When I was there they had to get two Chinese to mix the mustard with long-handled shovels. The shearing shed was so long the boss rode up and down the board on horse-back.'
1951 Ernestine Hill *The Territory* 445: *On the Speewaa* A legendary station of doughty deeds – 'I bet that happened on the Speewaa'. The original Speewaa Station is near Swan Hill on the Murray River, home of great men and tall tales in the very earlies.

1966 Bill Wannan *Crooked Mick of the Speewah and Other Tall Tales* [book title]
1979 *Courier-Mail* (Brisbane) 12 May 1: Each [contestant] must tell a speerwah, or bush yarn, for more than four minutes.

spell *n.* A period of rest, interrupting work [f. *spell* a turn of work taken by a person ... in relief of another OED 1625]
c. **1845** James Tucker *Ralph Rashleigh* (1952) 140: Ralph taking one of their tools, Bob took another and worked awhile, to give the children a *spell*.
1847 Alexander Harris *Settlers and Convicts* ed. C. M. H. Clark (1954) 137: We were both of us glad of a day's spell. Ibid. 240: We could get our bullocks over it if we gave them a good long spell in the afternoon.
1861 Horace Earle *Ups and Downs* 214: After the dray had departed Tom declared his intention 'to take a bit of a spell, and have a pipe.'
1870 Marcus Clarke *His Natural Life* ed. S. Murray-Smith (1970) 607: 'Take a spell,' says Frere; 'you overwork yourself.'
1886 John Farrell 'My Sundowner' *How He Died* (1913) 65: I proposed that we should take a spell in / The shade of a big tree that stood alone.
1896 Edward Dyson *Rhymes from the Mines* 65: 'Twas good when 'spell-oh' had been said.
1903 William Craig *My Adventures on the Australian Goldfields* 108: With only a small portion of his claim worked out, but unable longer to resist his intense craving for strong drink, he decided to take a 'spell.'
1918 Harley Matthews *Saints and Soldiers* 84: They sat on a hill during a spell in their practice manoeuvres.
1930 Vance Palmer *The Passage* 59: During the days that followed there was little chance of a spell for anyone.
1942 Gavin Casey *It's Harder for Girls* 171: You've worked hard for a long time and ought to be able to afford a spell.
1980 *Sun-Herald* 1 Jun. 63: Happy Landing would have one more run and then go for a spell.
spelling paddock
1982 *Australian* 2 Jul. 18: At an age when most people would have retired to the spelling paddocks, he was able to undertake such a daunting task so successfully.

spell *v.* To rest from work
1846 J. L. Stokes *Discoveries in Australia* ii 42: In order to spell the oars, we landed at a point on the east side. [Morris]
1865 Rachel Henning *Letters* ed. David Adams (1963) 199: He went down to Mr Paterson's ... to 'spell' his horses before starting on a long journey southward.

1877 Rolf Boldrewood *A Colonial Reformer* (1891) 328: 'There's a hundred and fifty stock horses there, spelling for next winter's work.'
1892 Harry Morant 'Paddy Magee' *Bulletin* 20 Feb. 14: What are you doing now, Paddy Magee? / Grafting, or spelling now, Paddy Magee?
1908 W. H. Ogilvie *My Life in the Open* 42: The shearers' horses, which have been spelling girth-deep in the river grass, are run up to the yard.
1926 K. S. Prichard *Working Bullocks* 101: When the team had spelled a day Red brought the big whim into action.
1975 Xavier Herbert *Poor Fellow My Country* 1314: By rights the horses should have been spelled for a couple of days before being pushed further.
1981 A. B. Facey *A Fortunate Life* 81: A dingo had killed one and was in the act of dragging it away. The dingo kept stopping as the goose was heavy and it had to keep spelling itself.

spider Brandy with lemonade or ginger beer; a fizzy soft drink with icecream added
1854 C. H. Spence *Clara Morison* ii 67: 'I must have a nobbler or a spider to put me to rights.'
1859 Frank Fowler *Southern Lights and Shadows* 52: A *Spider* Lemonade and brandy.
1888 E. Finn *Chronicles of Early Melbourne* ii 548: The favourite tipple of the bushman was mixed brandy and ginger-beer – a 'spider', as it was called – for which 1s. 6d. was charged.
1861 Horace Earle *Ups and Downs* 283: They are neat dancers, good for an hour's polkaing at a stretch, and up to unlimited 'spiders', or lemonade and sherry.
[1920] Graham McInnes *The Road to Gundagai* (1965) 14: She reached for a thick yellow glass and poured in the ginger beer ... an enormous dollop of ice-cream which she dropped into the ginger beer. 'There's your spider.'
1942 Gavin Casey *It's Harder for Girls* 233, 4: 'You've had your drink, so now you've got to buy us all a spider at Smith's.' ... I didn't want to go back and sit in Smith's and drink silly coloured muck with ice-cream floating in it.
1962 Criena Rohan *The Delinquents* 122: Mavis had Sharon Faylene, clad only in a damp napkin, on her hip, and both were enjoying a raspberry spider.
1970 *Coast to Coast 1969–1970* 52: 'This calls for a celebration,' Alf said. 'I'll get you another straw and you can suck up the other side of my iniquitous coke-spider.'
1974 *Festival* ed. B. Buckley and J. Hamilton 127: 'You used to strut into the milk bar as though you owned the place. "A lime spider, Harry." "Harry" you called me!'
1983 John K. Ewers *Long Enough for a Joke* 53: 'Come over to the tuckshop lunchtime, Tiny! I'll

shout you a spider!'

spiel *v.* To move quickly (of a horse): *obs.* [E. dial. *speel* to run quickly OED]
[**1859** Hotten: *Speel,* to run away, make off.]
1888 A. B. Paterson 'Old Pardon, the Son of Reprieve' in *Singer of the Bush* (1983) 62: If Pardon don't spiel like tarnation / And win the next heat – if he can – / He'll earn a disqualification.
1905 'The Broken-down Squatter' in *The Old Bush Songs* ed. A. B. Paterson 56: No more shall we muster the river for fats, / Or spiel on the Fifteen-mile plain.

spiel *n.* 1 The dishonest scheme of a **spieler** 1
1932 William Hatfield *Ginger Murdoch* 175: 'I reckon you were thinking you had shaken me off, and could go about your spiel, whatever it is.'
1954 T. A. G. Hungerford *Sowers of the Wind* 174: 'This isn't a spiel, Colonel,' McNaughton said desperately ... 'I know this bloke, and he's on the level.'
2 The utterance of a **spieler** 2, a prepared line of talk
1957 Judah Waten *Shares in Murder* 62: 'I get you Brummel. Go on with your spiel.'
1962 Alan Marshall *This is the Grass* 125: Spruikers in braided uniforms strutted up and down before foyers extolling the virtues of the pictures within ... I often stood watching them, listening to every word of their spiel.
1971 Robin Miller *Flying Nurse* 69: I delivered my spiel and looked around, feeling as embarrassed as on my first day as a trainee in a Perth hospital ward.
1973 Max Harris *The Angry Eye* 180: 'He must be pretty dim to have fallen for that kind of spiel.'
1981 *Australian* 22 Jul. 22: In his official welcome to delegates, Alderman Sutherland gave a spirited spiel about the beauties of Sydney.

spieler 1 Someone who lives by his wits; a gambler, 'con-man' [f. G. *spielen* to play U.S. 1891 Mathews]
1885 *The Australasian Printers' Keepsake* 72: Who eyed Bob very suspiciously, muttering 'spieler' and 'Murrumbidgee whaler'.
1896 Henry Lawson 'Stiffner and Jim' *Prose* i 124: He was cracked on the subject of spielers. He held that the population of the world was divided into two classes – one was the spielers and the other was the mugs.
1901 Rolf Boldrewood *In Bad Company* 7: 'Those larrikins and spielers, that come up partly for work, and more for gambling and stealing.'
1921 K. S. Prichard *Black Opal* 27: 'Which one of us,' George Woods inquired, 'if a mate'd been set on by a spieler in Sydney, would've let him stump

his way to Brinarra and foot it out here?'
1935 H. R. Williams *Comrades of the Great Adventure* 234: The spielers worked the three-card trick on the 'mugs'.
1944 Alan Marshall *These Are My People* 81: 'A good spieler can pick his man,' he said. 'It's the greedy bloke they catch; the bunny that wants something for nothing.'
1957 Judah Waten *Shares in Murder* 156: You could match your wits against smart con-men and spielers.
2 A 'barker' for a sideshow; anyone with a plausible tongue [U.S. 1891 Mathews]
1975 Max Williams *The Poor Man's Bean* 33: A spieler calls, 'Come in; come on; come over.'

spill In politics, the declaring of a number of offices in the party vacant as a result of one vacancy occurring
1956 J. T. Lang *I Remember* 311: There had to be an annual election of leader. That made it inevitable that some members would intrigue against the leader hoping for a Cabinet spill.
1975 *Australian* 18 Mar. 1: It will be left to Mr Fraser's supporters to force the issue and move against Mr Snedden through either a spill of leadership positions or a motion of no confidence.

spin 1 A piece of experience (always with an adjective: 'rough spin', 'fair spin', etc.) [? f. *spin* for the toss of a coin OED 1882, or *spin* in various uses implying duration OED 1856, 1875]
1917 Diary entry 10 Jan. cit. in Bill Gammage *The Broken Years* (1974) 259: Out of the line at last ... by jove she's been a crook spin this trip.
1919 W. H. Downing *Digger Dialects* 47: Spin See trot. *Trot* An experience (e.g., 'a rough trot', 'a bad time').
1929 K. S. Prichard *Coonardoo* 188: Mollie had had a crook spin when the children were little.
1934 Vance Palmer *Sea and Spinifex* 247: 'It's about time I had a bit of luck. Me and Mary – we've had a pretty rough spin up till now.'
1942 Leonard Mann *The Go-Getter* 243: 'I had a rough spin during the depression and bad luck since.'
1957 Ray Lawler *Summer of the Seventeenth Doll* 121: 'I know you've 'ad a bad spin and I know you're all on edge.'
1964 H. P. Tritton *Time Means Tucker* 113: When I remarked that he'd had a tough spin he grinned. 'Served me right for being such a blanky fool.'
1974 Desmond O'Grady *Deschooling Kevin Carew* 107: He knew Kevin had had a rough spin since the withdrawal of the Education Department scholarship.
2 £5, esp. in gambling
1941 Baker 70: *Spin, spinnaker £5.*
1949 Lawson Glassop *Lucky Palmer* 15: 'Not a five

bob. A spin,' said the carpenter, fishing a five pound note out.
1953 *Caddie A Sydney Barmaid* 225: 'Yer got a spin,' he said, as I picked up a five-pound note.
1962 Stuart Gore *Down the Golden Mile* 261: 'Backed Sweet Friday for a spin,' replied Tug. 'But it never run a drum.'

spin out, to In two-up, to throw tails [f. the rule that the spinner backs heads]
1983 *Sun-Herald* 23 Jan. 35: Bluey ... once spun 13 heads before spinning out (threw tails).

spine basher, spine bashing A loafer (World War II slang): *obsolescent*
1944 Lawson Glassop *We Were the Rats* 208: 'She's sweet,' I said. 'Go and do some spine bashing.' Ibid. 175: Jim was spine bashing.
1946 Rohan Rivett *Behind Bamboo* 399: *Spine-basher*, one always on his back, always resting.
1946 Kylie Tennant *Lost Haven* 343: 'A bit of drill and a lot of spine-bashing.'
1948 Sumner Locke Elliott *Rusty Bugles* in *Khaki, Bush and Bigotry* ed. Eunice Hanger (1968) 49: 'A man's got to have a rest day, hasn't he?' 'Except of course when he's been spine-bashing the whole week.'
1976 *Sydney Morning Herald* 20 Mar. 14: The elbow-benders, spine-bashers, eternal babblers keep one ear to the loudspeakers, an ear to the ground.

spinifex wire Equivalent of a **mulga wire** q.v. in the spinifex country
1938 H. Drake-Brockman *Men Without Wives* (1955) 12: 'Whatever's a spinifex wire?' 'That's the way we get our news up here ... you'd be surprised how quickly it travels sometimes ... seems like magic. So we say it comes by spinifex wire ... across on the spinifex grass, you know.'

spinner, come in The cry in two-up that clears the way for the tossing of the coins, all bets having been placed
1945 Tom Ronan *Strangers on the Ophir* 119: Cries of 'Another quid to see him go. Get set on the side. All set, come in Spinner.'
1951 Dymphna Cusack and Florence James *Come In Spinner* [book title]
1965 Leslie Haylen *Big Red* 101: Outside he could hear the gamblers: 'Come on, I want a dollar in the guts.' 'Who'll put a dollar in the guts.' Laughter, shouts, and then silence. 'Come in spinner.'
1975 Les Ryan *The Shearers* 97: 'All set?' Lofty asked. 'Set!' Sandy said. 'Come in, spinner!'

spit, go for the big To vomit (given currency by the Barry McKenzie comic strip)
1967 Frank Hardy *Billy Borker Yarns Again* 40:

Don't tell me the Gargler went for the bit spit.
1973 Alexander Buzo *Rooted* 43: 'Remember the time he got sick at Davo's twenty-first and went for the big spit? He said to me "Jees I feel crook", and then he raced across the room, shoved his head out of the window and burped a rainbow.'
1975 Richard Beilby *The Brown Land Crying* 225: 'Goin' for the big spit, was I? I don't remember.'

spit chips, to   1   To be extremely thirsty
1901 *The Bulletin Reciter* 108: While you're spitting chips like thunder ... / And the streams of sweat near blind you.
[**1904** Laura M. Palmer-Archer *A Bush Honeymoon* 349: *Spit sixpences* A sign of thirst.]
1946 Alan Marshall *Tell us about the Turkey, Jo* 142: I was spitting chips. God, I was dry!
2   To be in a state of anger and frustration
1947 John Morrison *Sailors Belong Ships* 189: 'Old Mick Doyle's with them. He's spitting chips because they're not using sea water.'
1954 Peter Gladwin *The Long Beat Home* 17: 'It's enough to make you spit chips when you think of Sydney – movies and vaudeville comedies and a decent musician once in two years.'
1965 Ivan Southall *Ash Road* 77: 'Not when I saw Mr Fairhall last. He was spittin' chips because Peter had gone away.'
1983 *Weekend Australian* 15 Jan. Mag. 11: My spies tell me that at least two commercial firms which had tried – and failed – to persuade Pavarotti to visit Oz were spitting chips when the Australian Opera finally succeeded in getting him to come.

split, the (great)   The split in the Labor Party in 1955 which was marked by the formation of the DLP
1970 Kylie Tennant *Evatt* 338: After the election Evatt was again elected leader of the Parliamentary Labour Party by 58 votes to 20 ... The Party was settling into shape after the split.
1977 Fred Daly *From Curtin to Kerr* 132: The Split [chapter heading]
1984 *Sydney Morning Herald* 30 Jun. 13: The Great Split has become the great hate of the Labor Party.

sport   A form of colloquial address
1923 George S. Beeby *Concerning Ordinary People* 305: 'All right, sport. No offence meant.'
1941 Kylie Tennant *The Battlers* 105: 'Now lay off, sport.'
1943 George Johnston *New Guinea Diary* 186: Before they have been there long they are calling them [the natives] 'sport', which seems to be the second A.I.F.'s equivalent for 'digger'.
1952 Eric Lambert *The Twenty Thousand Thieves* 38: 'Have a swig, sport.' He took the bottle ... and

helped himself to a mouthful. 'Thanks, sport.' He handed the bottle back and idly he noted that he never called a man 'sport' before.
1961 Hugh Atkinson *Low Company* 46: 'Whatyer tryin' to do, sport? Pull me leg?'
1975 Richard Beilby *The Brown Land Crying* 80: 'Come on, sport,' the doorman was saying patiently. 'You can't stop here. You've had a skinful.'

sport back on the front page, to get   Paraphrase of a remark by Mr Malcolm Fraser during the 1975 election campaign, to indicate a desirable state of political stability
1975 *National Times* 1 Dec. 12: On the Sydney radio station, 2SM, Mr Fraser responded to one question about the turbulence of the last three years by remarking on the placidity of the long Liberal regime. 'It may have been dull,' he said, 'but I'm not sure they didn't prefer to have a dull government so they could go straight to the sports pages and not have to worry about what the politicians were doing.'
1975 *Sun-Herald* 28 Dec. 21: During the election campaign he [Mr Fraser] said he wanted Australia again to become a place where people didn't need to snatch their morning newspapers to learn about the latest broadside from Canberra. He said he wanted a country where people could turn straight to the sporting pages without fear.
1980 *Weekend Australian* 26 Jan. 5: If Mr Fraser's determination to 'put sport on the front page' was regarded as something of a cynical exercise at the time it is certainly no less cynical than the demand by sporting leaders to keep 'politics out of sport'.
1982 *Sydney Morning Herald* 23 Oct. 13: After the 1975 election, when Fraser wanted to wind down an over-excited electorate, he expressed the hope that sport would return to the front page.
1984 *Weekend Australian* 28 Jan. 12: All right thinking, sports-minded, dinki-di Aussies should raise their arms in gratitude to the Prime Minister [Mr Hawke]. In less than 12 months, he has done what Malcolm Fraser vowed to do but failed to achieve in seven years – put sport back on the front page of our national dailies.

spruik   To hold forth like a showman [unexplained]
1915 C. J. Dennis *The Songs of a Sentimental Bloke* 42: 'E'll sigh and spruik, an' 'owl a love-sick vow – / (The silly cow!)
1916 C. J. Dennis *The Moods of Ginger Mick* 156: *Spruik* To deliver a speech, as a showman.
1920 Louis Esson 'The Woman Tamer' in *Dead Timber* 19: 'Don't be all day spruikin'.'
1934 Vance Palmer *The Swayne Family* 250: 'Wonder you didn't get a job spruiking for the pictures down there in town.'

1941 Kylie Tennant *The Battlers* 181: The ampster's is an easy job. He stands in the front row of the listening crowd registering intense interest and enthusiasm while the showman 'spruiks'.
1951 A. W. Upfield *The Widows of Broome* 31: 'Old Bilge's bound to do a bit of spruiking, but he isn't too bad.'
1975 Hal Porter *The Extra* 244: Hollow-chested men ... who sell agitated toys on street corners or spruik outside strip-tease joints.

spruiker A speaker attracting custom outside a theatre or sideshow; any loquacious person
1924 *Truth* 27 Apr. 6: *Spruiker* A speaker.
1934 Tom Clarke *Marriage at 6 a.m.* 46: *Spruiker* an announcer at the door of a theatre.
1951 Dal Stivens *Jimmy Brockett* 82: A spruiker outside was dressed up like a train conductor and he told you about the tour.
1962 Alan Marshall *This is the Grass* 125: Spruikers in braided uniforms strutted up and down before foyers extolling the virtues of the pictures within.
1964 H. P. Tritton *Time Means Tucker* 33: Madam Cora, a fortune teller, had a long line of people waiting their turn ... Her husband, a pudgy little man, was her spruiker.
1971 Craig McGregor *Don't Talk to me about Love* 159: He declaimed in the voice of a Royal Easter Show spruiker.
1981 *National Times* 11 Jan. 6: Not only has Ellicott contrived the new tax breaks to the advantage of film makers, he is also a spruiker extraordinaire for Australian movies ... Those who have attended showings at which Ellicott has acted as spruiker are hard put to decide which is more intoxicating: Ellicott's Methodist lay preacher eloquence or the cocktails which are served.

spud, not the clean see **potato**
1925 E. S. Sorenson *Murty Brown* 135: 'He wasn't the clean spud.'

spunk Someone attractive to the opposite sex, esp. a male [f. *spunk* semen]
1979 Kathy Lette and Gabrielle Carey *Puberty Blues* 5: It was Darren Peters – the top surfing spunk of sixth form.
1981 *Age* (Melbourne) 21 Aug. Weekender 11: The show attracts a lot of 'spunk mail' from younger viewers (i.e. Dear John, you are a real spunk, please send me a photo).
1982 *Sydney Morning Herald* 18 Sep. 1: Teenagers still rage at weekends, check out spunks of both sexes and try to avoid hassles with the olds.

spunky Attractive sexually
1975 Barry Humphries *A Nice Night's Entertainment* (1981) 149: 'I just intercepted a memo at the

Film Finance Council and they've okayed another eight grand for you to develop the synopsis of a film as yet unwritten. Isn't that spunky?'
1979 *National Times* 17 Nov. 54: 'When we were surfie chicks they used to drive past yelling sexual insults to us. Now we drive past and yell "Eh, spunky!"'
1984 *Sydney Morning Herald* 6 Oct. Mag. 28: Gynaecologists in Sydney have been known to leave their wives for younger, spunkier patients.

square dinkum see **dinkum**

squat To take up land like a **squatter** q.v.
1827 P. Cunningham *Two Years in New South Wales* ii 162: They have therefore nothing to lose and much to gain by new settlers 'squatting' near their locations.
1835 G. F. Moore *Diary of ... an Early Settler in Western Australia* (1884) 279: Old Mr Henty has 'squatted' himself on an unlocated district along the coast outside of this territory, at Portland Bay.
1836 *HRV* i 65: There are numerous settlers here called 'Squatters' who rear and graze large flocks of sheep in any part of the country they choose to occupy ... when the Sydney Government finally make a settlement here, these men will have to purchase from the Crown, at a great cost, the land they now live on, or else wander further in shore without the limits of the new colony, and 'squat' elsewhere.
1840 Let. in *No Place for a Nervous Lady* ed. Lucy Frost (1984) 90: Everything was most exorbitantly high when we 'squatted' (i.e. settling on Government land & not purchasing it –) and we determined not to get into debt.

squattage The holding of a squatter
1864 William Westgarth *The Colony of Victoria* 272: Here we are in ... the great Riverine district, which is one vast series of squattages, with a total area greater than that of Victoria twice told.
1883 W. A. Brodribb *Recollections of an Australian Squatter* 57: The squatters commenced to erect permanent improvements on their squattages, and they pushed further into the interior ... The traveller would meet highly respectable ladies with their families located on their squattages in comfortable houses, very happy and contented.
1901 Rolf Boldrewood *In Bad Company* 476: We pass Bungawannah, one of the large estates, formerly squattages, which alternate with the farms and smaller pastoral holdings.
1911 E. S. Sorenson *Life in the Australian Backblocks* 223: The majority [of selectors] took contracts to keep the pot boiling – working on the roads and squattages, droving, horse-breaking.
1928 Miles Franklin (Brent of Bin Bin) *Up the

Country 10: Philip would have been at variance with his generation and environment if, in weighing a slice of his father's squattage against that rare prize a comely maid, the scales had not gone down with a bump.

squatter 1 Someone taking up his abode in the bush and living by preying on the flocks of others, dealing in sly grog, etc. [f. *squatter* One who settles upon land, esp. public land, to which he has no legal title U.S. 1788 Mathews]

1830 J. Betts *An Account of the Colony of Van Diemen's Land* 39: The means of rooting out a class of people called 'Squatters'. These were generally emancipated convicts, or ticket-of-leave-men, who, having obtained a small grant, under the old system, or without any grant at all, sat themselves down in remote situations, and maintained large flocks, obtained, generally, in very nefarious ways, by having the run of all the surrounding country.

1833 W. H. Breton *Excursions in New South Wales* 442: There are likewise in the colony certain persons called 'squatters' (the term is American) who are commonly, it may be said always, of the lowest grade. These men establish themselves on some unlocated spot, where they cultivate enough land to supply them with grain, and not unfrequently pilfer whatever else they require, from the neighbouring farms.

1835 *Sydney Gazette* 28 Apr. 2: In every part of the country squatters without any reasonable means of maintaining themselves by honesty, have formed stations, and evidently pursued a predatory warfare against the flocks and herds in the vicinity.

2 A respectable pastoralist; a pastoralist occupying a tract of land with a licence from the Crown (from 1836)

1835 G. F. Moore *Diary of ... an Early Settler in Western Australia* (1884) 275: A squatter – that is a person who would go beyond the locations and occupy any ground that would answer his purpose – might do well here with a large flock, but he must be contented with a rude house or a tent, cultivate only such ground as would give him wheat and vegetables; live much upon the produce of his dogs and his guns; drive his surplus stock occasionally to market, with his wool also; and take back little necessaries, comforts and luxuries.

1840 Gov. Gipps to Lord Russell *HRA* xxi 130: A very large proportion of the land, which is to form the new district of Port Phillip, is already in the licensed occupation of the Squatters of New South Wales, a class of persons whom it would be wrong to confound with those who bear the same name in America, and who are generally persons of mean repute and small means, who have taken unauthorized possession of patches of land. Among the Squatters of New South Wales are the wealthiest of the Land, occupying with the permission of Government thousands and tens of thousands of acres; Young men of good Family and connexions in England, Officers of the Army and Navy, Graduates of Oxford and Cambridge are also in no small number amongst them.

1848 J. C. Byrne *Twelve Years' Wanderings in the British Colonies* i 186: Squatting in New South Wales, is the occupation without purchase of the Crown lands, within the boundaries of the colony, and of the vast extent of territory beyond the frontiers, or rather old line of demarcation. A squatter obtains his temporary right to what land he requires by producing a licence from the Crown land Commissioners in the colony, for which he pays annually, the sum of £10; besides being subject to a small annual assessment on his sheep, cattle and horses, for the support of a border police. The squatters are the great producing class of the colony: their vast herds and flocks out-number by many degrees the scanty numbers depastured on the purchased, or granted, land of the country.

1888 H. S. Russell *The Genesis of Queensland* 162–3: The circumstances of the time were combining in 1840 to compel the squatters of the northern district into some more genial climate ... Some who had bought stations there were already seeking, and at times, finding purchasers for what dissatisfied themselves: albeit held under the easy rent of an annual ten pound licence – for ever! as it seemed – with a small assessment upon their stock ... The term 'squatter', as applied to the class it now designates, was not in vogue until two years after this.

3 A pastoral magnate, whether occupying land as tenant of the Crown or as owner, regarded as one of the privileged or affluent

1900 Let. of 21 Sep. in *Audrey Tennyson's Vice-Regal Days* ed. Alexandra Hasluck (1978) 118: Squatters in the colonies are our aristocracy – as being the people who came out from home in early days. 'Oh he is an old squatter, or, she is a daughter of a squatter' means that nothing more need be asked.

1902 Henry Lawson 'Lord Douglas' *Prose* i 494: 'You're allers findin' excuses for blacklegs an' scabs, Mitchell,' said Barcoo-Rot ... 'Why, you'd find a white spot on a squatter.'

1908 E. S. Sorenson *The Squatter's Ward* 187: Mr Susman was a squatter, and as such to be held above suspicion.

1934 Tom Clarke *Marriage at 6 a.m.* 46: *Squatter* a station owner (corresponds almost to 'squire' in English).

1940 Arnold L. Haskell *Waltzing Matilda* 109: The majority of wealthy squatters (read 'landed gentry') have gained their first experience in this manner as jackaroos (read 'apprentices') on some vast station.

1958 H. D. Williamson *The Sunlit Plain* 42: She might have been a squatter's wife, the way she was dressed, Leo reflected.

squatterdom

1963 Xavier Herbert *Larger Than Life* 94: There is now no 'done thing' in the doings of squatterdom half so classy as an 'eagle shoot'.

squatter's chair A canvas-backed chair with the arm-rests extended to support the full length of the legs

1961 Noni Braham *The Interloper* 5: She flung herself into one of the squatters' chairs, stretched out her legs on its extended arms.

1982 *Sydney Morning Herald* 3 Jul. 29: Membership of the Queensland Club puts you at the top of Queensland's highly structured social heap. From the squatters' chairs on its balconies, one can look across Alice Street onto the Botanical Gardens, a riot of tropicality snuggling into a bend in the lolling Brisbane River.

squattocracy The squatters (senses 2 and 3) collectively regarded as a colonial aristocracy, often with a derogatory implication

1846 C. P. Hodgson *Reminiscences of Australia* 118: Throughout the Colony generally English are the most numerous, then the Scotch, then the Irish, amongst the squattocracy.

1852 William Hughes *The Australian Colonies* 124: The aristocracy (or the *squattocracy*) of the colonies.

1865 Henry Kingsley *The Hillyars and the Burtons* iii 265: A miserable and effete Squattocracy (with their wretched aping of the still more miserable and effete aristocracy of the old world).

1888 E. Finn *The Chronicles of Early Melbourne* ii 908: Though presented himself as a Colonial Emissary in England, he was veritably an agent of the 'squattocracy', of which he was one. On the Transportation question he lent himself to promote the interests of the few against the many.

1891 Francis Adams *Fortnightly Review* Sep. 398: One has not endured all these years the rule of the squattocracy, as voiced in a hopelessly subservient and corrupt legislature, for nothing.

1902 Mrs Campbell Praed *My Australian Girlhood* 217: My lady did not enter into effusive social relations with the selectors not specially accredited to her. The was perhaps hardly to be expected in one who, as a representative of the old order, was traditionally opposed to the inroads of agriculturalist upon privileges of the squattocracy.

1919 E. S. Sorenson *Chips and Splinters* 17: He talked like that at his timber-camp meetings, but the timber-getters noticed that he wore a different coat when he was among the squattocracy.

1939 Miles Franklin and Dymphna Cusack *Pion-*

eers on Parade 2–3: She had canonized anyone who held more than ten thousand acres, and lumped pure merinos and the poorer goats in the one romantic squirearchy known as the squattocracy.

1951 Dymphna Cusack and Florence James *Come In Spinner* 30: 'She's turning on the dentures for the benefit of some of the squattocracy in the Madrid Lounge.'

1975 Hal Porter *The Extra* 91: Here, you find Petty's Hotel, once the haunt of squattocracy, now a Red Cross Blood Transfusion Centre.

1982 *NT News* (Darwin) 11 Jan. 7: We do not need a taxpayers' subsidised squattocracy.

squib *n.* 1 A coward, or someone lacking in nerve [f. *squib* a mean, insignificant or paltry fellow OED 1586–1653 *obs.*]

1924 *Truth* 27 Apr. 6: *Squib* A coward.

1936 Archer Russell *Gone Nomad* 55: 'There's no place in this town for squibs', he was told.

1942 Gavin Casey *It's Harder for Girls* 200: 'He shut up, just like th' bloody squib he is.'

1959 Vance Palmer *The Big Fellow* 201: 'There's nothing I care a damn about', he said, 'except the charge of being a squib.'

1969 D'Arcy Niland *Dead Men Running* 26: 'You're a squib, son. You're yellow.'

1978 Richard Beilby *Gunner* 40: 'Anyone who wouldn't fight after two glasses of that is a squib', he pronounced gravely.

2 A horse without staying power, esp. in the expression 'speedy squib'

1923 Con Drew *Rogues & Ruses* 107: 'He's only a long-legged squib.'

1984 *Sun-Herald* 26 Feb. 78: It has been said, among other things, that the Golden Slipper is a race for speedy squibs.

squib *v.*

1938 Eric Lowe *Salute to Freedom* 222: 'Was there ever a more glaring example of squibbing?' ... He wanted to stand up and shout that it was Smoke not himself that had squibbed, but that would only make matters worse.

1959 Vance Palmer *The Big Fellow* 227: 'Not going to squib at the last moment, is he?'

1977 Vera Deacon in *Depression Down Under* ed. Len Fox 96: Mr Mac. would not let me 'squib' anything. Dare I hang back in sport, he would urge me to leap higher as basketball centre.

1984 *Sydney Morning Herald* 23 Feb. 9: The Treasury-types' eternal search for 'a politician with some guts' is futile. Mr Fraser looked tough enough at the time, but he squibbed.

squib it

1918 George Dale *The Industrial History of Broken Hill* 170: All the employers had agreed to fight the Union, but had squibbed it at the last moment.

1939 Herbert M. Moran *Viewless Winds* 43: In the decalogue of our Rugby there were two commandments on which you were judged and condemned. They were: 'Thou shalt not squib it', and again: 'Thou shalt not squeal'.

1949 Lawson Glassop *Lucky Palmer* 222: 'What, are yous squibbin' it?' asked the man incredulously.

1960 John Iggulden *The Storms of Summer* 95: 'Ya reckon I ought to squib it do ya?'

1978 Keith Garvey *Tales of My Uncle Harry* 22: Tiger's supporters couldn't believe that their champion had squibbed it.

squiz   An inquisitive look [? f. *squint + quiz*]

1913 C. J. Dennis *Backblock Ballads* 199: *Squiz* a glance.

1924 *Truth* 27 Apr. 6: *Squiz* A hurried look.

1946 Dal Stivens *The Courtship of Uncle Henry* 69: He put the chops down and took a squiz at me.

1948 K. S. Prichard *Golden Miles* 97: 'Was jest goin' to send for you to have a squiz at her.'

1968 Geoffrey Dutton *Andy* 282: 'You're mad, you blokes, not to go and have a decent squiz at it.'

1975 Don Townshend *Gland Time* 142: He put his hand in his pocket and produced a small box. 'Have a squiz at that.'

1978 Barry Humphries *A Nice Night's Entertainment* (1981) 174: I gets a sqizz through the curtain at first class and there's Rupert bloody Murdoch and Kerry Packer poncing around with glasses of champagne in their hands.

SS   Social Security i.e. the payments to the unemployed and others

1982 Jack Davis *The Dreamers* 132: 'Lend me five bucks.' 'Here you are. I don't mind collecting it out of your next SS.'

stack on   To put on, 'stage', perpetrate (usu.) an *act, blue, turn*

1949 Lawson Glassop *Lucky Palmer* 175: 'Don't stack on no blue', he said. 'I'm runnin' this game and I'm runnin' it proper.'

1952 T. A. G. Hungerford *The Ridge and the River* 21: 'I guess I must have stacked on a turn. I'm sorry.'

1969 Mena Calthorpe *The Defectors* 11: She was prettier than he had thought, swinging about on her heels and stacking on an act.

1970 Jack Hibberd *White with Wire Wheels* in Penguin *Plays* 159: 'How was she? Stacking on a turn?' 'Not Sue. She's as placid as they come.'

1981 *Weekend Australian* 21 Nov. Mag. 19: For reasons best known to himself, Mr Bjelke-Petersen stacked on a turn and the negotiations broke down.

staggering bob   see **bob**

stand   The place allocated to one man on the board of a shearing shed, with the accompanying equipment

1901 Rolf Boldrewood *In Bad Company* 21: 'It's hard on a chap, when he comes to a shed after travellin' three or four 'undred mile, to be told that all the stands is took up.'

1911 E. S. Sorenson *Life in the Australian Backblocks* 227: Stands are sometimes booked weeks and months prior to date of shearing, applications being accompanied in many cases with a sovereign as a guarantee of good faith.

1955 'I Don't Go Shearing Now' in *Australian Bush Ballads* ed. Stewart and Keesing 246: You will pay an early visit to the dear old shed, I'll bet – / Perhaps upon your own old stand the oil-rag's lying yet.

1964 Tom Ronan *Packhorse and Pearling Boat* 147: There was a shearing shed with eight stands rapidly disintegrating from the combined effects of white ants, rust and general neglect.

1973 John Morrison *Australian by Choice* 43: 'Last time I saw Colin he had a stand next to me on Quiremong.'

stand over *v.*   To extort money etc. by intimidation; to domineer over someone

1939 Kylie Tennant *Foveaux* 173: 'I just had Thompson in here and he stood over me for three quid.'

1950 *The Australian Police Journal* Apr. 119: *Stand over* To threaten, menace, or use duress on someone for the purpose of gain.

1952 T. A. G. Hungerford *The Ridge and the River* 209: 'Wilder'll be the poor down-trodden guy that's being stood over.'

1958 Frank Hardy *The Four-Legged Lottery* 192: We'll have to stand over him to get our money.

standover *n. & a.*   An intimidatory operation

1939 Kylie Tennant *Foveaux* 180: ''Struth, you earn your money on a stand over,' he told himself.

1954 L. H. Evers *Pattern of Conquest* 198: 'Don't come the stand-over tactics you used with Charlie.'

1957 Judah Waten *Shares in Murder* 63: 'He can't come this standover on me. He's got nothing on me and you know it.'

standover man   A criminal using force, or the threat of force, to intimidate or extort

1939 Kylie Tennant *Foveaux* 174: He didn't deserve to be a 'standover man' if he couldn't move quicker.

1951 Dymphna Cusack and Florence James *Come In Spinner* 355–6: It was Joe's bodyguard, Curly – stand-over man as well, they said.

1957 Judah Waten *Shares in Murder* 79: He might

end up as a common bully, a standover man.

1962 Alan Marshall *This is the Grass* 60: I guessed he was a stand-over merchant and that he had brought these two men with him like a hunter who goes out with his dogs.

1975 *Bulletin* 26 Apr. 44: The heavies (stand over men) and the bludgers who neither worked nor stole but were simply professional parasites.

stanza A half or quarter in a football match [U.S. Wentworth & Flexner]

1978 *Australian* 19 Jun. 25: St George ... were aided in their fightback by a huge 12–2 penalty count in the second stanza.

1981 *Canberra Times* 21 Sep. 16: Both sides looked nervous in the opening stanza.

1984 *Age* (Melbourne) 16 Apr. 24: Experience was going to tell. Well experience did, in the last stanza, but not in the way I'd imagined.

Star Hotel See quot. 1941

1905 E. C. Buley *Australian Life in Town and Country* 54: The rags that serve him for socks are 'Prince Alberts'; he lodges each night in 'The Moon and Stars Hotel, ground floor.'

1941 Baker 71: *Star Hotel, sleep in the* To sleep in the open.

1942 Charles Barrett *From a Bush Hut* 37: Spreading our blankets on stony ground – there wasn't a soft spot within miles – we slept at the Inn of Stars.

starve the bardies see **bardies**

starver A saveloy

1941 Baker 71: *Starver* A saveloy.

1959 D'Arcy Niland *The Big Smoke* 211: 'I know what the things I eat cost me. Starvers, crumpets, stale cakes, specked fruit, pies.'

State of Excitement Western Australia: slogan for vehicle registration plates adopted in 1979 in the 150th anniversary celebrations, replaced in 1983 by 'WA – Home of the America's Cup'

1979 *Herald* (Melbourne) 25 Apr. 2: Some West Australians are obviously finding things duller in their State than their slogan 'State of Excitement' would lead tourists to believe.

1982 *Sun-Herald* 5 Dec. 98: The West Australians who have cornered the cricket commentary market such as Ian Brayshaw, Dennis Cometti and Norm O'Neill, the last a New South Welshman who is still in a state of excitement following many years in Perth.

1983 Fay Zwicky *Hostages* 83: *This Week in Perth* tells you to 'Relax in a State of Excitement'.

station, there's movement at the Expression for hurried activity, esp. portending some imminent event [f. the opening line of A. B. Paterson's 'The Man from Snowy River' (There was movement at the station, for the word had passed around) 1895]

1918 George Dale *The Industrial History of Broken Hill* 79: He is still the rebel of yore, and is seen in the forefront of any movement on the station for the betterment of conditions.

1966 Tom Ronan *Once There was A Bagman* 225: There was movement on the station, of course, as soon as old Harry showed over the skyline.

1974 'Ah, now there's movement at the station' (racing broadcaster reporting signs that a race was about to begin).

1976 *Sun-Herald* 18 Jan. 84: Movement at the station. Mr Rex Palmer, 2GB's general manager for the past 18 months, left on Friday to head Adelaide's fledgling 'good music' station, 5AA.

1984 Paul Kelly *The Hawke Ascendancy* 339: By Monday 13 December Hayden had received sufficient reports to know trouble was brewing. Bowen had told him earlier: 'Watch it, there's movement at the station.'

statistics, the In football, the count of points scored, errors made, tackles completed, penalties awarded, scrum wins etc., according to the code

1978 David Williamson *The Club* 23: 'He only got twelve kicks last week. I saw the statistics.'

1979 *Advertiser* (Adelaide) 11 Jun. 14: Statistics illustrate his dominance – 35 hit outs, 11 marks, four hand-passes and 23 kicks.

1984 *Age* (Melbourne) 17 Sep. 23: An assessment of statistics at half-time indicated that Ezard, Neagle and Watson were the damaging players for Essendon.

steam Cheap wine; methylated spirits

1941 Baker 71: *Steam* Cheap wine, esp. laced with methylated spirits.

1953 T. A. G. Hungerford *Riverslake* 185: 'I've got a bottle of steam if you'd like a snort, Kerry.'

1958 H. D. Williamson *The Sunlit Plain* 145: 'Steam?' Smithy had never heard of it. 'Steam, yes. Plonk. Bombo. You sell it, don't you?'

1968 Stuart Gore *Holy Smoke* 60: 'Top quality plonk ... Not this round-the-world-for-a-dollar steam that *you* go for.'

1978 Max Richards *Sadie and Neco* in *Can't You Hear Me Talking to You?* ed. Alrene Sykes 147: *Neco* Is that bottle of steam still there? ... *Sadie* What bottle? *Neco* The Meths.

steamed up In a temper, in a state of excitement

1941 Baker 71: *Steamed up, get* To become angry or frenzied.

1953 T. A. G. Hungerford *Riverslake* 109: 'Holy cow, was he steamed up!'

1966 Roger Carr *Surfie* 80: I just sat around the kitchen thinking and getting all steamed up,

mostly at her folks pushing me around and making me stay the night.
1984 *Age* (Melbourne) 16 Apr. 24: 'We were prepared to see St Kilda come out steamed up after what happened last week', said Quade.

steamer   1   Kangaroo meat cooked with pork: *obs.*
1820 C. Jeffreys *Geographical ... Delineations of the Island of Van Diemen's Land* 69: Their meal consisted of the hind-quarters of a kangaroo cut into mince-meat, stewed in its own gravy, with a few rashers of salt pork, this dish is commonly called a steamer.
1834 George Bennett *Wanderings in New South Wales* i 289: The colonial dish called a steamer, consists of the flesh of this animal [kangaroo] dressed, with slices of ham.
1843 Charles Rowcroft *Tales of the Colonies* i 134: The tenderest parts, and those most free from the tendons and fibres with which the flesh of the kangaroo abounds, were carefully cut out, and chopped up fine; some slices of salt pork were added to this, and the whole put to steam slowly over the fire. This national dish of Van Diemen's Land bush is called a 'Steamer'.
2   Clash of two sporting teams marked by rough play
1978 *Sunday Telegraph* (Sydney) 9 Apr. 60: Cook takes 'steamer' off the boil [heading]

steam, like   Rapidly, vigorously, energetically
1905 Henry Lawson 'The Shearer's Dream' *Verse* ii 4: 'We was draftin' 'em out for the homeward track and sharin' 'em round like steam, / When I woke with my head in the blazin' sun to find 'twas a shearer's dream'.
1923 Con Drew *Rogues & Ruses* 180: 'Sparkle's got a break on the field and is leatherin' it out like steam.'
1944 Lawson Glassop *We Were the Rats* 129: 'We reefed watches and rings off 'em like steam.' Ibid. 179: 'She comes across. Turns it on like steam. She pulls her dress off.'
1969 Patsy Adam-Smith *Folklore of the Australian Railwaymen* 151: We'd been working like steam in the van to get things ready for our arrival.
1979 Bobbie Hardy *The World Owes Me Nothing* 102: I hammered at the door like steam and over he came and opened it.

Steel City   1   Newcastle, N.S.W. [f. steel industry]
1983 *Weekend Australian* 12 Feb. Mag. 16: A grim future faces thousands more families as BHP's retrenchments bite deeper into the heart of Australia's Steel City. Alan Goodall Reports from Newcastle.
2   Wollongong, N.S.W.
1982 *Sydney Morning Herald* 6 Nov. 30: Pullen

has been saying for a long time that tourism is Wollongong's only way out ... he aims to turn Steel City into a new Gold Coast.

Steelers, the   The Illawarra Rugby League Club, whose home ground is in Wollongong, 'the Steel City'
1982 *Sun-Herald* 7 Feb. 73: Lack of playing depth, and an inadequate home ground, will be two of the biggest problems for the Illawarra Rugby League Club in their first year in the Sydney premiership. The Steelers' home ground, Wollongong Showground, with a capacity of about 13,000, could be taxed to the limit at some home matches this season.

steer, the red   see **red**

sterks, the   The shits [see **sterky**]
1959 David Forrest *The Last Blue Sea* 24: 'He just gives me the sturks.'
1968 Stuart Gore *Holy Smoke* 26: 'You'd give a man the sterks, bludgin' there in bed as if it was the Palace Hotel.'

sterky   As for **packing them** q.v.: *rare* [abbr. of *stercoraceous*]
1944 Jean Devanny *By Tropic, Sea and Jungle* 162: The croc disappears, and there's Ernest, standing up to his waist in the water, looking for him – scared as hell, but too game to come out. He yells for us to come in ourselves, so my dad goes in. He's a bit sterky too.
1953 Baker 104: *sterky* frightened.

sterling   English immigrants, as distinct from the native born [see quot. 1827]
1827 P. Cunningham *Two Years in New South Wales* ii 53: Our colonial-born brethren are best known here by the name of *Currency*, in contradistinction to *Sterling*, or those born in the mother-country.
1844 Louisa Meredith *Notes and Sketches of New South Wales* 50: The natives (not the aborigines, but the 'currency', as they are termed, in distinction from the 'sterling', or British-born residents) are often very good-looking when young.
see **currency**

stick, more than one could poke (shake) a ~ at   An inordinate amount
1905 Joseph Furphy *Rigby's Romance* ed. R. G. Howarth (1946) 42: '"What the (adj. sheol) did you want fetchin' us out of Egypt, where we had as much meat and vegetables as you could shake a stick at?" says they.'
1944 Lawson Glassop *We Were the Rats* 104: 'I been in more drums than ya could poke a stick at', he said.

1958 H. D. Williamson *The Sunlit Plain* 142: 'I'm going bush for a month, and then I'll be back with more skins than you could poke a stick at.'
1967 Frank Hardy *Billy Borker Yarns Again* 15: Your tips have cost me more money than I could poke a stick at.

stick one's bib in   see **bib**

sticker licker   A parking policeman in S.A.
1982 *Bulletin* 2 Mar. 32: Sticker lickers in South Australia are called brown bombers in New South Wales.

sticks, the   The rural areas generally, or anywhere so regarded [*the sticks* the backwoods U.S. 1905 Mathews]
1958 Christopher Koch *The Boys in the Island* 101: 'Still,' he said with a chuckle, 'what can y' expect, way out here in the sticks? You would pick on a dame from back of beyond.'
1962 Criena Rohan *The Delinquents* 19: Back to the God-awful little town in the sticks.
1971 Frank Hardy *The Outcasts of Foolgarah* 5: A shire clerk's job in the sticks for three years' practice then back to the big smoke, into the big league.
1983 Fay Zwicky *Hostages* 85: It's the sticks. They have outside dunnies there.
see **scrub**

sticky   Inquisitive [abbr. of *stickybeak*]
1941 Baker 72: *Sticky* (adj.) Curious, inquisitive.
1974 David Ireland *Burn* 139: 'Have a gander. Perhaps your mates'd like a bit of sticky too.'

stickybeak *n.*   An inquisitive person (sticking his beak in)
1924 Steele Rudd *Me an' th' Son* 7: 'Did y' hurt yourself – sticky-beak?' he sez.
1926 J. Vance Marshall *Timely Tips for New Australians: Sticky-beak* A slang term denoting an inquisitive person.
1938 *Bulletin* 6 Jul. 48: 'Then you'll spoil your life and hers for what some old stickybeak and scandalcat has said.'
1947 Margaret Trist *Daddy* 262: 'Well, if he's not the biggest stickybeak of a man I've ever met,' Lydia murmured.
1953 *Caddie A Sydney Barmaid* 25: The sticky-beaks were dying to know who was the father of the baby, but Nellie wouldn't tell.
1961 Xavier Herbert *Soldier's Women* 471: This clever girl, who had probably spent her life lying to sticky-beaks interfering in her affairs, had it all worked out.
1980 *Mercury* (Hobart) 23 Jun. 6: Being natural stickybeaks, we also phoned the number to see what was so strange.

stickybeak *v.*   To act as a stickybeak, to pry into the affairs of others
1935 Kylie Tennant *Tiburon* 111: 'Ain't I got enough trouble,' he roared, 'with them sticky-beakin' round 'ere gettin' me up before the court.'
1945 Margaret Trist *Now That We're Laughing* 142: 'It's so good of them to come.' 'Why is it?' demanded Mrs Henderson. 'They only come to stickybeak.'
1957 Judah Waten *Shares in Murder* 83: 'Why don't you stop stickybeaking?'
1968 *Coast to Coast 1967–1968* 9: 'I don't have to put up with you and your sticky-beaking into my affairs.'

sticky nose   As for **stickybeak**
1966 H. F. Brinsmead *The Beat of the City* 62: 'At first I followed them in just to be a sticky nose.'

stiff   Out of luck
1919 W. H. Downing *Digger Dialects* 27: *Stiff* Unlucky.
1922 Arthur Wright *A Colt from the Country* 124: 'On'y just got cut out of second place,' declared Knocker. 'Ain't a man stiff?'
1945 Cecil Mann *The River* 137: It's damn' stiff you can't march this year, but you will next year.
1955 John Morrison *Black Cargo* 64: 'You're stiff,' cut in Boyd, 'my time's up at five.'
1970 Richard Beilby *No Medals for Aphrodite* 77: How stiff could you be? The truck gone, the bridge blown, and now her, packing up like this!
1980 *Sun-Herald* 23 Nov. 103: A man would be as stiff as a board not to get a lift home with one of the boys.

stiffen the lizards   see **lizards**

stilts   The piles on which houses stand in Queensland
1963 John Cantwell *No Stranger to the Flame* 11: Gus Bermann gazed with compassion at growers of cane and pineapples on the wire-screened verandahs of wooden houses on stilts.
1983 *Sydney Morning Herald* 17 Sep. 32: Queensland timber houses are unique, transplants from Russian country estates or British India. Nowhere else in Australia does one encounter these curious buildings on stilts.
see **stumps**

sting *n.*   1   A strong drink [f. *stingo* strong ale or beer OED 1635]
1929 K. S. Prichard *Coonardoo* 60: 'I'm through with prospectin'!' 'Misses his three square meals a day and sting,' Bob explained.
1954 T. A. G. Hungerford *Sowers of the Wind* 263: He drained his glass [of whisky], and filled it again immediately . . . 'Feel the need of a bit of sting, eh?'
1972 John de Hoog *Skid Row Dossier* 4: You can

share a bottle of sting (methylated spirits) down a lane.

2 Dope, esp. in racing

1950 *Australian Police Journal* Apr. 118: *Sting* Dope.

1958 Frank Hardy *The Four-Legged Lottery* 173: The 'smarties' soon found stings that didn't show on a swab.

sting *v.* **1** To exploit someone by extracting a loan; to overcharge

[**1812** Vaux: *Sting* To rob or defraud a person or place is called *stinging* them, as, that *cove* is too fly; he has been *stung* before; meaning that man is upon his guard, he has already been trick'd.]

1919 W. H. Downing *Digger Dialects* 47: *Sting* (vb.) Make a request for a loan or gift. So, also, 'Put in the stings'.

1928 Arthur Wright *A Good Recovery* 161: 'Suppose he wants to put the stings in for a few quid.'

1941 Baker 72: *Sting, to* To borrow money from someone.

1945 Kylie Tennant *Ride on Stranger* 63: 'In this world you've got to sting or get stung,' he pointed out.

1959 D'Arcy Niland *The Big Smoke* 206: 'Pay?' Georgie Barber said, taken aback. 'What would you sting me?'

1969 Alan O'Toole *The Racing Game* 69: 'I'm being stung for quite a bit of money, at a time when there's none coming in, and there's more bills on the way.'

1970 Patrick White *The Vivisector* 331: 'Who sold you the paintings?' he asked . . . 'Diacono? Then he must have stung you!'

2 (*give the sting*) To dope a racehorse

1949 Lawson Glassop *Lucky Palmer* 36: 'It's a moral. They're going to give it the sting. They'll hit it with enough dope to win a Melbourne Cup.'

stinker An oppressively hot day (f. *stinker* for anything unpleasant]

1941 Baker 72: *Stinker* A disagreeable, highly unpleasant and often humid day.

1950 Jon Cleary *Just Let Me Be* 17: 'Hullo, Mrs Brennan. Stinker of a day, ain't it?'

1959 Dorothy Hewett *Bobbin Up* 170: Already the sky was pale and smoky with the promise of 'another stinker'.

1976 *Sydney Morning Herald* 6 Nov. 11: A thick heat haze is covering the mountains. It's going to be a scorcher. A stinker.

stipe Stipendiary steward (controlling horse-racing) [abbr.]

[**1860** Hotten 228: *Stipe* a stipendiary magistrate. *Provincial.*]

1949 Lawson Glassop *Lucky Palmer* 163: 'You was

going to do all sorts of things to us. Going to call in the stipes and everything.'

1977 *Australian* 15 Jan. 20: The racing page screamed STIPES PROBE JOCKEY.

1983 *Newcastle Herald* 14 Jan. 14: The stipes have wide-ranging powers to banish undesirables from tracks, quiz jockeys about riding performances, hold inquiries into so-called 'form reversals' when a nag that had the staggers one week suddenly sprouts wings the next, and generally act as a bulwark against hanky-panky detrimental to the best interests of punters.

stir To act in a way provocative to authority or upholders of the status quo; to create a minor disturbance (juvenile) [? f. *stir the possum* q.v. or the proverb 'The more you stir a turd, the worse it stinks' 1546]

1972 John de Hoog *Skid Row Dossier* 110: Excitement was whipped up over the tiniest incident and when several youths went 'stirring' one day – riding up and down the lifts of large office blocks – conversations dwelt on and enlarged every action.

1973 H. Williams *My Love Had a Black Speed Stripe* 54: It was a pity we couldn't pack this pommy foreman Charlie up to Japan to stir it up with the workers there, where they would soon give him the old samurai treatment.

1978 Kevin Gilbert *Living Black* 38: When I started to stir, people began to wake up to what conditions we lived in.

stir the possum see **possum**

stirrer Someone given to 'stirring'

1971 Frank Hardy *The Outcasts of Foolgarah* 88: That'd be him, thought the Dean, a shit-stirrer from way back. Ibid. 109: The lurk men and stirrers weren't the only ones burning the midnight oil.

1973 H. Williams *My Love Had a Black Speed Stripe* 55: We were not to be led away by a few stirrers who had no regard for their own union but were just trying to stir it up for their own purposes.

1979 Bill Scott *Tough in the Old Days* 16: The new bloke was a stirrer, with all his talk at lunch time about how the lunchroom was too small.

1983 *Weekend Australian* 14 May 11: Mr Paul Everingham, in boots-and-all fashion, immediately claimed protests were motivated by stirrers, white radicals and those opposed to Northern Territory development.

stobie pole A telegraph pole made of concrete and steel (S.A.) [f. J. C. Stobie 1895–1953, the designer]

1984 *Sydney Morning Herald* 25 Aug. 19: Sex and the urge to paint electricity poles are recurring themes in Mr [Clifton] Pugh's life lately. About a month ago he painted a Stobie pole in Prospect, a suburb of Adelaide, and the controversy which followed virtually drove him to the bush in search of peace. A Stobie pole is a concrete power pole edged with steel girders (named after its South Australian inventor).

stone the crows   see **crows**

stonker   To defeat, thwart, put out of commission [cf. *stonk* the stake in a game EDD; *stunk* (stonk) to pant, gasp, groan with exertion SND]
   1917 Diary cit. in Patsy Adam-Smith *The Anzacs* (1978) 215: We just go into the line again and again until we get knocked ... Just in and out, in and out, and somebody stonkered every time.
   1919 W. H. Downing *Digger Dialects* 48: *Stonker* Exterminate; kill; strike out.
   1932 A. W. Upfield *A Royal Abduction* 250: 'Why don't they shut off the confounded thing?' 'Too stonkered with surprise, I'll bet.'
   1942 Sarah Campion *Bonanza* 42: 'Now you're stonkered all right, if Clancy ever gets on yer track.'
   1948 Robert S. Close *Morn of Youth* 99: She threw ... straight for the target, which suddenly fell down on the road. 'Cripes! You've stonkered it,' I said.
   1959 Peter Ryan *Fear Drive My Feet* 130: The most picturesque of the mechanics' repair jobs was the Stonkered Taxi Service – consisting of a nearly wrecked sedan car which had been put back on the road and which now served as an ambulance.
   1961 Jon Rose *At the Cross* 79: 'There's nothing I can do ... I'm stonkered.' Bella began to cry.
   1981 Dorothy Hewett *The Golden Oldies* 46: 'That was the day when I felt so stonkered and stayed in our suite.'

stoom, stoomer   see **stumer**

stores, on, off the   Applied to convicts either drawing rations from the government stores in Sydney, or subsisting independently of them
   1798 David Collins *An Account of the English Colony in New South Wales* ed. B. Fletcher (1975) i 193: Having taken himself off the stores to avoid working for the public, he was frequently distressed for food. Ibid. 392: All these depredations were chiefly committed by those public nuisances the people off the stores.
   1809 *HRNSW* vii 141: A general muster of male prisoners, on or off the stores ... will be taken on the following days.

stoush *v.*   To clout, punch [see *stoush n.*]
   1893 J. A. Barry *Steve Brown's Bunyip* 66: 'I'll get stoushed over this job yet. Brombee's got it in for me.'
   1896 Henry Lawson 'Shooting the Moon' *Prose* i 150: 'Now look here,' I said, shaking my fist at him, like that, 'if you say a word, I'll stoush yer!'
   1900–10 O'Brien and Stephens: *Stoush* to hit or punch.
   1911 Louis Stone *Jonah* 50: 'The Push stoushed 'im, an' then cleared.'
   1934 'Leslie Parker' *Trooper to the Southern Cross* (1966) 69: 'He had a bit of turn-up with the military policeman and stoushed him.'
   1959 Dorothy Hewett *Bobbin Up* 80: The boys still coming out at playtime in their wrinkled jeans, stoushing each other over the head.
   1965 Eric Lambert *The Long White Night* 79: 'Get out of that bloody car while I stoush yer!'

stoush *n.*   Fighting, violence [? f. *stashie* (*stash*) an uproar; a commotion, disturbance, quarrel EDD 1851]
   1908 Henry Fletcher *Dads and Dan between Smokes* 32: 'He looked as though he liked bein' hit an' took stoush fer breakfast every mornin'.'
   1916 C. J. Dennis *The Moods of Ginger Mick* 31: The Call of Stoush [poem title]
   1935 H. R. Williams *Comrades of the Great Adventure* 247: He returned to France and participated in some more 'real stoush' – as he called a battle – before the war came to an end.
   1939 Kylie Tennant *Foveaux* 247: Strikers who pounced into the tram compartments and began dealing out 'stouch' to the terrified passengers.
   1945 Robert S. Close *Love Me Sailor* 149: It was like the old days when I got Ernie into some stoush ashore just for the hell of fighting him out of it.
   1953 T. A. G. Hungerford *Riverslake* 122: 'I'd rather be with him than against him in any stoush.'
   1971 Frank Hardy *The Outcasts of Foolgarah* 82: Here they are now with their mob looking for a bit of stoush.
   1981 *Sun-Herald* 19 Apr. 135: Personally, I like a good stoush at Brookvale Oval, or wherever.

straight wire   see **wire**

streaker's defence   See quot. 1983
   1983 *Australian* 22 Apr. 1: The Attorney-General, Senator Evans, yesterday explained that his decision to allow RAAF spy flights over the Franklin dam had been taken because 'it seemed like a good idea at the time'. He told the National Press Club he had adopted what was known in legal circles as 'the streaker's defence: it seemed, your worship, like a good idea at the time.'
   1984 *Australian* 12 Jan. 2: To explain their tenancy of room 004 at the Sheraton they invoked the now-famous streaker's defence: It seemed like a good idea at the time.

street, to To outdistance, esp. in horseracing
1983 *Newcastle Herald* 20 Apr. 36: Rosebrook streeted the opposition in yesterday's $10,000 Rocket Stakes (900m) at Broadmeadow.

strength, the ~ of The essential facts about, reliable information upon [? f. *strength* the force, tenor, import (of a document) OED 1425–1602 *obs.*]
1904 Henry Fletcher *Dads Wayback: His Work* 34: 'About this forchin-tellin' game, it takes er bit o' knowin' ter get ther full strength of it.'
1916 C. J. Dennis *The Moods of Ginger Mick* 157: *Strength of it* The truth of it, the value of it.
1921 Ernest O'Ferrall *Bodger and the Boarders* 52: 'I see that Barnstormer bloke an' got the strength of the whole thing.'
1926 K. S. Prichard *Working Bullocks* 136: 'Now,' she continued ... 'I'll just give you the strength of Red Burke.'
1939 Kylie Tennant *Foveaux* 154: 'What's the strength of it? Any idea?'
1947 Vance Palmer *Hail Tomorrow* 20: 'You've about got the strength of it, Mick.'
1959 K. S. Prichard *N'Goola* 153–4: 'A trapper camped further along the road gave me the strength of them.'
see **strong**

strides Men's trousers, leggings [f. *strides* trousers EDD 1895; also listed by Partridge as theatrical]
1924 *Truth* 27 Apr. 6: *Strides* Trousers.
1932 Leonard Mann *Flesh in Armour* 291: His tunic and light coat were of the ultra fashionable style, and his strides would not have disgraced an officer of the Guards.
1940 Thomas Wood *Cobbers Campaigning* 54: 'But if ye'll just wait till I put on me strides I'll get ye there in two-ups.'
1959 D'Arcy Niland *The Big Smoke* 11: It's like taking your strides off and getting into bed, broke and finished.
1962 Jock Marshall and Russell Drysdale *Journey Among Men* 109: Most of us wore shorts, or khaki strides, and suede desert boots.
1975 Don Townshend *Gland Time* 54: Their sex life had come to an abrupt halt and Bluey said he hadn't dropped his strides with Gwenda for weeks.
1983 *Australian* 26 Jan. 9: Sir Jack Egerton, the *dernier cri* in Labor knights, has a fine military taste in strides and has been sporting a cherry-coloured pair in the bar of a flash Sydney club.

strife A 'literary' term often given a colloquial use
1931 Miles Franklin *Back to Bool Bool* 320: 'Laleen does not want to come back here and make strife amongst her relatives,' he said.
1944 Lawson Glassop *We Were the Rats* 113: 'Some blokes aren't nominated,' he said dismally.

'They cop all the strife that's goin'.'
1958 Barry Humphries *A Nice Night's Entertainment* (1981) 16: Had a bit of strife parking the vehicle.
1962 Nancy Phelan *The River and the Brook* 66: 'Probation ... they check up on you to see what you're doing. If you get into any more strife, then they put you in jail.'
1972 David Williamson *The Removalists* 105: 'You're in the shit I'm afraid, Ross ... You're in real strife, boy.'
1980 *Daily Telegraph* (Sydney) 12 Mar. 48: 'Biff' confession has Boyd in strife [heading] Manly international second-rower Les Boyd's 'I hit Artie' confession could have him facing disciplinary action from the NSW Rugby League on Monday night.

strike a blow see **blow**

strike paydirt see **paydirt**

string To form a string, move in a string, esp. of cattle [f. *string* to move or progress in a string or disconnected line OED 1824]
1887 W. S. S. Tyrwhitt *The New Chum in the Queensland Bush* 192: He sees through the darkness a line of cattle slowly stringing away across the flat.
1895 A. B. Paterson 'Clancy of the Overflow' *The Man from Snowy River* 21: As the stock are slowly stringing, Clancy rides behind them singing, / For the drover's life has pleasures that the townsfolk never know.
1900 Henry Lawson 'Thin Lips and False Teeth' *Prose* i 242: Brook ... found the road to the school by the children 'stringing' along in the opposite direction.
1905 E. C. Buley *Australian Life in Town and Country* 26: After the cutting out is done, the beasts have been sorted in mobs according to their classes, each mob is made to 'string' or move in single file, in order that a count may be made.

stringy bark An example (like *geebung*) of the name of the native flora being used to distinguish some denizen of the outback, as though embodying its uncouth indigenous qualities
1833 *New South Wales Magazine* Oct. 171: The workmanship of which I beg you will not scrutinize, as I am but, to use a colonial expression, 'a stringy-bark carpenter'. [Morris]
1836 J. F. O'Connell *A Residence of Eleven Years in New Holland* 49: Let us suppose the suitor an old 'stringy-bark', such being the soubriquet in which inland settlers rejoice.
1861 Horace Earle *Ups and Downs* 59: 'She would never have had the bad taste to prefer a stringy bark like me to such a fine-looking, first-class

fellow as yourself.'

1865 Henry Kingsley *The Hillyars and the Burtons* 58: 'Hallo!' said Burton. 'Are *you* Stringy Bark?' [an ex-convict] 'I am from Van Diemen's Land,' said the old man, quietly. 'But an emigrant.' The convict gave a grunt of disappointment.

1905 *The Old Bush Songs* ed. A. B. Paterson 43: 'The Stringy-bark Cockatoo [ballad title]. Ibid. xiii: The stringy-bark tree is an unfailing sign of poor land; and the minstrel was much worse treated when working for 'The Stringy-bark Cockatoo' than when he was a 'Squatter's man.'

Strip, the   See quot.

1984 *Sydney Morning Herald* 6 Feb. 3: The Strip – the few hundred metres of George Street, south of the Town Hall, which has two main attractions: movies and mass-production food.

strong, the ~ of   As for **the strength of**

1910 Arthur Wright *Under a Cloud* 31: 'Don't yer want to own up? Some reason for wantin' to preserve yer incog. I suppose. What's the strong of it?'

1938 Xavier Herbert *Capricornia* 566: 'What's the strong of you? What's the questioning for? I've done nuthin'.'

1946 K. S. Prichard *The Roaring Nineties* 294: 'What's the strong of it, Morrey?' he asked.

1959 Eric Lambert *Glory Thrown In* 161: 'What's the strong of this joint?' demanded Doc brusquely. 'Not an undertaker's is it?'

1968 Stuart Gore *Holy Smoke* 58: 'That's about the strong of 'em,' he agreed.

stroke, Government   see **Government**

stubby   **1**   A beer bottle smaller than the usual size, esp. 375 ml [f. shape]

1968 Frank Hardy *The Unlucky Australians* 49: He threw an empty stubby into the box and went to the refrigerator for a full one.

1979 *Courier-Mail* (Brisbane) 12 May 1: If you can roll a cigarette in one hand, play a gumleaf, saw or comb, crack a whip and drink a stubbie in 10 seconds, then make tracks for Winton and the Mr Outback quest.

1982 *NT News* (Darwin) 29 May 3: Beer drinkers are not pleased with a recent Carlton United decision to change the size of its small stubbies. The basic 375 ml capacity is the same but the shape is different ... The old stubby is 68 mm in diameter and fits firmly into the average cooler which has an inner diameter of 70 mm. The new stubbies are only 64 mm at the widest point, giving 6 mm of play and space for warm air to circulate.

2   *Stubbies* A brand of men's shorts

1977 *Australian* 7 Apr. 3: Stubbies – the football shorts with pockets – have become an inter-

national fashion ... Although the Stubby is a very Australian name – thought of in the context of short shorts to go with short bottles of beer – Mr Phillips is confident they will become as American as apple pie.

1982 *National Times* 25 Apr. 25: Perhaps the popular picture of the Aussie wearing Stubbies and swigging a tinny should be replaced by a svelte gay, sipping Perrier.

1983 David Foster *Plumbum* 176: Australian tourists ... are recognisable throughout Asia by their characteristic attire of thongs and stubbies, and their self-satisfied expressions.

stuck into, to get   **1**   To attack someone, physically or verbally

1942 Gavin Casey *It's Harder for Girls* 228: 'A bit o' peace after ... you an' Winch nearly getting stuck into each other at the pub.'

1953 T. A. G. Hungerford *Riverslake* 120–1: 'What was the trouble, Con? I saw you stuck into a Balt across the press as I come down.'

1973 Alexander Buzo *Rooted* 44: 'Then he tried to job Hammo. Well, Hammo got stuck into him, I can tell you.'

1977 Jeff Thomson *Sunday Telegraph* (Sydney) 27 Feb. 60: 'They're getting a bit cocky, the Poms. So I'd like to get stuck into 'em again.'

2   To apply oneself energetically to a task

1955 John Morrison *Black Cargo* 65: 'All right, grab those knives and get stuck into it.'

1970 Alexander Buzo *The Front Room Boys* in Penguin *Plays* 29: 'The back room boys are going to streamline this department, which means a few heads are going to roll, so get stuck into it.'

1975 Les Ryan *The Shearers* 124: 'Righto, you blue-tongues!' he bellowed out. 'Get stuck into it!'

3   To consume (food or drink) with gusto

1947 Gavin Casey *The Wits are Out* 89: 'Come on,' Syd said. 'What about getting stuck into it?' They gathered round the barrel for some serious drinking.

1955 D'Arcy Niland *The Shiralee* 26: 'Never mind that,' he grunted. 'Get stuck into your tucker.'

1963 D. H. Crick *Martin Place* 218: 'Let's get stuck into them prawns.'

1973 Alexander Buzo *Rooted* 30: 'Davo got stuck into the grog, didn't he?'

stud   See quot. [cf. *bull* 2]

1962 *Sydney Morning Herald* 24 Nov. 12: The contractor knows he has four or five 'stud' shearers (boss's men) on the board who will vote them dry.

students, the   The members of one of the University sporting teams in N.S.W.

1976 *Sunday Telegraph* (Sydney) 24 Oct. 76: Boycott thrashes Students [heading] Geoff

Boycott, the veteran English test batsman, scored a casual century for Waverley against University of NSW yesterday.

stumer, come a   To crash financially, come a cropper: *rare* [? f. *stummer* to stagger, stumble EDD 1793; or *stumer* a forged or dishonoured cheque OED 1890]
  1898 *Bulletin* 17 Dec. Red Page: *stoomey* broke; and a *stoomer* or *stumer* is a man without money.
  1900–10 O'Brien and Stephens: *Come a stoomer* stake a bet and lose everything.
  1936 A. B. Paterson 'The Shearer's Colt' in *Song of the Pen* (1983) 725: She . . . had been wondering how she would face her co-religionists if she brought them what is known in certain financial circles as a 'stumer'.
  1941 Baker 73: *Stumer, come a* To crash financially, esp. in a racing bet.

to stoom   To knock unconscious, kill: *rare*
  1908 E. S. Sorenson *Quinton's Rouseabout* 119: 'Seemed plain ter me as Garron 'ad left 'is team at the station an' rode 'ome; 'as a kick-up with the ole gerl over something – God knows wot – an' she stooms him out – accidental, as yer might say. Then she hits on the black stump as an orlright place ter hide 'im.'
  1925 E. S. Sorenson *Murty Brown* 68: 'Might a 'urt yer!' ''Urt me!' Charcoal snorted. 'Might a stoomed me out!'

stump, the black   see **black**

stumps   As for **stilts**, q.v.
  1959 Eleanor Dark *Lantana Lane* 42: In these parts most houses stand up on stumps high enough to provide room beneath the floorboards for innumerable things, including, of course, the family's motor vehicle.
  1983 Hugh Lunn *Weekend Australian* 7 May Mag. 2: It finally dawned on me why the first Queenslanders built their houses on stilts, or 'stumps' as they call them up here.
  1984 David Malouf *Harland's Half Acre* 144: The land sloped, so that the house . . . sat on stumps that were five feet high at the front and eighteen at the back.

stung   Drunk, tipsy [f. **sting** 1]
  1919 W. H. Downing *Digger Dialects* 48: *Stung* (adj. or p. part.) (1) Drunk; (2) having been induced to lend.
  1941 Baker 74: *Stung* Drunk.
  1952 T. A. G. Hungerford *The Ridge and the River* 62: 'The old bloke's stung already, and the pubs aren't even opened yet!'
  1965 William Dick *A Bunch of Ratbags* 219: We had arrived at Doreen's sister's wedding-reception about an hour ago and by now we were all half stung.
  1970 Kenneth Slessor *Bread and Wine* 154: To a total abstainer, the line 'I am stung, stung to the heart of me' would convey, I suppose, nothing so coarse as the associations which I find in it.
  1982 *National Times* 22 Aug. 11: To be drunk, I learn, is to be 'stung' or 'rotten'.

stunned mullet, like a   see **mullet**

Stupenda, La   The soprano Joan Sutherland [f. the applause (*È stupenda*, She's stupendous) when she sang Handel's *Alcina* at the Fenice Theatre, Venice, in February 1960]
  1960 *Daily Express* (London) 22 Feb. 4: Noel Goodwin flies to Italy and hears them call Joan Sutherland LA STUPENDA [heading] Pink carnations which decorated the boxes and galleries of the graceful Fenice Theatre . . . were showered last night on the woman the audience cheered as 'La Stupenda'. She was Joan Sutherland, Covent Garden's star soprano.
  1964 *Sydney Morning Herald* 14 Oct. 1: The Metropolitan Opera opened its eightieth season last night with one of the greatest accolades in its history for 'La Stupenda', Australian soprano Joan Sutherland.
  1984 *Sydney Morning Herald* 16 Feb. 16: La Stupenda, in a rare burst of public talking, reveals that, like Kate Fitzpatrick, she too enjoys a decent game of cricket.

style, ball of   see **ball**

subbie   A sub contractor
  1978 *Sun-Herald* 4 Jun. 21: Most owner-drivers or sub-contractors, as they are known in the business, have to overload if they want to make ends meet. For the independent 'subbie' a couple of extra tonnes over the legal limit is often the only thing separating a profitable run from a straight-out loss.
  1980 *Australian* 10 Apr. 15: 'The work escalated', Jack said. 'So we got subbies and we said right from the word go we would not rip them off.'
  1983 *Sydney Morning Herald* 28 Apr. 7: Implicit in this is the proposition that the people who use the services of sub-contractors share to some extent the savings which subbies make evading tax.

Such is life   An expression given a special Australian currency from being the supposed last words of Ned Kelly, and from being adopted by Joseph Furphy as the title of his famous novel
  1880 J. Jenkins *Diary of a Welsh Swagman* (1975) 100: Ned Kelly, the Bushranger was hanged today [9 Nov.] at 8 a.m. His last words at the scaffold were, 'Such is life'.

c. **1897** Joseph Furphy *Such is Life Being certain extracts from the diary of Tom Collins* (1903)
1969 *Such Was Life Select Documents in Australian Social History 1788–1850* ed. Russel Ward and John Robertson.

suds Beer
1945 Cecil Mann *The River* 139: By the look of you, Jim, you've put away a quart or two since last Day. Always were pretty good on the suds.
1978 *Weekend Australian* 23 Sep. Mag. 2: By placing oblivion beyond the average inebriate's grasp, Government ignores the role that spirits and suds have played in fostering (not to speak of tooheying) our national greatness.
1984 *Sunday Independent* (Perth) 29 Apr. 3: WA beer drinkers, faced tomorrow with the fifth price increase in a year, can take solace in the fact that suds-lovers in the eastern states pay quite a bit more.

sugar bag A nest of wild honey in a tree; honey [Pidgin]
1830 Robert Dawson *The Present State of Australia* 136: The strange native ... pointed with his tomahawk to the tree and nodding his head and smiling at me, repeated the words, 'Choogar-bag, choogar-bag, choogar-bag!' (sugar-bag) their English expression for honey, or anything sweet.
1851 John Henderson *Excursions and Adventures in New South Wales* 139–40: There is another mode, however, of hunting for sugar bags ... Having seen a bee alight on any twig or leaf, the black takes a little bit of the finest down ... cautiously steals upon the bee, and dexterously places the down upon his back ... Having traced the bee to its retreat ... he then, with his tomahawk, cuts his way up the tree, cuts into the hollow branch where the hive is.
1864 Rachel Henning *Letters* ed. David Adams (1963) 185: The other has been employing his energies in climbing gum-trees after 'sugar-bags', or wild honeycombs.
1901 F. J. Gillen *Diary* (1968) 288: Honey or as the blacks call it 'Sugar bag' appears to be fairly plentiful for the boys cut out two lots yesterday.
1908 E. S. Sorenson *The Squatter's Ward* 32: 'There's allers plenty of 'em pokin' about the bush lookin' for sugar-bags.'
1930 *Bulletin* 8 Jan. 20: The two new hands who were ringbarking on Blade's selection reported gleefully that they had found a bees' nest near the boundary fence. They had heard a lot about 'sugarbags', and had been wasting much of their boss's time looking up trees.
1941 Charles Barrett *Coast of Adventure* 109: Grigalalok already had found 'sugar bag' in a rock cavity, bringing a mass of dripping honeycomb to our conchologist.

sunbeam An item of cutlery or crockery laid on the table but not used, and so not needing to be washed up
1982 *Sydney Morning Herald* 24 Dec. 19: In Australian households sunbeams still lighten the washing up.

sunburnt country, the Australia [f. Dorothea Mackellar's poem: see quot. 1914]
1914 Dorothea Mackellar 'My Country' *The Witch Maid* 29: I love a sunburnt country / A land of sweeping plains.
1953 Ian Bevan ed. *The Sunburnt Country Profile of Australia* [book title]
1979 Thea Astley *Hunting the Wild Pineapple* 106: 'To stop the brain-drain, that's for what. Keep the old genius located right here in the sunburnt country.'
1981 *Australian* 3 Dec. 16: The sunburnt country's droughts and flooding rains have had a marked effect on the end-of-year result for our second largest pastoral company, Dalgety Australia.

Sunday too far away An expression given currency by a film of this title (see quot. 1975), but part of the lore of the shearer much earlier
1963 *Sydney Morning Herald* 17 Aug. 11: A lot of greasies (shearers) get hen trouble. Some shearers' wives reckon we shearer blokes are either too tired, too drunk, or too far away.
1975 *Times* (London) 20 May 9: The title [of the film] is from a song, the complaint of a shearer's loveless wife: 'Friday he's too tired, Saturday too drunk, and Sunday too far away.'
1984 *Sydney Morning Herald* 8 May 4: The jibes of Mick Young, who described the Thredbo weekend as 'Friday too tired, Saturday too drunk, Sunday too far away' ... did not hit home.

sundowner A swagman who arrives at a station at sundown, too late in the day to do any work, but in time to draw rations
[**1846** C. P. Hodgson *Reminiscences of Australia* 302: This day's work [climbing a tree to look around] is what is generally though not elegantly termed 'eye-balling' and its duration amounted in colonial phraseology to a 'Sundowner' (? a task requiring no great exertion which lasts until sundown), neither word is to be found I believe in an English dictionary, but both have very expressive meanings.]
1868 'The Song of the Sundowner' *Sydney Punch* 14 Nov. 198 repr. in *Old Bush Songs* ed. Stewart and Keesing (1957) 230: A visit at sundown I manage to pay, / And ask for my evening ration.
1887 W. S. S. Tyrwhitt *The New Chum in the Queensland Bush* 82: There is a class of men in Australia called 'sundowners' from the fact that

they always turn up at stations, nominally in search of work, at sundown, never coming in before for fear of having to work for their rations.
1890 Tasma *A Sydney Sovereign* 127: For the chance 'sundowner' who cast his tired eyes upon them, they could not signify much.
1901 Henry Lawson 'A Double Buggy at Lahey's Creek' *Prose* i 596: 'What do you want me to come at sunset for?' asked James. 'Do you want me to camp out in the scrub and turn up like a blooming sundowner?'
1913 John Sadleir *Recollections of a Victorian Police Officer* 109: 'Sundowners', swagmen who travelled without any settled purpose from station to station, obtaining fresh supplies of food at any station where they might chance to find themselves at sunset.

Sun King, the   Mr R. J. Hawke, Prime Minister 1983– [f. analogy with *Le Roi Soleil*, Louis XIV of France]
1984 *National Times* 27 Apr. 50: This week – a clash in perceptions between two Big Australians – BHP and the Prime Minister. It appears that the Sun King's visit to Peking in February was perhaps not the greatest diplomatic coup since Marco Polo.
1984 *Toorak Sunday* 10 Jun. 13: The other noteworthy tableau of knives flashing appears to be unfolding at the court of our very own Sun King, Bob the Magnificent.

Sunlamp (Suntan) Kid   Mr Andrew Peacock [f. tanned appearance]
1981 *Age* (Melbourne) 23 Jul. 5: Andrew Peacock, the man with the perennial tan, is known as the 'Sun Lamp Kid'.
1981 *Sun-Herald* 18 Oct. 21: A report from Melbourne tells of Andrew Peacock and his staff frantically engaged in an exercise campaign. The suggestion is that the fitter team will win the leadership battle between the Suntan Kid and the Prime Minister.
1983 *National Times* 2 Dec. 3: The light goes out on the Sunlamp Kid [heading] Andrew Peacock is in deep trouble as Liberal leader.

sunnies   Sunglasses
1981 *Sun-Herald* 11 Jan. 9: On his head was a top hat adorned with dark glasses ('sunnies').
1984 *Sydney Morning Herald* 4 Feb. 35: A mob in mirrored sunnies (essential accessories at Narara).

sunny New South   see **New South**

sunshine state, the   Queensland, in the language of tourist advertising
1962 Criena Rohan *The Delinquents* 128: 'If you

ask me, all Brisbane's full of coppers and all of them bastards,' she said, expressing in one concise sentence the full theory of central government of the sunshine state.
1970 *Coast to Coast 1969–1970* 115: 'We had such fun, remember? And somehow it never seemed to rain. Good old sunshine State.'
1974 *Nation Review* 7 Jun. 1117: The recent Queensland Festival of Arts has caused something of a crisis of identity in the Sunshine State. A Queensland festival of arts is, after all, something of a contradiction in terms.
1982 *Sunday Mail* (Brisbane) 19 Sep. 3: Once most definitely taboo in the Sunshine State, male strippers are now performing under the nose of the police and, according to promoters, they can't keep the girls away.

sunstruck bone, like a   Extremely dry, thirsty
1894 Henry Lawson 'Stiffner and Jim (Thirdly, Bill)' *Prose* i 123: We comes to Stiffner's Hotel ... with throats on us like sun-struck bones, and not the price of a stick of tobacco.
1962 Dymphna Cusack *Picnic Races* 168: 'Spend yer day riding round 9,000 bloody acres with a thirst on yer like a sunstruck bone, and the heat frying the brains under yer hat.'
1977 F. A. Reeder *Diary of a Rat* 39: Hot as a couple of hells, dry as a sunstruck bone, with huge sand hills everywhere.

super   **1**   The superintendent of a station [abbr.]
1857 F. Cooper *Wild Adventures in Australia* 59: 'Scotchy' ... introduced me as a particular friend to Wilder the owner of that run, under the impression that a 'super' was required, as Wilder had from some time spoken of his intention to reside in Brisbane.
1870 Henry Kendall 'Camped by the Creek' *Poetical Works* ed. T. T. Reed (1966) 386: But now let us stop for the 'super' / Will want us tomorrow by noon.
1873 Rolf Boldrewood 'The Fencing of Wanderowna' *A Romance of Canvas Town* (1898) 108: 'I wasn't always a super. I started with a tidy little capital when I first came to Australia, and I lost nine thousand sheep ... within six months.'
1888 'The Jackeroo' *Bulletin* 10 Mar. 14 repr. in *Old Bush Songs* ed. Stewart and Keesing (1957) 79: When I got to the station I saw the super there.
2   Superphosphate
1931 *Southern Cross Times* 25 Jul. cit. G. C. Bolton *A Fine Country to Starve In* (1972) 142: Oh, kind hearted creditors, / don't start repossessing the super bags yet!
1949 John K. Ewers *Harvest* 186: He flung the empty bag impatiently from him and repeated the process with the super.
1959 K. S. Prichard *N'Goola* 142: The bottom fell

out of the market for wheat. Prices were so low they would not pay for seed and super.

1975 *Australian* 12 Aug. 1: Restore super bounty, says IAC.

3   Petrol with an octane rating above 'standard'

4   Superannuation

1978 *Sydney Morning Herald* 20 Jun. 13: Super board funds $30m project [heading] The State Superannuation Board is to provide finance for Lend Lease Development Pty Ltd's new regional shopping centre at Campbelltown.

surf, surfie   A young habitué of the beaches, long-haired and given to surf-board-riding, seen as a cult figure

1963 *Sun-Herald* 10 Mar. 1: Police will maintain a constant alert today on Sydney's 15 beaches to prevent gang warfare between Rockers and Surfies.

1965 Barry Humphries *Times Literary Supplement* 16 Sep. 812: The Surfies, a repellent breed of sun-bronzed hedonists who actually hold chundering contests on the famed beaches of the Commonwealth.

1967 David Beal and Donald Horne *Southern Exposure* 51: On the ocean beaches the surfies drive hard and fast down the wall, with the soup curling behind them, or do a backside bottom turn on a big one about to tube.

1975 *National Times* 13 Jan. 40: If you are a 14-year-old schoolgirl and you have just discovered boys are not the same thing as your brothers, what really sends your heart into a turmoil is the sight of a blond, long-haired, blue-eyed, sun-bronzed surf wearing board shorts and bare feet.

1982 *Sun-Herald* 11 Apr. 15: 'People automatically think of a surfie as a brainless twirp with bleached blonde hair who takes drugs and sleeps around. It's such a terrible generalisation.'

Susso   Government sustenance for the unemployed during the depression; a man drawing this dole [abbr.]

1942 Leonard Mann *The Go-Getter* 10: Five shillings were five shillings and a handsome help to the sustenance. 'We're on the Susso now.' That was the song they knew and did not sing.

1947 Vance Palmer *Cyclone* 8: 'He thinks it puts hair on his chest knocking about with the sussos.'

1958 Frank Hardy *The Four-Legged Lottery* 44: Some of those who still had work looked down on the unemployed, the 'sussos' as they were contemptuously called.

1969 Patsy Adam-Smith *Folklore of the Australian Railwaymen* 190: When war was declared all our big 'susso' camps folded up overnight and the boys went to where they were sure to find work.

1973 Frank Huelin *Keep Moving* 67: 'We want to

see the mayor and council about susso.'

swag *n.*   1   Booty, plunder (as in English thieves' slang)

1812 Vaux: *The swag*, is a term used in speaking of any booty you have lately obtained, be it of what kind it may, except money.

2   A collection of legitimate belongings

c. **1845** James Tucker *Ralph Rashleigh* (1952) 125: The cart contained various articles of property of those kinds that generally constitute the bulk of a settler's swag. There were pipes, tobacco, the keg above named, a quantity of tea and sugar, two or three coarse cotton striped shirts, and a pair or two of duck trousers.

1852 G. C. Mundy *Our Antipodes* iii 285: A tall picturesque-looking sprig of the squattocracy has just pitched his 'swag' – a leathern valise – through the open skylight on to the cuddy table.

3   The pack carried by the traveller, usually some essential belongings rolled in a blanket

1853 John Rochfort *Adventures of a Surveyor* 49: Disregarding the state of the roads, on the 24th of August, 1852, we strapped on our 'swags',* consisting of a pair of blankets and a spare pair of trousers, and started for the diggings. *Swags, colonial word for pack.

1855 William Howitt *Land, Labour and Gold* i 297: Those who go up only with their swags, containing their blankets, tea, and sugar, have to buy all their stores all winter at digging prices.

1873 A. Trollope *Australia* ed. Edwards and Joyce (1967) 293: The man who travels on foot in Australia, whether he be miner, shepherd, shearer, or simply beggar, always carries his 'swag' with him, – which consists of his personal properties rolled up in a blanket.

1878 Rolf Boldrewood *An Australian Squire* repr. as *Babes in the Bush* (1901) 134: Dressed in the garb of a bushman and carrying upon his back the ordinary knapsack or 'swag' of the travelling labourer of the period as he strode along the path.

1887 W. S. S. Tyrwhitt *The New Chum in the Queensland Bush* 82: A man came up one evening, 'humping his swag', as the expression is for carrying a bundle.

1896 Henry Lawson 'Enter Mitchell' *Prose* i 132: It was a stout, dumpy swag, with a red blanket outside, and the edge of a blue blanket showing in the inner rings at the end ... It might have been hooped with decent straps, instead of bits of clothes-line and greenhide – but otherwise there was nothing the matter with it, as swags go.

1908 W. H. Ogilvie *My Life in the Open* 35: The rouseabouts and shed-hands come in from all quarters on foot, carrying their 'swags', i.e. blankets strapped in bundles across their shoulders.

swag, the dogs are pissing on   see **pull out**

swag, cigarette   see **cigarette**

swag it   To follow the swagman's life
1870 W. M. Finn *Glimpses of North-Eastern Victoria* (1971) 26: I was much surprised to see two able-bodied men, who informed me that for seventeen years they were swagging it from one place to another; indeed, they had travelled the colony, and had no notion of now abandoning their nomadic way of life ... They said they were not going to work for any master, and would eke out an existence for their remaining time in the world.
1875 J. Jenkins *Diary of a Welsh Swagman* (1975) 52: It is better than swagging the country ... searching for work.
1901 *The Bulletin Reciter* 5: And swagging up the long divide that leads to Daybreak Range / We came.
1903 Joseph Furphy *Such is Life* (1944) 198: No man must be allowed to swag the country, ragged and homeless, with the story in his mouth that he had been boundary riding on Avondale for ten years.
1936 Archer Russell *Gone Nomad* 58: 'Swagging it' to a sheep station on the Queensland border he secured a job as a boundary rider.

swaggie   A swagman q.v.
1896 Henry Lawson 'She Wouldn't Speak' *Prose* i 115: I thought a damp expression seemed to pass across her face when me and my mate sat down, but she served us and said nothing – we was only two dusty swaggies, you see.
1916 Joseph Furphy *Poems* 28: And across this fenced-in view, like our friend the well-sung Jew, / Goes the swaggy, with a frown upon his brow.
1926 K. S. Prichard *Working Bullocks* 158: He would ... fraternize with everyone he met, shouting all comers in the hotel bars, pick up any old swaggie and take him to dinner.
1961 Jack Danvers *The Living Come First* 25: 'My father was some roaming swaggy who wandered into an abo camp with a couple of bottles of plonk'.

swaggie's dog, all prick and ribs like a   see **all**

swagman   A tramp carrying his belongings in a 'swag'. The swagman is sometimes distinguished from the 'traveller', who is regarded as seeking work
1868 Marcus Clarke 'Swagmen' in *A Colonial City* ed. L. T. Hergenhan (1972) 32–3: The Wimmera district is noted for the hordes of vagabond 'loafers' that it supports, and has earned for itself the name of 'The Feeding Track.'
1875 A. J. Boyd *Old Colonials* (1882) 110–11: 'The Swagman' [chapter title]. He tramps across

the country ostensibly for work, and at the same time praying Heaven that he may not find it ... Idleness being the mainspring of the journeys of the Swagman (*anglice*, tramp).
1887 *All the Year Round* 30 Jul. 66: A 'swagman' is a different character. The name is given to any one tramping the country for work, or any other purpose, and carrying his worldly goods slung round him in a bundle, which is always known as his 'swag'.
1893 Henry Lawson 'Some Popular Australian Mistakes' *Prose* ii 24: Men tramping in search of a 'shed' are not called 'sundowners' or 'swaggies'; they are 'trav'lers'.

swallows flying out of one's backside   see **sparrows**

swamp v.   To act as an assistant to a bullock-driver; to travel on foot with a bullock-team, giving minor assistance or having one's swag carried; to obtain a lift for oneself and one's swag from any traveller [see *swamper*]
1926 K. S. Prichard *Working Bullocks* 101: Billy Williams the bullocky, and Ern Collins who was swamping for him, turned their team into the yards on the following Monday.
1937 Ernestine Hill *Ports of Sunset* 96: In they came, across the jagged Leopolds, or up from the desert, 'swamping' with a bullocky, staggering behind a pack donkey, or on Shanks' pony.
1944 M. J. O'Reilly *Bowyangs and Boomerangs* 6: My duties were to help to load and unload, bring the horses in the morning, to harness up, help to corduroy bad patches on the track, draw water for the horses at the soaks and wells, hobble out the horses at night, put the bells on, etc. These duties were then known as 'swamping' ... All this work for the privilege of having one's tucker, tools and swag carried on the waggon. Fortunately the chap I 'swamped' for was an exceptionally good sort.
1946 K. S. Prichard *The Roaring Nineties* 7: He was charging a man five pounds to throw a hundred-pound swag on the wagon and swamp along with the team [to the goldfield].
1951 Ernestine Hill *The Territory* 446: *Swamping* Originally travelling with bullock team to carry the swag, now joining up with the mailman or any regular traveller.
1964 Tom Ronan *Packhorse and Pearling Boat* 170: 'If I broke it for a tenner, I'd roll my swag and swamp my way back to Queensland.'

swamper   One engaged in the activities of swamping [f. *swamper* a road-breaker or clearer U.S. 1850; assistant to the driver of a mule team U.S. 1870 Mathews]
1901 May Vivienne *Travels in Western Australia* 284: A 'swamper' is a man tramping without his

swag, which he entrusts to a teamster to bring on his waggon. Arrived at the camping-place, . . . the swamper awaits the teamster's coming, . . . recovers his swag and spends the night at the camp. While on foot the swamper will generally leave the track, and prospect.

1900–10 O'Brien and Stephens: *Swamper* West Australian term for a traveller making his way on foot to the goldfields.

1929 Jules Raeside *Golden Days* 380: With many a swamper's swag on / And many a billy black.

1944 Randolph Bedford *Naught to Thirty-three* 200: A 'swamper' being a man [on the way to a gold rush] who pays for the carriage of his swag, and walks after the dray.

1956 F. B. Vickers *First Place to the Stranger* 125: I went as 'swamper' on a camel waggon bound for Gascoyne Junction with ten ton of stores.

1966 Tom Ronan *Once There Was a Bagman* 15: My fellow swamper tossed his swag off [the mail-man's truck] here; he was home.

Swans, the 1 The South Melbourne V.F.L. team
1975 *Sunday Telegraph* (Sydney) 7 Sep. 64: Bull-dogs race to big Rules win over Swans.
2 In N.S.W., the same team re-named the Sydney Swans
1982 *Australian* 25 Feb. 1: The Sydney Swans are 32 tall and muscular young men who up until yesterday went under the name of the South Melbourne Football Club.
3 In W.A., Swan Districts Australian Rules team
1980 *West Australian* (Perth) 19 May 60: Round One to Swans . . . Twelve wins straight, and un-defeated at the end of the first round this season – that is how Swan Districts stand.

swarm *n. & v.* A meeting of shearers, esp. a stop-work meeting
1962 *Sydney Morning Herald* 24 Nov. 12: After seeing them in the yards, the shearers 'swarmed' (held a meeting) and decided to ask the squatter for five bob a ram – away above the award.
1975 Les Ryan *The Shearers* 58–9: 'There's been a swarm. The shearers want to negotiate a complaint.'

sweet All right, in order, 'jake'
1898 *Bulletin* 17 Dec. Red Page: *sweet, roujig* and *not too stinkin'* are good.
1939 Kylie Tennant *Foveaux* 312: 'I brassed a mug yesterday,' he told her, 'and everything's sweet again.' He flashed a roll of notes as big as his fist.
1949 Lawson Glassop *Lucky Palmer* 242: 'Every-thing jake?' he asked. 'She's sweet,' said Max.
1959 Dorothy Hewett *Bobbin Up* 106: She made certain of her bonus that way and got in sweet with the foreman.

1962 Stuart Gore *Down the Golden Mile* 120: 'Might as well be in it. We'll be sweet for getting back.'
1975 Xavier Herbert *Poor Fellow My Country* 353: Mossie came in . . . to say cheerfully, 'She's sweet.'

sweetheart of song Miss Gladys Moncrieff, also known as 'Our Glad' q.v.
1972 Peter Mathers *The Wort Papers* 280: Nor I, sang Gladys Moncrieff, the sweetheart of song.

sweetheart agreement An industrial agreement negotiated directly by employers and employed, without reference to the arbitration court
1974 *Australian* 12 Nov. 3: Miss Martin said Mr Jones' description of the hostesses' and stewards' award as a sweetheart agreement was farcical. The award had been decided by arbitration, not by negotiation between Qantas and the unions.

Sweet Pea See quot.
1978 *Sydney Morning Herald* 22 Dec. 13: It appears that the Government's Special Youth Employment Training Program (SYETP, or 'Sweet Pea' as it's known in the trade) is at least partly responsible.

swifty An act of deception
1953 *Caddie A Sydney Barmaid* 224: 'You didn't work a swiftie on them, did you?' I asked suspiciously. For I was already aware that Bill was collecting three doles for himself.
1962 Ron Tullipan *March into Morning* 43: 'And if these mugs hadn't pulled a swifty they wouldn't have been working for me at all.'
1976 *Sydney Morning Herald* 9 Apr. 6: The Queensland Premier, who thinks there is a cen-tralist under every bed, is now worried that the Federal Treasury may be trying to pull a swiftie.
1982 Malcolm Mackerras *Sydney Morning Herald* 31 Jul. 13: The point needs explaining and repeat-ing so that the electorate will fully understand the 'swifty' being pulled by a double dissolution.

swill, the six o'clock The last minute rush for drinks in the pubs, occasioned by six o'clock closing (in N.S.W. 1916–55)
1951 A. W. Upfield *The New Shoe* 93: It wanted ten minutes to the fatal hour of six, and the enforced National Swill was in full flood.
1955 Alan Ross *Australia 55* 81: This evening ritual, known amongst Australians as the 'six o'clock swill'.
1961 Frank Hardy *The Hard Way* 73: The [prison] yard was filling steadily, mostly with drunks, and a few victims of the six-o'clock swill.
1970 Donald Horne *The Next Australia* 160: The 'six o'clock swill' before the lavatory-tiled bars

closed was one of the continuing tests of masculinity.

1980 *Sunday Mail* (Brisbane) 10 Feb. 12: Are southerners appalled at the one o'clock and six o'clock 'swills' which Queensland's two-session policy causes at some hotels?

1984 *Age* (Melbourne) 19 Mar. 13: There are some reading this who will not remember Melbourne's notorious six o'clock swill ... that as little as 28 years ago that daily antipodean wallow could be looked upon by the urbane traveller as a tribal rite of a backward nation.

swing the billy   The action required to settle the tea-leaves

1966 D. E. Charlwood *An Afternoon of Time* 46: He put in the tea and a gumleaf and swung the billy over his head.

1981 *Sydney Morning Herald* 2 May 42: Ken Esgate has been a bushie round these parts all his life, as was his father. Esgate gave James Mason a lesson in how to swing the billy.

sword swallower   Someone eating from his knife, esp. among shearers

1941 Baker 74: *Sword-swallowing* The practice of eating with one's knife.

swy   The game of two-up [G. *zwei* two]

1921 *Aussie* 15 Mar. 54: 'Just done me last dollar up at the swi school.'

1924 *Truth* 27 Apr. 6: *Swy* two.

1941 Baker 75: *Swy* The game of two-up (2) A sentence of two years' goal (3) A florin.

1961 Jack Danvers *The Living Come First* 106:

'Collecting their cut of the local swy-game.'

1981 *Weekend Australian* 26 Dec. 4: Swy school a declared gaming house, rules NSW judge [heading] Thommo's two-up school in Sydney is a declared gaming house – that's official.

Sydney or the bush   All or nothing (i.e. to make one's fortune, and live in the capital, or lose it all, and seek a livelihood in the bush)

1924 *Truth* 27 Apr. 6: *Sydney or the Bush* All or nothing.

1930 E. Shann *An Economic History of Australia* 365: 'Sydney or the bush!' cries the Australian when he gambles against odds, and the slogan betrays a heart turning ever towards the pleasant coastal capitals.

1945 Cecil Mann *The River* 45: He bet on a Sydney or the Bush basis; and now, to-morrow, it was the Bush.

1953 T. A. G. Hungerford *Riverslake* 127: 'Spin for five,' Murdoch suggested to Novikowsky. 'Sydney or the bush!'

1969 Mr David Fairbairn [challenging Mr Gorton for the leadership of the Liberal Party] *Bulletin* 15 Nov. 27: 'Well, gentlemen, the die is cast. For me it's Sydney or the bush – Kirribilli or Woomargama.'

1970 Richard Beilby *No Medals for Aphrodite* 34: 'Here we go,' Turk murmured grimly, climbing in behind the wheel. 'It's Sydney or the bush! Keep your fingers crossed.'

1983 *Sun* (Sydney) 30 Dec. 39: It's hard to pick a middle ground. The [investment] choices for next year appear to be boom or bust, Sydney or the bush.

tack, flat as a   see **flat**

tail   To tend and herd stock, esp. on foot; to pursue stock that have strayed
   1844 *Port Phillip Patriot* 5 Aug. 3: I know many boys, from the age of nine to sixteen years, tailing cattle. [Morris]
   1851 J. Henderson *Excursions and Adventures in New South Wales* ii 2: He was rather old and feeble, and not of much use ... He served, however, for hut-keeper, and did well enough taleing* cattle, or going for rations. *The term used to express looking after cattle on foot.
   1852 G. C. Mundy *Our Antipodes* i 314: The stockman, as he who tends cattle and horses is called, despises the shepherd as a grovelling, inferior creature, and considers 'tailing sheep' as an employment too tardigrade for a man of action and spirit.
   1861 Horace Earle *Ups and Downs* 10: Cattle require to be tailed, or followed, by the stockman for many months, before they become sufficiently acquainted with each other.
   1875 A. J. Boyd *Old Colonials* (1882) 56: See him in some bush township, tailing cattle for a pound-keeper.
   1887 W. S. S. Tyrwhitt *The New Chum in the Queensland Bush* 193: 'Tailing' is to cattle what shepherding is to sheep, all you have to do is to keep them together, and let them feed.
   1919 W. K. Harris *Outback in Australia* 17: Camels will wander miles away during the night, even though they are hobbled. 'Tailing' horses, bullocks or mules is mere play compared with the task of 'tailing' camels.
   1934 Steele Rudd *Green Grey Homestead* 65: You battle on, following the plough and the sun from day to day, tailing the dairy herd.

tailer
   1934 Mary Gilmore *Old Days: Old Ways* 242: You must not confuse the stockman with the 'tailer'. The tailer, and, for years the later rouseabout on the sheep-run, were no-account men. They were weaklings; they were menial; and could be asked to cut wood and would do it as part of their lowly, wretched, and good-for-nothing lot.

tailie   In two-up, a gambler who habitually backs tails
   1919 W. H. Downing *Digger Dialects* 49: *Tailie* A man who backs 'tails' in the game of two-up.
   1949 Lawson Glassop *Lucky Palmer* 176: 'Gents', he cried, 'now isn't there a tailie in the school?'

tail out of a peewee, couldn't pull the   see **couldn't**

Taj, the   See quot. 1979
   1979 *Sydney Morning Herald* 30 Mar. 7: Everyone calls it 'the Taj' – short for Taj Mahal – even loyal staff members of Premier Joh Bjelke Petersen. Its official title is the Queensland Parliamentary Annexe, it cost $20 million and it was opened amid the usual squabbling earlier this month.
   1980 *Sunday Mail* (Brisbane) 21 Sep. 3: It was old

boys' day at State Parliament last Wednesday. More than 150 of some of Queensland's most colorful pollies came back to see the 'Taj Mahal' and have lunch, at our expense.

take an early shower   see **shower**

take a look at   see **look**

take out   To win, esp. in sport
1976 *Australian* 15 Jul. 2: Helen Morse . . . takes out the Australian Film Institute's top actress award tomorrow night.
1979 *Advertiser* (Adelaide) 23 Jul. 7: Flautist takes out title [heading]
1980 *Daily Mirror* (Sydney) 31 Mar. 54: Atkins, who prepares his team at Toowoomba, is hoping the colt will take out the AJC Derby.
1984 *Sunday Telegraph* (Sydney) 8 Apr. 130: Falcons take out nailbiter [heading]

take to the bush   see **bush**

talent, the   Collective term for those who stand out in any group, esp. in their own estimation, hence a 'push' q.v.; likely-looking girls (to male observation) [cf. *the talent* the clever ones (racing slang) OED 1883; also *the fancy*]
1870 Rolf Boldrewood 'Shearing in Riverina' *Town and Country Journal* 29 Oct. 10: Upon the 'talent' also, consisting of men who can shear, and shear well, from fifty to seventy sheep more in a day than their fellows, the eye of watchfulness must be kept.
c. **1882** *The Sydney Slang Dictionary* 8: The Talent Low gamblers, sharpers, larrikins and their girls, confirmed prostitutes, and 'the fancy' generally who frequent their resorts.
1913 Henry Lawson 'Mateship' *Prose* i 725: Presently the word goes round that Frowsy Sal is stickin' ter Boko Bill and is received, for the most part, with blasphemous incredulity by the 'talent'.
1950 Jon Cleary *Just Let Me Be* 115: The thick-set detective looked after her, and Harry grinned at him. 'Not bad, eh?' he said, raising his eyebrow. 'That's a bit of the local talent.'
1953 Dymphna Cusack *Southern Steel* 31: He'd learn responsibility quicker married than he would knocking about the ports with the rest of the talent.
1959 Dorothy Hewett *Bobbin Up* 93: The boys hang round the entrance, stamping cigarette butts into the floor, swapping dirty jokes, eyes narrowed to survey the talent.
1968 Geoffrey Dutton *Andy* 222: 'I'll meet you in town at the Salamanca Hotel at 8 p.m. and you can inspect the local talent.'
1979 *Sun-Herald* 7 Oct. 97: There wasn't even any 'talent' to rescue us. All the men were married, or

about to be.

talk under water, wet cement, able to   Extremely vociferous
1976 Sam Weller *Bastards I have met* 2: He can talk under water and eat an ice cream at the same time.
1980 *Sun-Herald* 9 Nov. 103: Mr Hodgman is known among other things as 'The Mouth from the South', because of the fact that he is a Tasmanian who is articulate to point of garrulousness, in fact, it is generally believed that he would talk under wet cement.
1980 *Bulletin* 5 Feb. 43: McMahon was then a relatively junior minister, not that that would have bothered McMahon, of whom a contemporary once said admiringly, 'Billy can talk under wet concrete.'
1982 *Sydney Morning Herald* 2 Aug. Guide 1: One often gets the impression that John Tapp can talk under water; a trait he undoubtedly inherited when he was understudy to the late Ken Howard.

tall poppy   see **poppy**

tall timber, to take to the   To decamp, as in 'take to the scrub'
1919 W. H. Downing *Digger Dialects* 49: *Take to the tall timber* Abscond.
1954 T. A. G. Hungerford *Sowers of the Wind* 61: 'Head for the tall timber until the grog runs out.'

Tallarook, things are crook in   Catchphrase for any adverse situation [f. rhyme on place-name]. Other catchphrases include: There's no work at Bourke. Got the arse at Bulli Pass. No lucre at Echuca. In jail at Innisfall. Things are weak at Julia Creek. Things are crook at Muswellbrook. The girls are bandy at Urandangie.
1963 Lawson Glassop *The Rats in New Guinea* 217: 'He says things are crook in Tallarook. He's the only soldier on his foot in his weapon pit.'
1969 Leslie Haylen *Twenty Years' Hard Labor* 144: The workers loved it. They cheered hysterically at the glad news that things were crook in Tallarook and likely to remain so until there was a Labor government.
1978 *Weekend Australian* 23 Sep. 3: Things are crook in Tallarook . . . and even worse at Kingaroy. One of the country's best known families, the Bjelke-Petersens, is feeling the rural pinch.
1979 *Overland* 75 36: Things really are culturally crook in Tallarook and all the other places beyond the big cities.
1982 *Sun-Herald* 21 Nov. 86: The number of people who ring talk-back shows asking for financial advice must surely be a good indication that not all is well in Tallarook or the North Shore's normally comfortable Ben Ean belt either.

411

tally 1 'The last of a specified number forming a unit of computation, on the completion of which the tally-man calls "tally" and notes it down' (OED *tally sb.* 5d)

1875 Rolf Boldrewood *The Squatter's Dream* (1878) 222: Keeping tally ... is the notation of the hundreds, by pencil or notched stick, the counter being supposed only to concern himself with the units and tens.

1886 P. Clarke *New Chum in Australia* 175: As a 'hundred' is called, one of us calls out 'tally', and cuts one notch in a stick.

1911 E. S. Sorenson *Life in the Australian Backblocks* 180: The man in charge sits on his horse ... and at every hundred calls out 'tally', while the man next him, provided with a stick and a knife, cuts a notch to correspond.

1945 Tom Ronan *Strangers on the Ophir* 96: He counted the cattle as they strung over the first gap. 'Tally 982,' he told Vancouver.

2 The total number of sheep shorn by one man in a specified period

1870 Rolf Boldrewood 'Shearing in Riverina' *Town and Country Journal* 29 Oct. 10: At five o'clock the bell rings; the day's labour is over; the men wait to see the sheep counted, and to hear their 'tallies' – the sums total of the day's shearing – read aloud.

1905 *Old Bush Songs* ed. A. B. Paterson 26: I can do a respectable tally myself whenever I like to try, / But they know me round the back blocks as Flash Jack from Gundagai.

1911 E. S. Sorenson *Life in the Australian Backblocks* 241: The quality and weight of the fleeces, and the size and condition of the sheep, have also a lot to do with the fluctuations of tallies.

1919 A. B. Paterson 'The Cook's Dog' in *Song of the Pen* (1983) 409: Each shearer has his average tally – one is a hundred-a-day man, another can only do eighty, while some run up to a hundred and fifty and even more.

3 Any other total achieved by an individual or team

1957 Ray Lawler *Summer of the Seventeenth Doll* 21: 'Roo's one of the best men they've got – runs his own gang [of cane-cutters] – but even down here you never get him yappin' about his season's tally.'

1960 Nancy Cato *Green Grows the Vine* 24: 'You'd better help her fill her tins for the rest of the morning, to bring up her tally.'

1978 *Sunday Telegraph* (Sydney) 9 Jul. 43: Nevicata took Johnston's tally of winners for the season so far to a personal best of 108½.

1982 *Sun-Herald* 25 Jul. 63: Williams, 18, booted home four winners – a tally that could have been even higher.

Tambaroora (muster) See quots: *obs.* [f. place-name]

1882 A. J. Boyd *Old Colonials* 63: It may be that the exciting game of Tambaroora is not familiar to all my readers ... Each man of a party throws a shilling, or whatever sum may be mutually agreed upon, into a hat. Dice are then produced, and each man takes three throws. The Nut who throws highest keeps the whole of the subscribed capital, and out of it pays for the drinks of the rest. The advantage of the proceeding lies in this: Where drinks are charged at sixpence, the subscription is double that amount for each ... Thus if ten Nuts go in for a Tambaroora, with nobblers at sixpence, the winner pockets five shillings by the transaction.

1895 Cornelius Crowe *The Australian Slang Dictionary* 84: *Tambaroora*, a game of a shilling each in the hat and the winner shouts.

1897 *Bulletin* 18 Dec. Red Page: The essence of a present-day tambaroora is a sweep for the purchase of drinks – frequently on the principle that more liquor can be purchased wholesale for 1s. 6d. than six thirsty people can buy for 3d each. Hence 'tambaroora muster', when the droughty party musters all the coin it's possessed of, and one individual goes and bargains for the beer.

1901 *The Bulletin Reciter* 202: 'Tambaroora' [poem title]

tank A dam, formed by excavation

1903 Joseph Furphy *Such is Life* (1944) 330: On a well-managed station, like Runnymede, a tank is, whenever possible, excavated on the margin of a swamp. The clay extracted is formed into a strong wall, or enclosing embankment, a couple of yards back from the edge of the excavation; and under this wall, an iron pipe connects the swamp with the tank.

1910 C. E. W. Bean *On the Wool Track* 58: The night before last we were making for a tank [added in later editions:] that is to say, a big, low, open reservoir and dam.

1931 Vance Palmer *Separate Lives* 229–30: He had been a mate of Denison's thirty years before, and had helped him sink tanks along the stock-routes from Dawson to the Bree.

Tantanoola tiger An animal reported preying on sheep at Tantanoola, S.A. in 1889, sometimes identified with a large wild dog shot there in 1895, whose stuffed hide was preserved in a local hotel; any beast similarly reported

1907 Charles MacAlister *Old Pioneering Days in the Sunny South* 356: The old-time system of shepherding flocks, hurdling or yarding them together at night in the days when the prowling dingo was the 'Tantanoola Tiger' of the bush.

1958 Max Harris in *The Penguin Book of Australian Verse*, ed. Thompson, Slessor and Howarth

258: 'The Tantanoola Tiger' [poem title]
1966 D. E. Charlwood *An Afternoon of Time* 68: Various legends, some written, some stencilled with bale stencils: 'Barney Elder shore here – 1887', 'Gerry owes Percy 10/–', 'The Tantanoola Tiger as bin cort'.
1979 *Weekend Australian* 30 Jun. 11: Don't bother to call Premier Des Corcoran the Colonel any more. The Tantanoola Tiger may be more appropriate. He has been back on his old stamping ground, the scene of his first electoral success [where Tantanoola is located], better known as Corcoran Country.

tap, on See quot. 1984
1984 *Bulletin* 19 Jun. 68: The word in the Cross is that he is 'on tap' (dead) in Long Bay.

tar, thumbnail dipped in see **thumbnail**

tarp A tarpaulin [abbr.]
1917 Diary cit. Patsy Adam-Smith *The Anzacs* (1978) 205: Made a shelter out of boxes of ammunition with a tarp for roof. Bad luck if a shell lands near.
1919 W. H. Downing *Digger Dialects* 49: *Tarp* A tarpaulin.
1963 Alan Marshall *In Mine Own Heart* 174: 'They were open trucks with no tarps.'
1971 Frank Hardy *The Outcasts of Foolgarah* 183: 'There's plenty of tarps: we'll rig up a tent.'

tarpaulin muster See quots
1904 E. S. Emerson *A Shanty Entertainment* 26: Each one in the room to sing, recite, or shout all round, and if nobody reneged, a tarpaulin muster every half-hour for drinks, or smokes, just as the company cared.
1936 Daisy McWilliams in *Depression Down Under ed. Len Fox* (1977) 17: Knowing his plight, friends made a 'tarpaulin muster' and paid the fine for him.
1945 Elisabeth George *Two at Daly Waters* 102: As she had not brought a town outfit, Daly Waters had what we call in the bush a tarpaulin muster (the loan of everybody's best clothes).
1969 Arthur Fadden *They called me Artie* 9: A tarpaulin muster among my family enabled me to collect it the night before the ball.
1978 Wendy Lowenstein *Weevils in the Flour* 187: I rushed in there and took up a tarpaulin muster, and got enough to pay the bailiff and fix us up for another week.

tart A girl or woman. Not used in any derogatory sense, although women would not refer to themselves as 'tarts'. The juvenile 'jam tart' is obsolete [abbr. of *sweetheart*]
[**1865** Hotten 254: *Tart* a term of approval applied by the London lower orders to a young woman for whom some affection is felt. The expression is not generally employed by the young men, unless the female is in 'her best', with a coloured gown, red or blue shawl, and plenty of ribbons in her bonnet – in fact, made pretty all over, like the jam tarts in the swell bakers' shops.]
1899 W. T. Goodge *Hits! Skits! and Jingles!* 150: And his lady-love's his 'donah' / Or his 'clinah' or his 'tart'.
1910 Thomas E. Spencer *Why Doherty Died* 83: You're a bosker! You're a jewel! You're a tart! / You're the only gel as I was ever sweet on.
1915 C. J. Dennis *The Songs of a Sentimental Bloke* 34: A cove 'as got to think some time in life / An' get some decent tart, 'ere it's too late, / To be 'is wife.
1938 H. Drake-Brockman *Men Without Wives* 15: 'The old tart's impatient, and so'm I. There'll be no peace till she's gone.'
1942 Gavin Casey *It's Harder for Girls* 111: 'She's a stupid sort of tart, anyway.'
1968 Thomas Keneally *Three Cheers for the Paraclete* 114: 'The mortgage office, you've got no idea ... Little tarts with short haircuts running all over the place with folders.'
1979 Ted Schurmann *The Showie* 44: 'Look', Tommo said, 'Danny's got himself a tart.'
1983 Clem Gorman *A Night in the Arms of Raeleen* 25: 'You gotta bar that ... Swearin' in front of a tart.'
see **tom, tom tart**

tart, bachelor's see **bachelor**

tartplate Pillion seat on motorbike or motorscooter, for female passenger
1982 *Southerly* 439: There may have been no disrespect in calling the pillion seat on a motor cycle or motorscooter a *tartplate*.

tartshop, dragged screaming from the Applied to politicians who have come reluctantly to face an election [attributed to W. M. Hughes, but used earlier by Alfred Deakin]
1904 Alfred Deakin *Ballarat Courier* 23 Aug. cit. J. A. La Nauze *Alfred Deakin* (1965) 378: I do not propose to reply to him [W. M. Hughes] except by saying he presents to you as undignified a spectacle as does the ill-bred urchin whom one sees dragged from a tart-shop kicking and screaming as he goes.
1974 *Sydney Morning Herald* 11 Jan. 6: It's time for the Whitlam Government, in Billy Hughes's immortal words, to be dragged screaming from the tart shop.
1982 *Sydney Morning Herald* 24 Dec. 12: Why should retired politicians, whose superannuation is already generously subsidised from the public

purse, get free rides as well? The tart shop, it seems, is not just open to the railway unions.

Tasmanian bluey   A hard-wearing jacket for outdoor work
[1891 Wilberton Tilley *The Wild West of Tasmania* 29: For about half a mile from the Silver Queen workings Zeehan is very thickly populated ... Heavily laden drays, pack-horses and mules, form constant processions journeying to or from Dundas and Trial; miners with their swags, surveyors in their 'blueys'.]
1934 Thomas Wood *Cobbers* 86: Axemen ... dressed in the manner of the craft – a slouch hat, trousers tucked into heavy boots, and a seamless coat of 'Tasmanian bluey', cut low round the neck and under the arms.
1977 *Sunday Telegraph* (Sydney) 5 Jun. 27: A tough, all-wool weatherproof jacket could become the new 'uniform' of Sydney wharfies. The jacket is the Tasmanian bluey, first made in Hobart in 1905.

Tassie (Tassy)   Tasmania; a Tasmanian [abbr.]
1894 *The Argus* 26 Jan. 3: Today Tassy – as most Victorian cricketers and footballers familiarly term our neighbour over the straits – will send a team into the field. [Morris]
1898 G. T. Bell *Tales of Australian Adventure* 103: 'I ... am going away to dear old Tassy to see the folks and the girl I left behind me.'
1900–10 O'Brien and Stephens: *Tassy* slang abbreviation of Tasmania.
1905 *The Old Bush Songs* ed. A. B. Paterson 51: Once more the Maorilander and the Tassey will be seen / Cooking johnny cakes and jimmies on the plains of Riverine.
1915 Henry Lawson 'Fighting Hard' *Verse* iii 154: Fighting hard for little Tassy, where the apple orchards grow.
1934 'Leslie Parker' *Trooper to the Southern Cross* (1966) 2: Coming round the west coast of Tassie we ran into really bad weather.
1963 Bruce Beaver *The Hot Summer* 61: 'Maybe Perth, eh? Or Tassie?'
1976 Helen Hodgman *Blue Skies* 11: 'I've come over from the mainland to give it a go in Tassie.'
1981 *Weekend Australian* 21 Nov. Mag. 5: 'They're all ratbags – the politicians and the conservationists. Tassie's in a mess and all they do is bloody argue.'

Tatt's   Tattersall's sweep, first promoted on the Sydney Cup in 1881 by George Adams, proprietor since 1878 of Tattersall's Hotel in Pitt St Sydney (on the model of subscription betting conducted by Tattersall's in London)
1908 Henry Fletcher *Dads and Dan between Smokes* 51: 'Ther white savage plays two-up; a

little better, he puts half-a-crown on ther tote; a little better, he sends a crown to Tatt's.'
1926 K. S. Prichard *Working Bullocks* 69: 'I says, "my intentions is honourable, and my prospeks – a ticket in Tat's".'
1934 *A Ticket in Tatt's* [title of film directed by F. W. Thring, screened Melbourne, Brisbane and Sydney from 6 Jan.]
1942 John Shaw Neilson *Autobiography* (1978) 95: The accountant suggested we should take a ticket in tatt's. We did so & won £9 each [in 1917].
1945 Tom Ronan *Strangers on the Ophir* 156: 'If we were living in a story-book, it would be simple. I'd find another Broken Hill, or win Tatts, or be discovered by a rich uncle.'
1963 Alan Marshall *In Mine Own Heart* 202: 'You can build them up before they leave [the fortune-teller's tent] – give them a legacy from a relative or a win in Tatt's or something.'
1983 *Bulletin* 26 Jul. 101: Said Paul Harris: 'It's a bit like winning Tatt's.'

taws   The initial or basic position, esp. in such figurative expressions as 'right from taws', 'back to taws' [f. *taw* a marble, and the line from which play starts OED 1740]
1954 Tom Ronan *Vision Splendid* 165: Should anyone leave a pannikin away from the table ... the old fellow would, in the Character's words, 'Be at him from taws with his whiskers waving'.
1964 H. P. Tritton *Time Means Tucker* 18: I was under the impression that it was to be the usual sparring match, but he came at me from taws.
1977 Colleen Klein *The Heart in the Basket* 99: 'I'd gather a bunch of young architects ... and I'd start from taws.'
1985 *Sydney Morning Herald* 27 May Guide 15: If it comes down to taws, they still do make films like that from time to time.

taxi, black   see **black taxi**

taxidermist, see a   Get stuffed
1969 A. W. Fadden *They Called Me Artie* 39: On the Saturday before election day I met my old friend Ted Walsh who was also my opponent ... On the wall of the bar an expertly preserved crocodile was displayed ... Nellie ... asked how I expected to fare against Ted on polling day. I replied, 'I expect that Ted will do to me what the taxidermist has done to your poor crocodile.'
1981 *Weekend Australian* 10 Oct. 15: Earlier this year he [Mr Muldoon] suggested that the President of Nigeria, Mr Shagari, should see a taxidermist.
1981 *Sydney Morning Herald* 8 Oct. 6: The problem with hard-hearted economists such as John Stone is their belief that the poor countries should – to borrow a CHOGMesque phrase – see a

taxidermist.

tea-and-sugar burglar A swagman who begs or 'borrows' tea and sugar; a minor predator
  1899 Henry Lawson 'A Rough Shed' *Prose* i 463: 'Could I explain that I "jabbed trotters" and was a "tea-and-sugar burglar" between sheds.'
  1956 Tom Ronan *Moleskin Midas* 165: 'We're pulling off a big job soon ... We'll make these tea-and-sugar bushrangers around this shanty look like a mob of schoolgirls.'
see **frying-pan**

tea and sugar train Weekly train across the Nullarbor from Cook, S.A. to Parkeston, W.A. to service the fettlers and railway communities on the Trans-Australia line
  1937 Ernestine Hill *The Great Australian Loneliness* 225: The 'Trans' and its people are a little world sufficient to themselves ... with a weekly shopping orgy on the 'Tea and Sugar' train that brings their water and supplies.
  1969 Patsy Adam Smith *Folklore of the Australian Railwaymen* 150: We were at Wirraminna doing the inaugural run of Santa Claus to children of the railway settlements across the Nullarbor ... Commonwealth Railways had given us a workman's van to live in on the Tea and Sugar train.
  1980 *Daily News* (Perth) 11 Nov. 3: Paddy has been a fettler on the trans-line for more than 20 years. His only regular contact now with people is when his 'tea and sugar' train makes a brief stop near his house once a week, to supply him with food.

Teddy Bear A show-off, esp. a cricketer given to antics on the field [? rhyming slang for *lair* q.v.]
  1953 Baker 135: *teddy bear* A flashily dressed, exhibitionistic person; by rhyme on *lair*.
  1955 *Bulletin* 28 Dec. 9: Rhyming slang added two more syllables to the noun [lair] and made it 'teddy-bear', and our natural tendency to abbreviate everything knocked the last syllable off again. Thus the 'lair' of yesteryear became a 'Teddy'.
  1965 Wally Grout *My Country's 'Keeper* 55: Umpire Col Egar was so furious at this amateurish attempt at time-wasting that he snapped to the Pakistani bowler: 'Get up you Teddy Bear' (an Australian expression not meant to be complimentary). Ibid. 133: Dave, according to us, was not only a candidate for the Teddy Bear's Picnic, he was driving the bus. In other words, he was inclined to be something rather more than boastful.
  1973 Frank Huelin *Keep Moving* 180: *Teddy-bears, Lairs* Brash, vain young hoboes.
  1974 Keith Stackpole *Not Just for Openers* 128: When Parfitt made the catch Greig jumped in the air, and, as he landed, thumped his fist into the pitch ... I said to Greig as I walked past, 'You're nothing but a bloody Teddy Bear.' He returned the pleasantries.

telegraph, bush see **bush**

tell the time if the town hall clock fell on top of him, couldn't see **couldn't**

ten, ten, two, and a quarter A week's rations in the outback: ten pounds of flour, ten of meat, two of sugar, and a quarter-pound of tea (the quantities might vary within this framework)
  1867 John Morrison *Australia As It Is* 175: The rations for one man are the well-known weekly allowance of 10 lbs. of flour, 10 lbs. of meat, 2 lbs. of sugar, and a quarter of a pound of tea.
  1903 Joseph Furphy *Such is Life* (1944) 104: He [the boundary rider] has some hundreds of pounds lent out (without interest or security) though his pay is only fifteen shillings a week – with ten, ten, two, and a quarter.
  1905 *The Old Bush Songs* ed. A. B. Paterson 41: 'But I'll give ten-ten, sugar an' tea; / Ten bob a week, if you'll suit me.'
  1935 R. B. Plowman *The Boundary Rider* 186: *Ten, two, and a quarter.* Wherever there are sheep and boundary riders these cryptic words have a world of meaning ... for they are at the basis of the boundary-rider's existence. On every sheep and cattle station where men are provided with rations, one man's needs for a week are allotted on the basis of ten pounds of flour, two pounds of sugar, and a quarter of a pound of tea ... Meat is provided without being measured by the pound.
  1956 Tom Ronan *Moleskin Midas* 332: 'Give me a humpy down there on the creek and feed me on the old ten, ten, two and a quarter.'
  1964 H. P. Tritton *Time Means Tucker* 20: Most of the outback stations issued rations. It was not done as a charity ... but as a means of ensuring a plentiful supply of casual labour ... Most of the squatters did not stick strictly to the bare issue laid down by the Pastoralists' Union, which was ten pounds of flour, ten of meat, two of sugar and a quarter pound of tea.
  1978 John Hepworth *His Book* 155: There was the great tradition that you could always get a feed in the bush. Well, generally you managed, but it wasn't like it used to be in the good old days of ten, ten, two and a quarter.

Tench The convict barracks in Hobart: *obs.* [abbr. of *Penitentiary*]
  1859 Oliné Keese *The Broad Arrow* ii 432: 'Prisoners' barracks, sir – us calls it Tench.'
  1864 J. F. Mortlock *Experiences of a Convict* (1965) 89: The Prisoners' Barracks (commonly called the 'Tench') became the abode of myself and

hundreds more, who earned our food and lodging by stone-breaking, or other public labour.

tent embassy   see **embassy**

tent, were you born in a   Reproach to someone who has come in leaving the door open [Partridge lists *born in a barn* Canadian]
1979 *Sun-Herald* 11 Nov. 119: Now that the Olds are liberated, they'll probably stop locking doors. 'What were you, born in a tent?'

Territorian   1   An inhabitant of the Northern Territory
1882 William J. Sowden *The Northern Territory As It Is* 41: Past the racecourse – for the Territorians attempt races between the animated clothes-horses dubbed equines here – you come to Sailor's Gully.
1908 Mrs Aeneas Gunn *We of the Never-Never* 10: The Man-in-Charge smiled openly as he poured out the tea, proving thereby his kinship with all other Territorians.
1930 J. S. Litchfield *Far-North Memories* 57: Unfortunately, a number of Territorians considered they had a right to take forcible possession of any lubra that suited their fancy.
1941 Charles Barrett *Coast of Adventure* 121: Old Territorians, over a glass of beer at the 'pub', or pannikin of tea by the campfire, will tell yarns as long as you'll listen.
1968 Frank Hardy *The Unlucky Australians* 11: 'The old Territorian is a good bloke, rough as guts but his heart's in the right place.'
1975 *Australian* 27 Sep. 3: The Territorians – obviously attracted by the commissioners' informality and interest – responded by giving them a good – and welcome – earbashing.
1982 *Weekend Australian* 15 May 3: Each Territorian annually guzzles an average of 931 glasses of beer, 25 bottles of wine and 125 nips of hard spirits – a consumption twice the national average.
2   A resident of the A.C.T.
1981 *Canberra Times* 24 Jun. 21: The discovery that there is nascent shelter [from nuclear fallout] for 35,874 Territorians, or at best 150,911 of us is not especially cheering since there were 197,622 Territorians alive and kicking when the 1976 census was taken and may very well be 240,000 of us now.

Territory, the   The Northern Territory
1882 William J. Sowden *The Northern Territory As It Is* 48: Capital and skilled labour must be the watch-word for the Territory.
1898 A. B. Paterson *Bulletin* 31 Dec. 31: The man who once goes to the Territory always has a hankering to get back there.
1930 J. S. Litchfield *Far-North Memories* 207: It

is the exception to find the man who does not drink to excess in the Territory.
1933 F. E. Baume *Tragedy Track* 79: They are the rats of the Territory, men who refuse to work.
1951 Ernestine Hill *The Territory* [book title]
1975 *Australian* 27 Sep. 3: Commission gets down to earth on the Territory's troubles.
1981 *Australian* 22 Jul. 3: I was mystified by the bowl in the men's pissoir being way off-centre on its cubicle wall. Why? Denis Hornsby ... explained: 'So the users who are, ah, tired can lean against the wall.' They look after drinkers in the Territory.
Territory confetti
1982 *NT News* (Darwin) 14 Jan. 7: It's called 'Territory confetti' and it's scattered around the countryside ... the ring-pull tops from stubbies and cans.
Territory factor
1983 *NT News* (Darwin) 11 Jan. 7: Most of us have heard of the Territory factor – the indefinable excuse for charging more.
Territory rig
1983 *Australian* 4 Nov. 7: Mr Yunupingu, in what the tourist brochures call 'Territory rig' – open-neck shirt, shorts and long white socks.

that   Used to express qualification, tentative addition to a statement (cf. **like**)
1974 Keith Stackpole *Not Just for Openers* 22: Not patting ourselves on the back or that, I think the only sound sides over the last couple of years have been the sides chosen on tour. They've been chosen on form.
1977 *Weekend Australian* 3–4 Sep. Mag. 14: 'Now listen to what we're saying, Mick, because this will be bloody vital and that.'
1980 Rod Ansell *To Fight the Wild* 54: There wasn't much bush tucker in the area around my camp, in the way of fruit or that.

that'll be the day   see **day**

that's the issue   see **issue**

that's the shot   see **shot**

they were open   see **open**

thirds, on   See quots
1824 E. Curr *An Account of the Colony of Van Diemen's Land* 77–8: It is common practice for persons who have not sufficient land, or who cannot attend personally to their flocks, to give them in charge to another party, who receives one third of the increase for his trouble ... In this manner many persons have become possessed of considerable flocks, and if the party taking them for 'the thirds' be careful and trustworthy, it is

beneficial to both parties. The same method is adopted with cattle.

1826 *Hobart Town Gazette* 22 Apr. 3: A Gentleman, possessing an extensive Run for Sheep, will have no objection to Run on the Thirds to the Number of 1000 – None need apply but those of respectable Character.

1834 Let. in T. P. Besnard *A Voice from the Bush of Australia* (1839) 14: These sheep I have put out to graze, according to the custom of the country, on *thirds* – that is the person who grazes and takes care of the flock is entitled to ⅓ of the produce of the wool, and ⅓ of the lambs that are dropped.

1843 Charles Rowcroft *Tales of the Colonies* ii 109: I had prevailed on him to purchase ... a hundred ewes heavy with lamb, and to put them out 'on thirds'.

1852 G. C. Mundy *Our Antipodes* i 282: Take stock on the system of 'thirds', in which the working partner gets one third of the wool and of the increase, while the proprietary partner, as he may be called, follows some other profession, or his pleasures, or holds some Government appointment at the capital or elsewhere.

Thommo's A notorious two-up school operating near Sydney [f. Joe Thomas, the organizer]

1959 Dorothy Hewett *Bobbin Up* 69: The show folded up, Kel did all their savings at Thommo's. Ibid. 159: The cockatoos kept watch outside the dirty house in Reservoir Street, where Thommos two-up school did a roaring, open trade.

1966 Elwyn Wallace *Sydney and the Bush* 140: He did his ready at Tommo's game.

1973 *Sydney Morning Herald* 29 Jun. 6: Jack Brown ... ran a two-up school in the northern suburbs, as popular as Thommo's was in the City.

1976 *Sunday Telegraph* (Sydney) 13 Jun. 12: Police raid Thommo's: 15 charged on two-up Thommo's two-up school, the most famous and longest lasting game in Sydney, was raided by police early yesterday ... Thommo's two-up school was established during World War II and has flourished ever since. Successive police commissioners have denied the two-up school's existence, claiming it was a 'press myth'.

1979 *Sydney Morning Herald* 17 Jul. 10: Forty-one people were arrested on Saturday night when police from the 21 Special Squad CIB raided a two-up game at Thommo's in Darlinghurst ... Mr Roach told the court that the two-up school at Thommo's had been resurrected, Thommo himself had died a few years ago.

1981 *Sydney Morning Herald* 26 Dec. 3: Police have obtained a court order making Thommo's two-up school a 'declared gaming house' ... Police had recently made five raids on the first floor premises at 179 Oxford Street, Darlinghurst.

three-up A game which preceded two-up; see quot. 1859

[**1859** Hotten 108: *Three-up* a gambling game played by costers. Three half-pennies are thrown up, and when they all fall 'heads', or all 'tails', it is a mark; and the man who gets the greatest number of marks out of a given amount – three, five, or more – wins.]

1849 Alexander Harris *The Emigrant Family* ed. W. S. Ramson (1967) 335: A circle of spectators; in the midst of which was Oshee, face to face with an antagonist, whose pockets he was rapidly emptying by his skill, acquired through many a year's hard study of the evolutions of three penny pieces in the air; or, as he himself would have designated the game, 'three-up'.

1907 Charles MacAlister *Old Pioneering Days in the Sunny South* 191: Some of them were ... ardent followers of the 'three-up school'.

throat, to have the game by the To be in full control, in a position of advantage

1947 John Morrison *Sailors Belong Ships* 15: 'We're sailors, see? Two sailors. We got the game by the throat.'

1960 Ron Tullipan *Follow the Sun* 105: 'Think we'll get it done to-day?' 'Can't miss ... We have it by the throat now all right.'

1974 David Ireland *Burn* 58: 'So you got the game by the throat, eh?'

throw a map see **map**

throw a seven see **seven**

throw one's hat in first see **hat**

throw off To deride, ridicule; superseded by **sling off** q.v.

1812 Vaux: *Throw off* to talk in a sarcastical strain, so as to convey offensive allusions under a mask of pleasantry, or innocent freedom; but, perhaps, secretly venting that abuse which you would not dare to give in direct terms.

1911 E. S. Sorenson *Life in the Australian Back-blocks* 247: Some hard case is bound to 'throw-off' at him at such times.

1935 Kylie Tennant *Tiburon* 190: 'You're not being funny, are you? Sort of throwing off?'

1947 Margaret Trist *Daddy* 126: 'Of course, I do get annoyed when Geoff throws off about it.'

1962 Dymphna Cusack *Picnic Races* 183: 'You're like all the townies. Throwing off at people on the land.'

thumbnail dipped in tar, written with a Catch-phrase for rough penmanship, from Paterson's 'Clancy of the Overflow'

1895 A. B. Paterson *The Man from Snowy River*

20: And an answer came directed in a writing unexpected / (And I think the same was written with a thumb-nail dipped in tar); / 'Twas his shearing mate who wrote it, and *verbatim* I will quote it: / 'Clancy's gone to Queensland droving, and we don't know where he are.'

1984 Phillip Adams *Weekend Australian* 28 Apr. Mag. 2: My attention turned to home and, dipping my thumb nail in tar, I managed, I think, to evoke the cultural, social and spiritual reality for a typical suburbanite [in writing 'I Love this Bonzer Country' as a new national anthem].

Thursday or Anthony Horderns   An equivalent to 'Pitt Street or Christmas' or 'Tuesday or Bourke Street', q.v. [f. the former Sydney retail store]

1982 Nancy Keesing *Lily on the Dustbin* 127: More to the point is her brother's remark that she'd 'forget her head if it wasn't screwed on.' Her aunt sums up: 'You wouldn't know if it was Thursday or Anthony Horderns.'

ticket, pakapoo   see **pakapoo**

tickets, to have ~ on oneself   To be conceited [? f. sales tickets advertising a high price, or prize certificates at a show]

[**1915** C. J. Dennis *The Songs of a Sentimental Bloke* 28: 'E's taken tickets on 'is own 'igh worth; / Puffed up wiv pride.]

1941 Kylie Tennant *The Battlers* 20: 'Arr,' the busker said disgustedly, 'you've got tickets all over yourself.'

1953 Gwen Meredith *Beyond Blue Hills* 84: 'I know I'm not in the same class as Danny Marks,' he announced, 'I haven't got any tickets on myself.'

1965 Randolph Stow *The Merry-go-Round in the Sea* 132: 'You've got tickets on yourself,' he finished, lamely.

1970 Jack Hibberd *White with Wire Wheels* in *Plays* 227: 'You're the bastard that's always been smug and had tickets on himself.'

tiger   A toiler in a shearing-shed; any one doing rough work

1897 Henry Lawson 'The Green-hand Rouseabout' *Verse* i 322: Engine whistles. 'Go it, tigers!' and the agony begins.

c. **1910** *Old Bush Songs* ed. Stewart and Keesing (1957) 259: 'A Lot of Lachlan Tigers' [ballad title]

1956 F. B. Vickers *First Place to the Stranger* 135: 'You're going to see something now ... Those tigers (he meant the shearers) will make you dance.'

1959 C. V. Lawlor *All This Humbug* 23: 'If you don't mind, Missus, I'd like to be sure I'm not drinking out of the same cup as the new "Tiger".'

tigering   Working hard under adverse conditions;

roughing it

1880–1904 'The Banks of the Condamine' *Old Bush Songs* ed. Stewart and Keesing (1957) 257: Your delicate constitution / Is not equal unto mine, / To stand the constant tigering / On the banks of the Condamine.

1973 Roland Robinson *The Drift of Things* 385: He was a well-built young man, and a good worker as I was to find out; but then I had done my share of tigering and I reckoned I could hold my own.

tiger country   Rough, thickly wooded terrain feared by airmen; any primitive area

1945 Elisabeth George *Two at Daly Waters* 89: The territory a hundred and sixty miles west of Daly Waters and thence to the Western Australian coast is also dreaded by aviators and generally called by them 'tiger country'. Dwellings are from eighty to a hundred miles apart and there are no recognizable landmarks for the flyer who is bushed. Ibid. 115: What other aviators call tiger country – hills, thick scrub and probably only one chance in a hundred of landing without disaster.

1961 George Farwell *Vanishing Australians* 20: A Kimberley settler in the undeveloped 'tiger country', away on the wrong side of the rough-shod King Leopold Range.

1968 Patsy Adam-Smith *Tiger Country* [book title]

1974 *Australian* 12 Jan. 22: Mr Brown has spent a good part of his tenure as mayor chasing after new industries, urging them to come and settle where there are thousands of acres of Crown land, not wanted for agriculture or housing – 'tiger country', he calls it.

tiger, for work (punishment)   A 'demon' for work, someone with an insatiable appetite for it

1896 *Bulletin* 24 Oct. Red Page: His father thought a lot of Henry; he used to call him a tiger for work.

1935 William Hatfield *Black Waterlily* 15: 'Tiger for work, aren't you?' he smiled. 'A good fault, of course, if you don't carry it to extremes.'

1953 Dymphna Cusack *Southern Steel* 249: 'I'll hand it to you. You were always a tiger for work.'

1959 Dorothy Hewett *Bobbin Up* 79: 'He's a real tiger for his tucker,' Linnie said, smiling wanly through her tears.

1965 Eric Lambert *The Long White Night* 74: I patted her shoulder. 'Mum, you're a tiger for punishment!'

tiger, Tantanoola   see **Tantanoola**

Tigers, the   1   In N.S.W., the Balmain Rugby League team [f. black and gold colours, and club emblem]

1976 *Sun-Herald* 13 Jun. 52: Tigers' semi-final spot is on the line.

Tigertown   Balmain
1976 *Sunday Telegraph* (Sydney) 14 Nov. 160: Sir John Kerr might have moved out of Tigertown, but Kep Enderby has moved in. The former Attorney-General has ... bought a house in Balmain.
2   In Victoria, the Richmond V.F.L. team
1974 *Sunday Telegraph* (Sydney) 29 Sep. 108: Tigers knock the knockers.
3   In W.A., the Claremont Australian Rules team
1980 *West Australian* (Perth) 19 May 60: Runaway Tigers swamp Demons [heading] Claremont kicked their highest score for the season against Perth at Lathlain Park on Saturday.
4   In S.A., the Glenelg Australian Rules team
1979 *Advertiser* (Adelaide) 23 Apr. 13: Roosters' full back cages Tigers [heading]
5   In Queensland, the Easts Rugby League team
1979 *Courier-Mail* (Brisbane) 19 Apr. 21: Tigers captain-coach Des Morris confirmed that some of his players had complained of being bitten.
The Mayne Australian Rules team
1979 *Courier-Mail* (Brisbane) 28 May 18: It was a disappointing performance from the Tigers, who ... succumbed to the Kedron onslaught in the third quarter.
6   In N.T., the Nightcliff Australian Rules team
1979 *NT News* (Darwin) 17 Nov. 40: Tigers skin safe Too strong for Buffs [heading]
7   In Tasmania, the Hobart Australian Rules team
1980 *Mercury* (Hobart) 31 Mar. 28: The Tigers show that old snarl [heading]

Tilly Devine   Wine [rhyming slang]
1953 T. A. G. Hungerford *Riverslake* 35: 'Right now, he'd give you half next week's pay for a snort of Tilly Devine, I bet!'

time, couldn't tell the   see **couldn't**

timothy   A brothel
1953 Baker 124: *timothy*, a brothel.
1982 *NT News* (Darwin) 8 May 9. There were 17 men in the 'Timothy' when it 'went off'.

tin-arsed, tin-back, tin-bum   Lucky, a lucky person [? f. being impervious to kicks in the backside. Apparently unrelated to *tin* = money]
1899 W. T. Goodge *Hits! Skits! and Jingles!* 150: And a 'tin-back' is a party / Who's remarkable for luck.
1955 D'Arcy Niland *The Shiralee* 142: 'I come up with a stone worth five hundred quid ... Tin-bum, they call me.'
1971 R. F. Brissenden *Winter Matins* 25: This tin-arsed character / Hasn't been there six months before he starts / To fidget, gets to grizzling in his beer.
1975 Les Ryan *The Shearers* 79: 'Good on yer Joe. You always were a tin-arse.'

tin dog   An improvised rattle, used when travelling stock: *rare*
1911 L. St Clare Grondona *Collars and Cuffs* 76: I hastily procured a jam tin from the cook, and manufactured what is locally known as a 'tin dog' ... I put in some gravel, and whenever 'Nigger' fagged, which wasn't seldom, I rattled it for all I was worth.

Tin Hare   1   The mechanical hare used in dog racing
2   Nickname for a train, esp. a rail motor, with a rapid bobbing motion
1941 Kylie Tennant *The Battlers* 159: The 'Tin Hare's' whistle was heard in the distance.
1983 *Sydney Morning Herald* 8 Oct. 37: It is the last of the 'tin-hare' rail-motors.

tin-kettle, tin-kettling   The beating of dishes, etc. to celebrate a wedding or similar event
[**1875** A. J. Boyd *Old Colonials* (1882) 49–50: Watch them, when they have scented out a wedding. They collect all the kerosene-tins, pots and pans they can lay their hands on, and in the evening, if the luckless pair have not previously departed on a tour, their ears are assailed with a most atrocious din. Tins are battered under the windows, stones are thrown on the roof, and yells and cheers make the night hideous ... the maddened benedict rushes out and distributes either money or liquor.]
1892 Barcroft Boake 'Babs Malone' *Bulletin* 20 Feb. 21 repr. in *Where the Dead Men Lie* (1897) 103: What cheering and tin-kettling / Had they after at the 'settling'.
1898 D. W. Carnegie *Spinifex and Sand* 325–6: Christmas Eve is celebrated by a performance known as 'tin-kettling', in which all join. Each arms himself with a dish, or empty tin, which he beats violently with a stick. To the tune of this lovely music the party marches from house to house, and at each demands drink of some kind, which is always forthcoming.
1900 Henry Lawson 'The Songs They Used to Sing' *Prose* i 380: They married on the sly and crept into camp after dark; but the diggers got wind of it and rolled up with gold-dishes, shovels &c. &c., and gave them a real good tin-kettling in the old-fashioned style.
1931 A. W. Upfield *The Sands of Windee* 39: 'I hope you haven't forgotten that we are to tin-kettle the Fosters tomorrow night.'
1950 Vance Palmer *Coast to Coast 1949–50* 6: They had missed their chance of tin-kettling the parson on the night he had brought his bride home; it was a ceremony that was organized for couples when there was anything dubious about the marriage.
1964 *Sydney Morning Herald* 25 Apr. 11: At

Dalton ... a few weeks back there was a 'tin kettling' (first night after the honeymoon neighbours surround the house and bang tin utensils.)
1971 Frank Hardy *The Outcasts of Foolgarah* 200: 'We orta give the bludger a tin kettling.'
1980 Barney Roberts *The Penalty of Adam* 169: 'The boys have organised a tin kettling for Harry Eddington, tomorrow night.'

tin, kick the   see **kick**

tinlid   A kid [rhyming slang]
1954 T. A. G. Hungerford *Sowers of the Wind* 254: 'You got any tin-lids that you know of?'
1968 Stuart Gore *Holy Smoke* 110: *tin-lid* A 'kid'; a child.
1983 Barry Dickins *Australian Book Review* Jul. [inside front cover]: It says in the foreword that Bruce used to help out at his Dad's orchard as a tinlid.

tinned dog   Canned meat
1895 *Bulletin* 17 Aug. 27: We gave him some 'tinned dorg' and a drink.
1898 D. W. Carnegie *Spinifex and Sand* 14: A supply of the staple food of the country, 'Tinned Dog' – as canned provisions are designated.
1901 F. J. Gillen *Diary* (1968) 275: I'm afraid it will take us some days to settle down to damper and tinned dog.
1922 Edward Meryon *At Holland's Tank* 28: The jam stood on the table in its original tin, and the 'tinned dog' or tinned meat, was served likewise.
1946 K. S. Prichard *The Roaring Nineties* 7: Dinny induced the storekeeper to stake him for a few pounds of flour and sugar, tinned dog and tea.
1950 Gavin Casey *City of Men* 326: 'We'll be living in a tent and eating tinned dog. It's no place for a woman.'
1964 Nancy Cato *The Sea Ants* 13: The welcome change in diet, with fried fish instead of tinned-dog on the menu, only whetted their appetites for more.

tinnie   **1**   A can of beer, usu. 375 ml
1964 Barry Humphries *A Nice Night's Entertainment* (1981) 79: We all shacked up there with stacks of the old *glühwein*, a few crates of tinnies, a couple of little snow bunnies and no complications.
1978 *Sunday Telegraph* (Sydney) 19 Mar. 35: Low-price 'tinnies' woo drinkers away from bottles.
1982 *Sun-Herald* 11 Apr. 68: Television may encourage a generation of Norms, flaked in the easychair with a carton of tinnies.
1984 *Alice Springs Star* 7 Aug. 15: With ice cold tinnies at only $1 a good raging crowd is certain.
2   A boat with an aluminium hull (instead of fibreglass)
1979 *Herald* (Melbourne) 7 Jun. 35: The aluminium 'tinnie' has long been a major force in the Australian boat market for its low initial cost, durability and ease of use.
1982 *Sun-Herald* 5 Sep. 112: Tinnies offer value, fun [heading] Dollar for dollar it's hard to go past the simple aluminium dinghy as a versatile fun boat ... In price, there's a tinnie to suit most pockets. They can be bought secondhand with a small outboard, for as little as $500, while fully equipped new models can cost more than $2000.
1983 *Daily Mirror* (Sydney) 25 Feb. 22: The Quintrex Fish Nipper is a little more than a 3.5m (11ft 6in) 'tinnie'.

tinny *adj.*   As for **tin-arsed**
1919 W. H. Downing *Digger Dialects* 50: *Tinny* Lucky.
1950 Jon Cleary *Just Let Me Be* 54: 'Your mother won again, Joe. Six pounds.' 'She's tinny,' Joe said.
1962 *Australian One-Act Plays* ed. Eunice Hanger 20: 'Some people are always lucky. So tinny, they must wear tin pants.'
1981 Rev. Fred Nile *Sun-Herald* 27 Sep. 9: 'I developed a technique and skills in gambling and I reckon I could still win a lot of money. As it is, I'm what you might call tinny. The only time I ever pulled the handle of a poker machine after I was converted, I won a jackpot.'

tin, ring the   see **ring**

Tinsel Town   Sydney, esp. from a Melbourne standpoint [f. parallel with Hollywood]
1981 *National Times* 29 Mar. 38: Seems Tinsel Town won't support elegant theatre restaurants. The Tivoli cabaret in George St, Sydney closed after two months. Pinks in Goulburn Street ... is languishing.
1982 *Age* (Melbourne) 19 May 2: Sydney's gay community is ready to give the deeply moral American fundamentalist, the Reverend Jerry Falwell, a fun welcome when he arrives in tinsel town to begin his saving grace tour tomorrow.

Tin Shed, the Old   As for **the Old Barn** q.v.
1975 *Sun* (Sydney) 4 Dec. 28: The Old Tin Shed, the Stadium, long gone home of boxing heroes, wrestling bums, pop artists and jazz greats.

to and from   A Pom i.e. Englishman (rhyming slang]
1946 Rohan Rivett *Behind Bamboo* 399: *To-and-from* a Pommy, i.e. Englishman.
1978 *Daily Telegraph* (Sydney) 11 Mar. 17: The to-and-froms speak in a most peculiar way.
1982 *Weekend Australian* 6 Mar. Mag. 8: As a 'To-and-From', one of the things that baffled me ...

when I first arrived here many years ago was the esky routine.

toastrack A tram with external footboards instead of an internal corridor (discontinued in Sydney by 1960) [f. resemblance]
1941 Baker 77: *Toastrack* One of the old-style footboard trams still used in Sydney.
1961 Hugh Atkinson *Low Company* 113: The tram stop opposite where the faithful got down after riding the toast-rack trams from the smart areas uptown.
1966 Peter Mathers *Trap* 190: A tram now, it would be a toast-rack with ten or so compartments with the only physical intercommunication along the outside footboards, and the concertina doors.
1973 *Bulletin* 17 Nov. 44: Visitors there [the Sydney Tram Museum at Loftus] can ride on an authentic toastrack for 15 cents (children 10 cents).
1980 Clive James *Unreliable Memoirs* 96: The rest of us went by toast-rack tram to Rushcutter's Bay.

toby 1 A raddle stick for marking sheep not shorn to the employer's satisfaction
1912 'Goorianawa' *The Lone Hand* 1 Oct. 30 repr. in *Old Bush Songs* ed. Stewart and Keesing (1957) 273: I've been shearing on the Goulburn side and down at Douglas Park, / Where every day 'twas 'Wool away!' and toby did his work.
1964 H. P. Tritton *Time Means Tucker* 41: Till the 1902 strike, the owner had the right to raddle any sheep not shorn to his satisfaction and the shearer would not be paid for it. (Raddle was a stick of blue or yellow ochre, also called 'Toby').
2 A 'dab' at something: *rare*
1941 Baker 77: *Toby* A man silly of mind and clumsy of hand, but willing to do whatever asked.
1944 Alan Marshall *These Are My People* 155: 'I'm not much chop on pies, but I'm a toby on puddin's.'

toe Speed, esp. in horse racing
1889 A. B. Paterson 'The Scapegoat' in *Singer of the Bush* (1983) 103: He had what the racing men call 'too much toe' for him.
1923 Con Drew *Rogues & Ruses* 163: 'He has got two horses in the Handicap, and is bemoanin' his fate that both can't win. They're both got plenty of toe, and they're got about equal weights.'
1951 Dal Stivens *Jimmy Brockett* 166: It made me feel real good to hear that engine. It sounded as though it had plenty of toe.
1963 Lou Richards *Boots and All!* 75: He really had a ton of toe because he was a top professional foot-runner.
1981 *Sydney Morning Herald* 12 Jun. 33: Toey filly fully fit for classic final [heading] Back ail-

ment or not, the Brad Hanover youngster had enough toe to race without cover for the final 1,300 metres.
1983 *Sun-Herald* 23 Oct. 73: In Lawson and Hogg we have two penetrating fast bowlers who have enough 'toe' to keep any batsman honest.

toe-ragger 1 A swagman, an itinerant down-and-out [also English tramps' slang, as in Orwell's *Down and Out in Paris and London*]
[**1864** J. F. Mortlock *Experiences of a Convict* (1965) 83–4: Stockings being unknown, some luxurious men wrapped round their feet a piece of old shirting, called, in language more expressive than elegant, a 'toe-rag'.]
1896 *Truth* 12 Jan. 4: The bushie's favourite term of opprobrium 'a toe-ragger' is also probably from the Maori. [Morris]
1900–10 O'Brien and Stephens: *Toe-ragger* Person of no position, occupation, wealth or attainments.
1903 Joseph Furphy *Such is Life* (1944) 227: 'Come over to the wagon, and have a drink of tea,' says I. 'No, no,' says he, 'none of your toe-rag business.'
1941 Baker 77: *Toe ragger* a person of no position, wealth or attainments.
2 A prisoner with a short sentence
1918 J. Vance Marshall *Jail from Within* 45: 'Some o' you toeraggers (short-timers) take the cake.'

toey 1 Restive, fractious, touchy [? pawing ground]
1945 Baker 135: *toey* Worried or anxious.
1969 Patsy Adam Smith *Folklore of the Australian Railwaymen* 82–3: We were shunting at Marree and I had a toey crew on. I knew they had booze planted somewhere and they knew I knew.
1974 *Sydney Morning Herald* 1 Jan. 2: 'He's that toey he's got us all nervous, too.'
1983 *Sydney Morning Herald* 14 Jan. 1: Mr Wran returned from Lord Howe Island one day earlier than scheduled because, as he put it, 'I get toey: I was anxious to get back to work.'
2 Speedy
1973 Jack Hibberd *A Stretch of the Imagination* (1981) 43: 'A toey winger was rendered flat of foot by a long handball over his skull on to the half-forward line.'

togs Clothes esp. a bathing costume [f. thieves' slang OED 1809]
[**1812** Vaux: *Togs* or *Toggery* wearing-apparel in general.]
1857 Charles Thatcher *Colonial Songster* 18: In the colony I've just arrived, / My togs, I know, look rum.
1899 W. T. Goodge *Hits! Skits! and Jingles!* 151:

And his clothes he calls his 'clobber' / Or his 'togs'.
1918 *Kia Ora Coo-ee* 15 Apr. 7: Some of the Queenslanders are revelling in the opportunity of getting out in this hot weather in their bathing togs.
1924 Steele Rudd *Me an' th' Son* 9: The store-keeper hands us th' togs – a large set for me, an' a medium lot for th' son.
1945 Baker 183: Swimming costumes are variously known as *togs*, *bathers*.
1952 Jon Cleary *The Sundowners* 132: 'I get up in the morning, put on my togs and in three minutes I'm down in the surf.'
1960 John Iggulden *The Storms of Summer* 208: 'Why don't we have a swim?' asked Judy . . . 'Get your togs and wake up the others.'

tom, tom-tart A girl or woman. Not derogatory, but not used by women of themselves: *obsolescent* [? f. *tomrig* a strumpet OED 1668]
c. **1882** *The Sydney Slang Dictionary* 8: *Tom-tart* Sydney phrase for a girl or sweetheart.
1906 Edward Dyson *Fact'ry 'Ands* 55: 'There's a little tom in this flat who'd give er bit t' have you hers for keeps.'
1915 C. J. Dennis *The Songs of a Sentimental Bloke* 20: A squarer tom, I swear, I never seen, / In all me natchril, than this 'ere Doreen.
1933 Norman Lindsay *Saturdee* 181: 'Who's yer tom? She must be yer sweetheart. Why don't yer up an' kiss her?'
1951 Dal Stivens *Jimmy Brockett* 102: 'You did, darling,' one of the little social toms said. She was a nuggety little sheila.

tomahawk To cut sheep while shearing; to shear roughly
1859 Henry Kingsley *Recollections of Geoffry Hamlyn* ii 25: Shearers were very scarce, and the poor sheep got fearfully 'tomahawked' by the new hands.
1864 James Armour *The Diggings, the Bush, and Melbourne* 17: The latter were often brought to task for 'tomahawking', or leaving ridge-and-furrow shearmarks.
1878 G. H. Gibson *Southerly Busters* 179: I'm able for to shear 'em clean, / And level as a die; / But I prefers to 'tommy-hawk', / And make the 'daggers' fly.
1898 Roland Graeme *From English to the Backblocks* 189: 'I don't want small numbers,' he replied once to a squatter, who had been boasting of the high tallies his shearers made, 'but I won't have my sheep tomahawked.'
1925 E. S. Sorenson *Murty Brown* 105: 'They do a bit o' tommyhawkin' at shearin' time, an lay up with gammy wrists about three days a week.'
tomahawker
1964 H. P. Tritton *Time Means Tucker* 40: Toma-

hawkers were shearers whose sheep looked as though the wool had been chopped off with an axe.

Tomaris Sweep conducted in Darwin on the Melbourne Cup [f. Tom Harris, who founded it in 1934]
1979 *NT News* (Darwin) 6 Nov. 1: Darwin book-maker Gerry Monck has won the Tomaris. His last minute decision to gamble on 2000 tickets instead of his usual 1000 has won him $10,000.

Tom Collins see **Collins**

toms tits, toms, the The shits [rhyming slang: different from the English use (Franklyn, Partridge) in being always in the plural, and in not occurring as a verb]
1944 Lawson Glassop *We Were the Rats* 67: 'Break it down,' said the corporal. 'You'll give these blokes the tomtits before they get their first lot of C.B.'
1946 Rohan Rivett *Behind Bamboo* 399: *Tomtits* dysentery, diarrhoea.
1948 Sumner Locke Elliott *Rusty Bugles* in *Khaki, Bush and Bigotry* ed. Eunice Hanger (1968) 44: 'You blokes give me the tom-tits. Always belly-aching about something.'
1964 Thomas Keneally *The Place at Whitton* 51: 'This place,' Raddles, some way down the hall, grunted, 'and this silence business. It gives me the toms.'
1968 Geoffrey Dutton *Andy* 199: 'Yanks? Here? Don't give us the tom tits.'
1973 Patsy Adam Smith *The Barcoo Salute* 14: 'What's the matter, got the tom tits?'

tongs Hand shears [f. shape]
1908 W. H. Ogilvie *My Life in the Open* 36: Most of the . . . sheds in Australia are now fitted with machinery, but in many are still to be found the old-fashioned shears, or 'tongs' as they are familiarly called.
1910 C. E. W. Bean *On the Wool Track* 195: 'It's the same . . . whether they're working tongs or machines.'
1955 *Australian Bush Ballads* ed. Stewart and Keesing 247: There in crowded huts at night-time, drinking tea and rigging 'tongs'.
1961 George Farwell *Vanishing Australians* 93: Back in Jackie Howe's day there were many good men who could cut their 300 a day 'with the tongs'.

tonk A man with un-masculine characteristics; a male homosexual, esp. in the passive role: *derogatory* [unexplained]
1941 Baker 77: *Tonk* A simpleton or fool (2) A dude or fop (3) A general term of contempt.
1964 George Johnston *My Brother Jack* 65: 'You've got to get rid of those sonky bloody cobbers of yours,' he said to me one night. 'The way you lot

are heading you'll end up a bunch of tonks.'

1965 Hal Porter *Stars of Australian Stage and Screen* 280: During the last ten years or more, there have been imported a coterie of *untalented* English homosexuals, English tonks unheard of outside their home country, to dominate sections of the Australian theatrical scene.

1968 *Coast to Coast 1967–1968* 2: He had gone to agricultural college until he was eighteen, but like most farmers' sons tended to disguise the fact in his speech. One taunting cry of 'Tonk!' and country boys felt they were ruined for life.

1970 Richard Beilby *No Medals for Aphrodite* 32: 'You're a good bloke, Turk, but sometimes you talk like a tonk,' one of them had told him in a moment of bibulous candour. And so he took care not to talk like a tonk ... Instead, he had adopted their sloppy, profanity-riddled speech.

Top End The northern part of the Northern Territory

1933 F. E. Baume *Tragedy Track* 93: She looked around, stayed one day, and left again for the more human ... regions of the Top End, where at least one could drink fresh water occasionally.

1941 C. Barrett *Coast of Adventure* 13: He ... asked me casually what had brought me to the Top End of the Territory.

1945 Tom Ronan *Strangers on the Ophir* 37: 'Those Kimberley horse-buyers wouldn't give a fiver for Carbine unless you could show a receipt. And the top-end drovers do their own stealing.'

1951 Ernestine Hill *The Territory* 446: Top End The Territory north of Katherine.

1971 *Australian* 10 Oct. 35: The sell-off of Australia's Top End to overseas interests quickened last week with a $US7.6 million offer of shares.

1975 *Bulletin* 30 Aug. 10: May I protest the use of the term 'Top End' ... as applied to parts of North Queensland? This term has long been used to refer to – and only to – that portion of the Northern Territory north of Katherine, including Arnhem Land. Longtime residents of this part of the continent commonly use it with a hint of pride and manage to instil into it some feeling of the remoteness and special character of the region.

1982 Alan Powell *Far Country* 5: The Katherine-Darwin region, the 'Top End' to Territorians, finds its unity in climate and economic use. It is the area which looks to Darwin as the focal point of its human activities; it is the area which enjoys a high, reliable and strictly seasonal rainfall. The Top End lies between 11° and 15° South latitude, well within the tropics.

Top-ender

1941 C. Barrett *Coast of Adventure* 14: The old Top-ender drank beer, which, to the men up there, is more desirable than iced nectar is to gods.

1961 Tom Ronan *Only a Short Walk* 52: Any 'Top-Ender' who wanted an hotel booking, a tip for the races, or the loan of a fiver ... went to Billy.

1982 *Age* (Melbourne) 21 Jun. 22: Top Enders are a breed set apart ... Scratch a Top Ender and you scratch a visionary.

top-off *v. & n.* To inform to the police; an informer; *derogatory* [? f. *top* to put to death by hanging OED 1812]

1941 Kylie Tennant *The Battlers* 129: 'Who topped off Chigger Adams to the cops?' he shouted angrily.

1944 Lawson Glassop *We Were the Rats* 133: 'I haven't forgot ... how he pooled me with the Q.M. Just a top-off merchant, that's all he is.'

1950 *Australian Police Journal* Apr. 119: *Top-off, A* Informant.

1959 Dorothy Hewett *Bobbin Up* 104: Rosebery was a hybrid mixture of honest workers, top-off men and crawlers.

1966 Betty Collins *The Copper Crucible* 14: 'About four o'clock in the morning some top-off rings the cops.'

1970 Richard Beilby *No Medals for Aphrodite* 177: 'Go on, shout so they can all hear, you top-off bastard.'

top paddock, kangaroos in one's   see **kangaroos**

Tothersider 1 A person from Van Diemen's Land (Tasmania), from the standpoint of the mainland

[**1855** William Howitt *Land, Labour and Gold* ii 362: Scenery precisely like hundreds of miles which I have seen 'on the other side', as they call Victoria, and as the Victorians call Van Diemen's Land.]

1903 Joseph Furphy *Such is Life* (1944) 276: The ancient t'other-sider [Vandemonian Jack] oscillated his frame-saw.

2   In W.A., a person from the eastern states

1896 Henry Lawson *Letters* 62: W.A. is a fraud ... The old Sand-gropers are the best to work for or have dealings with. The Tothersiders are cutting each other's throats.

1929 Jules Raeside *Golden Days* 224: The population of Hannans, although mostly composed of t'othersiders, included not a small sprinkling of West Australians.

1950 K. S. Prichard *Winged Seeds* 30: 'Unemployed from all over the country swarmin' here, t'other siders as well as W.A. blokes.'

1963 Xavier Herbert *Disturbing Element* 2: My parents ... were what were called T'othersiders, meaning people who had come to West Australia from the other side of the continent.

1984 *Weekend Australian* 12 May 20: For 't'other siders' (local slang for anyone born east of the border) quokkas are a native marsupial and look a lot like miniature kangaroos.

touch of them, a   1   sc. the 'rats', the d.t.'s
1900 Henry Lawson 'The Hero of Redclay' *Prose* i 302: 'He's boozin' again,' someone whispered. 'He's got a touch of 'em.' 'My oath, he's ratty!' said someone else.
2   sc. the shits
1944 Lawson Glassop *We Were the Rats* 30: 'You tell me you're licked just because you've taken one on the chin in the first round. You give me a touch of 'em.'
1962 Gavin Casey *Amid the Plenty* 53: 'This place gives me a touch of 'em,' said Lenny.

tough as fencing wire   see **fencing wire**

towel up   To give someone a thrashing, verbal or physical
[**1859** Hotten 111: *Towel* to beat or whip. In *Warwickshire* an oaken stick is termed a *towel* ... *Towelling* a severe beating.]
1923 Con Drewe *Rogues & Ruses* 128: 'And you think Matt Barker will towel up Jumbo Lewis ... He might if he had an axe.'
1934 'Leslie Parker' *Trooper to the Southern Cross* (1966) 90: I knew I was in for trouble, but Celia wasn't the girl to let me down in public, however much she might towel me up in private.
1941 Baker 78: *Towel up, to* To beat, thrash.
1951 Dymphna Cusack and Florence James *Come In Spinner* 372: 'I think you deserve the V.C. for the way you towelled Old Mole up.'
1957 Ray Lawler *Summer of the Seventeenth Doll* 34: 'The kid towelled him up proper.'
1962 David Forrest *The Hollow Woodheap* 218: 'It wasn't me who towelled him up.'
1973 Alexander Buzo *Rooted* 42: 'Gary got his big serve working, I chipped in at the net, and we were laughing. Towelled them up in no time.'

towie   A tow-truck operator
1984 Robert Caswell *Scales of Justice* 38: 'Any of you towies got your Authorities signed?'

town bike, the   see **bike**

town hall clock, couldn't tell the time if the ~ fell on top of him   see **couldn't**

town, to go to   As for **go to market** q.v.
1952 T. A. G. Hungerford *The Ridge and the River* 80: 'Malise was going to town on them about their fire.'
1961 Nene Gare *The Fringe Dwellers* 142: 'Went ta town on em, e did ... E thinks that water got put on because he ticked off them pleecemen.'
1973 Henry Williams *My Love Had a Black Speed Stripe* 120: Rose came out of the house, all ready

to go, and she had really been to town on herself. Lipstick, eyeshadow, high heels, the lot.
1984 Rosemary Foot *National Times* 9 Mar. 18: I decided really to go to town on it when Wran made some public comments at the end of the last session about how we were a fairy floss Opposition.

trac   An intractable prisoner [abbr.]
1978 Kevin Gilbert *Living Black* 237: 'They're used to treating the tracs with the rough stuff and it rubs off on to the other prisoners so they get it rough, too, although not as rough as the tracs.'
1984 *National Times* 1 Jun. 15: Like when they sent me to the tracs and the Blockhouse.

Track, the   The Stuart Highway, joining Darwin to the south
1965 *Australian* 28 Jan. 10: Maps may tell you the thousand miles long black ribbon linking Darwin with Alice Springs and the south is the Stuart Highway. But up here it is 'the Track' or 'the Bitumen'.
1982 *Sydney Morning Herald* 13 Jul. Good Living 7: A morning spotting World War II's overgrown and rusted gun emplacements alongside the Track, the main highway down to Alice.
1984 *Age* (Melbourne) 16 Jun. Extra 11: They call the 1500 kilometres of bitumen south [of Darwin], the track. We went down the track to Noonamah.
track, down the   In the direction south of Darwin
1982 *NT News* (Darwin) 7 Apr. 1: There'll be a special full-page in color on where to go and what to see down the track.
see **Bitumen**

Track, the Bridle   see **Bridle**

track, on the   As for **on the wallaby track** q.v.
1896 Henry Lawson 'Some Day' *Prose* i 138: 'I've been knocking round for five years, and the last two years constant on the track, and no show of getting off it unless I go for good.'
1935 Kylie Tennant *Tiburon* 74: 'See 'ere, Mr Sullivan, I'm on the track, an' I'm down an' out.'
1953 *Caddie A Sydney Barmaid* 255: It would have been impossible for him to maintain the home on a dole ration ... He was going on the track.* *On the track – Tramping the back country in search of work.
1965 Eric Lambert *The Long White Night* 12: His clothes clearly proclaimed him as a man who had been on the track, one of that tattered, aimless, wandering band which the Depression threw up, who moved from town to town in the bush, drew their dole and then were moved on by the police.

track, wallaby   see **wallaby**

track with   To associate with, to cohabit with
1915 C. J. Dennis *The Songs of a Sentimental Bloke* 51: I swear I'll never track wiv 'er no more; / I'll never look on 'er side o' the street. Ibid. 126: *Track with* To woo; to go 'walking with'.
1924 *Truth* 27 Apr. 6: *Track with* To associate in love affairs.
1926 K. S. Prichard *Working Bullocks* 47: 'Combo's what they call a man tracks round with a gin in the nor'-west.'
1933 Norman Lindsay *Saturdee* 239: 'Who are you trackin' with now?'
1941 Baker 78: *Track with* To pay court to a girl or woman.
1954 T. A. G. Hungerford *Sowers of the Wind* 270: 'I bet it's that cross-eyed harlot he's been tracking with.'

track square with
1919 W. II. Downing *Digger Dialects* 50: *Track square* to pursue an amorous enterprise with honourable intentions.
1949 Alan Marshall *How Beautiful Are Thy Feet* 64: 'He wants me to track square with him. To look at him you'd never think he could talk seriously. He talked for a long while about tracking square.'
1952 Jon Cleary *The Sundowners* 148: 'Nobody ever said anything about us tracking square with one another! I'm free and over twenty one and how I spend me time is me own business!'
1964 George Johnston *My Brother Jack* 161: 'He's been at me for years about how irresponsible I am, and the first time I come back with a girl I'm tracking square with, I get hoisted!'

Tracy   The cyclone which devastated Darwin on 25 December 1974
1977 *Weekend Australian* 3 Sep. Mag. 5: John Waters explains how his house is three storeys high: 'It's the only one in Darwin. After Tracy everyone was building down, but I thought we'd go up as a mark of defiance.'
1979 *Herald* (Melbourne) 23 Jun. 9: The freebooters who arrived after Tracy, getting vast wages to reconstruct the town and often as not paying no tax on them, have drifted away.

trag   Teraglin [abbr.]
1984 *Sunday Telegraph* 5 Aug. 122: Tailor and teraglin could also put in an appearance, with the moon beginning to grow larger. One area which usually produces 'trags' is the Coogee ground.

train *n.*   See quot. 1976
1976 *National Times* 29 Nov. 10: How Women Are Trained: If It's Not Rape What Is It? [heading] A National Times team has interviewed a number of people in a small cane-growing community [Ingham] in North Queensland, where a sexual practice called 'the train' occurs . . . A train might begin at the Saturday night cabaret, as a couple left together. Other men made a yanking motion in the air, like a conductor pulling the cord, and shouted, 'Too-hoot' All aboard! And they would follow, and as many as 50 men would have sexual intercourse with the woman.

train *v.*
1976 See **train** *n.*
1978 Paul R. Wilson *The Other Side of Rape* 115: Hence the colloquial phrase for the rapes developed – *trains* – a term with more significance than simply the signalling mechanism reminiscent of the cane trains which shunt through the town during the cane season. A variety of derivations set the phrase in a more illuminating context – how women are trained, we want to train your woman, and so on.

train a choko vine over a country dunny, couldn't   see **couldn't**

train, tea and sugar   see **tea**

tram, on the wrong   Following the wrong tactics, mistaken, astray
1955 John Morrison *Black Cargo* 223: 'No, son, you're on the wrong tram with me'.
1963 Lou Richards *Boots and All!* 116: His theory of training . . . proved right in 1961 yet back-fired in 1962. I think we should let it go for another year before being too eager to say Kennedy is on the wrong tram.
1982 *Bulletin* 19 Jan. 27: What McMahon will be telling his former parliamentary colleagues is that the Fraser Government is, in his judgment, on the wrong tram economically.

trammie   A tram conductor or driver [abbr.]
1946 Margaret Trist *What Else is There?* 229: 'A blue uniform, that's air force, isn't it?' 'It depends,' replied Alf cautiously. 'Maybe it was a trammie.'
1959 Dorothy Hewett *Bobbin Up* 1: Shirl had a glimpse of the trammie, swinging on the footboard.
1963 Gunther Bahnemann *Hoodlum* 146: 'There won't be much dough in a trammie's bag, Rob. Shillings, pennies, and so on.'
1984 *Age* (Melbourne) 11 Aug. 2: The reluctant trammie [heading]

tramp   To give someone the sack: *rare*
1941 Baker 78: *Tramped* Dismissed from employment.
1953 T. A. G. Hungerford *Riverslake* 109: 'If you come in tanked at tea-time, he'll tramp you, sure as your ring points to the ground!'
1975 Les Ryan *The Shearers* 128: 'The next day I managed to get the pen I was offered, but only after another shearer had been tramped.'

tramper
1950 K. S. Prichard *Winged Seeds* 219: A mate who had been sacked on the trumped-up charge of an underground manager known as 'The Tramper'.

trannie   A portable transistor radio
1979 *Sun-Herald* 29 Apr. 18: The thought of the axe somehow working through the trannie and striking the likes of Des Hoysted plunk-dunk between the eyebrows had definite appeal.

Transed   The National Transition Education Scheme introduced by the Commonwealth in 1979 to assist school leavers with poor job prospects
1980 *Sydney Morning Herald* 24 Jun. 13: 'Transed' hit the education scheme at a time of high youth unemployment, and on the crest of a wave of urgency among politicians to offer something more constructive than the dole queue to young school leavers.

trap   A policeman; in the nineteenth century, esp. a mounted policeman: a survival in Australia of English thieves' slang ('One whose business is to 'trap' or catch offenders; a thief-taker; a detective or policeman; a sheriff's officer' 1705 OED)
1812 Vaux 274: *Traps*: Police officers or runners, are properly so called; but it is common to include constables of any description under this title.
1853 John Rochfort *Adventures of a Surveyor* 72: If he is taken by the 'traps', he will be sent to prison handcuffed to a common felon.
1882 Rolf Boldrewood *Robbery Under Arms* (World's Classics 1949) 2: Our 'bush telegraphs' were safe to let us know when the 'traps' were closing in on us.
1899 A. B. Paterson 'The "Bottle-oh" Man' in *Singer of the Bush* (1983) 332: I always says, for laying out of a trap, / Oh, there's nothing like an Empty Bottle, oh!
1911 Louis Stone *Jonah* 32: The police, variously named 'Johns', 'cops' and 'traps', were their natural enemies.
1945 Tom Ronan *Strangers on the Ophir* 229: 'I never thought I'd offer to shake hands with a trap, but give me a hold of your fist, Mike Devlin.'
1950 Frank Hardy *Power Without Glory* 30: Someone else shouted: 'There's traps in the back lane!'
1974 Ronald McKie *The Mango Tree* 146: They were sorry that Scanlon was dead and knew that he had been a good trap.

trap for young (amateur) players   A hazard for the unwary
1944 G .H. Fearnside *Sojourn in Tobruk* 60: 'This nuptial bliss stuff will get you in every time. It's a trap for young players.'

1957 R. S. Porteous *Brigalow* 18: I said something about the broken step being dangerous. 'That's right,' he agreed. 'She's a trap for young players.'
1962 Gavin Casey *Amid the Plenty* 80: 'You look out for the hire-purchase, that's a trap for young players, these days.'
1975 Les Ryan *The Shearers* 107: 'Don't be in it,' Lofty advised. 'It's a trap for young players.'

traveller   A tramp seeking work in the outback, sometimes distinguished from the 'swagman' and the 'sundowner', and sometimes classified with them; one of the itinerant unemployed in the depression
[**1859** Hotten 111: *Traveller* name given by one tramp to another.]
1868 Marcus Clarke 'Swagmen' in *A Colonial City* ed. L. T. Hergenhan (1972) 33: I remembered at one station, situated on the main road for 'travellers', that the unhappy cook was 'put on the fire' by a crowd of these gentry.
1873 Rolf Boldrewood 'The Fencing of Wanderowna' *A Romance of Canvas Town* (1898) 82: 'They'll lay baits for the swagmen and poor travellers next,' says he with a grim, unsmiling visage.
1875 A. J. Boyd *Old Colonials* (1882) 114–15: Before the swagsman became known, a traveller in search of employment was always sure of a hospitable reception at the hands of the squatter. I have lived on a station where it was invariably the custom to serve out two men's rations weekly for the benefit of travellers. All this is now done away with in the more settled parts of the colonies.
1893 Henry Lawson 'Some Popular Australian Mistakes' *Prose* ii 24: Men tramping in search of a 'shed' are not called 'sundowners' or 'swaggies'; they are 'trav'lers'.
1910 C. E. W. Bean *On The Wool Track* 65: Once a year, for a month or two, on horses, on bicycles, occasionally on foot, come by the 'travellers', shearers on their way from shed to shed.
1919 E. S. Sorenson *Chips and Splinters* 72: 'You seem to think a man's got nothing to do on these stations but cook for travellers.'
1941 Kylie Tennant *The Battlers* 23: Any sergeant will tell you that the 'locals' – that is, the unemployed residing in the town – are bad enough. But the 'travellers' – meaning the men with track-cards who wander the country in search of work, getting their food-orders from declared 'dole stations' in towns fifty of sixty miles apart – the travellers are worse.

travelling, a fine day for   See quot. 1951
1951 Ernestine Hill *The Territory* 306: 'It's a fine day for travellin',' they told him – the time-honoured phrase that all over the outback is notice to quit.
1953 *Daily Mirror* (Sydney) 18 Mar. 17: Finally,

the head stockman told him 'It's a fine day for travellin',' the time-honored phrase that means notice to quit all over the outback.

1962 David Forrest *The Hollow Woodheap* 214: He was going on a long, long journey, alone and torn in half, and ... looking out at the morning, decided it was as good a day as any for travelling.

trawler   See quot.

1947 C. K. Thompson *Yes, Your Honour!* xiv: The driver of the Black Maria, the 'trawler', or in polite language, the police patrol ... offered me a lift from the police-station to the court.

tray (trey) -bit   A threepenny piece (before decimal coinage, 1966)

1898 *Bulletin* 1 Oct. 14: 3d. a 'traybit'.

1906 Henry Lawson 'In the Height of Fashion' *Verse* ii 182: Then our country, cold and scornful, / Answered 'Go and get a beer!' / And it threw the tray bit at us / Just to stop our 'silly row'.

1911 Louis Stone *Jonah* 98: 'Well, a tray bit won't break me,' said Chook, producing threepence from his pocket.

1918 Harley Matthews *Saints and Soldiers* 103: Come, join the army, / Make no delay, / Front seats a deener, / Back seats a tray.

1949 Ruth Park *Poor Man's Orange* 68: She wanted to say something, to tell this silly old coot that what she knew about life could be written on a tray bit.

1980 Clive James *Unreliable Memoirs* 15: My mother had naturally spiced the pudding with sixpences and threepenny bits, called zacs and trays respectively.

trays, tray-bits, the   The shits [rhyming slang]

1952 T. A. G. Hungerford *The Ridge and the River* 24: 'Oscar's got a touch of the trays.'

treat with ignore   see **ignore**

trick, can't take a   To be constantly unsuccessful [f. card games]

1944 Lawson Glassop *We Were the Rats* 211: 'He tells us we might be Aussies but we can't take a trick. He says we got a canin' in Greece an' had to get out.'

1963 D. H. Crick *Martin Place* 192–3: 'Looks like curtains for you, pal. Can't take a trick.'

1977 *Bulletin* 5 Feb. 11: The ACTU leader can't take a trick.

Tricolours, the   The Eastern Suburbs (N.S.W.) Rugby League team (also the Roosters)

trifecta   A set of three successes, or exceptional events [f. *trifecta* betting, the selection of the first three place-getters in correct order]

1982 Nancy Keesing *Lily on the Dustbin* 62: A Sydney woman said of a friend's daughter that she had won the daily double but missed out on the trifecta: the young woman in question was having her wedding at the fashionable St Marks, Darling Point, the reception at the Royal Sydney Yacht Squadron, but had missed out on the honeymoon in Fiji.

1983 *Sun-Herald* 6 Mar. 130: If they're super Sloanes they'll have the trifecta – a wedding at St Mark's, the reception at THE Golf Club and a honeymoon in Fiji.

1984 *Bulletin* 20 Mar. 54: The south-west of New South Wales struck the trifecta last week – the Riverina Merino Field Day, the opening of the duck season and a visit by Prime Minister Bob Hawke.

1984 *Sun-Herald* 5 Aug. 130: Well, the trifecta's over for another season. The Black and White Committee has successfully presented the big three – Maria Finlay, Nellie Vida and Beril Jents, purveyors of fine frocks.

1984 *Age* (Melbourne) 20 Sep. 1: Sister Manion is not only a nun. She is also professor of fine arts at the University of Melbourne. And now she is a [hotel] licensee. I said to her later that this was a pretty good trifecta, and that if she owned a racehorse, she would have a quadrella hard to beat anywhere in the world.

trilogy, the   The set of three undertakings given by Mr R. J. Hawke in the course of the 1984 election campaign

1984 *Sydney Morning Herald* 5 Dec. 1: The so-called economic trilogy was the centrepiece of Labor's election campaign ... As spelled out most recently by Mr Hawke in a speech last week, the promises are that the Government over the next three years will:

• Not increase the overall level of taxes as a proportion of the Gross Domestic Product;
• Not increase the deficit as a proportion of GDP;
• Restrain Government spending increases to below the rate of economic growth.

triss   A homosexual

1967 Kylie Tennant *Tell Morning This* 157: 'Think I'm going round flapping my mouth to every silly triss that gets shoved in [the cell] with me?'

1982 Mike Carlton *Sydney Morning Herald* 4 Aug. 8: This is where Brideshead fails utterly; with the one exception of the scandalously trissy but minor character, Anthony Blanche, they are all such dreary people.

1983 Ron Saw *Bulletin* 14 Jun. 59: What on Earth's wrong with terms such as pouf, fag, fairy, dike, trizz, queer or pansy? Why 'gay'?

trizz   see **triss**

trizzie A threepenny piece

1942 *Salt* 2 Feb. 18: 3 pence a trey, or trizzie.

1959 Gerard Hamilton *Summer Glare* 31: My greatest pal now was John 'Trizzie' Peele ... He always had a threepeny bit in his pocket which gave him his nickname.

troppo Mentally or nervously affected by the privations of war service in the tropics; showing any signs of being similarly affected

1943 George Johnston *New Guinea Diary* 222: 'A man must be going troppo,' he remarks quietly.

1946 Rohan Rivett *Behind Bamboo* 399: *Troppo* mad, sunstruck, weak-minded, affected by captivity.

1948 Sumner Locke Elliott *Rusty Bugles* in *Khaki, Bush and Bigotry* ed. Eunice Hanger (1968) 88: 'They're taking him to the psychiatric ward.' ... 'What's that?' 'Where they take you when you go troppo.'

1954 L. H. Evers *Pattern of Conquest* 144: 'Troppo!' said the other man, 'mad as a hatter.'

1963 Lawson Glassop *The Rats in New Guinea* 197: Every time I held my hand out I noticed my fingers shaking ... My fingers shook against my lips as I took a draw at an imaginary cigarette. My God, I thought, I'm going troppo. I'm even smoking without cigarettes now.

1973 Roland Robinson *The Drift of Things* 266: Cecil tried to give me advice against the boredom which gripped everyone in the Territory ... 'Don't give way to going "Troppo", as most of our fellows do.'

1975 *Sun-Herald* 30 Nov. 131: Aunty Jack ... could bring a badly-needed fresh burst of local comedy (in a troppo way) to our screens.

1984 *Sydney Morning Herald* 16 Feb. 9: According to one person, 'Neville [Wran] is troppo about Barrie [Unsworth]. He is dedicated to stopping him.'

trot A sequence of chance events, esp. betokening good or ill fortune ('a good trot', 'a rough trot') esp. sporting

1911 Louis Stone *Jonah* 216: A trot or succession of seven tails followed, and the kip changed hands rapidly.

1919 W. H. Downing *Digger Dialects* 51: *Trot* An experience (e.g. 'a rough trot'; 'a bad time').

1922 Arthur Wright *A Colt from the Country* 147: 'Luck? Hang it, no. I'm having a bad trot. Lost to-day and again to-night.'

1949 Lawson Glassop *Lucky Palmer* 177: He was 'Lucky' Palmer, having a bad trot at the moment, admittedly, but still 'Lucky' Palmer.

1952 T. A. G. Hungerford *The Ridge and the River* 181: 'We didn't even hope that she'd last any longer, she had such a tough trot. But she hung on.'

1965 Wally Grout *My Country's 'Keeper* 166: Most

Pressmen I have found to be good coves who will lay off a player having a bad trot.

see **spin**

troubles!, my A dismissive expression, equivalent to 'Don't worry about me!': *obsolescent*

1895 Cornelius Crowe *The Australian Slang Dictionary* 89: *Troubles* 'my troubles' what do I care.

1905 Nathan Spielvogel *A Gumsucker on the Tramp* 90: Off again; round Leuwin Cape; rough seas; My Troubles! I'm coming home.

1911 E. M. Clowes *On the Wallaby through Victoria* 16: A shrug of the shoulders and the 'My troubles' are his response to any advice or sympathy you may offer.

1924 Vance Palmer *The Outpost* 84: 'I never got along with other women. Even the girls at school didn't like me, and weren't slow in showing it. My troubles, though!'

1934 'Leslie Parker' *Trooper to the Southern Cross* (1966) 134: 'I suppose you won't mind if he flirts with Celia,' said Mrs Dicky. 'His troubles,' I said, knowing Celia would turn him down well and truly.

1947 Gavin Casey *The Wits are Out* 44: 'You better lay off Kitty while the old man's about, or there'll be one more out-of-work motor salesman kicking round the city,' Syd suggested. 'My troubles!' Jerry jeered.

truckie A truck (i.e. lorry) driver [abbr.]

1958 *Coast to Coast 1957–1958* 201: The truckie looked upwards. 'Whaddya want, mate?'

1973 *Australian* 13 Apr. 1: 'Trucking is in my bones; I love being with truckies; I've always thought of myself as a truckie,' he [Mr Ken Thomas] said.

1983 *Sun-Herald* 25 Sep. 152: Because we think there is more to life than sitting around waiting for our men to come home we are forming the Truckies Wives' Association.

1984 *Australian* 24 May 16: Motorists, not truckies, to blame for road carnage [heading]

try it on, to To seek some advantage to which one is not entitled, esp. by bluff or presumption; to see what one can 'get away with' [f. *try on* to live by thieving OED 1811]

1812 Vaux: *Try it on* To make an attempt, or essay, where success is doubtful. So to *try it on with* a woman, signifies to attempt her chastity.

1845 C. Griffith *The Present State of Port Phillip* 77: Requiring a strict hand to keep them [ex-convicts] in order, as it is part of their system to impose (or as they term it to *try it on*) whenever they have a chance of success, which is of course most likely with new settlers.

1859 Oliné Keese *The Broad Arrow* i 257: 'No, no,

428

Miss Bridget; they [the convict servants] are only trying it on ... When you are more up to their ways, they'll leave you alone.'
1883 R. E. N. Twopeny *Town Life in Australia* 134: The upper forms have a disposition to 'try it on' when a new hand is set over them.
1900 Henry Lawson 'Joe Wilson's Courtship' *Prose* i 547: 'Oh, she tried it on, but it didn't go,' said Romany. 'I've met her sort before.'
1953 Bant Singer *You're Wrong Delaney* 136: 'Nugget caught Martini trying it on with Lily and shot him.'

a try on   'An attempt, esp. an attempt at imposition or deceit' (OED 1874)
1900 Henry Lawson 'A Daughter of Maoriland' *Prose* i 374: The girl's last 'try on' was to come down to the school fence, and ostentatiously sharpen a table-knife on the wires.
1910 C. E. W. Bean *On the Wool Track* 41: There almost always came a time when the boss's authority was at issue; not a continental rebellion, but some mean Anglo-Saxon 'try-on'.

tube   1   The downtube in a shearing shed to which the hand piece is connected
1963 *Sydney Morning Herald* 17 Aug. 11: Get off the tube (out of the game) while you are young enough.
2   A can of beer; given currency by the Barry McKenzie strip in the 1960s
1964 Barry Humphries *A Nice Night's Entertainment* (1981) 77: Oh, I was down by Manly pier / Drinking tubes of ice-cold beer / With a bucket full of prawns upon me knee.
1971 George Johnston *A Cartload of Clay* 137: 'A beer'd be just the shot,' said the Ocker. 'Never bin known to say no to a tube.'
1974 John Powers *The Last of the Knucklemen* 58: 'We got the old backslap routine, an' a few free tubes.'
1975 *Australian* 17 Feb. 3: Meat pies are not the only concession to Ockerism. Should Bazza Mackenzie arrive in Peking seeking a cold tube, Dr Fitzgerald [the ambassador] could cope with that as efficiently as he does the daily round of diplomatic consultations.
1976 *Sydney Morning Herald* 25 Jun. 12: They said 'Good on yer mate. Good on yer. Have a tube.'

tucker, to make   To gain an income sufficient only to cover such necessities as food
1861 Horace Earle *Ups and Downs* 336: 'Well, we shall perhaps make tucker* out of it,' was the reply ... for diggers never like to let their neighbours know the extent of their luck. *Food.
1875 A. J. Boyd *Old Colonials* (1882) 127: Patient and plodding ... often months without doing more than earning 'tucker', he [the digger] delves on

until he either makes his pile, or is laid up in ordinary.
1880 Rolf Boldrewood *The Miner's Right* (1890) 381: 'I believe you never would have made anything more than tucker – isn't that the expression? – if it hadn't been for your mates and your backers.'
1901 Henry Lawson 'The Golden Graveyard' *Prose* i 344: They 'drove' (tunnelled) inwards at right angles to the fence, and at a point immediately beneath it they were 'making tucker'; a few feet farther and they were making wages.
1933 F. E. Baume *Tragedy Track* 18: During the past year they could not be said to be making more than their tucker.
1944 Brian James *First Furrow* 8: They spoke to Tully and begged him to throw it in. They'd never make tucker, they said, on the job. They'd starve on it.
1954 Miles Franklin *Cockatoos* 120: 'The farms are not big enough to make tucker off.'
tucker dirt, tucker track
1896 Edward Dyson *Rhymes from the Mines* 74: Where gold was getting I was on the job, and early, – / Stuck some tucker dirt at Armstrong's, and just lived at Pleasant Creek.
1880–1914 'With My Swag All on My Shoulder' *Old Bush Songs* ed. Stewart and Keesing (1957) 226: It is the best of tucker tracks, / So I'll stay here till I die.

tucker bag, box   The bag in which the itinerant carries his rations
1893 Henry Lawson 'Some Popular Australian Mistakes' *Prose* ii 24: The nose (tucker) bag hangs over the other shoulder and balances the load nicely – when there's anything in the bag.
1908 W. H. Ogilvie *My Life in the Open* 52: The 'tucker box' is taken from one of the waggons, and there in the weird silence of the brooding Bush they take their evening meal.
1919 W. K. Harris *Outback in Australia* 143: He 'smoodges' round the cook, and if 'moved on' without his tucker-bags replenished, he does not scruple to do an injury.
1941 Charles Barrett *Coast of Adventure* 36: Old man Rogers enjoyed his supper, and stowed cold roast goose in the tucker-bag, for breakfast.
1968 Walter Gill *Petermann Journey* 82: Squatting on his 'nap', with his back to a tucker box.

Tuesday or Bourke Street   see **Bourke Street**

tug the coat   see **coat**

turfing   A form of **bastardization** q.v.
1983 *Australian* 17 May 1: Allegations of 'turfing' or bastardisation at Hawkesbury Agricultural College, NSW ... have been made to *The Austra-*

lian ... At least seven senior students, some women in their 50s, were subjected to serious turfing, involving vandalism of their rooms and belongings. Ibid. 2: Many found their rooms had been 'turfed' in their absence: their possessions, bedding, clothes and notes thrown about.

turkey 1 A swag: *rare*
1912 G. H. Gibson *Ironbark Splinters* 6: So you 'pack' your bloomin' turkey,[1] and you take the northern train. [1]'Turkey' – a bushman's slang for 'swag', a bundle of blankets and clothes. The term is sometimes also applied to a pack-horse.
2 In 'plain turkey', 'scrub turkey' etc., a swagman who tramps the plain country, the scrub [f. the birds inhabiting these regions]
1955 D'Arcy Niland *The Shiralee* 27: He had met plenty of these plain-turkeys, as they were known. They zoned themselves on the plains, wandering the roads and the back-tracks among the sheep stations and the wheat farms, doing the rounds year in and year out. They did the rounds from shed to shed at shearing time, ate a couple of good meals, had the tucker-bag filled, and moved on to the next place.
1955 Alan Marshall *I Can Jump Puddles* 152: Father had humped his bluey in Queensland and was familiar with the ways of swagmen. He always called them 'travellers'. The bearded men who kept to the bush he called 'Scrub Turkeys' and those came down from the plains he called 'Plain Turkeys'.
1964 H. P. Tritton *Time Means Tucker* 15: Many of these men never left the Plains, but between burr cutting and work in the shearing sheds managed to exist. The regulars were known as 'Plain Turkeys' and most of them were well up in years.
1973 Frank Huelin *Keep Moving* 178: *Scrub Turkey* Bagman who has gone Bush. Usually slightly mental or eccentric.

turkey, head over Head over heels [? f. *tuck* the stern of a boat OED 1625]
1906 Edward Dyson *Fact'ry 'Ands* 234: 'One was dumped down two flights, 'ead over tuck, with a fat punch.'
1915 C. J. Dennis *The Songs of a Sentimental Bloke* 43: 'E swallers lysol, throws a fancy fit, / 'Ead over turkey, an' 'is soul 'as flit.
1955 Alan Marshall *I Can Jump Puddles* 46: 'I knock Sir Frederick Salisbury, or whatever his name is, head over turkey into a clump of peacocks.'

turkey, on the 'A fit or spell of intoxication. *Slang. Obs.*' (U.S. 1846 Mathews)
1903 Joseph Furphy *Such is Life* (1944) 278: 'Gosh! you've been on the turkey; you'll be cutting

yourself some of these times.'

turn out To become a bushranger
1875 Rolf Boldrewood *The Squatter's Dream* repr. as *Ups and Downs* (1878) 165: 'I'm not sure that you won't get off light. You have had the good luck not to have killed anybody that I know of since you turned out.'
1899 G. E. Boxall *The Story of the Australian Bushrangers* 274: The reward offered for the capture of Thomas Clarke was raised to £1000, while £500 was offered for his brother John, who had just 'turned out'.

turps Liquor
1865 Henry Kingsley *The Hillyars and the Burtons* 294: 'They tossed for a go of turps and a hayband – I ask your ladyship's pardon, that means a glass of gin and a cigar.'
1962 J. Marshall and R. Drysdale *Journey Among Men* 84: The Sergeant alleged that Ah Fong was a notorious drunkard, forever on the 'turps'. Ibid. 131: 'He likes to hit the turps now and again, and you can't blame him.'
1973 John O'Grady *Survival in the Doghouse* 57: He's humping a dozen cans with him. Ice cold. And he gets a great welcome. Not only because of the turps, but because with him there we can have a four-handed game.
1982 *NT News* (Darwin) 13 Mar. 6: What about the rest who are going straight back on the turps the minute the stores do open?

twang Opium [unexplained]
1898 *Bulletin* 1 Oct. 14: Tobacco is 'snout', opium 'twang'.
1900–10 O'Brien and Stephens: *Twang* opium.
1945 Tom Ronan *Strangers on the Ophir* 68: The honest Chinese limits himself to his one pipe of 'Twang' per night.
1961 Ion L. Idriess *Tracks of Destiny* 94: This Chinaman was a 'runner' carrying smuggled 'twang' (opium) from Port Darwin to his compatriots in at the Creek.

tweeds Pants
1954 T. A. G. Hungerford *Sowers of the Wind* 116–17: 'I take my coat off every day, and it don't stop the flaming traffic!' 'Try taking your tweeds off, boof-head!'
1973 Alexander Buzo *Rooted* 85: 'Susan was a lovely girl. She never dropped her tweeds for anyone.'
1980 Murray Bail *Homesickness* 161: 'Should always lock the door, Shiel,' he said, giving his tweeds a hitch.

twenty-four door sedan A nightcart
1978 Encountered in conversation.

twisted sandshoe, head like a   see **head**

twist top   A beer bottle containing 250 ml [f. type of seal, which may be used on other sizes also]

two bob   The sum of money most often used in derogatory expressions like 'not worth two bob', 'silly as a two bob watch', 'two bob lair' [cf. U.S. 'two-bit']
1944 Lawson Glassop *We Were the Rats* 144: Bert was more the 'two-bob lair' type.
1948 K. S. Prichard *Golden Miles* 214: 'They're all scoundrels, would cut your throat for two bob.'
1954 *Coast to Coast 1953–1954* 122: 'Fifty flamin' quid! Why, it's not worth two bob.'
1958 H. D. Williamson *The Sunlit Plain* 257: 'Cunning, too – put it over his own cobbers – sell his wife fer two bob.'
1959 Dorothy Hewett *Bobbin Up* 142: 'One little wizened-up Pommy feller, you wouldn't give a two bob for 'im.'
1966 Elwyn Wallace *Sydney and the Bush* 83: 'There are not too many bloody two bob snobs on the track.'
1974 John Powers *The Last of the Knucklemen* 30: 'I don't get hustled into punch-ups with two-bob lairs.'
1978 Richard Beilby *Gunner* 91: 'We lived in a little two-bob town on the edge of the wheat-belt in West Australia, wheat and sheep, mixed.'
1984 *National Times* 23 Mar. 31: Curtis used to be a two-bob revolutionary, wearing a North Vietnam badge on his school uniform and clutching Martin Sharp's Oz.

two bob each way, to have   Not to commit oneself to either of two courses of action; to seek to profit from all contingencies [f. horseracing]
1973 Max Harris *The Angry Eye* 186: I suspect our elegant French trading friends are having two bob each-way in the Australian sex-aid market.
1977 *Sunday Telegraph* (Sydney) 11 Sep. 48: The ACTU and its president, Bob Hawke, appear to be taking an easy 'two bob each-way' attitude to the Government's decision to mine uranium.
1982 *Weekend Australian* 12 Jun. Mag. 10: Is the Australian Opera trying two bob each way? Pandering to the snobs and backslapping the plebs at the same time?
1984 *Age* (Melbourne) 16 Jul. 12: Mr Hawke has gone down in my estimation also, he seems to want two bob each way on this one [abortion].

two, four, six, eight; bog in, don't wait   A mock grace, esp. used by children
1936 Encountered in conversation.
1975 Les Ryan *The Shearers* 45: Clarrie stood nearby . . . disapproving of the two, four, six, eight, bog in don't wait, business going on.

1984 Helen Garner *The Children's Bach* 11: 'Two four six eight, bog in don't wait', said Dexter.

two kilometre law   Law in N.T. banning the drinking of liquor within 2 km of licensed premises, contentious because taken as curbing Aboriginal drinking in public places
1982 *Weekend Australian* 28 Aug. 13: It is known throughout the Territory as the two kilometre law, and it is due to come into force at the end of the month.
1984 *Bulletin* 10 Jul. 77: 'We had this magic thing happen,' she [the Mayor of Alice Springs] explains. 'Eighteen months ago the government brought in the two-kilometre law which makes it illegal for anyone to drink in a public place within two kilometres of a licensed outlet. Overnight it changed Alice Springs from the real rubbish dump it was becoming.'

two ones   see **ones**

two-pot screamer   see **screamer**

two-tooth   A sheep one year old; (as butcher's meat) hogget [? A New Zealandism rather than an Australianism, but reported in Australia]
1863 Samuel Butler *A First Year in Canterbury Settlement* ed. R. A. Streatfeild (1914) 39: Two teeth indicate one year old, four teeth two years, six teeth three years, eight teeth (or full mouthed) four years . . . The above teeth are to be looked for in the lower jaw and not the upper.
1933 Acland 359: After weaning a lamb becomes a (ram, etc.) hogget until shorn. After shearing he is usually called a shorn hogget until the next crop of lambs are weaned about the time he gets his first two-teeth. He is then called a two-tooth. Some people, however, call him a two-tooth as soon as he is shorn, whether his new teeth are up or not.
1935 R. B. Plowman *The Boundary Rider* 00. 'That's a nice young sheep . . . Looks like a well-grown two-tooth.'
1979 *Weekly Times* (Melbourne) 9 May 112: Fat sheep sold firm to $1 dearer while two-tooths remained firm.

two-up   A gambling game based on spinning two pennies, and wagering whether they fall as two heads or two tails
1898 W. T. Goodge 'Australia's Pride' *Bulletin* 3 Sep. 32: At 'loo he'd lately scooped the pool; / He'd simply smashed the two-up school.
1916 Official memo 10 Jan. cit. Patsy Adam-Smith *The Anzacs* (1978) 151: Gambling. The game known as Two-up is not to be played.
1926 J. Vance Marshall *Timely Tips for New Australians: Two-up* A prevalent method of gambling by tossing two pennies into the air.

1932 Leonard Mann *Flesh in Armour* 57: Once a bookmaker's clerk, and now a two-up king.
1959 Vance Palmer *The Big Fellow* 65: 'He showed me how I could do something better for the other fellows than keeping the two-up ring for them on Sunday mornings.'
1969 Bobbie Hardy *West of the Darling* 162: 'In 1883 in Silverton I noticed all sorts of games going on outside my Dad's hotel . . . And also around the back you would see a big two up school.'
see **grouter, heading them, kip, spinner, swy**

tyke, tike   A Roman Catholic: *derogatory*
1941 Baker 76: *Tike, tyke* A Roman Catholic.
1948 Ruth Park *The Harp in the South* 268: 'I'll do what I like when I like without the interference of any bone-headed tike.'
1961 Patrick White *Riders in the Chariot* 232: 'I would never ever of suspected you Rosetrees of being tykes. Only the civil servants are Roman Catholics here, and the politicians, if they are anything at all.'
1969 Jon Cleary *Remember Jack Hoxie* 86: 'I'm like you, a Tyke. A Catholic.'
1983 Patrick White *Netherwood* 21: 'Don't want ter listen to any of yer tyke arguments.'

tyranny of distance, the   Phrase applied by Geoffrey Blainey to the isolation of Australia, and the dispersion of settlement within it
1966 Geoffrey Blainey *The Tyranny of Distance* [book title]
1973 Henry Williams *My Love Had a Black Speed Stripe* 19: 'It is the tyranny of distance Ronald that makes the motor car such an important adjunct to living in this empty continent.'
1979 *Australian* 6 Jun. 3: Mr Staley said 'The tyranny of distance which has for so long added considerably to the costs of running a farm or property will be significantly overcome by these cuts [in telephone charges].'
1983 *National Times* 8 Apr. 15: A sense of isolation affects even long-time country residents. Few are immune to the tyranny of distance.

tyrants, the last of the   Lachlan Macquarie, Governor of New South Wales 1809–22 (in old-fashioned school textbooks)

Tyson, hungry (mean, rich, independent) as   Expressions referring to the millionaire pastoralist, James Tyson (1823–98)
[**1877** Marcus Clarke *A Colonial City* ed. L. T. Hergenhan (1972) 387: When the stranger hears that the magnificent and park-like lands through which he drives are the property of 'Scabby Moffatt', 'Hungry-man Tyson', and 'Pig-pig Carter', he is apt to understand why a witty barrister called the squattocracy of the colonies the wealthy lower orders.]
1890 *Bulletin* 4 Oct. 11: 'Hungry' Tyson gave £2000 to the Sydney Royal Naval Home.
1898 *Bulletin* 17 Dec. Red Page: 'As mean as Hungry Tyson' (used by people who know nothing of Tyson.)
1928 Arthur Wright *A Good Recovery* 8: 'Th' old bloke's as rich as Tyson.'
1950 *Coast to Coast 1949–1950* 190: 'No more bunging a job in at a minute's notice and walking off with a billycan and a roll of blankets, as independent as Tyson.'
1962 Tom Ronan *Deep of the Sky* 30: He never subscribed to the 'hungry Jimmy Tyson' legend.

U

uey, do a To make a U-turn
1976 *Bulletin* 28 Feb. 27: Ted Heath, like Fraser, began as a professed opponent of big government but was soon 'doing a youee' (U-turn) all over the place.

ugly as a hatful of arseholes see **hatful**

ump, umpy Umpire, esp. in Victoria [abbr.]
1973 Phillip Adams *Australian* 4 Aug. 18: Then there's our recreations / Like tossing cans at umpies / Or molesting Abo sheilas / And burning down their humpies.
1979 *Herald* (Melbourne) 2 Jun. 32: Umpy kicked: boy is outed [heading] A teenage footballer has been suspended until the 1981 season for kicking an umpire.
1981 *Sun-Herald* 18 Jan. 63: The ball was going so far down the legside Howarth must have thought someone had moved the stumps when he saw the umpy's finger go up.

uncle from Fiji see **Fiji**

underground mutton Rabbit, as an edible meat
1946 A. J. Holt *Wheat Farms of Victoria* 129: 'Underground mutton' (rabbit) is almost always available for those who like it.
1958 H. D. Williamson *The Sunlit Plain* 58: Underground mutton to a rabbit-trapper should be as pig-flesh to a Mohammedan.
1965 Eric Lambert *The Long White Night* 138: 'I

thought a feed of underground mutton would go all right for my tea.'
1972 G. C. Bolton *A Fine Country to Starve In* 225: It was apparently a plague season for rabbits, and ... this may have helped the unemployed and struggling farmers to eke out their diets with 'underground mutton'.
1981 *Bulletin* 22 Dec. 206: The rifle was for rabbits: we ate a lot of underground mutton in the 30s.

under someone's neck, go see **neck**

uni The university
1962 Alan Seymour *The One Day of the Year* 103. 'I think I might ditch my course. Leave Uni.'
1977 *Sydney Morning Herald* 26 Feb. 21: Sydney Uni spends up to welcome its students.
1982 Tim Winton *An Open Swimmer* 16: 'The Uni, eh?' The old man grinned. 'They tell yer anything at the Uni?'

unlock the lands The cry of those seeking to break the monopoly given to the squatters by the Order-in-Council of March 1847, esp. after the goldrush
1855 Raffaello Carboni *The Eureka Stockade* ed. Geoffrey Serle (1969) 75: The licence fee, and especially the disreputable mode of collecting it at the point of the bayonet, were *not* the only grievances the diggers complained of. They wanted to be represented in the Legislative Council; they wanted to 'unlock the lands'.

1862 Henry Brown *Victoria* 164: The cry was raised 'Unlock the lands to the people'.

1865 Henry Kingsley *The Hillyars and the Burtons* 325: There being undoubtedly a strong necessity to attend to the cry of 'unlock the lands', the Radicals brought in their bill.

up the duff   see **duff**

up a gum tree   see **gumtree**

up there, Cazaly   see **Cazaly**

up to pussy's bow   see **pussy's**

up who, who's (and who's paying the rent)   See quot. 1966: World War II slang
1966 Baker 172: *who's up who (and who's paying the rent)?* Just what is happening? Who's in control? e.g. 'Nobody knows who's up who' etc., said of a complete mess-up.
1970 Barry Oakley *Let's Hear it for Prendergast* 66: 'These days you don't know who's up who and who's paying the rent.'
1971 Frank Hardy *The Outcasts of Foolgarah* 162: Finer points, precedents, split straws, who's up who and who's paying for a strike within the meaning of the act.
1976 Robert Drewe *The Savage Crows* 258: Victor already knew, even here at the end of the world, who was up whom in this life.
1981 Maxwell Grant *Inherit the Sun* 356: It all had to do with who was up who, as far as Red could see, in this business world.

uphill   In difficulty
1945 Tom Ronan *Strangers on the Ophir* 184: 'Peter'll be a bit uphill getting Luke out of the cooler, won't he?'
1954 T. A. G. Hungerford *Sowers of the Wind* 141: 'He'll certainly be uphill now, trying to stack Lefevre for leave.'
1978 *Sun-Herald* 15 Jan. 44: The Opposition ... will be uphill in persuading the voters to reject this opportunity to have the Council democratically elected.

upside down, the hut that's   The symbol of the strange aspect which Australia presented to the immigrant from the antipodes (Christmas in midsummer, trees losing bark instead of leaves, etc.) with the underlying belief that the inhabitants on the bottom of the world must walk upside down [f. ballad with this refrain]
1957 *Old Bush Songs* ed. Stewart and Keesing 269: 'The Hut That's Upside-down' [ballad title]
1961 Judith Wright *Australian Letters* Jun. 30: The Upside-down Hut [essay title]

upside down, the only river in the world that flows   The Yarra river, Melbourne, from its brownish water: *jocular*
1953 Baker 275: *The only river in the world that flows upside down* a reference to the River Yarra which flows through Melbourne.
1965 Frank Hardy *The Yarns of Billy Borker* 43: Melbourne Mick and Sydney Sam might start making sly little jokes about the harbour bridge being an oversized coathanger, or the Yarra the only river in the world that flows upside down.
1966 Jan Smith *An Ornament of Grace* 51: Bet you're from Melbourne, the only city in the world where the river flows upside down with the mud on top.
1982 *Age* (Melbourne) 11 Jun. 3: Getting wet in the Yarra means taking your chances with a river that many believe flows upside down. It means sinking into black mud up to a metre deep and finding the odd oil slick slip past your face.
see **Little Muddy**

upter   No good at all [abbr. of 'up to putty' or 'up to shit']
1919 W. H. Downing *Digger Dialects* 52: *Upter* A corruption of 'Up to Putty'.
1951 Eric Lambert *The Twenty Thousand Thieves* 169: Go Through slapped Happy's shoulder. 'How are yer, Hap, old feller?' 'Up to shit' ['Upter' in 1963 edn], replied Happy.
1970 Richard Beilby *No Medals for Aphrodite* 174: 'How's the feet, Private Wilkinson?' 'Upta, sir. Can't get me boots on this mornin'.'

Urandangie, the girls are bandy at   see **Tallarook**

urger   1   A race tipster who seeks a bonus from the winnings of others
1924 *Truth* 27 Apr. 6: *Urger* A fraudulent race follower.
1930 L. W. Lower *Here's Luck* 85: Tip-slingers, urgers and whisperers slunk like jackals through the crowd.
1946 *Sun* (Sydney) 18 Aug. Suppl. 15: Bill's got more nerve than a Randwick urger.
1950 *Australian Police Journal* Apr. 120: *Urger* A nuisance on a racecourse who will prevail on a mug to back something, usually on the pretence that the urger's brother-in-law trains it, etc., or something similar, the object being that the mug might 'sling' if the horse wins.
1956 Tom Ronan *Moleskin Midas* 329: 'When I struck him first he was urger and knockdown man for Dupont the bookie.'
1967 Frank Hardy *Billy Borker Yarns Again* 14: 'An urger is a bloke who slings out tips and asks for a cut if one of them wins.'
1981 *Sunday Mail* (Brisbane) 25 Oct. 11: Last week urgers were a problem at Eagle Farm.

2 Any parasite or loafer, who incurs no risk himself

1952 T. A. G. Hungerford *The Ridge and the River* 155: 'Come on, you urgers!' he muttered. 'Sooner we get goin', the sooner we get across.'

1964 George Johnston *My Brother Jack* 325: 'I'm not saying you're an *urger* or anything like that, but this recruiting stuff, well, it *is* sort of urging in a way, don't you think?'

1972 G. C. Bolton *A Fine Country to Starve In* 231: The farmers ... resented the intrusion of pickets and urgers who came in from outside the district and attempted to run their campaign for them.

1983 Garry Sturgess and Bill Birnbauer *The Journalist who Laughed* 79: Clancy was a free enterprise man. He thought all unionists were urgers.

useful A general factotum in a business, pub etc. [**1866** Rachel Henning *Letters* ed. David Adams (1963) 219: There are three men employed about the place [a timber-logging business]. The bullock-driver, the puntman and a 'generally useful' man.]

1898 Alfred Joyce *A Homestead History* ed. G. F. James (1969) 41: Our friends had met with a trained carpenter in town, whom with his wife they had hired for £20 a year, the man as general useful, which would include his trade employment, and his wife as cook for the proprietors.

1900 Henry Lawson 'Middleton's Peter' *Prose* i 261: There were two rooms, of a sort, attached to the stables – one at each end. One was occupied by a man who was 'generally useful'.

1935 Kylie Tennant *Tiburon* 37: Roman stepped out of the room next to the laundry of O'Brien's Hotel, where he was barman, yardman and general useful.

1953 *Caddie A Sydney Barmaid* 6: The Missus called the useful to take over. A fight had started in the front parlour and women were biting and scratching in one mad mix up.

1962 Criena Rohan *The Delinquents* 31: 'I met Paddy Murphy, you know the 'useful' at your pub, and he had a look at it.'

useful/useless, as ~ as an ashtray on a motorbike, a glass door on a dunny, a handbrake on a Holden, a hip pocket in a singlet, the Yarra

1984 *Sydney Morning Herald* 9 Feb. 14: Like a bridge under troubled waters or an ashtray on a motorbike, some things come easily to lateral thinkers.

1981 *National Times* 25 Jan. 23: As useless as a glass door on a dunny.

1976 Sam Weller *Bastards I have met* 2: He's about as useful as a pocket in a singlet.

1983 *NT News* (Darwin) 29 Jan. 21: One day a man asked if she would like some help. She declined – and remarked to a friend sotto voce, 'I'd rather do it myself. He'd be as much help as a hip pocket in a singlet!'

1981 *National Times* 25 Jan. 23: 'As useless as the Yarra – too thick to swim in and too thin to plough!'

ute 1 A utility (vehicle combining the features of a sedan and a truck) [abbr.]

1951 Eric Lambert *The Twenty Thousand Thieves* 178: 'He gets pissed one night, pinches a ute from the transport lines.'

1961 Jack Danvers *The Living Come First* 17: 'Take the ute and drive in to Alice. The wire we ordered has arrived.'

1981 Dorothy Hewett *Susannah's Dreaming* 13: 'I'll give y' a lift 'ome in me ute.'

2 A brand of trousers

1979 *Sydney Morning Herald* 27 Jun. 3: FJ 'Utes'. The good looking trousers that work for a living. $32 Buys you enough toughness to work year-round in, enough good looks to go into town. Utes, the unique wool-rich work trousers. Washable, of course. At Fletcher Jones stores.

vag, on the   According to the provisions of the Vagrancy Act
1877 T. E. Argles *The Pilgrim* ii 21: She had got three months 'on the vag.' for making a sleeping place of a prominent doorstep.
1896 Edward Dyson *Rhymes from the Mines* 77: I needed tucker badly, / And this job, I think, just saved me being lumbered on the vag.
1916 C. J. Dennis *The Moods of Ginger Mick* 28: If I don't work they'd pinch me on the vag.
1951 Dymphna Cusack and Florence James *Come In Spinner* 300: 'If there's a police raid the girls are picked up under the Vag. and that's all there is to it.'
1959 K. S. Prichard *N'Goola* 148: 'Was you in the game, love? Or did they get you on the vag?'
vag   A vagrant
1895 Cornelius Crowe *The Australian Slang Dictionary* 91: *Vag* a vagrant.
1965 Xavier Herbert *Larger than Life* 40: 'We got a prisoner, eh?' The sergeant grunted. 'Just a vag.'

vagged, to be   To be arrested under the provisions of the Vagrancy Act
1930 *Bulletin* 9 Jul. 28: 'We can't have the public's mind polluted by abusive language. You're vagged.'
1941 Kylie Tennant *The Battlers* 11: 'I been vagged,' the Stray mentioned. 'Oh! you have? Well, there you are. If you ain't got any money, they run you in.'
1954 *Coast to Coast 1953–1954* 174: She'd beat

that consorting charge now; they couldn't vag her again either.
1972 David Ireland *The Flesheaters* 156: 'You can't go out alone and penniless *these* days ... You can be vagged if you've got no money.'

Van Diemen's Land   See quot.
1982 Kathy Lette *Sydney Morning Herald* 10 Dec. 12: Australian males, in their more imaginative moments, refer to the female pubic area – because of their similar shapes – as 'Van Demiens [sic] Land'.

Vandemonian *n.* & *a.* 1 Tasmanian [f. Van Diemen's Land, the original name of Tasmania]
1832 *The Currency Lad* 25 Aug. [2]: We are no advocates for the unlimited admission of Vandemonian wheat to our market.
1840 G. Arden *Australia Felix* 9: A shrewd old Vandemonian colonist.
1903 Joseph Furphy *Such is Life* (1944) 273: Vandemonian Jack, aged about a century, was mechanically sawing firewood in the hot, sickly sunshine.
2   An ex-convict from Van Diemen's Land
[**1847** Let. 31 Oct. cit. *No Place for a Nervous Lady* ed. Lucy Frost (1984) 175: Nearly all the men about this part are old Vandemonian convicts and a notable set they are, but I trust their days of extortion and impudence are nearly over.]
1855 Raffaello Carboni *The Eureka Stockade* ed. G. Serle (1969) 90: A sulky ruffian ... [of] the

known cast, as called here in this colony, of a 'Vandemonian', made up of low, vulgar manners and hard talk.

1899 G. E. Boxall *The Story of the Australian Bushrangers* 139: It was popularly supposed that these bushrangers were all convicts from 'Van Diemen's Land', hence they were known as 'Van Demonians', 'Derwenters' from the River Derwent, and 'Tother siders'.

Vaseline Valley   See quot.

1982 *Sydney Morning Herald* 10 Apr. 31: When Capriccios, or International Vanities as it was sometimes known, opened its doors in the early 1970s, it started the gay development along the stretch of Oxford Street that is now known as 'The Golden Mile', or, in a cruder vernacular form, as 'Vaseline Valley'.

Vee-dub   A Volkswagen car [f. abbr. VW]

1970 Alexander Buzo *The Front Room Boys* in Penguin *Plays* 48–9: 'They've got all the defects of the Vee Dub fifteen hundred and none of its virtues'.

1981 *Sydney Morning Herald* 14 Feb. 40: 'It's got a little bit of rust but nothing major and like all Veedubs the engine just keeps on going.'

Vegemite   Trade name of a yeast extract, with a status like that of the meat pie or the smell of gumleaves as something typically Australian

1980 Thomas Keneally in *Days of Wine and Rage* ed. Frank Moorhouse 249: It was ... like seeing something tribal, Vegemite say, in the window of NSW House in the Strand.

1985 *Sydney Morning Herald* 9 Feb. 59: A few hours of conversation with Holmes a Court are more than enough to instil the conviction that he sees himself as being as Australian as Vegemite.

velvet, black   see **black**

verandah (under the)   An exchange market conducted on a city pavement, under an awning, in Victoria; title of a serial column in the Melbourne *Leader* from the 1860s: *obs.*

1868 Marcus Clarke *A Colonial City* ed. L. T. Hergenhan (1972) 18: The Victorian broker ... begins to be known, he is seen under the 'Verandah' [illustration on facing page], and lunches at the Criterion.

1873 A. Trollope *Australia* ed. Edwards and Joyce (1967) 403: The verandah is a kind of open exchange – some place on the street pavement apparently selected by chance, on which dealers in mining shares congregate. What they do, or how they carry on their business when there, I am unable to explain.

1898 Morris 489: Verandahs ... are an architec-

tural feature of ... most city shops, where they render the sidewalks an almost continuous arcade. 'Under the Verandah' has acquired the meaning 'where city men most do congregate.'

Viceroy, the old   Lachlan Macquarie, Governor of New South Wales 1809–22, so termed by his supporters after his resignation

1824 Michael Massey Robinson *The Colonist* 5 Feb. 1835 46: 'The Old Viceroy' [song title]

Vietnamatta   The Cabramatta-Fairfield area, as populated by Indo-Chinese refugees

1981 *Sydney Morning Herald* 11 Feb. 10: 'Vietnamatta', or 'Saigon City', are the terms used by local people to describe the changing face of Cabramatta.

1982 *Sydney Morning Herald* 23 Sep. 7: A sign at Cabramatta station identifying the place has been crossed out and replaced by the word Vietnamatta. Vietnamese refugees have made a new home in Cabramatta. It's called Little Saigon by the locals.

village, the place for a   The site of Melbourne, as indicated by John Batman in his diary after concluding an agreement with the Aborigines giving him possession of 500,000 acres in the vicinity of the Yarra Yarra, Port Phillip

1835 John Batman Diary MS [La Trobe Library] 8 Jun: This will be the place for a village.

1959 Barry Humphries *A Nice Night's Entertainment* (1981) 20: Who has not heard of his [Batman's] famous statement: 'This is the spot for a village', or 'This is the village for a spot', as they say in the classics.

1965 Agnes Paton Bell *Melbourne John Batman's Village* [book title]

1984 *Weekend Australian* 17 Nov. Mag. 8: 150 years later, is Melbourne a good place for a suburb? [heading]

Vinnie's   The Society of St Vincent de Paul, as an outlet for used clothing, etc.

1984 *Sydney Morning Herald* 7 Sep. Metro 15: Cardier ... in a suit fresh from St Vinnies' and a hat pulled low like the gangster he sometimes portrays.

1984 *Southerly* 390: 'I'll go down to Vinny's and see what they've got.'

1985 *Australian* 24 Jan. 8: It is only possible to live healthily on this budget by supermarket shopping late on Saturday mornings to take advantage of reductions on perishables and by scouring the racks at 'Vinnies' for clothes.

vision splendid, the   Any splendid prospect, esp. of the future (from A. B. Paterson's 'Clancy of the Overflow' and Wordsworth's 'Immortality' ode)

437

1895 A. B. Paterson *The Man from Snowy River* 21: And he sees the vision splendid of the sunlit plains extended, / And at night the wondrous glory of the everlasting stars.

1951 Ernestine Hill *The Territory* 294: Prose and poetry glorify the drover's life into 'vision splendid of the sunlit plains extended.'

1954 Tom Ronan *Vision Splendid* [book title]

1959 Xavier Herbert *Seven Emus* 110: Such was his acting that he took in his audience along with himself, made them share his optimism, his vision splendid, even . . . against their better judgement.

1972 *Sun-Herald* 19 Nov. 11: Scratch the surface of Gough Whitlam's promises of the vision splendid and you quickly run up against some very strange political promises.

1972 Ian Moffitt *The U-Jack Society* 199: I sat obediently and listened, and Sir Phillip spread his vision splendid of electricity extended with nuclear power.

1984 Mike Carlton *Sydney Morning Herald* 21 Nov. 12: We were treated to the choking sob and the glint of a tear as the Prime Minister was overcome by his vision splendid of electoral gains extended.

Volvo set, the Well-to-do environmentalists, as described by Mr Barrie Unsworth, secretary of the N.S.W. Labor Council, in the debate over the logging of rainforests in N.S.W. in 1982

1982 Barrie Unsworth *Sydney Morning Herald* 22 Oct. 1: 'The phrase Volvo set was coined by Rod Muir of 2-Day FM to describe the chic, trendy set of the middle class. What I said to the Premier on Monday was that while he is looking after the Volvo set he didn't want to lose the support of the Holden Kingswood set.'

1982 *Sydney Morning Herald* 23 Oct. 12: The image often conjured up of people lounging on their Paddington patios, drinking white wine and feeling emotional about trees – the middle-class, Volvo set, in Unsworth's terms.

1984 *Sydney Morning Herald* 1 Dec. 5: The 'Volvo set' catches up with Trades Hall [heading] The Minister for Transport, Mr Barrie Unsworth, might well blush when he passes his alma mater, the old Sydney Trades Hall in Goulburn Street. There may not be much evidence of the 'Volvo set', as he once tagged environmentalists, but the fine old structure itself has been claimed by the trendy conservationists.

vomit, Burdekin see **Burdekin**

waddy   A wooden club, often improvised [Ab. 1788 Ramson 126]

1899 Steele Rudd *On Our Selection* 19: We each carried a kerosene tin, slung like a kettle-drum, and belted it with a waddy – Dad's idea.

1930 K. S. Prichard *Haxby's Circus* 236: The men grabbed seats, started to smash them up, and use them as waddies.

1939 Miles Franklin and Dymphna Cusack *Pioneers on Parade* 141: 'No danger,' said William, selecting a waddy.

1947 Vance Palmer *Cyclone* 79: 'They're planning to march out to the camp some night and deal it out to the lot of us with waddies.'

1973 Frank Huelin *Keep Moving* 114: 'The only ones who wait for us are railway demons with boots and waddies.'

wadgella   A white man, in W.A. [pidgin version of *whitefellow*]

1927 A. G. Bolam *The Trans-Australia Wonderland* 79: 'Waijela bool-ga munda?' (White fellow dig big earth?)

1969 Lyndall Hadow *Full Cycle* 157: 'Sister Merry Christmas only Waigella[2]!' [2]Corruption of 'white fella'.

1978 Nene Gare *Bend to the Wind* 126–7: 'Oh, my people. Loveliest people in the world. Easy ta get along with. Easy going. They must be or they wouldn't a put up with the wadgellas fa so many years.'

1979 Kirk Weller *The Dwarf* ed. Noni Braham 29:

These Wadgulas have got funny tricks.

1981 Archie Weller *The Day of the Dog* 45: 'Susan Smith was raped by two wadgula boys out at Scarborough beach.' Ibid. 167: *wadgula* white people.

wage-plug   A worker for wages [cf. *plug* a slow horse U.S. 1860 Mathews; *wage slave* OED 1886]

1918 George Dale *The Industrial History of Broken Hill* 200: The wage-plug on the surface is keeping in motion the machines of production.

1921 *NSW Police News* 7 Dec. 41: He was a mercilessly down-trodden wage-plug.

1931 Miles Franklin *Back to Bool Bool* 154: 'The Australian working-man is the richest wage plug on God's earth, and the most leisured.'

1951 Ernestine Hill *The Territory* 392: 'Our sons an' daughters'll be wage-plugs workin' for them strangers, an' getting' the sack.'

1971 Frank Hardy *The Outcasts of Foolgarah* 22: A grand place to live is Foolgarah, even for wage-plugs.

1983 *Newcastle Herald* 19 Apr. 2: This package of extras ... makes sure that the actual level of salary is less important to the MP than it is to the ordinary wage plug.

Wagga blanket, rug   A covering made from corn sacks, chaff bags or similar material [f. place-name Wagga Wagga, N.S.W.: otherwise unexplained]

1893 Henry Lawson 'The Darling River' *Prose* i 86–7: The live cinders from the firebox ... fell in showers on deck. Every now and then a spark would burn through the 'Wagga rug' of a sleeping shearer, and he'd wake up suddenly and get up and curse.

1938 Xavier Herbert *Capricornia* 454: The nap ... consisted of two greasy bran-sacks, or, as bushmen call them, Wagga Rugs.

1944 Jean Devanny *By Tropic, Sea and Jungle* 156: When you crawl under your wagga you get in one position and aren't game to move, it hurts so much.

1951 Simon Hickey *Travelled Roads* 52: Any bush worker in the West knows that a Wagga rug is made by top-sewing two cornsacks together, which, with any sort of blanket underneath, would keep out the cold, or even rain, at a pinch.

1962 Ron Tullipan *March into Morning* 22: A blanket under him, another on top, and over that again a big bush wagga of stitched cornsacks.

1969 Lyndall Hadow *Full Cycle* 248: She went to his camp bed. 'Take your wagga, then.' 'No, it's too heavy.' Besides, he was tired of the prickly corn-sacks, half a dozen of them opened out and sewn together that had formed his bedclothes for a long time now.

1979 Justina Williams *White River* 14: Dulcie and Hew were already asleep under super-bag waggas in the dray, a covering stiff as boards but warm nevertheless.

1983 John K. Ewers *Long Enough for a Joke* 92: It contained his bunk covered with a couple of new cornsacks which he called his 'wagga'.

Wagga grip   see **monkey** 2

waigella   see **wadgella**

waist, lady's   see **lady's**

wake up to, to be a   To be fully apprised of a situation; to be alert to possible deception [f. thieves' slang: see quot. 1812]

1812 Vaux: *Awake:* an expression used ... as a thief will say to his accomplice, on perceiving the person they are about to rob is aware of their intention, and up on his guard, *stow it,* the *cove's awake.* To be awake to any scheme, deception, or design, means, generally, to see through it or comprehend it.

1924 *Truth* 27 Apr. 6: *Awake* To know all.

1932 Leonard Mann *Flesh in Armour* 237: She would see, then, that he was no fool, and take a full wake-up to it.

1945 *Coast to Coast 1944* 85: 'When did you become a wake-up?' 'A wake-up to what?' 'To the papers.'

1957 Ray Lawler *Summer of the Seventeenth Doll* 17: 'She shakes them down for all they're worth the whole time they're here. 'Course they're a

wake up, but they don't seem to mind.'

1963 Alan Marshall *In Mine Own Heart* 64: 'The trouble is that Florrie's a wake-up to me. She doesn't believe half the lies I tell her.'

1975 Xavier Herbert *Poor Fellow My Country* 592: 'I got a feelin' he's a wake-up. Still, don't worry. We'll beat him.'

Waler   'An Anglo-Indian name for an Australian horse imported from New South Wales into India, especially for the cavalry. Afterwards used for any horse brought from Australia.' (Morris)

1863 B. A. Heywood *Vacation Tour at the Antipodes* 134: I have heard men from Bengal talk of the 'Walers', meaning horses from New South Wales.

1874 Rolf Boldrewood *My Run Home* (1897) 330: 'I can't imagine any horse but an English thorough-bred worthy to be named in the same day with a high-caste Arab ...' 'I'll show you a "Waler" ["whaler" in 1897] to-morrow that may convert you.'

1900 Henry Lawson 'The Ballad of the Cornstalk' *Verse* i 380: He mounted his waler and rode to the sea.

1964 H. P. Tritton *Time Means Tucker* 90: The horses were bred specially for the Indian Army and known as 'Walers' (because they came from New South Wales).

1966 Tom Ronan *Strangers on the Ophir* 48: That old original waler strain than which no greater or gamer breed of horse ever sniffed the wind.

1983 *Australian* 9 May 9: In Sydney opposite the State Library stands a modest memorial to our 'gallant horses', the Walers of World War I, which carried our boys from the Pyramids to Jerusalem.

walkabout   1   Temporary migration from one's normal habitat (originally applied to the movements of Aboriginals); any journey away from a home base [Pidgin]

1828 *Sydney Gazette* 2 Jan. 3: When the execu-tioner had adjusted the rope, and was about to pull the cap over his eyes ... he said, in a tone of deep feeling, which it was impossible to hear without strong emotion, 'Bail more walk about', meaning that his wanderings were all over.

1908 Mrs Aeneas Gunn *We of the Never-Never* 218: The day after that was filled in with prepara-tions for a walk-about, and the next again found us camped at Bitter Springs.

1930 Vance Palmer *The Passage* 24: 'Tired of the smell of fish,' he would explain, 'only a cat could stand it so long on end. I'm going for a walkabout – there's plenty doing up in the orchards now the oranges are on.'

1941 Charles Barrett *Coast of Adventure* 14: As an old man whose walkabouts were made in an old-fashioned vehicle, the Doctor understood

440

natives.

1969 William Dick *Naked Prodigal* 10: 'Hold the fort men. I'm going walkabout,' yelled Arthur, throwing down his trolley with a clang.

1976 *Sydney Morning Herald* 17 May 6: His answers to questions were garbled and grammatically walkabout.

2 A 'meet-the-people' stroll by royalty or other notable (first used of Queen Elizabeth on 12 Mar. 1970 Auckland N.Z.)

1977 *Australian* 24 Mar. 5: A fair-haired 16-year-old girl . . . was the other star of the walkabout. She presented the flowers then popped her head up and kissed the Queen on the cheek.

1981 *Sydney Morning Herald* 25 Jul. 10: Lady Diana takes Royal walkabout in her stride.

walk off, do a walk   To abandon a rural property through inability to make it pay

1939 Leonard Mann *Mountain Flat* 76 7: 'The one who doesn't get Suttons' will have to walk off.'

1958 E. O. Schlunke *The Village Hampden* 114: 'They're so much in debt that, if the Government Relief Board wasn't carrying them on, they'd all have to walk off their farms tomorrow.'

1959 C. V. Lawlor *All That Humbug* 87: Almost every week one heard of yet another farmer who had 'walked off' in the south-west area of N.S.W. Sad hearts and bitter; moneyless pockets; an obscure future; machinery left behind that could not be paid for.

1964 Arthur Staples *Paddo* 21: 'He drank everything away, and we had to walk off the place.'

1970 *Sydney Morning Herald* 21 Jul. 6: The manager of the Bourke Rural Bank can recall four graziers who have 'done a walk', leaving the bank to use the properties as best it could to recover the graziers' debts.

Walla Walla, further behind than   At a disadvantage [see quot. 1978]

1953 T. A. G. Hungerford *Riverslake* 161: 'Chuck over that pair of strides, will you – I'm further behind than Walla Walla.'

1967 Frank Hardy *Billy Borker Yarns Again* 19–20: 'Not much use backing a two-to-one winner at this stage. You're further behind than Walla Walla.'

1978 *Sydney Morning Herald* 21 Nov. 27: Walla Walla the great pacer after whom the phrase . . . was coined because he won from seemingly impossible handicaps.

Wallabies, the   The Rugby Union team representing Australia internationally [f. analogy with the Kangaroos, the Rugby League team]

1976 *Australian* 22 Oct. 20: Wallabies flop in the wet.

wallaby, on the ~ track   Tramping the outback in search of work (as though following the track made by the wallabies)

1861 Horace Earle *Ups and Downs* 208: He had started on the Wallaby track* more than once. *Wallaby track – tramping in search of employment.

1865 E. J. Overbury 'The Wallaby Track' *Old Bush Songs* ed. Stewart and Keesing (1957) 232: There are others who stick during shearing, / Then shoulder their swags on their back; / For the rest of the year they'll be steering / On their well-beloved Wallaby Track.

1870 W. M. Finn *Glimpses of North-Eastern Victoria* (1917) 26: On a sunny day the banks of the river will be covered with clothes of those men who are tramps, and are on what is colonially known as the 'Wallaby Track'.

1876 Rolf Boldrewood *A Colonial Reformer* (1891) 82: 'What is the meaning of "out on the wallaby"? asked Ernest. 'Well, it's bush slang, sir, for men just as you or I might be now, looking for work or something to eat; if we can't get work, living on the country, till things turn round a little.'

1887 *All the Year Round* 20 Jul. 66: He perambulates the country, going 'on the Wallaby', as it is strangely termed, nightly receiving the hospitality of the farmers and station-managers whom he honours with his presence.

1891 Henry Lawson *Verse* i 134: 'On the Wallaby' [poem title]

1905 Joseph Furphy *Rigby's Romance* ed. R. G. Howarth (1946) 69: 'I'll live and die on the wallaby. I'm like that character in the Bible . . . always going to and fro on the earth, and walking up and down in it.'

1919 W. K. Harris *Outback in Australia* 146: All the . . . celebrities of the day were 'on the wallaby', 'humping bluey'.

1934 Brian Penton *Landtakers* 382: 'The last time I saw a sky like this was in 'Thirty-nine. A lot of good men were on the wallaby after that.'

1961 George Farwell *Vanishing Australians* 107: Since then it has been de rigueur with every bushman on the wallaby.

walloper   A policeman [f. *wallop*]

1945 Baker 137: We also call a policeman . . . a *walloper*.

1950 *Australian Police Journal* Apr. 120: *Wallopers* Police.

1951 Frank Hardy *Power Without Glory* 33: 'Police! Everyone out! The bloody wallopers are on their way!'

1954 *Coast to Coast 1953–1954* 175: He'd kept pretty clear of courts though . . . Always two jumps ahead of the wallopers.

1960 Ron Tullipan *Follow the Sun* 125: 'The wallopers collected him. They got here just as the blue was finished and took him away in the ghost truck.'

1969 Osmar White *Under the Iron Rainbow* 117: 'Brownie never did anything that you wallopers would want him for.'

1972 Alexander Macdonald *The Ukelele Player under the Red Lamp* 237: I saw this enormous walloper leaning affectionately over the driver's window.

1975 *Nation Review* 5 Dec. 212: His [Ned Kelly's] skull was round for a long while being used as an ashtray by a sensitive and softly spoken walloper.

1980 *NT News* (Darwin) 23 Feb. 7: After being allowed through the door [of the casino], our man was pounced upon by the eagle-eyed security walloper.

waltzing Matilda   see **Matilda**

waratah   A celebration, festival [? f. the Waratah Festival in N.S.W., for which the waratah is the State flower]

1975 Evonne Goolagong *Evonne* 189: When would they stop clapping? Not for five minutes, according to the journalists who timed it. It was a regular waratah (party) in the stadium.

warb   1   Someone of little acumen, or of disreputable appearance [see *warby*]

1941 Baker 80: *Warb* A low-paid manual worker.

1953 Baker 135: *warb* A dirty or untidy person; also (by rhyme) *wattle and daub*; whence, *warby*, dirty or untidy.

1956 Ruth Park and D'Arcy Niland *The Drums Go Bang!* 126: Alongside this masterpiece he felt the warbiest of the warbs.

1967 Kylie Tennant *Tell Morning This* 201: 'But it's a no-hoper's jail – a lot of old warbs and kids mixed up with coves like Amos the Cannibal and chaps that razors bounce off.'

1984 *Sydney Morning Herald* 4 Feb. 37: In Moore Park Road, she picks up an intoxicated person (police call them warbs, slang passed down from they don't know where).

2   An unskilled circus hand

1945 Baker 249: *warb*, a circus labourer.

1956 Ruth Park and D'Arcy Niland *The Drums Go Bang!* 174: I'm classed as a warb, but I do everything. I help pull down and put up the Big Top, play recorded music, bang the cymbals.

1967 John Yeomans *The Scarce Australians* 30: There are four general hands (known in Australian circus slang as worbs).

warby   Unprepossessing in appearance or disposition; decrepit, unkempt, 'drack' [cf. *warbie* a maggot bred in the skin of cattle EDD]

1941 Kylie Tennant *The Battlers* 264: 'Of all the warby ideas,' he said . . . 'the warbiest is you going

on your own.'

1949 Ruth Park *Poor Man's Orange* 181: Yeah, there she was, in a warby kind of blue dress, and low-heeled shoes.

1959 D'Arcy Niland *The Big Smoke* 183: A warby unshaven young man in working clothes walked through and right up to him at the back.

1964 Tom Ronan *Packhorse and Pearling Boat* 81: Billy Bunter [in *The Magnet*] was considered worthy neither of dislike nor blame. We had a few similar warby types among ourselves.

1965 Eric Lambert *The Long White Night* 135: 'That was one of the funniest sights the main street ever saw – my old man's warby old Model A towing Foran's dirty big gleaming new Packard!'

1973 Jim McNeil *The Old Familiar Juice* 74: 'He's down there whackin' up bumpers with a couple of 'is warby mates.'

Warder, Johnny   See quot. 1882: *obs.*

1872 *Punch Staff Papers* 218: On the kerbstone sat one of those amiable old ladies who are popularly known as 'Johnny Warders'. She was very drunk.

c. **1882** *The Sydney Slang Dictionary* 5: *Johnny Warder* An idle drunkard who hangs about public-house corners looking for a drink (called after a publican named John Ward who formerly kept a low house in Sydney noted for that species).

warm inner glow, the politics of   The ideology of the Left in the Australian Labor Party, from the standpoint of the Right: any reformist programme which seems unrealistic to its opponents [see quot. 1984]

1982 *Australian* 15 Jun. 1: The politics of the 'warm inner glow' – the right-wingers' derisive phrase for the social concerns of the Left – received a hefty beating over the holiday weekend . . . 'What we have here are the politics of the warm inner glow – making people feel good', Mr Keating said.

1982 *Sun-Herald* 4 Jul. 152: Notice how the phrase 'the politics of the warm inner glow' has caught on lately? It describes an action which means nothing but makes the perpetrator feel good. Paul Keating was said to have coined it to describe NSW left wingers. But the author was former Senator Diamond Jim McClelland, now a judge of the NSW Land and Environment Court.

1983 *Sydney Morning Herald* 26 Feb. 13: Hawke's personal following is the same as Chipp's, caring, ideologically soft middle Australia, the 'warm inner glow' constituency which has taken its heart off its sleeve and put it in a rubber raft on the Franklin River.

1983 Patrick Cook *National Times* 10 Jan. 13: If it wasn't in poor taste, the policy of unilateral disarmament could be described as the politics of the warm inner glow.

1984 James McClelland *Weekend Australian* 15 Dec. Mag. 14: A few years ago when I was a practising politician I coined a phrase to describe the philosophy of those for whom the ultimate test of a policy is the feeling of personal virtuousness to be derived from its espousal: the politics of the warm inner glow.

warrigal 1 Aboriginal term for dog
1793 J. Hunter *Historical Journal* ed. J. Bach (1968) 274: *Waregal*, A large dog.
2 An untamed creature (e.g. horse, native); and outlaw
1875 Rolf Boldrewood *The Squatter's Dream* repr. as *Ups and Downs* (1878) 249: 'He's a good shot, and these warrigal devils [natives] knows it, or they'd have rushed the place long enough before now.'
1885 'The Cabbage-tree Tile' *The Melbourne Vocalist* 71 repr. in *Old Bush Songs* ed. Stewart and Keesing (1957) 164: I'm a warragle fellow that long hath dwelt / In the wild interior, nor hath felt, / Nor heard, nor seen the pleasures of town.
1892 Gilbert Parker *Round the Compass in Australia* 44: Six wild horses – warrigals or brombies, as they are called – have been driven down, corralled, and caught.'
1903 Joseph Furphy *Such is Life* (1944) 17: 'Well, you know, ole Martin, the head boundary man, he's about as nice a varmin as Warrigal Alf.'
[1916] Oliver Hogue *Trooper Bluegum at the Dardanelles* 25: Some of the kind-hearted station folk in the backblocks had sent down some wild warrigals of the West . . . old outlaws off the grass that the station hands could never master.
1939 Kylie Tennant *Foveaux* 410: The people of Foveaux were Kingston's 'Warrigals', as he said with a contemptuous affection.
1948 K. S. Prichard *Golden Miles* 244: He was toddling now, a sturdy, obstreperous youngster with a shock of dark hair, and 'the wicked look in his eye of a regular young warrigul,' Dinny said.
1959 Ian Mudie 'Outside the Fences' *Blue Crane* 47: Out beyond the fences of convention / where we mangy and flea-bitten warrigals run.

washer A face-washer, a 'flannel'
1951 Dymphna Cusack *Say No to Death* 194: Doreen had given her a washer and a drop of warm water to wash the sleep out of her eyes.
1962 *Southerly* 97: We add to *washer* the meaning of *face-cloth*.
1970 Patrick White *The Vivisector* 236: He was reminded of an old face-washer, often grubby, one of the maids had crocheted for him, in wide mesh.
1974 Alexander Buzo *Coralie Lansdowne Says No* 71: 'I'll get you a cold washer.'

watch, silly (crazy) as a two-bob Extremely silly
1954 Peter Gladwin *The Long Beat Home* 72: 'There now, I clean forgot. I'm getting silly as a two-bob watch.'
1964 George Johnston *My Brother Jack* 58: He would describe somebody as being 'as silly as a two-bob watch.'
1972 John de Hoog *Skid Row Dossier* 75: 'Don't buy him a beer, Johnny, he's silly as a two bob watch,' someone advised as he tapped me on the shoulder.

water, able to talk under see **talk**

water, over the In Van Diemen's Land (Tasmania), from the standpoint of the mainland: *obs.*
1859 Henry Kingsley *Recollections of Geoffry Hamlyn* ii 23: 'Indeed' said I; 'and is he in the colony?' 'No, he's over the water, I expect.' 'In Van Diemen's Land, you mean?'

Watsons, to bet like the To wager large amounts [derived by Baker (1966: 73–4) from the Watson brothers, noted betters]
1945 *Argus* 12 Jun. 15: I have been asked for the origin of the expression 'Betting like the Watsons'. Thinking back, I seem to remember a previous controversy as to who were the Watsons so famous for their betting activities.
1949 Lawson Glassop *Lucky Palmer* 163: 'Bet well? You bet like the Watsons.'
1954 Tom Ronan *Vision Splendid* 76: 'The survey-party is chequed-up to the skies and while they've got it they'll bet like the Watsons.'
1967 Frank Hardy *Billy Borker Yarns Again* 140: 'That Frank Duval must be a game puntor, Billy.' 'I'd bet like the Watsons meself if I had a million quid in the bank.'

wayback 1 The regions remote from settlement
1901 F. J. Gillen *Diary* (1968) 277: Like most stock stations in the 'wayback' there has been no attempt made to improve the appearance of the surroundings.
1929 Jules Raeside *Golden Days* 344: The episode reminded me of a boarding-house where I once stayed at in the way-back.
1973 Margaret Carnegie *Friday Mount* 218: No wonder some of the way-back towns had that look.
2 An inhabitant of the 'wayback' regions, unused to city life
1904 Henry Fletcher *Dads Wayback: His Work* [book title]
1912 R. S. Tait *Scotty Mac, Shearer* 125: At a group in front of him a thimble-rigger was expending much eloquence to induce a party of waybacks to relieve him of his surplus cash.
1924 *Truth* 27 Apr. 6: *Wayback* An Australian resident living far removed from townships and

not versed in city customs.
1931 Miles Franklin *Back to Bool Bool* 54: 'The real old way-backs. You can't change 'em.'
1956 Tom Ronan *Moleskin Midas* 165: 'I'm only a wayback meself with no schoolin' so I wouldn't know.'

weak as gin's piss   see **gin's piss**

weegie   see **widgie**

weekender   See quot. 1941
1941 Baker 81: *Weekender* A week-end cottage or shack.
1944 Lawson Glassop *We Were the Rats* 266: It was just a 'week-ender', just like any of the other thousands scattered sparsely around the edge of Lake Carraday.
1951 Dymphna Cusack and Florence James *Come In Spinner* 168: No mere week-ender this, but a house of character and impressive solidity.
1961 Hugh Atkinson *Low Company* 123: 'It used to be so quiet here. Weekenders and holiday cottages, mostly. Now it's a real little suburbia.'
1976 *Australian* 23 Feb. 9: Remember the week-ender? They haven't been building too many of them in recent years. It used to be a glorified garage ... a kilometre from the nearest sealed road, ten kilometres from running water and 100 kilometres from the nearest sewer pipe.

Weetbix packet   see **where did you get your licence?**

weight is right   As for **correct weight** q.v.

well in   Well established financially, prosperous, affluent
1845 Thomas McCombie *Arabin* 241: They had a pretty little farm, and were well in.
1874 Marcus Clarke *A Colonial City* ed. L. T. Hergenhan (1972) 331: When we wished to give a man the highest praise, we spoke of him as being 'well-in', or 'having made his pile'.
1883 Rolf Boldrewood *Robbery Under Arms* (World's Classics 1949) 568: 'My word, he's well in, is the cove' says the horse-driver; 'he's got half-a dozen stations besides this one. He'll be one of the richest men in Australia yet.'
1899 Steele Rudd *On Our Selection* 84: He was reputed to be well-in, though some said that if everybody had their own he wouldn't be worth much.
1922 Arthur Wright *A Colt from the Country* 83: 'Said to be well in, is he not?' queried Mrs Whinston.
1936 H. Drake-Brockman *Sheba Lane* 139–40: 'I told you we were pretty well in. Emily had all the things a girl likes.'

1948 K. S. Prichard *Golden Miles* 15: 'I'm not much to look at, ma'am,' Paddy protested. 'But I'm well in.'
1954 T. A. G. Hungerford *Sowers of the Wind* 35: 'He was an architect before the war, and pretty well in.'
1960 Donald McLean *The Roaring Days* 218: 'I might look up some of my father's people; they're pretty well-in over there, I'm told.'
1976 David Ireland *The Glass Canoe* 180: Someone saw her at the trots with some of the trotting men who were really well in, and she was regarded with awe ever after.

welter of it, make a   To do something to excess [*welter* Something exceptionally big or heavy of its kind 1865 OED]
1918 *Kia Ora Coo-ee* 15 May 5: My oath! he was making a welter of it.
1932 Myrtle Rose White *No Roads Go By* 141: The Boss was away, and now was his chance to make a welter of it.
1947 Gavin Casey *The Wits Are Out* 55: 'He goes the slops too heavy, though ... he makes a welter of it.'
1952 Jon Cleary *The Sundowners* 196: 'Now I don't want you to make a welter of it,' she said as she walked in behind the bar ... 'Any-one who gets noisy drunk or tries to start a fight gets locked up until he sobers up.'
1979 *National Times* 17 Feb. 10: Whitlam lists the works of art purchased by the National Gallery that were ordered to be hung at Yarralumla ... The Kerrs made a bit of a welter of it.
1984 David Marr *The Ivanov Trail* 300: Barker was able to demonstrate that Hawke had no grounds on which to argue that Combe had or would make a welter of his party connections.

westie   See quot. 1981
1979 *NT News* (Darwin) 24 Nov. 14: Westie: A person from the western suburbs.
1981 *Sydney Morning Herald* 20 Oct. 13: Bondi attracts all sorts. The eastern suburbs trendies, the 'westies' (anyone who lives west of the Har-bour Bridge), the families, the migrants, the vagrants ...
1984 *Sydney Morning Herald* 19 Jun. 1: Westie-bashing is alive and well and living in State Parliament. After the Labor member for Black-town, Mr John Aquilina, told the House he was proud to represent the people of Blacktown, the National Party member for Coffs Harbour, Mr Matt Singleton, replied: 'Yes, because you have 90 per cent of the drones, drongos and idiots in the community voting for you ... There are plenty of these people out around Blacktown so easily 90 per cent of them would vote for you.'

wet 1 Annoyed, irritated

1898 *Bulletin* 17 Dec. Red Page: To *get narked* is to lose your temper; also expressed by *getting dead wet.*

1915 C. J. Dennis *The Songs of a Sentimental Bloke* 42: Quite natchril, Romeo gits wet as 'ell. / 'It's me or you' 'e 'owls, and wiv a yell, / Plunks Tyball through the gizzard wiv 'is sword.

1924 *Truth* 27 Apr. 6: *Wet, to get* Become annoyed.

1941 Baker 81: *Wet, get* To become angry or irritable.

2 Used in a special sense of sheep being shorn, when any dampness in the fleece is thought by shearers to cause cramps, rheumatism or poisoning: if the sheep are voted 'wet', shearing will cease

1910 C. E. W. Bean *On the Wool Track* 181: A shearer halfway down the board stopped and hung up his machine. The slip of a boy shearing next to him looked up. 'Reckon they're wet?' he asked. The first shearer was putting on his coat. He nodded. 'I've been thinking so too, this half-hour', said the youngster. It spread down the shed just like fire in stubble.

1962 *Sydney Morning Herald* 24 Nov. 12: When it rains they get square on 'the bloody cocky' by voting 'em wet.

1966 D. E. Charlwood *An Afternoon of Time* 55: The shearers . . . felt the ewes and lambs, declared them 'wet' and knocked off.

wet, the The rainy season in N.W. Australia (cf. 'the Dry')

1908 Mrs Aeneas Gunn *We of the Never-Never* 292: 'Not too bad, though,' he said, reviewing the year's work, after fixing up a sleeping-camp for the wet.

1938 Xavier Herbert *Capricornia* 115: People scoffed at O'Cannon's cotton, saying at first that it would never see the Wet through, then that it would never live through the Dry.

1941 Charles Barrett *Coast of Adventure* 14: It was just before The Wet sent over Darwin a reminder that it would take over soon from The Dry: a storm that flooded streets in five minutes.

1953 Nevil Shute *In the Wet* [novel title]

1969 Christopher Bray *Blossom Like a Rose* 14: 'Oh, it's the Wet coming on. That's what does it. Makes people edgy as can be.'

1983 *Weekend Australian* 5 Feb. Mag. 1: 'Thou shalt not kill – except coons in the wet', said the barmaid, laughing.

wet cement, able to talk under   see **talk**

wet enough to bog a duck   see **duck**

whale   See quot. 1905

[**1895** A. B. Paterson *The Man from Snowy River*

182: Tramping along in the dust and sand, / Humping his well-worn swag. / He would camp for days in the river-bed, / And loiter and 'fish for whales'.]

1905 'Flash Jack from Gundagai' *The Old Bush Songs* ed. A. B. Paterson 27 and note: I've been whalin' up the Lachlan, and I've dossed on Cooper's Creek. 'Whalin' up the Lachlan' – In the old days there was an army of 'sundowners' or professional loafers who walked from station to station, ostensibly to look for work, but without any idea of accepting it. These nomads often followed up and down certain rivers, and would camp for days and fish for cod in the bends of the river. Hence whaling up the Lachlan.

1911 E. J. Brady *River Rovers* 90: Seven years had he 'whaled' the Darling and the Lower Murray, and now he was trekking upstream with his dog for companion.

whale in the bay, a   An extraordinary situation

1984 *Australian* 14 Nov. 3: Mr Read said he had thought there was something suspicious about the race, and had told his staff the only way such a poor horse [Fine Cotton] could possibly win such a race was 'by a ring-in'. 'I knew there had to be some kind of whale in the bay for this kind of activity to go on,' he said.

whaler   A bush nomad, managing to subsist without work

1883 R. E. N. Twopeny *Town Life in Australia* 244–5: A 'waler' is a bushman who is 'on the loaf'. He 'humps his drum', or 'swag', and 'starts on the wallaby track'.

1886 Frank Cowan *Australia: A Charcoal Sketch* 31: The Whalers of the Murrumbidgee and the Darling: when it suits his pleasure and convenience, a dolce-far-niente outcast in the fertile valleys of the rivers named, beyond the running of a warrant or a writ; a fisher, hunter, cut-throat, thief or what he will, time, place and circumstance suggesting and determining.

1900 Henry Lawson 'The Darling River' *Prose* i 84: They grow weary of seeing the same old 'whaler' drop his swag on the bank opposite whenever the boat ties up for wood; they get tired of lending him tobacco, and listening to his ideas, which are limited in number and narrow in conception.

1903 Joseph Furphy *Such is Life* (1944) 4: Willoughby, who was travelling loose with Thompson and Cooper, was a whaler.

1911 E. J. Brady *River Rovers* 90: It was a wrinkled whaler that we camped beside on a sandspit next night . . . A wise old vagabond was this who had bearded many station cooks in his day.

1919 W. K. Harris *Outback in Australia* 144: On

the Murrumbidgee we asked several questions of an old 'whaler'* as to roads and grass and water ahead. *On the Outback rivers sundowners are known as 'whalers'.

1927 R. S. Browne *A Journalist's Memories* 76: In the shearer's huts in the West, on mustering camps and at those little meetings of 'billabong whalers' where two or three were gathered together, the name of 'Billy' Lane was reverenced.

1947 Vance Palmer *Hail Tomorrow* 2: 'There's too many of these billabong whalers, like Tom says, just wandering in for the company and the rations.'

1963 Alan Marshall *In Mine Own Heart* 164: The whaler, a term that had originated from the name given to those swagmen who in the early days spent their time moving up and down the Murrumbidgee River getting handouts from the stations on its banks, now applied to those who walked from town to town in preference to jumping trains. They were generally older men.

whaler, Murrumbidgee   see **Murrumbidgee**

wharfie   A waterside worker, docker, longshoreman [abbr. of *wharf-labourer*]

1912 *The Lone Hand* 1 May 40: The best testimonial to Hughes' ability is the fact that he has so often swayed the unruly 'wharfies', and controlled their organisation for so long.

1923 George S. Beeby *Concerning Ordinary People* 152: 'Some o' the neighbours is already beginning to look down on us because you're only a wharfie.'

1948 K. S. Prichard *Golden Miles* 239: 'The wharfies and returned soldiers have been warned against giving them any excuse for a brawl.'

1955 John Morrison *Black Cargo* 229: 'As long as I'm secretary of the Melbourne Branch of the Waterside Workers I'll continue to put the interests of wharfies first.'

1971 Frank Hardy *The Outcasts of Foolgarah* 7–8: Every job has its perquisites ... the business executive has the expense account, the wharfie has the busted crate of cigarettes.

1981 *Sunday Telegraph* (Sydney) 8 Feb. 30: The Premier, Mr Wran, can swear like a Balmain wharfie, according to Graham Richardson, secretary of the NSW branch of the ALP.

wheel, to be on someone's   As for **on someone's hammer** q.v. [? f. cycle racing]

1954 Vince Kelly *The Shadow* 89: 'I'm going back to Melbourne. Down there the cops'll give you a go. Here they're on your wheel all the time.'

1959 A. W. Upfield *Bony and the Mouse* 104: 'I'll be ready for it. I'm going to be right on Tony's wheel when it happens.'

1969 Osmar White *Under the Iron Rainbow* 118:

'The inspector's been on my wheel to trace him.'

wheel, silly as a   Extremely silly

1952 T. A. G. Hungerford *The Ridge and the River* 57: Oscar was sound, but silly as a wheel.

1965 William Dick *A Bunch of Ratbags* 124: 'She hasn't changed one bit, she's as silly as a wheel, she's like her mother was.'

1966 *Coast to Coast 1965–1966* 157: 'She was as silly as a wheel, too, but a man's got to do what he can to protect his daughters.'

Whelan the Wrecker   Trading-name of a firm of demolition specialists, generalized to any demolition team

1964 George Johnston *My Brother Jack* 347: One frontage was boarded up and it was in process of demolition, and there was a big sign on one wall that said WHELAN THE WRECKER IS HERE.

1976 W. K. Hancock *Professing History* 124: The government might cut its losses and call in Whelan the Wrecker to clear away the mess on Black Mountain.

1982 *NT News* (Darwin) 10 Aug. 3: John Holland (Constructions) won the $172050 contract and sub-contracted it to Whelan the Wrecker.

Where did you get your licence?   An allegation of incompetence, with varying explanations

1971 Colin Simpson *The New Australia* 110: Our taximan leans out of his window: 'And where did you ever get a bloody driver's licence – out of a Weetbix packet?'

1971 John O'Grady *Aussie Etiket* 56: Because you are driving safely, you will be abused with sentences like ... 'Where did you get your bloody licence, Woolworth's?'

1982 *Sun-Herald* 4 Apr. 87: The bloke beside me yelled out ... 'Where'd you get a ticket, ref, out of a cornflakes packet?'

1984 *Australian* 19 Jan. 6: Mr Wran talks of bringing in overseas doctors. As an ex-merchant seaman, I've been to a few port doctors overseas and I am sure some of them got their degrees from Woolies.

whinge   To complain, gripe, protest [f. *whinge* to whine 1150 OED: Sc. and northern dial.]

1951 Dal Stivens *Jimmy Brockett* 279: Old Misery Guts and Fuller whinged when I told them what we had to do.

1965 John Beede *They Hosed Them Out* 178: Even though I wasn't going home, I was alive and well. What did I have to winge about?

1973 Henry Williams *My Love Had a Black Speed Stripe* 23: That's a thing that gets me with sheilas: whenever they start whinging they always try and make out how reasonable they are.

1984 *West Australian* (Perth) 7 Feb. 20: Australia's farmers are weary of being seen by their city cousins as whingeing conservatives dependent on government help to keep them in clover.

whinger One who whinges
1965 John Beede *They Hosed Them Out* 210: I said, 'Doc, I'm no winger but I can't sleep with this damn thing.'
1979 Dorothy Hewett *The Man from Mukinupin* 106: 'Don't whinge. I can't stand a whinger.'
1983 *Sydney Morning Herald* 5 Aug. 9: His [Andrew Peacock's] supporters believe that constant criticisms of the Government would easily leave him open to the charge of being a 'whinger' – a tag Malcolm Fraser successfully pinned on the luckless Bill Hayden.
1984 *National Times* 27 Jan. 34: 'As you know, cockies are the greatest whingers in the world.'
see **Pommy, whingeing**

whip, a fair crack of the Fair treatment or opportunity, a 'fair go' [listed by Partridge as 'North Country miners': late C.19–20']
1929 K. S. Prichard *Coonardoo* 179: 'I'll see you get a fair crack of the whip now, Mr Watt.'
1944 Lawson Glassop *We Were the Rats* 2: 'I am sorry to have to tell you that the Lord's had a fair crack of the whip and He's missed the bus.'
1951 Frank Hardy *Power Without Glory* 43: 'I'll give the punters the best crack of the whip.'
1961 Ray Lawler *The Piccadilly Bushman* 72: 'Big slangy stuff like – "Don't come the raw prawn" and "Fair crack of the whip".'
1968 Geoffrey Dutton *Andy* 116: 'Shut up, youse animals,' shouted the sergeant. 'Fair crack of the whip, Sarge.'
1983 *National Times* 3 Jun. 14: Give sadists a fair crack of the whip [graffito]

whippy The wallet, the pocket
1977 Jim Ramsay *Cop It Sweet* 96: Whippy: Pocket.
1980 *Sun-Herald* 27 Jan. 66: Fair dinkum, if a man had enough in the willy, I mean whippy ...
1984 *Sunday Telegraph* (Sydney) 8 Apr. 63: The going has been tough on the punt lately and the whippy was looking pretty bare.

whips of An abundance [f. *whips* plenty, lots EDD 1894; cf. *lashings of*]
1905 *The Old Bush Songs* ed. A. B. Paterson 24: We'd whips and whips of Rhino as we meant to push about.
1906 G. M. Smith *Days of Cobb & Co.* 19: I had whips of strength and energy.
1918 Bernard Cronin *The Coastlanders* 123: 'They's whips of feed and the water's not bad.'
1934 Steele Rudd *Green Grey Homestead* 97: 'And tell him I've got whips of room for him.'

1955 Alan Marshall *I Can Jump Puddles* 19: 'There's whips of feed on the creek flats yet.'
1961 George Farwell *Vanishing Australians* 182: 'Then you want capital – whips of it.'

white ants, to have To be eccentric, crazy
1900–10 O'Brien and Stephens: *White ants* silliness, madness. Any person of weak intellect or peculiar in their manner as if insane is said to have white ants.
1908 Henry Fletcher *Dads and Dan between Smokes* 64: It wants a fool or a very sane cove indeed ter live in ther lonely bush an' keep ther white ants out o' his napper.
1926 L. C. E. Gee *Bushtracks and Goldfields* 65: And so he rambles on ... and in the unsteady glance of his honest, old eyes and his disconnected speech, I read the mark of the Australian solitudes – 'white ants' they call it up north.
1938 H. Drake-Brockman *Men Without Wives* 27: '"Get the white ants?" What do you mean?' 'Go ratty. Mad.'
1951 Ernestine Hill *The Territory* 446: White ants in the billy: Crazy.

white lady Methylated spirits, sometimes mixed with something else
1935 Kylie Tennant *Tiburon* 19: Two old men in the corner lying stupefied over a mixture of 'white lady' – boiled methylated spirit with a dash of boot polish and iodine.
1949 Judith Wright *Woman to Man* 35: His white and burning girl, his woman of fire, / creeps to his heart and sets a candle there.
1962 Ron Tullipan *March into Morning* 57: 'What is it?' Chapple asked, eying the bottle with suspicion, 'metho?' 'The white lady.'
1975 Richard Beilby *The Brown Land Crying* 225: 'Ya was on the White Lady at the finish, mixin' it with Coke' ... 'But jees, meths'n Coca Cola.'
1982 Jack Davis *The Dreamers* 109: White lady methylate / Keep us warm and from crying.

white leghorn See quot.
1975 Les Ryan *The Shearers* 135: *White leghorn* Colloquial term for a woman bowler.
1984 David McNicoll *Bulletin* 3 Apr. 50: I wrote recently about lawn bowlers, known affectionately as the 'White Leghorns'. Gwen Dunn, of Blakehurst, NSW, writes to tell me that they are now wearing 'mini-beige' instead of white.

Whitely King See quots
1902 *Bulletin* 1 Feb 16: A billy fashioned from a fruit tin is universally known as a 'Whitely King' from the secretary of the Pastoralists' Union, who, during the shearing troubles, sent out bands of non-unionists furnished with these impromptu utensils. They are accordingly despised.

1911 E. S. Sorenson *Life in the Australian Back-blocks* 278: An improvised billy made from a fruit-tin, with a bit of fencing wire for handle ... is known as a 'Whitely King' from the fact that the Secretary of the Pastoralists' Union, during a shearers' strike, sent out a bank of non-unionists furnished with this kind of utensil.

white, a ~ man Term of highest commendation, making any other comment unnecessary [U.S. 1865 Mathews]
1883 Rolf Boldrewood *Robbery Under Arms* (World's Classics 1949) 503: He was always the same. The whitest man I ever knew, or ever shall – that I say and stick to.
1892 Henry Lawson 'Jack Dunn of Nevertire' *Verse* i 222: There is no whiter man than Jack – no straighter south the line, / There is no hand in all the land I'd sooner grip in mine.
1911 Louis Stone *Jonah* 190: 'Yous are a white man, an' I always knew it.'
1918 Let. in Bill Gammage *The Broken Years* (1974) 249: One could not find a whiter man in the whole world. He would never let a pal down ... and would never allow a word to be said against me, whether I was right or wrong.
1929 Jules Raeside *Golden Days* 314: I knew Treffene personally, and found him every inch a white man.
1939 H. M. Moran *Viewless Winds* 173: Our commanding officer, who was of the Irish ascendancy class, a Protestant, a friend, and, what we call in Australia, a white man.
1942 John Shaw Neilson *Autobiography* (1978) 96: My boss was as white a man as ever I worked for and he was very anxious that I should keep on.
1951 Frank Hardy *Power Without Glory* 366: 'Everyone knows', Scott concluded, pointing dramatically at John West, 'that our host to-day is a real white man!'

white, the man in The referee or umpire in football [f. dress]
1973 *Sun-Herald* 16 Sep. 63: Refereeing continued to be a pain in the neck, with the public asking only one thing from the men in white – consistency.
1973 Alexander Buzo *The Roy Murphy Show* 107: 'It's all very well to knock the men in white, Mike, but you must bear in mind that referees have many difficulties confronting them.'
1982 *NT News* (Darwin) 31 Dec. 13: 12 women umpires have been sharing the solitary shower at the Gardens Oval with the men in white (not all at the same time) while waiting for extra showers to be installed.
1984 *Sun* (Melbourne) 16 Jul. 68: An earlier incident involving Footscray skipper Jim Edmond and Swans defender David Ackerley went unseen by the men in white.

white virgin See quot.
1983 *Sydney Morning Herald* 23 Nov. 1: A white police van, 'the white virgin', picks up Aboriginal drinkers who are not too far gone ... and gives them a lift home, rather than locking them into cells.

whitewash The overwhelming defeat of one sporting team by another, esp. when the losing side fails to score [also U.S.]
1977 *Australian* 24 Jan. 16: Australia ... completed a 5–0 whitewash of the eastern zone semi-final against India at Royal Kings Park in Perth.
1980 *Sydney Morning Herald* 6 Feb. 52: Australia will inevitably win to complete a clean sweep of the series – the first time it has happened since Warwick Armstrong's Australians whitewashed Johnny Douglas's England team in 1920–21.

whizz off As for **race off** q.v.
1963 Lawson Glassop *The Rats in New Guinea* 87: 'You might have been the Wizard of Nerridale but I was the Whizzer of Nerridale.'
1978 Richard Beilby *Gunner* 308: 'Good on ya, Digger! Whizz 'er off while she's hot.'

who's robbing this coach see **coach**

who's up who and who's paying the rent see **up**

Wicks, the The Randwick, N.S.W., Rugby Union team [abbr.]
1984 *Sunday Telegraph* (Sydney) 8 Apr. 127: Wicks go down in shocker [heading]

wide brown land, the Australia, from Dorothea Mackellar's 'My Country'
1914 Dorothea Mackellar *The Witch Maid* 29: Her beauty and her terror – / The wide brown land for me.
1934 *The Wide Brown Land: a new Anthology of Australian Verse* chosen by Joan Mackaness and George Mackaness.
1966 Jan Smith *An Ornament of Grace* 33: A nice myth to be dusted off every Anzac Day, about bronzed heroes of the wide brown land.
1970 *Sunday Telegraph* (Sydney) 9 Aug. 30: The wide brown land is up for sale.
1973 *Australian* 4 May 11: Migrants are staying away in droves from the widest and brownest part of this wide, brown land.

wider the brim, the smaller the property see **brim**

widgie Female counterpart of the **bodgie** q.v.
1950 *Sun* (Sydney) 5 Jul. 19: A benefit dance will be held on Friday at the Gaiety Ballroom, Oxford

Street ... There'll be competitions for jitter-bugging, Charleston, and prizes for the most color-fully dressed 'bodgy' and 'weegie'. Mo and Hal Lashwood will be the judges.
1951 *Sydney Morning Herald* 1 Feb. 1: What with 'bodgies' growing their hair long and getting round in satin shirts, and 'weegies' cutting their hair short and wearing jeans, confusion seems to be arising about the sex of some Australian adolescents.
1963 Gunther Bahnemann *Hoodlum* 48: His milk bar was the biggest assembling place for the bodgies and widgies in town, particularly after the pictures were out.
1965 William Dick *A Bunch of Ratbags* 248: I had never seen so many bodgies and widgies all together at one time before.

wild colonial boy see **colonial**

wild white man, the William Buckley (1780–1856), the convict who escaped and lived for thirty-two years with the natives, being eventually returned to the white community
1856 James Bonwick *William Buckley, the Wild White Man* [book title]
1871 Marcus Clarke *Old Tales of a Young Country* 18: William Buckley, The 'Wild White Man' [essay title]

Wilcannia shower see **shower**

willy A supply of money for betting; money (in criminal slang)
1949 Lawson Glassop *Lucky Palmer* 36: 'Two quid? Break it down. That's me willie. That's all I got.'
1975 *Bulletin* 26 Apr. 46: It was this woman who was guarding the willy (money) and the success of the operation rested on the Limp distracting her attention.
1977 Jim Ramsay *Cop it Sweet* 96: *Willy* Supply of betting money; Wallet.

willy willy On land, a spiralling dusty wind; at sea, a minor cyclone: esp. N.W. Australia
1894 *The Age* 20 Jan. 13: The willy willy is the name given to these periodical storms by the natives of the north-west. [Morris]
1898 D. W. Carnegie *Spinifex and Sand* 254: Large tracts of burnt country had to be crossed from which clouds of dust and ashes were continu-ally rising, blown up by 'Willy-Willies' (spiral winds).
1929 Sir Hal Colebatch *A Story of a Hundred Years* 168: The [pearling] industry requires that capital be risked; it takes its toll of life even in ordinary working, and in cyclones or 'willy willys' many lives and much property have been lost.

1942 Gavin Casey *It's Harder for Girls* 113: A corkscrew of sand, the beginning of a willy-willy, danced through the yard, tugging at her skirts as it went and making her drop the wood as she grabbed at the garment with both hands.
1955 F. B. Vickers *The Mirage* 120: Mrs Gordon, sitting under the poinciana tree, watched these willy-willies, the whirlpools of wind and dust, go staggering about the plain as if they were drunk with their own force.
1962 J. Marshall and R. Drysdale *Journey Among Men* 114: A willy-willy is what is called a dust devil in many countries. It is a rotary vortex of air that appears suddenly when a gentle breeze is blowing across a blazing desert. A willy-willy can dump a man on to the ground; it can tear through a camp ... it can carry dust and other debris more than a thousand feet in the air.
1980 *National Times* 27 Apr. 28: Again and again we see 'willy-willys' which dance friskily in the parched landscape, often more than 100 metres high. They are almost solid with sand.

Windies, the The West Indies cricket team
1965 Wally Grout *My Country's 'Keeper* 69: The Australian public was enchanted and took the 'Windies' to their hearts from that moment.
1976 *Sunday Telegraph* (Sydney) 4 Jan. 52: Windies roll with brutal pace beating.

wine dot See quot. 1966
1953 T. A. G. Hungerford *Riverslake* 35: 'Is he a wine-dot?' 'Is he hell! ... He's never off it.'
1966 Baker 226: Addicts of cheap wine are known variously as *winedots* (a play on Wyandottes, domestic fowls of a U.S. breed).
1976 Dorothy Hewett *This Old Man Comes Roll-ing Home* 11: 'Gawd, you smell like an old wine dot, Laurie.'

wingy Nickname for someone who has lost an arm [f. *wing* to wound ... in the arm or shoulder *OED* 1802]
[**1895** Cornelius Crowe *The Australian Slang Dictionary* 96: *Winged* one-armed, or wounded.]
1910 Henry Lawson 'The Rising of the Court' *Prose* i 660: Wingy, by the way, is a ratty little one-armed man, whose case is usually described in the headline, 'A 'Armless Case', by one of our great dailies.
1932 Leonard Mann *Flesh in Armour* 8: The figure of Nelson ... on the top of the column, was hardly discernible in the dirty mist ... Bill Potter waved a nonchalant greeting with 'Good-day Nelson,' 'Eh?' asked his companion. 'Just passing the day to old Wingie.'
1945 *Coast to Coast 1944* 32: The only thing I haven't is a left arm ... they can call me Wingy now.

1964 Tom Ronan *Packhorse and Pearling Boat* 129: As Dad later referred to him as 'Wingy' Collins I presume that he had one arm amputated, or some similar disability.

1971 Keith Willey *Boss Drover* 150: One of the most unlikely fighters I knew in the bush was Wingy Collins. He was a big fellow and he took his name from the fact that one arm was twisted, although it still had plenty of strength in it.

1982 *Sydney Morning Herald* 24 Jul. 13: John Hyde, the West Australian wheat farmer who lost an arm in a tractor accident and is called 'Wingie', is the Dries' cavalier and strategist who leads the charges on Cabinet.

wipe To dismiss from consideration, wash one's hands of [f. *to wipe one's hands of* OED 1785]

1941 Kylie Tennant *The Battlers* 196: Giving her money ... in the casual manner that wiped her from all consideration as a human being.

1946 *Coast to Coast 1945* 123: 'Listen pal – your girl wiped you, didn't she?'

1948 Ruth Park *The Harp in the South* 269: 'From now on he's wiped. I never want to see him again.'

1954 T. A. G. Hungerford *Sowers of the Wind* 162: 'She dumped me, wiped me like a dirty nose.'

1962 David Forrest *The Hollow Woodheap* 149: 'She wiped you like last week's bath mat.'

1965 Eric Lambert *The Long White Night* 64: 'We'll have a drink,' I told them. 'Then I'm wiping you two like a dirty floor.'

1975 Richard Beilby *The Brown Land Crying* 295: 'You can wipe that idea, if that's what you're thinking.'

1983 Patrick White *Netherwood* 36: 'Suspended once – but they didn't wipe me.'

wire, mulga, spinifex see **mulga, spinifex**

wire, straight Fair dinkum, on the level: *obs.*

1892 William Lane *The Workingman's Paradise* 203: 'When it's all over you'll remember what I say and know it's the straight wire.'

1909 Arthur Wright *A Rogue's Luck* 70: 'Now, no kid, Harry,' said Ned anxiously. 'Straight wire, did you beat him?'

1915 C. J. Dennis *The Songs of a Sentimental Bloke* 59: Say, ain't it bonzer makin' up agen? / Straight wire, it's almost worth ... Ar, I'm a cow!

1936 Miles Franklin *All That Swagger* 394: 'Straight wire, I will.'

within a bull's roar see **bull's roar**

within cooee see **cooee**

Wollongong Races See quot.

1849 J. P. Townsend *Rambles and Observations in New South Wales* 152: He is bound for the 'Wollon-gong Races', otherwise the Court of Requests, which bears this name by reason of the numbers who hurry to it from all quarters.

Wolseley The name of the shearing machine which came into use in the late 1880s and the 1890s, patented 1877 [f. F. Y. Wolseley the inventor]

1897 Henry Lawson 'The Boss's Boots' *Verse* i 321: Bogan laid his 'Wolseley' down and knocked the rouser out.

1905 'Flash Jack from Gundagai' *The Old Bush Songs* ed. A. B. Paterson 27 and note: I've pinked 'em with the Wolseleys and I've rushed with B-bows, too. Wolseleys and B-bows are respectively machines and hand shears.

1964 H. P. Tritton *Time Means Tucker* 60: The old type Wolseleys, if the tension screw was a bit tight, would run hot: when jammed onto thin pants it was somewhat startling.

wombat 1 Used in expressions suggesting torpor or stupidity

1896 Edward Dyson *Rhymes from the Mines* 124: I was sullen as a wombat on such still, wan days as these.

1917 A. B. Paterson *Three Elephant Power* 31: Dooley, better known as The Wombat because of his sleepy disposition, was a man of great strength.

2 Nickname for an unappreciative male [cf. *root v.* 1]

1982 *Weekend Australian* 4 Dec. Mag. 11: 'Could be he's what us girls call a wombat!' An animal that eats roots and leaves.

see **koala** 2

3 See quot. 1984 [? f. animal's burrowing habit]

1984 *Bulletin* 13 Nov. 32: Men known colloquially as 'wombats', says Costigan, illegally transmit prices to an operator outside racetracks by talking into radio devices in their pockets. This information is passed in turn to an operational base and then phoned to SP operators.

wongi 1 A friendly yarn, esp. in N.W. Australia [Ab.]

[**1835** G. F. Moore *Diary of ... an Early Settler in Western Australia* (1884) 271: Weeip ... asked me to 'paper wonga' the Governor about it. *Descriptive Vocabulary* 73: Wangow – To speak; to talk.]

1916 Arthur Wilson *Mining, Lays, Tales and Folk Lore* (1944) 78: I gave them a 'good luck greeting', and then, somehow, we all fell to a wongi.

1938 Xavier Herbert *Capricornia* 386: 'By cripes, Andy, that was a great wongi.'

1948 K. S. Prichard *Golden Miles* 91: 'All he wanted to do was to go home to his missus, or have a pot and a wongie with his mates.'

1957 Randolph Stow *The Bystander* 186: 'I just wanted a bit of a wongi with you. You know how it

450

is, a joker gets the urge to talk sometimes.'
1969 Lyndall Hadow *Full Cycle* 178: 'If he asks you to have one . . . well, he's out for a wongi.'
1984 *Sunday Independent* (Perth) 28 Oct. 8: Senator Withers plays down his role and dislikes the term 'Peacock's right-hand man'. 'Call me his "Wongi man" – I'm just someone he can have a chat with at the end of the day', he said with a smile.
2   A native of the Kalgoorlie region
1950 K. S. Prichard *Winged Seeds* 161: 'Bob Brown'd never forgive us if he heard we'd been calling on the wongi and hadn't paid him and his missus a visit'.
1981 Archie Weller *The Day of the Dog* 61: Charley's woman, a shy dark wongi from Kalgoorlie, comes out and takes the baby. Ibid. 167: *wongi* really the people from Kalgoorlie way, but any full-blood Aboriginal.

wonk   1   Aboriginal term for a white: *derogatory*
1938 Xavier Herbert *Capricornia* 252: He went to the Dagoes and Roughs of second-class and won their friendship by buying them liquor and telling them how he had been cast out by the Wonks of the saloon.
1958 Elizabeth Webb *Into the Morning* 116: I began remembering dirty words the boys at the River Camp used to call whites. I said aloud: 'A lot of bloody wonks – I don't care. I don't bloody well care . . . a lot of dirty wonks.'
2   A male homosexual
1945 Baker 123: An effeminate male is a . . . *wonk*.
1970 Patrick White *The Vivisector* 213: 'I'd have to have a chauffeur to drive me about – with a good body – just for show, though. I wouldn't mind if the chauffeur was a wonk.'

wood-and-water joey   Someone given the menial tasks on a station, etc., having no special skills of his own [f. 'hewers of wood and drawers of water' *Joshua* 9:21]
1882 Rolf Boldrewood *Robbery Under Arms* (World's Classics 1949) 313: 'It's all devilish fine for you . . . to go flashin' about the country and sporting your figure on horse-back, while I'm left alone to do the housekeepin' in the Hollow. I'm not going to be wood-and-water Joey, I can tell ye, not for you nor no other men.'
1887 *All the Year Round* 30 Jul. 67: A 'wood-and-water Joey' is a hanger about the hotels, and a doer of odd jobs.
1901 *The Bulletin Reciter* 15: Next, the wood-and-water joey fell a victim to his bowie, / And the boss's weeping widow got a gash from ear to ear.
1906 T. E. Spencer *How M'Dougall Topped the Score* 128: He was wood-and-water Joey at the 'Star' / Where she waited, and assisted at the bar.

c. 1926 Alpha *Reminiscences of the Goldfields* 58: She was the only single girl on the creek – sweet seventeen at that – for whom I sometimes acted as wood and water 'joey'.
1935 A. B. Paterson *The World of 'Banjo' Paterson* ed. C. Semmler (1967) 24: 'I'm a fireman,' he says, 'not a wood-and-water joey'.
1955 E. O. Schlunke *The Man in the Silo* 205: A Furphy water-cart, with the wood-and-water Joey sitting unhappily on the shaft.

Woodbine   See quot. 1919
1919 W. H. Downing *Digger Dialects* 54: *Woodbine* An English soldier, so called from the name of a cheap brand of cigarettes favored by Englishmen.
1934 Vance Palmer *Sea and Spinifex* 150: 'He's in with those woodbines on the first floor.'
1937 Ernestine Hill *Water into Gold* 192: Bagtown became 'Woodbine Ave' . . . so-called for the number of English settlers in residence.
1978 Richard Beilby *Gunner* 43: 'Ingelesi', he grinned. 'Pommies. Chooms. 'Bines. That's what we call them.'

wood duck   See quot. 1984 [f. the proverbial stupidity of the woodcock]
1984 *Bulletin* 19 Jun. 69: The bigger suppliers sit back in luxurious harbourside apartments and rely instead on a network of couriers (known as wood ducks or woodies) to run all the risks in contacting and selling to users in the street.

wooden   To fell, knock out [cf. *stiffen*]
[**1908** Henry Fletcher *Dads and Dan between Smokes* 39: When misfochin' as yous can't prevent lands yer a woodener, take it smilin'.]
1911 Steele Rudd *The Dashwoods* 25: 'I never saw him any more till I see you going to wooden him with the furniture.'
1936 A. B. Paterson 'The Shearer's Colt' in *Song of the Pen* (1983) 721: Some poor inoffensive Chinaman had come into the yard . . . and his wife had 'woodened' him without giving him a chance to explain.
1957 A. W. Upfield *Bony Buys a Woman* 124: 'We're all stonkered by now, but that fool Jimmy Wall Eye makes a swipe at Arnold and Arnold woodens him.'
1974 *Southerly* 145: 'If you can't wooden 'em [kangaroos] at a 'undred yards with one I.C.I. bullet, you're not tryin'!'
1981 A. B. Facey *A Fortunate Life* 70: He had picked up a stick about four feet long and one and a half inches thick, and intended to wooden me out.

wood, have the ~ on   To hold an advantage
1941 S. J. Baker *New Zealand Slang* 53: *to have the*

wood on a person to have an advantage over someone.

1949 Lawson Glassop *Lucky Palmer* 156: 'She's got you taped, too, kid. She's got the wood on all of us.'

1954 T. A. G. Hungerford *Sowers of the Wind* 264: 'Can't you realize I've got the wood on you? You've got two minutes.'

1965 Leslie Haylen *Big Red* 55: It was another of his occasions of fear: she liked having the wood on you.

1973 *Sunday Telegraph* (Sydney) 16 Sep. 47: The Swans hold the wood on the Magpies in finals matches.

1984 Ned Manning *Us or Them* 46: 'We've got the wood on Wilkie and McKenzie . . . I caught them smoking pot in the out-of-bounds area.'

woodie   see **wood duck**

Woods, the   1   In N.S.W., the Eastwood Rugby Union team [abbr.]

1975 *Sunday Telegraph* (Sydney) 17 Aug. 57: Woods as premiers? Forget it.

2   In Victoria, the Collingwood V.F.L. team (more often 'the Magpies')

1977 *Sunday Telegraph* (Sydney) 25 Sep. 75: Once a Woodsman always a Woodsman is the rule at Collingwood – and that's the way it will always be so long as blokes play football in black and white striped jumpers.

Woodser, Jimmy   A person drinking alone at a bar; a drink taken alone [see quots 1933, 1982]

1892 Barcroft Boake 'Jimmy Wood' *Bulletin* 7 May 17: Who drinks alone, drinks toast to Jimmy Wood, sir.* *A man drinks by himself is said to take a 'Jimmy Woodser'.

1895 Cornelius Crowe *Australian Slang Dictionary* 40: *Johnnie Woodser* taking a solitary drink at the bar.

1898 *Bulletin* 17 Dec. Red Page: *Jimmy-Woodser* a solitary drinker.

1900 Henry Lawson 'They Wait on the Wharf in Black' *Prose* i 286: 'I wanted to score a drink!' he said. 'I thought he wanted one and wouldn't like to be a Jimmy Woodser.'

1924 *Truth* 27 Apr. 6: *Jimmy Woodser* One who drinks alone.

1933 Acland: *Jimmy* or *Johnny Woodser* Slang. A drink by yourself . . . A correspondent tells me that James Woods was a shearer on the Darling River, New South Wales, in the 'eighties. He spent the off season in Bourke. He was fond of a glass of beer but was never known to shout. He always drank on his own, so that when the shearers saw any one go to the bar by himself they always said he was having a *J.W.* Hence the saying.

1963 Frank Hardy *Legends from Benson's Valley* 150: The fact that his unexpected wealth purchased a welcome in our school instead of drinking Jimmy Woodsers' pleased him no end.

1971 Hal Porter *The Right Thing* 34: 'I had three with Pauline Ashburn before she whizzed off, and a Jimmy Woodser after. No – two Jimmy Woodsers!'

1982 Heather M. Hassall *Bulletin* 27 Jul. 8: 'Jimmy' Wood was the son of James Wood who, in 1716, founded the Gloucester City Old Bank, the most ancient banking house in England with the exception of Messrs Child of Fleet Street. 'Jimmy' was a miser who, although generous to the poor – such as a gift of £200,000 to the impoverished of the City of Gloucester – was exceedingly frugal in his own living habits. His always drinking alone, led to the term 'Jimmy Woodser' for mean people who adopted the same practice. I can vouch for the accuracy of the above statements as I am connected with the Wood family.

Woolworth's   see **where did you get your licence?**

Woop Woop   Imaginary place which is a byword for backwardness and remoteness. Sometimes defined as 'where the crows fly backward, to keep the dust out of their eyes'

1923 A. B. Paterson 'Shakespeare on the Turf' in *Song of the Pen* (1983) 436: On the Woop Woop course he ran a mile / In less than forty with his irons on!

1926 J. Vance Marshall *Timely Tips for New Australians: Woop Woop* A humorous method of alluding to the country districts, used most frequently in New South Wales.

1928 Arthur Wright *A Good Recovery* 34: 'They're chasin' Murraba out along the Woop Woop Road, or somewhere.'

1949 Lawson Glassop *Lucky Palmer* 94: 'I don't come from Woop Woop. Harry Hughes is known on every racecourse in New South Wales.'

1959 Hal Porter 'Country Town' *A Bachelor's Children* (1962) 281: Oh, a local, a yokel, a hick, a peasant, a simple boy from Woop Woop! Had I heard of wireless?

1970 Sumner Locke Elliott *Edens Lost* 90: 'I was all over the country. You could drive hundreds of miles back of the beyond out into Woop-Woop or Buggeryville and there I was.'

1980 *Daily News* (Perth) 5 Nov. 68: Doesn't matter which race . . . could be the Hanging Rock Cup or the Woop Woop welter . . . the ritual is the same. Only the baloney is different.

woop   Someone from the remote regions

1939 Miles Franklin and Dymphna Cusack *Pioneers on Parade* 31: 'A glorified woop.' Ibid. 155: 'Every woop from woop-woop.'

1950 *Coast to Coast 1949–50* 201: 'I'll make a fair dinkum woop-woop out of you in no time.'

452

word   To inform someone privately, tip off
1915 C. J. Dennis *The Songs of a Sentimental Bloke* 50: I met 'im on the quiet, / 'An worded 'im about a small affair.
1928 Arthur Wright *A Good Recovery* 26: 'Here's a few bob to go on with. I'll word the landlord to look after y'.'
1939 Kylie Tennant *Foveaux* 349–50: 'You word the paper-boy to send your paper up to Central.'
1941 Baker 83: *Word up, to* To advise, 'tip off' a person.
1949 Lawson Glassop *Lucky Palmer* 212: 'Joyce Butler's on the switch and you can word her up to make a date for you.'
1951 Dymphna Cusack and Florence James *Come In Spinner* 306: 'Somebody worded me you was round here in the side lift.'
1967 K. S. Prichard *Subtle Flame* 234: 'Ted worded a mate of his on the *Western Star*.'

work in an iron lung   see **iron lung**

working off a dead horse   see **dead horse**

workingman's paradise, the   Australia
1859 Henry Kingsley *Recollections of Geoffry Hamlyn* i 103–4: That was what they saw, and what any man may see to-day for himself in his own village, whether in England or Australia, that working man's paradise.
1873 Anthony Trollope *Australia* ed. P. D. Edwards and R. B. Joyce (1967) 524: I must say of this colony [Tasmania], as I have and shall say of all the others, that it is a Paradise for a working man as compared with England.
1892 William Lane *The Workingman's Paradise: An Australian Labour Novel* 38: In Sydney, in 1889, in the working-man's paradise, she stood on the kerb, this blind girl, and begged.
1901 Rolf Boldrewood *In Bad Company* 288: This Australian land of ours. The workman's Paradise!
1911 E. M. Clowes *On the Wallaby through Victoria* 253: Victoria, and indeed Australia as a whole, has been spoken of as the 'paradise of the workingman'.
1915 F. C. Spurr *Five Years under the Southern Cross* 103: 'The working man's paradise' they call Australia, and not without good reason.
1938 Xavier Herbert *Capricornia* 375: 'They can't export it, because, Australia bein' a workin' man's paradise . . . their cost of production is too high for competition with countries where labour is sweated.'
1962 *Australian Civilization* ed. Peter Coleman 58: The nineteenth-century conviction that Australia was to be a 'working man's paradise'.
1978 *Overland* 71 42: It conjures up the old image of Queensland as a workers' paradise – a kind of Australian deep south and California wrapped into one.

worries, my   As for **my troubles** q.v.
1949 Alan Marshall *How Beautiful Are Thy Feet* 50: 'My worries,' said Correll, contemptuously gesturing, 'She's got nothing on me.'
1953 T. A. G. Hungerford *Riverslake* 174: 'And you're on the outer for sticking up for him?' 'My worries.'
1963 A. W. Upfield *Madman's Bend* 83: 'It's going to be another fine day, isn't it?' 'My worries if it's fine or wet.'

worries, no   i.e. there is no problem, no difficulty [f. *not to worry*]
1966 Roger Carr *Surfie* 100: I went over to the boarding house to her room. Only she wasn't there either. No worries, she'd be back.
1974 Jack Hibbert *Dimboola* 14: 'How are you shaping up, Morris?' 'No worries.'
1979 *Age* (Melbourne) 30 Aug. 20: We had a mound of luggage but the taxi driver who swept it into his cab said 'No worries, she's apples.' We were back once more in the no-worries country.
1981 Garry Disher *Approaches* 117: There was this bloke who walks into a pub and asks barman if he wants to hear an Irish joke. 'I'm Irish', says the barman. 'No worries', says the bloke, 'I'll tell it slow.'

wouldn't it?   Expression of exasperation [see quot. 1945 and *root v.* 2]
1941 Baker 83: *Wouldn't it!* Abbreviation of 'Wouldn't it make you sick?' or 'Wouldn't it make you mad?' etc.
1944 Lawson Glassop *We Were the Rats* 162: 'Do you know our divisions have even got a mobile laundry, decontamination unit? Wouldn't it rip you?' Ibid. 135: 'Well wouldn't it rotate you?' said Eddie.
1945 Baker 152n: The authentic digger form is *Wouldn't it root you!*
1951 Dymphna Cusack and Florence James *Come In Spinner* 382: Guinea kicked a hassock across the room. 'Wouldn't it!' she muttered furiously, 'wouldn't it!'
1955 Mary Durack *Keep Him My Country* 161: 'Hell,' Tex groaned. 'Wouldn't it, eh? You can just imagine how this makes me feel.'

wouldn't read about it   see **read**

wouldn't work in an iron lung   see **iron lung**

wowser   A censorious person; a killjoy [? f. *wow* To whine; to grumble, make complaint EDD 1876]
1899 *Truth* 8 Oct. 5: The Parraween Push / A

Partisan Protest / Willoughby 'Wowsers' Worried / The 'Talent' get a 'Turn' On Thursday week at the North Sydney Police Court . . . ten young men were fined sums varying from £2 with costs to 7/6 with costs . . . for having behaved in a riotous manner on the Military Rd.

1911 Henry Lawson 'The Song of the Heathen' *Verse* iii 65: O this is the Wowsers' land, / And the laughing days are o'er, / For most of the things that we used to do / We must not do any more!

1916 Joseph Furphy *Poems* 13: The gnats at which the Wowsers strain, / The camels that they entertain / Sectarian bigotry insane.

1925 Seymour Hicks *Hullo Australians* 93: 'I am a teetotaller at meals. It looks better in front of the wowzers.'

1930 J. S. Litchfield *Far-North Memories* 182: The wife was undeniably a 'wowser'. One could read her character in the square-toed, thick-soled boots she wore, in her thick black woollen stockings, and in her stiff black hat.

1936 H. Drake-Brockman *Sheba Lane* 41: 'He drinks, doesn't he?' 'Used to . . . But he's apparently chucked it now. Quite a wowser, in fact.'

1942 Leonard Mann *The Go-Getter* 201: 'A few years ago the age [of consent] was seventeen, but some old women got a wowser government to increase the age.'

1955 E. O. Schlunke *The Man in the Silo* 168: 'I'll buy a nine-gallon keg with my bonus and get that old wowser Weismann drunk!'

1965 Hal Porter *The Cats of Venice* 59: 'A sawn-off little wowser. No confidence.'

1976 *Sydney Morning Herald* 14 Aug. 10: Mr Nile does not see the Festival of Light as a puritanical neo-wowser movement.

1981 Roger Pulvers *Age* (Melbourne) 10 Aug. 11: 'I love Melbourne because it's the only city with a radical tradition in Australia, as well as being the home base for the wowsers.'

wowserdom, wowserish, wowserism

1984 *Bulletin* 17 Apr. 47: As a veteran student of wowserdom, I will watch his progress with devoted interest.

1933 Frank Clune *Try Anything Once* 122: They looked much the same although it seemed to me they had lost their dash and grown wowserish.

1918 George Dale *The Industrial History of Broken Hill* 229: Brookfield . . . had arrayed against him every device known to both Capitalism and wowserism.

1947 Norman Lindsay *Halfway to Anywhere* 191: Oral tradition is probably still busy immortalizing it, such is the spiritual need to make some ribald retort to wowserism's restrictions.

1980 *Sunday Mail* (Brisbane) 28 Sep. 2: Syd Williams says Brisbane is boring. He says the city dies after 8 p.m. That there is an air of wowserism about the place. That there's nothing to do.

wrap (up) *n.* A flattering account (interchangeable with **rap (up)** q.v.)

1949 Lawson Glassop *Lucky Palmer* 54: 'Do you want a cigarette paper?' 'Cigarette paper? No, I've got the makings.' 'I thought you wanted to give yourself another wrap up.'

1958 Frank Hardy *The Four-Legged Lottery* 177: Ronnie Hutchison, a specialist in long distance races, getting the wrap up from his mates, Des Hoysted and Frank O'Brien – 'ridden in copy-book style by Hutchie.'

1963 Criena Rohan *Down by the Dockside* 155: 'I've got to have a job and a respectable address and someone to give me the big wrap-up.'

1973 *Australian* 7 Aug. 22: When I was at Ipswich I thought it was a great 'wrap' to be picked to play for Queensland.

1975 Xavier Herbert *Poor Fellow My Country* 324: 'Quite a wrap-up, isn't it . . . only much more what I'd like to be than what I am.'

1980 *Sunday Mail* (Brisbane) 22 Jun. 40: The Brisbane players destroyed the reputations of several Manly players who came to Brisbane with huge 'wraps' on them.

wrap (up) *v.* To praise (interchangeable with **rap (up)** q.v.)

1973 *Sun* 1 May 78: Last week I wrapped him over his display of whistle blowing in the Easts-Manly game. This was virtually the 'kiss of death'. Anytime referees get a wrap they seem to get banished to the suburbs.

1975 Xavier Herbert *Poor Fellow My Country* 875: 'Does she wrap you up! Look . . . "This sweet and lovely creature".'

wrapped Overjoyed with something (interchangeable with **rapt** q.v.)

1963 Criena Rohan *Down by the Dockside* 212: 'She gave me a quid now and then. I never stood over her for it. She's wrapped in me, see?'

1976 *Sydney Morning Herald* 21 Jan. 1: $1,210 a week to play cricket 'I'm just wrapped,' Thomson said. 'The offer is a fantastic one which never in my wildest dreams did I expect.'

Wrecker, Whelan the see **Whelan**

wrestling, mobile, open-air Rugby football, from the standpoint of an Australian Rules player

1971 Colin Simpson *The New Australia* 215: Rules fans call Rugby 'open-air wrestling'.

1980 *Weekend Australian* 20 Dec. 14: You know the old chestnut. To Melburnians, rugby is no more than mobile wrestling.

wrong tram, on the see **tram**

wrong, you're not An expression of agreement

1981 Buzz Kennedy *Weekend Australian* 18 Jul.

Mag. 4: Just as one would not wear spats, so one does not wish to say, 'You're right' when the argot of the day dictates, 'You're not wrong.'

1984 *Sunday Independent* (Perth) 9 Sep. 38: Robin Leach, who fronts the programme, says: 'My show is *Dallas* come to life.' You're not wrong old son.

wurley, wurlie   An Aboriginal hut (1847 OED), extended to any similar rude shelter constructed by a white

1917 F. J. Mills *Dinkum Oil* 66: And 'wurlie' cigarettes (you have all sniffed those fearful cigarettes, which effluviate like a wurlie).

1937 Ernestine Hill *The Great Australian Loneliness* 11: I have interviewed men living in wurlies of paper-bark who read Gibbon and wrote Greek.

yabber *n.* Talk [Ab.]
1855 Raffaello Carboni *The Eureka Stockade* ed. G. Serle (1969) 7: There was further a great waste of yabber-yabber about the diggers not being represented in the Legislative Council.
1885 *The Australasian Printers' Keepsake* 71: This was argued out ... with much vehemence, if not rancour, till I got thoroughly sick of their yabber.
1901 *Bulletin Reciter* 37: Here's the landlord for orders – I'm dry with this yabber.
1908 *The Australian Magazine* 1 Nov. 1252: Others [aboriginal words] have remained, and are likely to remain in the category of slang, such as ... yabber (yabba) talk.
1975 Les Ryan *The Shearers* 155: *Yabber* Unnecessary talk.

yabber *v.* To talk
1848 H. W. Haygarth *Recollections of Bush Life in Australia* 102: The most loquacious of them all would bear little comparison with an Australian 'gin' when fairly moved to 'yabber'.
1877 Rolf Boldrewood *A Colonial Reformer* (1890) 334: 'Well, what did you see?' pursued his master. 'You can yabber fast enough when you like.'
1890 Jane I. Watts *Family Life in South Australia* 190: He told me that he heard my father 'Plenty yabber, yabber.' I could not understand what he meant till he held up his hands, and in a serious tone uttered words as though he were reading. It then dawned across me that he was mimicking my father reading the Bible.
1903 Joseph Furphy *Such is Life* (1944) 238: 'Nobody could yabber with her but Bob.'
1917 A. B. Paterson *Three Elephant Power* 24: 'Now let's hear him yabber.'

yabber, paper A letter
1888 Overlander *Australian Sketches* 24: I determined to send him [a native] off first with a paper yabber to the other stockman, telling him where we had gone.
1901 F. J. Gillen *Diary* (1968) 303: The letter is carried securely tied in a cleft stick ... The blacks regard messengers of this sort as sacred; they probably have an idea that if they interfered with a 'paper yabber' some evil magic would result.
1908 Mrs Aeneas Gunn *We of the Never-Never* 257: 'Paper yabber!' he added curtly, passing a letter to the Maluka.
1933 R. B. Plowman *The Man from Oodnadatta* 131: 'I said to tell Billy to send a paper-yabber (letter) by the boy that comes for the flour.'
1935 H. H. Finlayson *The Red Centre* 74: In the bad old days of early settlement undesirable bucks were got rid of by giving them 'paper yabbers' to deliver to distant neighbours.

yabbie, yabby A small freshwater crayfish (*Parachaeraps bicarinatus*) [Ab.]
1894 *Argus* 6 Oct. 11: Small crayfish, called 'yabbies' ... may be found all over Australia, both in large and small lagoons. These creatures, whilst

nearing a drought, and as the supply of water is about to fail, burrow deeply in the beds of the lagoons, water-holes, or swamps. [Morris]

1941 Baker 83: *Yabbie* A small freshwater crayfish.

1960 John Iggulden *The Storms of Summer* 182: 'We used to catch yabbies this way when I was a kid.'

1965 Graham McInnes *The Road to Gundagai* 142: Down the hill came running McLachlan kids ready to go fishing for yabbies. These small fresh water crayfish, which inhabited every muddy pool in the bush, were the easiest things to catch in the world.

1979 *Advertiser* (Adelaide) 8 Mar. 30: Fresh yabbies are at the Grote Street fishmongers for the first time in many months. Freshly cooked yabbies are $3.70 a kilogram, $1.90 less than prawns.

1982 *Sydney Morning Herald* 4 Jun. 8: To cook them, Mr Ruello drops live yabbies into boiling salted water flavoured with dill for five minutes, before trailing them in a seafood cocktail sauce. He recommends grilled or barbecued yabbies in a tomato and oregano-based sauce. Patrick Juillet, chef-proprietor of Le Cafe restaurant, Manly, only uses live yabbies and buys 10 kilograms every Thursday from the fish markets.

yabbying

1962 Dymphna Cusack *Picnic Races* 12–13: In the old days he used to go birds-nesting on the hill-side and yabbying in the creek.

see **crabhole, gilgie**

yachtie A yachtsman, esp. if engaged in yacht racing

1979 *Weekend Australian* 14 Jul. Mag. 15: He admits to being a fanatic 'yachtie' and said: 'I love sailing. I live it. In fact I'd be happy to die on the boat.'

1984 *Weekend Australian* 21 Apr. Mag. 20: Yachties look for cash from the Auld Mug [heading]

yack, yacker (yakkitty-yak) *n. & v.* Talk [*yack* a syllable imitative of a snapping sound; hence as vb. OED 1861]

c. 1882 *Sydney Slang Dictionary* 9: *Yacker* Talk.

1941 Baker 83: *Yacker* Talk.

1959 *Daily Telegraph* (Sydney) 7 Mar. 2: He was a travelling yakitty-yak man in the ubiquitous presence of Mr Graham Webb.

1969 William Dick *Naked Prodigal* 16: All the girls ... yacking about clothes or some woman who'd just had her twentieth kid.

1971 Frank Hardy *The Outcasts of Foolgarah* 198: Borky yakked on.

1976 Gwen Kelly *The Middle-Aged Maidens* 110: He got up. 'Can't spend any more time yacketing away with women,' he said.

1980 Murray Bail *Homesickness* 162: 'They were all yacking in some other lingo.'

yakker (yakka, yacker) Work [Ab.]

1866 W. Ridley *Kamilaroi* 171: work *yakka*.

1888 *Boomerang* 14 Jan. 13: The Brisbane wharf labourers ... are so accustomed to hard yacker that they can't be happy for a single day without it.

1908 *The Australian Magazine* 1 Nov. 1251: Others [aboriginal words] ... are likely to remain in the category of slang, such as ... yacker (yakka), work.

1914 Edward Dyson *Spats' Fact'ry* 124: 'But iv yeh don't do yeh fair share iv yacker this after, I'll punt the slacks off yeh.'

1924 *Truth* 27 Apr. 6: *Yacker* Hard work.

1936 Archer Russell *Gone Nomad* 74: Two days later Adams packed his blanket and his Shake-speare and left for the South ... No more 'bush yacker' for him.

1946 A. W. Upfield *Death of a Swagman* 87: 'Give us the shovel, Mr Jason,' suggested Harry Hudson. 'I'm used to hard yakka.'

1953 T. A. G. Hungerford *Riverslake* 89: 'One week, maybe twelve pounds. But hard yakka. Still ... I am young.'

1962 Stuart Gore *Down the Golden Mile* 127: 'I'm not scared of a bit of hard yakka.'

1983 Janise Beaumont *Sun-Herald* 25 Sep. 136: The overall feeling as one watched the bejewelled matrons was that a great deal of yakka had gone into redistributing flesh and tarting up faces and hair.

yamidgee An Aboriginal: W.A.

1965 Randolph Stow *The Merry-go-Round in the Sea* 186: 'What's yamidgees?' said the boy. 'Boongs. Noogs. Coloured folk.'

1983 G. E. P. Wellard *Bushlore* 55: I was standing outside the humpy discussing the day's work with three of the Yamagee musterers. I use the word 'Yamagee' because that is the name they call themselves in that district. They never say 'Black-man' or 'Aborigine', it is always 'Yamagee'.

Yan Yean The water supply to Melbourne from the Yan Yean reservoir (originally as distinct from tank water)

1871 Dogberry Dingo *Australian Rhymes and Jingles* 8: I'll go and take a bath, / And at the weather scoff; / O horror, what is this I find? / The Yan Yean is turned off.

1873 Anthony Trollope *Australia* ed. P. D. Edwards and R. B. Joyce (1967) 386: During the very heart of the summer of 1871 ... I moved from a house in the town to a friend's residence in the country; and neither at the one nor the other could a bath be filled. The Yan Yean was not 'running'.

1885 *The Australasian Printers' Keepsake* 26:

Each lovely river, with its margins green, / All will be water-trust or else Yan Yean.
1945 Baker 196: *Yan Yean* Melbourne water supply.

yandy To winnow, now in a tin-mining process [Ab.]
1929 *The Inlander* Nov. 25: A few miles from the 'Bar,' we saw for the first time the native women 'yandying' tin ore. 'Yandying' is a delicate science, which only the women of the tribes seem able to master.
1937 Ernestine Hill *The Great Australian Loneliness* 49: All along the river-bed the blacks are yandying tin.
1944 M. J. O'Reilly *Bowyangs and Boomerangs* 48: Yandying, in black-fellow language, means shake-about. It is the natives' method of separating the grass seeds from the husks.
1959 Donald Stuart *Yandy* 158: *Yandy, tjardoo:* Long shallow oval dish, of wood sometimes, but now almost always of sheet-iron, in which mineral is separated from the alluvial rubbish by means of a complicated rocking action. A skill, the working of a yandy, which is almost exclusively aboriginal.
1971 Robin Miller *Flying Nurse* 76: They all lived by collecting tin from the creek beds. The pieces of metal were separated from extraneous matter by a process known as 'yandying', which entailed placing the material in a curved sheet iron container and shaking it expertly until the metal was at one end and the discard at the other.
1976 Roland Robinson *The Shift of Sands* 360: Maudie's yandy is an oval, concave piece of galvanised iron, coolamon shaped. With a constant yandying motion, throwing the sand into the air towards her, a backwards and forwards and sideways motion, Maudie separates the mineral sand in the yandy and pours it out.

yarra Insane [f. mental asylum at Yarra Bend, Victoria]
[**1921** Mary E. Fullerton *Bark House Days* 119: His monomania sent him at last to 'Yarra Bend', where as was gruesomely said, he walked round and round in a circle each day, whim-horse to his own imaginary invention.]
1943 Baker 89: *Yarra* (adj.): Stupid, crazy.
1973 Jim McNeil *The Chocolate Frog* 50: 'Whats'er matter? You gone yarra, or somethin'?'
1980 *Sydney Morning Herald* 20 Oct. 26: 'Kingston Town is a good horse, . . . but in my opinion he would not have lived with Phar Lap. I know a lot of people will say I'm "Yarra"; but that's my belief.'

Yarra, useful as the see **useful**

Yarra-banker A soapbox orator [f. Yarra River, Victoria]

[**1895** Cornelius Crowe *The Australian Slang Dictionary* 98: *Yarra Bankers* vagrants living on the banks of the Yarra.]
1912 Louis Esson *The Time is not Yet Ripe* ed. P. Parsons (1973) 32: 'The man's an agitator, a red-flagger, a Yarra-banker.'
[**1913**] Turner O. Lingo *The Australian Comic Dictionary* 6: *Yarra Banker* Usually a man who stands on a soap box telling the great unwashed how 'dirty' the rich man is.
1973 Dr J. Cairns *Bulletin* 8 Dec. 13: I think that Parliament is a sort of elevated Yarra bank.

yarraman Aboriginal term for horse, used also by whites: *obs.*
1860 Mrs A. Macpherson *My Experiences of Australia* 50: [He] was told by his black guide 'Bail yarraman (no horse) only white fellow.'
1866 W. Ridley *Kamilaroi* 20: *Horse* yaraman* *All the Australians use this name – probably from the neighing of the horse.
1875 A. J. Boyd *Old Colonials* (1882) 69: 'Then there's seventeen yarramen – call 'em thirty pounds a head.'
1891 H. Patchett Martin *Coo-ee: Tales of Australian Life* 280: He just clapped spurs to his old yarraman (horse), and never pulled up out of a gallop till he had got over the range.
1905 Joseph Furphy *Rigby's Romance* ed. R. G. Howarth (1946) 21: 'He needn't be frightened o' these yarramans. I got 'em like lambs.'
1908 Giles Seagram *Bushmen All* 20: 'You accuse me of taking the yarramen. Of course I did. It was our only hope.'

yartz, the The arts, in Australia [invention of the Barry Humphries persona Les Patterson, Australian Cultural Attaché]
1978 Barry Humphries *A Nice Night's Entertainment* (1981) 183: This pome is dedicated to something Australians hold very precious beginning with Y – 'the Yartz'.
1983 *Sydney Morning Herald* 2 Mar. 24: Only a cultural philistine would disapprove of such generosity to the yartz.
1984 *Age* (Melbourne) 5 May 3: Horne looks forward to the end of the yartz [heading]

yeller fella Male half-caste in N.W. Australia [f. colour]
1937 Ernestine Hill *The Great Australian Loneliness* 206: The attitude of the lubras to these children is problematic. In some instances they treasure the 'little yellafella' as they call him.
1938 Xavier Herbert *Capricornia* 37: What if people found out? . . . A half-caste – a yeller-feller!
1959 Donald Stuart *Yandy* 12: No future in being a yeller feller, down this end, or further north.
1971 Keith Willey *Boss Drover* 29: Part-

Aborigines, or yeller-fellers as we called them in the old days, had a hard life.
1977 Kenneth Cook *The Man Underground* 137: 'The boongs and the yella fellas are lousing up this town so fast that it's no longer safe for a decent white woman to walk down the street.'

Yellow Monday A variety of cicada [f. colouring]
1951 Dymphna Cusack and Florence James *Come In Spinner* 163: She uncurled her fingers and showed the jewelled head of a cicada. 'He's a Yellow Mundy.'
1959 Anne von Bertouch *February Dark* 124: Through the shimmer of heat and the drilling song Helen saw the beautiful cicadas of childhood, the Black Prince, the Greengrocer, the Yellow Monday, held on a child's small hand.
1976 Douglas Stewart *Southerly* 177: They have caught a Yellow Monday / Slipped it down Anita's blouse.
1981 *Bulletin* 24 Nov. 110: In the unlikely event that I get to heaven, there will be no angels strumming harps. Just a band of Yellow Mondays playing summer's old sweet song and McGilvray giving cricket commentaries between the breaks.

Yellow Peril, the The 20-tonne sculpture 'Vault' by Ron Robertson-Swann
1980 *National Times* 30 Nov. 42: The fate of the controversial sculpture chosen for Melbourne's City Square – dubbed the 'Yellow Peril' – was officially sealed last week. The Board of Works approved an application by Melbourne City Council to relocate the work in the proposed Batman Park at the docks end of the Yarra.
1984 *Age* (Melbourne) 20 Aug. 2: Can this be the city that threw the 'Yellow Peril' out of the Square? Melbourne will become quite the sculpture capital of the southern hemisphere from November.

Yellowcake Bob R. J. Hawke, Prime Minister 1983– [f. policy on mining uranium]
1984 *Sydney Morning Herald* 19 Jan. 1: Mr Hugh Morgan, executive director of Western Mining Corporation, told a large contingent of Australian financial leaders in London that the mantle of Pig Iron Bob Menzies had been taken over by Yellowcake Bob Hawke ... Mr Morgan attracted the biggest crowd ever to attend an Australian Business and Businessmen in Europe (ABBE) luncheon at the Savoy Hotel for his address, titled, Australia under Yellowcake Bob – a study in pragmatism.

yike A heated argument, a disturbance [unexplained]
1941 Baker 84: *Yike* A row or argument (2) A fight.

1945 Roy Rene *Mo's Memoirs* 186: 'There's that tram connie having a yike with a drunk.'
1951 Dal Stivens *Jimmy Brockett* 86: It was a pretty good yike while it lasted.
1960 Ron Tullipan *Follow the Sun* 32: 'Chow doesn't need that much of an excuse to put on a yike, even on his most peaceful days.'
1964 George Johnston *My Brother Jack* 244: 'Sorry your party ended up in a yike.'
1980 *National Times* 12 Oct. 61: I think of my grandmother, who came from Hopetoun in the Mallee and whose utterances were few ... An argument she referred to as a 'yike', a serious disagreement 'a decent yike'.
yike To argue, fight
1952 T. A. G. Hungerford *The Ridge and the River* 213: 'Don't let's yike about it, Jim.'

yolk Suint, the natural grease in sheep's wool (OED 1607)
1824 R. S. Macarthur-Onslow *Some Early Records of the Macarthurs of Camden* (1914) 405: Send home the fleeces for the future in much brighter condition and nearly free from yolk.
1853 S. Mossman and T. Banister *Australia, Visited and Revisited* 76: Here they [the sheep] remained until the fleece dried, and the yolk or natural oil of the wool began to rise, after which they were considered to be ready for shearing.
1897 Henry Lawson 'The Green-hand Rouseabout' *Verse* i 321: Blinded by the yolk of wool, and shirt and trousers stiff with grease.
1912 G. H. Gibson *Ironbark Splinters* 43: While we was grimed from top to toe / With blood, an' yolk, an' tar.
1921 K. S. Prichard *Black Opal* 116: Grey flannel shirts and dungarees, blood-splashed, grimy, and greasy with the 'yolk' of fleeces they had been handling.

yonnie A stone, esp. of a size for throwing
1941 Baker 84: *Yonnie* A small stone, a pebble.
1979 *Sun-Herald* 18 Mar. 79: There were two lamp posts ... each equipped with an electric bulb. I'd say about 45 watts. Young couples courting would smash each of them with a well-aimed 'yonnie' on pay night.
1980 *Sun-Herald* 27 Jan. 66: Yonnies are stones to Victorians. A Sydneysider will look at you blankly.

you beaut see **beaut**

youee see **uey**

you'll be sorry see **sorry**

young and old, it was on for see **on**

young Harry, cop this see **cop**

young (amateur) players, a trap for   see **trap**

you're not wrong   see **wrong**

yous, youse   Perhaps derived from *yez* [You (said to more than one) *Anglo-Irish* OED 1804], but in Australia not necessarily a plural
  1908 Henry Fletcher *Dads and Dan between Smokes* 39: When misfochin' as yous can't prevent lands yer a woodener, take it smilin'.
  1911 Louis Stone *Jonah* 190: 'Yous are a white man, an' I always knew it'.
  1944 Lawson Glassop *We Were the Rats* 81: 'Glad ter know yous both', said Jim awkwardly.
  1955 E. O. Schlunke *The Man in the Silo* 206: 'Pity one of yous wasn't here to crawl up the steamer'.
  1969 Christopher Bray *Blossom Like a Rose* 165: 'I don't mean to piss in yer pockets, but youse blokes are all right'.
  1973 Frank Huelin *Keep Moving* 83: 'Yous got your ideas and I've got mine. Let it go at that'.
  1984 Jack Hibberd *Squibs* 226: 'Mr Prime Minister . . . How would youse like your grapefruit this corker of a morn?'

yow, to keep   To **keep nit** q.v.
  1942 Eve Langley *The Pea-Pickers* 283: 'You keep yow', she said in a muffled voice, 'and whistle "The Prisoner's Song" if anyone comes along.'

yowie   Supposed Australian counterpart to the Yeti or Abominable Snowman, sometimes connected with Aboriginal legend: described as a hairy creature about two metres high
  1975 Rex Gilroy *Sun-Herald* 14 Dec. 126: Australia has its own version of 'Bigfoot', known to the Aborigines for thousands of years as the Yowie ('Great Hairy Man'). The beast has the appearance of an ape. It is described as a hairy, man-like ape-like creature standing from 6ft to 8ft tall. It is stooped and moves with a loping gait, emitting a screeching sound if disturbed. It inhabits trees and caves, but always in the denser and generally inaccessible mountainous forest regions.
  1979 *Sydney Morning Herald* 20 Apr. 1: There's talk that the Yowie – Australia's answer to the Abominable Snowman – has been spotted on the desolate Newell Highway between Coonabarabran and Narrabri.
  1979 *Advertiser* (Adelaide) 23 May 24: Rex's [Rex Gilroy's] main grudge against Australian academics is not that they don't believe in Yowies but that they condemn his theories without considering his research or evidence . . . 'If you could get a Yowie to tap-dance with hat and cane in front of one of these people, there is still no guarantee they'd accept it.'
  1984 *Sydney Morning Herald* 7 Jan. 4: Rather frightening being out in a pitch black night on a river bank in a thunderstorm. It's the sort of time when the Yowie monster of Aboriginal legend is likely to come and get you.

Yugo   A Yugoslavian migrant [abbr.]
  1973 Henry Williams *My Love Had a Black Speed Stripe* 46: We filled him in about Johnny, the young Yugo.
  1981 *National Times* 13 Sep. 22: 'What we call Yugos', he said, 'they seem to mix in a bit better, they come in here and have a drink.'

yummie   Term invented by the Sydney stockbroking firm Bridges Son and Shepherd, as a variant of *yuppie*: see quot. 1985
  1985 *Weekend Australian* 27 Apr. 19: Bridges believes people aged 35 and over have been ignored in the rush to service Australia's Yuppies . . . Bridges has labelled those investors 35 and over, Yummies. 'Yummies are mature people who are becoming more and more enterprising with their money', Bridges' senior partner, Mr Michael Shepherd, said . . . Bridges had put together four investment packages to suit investors in the wealthy over 35 bracket.

zack   Sixpence: *obsolescent* [? Yiddish (G. *sechs* six)]
  1898 *Bulletin* 1 Oct. 14: 6d. a 'zack'
  1928 A. W. Upfield *The House of Cain* 89: 'When I throw a seven (die), I won't have a zac on me.'
  1949 Ruth Park *Poor Man's Orange* 105: Miserable grey sausage, which could be sold at a 'frippence-worf' and a 'zack's worf', filled the glass window of the refrigerator.
  1958 Frank Hardy *The Four-Legged Lottery* 215: 'It's mortgaged, Jim. Not worth a zac.'
  1961 George Farwell *Vanishing Australians* 94: 'He never spent more than a zac on a feed in his life.'
  1983 *Australian* 14 Jul. 5: I would be a rich man if I had a zack for every time I heard someone in ethnic broadcasting make a disparaging remark about the Public Service.

zambuck   Ambulance or first aid man, esp. at a sporting fixture: *obsolescent* [f. brand name of an ointment]
  1943 Baker 90: *Zambuck* A first-aid man in attendance at a sporting contest.
  1956 Ruth Park and D'Arcy Niland *The Drums Go Bang* 146–7: 'I might have come home just in time to see the zambucks carting you two off in the ambulance.'
  1972 Peter Mathers *The Wort Papers* 95: They even supplied the zambuck, a priest with brown attaché case containing oils and waters for extreme unction.

  1976 *Sun-Herald* 5 Sep. 70: If you asked the kids of to-day what a zambuck was, they would probably tell you that he was some type of South African antelope.
  1984 *Bulletin* 6 Mar. 43: If you don't know what a Zambuck is, it's someone in the black and white uniform of the St John Ambulance Brigade doing honorary duty at a sports arena, ready to dash on the field with everything from liniment to stretcher.

Z cars   1   The Z class trams in Melbourne, painted orange instead of the former green
  1982 *Age* (Melbourne) 25 May 11: The Tramways Board is now, after seven years, still forced to conduct a defence of the Z cars.
  2   As for **black taxis** q.v.
  1983 *Australian* 13 Jan. 7: The car was among official Ford limos known to Canberrans as 'Z-cars', for the red Z prefix on the number plates.

ziff   A beard [unexplained]
  1919 W. H. Downing *Digger Dialects* 54: *Ziff* A beard.
  1924 C. J. Dennis *Rose of Spadgers* 137: 'E lobbed in on us sudden, ziff an' all.
  1939 Miles Franklin and Dymphna Cusack *Pioneers on Parade* 88: Lord Cravenburn regretted his ziff.
  1947 John Morrison *Sailors Belong Ships* 97: 'We all called him The Prophet. He had a long ziff.'
  1955 F. B. Vickers *The Mirage* 114: 'Wears a ziff,

461

black 'un, black as the hair on his chest.'

1961 Robert Close *Hooves of Brass* 22: He was glad now that he'd let his mates kid him into growing a ziff.

1981 Gwen Kelly *Always Afternoon* 211: 'Better get rid of that ziff', she said pointing to his embryonic beard.

zoo, feeding-time at the   An undisciplined assault on food and drink; any disorderly but excited scene

1951 Dymphna Cusack and Florence James *Come In Spinner* 33: 'The Public Bar gets more like Taronga Zoo at feeding time every day.'

1970 Richard Beilby *No Medals for Aphrodite* 68–9: 'Gawd, you should get on that crowd . . . It's like feeding time at the zoo.'

1975 *Sydney Morning Herald* 23 Oct. 6: At question time, the Prime Minister gives a daily performance. It's the highlight of the day – feeding time at the zoo. Just about every question thrown at him he appears to greet with relish.

Zorba   Nickname for anyone of Greek background, esp. the N.S.W. sports commentator Peter Peters [f. the novel by Nikos Kazantzakis *Zorba the Greek*, also a film]

1985 *Sun-Herald* 7 Apr. 66: An afternoon in the commentary box with Greg 'Hollywood' Hartley and Peter 'Zorba' Peters is all about entertainment.

Appendix I

Terms Assumed to be Australianisms

The following terms have all been claimed as part of Australian English. While they may be used in Australia, I can find no evidence that they are of Australian origin, or that they have acquired special senses in Australia, or that they have survived here while falling into disuse elsewhere. These are the requirements for the inclusion of a colloquialism in the Dictionary. It also includes some items shared with English elsewhere (e.g. *bloody, mate, sav*) which have become part of the Australian ethos. The following expressions fall outside all these categories. When, for example, *bobby-dazzler* is recorded in the OED in 1866 as a Lancashire word, and as used in 1913 by D. H. Lawrence and in 1959 by John Braine, one Australian citation (1931, Vance Palmer) out of the nine does not qualify it as an Australianism. This is the principle followed in drawing up the list. It may be that other items at present in the Dictionary, not so well documented as *bobby-dazzler*, may need to be consigned to the Appendix when more information comes to hand.

Expressions based on rhyming slang are in Appendix II.

all serene   everything in order; no problems
all the go   fashionable, popular, in demand
all there   sensible, shrewd, alert
all wool and a yard wide   genuine
also ran   an unsuccessful competitor; person of no account
argue the toss   to dispute
arse about   to act the fool
axed, to be   to be dismissed, dispensed with

back, on someone's   to be officious, nagging, harassing
back of beyond   regions remote from civilization
backhander   a sling, bribe
bag   to appropriate, secure for oneself
bag, in the   certain in advance
bagman   a commercial traveller
ball, have a   to enjoy oneself
balls   nonsense

balls up   a mess, blunder
banana, top   in the leading role
bang   to copulate (of a woman) e.g. 'she bangs like a shithouse door'
bangers   sausages
bark, to keep a dog and ~ oneself   to do the work for which a subordinate is employed
barmy   weak-minded, eccentric, mad
bash   copulation e.g. 'good for a quick bash'
bat out of hell, like a   at high speed
beak   a magistrate
beano   a feast, jollification
bee from a bull's foot, not to know a   to be ignorant, incompetent
beef   to complain, grouch
belly thinks your throat's cut, your   to be hungry
belt up   to stop talking
bender, on a   on a spree
berries, the   something outstanding in its class
Bibles, to swear on a stack of   to insist that an assertion is true
bickie   a biscuit
binge   a drinking spree
bint   a girl or woman
bird   a girl or woman
bird, give the   to hiss off the stage, treat with derision
blinder   an outstanding performance, esp. in sport
blink, on the   defective, not working
bloke   a chap, ordinary fellow
blotto   drunk
blow   to spend money, or other resources
blue rinse set   women, esp. middle-aged, classified socially by their tinted hair
blunt   money
boat race   a race that is 'rigged'
bobby dazzler   something exceptional in its class
bog   a lavatory; excrement
boiler   a woman no longer young
boko   the nose
bollicky   naked
bomb   to fail
bomb, go like a   to perform well

bone   to steal, purloin

bone, give it a   a request to stop harping on a theme

boob   prison

booboo   a blunder

boobs   women's breasts

boodle   money; loot

booze-up   a drinking party

bounce   self-assertion, self-confidence

bouncer   a chucker-out

brass   money

brass monkey, cold enough to freeze the balls off a   extremely cold

bread   money

brewer's droop   temporary impotence from alcohol

brickie   a bricklayer

brief   a ticket

Brit   a native of the United Kingdom

browned off   fed up, disillusioned

bucket, kick the   to die

buckshee   free, gratis

bugle   the nose

bullet, get the   to be dismissed

bumf   official memoranda, instructions etc. [f. bumfodder]

bunch of fives   a clenched fist

bun in the oven   pregnant

bunce   a bonus, benefit received above the contract

bundle   a large sum of money

bunfight   a party, celebration, assembly

bung   to throw

bunghole   cheese (thought of as causing constipation)

bunk, do a   to decamp, abscond

burgoo   porridge

burk   to avoid

buster   a fall

buzz   a thrill, stimulus (buzz word = vogue word)

cake, to take the   to be pre-eminent, esp. in an outrageous way

cakehole   mouth

can   1) prison 2) lavatory

cat, like something the ~ dragged in   very dishevelled and disreputable

char   tea

charlie   a fool

charlies   women's breasts

chat   a louse

chat up   to strike up a relationship

cheesed off   disgruntled, disillusioned, annoyed

cheese, the   the fashion, the preferred

cheese, hard   bad luck

chip   to reprove, tease

chips, to have had (done) one's   to have lost one's money, forfeited one's prospects

chiv   a knife

chop   share, allocation ('get in for your chop')

choppers   the teeth

chronic   objectionable, severe, disagreeable

chump, off one's   unbalanced, deranged

claret   blood

cleaners, to be taken to   to be defrauded of all one's money

clever, not too   indisposed

clink   gaol

clippie   a bus or tram conductress

clued up   well informed, alert

clueless   ill informed, stupid

cock-up   a blunder, mess, debacle

codger   an old man

codswallop, a load of   a lot of nonsense

come across   to consent to sex (of a woman)

come on   an enticement

conk   the nose

cooler   gaol

coop, fly the   escape, depart

coot   someone contemptuously regarded

coot, bald as a   quite bald [f. the bird]

crash   to sleep, pass out

create   to make a fuss

creek, up the ~ without a paddle   in difficulties, stranded without resources

croak   to die

cross, on the   dishonest (opp. of on the square)

crow, a ~ to pick   a bone of contention

crumpet   a woman, viewed sexually

crunch, the   the critical stage, the showdown

crying out loud, for   a protest at an unreasonable claim

cuppa   a cup of tea

curse, the   menstruation

cut it out   stop it, desist

dago   an Italian

daisies, to push up the   to be dead and buried

daks   a brand of trousers; trousers generally

damage, the   the charge incurred

dead ringer   of identical appearance

deck   to knock to the floor

dekko   a glance, look

demo   a political demonstration

dial   the face

dingaling   a fool

dip the wick   to copulate (of men)

dirty   used as an intensive e.g. 'dirty big'

dirty water off one's chest, to get the   expression for male copulation after period of abstinence

divvy up   to divide, share out

dog-end   a cigarette butt

dog, to put on   to behave pretentiously, put on airs

dog's balls, stick out like a   to be glaringly obvious

dog's dinner (breakfast), like a   in disorder or confusion

dolled up   dressed up for an occasion

donnybrook   an argument, fight

dook the hand, fist
doover a thingummy
dose a venereal infection
dough money
down on, get to steal, appropriate
DP displaced person
drummer a commercial traveller
dummy, to sell the to deceive an opponent with a
  pretend pass (sporting)
dump any place viewed with disfavour
dyke a lesbian

edge an advantage, element of superiority
elbow, to bend the to be given to drinking
elbow, to get the to be thrust aside, discharged
enemy, the the time
even Stephen equally
Eyetie an Italian

fag a cigarette
fairy a male homosexual
fat cat someone affluent
filthy big as for *dirty big*
finger, to pull one's ~ out to get on with the job
flack, flak press secretary, public relations
  officer
flake (out) to collapse, fall into bed
fleapit a cinema, theatre etc.
flicks, the the pictures i.e. cinema
flog to sell or barter (often illicitly)
fly a kite, to 1) to pass a worthless cheque 2) to
  make a tentative offer or to 'leak' an announcement in order to test the reaction
frig about, to to mess around, do nothing decisive
frog a Frenchman
frost unwelcome reception, a washout
fruitcake, nutty as a eccentric
fuzz, the the police

gander, take a ~ at to have a look at
gang-bang a number of men having intercourse
  successively with one woman
gargle any alcoholic drink
gasper a cigarette
gawk an awkward or clumsy person
gear clothing, accessories
gen reliable information (Services slang)
gigglesuit fatigue dress (Services slang)
glim a light
go for, to 1) to attack 2) to be keen on
go for broke, to to make an all-out effort
go in for, to to devote one's attention to, take up
  as a vocation
go it alone, to to act without support
go off, to 1) to begin to dislike 2) to experience
  orgasm
go off at, to to rebuke, reprimand angrily
go on! expression of mild disbelief
go through to copulate with (the male role)

goatrider a Freemason
goog an egg
gooney bird DC3 aircraft
gormless stupid, clumsy
grey power the pensioner vote
griff, griffin reliable information
grotty unattractive, dilapidated
grub food
gum-up, a a mess, blunder, confusion
gun, in the exposed to danger, held to account
gunny sack a coarse sack
gutsache a complaining or disagreeable person
gyp to cheat, deceive
gyp, to give someone to cause pain
Gyppo an Egyptian

hack to cope with, manage, tolerate
hairy difficult, unpromising
hang out to reside
hard case an incorrigible
have it off with to have sexual relations with
hay, hit the go to bed
heap an old or unreliable car
heave ho, the dismissal
hiding to nothing, on a with no way of winning,
  whatever the outcome
hobo a tramp
home on the pig's back successfully concluding
  some enterprise
homo a homosexual, esp. male
hook, get off the to extricate oneself from difficulty, escape the consequences
hoot, not to give a not to care at all
hops, the beer
horn an erection
humdinger something exceptional of its kind

idiot box the television set
imshi be off!
info reliable information

jack a policeman
jailbait a girl below the age of consent
jar a glass of beer
Jerusalem, since Christ played fullback for a long
  time in the past
jimjams the DTs
job, do a to defecate (juvenile)
jobs for the boys appointments made by political
  influence
joint a place, building
jug prison
jumper a pullover
junk salt meat

kangaroo court legal proceedings improperly
  conducted
kerfuffle fuss, confusion
kybosh, put the ~ on to put a stop to

465

kick   the pocket, wallet
kick in   to contribute
kick the bucket   to die
kip   sleep
kite, fly a   see *fly*
kitty   fund
knackered   exhausted
knackers   testicles
knee trembler   intercourse performed standing up, esp. with a prostitute
knock, take the   to fail to pay one's debts, esp. in betting
knocked up   exhausted
knockers   women's breasts
knotted, get   go to hell
knots, at the rate of   very fast

lamp   to look at
latch on to   to seize, understand
layoff   a period off work
lead in one's pencil, to put some   to take measures to ensure a vigorous sexual performance (of a man)
leak, to have a   to urinate
left-footer   a Roman Catholic
lift   to purloin, steal
limey   an Englishman
lip   cheek, impudence
loan of, to take a   to take a rise out of, to delude
log   a stupid person
lolly   money
lousy   mean
lug   ear
lush, lushington   a drunkard

Mackay, the real   the genuine article
mazooma   money
mickey, slip a   to drug someone surreptitiously
mickey, take the   to taunt, deride
mitt   hand
moggy   cat
molo   drunk
monicker   name
month of Sundays, not in a   never
moolah   money
moonlight   to have a second job, illicitly
moush   face
muck about   mess around, behave irresponsibly
mug   face

napoo   finished, destroyed
nelly, not on your   on no account, in no circumstances
nerd   a simpleton, a dill
nervous Nelly   a timorous person
nest, on the   exercising conjugal rights
never never   hire purchase
nipper   a child; assistant to a group of workmen
Nips   the Japanese [f. *Nippon*]

nit   simpleton, fool [f. *nitwit*]
nobble   to tamper with (esp. a racehorse)
nod, get the   to win approval, selection
nut   the head, brain

office, give the   to hint or signal
one-off   for the one occasion only
onions, to know one's   to be shrewd, competent, proficient
oont   a camel
oracle, to work the   to gain one's end by underhand means

pace, to go the   to live recklessly
packet   as for *bundle*
pad   an apartment, lodging, etc.
pad the hoof   to travel on foot
pansy   an effeminate boy or man
peg out   to die
penciller   bookmaker's assistant
perform   to make a fuss
piece of cake   something easily accomplished
pigs   the police
pile, to make one's   to make one's fortune
pill   someone hard to take
pinch   1) to steal 2) to arrest
pissed   drunk
piss off, to   to depart
pissed off   fed up, disgruntled
piss and wind, all ~ like the barber's cat   all talk and no do
pits, the   the ultimate in unattractiveness
P.O.Q.   piss off quick
pot, go to   to deteriorate
powder, to take a   to depart, disappear
prad   a horse
prang   a crash or accident (esp. automobile)
pull in (down)   to earn
pull oneself off   to masturbate (of a man)
pup, to sell someone a   to swindle, deceive
pussy   the vulva
put down   to denigrate
put out, to   to make oneself available sexually (of a woman)

queen   a male homosexual
queer   a homosexual
quod   gaol
Q.T., on the   confidentially, secretly

rabbit-catcher   a midwife
rag, chew the   to yarn, argue
rag out, to get one's   to lose one's temper
rags, have the ~ on   to be menstruating
ramp   a swindle
rantan   a spree
ready, the   cash, money
recap, to   to recapitulate
red, in the   in deficit

466

redeye special   overnight train, plane etc.
rhino   money
ring a bell, to   to prompt a recollection
ring-in   a fraudulent substitute
ringer   see *dead ringer*
rip off   to exploit
robbed, we was   complaint by a losing team
roll   a wad of money
rough it   to live or work under rough conditions
rumble   a fight, disturbance

sauce   liquor
savvy   to know, understand
sawney   stupid or inept person
scab   blackleg
scalded cat, like a   very quickly
scorcher   a hot day
scotty   angry, annoyed
scran   food
screw   1) prison warder 2) a regular wage 3) an
   unsound horse 4) act of copulation 5) glance, look
scrub   to cancel
scrubber   a prostitute; an unattractive woman
sewn up, to have it   to have something under
   control
SFA   sweet Fanny Adams; sweet fuck all
shag   to fornicate
**shake hands with the unemployed, the wife's best
   friend**   to urinate
shakedown   an improvised bed
shanghai   to abduct
Shanks' pony (mare), on   on foot
sheik   a handsome man; a Don Juan
shekels   money
shindy   a disturbance
shine, take a ~ to   to take a liking to, be impressed
   by
shirty   annoyed, angry
shot   drunk
sissy   an effeminate boy or man
skinful, to have a   to be drunk
skirt   a woman
slip one's wind   to die
slate   criticize severely
slit   the vagina
slob   person of sloppy habits and appearance
slope *v.*   to decamp
slope *n.*   an Asiatic
sloshed   drunk
slummocky   slovenly in dress or posture
snaffle (snavvle)   to steal, appropriate
snag   a hindrance
snatch   the vulva
snide   sneering, underhand
snooty   supercilious
snow-dropper   someone stealing from a clothes-
   line
so long   farewell
soft soap   to flatter, ingratiate oneself

souped up   with increased power (of an engine)
spadger   a sparrow
sparrowfart   dawn
sparrow-starver   someone who collects horse-
   droppings in the street
specks   damaged fruit
spondulics   money
spud   potato
square   1) honest ('on the square') 2) conventional
squeal   1) to complain 2) to inform upon
stash   to hide, conceal
stick   punishment (opposite to *carrot*)
stiver   a skerrick, fragment
stop   to knock out (boxing)
strain yourself, don't   sarcastic comment on
   unwilling help or effort
strain the potatoes   to urinate
strapped   out of funds
stuff   money
stuffed, get   insulting advice
sugar   money
**sun shines out of the seat of his pants, she thinks
   the**   to have an infatuated view of
sweat on   to await impatiently
swing the lead   to be idle, to avoid work

tailormade   a machine-produced cigarette
tanked   drunk
taped, to have it   to have it under control
tart up   to make superficially attractive
tats   teeth
tatty   shabby, of disreputable appearance
tee up   to make arrangements for
three-ring circus   a state of confusion, disorder
throw *n.*   apiece ('a dollar a throw')
throw *v.*   to disconcert, defeat, upset
tick, on   on credit
tight   1) drunk 2) miserly
tighter than a fish's arse   very tight
tile   a hat
tin   money
tinpot   smalltime, of little account
titter   a girl
ton   one hundred
toss   as for *throw v.*
tossup   an even chance
tonk   to strike, esp. a cricket ball
touch   to make an attempt to borrow
tracks, make   to move off, travel
trot, on the   in succession
trots, the   diarrhoea
turn-up   a reversal
twicer   someone deceitful
twig   to apprehend, perceive, 'wake up' to
twig, hop the   to die
twist, round the   deranged, mad

upcountry   away from the city
upstairs, to kick   to promote an incompetent

wacker someone stupid or ineffectual

wag it to play truant (juvenile)

walkover an easy victory

wallah a chap, fellow

wanker someone given 1) to masturbation 2) to self-deception

watering-hole pub or bar

weed tobacco

welsh to renege, default

wet stupid

wet the baby's head to celebrate the birth of a child; stand a round of drinks

whack share, portion

whacked exhausted

whacko expression of enthusiasm

whimwham to bridle a goose nonsense reply to a child's enquiry e.g. 'What's that you're making?'

white-ant to undermine, sabotage

white collar job not involving physical labour

white-haired boy someone favoured or cherished

wind up, have the to be scared

wire in to eat heartily, take part energetically

wog foreigner, esp. from Middle East

wooden spoon reward of the team coming last in a competition

Wop an Italian

wrinkle a useful hint

yellow peril threat of the yellow races overwhelming the white

yid a Jew

yob, yobbo an uncouth person (*boy* reversed)

yuppie young upwardly mobile (or urban) professional

Appendix II
Rhyming
Slang

Although rhyming slang was being recorded in Australia in the nineteenth century, most of it came from England, and it is still difficult now to identify terms which are distinctively Australian, and even more difficult to ascertain their currency. Rhyming slang seems to have had a fitful existence in Australia, generating more terms than have survived, and owing much to influences like those of particular columnists and entertainers.

List A includes a relatively small number of terms (e.g. *john* or *johnhop* for *cop*, *rubbity* or *rubbity-dub* for *pub*) which have become fairly well established in Australian English. Further illustrations of their use will be found in the main Dictionary. The list also includes a larger number of terms whose vogue is more uncertain. Some are localized (*Jim Gerald* refers to the *Herald* in Melbourne, not Sydney); some are old-fashioned, and likely to be unfamiliar to anyone younger than fifty (e.g. *amster*); and others are so specialized (e.g. *Gordon and LKS* for *Scotch and water*) that only a minority could understand them.

List B attempts to identify items of rhyming slang which are used in Australia but have no claim to be regarded as Australianisms. Discrimination is difficult, as *butcher's hook* for *look* is English, while *butcher's hook* for *crook* is Australian. My guide to what is English has been Julian Franklyn's *A Dictionary of Rhyming Slang* (2nd edn, 1961).

List A (Australian)

Adrian Quist pissed
A.I.F. deaf
Al Capone telephone
amster, amsterdam ram (trickster's confederate)
Arthur, Arthur Murray a hurry
babbler, babbling brook cook
Beecham's Pill dill
Bondi, Bondi Junction function
Botany Bay run away
bread and jam tram
bugs bunny money
butcher's, butcher's hook crook
Charlie, Charlie Wheeler sheila

comics, comic cuts guts
copper, copper jug mug
Dad and Dave shave
Donald, Donald Duck truck, fuck
Edgar Britt a shit
egg, egg and spoon hoon
fiddley, fiddley-did a quid
Flemington races braces
forby, four by two a Jew
freddo, freddo frog wog
fried, fried rice ice
Germaine Greer beer
gingerbeers engineers (Army)
Gordon, Gordon and Gotch a Scotch (drink)
Gregory, Gregory Peck neck
hammer, hammer and tack back ('on your hammer')
Hawkesbury Rivers the shivers
Hedy, Hedy Lamarr car
hollow log dog
Huckleberry, Huckleberry Finn gin
Jack Lang slang
Jersey Flegg leg
Jim Gerald *Herald* (Melbourne)
Jimmy Britts the shits
Jimmy Dancer cancer
Jimmy, Jimmy Grant an immigrant
Joe Blake a snake
Joe Blakes shakes (DTs)
John, John Freer beer
john, john hop a cop
kanga, kangaroo screw (prison warder, wage)
Kembla, Kembla Grange change
Lady, Lady Godiva driver (golf)
lemon, lemon spread head
Leonard, Leonard Teale a deal
Lionel, Lionel Rose nose
L.K.S. (L.K.S. McKinnon Stakes, run over a mile and a quarter) water
mad mick a pick
Mahatma, Mahatma Ghandi handy
mallee root prostitute
Marie Corelli belly
Mary Lou, on the on the blue (bet on credit)

469

moan and wail   gaol
Moreton, Moreton Bay fig   fizz, fizzgig (informer)
Murray, Murray Cod, on the   on the nod
murrum, Murrumbeena   a deener
Ned Kelly   the belly
Noah, Noah's ark   a shark
onka, onkaparinga   finger
Oscar, Oscar Asche   cash
Pat, Pat Malone   alone
Perce, Perce Galea   ear
pork and bean   queen (homosexual)
Port Melbourne Pier   ear
red hots   trots (racing)
Reginalds, Reg Grundies   undies
rubbity, rubbity dub   pub
sausage roll   goal
septic, septic tank   Yank
Slapsie, Slapsie Maxie   a taxi
slotma, slot machine   green (golf)
snake's, snake's hiss   piss
steak and kidney   Sydney
Steele Rudds   spuds
St Louis, St Louis blues   shoes
super, supersonic   tonic (water)
teddy, teddy bear   a lair
ten (ten furlongs = a mile and a quarter)   water
Tilly Devine   wine
tin lid   kid
to and from   a Pom
tom, tom tart   a girl
toms, tom tits   the shits
trays, tray bits   the shits
Tyrone, Tyrone Power   shower
Warwicks, Warwick Farms   the arms
Werris, Werris Creek   a Greek
wide opens, wide open spaces   races

almonds, almond rocks   socks
arris, aristotle   a bottle
bag of fruit   suit
bristols, Bristol Cities   titties
butcher's, butcher's hook   look
Cain and Abel   table
Captain Cook   a look
cheese, cheese and kisses   missus
chevy chase   face
china, china plate   mate
cobbler's, cobbler's awls   balls
eau de Cologne   see *odi*
elephant's, elephant's trunk   drunk
Errol, Errol Flynn   chin
frog and toad   road
God forbids   kids
Gordon and Gotch   a watch
horse's hoof   poof
iron, iron hoof   poof
Jimmy Riddle   a piddle
Khyber, Khyber Pass   arse
mince pies   eyes
north and south   mouth
odi, eau de Cologne   phone
Oxford Scholar   dollar
plates, plates of meat   feet
Richard, Richard the Third   bird; turd
Rory, Rory O'Moore   the door
saucepan, saucepan lid   kid
scarper, Scapa Flow   go
tealeaf   thief
titfer, tit for tat   hat
trouble and strife   wife
Uncle Willy   silly